Portable Literature

Reading • Reacting • Writing

Tenth Edition

2021 MLA Update Edition

Laurie G. Kirszner
St. Joseph's University, Emerita

Stephen R. Mandell
Drexel University, Emeritus

Australia • Brazil • Canada • Mexico • Singapore • United Kingdom • United States

Portable Literature: Reading, Reacting, Writing, Tenth Edition 2021 MLA Update Edition
Laurie G. Kirszner, Stephen R. Mandell

SVP, Product: Cheryl Costantini

VP, Product: Thais Alencar

Portfolio Product Director: Laura Ross

Portfolio Product Manager: Matt Filimonov

Product Assistant: Beth Matracia

Content Manager: Jessica Blevins

Learning Designer: Jacqueline Czel

Subject Matter Expert: Anne Alexander

Digital Project Manager: Matt Altieri

Sr. Manager, Content Acquisition Operations: Alexandra Ricciardi

Content Acquisition Analyst: Erin McCullough

Production Service/ Compositor: Straive

Cover/Text Designer: Felicia Bennett

Cover Image: Milena Sabeva / Shutterstock.com

Library of Congress Control Number: 2023903918

ISBN: 978-0-357-79385-5

Cengage
200 Pier 4 Boulevard
Boston, MA 02210
USA

Printed in the United States of America
Print Number: 01 Print Year: 2023

Brief Contents

Contents

Robert Frost

Sample student essay

3 Writing Literary Arguments 45

Alice Walker

4 Using Sources in Your Writing 58

Collins 5

Works Cited

Bartel, Roland. "Life and Death in Eudora Welty's 'A Worn Path.'" *Studies in Short Fiction*, vol. 14, no. 1, 1977, pp. 288–90.

Bethea, Dean. "Phoenix Has No Coat: Historicity, Eschatology, and Sins of Omission in Eudora Welty's 'A Worn Path.'" *International Fiction Review*, vol. 27, no. 5, 2001, pp. 32–38, journals.lib.unb.ca/index.php/ifr/article/view/7689/8746.

Howard, Zelma T. *The Rhetoric of Eudora Welty's Short Stories*. UP of Mississippi, 1973.

Piwinski, David J. "Mistletoe in Eudora Welty's 'A Worn Path.'" *ANQ: A Quarterly Journal of Short Articles, Notes and Reviews*, vol. 16, no. 1, 2003, pp. 40–43. *Taylor and Francis Online*, doi:10.1080/08957690309598188.

Saunders, James Robert. "'A Worn Path': The Eternal Quest of Welty's Phoenix Jackson." *Southern Literary Journal*, vol. 25, no. 1, 1992, pp. 62–73.

Welty, Eudora. Interview by Beth Henley. *The Heinle Original Film Series in Literature: Eudora Welty's "A Worn Path."* Directed by Bruce R. Schwartz, Wadsworth, 2003.

---. "A Worn Path." *Portable Literature: Reading, Reacting, Writing*, edited by Laurie G. Kirszner and Stephen R. Mandell, 10th ed., Cengage, 2024, pp. 370–37.

Sample MLA Works-Cited list

5 Documenting Sources and Avoiding Plagiarism 74

Sample MLA works-cited entries

Part 2 Fiction 91

6 Understanding Fiction 92

Ernest Hemingway

7 Fiction Sampler: The Short-Short Story 107

Ed Park

8 Fiction Sampler: Graphic Fiction 123

Franz Kafka

9 Plot 146

Kate Chopin

10 Character 175

Zadie Smith

11 Setting 211

Alberto Álvaro Ríos

12 Point of View 236

Chitra Banerjee Divakaruni

13 Style, Tone, and Language 288

James Joyce

14 Symbol, Allegory, and Myth 330

Shirley Jackson

15 Theme 365

Stephen Crane

16 Fiction for Further Reading 412

Louise Erdrich

Part 3 Poetry 481

17 Understanding Poetry 482

Billy Collins

18 Voice 495

Langston Hughes

Walt Whitman

20 Imagery 544

William Shakespeare

21 Figures of Speech 559

N. Scott Momaday

22 Sound 590

Adrienne Rich

23 Form 612

Yusef Komunyakaa

24 Symbol, Allegory, Allusion, Myth 646

William Butler Yeats

25 Discovering Themes in Poetry 669

Dylan Thomas

Emily Dickinson

Anton Chekhov

28 Drama Sampler: Ten-Minute Plays 783

José Rivera

29 Plot 815

Arthur Miller

30 Character 945

Tennessee Williams

31 Staging 1115

Milcha Sanchez-Scott

32 Theme 1185

August Wilson

Appendix Using Literary Criticism in Your Writing 1278

About the Authors

Laurie G. Kirszner
St. Joseph's University, Emerita

Stephen R. Mandell
Drexel University, Emeritus

Laurie G. Kirszner and Stephen R. Mandell are best-selling authors who are well known nationally and have written best sellers for nearly every English market. They have the deepest publishing record of any literature anthology author team and have successfully published up and down the curriculum from developmental to literature.

Preface

In Alice Walker's short story "Everyday Use" (p. 346), two sisters—one rural and traditional, one urban and modern—compete for possession of two quilts that have been in their family for years. At the end of the story, the narrator's description of the quilts suggests their significance—as a link between the old and the new, between what was and what is:

> One was in the Lone Star pattern. The other was Walk Around the Mountain. In both of them were scraps of dresses that Grandma Dee had worn fifty and more years ago. Bits and pieces of Grandpa Jarrell's Paisley shirts. And one teeny faded blue piece, about the size of a penny matchbox, that was from Great Grandpa Eza's uniform that he wore in the Civil War. (350)

In a sense, *Portable Literature: Reading, Reacting, Writing* is a kind of literary quilt, one that places nontraditional works alongside classics, integrates the familiar with the unfamiliar, and invites students to see well-known works in new contexts. To convey this message, each edition of the book integrates imagery from a handmade quilt. The quilt designed for this new edition uses contemporary as well as traditional quilting techniques to reflect our own increased focus on contemporary and emerging writers as well as on writers from diverse cultures and backgrounds.

The tenth edition of *Portable Literature: Reading, Reacting, Writing*, like the previous editions, is designed to demystify the study of literature and to prepare students to explore the literary works collected here. Our goal in this edition remains what it has been from the start: to expand students' personal literary boundaries. To this end, we have fine-tuned the reading selections and expanded the pedagogical features that support the study of literature, acting in response to thoughtful comments from our reviewers and from our students. Having class-tested this book in our own literature classrooms, we have learned what kinds of selections and features best help our students to read, think about, understand, and write about literature in ways that make it meaningful to their lives in the twenty-first century.

To help instructors engage their students with literature and guide them in becoming better thinkers and writers, we have added new readings and enhanced key elements that have made *Portable Literature: Reading, Reacting, Writing* a classroom success.

Unparalleled Writing Coverage

The first college literature anthology to address writing as a major component of the introductory literature course, *Portable Literature: Reading, Reacting, Writing* begins with a comprehensive writing guide. **Part 1, "A Guide to Writing about Literature,"** consists of five chapters that help students see writing about literature as a process of discovering, testing, and arguing about ideas. In addition, comprehensive writing coverage is integrated throughout the book in the following features:

- **An introduction to understanding literature** Chapter 1, "Understanding Literature," gives students an overview of the themes, genres, conventions, and interpretive possibilities that influence how they read and write about literature.

- **An introduction to the writing process** Chapter 2, "Reading and Writing about Literature," explains and illustrates the process of planning, drafting, and revising essays about literary works, concluding with three model student essays—one focusing on a short story, one comparing two poems, and one analyzing a short play.

- **A chapter on literary argument** Chapter 3, "Writing Literary Arguments," helps students to think critically about their writing and build convincing and insightful arguments about literary works. Chapter 3 takes students through the process of writing a literary argument and concludes with an annotated student essay.

- **A chapter on using appropriate sources** Chapter 4, "Using Sources in Your Writing" includes extensive advice for conducting research both online and in print, making use of the latest technologies in libraries and on the web.

- **Extensive research and documentation coverage** Chapter 5, "Documenting Sources and Avoiding Plagiarism," includes strategies for avoiding plagiarism. This chapter also includes the updated documentation guidelines set forth in the ninth edition of the *MLA Handbook* (2021). Using the concept of "containers," the chapter gives students the tools to document a wide variety of source types. At the same time the updated chapter presents numerous examples of model citations.

- **Five complete model student essays** Because our own experience in the classroom has shown us that students often learn most easily from models, the text includes five model student essays written in response to the kinds of topics that are typically assigned in Introduction to Literature classes.

- **Checklists** Most chapter introductions end with a checklist designed to help students measure their understanding of concepts introduced in the chapter. These checklists can also guide students as they generate, explore, focus, and organize ideas for writing about works of literature.

- **Writing suggestions** Imaginative suggestions for essay topics are included at the end of each chapter to spark students' interest and inspire engaged writing.

Fresh, Balanced Selections

The short stories, poems, and plays collected in this book represent a balance of old and new as well as a wide variety of nations and cultures and a full range of writing styles.

- **Extensive selection of fiction** The fiction section includes not only perennial classics ("The Lottery," "A Rose for Emily," "The Cask of Amontillado") and stories we introduced to readers in the first edition, such as David Michael Kaplan's "Doe Season" and Charles Baxter's "Gryphon," but also a number of works never previously collected in a college literature anthology. Stories that may be new to many instructors include several popular contemporary works, such as Neil Gaiman's "How to Talk to Girls at Parties" and Ed Park's "Slide to Unlock." In addition, Chapter 8, "Fiction Sampler: Graphic Fiction," engages students by juxtaposing a short story by Franz Kafka with a graphic version of the story by R. Crumb.

- **Blend of contemporary and classic poetry** The poetry section balances works by classic poets (such as Robert Frost, Emily Dickinson, and Langston Hughes) with works by more contemporary poets (such as Allen Ginsberg and Rafael Campo) and also introduces students to exciting twenty-first-century poetry. Now offering an even broader range of diverse selections, the poetry section has been expanded with poems by Agha Shahid Ali, Gwendolyn Brooks, David Trinidad, Kobayashi Issa, Rhina Espaillat, David Hernandez, Nancy Mercado, Deborah Paredez, Sylvia Plath, Lola Ridge, Jacob Saenz, Carl Sandburg, Virgil Suárez, May Swenson, Jean Toomer, Claude McKay, and many others. In addition, unique visual glossary items appear throughout the poetry section, clarifying and illuminating unfamiliar terms and concepts within poems.

- **Varied selection of plays** The drama section juxtaposes classic selections—William Shakespeare's *Hamlet*, August Wilson's *Fences*, Milcha Sanchez-Scott's *The Cuban Swimmer*—with contemporary plays, such as Jeni Mahoney's *Come Rain or Shine* and James McLindon's *Choices*. Six plays are new to the tenth edition, including Arthur Miller's *All My Sons* and Tennessee Williams's *The Glass Menagerie*.

- **Innovative "sampler" chapters** Chapter 7, "Fiction Sampler: The Short-Short Story"; Chapter 8, "Fiction Sampler: Graphic Fiction"; and Chapter 28, "Drama Sampler: Ten-Minute Plays," showcase representative selections from three popular literary subgenres, introducing students to the variety and diversity of literature with brief, accessible works.

Thorough Background Information

As we have learned in our classrooms over the years, part of helping students to demystify literature is helping them to understand the context in which the stories, poems, and plays were written. To achieve this goal, we continue to include contextual and background materials throughout the book in various forms:

- **Cultural context notes** A cultural context section follows each author headnote in the fiction and drama sections, providing vital background about the social and historical climate in which the work was written.
- **Accessible discussion of literary history** "Origins of Modern Fiction" in Chapter 6, "Understanding Fiction"; "Origins of Modern Poetry" in Chapter 17, "Understanding Poetry"; and "Origins of Modern Drama" in Chapter 27, "Understanding Drama," are fully illustrated with visuals that trace each genre's development and bring the history of literature to life.

What's New to This Edition

- The writing guide at the beginning of the book, Chapters 1-5, has been revised and expanded. This section now includes five chapters of in-depth instruction to help students see writing about literature as a process of discovering, testing, and arguing about ideas.
- The new Chapter 1: Understanding Literature gives students an overview of the themes, genres, conventions, and interpretive possibilities that influence how they read and write about literature.
- The new Chapter 4: Using Sources in Your Writing offers extensive advice for conducting research both online and in print, making use of the latest technologies in libraries and on the web.
- Throughout, we now include more than 30 new readings that widen the book's appeal, including compelling short stories, poems, and plays that represent a balance of old and new as well as a wide variety of nations and cultures and a full range of writing styles. Writers now represented include Chitra Banerjee Divakaruni, Junot Diaz, Zora Neale Hurston, and Alberto Álvaro Ríos in fiction; Ada Limón, Joy Harjo, and Naomi Shihab Nye in poetry; and José Rivera and Tennessee Williams in drama.
- Each chapter includes refreshed, imaginative suggestions for essay topics to spark students' interest and inspire engaged writing.
- The updated and expanded appendix, "Using Literary Criticism in Your Writing," now includes three new schools of literary criticism (ecocriticism, posthumanism, and postmodernism), with a historical overview, textual analysis and relevant resources for further reading for each.

Other Pedagogical Features

A number of other pedagogical features appear throughout the text to prompt students to think critically about reading and to stimulate class discussions and energetic, thoughtful writing:

- **Reading and Reacting questions** Reading and Reacting questions, including journal prompts, follow many selections throughout the text. These questions ask students to interpret and evaluate what they have read—sometimes encouraging them to make connections between the literary work being studied and other works in the text.
- **Critical Perspectives** Critical Perspective questions (included in most sets of Reading and Reacting questions) ask students to respond to analytical, interpretative, or evaluative comments that writers and critics have made about the work. This feature encourages students to apply their own critical thinking skills to literary criticism as well as to the work of literature itself.
- **Literary criticism appendix** The newly updated and expanded appendix, "Using Literary Criticism in Your Writing," explains and illustrates the key schools of literary criticism and shows how each can be applied to a typical student writing assignment inspired by a literary work.
- **Related Works** A Related Works section following the Reading and Reacting questions lists works linked (by theme, author, or genre) to the particular work under study. This feature encourages students to see connections between works by different writers, between works in different genres, or between two themes—connections they can explore in class discussion and in writing.

A Full Package of Supplementary Materials

To support students and instructors who use the tenth edition of *Portable Literature: Reading, Reacting, Writing*, these ancillary materials are available from Cengage:

- **Instructor Resources** Additional instructor resources for this product are available online. Instructor assets include an Instructor's Manual, Educator's Guide, Sample Syllabi and PowerPoint® slides. Sign up or sign in at www.cengage.com to search for and access this product and its online resources.
- **MindTap®** Today's leading online learning platform, MindTap offers a personalized, engaging learning experience that challenges students, builds confidence and elevates performance.

MindTap introduces students to core concepts from the beginning of the course using a simplified learning path that progresses from understanding to application and delivers access to eTextbooks, study tools, interactive media, auto-graded assessments and performance analytics.

Acknowledgments

From start to finish, this book has been a true collaboration, not only with each other, but also with our students and colleagues. We have worked hard on this book, and many people have worked hard along with us.

We'd like to begin by thanking our Content Manager, Jessica Blevins. Her attention to detail, her keen insights, and her helpful suggestions have been truly amazing. We didn't know her before we began this revision, but we hope that we get to work with her again in the future. We'd also like to thank Matt Filimonov, Senior Portfolio Product Manager at Cengage, whose support and guidance made our work on this project a lot easier. Special mention goes to Brian Malone, Consulting Editor, whose discerning comments helped us shape our discussions about literature and its societal impact. At Cengage, we'd also like to thank Beth Matracia, Product Assistant; Anne Alexander, Subject Matter Expert; Jacqueline Czel, Learning Designer; Erin McCullough, Content Acquisition Analyst; Matt Altieri, Digital Product Manager; Felicia Bennett, Designer. We also thank the teams at Straive Publisher Services, Lumina Datamatics, and MPS Limited.

We would like to thank the following reviewers of the tenth edition: Valrie Martin Buchanan, Palm Beach State College; Mackinzee Escamilla, South Plains College; Christie Harper, LeMoyne-Owen College; Katherine Jackson, South Plains College; Fayaz Kabani, Allen University; Harry Manos, Los Angeles City College; Carol Martinson, Polk State College; Dr. Jim Richey, Tyler Junior College; and Joan Reeves, Northeast Alabama Community College.

We would also like to thank our families for being there when we needed them. And finally, we each thank the person on the other side of the ampersand for making our collaboration work one more time.

Part 1

A Guide to Writing about Literature

Chapter

1

Understanding Literature

Westminster Bridge, London (1886) by Claude Thomas Stanfield Moore
Source: Fine Art Photographic/Getty Images

Learning Objectives

After reading this chapter, you will be able to. . .

- Identify genres of imaginative literature.
- Describe conventional themes in a work of literature.
- Recognize how works are included and excluded from the literary canon.
- Interpret a literary work.
- Evaluate a literary work.
- Identify the use of literary criticism and its purpose in evaluating literature.
- Evaluate literary criticism.

Imaginative Literature

Imaginative literature begins with a writer's need to convey a personal vision to readers. Consider, for example, how William Wordsworth uses language in these lines from his poem "Composed upon Westminster Bridge, September 3, 1802" (p. 744):

> This City now doth, like a garment, wear
> The beauty of the morning; silent, bare,
> Ships, towers, domes, theatres, and temples lie
> Open unto the fields, and to the sky;
> All bright and glittering in the smokeless air.

Wordsworth does not try to present a picture of London that is topographically or sociologically accurate. Instead, by comparing the city at dawn to a person wearing a beautiful garment, he creates a striking picture that has its own kind of truth. By using a vivid, original comparison, the poet suggests the oneness of the city, nature, and himself.

Even when writers of imaginative literature use factual material—historical documents, newspaper stories, or personal experience, for example—their primary purpose is to present their own unique view of experience, one that has significance beyond the moment. (As the poet Ezra Pound said, "Literature is the news that *stays* news.") To convey their views of experience, these writers often manipulate facts—changing dates, creating characters and events, and inventing dialogue. For example, when Herman Melville wrote his nineteenth-century novella *Benito Cereno*, he drew many of his facts from an 1817 account of an actual slave rebellion. In his story, he reproduces court records and uses plot details from this primary source—Amasa Delano's *Narrative of Voyages and Travels, in the Northern and Southern Hemispheres*—but he leaves out some incidents, and he adds material of his own. The result is an original work of literature. Wanting to do more than retell the original story, Melville used the factual material as "a skeleton of actual reality" on which he built a story that attacks the institution of slavery and examines the nature of truth.

Imaginative literature is more likely than other types of writing to include words chosen not only because they communicate the writer's ideas but also because they are memorable. Using vivid imagery and evocative comparisons, writers of imaginative literature often stretch language to its limits. By relying on the multiple connotations of words and images, a work of imaginative literature encourages readers to see the possibilities of language and move beyond the factual details of an event.

Even though imaginative literature can be divided into types called **genres**—fiction, poetry, and drama, for example—the nature of literary genres varies greatly from culture to culture. In fact, some literary forms that Western readers take for granted are alien to other literary traditions. The sonnet, a fairly common poetic form in the West, is not a conventional literary form in

Kabuki performance of Shakespeare's *Twelfth Night*
Geraint Lewis/Alamy Stock Photo

Chinese or Arabic poetry. Similarly, the most popular theatrical entertainment in Japan since the mid-seventeenth century, the **Kabuki play**, has no counterpart in the West. (In a Kabuki play, which includes stories, scenes, dances, music, acrobatics, and elaborate costumes and stage settings, all the actors are men, some of whom play female roles. Many Kabuki plays have little plot and seem to be primarily concerned with spectacle. One feature of this form of drama is a walkway that extends from the stage through the audience to the back of the theater.)

Conventions of narrative organization and character development can also vary considerably from culture to culture, especially in literature derived from oral traditions. For example, narrative organization in some Native American stories (and, even more commonly, in some African stories) can be very different from what contemporary Western readers are accustomed to. Events may be arranged spatially instead of chronologically: first, a story presents all the events that happened in one place, then it presents everything that happened in another location, and so on. Character development is also much less important in some traditional African and Native American stories than it is in modern short fiction. In fact, a character's name, description, and personality can change dramatically (and without warning) during the course of a story.

Despite such differences, the imaginative literature of all cultures has similar effects on readers: memorable characters, vivid descriptions, imaginative use of language, and compelling plots can fascinate and delight. Literature can take readers where they have never been before and, in so doing, can create a sense of adventure and wonder.

At another level, however, readers can find more than just pleasure or escape in literature. Beyond transporting readers out of their own lives and times, literature can enable them to see their lives and times more clearly. Whether a work of imaginative literature depicts a young girl as she experiences the disillusionment of adulthood for the first time, as in David Michael Kaplan's "Doe Season" (p. 378), or the thoughts and feelings of a soldier as he tries to come to terms with what he did during the Boer War, as in Thomas Hardy's "The Man He Killed" (p. 505), it can help readers to understand their own experiences and the experiences of others. In this sense, literature offers readers increased insight into the human condition. As the Chilean poet Pablo Neruda said, works of imaginative literature fulfill "the most ancient rites of our conscience in the awareness of being human and of believing in a common destiny."

Conventional Themes

The **theme** of a work of literature—its central or dominant idea—is seldom explicitly stated. Instead, it is conveyed through the selection and arrangement of details; through the emphasis of certain words, events, or images; and through the actions and reactions of characters.

Although one central theme may dominate a literary work, many works explore a number of different themes or ideas. For example, the central theme of Mark Twain's *Adventures of Huckleberry Finn* might be the idea that an individual's innate sense of right and wrong is superior to society's artificial and sometimes unnatural values. The main character, Huck, gains a growing awareness of this idea by witnessing feuds, duels, and all manner of human folly. As a result, he decides to help his friend Jim escape from slavery despite the fact that society, as well as his own conscience, condemns this action. However, *Huckleberry Finn* also examines other themes. Throughout his novel, Twain criticizes many of the ideas that prevailed in the pre–Civil War South, such as the racism and religious hypocrisy that pervaded the towns along the Mississippi.

On the Raft, illustration from Mark Twain's *Adventures of Huckleberry Finn*

Source: Historical/Getty Images

A literary work can explore any theme; however, certain themes have become **conventions**—that is, they have reoccurred so often over the years that they have become familiar and accepted. One conventional theme—a character's loss of innocence—appears in the biblical story of Adam and Eve and later finds its way into works such as Nathaniel Hawthorne's 1835 short story "Young Goodman Brown" (p. 354) and James Joyce's 1914 short story "Araby" (p. 296).

Another conventional theme—the conflict between an individual's values and the values of society—is examined in the ancient Greek play *Antigone* (p. 1191) by Sophocles. Almost two thousand years later, Norwegian playwright Henrik Ibsen deals with the same theme in *A Doll's House* (p. 834).

Other conventional themes examined in literary works include the individual's quest for spiritual enlightenment, the *carpe diem* ("seize the day") philosophy, the making of the artist, the nostalgia for a vanished past, the disillusionment of adulthood, the pain of love, the struggle for equality, the conflict between parents and children, the clash between civilization and the wilderness, the evils of unchecked ambition, the inevitability of fate, the impact of the past on the present, the conflict between human beings and machines, and the tension between the ideal and actual realms of experience.

Many cultures explore similar themes, but writers from different cultures may develop these themes differently. A culture's history, a particular region's geography, or a country's social structure can suggest unique ways of developing conventional themes. In addition, the assumptions, concerns, values, ideals, and beliefs of a particular country or society—or of a particular group within that society—can help to determine the themes writers choose to explore and the manner in which they do so.

Detail of fresco showing expulsion of Adam and Eve from the Garden of Eden
Print Collector/Hulton Archive/Getty Images

In American literature, for example, familiar themes include the loss of innocence, rites of passage, childhood epiphanies, and the ability (or inability) to form relationships. American writers from traditionally marginalized groups—for example, Richard Wright in "Big Black Big Man" (p. 246) or Zadie Smith in "The Girl with Bangs" (p. 204)—may use these themes to express their frustration with racism or to celebrate their identities. For example, the theme of loss of innocence may be presented as a first encounter with racial prejudice; a conflict between the individual and society may be presented as a conflict between a minority view and the values of the dominant group; and the theme of failure or aborted relationships may be explored in a work about cultural misunderstandings.

Finally, modern works of literature sometimes treat conventional themes in new ways. For example, in *1984* George Orwell explores the consequences of unchecked power by creating a nightmare world in which the government controls and dehumanizes a population. Even though Orwell's novel is set in an imaginary future (it was written in 1948), its theme echoes ideas frequently examined in the plays of both Sophocles and Shakespeare.

The Literary Canon

Originally, the term *canon* referred to the accepted list of books that made up the Christian Bible. More recently, the term **literary canon** has come to denote a group of works generally agreed upon by writers, teachers, and critics to be worth reading and studying. Over the years, as standards have changed, the definition of "good" literature has also changed, and the literary canon has been modified accordingly. For example, at various times, critics have characterized Shakespeare's plays as mundane, immoral, commonplace, and brilliant. The eighteenth-century critic Samuel Johnson said of Shakespeare that "in his comick scenes he is seldom very successful" and in tragedy "his performance seems constantly to be worse, as his labor is more." Many people find it difficult to believe that a writer whose name today is synonymous with great literature could ever have been judged so harshly. Like all aesthetic works, however, the plays of Shakespeare affect individuals in different periods of history and in different societies in different ways.

Some educators and literary scholars believe that the traditional literary canon, like a restricted club, arbitrarily admits some authors and excludes others. This fact is borne out, they say, by an examination of the literature curriculum that, until recently, was standard at many North American universities. This curriculum typically began with Homer, Plato, Dante, and Chaucer; progressed to Shakespeare, Milton, the eighteenth-century novel, the Romantics, and the Victorians; and ended with some of the "classics" of modern British and American literature. Most of the authors of these works are White men, and their writing for the most part reflects Western values.

Missing from the literature courses in North American universities for many years were Latin American, Caribbean, African, and Asian writers. Students of American literature were not encouraged to consider the perspectives of women, LGBTQ, or Latin Americans, Native Americans, or other ethnic or racial groups. During the past four decades, however, most universities have expanded the traditional canon by including more works by women, people of color, and writers from a variety of cultures and backgrounds. These additional works, studied alongside those representing the traditional canon, have opened up the curriculum and redefined the standards by which literature is judged.

One example of a literary work that challenged the traditional canon is "All about Suicide" by Luisa Valenzuela, an Argentinean writer. Currently, she is one of the most widely translated South American writers. This brief story is part of a large and growing body of literature from around the world that purposely violates our standard literary expectations to make its point—in this case, a point about the political realities of Argentina in the 1960s.

Luisa Valenzuela (1938–)

All about Suicide (1967)

Translated by Helen Lane

Ismael grabbed the gun and slowly rubbed it across his face. Then he pulled the trigger and there was a shot. Bang. One more person dead in the city. It's getting to be a vice. First he grabbed the revolver that was in a desk drawer, rubbed it gently across his face, put it to his temple, and pulled the trigger. Without saying a word. Bang. Dead.

Let's recapitulate: the office is grand, fit for a minister. The desk is ministerial too, and covered with a glass that must have reflected the scene, the shock. Ismael knew where the gun was, he'd hidden it there himself. So he didn't lose any time, all he had to do was open the right-hand drawer and stick his hand in. Then he got a good hold on it and rubbed it over his face with a certain pleasure before putting it to his temple and pulling the trigger. It was something almost sensual and quite unexpected. He hadn't even had time to think about it. A trivial gesture, and the gun had fired.

There's something missing: Ismael in the bar with a glass in his hand thinking over his future act and its possible consequences.

We must go back farther if we want to get at the truth: Ismael in the cradle crying because his diapers are dirty and nobody is changing him.

Not that far. 5

Ismael in the first grade fighting with a classmate who'll one day become a minister, his friend, a traitor.

No, Ismael in the ministry without being able to tell what he knew, forced to be silent. Ismael in the bar with the glass (his third) in his hand, and the irrevocable decision: better death.

Ismael pushing the revolving door at the entrance to the building, pushing the swinging door leading to the office section, saying good morning to the guard, opening the door of his office. Once in his office, seven steps to his desk. Terror, the act of opening the drawer, taking out the revolver, and rubbing it across his face, almost a single gesture and very quick. The act of putting it to his temple and pulling the trigger—another act, immediately following the previous one. Bang. Dead. And Ismael coming out of his office (the other man's office, the minister's) almost relieved, even though he can predict what awaits him.

* * *

In "All about Suicide," the author not only undercuts the reader's assumptions about the story but also about fiction itself. Is the story about suicide, as the title implies, or is it about something else? Should readers trust their preconceptions about the conventions of fiction, or should they begin to question the "rules"? By addressing questions such as these, Venezuela expands the boundaries of literature and invites readers to abandon easy assumptions about their world and their place within it.

Certainly, canon revision is not without problems—for example, the possibility of including a work more for political or sociological reasons than for literary merit. Nevertheless, if the debate about the literary canon has accomplished anything, it has revealed that the canon is not fixed and that many works formerly excluded—African American slave narratives and eighteenth-century women's diaries, for example—deserve to be read.

Interpreting Literature

When you **interpret** a literary work, you explore its possible meanings. One commonly held idea about reading a literary work is that its meaning lies buried somewhere within it, waiting to be unearthed. This reasoning suggests that a clever reader has only to discover the author's intent to find out what a story or poem means, and that the one actual meaning of a work is hidden "between the lines," unaffected by a reader's experiences or interpretations. More recently, however, a different model of the reading process—one that takes into consideration the reader as well as the work the reader is interpreting—has emerged.

Many contemporary critics see the reading process as **interactive**. In other words, meaning is created through the reader's interaction with a text. Thus, the meaning of a particular work comes alive in the imagination of an individual reader, and no reader can determine a work's meaning without considering their own reaction to the text. Meaning, therefore, is created partly by what is supplied by a work and partly by what is supplied by the reader.

The most obvious thing a work supplies is **facts**, the information that enables a reader to follow the plot of a story, the action of a play, or the development of a poem. The work itself will provide factual details about the setting; about the characters' names, ages, and appearances; about the sequence of events; and about the emotions and attitudes of a poem's speaker, a story's narrator, or the characters in a play or story. This factual information cannot be ignored: if a play's stage directions identify its setting as nineteenth-century Norway or the forest of Arden, that is where the play is set.

In addition to facts, a work also conveys the social, political, class, and gender **attitudes** of the writer. Thus, a work may reflect overtly feminist or working-class attitudes or a subtle (or obvious) political agenda; it may confirm or challenge contemporary attitudes; it may communicate a writer's nostalgia for a vanished past or outrage at a corrupt present; it may take an elitist, distant view of characters and events or present a sympathetic perspective. A reader's understanding of these attitudes will contribute to their own interpretation of the work.

Finally, a work also includes **assumptions** about literary conventions. A poet, for example, may have definite ideas about whether a poem should be rhymed or unrhymed or about whether a particular subject is appropriate or inappropriate for poetic treatment. Therefore, a knowledge of the literary conventions of a particular period or the preferences of a particular writer can provide a starting point for your interpretation of literature.

As a reader, you bring to a work your own **personal perspectives**. Your experiences, your beliefs, your ideas about the issues discussed in the work, and your assumptions about literature color your interpretations. In fact, nearly every literary work has somewhat different meanings for different people, depending on their age, gender, sexual orientation, nationality, political and religious beliefs, ethnic background, social and economic class, education, knowledge, and personal experiences. Depending on your religious beliefs, for example, you can react to a passage from the Old Testament as literal truth, symbolic truth, or fiction. Depending on your race, where you live, your biases, and the nature of your experience, a story about racial discrimination can strike you as accurate and realistic, exaggerated and unrealistic, or understated and restrained.

In a sense, then, the process of determining meaning is like a conversation, one in which both you and the text have a voice. Sometimes, by clearly dictating the terms of the discussion, the text determines the direction of the conversation; at other times, by using your knowledge and experience to interpret the text, you dominate. Thus, because every reading of a literary work is actually an interpretation, it is a mistake to look for a single "correct" reading.

The 1923 poem "Stopping by Woods on a Snowy Evening," by the American poet Robert Frost, illustrates how a single work can have more than one interpretation.

Robert Frost (1874–1963)

Stopping by Woods on a Snowy Evening (1923)

Whose woods these are I think I know.
His house is in the village though;
He will not see me stopping here
To watch his woods fill up with snow.

My little horse must think it queer
To stop without a farmhouse near
Between the woods and frozen lake
The darkest evening of the year.

He gives his harness bells a shake
To ask if there is some mistake.

The only other sound's the sweep
Of easy wind and downy flake.

The woods are lovely, dark and deep,
But I have promises to keep,
And miles to go before I sleep,
And miles to go before I sleep.

Readers may interpret the poem as being about the inevitability of death, as suggesting that the poet is tired or world weary, as making a comment about duty and the need to persevere, or about the conflicting pulls of life and art. Beyond these possibilities, readers' own associations of snow with quiet and sadness could lead them to define the mood of the poem as sorrowful or melancholy. Information about Robert Frost's life or his ideas about poetry could add to readers' understanding of the poem, and they might even develop ideas about the poem that are quite different from the poet's. In fact, on several occasions, Frost himself gave strikingly different—even contradictory—interpretations of "Stopping by Woods on a Snowy Evening," sometimes insisting that the poem had no hidden meaning and at other times saying that it required a good deal of explication. (Literary critics also disagree about its meaning.) When reading a work of literature, then, keep in mind that the meaning of the text is not fixed. Your best strategy is to open yourself up to the text's many possibilities and explore the full range of your responses.

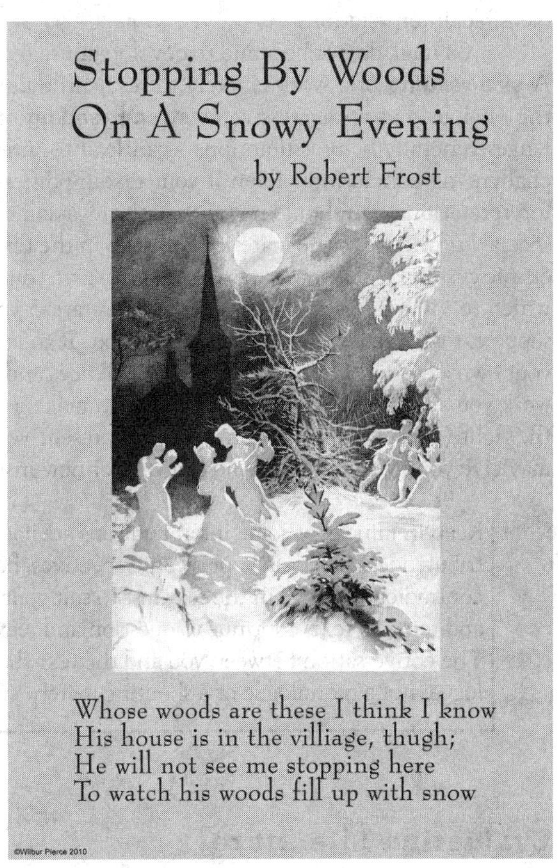

Stopping By Woods
On A Snowy Evening
by Robert Frost
Whose woods are these I think I know
His house is in the villiage, thugh;
He will not see me stopping here
To watch his woods fill up with snow
©Wilbur Pierce 2010

Opening pages from Susan Jeffers's illustrated children's book *Stopping by Woods on a Snowy Evening* (1978)
akg-images/Universal Images Group

Although no single reading of a literary work is "correct," some readings are more defensible than others. Like a scientific theory, a literary interpretation must have a basis in fact, and the text supplies the facts against which your interpretation should be judged. For example, after you read Shirley Jackson's "The Lottery" (p. 337), a 1948 short story in which a randomly chosen victim is stoned to death by her neighbors, it would be reasonable to conclude that the ceremonial aspects of the lottery suggest an ancient ritual. Your understanding of what a ritual is, combined with your observation that a number of details in the text suggest ancient fertility rites, might lead you to this conclusion. Another possibility is that "The Lottery" provides a commentary on mob psychology. The way characters reinforce one another's violent tendencies lends support to this interpretation. However, the interpretation that the ritual of the lottery is a thinly veiled attack on the death penalty would be difficult to support. Certainly, a character in the story is killed, but she is not accused of a crime nor is she tried or convicted; in fact, the killing is random and seemingly without motivation. Still, although seeing "The Lottery" as a comment on the death penalty may be far-fetched, this interpretation could be a starting point. A second, closer reading of the story would allow you to explore other, more plausible, interpretations.

As you read, do not be afraid to develop unusual or creative interpretations. A **safe reading** of a work is likely to result in a dull essay that simply states the obvious, but an aggressive or **strong reading** of a work—one that challenges generally held assumptions—can lead to interesting and intellectually challenging conclusions. Even if your reading differs from established critics' interpretations, you should not automatically assume it has no merit. Your own special knowledge of the material discussed in the text—a regional practice, an ethnic custom, a personal experience—may give you a unique perspective from which to view the work. Whatever interpretation you make, be sure that you support it with specific references to the text. If your interpretation is based on your own experiences, explain those experiences and relate them clearly to the work you are discussing. As long as you can make a reasonable case, you have the right (and perhaps the obligation) to present your ideas. By doing so, you may give your fellow students and instructor new insight into the work.

Note Keep in mind that some interpretations are *not* reasonable. You may contribute ideas based on your own perspectives, but you cannot ignore or contradict evidence in the text just to suit your own biases. As you read and reread a text, continue to question and reexamine your judgments. The conversation between you and the text should be an ongoing dialogue, not a monologue or a shouting match.

Evaluating Literature

When you **evaluate** a work of literature, you do more than interpret it; you make a judgment about it. You reach conclusions not simply about whether the work is "good" or "bad" but also about how effectively the work presents itself to you, the reader. To evaluate a work, you **analyze** it, breaking it apart and considering its individual elements. As you evaluate a work of literature, remember that different works are designed to fulfill different needs—entertainment, education, or enlightenment, for example. Before you begin to evaluate a work, be sure you understand its purpose, then follow these guidelines:

- ***Consider how various literary elements function within a work.*** Fiction may be divided into chapters and use flashbacks and foreshadowing; plays may be divided into scenes and acts and include dialogue and special staging instructions; poems may be divided into stanzas and use poetic devices such as rhyme and meter. Understanding the choices writers make about these and other literary conventions can help you form judgments about a work. For example, why does Alberto Alvaro Ríos use a first-person narrator in his story "The Secret Lion" (p. 222)? Would the story have been different had it been told in the third person by a narrator who was not a character in the story? How does unusual staging contribute to the effect Milcha Sanchez-Scott achieves in her play *The Cuban Swimmer* (p. 1122)? How would a more realistic setting change the play? Naturally, you cannot focus on every element of a particular story, poem, or play. But you can and should focus on those aspects that determine your responses to a work. For this reason, elements such as the unusual stanzaic form in Laurence Ferlinghetti's poem "Constantly Risking Absurdity" (p. 562) and the very specific stage directions in August Wilson's play *Fences* (p. 1222) should be of special interest to you.

  As you read, then, you should ask questions. Do the characters in a short story seem real, or do they seem like cardboard cutouts? Are the images in a poem original and thought provoking, or are they clichéd? Are the stage directions of a play minimal or very detailed? The answers to these and other questions will help you to shape your evaluation.
- ***Consider whether the literary elements of a work interact to achieve a common goal.*** Good writers are like master cabinetmakers: their skill disguises the work that has gone into the process of creation. Thus, the elements of a well-crafted literary work often fit together in a way that conceals the craft of the writer. Consider the subtlety of the following stanza from the 1862 poem "Echo" by Christina Rossetti:

  Come to me in the silence of the night;
      Come to me in the speaking silence of a dream;
  Come with soft round cheeks and eyes as bright
      As sunlight on a stream;
          Come back in tears,
  O memory, hope, love of finished years.

  Throughout this stanza, Rossetti repeats words ("Come to me . . . / Come with soft . . . / Come back . . .") and initial consonants ("speaking silence"; "sunlight on a stream"), using sound to create an almost hypnotic mood.

The rhyme scheme (*night/bright*, *dream/stream*, and *tears/years*) reinforces the mood by establishing a musical undercurrent that extends throughout the poem. Thus, this stanza is effective because its repeated words and sounds work together to create a single lyrical effect.

The chorus in *Oedipus the King* by Sophocles (p. 1137) also illustrates how the elements of a well-crafted work of literature function together. In ancient Greece, plays were performed by masked male actors who played both male and female roles. A chorus of fifteen men remained in a central circle called the *orchestra* and commented on and reacted to the action taking place around them. The chorus expressed the judgment of the community and acted as a moral guide for the audience. Once modern audiences grow accustomed to the presence of the chorus, it becomes an important part of the play. It neither distracts the audience nor intrudes on the action. In fact, eliminating the chorus would diminish the impact of the play.

- ***Consider whether a work reinforces or calls into question your ideas about the world.*** Some works of fiction do little more than reassure readers that what they believe is correct. Catering to people's desires (for adventure, love, or success, for example), to their prejudices, or to their fears, these works serve as escapes from life. Other works of fiction, however, cut against the grain, challenging cherished beliefs and leading readers to reexamine long-held assumptions. For example, in the 1957 short story "Big Black Good Man" (p. 246), Richard Wright's protagonist, a night porter at a hotel, struggles with his consuming yet irrational fear of a "big black" sailor and with his inability to see beyond the sailor's size and skin color. Only at the end of the story do many readers see that they, like the night porter, have stereotyped and dehumanized the sailor.
- ***Consider whether a work is intellectually challenging.*** The extended comparison between the legs of a compass and two people in love in "A Valediction: Forbidding Mourning" (p. 568) by the seventeenth-century English poet John Donne illustrates how effectively an image can communicate complex ideas to readers. Compressed into this comparison are ideas about the perfection of love, the pain of enforced separation, and the difference between sexual and spiritual love. As intellectually challenging as this extended comparison is, it is nonetheless accessible to the careful reader. After all, many people have used a compass to draw a circle and, therefore, are able to understand the relationship between the two arms of the compass (and the two lovers).

A fine line exists, however, between works that are intellectually challenging and those that are intentionally obscure. An intellectually challenging work requires effort from readers to unlock ideas that enrich and expand their understanding of themselves and the world. Although complex, the work gives readers a sense that they have gained something by putting forth the effort to interpret it. An intentionally obscure work exists solely to display a writer's erudition or intellectual idiosyncrasies. Allusions to other works and events are so numerous and confusing that the work may seem more like a private code than an effort to enlighten readers. Consider the following excerpt from "Canto LXXVI" by the twentieth-century American poet Ezra Pound:

Le Paradis n'est pas artificiel
    States of mind are inexplicable to us.
    δακρύων δακρύων δακρύων
L. P. gli onesti
        J'ai eu pitié des autres
probablement pas assez, and at moments that suited my own
    convenience
        Le paradis n'est pas artificiel,
            l'enfer non plus.
Came Eurus as comforter
and at sunset la pastorella dei suini
    driving the pigs home, benecomata dea
        under the two-winged cloud
        as of less and more than a day

This passage contains lines in French, Greek, and Italian, as well as a reference to Eurus, the ancient Greek personification of the east wind, and the initials L. P. (Loomis Pound?). It demands a lot from readers; the question is whether the reward is worth the effort.

No hard-and-fast rule exists for determining whether a work is intellectually challenging or simply obscure. Just as a poem has no fixed meaning, it also has no fixed value. Some readers would say that the passage from "Canto LXXVI" is good, even great, poetry. Others would argue that those lines do not yield enough pleasure and insight to justify the effort needed to analyze them. As a reader, you must draw your own conclusions and justify them in a clear and reasonable way. Do not assume that just because a work is difficult, it is obscure. (Nor should you assume that all difficult works are great literature or that all accessible literature is trivial.) Some of the most beautiful and inspiring literary works demand a great deal of effort. Many readers would agree, however, that the time spent exploring such works yields tremendous rewards.

- ***Consider whether a work gives you pleasure.*** One of the primary reasons literature endures is that it gives readers enjoyment. As subjective as this assessment is, it is a starting point for critical judgment. When readers ask themselves what they liked about a work, why they liked it, or what they learned, they begin the process of evaluation. Although this process is largely uncritical, it can lead to an involvement with the work and to a valid critical response. When you encounter great literature, with all its complexities, you may lose sight of the idea of literature as a source of pleasure. But literature should touch you on a deep emotional or intellectual level. If it does not—despite its technical perfection—it fails to achieve one of its primary aims.

Using Literary Criticism

Sometimes your personal reactions and knowledge cannot give you enough insight into a literary work. For example, archaic language, references to mythology, historical allusions, and textual inconsistencies can make a work difficult or even inaccessible. Similarly, an intellectual or philosophical movement such as Darwinism, Marxism, naturalism, structuralism, or feminism may influence a work, and if this is the case, you need some knowledge of the movement before you can interpret the work. In addition, you may not have the background to appreciate the technical or historical dimensions of a work. To increase your understanding, you may choose to read **literary criticism**—books and journal articles written by experts who describe, analyze, interpret, or evaluate a work of literature (see the appendix: "Using Literary Criticism in Your Writing"). Reading literary criticism enables you to expand your knowledge of a particular work and participate in ongoing critical discussions about literature. In a sense, when you read literary criticism, you become part of a community of scholars who share their ideas and who are connected to one another through their writing.

Literary criticism is written by experts, but this does not mean you must always agree with it. You have to evaluate literary criticism just as you would any new opinion that you encounter. Not all criticism is sound, timely, or responsible (and not all literary criticism is pertinent to your assignment or useful for your purposes). Some critical comments will strike you as plausible; others will seem far-fetched or biased.

Quite often, two critics will reach strikingly different conclusions about the quality or significance of the same work or writer, or they will interpret a character, a symbol, or even the entire work quite differently. Although critics may disagree, their conflicting ideas can help you reach your own conclusions about a work. It is up to you to sort out the various opinions and decide which have merit and which do not.

Note If you use literary criticism in your own writing, keep in mind that your ideas, not the ideas of the critics, should dominate the discussion. The critical opinions you include should support your points and strengthen your argument. Also, remember that you must document all words and ideas that you borrow from your sources. If you do not, you will be committing **plagiarism**—presenting another person's words or ideas as if they were your own. (See Chapter 5 for information on documenting sources and avoiding plagiarism.)

Checklist Evaluating Literary Criticism

To help you evaluate literary criticism, consider the following questions:

- What is the main point of the text you are reading?
- Does the critic supply enough examples to support their conclusions?
- Does the critic acknowledge and refute the most obvious opposing arguments?
- Does the critic ignore any information in the text that might call their conclusions into question?
- Does the critic present historical information? biographical information? literary information? How does this information shed light on the work or works being discussed?
- Does the critic hold any beliefs that might interfere with their critical judgment?
- Does the critic slant the facts, or does the critic approach the text critically and objectively?
- Does the critic support conclusions with references to other sources? Does the critic provide documentation and a list of works cited?
- Does the critic take into consideration the most important critical books and articles? Are there works that should have been mentioned but were not?
- Do other critics mention the source you are reading? Do they agree or disagree with its conclusions?
- Is the critic identified with a particular critical school of thought—deconstruction or Marxism, for example? What perspective does this school of thought provide?
- Is the critic well known and respected?
- Is the critical work's publication date of any significance?

Chapter

2

Reading and Writing about Literature

Learning Objectives

After reading this chapter, you will be able to. . .

- Demonstrate the active reading process.
- Preview a work of literature
- Highlight and annotate a work of literature.
- Identify various purposes for writing an essay about literature.
- Choose a topic for an essay about literature, and find ideas to write about.
- Develop a thesis statement for your essay.
- Draft an essay that effectively supports your thesis using relevant outside sources where necessary.
- Revise and edit your essay.

Reading Literature

Reading is often a passive process; readers expect the text to give them everything they need, and they do not expect to contribute much to the reading process. In contrast, **active reading** means participating in the reading process: thinking about what you read, asking questions, challenging ideas, and forming opinions and judgments. For this reason, active reading is excellent preparation for the writing you will do and the discussions you will have in college literature classes. Moreover, because it helps you understand and appreciate the works you read, active reading will continue to be of value to you long after your formal classroom study of literature has ended.

Previewing

You begin the active reading process by **previewing** a work, skimming it to get a general idea of what to look for later on when you read it more carefully.

Start previewing by considering the work's most obvious structural characteristics. How long is a short story? How many acts and scenes does a play have? Is a poem divided into stanzas? The answers to these and similar questions will guide you as you begin to notice more subtle aspects of the work's form. For example, previewing may reveal that a contemporary short story is presented entirely in a question-and-answer format, that it is organized as diary entries, or that it is divided into sections by headings. Previewing may identify poems that seem to lack formal structure, such as E. E. Cummings's unconventional "l(a" (p. 492); poems written in traditional forms (such as **sonnets**) or in experimental forms, such as Yusef Komunyakaa's **prose poem** "Nude Interrogation" (p. 640); or **concrete poems**, such as George Herbert's 1663 poem "Easter Wings" (p. 643). Identifying these and other distinctive features at this point may help you gain insight into a work later on.

Perhaps the first thing you will notice about a work is its title. Not only can the title give you a general idea of what the work is about, as straightforward titles like "Miss Brill" (p. 185) and "The Cask of Amontillado" (p. 258) do, but it can also call attention to a word or phrase that emphasizes an important idea. For example, the title of Amy Tan's short story "Two Kinds" (p. 471) refers to two kinds of daughters—Chinese and American—identifying the two perspectives that create the story's conflict. A title can also be an allusion to another work. Thus, *The Sound and the Fury*, the title of a novel by William Faulkner, alludes to a speech from Shakespeare's *Macbeth* that reinforces a major theme of the novel. Finally, a title can introduce a symbol that will gain meaning in the course of a work—as the quilt does in Alice Walker's "Everyday Use" (p. 346).

As you preview a text, you may notice other elements—such as paragraphing, capitalization, italics, and punctuation—that provide clues about how to read a work. Such features may or may not be important. At this stage, your goal is to observe, not to analyze or evaluate.

Previewing is a useful strategy not because it provides answers but because it suggests questions to ask later, as you read more closely. For example, *why* does Faulkner's title refer to Shakespeare, and *why* does Herbert shape his poem like a pair of wings? Features such as those described will gain significance as you read more carefully.

Highlighting

When you read a work closely, you will notice additional, more subtle, elements that you may want to examine further. At this point, you should begin **highlighting**—physically marking the text to identify key words or details and note relationships among ideas.

For example, you might notice that particular words or phrases are repeated, as in "The Things They Carried," Tim O'Brien's 1986 short story about the Vietnam War, in which the word *carried* appears again and again. Because this word appears so frequently and because it appears at key points in the story, it helps to reinforce a key theme: that soldiers carry heavy burdens and responsibilities in wartime. Repeated words and phrases are particularly important in poetry. In Dylan Thomas's "Do not go gentle into that good night" (p. 676), for example, the repetition of two of the poem's nineteen lines four times each enhances the poem's rhythmic, almost monotonous, cadence. As you read, you should highlight your text to identify such repeated words and phrases. Later, you can consider *why* these elements are repeated.

During the highlighting stage, you might also pay particular attention to **patterns of imagery** that can help you to interpret the work. When highlighting Robert Frost's "Stopping by Woods on a Snowy Evening" (p. 10), for example, you might identify the related images of silence, cold, and darkness. Later, you can consider their significance.

Checklist Using Highlighting Symbols

When you highlight a text, try these strategies:

- Underline important ideas.
- Box or circle words, phrases, or images that you want to think more about.
- Put question marks beside confusing passages, unfamiliar references, or words that need to be defined.
- Circle related words, ideas, or images and draw lines or arrows to connect them.
- Number incidents that occur in sequence.
- Mark a key portion of the text with a vertical line in the margin.
- Star particularly important ideas.

Annotating

As you highlight a text, you should also **annotate** it, recording your reactions in the form of notes between lines or in the margins. In these notes, you may define new words, identify **allusions** and patterns of language or imagery, summarize key events, list a work's possible themes, suggest a character's motivation, examine the possible significance of a particular symbol, or record questions that occur to you as you read. Ideally, your annotations will help you discover ideas to write about.

The following paragraph from John Updike's 1961 short story "A&P" (p. 179) was highlighted and annotated by a student in an Introduction to Literature course who was responding to the question, "Why does Sammy really quit his job?"

Lengel sighs and begins to look very patient and old and gray. He's been a friend of my parents for years. "Sammy, you don't want to do this to your Mom and Dad," he tells me. It's true, I don't. But it seems to me that once you begin a gesture it's fatal not to go through with it. I fold the apron, "Sammy" stitched in red on the pocket, and put it on the counter, and drop the bow tie on top of it. The bow tie is theirs, if you've ever wondered. "You'll feel this for the rest of your life," Lengel says, and I know that's true, too, but remembering how he made the pretty girl blush makes me so scrunchy inside I punch the No Sale tab and the machine whirs "pee-pul" and the drawer splats out. One advantage to this scene taking place in summer, I can follow this up with a clean exit, there's no fumbling around getting your coat and galoshes, I just saunter into the electric eye in my white shirt that my mother ironed the night before, and the door heaves itself open, and outside the sunshine is skating around on the asphalt.

Is this why he quits?

Sammy reacts to the girl's embarrassment.

Need for a clean exit—Romantic idea.

Does he feel confident? Or is this an act?

Because the instructor had discussed the story in class and given students a specific assignment, these annotations are quite focused. In addition to highlighting important information, the student notes some reactions to the story and tries to interpret the main character's actions.

Often, however, you highlight and annotate a work before you have decided on a topic. In fact, the process of reading and responding to the text can help you find a topic to write about. If you don't yet have a topic, your annotations are likely to be somewhat unfocused, so you will probably need to make additional annotations when your essay's direction is clearer.

Writing about Literature

Writing about literature—or about anything else—is an idiosyncratic process during which many activities occur at once: as you write, you think of ideas; as you think of ideas, you clarify the focus of your essay; and as you clarify your focus, you reshape your paragraphs and sentences and refine your word choice. Even though this process may sound disorganized, it has three distinct stages: *planning*, *drafting*, and *revising and editing*.

Planning an Essay

Considering Your Audience

Sometimes you write primarily for yourself—for example, when you write a journal entry. At other times, you write for others. As you write an essay, consider the special requirements of your **audience**. Is your audience your classmates or just your instructor? Can you assume your readers are familiar with your essay's topic and with any technical terms you will use, or should you include brief plot summaries or definitions of key terms? When you write for your instructors, remember that they are representatives of a larger academic audience that expects accurate information, logical arguments, and a certain degree of stylistic fluency, as well as standard English and correct grammar, mechanics, and spelling. In addition, your instructors expect you to support your statements with specific information, to express yourself clearly and unambiguously, and to document your sources. In short, your instructors want to see how clearly you think and whether you are able to arrange your ideas into a well-organized, coherent essay.

In addition to being members of a general academic audience, your instructors are also members of a particular community of scholars—in this case, those who study literature. By writing about literature, you engage in a dialogue with this community. For this reason, you need to follow certain specific **conventions**—procedures that have become accepted practice due to habitual use. Many of the conventions that apply specifically to writing about literature—matters of style, format, and the like—are discussed in this book. (The checklist on pages 34-35 addresses some of these conventions.)

Understanding Your Purpose

Sometimes you write with a single **purpose** in mind. At other times, you may have more than one purpose. In general terms, you may write for any of the following three reasons:

1. ***Writing to respond*** When you write to **respond**, your goal is to discover and express your reactions to a work. To record your responses, you engage in relatively informal activities, such as *brainstorming* and *journal writing* (see pp. 24-25). As you write, you explore your own ideas, forming and re-forming your impressions of the work.

2. ***Writing to interpret*** When you write to **interpret**, your aim is to explain a work's possible meanings. As you interpret a work of literature, you may summarize, give examples, or compare and contrast the work with other works or with your own experiences. Then, you may go on to analyze the work: as you discuss each of its elements, you put complex statements into your own words, define difficult concepts, and place ideas in context.

3. ***Writing to evaluate*** When you write to **evaluate**, your purpose is to assess a work's literary merits. You may consider not only its aesthetic appeal but also the likelihood that it will retain that appeal over time and across national or

cultural boundaries. As you write, you use your own critical sense and the opinions of experts to help you make judgments about the work.

Note When you write a **literary argument**, your purpose is to **persuade**. See Chapter 3.

Choosing a Topic

Before you begin writing an essay about literature, you should make certain that you understand your assignment. Do you know how much time you have to complete your essay? Are you expected to rely on your own ideas, or are you able to consult outside sources? Is your essay to focus on a specific work or on a particular element of literature? Do you have to write on an assigned topic, or are you free to choose a topic? About how long should your essay be? Do you understand exactly what the assignment is asking you to do? Do you know what format to use?

Sometimes your assignment limits your options by telling you what you should discuss:

- Analyze Thomas Hardy's use of irony in his poem "The Man He Killed."
- Discuss Hawthorne's use of allegory in his short story "Young Goodman Brown."
- Explain Nora's actions at the end of Ibsen's *A Doll's House*.

At other times, your instructor may give you few guidelines other than an essay's required length and format. In such situations, when you must choose a topic on your own, you can often find a topic by brainstorming or writing journal entries. As you engage in these activities, keep in mind that you have many options to choose from:

- You can **explicate** a poem or a passage of a play or short story, doing a close reading and analyzing the text.
- You can **compare two works** of literature. (The Related Works lists that follow many of the selections in this book suggest possible connections.)
- You can **compare two characters** or discuss some trait those characters share.
- You can **trace a common theme**—jealousy, revenge, power, coming of age—in two or more works.
- You can **discuss a common subject**—war, love, nature—in two or more works.
- You can **analyze a single literary element** in one or more works—for example, plot, point of view, or character development.
- You can **focus on a single aspect** of a literary element, such as the use of flashbacks, the effect of a shifting narrative perspective, or the role of a minor character.
- You can **apply a critical theory** to a work of literature—for example, you might apply a feminist perspective to Tillie Olsen's "I Stand Here Ironing" (p. 227).

- You can **consider a work's cultural context**, examining connections between an issue treated in a work of literature—for example, you could discuss racism in Richard Wright's "Big Black Good Man" (p. 246) or postpartum psychosis in Charlotte Perkins Gilman's "The Yellow Wallpaper" (p. 315)—and that same issue as it is treated in professional journals or in the popular press.
- You can **examine some aspect of history or biography** and consider its relationship to a literary work—for example, the influence of World War I on Wilfred Owen's poems.
- You can **explore a problem within a work and propose a possible solution**—for example, you might consider Montresor's possible motives for killing Fortunato in Edgar Allan Poe's "The Cask of Amontillado" (p. 258) and suggest the most likely one.
- You can **compare fiction and film**, exploring similarities and differences between a literary work and a film version of the work—for example, the different endings in Joyce Carol Oates's short story "Where Are You Going, Where Have You Been?" (p. 447) and *Smooth Talk*, the 1985 film version of the story.

Finding Something to Say

Once you have a topic, you have to find something to say about it. The ideas you came up with as you highlighted and annotated can help you formulate a statement that will be the central idea of your essay and can also help you find material that can support that statement.

You can use a variety of strategies to find supporting material:

- You can **freewrite**—that is, write on a topic for a given period of time without pausing to consider style, structure, or content.
- You can discuss ideas with others—friends, classmates, coworkers, instructors, family members, and so on.
- You can do research.

Two additional strategies—*brainstorming* and *keeping a journal*—are especially helpful at this stage of the writing process.

Brainstorming When you **brainstorm**, you record ideas—single words, phrases, or sentences (in the form of statements or questions)—as they occur to you, moving as quickly as possible. Your starting point may be a general assignment, a particular work (or works) of literature, or a specific topic. You can brainstorm at any stage of the writing process—alone or with other students—and you can repeat this activity as often as you like.

A student preparing to write an essay on the relationships between children and parents in four poems brainstormed about each poem. The following excerpt from their notes shows their preliminary reactions to one of the four poems, Adrienne Rich's "A Woman Mourned by Daughters."

Memory: then and now

Then: leaf, straw, dead insect (= light);
ignored

Now: swollen, puffed up, weight (= heavy);
focus of attention controls their
movements.

* Kitchen = a "universe"

Teaspoons, goblets, etc. = concrete
representations of mother; also =
obligations, responsibilities (like
plants and father)

(weigh on them, keep them under her spell)

Milestones of past: weddings, being fed as
children, "You breathe upon us now"

PARADOX? (Dead, she breathes, has weight,
fills house and sky. Alive, she was a dead
insect, no one paid attention to her.)

Keeping a Journal You can record ideas in a journal (a notebook, a small notepad, or a computer file)—and, later, you can use these ideas in your essay. In a **journal**, you can expand your marginal annotations, recording your responses to works you have read, noting questions, exploring emerging ideas, experimenting with possible essay topics, trying to paraphrase or summarize difficult concepts, or speculating about a work's ambiguities. A journal is the place to take chances, to try out ideas that may initially seem frivolous or irrelevant; here you can write until connections become clear or ideas crystallize.

In preparation for writing an essay analyzing the role of Jim—the "gentleman caller" who is invited to meet Laura—the shy, lonely sister of the protagonist in Tennessee Williams's *The Glass Menagerie* (p. 958), a student explored ideas in the following journal entry.

When he tells Laura that being disappointed is not the same as being discouraged, and that he's disappointed but not discouraged, Jim reveals his role as a symbol of the power of newness and change—a "bulldozer" that will clear out whatever is in its path, even delicate people like Laura. But the fact that he is disappointed shows Jim's human side. He has run into problems since high school, and these problems have blocked his progress toward a successful future. Working at the warehouse, Jim needs Tom's friendship to remind him of what he used to be (and what he still can be?), and this shows his insecurity. He isn't as sure of himself as he seems to be.

Seeing Connections

As you review your notes, you try to discover patterns—to see repeated images, similar characters, recurring words and phrases, and interrelated themes or ideas. Identifying these patterns can help you to decide which points to make in your essay and what information you will use to support these points.

A student preparing an essay about D. H. Lawrence's 1920 short story "The Rocking-Horse Winner" made the following list of related ideas.

Secrets

Mother can't feel love
Young son gambles
Son gives mother money
Family lives beyond means
Son gets information from horse

Religion

Gambling becomes like a religion
They all worship money
Specific references: "serious as a church"; "It's as if he had it from heaven"; "secret, religious voice"

Luck

Father is unlucky
Mother is desperate for luck
Son is lucky (ironic)

Deciding on a Thesis

When you are ready, you will express the main idea of your emerging essay in a **thesis statement**—an idea, often expressed in a single sentence, that the rest of your essay will support. This idea should emerge logically out of your highlighting, annotating, brainstorming notes, journal entries, and lists of related ideas. Eventually, you will write a **thesis-and-support essay**: stating your thesis in your introduction, supporting the thesis in the body paragraphs of your essay, and reinforcing the thesis in your conclusion.

An effective thesis statement tells readers what your essay will discuss and how you will approach your material. For this reason, it should be precisely worded, making its point clear to your readers, and it should contain no vague words or imprecise phrases that will make it difficult for readers to follow your discussion.

In addition to being specific, your thesis statement should give your readers an accurate sense of the scope and direction of your essay. It should not make promises that you do not intend to fulfill or include extraneous details that might confuse your readers. If, for example, you are going to write an essay about the dominant image in a poem, your thesis should not imply that you will focus on the poem's setting or tone.

Remember that as you organize your ideas and as you write, you will probably modify and sharpen your thesis. Sometimes you will even begin planning your essay with one thesis in mind and end up with an entirely different one. If this happens, be sure to revise your body paragraphs so that they support your new thesis statement. If you find that your ideas about your topic are changing, don't be concerned; this is how the writing process works. (See pp. 46 for more on stating a thesis.)

Preparing an Outline

Once you have decided on a thesis and have some idea how you will support it, you can begin to plan your essay's structure. At this stage of the writing process, an **outline** can help you to clarify your ideas and show how these ideas relate to one another.

A **scratch outline** is perhaps the most useful kind of outline for a short essay. An informal list of the main points you will discuss in your essay, a scratch outline is more focused than a simple list of related ideas because it presents ideas in the order in which they will be introduced. As its name implies, however, a scratch outline lacks the detail and degree of organization of a more formal outline. The main purpose of a scratch outline is to give you a sense of the shape and order of your essay and thus enable you to begin writing.

A student writing a short essay on Edwin Arlington Robinson's use of irony in his 1910 poem "Miniver Cheevy" used the following scratch outline as a guide.

<u>Speaker's Attitude</u>

Ironic
Cynical
Critical

<u>Diction</u>

Formal
Detached

<u>Allusions</u>

Thebes
Camelot
Priam
Medici

<u>Repeated Words</u>

"Miniver"
"thought"

<u>Regular Rhyme Scheme</u>

Drafting an Essay

A first draft is a preliminary version of your essay, something to react to and revise. Even before you actually begin drafting your essay, however, you should review the material you have collected. To make sure you are ready to begin drafting, take the following three steps:

1. ***Make sure you have collected enough information to support your thesis.*** The points you make are only as convincing as the evidence you present to support them. As you read and take notes, you collect supporting examples from the work or works about which you are writing. How many of these examples you need to use in your draft depends on the scope of your thesis. In general, the broader your thesis, the more material you need to support it. For example, if you were supporting the rather narrow thesis that the speech of a certain character in one scene of a play reveals important information about his motivation, only a few examples would be needed. However, if you wanted to support the broader thesis that Nora and Torvald Helmer in Henrik Ibsen's *A Doll's House* (p. 834) are trapped in their roles, you would need to present a wide range of examples.
2. ***See if the work includes any details that contradict your thesis.*** Before you begin writing, test the validity of your thesis by looking for details that contradict it. For example, if you plan to support the thesis that in *A Doll's House*, Ibsen makes a strong case for the rights of women, you should look for counterexamples. Can you find subtle hints in the play that suggest women should remain locked in their traditional roles and continue to defer to their fathers and husbands? If so, you will want to modify your thesis accordingly.
3. ***Consider whether you need to use outside sources to help you support your thesis.*** You could, for example, strengthen the thesis that *A Doll's House* challenged contemporary attitudes about marriage by including the information that when the play first opened, Ibsen was convinced by an apprehensive theater manager to write an alternative ending. In this new ending, Ibsen had Nora decide, after she stopped briefly to look in at her sleeping children, that she could not leave her family. Sometimes information from a source can even lead you to change your thesis. For example, after reading *A Doll's House*, you might have decided that Ibsen's purpose was to make a strong case for the rights of women. In class, however, you might learn that Ibsen repeatedly said that his play was about the rights of all human beings, not just of women. This information could lead you to a thesis that suggests Torvald is just as trapped in his role as Nora is in hers. Naturally, Ibsen's interpretation of his own work does not invalidate your first judgment, but it does suggest another possible conclusion that is worth investigating.

After carefully evaluating the completeness, relevance, and validity of your supporting material, you can begin drafting your essay, using your scratch outline as a guide. In this first draft, your focus should be on the body of your essay; this is not the time to worry about constructing the "perfect" introduction and conclusion. (In fact, many writers, knowing that their ideas will change as they write, postpone writing these paragraphs until a later draft, preferring instead to begin simply by stating their thesis.) As you write, remember that your first draft will probably not be as clear as you would like it to be; still, it will enable you to see your ideas begin to take shape.

Revising and Editing an Essay

Revision

When you **revise**, you literally "re-see" your draft; sometimes you then go on to reorder and rewrite substantial portions of your essay. Before you are satisfied with your essay, you will probably write several drafts—each more closely focused and more coherent than the previous one.

Strategies for Revision

Two strategies can help you to revise your drafts: *peer review* and *a dialogue with your instructor*.

1. **Peer review** is a process in which students assess each other's work-in-progress. This activity may be carried out in informal sessions during which one student comments on another's draft, or it may be a formal process in which students respond to specific questions posed by the instructor in class or in a discussion online. In either case, one student's reactions can help another student revise.
2. **A dialogue with your instructor**—in a conference or by email—can give you a sense of how to proceed with your revision. Establishing such an oral or written dialogue can help you learn how to respond critically to your own writing, and your reactions to your instructor's comments on any draft can help you to clarify your essay's goals and write drafts that are increasingly consistent with these goals. (If your instructor is not available, try to schedule a conference with a writing center tutor.)

As you move through successive drafts, the task of revising your essay will be easier if you follow a systematic process. As you read and react to your essay, begin by assessing the effectiveness of the larger elements—for example, your thesis statement and key supporting ideas—and then move on to examine increasingly smaller elements.

Thesis Statement First, reconsider your **thesis statement**. Is it carefully and precisely worded? Does it provide a realistic idea of what your essay will cover? Does it make a point that is worth supporting?

Vague: Many important reasons exist to explain why Margot Macomber's shooting of her husband was probably intentional.

Revised: Although Hemingway's text states that Margot Macomber "shot at the buffalo," a careful analysis of her relationship with her husband suggests that in fact she intended to kill him.

Vague: Dickens's characters are a lot like those of Addison and Steele.

Revised: With their familiar physical and moral traits, Charles Dickens's minor characters are similar to the "characters" created by the eighteenth-century essayists Joseph Addison and Richard Steele for the newspaper the *Spectator.*

Supporting Ideas Next, assess the appropriateness of your **supporting ideas**, considering whether you present enough support for your thesis and whether all the details you include are relevant to that thesis. Make sure you have supported your key points with specific, concrete examples from the work or works you are discussing, briefly summarizing key events, quoting dialogue or description, and describing characters or settings. Make certain, however, that your own ideas are central to the essay and that you have not substituted plot summary for analysis and interpretation. Your goal is to draw a conclusion about one or more works and to support that conclusion with pertinent details. If an event in a story you are analyzing supports a point you wish to make, include a *brief* summary then explain its relevance to the point you are making.

In the following excerpt from an essay on a short story by James Joyce, the first sentence briefly summarizes a key event, and the second sentence explains its significance.

> At the end of James Joyce's "Counterparts," when Farrington returns home after a day of frustration and abuse at work, his reaction is to strike out at his son Tom. This act shows that although he and his son are similarly victimized, Farrington is also the counterpart of his tyrannical boss.

Topic Sentences Now, turn your attention to the **topic sentences** that present the main ideas of your body paragraphs. Make sure that each topic sentence is clearly worded and that it signals the direction of your discussion.

Be especially careful to avoid abstractions and vague generalities in topic sentences. Also avoid words and phrases such as *involves*, *deals with*, *concerns*, *revolves around*, and *pertains to*, which are likely to make your topic sentences wordy and imprecise.

Vague: One similarity involves the dominance of the men by women. (What is the similarity?)

Revised: In both stories, a man is dominated by a woman.

Vague: There is one reason for the fact that Jay Gatsby remains a mystery. (What is the reason?)

Revised: Because *The Great Gatsby* is narrated by the outsider Nick Carraway, Jay Gatsby himself remains a mystery.

When revising topic sentences that are intended to move readers from one point (or one section of your essay) to another, be sure the relationship between the ideas they link is clear. A topic sentence should include transitions that look back at the previous paragraphs as well as ahead to the paragraph it introduces.

Unclear: Now, the poem's imagery will be discussed.

Revised: Another reason for the poem's effectiveness is its unusual imagery.

Unclear: The sheriff's wife is another interesting character in *Trifles*.

Revised: Like her friend Mrs. Hale, the sheriff's wife in *Trifles* also has mixed feelings about what Mrs. Wright has done.

Introduction and Conclusion When you are satisfied with the body of your essay, you can turn your attention to your essay's *introduction* and *conclusion*.

The **introduction** of an essay about literature should identify the works to be discussed and their authors and indicate the emphasis of the discussion to follow. Depending on your purpose and on your essay's topic, you may want to provide some historical background or biographical information or briefly discuss the work in relation to similar works. Like all introductions, the one you write for an essay about literature should create interest in your topic and include a clear thesis statement.

The following introduction, though acceptable for a first draft, needs revision.

Draft: *Revenge*, which is defined as "the chance to retaliate, get satisfaction, take vengeance, or inflict damage or injury in return for an injury, insult, etc.," is a major theme in many of the stories we have read. The stories that will be discussed here deal with a variety of ways to seek revenge. In my essay, I will consider some of these differences.

Although the student clearly identifies her essay's topic, neither the works that will be discussed nor the particular point to be made about revenge is identified. The tired opening strategy, a dictionary definition, is not likely to create interest in the topic, and the announcement of the writer's intention in the last sentence is awkward and unnecessary. The following revised introduction is much more effective.

Revised: In Edgar Allan Poe's "The Cask of Amontillado," Montresor vows revenge on Fortunato for an unspecified "insult"; in Ring Lardner's "Haircut," Paul, a young man with an intellectual disability, gets even with a cruel practical joker who has taunted him for years. Both of these stories present characters who seek revenge, and both stories end in murder. However, the murderers' motivations are presented very differently. In "Haircut," the narrator is unaware of the significance of many events, and his ignorance helps to create sympathy for the murderer; in "The Cask of Amontillado," where the narrator is actually the murderer, Montresor's inability to offer a convincing motive turns the reader against him.

In your **conclusion**, you reinforce your thesis and perhaps sum up your essay's main points, then you make a graceful exit.

The conclusion that follows is acceptable for a first draft, but it needs further development.

Draft: Although the characters of Montresor and Paul were created by different authors at different times, they do have similar motives and goals. However, they are portrayed very differently.

The following revised conclusion reinforces the essay's main point, effectively incorporating a brief quotation from "The Cask of Amontillado":

Revised: What is significant is not whether each murderer's act is justified but rather how each murderer, and each victim, is portrayed by the narrator. Montresor—driven by a thirst to avenge a "thousand injuries" as well as a final insult—is shown to be sadistic and unrepentant; in "Haircut," it is Jim, the victim, whose sadism and lack of remorse are eventually revealed to the reader.

Sentences and Words Now, focus on the individual sentences and words of your essay. Begin by evaluating your **transitions**, the words and phrases that link sentences and paragraphs. Be sure that every necessary transitional element has been supplied and that each word or phrase you have selected accurately conveys the exact relationship (sequence, contradiction, and so on) between ideas.

When you are satisfied with the clarity and appropriateness of your essay's transitions, consider sentence variety and word choice:

- Be sure you have varied your sentence structure. You will bore your readers if all your sentences begin with the subject ("He … He …"; "The story … The story…").
- Make sure that all the words you have selected communicate your ideas accurately and that you have not used vague, inexact diction. For example, saying that a character is *bad* is not as helpful as describing that character as *ruthless*, *conniving*, or *malicious*.
- Eliminate subjective expressions, such as *I think*, *in my opinion*, *I believe*, *it seems to me*, and *I feel*. These phrases weaken your essay by suggesting that its ideas are "only" your opinions and have no objective validity.

Documentation Make certain that all references to sources are integrated smoothly into your sentences and that all information that is not your own is documented appropriately. For specific information on using and documenting sources, see Chapter 5.

Checklist Using Sources

When you incorporate source material into your essays, follow these guidelines:

- Acknowledge all material from sources, including the literary work or works under discussion, using the documentation style of the Modern Language Association (MLA).
- Combine paraphrases, summaries, and quotations with your own interpretations, weaving quotations smoothly into your essay. Introduce the words or ideas of others with a phrase that identifies their source ("According to Richard Wright's biographer..."), and end with appropriate parenthetical documentation.
- Use quotations *only* when something vital would be lost if you did not reproduce the author's exact words.
- Integrate short quotations (four lines or fewer of prose or three lines or fewer of poetry) smoothly into your essay. Use a slash (/) with one space on either side to separate lines of poetry. Be sure to enclose quotations in quotation marks.
- Set off quotations of more than four lines of prose or more than three lines of poetry by indenting one-half inch from the left-hand margin. Double-space, and do not use quotation marks. If you are quoting just one paragraph, do not indent the first line.
- Use ellipses—three spaced periods—to indicate that you have omitted material within a quotation (but never use ellipses at the beginning of a quoted passage).
- Use brackets to indicate that you have added words to a quotation: As Earl notes, "[Willie] is a modern-day Everyman" (201). Use brackets to alter a quotation so that it fits grammatically into your sentence: Wilson says that Miller "offer[s] audiences a dark view of the present" (74).
- Place commas and periods *inside* quotation marks: According to Robert Coles, the child could "make others smile."
- Place punctuation marks other than commas and periods *outside* quotation marks: What does Frost mean when he says, "a poem must ride on its own melting"? However, if the punctuation mark is part of the quoted material, place it *inside* the quotation marks: In "Mending Wall," Frost asks, "Why do they make good neighbors?"

- When citing part of a short story or novel, supply the page number (143). For a poem, supply line numbers (3–5), including the word *line* or *lines* in just the first reference. For a play, supply act, scene, and line numbers in arabic numerals (2.2.17-22).
- Include a works-cited list.

Editing and Proofreading

Once you have finished revising, you **edit**—that is, you make certain that your essay's grammar, punctuation, spelling, and mechanics are correct. Always run a spell check but remember that you still have to **proofread**, looking carefully for errors that the spell checker will not identify. These include homophones (*brake* incorrectly used instead of *break*), typos that create correctly spelled words (*work* instead of *word*), and words (such as a technical or foreign term or a writer's name) that may not be in your computer's dictionary. If you use a grammar checker, remember that although grammar programs may identify potential problems—long sentences, for example—they may not be able to determine whether a particular long sentence is grammatically correct (let alone stylistically pleasing). Be sure to double-check any problems a spell checker or grammar checker highlights in your writing.

As you edit, pay particular attention to the special conventions of literary essays, some of which are addressed in the following checklist. When your editing is complete, give your essay a descriptive title. Before you print your final copy, be sure that its format conforms to your instructor's requirements.

Checklist Conventions of Writing about Literature

When you write about works of literature, follow these guidelines:

- Use present-tense verbs when discussing works of literature: "The character of Mrs. Mallard's husband is not developed. . . ."
- Use past-tense verbs only when discussing historical events ("Owen's poem conveys the destructiveness of World War I, which at the time the poem **was** written **was** considered to be . . ."); when presenting historical or biographical data ("Her first novel, which **was** published in 1811 when Austen **was** thirty-six, . . ."); or when identifying events that occurred prior to the time of the story's main action ("Miss Emily is a recluse; since her father's death she **has lived** alone except for a servant").
- Avoid unnecessary plot summary. Your goal is to draw a conclusion about one or more works and to support that conclusion with pertinent details. If a plot detail supports a point you wish to make, a *brief*

summary is acceptable. Remember, however, that plot summary is no substitute for analysis.

- Use literary terms accurately. For example, be careful not to confuse *narrator* or *speaker* with *author;* feelings or opinions expressed by a narrator or character do not necessarily represent those of the author. You should not say, "In the poem's last stanza, *Frost* expresses his indecision" when you mean that the poem's *speaker* is indecisive.
- Italicize titles of novels and plays; place titles of short stories and poems within quotation marks.
- Refer to authors of literary works by their full names (*Edgar Allan Poe*) in your first reference to them and by their last names (*Poe*) in subsequent references. Never refer to authors by their first names, and never use titles that indicate marital status (*Flannery O'Connor* or *O'Connor*, never *Flannery* or *Miss O'Connor*).
- Be careful not to make sweeping or unrealistic claims. Remember that the support you present cannot "prove" that what you are saying is true, so choose verbs like *demonstrate, show, suggest,* and *indicate* rather than *prove*.

Three Model Student Essays

The three papers in this section were written by students in an Introduction to Literature course. The first, by John Frei, analyzes the short story "The Secret Lion" (p. 222); the second, by Catherine Whittaker, compares the poems "Those Winter Sundays" (p. 672) and "Digging" (p. 673); the third, by Kimberly Allison, discusses the play *Trifles* (p. 820). As they planned, drafted, and revised these essays, the students followed the writing process described in this chapter.

Frei 1

John Frei

Professor Nyysola

English 102

14 January 2023

"The Secret Lion": Everything Changes

The first paragraph of Alberto Alvaro Ríos's "The Secret Lion" presents a twelve-year-old's view of growing up: everything changes. When the magician pulls a tablecloth out from under a pile of dishes,

Opening paragraph identifies work and author.

Parenthetical documentation identifies source of quotation.

Frei 2

the child is amazed at the "staying-the-same part" (222); adults focus on the tablecloth. As adults, we have the benefit of experience; we know the trick will work as long as the technique is correct.

When we become adults, we gain confidence, but we lose our innocence, and we lose our sense of wonder. The price we pay for knowledge is a permanent sense of loss, and this trade-off is central to "The Secret Lion," a story whose key symbols reinforce its central theme: that change is inevitable and always accompanied by loss.

Thesis statement

The golf course is one symbol that helps to convey this theme. When the boys first see the golf course, it is "heaven" (225). Lush and green and carefully tended, it is very different from the dry, brown Arizona landscape and the polluted arroyo. In fact, to the boys it is another world, as exotic as Oz and ultimately as unreal. Before long, the Emerald City becomes black and white again. They learn that there is no such thing as a "Coke-holder," that their "acting 'rich'" is just an act, and that their heaven is only a golf course (225). As the narrator acknowledges, "Something got taken away from us that moment. Heaven" (226).

Topic sentence identifies one key symbol.

The arroyo, a dry gulch that can fill up with water, is another symbol that reflects the idea of the inevitability of change and of the loss that accompanies change. It is a special, Edenlike place for the boys—a place where they can rebel by shouting forbidden words and by swimming in forbidden waters. Although it represents a retreat from the disillusionment of the golf course, and it is clearly second choice, it is still their "personal Mississippi" (222), full of possibilities. Eventually, though, the arroyo too disappoints the boys, and they stop going there. As the narrator says, "Nature seemed to keep pushing us around one way or another, teaching us the same thing every place we ended up" (223). The lesson they keep learning is that nothing is permanent.

Topic sentence identifies another key symbol.

The grinding ball, round and perfect, suggests permanence and stability. When the boys find it, however, they realize at once that they cannot keep it forever, just as they cannot remain balanced forever between childhood and adulthood. Like a child's life, the ball is perfect but temporary. Burying it is their desperate attempt to stop time, to preserve perfection in an imperfect world, innocence in an adult world.

Topic sentence identifies another key symbol.

Frei 3

However, the boys are already twelve years old, and they have learned nature's lesson well enough to know that this action will not work.

Even if they had been able to find the ball, the perfection and the innocence it suggests to them would still be unattainable. Perhaps that is why they do not try very hard to find it.

Like the story's other symbols, the secret lion itself suggests the most profound kind of change: the movement from innocence to experience, from childhood to adulthood, from expectation to disappointment to resignation. The narrator explains that when he was twelve, "something happened that we didn't have a name for, but it was there nonetheless like a lion, and roaring, roaring that way the biggest things do. Everything changed" (222). School was different, girls were different, language was different. Despite its loud roar, the lion remained paradoxically "secret," unnoticed until it passed. Like adolescence, the secret lion is a roaring disturbance that unsettles everything for a brief time and then passes, leaving everything changed.

Topic sentence identifies final (and most important) symbol.

In an attempt to make things stay the same, to make time stand still, the boys bury the grinding ball "because it was perfect ... It was the lion" (226). The grinding ball is "like that place, that whole arroyo" (223): secret and perfect. The ball, arroyo, and lion are all perfect, but all, ironically, are temporary. The first paragraph of "The Secret Lion" tells us, "Everything changed" (222); by the last paragraph, we learn what this change means: "Things get taken away" (226). In other words, change implies loss. Heaven turns out to be just a golf course; the round, perfect object is only "a cannonball thing used in mining" (223); the arroyo is just a polluted stream; and childhood is just a phase. "Things get taken away," and this knowledge that things do not last is the lion, secret yet roaring.

Conclusion

Frei 4

Works Cited

Ríos, Alberto Alvaro. "The Secret Lion." *Portable Literature: Reading, Reacting, Writing*, edited by Laurie G. Kirszner and Stephen R. Mandell, 10th ed., Cengage, 2024, pp. 222-226.

Whittaker 1

Catherine Whittaker

Professor Jackson

English 102

5 January 2023

Digging for Memories

Robert Hayden's "Those Winter Sundays" and Seamus Heaney's "Digging" are two poems that are tributes to the speakers' fathers. Although the depiction of the families and the tones of the two poems are different, the common thread of love between fathers and children extends through the two poems, and each speaker is inspired by his father's example.

Introduction

Thesis statement

Many other poets have written about children and their fathers. Some of these poems express regret and gratitude. For example, Judith Ortiz Cofer in "My Father in the Navy: A Childhood Memory" writes a touching tribute to her father, whose homecomings were so eagerly awaited. In other poems, such as Theodore Roethke's "My Papa's Waltz," fathers are depicted as imperfect, vulnerable people who try to cope with life as well as possible.

References to poems include complete authors' names and titles.

As these and other poems reveal, reflections on childhood can bring complex memories to light, as they do for Hayden's and Heaney's speakers. Now adults, they reminisce about their childhoods with a mature sense of enlightenment not found in children. Both speakers describe their fathers' hard work and dedication to their families. For example, Hayden's speaker remembers that even after working hard all week, his father would get up early on Sunday to warm the house for his sleeping children. The speaker vividly portrays his father's hands, describing "cracked hands that ached / from labor in the weekday weather" (lines 3-4). Still, these same hands not only built the fires that drove out the cold but also polished his children's good shoes. In a similar way, Heaney's speaker reminisces about his father's and grandfather's digging of soil and sod, pointing out their skill and their dedication to their tasks.

First point of similarity: both poems focus on memory.

First reference to lines of poetry includes *line* or *lines*. Subsequent references include just line numbers.

Whittaker 2

The fathers in these poems appear to be hard workers, laborers who struggled to support their families. Not only were they dedicated to their work, but they also loved their children. Looking back, Hayden's speaker realizes that, although his childhood may not have been perfect and his family life was not entirely without problems, his father loved him. Heaney's description of the potato digging allows us to imagine a loving family led by a father and grandfather who worked together and included the children in both work and celebration. Heaney's speaker grows into a man who has nothing but respect for his father and grandfather, wishing to be like them and to somehow fill their shoes.

Second point of similarity: both fathers are hard workers.

Although some similarities exist between the fathers (and the sons) in the poems, the family life the two poems depict is very different. Perhaps it is the tone of each poem that best reveals the family atmosphere. The tone of "Digging" is wholesome, earthy, natural, and happy, emphasizing the healthy and caring nature of the speaker's childhood. Heaney's speaker seems to have no bad memories of his father or family. In contrast, the tone of Hayden's poem is very much like the coldness of the Sunday mornings he remembers. Even though the father warmed the house, the "chronic angers of that house" (9) did not leave with the cold. As a child, the speaker seems to have resented his father, blaming him for the family's problems. The warm relationship readers see between the father and the son in Heaney's poem is absent in Hayden's.

Focus shifts to contrast between the two poems.

In spite of these differences, readers cannot go away from either poem without the impression that both speakers learned important lessons from their fathers. Both fathers had a great amount of inner strength and were dedicated to their families. As the years have passed, Hayden's speaker has come to realize the depth of his father's devotion to his family. He uses the image of the "blueblack cold" (2) that was splintered and broken by the fires lovingly prepared by his father to suggest the father's efforts to keep his family free from harm. The cold suggests the tensions of the family, but the father is determined to force these tensions out of the house through his "austere and lonely offices" (14).

Focus returns to parallels between the two poems. Third point of similarity: both speakers learn from fathers (discussed in two paragraphs).

Whittaker 3

In Heaney's poem, the father—and the grandfather—also had a profound impact on the young speaker. As the memories come pouring back, the speaker's admiration for the men who came before him forces him to reflect on his own life and work. He realizes that he will never have the ability (or the desire) to do the physical labor of his relatives: "I've no spade to follow men like them" (28). However, just as the spade was the tool of his father and grandfather, the pen will be the tool with which the speaker will work. The shovel suggests the hard work, effort, and determination of the men who came before him, and the pen is the literary equivalent of the shovel. Heaney's speaker has been inspired by his father and grandfather, and he hopes to accomplish with a pen in the world of literature what they accomplished with a shovel on the land.

"Digging" and "Those Winter Sundays" are poems written from the perspective of adult sons who admire and appreciate their fathers. Childhood memories not only evoke vivid images of the past but also lead the speakers to insight and enlightenment. Long after childhood, the fathers' influence over their sons is evident; only now, however, do the speakers appreciate its true importance.

Conclusion reinforces thesis.

Whittaker 4

Works Cited

Hayden, Robert. "Those Winter Sundays." Kirszner and Mandell, pp. 672-73.

Heaney, Seamus. "Digging." Kirszner and Mandell, pp. 673-74.

Kirszner, Laurie G., and Stephen R. Mandell, editors. *Portable Literature: Reading, Reacting, Writing*. 10th ed., Cengage, 2024.

Allison 1

Kimberly Allison

Professor Johnson

English 1013

3 January 2023

Desperate Measures: Acts of Defiance in *Trifles*

Susan Glaspell wrote her best-known play, *Trifles*, in 1916, at a time when married women were beginning to challenge their socially defined roles, realizing that their identities as wives kept them in a subordinate position in society. Because women were demanding more autonomy, traditional institutions such as marriage, which confined women to the home and made them mere extensions of their husbands, were beginning to be re-examined.

Opening sentence identifies author and work.

Introduction places play in historical context.

Evidently touched by these concerns, Glaspell chose as her play's protagonist a married woman, Minnie Wright, who challenged society's expectations in a very extreme way: by murdering her husband. Minnie's defiant act has occurred before the action begins; during the play, two women, Mrs. Peters and Mrs. Hale, who accompany their husbands on an investigation of the murder scene, piece together the details of the situation surrounding the murder. As the events unfold, however, it becomes clear that the focus of *Trifles* is not on who killed John Wright but on the themes of the subordinate role of women, the confinement of the wife in the home, and the experiences all women share. With these themes, Glaspell shows her audience the desperate measures women had to take to achieve autonomy.

Thesis statement

The subordinate role of women, particularly Minnie's role in her marriage, becomes evident in the first few minutes of the play, when Mr. Hale observes that the victim, John Wright, had little concern for his wife's opinions: "I didn't know as what his wife wanted made much difference to John—" (821). Here Mr. Hale suggests that Mrs. Wright was powerless to resist the wishes of her husband. Indeed, as these characters imply, Mrs. Wright's every act and thought was controlled by her husband, who tried to break her spirit by forcing her to stay alone in the house, performing repetitive domestic chores. Mrs. Wright's only source

Topic sentence identifies first point essay will discuss: women's subordinate role.

Allison 2

of power in the household was her kitchen work, a situation that Mrs. Peters and Mrs. Hale understand because their own behavior is also determined by their husbands. Therefore, when Sheriff Peters makes fun of Minnie's concern about her preserves, saying, "Well, can you beat the women! Held for murder and worryin' about her preserves" (823), he is actually criticizing all three of the women for focusing on domestic matters rather than on the murder that has been committed. Indeed, the sheriff's comment suggests that he assumes women's lives are trivial, an attitude that influences the thoughts and speech of all three men.

Mrs. Peters and Mrs. Hale are similar to Minnie Wright in another way as well: throughout the play, they are confined to the kitchen of the Wrights' house. As a result, the kitchen becomes the focal point of the play—and, ironically, the women find that the kitchen holds the clues to Mrs. Wright's loneliness and to the details of the murder. Mrs. Peters and Mrs. Hale remain confined to the kitchen while their husbands enter and exit the house at will. This situation mirrors Minnie Wright's daily life, as she remained in the home while her husband went to work and into town. As they move about the kitchen, the two women discuss Minnie Wright's isolation: "Not having children makes less work—but it makes a quiet house, and Wright out to work all day, and no company when he did come in" (828). Beginning to identify with Mrs. Wright's loneliness, Mrs. Peters and Mrs. Hale recognize that, busy in their own homes, they have participated in isolating and confining Minnie Wright. Mrs. Hale declares, "Oh, I *wish* I'd come over here once in a while! That was a crime! That was a crime! Who's going to punish that? ... I might have known she needed help!" (831).

Topic sentence introduces second point essay will discuss: women's confinement in the home.

Soon the two women discover that Mrs. Wright's only connection to the outside world was her bird, the symbol of her confinement; she herself was a caged bird who was kept from singing and communicating with others because of her husband. Piecing together the evidence—the disorderly kitchen, the misstitched quilt pieces, and the dead canary—the women come to believe that John Wright broke the bird's neck, just as he had broken his wife's spirit. At this point, Mrs. Peters and Mrs. Hale understand the connection between the dead canary and Minnie Wright's

Transitional paragraph discusses women's observations and conclusions.

motivation. The stage directions describe the moment when the women become aware of the truth behind the murder: "*Their eyes meet,*" and the women share "*A look of growing comprehension, of horror*" (829).

Through their observations and discussions in Mrs. Wright's kitchen, Mrs. Hale and Mrs. Peters come to understand the commonality of women's experiences. Mrs. Hale speaks for both of them when she says, "I know how things can be—for women ... We all go through the same thing—it's all just a different kind of the same thing" (831). And once the two women realize the experiences they share, they begin to recognize that they must join together to challenge their male-oriented society; although their experiences may seem trivial to the men, the "trifles" of their lives are significant to them. They realize that Minnie's independence and identity were crushed by her husband and that their own husbands also believe that women's lives are trivial and unimportant. These realizations lead them to commit an act as defiant as the one that got Minnie into trouble: they conceal their discovery from their husbands and from the law.

Topic sentence introduces third point essay will discuss: experiences women share.

Significantly, Mrs. Peters does acknowledge that "the law is the law" (826), yet she still seems to believe that because Mr. Wright treated his wife badly, she was justified in killing him. They also realize, however, that for men the law is black and white and that an all-male jury will not consider the extenuating circumstances that prompted Minnie Wright to kill her husband. Even if Mrs. Wright were allowed to communicate to the all-male court the psychological abuse she has suffered, the law would undoubtedly view her experience as trivial because a woman who complained about how her husband treated her would be seen as ungrateful.

Nevertheless, because Mrs. Hale and Mrs. Peters empathize with Mrs. Wright's situation, they suppress the evidence they find, enduring their husbands' condescension rather than standing up to them. Through this desperate action, the women break through the boundaries of their social role, just as Minnie Wright has done. Although Mrs. Wright is imprisoned for her crime, she has freed herself; and although Mrs. Peters and Mrs. Hale conceal their knowledge, fearing the men will laugh at them, these women are really challenging society and thus freeing themselves as well.

Allison 4

In *Trifles,* Susan Glaspell addresses many of the problems shared by early-twentieth-century women, including their subordinate status and their confinement in the home. To emphasize the pervasiveness of these problems and the desperate measures women had to take to break out of restrictive social roles, Glaspell does more than focus on the plight of a woman who has ended her isolation and loneliness by committing a heinous crime against society. By presenting characters who demonstrate the vast differences between male and female experience, she illustrates how men define the roles of women and how women must challenge these roles in search of their own significance in society and their eventual independence.

Conclusion places play in historical context.

Allison 5

Work Cited

Glaspell, Susan. *Trifles. Portable Literature: Reading, Reacting, Writing,* edited by Laurie G. Kirszner and Stephen R. Mandell, 10th ed., Cengage, 2024 pp. 820-833.

Chapter

3

Writing Literary Arguments

Learning Objectives

After reading this chapter, you will be able to. . .

- Define the purpose of a literary argument.
- Develop a suitable topic for a literary argument.
- Recognize the qualities of a debatable thesis.
- Identify the need for solid evidence to convince a skeptical audience.
- Respond to opposing views.
- Explain the need to be fair and unbiased.
- Define the six elements of a literary argument.

Many of the essays you write about literature are **expository**—that is, you write to give information to readers. For example, you might discuss the rhyme or meter of a poem or examine the interaction of two characters in a play. Other essays you write, however, may be **arguments**—that is, you take a debatable position on a literary topic and attempt to change readers' minds about it. For example, you might argue that the boy's quest in James Joyce's short story "Araby" (p. 296) has symbolic meaning or that Sammy, the main character in John Updike's short story "A&P" (p. 179), is sexist.

When you write a literary argument, you follow the same process you do when you write any essay about a literary topic. However, because the purpose of an argument is to convince readers, you need to use some additional strategies to present your ideas.

Planning a Literary Argument

Choosing a Topic

Your first step in writing a literary argument will be to decide on a topic to write about. Ideally, your topic should be one that you want to explore further. It stands to reason that the more your topic interests you, the more willing you will be to do some serious research and some hard thinking.

Your topic should also be narrow enough for you to develop within your page limit. After all, in an argumentative essay, you will have to present your own ideas and supply convincing support while also addressing opposing arguments. If your topic is too broad, you will not be able to discuss it in enough detail.

Finally, your topic should be interesting to your readers. Keep in mind that some topics—such as the significance of the two roads in Robert Frost's poem "The Road Not Taken" (p. 605)—have been written about so often that you will probably not be able to say anything new or interesting about them. Instead, choose a topic that allows you to say something original.

Developing an Argumentative Thesis

After you have chosen a topic, your next step is to develop a **thesis**—one that takes a stand on an issue. Because an argumentative essay attempts to change the way readers think, it should focus on a thesis about which reasonable people may disagree. In other words, it must be **debatable**; that is, it must have at least two sides. A factual statement is therefore not appropriate as a thesis.

Factual Statement: Nora is Torvald Helmer's long-suffering wife in Henrik Ibsen's play *A Doll's House*.

Debatable Thesis: More than a stereotypical long-suffering wife, Nora Helmer in Henrik Ibsen's play *A Doll's House* is a complex character.

One way to make sure that your thesis takes a stand is to try to formulate an **antithesis**—a statement that takes an arguable position opposite from yours. If you can construct an antithesis, you can be certain that your thesis statement is debatable. If you cannot, your thesis statement needs further revision.

Thesis Statement: The last line of Richard Wright's short story "Big Black Good Man" indicates that Jim was fully aware all along of Olaf's deep-seated racial prejudice.

Antithesis: The last line of Richard Wright's short story "Big Black Good Man" indicates that Jim remained unaware of Olaf's feelings toward him.

Note Keep in mind that you can never prove an argumentative thesis conclusively. If you could, there would be no argument. The best you can do is provide enough evidence to establish a high probability that your thesis is reasonable.

Checklist Developing an Argumentative Thesis

To make sure you have an effective argumentative thesis, consider these questions:

- Does your thesis statement make clear to readers what position you are taking?
- Can you formulate an antithesis?
- Can you support your thesis with evidence from the text and from research?

Defining Your Terms

You should always define the key terms you use in your argument. For example, if you are using the term *narrator* in an essay, make sure that readers know whether you are referring to a first-person or a third-person narrator. In addition, you may need to clarify the difference between an **unreliable narrator**—someone who misrepresents or misinterprets events—and a **reliable narrator**—someone who accurately describes events. Without a clear definition of these terms, readers would have a difficult time understanding the point you are making.

Defining Your Terms

Be especially careful to use precise terms in your thesis statement. Avoid vague and judgmental words, such as *wrong, bad, good, right,* and *immoral.*

Vague: The poem "Birmingham Sunday (September 15, 1963)" by Langston Hughes shows how bad racism can be.

Clearer: The poem "Birmingham Sunday (September 15, 1963)" by Langston Hughes makes a moving statement about how pervasive and dehumanizing racism can be.

Considering Your Audience

As you plan your essay, keep your audience in mind. For example, if you are writing about a work that has been discussed in class, you can assume that your readers are familiar with it; include plot summary only when it is needed to illustrate a point you are making. Keep in mind that you will be addressing an academic audience—your instructor and possibly some students. For this reason, be sure to follow the conventions of writing about literature as well as the conventions of standard written English. (For information on the conventions of writing about literature, see the checklist in Chapter 2, pp. 34–35.)

When you write an argumentative essay, you should assume that you are addressing a **skeptical audience**—one that questions and needs to be convinced. Remember, your thesis is debatable, so not everyone will agree with you. And even if your readers are sympathetic to your position, you cannot assume that they will simply accept your ideas without question.

The strategies you use to convince your readers will vary according to how they respond to your thesis. Somewhat skeptical readers may need to see only that your argument is logical and that your evidence is solid. More skeptical readers, however, may need to see that you understand their reservations and that you concede some of your points. Of course, you may never be able to convince hostile readers that your position is reasonable. The best you can hope for is that these readers will acknowledge the strengths of your argument even if they do not accept your conclusion.

Refuting Opposing Arguments

As you develop your literary argument, you may need to **refute**—disprove or raise doubts about—opposing arguments by demonstrating that they are false, misguided, exaggerated, or illogical. By summarizing and refuting opposing views, you make opposing arguments seem less credible; thus, you strengthen your case. When an opposing argument is so strong that it cannot be dismissed, you should concede its strength and then discuss its limitations.

Notice in the following paragraph how a student refutes the argument that Homer Barron, a character in William Faulkner's short story "A Rose for Emily," is a gay man.

Summary of opposing argument

A number of critics have suggested that Homer Barron, Miss Emily's suitor, is a gay man. Actually, there is some evidence in the story to support this interpretation. For example, the narrator points out that Homer "liked men" and that

Acknowledgment of argument's strengths

he was not "a marrying man" (Faulkner 224). In addition, the narrator describes Homer as wearing yellow gloves when he took Emily for drives. According to the critic William Greenslade, in the 1890s yellow was associated with being gay (24). This evidence does not in itself establish that Homer is a gay male, however.

Refutation

During the nineteenth century, many men preferred the company of other men (as many do today). This, in itself, did not mean they were sexually attracted to other men. Neither does the fact that Homer wore yellow gloves. According to the narrator, Homer was a man who liked to dress well. It is certainly possible that he wore these gloves to impress Miss Emily, a woman he was trying to attract.

Using Evidence Effectively

Supporting Your Literary Argument

Many literary arguments are built on **assertions**—statements made about a debatable topic—backed by **evidence**—supporting examples in the form of references to the text, quotations, and the opinions of literary critics. For example, if you stated that Torvald Helmer, Nora's husband in Henrik Ibsen's play *A Doll's House*, is as much a victim of society as his wife is, you could support this assertion with quotations and examples from the play. You could also paraphrase, summarize, or quote the ideas of literary critics who also hold this opinion. Remember, only assertions that are **self-evident** ("All plays include characters and dialogue.") or **factual** ("*A Doll's House* was published in 1879.") need no supporting evidence. All other kinds of assertions require support.

Establishing Credibility

Some people bring **credibility** with them whenever they write. When a well-known literary critic evaluates the contributions of a particular writer, you can assume that the critic speaks with authority. (Although you might question the critic's opinions, you do not question the critic's expertise.) But most people do not have this kind of credibility. When you write a literary argument, you must constantly work to establish credibility. You do this by *demonstrating knowledge*, *maintaining a reasonable tone*, and *presenting yourself as someone worth listening to*.

Demonstrating Knowledge

One way to establish credibility is by presenting your own ideas about a subject. A clear argument and compelling support can demonstrate to readers that you know what you are talking about.

You can also show readers that you have thoroughly researched your subject. By including important research sources and by providing accurate documentation, you demonstrate that you have done the necessary background reading. Including a range of sources—not just one or two—suggests that you are well acquainted with your subject. Remember, however, that questionable sources, inaccurate (or missing) documentation, and factual and grammatical errors can undermine your credibility. For some readers, an undocumented quotation or even a misspelled name can call an entire argument into question.

Maintaining a Reasonable Tone

Your **tone**—your attitude toward your readers or subject—is almost as important as the information you present. Talk *to* your readers, not *at* them. If you lecture your readers or appear to talk down to them, you will alienate them. Generally speaking, readers are more likely to respond to a writer who seems fair and respectful than one who seems strident or condescending.

As you write, use moderate language, and qualify your statements so that they seem reasonable. Avoid absolutes such as *all*, *never*, *always*, *definitely*, and *in every case*, which can make your statements seem simplistic, exaggerated, or unrealistic. For example, the statement, "In 'Doe Season,' the ocean definitely symbolizes Andy's attachment to her mother," leaves no room for other interpretations. A more measured and accurate statement might be, "In 'Doe Season,' the use of the ocean as a symbol suggests Andy's identification with her mother and her realization that she is becoming a woman."

Presenting Yourself as Someone Worth Listening To

When you write a literary argument, present yourself as someone worth listening to. Make your points confidently, and don't apologize for your views. For example, do not use phrases such as "In my opinion," "It seems to me," and "Although I am not an expert," which undercut your credibility. Finally, avoid slang and colloquialisms (unless you are quoting dialog).

Being Fair

Because argument promotes one position over all others, it is seldom objective. However, college writing requires that you stay within the bounds of fairness and avoid **bias**—opinions based on preconceived ideas rather than on evidence. To make sure that your argument is not misleading or distorted, follow these guidelines:

- ***Avoid misrepresenting evidence.*** You **misrepresent evidence** when you exaggerate the extent to which critical opinion supports your thesis. For example, don't try to make a weak case stronger by saying that "many critics" think that something is so when only one does.
- ***Avoid quoting out of context.*** You **quote out of context** when you take a passage out of its original setting in order to distort its meaning. For example, you are quoting out of context if you say, "Emily Dickinson's poems are so idiosyncratic that they do not appeal to readers" when your source says, "Emily Dickinson's poems are so idiosyncratic that they do not appeal to readers *who are accustomed to safe, conventional subjects*." By eliminating a key portion of the sentence, you alter the meaning of the original.
- ***Avoid slanting.*** When you select only information that supports your case and ignore information that does not, you are guilty of **slanting**. You can eliminate this problem by including a full range of examples, not just the one or two that support your thesis. Be sure to consult books and articles that represent a cross-section of critical opinion about your subject.

- ***Avoid using unfair appeals.*** Writers of arguments typically use three types of appeals to influence readers: **logical appeals**, which rely on reason and logic; **emotional appeals**, which rely on emotions; and **ethical appeals**, which rely on the credibility of the writer. Problems arise, however, when these appeals are used unfairly. For example, writers can use **logical fallacies**—flawed arguments—to fool readers into thinking a conclusion is logical when it is not. Writers can also use inappropriate appeals—appeals to prejudice, for example—to influence readers. And finally, writers can undercut their credibility by using questionable support—books and articles written by people who have little or no expertise. This is especially true when information is obtained from the internet, where the credentials of the writer may be difficult or impossible to assess. If you want your readers to accept your position, be sure to avoid logical fallacies and unfair appeals.

Using Visuals as Evidence

Because **visuals**—pictures, drawings, and diagrams—can be very persuasive, they can make a strong literary argument even stronger. In a sense, visuals are a type of evidence that can support your thesis. For example, suppose you are writing an essay about the play *Trifles* in which you argue that Mrs. Wright's quilt is an important symbol. In fact, you make the point that the process of creating the quilt with a log cabin pattern parallels the process by which the two female characters determine why Mrs. Wright murdered her husband. The addition of a photograph of a quilt with a log cabin pattern could not only support your conclusion but also eliminate a paragraph of description.

Before using a visual, however, make certain it actually supports the point you want to make. If it does not, it will distract readers and undercut your argument. To ensure that readers understand the purpose of the visual, introduce it with a sentence that establishes its context; then, discuss its significance, paying particular attention to how it supports your point. Finally, be sure to include full documentation for any visual that is not your original creation. (See pp. 54 and 55 for examples of visuals used as evidence in student essays.)

Organizing a Literary Argument

In its simplest form, a literary argument—like any argumentative essay—consists of a thesis statement and supporting evidence. Literary arguments, however, frequently use additional strategies to convince readers and overcome potential opposition.

Elements of a Literary Argument

- **Introduction:** The introduction should present the issue you will discuss and explain its significance.
- **Thesis statement:** In most literary arguments, you state your thesis in your introduction. However, if you think your readers may not be familiar with the issue you are discussing (or if it is very controversial), you may want to state your thesis later in the essay.
- **Background:** In this section, you can summarize critical opinion about your topic, perhaps pointing out the shortcomings of these opinions. You can also define key terms, review basic facts, or summarize the plot of the work or works you will discuss.
- **Arguments in support of your thesis:** Here you present your arguments and the evidence to support them. It makes sense to move from the least controversial to the most controversial point or from the most familiar to the least familiar idea. In other words, you should begin with arguments that your readers are most likely to accept and then deal with those that require more discussion later.
- **Refutation of opposing arguments:** In a literary argument, you should summarize and refute the most obvious arguments against your thesis. If the opposing arguments are relatively weak, refute them after you have presented your own arguments. However, if the opposing arguments are strong, you may want to concede their strengths and discuss their limitations *before* you present your own arguments.
- **Conclusion:** In your conclusion you often restate your thesis as well as the major arguments you have made in support of it. Your conclusion can also summarize key points, remind readers of the weaknesses of opposing arguments, or underscore the logic of your position. Many writers like to end their essays with a quotation or a memorable statement that they hope will stay with readers after they finish the essay.

Writing a Literary Argument

The following student essay presents literary arguments, focusing on Dee, a character in Alice Walker's short story "Everyday Use." The student writer, Margaret Chase, supports her thesis with ideas she developed as she read the story and watched a film version of the story. She also includes information she found when she did research. (Note that her essay includes two visuals from the film.)

Chase 1

Margaret Chase

Professor Sierra

English 1001

6 January 2023

The Politics of "Everyday Use"

Introduction

Alice Walker's "Everyday Use" focuses on a mother, Mrs. Johnson, and her two daughters, Maggie and Dee, and how they view their Black American heritage. The story's climax comes when Mrs. Johnson rejects Dee's request to take a hand-stitched quilt with her so that she can hang it on her wall. Knowing that Maggie will put the quilt to "everyday use," Dee is horrified, and she tells her mother and Maggie that they do not understand their heritage. Although many literary critics see Dee's desire for the quilt as materialistic and shallow, a closer examination of this story, written in 1973, suggests a more positive interpretation of Dee's character.

Thesis statement

Background

On the surface, "Everyday Use" is about two sisters, Dee and Maggie, and Mrs. Johnson, their mother. Mrs. Johnson tells the reader that "Dee... would always look anyone in the eye. Hesitation was no part of her nature" (347). Unlike her sister Dee, Maggie is shy and introverted. She is described as looking like a lame animal that has been run over by a car (347). According to the narrator, "She has been like this, chin on chest, eyes on ground, feet in shuffle" (347) ever since she was burned in a fire.

Unlike Dee, Mrs. Johnson never got an education. After second grade, she explains, the school closed down. She says, "Don't ask me why: in 1927 colored asked fewer questions than they do now" (348). Mrs. Johnson admits that she accepts the status quo even though she knows that it is unjust. This admission further establishes the difference between Mrs. Johnson and Dee: Mrs. Johnson has accepted her circumstances, while Dee has worked to change hers. Their differences are illustrated in a film version of the story by their contrasting styles of dress. As shown in Figure 1, Dee and her boyfriend Hakim, a barber, dress in clothes that celebrate their African heritage while Mrs. Johnson and Maggie dress in plain, conservative clothing.

Chase 2

Figure 1. Dee and Hakim-a-barber arrive at the family home; *The Wadsworth Original Film Series in Literature: "Everyday Use,"* directed by Bruce R. Schwartz, Wadsworth, 2005.
Denna Bendall/Worn Path Productions

When Dee arrives home with her new boyfriend, other differences soon become obvious. As she surveys her mother's belongings and asks Mrs. Johnson if she can take the top of the butter churn home with her, it is clear that she is materialistic. However, her years away from home have also politicized her. Dee now wants to be called "Wangero" because she believes (although mistakenly) that her given name is a slave name that has been passed down. In addition, she talks about how a new day is dawning for Black Americans.

Background continued

The importance of Dee's decision to adopt an African name and wear African clothing cannot be fully appreciated without a knowledge of the social and political context in which Walker wrote this story. Walker's own comments about this time period explain Dee's behavior and add meaning to it. In her interview with Evelyn C. White, Walker explains that the late 1960s was a time of cultural and intellectual awakening for Black Americans. Many turned ideologically and culturally to Africa, adopting the dress, hairstyles, and even the names of their African ancestors. Walker admits that as a young woman she too became interested in discovering her African heritage. (In fact, she herself was given the name *Wangero* during a visit to Kenya in the late 1960s.) Walker tells White that she considered keeping this new name but eventually realized that to do so would be to "dismiss" her family and her American heritage. When she researched her American family, she found that her great-great-grandmother had walked from Virginia to

First argument in support of thesis

Georgia carrying two children. "If that's not a Walker," she says, "I don't know what is." Thus, Walker realized that, over time, Black Americans had actually transformed the names they had originally taken from their enslavers. To respect the ancestors she knew, Walker says, she decided it was important to keep her given name.

Second argument in support of thesis

Along with adopting symbols of their African heritage, many Black Americans also elevated these symbols, such as the quilt shown in Figure 2, to the status of art. One way of doing this was to put these objects in museums; another was to hang them on the walls of their homes. Such acts were aimed at convincing European Americans that Black Americans had an old and rich culture and that, consequently, they deserved respect. These gestures were also meant to improve self-esteem and pride within Black American communities (Salaam 42-43).

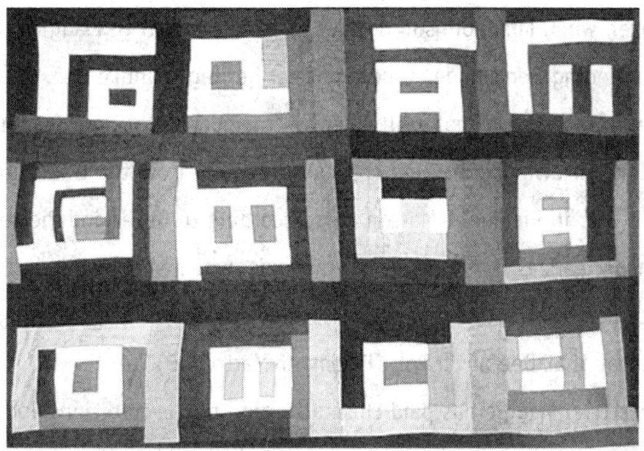

Figure 2. Traditional hand-stitched quilt; Evelyn C. White, "Alice Walker: Stitches in Time," interview, *The Wadsworth Original Film Series in Literature: "Everyday Use,"* directed by Bruce R. Schwartz, Wadsworth, 2005.
Suzanne English/Worn Path Productions

Summary and refutation of opposing argument

Admittedly, as some critics have pointed out, Dee is more materialistic than political. For example, although Mrs. Johnson makes several statements throughout the story that suggest her admiration of Dee's defiant character, she also identifies incidents that highlight Dee's materialism and selfishness. When their first house burned down, Dee watched it burn while she stood under a tree with "a look of concentration" (347) rather than grief. Mrs. Johnson knows that Dee hated their small, dingy house, and she knows too that Dee was glad to see it destroyed. Furthermore, Walker acknowledges in an interview that, as she was writing the story, she imagined that Dee might even have set the fire that destroyed the house and scarred her sister (White). Even now, Dee is ashamed of the tin-roofed house her family lives in, and she has said that she would never bring her friends there. Mrs. Johnson has always known that Dee wanted "nice things" (347); even at sixteen, "she had a style of her own, and knew what style was" (348). However, although Dee is materialistic and self-serving, she is also proud and strong willed. Knowing that she will encounter opposition wherever she goes, she works to establish power. Thus, her desire for the quilt can be seen as an attempt to establish herself and her Black American culture in a society dominated by White, European Americans.

Analysis of Mrs. Johnson's final act

Even though Mrs. Johnson knows Dee wants the quilt, she gives it to Maggie. According to literary critics Houston Baker and Charlotte Pierce-Baker, when Mrs. Johnson decides to give the quilt to Maggie, she is challenging Dee's understanding of her heritage. Unlike Dee, Mrs. Johnson recognizes that quilts signify "sacred generations of women who have made their own special kind of beauty separate from the traditional artistic world" (qtd. in Piedmont-Marton 45). According to Baker and Pierce-Baker, Mrs. Johnson realizes that her daughter Maggie, whom she has long dismissed because of her quiet nature and shyness, understands the true meaning of the quilt in a way that Dee never will (Piedmont-Marton 45).

Unlike Dee, Maggie has paid close attention to the traditions and skills of her mother and grandmother: she has learned to quilt. More importantly, by staying with her mother instead of going to school, she has gotten to know her family. She underscores this fact when she tells her mother that Dee can have the quilt because she does not need it to remember her grandmother. Even though Maggie's and Mrs. Johnson's understanding of heritage may be more emotionally profound than Dee's, it is important not to dismiss Dee's interest in elevating the quilt to the level of art. The political stakes of defining an object as art in the late 1960s and early 1970s were high, and the fight for equality went beyond basic civil rights.

Chase 5

Although there is much in the story that indicates Dee's materialism, her desire to hang the quilt should not be dismissed as selfish. Like Mrs. Johnson and Maggie, Dee is a complicated character. In 1973, when "Everyday Use" was written, displaying the quilt would have been not only a personal act, but also a political act—an act with important implications. The final message of "Everyday Use" may just be that an accurate understanding of the quilt (and, by extension, of Black American culture) requires both views—Maggie's and Mrs. Johnson's "everyday use" and Dee's elevation of the quilt to art.

Conclusion (restating thesis)

Chase 6

Works Cited

Piedmont-Marton, Elisabeth. "An Overview of 'Everyday Use." *Short Stories for Students*, vol. 2, 1997, pp. 42-45. *Gale Literature Resource Center*, https://link.gale.com/apps/doc/H1420002698/LitRC?u=gale&sid=bookmark-LitRC&xid=762d70ad.

Salaam, Kalamu Ya. "A Primer of the Black Arts Movement: Excerpts from *The Magic of Juju: An Appreciation of the Black Arts Movement." Black Renaissance/Renaissance Noire*, 2002, pp. 40-59.

Walker, Alice. "Alice Walker: Stitches in Time." Interview by Evelyn C. White. *The Wadsworth Original Film Series in Literature: "Everyday Use,"* directed by Bruce R. Schwartz, Wadsworth, 2005.

---. "Everyday Use." *Portable Literature: Reading, Reacting, Writing,* edited by Laurie G. Kirszner and Stephen R. Mandell, 10th ed., Cengage, 2024, pp. 346-52.

Chapter

4

Using Sources in Your Writing

Learning Objectives

After reading this chapter, you will be able to. . .

- Identify the purpose of exploratory research.
- Describe how to narrow a topic and conduct focused research.
- Search for sources in a library database.
- Identify frequently used databases and search engines for literary research.
- Evaluate a source for its usefulness and reliability.
- Explain how to paraphrase and summarize a source.
- Integrate direct quotations into an essay.
- Draft and revise a literary essay.

When you write an essay about a literary topic, you often do **research**, supplementing your own interpretations with information from other sources. These sources may include works of literature as well as books and journal articles by literary critics (see p. 60). You may get this information from print sources, from electronic databases in the library, or from the internet. When you write an essay that uses sources, follow the process discussed in this chapter.

Choosing a Topic

Your instructor may assign a topic or allow you to choose one. If you choose a topic, make sure it is narrow enough for your essay's length, the amount of time you have for writing, and the number of sources your instructor expects you to use.

Daniel Collins, a student in an Introduction to Literature course, was given three weeks to write a four- to six-page essay on one of the short stories the class had read. Daniel chose to write about Eudora Welty's short story "A Worn Path" because the main character, Phoenix Jackson, interested him. He knew, however, that he would have to narrow his topic before he could begin. In class, Daniel's instructor had asked some provocative questions about the significance of Phoenix Jackson's journey. Daniel thought that this topic might work well because he could explore it in a short essay and could complete the essay within the three-week time limit.

Doing Exploratory Research

To see whether you will be able to find enough material about your topic, you should do some **exploratory research** by taking a quick survey of possible sources. Your goal at this stage is to formulate a **research question**, the question that you want your research to answer. This question will help you decide which sources to look for, which to examine first, and which to skip entirely.

You can begin your exploratory research by consulting your library's **webpage**, which will give you access to the library's online **catalog** as well as a number of electronic databases, such as *Readers' Guide to Periodical Literature Index* and *Humanities Index*. Then, if necessary, consult **general reference works** like encyclopedias and specialized dictionaries and browse your search engine's subject guides to get an overview of your subject. You should also see what resources are available on the internet. Try using more than one search engine or a meta search engine like *DuckDuckGo* or *MetaCrawler*, which gathers results from several search engines, to determine if you can find appropriate materials for your project.

When he surveyed his library's resources, Daniel saw that his library had several books and articles on Eudora Welty. He also found two journal articles that discussed the significance of Phoenix Jackson's journey, and he hoped they would help him to understand why this character continued her journey despite all the hardships she encountered. However, he knew that he would have to do more than just summarize his sources; he would have to make a point about Phoenix's journey, one that he could support with examples from the story as well as from his research.

After looking at some additional sources on the internet, Daniel came up with the following research question:

> What enabled Phoenix Jackson to continue her journey despite the many obstacles she faced?

Narrowing Your Topic

As you survey your library and internet resources, the titles of books and articles as well as discussions in general encyclopedias should help you to narrow your topic.

Doing Focused Research

Once you have completed your exploratory research and formulated your research question, you are ready to begin **focused research**—the process of looking in the library and on the internet for the specific information you need.

Library Research

When it comes to finding trustworthy, high-quality, and authoritative sources, nothing surpasses your college library. A modern college library offers reliable resources (that have been curated by librarians) that you cannot find on the internet. In the long run, you will save a good deal of time and effort if you begin your research by consulting your library's print and electronic resources.

Using the Library

The best way to start your focused research is the visit your college library's website, which gives you access to the library's online catalogue as well as the digital databases to which the library subscribes. Many college libraries now have a **discovery service**, an online searching tool that enables you to use a single search box to access the physical items held by the library as well as journal articles, government documents, and electronic databases. The results of your search are listed according to their relevancy to your search terms.

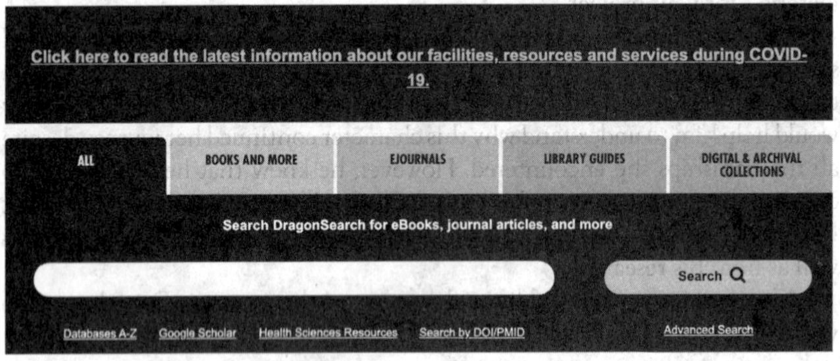

Search Box from the Homepage of Drexel University's Library

Locating Library Sources

When you hunt for sources using the library's discovery service (or the online catalog), you can do either a *keyword search* or a *subject search*.

- **Doing a Keyword Search** When you do a **keyword search**, you enter into the search box of the discovery service or the online catalog a word (or words) associated with your topic. (These key-words can be an author's name, the title of a journal article, or an idea associated with your topic.) The computer then displays a list of entries that contain these words. The more precise your keywords, the more specific and useful the information you retrieve will be. For example, the keywords *"A Worn Path"* will yield thousands of entries; *Phoenix Jackson's journey in "A Worn Path"* will yield far fewer.

- **Doing a Subject Search** When you do a **subject search**, you enter a subject heading into the search box of the discovery service or the online catalog. Many online catalogs have a list of subject headings to help you identify the exact words that you will need for your subject search.

Searching the Library's Databases

Through your library's website, you can access the electronic periodical databases to which your library subscribes. A **periodical** is a publication that appears at regular intervals, for example, weekly, monthly, or quarterly. **Periodical databases** are collections of digital information—such as newspaper, magazine, and journal articles—arranged for easy retrieval. (You search these databases the same way you search the library's discovery service or its online catalog.) These databases enable you to access information from scholarly journals, abstracts, books, government reports, magazines, and newspapers.

Assuming your library offers a variety of databases, how do you know which ones will be best for your research?

- *First, find out to which databases your library subscribes.* You can usually find a list of these databases on your library's website. If necessary, ask a reference librarian for help.
- *Next, determine the level of the articles listed in the database.* **Scholarly journals** publish articles written by experts in a field and usually provide in-depth analysis of a topic as well as documentation of sources. They are usually the most reliable sources you can find on a particular subject area. However, because journal articles are aimed at experts, they can be difficult for general readers to understand. **Popular periodicals** are magazines and newspapers that publish articles aimed at general readers. Although these articles are more accessible, they can be less reliable than scholarly journals. However, assuming they are written by reputable authors, articles from some popular publication—such as *The Atlantic* or *Scientific American*—may be appropriate for your research. Ask your instructor or librarian if the popular source you wish to use is reputable enough for your research.
- *Finally, look for a database that is suitable for your topic.* Each database has a different focus and lists different magazines or journals. In addition, some databases include only citations while others contain the full text of articles. For these reasons, using the wrong database can result

in wasted time and frustration. For example, searching a database that focuses on business will not help you if you are looking for information about a literary topic.

Frequently Used Databases for Literary Research

- **EBSCOhost** Includes thousands of periodical articles on many subjects, including literature.
- **Gale Literary Sources** Full text of poems, stories, and novels. Cross-searches Gale Virtual Reference Library, literature Criticism Online, and Literary Resource Center.
- **ProQuest** Access to more than 400 humanities journals and weekly magazines as well as the full text of many journal articles.
- **JSTOR** Full-text issues of selected peer-reviewed journals in a wide variety of humanities and social sciences fields.
- **Literature Resource Central** Gale's Literature Resource Center covers 2,000 of the most studied authors.
- **ProQuest** Central General reference database for more than 175 subjects from magazines, journals, and newspapers, including scholarly works.

Evaluating Library Sources

Whenever you find a library source, print or electronic, take the time to **evaluate** it—to assess its usefulness and reliability.

Checklist Evaluating Library Sources

To help you evaluate sources you find in the library, consider the following questions:

- *Does the source treat your topic in enough detail?* To be of real help, a book should include a section or a chapter on your topic. An article should have your topic as its central subject or at least one of its main concerns.
- *Is the source current?* Although currency is not as important for literary research as it is in the sciences, it should still be a consideration. Check the date of publication to see whether the information in a book or article is up to date. A review of current literary scholarship can help you to make this assessment.

- *Is the source respected?* Is the author a recognized expert? Is the publisher reputable? You can consult reviews in *Book Review Digest*, available in print and online, to make this determination.
- *Is the source reliable?* Does the author support their opinions? Does the author include documentation? Does the author have a particular agenda to advance? Compare a few statements with a more neutral source—an encyclopedia or a textbook, for example—to see whether the author seems to be slanting facts. If you have difficulty making this assessment, ask your instructor or a reference librarian for help.
- *Is the source balanced?* Does the writer present a balanced discussion? Do you detect bias? If so, does this bias undermine the author's credibility? You can make this determination by looking at the writer's word choice and seeing if the writer's assumptions are justified by the story, poem, or play being discussed.

Web Research

When most people refer to the internet, they actually mean the web, which is part of the internet.

Searching the Web

The web has revolutionized the way scholars conduct research. Keep in mind, however, that the web does not give you access to the large number of reliable print and electronic sources that you can find in your college library. Because anyone can post information on the web, it is often difficult to know who, if anyone, has reviewed the information for accuracy, and for this reason, web-based sources need to be evaluated carefully.

Of course, there are trustworthy sources of information on the web. Google Scholar provides links to some sources that can also be found in your college library. (Even so, you have to be careful: some articles accessed through Google Scholar are pay-per-view, and others are not current or comprehensive.) In addition, the Directory of Open Access Journals (doaj.org) lists thousands of open-access (free, digital online information) scientific and scholarly journals in its directories.

Locating Web Sources

When you search the web, you can do either a *keyword search* or paste a URL or DOI.

- *Doing a keyword search.* You look for web sources the same way you look for library sources (see p. 60). You enter keywords into your search engine's search bar and select the option to search. This will display your search results in a list. The more specific your keywords, the more likely you will be to retrieve information on your topic.

- *Pasting a URL* or *DOI.* Every page on the internet has an electronic address called a URL (uniform resource locator) or DOI (digital object identifier). When you copy and paste a URL or DOI into your search engine's location field and select the option to search, you will be connected to the website you want.

To carry out a web search, you need a search engine—an application like Google or Bing. The most widely used search engines are **general purpose** and focus on a wide variety of topics. Some of these search engines are more user friendly than others; some are updated more frequently; and some are more comprehensive. As you try out various search engines, you will eventually settle on one (or ones) that you will turn to when you need to find information.

Some General-Purpose Search Engines

Google	Currently, the best search engine available. This tool accesses a large database that enables you to search for websites, images, discussion groups, and news stories.
YouTube	The best search engine for videos. It is the second largest search engine in the world, after Google.
Bing	The third most-used search engine on the web. It has a variety of specialized functions that sort responses into categories. By clicking on progressively narrower categories, you get more and more specific results. For some searches, a single "Best Match" response may appear. This tool has excellent image and video search functions.
Yahoo!	A search engine that is a credible alternative to Google. This tool searches its own indexes as well as the web and suggests search queries as you type.
DuckDuckGo	The seventh largest search engine in the world. It is a metasearch engine that gives results from several search engines at once. Unlike other search engines, it does not track, collect, or store a user's data.

In addition to the previously listed general-purpose search engines, you can use **specialized search engines**—search sites that are especially useful during focused research when you are looking for in-depth information about a specific topic.

Some Specialized Search Engines	
Directory of Open-Access Journals <doaj.org>	This site offers access to more than 2,000 free, full-text, open-access journals.
Microsoft Academic Search	This high-quality, reliable search engine is designed for academic research.
Thinkers.net <thinkers.net>	This search engine gives access to reliable discussions on literature and information about publishing.
RefSeek <refseek.com>	This search engine removes results not related to science, academia, and research.
Voice of the Shuttle <vos.ucsb.edu>	This search engine gives access to reliable, in-depth research in the humanities.

Evaluating Websites

Because information on websites can often be unreliable, it is important to determine the quality of a website before you use material from it. Asking the questions below will help you evaluate websites and the information they contain.

Checklist Evaluating Websites

To help you evaluate websites, consider the following questions:

- *How credible is the person or organization responsible for the site?* Does the site list an author? Can you determine the author's expertise?
- *How accurate is the information on the website?* Is it free of factual, spelling, and grammatical errors? Can you verify the information by checking other sources? Does the site include documentation?
- *How balanced does the information on the website seem?* Does a business, political organization, or special interest group sponsor the site? Does the site express only one viewpoint?

- *How comprehensive is the website?* Does the site provide in-depth coverage, or is the information largely common knowledge?
- *How well maintained is the website?* Has it been active for a long period of time? Has the site been updated recently?
- *How current is the website?* Does the site display the date it was last updated? Are the links to other sites all working?

Daniel Collins, the student writing about Phoenix Jackson's journey, located everything he needed in his college library. He found two print articles about the Welty story, and he found two more articles in the *Humanities Index*, which he accessed through the ProQuest database. Finally, a search of his library's online catalog revealed that among the library's holdings was a DVD dramatization of "A Worn Path" that included an interview with the author.

Taking Notes

Once you have located your sources, you should record information that you think will be useful. There is no single correct way to take notes. Some writers store information in a computer file; others keep their notes on index cards. Still others take notes using an electronic note-taking application like *Evernote* or *Simplenote*. Whatever system you use, be sure to record the author's full name, *complete* publication information, and the URL or DOI for electronic sources. You will need this information later to compile your works-cited list (see p. 82).

When you take notes from a source, you have three options: you can *paraphrase*, *summarize*, or *quote*.

When you **paraphrase**, you put the author's main points into your own words, keeping the emphasis of the original. You paraphrase when you want to make a difficult or complex discussion accessible to readers so that you can comment on it or use it to support your own points. For this reason, a paraphrase can sometimes be longer than the original. Here is a passage from a critical article, followed by Daniel's paraphrase.

Original: The assumption that the grandson is dead helps explain Phoenix Jackson's stoical behavior in the doctor's office. She displays a "ceremonial stiffness" as she sits "bolt upright" staring "straight ahead, her face solemn and withdrawn into rigidity." This passiveness suggests her psychological dilemma—she cannot explain why she made the journey. Her attempt to blame the lapse of memory on her illiteracy is unconvincing. Her lack of education is hardly an excuse for forgetting her grandson, but it goes a long way toward explaining her inability to articulate her subconscious motives for her journey. (Bartel, Roland. "Life and Death in Eudora Welty's 'A Worn Path.'")

Paraphrase: As Roland Bartel points out in "Life and Death in Eudora Welty's 'A Worn Path,'" Phoenix Jackson's "stoical behavior" at the doctor's office makes sense if her grandson is actually dead. Although she says that her forgetfulness is due to her lack of education, Bartel does not accept this excuse. According to him, the fact that Phoenix is uneducated cannot fully explain her forgetting about her grandson—although it might explain why she cannot communicate her reasons for her trip (289).

When you write a **summary**, you also put an author's ideas into your own words, but in this case, you convey just the main idea of a passage. For this reason, a summary is always much shorter than the original. Here is Daniel's Collins's summary of the passage from Bartel's article.

Summary: As Roland Bartel points out in "Life and Death in Eudora Welty's 'A Worn Path,'" Phoenix Jackson's actions make sense if we assume that her grandson is dead and that she does not have the verbal skills to explain why she made the trip (289).

When you **quote**, you reproduce a passage exactly, word-for-word and punctuation mark-for-punctuation mark, enclosing the entire passage in quotation marks. Because including too many quotations will distract readers, use a quotation only when you think that the author's words will add something—memorable wording, for example—to your essay.

Quotation: According to Roland Bartel, Phoenix Jackson's lack of education helps explain "her inability to articulate her subconscious motives" (289).

Note Remember to document all paraphrases, summaries, and quotations that you use in your essays. (See Chapter 5, Documenting Sources and Avoiding Plagiarism.)

Integrating Sources

To integrate a paraphrase, summary, or quotation smoothly into your essay, use a phrase that introduces your source and its author—*Bartel points out*, *according to Bartel*, *Bartel claims*, or *Bartel says*, for example. You can place this identifying phrase at various points in a sentence.

According to Roland Bartel, "The assumption that the grandson is dead helps explain Phoenix Jackson's stoical behavior in the doctor's office" (289).

"The assumption that the grandson is dead helps explain Phoenix Jackson's stoical behavior in the doctor's office," observes Roland Bartel in his article "Life and Death in Eudora Welty's 'A Worn Path'" (289).

"The assumption that the grandson is dead," notes the literary critic Roland Bartel, "helps explain Phoenix Jackson's stoical behavior in the doctor's office" (289).

EXERCISE Integrating Quotations

For each of the quotations below, write three sentences: one that integrates the complete quotation into your sentence, one that integrates part of the quotation into your sentence, and one that quotes just a distinctive word or phrase.

Example

- **Original quotation:** "But it seems to me that once you begin a gesture it's fatal not to go through with it" (Updike 183).
- **Sentence integrating complete quotation:** Readers understand Sammy's determination to stand up to Lengel when he says, "But it seems to me that once you begin a gesture it's fatal not to go through with it" (Updike 183).
- **Sentence integrating part of the quotation:** Sammy has mixed feelings about quitting his job but feels that "once you begin a gesture it's fatal not to go through with it" (Updike 183).
- **Sentence quoting one distinctive word:** Sammy considers changing his mind but decides that to do so would be "fatal" (Updike 183).

Quotations

- "We remembered all the young men her father had driven away, and we knew that with nothing left she would have to cling to that which had robbed her, as people will" (Faulkner 169).
- "That moment she was mine, mine, fair" (Browning, line 36)
- "But I have promises to keep, / And miles to go before I sleep / and miles to go before I sleep" (Frost, lines 14–16).
- "We live close together and we live far apart. We all go through the same things—it's just a different kind of the same thing" (Glaspell 831).

Developing a Thesis Statement

After you have taken notes, review the information you have gathered, and use it to help draft a **thesis statement**—usually a single sentence that states the main idea of your essay. You should support this thesis with a combination of your own ideas and the ideas you have gotten from your research.

After reviewing his notes, Daniel developed the following thesis statement about Eudora Welty's "A Worn Path."

Thesis Statement: What is most important in the story is the spiritual and emotional strength of Phoenix Jackson and how this strength enables her to continue her journey.

As you draft and revise your essay, your thesis statement will probably change. At this point in the writing process, however, it gives your ideas focus and enables you to organize them into an outline.

Constructing a Formal Outline

Once you have a thesis statement, you can construct a **formal outline** that presents your main points and supporting details in the order you will discuss them. Begin by writing your thesis statement at the top of the page. Then, review your notes, and arrange them in the order in which you plan to use them. As you construct your outline, group these points under appropriate headings.

When it is completed, your formal outline will show you how much support you have for each of your points, and it will guide you as you write a draft of your essay. Your outline, which covers the body paragraphs of your essay, can be a **sentence outline**, in which each idea is expressed as a sentence, or a **topic outline**, in which each idea is expressed in a word or a short phrase.

After reviewing his notes, Daniel constructed the following topic outline. Notice that he uses Roman numerals for first-level headings, capital letters for second-level headings, and Arabic numerals for third-level headings. Notice too that all points in the outline are expressed in parallel terms and that every heading has at least two subheadings.

Thesis Statement: What is most important in the story is the spiritual and emotional strength of Phoenix Jackson and how this strength enables her to continue her journey.

I. Critical interpretations of "A Worn Path"
  A. Heroic act of sacrifice
  B. Journey of life
  C. Religious pilgrimage
II. Focus on journey
  A. Jackson and her grandson
  B. Nurse's question
  C. Jackson's reply
III. Jackson's character
  A. Interaction between Jackson's character and journey
    1. Significance of Jackson's first name
    2. Jackson as a complex character
  B. Jackson's physical problems
    1. Failing eyesight
    2. Difficulty walking
IV. Jackson's spiritual strength
  A. Belief in God
  B. Child of nature
V. Jackson's emotional strength
  A. Love for grandson
  B. Fearlessness and selflessness
  C. Determination

Note Microsoft Word and Google Documents will automatically create outlines for you and even enable you to create your own outline templates.

Drafting Your Essay

Once you have constructed your outline, you are ready to draft your essay. Follow your outline as you write, using your notes as the need arises.

- Your essay's **introduction** will usually be a single paragraph. In addition to identifying the work (or works) you are writing about and stating your thesis, the introduction may present an overview of your topic or provide necessary background information.
- The **body** of your essay supports your thesis statement, with each of your body paragraphs developing a single point. Support your points with examples from the literary work you are discussing as well as with summaries, paraphrases, and quotations from your sources. In addition, be sure to include your own observations and inferences. Keep in mind, your ideas, not those of your sources, should lead the discussion.
- Your essay's **conclusion**, usually a single paragraph (but sometimes more), restates your main points and reinforces your thesis statement.

Remember, the purpose of your first draft is to get ideas down on paper so that you can react to them. You should expect to revise, possibly writing several drafts.

The final draft of Daniel Collins's essay on Eudora Welty's "A Worn Path" (p. 370) appears on the pages that follow.

Model Essay with MLA Documentation

Collins 1

Daniel Collins

Professor Smith

English 201

20 January 2023

And Again She Makes the Journey: Character and Action in Eudora Welty's "A Worn Path"

Since it was published in 1940, Eudora Welty's "A Worn Path," the tale of an older Black woman, Phoenix Jackson, traveling to the city to obtain medicine for her sick grandson, has been the subject of much critical interpretation. Critics have wondered about the meaning of the many death and rebirth symbols, including the scarecrow, which Phoenix believes is a ghost; the buzzard who watches her travel; the skeleton-like branches that reach out to slow her; and her first name, Phoenix. Various critics have concluded that

"A Worn Path" is either a "heroic act of sacrifice," "a parable for the journey of life," or "a religious pilgrimage" (Piwinski 40). It is certainly true that Phoenix Jackson's journey has symbolic significance. However, what is most important in the story is Phoenix Jackson's spiritual and emotional strength—and how this strength enables her to continue her journey.

Eudora Welty discusses Phoenix Jackson in an interview with Beth Henley. Welty points out that Jackson's first name refers to a mythical bird that dies and is reborn every five hundred years. She explains, however, that despite her symbolic name, Phoenix Jackson is more than a symbol: she is a complex character with human frailties and emotions.

Phoenix Jackson has a number of physical problems that make it difficult for her to perform daily tasks. Because of her age, she has failing eyesight, which distorts her perception of the objects she encounters during her journey. For example, Phoenix mistakes a patch of thorns for "a pretty little *green* bush" (371), and she believes a scarecrow is the ghost of a man. She also has difficulty walking, so she must use a cane; at one point, she is unable to bend and tie her own shoes. Because of these physical problems, readers might expect her to fail in her attempt to reach town. As the narrator points out, the journey is long and difficult. So what gives Phoenix Jackson the energy and endurance for the journey?

Although Phoenix Jackson's body is weak, she has great spiritual and emotional strength. According to James Saunders, her oneness with nature helps her overcome the challenges that she encounters (67). Because Phoenix Jackson is "a child of nature," her impaired vision, although it slows her journey, does not stop it. As Saunders explains, "mere human vision would not have been sufficient for the journey" (67). Instead, Phoenix Jackson relies on her spiritual connection with nature; thus, she warns various animals to "Keep out from under these feet . . ." (371). Her spiritual strength also comes from her belief in God—a quality seen when she refers to God watching her steal the hunter's nickel.

Phoenix Jackson's spiritual strength is matched by her emotional strength. Her love for her grandson drives her to endure any difficulty and to defy any danger. Therefore, throughout her journey, she demonstrates fearlessness and selflessness. For example, when the hunter threatens her with his gun, she tells him that she has faced worse dangers. And, despite her need for new shoes, she buys a paper windmill for her grandson instead.

In her interview with Beth Henley, Eudora Welty explains how she created Phoenix Jackson—outwardly frail and inwardly strong. Welty tells how she noticed an "old lady" slowly making her way across a "silent horizon,"[1] driven by an overwhelming need to reach her destination. As Welty says, "she had a purpose." Welty created Phoenix Jackson in the image of this determined woman. In order to underscore the character's strength, Welty had her make the journey to Natchez to get medication for her grandson. Because the act had to be performed repeatedly, the journey became a ritual that had to be completed at all costs. Thus, as Welty explains in the interview, the act of making the journey—not the journey itself—is the most significant element in the story.

In order to emphasize the importance of the journey, Welty gives little information about the daily life of the boy and his grandmother or about the illness for which the boy is being treated. Regardless of the boy's condition—or even whether he is alive or dead—Jackson must complete her journey. The nurse's statement—"The doctor said as long as you came to get [the medicine], you could have it" (376)—reinforces the ritualistic nature of Jackson's journey, a journey that Bartel suggests is a "subconscious" act (289). Thus, Phoenix Jackson cannot answer the nurse's questions because she does not consciously know what forces her to make the journey. Nevertheless, next Saturday, Phoenix Jackson will again walk, and "will continue to do so, regardless of the difficulties facing her, along the worn path that leads through the wilderness of the Natchez Trace, cheerfully performing her labor of love" (Howard 84).

Clearly, the interaction of character (Phoenix Jackson) and act (the ritual journey in search of medication) is the most important element of Welty's story. By describing Phoenix Jackson's difficult encounters during her ritual journey to town, Welty emphasizes how spiritual and emotional strength can overcome physical frailty and how determination and fearlessness can overcome danger (Bethea 37). These moral messages become clear by the time Jackson reaches the doctor's office. The image of the older woman determinedly walking across the horizon, the image that prompted Welty to write the story, remains in the minds of readers.

Collins 4

Note

1. Unlike the written version of "A Worn Path," the film version of the short story ends not at the doctor's office but with a vision similar to the one that inspired Welty to write the story: an older African American woman silently walking along the horizon at dusk.

Collins 5

Works Cited

Bartel, Roland. "Life and Death in Eudora Welty's 'A Worn Path.'" *Studies in Short Fiction*, vol. 14, no. 1, 1977, pp. 288–90.

Bethea, Dean. "Phoenix Has No Coat: Historicity, Eschatology, and Sins of Omission in Eudora Welty's 'A Worn Path.'" *International Fiction Review*, vol. 27, no. 5, 2001, pp. 32–38, journals.lib.unb.ca/index.php/ifr/article/view/7689/8746.

Howard, Zelma T. *The Rhetoric of Eudora Welty's Short Stories*. UP of Mississippi, 1973.

Piwinski, David J. "Mistletoe in Eudora Welty's 'A Worn Path.'" *ANQ: A Quarterly Journal of Short Articles, Notes and Reviews*, vol. 16, no. 1, 2003, pp. 40–43. *Taylor and Francis Online*, doi:10.1080/08957690309598188.

Saunders, James Robert. "'A Worn Path': The Eternal Quest of Welty's Phoenix Jackson." *Southern Literary Journal*, vol. 25, no. 1, 1992, pp. 62–73.

Welty, Eudora. Interview by Beth Henley. *The Heinle Original Film Series in Literature: Eudora Welty's "A Worn Path."* Directed by Bruce R. Schwartz, Wadsworth, 2003.

---. "A Worn Path." *Portable Literature: Reading, Reacting, Writing*, edited by Laurie G. Kirszner and Stephen R. Mandell, 10th ed., Cengage, 2024, pp. 370–377.

Chapter 5

Documenting Sources and Avoiding Plagiarism

Learning Objectives

After reading this chapter, you will be able to. . .

- Determine which sources need to be documented and which sources do not need to be documented.
- Identify and avoid plagiarism.
- Format and punctuate in-text citations following MLA documentation guidelines.
- Format the entries on a works-cited list.

Documentation is the formal acknowledgment of the sources in an essay. This chapter explains and illustrates the documentation style recommended by the Modern Language Association (MLA), 9th edition, the style used by students of literature.

What to Document

In general, you must document the following types of information from a source (print or electronic):

- ***All word-for-word quotations from a source.*** Whenever you use a writer's exact words, you must document them. Even if you quote only a word or two within a paraphrase or summary, you must document the quoted words separately, after the final quotation marks.
- ***All ideas from a source that you put into your own words.*** Be sure to document all paraphrases or summaries of a source's ideas, including the author's judgments, conclusions, and debatable assertions.
- ***All visuals—tables, charts, and photographs—from a source.*** Because visuals are almost always someone's original creation, they must be documented.

Note Certain items do not require documentation: **common knowledge** (information most readers probably know), facts available from a variety of reference sources, passing mentions of a work or an author, familiar sayings and well-known quotations, and your own ideas and conclusions.

Avoiding Plagiarism

Plagiarism is the presentation of another person's words or ideas as if they were your own. Most plagiarism is **unintentional plagiarism**—for example, pasting a passage from a downloaded document directly into your essay and forgetting to include quotation marks and documentation. However, there is a difference between an honest mistake and **intentional plagiarism**—for example, copying sentences from a journal article or submitting as your own an essay that someone else has written. The penalties for unintentional plagiarism may sometimes be severe, but intentional plagiarism is intellectual theft and is almost always dealt with harshly.

The guidelines that follow can help you avoid the most common mistakes that lead to unintentional plagiarism.

Document All Material That Requires Documentation

Original: In Oates's stories there are no safe relationships, but the most perilous of all possibilities is sex. Sex is always destructive. (Tierce, Mike, and John M. Crafton. "Connie's Tambourine Man: A New Reading of Arnold Friend.")

Plagiarism: In many of Oates's stories, relationships—especially sexual relationships—are dangerous.

In the previous example, the writer uses an idea from a source but does not include documentation. As a result, readers are given the mistaken impression that the source's idea is actually the writer's.

Correct: Tierce and Crafton point out that in many of Oates's stories, relationships—especially sexual relationships—are dangerous (220).

Enclose Borrowed Words in Quotation Marks

Original: "The Yellow Wallpaper," which Gilman herself called "a description of a case of nervous breakdown," recalls in the first person the experiences of a woman who is evidently suffering from postpartum psychosis. (Gilbert, Sandra M., and Susan Gubar. *The Madwoman in the Attic: The Woman Writer and the Nineteenth-Century Literary Imagination.*)

Plagiarism: As Gilbert and Gubar point out, the narrator in "The Yellow Wallpaper" is evidently suffering from postpartum psychosis (212).

Even though the writer documents the passage the source's exact words are used without putting them in quotation marks.

Correct: As Gilbert and Gubar point out, the narrator in "The Yellow Wallpaper" is "evidently suffering from postpartum psychosis" (212).

Do Not Imitate a Source's Syntax and Phrasing

Original: Tennessee Williams's *The Glass Menagerie*, though it has achieved a firmly established position in the canon of American plays, is often distorted, if not misunderstood, by readers, directors, and audiences. (King, Thomas. "Irony and Distance in *The Glass Menagerie*.")

Plagiarism: Although *The Glass Menagerie* has a well-established place in the American theater, it is frequently misinterpreted by those who read it, direct it, and see it (King 125).

Although the student does not use the exact words of the source, the sentence structure closely follows the original and simply substitutes synonyms for the writer's keywords. Remember, acceptable paraphrases and summaries do more than change words; they use original phrasing and syntax to convey the source's meaning.

Correct: According to Thomas King, although *The Glass Menagerie* has become an American classic, it is still not fully appreciated (125).

Differentiate Your Words from Those of Your Source

Original: Learning to correctly pronounce other people's names to the best of our individual abilities is an important part of respecting their identity. Having your name butchered every time you meet a new person can be exhausting and invalidating ... remember that there is no such thing as "difficult names" or "easy names," there are simply names you are familiar with and names you have yet to come across—and there are certainly more of the latter than the former" (Imani, Blair. *Read This to Get Smarter*).

Plagiarism: When you're meeting someone new, it's a sign of respect to try your best to pronounce their name correctly. After all, there "is no such thing as 'difficult names' or 'easy names,'" but only "names you are familiar with and names you have yet to come across" (Imani 7-8).

It appears that only the two quotations in the last sentence are borrowed when, in fact, the first sentence also borrows ideas from the original. The student should have identified the boundaries of the borrowed material by introducing it with an identifying phrase and ending with documentation. (Note that a quotation always requires its own documentation.)

Correct: Imani advises that when meeting someone new, it is respectful to try your best to pronounce that person's name correctly (7). After all, she reminds us, "there is no such thing as 'difficult names' or 'easy names,'" but only "names you are familiar with and names you have yet to come across" (8).

Note It is easy to become overwhelmed by any research project. For example, you can run out of time, lose track of your sources, or confuse your own ideas with those of your sources.

Checklist Avoiding Unintentional Plagiarism

Any of these problems can result in unintentional plagiarism—to avoid this problem, keep the following suggestions in mind:

- *Formulate a research plan.* List the steps you intend follow and estimate how much time they will take.
- *Set up a schedule.* Set up a realistic schedule that allows you enough time to complete your assignment. Include extra time just in case any unexpected problems occur.
- *Ask for help.* If you run into trouble, don't panic; ask your instructor or a college reference librarian for help.
- *Don't paste downloaded text directly into your essay.* Summarize or paraphrase downloaded material that you intend to use. Boldface or highlight quotation marks to remind you that you are using the exact words of your sources.
- *Keep track of your sources.* Create one set of files for downloaded material and another set of files for your notes. Make sure you label and date these files so that you'll know what they contain and when they were created.
- *Record full documentation information for every source.* Make sure you have all the source information you will need to create your works-cited list.
- *Document your sources.* As you write your first draft, document each piece of information that comes from a source. Don't make the mistake of thinking you will be able to find this information later. If you don't keep track of your sources as you write, you could easily forget which words and ideas are your own compared to which are from your sources and require documentation.
- *Keep a list of the sources you are using.* Keep an up-to-date list of all the sources you are using, and keep updating it as you add and delete sources. This list will enable you to create a works-cited list when you have finished writing your essay.

Documenting Sources

MLA documentation has two main parts: ***in-text citations*** and a ***works-cited list***.* In addition, there may be ***content notes***.

In-Text Citations

MLA documentation style uses in-text citations to refer to an alphabetical works-cited list at the end of the essay. An in-text citation should contain just enough information to guide readers to the appropriate entry in your works-cited list.

A typical in-text citation consists of the author's last name and a page number.

> Gwendolyn Brooks uses the sonnet form to create poems that have a wide social and aesthetic range (Williams 972).

Checklist Guidelines for Punctuating In-Text Citations

To punctuate in-text citations correctly, follow these guidelines:

Paraphrases and Summaries

- Place the in-text citation *after* the last word of the sentence and *before* the final punctuation.

  In her poems, Brooks combines the pessimism of modernist poetry with the optimism of the Harlem Renaissance (Smith 978).

Quotations of Four Lines or Less

- Quotations of four lines or less should be included in the text of your essay. Place the in-text citation *after* the quotation marks and *before* the final punctuation.

  According to Gary Smith, Brooks' *A Street in Bronzeville* "conveys the primacy of suffering in the lives of poor Black women" (980).

  According to Gary Smith, the poems in *A Street in Bronzeville* "served notice that Brooks had learned her craft . . ." (978).

  Along with Thompson, we must ask, "Why did it take so long for critics to acknowledge that Gwendolyn Brooks is an important voice in twentieth-century American poetry" (123)?

*For more information, see the *MLA Handbook*, 9th ed. (MLA, 2021). You can also consult the MLA website at style.mla.org.

Quotations of More than Four Lines

- Quotations of more than four lines should be set off from the text as a block, one half inch from the left margin. Do not indent the first line or include quotation marks. Place the in-text citation *after* the final punctuation.

  For Gary Smith, the identity of Brooks' African American women is inextricably linked with their sense of race and poverty:

  For Brooks, unlike the Renaissance poets, the victimization of poor Black women becomes not simply a minor chord but a predominant theme of *A Street in Bronzeville.* Few, if any, of her female characters are able to free themselves from a web of poverty that threatens to strangle their lives. (980)

If you mention the author's name or the title of the work in your essay, only a page reference is needed.

> According to Gladys Margaret Williams in "Gwendolyn Brooks's Way with the Sonnet," Brooks combines a sensitivity to poetic forms with a depth of emotion appropriate for her subject matter (972-73).

If you use more than one source by the same author, include a shortened title in the in-text citation.

> Brooks knows not only Shakespeare, Spenser, and Milton, but also the full range of African American poetry (Williams, "Brooks's Way" 972).

Sample In-Text Citations

An entire work

When citing an entire work, state the name of the author in your essay instead of in an in-text citation.

August Wilson's play *Fences* treats many themes frequently expressed in modern drama.

A work by two authors

Myths cut across boundaries and cultural spheres and reappear in strikingly similar forms from country to country (Feldman and Richardson 124).

A work by three or more authors

State the last name of the first author, and use the abbreviation *et al.* (Latin for "and others") for the rest.

Hawthorne's short stories frequently use a combination of allegorical and symbolic methods (Guerin et al. 91).

A work in an anthology

In his essay "Flat and Round Characters," E. M. Forster distinguishes between one-dimensional characters and those that are well developed (Stevick 223-31).

Note that the in-text citation includes the anthology (edited by Stevick) that contains Forster's essay; full information about the anthology appears in the works-cited list.

A work with volume and page numbers

Critics consider *The Zoo Story* to be one of Albee's best plays (Eagleton 2: 17).

An indirect source

Use the abbreviation *qtd. in* ("quoted in") to indicate that the quoted material was not taken directly from the original source.

Wagner observed that myth and history stood before him "with opposing claims" (qtd. in Winkler 10).

A play with numbered lines

The in-text citation should contain the act, scene, and line numbers, separated by periods. Titles of books of the Bible and well-known literary works are often abbreviated—Gen. for Genesis and *Ham.* for *Hamlet*, for example.

"Give thy thoughts no tongue," says Polonius, "Nor any unproportioned thought his act" (*Ham.* 1.3.64-65).

Note that in general, titles of books of the Bible are not italicized.

A poem

Use a slash (/) to separate lines of poetry run in with the text. (The slash is preceded and followed by one space.) Use a double slash (//) to separate stanzas. The in-text citation should include the lines quoted. Include the word *line* or *lines* in the first reference but just numbers in subsequent references.

"I muse my life-long hate, and without flinch / I bear it nobly as I live my part," says the speaker in Claude McKay's bitterly ironic poem "The White City" (lines 3-4).

An electronic source

If you are citing a source from the internet or from an online database, use page numbers when available. If the source uses paragraph, section, or screen numbers, use the abbreviation *par.* or *sec.* or the full word screen.

The earliest type of movie censoring came in the form of licensing fees, and in Deer River, Minnesota, "a licensing fee of $200 was deemed not excessive for a town of 1000" (Ernst, par. 20).

If an internet source has no page, paragraph, section, or screen markers, cite the entire work.

In her article "Limited Horizons," Lynne Cheney says that schools do best when students read literature not for practical information but for its insights into the human condition.

Because of its parody of communism, the film *Antz* is actually an adult film masquerading as a child's tale (Clemin).

The Works-Cited List

In-text citations refer to a **Works-Cited List** that includes all the sources you refer to in your essay:

- Begin the works-cited list on a new page, continuing the page numbers of the essay. For example, if the text of the essay ends on page 6, the works-cited list will begin on page 7.
- Center the title, "Works Cited" one inch from the top of the page.
- Arrange entries alphabetically, according to the last name of each author. Use the first word of the title if the author is unknown (articles—*a*, *an*, and *the*—at the beginning of a title are not considered first words).
- Double-space the entire works-cited list between and within entries.
- Begin typing each entry at the left margin, and indent subsequent lines one-half inch.

The entries on the works-cited list are created using a template called a "container." To use this template, you fill in each element relevant to your source. If a source is part of a larger whole, that larger part is the container. For example, when citing a short story in anthology, the anthology would be the container. In the same respect, if you were citing an article in a journal, the journal would be the container.

Following are the basic elements of a container. (Remember, that all elements may not be present for each entry.) The first two elements—author and title—are needed for most sources and are followed by periods. Next is the "container," the larger work that contains the source you are citing.

Author (s). "Title of the Source." *Title of container*, other contributors, version, number, publisher, publication date, location.

The following is a directory listing the sample MLA works-cited list entries that begin on page 83.

Directory of MLA Works-Cited List Entries

Print Sources: Entries for Articles

1. An article in a scholarly journal
2. An article in a magazine
3. An article in a daily newspaper
4. An article in a reference book

Print Sources: Entries for Books

5. A book by a single author
6. A book by two authors
7. A book by three or more authors
8. Two or more works by the same author
9. An edited book
10. A book with a volume number
11. A short story, poem, or play in a collection of the author's work
12. A short story in an anthology
13. A poem in an anthology
14. A play in an anthology
15. An essay in an anthology
16. More than one item from the same anthology
17. An e-book
18. A translation

Entries for Other Sources

19. An interview
20. A lecture or an address

Electronic Sources: Entries from Websites

21. An article in a scholarly journal from a website
22. An article in an encyclopedia from a website
23. An article in a newspaper from a website
24. An article in a magazine from a website
25. A book from a website
26. A painting or photograph from a website
27. An email
28. A blog or online forum

Electronic Sources: Entries from Online Databases

29. A scholarly journal article from an online database
30. A monthly magazine article from an online database
31. A newspaper article from an online database
32. A reference book article from an online database
33. A dictionary definition from an online database

Entries for Other Electronic Sources

34. A *YouTube* video
35. A *TED Talk*
36. A film, videocassette, DVD, or CD-ROM

MLA • Print Sources: Entries for Articles

Article citations include the author's name; the title of the article (in quotation marks); the name of the periodical (italicized); the volume and issue numbers (if applicable; see below); the month, if applicable (abbreviated, except for May, June, and July); the year; and the pages on which the full article appears (with the abbreviations *p.* or *pp.*).

1. **An article in a scholarly journal**

Grossman, Robert. "The Grotesque in Faulkner's 'A Rose for Emily.'" *Mosaic*, vol. 20, no. 3, 1987, pp. 40–55.

In this citation, *no. 3* signifies issue 3. Note that some scholarly journals do not have volume numbers.

2. An article in a magazine

Milosz, Czeslaw. "A Lecture." *The New Yorker*, 22 June 1992, p. 32.

An article with no listed author is entered by title in the works-cited list.

"Solzhenitsyn: An Artist Becomes an Exile." *Time*, 25 Feb. 1974, pp. 34+.

Note that *34+* indicates that the article appears on pages that are not consecutive; in this case, the article begins on page 34 and continues on page 37.

3. An article in a daily newspaper

Oates, Joyce Carol. "When Characters from the Page Are Made Flesh on the Screen." *The New York Times*, late ed., 23 Mar. 1986, pp. C1+.

Note that *C1+* indicates that the article begins on page 1 of Section C and continues on a subsequent page.

4. An article in a reference book

If the entries are arranged alphabetically, do not include page numbers or volume numbers. When citing a well-known encyclopedia, include only the edition and year. (If the article's author is given, include that too.) For lesser-known encyclopedias, include publication information.

"Dance Theatre of Harlem." *The New Encyclopaedia Britannica: Micropaedia*, Encyclopaedia Britannica, 2008.

Grimstead, David. "Fuller, Margaret Sarah." *Encyclopedia of American Biography*, edited by John A. Garraty, HarperCollins, 1996.

MLA • Print Sources: Entries for Books

Book citations include the author's name; book title and subtitle (italicized); and publication information (place, only if relevant; publisher; and date). Capitalize all major words in the title except articles, prepositions, and the *to* of an infinitive (unless it is the first or last word of the title or subtitle). Abbreviate publishers' names, and with academic presses, replace *University Press* with *UP* (or, if the words are separated by other words, replace them with *U* and *P*: *U of Chicago P*.

5. A book by a single author

Kingston, Maxine Hong. *The Woman Warrior: Memoirs of a Girlhood among Ghosts*. Alfred A. Knopf, 1976.

6. A book by two authors

Feldman, Burton, and Robert D. Richardson. *The Rise of Modern Mythology*. Indiana UP, 1972.

Note that only the *first* author's name is in reverse order.

7. A book by three or more authors

List only the first author, last name first, followed by the abbreviation et al. ("and others").

Guerin, Wilfred, et al., editors. *A Handbook of Critical Approaches to Literature.* 6th ed., Oxford UP, 2011.

8. Two or more works by the same author

List two or more works by the same author alphabetically, by *title*. Include the author's full name in the first entry; use three *unspaced* hyphens followed by a period to take the place of the author's name in second and subsequent entries.

Novoa, Juan-Bruce. *Chicano Authors: Inquiry by Interview.* U of Texas P, 1980.

---. "Themes in Rudolfo Anaya's Work." Literature Colloquium, New Mexico State U, Las Cruces, 11 Apr. 2002. Address.

9. An edited book

If your focus is on the *editor*, list the editor's name first, followed by *editor* or *editors*.

Stauffer, John, editor. *The Portable Frederick Douglass.* Penguin Classics, 2016.

If your focus is on the *author*, include the editor's name, preceded by *Edited by*.

Douglass, Frederick. *The Portable Frederick Douglass.* Edited by John Stauffer, Penguin Classics, 2016.

10. A book with a volume number

When all the volumes of a multivolume work have the same title, list the number of the volume you used.

Eagleton, T. Allston. *A History of the New York Stage.* Vol. 2, Prentice Hall, 1987.

When each volume of a multivolume work has a separate title, list the title of the volume you used.

Durant, Will, and Ariel Durant. *The Age of Napoleon: A History of European Civilization from 1789 to 1815.* Simon & Schuster, 1975.

(*The Age of Napoleon* is volume 2 of *The Story of Civilization*. You need not provide documentation for the entire multivolume work unless this information is relevant to your essay.)

11. A short story, poem, or play in a collection of the author's work

Gordimer, Nadine. "Once upon a Time." *"Jump" and Other Stories,* Farrar, Straus and Giroux, 1991, pp. 23–30.

12. A short story in an anthology

Salinas, Marta. "The Scholarship Jacket." *Nosotras: Latina Literature Today,* edited by Maria del Carmen Boza et al., Bilingual, 1986, pp. 68–70.

13. A poem in an anthology

Simmerman, Jim. "Child's Grave, Hale County, Alabama." *The Pushcart Prize, X: Best of the Small Presses,* edited by Bill Henderson, Penguin, 1986, pp. 198–99.

14. A play in an anthology

Hughes, Langston. *Mother and Child. Black Drama Anthology*, edited by Woodie King and Ron Miller, New American Library, 1986, pp. 399–406.

15. An essay in an anthology

Forster, E. M. "Flat and Round Characters." *The Theory of the Novel*, edited by Philip Stevick, Free Press, 1980, pp. 223–31.

16. More than one item from the same anthology

If you are using more than one selection from an anthology, cite the anthology in a separate entry. Then, list each individual selection separately, including the author and title of the selection, the anthology editor's last name, and the included page numbers.

Baxter, Charles. "Gryphon." Kirszner and Mandell, pp. 191–203.

Kirszner, Laurie G., and Stephen R. Mandell, editors. *Portable Literature: Reading, Reacting, Writing.* 10th ed., Cengage, 2024.

Rich, Adrienne. "Living in Sin." Kirszner and Mandell, pp. 528–529.

17. An E-Book

Kirszner, Laurie G., and Stephen R. Mandell, editors. *Portable Literature: Reading, Reacting, Writing.* 10th ed., e-book ed., Cengage, 2024.

18. A translation

Carpentier, Alejo. *Reasons of State.* Translated by Francis Partridge, W. W. Norton, 1976.

Entries for Other Sources

19. An interview

Brooks, Gwendolyn. "An Interview with Gwendolyn Brooks." *Triquarterly*, no. 60, 1984, pp. 405-10.

20. A lecture or an address

Novoa, Juan-Bruce. "Themes in Rudolfo Anaya's Work." Literature Colloquium, 11 Apr. 2002, New Mexico State U, Las Cruces.

MLA • Electronic Sources: Entries from Websites

Full publication information is not always available for sources accessed from websites. Include in your citation whatever information you can reasonably obtain: the author or editor of the source (if available); the title of site (italicized); the version number of the source (if applicable); the name of the publisher (if available); and the date of electronic publication. Include digital object identifiers (DOIs) or URLs, preferably permalinks (stable internet addresses), in the works-cited list. The date of access may be included if there is a possibility that the source may change or be removed from the site, or if the source does not specify the publication date.

21. **An article in a scholarly journal from a website**

DeKoven, Marianne. "Utopias Limited: Post-Sixties and Postmodern American Fiction." *Modern Fiction Studies*, vol. 41, no. 1, 1995, pp. 75–97. *Project Muse*, https://doi.org/10.1353/mfs.1995.0002.

22. **An article in an encyclopedia from a website**

"Hawthorne, Nathaniel." *Encyclopaedia Britannica Online*, 2010, www.britannica.com/biography/Nathaniel-Hawthorne.

23. **An article in a newspaper from a website**

Cave, Damien. "Election Day May Look Familiar." *The New York Times*, 28 Apr. 2008, www.nytimes.com/2008/04/28/us/politics/28voting.html

24. **An article in a magazine from a website**

Anolik, Lili. "How Joan Didion the Writer Became Joan Didion the Legend." *Vanity Fair*, Feb. 2016, www.vanityfair.com/culture/2016/02/joan-didion-writer-los-angeles.

25. **A book from a website**

Douglass, Frederick. *My Bondage and My Freedom*. Boston, 1855. *Google Book Search*, hwww.google.com/books/edition/My_Bondage_and_My_Freedom/G8t0AgAAQBAJ?hl=en&gbpv=0

26. **A painting or photograph from a website**

Lange, Dorothea. *John, San Francisco*. 1931, *MOMA*, New York. *MoMA*, www.moma.org/collection/works/56378.

27. **An email**

Mauk, Karen. E-Mail to the author. 3 Mar. 2016.

28. **A blog or online forum**

Berg, Kirsten. "Bright Angel." *PowellsBooks.Blog*, 17 June 2009, www.powells.com/post/rare-books/bright-angel.

MLA • Electronic Sources: Entries from Online Databases

To cite information from an online database, supply the publication information (including page numbers, if available) followed by the italicized name of the database and the DOI or URL.

Witze, Alexandra. "Climate Change: Losing Greenland." *Nature*, 17 Apr. 2008, pp. 798–802. *ProQuest*, https://doi.org/10.1038/452798a.

29. A scholarly journal article from an online database

Schaefer, Richard J. "Editing Strategies in Television News Documentaries." *Journal of Communication*, vol. 47, no. 4, 1997. pp. 69–89. *InfoTrac OneFile Plus*, https://doi.org/10.1111/j.1460-2466.1997.tb02726.x.

30. A monthly magazine article from an online database

"Produce sans plastic labels." *National Geographic*, vol. 241, no. 4, Apr. 2022, p. 22. *Gale OneFile: Popular Magazines,* http://www.link.gale.com/apps/doc/A700235245/PPPM?u=gale&sid=bookmark-PPPM&xid=71c36bc4. Accessed 3 June 2022.

31. A newspaper article from an online database

"HG Semiconductor Enters into Cooperation Framework Agreement with China Titans Energy." *ACN Newswire*, 2 June 2022, *Gale OneFile: News*, link.gale.com/apps/doc/A705766211/STND?u=gale&sid=bookmark-STND&xid=42f8e44a. Accessed 3 June 2022.

32. A reference book article from an online database

"Embroidery from Iraq." *Encyclopedia of Embroidery from the Arab World*, 2016, *What Do I Read Next? Online*, Gale, 2021. *Gale Books and Authors*, link.gale.com/apps/doc/M1300234390/BNA?u=gale&sid=bookmark-BNA&xid=34a20d30. Accessed 3 June 2022.

33. A dictionary definition from an online database

Tian, Xiaofei. "Xu Ling (507-583)." *Classical Chinese Writers of the Pre-Tang Period, Gale Literature Dictionary of Literary Biography.*

MLA • Electronic Sources: Entries for Other Electronic Sources

34. A *YouTube* Video

"Intro to Literary Theory." *YouTub*e, uploaded by Leah Plath, 20 Sept. 2020, www.youtube.com/watch?v=FKGcwY9TyNE

35. A *Ted Talk*

Abani, Chris. "Telling Stories from Africa." *TED*, June 2007, https://www.ted.com/talks/chris_abani_telling_stories_from_africa

36. A film, videocassette, DVD, or CD-ROM

The Heinle Original Film Series in Literature: Eudora Welty's "A Worn Path." Directed by Bruce R. Schwartz, DVD ed., Wadsworth, 2003.

Note Using information from a website (especially anonymous websites, blogs, and online forums) can be risky. Contributors are not necessarily experts. Unless you can verify that the information you are obtaining from these sources is reliable, do not use it. You can check the reliability of an online source by asking your instructor or librarian for guidance.

Content Notes

Use **content notes**, indicated by a superscript (a raised number) in the text, to cite several sources at once or to provide commentary or explanations that do not fit smoothly into your essay. The full text of these notes appears on the first numbered page following the last page of the essay. (If your essay has no content notes, the works-cited list follows the last page of the essay.) Like works-cited entries, content notes are double-spaced within and between entries. However, the first line of each explanatory note is indented one-half inch, and subsequent lines are flush with the left-hand margin.

To Cite Several Sources

In the essay: Surprising as it may seem, there have been many attempts to define literature.[1]

In the note: 1. For an overview of critical opinion, see Arnold 72; Eagleton 1–2; Howe 43–44; and Abrams 232–34.

To Provide Explanations

In the essay: In recent years, gothic novels have achieved great popularity.[3]

In the note: 3. Gothic novels, works written in imitation of medieval romances, originally relied on supernatural occurrences. They flourished in the late eighteenth and early nineteenth centuries.

Part 2

Fiction

Chapter

6

Understanding Fiction

Learning Objectives

After reading this chapter, you will be able to. . .

- Understand the origins of fiction and its development.
- Describe the evolution of the novel over time.
- Identify major literary movements throughout history.
- Explain the evolution of the short story genre.
- Outline the elements of a short story.
- Compare the different types of fiction.
- Outline alternative forms of short fiction.

A **narrative** tells a story by presenting events in some logical or orderly way. A work of **fiction** is a narrative that originates in the imagination of the author rather than in history or fact. Of course, some fiction—historical or autobiographical fiction, for example—focuses on real people and is grounded in actual events, but the way the characters interact, what they say, and how the plot unfolds are largely the author's invention.

Even before they know how to read, most people learn how narratives are structured. As children learn how to tell a story, they start to experiment with its form, learning the value of exaggerating, adding, or deleting details; rearranging events; and bending facts. In other words, they learn how to *fictionalize* a narrative to achieve a desired effect. This kind of informal personal narrative is similar in many respects to more structured literary narratives.

Origins of Modern Fiction

People have always had stories to tell, and as we evolved, so did our means of self-expression. Our early ancestors depicted the stories of their daily lives and beliefs in primitive drawings that used pictures as symbols. As language evolved, so too did our means of communicating—and our need to preserve what we understood to be our past.

Stories and songs emerged as an oral means of communicating and preserving the past: tales of heroic battles or struggles, myths, or religious beliefs. In a society that was not literate and in a time before mass communication, the oral tradition enabled people to pass down these stories, usually in the form of long rhyming poems. These poems used various literary devices—including **rhyme** and **alliteration** as well as **anaphora** (the repetition of key words or phrases)—to make them easier to remember. Thus, the earliest works of fiction were, in fact, poetry.

Engraving of Ulysses slaying Penelope's suitors, from Homer's *Odyssey*
Bettmann/Getty Images

Eventually written down, these extended narratives developed into **epics**—long narrative poems about heroic figures whose actions determined the fate of a nation or of an entire race. Homer's *Iliad* and *Odyssey*, the ancient Babylonian *Epic of Gilgamesh*, the Hindu *Bhagavad Gita*, and the Anglo-Saxon *Beowulf* are examples of epics. Many of the tales of the Old Testament also came out of this tradition. The setting of an epic is vast—sometimes worldwide or cosmic, including heaven and hell—and the action commonly involves a battle or perilous journey. Quite often, divine beings participate in the action and influence the outcome of events, as they do in the Trojan War in the *Iliad* and in the founding of Rome in Virgil's *Aeneid*.

During the Middle Ages, these early epics were supplanted by the **romance**. Written initially in verse and later in prose, the romance replaced the gods, goddesses, and central heroic characters of the epic with knights, kings, and damsels in distress. Events were controlled by enchantments rather than by the will of divine beings. The anonymously written *Sir Gawain and the Green Knight* and Thomas Malory's *Le Morte d'Arthur* are romances based on the legend of King Arthur and the Knights of the Round Table.

Other significant texts of the Middle Ages include Geoffrey Chaucer's *The Canterbury Tales* and Giovanni Boccaccio's *The Decameron*, both written in the fourteenth century. These two works are made up of poems and stories, respectively, integrated into a larger narrative framework. They share similarities with modern collections of linked short stories—stories set in the same town or featuring the same characters, such as Sherwood Anderson's 1919 *Winesburg, Ohio* and Amy Tan's 1989 *The Joy Luck Club*.

Engraving of the Trojan horse from Homer's *Odyssey*
Bettmann/Getty Images

Portrait of Queen Guinevere, King Arthur's wife and Sir Lancelot's mistress
Bettmann/Getty Images

The History of the Novel

The evolution of the **novel** has been a gradual but steady process. Early forms of literature share many of the characteristics of the novel (although not necessarily sharing its recognizable form). Epics and romances, for example, often had unified plots, developed characters, and complex themes, and in this way, they were precursors of what today we call the novel.

Perhaps the most notable event in the development of the novel, and of literature as a whole, was the invention of the printing press by Johannes Gutenberg in 1440. Before this milestone, monks working in monasteries painstakingly copied texts by hand. Most books were religious in nature, and because they were difficult to produce, they were extremely expensive and quite rare. (Accessing a particular book often meant travelling a great distance to where it was kept.) The printing press and the attendant rise in literacy made the production and distribution of books a practical possibility and forever expanded the scope of what we consider literature to be—and how we access it. In fact, the printing press was one of the factors that made the Renaissance possible. During this period, books became widely available, and as a result, philosophy, science, literature, and the arts flowered. The **pastoral romance**, a prose tale set in an idealized rural world, and the **character**, a brief satirical sketch illustrating a type of personality, both became popular in Renaissance England. The **picaresque novel**, an episodic, often satirical work about a rogue or rascal (such as Miguel de Cervantes's *Don Quixote*), emerged in seventeenth-century Spain. Other notable Renaissance-era texts included Sir Philip Sidney's

Arcadia, Edmund Spenser's *The Faerie Queen*, and John Bunyan's *The Pilgrim's Progress*. Each of these texts included features now associated with the novel—longer narratives, extended plots, the development of characters over time, and a hero/protagonist.

The First Printing Press.
Nineteenth-century woodcut depicting Johannes Gutenberg's printing press
North Wind Picture Archives/Alamy Stock Photo

The English writer Daniel Defoe is commonly given credit for writing the first novel. His *Robinson Crusoe* (1719) is an episodic narrative similar to a picaresque but unified by a single setting as well as by a central character. Another early novel, Jonathan Swift's *Gulliver's Travels* (1726), is a satirical commentary on human nature and the shortcomings of society. During this time, the **epistolary novel,** in which a story is conveyed indirectly to readers through letters or other documents, also flourished. Samuel Richardson's *Clarissa* (1748) is an example from the eighteenth century; a contemporary example is Alice Walker's *The Color Purple* (1982).

By the nineteenth century, the novel had reached a high point in its development, and its influence and importance were widespread. During the Victorian era in England (1837–1901), many novels reflected the era's

An 1863 engraving by Gustave Doré depicting a scene from Miguel de Cervantes's *Don Quixote*
Timewatch Images/Alamy Stock Photo

Nineteenth-century woodcut by J. Mahoney depicting a scene from Charles Dickens's *Oliver Twist*
Source: Bettmann/Getty Images

preoccupation with propriety and manners. The most notable examples of these **novels of manners** were Jane Austen's *Sense and Sensibility* (1811) and *Pride and Prejudice* (1813). Beyond the world of the aristocracy, members of the expanding middle class clamored for novels that mirrored their own experiences, and writers such as George Eliot, Charles Dickens, William Thackeray, and Charlotte and Emily Brontë appealed to this desire by creating large fictional worlds populated by many different characters who reflected the complexity—and, at times, the melodrama—of Victorian society. Other writers addressed the dire consequences of science and ambition, as Mary Wollstonecraft Shelley did in her Gothic tale *Frankenstein* (1817).

Scene from the 1931 film *Frankenstein*
Source: Bettmann/Getty Images

In the United States, the early nineteenth century was marked by novels that reflected the concerns of a rapidly expanding country with burgeoning interests. James Fenimore Cooper (*Last of the Mohicans*) and Nathaniel Hawthorne (*The Scarlet Letter*) wrote historical fiction, while Herman Melville (*Moby-Dick*) examined good and evil, the limits of knowledge, obsession, and the exploitive nature of whaling. **Realism**, which strove to portray everyday events and people in realistic ways, began in France with

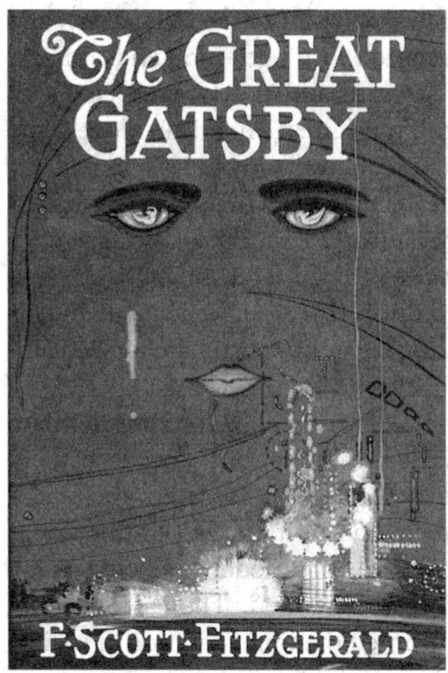

Source: Courtesy, Charles Scribner's Sons, an imprint of Simon & Schuster

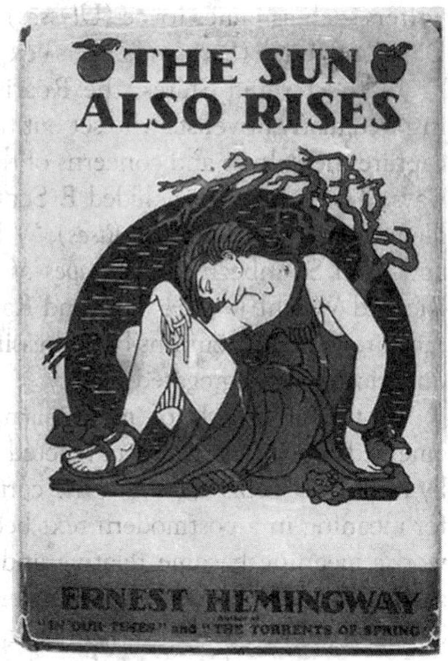

Cover images of *The Great Gatsby, The Sun Also Rises*, and *The Sound and the Fury*

Source: Courtesy, Charles Scribner's Sons, an imprint of Simon & Schuster

Courtesy of Royal Books

Honoré de Balzac and Gustav Flaubert and spread to the United States, influencing writers such as Henry James, Stephen Crane, and Mark Twain. Other nineteenth-century writers addressed social and even feminist themes in their work. In the United States, writers who addressed such concerns included Harriet Beecher Stowe (*Uncle Tom's Cabin*) and Kate Chopin (*The Awakening*). Meanwhile, in Russia, novelists such as Fyodor Dostoyevsky (*Crime and Punishment*) and Leo Tolstoy (*War and Peace*) examined the everyday lives, as well as the larger political struggles and triumphs, of their people.

The early twentieth century marked the beginning of a literary movement known as **modernism**, in which writers reacted to the increasing complexity of a changing world and mourned the passing of old ways under the pressures of modernity. World War I, urbanization, and the rise of industrialism all contributed to a sense that new ideas needed to be expressed in new ways, and writers such as James Joyce (*Ulysses*), Virginia Woolf (*To the Lighthouse*), and D. H. Lawrence (*Sons and Lovers*) experimented with both form and content.

In the United States, the Roaring Twenties and the Great Depression inspired many novelists who set out to write the "Great American Novel" and capture the culture and concerns of the times, often in very gritty and realistic ways. These authors included F. Scott Fitzgerald (*The Great Gatsby*), Ernest Hemingway (*The Sun Also Rises*), William Faulkner (*The Sound and the Fury*), and John Steinbeck (*The Grapes of Wrath*). A little later, novelists such as Richard Wright (*Native Son*) and Ralph Ellison (*Invisible Man*) made important literary contributions by addressing the sociopolitical climate for African-Americans in a segregated society.

In the aftermath of modernism, a movement called **postmodernism** emerged. Postmodern artists reacted against the limitations placed on them by modernist ideas as well as the carnage of World War II. Often, the search for meaning in a postmodern text became an end in itself, and in this way, a work's meaning became relative and subjective. Postmodern novelists, such as Donald Barthelme, J. D. Salinger, Margaret Atwood, Thomas Pynchon, Salman Rushdie, and Kurt Vonnegut, confronted the fragmentation of society and rejected the idea of a unified plot or the possibility of a reliable narrator.

Contemporary fiction has been marked and influenced by the developments of the latter part of the twentieth century, including globalization and the advent of the internet and the Age of Communication. As our ability to interact and communicate with other societies has increased exponentially, so too has our access to the literature of other cultures. Contemporary fiction is a world that mirrors the diversity of its participants in terms of form, content, theme, style, and language. There are many writers worthy of mention, as each culture makes its own invaluable contributions. Some particularly noteworthy contemporary writers include Nobel Prize-winning novelists Orhan Pamuk, José Saramago, Doris Lessing, Gabriel García Márquez, Nadine Gordimer, Saul Bellow, Toni Morrison, V. S. Naipul, Mo Yan, and Abdulrazak Gurnah.

Fiction of the twenty-first century continues to grapple with current events, political movements, the legacy of the past, the search for identity, and what it means to live in a multicultural, interconnected world. For example, Louise Erdrich in *The Night Watchman* (2020) tells the story of her grandfather's fight against Native American land dispossession in the 1950s in rural North Dakota; in her graphic novel *Fun Home: A Family Tragicomic* (2007), Alison Bechdel traces her journey to young adulthood as she comes to grips with her sexuality; and in *Nickel Boys* (2019), Colson Whitehead explores abuse at a reform school in Jim-Crow era Florida. Additionally, recent scientific advances have led writers to speculate about what the future holds for humankind. In so doing, they try to make sense of how technological developments—such as artificial intelligence, virtual reality, DNA manipulation, and mass surveillance—will affect how we live and interact. For example, in *Ready Player One* (2011), Ernest Cline depicts a society in which everyone escapes reality by plugging into a vast computer-generated universe, and in *Klara and the Sun* (2021), Nobel Prize-winning author Kazuo Ishiguro examines the human condition through the eyes of a solar-powered android. As we continue through the twenty-first century, the only thing that remains certain about the future of the novel, and of fiction in general, is that it will continue to evolve in new and often unexpected ways.

The History of the Short Story

Early precursors of the short story include **anecdotes**, **parables**, **fables**, **folktales**, and **fairy tales**. What all of these forms have in common is brevity and a moral. The ones that have survived, such as "Cinderella" and *Aesop's Fables*, are contemporary versions of old, even ancient, tales that can be traced back centuries through many different cultures.

Folktales and fairy tales share many characteristics. First, they feature simple characters who illustrate a quality or trait that can be summed up in a few words. Much of the appeal of "Cinderella," for example, depends on the contrast between the selfish, sadistic stepsisters and the poor, gentle, victimized Cinderella. In addition, the folktale or fairy tale has an obvious theme or **moral**—good triumphing over evil or virtue triumphing over vice, for example. The stories move directly to their conclusions, never interrupted by ingenious or unexpected plot twists. (Love is temporarily thwarted, but the prince eventually finds Cinderella and marries her.) Finally, these tales are anchored not in specific times or places but in "once upon a time" settings, green worlds of prehistory filled with royalty, talking animals, and magic.

The thematically linked stories in Giovanni Boccaccio's *The Decameron* and Geoffrey Chaucer's *The Canterbury Tales*, both written in the fourteenth century, were precursors of the modern short story. *Grimm's Fairy Tales* (1824–1826), an early collection of short narratives and folk stories, also helped to pave the way for the development of the genre, but it was not until the nineteenth century that the contemporary version of the short story emerged.

Undated woodcut of Cinderella
Source: Bettmann/Getty Images

During the last quarter of the nineteenth century, a proliferation of literary and popular magazines and journals created a demand for short fiction (between 3,000 and 15,000 words) that could be published in their entirety rather than in serial installments, as most novels at the time were. Nathaniel Hawthorne's *Twice Told Tales* (1842) and Edgar Allan Poe's *Tales of the Grotesque and Arabesque* (1836) were early collections of short stories. Americans in particular hungrily consumed the written word, and short stories soared in popularity. In fact, because the short story was embraced so readily and developed so quickly in the United States, it is commonly (although not quite accurately) thought of as an American literary form.

Defining the Short Story

Like the novel, the short story evolved from various forms of narrative and has its roots in an oral tradition. However, whereas the novel is an extended piece of narrative fiction, the **short story** is distinguished by its relative brevity, which creates a specific set of expectations and possibilities as well as certain limitations. Unlike the novelist, the short story writer cannot devote a great deal of space to developing a complex plot or a large number of characters. As a result, the short story often begins close to or at the height of action and involves a limited number of characters. Usually focusing on a single incident, the writer develops one or more characters by showing their reactions to events. This attention to character development, as well as its detailed description of setting, is what distinguishes the short story from earlier short narrative forms.

In many contemporary short stories, a character experiences an **epiphany**, a moment of illumination in which something hidden or not understood becomes immediately clear. In other short stories, the thematic significance, or meaning, is communicated through the way in which characters develop, or react. Regardless of its format or its theme, a short story offers readers an open window to a world that they can enter—if only briefly.

The short story that follows, Ernest Hemingway's "Hills Like White Elephants" (1927), illustrates many of the characteristics of the **modern short story**. Although it is so brief that it might be more accurately called a **short-short story**, it uses its limited space to establish a distinct setting and to develop two characters. From the story's first paragraph, readers know where the story takes place and whom it is about: "The American and the girl with him sat at a table in the shade, outside the building. It was very hot and the express from Barcelona would come in forty minutes." As time passes and the man and woman wait for the train to Madrid, their strained dialogue reveals the tension between them and hints at the serious conflict they must resolve.

Ernest Hemingway Photograph Collection, John F. Kennedy Presidential Library and Museum, Boston.

ERNEST HEMINGWAY (1898–1961) grew up in Oak Park, Illinois, and after high school graduation began his writing career as a reporter on the *Kansas City Star*. While working as a volunteer ambulance driver in World War I, eighteen-year-old Hemingway was wounded. As Hemingway himself told the story, he was hit by machine-gun fire while carrying an Italian soldier to safety. (Hemingway biographer Michael Reynolds, however, reports that Hemingway was wounded when a mortar shell fell and killed the man next to him.)

Recognition for Hemingway came early, with publication of the short story collection *In Our Time* (1925) and his first and most acclaimed novel, *The Sun Also Rises* (1926), a portrait of a postwar "lost generation" of Americans adrift in Europe. This novel established Hemingway as a writer who was able to create fiction out of his own life experiences. Shortly after his return to the United States, Hemingway published *Men Without Women* (1927) and *A Farewell to Arms* (1929). *For Whom the Bell Tolls* (1940) emerged out of his experiences as a journalist in Spain during the Spanish Civil War. Later in life, he made his home in Key West, Florida, and then in Cuba, where he wrote *The Old Man and the Sea* (1952), a novella that won the Pulitzer Prize. In 1954, he won the Nobel Prize in Literature. In 1961, plagued by poor health and mental illness—and perhaps also by the difficulty of living up to his own image—Hemingway took his own life. His book about life in Paris, *A Moveable Feast* (1964), was published after his death. Today, Hemingway is widely regarded as one of America's greatest authors.

Cultural Context At the time this story was written, Ernest Hemingway was part of a group of American expatriates living in Paris. Disillusioned by World War I and seeking a more bohemian lifestyle, free from the concerns of American materialism, this group of artists, intellectuals, poets, and writers were known as the "Lost Generation." Some of the group's most famous members included F. Scott Fitzgerald, Gertrude Stein, and John Dos Passos. The literary legacy they left behind is arguably one of the greatest of the twentieth century.

Hills Like White Elephants (1927)

The hills across the valley of the Ebro[1] were long and white. On this side there was no shade and no trees and the station was between two lines of rails in the sun. Close against the side of the station there was the warm shadow of the building and a curtain, made of strings of bamboo beads, hung across the open door into the bar, to keep out flies. The American and the girl with him sat at a table in the shade, outside the building. It was very hot and the express from Barcelona would come in forty minutes. It stopped at this junction for two minutes and went on to Madrid.

"What should we drink?" the girl asked. She had taken off her hat and put it on the table.

"It's pretty hot," the man said.

"Let's drink beer."

"Dos cervezas," the man said into the curtain.

"Big ones?" a woman asked from the doorway.

"Yes. Two big ones."

The woman brought two glasses of beer and two felt pads. She put the felt pads and the beer glasses on the table and looked at the man and the girl. The girl was looking off at the line of hills. They were white in the sun and the country was brown and dry.

"They look like white elephants," she said.

"I've never seen one," the man drank his beer.

"No, you wouldn't have."

---

[1] *Ebro:* A river in northern Spain.

"I might have," the man said. "Just because you say I wouldn't have doesn't prove anything."

The girl looked at the bead curtain. "They've painted something on it," she said. "What does it say?"

"Anis del Toro.[2] It's a drink."

"Could we try it?" 15

The man called "Listen" through the curtain. The woman came out from the bar.

"Four reales."[3]

"We want two Anis del Toro."

"With water?"

"Do you want it with water?" 20

"I don't know," the girl said. "Is it good with water?"

"It's all right."

"You want them with water?" asked the woman.

"Yes, with water."

"It tastes like licorice," the girl said and put the glass down. 25

"That's the way with everything."

"Yes," said the girl. "Everything tastes of licorice. Especially all the things you've waited so long for, like absinthe."[4]

"Oh, cut it out."

"You started it," the girl said. "I was being amused. I was having a fine time."

"Well, let's try and have a fine time." 30

"All right. I was trying. I said the mountains looked like white elephants. Wasn't that bright?"

"That was bright."

"I wanted to try this new drink. That's all we do, isn't it—look at things and try new drinks?"

"I guess so."

The girl looked across at the hills. 35

"They're lovely hills," she said. "They don't really look like white elephants. I just meant the coloring of their skin through the trees."

"Should we have another drink?"

"All right."

The warm wind blew the bead curtain against the table.

"The beer's nice and cool," the man said. 40

"It's lovely," the girl said.

"It's really an awfully simple operation, Jig," the man said. "It's not really an operation at all."

The girl looked at the ground the table legs rested on.

---

[2] *Anis del Toro*: Spanish for *bull's anisette*, a dark alcoholic drink made from anise, an herb that tastes like licorice.

[3] *reales:* Spanish coins.

[4] *absinthe:* A green alcoholic drink made from wormwood, anise, and other herbs.

"I know you wouldn't mind it, Jig. It's really not anything. It's just to let the air in."

The girl did not say anything.

"I'll go with you and I'll stay with you all the time. They just let the air in and then it's all perfectly natural."

"Then what will we do afterward?"

"We'll be fine afterward. Just like we were before."

"What makes you think so?"

"That's the only thing that bothers us. It's the only thing that's made us unhappy."

The girl looked at the bead curtain, put her hand out and took hold of two of the strings of beads.

"And you think then we'll be all right and be happy."

"I know we will. You don't have to be afraid. I've known lots of people that have done it."

"So have I," said the girl. "And afterward they were all so happy."

"Well," the man said, "if you don't want to you don't have to. I wouldn't have you do it if you didn't want to. But I know it's perfectly simple."

"And you really want to?"

"I think it's the best thing to do. But I don't want you to do it if you don't really want to."

"And if I do it you'll be happy and things will be like they were and you'll love me?"

"I love you now. You know I love you."

"I know. But if I do it, then it will be nice again if I say things are like white elephants, and you'll like it?"

"I'll love it. I love it now but I just can't think about it. You know how I get when I worry."

"If I do it you won't ever worry?"

"I won't worry about that because it's perfectly simple."

"Then I'll do it. Because I don't care about me."

"What do you mean?"

"I don't care about me."

"Well, I care about you."

"Oh, yes. But I don't care about me. And I'll do it and then everything will be fine."

"I don't want you to do it if you feel that way."

The girl stood up and walked to the end of the station. Across, on the other side, were fields of grain and trees along the banks of the Ebro. Far away beyond the river, were mountains. The shadow of a cloud moved across the field of grain and she saw the river through the trees.

"And we could have all this," she said. "And we could have everything and every day we make it more impossible."

"What did you say?"

"I said we could have everything."

"We can have everything."

"No, we can't." 75

"We can have the whole world."

"No, we can't."

"We can go everywhere."

"No, we can't. It isn't ours any more."

"It's ours." 80

"No, it isn't. And once they take it away, you never get it back."

"But they haven't taken it away."

"We'll wait and see."

"Come on back in the shade," he said. "You mustn't feel that way."

"I don't feel any way," the girl said. "I just know things." 85

"I don't want you to do anything that you don't want to do—."

"Nor that isn't good for me," she said. "I know. Could we have another beer?"

"All right. But you've got to realize—"

"I realize," the girl said. "Can't we maybe stop talking?"

They sat down at the table and the girl looked across at the hills on the dry side of the valley and the man looked at her and at the table. 90

"You've got to realize," he said, "that I don't want you to do it if you don't want to. I'm perfectly willing to go through with it if it means anything to you."

"Doesn't it mean anything to you? We could get along."

"Of course it does. But I don't want anybody but you. I don't want any-one else. And I know it's perfectly simple."

"Yes, you know it's perfectly simple."

"It's all right for you to say that, but I do know it." 95

"Would you do something for me now?"

"I'd do anything for you."

"Would you please please please please please please stop talking?"

He did not say anything but looked at the bags against the wall of the station. There were labels on them from all the hotels where they had spent nights.

"But I don't want you to," he said, "I don't care anything about it." 100

"I'll scream," the girl said.

The woman came out through the curtains with two glasses of beer and put them down on the damp felt pads. "The train comes in five minutes," she said.

"What did she say?" asked the girl.

"That the train is coming in five minutes."

The girl smiled brightly at the woman, to thank her. 105

"I'd better take the bags over to the other side of the station," the man said. She smiled at him.

"All right. Then come back and we'll finish the beer."

He picked up the two heavy bags and carried them around the station to the other tracks. He looked up the tracks but could not see the train. Coming back, he walked through the barroom, where people waiting for the train were drinking. He drank an Anis at the bar and looked at the people. They were all waiting reasonably for the train. He went out through the bead curtain. She was sitting at the table and smiled at him.

"Do you feel better?" he asked.

"I feel fine," she said. "There's nothing wrong with me. I feel fine."

* * *

Like many short stories, "Hills Like White Elephants" has a single setting, contains a straightforward plot, involves few characters, starts at the height of the action, and reaches its climax quickly. Even so, this story is anything but simple. From the beginning, readers can sense the tension that exists between the two unnamed characters, "the girl" and "the American." For almost half the story, they talk about anything except what concerns them most—the question of whether the girl should have an unspecified "simple operation"—presumably an abortion. When they finally confront the issue, the man trivializes the situation by saying that the procedure is "natural" and "not really an operation at all." Eventually, the girl pleads, "Would you please please please please please please please stop talking?" She is clearly hurt by the American's condescending tone and is frightened by her circumstances. Although at the end of the story she assures him that she is "fine," they both sense that no matter what she decides to do, their relationship will never be the same. In this brief, deceptively uncomplicated story, Hemingway manages to convey, almost entirely through dialogue, the inability of the two main characters to communicate, as well as the moral bankruptcy of their world.

The Boundaries of Fiction

As previously noted, a **short story** is a work of fiction that is marked by its brevity, its relatively limited number of characters, its short time frame, and its ability to achieve thematic significance in a relatively short space. A **novella** (such as Franz Kafka's "The Metamorphosis" and Herman Melville's "Bartleby, the Scrivener") is an extended short story that shares some characteristics (for example, concentrated action) with a short story while retaining some qualities of a novel, including greater character development. At the other end of the spectrum are **short-short stories**, which are under 1,500 words (about five pages) in length. (Examples of those very brief stories are included in Chapter 7.) **Prose poems**, such as Yusef Komunyakaa's "Nude Interrogation" (p. 640), are hybrid versions of literature that have characteristics of both prose (being written in paragraphs) and poetry (being written in verse form, often using imagery, meter, and rhyme to create lyrical beauty). In addition, **graphic stories**—sometimes complete in themselves, sometimes part of longer works of **graphic fiction**—have proliferated in recent years. (An example of graphic fiction is included in Chapter 8.)

Finally, the internet—along with computers, smartphones, and tablets—offers numerous possibilities for arranging and disseminating texts. Currently, writers are experimenting with fictional forms that are every bit as revolutionary as those modernist works created by James Joyce, John Dos Passos, Virginia Woolf, and Gertrude Stein nearly a century ago. For example, "Black Box" (an excerpt appears below), a science fiction short story written by Pulitzer Prize-winning author Jennifer Egan, was originally presented as tweets over a ten-night period.

> Some powerful men actually call their beauties "Beauty."
>
> Contrary to reputation, there is a deep camaraderie among beauties.
>
> If your Designated Mate is widely feared, the beauties at the house party where you've gone undercover to meet him will be especially kind.
>
> Kindness feels good, even when it's based on a false notion of your identity and purpose.

Egan has also written a story in the form of a PowerPoint presentation. The writer Alex Epstein has created a story made up of Facebook photos, and other writers are experimenting with blog-post fiction as well as with stories on websites devoted to specific kinds of fiction—for example, **flash fiction** (fiction consisting of a very few words) or graphic short stories. Perhaps the most experimental fictional form is **hypertext fiction**—stories, such as Catlin Fisher's "These Waves of Girls" and Paul La Farge's "Luminous Airplanes," that contains text and links to pictures, film clips, and other texts. Readers create "paths" through hypertext stories by following links in any order they choose. In this way, a single work of hypertext fiction can contain many possible plots, and readers can move through them at will.

There are, it seems, as many different ways to tell a story as there are stories to be told. A short story may be comic or tragic; its subject may be growing up, marriage, crime and punishment, war, sexual awakening, death, or any number of other human concerns. The setting can be an imaginary world, the old West, rural America, the jungles of Uruguay, nineteenth-century Russia, precommunist China, or modern Egypt. The story may have a conventional form, with a definite beginning, middle, and end, or it may be structured as a letter, as a diary entry, or even as a collection of random notes. The story may use just words or it may juxtapose conventional text with symbols, pictures, or empty space. The narrator of a story may be trustworthy or unreliable, involved in the action or a disinterested observer, sympathetic or deserving of scorn, extremely ignorant or highly insightful, limited in vision or able to see inside the minds of all the characters. As the selections in this anthology show, the possibilities of the short story are almost endless.

Chapter

7

Fiction Sampler: The Short-Short Story

Sandra Cisneros
Beowulf Sheehan/ZUMA Press/New York/NY/USA/Newscom

Jamaica Kincaid
Taro Yamasaki//Time Life Pictures/Getty Images

Stephen Graham Jones
Gary Isaacs

Ed Park
Carolyn Cole/Los Angeles Times/Getty Images

Learning Objectives

After reading this chapter, you will be able to. . .

- Describe the characteristics of the short-short story.
- Classify short-short stories as conventional or experimental.
- Compare the different types of short-short stories.
- Write an essay about one or more short-short stories.

This chapter focuses on the **short-short story**, a short story that is fewer than 1,500 words in length. Short-shorts are often divided into subcategories according to their overall length. For example, **micro fiction**, at approximately 250 words or fewer, is one of the shortest kinds of short-short fiction, followed by **flash fiction** (fewer than approximately 1,000 words), and then by **sudden fiction** (fewer than approximately 1,500 words). Short-shorts are sometimes also categorized according to how long they take to read or to write. Regardless of their individual characteristics, all short-short stories compress ideas into a small package and, to varying degrees, test the limits of the short story genre. Some short-shorts are quite conventional (that is, they include recognizable characters and have an identifiable beginning, middle, and end); others are experimental, perhaps lacking a definite setting or a clear plot. As defined by Robert Shapard (who, along with James Thomas, edited the short-short story collections *Sudden Fiction* and *New Sudden Fiction*), short-short stories are "Highly compressed, highly charged, insidious, protean, sudden, alarming, tantalizing;" they can "confer form on small corners of chaos, can do in a page what a novel does in two hundred." One of the most extreme examples is Ernest Hemingway's famous six-word story: "For sale: baby shoes, never worn."

The stories in this sampler represent a wide range of short-short fiction. Of the seven stories collected here, Bret Anthony Johnston's "Encounters with Unexpected Animals" perhaps most closely resembles a traditional short story in that it develops familiar characters in a recognizable setting. Similarly, Sandra Cisneros's "Geraldo No Last Name" explores a theme that is familiar in literary works: a character's attempt to make sense of an event from the past.

Other stories in this sampler are somewhat more experimental. Although their plots may unfold in conventional ways, their treatment of time is sometimes surprising. For example, in "Discovering America," Stephen Graham Jones summarizes the events of several years of the narrator's life in three pages, while George Saunders's two-paragraph "Sticks" covers several decades, and Ed Park's "Slide to Unlock" unfolds in just a few minutes. Dave Eggers's "Accident" is perhaps even more unpredictable. Although it resembles a conventional short story in some respects, it maintains an unusual narrative distance through its unexpected point of view. Finally, Jamaica Kincaid's "Girl," a **stream-of-consciousness monologue**, is unique in its style and form (the entire story is a single sentence).

Despite their brevity, the stories in this chapter have much in common with the stories that appear elsewhere in this book. Each, in its own distinctive way, "tells a story."

* * *

Beowulf Sheehan/ZUMA Press/New York/NY/USA/Newscom

SANDRA CISNEROS (1954–) was born and raised in Chicago. Her fiction, poems, and essays for adults and children explore Mexican American heritage and identity. Her recent publications—the poetry collection *Women Without Shame* (2022); the novel *Martita, I Remember You* (2021); the chapbook *Puro Amor* (2018); and the essay collection, *A House of My Own* (2015)—represent the wide range of genres in which she publishes. Her novel *The House on Mango Street* (1984) won the American Book Award, one of many prestigious awards and fellowships Cisneros has received. Other accolades include the National Medal of the Arts, a MacArthur Foundation Fellowship, and two National Endowment of the Arts Fellowships for fiction and poetry. Cisneros earned her MFA in Creative Writing in 1978, and she is the founder of the Macondo Foundation.

Geraldo No Last Name (1984)

She met him at a dance. Pretty too, and young. Said he worked in a restaurant, but she can't remember which one. Geraldo. That's all. Green pants and Saturday shirt. Geraldo. That's what he told her.

And how was she to know she'd be the last one to see him alive. An accident, don't you know. Hit and run. Marin, she goes to all those dances. Uptown. Logan. Embassy. Palmer. Aragon. Fontana. The manor. She likes to dance. She knows how to do cumbias and salsas and rancheras even. And he was just someone she danced with. Somebody she met that night. That's right.

That's the story. That's what she said again and again. Once to the hospital people and twice to the police. No address. No name. Nothing in his pockets. Ain't it a shame.

Only Marin can't explain why it mattered, the hours and hours, for somebody she didn't even know. The hospital emergency room. Nobody but an intern working all alone. And maybe if the surgeon would've come, maybe if he hadn't lost so much blood, if the surgeon had only come, they would know who to notify and where.

But what difference does it make? He wasn't anything to her. He wasn't her boyfriend or anything like that. Just another *brazer* who didn't speak English. Just another wetback. You know the kind. The ones who always look ashamed. And what was she doing out at 3:00 A.M. anyway? Marin who was sent home with her coat and some aspirin. How does she explain? 5

She met him at a dance. Geraldo in his shiny shirt and green pants. Geraldo going to a dance.

What does it matter?

They never saw the kitchenettes. They never knew about the two-room flats and sleeping rooms he rented, the weekly money orders sent home, the currency exchange. How could they?

His name was Geraldo. And his home is in another country. The ones he left behind are far away, will wonder, shrug, remember. Geraldo—he went north . . . we never heard from him again.

* * *

David Levenson/Getty Images Entertainment/Getty Images

DAVE EGGERS (1970–) is the author of many books, among them *The Circle, The Every, The Monk of Mokha, A Hologram for the King, What Is the What,* and *The Museum of Rain.* He is a cofounder of 826 National, a network of youth writing centers, and *Voice of Witness,* an oral history book series that illuminates the stories of those impacted by human rights crises. He has been a finalist for the Pulitzer Prize, the National Book Award, and the National Book Critics Circle Award, and is the recipient of the Dayton Literary Peace Prize and the American Book Award. He has attended the JetPack Aviation academy in Moorpark, California, but is not yet certified to fly off-tether. Born in Boston and raised in Illinois, he has now lived in the San Francisco Bay Area for three decades. He and his family often consider leaving, but they do not leave.

Accident (2005)

You all get out of your cars. You are alone in yours, and there are three teenagers in theirs, an older Camaro in new condition. The accident was your fault, and you walk over to tell them this. Walking to their car, which you have ruined, it occurs to you that if the three teenagers are angry teenagers, this encounter could be unpleasant. You pulled into an intersection, obstructing them, and their car hit yours. They have every right to be upset, or livid, or even contemplating violence. As you approach, you see that their driver's side door won't open. The driver pushes against it, and you are reminded of scenes where drivers are stuck in submerged cars. Finally they all exit through the passenger side door and walk around the Camaro, inspecting the damage. None of them is hurt, but the car is wrecked. "Just bought this today," the driver says. He is 18, blond, average in all ways. "Today?" you ask. You are a wretched, reckless person, you think. You also think: what a strange car for a teenager to buy in 2005. "Yeah, today," he says, then sighs. You tell him that you are sorry. That you are so, so sorry. That it was your fault and that you will cover all costs. You exchange insurance information, and you find yourself, minute by minute, ever more thankful that none of these teenagers has punched you, or even made a remark about your being drunk, which you are not, or being stupid, which you are, often. You become more friendly with all of them, and you realize that you are much more connected to them, particularly to the driver, than possible in perhaps any other way. You have done him and his friends harm, you jeopardized their health, and now you are so close you feel like you share a heart. The driver knows your name and you know his, and you almost killed him but, because you got so close to doing so but didn't, you want to fall on him, weeping, because you are so lonely, so lonely always, and all contact is contact, and all contact makes us so grateful we want to cry and dance and cry and cry. In a moment of clarity, you finally understand why boxers, who want so badly to hurt each other, can rest their heads on the shoulders of their opponents, can lean against one another like tired lovers, so thankful for a moment of peace.

* * *

Brian Birzer/Getty Images

BRET ANTHONY JOHNSTON (1971–) is the author of the story collection *Corpus Christi* (2004), the documentary *Waiting for Lightning* (2012), and the novel *Remember Me Like This* (2014), as well as the editor of *Naming the World and Other Exercises for the Creative Writer* (2008). His work also appears in many top-tier literary magazines. Director of the Michener Center for Writers at the University of Texas in Austin and former director of creative writing at Harvard University, Johnston has received several honors and prizes, including the Pushcart Prize, a National Endowment for the Arts Literature Fellowship, the James Michener Fellowship, and the National Book Foundation 5 Under 35 award.

Encounters with Unexpected Animals (2012)

Lambright had surprised everyone by offering to drive his son's girlfriend home. The girl was three months shy of seventeen, two years older than Robbie. She'd been held back in school. Her driver's license was currently suspended. She had a reputation, a body, and a bar code tattooed on the back of her neck. Lambright sometimes glimpsed it when her green hair was ponytailed. She'd come over for supper this evening, and though she volunteered to help Robbie and his mother with the dishes, Lambright had said he'd best deliver her home, it being a school night. He knew this pleased his wife and Robbie, the notion of him giving the girl another chance.

Driving, Lambright thought the moon looked like a fingerprint of chalk. They headed south on Airline Road. A couple of miles and he'd turn right on Saratoga, then left onto Everhart, and eventually they'd enter Kings Crossing, the subdivision with pools and sprinkler systems. At supper, Robbie and the girl had told, in tandem, a story about playing hide-and-seek on the abandoned country club golf course. Hide-and-seek, Lambright thought, is that what y'all call it now? Then they started talking about wildlife. The girl had once seen a blue-and-gold macaw riding on the headrest of a man's passenger seat, and another time, in a pasture in the Rio Grande Valley, she'd spotted zebras grazing among cattle. Robbie's mother recalled finding goats in the tops of peach trees in her youth. Robbie told the story of visiting the strange neighborhood in San Antonio where the muster of peacocks lived, and it led the girl to confess her desire to get a fan of peacock feathers tattooed on her lower back. She wanted a tattoo of a busted magnifying glass hovering over the words FIX ME.

Lambright couldn't figure what she saw in his son. Until the girl started visiting, Robbie had superhero posters on his walls and a fleet of model airplanes suspended from the ceiling with fishing wire. Lambright had actually long been skeptical of the boy's room, worrying it looked too childish, worrying it confirmed what might be called "softness" of character. But now the walls were stripped and all that remained of the fighter fleet was the fishing-wire stubble on the ceiling.

Two weeks ago, one of his wife's necklaces disappeared. Last week, a bottle of her nerve pills. Then, over the weekend, he'd caught Robbie and the girl with a flask of whiskey in the backyard. She'd come to supper tonight to make amends.

Traffic was light. When he stopped at the intersection of Airline and Saratoga, the only headlights he saw were far off, like buoys in the bay. The turn signal dinged. He debated, then clicked it off. He accelerated straight across Saratoga. 5

"We were supposed to turn—"

"Scenic route," he said. "We'll visit a little."

But they didn't. There was only the low hum of the tires on the road, the noise of the truck pushing against the wind. Lambright hadn't contributed anything to the animal discussion earlier, but now he considered mentioning what he'd read a while back, how bald-eagle nests are often girded with cat collars, strung with the little bells and tags of lost pets. He stayed quiet, though. They were out near the horse stables now. The air smelled of alfalfa and manure. The streetlights had fallen away.

The girl said, "I didn't know you could get to Kings Crossing like this."

They crossed the narrow bridge over Oso Creek, then came into a clearing, a swath of clay and patchy brush, gnarled mesquite trees. 10

He pulled onto the road's shoulder. Caliche pinged against the truck's chassis. He doused his headlights, and the scrub around them silvered, turned to moonscape. They were outside the city limits, miles from where the girl lived. He killed the engine.

"I know you have doubts about me. I know I'm not—"

"Cut him loose," Lambright said.

"Do what?"

"Give it a week, then tell him you've got someone else." 15

Her eyes scanned the night through the windshield. Maybe she was getting her bearings, calculating how far out they were. Cows lowed somewhere in the darkness. She said, "I love Rob—"

"You're a pretty girl. You've been to the rodeo a few times. You'll do all right. But not with him."

The chalky moon was in and out of clouds. A wind buffeted the truck and kicked up the odor of the brackish creek. The girl was picking at her cuticles, which made her look docile.

"Is there anything I can say here? Is there something you're wanting to hear?"

You can say you'll quit him," Lambright said. "I'd like to have your word on that subject." 20

"And if I don't, you'll leave me on the side of the road?"

"We're just talking. We're sorting out a problem."

"Or you'll beat me up and throw me in the creek?"

"You're too much for him. He's overmatched."

"And so if I don't dump him, you'll, what, rape me? Murder me? Bury me in the dunes?" 25

"Lisa," he said, his tone pleasingly superior. He liked how much he sounded like a father.

Another wind blew, stiff and parched, rustling the trees. To Lambright, they appeared to shiver, like they'd gotten cold. A low cloud unspooled on the horizon. The cows were quiet.

"I see how you look at me, you know," she said, shifting toward him. She unbuckled her seat belt, the noise startlingly loud in the truck. Lambright's eyes went to the rearview mirror: no one around. She scooted an inch closer. Two inches. Three. He smelled lavender, her hair or cool skin. She said, "Everyone sees it. Nobody'll be surprised you drove me out here."

"I'm telling you to stay away from my son."

"In the middle of the night, in the middle of nowhere."

"There's no mystery here," Lambright said.

"Silly," she said.

"Do what?"

"I said you're silly. There's mystery all around us. Goats in trees. Macaws in cars."

Enough, Lambright thought. He cranked the ignition, switched on his headlights.

"A man who drives his son's underage girl into remote areas, that's awfully mysterious."

"Just turn him loose," he said.

"A girl who flees the truck and comes home dirty and crying. What will she tell her parents? Her boyfriend? The man's depressed wife?"

"Just leave him be," he said. "That's the takeaway tonight."

"Will the police be called? Will they match the clay on her shoes to his tires?"

"Lisa—"

"Or will she keep it to herself? Will it be something she and the man always remember when they see each other? When she marries his son, when she bears his grandbabies? These are bona fide mysteries, Mr. Lambright."

"Lisa," he said. "Lisa, let's be clear."

But she was already out of the truck, sprinting toward the creek. She flashed through the brush and descended the bank, and Lambright was shocked by the languid swiftness with which she crossed the earth. Blood was surging in his veins, like he'd swerved to miss something in the road and his truck had just skidded to a stop and he didn't yet know if he was hurt, if the world was changed. The passenger door was open, the interior light burning, pooling. The girl jumped across the creek and bolted alongside it. She cut to and fro. He wanted to see her as an animal he'd managed to avoid, a rare and dangerous creature he'd describe for Robbie when he got home, but really her movement reminded him of a trickle of water tracking through pebbles. It stirred in him a floating sensation, the curious and scattered feeling of being born on waves or air or wings. He was disoriented, short of breath. He knew he was at the beginning of something, though just then he couldn't say exactly what.

* * *

Gary Isaacs

STEPHEN GRAHAM JONES (1972–) is a Blackfoot Native American who grew up in Texas. Currently a professor of English at the University of Colorado at Boulder, Jones has published nearly thirty novels, collections, novellas, and comic books. Jones has been an NEA recipient and has won the Texas Institute of Letters Award for Fiction, the LA Times Ray Bradbury Prize, the Mark Twain American Voice in Literature Award, the Independent Publishers Award for Multicultural Fiction, and numerous other awards. His works include *Mongrels* (2016), *The Only Good Indians* (2020), and *My Heart is a Chainsaw* (2021).

Discovering America (2001)

Because I'm Indian in Tallahassee Florida the girl behind the counter feels compelled to pull the leather strap ($1.19 per foot) around her neck, show me her medicine pouch, how authentic it is. "Yeah," I say, "hmm," and don't tell her about the one-act play I'm writing, about this Indian in the gift shop at the bottom of Carlsbad Caverns. His name isn't Curio but that's what the lady calls him when she sighs into line with her Germanic accent and her Karl May[1] childhood. "You should do a rain dance or something," she tells him, she's never seen heat like this, like New Mexico. In the play she's sweating, he's sweating, and there's uncounted tons of rock above them, all this pressure.

In Tallahassee it rained all the time.

I stayed there for eleven months, nineteen days, and six hours.

Because I'm Indian at a party in Little Rock Arkansas, a group of students approaches me out of a back room of the house, ceremony still thick on their breath. In a shy voice their leader asks me what kind of animal my spirit helper is, and when I can't quite get enough tact into my mouth to answer, they make a show of respect, say they understand if I can't tell them, really. They tell me theirs, though: a grasshopper, a dragonfly, three wolves, and somewhere in there I become that tall, silent Indian in Thomas Pynchon's "Mortality and Mercy in Vienna," right before he goes cannibalistic in the middle of an otherwise happening party. The working title of the play I'm still writing is *The Time That Indian Started Killing Everybody*, and standing there with my beer I don't revise it.

In Little Rock there were all kinds of bugs I hadn't seen before. 5

I stayed there for five months, four days, and twenty-two hours.

Because I'm Indian in Odessa Texas the guy who picks me up off the side of the road asks me what kind. He's an oilfield worker. His dashboard is black with it. When I say *Blackfeet* he finishes for me with *Montana*, says yeah, he drilled

---

[1] *Karl May:* German author (1842–1912).

up there for a while. Cold as hell. "Yeah," I say, thinking this is going to be an all right ride. He drives and tells me how when he was up there he used to ride a helicopter to the rig every morning, it was *that* cold. In trade I tell him how the National Guard had to airlift hay and supplies a couple of winters back. He nods as if this is all coming back to him, and then, with both arms draped over the wheel real casual, asks me if they still run over Indians up there? I turn to him and he explains the sport, even hangs a tire into the ditch to show me how it's done.

In Odessa the butane pumps go all night, and it's hard to sleep.

I stayed there for three months, fourteen days, and fourteen hours.

Because I'm Indian the guys at the warehouse in Clovis New Mexico add a single feather to the happy face that's been carved into the back of my locker ever since I got there. It's not like looking in a mirror. Every time it's not like looking in a mirror. My second week there we're sweeping rat droppings into huge piles, and when I lean over one to see what Butch is pointing at he slams his broom down, drives it all into my face. That weekend I start coughing it all up, become sure it's the hantavirus that's been killing Indians all over. My whole check goes into the pay phone, calling everyone, talking to them one last time, reading them my play, the part where Curio kills one of the gift-shop people the old way, which means he hits him across the face with a log of Copenhagen, then follows him down to finish it, out of mercy.

In Clovis they don't turn their trucks off so you can talk on the phone, so you have to scream. 10

I stayed there for four weeks, one day, and two and a half hours.

Because I'm Indian in Carlsbad New Mexico the crew I'm working with calls me Chief, motions me over every time there's another animal track in the dirt. "I don't know," I tell them about the tracks, even though I do, and for a couple of hours we work in silence, up one row, down another. Once I find strange and cartoonish tracks in my row—traced with the sharp corner of a hoe—but I pretend to miss them, pretend no one's watching me miss them. All this pretending. Towards the end of the day I pass one of the crew and, without looking up, he asks if I've scalped anybody today, Chief?

I unplant a weed from his row, look up for the briefest moment, long enough to say it: "Nobody you know." He doesn't laugh, and neither do I, and then later that night in a gas station I finish the play I started writing in Florida. It starts when the clerk wipes the sweat from his forehead, says how damn hot it is. And dry. I neither nod nor don't nod, just wait for him to say it.

In Carlsbad New Mexico the law is sluggish, slow to respond.

I stay there for sixteen hours, nine minutes, and fifty-two seconds, and when the rain comes it's not because I danced it up, but because I brought it with me.

* * *

Source: Taro Yamasaki//Time Life Pictures/Getty Images

JAMAICA KINCAID (1949–) was born Elaine Potter Richardson on the island of Antigua, where she received a British education and was often at the top of her class. In 1973, after having begun her writing career in the United States, she changed her name to Jamaica Kincaid because her family disapproved of her writing. She soon began writing a regular column for the *New Yorker.* Author of a dozen books of short stories, novels, memoir, and nonfiction, Kincaid's novel *Annie John* (1986) has likely been translated more than any other book by an Antiguan author. Her nonfiction book *A Small Place* (1988) criticizes British Colonialism in Antigua, and her memoir *My Brother* (1997) recounts the loss of her brother to AIDS. Her most recent novel is *See Now Then* (2013). Kincaid's literary achievements include having won a Guggenheim Fellowship and election to both the American Academy of Arts and Sciences as well as the American Academy of Arts and Letters. Twice a finalist for the PEN/Faulkner Award for Fiction, Kincaid has also won the Prix Femina étranger, the Before Columbus Foundation American Book Award, and, most recently, *The Paris Review* Hadada Award for Lifetime Achievement.

Girl (1984)

Wash the white clothes on Monday and put them on the stone heap; wash the color clothes on Tuesday and put them on the clothesline to dry; don't walk barehead in the hot sun; cook pumpkin fritters in very hot sweet oil; soak your little clothes right after you take them off; when buying cotton to make yourself a nice blouse, be sure that it doesn't have gum on it, because that way it won't hold up well after a wash; soak salt fish overnight before you cook it; is it true that you sing benna[1] in Sunday School?; always eat your food in such a way that it won't turn someone else's stomach; on Sundays try to walk like a lady and not like the slut you are so bent on becoming; don't sing benna in Sunday School; you mustn't speak to wharf-rat boys, not even to give directions; don't eat fruits on the street—flies will follow you; *but I don't sing benna on Sundays at all and never in Sunday school;* this is how to sew on a button; this is how to make a buttonhole for the button you have just sewed on; this is how to hem a dress when you see the hem coming down and so to prevent yourself from looking like the slut I know you are so bent on becoming; this is how you iron your father's khaki shirt so that it doesn't have a crease; this is how you iron your father's khaki pants so that they don't have a crease; this is how you grow okra—far from the house, because okra tree harbors red ants; when you are growing dasheen, make sure it gets plenty of water or else it makes your throat itch when you are eating it; this is how you sweep a corner; this is how you sweep a whole house; this is how you sweep a yard; this is how you smile to someone you don't like too

[1]*benna:* Calypso music.

much; this is how you smile to someone you don't like at all; this is how you smile to someone you like completely; this is how you set a table for tea; this is how you set a table for dinner; this is how you set a table for dinner with an important guest; this is how you set a table for lunch; this is how you set a table for breakfast; this is how to behave in the presence of men who don't know you very well, and this way they won't recognize immediately the slut I have warned you against becoming; be sure to wash every day, even if it is with your own spit; don't squat down to play marbles—you are not a boy, you know; don't pick people's flowers—you might catch something; don't throw stones at blackbirds, because it might not be a blackbird at all; this is how to make a bread pudding; this is how to make doukona;[2] this is how to make pepper pot; this is how to make a good medicine for a cold; this is how to make a good medicine to throw away a child before it even becomes a child; this is how to catch a fish; this is how to throw back a fish you don't like, and that way something bad won't fall on you; this is how to bully a man; this is how a man bullies you; this is how to love a man, and if this doesn't work there are other ways, and if they don't work don't feel too bad about giving up; this is how to spit up in the air if you feel like it, and this is how to move quick so that it doesn't fall on you; this is how to make ends meet; always squeeze bread to make sure it's fresh; *but what if the baker won't let me feel the bread?*; you mean to say that after all you are really going to be the kind of woman who the baker won't let near the bread?

* * *

Carolyn Cole/Los Angeles Times/ Getty Images

ED PARK (1970–) teaches in the graduate writing program at Columbia University. An avid blogger and tweeter, Park has published numerous stories and short works of creative nonfiction. Recognized as one of *Time*'s top ten fiction books of the year and one of *The Atlantic*'s top ten pop culture moments of the decade, his 2008 novel *Personal Days* was a finalist for the PEN Hemingway Award, the Asian American Literary Award, and the John Sargent Sr. First Novel Prize. Besides his writing, Park has also worked as an editor for the *Voice Literary Supplement* and the Poetry Foundation. He is the founding editor of the magazine *The Believer,* which has been a finalist for the National Magazine Award twelve times.

Slide to Unlock (2013)

You cycle through your passwords. They tell the secret story. What's most important to you, the things you think can't be deciphered. Words and numbers stored in the lining of your heart.

Your daughter's name.

Your daughter's name backward.

[2]*doukona:* Spicy plantain pudding.

Your daughter's name backward plus the year of her birth.

Your daughter's name backward plus the last two digits of the year of her birth.

Your daughter's name backward plus the current year.

They keep changing. They blur in the brain. Every day you punch in three or four of these memory strings to access the home laptop, the work laptop. The e-mail, the Facebook, the voice mail. Frequent-flyer account. Every week, you're asked to change at least one, to increase the security. You feel virtuous when the security meter changes from red to green.

Your home town backward.

Your home town plus the year you were born.

Your home town backward plus the year you were born.

Olaf Fub 1970.

There are hints when you forget. Mother's maiden name. First car, favorite color, elementary school.

First girl you kissed—that should be one.

First boy.

Can the hints just be the passwords?

Stop stalling.

First sex. You remember the day, month, year. The full year or just the last two digits?

First concert you attended.

Name of hospital where you were born.

You wonder who writes these prompts. Someone has to write them.

Tip: Never use the same password for more than one account.

Last four digits of first phone number.

Last four digits of first work number.

Your daughter's best friend's name backward.

Your boss's first name.

Your first boss's last name plus the year you were born.

If you could type out all your passwords, their entire silent history, they would fill a book you could read in a minute.

Last four digits of your cell backward.

Favorite sports team.

Favorite sports team backward.

Serbas.

Pet's name.

You knew a guy who had a dog named Serbas. You knew two guys with dogs named Serbas. They didn't like each other. The guys, that is. The dogs, who knows. You're pretty sure one was female, the other male.

Pet's name backward plus current year.

Favorite sibling—sibling who never let you down—plus last two digits of current year.

Mix of capitals and lowercase.

Six to eight characters long.

Ten to fourteen.

Stop stalling.

Mix of numerals and letters.

At least one symbol: #, %,*,!.!

Father's home town.

Mother's maiden name backward.

The girl at work you can't stop thinking about.

The girl at work plus current year.

The girl at work backward.

The girl at work backward and lowercase plus last two digits of current year.

Passwords mean nothing to the machine. The machine lets you in to do what you need to do. It doesn't judge. It doesn't care.

Your password appears as a row of dots.

Favorite film. But that keeps changing.

"Vertigo." "Groundhog Day."

Favorite actor.

Actress who first made you hard, backward, plus current year.

Best friend from high school.

Best friend from college.

Stop stalling.

Year you last saw your daughter.

Year you last saw your daughter plus her name.

There's a file on your work computer called PASSWORDS. But what if you forget the password to get into your work computer?

Her favorite toy.

What she named her bike.

First girl you dated in college backward and lowercase.

"The Shop Around the Corner." "Buffalo '66."

Date of first death in the family.

Grandfather's name backward plus birth year.

Year you finally started getting your shit together.

"Citizen Kane." "Ace Ventura: Pet Detective."

Year of First Communion plus name of priest.

Stop stalling.

Favorite author backward and lowercase with middle letter capped for no reason save randomness.

Street address of the house you grew up in.

Sibling you don't talk to.

Spouse of sibling you don't talk to, whom you text when you're drunk.

Stop stalling.

Your last name backward plus the day, month, and year you find yourself at an A.T.M. at the ass end of Hertel Avenue with the tip of a gun pressed between your shoulder blades, the gun in the hand of the guy who followed you from down the street, affecting a limp, a big guy in a black windbreaker and a Bills Starter cap, who stepped behind you, quiet as a shadow, the big guy with dead eyes behind five-dollar sunglasses who already has your phone and wallet and the bottle of wine you thought it would be a good idea to run out and get, at ten in the evening, she said she'd stay inside and you said you would hurry, and it was a good night for a walk, so, while you're at it, taking in the cool night air, why not get some cash for the week to come?

The big guy with the very hard gun who is saying *Password* and *Right now* and *Stop stalling.* 75

* * *

Eamonn McCabe/Popperfoto/Getty Images

GEORGE SAUNDERS (1958–) teaches in the MFA program at Syracuse University and was named one of *Time*'s 100 most influential people in the world. He has published several story and essay collections, including *Tenth of December* (2013), in which the following story appeared. Saunders is the recipient of MacArthur and Guggenheim Fellowships, and he is a member of the American Academy of Arts and Letters as well as the American Academy of Arts and Sciences. His book *Lincoln in the Bardo* (2017) won the prestigious Man Booker Prize and later became a finalist for the decade's Golden Man Booker award.

Sticks (1995)

Every year Thanksgiving night we flocked out behind Dad as he dragged the Santa suit to the road and draped it over a kind of crucifix he'd built out of metal pole in the yard. Super Bowl week the pole was dressed in a jersey and Rod's helmet and Rod had to clear it with Dad if he wanted to take the helmet off. On Fourth of July the pole was Uncle Sam, on Veterans Day a soldier, on Halloween a ghost. The pole was Dad's one concession to glee. We were allowed a single Crayola from the box at a time. One Christmas Eve he shrieked at Kimmie for wasting an apple slice. He hovered over us as we poured ketchup, saying, Good enough good enough good enough. Birthday parties consisted of cupcakes, no ice cream. The first time I brought a date over she said, What's with your dad and that pole? and I sat there blinking.

We left home, married, had children of our own, found the seeds of meanness blooming also within us. Dad began dressing the pole with more complexity and less discernible logic. He draped some kind of fur over it on Groundhog Day and lugged out a floodlight to ensure a shadow. When an earthquake struck Chile he laid the pole on its side and spray-painted a rift in the earth. Mom died and he dressed the pole as Death and hung from the crossbar photos of

Mom as a baby. We'd stop by and find odd talismans from his youth arranged around the base: army medals, theater tickets, old sweatshirts, tubes of Mom's makeup. One autumn he painted the pole bright yellow. He covered it with cotton swabs that winter for warmth and provided offspring by hammering in six crossed sticks around the yard. He ran lengths of string between the pole and the sticks, and taped to the string letters of apology, admissions of error, pleas for understanding, all written in a frantic hand on index cards. He painted a sign saying LOVE and hung it from the pole and another that said FORGIVE? and then he died in the hall with the radio on and we sold the house to a young couple who yanked out the pole and left it by the road on garbage day.

* * *

Reading and Reacting

1. Which of the stories in this chapter do you see as the most conventional? Which seems the *least* conventional? Why?
2. Does every story seem complete? What, if anything, seems to be missing from each story that might be present in a longer story?
3. If you were going to add material to "Sticks," what would you add? Why?
4. Some stories in this chapter—for example, "Encounters with Unexpected Animals"—include dialogue; others include none (or very little). How would these stories be different if dialogue (or more dialogue) were added? What kind of dialogue would be useful?
5. **Critical Perspective** Writing for *Studies in Short Fiction*, William C. Hamlin describes the essential characteristics of the short-short story:

   > Perhaps in no kind of fiction other than the short-short can Poe's "rules" for the "tale" be so fully adapted and realized. He wrote about organic unity and singleness of effect and the totality of that effect. In the short-short there is simply no room for sub-plotting, for Jamesian penetration, for slowly developing tensions, for any kind of byplay. The writer is trying to go from A to B in the shortest time consistent with purpose and reason. If he or she is successful, then the reader is richer by a minor masterpiece.

   Do you think all the stories in this sampler meet Hamlin's criteria for success? Why or why not?

WRITING SUGGESTIONS: The Short-Short Story

1. Write a **response** expressing your reactions to the ending of "Discovering America" or "Slide to Unlock."
2. Write an **explication** of any short-short story in this chapter—or of a short-short story located elsewhere in this book—for example, Kate Chopin's "The Story of an Hour" (p. 151).

3. Write a character analysis of the narrator in "Girl" or "Accident."
4. Write a **comparison-contrast essay** comparing "Encounters with Unexpected Animals" to Joyce Carol Oates's "Where Are You Going, Where Have You Been?" (p. 447).
5. Write an essay about the **cultural context** of "Geraldo No Last Name" or "Discovering America."

Chapter

8

Fiction Sampler: Graphic Fiction

Franz Kafka
Hulton Archive/Archive Photos/Getty Images

R. Crumb
Oscar White/Corbis Historical/Getty Images

Learning Objectives

After reading this chapter, you will be able to. . .

- Describe the characteristics of graphic fiction.
- Identify the most popular types of graphic fiction.
- Summarize the history of graphic fiction and its evolution over time.
- Explain how images and words work together in a work of graphic fiction.
- Identify the visual elements that establish setting in a work of graphic fiction.

The term *graphic fiction* can be applied to a wide range of visual material, including individual and collected comics and cartoons. As graphic novelist Ivan Brunetti explains, when creating graphic fiction, "The cartoonist uses his own particular set of marks (or 'visual handwriting') to establish a consistent visual vocabulary in which to communicate experience, memory, and imagination—in short, the stuff of narratives."

Like the **short-short stories** (see p. 107), works of graphic fiction pack ideas into small spaces (in this case, the "cells" or "panels" on a page). While many graphic works are fictional narratives, others—such as graphic essays, biographies, memoirs, historical accounts, and journalistic pieces—actually qualify as nonfiction. Works of graphic fiction appear in printed books, magazines, newspapers, and pamphlets, and many are published online as **Web comics**.

Two of today's most popular kinds of graphic fiction are *manga* and *superhero comic books*. **Manga**, Japanese comics (many of which are translated into English), are extremely popular in Japan, where the term refers to animation as well as comics in print and digital form and includes works of romance, science fiction, adventure, and many other genres. **Superhero comic books**, which have their roots in the Superman comic books first published in 1938, continue to increase in popularity with the rise of Marvel's numerous superhero comics as well as film franchises, such as *X-Men*, *Black Panther*, *Captain Marvel*, and *Guardians of the Galaxy*. In recent years, superhero comics and the movies based on them have become more diverse and now feature protagonists who are female, LGBTQ, or members of other groups formerly not represented in the genre.

In its volatile history, graphic fiction has taken various forms, appealing to popular and literary audiences alike. In fact, the genre is constantly being redefined. As graphic novelist Eddie Campbell argues, the graphic novel genre "signifies a movement rather than a form" as it strives "to take the form of the comic book, which has become an embarrassment, and raise it to a more ambitious and meaningful level."

Graphic fiction had its origins in comic strips. In the late nineteenth and early twentieth centuries, American newspapers started to feature comic strips that ranged in variety from popular, slapstick, and science fiction (*The Yellow Kid*, 1895; *Happy Hooligan*, 1900; *Thimble Theatre* [later renamed *Popeye*], 1929; *Flash Gordon*, 1934) to literary and artistic (*Little Nemo*, 1905; *Krazy Kat*, 1913). Comic books, or collections of previously published comic strips, appeared in the mid-1930s, and shortly thereafter the superhero comic emerged and exploded. Comic book characters like Superman, Batman, Wonder Woman, and Captain Marvel began to dominate the genre in the 1940s, and contemporary superhero comics such as *Spider-Man* (1962) and *X-Men* (1963) have achieved international fame both in traditional print formats and in major motion pictures.

In response to the superhero subgenre, **underground** or **alternative comics** appeared in the 1960s, challenging the status quo and depicting taboo topics such as drugs and sex. These unconventional comics, created by artists such as Robert Crumb (1943–) and S. Clay Wilson (1941–2021), have experienced ups and downs throughout their sales history, unlike their consistently best-selling superhero counterparts. Alternative comics helped usher in the more

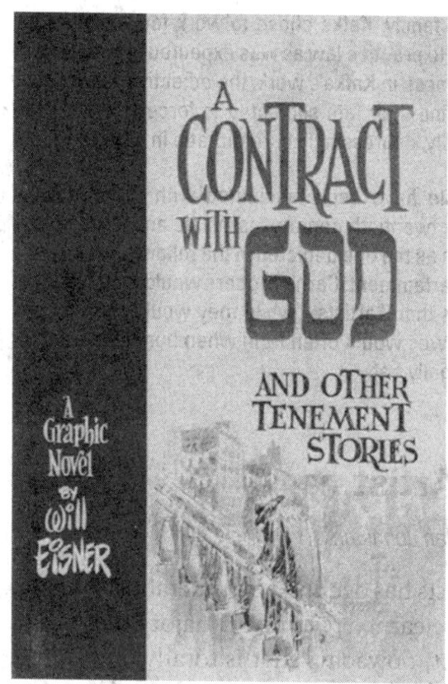

Cover image of the first graphic novel, Eisner's *A Contract with God* (1978)

Source: Baronet Books 1978

acclaimed literary graphic novels of the 1980s and 1990s, including Alison Bechdel's memoir *Fun Home* (2006) and Daniel Clowes's *Ghost World* (1993).

Will Eisner's *A Contract with God* (1978) is generally acknowledged to be the first graphic novel. Actually a collection of four short stories, the book displayed the label "graphic novel" on its cover, establishing this new genre as a literary form fundamentally different from mainstream comics.

The graphic novel continues to evolve today in its attempt to contribute in fresh, new ways to the changing literary canon. For example, Max Brooks's *The Harlem Hellfighters* (2014) recounts the struggles and triumphs of an African American army regiment in World War I, juxtaposing the men's courage in combat with the discrimination they faced at home. Marjane Satrapi's *Persepolis* (2003) presents an account of her life as a rebellious child in Iran during the Islamic Revolution; in his Pulitzer Prize–winning book *Maus: A Survivor's* Tale (1986), Art Spiegelman reimagines episodes from the life of his father, a Polish Jew who survived the Holocaust. More recently, Gene Luen Yang's *American Born Chinese* (2006) explores the familiar American theme of reinvention through a young boy's struggles with his identity.

In the pages that follow, this chapter juxtaposes a classic short story, Franz Kafka's "A Hunger Artist," with R. Crumb's work of graphic fiction based on it.

Hulton Archive/Archive Photos/Getty Images

FRANZ KAFKA (1883–1924) Before dying of tuberculosis, the still young and relatively obscure Franz Kafka, who had devoted himself to an excruciating overnight writing routine between his shifts at work and his family obligations, asked his friend, the writer Max Brod, to burn his unpublished work. Brod ignored Kafka's dying wish, and thanks to Brod's decision to have Kafka's work published posthumously, Kafka has become one of the world's most renowned authors. Perhaps most famous for his story "The Metamorphosis," Kafka has produced an impressive collection of stories and nonfiction as well as the novels *The Trial* (1925), *The Castle* (1926), and *Amerika* (1927).

Born to an intense and emotionally volatile family, Kafka chose to work for an insurance company and leave time for his writing rather than to practice law as was expected of him. So pronounced is the sense of alienation and powerlessness in Kafka's work, the adjective *Kafkaesque* has come to refer to situations in which people find their fate subjected to forces beyond their control—especially when those forces are absurdly, depressingly bureaucratic in nature.

Cultural Context Throughout history, people have been fascinated with the effects of fasting on the human body and mind. In the early twentieth century, carnivals and freak shows throughout Europe featured "hunger artists," such as the one depicted in the following story, who voluntarily starved themselves for the public's entertainment. Carnival goers would watch hunger artists, who were considered to be more oddities than "artists," while they would sit in a cage and do menial tasks—or nothing at all. Large crowds would often form when hunger artists, for whatever reason, decided to end their fast and finally eat.

A Hunger Artist (1924)

Translated by Ian Johnston

In the last decades interest in hunger artists has declined considerably. Whereas in earlier days there was good money to be earned putting on major productions of this sort under one's own management, nowadays that is totally impossible. Those were different times. Back then the hunger artist captured the attention of the entire city. From day to day while the fasting lasted, participation increased. Everyone wanted to see the hunger artist at least daily. During the final days there were people with subscription tickets who sat all day in front of the small barred cage. And there were even viewing hours at night, their impact heightened by torchlight. On fine days the cage was dragged out into the open air, and then the hunger artist was put on display particularly for the children. While for grown-ups the hunger artist was often merely a joke, something they participated in because it was fashionable, the children looked on amazed, their mouths open, holding each other's hands for safety, as he sat there on scattered straw—spurning a chair—in black tights, looking pale, with his ribs sticking out prominently, sometimes nodding politely, answering questions with a forced smile, even sticking his arm out through the bars to let people feel how emaciated he was, but then completely sinking back into himself, so that he paid no attention to anything, not even to what was so important to him, the striking of the clock, which was the single furnishing in the cage, merely looking out in front of him with his eyes almost shut and now and then sipping from a tiny glass of water to moisten his lips.

Apart from the changing groups of spectators there were also constant observers chosen by the public—strangely enough they were usually butchers—who, always three at a time, were given the task of observing the hunger artist day and night, so that he didn't get something to eat in some secret manner. It was, however, merely a formality, introduced to reassure the masses, for those who understood knew well enough that during the period of fasting the hunger artist would never, under any circumstances, have eaten the slightest thing, not even if compelled by force. The honour of his art forbade it. Naturally, none of the watchers understood that. Sometimes there were nightly groups of watchers who carried out their vigil very laxly, deliberately sitting together in a distant corner and putting all their attention into playing cards there, clearly intending to allow the hunger artist a small refreshment, which, according to their way of thinking, he could get from some secret supplies. Nothing was more excruciating to the hunger artist than such watchers. They depressed him. They made his fasting terribly difficult.

Sometimes he overcame his weakness and sang during the time they were observing, for as long as he could keep it up, to show people how unjust their suspicions about him were. But that was little help. For then they just wondered among themselves about his skill at being able to eat even while singing. He much preferred the observers who sat down right against the bars and, not satisfied with the dim backlighting of the room, illuminated him with electric flashlights. The glaring light didn't bother him in the slightest. Generally he couldn't sleep at all, and he could always doze under any lighting and at any hour, even in an overcrowded, noisy auditorium. With such observers, he was very happily prepared to spend the entire night without sleeping. He was very pleased to joke with them, to recount stories from his nomadic life and then, in turn, to listen to their stories—doing everything just to keep them awake, so that he could keep showing them once again that he had nothing to eat in his cage and that he was fasting as none of them could.

He was happiest, however, when morning came and a lavish breakfast was brought for them at his own expense, on which they hurled themselves with the appetite of healthy men after a hard night's work without sleep. True, there were still people who wanted to see in this breakfast an unfair means of influencing the observers, but that was going too far, and if they were asked whether they wanted to undertake the observers' night shift for its own sake, without the breakfast, they excused themselves. But nonetheless they stood by their suspicions.

However, it was, in general, part of fasting that these doubts were inextricably associated with it. For, in fact, no one was in a position to spend time watching the hunger artist every day and night, so no one could know, on the basis of his own observation, whether this was a case of truly uninterrupted, flawless fasting. The hunger artist himself was the only one who could know that and, at the same time, the only spectator capable of being completely satisfied with his own fasting. But the reason he was never satisfied was something different. Perhaps it was not fasting at all which made him so very emaciated that many people, to their own regret, had to stay away from his performance, because they couldn't bear to look at him. For he was also so skeletal out of dissatisfaction with himself, because he alone knew something that even initiates didn't know—how easy it was to fast. It was the easiest thing in the world. About this he did not remain silent, but people did not believe him. At best they thought he was being modest. Most of them, however, believed he was a publicity seeker or a total swindler, for whom, at all events, fasting was easy, because he understood how to make it easy, and then had the nerve to half admit it. He had to accept all that. Over the years he had become accustomed to it. But this dissatisfaction kept gnawing at his insides all the time and never yet—and this one had to say to his credit—had he left the cage of his own free will after any period of fasting.

The impresario had set the maximum length of time for the fast at forty days—he would never allow the fasting to go on beyond that point, not even in the cosmopolitan cities. And, in fact, he had a good reason. Experience had shown that for about forty days one could increasingly whip up a city's interest by gradually increasing advertising, but that then the people turned away—one could demonstrate a significant decline in popularity. In this respect, there were, of course, small differences among different towns and among different countries, but as a rule it was true that forty days was the maximum length of time.

So then on the fortieth day the door of the cage—which was covered with flowers—was opened, an enthusiastic audience filled the amphitheatre, a military band played, two doctors entered the cage, in order to take the necessary measurements of the hunger artist, the results were announced to the auditorium through a megaphone, and finally two young ladies arrived, happy about the fact that they were the ones who had just been selected by lot, seeking to lead the hunger artist down a couple of steps out of the cage, where on a small table a carefully chosen hospital meal was laid out. And at this moment the hunger artist always fought back. Of course, he still freely laid his bony arms in the helpful outstretched hands of the ladies bending over him, but he did not want to stand up. Why stop right now after forty days? He could have kept going for even longer, for an unlimited length of time. Why stop right now, when he was in his best form, indeed, not yet even in his best fasting form? Why did people want to rob him of the fame of fasting longer, not just so that he could become the greatest hunger artist of all time, which he probably was already, but also so that he could surpass himself in some unimaginable way, for he felt there were no limits to his capacity for fasting. Why did this crowd, which pretended to admire him so much, have so little patience with him? If he kept going and kept fasting longer, why would they not tolerate it? Then, too, he was tired and felt good sitting in the straw. Now he was supposed to stand up straight and tall and go to eat, something which, when he just imagined it, made him feel nauseous right away. With great difficulty he repressed mentioning this only out of consideration for the women. And he looked up into the eyes of these women, apparently so friendly but in reality so cruel, and shook his excessively heavy head on his feeble neck.

But then happened what always happened.

The impresario came and in silence—the music made talking impossible—raised his arms over the hunger artist, as if inviting heaven to look upon its work here on the straw, this unfortunate martyr, something the hunger artist certainly was, only in a completely different sense, then grabbed the hunger artist around his thin waist, in the process wanting with his exaggerated caution to make people believe that here he had to deal with something fragile, and handed him over—not without secretly shaking him a little, so that the hunger artist's legs and upper body swung back and forth uncontrollably—to the women, who had in the meantime turned as pale as death. At this point, the hunger artist endured everything. His head lay on his chest—it was as if it had inexplicably rolled around and just stopped there—his body was arched back, his legs, in an impulse of self-preservation, pressed themselves together at the knees, but scraped the ground, as if they were not really on the floor but were looking for the real ground, and the entire weight of his body, admittedly very small, lay against one of the women, who appealed for help with flustered breath, for she had not imagined her post of honour would be like this, and then stretched her neck as far as possible, to keep her face from the least contact with the hunger artist, but then, when she couldn't manage this and her more fortunate companion didn't come to her assistance but trembled and remained content to hold in front of her the hunger artist's hand, that small bundle of knuckles, she broke into tears, to the delighted laughter of the auditorium, and had to be relieved by an attendant who had been standing ready for some time. Then came the meal. The impresario put a little food into the mouth of the hunger artist, now half unconscious, as if fainting, and kept up a cheerful patter designed to divert attention away from the hunger artist's condition. Then a toast was proposed to the public, which was supposedly whispered to the impresario by the hunger artist, the orchestra confirmed everything with a great fanfare, people dispersed, and no one had the right to be dissatisfied with the event, no one except the hunger artist—he was always the only one.

He lived this way, taking small regular breaks, for many years, apparently in the spotlight, honoured by the world, but for all that his mood was usually gloomy, and it kept growing gloomier all the time, because no one understood how to take him seriously. But how was he to find consolation? What was there left for him to wish for? And if a good-natured man who felt sorry for him ever wanted to explain to him that his sadness probably came from his fasting, then it could happen that the hunger artist responded with an outburst of rage and began to shake the bars like an animal, frightening everyone. But the impresario had a way of punishing moments like this, something he was happy to use. He would make an apology for the hunger artist to the assembled public, conceding that the irritability had been provoked only by his fasting, something quite intelligible to well-fed people and capable of excusing the behaviour of the hunger artist without further explanation.

From there he would move on to speak about the equally hard to understand claim of the hunger artist that he could go on fasting for much longer than he was doing. He would praise the lofty striving, the good will, and the great self-denial no doubt contained in this claim, but then would try to contradict it simply by producing photographs, which were also on sale, for in the pictures one could see the hunger artist on the fortieth day of his fast, in bed, almost dead from exhaustion. Although the hunger artist was very familiar with this perversion of the truth, it always strained his nerves again and was too much for him. What was a result of the premature ending of the fast people were now proposing as its cause! It was impossible to fight against this lack of understanding, against this world of misunderstanding. In good faith he always listened eagerly to the impresario at the bars of his cage, but each time, once the photographs came out, he would let go of the bars and, with a sigh, sink back into the straw, and a reassured public could come up again and view him.

When those who had witnessed such scenes thought back on them a few years later, often they were unable to understand themselves. For in the meantime that change mentioned above had set in. It happened almost immediately. There may have been more profound reasons for it, but who bothered to discover what they were? At any rate, one day the pampered hunger artist saw himself abandoned by the crowd of pleasure seekers, who preferred to stream to other attractions. The impresario chased around half of Europe one more time with him, to see whether he could still re-discover the old interest here and there. It was all futile. It was as if a secret agreement against the fasting performances had developed everywhere. Naturally, it couldn't really have happened all at once, and people later remembered some things which in the days of intoxicating success they hadn't paid sufficient attention to, some inadequately suppressed indications, but now it was too late to do anything to counter them. Of course, it was certain that the popularity of fasting would return once more someday, but for those now alive that was no consolation. What was the hunger artist to do now? A man whom thousands of people had cheered on could not display himself in show booths at small fun fairs. The hunger artist was not only too old to take up a different profession, but was fanatically devoted to fasting more than anything else. So he said farewell to the impresario, an incomparable companion on his life's road, and let himself be hired by a large circus. In order to spare his own feelings, he didn't even look at the terms of his contract at all.

A large circus with its huge number of men, animals, and gimmicks, which are constantly being let go and replenished, can use anyone at any time, even a hunger artist, provided, of course, his demands are modest. Moreover, in this particular case it was not only the hunger artist himself who was engaged, but also his old and famous name.

In fact, given the characteristic nature of his art, which was not diminished by his advancing age, one could never claim that a worn out artist, who no longer stood at the pinnacle of his ability, wanted to escape to a quiet position in the circus. On the contrary, the hunger artist declared that he could fast just as well as in earlier times—something that was entirely credible. Indeed, he even affirmed that if people would let him do what he wanted—and he was promised this without further ado—he would really now legitimately amaze the world for the first time, an assertion which, however, given the mood of the time, which the hunger artist in his enthusiasm easily overlooked, only brought smiles from the experts.

However, basically the hunger artist had not forgotten his sense of the way things really were, and he took it as self-evident that people would not set him and his cage up as the star attraction somewhere in the middle of the arena, but would move him outside in some other readily accessible spot near the animal stalls. Huge brightly painted signs surrounded the cage and announced what there was to look at there. During the intervals in the main performance, when the general public pushed out towards the menagerie in order to see the animals, they could hardly avoid moving past the hunger artist and stopping there a moment. They would perhaps have remained with him longer, if those pushing up behind them in the narrow passage way, who did not understand this pause on the way to the animal stalls they wanted to see, had not made a longer peaceful observation impossible. This was also the reason why the hunger artist began to tremble at these visiting hours, which he naturally used to long for as the main purpose of his life. In the early days he could hardly wait for the pauses in the performances. He had looked forward with delight to the crowd pouring around him, until he became convinced only too quickly—and even the most stubborn, almost deliberate self-deception could not hold out against the experience—that, judging by their intentions, most of these people were, again and again without exception, only visiting the menagerie. And this view from a distance still remained his most beautiful moment. For when they had come right up to him, he immediately got an earful from the shouting of the two steadily increasing groups, the ones who wanted to take their time looking at the hunger artist, not with any understanding but on a whim or from mere defiance—for him these ones were soon the more painful—and a second group of people whose only demand was to go straight to the animal stalls.

Once the large crowds had passed, the late comers would arrive, and although there was nothing preventing these people any more from sticking around for as long as they wanted, they rushed past with long strides, almost without a sideways glance, to get to the animals in time.

And it was an all-too-rare stroke of luck when the father of a family came by with his children, pointed his finger at the hunger artist, gave a detailed explanation about what was going on here, and talked of earlier years, when he had been present at similar but incomparably more magnificent performances, and then the children, because they had been inadequately prepared at school and in life, always stood around still uncomprehendingly. What was fasting to them? But nonetheless the brightness of the look in their searching eyes revealed something of new and more gracious times coming. Perhaps, the hunger artist said to himself sometimes, everything would be a little better if his location were not quite so near the animal stalls. That way it would be easy for people to make their choice, to say nothing of the fact that he was very upset and constantly depressed by the stink from the stalls, the animals' commotion at night, the pieces of raw meat dragged past him for the carnivorous beasts, and the roars at feeding time. But he did not dare to approach the administration about it. In any case, he had the animals to thank for the crowds of visitors among whom, here and there, there could be one destined for him. And who knew where they would hide him if he wished to remind them of his existence and, along with that, of the fact that, strictly speaking, he was only an obstacle on the way to the menagerie.

A small obstacle, at any rate, a constantly diminishing obstacle. People got used to the strange notion that in these times they would want to pay attention to a hunger artist, and with this habitual awareness the judgment on him was pronounced. He might fast as well as he could—and he did—but nothing could save him any more. People went straight past him. Try to explain the art of fasting to anyone! If someone doesn't feel it, then he cannot be made to understand it. The beautiful signs became dirty and illegible. People tore them down, and no one thought of replacing them. The small table with the number of days the fasting had lasted, which early on had been carefully renewed every day, remained unchanged for a long time, for after the first weeks the staff grew tired of even this small task. And so the hunger artist kept fasting on and on, as he once had dreamed about in earlier times, and he had no difficulty succeeding in achieving what he had predicted back then, but no one was counting the days—no one, not even the hunger artist himself, knew how great his achievement was by this point, and his heart grew heavy. And when once in a while a person strolling past stood there making fun of the old number and talking of a swindle, that was in a sense the stupidest lie which indifference and innate maliciousness could invent, for the hunger artist was not being deceptive—he was working honestly—but the world was cheating him of his reward.

Many days went by once more, and this, too, came to an end.

Finally the cage caught the attention of a supervisor, and he asked the attendant why they had left this perfectly useful cage standing here unused with rotting straw inside. Nobody knew, until one man, with the help of the table with the number on it, remembered the hunger artist. They pushed the straw around with a pole and found the hunger artist in there. "Are you still fasting?" the supervisor asked. "When are you finally going to stop?" "Forgive me everything," whispered the hunger artist. Only the supervisor, who was pressing his ear up against the cage, understood him. "Certainly," said the supervisor, tapping his forehead with his finger in order to indicate to the spectators the state the hunger artist was in, "we forgive you." "I always wanted you to admire my fasting," said the hunger artist. "But we do admire it," said the supervisor obligingly. "But you shouldn't admire it," said the hunger artist. "Well then, we don't admire it," said the supervisor, "but why shouldn't we admire it?" "Because I had to fast. I can't do anything else," said the hunger artist. "Just look at you," said the supervisor, "why can't you do anything else?" "Because," said the hunger artist, lifting his head a little and, with his lips pursed as if for a kiss, speaking right into the supervisor's ear so that he wouldn't miss anything, "because I couldn't find a food which I enjoyed. If had found that, believe me, I would not have made a spectacle of myself and would have eaten to my heart's content, like you and everyone else." Those were his last words, but in his failing eyes there was the firm, if no longer proud, conviction that he was continuing to fast.

"All right, tidy this up now," said the supervisor. And they buried the hunger artist along with the straw. But in his cage they put a young panther. Even for a person with the dullest mind it was clearly refreshing to see this wild animal throwing itself around in this cage, which had been dreary for such a long time. It lacked nothing. Without thinking about it for any length of time, the guards brought the animal food. It enjoyed the taste and never seemed to miss its freedom. This noble body, equipped with everything necessary, almost to the point of bursting, also appeared to carry freedom around with it. That seemed to be located somewhere or other in its teeth, and its joy in living came with such strong passion from its throat that it was not easy for spectators to keep watching. But they controlled themselves, kept pressing around the cage, and had no desire to move on.

Reading and Reacting

1. What information does the story's first sentence give readers? What other **exposition** is provided?
2. What do we know about the hunger artist? What more would you like to know? Why?
3. List the characters (besides the hunger artist himself) who appear in this story. What role does each play? Are they all necessary?
4. In what sense is fasting a "profession"? What other designation might apply?
5. What transitional words and phrases does the writer use to move readers from one event or period to the next?
6. This story is fictional, but it is based on fact. Does the story seem real to you, or does it seem like fantasy? Why?
7. Do you see the title character as a mentally ill fanatic or as a man of high principles? In what sense do you see him as an "artist"? How is he different from the people who come to see him?
8. **Journal Entry** Is the ending of this story logical? Surprising? Tragic? Explain your reaction.
9. **Critical Perspective** Writing in *The Brooklyn Rail*, artist Betsy Kaufman discusses the meaning of "A Hunger Artist":

   > Critics differ about the meaning of this allegory—some saying it's about the hunger artist's asceticism, his "saintly or even Christ-like" characteristics. But I can't imagine an artist reading this story who doesn't identify with the character—one

who embodies a creative ideal with passion and commitment. Do you see the hunger artist as a "Christ-like" figure? Do you see him as a performer playing a role in front of an audience? Or, do you see him as a true artist, obsessed with his craft?

Related Works: "A Rose for Emily" (p. 166), "The Lottery" (p. 337), "The Tell-Tale Heart (p. 459), "Not Waving But Drowning" (p. 738), *Trifles* (p. 820)

Oscar White/Corbis Historical/Getty Images

R. CRUMB (1943–) is widely acknowledged as the founder of the underground or alternative comics movement, which emerged in the 1960s as a reaction against the popular superhero comics that had, until then, dominated and defined the comic book genre. Crumb and his underground contemporaries, including Art Spiegelman, depicted taboo topics such as drugs and sex in a medium that had previously been perceived as a children's genre. He created the infamously risqué illustrated character Fritz the Cat, among others. With works such as *Introducing Kafka* (1993), in which he illustrates Franz Kafka's life and work and from which the following selection is excerpted, and *The Book of Genesis* (2009), Crumb helped to raise the graphic novel to the level of high art. His work appears in numerous collections, including the *R. Crumb Sketchbook* volumes (1978, 1981, 2005), *The Complete Crumb* volumes (2005 and 2013), and *The Sweeter Side of R. Crumb* (2010).

Cultural Context Crumb's graphic telling of "A Hunger Artist" first appeared in *Introducing Kafka* in 1993 alongside Crumb's sketches of Kafka's stories and biography. *Introducing Kafka* has moved through multiple editions as *R. Crumb's Kafka* (2005) and, since 2007, has simply been titled *Kafka.* Evidence of Robert Crumb's enduring legacy among counterculture storytellers who use comic and graphic illustration as their medium, his work drew praise from longstanding comic book publisher Larry Reid, who wrote of "The Hunger Artist" on his blog, *Re/Read*, "I maintain these illustrated stories represent Crumb's strongest work to date." That Crumb converted this Kafka story from the early twentieth century into a graphic format that continues to engage new readers nearly a century after its original publication is a testament to the influence of comics as a medium for storytelling—and especially to Crumb's influence on the form.

A Hunger Artist (1993)

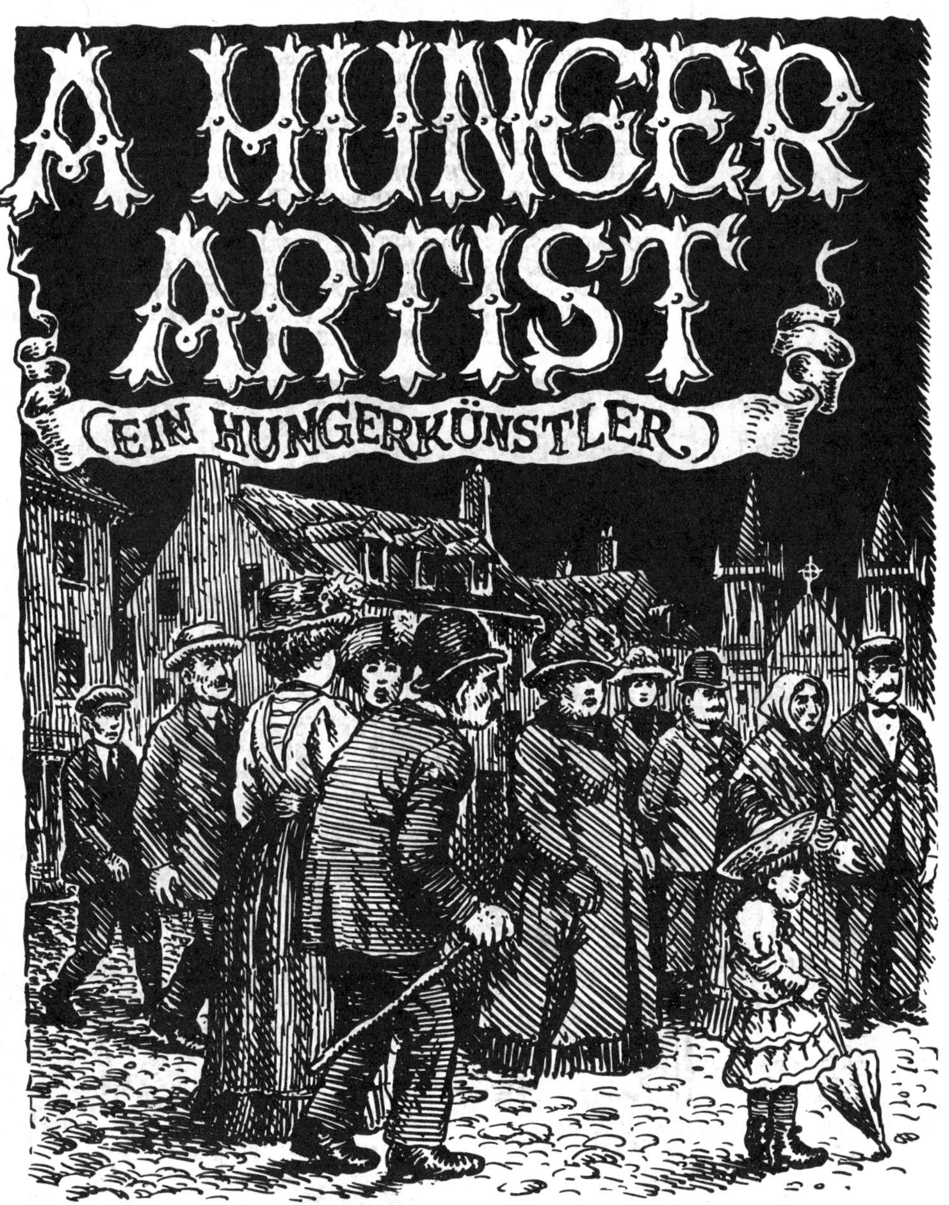

Source: 1993 R. Crumb. Used by permission of Totem Books.

IN THE LAST FEW DECADES, THE INTEREST IN PROFESSIONAL HUNGER-ARTISTRY HAS GREATLY DIMINISHED. ONCE THE WHOLE TOWN CAME OUT TO SEE THE HUNGER-ARTIST. SOME EVEN BOUGHT SEASON TICKETS, AND AT NIGHT THE SCENE WAS BATHED IN THE LIGHT OF TORCHES.
GROUPS OF PROFESSIONAL WATCHERS, USUALLY BUTCHERS, WERE SENT TO WATCH HIM, IN CASE HE HAD SOME SECRET CACHE OF NOURISHMENT. BUT, DURING HIS FAST THE ARTISTE WOULD NEVER, EVEN UNDER COMPULSION, SWALLOW THE SMALLEST BIT OF FOOD; HIS PROFESSIONAL HONOR FORBADE IT. HE ALONE KNEW WHAT THE OTHERS DIDN'T: FASTING WAS THE EASIEST THING IN THE WORLD.
TICKETS
SEE THE HUNGER ARTIST

Source: 1993 R. Crumb. Used by permission of Totem Books.

THE PERIOD OF FASTING WAS SET BY HIS IMPRESARIO AT FORTY DAYS MAXIMUM, BECAUSE AFTER THAT TIME THE PUB-LIC BEGAN TO LOSE INTEREST. SO, ON THE FORTIETH DAY, WITH AN EXCITED CROWD FILLING THE ARENA AND A MILITARY BAND PLAYING, TWO YOUNG LADIES CAME TO LEAD THE HUNGER-ARTIST OUT OF HIS CAGE. WHEN THIS HAPPENED HE ALWAYS PUT UP SOME RESISTANCE... WHY STOP AFTER ONLY FORTY DAYS?!? WHY SHOULD THEY TAKE FROM HIM THE GLORY OF FASTING EVEN LONGER, OF SURPASSING EVEN HIMSELF TO REACH UNIMAGINABLE HEIGHTS, FOR HE SAW HIS ABILITY TO GO ON FASTING AS UNLIMITED!

Source: 1993 R. Crumb. Used by permission of Totem Books.

Source: 1993 R. Crumb. Used by permission of Totem Books.

HE LIVED THIS WAY FOR MANY YEARS, HONORED BY ALL THE WORLD, YET TROUBLED IN HIS SOUL, DEEPLY FRUSTRATED THAT THEY WOULD NOT ALLOW HIS FASTING TO EXCEED FORTY DAYS. HE SPENT MOST OF HIS TIME IN A GLOOMY MOOD, AND WHEN SOME KIND-HEARTED PERSON WOULD TRY TO EXPLAIN THAT HIS DEPRESSION WAS THE RESULT OF THE FASTING, HE WOULD SOMETIMES FLY INTO A RAGE AND BEGIN RATTLING THE BARS OF HIS CAGE LIKE AN ANIMAL.

Source: 1993 R. Crumb. Used by permission of Totem Books.

Source: 1993 R. Crumb. Used by permission of Totem Books.

Source: 1993 R. Crumb. Used by permission of Totem Books.

Source: 1993 R. Crumb. Used by permission of Totem Books.

Source: 1993 R. Crumb. Used by permission of Totem Books.

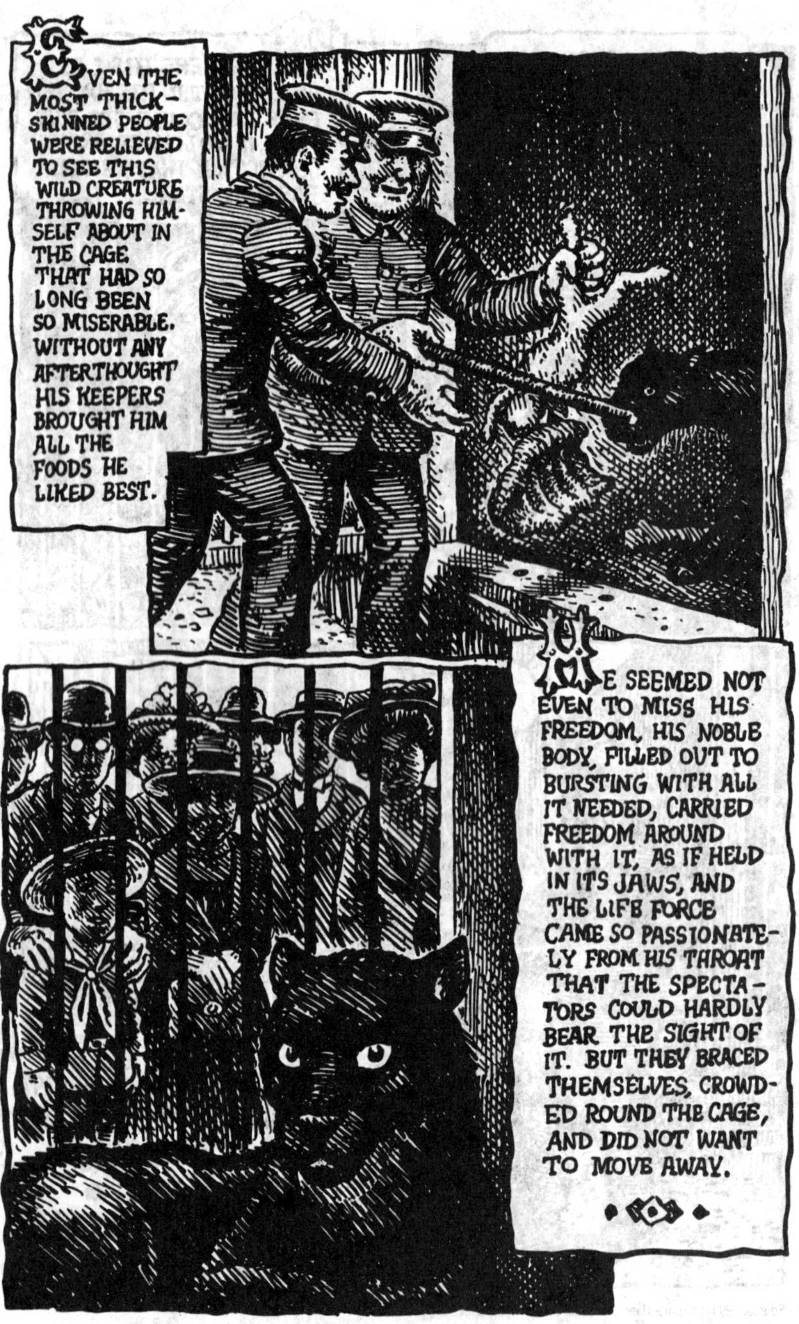
EVEN THE MOST THICK-SKINNED PEOPLE WERE RELIEVED TO SEE THIS WILD CREATURE THROWING HIMSELF ABOUT IN THE CAGE THAT HAD SO LONG BEEN SO MISERABLE. WITHOUT ANY AFTERTHOUGHT HIS KEEPERS BROUGHT HIM ALL THE FOODS HE LIKED BEST.
HE SEEMED NOT EVEN TO MISS HIS FREEDOM, HIS NOBLE BODY, FILLED OUT TO BURSTING WITH ALL IT NEEDED, CARRIED FREEDOM AROUND WITH IT, AS IF HELD IN ITS JAWS, AND THE LIFE FORCE CAME SO PASSIONATELY FROM HIS THROAT THAT THE SPECTATORS COULD HARDLY BEAR THE SIGHT OF IT. BUT THEY BRACED THEMSELVES, CROWDED ROUND THE CAGE, AND DID NOT WANT TO MOVE AWAY.

Reading and Reacting

1. How does this work of graphic fiction use images as well as words to move readers from one event, time period, or scene to the next?
2. What specific visual elements establish the story's setting? Is the setting depicted here consistent with the mood and atmosphere Kafka establishes in the original story?
3. What language did Crumb retain from the Kafka story? Why did he choose to keep those words and phrases and not others?
4. In a few sentences, describe the appearance of the hunger artist as imagined by Crumb. Is this how you pictured him after reading Kafka's story? Explain.
5. What is an *impresario*? Is the image of the impresario pictured here consistent with that definition?
6. **Journal Entry** How does Crumb's depiction of the hunger artist change as the story unfolds? How do you account for these changes?
7. **Critical Perspective** In an interview with R. Crumb for *The Guardian*, Nadja Sayej makes the following comments:

    - "Some have called Crumb's comics a comment on the American condition,…"
    - "Crumb's comics have often been a critique of modern society, with waves of nihilism to sarcasm and disillusionment,…"

However, during the interview, Crumb himself says, "I'm just a crazy artist. I can't be held to account for what I draw." Based on your reading of R. Crumb's version of the Kafka story, which of the above interpretations makes the most sense to you?

WRITING SUGGESTION: Graphic Fiction

Write a **comparison-contrast essay** comparing Kafka's story to R Crumb's. In your essay, you might consider the following questions:

- How are the two stories alike? How are they different?
- What content and language did R Crumb retain? What did he modify or delete?
- Is the character of the hunger artist portrayed more fully in one version of the story than in the other?
- What are the advantages and disadvantages of telling a story in graphic form?

Chapter
9

Plot

William Faulkner
AP Images

Kate Chopin
Courtesy of Louisiana State University

Neil Gaiman
Allstar Picture Library Ltd/Alamy Stock Photo

Learning Objectives

After reading this chapter, you will be able to. . .

- Explain the elements of a story's plot.
- Explain how interactions between characters and juxtaposition of events shape a story's plot.
- Identify the central conflict in a work of fiction.

- Identify exposition in a work of fiction.
- Explain the use of order and sequence in a story's plot.
- Analyze the use of foreshadowing and its effect on a work of fiction.

Alfred Hitchcock's classic 1951 film *Strangers on a Train*, based on a suspense novel by Patricia Highsmith, offers an intriguing premise: two men, strangers, each can murder someone the other wishes dead; because they have no apparent connection to their victims, both can escape suspicion. Many people would describe this ingenious scheme as the film's "plot," but in fact it is simply the gimmick around which the complex plot revolves. Certainly, a clever twist can be an important ingredient of a story's plot, but **plot** is more than "what happens": it is how what happens is revealed, the way in which a story's events are arranged.

Scene from Alfred Hitchcock's 1951 film *Strangers on a Train*
Album/Alamy Stock Photo

Plot is shaped by causal connections (historical, social, and personal), by the interaction between characters, and by the juxtaposition of events. In *Strangers on a Train*, the plot that unfolds is complex: one character directs the events and determines their order while the other character is drawn into the action against his will. The same elements that enrich the plot of the film—unexpected events, conflict, suspense, flashbacks, foreshadowing—can also enrich the plot of a work of short fiction.

Conflict

Readers' interest and involvement are heightened by a story's **conflict**, the struggle between opposing forces that emerges as the action develops. This conflict is a clash between the **protagonist**, a story's principal character, and an

antagonist, someone or something presented in opposition to the protagonist. Sometimes the antagonist is a villain; more often, it is a character who represents a conflicting point of view or advocates a course of action different from the one the protagonist follows. Sometimes the antagonist is not a character at all but a situation (for example, war or poverty) or an event (for example, a natural disaster, such as a flood or a storm) that challenges the protagonist. In some stories, the protagonist may struggle against a supernatural force, or the conflict may occur within a character's mind. It may, for example, be a struggle between two moral choices, such as whether to stay at home and care for an aging parent or to leave and make a new life.

Stages of Plot

A work's plot explores one or more conflicts, moving from *exposition* through a series of *complications* to a *climax* and, finally, to a *resolution*.

During a story's **exposition**, the writer presents the basic information readers need to understand the events that follow. Typically, the exposition sets the story in motion: it establishes the scene, introduces the major characters, and perhaps suggests the major events or conflicts to come.

Sometimes a single sentence can present a story's exposition clearly and economically, giving readers information vital to their understanding of the plot that will unfold. For example, the opening sentence of Amy Tan's "Two Kinds" (p. 471)—"My mother believed you could be anything you wanted to be in America"—reveals an important trait of a central character. Similarly, the opening sentence of Shirley Jackson's "The Lottery" (p. 337)—"The morning of June 27th was clear and sunny, with the fresh warmth of a full-summer day; the flowers were blossoming profusely and the grass was richly green"—introduces the picture-perfect setting that is essential to the story's irony. At other times, as in John Updike's "A&P" (p. 179), a more fully developed exposition section establishes the story's setting, introduces the main characters, and suggests possible conflicts. Finally, in some experimental stories, a distinct exposition component may be absent, as it is in Jamaica Kincaid's "Girl" (p. 116).

As the plot progresses, the story's conflict unfolds through a series of complications that eventually lead readers to the story's climax. As it develops, the story may include several crises. A **crisis** is a peak in the story's action, a moment of considerable tension or importance. The **climax** is the point of greatest tension or importance, the scene that presents a story's decisive action or event.

The final stage of plot, the **resolution** or **denouement** (French for "untying of the knot"), draws the action to a close and accounts for any remaining loose ends. Sometimes this resolution is achieved with the help of a *deus ex machina* (Latin for "god from a machine"), an intervention of some force or agent previously extraneous to the story—for example, the sudden arrival of a long-lost relative or a fortuitous inheritance, the discovery of a character's true identity, or a surprise last-minute rescue. Usually, however, the resolution is more plausible: all the events lead logically and convincingly (though not necessarily predictably) to the resolution. Sometimes the ending of a story is indefinite—that is, readers are not quite sure what the protagonist will do or what will happen next. This kind of resolution, although it may leave some readers feeling cheated, has its advantages: it mirrors the complexity of life, where closure rarely occurs, and it can keep readers involved in the story as they try to understand the significance of its ending or decide how conflicts should have been resolved.

Order and Sequence

A writer may introduce a story's events in strict chronological order, presenting each event in the sequence in which it actually takes place. More often, however, especially in relatively modern fiction, writers do not introduce events chronologically. Instead, they present incidents out of expected order, or in no apparent order. For example, a writer may choose to begin *in medias res* (Latin for "in the midst of things"), starting with a key event and later going back in time to explain events that preceded it, as Tillie Olsen does in "I Stand Here Ironing" (p. 227). Or, a writer can decide to begin a work of fiction at the end and then move back to reconstruct events that led up to the final outcome, as William Faulkner does in "A Rose for Emily" (p. 166). Many sequences are possible as the writer manipulates events to create interest, suspense, confusion, surprise, or some other effect.

Writers who wish to depart from strict chronological order can use *flashbacks* and *foreshadowing*. A **flashback** moves out of sequence to examine an event or a situation that occurred before the time in which the story's action takes place. A character can remember an earlier event, or a story's narrator can re-create an earlier situation. For example, in Alberto Alvaro Ríos's "The Secret Lion" (p. 222), the adult narrator looks back at events that occurred when he was twelve years old and then moves further back in time to consider related events that occurred when he was five. In Edgar Allan Poe's "The Cask of Amontillado" (p. 258), the entire story is told as a flashback. Flashbacks are valuable because they can substitute for or supplement formal exposition by presenting background readers need to understand a story's events. One disadvantage of flashbacks is that if they interrupt the natural flow of events, they may be intrusive or distracting. Such distractions, however, can be an advantage if the writer wishes to reveal events gradually and subtly or to obscure causal links.

Foreshadowing is the introduction early in a story of comments, situations, events, characters, or objects that hint at things to come. Typically, a seemingly simple element—a chance remark, a natural occurrence, a trivial event—is eventually revealed to have great significance. For example, a dark cloud passing across the sky during a wedding can foreshadow future problems for the marriage. Foreshadowing allows a writer to hint provocatively at what is to come so that readers only gradually become aware of a particular detail's role in a story. Thus, foreshadowing helps readers sense what will occur and grow increasingly involved as they come to see the likelihood (or even the inevitability) of a particular outcome.

In addition to using conventional techniques like flashbacks and foreshadowing, writers may experiment with sequence by substantially tampering with—or even dispensing with—chronological order. (An example is the scrambled chronology of "A Rose for Emily.") In such instances, the experimental form enhances interest and encourages readers to become involved with the story as they work to untangle or reorder the events and determine their logical and causal connections.

Today, the internet gives a new fluidity to the nature of plot, with readers actually able to participate in creating a story's plot. For more on such innovations, see page 106.

Checklist Writing about Plot

- What happens in the story?
- Where does the story's formal exposition section end? What do readers learn about characters in this section? What do readers learn about setting? What possible conflicts are suggested here?
- What is the story's central conflict? What other conflicts are presented? Who is the protagonist? Who (or what) serves as the antagonist?
- Identify the story's crisis or crises.
- Identify the story's climax.
- How is the story's central conflict resolved? Is this resolution plausible? satisfying?
- Which part of the story constitutes the resolution? Do any problems remain unresolved? Does any uncertainty remain? If so, does this uncertainty strengthen or weaken the story? Would another ending be more effective?
- How are the story's events arranged? Are they presented in chronological order? What events are presented out of logical sequence? Does the story use foreshadowing? flashbacks? Are the causal connections between events clear? logical? If not, can you explain why?

Source: Courtesy of Louisiana State University

KATE CHOPIN (1851–1904) was born Katherine O'Flaherty, the daughter of a wealthy Irish-born merchant and his aristocratic Creole wife. She was married at nineteen to Oscar Chopin, a Louisiana cotton broker, who took her to live first in New Orleans and later a plantation in central Louisiana. Chopin's representations of the Cane River region and its people in two volumes of short stories—*Bayou Folk* (1894) and *A Night in Arcadie* (1897)—are the foundation of her reputation as a local colorist, a writer dedicated to creating an accurate picture of a particular region and its people.

Her honest, sexually frank stories (many of them out of print for more than half a century) were rediscovered in the 1960s and 1970s, influencing a new generation of writers. Though she was a popular contributor of stories and sketches to the magazines of her day, Chopin scandalized many critics with her outspoken novel *The Awakening* (1899), in which a woman seeks sexual and emotional fulfillment with a man who is not her husband. The book was removed from the shelves of the public library in St. Louis, where Chopin was born.

"The Story of an Hour" depicts a brief event in a woman's life, but in this single hour, Chopin reveals both a lifetime's emotional torment and the momentary joy of freedom.

Cultural Context During her marriage, Chopin lived in Louisiana, the only civil-law state in the United States. Whereas the legal systems of all other states are based on common law, the laws of Louisiana have their roots in the Napoleonic Code, the civil code enacted in France in 1804 to regulate issues of property, marriage, and divorce. This patriarchal code favored the husband in all domestic affairs and left women without many legal or fiscal rights. In "The Story of an Hour," the concept of freedom is closely tied to the prospect of escaping these restrictions.

The Story of an Hour (1894)

Knowing that Mrs. Mallard was afflicted with a heart trouble, great care was taken to break to her as gently as possible the news of her husband's death.

It was her sister Josephine who told her, in broken sentences, veiled hints that revealed in half concealing. Her husband's friend Richards was there, too, near her. It was he who had been in the newspaper office when intelligence of the railroad disaster was received, with Brently Mallard's name leading the list of "killed." He had only taken the time to assure himself of its truth by a second telegram, and had hastened to forestall any less careful, less tender friend in bearing the sad message.

She did not hear the story as many women have heard the same, with a paralyzed inability to accept its significance. She wept at once, with sudden, wild abandonment, in her sister's arms. When the storm of grief had spent itself she went away to her room alone. She would have no one follow her.

There stood, facing the open window, a comfortable, roomy armchair. Into this she sank, pressed down by a physical exhaustion that haunted her body and seemed to reach into her soul.

She could see in the open square before her house the tops of trees that were all aquiver with the new spring life. The delicious breath of rain was in the air. In the street below a peddler was crying his wares. The notes of a distant song which some one was singing reached her faintly, and countless sparrows were twittering in the eaves. 5

There were patches of blue sky showing here and there through the clouds that had met and piled one above the other in the west facing her window.

She sat with her head thrown back upon the cushion of the chair, quite motionless, except when a sob came up into her throat and shook her, as a child who has cried itself to sleep continues to sob in its dreams.

She was young, with a fair, calm face, whose lines bespoke repression and even a certain strength. But now there was a dull stare in her eyes, whose gaze was fixed away off yonder on one of those patches of blue sky. It was not a glance of reflection, but rather indicated a suspension of intelligent thought.

There was something coming to her and she was waiting for it, fearfully. What was it? She did not know; it was too subtle and elusive to name. But she felt it, creeping out of the sky, reaching toward her through the sounds, the scents, the color that filled the air.

Now her bosom rose and fell tumultuously. She was beginning to recognize this thing that was approaching to possess her, and she was striving to beat it back with her will—as powerless as her two white slender hands would have been. 10

When she abandoned herself a little whispered word escaped her slightly parted lips. She said it over and over under her breath: "Free, free, free!" The vacant stare and the look of terror that had followed it went from her eyes. They stayed keen and bright. Her pulses beat fast, and the coursing blood warmed and relaxed every inch of her body.

She did not stop to ask if it were not a monstrous joy that held her. A clear and exalted perception enabled her to dismiss the suggestion as trivial.

She knew that she would weep again when she saw the kind, tender hands folded in death; the face that had never looked save with love upon her, fixed and gray and dead. But she saw beyond that bitter moment a long procession of years to come that would belong to her absolutely. And she opened and spread her arms out to them in welcome.

There would be no one to live for during those coming years; she would live for herself. There would be no powerful will bending her in that blind persistence with which men and women believe they have a right to impose a private will upon a fellow creature. A kind intention or a cruel intention made the act seem no less a crime as she looked upon it in that brief moment of illumination.

And yet she had loved him—sometimes. Often she had not. What did it matter! What could love, the unsolved mystery, count for in the face of this possession of self-assertion which she suddenly recognized as the strongest impulse of her being. 15

"Free! Body and soul free!" she kept whispering.

Josephine was kneeling before the closed door with her lips to the key-hole, imploring for admission. "Louise, open the door! I beg; open the door—you will make yourself ill. What are you doing, Louise? For heaven's sake open the door."

"Go away. I am not making myself ill." No; she was drinking in a very elixir of life through that open window.

Her fancy was running riot along those days ahead of her. Spring days, and summer days, and all sorts of days that would be her own. She breathed a quick prayer that life might be long. It was only yesterday she had thought with a shudder that life might be long.

She arose at length and opened the door to her sister's importunities. There was a feverish triumph in her eyes, and she carried herself unwittingly like a goddess of Victory. She clasped her sister's waist, and together they descended the stairs. Richards stood waiting for them at the bottom. 20

Some one was opening the front door with a latchkey. It was Brently Mallard who entered, a little travel-stained, composedly carrying his grip-sack and umbrella. He had been far from the scene of the accident, and did not even know there had been one. He stood amazed at Josephine's piercing cry; at Richards' quick motion to screen him from the view of his wife.

But Richards was too late.

When the doctors came they said she had died of heart disease—of joy that kills.

Reading and Reacting

1. The story's basic exposition is presented in its first two paragraphs. What additional information about character or setting would you like to know? Why do you suppose Chopin does not supply this information?
2. "The Story of an Hour" is a very economical story, with little action or dialogue. Do you see this economy as a strength or a weakness? Explain.
3. When "The Story of an Hour" was first published in *Vogue* magazine in 1894, the magazine's editors titled it "The Dream of an Hour." A film version, echoing the last words of the story, is called *The Joy That Kills*. Which of the three titles do you believe most accurately represents what happens in the story? Why?
4. Do you think Brently Mallard physically abused his wife? Did he love her? Did she love him? Exactly why was she so relieved to be rid of him? Can you answer any of these questions with certainty?
5. What is the nature of the conflict in this story? Who, or what, do you see as Mrs. Mallard's antagonist?
6. What emotions does Mrs. Mallard experience during the hour she spends alone in her room? What events do you imagine take place during this same period outside her room? outside her house?
7. Do you find the story's ending satisfying? believable? contrived?
8. Was the story's ending unexpected, or were you prepared for it? What elements in the story foreshadow this ending?

9. **Journal Entry** Rewrite the story's ending, substituting a few paragraphs of your own for the last three paragraphs.
10. **Critical Perspective** Kate Chopin is widely viewed today as an early feminist writer whose work often addressed the social injustices and inequalities that women faced during the second half of the nineteenth century. According to literary critic Elaine Showalter, "The Story of an Hour" was written during a period in which women writers were able to "reject the accommodating postures of femininity and to use literature to dramatize the ordeals of wronged womanhood."

    Do you think this story rejects the "postures of femininity"? What "ordeals of wronged womanhood" are being dramatized here?

Related Works: "The Storm" (p. 216), "The Disappearance" (p. 280), "The Yellow Wallpaper" (p. 315), "If I should learn, in some quite casual way" (p. 574), *Trifles* (p. 820), *A Doll's House* (p. 834), *The Glass Menagerie* (p. 958)

Allstar Picture Library Ltd/Alamy Stock Photo

NEIL GAIMAN (1960–) grew up in England and currently lives in Minnesota. The author of numerous critically acclaimed stories, novels, and works of graphic fiction for children and adults, Gaiman is also a screenwriter, film director, and essayist. Largely dealing with fantasy and science fiction subjects, his work has been translated into numerous languages. Gaiman has won several World Fantasy, Hugo, Locus, Stoker, and Nebula Awards as well as accolades that include the Newbury Medal and many international prizes. In discussing his novel *Anansi Boys* (2005), Gaiman provides a description that applies to much of his work: "It's a scary, funny sort of a story, which isn't exactly a thriller, and isn't really horror, and doesn't quite qualify as a ghost story (although it has at least one ghost in it), or a romantic comedy (although there are several romances in there, and it's certainly a comedy, except for the scary bits)." Gaiman's works include *Neverwhere* (1996), *American Gods* (2001), *Coraline* (2002), *The Ocean at the End of the Lane* (2013), and *Norse Mythology* (2017). Gaiman is also the author of the award-winning comics series *Sandman*.

Cultural Context The concept of "aliens living among us" is a popular subject in the science fiction genre. Classic science fiction films that explore this theme include *The Day the Earth Stood Still* (originally released in 1951 and remade in 2008), *The Thing* (originally released in 1951 and remade in 1982 and 2011), *Invasion of the Body Snatchers* (originally released in 1956 and remade in 1978), and *The Blob* (1958). More recent "aliens among us" films include *E.T.: The Extra-Terrestrial* (1982) and the *Men in Black* movies (1997, 2002, and 2012). While the classics tend to depict aliens as evil and scary, some of the newer films show the "human" side of our alien counterparts. In "How to Talk to Girls at Parties," Gaiman builds on this science fiction tradition by depicting young, enticing girls as aliens who forever change the male protagonists' attitudes toward lust and temptation. (A film version of this story, starring Nicole Kidman and Elle Fanning, was released in 2017.)

How to Talk to Girls at Parties (2007)

"Come on," said Vic. "It'll be great."

"No, it won't," I said, although I'd lost this fight hours ago, and I knew it.

"It'll be brilliant," said Vic, for the hundredth time. "Girls! Girls! Girls!" He grinned with white teeth.

We both attended an all-boys' school in South London. While it would be a lie to say that we had no experience with girls—Vic seemed to have had many girlfriends, while I had kissed three of my sister's friends—it would, I think, be perfectly true to say that we both chiefly spoke to, interacted with, and only truly understood, other boys. Well, I did, anyway. It's hard to speak for someone else, and I've not seen Vic for thirty years. I'm not sure that I would know what to say to him now if I did.

We were walking the back streets that used to twine in a grimy maze behind East Croydon station—a friend had told Vic about a party, and Vic was determined to go whether I liked it or not, and I didn't. But my parents were away that week at a conference, and I was Vic's guest at his house, so I was trailing along beside him. 5

"It'll be the same as it always is," I said. "After an hour you'll be off somewhere snogging the prettiest girl at the party, and I'll be in the kitchen listening to somebody's mum going on about politics or poetry or something."

"You just have to *talk* to them," he said. "I think it's probably that road at the end here." He gestured cheerfully, swinging the bag with the bottle in it.

"Don't you know?"

"Alison gave me directions and I wrote them on a bit of paper, but I left it on the hall table. S'okay. I can find it."

"How?" Hope welled slowly up inside me. 10

"We walk down the road," he said, as if speaking to an idiot child. "And we look for the party. Easy."

I looked, but saw no party: just narrow houses with rusting cars or bikes in their concreted front gardens; and the dusty glass fronts of newsagents, which smelled of alien spices and sold everything from birthday cards and second-hand comics to the kind of magazines that were so pornographic that they were sold already sealed in plastic bags. I had been there when Vic had slipped one of those magazines beneath his sweater, but the owner caught him on the pavement outside and made him give it back.

We reached the end of the road and turned into a narrow street of terraced houses. Everything looked very still and empty in the Summer's evening. "It's all right for you," I said. "They fancy you. You don't actually *have* to talk to them." It was true: one urchin grin from Vic and he could have his pick of the room.

"Nah. S'not like that. You've just got to talk."

The times I had kissed my sister's friends I had not spoken to them. They had been around while my sister was off doing something elsewhere, and they had drifted into my orbit, and so I had kissed them. I do not remember any talking. I did not know what to say to girls, and I told him so. 15

"They're just girls," said Vic. "They don't come from another planet."

As we followed the curve of the road around, my hopes that the party would prove unfindable began to fade: a low pulsing noise, music muffled by walls and doors, could be heard from a house up ahead. It was eight in the evening, not that early if you aren't yet sixteen, and we weren't. Not quite.

I had parents who liked to know where I was, but I don't think Vic's parents cared that much. He was the youngest of five boys. That in itself seemed magical to me: I merely had two sisters, both younger than I was, and I felt both unique and lonely. I had wanted a brother as far back as I could remember. When I turned thirteen, I stopped wishing on falling stars or first stars, but back when I did, a brother was what I had wished for.

We went up the garden path, crazy paving leading us past a hedge and a solitary rose bush to a pebble-dashed facade. We rang the doorbell, and the door was opened by a girl. I could not have told you how old she was, which was one of the things about girls I had begun to hate: when you start out as kids you're just boys and girls, going through time at the same speed, and you're all five, or seven, or eleven, together. And then one day there's a lurch and the girls just sort of sprint off into the future ahead of you, and they know all about everything, and they have periods and breasts and makeup and God-only-knew-what-else—for I certainly didn't. The diagrams in biology textbooks were no substitute for being, in a very real sense, young adults. And the girls of our age were.

Vic and I weren't young adults, and I was beginning to suspect that even when I started needing to shave every day, instead of once every couple of weeks, I would still be way behind.

The girl said, "Hello?"

Vic said, "We're friends of Alison's." We had met Alison, all freckles and orange hair and a wicked smile, in Hamburg, on a German Exchange. The exchange organizers had sent some girls with us, from a local girls' school, to balance the sexes. The girls, our age, more or less, were raucous and funny, and had more or less adult boyfriends with cars and jobs and motorbikes and—in the case of one girl with crooked teeth and a raccoon coat, who spoke to me about it sadly at the end of a party in Hamburg, in, of course, the kitchen—a wife and kids.

"She isn't here," said the girl at the door. "No Alison,"

"Not to worry," said Vic, with an easy grin. "I'm Vic. This is Enn." A beat, and then the girl smiled back at him. Vic had a bottle of white wine in a plastic bag, removed from his parents' kitchen cabinet. "Where should I put this, then?"

She stood out of the way, letting us enter. "There's a kitchen in the back," she said. "Put it on the table there, with the other bottles." She had golden, wavy hair, and she was very beautiful. The hall was dim in the twilight, but I could see that she was beautiful.

"What's your name, then?" said Vic.

She told him it was Stella, and he grinned his crooked white grin and told her that that had to be the prettiest name he had ever heard. Smooth bastard. And what was worse was that he said it like he meant it.

Vic headed back to drop off the wine in the kitchen, and I looked into the front room, where the music was coming from. There were people dancing in there. Stella walked in, and she started to dance, swaying to the music all alone, and I watched her.

This was during the early days of punk. On our own record players we would play the Adverts and the Jam, the Stranglers and the Clash and the Sex Pistols. At other people's parties you'd hear ELO or 10cc or even Roxy Music. Maybe some Bowie, if you were lucky. During the German Exchange, the only LP that we had all been able to agree on was Neil Young's *Harvest*, and his song "Heart of Gold" had threaded through the trip like a refrain; *I crossed the ocean for a heart of gold. . . .*

The music playing in that front room wasn't anything I recognized. It sounded a bit like a German electronic pop group called Kraftwerk, and a bit like an LP I'd been given for my last birthday, of strange sounds made by the BBC Radiophonic Workshop. The music had a beat, though, and the half-dozen girls in that room were moving gently to it, although I only looked at Stella. She shone. 30

Vic pushed past me, into the room. He was holding a can of lager. "There's booze back in the kitchen," he told me. He wandered over to Stella and he began to talk to her. I couldn't hear what they were saying over the music, but I knew that there was no room for me in that conversation.

I didn't like beer, not back then. I went off to see if there was something I wanted to drink. On the kitchen table stood a large bottle of Coca-Cola, and I poured myself a plastic tumblerful, and I didn't dare say anything to the pair of girls who were talking in the underlit kitchen. They were animated and utterly lovely. Each of them had very black skin and glossy hair and movie star clothes, and their accents were foreign, and each of them was out of my league.

I wandered, Coke in hand.

The house was deeper than it looked, larger and more complex than the two-up two-down model I had imagined. The rooms were underlit—I doubt there was a bulb of more than forty watts in the building—and each room I went into was inhabited: in my memory, inhabited only by girls. I did not go upstairs.

A girl was the only occupant of the conservatory. Her hair was so fair it was white, and long, and straight, and she sat at the glass-topped table, her hands clasped together, staring at the garden outside, and the gathering dusk. She seemed wistful. 35

"Do you mind if I sit here?" I asked, gesturing with my cup. She shook her head, and then followed it up with a shrug, to indicate that it was all the same to her. I sat down.

Vic walked past the conservatory door. He was talking to Stella, but he looked in at me, sitting at the table, wrapped in shyness and awkwardness, and he opened and closed his hand in a parody of a speaking mouth. *Talk*. Right.

"Are you from around here?" I asked the girl.

She shook her head. She wore a low-cut silvery top, and I tried not to stare at the swell of her breasts.

I said, "What's your name? I'm Enn."

"Wain's Wain," she said, or something that sounded like it. "I'm a second."

"That's uh. That's a different name."

She fixed me with huge liquid eyes. "It indicates that my progenitor was also Wain, and that I am obliged to report back to her. I may not breed."

"Ah. Well. Bit early for that anyway, isn't it?"

She unclasped her hands, raised them above the table, spread her fingers. "You see?" The little finger on her left hand was crooked, and it bifurcated at the top, splitting into two smaller fingertips. A minor deformity. "When I was finished a decision was needed. Would I be retained, or eliminated? I was fortunate that the decision was with me. Now, I travel, while my more perfect sisters remain at home in stasis. They were firsts. I am a second.

"Soon I must return to Wain, and tell her all I have seen. All my impressions of this place of yours."

"I don't actually live in Croydon," I said. "I don't come from here." I wondered if she was American. I had no idea what she was talking about.

"As you say," she agreed, "neither of us comes from here." She folded her six-fingered left hand beneath her right, as if tucking it out of sight. "I had expected it to be bigger, and cleaner, and more colorful. But still, it is a jewel."

She yawned, covered her mouth with her right hand, only for a moment, before it was back on the table again. "I grow weary of the journeying, and I wish sometimes that it would end. On a street in Rio, at Carnival, I saw them on a bridge, golden and tall and insect-eyed and winged, and elated I almost ran to greet them, before I saw that they were only people in costumes. I said to Hola Colt, 'Why do they try so hard to look like us?' and Hola Colt replied, 'Because they hate themselves, all shades of pink and brown, and so small.' It is what I experience, even me, and I am not grown. It is like a world of children, or of elves." Then she smiled and said, "It was a good thing they could not any of them see Hola Colt."

"Um," I said, "do you want to dance?"

She shook her head immediately. "It is not permitted," she said. "I can do nothing that might cause damage to property. I am Wain's."

"Would you like something to drink, then?"

"Water," she said.

I went back to the kitchen and poured myself another Coke, and filled a cup with water from the tap. From the kitchen back to the hall, and from there into the conservatory, but now it was quite empty.

I wondered if the girl had gone to the toilet, and if she might change her mind about dancing later. I walked back to the front room and stared in. The room was filling up. There were more girls dancing, and several lads I didn't know, who looked older than me and Vic. The lads and the girls all kept their distance, but Vic was holding Stella's hand as they danced, and when the song ended he put an arm around her, casually, almost proprietorially, to make sure that nobody else cut in.

I wondered if the girl I had been talking to in the conservatory was now upstairs, as she did not appear to be on the ground floor.

I walked into the living room, which was across the hall from the room where the people were dancing, and I sat down on the sofa. There was a girl sitting there already. She had dark hair, cut short and spiky, and a nervous manner.

Talk, I thought. "Um, this mug of water's going spare," I told her, "if you want it?"

She nodded, and reached out her hand and took the mug, extremely carefully, as if she were unused to taking things, as if she could trust neither her vision nor her hands.

"I love being a tourist," she said, and smiled hesitantly. She had a gap between her two front teeth, and she sipped the tap water as if she were an adult sipping a fine wine. "The last tour, we went to sun, and we swam in sunfire pools with the whales. We heard their histories and we shivered in the chill of the outer places, then we swam deepward where the heat churned and comforted us.

"I wanted to go back. This time, I wanted it. There was so much I had not seen. Instead we came to world. Do you like it?"

"Like what?"

She gestured vaguely to the room—the sofa, the armchairs, the curtains, the unused gas fire.

"It's all right, I suppose."

"I told them I did not wish to visit world," she said, "My parent-teacher was unimpressed. 'You will have much to learn,' it told me. I said 'I could learn more in sun, again. Or in the deeps. Jessa spun webs between galaxies. I want to do that.'

"But there was no reasoning with it, and I came to world. Parent-teacher engulfed me, and I was here, embodied in a decaying lump of meat hanging on a frame of calcium. As I incarnated I felt things deep inside me, fluttering and pumping and squishing. It was my first experience with pushing air through the mouth, vibrating the vocal cords on the way, and I used it to tell parent-teacher that I wished that I would die, which it acknowledged was the inevitable exit strategy from world."

There were black worry beads wrapped around her wrist, and she fiddled with them as she spoke. "But knowledge is there, in the meat," she said, "and I am resolved to learn from it."

We were sitting close at the center of the sofa now. I decided I should put an arm around her, but casually. I would extend my arm along the back of the sofa and eventually sort of creep it down, almost imperceptibly, until it was touching her. She said, "The thing with the liquid in the eyes, when the world blurs. Nobody told me, and I still do not understand. I have touched the folds of the Whisper and pulsed and flown with the tachyon[1] swans, and I still do not understand."

She wasn't the prettiest girl there, but she seemed nice enough, and she was a girl, anyway. I let my arm slide down a little, tentatively, so that it made contact with her back, and she did not tell me to take it away.

Vic called to me then, from the doorway. He was standing with his arm around Stella, protectively, waving at me. I tried to let him know, by shaking my head, that I was onto something, but he called my name, and, reluctantly, I got up from the sofa, and walked over to the door. "What?" 70

"Er. Look. The party," said Vic, apologetically. "It's not the one I thought it was. I've been talking to Stella and I figured it out. Well, she sort of explained it to me. We're at a different party."

"Christ. Are we in trouble? Do we have to go?"

Stella shook her head. He leaned down and kissed her, gently, on the lips. "You're just happy to have me here, aren't you darlin'?"

"You know I am," she told him.

He looked from her back to me, and he smiled his white smile: roguish, loveable, a little bit Artful Dodger, a little bit wide-boy Prince Charming. "Don't worry. They're all tourists here anyway. It's a foreign exchange thing, innit? Like when we all went to Germany." 75

"It is?"

"Enn. You got to *talk* to them. And that means you got to listen to them too. You understand?"

"I *did*. I already talked to a couple of them."

"You getting anywhere?"

"I was till you called me over." 80

"Sorry about that. Look, I just wanted to fill you in. Right?"

And he patted my arm and he walked away with Stella. Then, together, the two of them went up the stairs.

Understand me, all the girls at that party, in the twilight, were lovely; they all had perfect faces, but, more important than that, they had whatever strangeness of proportion, of oddness or humanity it is that makes a beauty something more than a shop-window dummy. Stella was the most lovely of any of them, but she, of course, was Vic's, and they were going upstairs together, and that was just how things would always be.

There were several people now sitting on the sofa, talking to the gap-toothed girl. Someone told a joke, and they all laughed. I would have had to push my way in there to sit next to her again, and it didn't look like she was expecting me back, or cared that I had gone, so I wandered out into the hall.

[1] *tachyon:* A hypothetical particle moving faster than light.

I glanced in at the dancers and found myself wondering where the music was coming from. I couldn't see a record player or speakers.

From the hall I walked back to the kitchen. 85

Kitchens are good at parties. You never need an excuse to be there, and, on the good side, at this party I couldn't see any signs of someone's mum. I inspected the various bottles and cans on the kitchen table, then I poured a half an inch of Pernod into the bottom of my plastic cup, which I filled to the top with Coke. I dropped in a couple of ice cubes, and took a sip, relishing the sweet-shop tang of the drink.

"What's that you're drinking?" A girl's voice.

"It's Pernod," I told her. "It tastes like aniseed balls, only it's alcoholic." I didn't say that I only tried it because I'd heard someone in the crowd ask for a Pernod on a live Velvet Underground LP.

"Can I have one?" I poured another Pernod, topped it off with Coke, passed it to her. Her hair was a coppery auburn, and it tumbled around her head in ringlets. It's not a hair style you see much now, but you saw it a lot back then.

"What's your name?" I asked. 90

"Triolet," she said.

"Pretty name," I told her, although I wasn't sure that it was. She was pretty, though.

"It's a verse form," she said, proudly. "Like me."

"You're a poem?"

She smiled and looked down and away, perhaps bashfully. Her profile was almost flat—a perfect Grecian nose that came down from her forehead in a straight line. We did *Antigone* in the school theater the previous year. I was the messenger who brings Creon the news of Antigone's death. We wore half-masks that made us look like that. I thought of that play, looking at her face, in the kitchen, and I thought of Barry Smith's drawings of women in the *Conan* comics: five years later I would have thought of the Pre-Raphaelites, of Jane Morris and Lizzie Siddall. But I was only fifteen, then. 95

"You're a poem?" I repeated.

She chewed her lower lip. "If you want. I am a poem, or I am a pattern, or a race of people whose world was swallowed by the sea."

"Isn't it hard to be three things at the same time?"

"What's your name?"

"Enn." 100

"So you are Enn," she said. "And you are a male. And you are a biped. Is it hard to be three things at the same time?"

"But they aren't different things. I mean, they aren't contradictory." It was a word I had read many times but never said aloud before that night, and I put the stresses in the wrong places. Con*tradict*ory.

She wore a thin dress, made of a white, silky fabric. Her eyes were a pale green, a color that would now make me think of colored contact lenses; but this was thirty years ago; things were different then. I remember wondering about Vic and Stella, upstairs. By now, I was sure that they were in one of the bedrooms, and I envied Vic so much it hurt.

Still, I was talking to this girl, even if we were talking nonsense, even if her name wasn't really Triolet (my generation had not been given hippie names: all the Rainbows and the Sunshines and the Moons, they were only six, seven, eight years old back then). She said, "We knew that it would soon be over, and so we put it all into a poem, to tell the universe who we were, and why we were here, and what we said and did and thought and dreamed and yearned for. We wrapped our dreams in words and patterned the words so that they would live forever, unforgettable. Then we sent the poem as a pattern of flux, to wait in the heart of a star, beaming out its message in pulses and bursts and fuzzes across the electromagnetic spectrum, until the time when, on worlds a thousand sun systems distant, the pattern would be decoded and read, and it would become a poem once again."

"And then what happened?" 105

She looked at me with her green eyes, and it was as if she stared out at me from her own Antigone half-mask; but as if her pale green eyes were just a different, deeper, part of the mask. "You cannot hear a poem without it changing you," she told me. "They heard it, and it colonized them. It inherited them and it inhabited them, its rhythms becoming part of the way that they thought; its images permanently transmuting their metaphors; its verses, its outlook, its aspirations becoming their lives. Within a generation their children would be born already knowing the poem, and, sooner rather than later, as these things go, there were no more children born. There was no need for them, not any longer. There was only a poem, which took flesh and walked and spread itself across the vastness of the known."

I edged closer to her, so I could feel my leg pressing against hers. She seemed to welcome it: she put her hand on my arm, affectionately, and I felt a smile spreading across my face.

"There are places that we are welcomed," said Triolet, "and places where we are regarded as a noxious weed, or as a disease, something immediately to be quarantined and eliminated. But where does contagion end and art begin?"

"I don't know," I said, still smiling. I could hear the unfamiliar music as it pulsed and scattered and boomed in the front room.

She leaned into me then and—I suppose it was a kiss. . . . I suppose. She pressed her lips to my lips, anyway, and then, satisfied, she pulled back, as if she had now marked me as her own. 110

"Would you like to hear it?" she asked, and I nodded, unsure what she was offering me, but certain that I needed anything she was willing to give me.

She began to whisper something in my ear. It's the strangest thing about poetry—you can tell it's poetry, even if you don't speak the language. You can hear Homer's Greek without understanding a word, and you still know it's poetry. I've heard Polish poetry, and Iniut poetry, and I knew what it was without knowing. Her whisper was like that. I didn't know the language, but her words washed through me, perfect, and in my mind's eye I saw towers of glass and diamond; and people with eyes of the palest green; and, unstoppable, beneath every syllable, I could feel the relentless advance of the ocean.

Perhaps I kissed her properly. I don't remember. I know I wanted to.

And then Vic was shaking me violently. "Come on!" he was shouting. "Quickly. Come on!"

In my head I began to come back from a thousand miles away. 115

"Idiot. Come on. Just get a move on," he said, and he swore at me. There was fury in his voice.

For the first time that evening I recognized one of the songs being played in the front room. A sad saxophone wail followed by a cascade of liquid chords, a man's voice singing cut-up lyrics about the sons of the silent age. I wanted to stay and hear the song.

She said, "I am not finished. There is yet more of me."

"Sorry love," said Vic, but he wasn't smiling any longer. "There'll be another time," and he grabbed me by the elbow and he twisted and pulled, forcing me from the room. I did not resist. I knew from experience that Vic could beat the stuffing out me if he got it into his head to do so. He wouldn't do it unless he was upset or angry, but he was angry now.

Out into the front hall. As Vic pulled open the door, I looked back one last time, over my shoulder, hoping to see Triolet in the doorway to the kitchen, but she was not there. I saw Stella, though, at the top of the stairs. She was staring down at Vic, and I saw her face. 120

This all happened thirty years ago. I have forgotten much, and I will forget more, and in the end I will forget everything; yet, if I have any certainty of life beyond death, it is all wrapped up not in psalms or hymns, but in this one thing alone: I cannot believe that I will ever forget that moment, or forget the expression on Stella's face as she watched Vic hurrying away from her. Even in death I shall remember that.

Her clothes were in disarray, and there was makeup smudged across her face, and her eyes—

You wouldn't want to make a universe angry. I bet an angry universe would look at you with eyes like that.

We ran then, me and Vic, away from the party and the tourists and the twilight, ran as if a lightning storm was on our heels, a mad helterskelter dash down the confusion of streets, threading through the maze, and we did not look back, and we did not stop until we could not breathe; and then we stopped and panted, unable to run any longer. We were in pain. I held onto a wall, and Vic threw up, hard and long, in the gutter.

He wiped his mouth. 125

"She wasn't a—" He stopped.

He shook his head.

Then he said, "You know . . . I think there's a thing. When you've gone as far as you dare. And if you go any further, you wouldn't be *you* anymore? You'd be the person who'd done *that*? The places you just can't go . . . I think that happened to me tonight."

I thought I knew what he was saying, "Screw her, you mean?" I said.

He rammed a knuckle hard against my temple, and twisted it violently. I wondered if I was going to have to fight him—and lose—but after a moment he lowered his hand and moved away from me, making a low, gulping noise. 130

I looked at him curiously, and I realized that he was crying: his face was scarlet; snot and tears ran down his cheeks. Vic was sobbing in the street, as unselfconsciously and heartbreakingly as a little boy.

He walked away from me then, shoulders heaving, and he hurried down the road so he was in front of me and I could no longer see his face. I wondered what had occurred in that upstairs room to make him behave like that, to scare him so, and I could not even begin to guess.

The streetlights came on, one by one. Vic stumbled on ahead, while I trudged down the street behind him in the dusk, my feet treading out the measure of a poem that, try as I might, I could not properly remember and would never be able to repeat.

Reading and Reacting

1. Consider the story's exposition. Where does it take place? What do we know about Enn? about Vic?
2. What is Enn's impression of Vic at the beginning of the story? Has it changed by the end? Explain.
3. In paragraph 7, Vic tells Enn that he needs to *talk* to girls if he is going to make any headway with them. Does Enn follow Vic's advice? Does the story actually explain or illustrate "how to talk to girls at parties"?
4. In paragraph 16, Vic says, "They're just girls, ... They don't come from another planet." How does this statement foreshadow the events to come? What other instances of foreshadowing can you identify?
5. What is your initial reaction to Wain? to the dark-haired girl? to Triolet? How do your own reactions differ from Enn's? How do you explain why you respond differently?
6. Reread paragraph 119. Do you think the narrator is exaggerating when he says he will remember forever the expression on Stella's face?
7. In what respects is this a realistic story? In what respects is it *not* realistic? Is it an initiation story? Is it a horror story?
8. What, if anything, does this story say about the differences between male and female college students? about college parties? Is the story about college students' social interactions, or is it about something else entirely?
9. **Journal Entry** What do you think Vic sees at the end of the story that upsets him so much?

10. **Critical Perspective** Literary critic David Rudd describes Gaiman's children's novel *Coraline* (2003) as: "a rich and powerful work that explores areas seen by many as inappropriate for children, although other critics, such as Bruno Bettelheim in *The Uses of Enchantment* (1976), argue that children not only *want* to but *need* to explore matters that affect their lives, albeit in their own time and fashion (issues to do with death, sex, ontology, evil, desire, violence, and so on)."

    How do Enn and Vic express their "need to explore matters that affect their lives" in "How to Talk to Girls at Parties"? How does this need help to drive the story's plot?

Related Works: "Gryphon" (p. 191), "The Secret Lion" (p. 222), "Young Goodman Brown" (p. 354), "Greasy Lake" (p. 419), *Beauty* (p. 785)

AP Images

WILLIAM FAULKNER (1897–1962), winner of the 1949 Nobel Prize in Literature and the 1955 and 1963 Pulitzer Prizes for fiction, was a Southern writer whose work transcends the regional label. His nineteen novels, notably *The Sound and the Fury* (1929), *As I Lay Dying* (1930), *Light in August* (1932), *Absalom, Absalom!* (1936), and *The Reivers* (1962), explore a wide range of human experience—from high comedy to tragedy—as seen in the life of one community, the fictional Yoknapatawpha County (modeled on the area around Faulkner's own hometown of Oxford, Mississippi). Faulkner's Yoknapatawpha stories—a fascinating blend of complex Latinate prose and primitive Southern dialect—paint an extraordinary portrait of a community bound together by ties of blood, by a shared belief in moral "verities," and by an old grief (the Civil War). Faulkner's grandfather raised "Billy" on Civil War tales and local legends, including many about the "Old Colonel," the writer's great-grandfather, who was a Confederate officer (and also a slaveowner). Although Faulkner's stories elegize the agrarian virtues of the Old South, they look unflinchingly at that world's tragic flaw: the institution of slavery.

Local legends and gossip frequently served as the spark for Faulkner's stories. As John B. Cullen, writing in *Old Times in Faulkner Country*, notes, "A Rose for Emily," Faulkner's first nationally published short story, was based on the tale of Oxford's aristocratic "Miss Mary" Neilson, who married Captain Jack Hume, the charming Yankee foreman of a street-paving crew, over her family's shocked protests. According to Cullen, one of Faulkner's neighbors said he created his story "out of fears and rumors"—the dire predictions of what *might* happen if Mary Neilson married her Yankee.

Cultural Context For many years, the pre–Civil War South was idealized as a land of prosperous plantations, large white houses, cultured and gracious people, and a stable economy based on farming. Central to the myth of the Old South was an adherence to the code of chivalry and a belief in the natural superiority of the white aristocracy, led by men who made their fortunes by owning and running plantations that depended on slave labor. Once the South lost the Civil War, the idealized image of the Old South fell by the wayside, making room for the New South, which, like the North, was industrialized. In this story, Faulkner contrasts notions of the Old South and its decaying values with the newer ideas and innovations of the post-Reconstruction South.

A Rose for Emily (1930)

I

When Miss Emily Grierson died, our whole town went to her funeral: the men through a sort of respectful affection for a fallen monument, the women mostly out of curiosity to see the inside of her house, which no one save an old manservant—a combined gardener and cook—had seen in at least ten years.

It was a big, squarish frame house that had once been white, decorated with cupolas[1] and spires[2] and scrolled balconies in the heavily lightsome style of the seventies, set on what had once been our most select street. But garages and cotton gins had encroached and obliterated even the august names of that neighborhood; only Miss Emily's house was left, lifting its stubborn and coquettish decay above the cotton wagons and the gasoline pumps—an eyesore among eyesores. And now Miss Emily had gone to join the representatives of those august names where they lay in the cedar-bemused cemetery among the ranked and anonymous graves of Union and Confederate soldiers who fell at the battle of Jefferson.

Alive, Miss Emily had been a tradition, a duty, and a care; a sort of hereditary obligation upon the town, dating from that day in 1894 when Colonel Sartoris, the mayor—he who fathered the edict that no Negro woman should appear on the streets without an apron—remitted her taxes, the dispensation dating from the death of her father on into perpetuity. Not that Miss Emily would have accepted charity. Colonel Sartoris invented an involved tale to the effect that Miss Emily's father had loaned money to the town, which the town, as a matter of business, preferred this way of repaying. Only a man of Colonel Sartoris' generation and thought could have invented it, and only a woman could have believed it.

When the next generation, with its more modern ideas, became mayors and aldermen, this arrangement created some little dissatisfaction. On the first of the year they mailed her a tax notice. February came, and there was no reply. They wrote her a formal letter, asking her to call at the sheriff's office at her convenience. A week later the mayor wrote her himself, offering to call or to send his car for her, and received in reply a note on paper of an archaic shape, in a thin, flowing calligraphy in faded ink, to the effect that she no longer went out at all. The tax notice was also enclosed, without comment.

They called a special meeting of the Board of Aldermen. A deputation waited upon her, knocked at the door through which no visitor had passed since she ceased giving china-painting lessons eight or ten years earlier.

---

[1] *cupolas:* Rounded structures on roofs.

[2] *spires:* Tapered structures on roofs.

They were admitted by the old Negro into a dim hall from which a stairway mounted into still more shadow. It smelled of dust and disuse—a close, dank smell. The Negro led them into the parlor. It was furnished in heavy, leather-covered furniture. When the Negro opened the blinds of one window, they could see that the leather was cracked; and when they sat down, a faint dust rose sluggishly about their thighs, spinning with slow motes in the single sun-ray. On a tarnished gilt easel before the fireplace stood a crayon portrait of Miss Emily's father. 5

They rose when she entered—a small, fat woman in black, with a thin gold chain descending to her waist and vanishing into her belt, leaning on an ebony cane with a tarnished gold head. Her skeleton was small and spare; perhaps that was why what would have been merely plumpness in another was obesity in her. She looked bloated, like a body long submerged in motionless water, and of that pallid hue. Her eyes, lost in the fatty ridges of her face, looked like two small pieces of coal pressed into a lump of dough as they moved from one face to another while the visitors stated their errand.

She did not ask them to sit. She just stood in the door and listened quietly until the spokesman came to a stumbling halt. Then they could hear the invisible watch ticking at the end of the gold chain.

Her voice was dry and cold. "I have no taxes in Jefferson. Colonel Sartoris explained it to me. Perhaps one of you can gain access to the city records and satisfy yourselves."

"But we have. We are the city authorities, Miss Emily. Didn't you get a notice from the sheriff, signed by him?"

"I received a paper, yes," Miss Emily said. "Perhaps he considers himself the sheriff . . . I have no taxes in Jefferson." 10

"But there is nothing on the books to show that, you see. We must go by the—"

"See Colonel Sartoris. I have no taxes in Jefferson."

"But, Miss Emily—"

"See Colonel Sartoris." (Colonel Sartoris had been dead almost ten years.) "I have no taxes in Jefferson. Tobe!" The Negro appeared. "Show these gentlemen out."

II

So she vanquished them, horse and foot, just as she had vanquished their fathers thirty years before about the smell. That was two years after her father's death and a short time after her sweetheart—the one we believed would marry her—had deserted her. After her father's death she went out very little; after her sweetheart went away, people hardly saw her at all. A few of the ladies had the temerity to call, but were not received, and the only sign of life about the place was the Negro man—a young man then—going in and out with a market basket. 15

"Just as if a man—any man—could keep a kitchen properly," the ladies said; so they were not surprised when the smell developed. It was another link between the gross, teeming world and the high and mighty Griersons.

A neighbor, a woman, complained to the mayor, Judge Stevens, eighty years old.

"But what will you have me do about it, madam?" he said.

"Why, send her word to stop it," the woman said. "Isn't there a law?"

"I'm sure that won't be necessary," Judge Stevens said. "It's probably just a snake or a rat that nigger of hers killed in the yard. I'll speak to him about it." 20

The next day he received two more complaints, one from a man who came in diffident deprecation. "We really must do something about it, Judge. I'd be the last one in the world to bother Miss Emily, but we've got to do something." That night the Board of Aldermen met—three graybeards and one younger man, a member of the rising generation.

"It's simple enough," he said. "Send her word to have her place cleaned up. Give her a certain time to do it in, and if she don't . . ."

"Dammit, sir," Judge Stevens said, "will you accuse a lady to her face of smelling bad?"

So the next night, after midnight, four men crossed Miss Emily's lawn and slunk about the house like burglars, sniffing along the base of the brickwork and at the cellar openings while one of them performed a regular sowing motion with his hand out of a sack slung from his shoulder. They broke open the cellar door and sprinkled lime there, and in all the outbuildings. As they recrossed the lawn, a window that had been dark was lighted and Miss Emily sat in it, the light behind her, and her upright torso motionless as that of an idol. They crept quietly across the lawn and into the shadow of the locusts that lined the street. After a week or two the smell went away.

That was when people had begun to feel really sorry for her. People in our town, remembering how old lady Wyatt, her great-aunt, had gone completely crazy at last, believed that the Griersons held themselves a little too high for what they really were. None of the young men were quite good enough for Miss Emily and such. We had long thought of them as a tableau, Miss Emily a slender figure in white in the background, her father a spraddled silhouette in the foreground, his back to her and clutching a horsewhip, the two of them framed by the back-flung front door. So when she got to be thirty and was still single, we were not pleased exactly, but vindicated; even with insanity in the family she wouldn't have turned down all of her chances if they had really materialized. 25

When her father died, it got about that the house was all that was left to her; and in a way, people were glad. At last they could pity Miss Emily. Being left alone, and a pauper, she had become humanized. Now she too would know the old thrill and the old despair of a penny more or less.

The day after his death all the ladies prepared to call at the house and offer condolence and aid, as is our custom. Miss Emily met them at the door, dressed as usual and with no trace of grief on her face. She told them that her father was not dead. She did that for three days, with the ministers calling on her, and the doctors, trying to persuade her to let them dispose of the body. Just as they were about to resort to law and force, she broke down, and they buried her father quickly.

We did not say she was crazy then. We believed she had to do that. We remembered all the young men her father had driven away, and we knew that with nothing left, she would have to cling to that which had robbed her, as people will.

III

She was sick for a long time. When we saw her again, her hair was cut short, making her look like a girl, with a vague resemblance to those angels in colored church windows—sort of tragic and serene.

The town had just let the contracts for paving the sidewalks, and in the summer after her father's death they began the work. The construction company came with niggers and mules and machinery, and a foreman named Homer Barron, a Yankee—a big, dark, ready man, with a big voice and eyes lighter than his face. The little boys would follow in groups to hear him cuss the niggers, and the niggers singing in time to the rise and fall of picks. Pretty soon he knew everybody in town. Whenever you heard a lot of laughing anywhere about the square, Homer Barron would be in the center of the group. Presently we began to see him and Miss Emily on Sunday afternoons driving in the yellow-wheeled buggy and the matched team of bays from the livery stable. 30

At first we were glad that Miss Emily would have an interest, because the ladies all said, "Of course a Grierson would not think seriously of a Northerner, a day laborer." But there were still others, older people, who said that even grief could not cause a real lady to forget *noblesse oblige*[3]—without calling it *noblesse oblige*. They just said, "Poor Emily. Her kinsfolk should come to her." She had some kin in Alabama; but years ago her father had fallen out with them over the estate of old lady Wyatt, the crazy woman, and there was no communication between the two families. They had not even been represented at the funeral.

And as soon as the old people said, "Poor Emily," the whispering began. "Do you suppose it's really so?" they said to one another. "Of course it is. What else could . . ." This behind their hands; rustling of craned silk and satin behind jalousies[4] closed upon the sun of Sunday afternoon as the thin, swift clop-clop-clop of the matched team passed: "Poor Emily."

She carried her head high enough—even when we believed that she was fallen. It was as if she demanded more than ever the recognition of her dignity as the last Grierson; as if it had wanted that touch of earthiness to reaffirm her imperviousness. Like when she bought the rat poison, the arsenic. That was

---

[3]*noblesse oblige:* The obligation of those of high birth or rank to behave honorably.

[4]*jalousies:* Blinds or shutters with adjustable horizontal slats.

over a year after they had begun to say "Poor Emily," and while the two female cousins were visiting her.

"I want some poison," she said to the druggist. She was over thirty then, still a slight woman, though thinner than usual, with cold, haughty black eyes in a face the flesh of which was strained across the temples and about the eye-sockets as you imagine a lighthouse-keeper's face ought to look. "I want some poison," she said.

"Yes, Miss Emily. What kind? For rats and such? I'd recom—" 35

"I want the best you have. I don't care what kind."

The druggist named several. "They'll kill anything up to an elephant. But what you want is—"

"Arsenic," Miss Emily said. "Is that a good one?"

"Is . . . arsenic? Yes, ma'am. But what you want—"

"I want arsenic." 40

The druggist looked down at her. She looked back at him, erect, her face like a strained flag. "Why, of course," the druggist said. "If that's what you want. But the law requires you to tell what you are going to use it for."

Miss Emily just stared at him, her head tilted back in order to look him eye for eye, until he looked away and went and got the arsenic and wrapped it up. The Negro delivery boy brought her the package; the druggist didn't come back. When she opened the package at home there was written on the box, under the skull and bones: "For rats."

IV

So the next day we all said, "She will kill herself"; and we said it would be the best thing. When she had first begun to be seen with Homer Barron, we had said, "She will marry him." Then we said, "She will persuade him yet," because Homer himself had remarked—he liked men, and it was known that he drank with the younger men in the Elks' Club—that he was not a marrying man. Later we said, "Poor Emily" behind the jalousies as they passed on Sunday afternoon in the glittering buggy, Miss Emily with her head high and Homer Barron with his hat cocked and a cigar in his teeth, reins and whip in a yellow glove.

Then some of the ladies began to say that it was a disgrace to the town and a bad example to the young people. The men did not want to interfere, but at last the ladies forced the Baptist minister—Miss Emily's people were Episcopal—to call upon her. He would never divulge what happened during that interview, but he refused to go back again. The next Sunday they again drove about the streets, and the following day the minister's wife wrote to Miss Emily's relations in Alabama.

So she had blood-kin under her roof again and we sat back to watch developments. At first nothing happened. Then we were sure that they were to be married. We learned that Miss Emily had been to the jeweler's and ordered a man's toilet set in silver, with the letters H. B. on each piece. Two days later we learned that she had bought a complete outfit of men's clothing, including a nightshirt, and we said, "They are married." We were really glad. We were glad because the two female cousins were even more Grierson than Miss Emily had ever been. 45

So we were not surprised when Homer Barron—the streets had been finished some time since—was gone. We were a little disappointed that there was not a public blowing-off, but we believed that he had gone on to prepare for Miss Emily's coming, or to give her a chance to get rid of the cousins. (By that time it was a cabal, and we were all Miss Emily's allies to help circumvent the cousins.) Sure enough, after another week they departed. And, as we had expected all along, within three days Homer Barron was back in town. A neighbor saw the Negro man admit him at the kitchen door at dusk one evening.

And that was the last we saw of Homer Barron. And of Miss Emily for some time. The Negro man went in and out with the market basket, but the front door remained closed. Now and then we would see her at a window for a moment, as the men did that night when they sprinkled the lime, but for almost six months she did not appear on the streets. Then we knew that this was to be expected too; as if that quality of her father which had thwarted her woman's life so many times had been too virulent and too furious to die.

When we next saw Miss Emily, she had grown fat and her hair was turning gray. During the next few years it grew grayer and grayer until it attained an even pepper-and-salt iron-gray, when it ceased turning. Up to the day of her death at seventy-four it was still that vigorous iron-gray, like the hair of an active man.

From that time on her front door remained closed, save for a period of six or seven years, when she was about forty, during which she gave lessons in china-painting. She fitted up a studio in one of the downstairs rooms, where the daughters and granddaughters of Colonel Sartoris' contemporaries were sent to her with the same regularity and in the same spirit that they were sent to church on Sundays with a twenty-five-cent piece for the collection plate. Meanwhile her taxes had been remitted.

Then the newer generation became the backbone and the spirit of the town, and the painting pupils grew up and fell away and did not send their children to her with boxes of color and tedious brushes and pictures cut from the ladies' magazines. The front door closed upon the last one and remained closed for good. When the town got free postal delivery, Miss Emily alone refused to let them fasten the metal numbers above her door and attach a mailbox to it. She would not listen to them. 50

Daily, monthly, yearly we watched the Negro grow grayer and more stooped, going in and out with the market basket. Each December we sent her a tax notice, which would be returned by the post office a week later, unclaimed. Now and then we would see her in one of the downstairs windows—she had evidently shut up the top floor of the house—like the carven torso of an idol in a niche, looking or not looking at us, we could never tell which. Thus she passed from generation to generation—dear, inescapable, impervious, tranquil, and perverse.

And so she died. Fell ill in the house filled with dust and shadows, with only a doddering Negro man to wait on her. We did not even know she was sick; we had long since given up trying to get any information from the Negro. He talked to no one, probably not even to her, for his voice had grown harsh and rusty, as if from disuse.

She died in one of the downstairs rooms, in a heavy walnut bed with a curtain, her gray head propped on a pillow yellow and moldy with age and lack of sunlight.

V

The Negro met the first of the ladies at the front door and let them in, with their hushed, sibilant voices and their quick, curious glances, and then he disappeared. He walked right through the house and out the back and was not seen again.

The two female cousins came at once. They held the funeral on the second day, with the town coming to look at Miss Emily beneath a mass of bought flowers, with the crayon face of her father musing profoundly above the bier and the ladies sibilant and macabre; and the very old men—some in their brushed Confederate uniforms—on the porch and the lawn, talking of Miss Emily as if she had been a contemporary of theirs, believing that they had danced with her and courted her perhaps, confusing time with its mathematical progression, as the old do, to whom all the past is not a diminishing road but, instead, a huge meadow which no winter ever quite touches, divided from them now by the
narrow bottle-neck of the most recent decade of years. 55

Already we knew that there was one room in that region above stairs which no one had seen in forty years, and which would have to be forced. They waited until Miss Emily was decently in the ground before they opened it.

The violence of breaking down the door seemed to fill this room with pervading dust. A thin, acrid pall as of the tomb seemed to lie everywhere upon this room decked and furnished as for a bridal: upon the valance curtains of faded rose color, upon the rose-shaded lights, upon the dressing table, upon the delicate array of crystal and the man's toilet things backed with tarnished silver, silver so tarnished that the monogram was obscured. Among them lay collar and tie, as if they had just been removed, which, lifted, left upon the surface a pale crescent in the dust. Upon a chair hung the suit, carefully folded; beneath it the two mute shoes and the discarded socks.

The man himself lay in the bed.

For a long while we just stood there, looking down at the profound and fleshless grin. The body had apparently once lain in the attitude of an embrace, but now the long sleep that outlasts love, that conquers even the grimace of love, had cuckolded him. What was left of him, rotted beneath what was left of the nightshirt, had become inextricable from the bed in which he lay; and upon him and upon the pillow beside him lay that even coating of the patient and biding dust.

Then we noticed that in the second pillow was the indentation of a head. One of us lifted something from it, and leaning forward, that faint and invisible dust dry and acrid in the nostrils, we saw a long strand of iron-gray hair. 60

Reading and Reacting

1. Arrange these events in the sequence in which they occur: Homer's arrival in town, the aldermen's visit, Emily's purchase of poison, Colonel Sartoris's decision to remit Emily's taxes, the development of the odor around Emily's house, Emily's father's death, the arrival of Emily's relatives, Homer's disappearance. Then, list the events in the sequence in which they are introduced in the story. Why do you suppose Faulkner presents these events out of their actual chronological order?
2. Despite the story's confusing sequence, many events are foreshadowed. Give some examples of this technique. What does this use of foreshadowing contribute to the story?
3. Where does the exposition end and the movement toward the story's climax begin? Where does the resolution stage begin?
4. Emily is clearly the story's protagonist. In the sense that he opposes her wishes, Homer is the antagonist. What other characters—or what larger forces—are in conflict with Emily?
5. Explain how each of these phrases moves the story's plot along: "So she vanquished them, horse and foot. . . ." (par. 15); "After a week or two the smell went away" (par. 24); "And that was the last we saw of Homer Barron" (par. 47); "And so she died" (par. 52); "The man himself lay in the bed" (par. 58).
6. The narrator of the story is an observer, not a participant. Who might this narrator be? Do you think the narrator is male or female? How do you suppose the narrator might know so much about Emily? Why do you think the narrator uses *we* instead of *I*?
7. The original version of "A Rose for Emily" included a two-page deathbed scene revealing that Tobe, Emily's servant, has shared her terrible secret all these years and that Emily has left her house to him. Why do you think Faulkner deleted this scene? Do you think he made the right decision?
8. Some critics have suggested that Miss Emily Grierson is a kind of symbol of the Old South, with its outdated ideas of chivalry, formal manners, and tradition. In what sense is she also a victim of those values?
9. **Journal Entry** When asked at a seminar at the University of Virginia about the meaning of the title "A Rose for Emily," Faulkner replied, "Oh, it's simply the poor woman had no life at all. Her father had kept her more or less locked up and then she had a lover who was about to quit her, she had to murder him. It was just 'A Rose for Emily'—that's all." In another interview, asked the same question, he replied, "I pitied her and this was a salute, just as if you were to make a gesture, a salute, to anyone; to a woman you would hand a rose, as you would lift a cup of *sake* to a man." What do you make of Faulkner's responses? What else might the title suggest?

10. **Critical Perspective** In his essay "William Faulkner: An American Dickens," literary critic Leslie A. Fiedler characterizes Faulkner as "primarily . . . a sentimental writer; not a writer with the occasional vice of sentimentality, but one whose basic mode of experience is sentimental." Fiedler continues, "In a writer whose very method is self-indulgence, that sentimentality becomes sometimes downright embarrassing." Fiedler also notes Faulkner's "excesses of maudlin feelings and absurd indulgences in overripe rhetoric."

    Do you think these criticisms apply to "A Rose for Emily"? If so, does the "vice of sentimentality" diminish the story, or do you agree with Fiedler—who calls Faulkner a "supereminently good 'bad' writer"—that the author is able to transcend these excesses?

Related Works: "Miss Brill" (p. 185), "Barn Burning" (p. 265), "Porphyria's Lover" (p. 514), "Richard Cory" (p. 734), *Trifles* (p. 820)

WRITING SUGGESTIONS: Plot

1. Write a sequel to "The Story of an Hour," telling the story in the voice of Brently Mallard. Use flashbacks to provide information about his view of the Mallards' marriage.
2. Find a newspaper or magazine article that presents a story that you find disturbing. Then, write a fictionalized version of the article in which you retell the story's events in a detached tone, without adding analysis or commentary. Expand the original article by creating additional characters and settings.
3. "The Story of an Hour" includes a *deus ex machina*, an outside force or agent that suddenly appears to change the course of events. Consider the possible effects of a *deus ex machina* on the two other stories in this chapter. What might this outside force be in each story? How might it change the story's action? How plausible would such a dramatic turn of events be in each case?
4. Both "The Story of an Hour" and "How to Talk to Girls at Parties" create a dreamlike, disorienting atmosphere that has an unsettling effect on the protagonists. However, "The Story of an Hour" is essentially a realistic story while "How to Talk to Girls at Parties" is something quite different. Compare and contrast these two stories, focusing on how the stories' events affect the two protagonists and their perceptions of reality.

Chapter

10

Character

Zadie Smith
AP Images/Sang Tan

Katherine Mansfield
Bettmann/Getty Images

John Updike
Rick Friedman/Corbis Entertainment/Getty Images

Charles Baxter
AP Images/Janet Hostetter

Learning Objectives

After reading this chapter, you will be able to. . .

- Explain how characterization functions in a work of fiction.
- Classify fictional characters as either round or flat.
- Identify a fictional character who functions as a foil.
- Classify fictional characters as either dynamic or static.
- Explain a fictional character's motivation.
- Compare and contrast characters in literary works.

A **character** is a fictional representation of a person—usually (but not necessarily) a psychologically realistic depiction. Writers may develop characters through their actions, through their reactions to situations or to other characters, through their physical appearance, through their speech and gestures and expressions, and even through their names.

Generally speaking, characters' personality traits, as well as their appearances, feelings, and beliefs, are communicated to readers in two ways. First, readers can be *told* about characters. Third-person narrators can provide information about what characters are doing, saying, and thinking; what experiences they have had; what they look like; how they are dressed; and so on. Sometimes these narrators also offer analysis of and judgments about a character's behavior or motivation. Similarly, first-person narrators can tell us about themselves or about other characters. Thus, Sammy in John Updike's "A&P" (p. 179) tells readers what he thinks about his job and about the girls who come into the supermarket where he works. He also tells us what various characters look like and describes their actions, attitudes, speech, and gestures. (For more information about first-person narrators, see Chapter 12, "Point of View.")

Alternatively, aspects of a character's personality and beliefs may be revealed through their actions, words, or thoughts. For example, Sammy's vivid fantasies and his disapproval of his customers' lives suggest to readers that he is something of a nonconformist; however, Sammy himself does not actually tell us this.

Round and Flat Characters

In his influential 1927 work *Aspects of the Novel*, English novelist E. M. Forster classifies characters as either **round** (well developed, closely involved in, and responsive to the action) or **flat** (barely developed or stereotypical). To a great extent, these categories are still useful today. In an effective story, the major characters are usually complex and fully developed; if they are not, readers will not care what happens to them. Sometimes readers are encouraged to become involved with the characters, even to identify with them, and this empathy is possible only when we know something about the characters—their strengths and weaknesses, their likes and dislikes. In some cases, of course, a story can be effective even when its central characters are not well developed. Sometimes, in fact, a story's effectiveness is enhanced by an *absence* of character development, as in Shirley Jackson's "The Lottery" (p. 337).

Readers often expect characters to behave as "real people" in their situation might behave. Real people are not perfect, and realistic characters cannot be perfect either. The flaws that are revealed as round characters are developed—greed, gullibility, naïveté, shyness, a quick temper, or a lack of insight or judgment or tolerance or even intelligence—make them believable. In modern fiction, protagonists are seldom if ever the noble "hero"; more often, they are at least partly victims, people to whom unpleasant things happen and who are sometimes ill-equipped to cope with events.

Unlike major characters, minor characters are frequently not well developed. Often they are flat, perhaps acting as *foils* for the protagonist. A **foil** is a supporting character whose role in the story is to highlight a major character by introducing someone with contrasting traits and behavior. For example, in "A&P," Stokesie, another young checkout clerk, is a foil for Sammy. Because he is a little older than Sammy and seems to have none of Sammy's imagination, restlessness, or nonconformity, Stokesie suggests what Sammy might become if he were to continue to work at the A&P. Some flat characters are **stock characters**, easily identifiable types who behave so predictably that readers can readily recognize them. The kindly old priest, the tough young bully, the ruthless business executive, and the reckless adventurer are all stock characters. Some flat characters can even be **caricatures**, characterized by a single dominant trait, such as miserliness, or even by one physical trait, such as near-sightedness.

Dynamic and Static Characters

Characters may also be classified as either *dynamic or static*. A **dynamic character** grows and changes in the course of a story, developing in response to events and to other characters. In "A&P," for example, Sammy's decision to speak out in defence of the girls—as well as the events that led him to do so—changes him. His view of the world has changed at the end of the story, and as a result his position in the world may change too. A **static character** may face the same challenges a dynamic character might face but will remain essentially unchanged: a static character who was selfish and arrogant will remain selfish and arrogant, regardless of the nature of the story's conflict. In the fairy tale "Cinderella," for example, the title character is as sweet and good-natured at the end of the story—despite her mistreatment by her family—as she is at the beginning. Her situation may have changed, but her character has not.

Whereas round characters tend to be dynamic, flat characters tend to be static. But even a very complex, well-developed major character may be static; sometimes, in fact, the point of a story may hinge on a character's inability to change. A familiar example is the title character in William Faulkner's "A Rose for Emily" (p. 166), who lives a wasted, empty life, at least in part because she is unwilling or unable to accept that the world around her and the people in it have changed.

A story's minor characters are often static; their growth is not usually relevant to the story's development. Moreover, we usually do not learn enough about a minor character's traits, thoughts, actions, or motivation to determine whether the character changes significantly.

Motivation

Because round characters are complex, they are not always easy to understand. They may act unpredictably, just as real people do. They wrestle with decisions, resist or succumb to temptation, make mistakes, ask questions, search for answers, hope and dream, rejoice and despair. What is important is not whether we approve of a character's actions but whether those actions are *plausible*—whether the actions make sense in light of what we know about the character. We need to understand characters' **motivation**—the reasons behind their behavior—or we will not believe or accept that behavior. In "A&P" for example, given Sammy's age, his dissatisfaction with his job, and his desire to impress the young woman he calls Queenie, the decision he makes at the end of the story is perfectly plausible. Without having established his motivation, Updike could not have expected readers to accept Sammy's actions.

Of course, even when readers get to know a character, they still are not able to predict how a complex, round character will behave in a given situation; only a flat character is predictable. The tension that develops as readers wait to see how a character will act or react, and thus how a story's conflict will be resolved, is what holds readers' interest and keeps them involved as a story's action unfolds.

Checklist Writing about Character

- Who is the story's main character? Who are the other major characters?
- Who are the minor characters? What roles do they play in the story? How would the story be different without them?
- What do the major characters look like? Is their physical appearance important?
- What are the major characters' most notable personality traits?
- What are the major characters' likes and dislikes? their strengths and weaknesses?
- What are the main character's most strongly held feelings and beliefs?
- What are we told about the major characters' backgrounds and prior experiences? What can we infer?
- Are the characters round or flat?
- Are the characters dynamic or static?
- Does the story include any stock characters? Does any character serve as a foil?
- Do the characters act in a way that is consistent with how readers expect them to act?
- With which characters are readers likely to be most sympathetic? least sympathetic?

Source: Rick Friedman/Corbis Entertainment/ Getty Images

JOHN UPDIKE (1932–2009) was a prolific writer of novels, short stories, essays, poems, plays, and children's tales. Updike's earliest ambition was to be a cartoonist for the *New Yorker*. He attended Harvard hoping to draw cartoons for the *Harvard Lampoon*, studied drawing and fine art at Oxford, and in 1955 went to work for the *New Yorker*—not as a cartoonist but as a "Talk of the Town" reporter. Updike left the *New Yorker* after three years to write full time but continued to contribute stories, reviews, and essays to the magazine for over forty years. Among his novels are *Rabbit, Run* (1960), *The Centaur* (1963), *Rabbit Redux* (1971), *Rabbit Is Rich* (1981), *The Witches of Eastwick* (1985), and *Rabbit at Rest* (1990). His last novels are *Seek My Face* (2002), *Villages* (2004), *Of the Farm* (2004), *Terrorist* (2006), and *The Widows of Eastwick* (2008). In 1998, Updike received the National Book Foundation Medal for Distinguished Contribution to American Letters.

In early stories such as "A&P" (1961), Updike draws on memories of his childhood and teenage years for the sort of "small" scenes and stories for which he quickly became famous. "There is a great deal to be said about almost anything," Updike comments in an interview in *Contemporary Authors*. "All people can be equally interesting. . . . Now either nobody is a hero or everybody is. I vote for everybody. My subject is the American Protestant small-town middle class. I like middles. It is in middles that extremes clash."

Cultural Context The 1950s were a decade of prosperity for many in the United States. Soldiers returned from World War II, women who had worked in defense plants returned to their homes, and the population soared as a result of a "baby boom." Part of this prosperity manifested itself materially: middle-class Americans tried to "keep up with the Joneses" in terms of their possessions, and manufacturers raced to produce the latest consumer goods. Conformity became the norm, with the advent of mass-produced suburban tract houses and a conservative code of dress and behavior that dictated what was appropriate. This atmosphere is the context for the manager's disapproval in "A&P"—and Sammy's reaction foreshadows the mood of the rebellious generation to come.

A&P (1961)

In walks these three girls in nothing but bathing suits. I'm in the third check-out slot, with my back to the door, so I don't see them until they're over by the bread. The one that caught my eye first was the one in the plaid green two-piece. She was a chunky kid, with a good tan and a sweet broad soft-looking can with those two crescents of white just under it, where the sun never seems to hit, at the top of the backs of her legs. I stood there with my hand on a box of Hi Ho crackers trying to remember if I rang it up or not. I ring it up again and the customer starts giving me hell. She's one of these cash-register-watchers, a witch about fifty with rouge on her cheekbones and no eyebrows, and I know it made her day to trip me up. She'd been watching cash registers for fifty years and probably never seen a mistake before.

By the time I got her feathers smoothed and her goodies into a bag—she gives me a little snort in passing, if she'd been born at the right time they would have burned her over in Salem—by the time I get her on her way the girls had circled around the bread and were coming back, without a push-cart, back my way along the counters, in the aisle between the check-outs and the Special bins. They didn't even have shoes on. There was this chunky one, with the two-piece—it was bright green and the seams on the bra were still sharp and her belly was still pretty pale so I guessed she just got it (the suit)—there was this one, with one of those chubby berry-faces, the lips all bunched together under her nose, this one, and a tall one, with black hair that hadn't quite frizzed right, and one of these sunburns right across under the eyes, and a chin that was too long—you know, the kind of girl other girls think is very "striking" and "attractive" but never quite makes it, as they very well know, which is why they like her so much—and then the third one, that wasn't quite so tall. She was the queen. She kind of led them, the other two peeking around and making their shoulders round. She didn't look around, not this queen, she just walked straight on slowly, on these long white prima-donna legs. She came down a little hard on her heels, as if she didn't walk in her bare feet that much, putting down her heels and then letting the weight move along to her toes as if she was testing the floor with every step, putting a little deliberate extra action into it. You never know for sure how girls' minds work (do you really think it's a mind in there or just a little buzz like a bee in a glass jar?) but you got the idea she had talked the other two into coming in here with her, and now she was showing them how to do it, walk slow and hold yourself straight.

She had on a kind of dirty-pink—beige maybe, I don't know—bathing suit with a little nubble all over it and, what got me, the straps were down. They were off her shoulders looped loose around the cool tops of her arms, and I guess as a result the suit had slipped a little on her, so all around the top of the cloth there was this shining rim. If it hadn't been there you wouldn't have known there could have been anything whiter than those shoulders. With the straps pushed off, there was nothing between the top of the suit and the top of her head except just *her*, this clean bare plane of the top of her chest down from the shoulder bones like a dented sheet of metal tilted in the light. I mean, it was more than pretty.

She had sort of oaky hair that the sun and salt had bleached, done up in a bun that was unravelling, and a kind of prim face. Walking into the A&P with your straps down, I suppose it's the only kind of face you *can* have. She held her head so high her neck, coming up out of those white shoulders, looked kind of stretched, but I didn't mind. The longer her neck was, the more of her there was.

She must have felt in the corner of her eye me and over my shoulder Stokesie in the second slot watching, but she didn't tip. Not this queen. She kept her eyes moving across the racks, and stopped, and turned so slow it made my stomach rub the inside of my apron, and buzzed to the other two, who kind of huddled against her for relief, and they all three of them went up the cat-and-dog-food-breakfast-cereal-macaroni-rice-raisins-seasonings-spreads-spaghetti-soft-drinks-crackers-and-cookies aisle. From the third slot I look straight up this aisle to the meat counter, and I watched them all the way. The fat one with the tan sort of fumbled with the cookies, but on second thought she put the packages back. The sheep pushing their carts down the aisle—the girls were walking against the usual traffic (not that we have one-way signs or anything)—were pretty hilarious. You could see them, when Queenie's white shoulders dawned on them, kind of jerk, or hop, or hiccup, but their eyes snapped back to their own baskets and on they pushed. I bet you could set off dynamite in an A&P and the people would by and large keep reaching and checking oatmeal off their lists and muttering "Let me see, there was a third thing, began with A, asparagus, no, ah, yes, applesauce!" or whatever it is they do mutter. But there was no doubt, this jiggled them. A few houseslaves in pin curlers even looked around after pushing their carts past to make sure what they had seen was correct. 5

You know, it's one thing to have a girl in a bathing suit down on the beach, where what with the glare nobody can look at each other much anyway, and another thing in the cool of the A&P, under the fluorescent lights, against all those stacked packages, with her feet paddling along naked over our checkerboard green-and-cream rubber-tile floor.

"Oh Daddy," Stokesie said beside me. "I feel so faint."

"Darling," I said. "Hold me tight." Stokesie's married, with two babies chalked up on his fuselage already, but as far as I can tell that's the only difference. He's twenty-two, and I was nineteen this April.

"Is it done?" he asks, the responsible married man finding his voice. I forgot to say he thinks he's going to be manager some sunny day, maybe in 1990 when it's called the Great Alexandrov and Petrooshki Tea Company or something.

What he meant was, our town is five miles from a beach, with a big summer colony out on the Point, but we're right in the middle of town, and the women generally put on a shirt or shorts or something before they get out of the car into the street. And anyway these are usually women with six children and varicose veins mapping their legs and nobody, including them, could care less. As I say, we're right in the middle of town, and if you stand at our front doors you can see two banks and the Congregational church and the newspaper store and three real-estate offices and about twenty-seven old freeloaders tearing up Central Street because the sewer broke again. It's not as if we're on the Cape; we're north of Boston and there's people in this town haven't seen the ocean for twenty years. 10

The girls had reached the meat counter and were asking McMahon something. He pointed, they pointed, and they shuffled out of sight behind a pyramid of Diet Delight peaches. All that was left for us to see was old McMahon patting his mouth and looking after them sizing up their joints. Poor kids, I began to feel sorry for them, they couldn't help it.

Now here comes the sad part of the story, at least my family says it's sad but I don't think it's sad myself. The store's pretty empty, it being Thursday afternoon, so there was nothing much to do except lean on the register and wait for the girls to show up again. The whole store was like a pinball machine and I didn't know which tunnel they'd come out of. After a while they come around out of the far aisle, around the light bulbs, records at discount of the Caribbean Six or Tony Martin Sings or some such gunk you wonder they waste the wax on, sixpacks of candy bars, and plastic toys done up in cellophane that fall apart when a kid looks at them anyway. Around they come, Queenie still leading the way, and holding a little gray jar in her hand. Slots Three through Seven are unmanned and I could see her wondering between Stokes and me, but Stokesie with his usual luck draws an old party in baggy gray pants who stumbles up with four giant cans of pineapple juice (what do these bums *do* with all that pineapple juice? I've often asked myself) so the girls come to me. Queenie puts down the jar and I take it into my fingers icy cold. Kingfish Fancy Herring Snacks in Pure Sour Cream: 49. Now her hands are empty, not a ring or a bracelet, bare as God made them, and I wonder where the money's coming from. Still with that prim look she lifts a folded dollar bill out of the hollow at the center of her nubbled pink top. The jar went heavy in my hand. Really, I thought that was so cute.

Then everybody's luck begins to run out. Lengel comes in from haggling with a truck full of cabbages on the lot and is about to scuttle into that door marked **MANAGER** behind which he hides all day when the girls touch his eye. Lengel's pretty dreary, teaches Sunday school and the rest, but he doesn't miss that much. He comes over and says, "Girls, this isn't the beach."

Queenie blushes, though maybe it's just a brush of sunburn I was noticing for the first time, now that she was so close. "My mother asked me to pick up a jar of herring snacks." Her voice kind of startled me, the way voices do when you see the people first, coming out so flat and dumb yet kind of tony, too, the way it ticked over "pick up" and "snacks." All of a sudden I slid right down her voice into her living room. Her father and the other men were standing around in ice-cream coats and bow ties and the women were in sandals picking up herring snacks on toothpicks off a big plate and they were all holding drinks the color of water with olives and sprigs of mint in them. When my parents have somebody over they get lemonade and if it's a real racy affair Schlitz in tall glasses with "They'll Do It Every Time" cartoons stencilled on.

"That's all right," Lengel said. "But this isn't the beach." His repeating this struck me as funny, as if it had just occurred to him, and he had been thinking all these years the A&P was a great big dune and he was the head lifeguard. He didn't like my smiling—as I say he doesn't miss much—but he concentrates on giving the girls that sad Sunday-school-superintendent stare. 15

Queenie's blush is no sunburn now, and the plump one in plaid, that I liked better from the back—a really sweet can—pipes up, "We weren't doing any shopping. We just came in for the one thing."

"That makes no difference," Lengel tells her, and I could see from the way his eyes went that he hadn't noticed she was wearing a two-piece before. "We want you decently dressed when you come in here."

"We *are* decent," Queenie says suddenly, her lower lip pushing, getting sore now that she remembers her place, a place from which the crowd that runs the A&P must look pretty crummy. Fancy Herring Snacks flashed in her very blue eyes.

"Girls, I don't want to argue with you. After this come in here with your shoulders covered. It's our policy." He turns his back. That's policy for you. Policy is what the kingpins want. What the others want is juvenile delinquency.

All this while, the customers had been showing up with their carts but, you know, sheep, seeing a scene, they had all bunched up on Stokesie, who shook open a paper bag as gently as peeling a peach, not wanting to miss a word. I could feel in the silence everybody getting nervous, most of all Lengel, who asks me, "Sammy, have you rung up this purchase?" 20

I thought and said "No" but it wasn't about that I was thinking. I go through the punches, 4, 9, **GROC, TOT**—it's more complicated than you think, and after you do it often enough, it begins to make a little song, that you hear words to, in my case "Hello *(bing)* there, you *(gung)* hap-py *pee*-pul *(splat)*!"—the *splat* being the drawer flying out. I uncrease the bill, tenderly as you may imagine, it just having come from between the two smoothest scoops of vanilla I had ever known were there, and pass a half and a penny into her narrow pink palm, and nestle the herrings in a bag and twist its neck and hand it over, all the time thinking.

The girls, and who'd blame them, are in a hurry to get out, so I say "I quit" to Lengel quick enough for them to hear, hoping they'll stop and watch me, their unsuspected hero. They keep right on going, into the electric eye; the door flies open and they flicker across the lot to their car, Queenie and Plaid and Big Tall Goony-Goony (not that as raw material she was so bad), leaving me with Lengel and a kink in his eyebrow.

"Did you say something, Sammy?"

"I said I quit."

"I thought you did." 25

"You didn't have to embarrass them."

"It was they who were embarrassing us."

I started to say something that came out "Fiddle-de-doo." It's a saying of my grandmother's, and I know she would have been pleased.

"I don't think you know what you're saying," Lengel said.

"I know you don't," I said. "But I do." I pull the bow at the back of my apron and start shrugging it off my shoulders. A couple customers that had been heading for my slot begin to knock against each other, like scared pigs in a chute. 30

Lengel sighs and begins to look very patient and old and gray. He's been a friend of my parents for years. "Sammy, you don't want to do this to your Mom and Dad," he tells me. It's true, I don't. But it seems to me that once you begin a gesture it's fatal not to go through with it. I fold the apron, "Sammy" stitched in red on the pocket, and put it on the counter, and drop the bow tie on top of it. The bow tie is theirs, if you've ever wondered. "You'll feel this for the rest of your life," Lengel says, and I know that's true, too, but remembering how he made that pretty girl blush makes me so scrunchy inside I punch the No Sale tab and the machine whirs "pee-pul" and the drawer splats out. One advantage to this scene taking place in summer, I can follow this up with a clean exit, there's no fumbling around getting your coat and galoshes, I just saunter into the electric eye in my white shirt that my mother ironed the night before, and the door heaves itself open, and outside the sunshine is skating around the asphalt.

I look around for my girls, but they're gone, of course. There wasn't anybody but some young married screaming with her children about some candy they didn't get by the door of a powder-blue Falcon station wagon. Looking back in the big windows, over the bags of peat moss and aluminum lawn furniture stacked on the pavement, I could see Lengel in my place in the slot, checking the sheep through. His face was dark gray and his back stiff, as if he'd just had an injection of iron, and my stomach kind of fell as I felt how hard the world was going to be to me hereafter.

Reading and Reacting

1. Summarize the information Sammy gives readers about his tastes and background. Why is this exposition vital to the story's development?
2. List some of the most obvious physical characteristics of the A&P's customers. How do these characteristics make them foils for Queenie and her friends?
3. What is it about Queenie and her friends that appeals to Sammy?
4. Is Queenie a stock character? Why or why not?
5. What rules and conventions are customers expected to follow in a supermarket? How does the behavior of Queenie and her friends violate these rules?
6. Is the supermarket setting vital to the story? Could the story have been set in a car wash? in a fast-food restaurant? in a business office?
7. How accurate are Sammy's judgments about the other characters? How might the characters be portrayed if the story were told by Lengel?
8. Given what you learn about Sammy as the story unfolds, what do you see as his *primary* motivation for quitting his job? What other factors motivate him?
9. **Journal Entry** Where do you think Sammy will find himself in ten years? Why?
10. **Critical Perspective** In *The Necessary Blackness*, critic Mary Allen observes, "Updike's most tender reverence is reserved for women's bodies. The elegant style with which he describes female anatomy often becomes overwrought, as his descriptions do generally. But it always conveys wonder."

    In what passages in "A&P" does Updike (through Sammy) convey this sense of wonder? Do you think today's audience, reading the story more than sixty years after Updike wrote it, and over fifty years after Allen's essay was published, would still see such passages as conveying "tender reverence"? Or do you think readers might now see Sammy (and, indeed, Updike) as crossing a line? How do you react to these passages?

Related Works: "How to Talk to Girls at Parties" (p. 155), "Araby" (p. 296), "A Supermarket in California" (p. 586), "The Road Not Taken" (p. 605), *Beauty* (p. 785), *The Glass Menagerie* (p. 958)

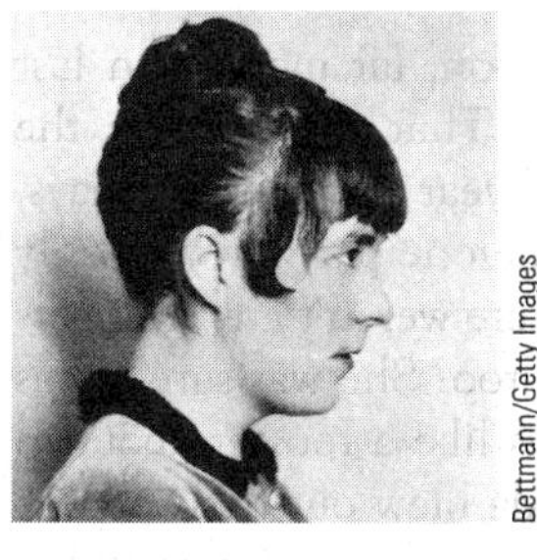
Bettmann/Getty Images

KATHERINE MANSFIELD (1888–1923), one of the pioneers of the modern short story, was born in New Zealand and educated in England. Very much a "modern young woman," she began living on her own in London at the age of nineteen, soon publishing stories and book reviews in many of the most influential literary magazines of the day.

A short story writer of great versatility, Mansfield produced sparkling social comedies as well as more intellectually and technically complex works intended for "perceptive readers." According to one critic, her best works "[w]ith delicate plainness . . . present elusive moments of decision, defeat, and small triumph." Her last two story collections—*Bliss and Other Stories* (1920) and *The Garden Party and Other Stories* (1922)—were met with immediate critical acclaim, but Mansfield's career was cut short in 1923 when she died of complications from tuberculosis at the age of thirty-five.

One notable theme in Mansfield's work is the *dame seule*, the "woman alone," which provides the basis for the poignant "Miss Brill."

Cultural Context During the nineteenth century, the task of spinning wool was typically given to unmarried women as a way for them to earn their keep in the home. Thus, the term *spinster* came into existence. Over time, the word acquired a negative stereotype, conjuring up the image of a lonely, childless, frumpy middle-aged woman who longs to be like other "normal" women—wives and mothers. Today, the word *spinster* is rarely used, reflecting the changed perception of unmarried women and the wider lifestyle choices open to them.

Miss Brill (1922)

Although it was so brilliantly fine—the blue sky powdered with gold and great spots of light like white wine splashed over the Jardins Publiques[1]—Miss Brill was glad that she had decided on her fur. The air was motionless, but when you opened your mouth there was just a faint chill, like a chill from a glass of iced water before you sip, and now and again a leaf came drifting—from nowhere, from the sky. Miss Brill put up her hand and touched her fur. Dear little thing! It was nice to feel it again. She had taken it out of its box that afternoon, shaken out the moth-powder, given it a good brush, and rubbed the life back into the

[1] *Jardins Publiques:* "Public Gardens" (French).

dim little eyes. "What has been happening to me?" said the sad little eyes. Oh, how sweet it was to see them snap at her again from the red eiderdown! . . . But the nose, which was of some black composition, wasn't at all firm. It must have had a knock, somehow. Never mind—a little dab of black sealing-wax when the time came—when it was absolutely necessary. . . . Little rogue! Yes, she really felt like that about it. Little rogue biting its tail just by her left ear. She could have taken it off and laid it on her lap and stroked it. She felt a tingling in her hands and arms, but that came from walking, she supposed. And when she breathed, something light and sad—no, not sad, exactly—something gentle seemed to move in her bosom.

There were a number of people out this afternoon, far more than last Sunday. And the band sounded louder and gayer. That was because the Season had begun. For although the band played all year round on Sundays, out of season it was never the same. It was like some one playing with only the family to listen; it didn't care how it played if there weren't any strangers present. Wasn't the conductor wearing a new coat, too? She was sure it was new. He scraped with his foot and flapped his arms like a rooster about to crow, and the bandsmen sitting in the green rotunda blew out their cheeks and glared at the music. Now there came a little "flutey" bit—very pretty!—a little chain of bright drops. She was sure it would be repeated. It was; she lifted her head and smiled.

Only two people shared her "special" seat: a fine old man in a velvet coat, his hands clasped over a huge carved walking-stick, and a big old woman, sitting upright, with a roll of knitting on her embroidered apron. They did not speak. This was disappointing, for Miss Brill always looked forward to the conversation. She had become really quite expert, she thought, at listening as though she didn't listen, at sitting in other people's lives just for a minute while they talked round her.

She glanced, sideways, at the old couple. Perhaps they would go soon. Last Sunday, too, hadn't been as interesting as usual. An Englishman and his wife, he wearing a dreadful Panama hat and she button boots. And she'd gone on the whole time about how she ought to wear spectacles; she knew she needed them; but that it was no good getting any; they'd be sure to break and they'd never keep on. And he'd been so patient. He'd suggested everything—gold rims, the kind that curved round your ears, little pads inside the bridge. No, nothing would please her. "They'll always be sliding down my nose!" Miss Brill wanted to shake her.

The old people sat on the bench, still as statues. Never mind, there was always the crowd to watch. To and fro, in front of the flower-beds and the band rotunda, the couples and groups paraded, stopped to talk, to greet, to buy a handful of flowers from the old beggar who had his tray fixed to the railings. Little children ran among them, swooping and laughing; little boys with big white silk bows under their chins, little girls, little French dolls, dressed up in velvet and lace. And sometimes a tiny staggerer came suddenly rocking into the open from under the trees, stopped, stared, as suddenly sat down "flop," until its small high-stepping mother, like a young hen, rushed scolding to its rescue. Other people sat on the benches and green chairs, but they were nearly always the same, Sunday after Sunday, and—Miss Brill had often noticed—there was something funny about nearly all of them. They were odd, silent, nearly all old, and from the way they stared they looked as though they'd just come from dark little rooms or even—even cupboards! 5

Behind the rotunda the slender trees with yellow leaves down drooping, and through them just a line of sea, and beyond the blue sky with gold-veined clouds.

Tum-tum-tum tiddle-um! tiddle-um! tum tiddley-um tum ta! blew the band.

Two young girls in red came by and two young soldiers in blue met them, and they laughed and paired and went off arm-in-arm. Two peasant women with funny straw hats passed, gravely, leading beautiful smoke-colored donkeys. A cold, pale nun hurried by. A beautiful woman came along and dropped her bunch of violets, and a little boy ran after to hand them to her, and she took them and threw them away as if they'd been poisoned. Dear me! Miss Brill didn't know whether to admire that or not! And now an ermine toque[2] and a gentleman in grey met just in front of her. He was tall, stiff, dignified, and she was wearing the ermine toque she'd bought when her hair was yellow. Now everything, her hair, her face, even her eyes, was the same color as the shabby ermine, and her hand, in its cleaned glove, lifted to dab her lips, was a tiny yellowish paw. Oh, she was so pleased to see him—delighted! She rather thought they were going to meet that afternoon. She described where she'd been—everywhere, here, there, along by the sea. The day was so charming—didn't he agree? And wouldn't he, perhaps? . . . But he shook his head, lighted a cigarette, slowly breathed a great deep puff into her face, and, even while she was still talking and laughing, flicked the match away and walked on. The ermine toque was alone; she smiled more brightly than ever. But even the band seemed to know what she was feeling and played more softly, played tenderly, and the drum beat, "The Brute! The Brute!" over and over. What would she do? What was going to happen now? But as Miss Brill wondered, the ermine toque turned, raised her hand as though she'd seen some one else, much nicer, just over there, and pattered away. And the band changed again and played more quickly, more gaily than ever, and the old couple on Miss Brill's seat got up and marched away, and such a funny old man with long whiskers hobbled along in time to the music and was nearly knocked over by four girls walking abreast.

Oh, how fascinating it was! How she enjoyed it! How she loved sitting here, watching it all! It was like a play. It was exactly like a play. Who could believe the sky at the back wasn't painted? But it wasn't till a little brown dog trotted on solemn and then slowly trotted off, like a little "theatre" dog, a little dog that had been drugged, that Miss Brill discovered what it was that made it so exciting. They were all on the stage. They weren't only the audience, not only looking on; they were acting. Even she had a part and came every Sunday.

---

[2]*ermine toque:* Small, close-fitting woman's hat made from the fur of an ermine, a type of weasel.

No doubt somebody would have noticed if she hadn't been there; she was part of the performance after all. How strange she'd never thought of it like that before! And yet it explained why she made such a point of starting from home at just the same time each week—so as not to be late for the performance—and it also explained why she had quite a queer, shy feeling at telling her English pupils how she spent her Sunday afternoons. No wonder! Miss Brill nearly laughed out loud. She was on the stage. She thought of the old invalid gentleman to whom she read the newspaper four afternoons a week while he slept in the garden. She had got quite used to the frail head on the cotton pillow, the hollowed eyes, the open mouth and the high pinched nose. If he'd been dead she mightn't have noticed for weeks; she wouldn't have minded. But suddenly he knew he was having the paper read to him by an actress! "An actress!" The old head lifted; two points of light quivered in the old eyes. "An actress—are ye?" And Miss Brill smoothed the newspaper as though it were the manuscript of her part and said gently: "Yes, I have been an actress for a long time."

The band had been having a rest. Now they started again. And what they played was warm, sunny, yet there was just a faint chill—a something, what was it?—not sadness—no, not sadness—a something that made you want to sing. The tune lifted, lifted, the light shone; and it seemed to Miss Brill that in another moment all of them, all the whole company, would begin singing. The young ones, the laughing ones who were moving together, they would begin, and the men's voices, very resolute and brave, would join them. And then she too, she too, and the others on the benches—they would come in with a kind of accompaniment—something low, that scarcely rose or fell, something so beautiful—moving. . . . And Miss Brill's eyes filled with tears and she looked smiling at all the other members of the company. Yes, we understand, we understand, she thought—though what they understood she didn't know. 10

Just at that moment a boy and a girl came and sat down where the old couple had been. They were beautifully dressed; they were in love. The hero and heroine, of course, just arrived from his father's yacht. And still soundlessly singing, still with that trembling smile, Miss Brill prepared to listen.

"No, not now," said the girl. "Not here, I can't."

"But why? Because of that stupid old thing at the end there?" asked the boy. "Why does she come here at all—who wants her? Why doesn't she keep her silly old mug at home?"

"It's her fu-fur which is so funny," giggled the girl. "It's exactly like a fried whiting."[3]

"Ah, be off with you!" said the boy in an angry whisper. Then: "Tell me, my petite chérie—"[4] 15

"No, not here," said the girl. "Not *yet*."

On her way home she usually bought a slice of honeycake at the baker's. It was her Sunday treat. Sometimes there was an almond in her slice, sometimes

---

[3] *whiting:* Food fish related to the cod.

[4] *petite chérie:* "Little darling" (French).

not. It made a great difference. If there was an almond it was like carrying home a tiny present—a surprise—something that might very well not have been there. She hurried on the almond Sundays and struck the match for the kettle in quite a dashing way.

But to-day she passed the baker's by, climbed the stairs, went into the little dark room—her room like a cupboard—and sat down on the red eiderdown. She sat there for a long time. The box that the fur came out of was on the bed. She unclasped the necklet quickly; quickly, without looking, laid it inside. But when she put the lid on she thought she heard something crying.

Reading and Reacting

1. What specific details can you infer about Miss Brill's character (and, perhaps, about her life) from this statement: "She had become really quite expert, she thought, at listening as though she didn't listen, at sitting in other people's lives just for a minute while they talked round her" (par. 3)?
2. How do Miss Brill's observations of the people around her give us insight into her own character? Why do you suppose she doesn't interact with any of the people she observes?
3. In paragraph 9, Miss Brill realizes that the scene she observes is "exactly like a play" and that "Even she had a part and came every Sunday." What part does Miss Brill play? Is she a stock character in this play, or is she a three-dimensional character? Does she play a lead role or a supporting role?
4. What do you think Miss Brill means when she says, "I have been an actress for a long time" (par. 9)? What does this comment reveal about how she sees herself? Is her view of herself similar to or different from the view the other characters have of her?
5. What role does Miss Brill's fur piece play in the story? In what sense, if any, does it function as a character?
6. What happens in paragraphs 11–16 to break Miss Brill's mood? Why is the scene she observes so upsetting to her?
7. At the end of the story, has Miss Brill changed as a result of what she has overheard, or is she the same person she was at the beginning? Do you think she will return to the park the following Sunday?
8. The story's last paragraph describes Miss Brill's room as being "like a cupboard." Where else has this image appeared in the story? What does its reappearance in the conclusion tell us?
9. **Journal Entry** Write a character sketch of Miss Brill, inventing a plausible family and personal history that might help to explain the character you see in the story.
10. **Critical Perspective** Critic Gillian Boddy, in *Katherine Mansfield: The Woman, The Writer*, offers the following analysis of Mansfield's fiction:

    The story evolves through the characters' minds. The external narrator is almost eliminated. As so often in her work, the reader is dropped into the story and

> simply confronted by a particular situation. There is no preliminary establishing and identification of time and place. The reader is immediately involved; it is assumed that he or she has any necessary prerequisite knowledge and is, in a sense, part of the story too.

Do you see this absence of conventional exposition as a problem in "Miss Brill"? Do you think the story would be more effective if Mansfield had supplied more preliminary information about setting and character? Or do you believe that what Boddy calls Mansfield's "concentration on a moment or episode" is a satisfactory substitute for the missing exposition, effectively shifting interest from "*what* happens" to "*why* it happens"?

Related Works: "Rooming houses are old women" (p. 563), "Aunt Jennifer's Tigers" (p. 598), *Trifles* (p. 820)

Source: AP Photo/Janet Hostetter

CHARLES BAXTER (1947–) was born in Minneapolis and educated at Macalester College and at the State University of New York, Buffalo. Recently retired from teaching in the creative writing program at the University of Minnesota, Baxter is the author of critically praised collections of short stories, including *Through the Safety Net* (1985), *A Relative Stranger: Stories* (1990), *Gryphon: New and Selected Stories* (2011), and *There's Something I Want You to Do* (2014). His novels include *First Light* (1987), *Shadow Play* (1993), *The Feast of Love* (2002), *Saul and Patsy* (2003), and *The Sun Collective* (2020), and he has also published a book of poetry, *Imaginary Paintings and Other Poems* (1989). Baxter has also written about the craft of writing in his books *Burning Down the House* (1997) and *The Art of Subtext* (2007). An essay collection, *Wonderlands: Essays on the Life of* Literature was published in 2022. A recipient of Guggenheim and NEA fellowships, Baxter's work has won awards from the American Academy of Arts and Letters, and his novel, *Feast of Love* was a finalist for the National Book Award.

Baxter's critics often mention the compassion he shows in writing about his fictional characters: a couple who lose their child, a hospital worker who wants to be famous, a tired businessman who really wants to paint. In many of his short stories in *Through the Safety Net* (in which "Gryphon" appeared), unexpected events jar Baxter's characters out of their routines, forcing them to consider different choices, to call on inner strength, or to swim against the tide of "middle America's" conventions.

Cultural Context One of the key elements of this story is a character's use of a deck of tarot cards to predict the future. Originating more than 500 years ago in northern Italy in a game called "Triumphs," the Tarot was quickly adopted as a tool for divining the future. With deep roots in the symbolism of medieval and Renaissance Europe, the Tarot is today the singular most popular tool for spiritual introspection and prophesy. While the death card is often feared, many interpreters argue that it hardly ever points to literal death but rather symbolizes the ending of something significant and the beginning of something new. In "Gryphon," the accuracy of the Tarot's prediction is less important than the young students' reactions to it.

Gryphon (1985)

On Wednesday afternoon, between the geography lesson on ancient Egypt's hand-operated irrigation system and an art project that involved drawing a model city next to a mountain, our fourth-grade teacher, Mr. Hibler, developed a cough. This cough began with a series of muffled throat clearings and progressed to propulsive noises contained within Mr. Hibler's closed mouth. "Listen to him," Carol Peterson whispered to me. "He's gonna blow up." Mr. Hibler's laughter—dazed and infrequent—sounded a bit like his cough, but as we worked on our model cities we would look up, thinking he was enjoying a joke, and see Mr. Hibler's face turning red, his cheeks puffed out. This was not laughter. Twice he bent over, and his loose tie, like a plumb line, hung down straight from his neck as he exploded himself into a Kleenex. He would excuse himself, then go on coughing. "I'll bet you a dime," Carol Peterson whispered, "we get a substitute tomorrow."

Carol sat at the desk in front of mine and was a bad person—when she thought no one was looking she would blow her nose on notebook paper, then crumble it up and throw it into the wastebasket—but at times of crisis she spoke the truth. I knew I'd lose the dime.

"No deal," I said.

When Mr. Hibler stood us up in formation at the door just prior to the final bell, he was almost incapable of speech. "I'm sorry, boys and girls," he said. "I seem to be coming down with something."

"I hope you feel better tomorrow, Mr. Hibler," Bobby Kryzanowicz, the faultless brown-noser said, and I heard Carol Peterson's evil giggle. Then Mr. Hibler opened the door and we walked out to the buses, a clique of us starting noisily to hawk and cough as soon as we thought we were a few feet beyond Mr. Hibler's earshot. 5

Five Oaks being a rural community, and in Michigan, the supply of substitute teachers was limited to the town's unemployed community college graduates, a pool of about four mothers. These ladies fluttered, provided easeful class days, and nervously covered material we had mastered weeks earlier. Therefore it was a surprise when a woman we had never seen came into the class the next day, carrying a purple purse, a checkerboard lunchbox, and a few books. She put the books on one side of Mr. Hibler's desk and the lunchbox on the other, next to the Voice of Music phonograph. Three of us in the back of the room were playing with Heever, the chameleon that lived in the terrarium and on one of the plastic drapes, when she walked in.

She clapped her hands at us. "Little boys," she said, "why are you bent over together like that?" She didn't wait for us to answer. "Are you tormenting an animal? Put it back. Please sit down at your desks. I want no cabals this time of the day." We just stared at her. "Boys," she repeated, "I asked you to sit down."

I put the chameleon in his terrarium and felt my way to my desk, never taking my eyes off the woman. With white and green chalk, she had started to draw a tree on the left side of the blackboard. She didn't look usual. Furthermore, her tree was outsized, disproportionate, for some reason.

"This room needs a tree," she said, with one line drawing the suggestion of a leaf. "A large, leafy, shady, deciduous . . . oak."

Her fine, light hair had been done up in what I would learn years later was called a chignon, and she wore gold-rimmed glasses whose lenses seemed to have the faintest blue tint. Harold Knardahl, who sat across from me, whispered "Mars," and I nodded slowly, savoring the imminent weirdness of the day. The substitute drew another branch with an extravagant arm gesture, then turned around and said, "Good morning. I don't believe I said good morning to all of
you yet." 10

Facing us, she was no special age—an adult is an adult—but her face had two prominent lines, descending vertically from the sides of her mouth to her chin. I knew where I had seen those lines before: *Pinocchio*. They were marionette lines. "You may stare at me," she said to us, as a few more kids from the last bus came into the room, their eyes fixed on her, "for a few more seconds, until the bell rings. Then I will permit no more staring. Looking I will permit. Staring, no. It is impolite to stare, and a sign of bad breeding. You cannot make a social effort while staring."

Harold Knardahl did not glance at me, or nudge, but I heard him whisper "Mars" again, trying to get more mileage out of his single joke with the kids who had just come in.

When everyone was seated, the substitute teacher finished her tree, put down her chalk fastidiously on the phonograph, brushed her hands, and faced us. "Good morning," she said. "I am Miss Ferenczi, your teacher for the day. I am fairly new to your community, and I don't believe any of you know me. I will therefore start by telling you a story about myself."

While we settled back, she launched into her tale. She said her grandfather had been a Hungarian prince; her mother had been born in some place called Flanders, had been a pianist, and had played concerts for people Miss Ferenczi referred to as "crowned heads." She gave us a knowing look. "Grieg," she said, "the Norwegian master, wrote a concerto for piano that was," she paused, "my mother's triumph at her debut concert in London." Her eyes searched the ceiling. Our eyes followed. Nothing up there but ceiling tile. "For reasons that I shall not go into, my family's fortunes took us to Detroit, then north to dreadful Saginaw, and now here I am in Five Oaks, as your substitute teacher, for today, Thursday, October the eleventh. I believe it will be a good day: All the forecasts coincide. We shall start with your reading lesson. Take out your reading book. I believe it is called *Broad Horizons*, or something along those lines."

Jeannie Vermeesch raised her hand. Miss Ferenczi nodded at her. "Mr. Hibler
always starts the day with the Pledge of Allegiance," Jeannie whined. 15

"Oh, does he? In that case," Miss Ferenczi said, "you must know it *very* well by now, and we certainly need not spend our time on it. No, no allegiance pledging on the premises today, by my reckoning. Not with so much sunlight coming into the room. A pledge does not suit my mood." She glanced at her watch. "Time *is* flying. Take out *Broad Horizons*."

She disappointed us by giving us an ordinary lesson, complete with vocabulary word drills, comprehension questions, and recitation. She didn't seem to care for the material, however. She sighed every few minutes and rubbed her glasses with a frilly perfumed handkerchief that she withdrew, magician style, from her left sleeve.

After reading we moved on to arithmetic. It was my favorite time of the morning, when the lazy autumn sunlight dazzled its way through ribbons of clouds past the windows on the east side of the classroom, and crept across the linoleum floor. On the playground the first group of children, the kindergartners, were running on the quack grass just beyond the monkey bars. We were doing multiplication tables. Miss Ferenczi had made John Wazny stand up at his desk in the front row. He was supposed to go through the tables of six. From where I was sitting, I could smell the Vitalis soaked into John's plastered hair. He was doing fine until he came to six times eleven and six times twelve. "Six times eleven," he said, "is sixty-eight. Six times twelve is . . ." He put his fingers to his head, quickly and secretly sniffed his fingertips, and said, "seventy-two." Then he sat down.

"Fine," Miss Ferenczi said. "Well now. That was very good."

"Miss Ferenczi!" One of the Eddy twins was waving her hand desperately in the air. "Miss Ferenczi! Miss Ferenczi!"

"Yes?"

"John said that six times eleven is sixty-eight and you said he was right!"

"*Did* I?" She gazed at the class with a jolly look breaking across her marionette's face. "Did I say that? Well, what *is* six times eleven?"

"It's sixty-six!"

She nodded. "Yes. So it is. But, and I know some people will not entirely agree with me, at some times it is sixty-eight."

"When? When is it sixty-eight?"

We were all waiting.

"In higher mathematics, which you children do not yet understand, six times eleven can be considered to be sixty-eight." She laughed through her nose. "In higher mathematics numbers are . . . more fluid. The only thing a number does is contain a certain amount of something. Think of water. A cup is not the only way to measure a certain amount of water, is it?" We were staring, shaking our heads. "You could use saucepans or thimbles. In either case, the water *would be the same*. Perhaps," she started again, "it would be better for you to think that six times eleven is sixty-eight only when I am in the room."

"Why is it sixty-eight," Mark Poole asked, "when you're in the room?"

"Because it's more interesting that way," she said, smiling very rapidly behind her blue-tinted glasses. "Besides, I'm your substitute teacher, am I not?" We all nodded. "Well, then, think of six times eleven equals sixty-eight as a substitute fact."

"A substitute fact?"

"Yes." Then she looked at us carefully. "Do you think," she asked, "that anyone is going to be hurt by a substitute fact?"

We looked back at her.

"Will the plants on the windowsill be hurt?" We glanced at them. There were sensitive plants thriving in a green plastic tray, and several wilted ferns in small clay pots. "Your dogs and cats, or your moms and dads?" She waited. "So," she concluded, "what's the problem?"

"But it's wrong," Janice Weber said, "isn't it?" 35

"What's your name, young lady?"

"Janice Weber."

"And you think it's wrong, Janice?"

"I was just asking."

"Well, all right. You were just asking. I think we've spent enough time on this matter by now, don't you, class? You are free to think what you like. When your teacher, Mr. Hibler, returns, six times eleven will be sixty-six again, you can rest assured. And it will be that for the rest of your lives in Five Oaks. Too bad, eh?" She raised her eyebrows and glinted herself at us. "But for now, it wasn't. So much for that. Let us go to your assigned problems for today, as painstakingly outlined, I see, in Mr. Hibler's lesson plan. Take out a sheet of paper and write your names in the upper left-hand corner." 40

For the next half hour we did the rest of our arithmetic problems. We handed them in and went on to spelling, my worst subject. Spelling always came before lunch. We were taking spelling dictation and looking at the clock. "Thorough," Miss Ferenczi said. "Boundary." She walked in the aisles between the desks, holding the spelling book open and looking down at our papers. "Balcony." I clutched my pencil. Somehow, the way she said those words, they seemed foreign, Hungarian, mis-voweled and mis-consonanted. I stared down at what I had spelled. *Balconie*. I turned my pencil upside down and erased my mistake. *Balconey*. That looked better, but still incorrect. I cursed the world of spelling and tried erasing it again and saw the paper beginning to wear away. *Balkony*. Suddenly I felt a hand on my shoulder.

"I don't like that word either," Miss Ferenczi whispered, bent over, her mouth near my ear. "It's ugly. My feeling is, if you don't like a word, you don't have to use it." She straightened up, leaving behind a slight odor of Clorets.

At lunchtime we went out to get our trays of sloppy joes, peaches in heavy syrup, coconut cookies, and milk, and brought them back to the classroom, where Miss Ferenczi was sitting at the desk, eating a brown sticky thing she had unwrapped from tightly rubber-banded wax paper. "Miss Ferenczi," I said, raising my hand. "You don't have to eat with us. You can eat with the other teachers. There's a teachers' lounge," I ended up, "next to the principal's office."

"No, thank you," she said. "I prefer it here."

"We've got a room monitor," I said. "Mrs. Eddy." I pointed to where Mrs. Eddy, Joyce and Judy's mother, sat silently at the back of the room, doing her knitting. 45

"That's fine," Miss Ferenczi said. "But I shall continue to eat here, with you children. I prefer it," she repeated.

"How come?" Wayne Razmer asked without raising his hand.

"I talked with the other teachers before class this morning," Miss Ferenczi said, biting into her brown food. "There was a great rattling of the words for the fewness of ideas. I didn't care for their brand of hilarity. I don't like ditto machine jokes."

"Oh," Wayne said.

"What's that you're eating?" Maxine Sylvester asked, twitching her nose. "Is it food?"

"It most certainly *is* food. It's a stuffed fig. I had to drive almost down to Detroit to get it. I also bought some smoked sturgeon. And this," she said, lifting some green leaves out of her lunchbox, "is raw spinach, cleaned this morning before I came out here to the Garfield-Murry school."

"Why're you eating raw spinach?" Maxine asked.

"It's good for you," Miss Ferenczi said. "More stimulating than soda pop or smelling salts." I bit into my sloppy joe and stared blankly out the window. An almost invisible moon was faintly silvered in the daytime autumn sky. "As far as food is concerned," Miss Ferenczi was saying, "you have to shuffle the pack. Mix it up. Too many people eat . . . well, never mind."

"Miss Ferenczi," Carol Peterson said, "what are we going to do this afternoon?"

"Well," she said, looking down at Mr. Hibler's lesson plan, "I see that your teacher, Mr. Hibler, has you scheduled for a unit on the Egyptians." Carol groaned. "Yessss," Miss Ferenczi continued, "that is what we will do: the Egyptians. A remarkable people. Almost as remarkable as the Americans. But not quite." She lowered her head, did her quick smile, and went back to eating her spinach.

After noon recess we came back into the classroom and saw that Miss Ferenczi had drawn a pyramid on the blackboard, close to her oak tree. Some of us who had been playing baseball were messing around in the back of the room, dropping the bats and the gloves into the playground box, and I think that Ray Schontzeler had just slugged me when I heard Miss Ferenczi's high-pitched voice quavering with emotion. "Boys," she said, "come to order right this minute and take your seats. I do not wish to waste a minute of class time. Take out your geography books." We trudged to our desks and, still sweating, pulled out *Distant Lands and Their People*. "Turn to page forty-two." She waited for thirty seconds, then looked over at Kelly Munger. "Young man," she said, "why are you still fossicking in your desk?"

Kelly looked as if his foot had been stepped on. "Why am I what?"

"Why are you . . . burrowing in your desk like that?"

"I'm lookin' for the book, Miss Ferenczi."

Bobby Kryzanowicz, the faultless brown-noser who sat in the first row by choice, softly said, "His name is Kelly Munger. He can't ever find his stuff. He always does that."

"I don't care what his name is, especially after lunch," Miss Ferenczi said. "*Where is your book?*"

"I just found it." Kelly was peering into his desk and with both hands pulled at the book, shoveling along in front of it several pencils and crayons, which fell into his lap and then to the floor.

"I hate a mess," Miss Ferenczi said. "I hate a mess in a desk or a mind. It's . . . unsanitary. You wouldn't want your house at home to look like your desk at school, now, would you?" She didn't wait for an answer. "I should think not. A house at home should be as neat as human hands can make it. What were we talking about? Egypt. Page forty-two. I note from Mr. Hibler's lesson plan that you have been discussing the modes of Egyptian irrigation. Interesting, in my view, but not so interesting as what we are about to cover. The pyramids and Egyptian slave labor. A plus on one side, a minus on the other." We had our books open to page forty-two, where there was a picture of a pyramid, but Miss Ferenczi wasn't looking at the book. Instead, she was staring at some object just outside the window.

"Pyramids," Miss Ferenczi said, still looking past the window. "I want you to think about the pyramids. And what was inside. The bodies of the pharaohs, of course, and their attendant treasures. Scrolls. Perhaps," Miss Ferenczi said, with something gleeful but unsmiling in her face, "these scrolls were novels for the pharaohs, helping them to pass the time in their long voyage through the centuries. But then, I am joking." I was looking at the lines on Miss Ferenczi's face. "Pyramids," Miss Ferenczi went on, "were the repositories of special cosmic powers. The nature of a pyramid is to guide cosmic energy forces into a concentrated point. The Egyptians knew that; we have generally forgotten it. Did you know," she asked, walking to the side of the room so that she was standing by the coat closet, "that George Washington had Egyptian blood, from his grandmother? Certain features of the Constitution of the United States are notable for their Egyptian ideas."

Without glancing down at the book, she began to talk about the movement of souls in Egyptian religion. She said that when people die, their souls return to Earth in the form of carpenter ants or walnut trees, depending on how they behaved—"well or ill"—in life. She said that the Egyptians believed that people act the way they do because of magnetism produced by tidal forces in the solar system, forces produced by the sun and by its "planetary ally," Jupiter. Jupiter, she said, was a planet, as we had been told, but had "certain properties of stars." She was speaking very fast. She said that the Egyptians were great explorers and conquerors. She said that the greatest of all the conquerors, Genghis Khan, had had forty horses and forty young women killed on the site of his grave. We listened. No one tried to stop her. "I myself have been in Egypt," she said, "and have witnessed much dust and many brutalities." She said that an old man in Egypt who worked for a circus had personally shown her an animal in a cage, a monster, half bird and half lion. She said that this monster was called a gryphon and that she had heard about them but never seen them until she traveled to the outskirts of Cairo. She said that Egyptian astronomers had discovered the planet Saturn, but had not seen its rings. She said that the Egyptians were the first to discover that dogs, when they are ill, will not drink from rivers, but wait for rain, and hold their jaws open to catch it.

* * *

"She lies."

We were on the school bus home. I was sitting next to Carl Whiteside, who had bad breath and a huge collection of marbles. We were arguing. Carl thought she was lying. I said she wasn't, probably.

"I didn't believe that stuff about the bird," Carl said, "and what she told us about the pyramids? I didn't believe that either. She didn't know what she was talking about."

"Oh yeah?" I had liked her. She was strange. I thought I could nail him. "If she was lying," I said, "what'd she say that was a lie?"

"Six times eleven isn't sixty-eight. It isn't ever. It's sixty-six, I know for a fact."

"She said so. She admitted it. What else did she lie about?"

"I don't know," he said. "Stuff."

"What stuff?"

"Well." He swung his legs back and forth. "You ever see an animal that was half lion and half bird?" He crossed his arms. "It sounded real fakey to me."

"It could happen," I said. I had to improvise, to outrage him. "I read in this newspaper my mom bought in the IGA about this scientist, this mad scientist in the Swiss Alps, and he's been putting genes and chromosomes and stuff together in test tubes, and he combined a human being and a hamster." I waited, for effect. "It's called a humster."

"You never." Carl was staring at me, his mouth open, his terrible bad breath making its way toward me. "What newspaper was it?"

"The *National Enquirer*," I said, "that they sell next to the cash registers." When I saw his look of recognition, I knew I had bested him. "And this mad scientist," I said, "his name was, um, Dr. Frankenbush." I realized belatedly that this name was a mistake and waited for Carl to notice its resemblance to the name of the other famous mad master of permutations, but he only sat there.

"A man and a hamster?" He was staring at me, squinting, his mouth opening in distaste. "Jeez. What'd it look like?"

When the bus reached my stop, I took off down our dirt road and ran up through the back yard, kicking the tire swing for good luck. I dropped my books on the back steps so I could hug and kiss our dog, Mr. Selby. Then I hurried inside. I could smell Brussels sprouts cooking, my unfavorite vegetable. My mother was washing other vegetables in the kitchen sink, and my baby brother was hollering in his yellow playpen on the kitchen floor.

"Hi, Mom," I said, hopping around the playpen to kiss her, "Guess what?"

"I have no idea."

"We had this substitute today, Miss Ferenczi, and I'd never seen her before, and she had all these stories and ideas and stuff."

"Well. That's good." My mother looked out the window behind the sink, her eyes on the pine woods west of our house. Her face and hairstyle always reminded other people of Betty Crocker, whose picture was framed inside a gigantic spoon on the side of the Bisquick box; to me, though, my mother's face just looked white. "Listen, Tommy," she said, "go upstairs and pick your clothes off the bathroom floor, then go outside to the shed and put the shovel and ax away that your father left outside this morning."

"She said that six times eleven was sometimes sixty-eight!" I said. "And she said she once saw a monster that was half lion and half bird." I waited. "In Egypt, she said."

"Did you hear me?" my mother asked, raising her arm to wipe her forehead with the back of her hand. "You have chores to do."

"I know," I said. "I was just telling you about the substitute."

"It's very interesting," my mother said, quickly glancing down at me, "and we can talk about it later when your father gets home. But right now you have some work to do."

"Okay, Mom." I took a cookie out of the jar on the counter and was about to go outside when I had a thought. I ran into the living room, pulled out a dictionary next to the TV stand, and opened it to the G's. *Gryphon*: "variant of griffin." *Griffin*: "a fabulous beast with the head and wings of an eagle and the body of a lion." Fabulous was right. I shouted with triumph and ran outside to put my father's tools back in their place.

Miss Ferenczi was back the next day, slightly altered. She had pulled her hair down and twisted it into pigtails, with red rubber bands holding them tight one inch from the ends. She was wearing a green blouse and pink scarf, making her difficult to look at for a full class day. This time there was no pretense of doing a reading lesson or moving on to arithmetic. As soon as the bell rang, she simply began to talk.

She talked for forty minutes straight. There seemed to be less connection between her ideas, but the ideas themselves were, as the dictionary would say, fabulous. She said she had heard of a huge jewel, in what she called the Antipodes, that was so brilliant that when the light shone into it at a certain angle it would blind whoever was looking at its center. She said that the biggest diamond in the world was cursed and had killed everyone who owned it, and that by a trick of fate it was called the Hope diamond. Diamonds are magic, she said, and this is why women wear them on their fingers, as a sign of the magic of womanhood. Men have strength, Miss Ferenczi said, but no true magic. That is why men fall in love with women but women do not fall in love with men; they just love being loved. George Washington had died because of a mistake he made about a diamond. Washington was not the first *true* President, but she did not say who was. In some places in the world, she said, men and women still live in the trees and eat monkeys for breakfast. Their doctors are magicians. At the bottom of the sea are creatures thin as pancakes which have never been studied by scientists because when you take them up to the air, the fish explode. 90

There was not a sound in the classroom, except for Miss Ferenczi's voice, and Donna DeShano's coughing. No one even went to the bathroom.

Beethoven, she said, had not been deaf; it was a trick to make himself famous, and it worked. As she talked, Miss Ferenczi's pigtails swung back and forth. There are trees in the world, she said, that eat meat: their leaves are sticky and close up on bugs like hands. She lifted her hands and brought them together, palm to palm. Venus, which most people think is the next closest planet to the sun, is not always closer, and, besides, it is the planet of greatest mystery because of its thick cloud cover. "I know what lies underneath those clouds," Miss Ferenczi said, and waited. After the silence, she said, "Angels. Angels live under those clouds." She said that angels were not invisible to everyone and were in fact smarter than most people. They did not dress in robes as was often claimed but instead wore formal evening clothes, as if they were about to attend a concert. Often angels *do* attend concerts and sit in the aisles where, she said, most people pay no attention to them. She said the most terrible angel had the shape of the Sphinx. "There is no running away from that one," she said. She said that unquenchable fires burn just under the surface of the earth in Ohio, and that the baby Mozart fainted dead away in his cradle when he first heard the sound of a trumpet. She said that someone named Narzim al Harrardim was the greatest writer who ever lived. She said that planets control behavior, and anyone conceived during a solar eclipse would be born with webbed feet.

"I know you children like to hear these things," she said, "these secrets, and that is why I am telling you all this." We nodded. It was better than doing comprehension questions for the readings in *Broad Horizons*.

"I will tell you one more story," she said, "and then we will have to do arithmetic." She leaned over, and her voice grew soft. "There is no death," she said. "You must never be afraid. Never. That which is, cannot die. It will change into different earthly and unearthly elements, but I know this as sure as I stand here in front of you, and I swear it: you must not be afraid. I have seen this truth with these eyes. I know it because in a dream God kissed me. Here." And she pointed with her right index finger to the side of her head, below the mouth, where the vertical lines were carved into her skin.

Absent-mindedly we all did our arithmetic problems. At recess the class was out on the playground, but no one was playing. We were all standing in small groups, talking about Miss Ferenczi. We didn't know if she was crazy, or what. I looked out beyond the playground, at the rusted cars piled in a small heap behind a clump of sumac, and I wanted to see shapes there, approaching me. 95

On the way home, Carl sat next to me again. He didn't say much, and I didn't either. At last he turned to me. "You know what she said about the leaves that close up on bugs?"

"Huh?"

"The leaves," Carl insisted. "The meat-eating plants. I know it's true. I saw it on television. The leaves have this icky glue that the plants have got smeared all over them and the insects can't get off, 'cause they're stuck. I saw it." He seemed demoralized. "She's tellin' the truth."

"Yeah."

"You think she's seen all those angels?"

I shrugged.

"I don't think she has," Carl informed me. "I think she made that part up."

"There's a tree," I suddenly said. I was looking out the window at the farms along County Road H. I knew every barn, every broken windmill, every fence, every anhydrous ammonia tank, by heart. "There's a tree that's . . . that I've seen . . ."

"Don't you try to do it," Carl said. "You'll just sound like a jerk."

I kissed my mother. She was standing in front of the stove. "How was your day?" she asked.

"Fine."

"Did you have Miss Ferenczi again?"

"Yeah."

"Well?"

"She was fine. Mom," I asked, "can I go to my room?"

"No," she said, "not until you've gone out to the vegetable garden and picked me a few tomatoes." She glanced at the sky. "I think it's going to rain. Skedaddle and do it now. Then you come back inside and watch your brother for a few minutes while I go upstairs. I need to clean up before dinner." She looked down at me. "You're looking a little pale, Tommy." She touched the back of her hand to my forehead and I felt her diamond ring against my skin. "Do you feel all right?"

"I'm fine," I said, and went out to pick the tomatoes.

Coughing mutedly, Mr. Hibler was back the next day, slipping lozenges into his mouth when his back was turned at forty-five minute intervals and asking us how much of the prepared lesson plan Miss Ferenczi had followed. Edith Atwater took the responsibility for the class of explaining to Mr. Hibler that the substitute hadn't always done exactly what he would have done, but we had worked hard even though she talked a lot. About what? he asked. All kinds of things, Edith said. I sort of forgot. To our relief, Mr. Hibler seemed not at all interested in what Miss Ferenczi had said to fill the day. He probably thought it was woman's talk; unserious and not suited for school. It was enough that he had a pile of arithmetic problems from us to correct.

For the next month, the sumac turned a distracting red in the field, and the sun traveled toward the southern sky, so that its rays reached Mr. Hibler's Halloween display on the bulletin board in the back of the room, fading the scarecrow with a pumpkin head from orange to tan. Every three days I measured how much farther the sun had moved toward the southern horizon by making small marks with my black Crayola on the north wall, ant-sized marks only I knew were there, inching west.

And then in early December, four days after the first permanent snowfall, she appeared again in our classroom. The minute she came in the door, I felt my heart begin to pound. Once again, she was different: this time, her hair hung straight down and seemed hardly to have been combed. She hadn't brought her lunchbox with her, but she was carrying what seemed to be a small box. She greeted all of us and talked about the weather. Donna DeShano had to remind her to take her overcoat off. 115

When the bell to start the day finally rang, Miss Ferenczi looked out at all of us and said, "Children, I have enjoyed your company in the past, and today I am going to reward you." She held up the small box. "Do you know what this is?" She waited. "Of course you don't. It is a tarot pack."

Edith Atwater raised her hand. "What's a tarot pack, Miss Ferenczi?"

"It is used to tell fortunes," she said. "And that is what I shall do this morning. I shall tell your fortunes, as I have been taught to do."

"What's fortune?" Bobby Kryzanowicz asked.

"The future, young man. I shall tell you what your future will be. I can't do your whole future, of course. I shall have to limit myself to the five-card system, the wands, cups, swords, pentacles, and the higher arcanes. Now who wants to be first?" 120

There was a long silence. Then Carol Peterson raised her hand.

"All right," Miss Ferenczi said. She divided the pack into five smaller packs and walked back to Carol's desk, in front of mine. "Pick one card from each of these packs," she said. I saw that Carol had a four of cups, a six of swords, but I couldn't see the other cards. Miss Ferenczi studied the cards on Carol's desk for a minute. "Not bad," she said. "I do not see much higher education. Probably an early marriage. Many children. There's something bleak and dreary here, but I can't tell what. Perhaps just the tasks of a housewife life. I think you'll do very well, for the most part." She smiled at Carol, a smile with a certain lack of interest. "Who wants to be next?"

Carl Whiteside raised his hand slowly.

"Yes," Miss Ferenczi said, "let's do a boy." She walked over to where Carl sat. After he picked his five cards, she gazed at them for a long time. "Travel," she said. "Much distant travel. You might go into the Army. Not too much romantic interest here. A late marriage, if at all. Squabbles. But the Sun is in your major arcana, here, yes, that's a very good card." She giggled. "Maybe a good life."

Next I raised my hand, and she told me my future. She did the same with Bobby Kryzanowicz, Kelly Munger, Edith Atwater, and Kim Foor. Then she came to Wayne Razmer. He picked his five cards, and I could see that the Death card was one of them. 125

"What's your name?" Miss Ferenczi asked.

"Wayne."

"Well, Wayne," she said, "you will undergo a *great* metamorphosis, the greatest, before you become an adult. Your earthly element will leap away, into thin air, you sweet boy. This card, this nine of swords here, tells of suffering and desolation. And this ten of wands, well, that's certainly a heavy load."

"What about this one?" Wayne pointed to the Death card.

"That one? That one means you will die soon, my dear." She gathered up the cards. We were all looking at Wayne. "But do not fear," she said. "It's not really death, so much as change." She put the cards on Mr. Hibler's desk. "And now, let's do some arithmetic."

At lunchtime Wayne went to Mr. Faegre, the principal, and told him what Miss Ferenczi had done. During the noon recess, we saw Miss Ferenczi drive out of the parking lot in her green Rambler. I stood under the slide, listening to the other kids coasting down and landing in the little depressive bowl at the bottom. I was kicking stones and tugging at my hair right up to the moment when I saw Wayne come out to the playground. He smiled, the dead fool, and with the fingers of his right hand he was showing everyone how he had told on Miss Ferenczi.

I made my way toward Wayne, pushing myself past two girls from another class. He was watching me with his little pinhead eyes.

"You told," I shouted at him. "She was just kidding."

"She shouldn't have," he shouted back. "We were supposed to be doing arithmetic."

"She just scared you," I said. "You're a chicken. You're a chicken, Wayne. You are. Scared of a little card," I singsonged.

Wayne fell at me, his two fists hammering down on my nose. I gave him a good one in the stomach and then I tried for his head. Aiming my fist, I saw that he was crying. I slugged him.

"She was right," I yelled. "She was always right! She told the truth!" Other kids were whooping. "You were just scared, that's all!"

And then large hands pulled at us, and it was my turn to speak to Mr. Faegre.

In the afternoon Miss Ferenczi was gone, and my nose was stuffed with cotton clotted with blood, and my lip had swelled, and our class had been combined with Mrs. Mantei's sixth-grade class for a crowded afternoon science unit on insect life in ditches and swamps. I knew where Mrs. Mantei lived: she had a new house trailer just down the road from us, at the Clearwater Park. She was no mystery. Somehow she and Mr. Bodine, the other fourth-grade teacher, had managed to fit forty-five desks into the room. Kelly Munger asked if Miss Ferenczi had been arrested, and Mrs. Mantei said no, of course not. All that afternoon, until the buses came to pick us up, we learned about field crickets and two-striped grasshoppers, water bugs, cicadas, mosquitoes, flies, and moths. We learned about insects' hard outer shell, the exoskeleton, and the usual parts of the mouth, including the labrum, mandible, maxilla, and glossa. We learned about compound eyes and the four-stage metamorphosis from egg to larva to pupa to adult. We learned something, but not much, about mating. Mrs. Mantei drew, very skillfully, the internal anatomy of the grasshopper on the blackboard. We learned about the dance of the honeybee, directing other bees in the hive to pollen. We found out about which insects were pests to man, and which were not. On lined white pieces of paper we made lists of insects we might actually see, then a list of insects too small to be clearly visible, such as fleas; Mrs. Mantei said that our assignment would be to memorize these lists for the next day, when Mr. Hibler would certainly return and test us on our knowledge.

Reading and Reacting

1. In classical mythology, a gryphon (also spelled *griffin*) is a monster that has the head and wings of an eagle and the body of a lion. Why is this story called "Gryphon"?
2. Describe Miss Ferenczi's physical appearance. Why is her appearance important to the story? How does it change as the story progresses?
3. How is Miss Ferenczi different from other teachers? from other substitute teachers? from other people in general? How is her differentness communicated to her pupils? to the story's readers?
4. What is the significance of the narrator's comment, in paragraph 11, that the lines on Miss Ferenczi's face remind him of Pinocchio?
5. Is Miss Ferenczi a round or a flat character? Explain.
6. In what sense is the narrator's mother a foil for Miss Ferenczi?
7. Why does the narrator defend Miss Ferenczi, first in his argument with Carl Whiteside and later on the playground? What does his attitude toward Miss Ferenczi reveal about his own character?
8. Are all of Miss Ferenczi's "substitute facts" lies, or is there some truth in what she says? Is she correct when she says that substitute facts cannot hurt anyone? Could it be argued that much of what is taught in schools today could be viewed as "substitute facts"?
9. **Journal Entry** Is Miss Ferenczi a good teacher? Why or why not?
10. **Critical Perspective** Writing in the *New York Times Book Review*, critic William Ferguson characterizes *A Relative Stranger*, a more recent collection of Baxter's short stories than the one in which "Gryphon" appeared, as follows:

    > The thirteen stories in *A Relative Stranger*, in all quietly accomplished, suggest a mysterious yet fundamental marriage of despair and joy. Though in one way or another each story ends in disillusionment, the road that leads to that dismal state is so richly peopled, so finely drawn, that the effect is oddly reassuring.

    Do you think this characterization of Baxter's work in *A Relative Stranger* applies to "Gryphon" as well? For example, do you see a "marriage of despair and joy"? Do you find the story reassuring in any way, or does it convey only a sense of disillusionment?

Related Works: "A&P" (p. 179), "The Secret Lion" (p. 222), "A Worn Path" (p. 370), "When I Heard the Learn'd Astronomer" (p. 526), "On First Looking into Chapman's Homer" (p. 619), "Isla" (p. 654)

Source: AP Photo/Sang Tan

ZADIE SMITH (1975–), born in London as Sadie Smith, changed her name at a young age "because," she said in an interview, "it seemed right, exotic, different." A renowned novelist, essayist, and short story writer, Smith is the author of the novels *White Teeth* (2000), *The Autograph Man* (2002), *On Beauty* (2005), *NW* (2012), and *Swing Time* (2016). She also published the essay collections *Changing My Mind* (2009) and *Feel Free* (2018), as well as *Intimations* (2020), which explores her life in New York City early in the COVID-19 pandemic. Smith also wrote a short story collection, *Grand Union* (2019). A professor at NYU, her achievements include her election as a Fellow to the Royal Society of Literature and to the American Academy of Arts and Letters. *White Teeth* won multiple awards, and *On Beauty*, shortlisted for the prestigious Man Booker Prize, also won the Orange Prize for Fiction. Smith wrote "The Girl with Bangs" in response to the song "Bangs" by They Might Be Giants.

Cultural Context As a cultural trend, bangs have come and gone and come again with American women throughout the latter part of the twentieth century and into the twenty-first century. The hairstyle has evolved from the long "mall bangs" of the 1960s, which start at the crown of the head, to a range of subtler styles used to frame the face. Today, popular styles of bangs among twenty- and thirty-something women include side-swept bangs, angled bangs, short choppy bangs, classic blunt bangs, straight bangs, super-short bangs, curly bangs, and eyebrow-skimming bangs. Well-known people who have worn bangs include everyone from Audrey Hepburn, Jacqueline Kennedy, Diana Ross, and Tina Turner to the Beatles.

The Girl with Bangs (2001)

I fell in love with a girl once. Some time ago, now. She had bangs. I was twenty years old at the time and prey to the usual rag-bag of foolish ideas. I believed, for example, that one might meet some sweet kid and like them a lot—maybe even marry them—while all the time allowing that kid to sleep with other kids, and that this could be done with no fuss at all, just a chuck under the chin, and no tears. I believed the majority of people to be bores, however you cut them; that the mark of their dullness was easy to spot (clothes, hair) and impossible to avoid, running right through them like a watermark. I had made mental notes, too, on other empty notions—the death of certain things (socialism, certain types of music, old people), the future of others (film, footwear, poetry)—but no one need be bored with those now. The only significant bit of nonsense I carried around in those days, the only one that came from the gut, if you like, was this feeling that a girl with soft black bangs falling into eyes the color of a Perrier bottle must be good news. Look at her palming the bangs away from her face, pressing them back along her hairline, only to have them fall forward again! I found this combination to be good, *intrinsically* good in both form and content, the same way you think of cherries (life is a bowl of; she was a real sweet) until the very center of one becomes lodged in your windpipe. I believed Charlotte Greaves and her bangs to be good news. But Charlotte was emphatically bad news, requiring only eight months to take me entirely apart; the kind of clinically efficient dismembering you see when a bright child gets his hand on some toy he assembled in the first place. I'd never dated a girl before, and she was bad news the way boys can never be, because with boys it's always possible to draw up a list of pros and cons, and see the matter rationally, from either side. But you could make a list of cons on Charlotte stretching to Azerbaijan,[1] and "her bangs" sitting solitary in the pros column would outweigh all objections. Boys are just boys after all, but sometimes girls *really seem to be* the turn of a pale wrist, or the sudden jut of a hip, or a clutch of very dark hair falling across a freckled forehead. I'm not saying that's what they really are. I'm just saying sometimes it seems that way, and that those details (a thigh mole, a full face flush, a scar the precise shape and size of a cashew nut) are so many hooks waiting to land you. In this case, it was those bangs, plush and dramatic, curtains opening on to a face one would queue up to see. All women have a backstage, of course, of course. Labyrinthine, many-roomed, no doubt, no doubt. But you come to see the show, that's all I'm saying.

I first set eyes on Charlotte when she was seeing a Belgian who lived across the hall from me in college. I'd see her first thing, shuffling around the communal bathroom looking a mess—undone, always, in every sense—with her T-shirt tucked in her knickers, a fag[2] hanging out of her mouth, some kind of toothpaste or maybe mouthwash residue by her lips and those bangs in her eyes. It was hard to understand why this Belgian, Maurice, had chosen to date her. He had this great accent, Maurice, *elabo-rately* French, like you couldn't *be* more French, and a jaw line that seemed in fashion at the time, and you could tick all the boxes vis-à-vis personal charms; Maurice was an impressive kind of a guy. Charlotte was the kind of woman who has only two bras, both of them gray. But after a while, if you paid attention, you came to realize that she had a look about her like she just got out of a bed, no matter what time of day you collided with her (she had a stalk of a walk, never looked where she was going, so you had no choice) and this tendency, if put under the heading "QUALITIES THAT GIRLS SOMETIMES HAVE," was a kind of poor relation of "BEDROOM EYES" or "LOOKS LIKE SHE'S THINKING ABOUT SEX ALL THE TIME"—and it worked. She seemed always to be stumbling away from someone else, toward you. A limping figure smiling widely, arms outstretched, dressed in rags, a smouldering city as backdrop. I had watched too many films, possibly. But still: a bundle of precious things thrown at you from a third-floor European window, wrapped loosely in a blanket, chosen frantically and at random by the well-meaning owner slung haphazardly from a burning building; launched at you; it could hurt, this bundle, but look! You have caught it! A little chipped, but otherwise fine. Look what you have saved! (You understand me, I know. This is how it feels. What is the purpose of metaphor, anyway, if not to describe women?)

---

[1] *Azerbaijan:* Country on the coast of the Caspian Sea, bordered by Russia, Armenia, and Iran.
[2] *fag:* Cigarette.

Now, it came to pass that this Maurice was offered a well-paid TV job in Thailand as a newscaster, and he agonized, and weighed Charlotte in one hand and the money in the other and found he could not leave without the promise that she would wait for him. This promise she gave him, but he was still gone, and gone is gone, and that's where I came in. Not immediately—I am no thief—but by degrees, studying near her in the library, watching her hair make reading difficult. Sitting next to her at lunch watching the bangs go hither, and, I suppose, thither, as people swished by with their food trays. Befriending her friends and then her; making as many nice noises about Maurice as I could. I became a boy for the duration. I stood under the window with my open arms. I did all the old boy tricks. These tricks are not as difficult as some boys will have you believe, but they are indeed slow, and work only by a very gradual process of accumulation. You have sad moments when you wonder if there will ever be an end to it. But then, usually without warning, the hard work pays off. With Charlotte it went like this: she came by for a herbal tea one day, and I rolled a joint and then another and soon enough she was lying across my lap, spineless as a mollusk, and I had my fingers in those bangs—teasing them, as the hairdressers say—and we had begun.

Most of the time we spent together was in her room. At the beginning of an affair you've no need to be outside. And it was like a filthy cocoon, her room, ankle deep in rubbish; it was the kind of room that took you in and held you close. With no clocks and my watch lost and buried, we passed time by the degeneration of things, the rotting of fruit, the accumulation of bacteria, the rising-tideline of cigarettes in the vase we used to put them out. It was a quarter past this apple. The third Saturday in the month of that stain. These things were unpleasant and tiresome. And she was no intellectual; any book I gave her she treated like a kid treats a Christmas present—fascination for a day and then the quick pall of boredom; by the end of the week it was flung across the room and submerged; weeks later when we made love I'd find the spine of the novel sticking into the small of my back, paper cuts on my toes. There was no bed to speak of. There was just a bit of the floor that was marginally clearer than the rest of it. (But wait! Here she comes, falling in an impossible arc, and here I am by careful design in just the right spot, under the window, and here she is, landing and nothing is broken, and I cannot believe my luck. You understand me. Every time I looked at the bangs, the bad stuff went away.)

Again: I know it doesn't sound great, but let's not forget the bangs. Let us not forget that after a stand-up row, a real screaming match, she could look at me from underneath the distinct hairs, separated by sweat, and I had no more resistance. *Yes, you can leave the overturned plant pot where it is. Yes, Rousseau is an idiot if you say so.* So this is what it's like being a boy. The cobbled street, the hopeful arms hugging air. There is nothing you won't do. 5

Charlotte's exams were coming up. I begged her to look through her reading list once more, and plan some strategic line of attack, but she wanted to do it her way. Her way meant reading the same two books—Rousseau's *Social*

Contract and Plato's *Republic* (her paper was to be on people, and the way they organize their lives, or the way they did, or the way they should, I don't remember; it had a technical title, I don't remember that either)—again and again, in the study room that sat in a quiet corner of the college. The study room was meant to be for everyone but since Charlotte had moved in, all others had gradually moved out. I recall one German graduate who stood his ground for a month or so, who cleared his throat regularly and pointedly picked up things that she had dropped—but she got to him, finally. Charlotte's papers all over the floor, Charlotte's old lunches on every table, Charlottes clothes and my clothes (now indistinguishable) thrown over every chair. People would come up to me in the bar and say, "Look, Charlotte did X. Could you please, for the love of God, stop Charlotte doing X, *please*?" and I would try, but Charlotte's bangs kept Charlotte in the world of Charlotte and she barely heard me. And now, please, before we go any further: tell me. Tell me if you've ever stood under a window and caught an unworthy bundle of chintz.[3] Gold plating that came off with one rub; faked signatures, worthless trinkets. Have you? Maybe the bait was different—not bangs, but deep pockets either side of the smile or unusually vivid eye pigmentation. Or some other bodily attribute (hair, skin, curves) that recalled in you some natural phenomenon (wheat, sea, cream). Some difference. So: have you? Have you ever been out with a girl like this?

Some time after Charlotte's exams, after the 2.2 that had been stalking her for so long finally pounced, there was a knock on the door. My door—I recall now that we were in my room that morning. I hauled on a dressing-gown and went to answer it. It was Maurice, tanned and dressed like one of the Beatles when they went to see the Maharashi,[4] a white suit with a Nehru collar, his own bangs and tousled hair, slightly long at the back. He looked terrific. He said, "Someone in ze bar says you might have an idea where Charlotte is. I need to see 'er—it is very urgent. Have you seen 'er?" I had seen her. She was in my bed, about five feet from where Maurice stood, but obscured by a partition wall. "No . . ." I said. "No, not this morning. She'll probably be in the hall for breakfast though, she usually is. So, Maurice! When did you get back?" He said, "All zat must come later. I 'ave to find Charlotte. I sink I am going to marry 'er." And I thought, *Christ, which bad movie am I in?*

I got Charlotte up, shook her, poured her into some clothes, and told her to run around the back of the college and get to the dining hall before Maurice. I saw her in my head, the moment the door closed—no great feat of imagination, I had seen her run before, like a naturally uncoordinated animal (a panda?) that somebody has just shot—I saw her dashing incompetently past the ancient walls, catching herself on ivy, tripping up steps, and finally falling through the swing doors, looking wildly round the dining hall like those

---

[3] *chintz:* A usually brightly printed and glazed cotton fabric.

[4] *Maharashi:* Maharishi Mahesh Yogi (1918–2008), Hindu religious leader revered by the British rock group the Beatles.

movie time-travellers who know not in which period they have just landed. But still she managed it, apparently she got there in time, though as the whole world now knows, Maurice took one look at her strands matted against her forehead, running in line with the ridge-ways of sleep left by the pillows, and said, "You're sleeping with her?" (Or maybe, "You're sleeping with *her?*"—I don't know; this is all reported speech) and Charlotte, who, like a lot of low-maintenance women, cannot tell a lie, said "Er . . . yes. Yes" and then made that signal of feminine relief; bottom lip out, air blown upward; bangs all of a flutter.

Later that afternoon, Maurice came back round to my room, looking all the more noble, and seemingly determined to have a calm man-to-man "you see, I have returned to marry her / I will not stand in your way" type of a chat, which was very reasonable and English of him. I let him have it alone. I nodded when it seemed appropriate; sometimes I lifted my hands in protest but soon let them fall again. You can't fight it when you've been replaced: a simple side-step and here is some old/new Belgian guy standing in the cobbled street with his face upturned, and his arms wide open, judging the angles. I thought of this girl he wanted back, who had taken me apart piece by piece, causing me nothing but trouble, with her bangs and her antisocial behaviour. I was all (un)done, I realized. I sort of marvelled at the devotion he felt for her. From a thousand miles away, with a smoldering city as a backdrop, I watched him beg me to leave them both alone; tears in his eyes, the works. I agreed it was the best thing, all round. I had the impression that here was a girl who would be thrown from person to person over years, and each would think they had saved her by some miracle when in actual fact she was in no danger at all. Never even for a second.

He said, "Let us go, zen, and tell 'er the decision we have come to," and I said yes, let's, but when we got to Charlotte's room, someone else was putting his fingers through her curls. Charlotte was always one of those people for whom sex is available at all times—it just happens to her, quickly, and with a minimum of conversation. This guy was some other guy that she'd been sleeping with on the days when she wasn't with me. It had been going on for four months. This all came out later, naturally.

Would you believe he married her anyway? And not only that, he married her after she'd shaved her head that afternoon just to spite us. All of us—even the other guy no one had seen before. Maurice took a bald English woman with a strange lopsided walk and a temper like a gorgon back to Thailand and married her despite friends' complaints and the voluble protest of Aneepa Kapoor, who was the woman he read the news with. The anchorwoman, who had that Hitchcock style: hair tied back tight in a bun, a spiky nose and a vicious red mouth. The kind of woman who doesn't need catching. "Maurice," she said, "you *owe* me. You can't just throw four months away like it wasn't worth a bloody thing!" He emailed me about it. He admitted that he'd been stringing Aneepa along for a while, and she'd been expecting something at the end of it. For in the real world, or so it seems to me, it is almost always women and not men who are waiting under windows, and they are almost always disappointed. In this matter, Charlotte was unusual.

Reading and Reacting

1. At what point did you realize that the narrator was female? Do you think her feelings and behavior would have been any different if she were male?
2. What exactly is it about Charlotte that fascinates the narrator? Do you share this fascination?
3. What do we learn in paragraph 1 about the narrator's tastes, feelings, and beliefs? Is this information enough to explain her obsession with Charlotte?
4. Why do you think the narrator focuses on Charlotte's bangs? What other physical traits does Charlotte have?
5. In paragraph 2, the narrator characterizes Charlotte as "the kind of woman who has only two bras, both of them gray." What does this tell readers about Charlotte? About the narrator? What does the description of Charlotte's room in paragraph 4 reveal about her?
6. What role does Maurice play in the story? What do we know about him? Is he a flat or a round character? Is he essential to the story?
7. At the end of paragraph 4, the narrator tells us, "Every time I looked at the bangs, the bad stuff went away." What do you think this "bad stuff" is?
8. In the story's last lines, the narrator explains that "in the real world, or so it seems to me, it is almost always women and not men who are waiting under windows, and they are almost always disappointed. In this matter, Charlotte was unusual." What does the narrator mean? How do these words help to explain her infatuation with Charlotte?
9. Find the lyrics of the They Might Be Giants song "Bangs" online. What insights do these lyrics (which Smith said inspired her story) give you about the narrator's feelings for Charlotte?
10. **Journal Entry** Write a farewell email to the narrator from Charlotte. Try to explain her feelings for the narrator as well as her motivation for shaving her head and for deciding to marry Maurice.
11. **Critical Perspective** Writing about Zadie Smith's novel *On Beauty*, Max Watman makes the following comments:

    > Smith's characters are expertly portrayed . . . She can blow them up in all their chalky whites and lively pinks. She is one of the best character writers working . . . *On Beauty* is one of the few contemporary novels that feels as if it is stuffed with fully formed people rather than tics and mannerisms.

    Do you think Charlotte in "The Girl with Bangs" is depicted as a "fully formed" person, or do you think she is really just "tics and mannerisms"?

Related Works: "Araby" (p. 296), "My mistress' eyes are nothing like the sun" (p. 557), "Love is not all" (p. 620), "General Review of the Sex Situation" (p. 686), "She Walks in Beauty" (p. 706), *Beauty* (p. 785)

WRITING SUGGESTIONS: Character

1. In both "A&P" and "Gryphon," the main characters (Sammy and Tommy, respectively) struggle against rules, authority figures, and inflexible social systems. Compare and contrast the struggles in which these two characters are engaged.
2. Write an essay in which you contrast the character of Miss Brill (p. 185) with Emily Grierson in "A Rose for Emily" (p. 166) or with Phoenix Jackson in "A Worn Path" (p. 370). Consider how each character interacts with those around her as well as how each seems to see her role or mission in the world.
3. Sammy, Miss Brill, and Miss Ferenczi all use their active imaginations to create scenarios that help get them through the day. None of them can sustain the illusion, however. As a result, all three find out how harsh reality can be. How are these scenarios alike, and how are they different? What steps could these three characters take to fit more comfortably into the worlds they inhabit? *Should* they take such steps? Are they able to do so?
4. Write an analysis of a minor character in one of this chapter's stories—for example, Stokesie in "A&P" or Maurice in "The Girl with Bangs."
5. In "A&P," "Gryphon," and "The Girl with Bangs," each narrator is fascinated by another character—Queenie, Miss Ferenczi, and Charlotte, respectively. What exactly is each narrator attracted to? How do you account for these almost obsessive attachments?

Chapter

11

Setting

Alberto Álvaro Ríos
Courtesy of Alberto Avaro Ríos

Kate Chopin
Courtesy of Louisiana State University

Tillie Olsen
Chris Felver/Archive Photos/Getty Images

Learning Objectives

After reading this chapter, you will be able to. . .

- Explain how setting functions in a work of fiction.
- Explain why an author might choose to set a work in a particular place and time.
- Identify geographical settings in works of fiction.
- Outline how physical setting can create atmosphere and mood in a work of fiction.
- Consider the significance of setting to characters and events in a specific work of fiction.

The **setting** of a work of fiction establishes its historical, geographical, and physical context. *Where* a work is set—on a tropical island, in a dungeon, at a crowded party, in the woods—influences our reactions to the story's events and characters. *When* a work takes place—during the French Revolution, during the Vietnam War, today, or in the future—is equally important. Setting, however, is more than just the approximate time and place in which a work is set; setting also encompasses a wide variety of other elements.

Clearly, setting is more important in some works than in others. In some stories, no time or place is specified or even suggested, perhaps because the writer does not consider a specific setting to be important or because the writer wishes the story's events to seem timeless and universal. In other stories, a writer may provide only minimal information about setting, telling readers little more than where and when the action takes place. In many cases, however, a particular setting is vital to the story, perhaps even influencing characters' feelings or behavior, as it does in the stories in this chapter.

Sometimes a story's central conflict is between the protagonist and the setting—for example, *Alice in Wonderland*, a northerner in the South, an unsophisticated American tourist in an old European city, a sane person in a psychiatric hospital, a moral person in a corrupt environment, an immigrant in a new world, or a city dweller in the country. Such a conflict may drive the story's plot and also help to define the characters. A conflict between *events* and setting—for example, the arrival of a mysterious stranger in a typical suburban neighborhood, the intrusion of modern social ideas into an old-fashioned world, or the intrusion of a brutal murder into a peaceful village—can also enrich a story.

Historical Setting

A particular historical period, and the events and customs associated with it, can be important to your understanding of a story; therefore, some knowledge of the period in which a story is set may be useful (or even essential) for readers. The historical setting establishes a story's social, cultural, economic, and political environment. Knowing, for example, that Charlotte Perkins Gilman's "The Yellow Wallpaper" (p. 315) was written in the late nineteenth century, when doctors treated women as delicate and dependent creatures, helps to explain the narrator's emotional state. Likewise, it may be important to know that a story is set during a particularly volatile (or static) political era, during a time of permissive (or repressive) attitudes toward sex, during a war, or during a period of economic prosperity or recession. Any one of these factors may help to explain why events occur as well as why characters act (and react) as they do. Historical events or cultural norms may, for example, limit or expand a character's options, and our knowledge of history may reveal to us certain characters' incompatibility with their milieu. For example, in F. Scott Fitzgerald's 1920 short story "Bernice Bobs Her Hair," set in the 1920s in a midwestern town, a young girl is goaded into cutting her long hair. To understand the significance of Bernice's act—and to understand the reactions of others to that act—readers must know that during that era only racy "society vampires," not nice girls from good families, bobbed their hair.

Knowing the approximate year or historical period during which a story takes place can help readers to better understand characters and events. This knowledge can explain forces that act on characters and account for their behavior, clarify circumstances that influence the story's action, and justify a writer's use of plot devices that might otherwise seem improbable. Thus, stories set before the development of modern transportation and communication networks may hinge on plot devices readers would not accept in a modern story. For example, in "Paul's Case," a 1904 story by Willa Cather, a young man who steals a large sum of money in Pittsburgh is able to spend several days enjoying his newfound wealth before the news of the theft reaches New York, where he has fled. In other stories, we see characters threatened by diseases that have now been eradicated (or subjected to outdated medical or psychiatric treatment) or constrained by social conventions very different from those that operate in our own society.

Geographical Setting

In addition to knowing *when* a work takes place, readers need to know *where* it takes place. Knowing whether a story is set in the United States, in Europe, or in a developing nation can help to explain anything from why language and customs are unfamiliar to us to why characters act in ways we find surprising or hold beliefs that are alien to us. Even in stories set in the United States, regional differences may account for differences in plot development and characters' motivation. For example, knowing that William Faulkner's "A Rose for Emily" (p. 166) is set in the post–Civil War American South helps to explain why the townspeople are so chivalrously protective of Miss Emily. Similarly, the fact that Bret Harte's classic story "The Outcasts of Poker Flat" (1869) is set in a California mining camp accounts for its varied cast of characters—including a gambler, a prostitute, and a traveling salesman.

The size of the town or city in which a story takes place may also be important. In a small town, for example, a character's problems are more likely to be subjected to intense scrutiny by other characters, as they are in stories of small-town life such as "A Rose for Emily." In a large city, characters may be more likely to be isolated and anonymous, like Mrs. Miller in Truman Capote's gothic short story "Miriam" (1945), who is so lonely that she invents an imaginary companion. Characters may also be alienated by their big-city surroundings, as Gregor Samsa is in Franz Kafka's classic 1915 novella, *The Metamorphosis*, about a man who turns into a bug.

Of course, a story may not have a recognizable geographical setting: its location may not be specified, or it may be set in a fantasy world. Choosing unusual settings may free writers from the constraints placed on them by familiar environments, thus allowing them to experiment with situations and characters, unaffected by readers' expectations or associations with familiar settings.

Physical Setting

Physical setting can influence a story's mood as well as its development. For example, *time of day* can be important. The gruesome murder described in Edgar Allan Poe's "The Cask of Amontillado" (p. 258) takes place in an appropriate setting: not just underground but in the darkness of night. Conversely, the horrifying events of Shirley Jackson's "The Lottery" (p. 337) take place in broad daylight, contrasting dramatically with the darkness of the society that permits—and even participates in—a shocking ritual. Many stories, of course, move through several time periods as the action unfolds, and changes in time may also be important. For example, the approach of evening (or of dawn) can signal the end of a crisis in the plot.

Whether a story is set primarily *indoors* or *out-of-doors* may also be significant: characters may be physically constrained by a closed-in setting or liberated by an expansive landscape. Some interior settings may be psychologically limiting. For example, the narrator in "The Yellow Wallpaper" feels suffocated by her room, whose ugly wallpaper comes to haunt her. In many of Poe's stories, the central character is trapped, physically or psychologically, in a confined, suffocating space. In other stories, an interior setting may have a symbolic function. For example, in "A Rose for Emily," the house is for Miss Emily a symbol of the South's past glory as well as a refuge, a fortress, and a hiding place. Similarly, a building may represent society, with its rules, norms, and limitations, as in John Updike's "A&P" (p. 179), where the supermarket establishes social as well as physical limits.

Conversely, an outdoor setting can free a character from social norms of behavior, as it does for Ernest Hemingway's Nick Adams, a war veteran who, in "Big Two-Hearted River" (1925), finds order, comfort, and peace only when he is away from civilization. An outdoor setting can also expose characters to physical dangers, such as untamed wilderness, uncharted seas, and frighteningly empty open spaces, as is the case in Stephen Crane's "The Open Boat" (p. 391).

Weather can be another important aspect of setting. A storm can threaten a character's life or just make the character—and readers—*think* danger is present, distracting us from other, more subtle threats. Extreme weather conditions can make characters act irrationally or uncharacteristically, as in Kate Chopin's "The Storm" (p. 216), where a storm provides the story's complication and sets in motion the characters' actions. In numerous stories set in hostile landscapes, where extremes of heat and cold influence the action, weather may serve as a test for characters, as it does in Jack London's "To Build a Fire" (1908), in which the main character struggles unsuccessfully against the brutally cold, hostile environment of the Yukon.

The various physical attributes of setting combine to create a story's **atmosphere** or **mood**. In "The Cask of Amontillado," for example, several factors work together to create the story's eerie, intense atmosphere: it is nighttime; it is the hectic carnival season; and the catacombs are dark, damp, and filled with the bones of the narrator's ancestors. Sometimes the mood or atmosphere that is created helps to convey a story's central theme—as the ironic contrast between the pleasant atmosphere and the shocking events that unfold communicates the theme of "The Lottery." A story's atmosphere may also be linked to a character's mental state, perhaps reflecting their mood. For example, darkness and isolation can reflect a character's depression, whereas an idyllic, peaceful atmosphere can express a character's joy. And, of course, a story's atmosphere can also *influence* the characters' state of mind, causing them to react one way in a crowded, hectic city but to react very differently in a peaceful, rural atmosphere.

Checklist Writing about Setting

- Is the setting specified or unspecified? Is it fully described or only suggested?
- Is the setting just background, or is it a key force in the story?
- Are any characters in conflict with their environment?
- How does the setting influence the story's plot? Does it cause characters to act?
- In what historical period does the story take place? How can you tell? What social, political, or economic situations or events of that historical period might influence the story?
- In what geographical location is the story set? Is this location important to the story?
- At what time of day is the story set? Is time important to the development of the story?
- Is the story set primarily indoors or out-of-doors? What role does this aspect of the setting play in the story?
- What role do weather conditions play in the story?
- What kind of atmosphere or mood does the physical setting create?
- How does the story's atmosphere influence the characters? Does it affect (or reflect) their emotional state? Does it help to explain their motivation?
- Does the atmosphere change as the story progresses? Is this change significant?

Courtesy of Louisiana State University.

KATE CHOPIN (1851–1904) (picture and biography on p. 151) wrote in a realistic, yet dense and sensual style that was perhaps, in part, her artistic response to her memories of the exotic Louisiana bayou country. Like her French contemporary Gustave Flaubert (Chopin's short novel *The Awakening*, published in 1899, has often been called a "Creole Bovary" in reference to Flaubert's classic *Madame Bovary*), Chopin used the physical world—as in the charged atmosphere of "The Storm"—to symbolize the inner truths of her characters' minds and hearts. Unlike Flaubert, however, she depicted sex not as a frantic and destructive force but as a joyous, elemental part of life. Apparently, Kate Chopin knew how daring "The Storm" was: she never submitted it for publication.

Cultural Context In the following story, which presumably takes place in Louisiana, the character Calixta expresses fear that the powerful storm will break the levees, the raised embankments kept in place to prevent the river from overflowing. In August 2005, more than one hundred years after this story was written, the levees in New Orleans gave way to the sheer force of Hurricane Katrina, which flooded the city, destroyed the area's economic and cultural foundation, and displaced hundreds of thousands of residents.

The Storm (c. 1899)

I

The leaves were so still that even Bibi thought it was going to rain. Bobinôt, who was accustomed to converse on terms of perfect equality with his little son, called the child's attention to certain sombre clouds that were rolling with sinister intention from the west, accompanied by a sullen, threatening roar. They were at Friedheimer's store and decided to remain there till the storm had passed. They sat within the door on two empty kegs. Bibi was four years old and looked very wise.

"Mama'll be 'fraid, yes," he suggested with blinking eyes.

"She'll shut the house. Maybe she got Sylvie helpin' her this evenin'," Bobinôt responded reassuringly.

"No; she ent got Sylvie. Sylvie was helpin' her yistiday," piped Bibi.

Bobinôt arose and going across to the counter purchased a can of shrimps, of which Calixta was very fond. Then he returned to his perch on the keg and sat stolidly holding the can of shrimps while the storm burst. It shook the wooden store and seemed to be ripping great furrows in the distant field. Bibi laid his little hand on his father's knee and was not afraid. 5

II

Calixta, at home, felt no uneasiness for their safety. She sat at a side window sewing furiously on a sewing machine. She was greatly occupied and did not notice the approaching storm. But she felt very warm and often stopped to mop her face on which the perspiration gathered in beads. She unfastened her white sacque at the throat. It began to grow dark, and suddenly realizing the situation she got up hurriedly and went about closing windows and doors.

Out on the small front gallery she had hung Bobinôt's Sunday clothes to air and she hastened out to gather them before the rain fell. As she stepped outside, Alcée Laballière rode in at the gate. She had not seen him very often since her marriage, and never alone. She stood there with Bobinôt's coat in her hands, and the big rain drops began to fall. Alcée rode his horse under the shelter of a side projection where the chickens had huddled and there were plows and a harrow piled up in the corner.

"May I come and wait on your gallery till the storm is over, Calixta?" he asked.

"Come 'long in, M'sieur Alcée."

His voice and her own startled her as if from a trance, and she seized Bobinôt's vest. Alcée, mounting to the porch, grabbed the trousers and snatched Bibi's braided jacket that was about to be carried away by a sudden gust of wind. He expressed an intention to remain outside, but it was soon apparent that he might as well have been out in the open: the water beat in upon the boards in driving sheets, and he went inside, closing the door after him. It was even necessary to put something beneath the door to keep the water out. 10

"My! what a rain! It's good two years sence it rain' like that," exclaimed Calixta as she rolled up a piece of bagging and Alcée helped her to thrust it beneath the crack.

She was a little fuller of figure than five years before when she married; but she had lost nothing of her vivacity. Her blue eyes still retained their melting quality; and her yellow hair, dishevelled by the wind and rain, kinked more stubbornly than ever about her ears and temples.

The rain beat upon the low, shingled roof with a force and clatter that threatened to break an entrance and deluge them there. They were in the dining room—the sitting room—the general utility room. Adjoining was her bed room, with Bibi's couch along side her own. The door stood open, and the room with its white, monumental bed, its closed shutters, looked dim and mysterious.

Alcée flung himself into a rocker and Calixta nervously began to gather up from the floor the lengths of a cotton sheet which she had been sewing.

"If this keeps up, *Dieu sait*[1] if the levees[2] goin' to stan' it!" she exclaimed. 15

"What have you got to do with the levees?"

"I got enough to do! An' there's Bobinôt with Bibi out in that storm—if he only didn't left Friedheimer's!"

---

[1]*Dieu sait:* "God knows" (French).

[2]*levees:* Raised embankments designed to keep a river from overflowing.

"Let us hope, Calixta, that Bobinôt's got sense enough to come in out of a cyclone."

She went and stood at the window with a greatly disturbed look on her face. She wiped the frame that was clouded with moisture. It was stiflingly hot. Alcée got up and joined her at the window, looking over her shoulder. The rain was coming down in sheets obscuring the view of far-off cabins and enveloping the distant wood in a gray mist. The playing of the lightning was incessant. A bolt struck a tall chinaberry tree at the edge of the field. It filled all visible space with a blinding glare and the crash seemed to invade the very boards they stood upon.

Calixta put her hands to her eyes, and with a cry, staggered backward. Alcée's arm encircled her, and for an instant he drew her close and spasmodically to him. 20

"*Bonté!*"[3] she cried, releasing herself from his encircling arm and retreating from the window, "the house'll go next! If I only knew w'ere Bibi was!" She would not compose herself; she would not be seated. Alcée clasped her shoulders and looked into her face. The contact of her warm, palpitating body when he had unthinkingly drawn her into his arms, had aroused all the old-time infatuation and desire for her flesh.

"Calixta," he said, "don't be frightened. Nothing can happen. The house is too low to be struck, with so many tall trees standing about. There! aren't you going to be quiet? say, aren't you?" He pushed her hair back from her face that was warm and steaming. Her lips were as red and moist as pomegranate seed. Her white neck and a glimpse of her full, firm bosom disturbed him powerfully. As she glanced up at him the fear in her liquid blue eyes had given place to a drowsy gleam that unconsciously betrayed a sensuous desire. He looked down into her eyes and there was nothing for him to do but to gather her lips in a kiss. It reminded him of Assumption.

"Do you remember—in Assumption, Calixta?" he asked in a low voice broken by passion. Oh! she remembered; for in Assumption he had kissed her and kissed and kissed her; until his senses would well nigh fail, and to save her he would resort to a desperate flight. If she was not an immaculate dove in those days, she was still inviolate; a passionate creature whose very defenselessness had made her defense, against which his honor forbade him to prevail. Now—well, now—her lips seemed in a manner free to be tasted, as well as her round, white throat and her whiter breasts.

They did not heed the crashing torrents, and the roar of the elements made her laugh as she lay in his arms. She was a revelation in that dim, mysterious chamber; as white as the couch she lay upon. Her firm, elastic flesh that was knowing for the first time its birthright, was like a creamy lily that the sun invites to contribute its breath and perfume to the undying life of the world.

---

[3]*Bonté:* "Goodness!" (French).

The generous abundance of her passion, without guile or trickery, was like a white flame which penetrated and found response in depths of his own sensuous nature that had never yet been reached.

When he touched her breasts they gave themselves up in quivering ecstasy, inviting his lips. Her mouth was a fountain of delight. And when he possessed her, they seemed to swoon together at the very borderland of life's mystery.

He stayed cushioned upon her, breathless, dazed, enervated, with his heart beating like a hammer upon her. With one hand she clasped his head, her lips lightly touching his forehead. The other hand stroked with a soothing rhythm his muscular shoulders.

The growl of the thunder was distant and passing away. The rain beat softly upon the shingles, inviting them to drowsiness and sleep. But they dared not yield.

The rain was over; and the sun was turning the glistening green world into a palace of gems. Calixta, on the gallery, watched Alcée ride away. He turned and smiled at her with a beaming face; and she lifted her pretty chin in the air and laughed aloud.

III

Bobinôt and Bibi, trudging home, stopped without at the cistern to make themselves presentable.

"My! Bibi, w'at will yo' mama say! You ought to be ashame'. You oughtn' put on those good pants. Look at 'em! An' that mud on yo' collar! How you got that mud on yo' collar, Bibi? I never saw such a boy!" Bibi was the picture of pathetic resignation. Bobinôt was the embodiment of serious solicitude as he strove to remove from his own person and his son's the signs of their tramp over heavy roads and through wet fields. He scraped the mud off Bibi's bare legs and feet with a stick and carefully removed all traces from his heavy brogans. Then, prepared for the worst—the meeting with an over-scrupulous housewife, they entered cautiously at the back door.

Calixta was preparing supper. She had set the table and was dripping coffee at the hearth. She sprang up as they came in.

"Oh, Bobinôt! You back! My! but I was uneasy. W'ere you been during the rain? An' Bibi? he ain't wet? he ain't hurt?" She had clasped Bibi and was kissing him effusively. Bobinôt's explanations and apologies which he had been composing all along the way, died on his lips as Calixta felt him to see if he were dry, and seemed to express nothing but satisfaction at their safe return.

"I brought you some shrimps, Calixta," offered Bobinôt, hauling the can from his ample side pocket and laying it on the table.

"Shrimps! Oh, Bobinôt! you too good fo' anything!" and she gave him a smacking kiss on the cheek that resounded. "*J'vous réponds*,[4] we'll have a feas' tonight! umph-umph!"

[4] *J'vous réponds:* "I tell you" (French).

Bobinôt and Bibi began to relax and enjoy themselves, and when the three seated themselves at table they laughed much and so loud that anyone might have heard them as far away as Laballière's.

IV

Alcée Laballière wrote to his wife, Clarisse, that night. It was a loving letter, full of tender solicitude. He told her not to hurry back, but if she and the babies liked it at Biloxi, to stay a month longer. He was getting on nicely; and though he missed them, he was willing to bear the separation a while longer—realizing that their health and pleasure were the first things to be considered.

V

As for Clarisse, she was charmed upon receiving her husband's letter. She and the babies were doing well. The society was agreeable; many of her old friends and acquaintances were at the bay. And the first free breath since her marriage seemed to restore the pleasant liberty of her maiden days. Devoted as she was to her husband, their intimate conjugal life was something which she was more than willing to forego for a while.

So the storm passed and everyone was happy.

Reading and Reacting

1. Trace the progress of the storm through the five parts of the story. Then trace the stages of the story's plot. How does the progress of the storm parallel the developing plot?
2. How does the weather help to create the story's atmosphere? How would you characterize this atmosphere?
3. In Part I, the "sombre clouds … rolling with sinister intention" introduce the storm. In what sense does this description introduce the story's action as well?
4. In what respects does the storm *cause* the events of the story? List specific events that occur because of the storm. Is the presence of the storm essential to the story?
5. In what sense does the storm act as a character in the story?
6. The weather is the most obvious element of the story's setting. What other aspects of setting are important to the story?
7. After Part II, the storm is not mentioned again until the story's last line. What signs of the storm remain in Parts III, IV, and V?
8. Besides referring to the weather, what else might the title suggest?
9. **Journal Entry** The storm sets in motion the chain of events that leads to the characters' adultery. Do you think the storm excuses the characters in any way from responsibility for their actions?
10. **Critical Perspective** Kate Chopin is widely considered to be a regional, or "local color," writer. This term refers to writing in which descriptions

of a particular geographic region are prominent. Local color writers strive to incorporate accurate speech patterns and dialects—as well as descriptions of local scenery, dress, and social customs—into their writing. Writing for the *Southern Literary Journal* and quoting Chopin critic Helen Taylor, Sylvia Bailey Shurbutt notes, "Of the regional stories, Taylor writes, '[Chopin's] ironic and resonant use of historical, topographical, and mythical Louisiana materials . . . functions to interrogate both the Southern ideology of womanhood and contradictory constructions of Southern femininity in the 1890's.'"

In what respects is "The Storm" an example of "local color" writing? How does it challenge "the southern ideology of womanhood"?

Related Works: "Hills Like White Elephants" (p. 101), "Love is not all" (p. 620), "What lips my lips have kissed" (p. 684), "General Review of the Sex Situation" (p. 686)

Courtesy of Alberto Avaro Ríos

ALBERTO ÁLVARO RÍOS (1952–) was born and raised in the border town of Nogales, Arizona, the son of a Mexican father and an English mother. He is the author of eleven books and chapbooks of poetry, including *Whispering to Fool the Wind* (1982), which won the American Academy of Poets Walt Whitman Award; *Teodoro Luna's Two Kisses* (1990); *The Smallest Muscle in the Human Body* (2002), which was a finalist for the National Book Award; *The Theater of Night* (2005); and *The Dangerous Shirt* (2009). His collections of short stories include *The Iguana Killer: Twelve Stories of the Heart* (1984), in which "The Secret Lion" appeared; *Pig Cookies and Other Stories* (1995); and *The Curtain of Trees* (1999). *Capirotada,* which was published in 1999, is a memoir about growing up on the Mexican border. His other literary awards include a Guggenheim Fellowship and a National Endowment of the Arts Fellowship. Ríos is presently Regents' Professor of English at Arizona State University as well as Arizona's first-ever poet laureate.

Reviewer Mary Logue, writing in the *Village Voice Literary Supplement,* observes that Ríos's writings "carry the feel of another world.... Ríos's tongue is both foreign and familiar," reflecting an upbringing "where one is neither in this country nor the other." In many of his stories, Ríos expresses the seeming "other-ness" of Anglo culture as seen through the eyes of Chicano children: a little boy frightened by the sight of his first snowfall or (as in "The Secret Lion") boys amazed by the otherworldly sight of "heaven." Through Ríos's children, we see our own world with new eyes.

Cultural Context With their rolling hills, freshwater ponds, lush greens, and fastidiously trimmed turf, golf courses are designed to convey a sense of wealth and comfort, typically providing recreation for the middle and upper classes. In a dry region—or even in a densely populated city—an irrigated, sculpted golf course may look like an oasis in the desert. The golf course that plays a role in this story is probably (like many others) part of a privately owned, exclusive country club.

The Secret Lion (1984)

I was twelve and in junior high school and something happened that we didn't have a name for, but it was there nonetheless like a lion, and roaring, roaring that way the biggest things do. Everything changed. Just that. Like the rug, the one that gets pulled—or better, like the tablecloth those magicians pull where the stuff on the table stays the same but the gasp! from the audience makes the staying-the-same part not matter. Like that.

What happened was there were teachers now, not just one teacher, teach-erz, and we felt personally abandoned somehow. When a person had all these teachers now, he didn't get taken care of the same way, even though six was more than one. Arithmetic went out the door when we walked in. And we saw girls now, but they weren't the same girls we used to know because we couldn't talk to them anymore, not the same way we used to, certainly not to Sandy, even though she was my neighbor, too. Not even to her. She just played the piano all the time. And there were words, oh there were words in junior high school, and we wanted to know what they were, and how a person did them—that's what school was supposed to be for. Only, in junior high school, school wasn't school, everything was backward-like. If you went up to a teacher and said the word to try and find out what it meant you got in trouble for saying it. So we didn't. And we figured it must have been that way about other stuff, too, so we never said anything about anything—we weren't stupid.

But my friend Sergio and I, we solved junior high school. We would come home from school on the bus, put our books away, change shoes, and go across the highway to the arroyo. It was the one place we were not supposed to go. So we did. This was, after all, what junior high had at least shown us. It was our river, though, our personal Mississippi, our friend from long back, and it was full of stories and all the branch forts we had built in it when we were still the Vikings of America, with our own symbol, which we had carved everywhere, even in the sand, which let the water take it. That was good, we had decided; whoever was at the end of this river would know about us.

At the very very top of our growing lungs, what we would do down there was shout every dirty word we could think of, in every combination we could come up with, and we would yell about girls, and all the things we wanted to do with them, as loud as we could—we didn't know what we wanted to do with them, just things—and we would yell about teachers, and how we loved some of them, like Miss Crevelone, and how we wanted to dissect some of them, making signs of the cross, like priests, and we would yell this stuff over and over because it felt good, we couldn't explain why, it just felt good and for the first time in our lives there was nobody to tell us we couldn't. So we did.

One Thursday we were walking along shouting this way, and the railroad, the Southern Pacific, which ran above and along the far side of the arroyo, had dropped a grinding ball down there, which was, we found out later, a cannonball thing used in mining. A bunch of them were put in a big vat which turned around and crushed the ore. One had been dropped, or thrown—what do caboose men do when they get bored—but it got down there regardless and as we were walking along yelling about one girl or another, a particular Claudia, we found it, one of these things, looked at it, picked it up, and got very very excited, and held it and passed it back and forth, and we were saying "Guythisis, this is, geeGuythis ...": we had this perception about nature then, that nature is imperfect and that round things are perfect: we said "GuyGodthis is perfect, thisisthis is perfect, it's round, round and heavy, it'sit's the best thing we'veeverseen. Whatisit?" We didn't know. We just knew it was great. We just, whatever, we played with it, held it some more. 5

And then we had to decide what to do with it. We knew, because of a lot of things, that if we were going to take this and show it to anybody, this discovery, this best thing, was going to be taken away from us. That's the way it works with little kids, like all the polished quartz, the tons of it we had collected piece by piece over the years. Junior high kids too. If we took it home, my mother, we knew, was going to look at it and say "throw that dirty thing in the, get rid of it." Simple like, like that. "But ma it's the best thing I" "Getridofit." Simple.

So we didn't. Take it home. Instead, we came up with the answer. We dug a hole and buried it. And we marked it secretly. Lots of secret signs. And came back the next week to dig it up and, we didn't know, pass it around some more or something, but we didn't find it. We dug up that whole bank, and we never found it again. We tried.

Sergio and I talked about that ball or whatever it was when we couldn't find it. All we used were small words, neat, good. Kid words. What we were really saying, but didn't know the words, was how much that ball was like that place, that whole arroyo: couldn't tell anybody about it, didn't understand what it was, didn't have a name for it. It just felt good. It was just perfect in the way it was that place, that whole going to that place, that whole junior high school lion. It was just iron-heavy, it had no name, it felt good or not, we couldn't take it home to show our mothers, and once we buried it, it was gone forever.

The ball was gone, like the first reasons we had come to that arroyo years earlier, like the first time we had seen the arroyo, it was gone like everything else that had been taken away. This was not our first lesson. We stopped going to the arroyo after not finding the thing, the same way we had stopped going there years earlier and headed for the mountains. Nature seemed to keep pushing us around one way or another, teaching us the same thing every place we ended up. Nature's gang was tough that way, teaching us stuff.

When we were young we moved away from town, me and my family. Sergio's was already out there. Out in the wilds. Or at least the new place seemed like the wilds since everything looks bigger the smaller a man is. I was five, I guess, and we had moved three miles north of Nogales where we had lived, three miles north of the Mexican border. We looked across the highway in one direction and there was the arroyo; hills stood up in the other direction. Mountains, for a small man. 10

When the first summer came the very first place we went to was of course the one place we weren't supposed to go, the arroyo. We went down in there and found water running, summer rain water mostly, and we went swimming. But every third or fourth or fifth day, the sewage treatment plant that was, we found out, upstream, would release whatever it was that it released, and we would never know exactly what day that was, and a person really couldn't tell right off by looking at the water, not every time, not so a person could get out in time. So, we went swimming that summer and some days we had a lot of fun. Some days we didn't. We found a thousand ways to explain what happened on those other days, constructing elaborate stories about the neighborhood dogs, and hadn't she, my mother, miscalculated her step before, too? But she knew something was up because we'd come running into the house those days, wanting to take a shower, even—if this can be imagined—in the middle of the day.

That was the first time we stopped going to the arroyo. It taught us to look the other way. We decided, as the second side of summer came, we wanted to go into the mountains. They were still mountains then. We went running in one summer Thursday morning, my friend Sergio and I, into my mother's kitchen, and said, well, what'zin, what'zin those hills over there—we used her word so she'd understand us—and she said nothingdon'tworryaboutit. So we went out, and we weren't dumb, we thought with our eyes to each other, ohhoshe'strying tokeepsomethingfromus. We knew adults.

We had read the books, after all; we knew about bridges and castles and wildtreacherousraging alligatormouth rivers. We wanted them. So we were going to go out and get them. We went back that morning into that kitchen and we said, "We're going out there, we're going into the hills, we're going away for three days, don't worry." She said, "All right."

"You know," I said to Sergio, "if we're going to go away for three days, well, we ought to at least pack a lunch."

But we were two young boys with no patience for what we thought at the time was mom-stuff: making sa-and-wiches. My mother didn't offer. So we got out little kid knapsacks that my mother had sewn for us, and into them we put the jar of mustard. A loaf of bread. Knivesforksplates, bottles of Coke, a can opener. This was lunch for the two of us. And we were weighed down, humped over to be strong enough to carry this stuff. But we started walking anyway, into the hills. We were going to eat berries and stuff otherwise. "Goodbye." My mom said that. 15

After the first hill we were dead. But we walked. My mother could still see us. And we kept walking. We walked until we got to where the sun is straight overhead, noon. That place. Where that is doesn't matter; it's time to eat.

The truth is we weren't anywhere close to that place. We just agreed that the sun was overhead and that it was time to eat, and by tilting our heads a little we could make that the truth.

"We really ought to start looking for a place to eat."

"Yeah. Let's look for a good place to eat." We went back and forth saying that for fifteen minutes, making it lunchtime because that's what we always said back and forth before lunchtimes at home. "Yeah, I'm hungry all right." I nodded my head. "Yeah, I'm hungry all right too. I'm hungry." He nodded his head. I nodded my head back. After a good deal more nodding, we were ready, just as we came over a little hill. We hadn't found the mountains yet. This was a little hill.

And on the other side of this hill we found heaven.

It was just what we thought it would be. 20

Perfect. Heaven was green, like nothing else in Arizona. And it wasn't a cemetery or like that because we had seen cemeteries and they had gravestones and stuff and this didn't. This was perfect, had trees, lots of trees, had birds, like we had never seen before. It was like *The Wizard of Oz*, like when they got to Oz and everything was so green, so emerald, they had to wear those glasses, and we ran just like them, laughing, laughing that way we did that moment, and we went running down to this clearing in it all, hitting each other that good way we did.

We got down there, we kept laughing, we kept hitting each other, we unpacked our stuff, and we started acting "rich." We knew all about how to do that, like blowing on our nails, then rubbing them on our chests for the shine. We made our sandwiches, opened our Cokes, got out the rest of the stuff, the salt and pepper shakers. I found this particular hole and I put my Coke right into it, a perfect fit, and I called it my Coke-holder. I got down next to it on my back, because everyone knows that rich people eat lying down, and I got my sandwich in one hand and put my other arm around the Coke in its holder. When I wanted a drink, I lifted my neck a little, put out my lips, and tipped my Coke a little with the crook of my elbow. Ah.

We were there, lying down, eating our sandwiches, laughing, throwing bread at each other and out for the birds. This was heaven. We were laughing and we couldn't believe it. My mother was keeping something from us, ah ha, but we had found her out. We even found water over at the side of the clearing to wash our plates with—we had brought plates. Sergio started washing his plates when he was done, and I was being rich with my Coke, and this day in summer was right.

When suddenly these two men came, from around a corner of trees and the tallest grass we had ever seen. They had bags on their backs, leather bags, bags and sticks.

We didn't know what clubs were, but I learned later, like I learned about the grinding balls. The two men yelled at us. Most specifically, one wanted me to take my Coke out of my Coke-holder so he could sink his golf ball into it. 25

Something got taken away from us that moment. Heaven. We grew up a little bit, and couldn't go backward. We learned. No one had ever told us about golf. They had told us about heaven. And it went away. We got golf in exchange.

We went back to the arroyo for the rest of that summer, and tried to have fun the best we could. We learned to be ready for finding the grinding ball. We loved it, and when we buried it we knew what would happen. The truth is, we didn't look so hard for it. We were two boys and twelve summers then, and not stupid. Things get taken away.

We buried it because it was perfect. We didn't tell my mother, but together it was all we talked about, till we forgot. It was the lion.

Reading and Reacting

1. Identify and briefly describe the story's geographical, physical, and historical settings. What role does each type of setting play in the story? Which do you think is most important? Why?
2. The boys are five years old when they first discover the golf course. What is their initial reaction to this discovery? Why do you think they react this way?
3. When recreating the boys' speech, the narrator sometimes runs words together ("knivesforksplates") or stretches out sounds ("sa-and-wiches"). Identify some other examples of this style. Why does the narrator present the boys' speech like this?
4. What is an *arroyo*? What is a grinding ball? What is a "Coke-holder"? How does each function as a symbol in the story?
5. How (and why) does the narrator's view of the golf course, the grinding ball, and the arroyo change as he grows older?
6. Is Sergio necessary to the story, or would the events described be the same without him? Explain.
7. At the end of the story, the narrator says, "Something got taken away from us that moment. Heaven" (par. 26). What does he mean?
8. **Journal Entry** What is the secret lion? Why is it a secret? How is it like a lion?
9. **Critical Perspective** During a visit to a web-based English composition class, when asked about his use of symbols in his writing, Rios gave this answer:

   > Do I use events, locations, and symbols to further the meanings in my stories? . . . That is one big reason I write about the border so much, for example. As a place, it's simply one more point of geography. But a border has many, many meanings as a symbol, and I base much of my writing on that edge.

   What symbolic meanings do you think the U.S.-Mexican border might have? In what sense does the border give Rios "that edge" in "The Secret Lion"?

Related Works: "Gryphon" (p. 191), "Araby" (p. 296), "Doe Season" (p. 378), "Nothing Gold Can Stay" (p. 553), "Where the Sidewalk Ends" (p. 607)

Chris Felver/Archive Photos/Getty Images

TILLIE OLSEN (1912 or 1913–2007) is known for her works of fiction about working-class Americans. Her short stories and one novel are inhabited by those she called the "despised people"—coal miners, farm laborers, packinghouse butchers, and housewives. Olsen was born in Nebraska into a working-class family. According to an account in her nonfiction work *Silences* (1978), she was inspired at age fifteen to write about working-class people when she read Rebecca Harding Davis' *Life in the Iron Mills*, a tale of the effects of industrialization on workers, in an 1861 issue of *Atlantic Monthly* bought for ten cents in a junk shop.

Shortly after she left high school, Olsen was jailed for helping to organize packinghouse workers. Motivated by her experiences, she began to write a novel, *Yonnondio*. Under her maiden name, Tillie Lerner, she published two poems, a short story, and part of her novel during the 1930s. After her marriage, she did not publish again for twenty-two years, spending her time raising four children and working at a variety of jobs. The collection of short stories *Tell Me a Riddle* (1961), which includes "I Stand Here Ironing" (originally titled "Help Her to Believe"), was published when she was fifty. Her only other work of fiction is *Yonnondio*, which she pieced together from drafts she wrote in the 1930s and edited for publication in 1974.

In 1984, she edited *Mother to Daughter, Daughter to Mother: Mothers on Mothering*, a collection of poems, letters, short fiction, and diary excerpts written by famous and not-so-famous women, and in 1987, she collaborated with photographer Estelle Jussim on *Mothers & Daughters: An Exploration in Photographs*.

Cultural Context During the Great Depression of the 1930s, jobs were scarce throughout the United States, and many people who managed to keep their jobs were forced to take pay cuts. At the height of the Depression in 1933, almost twenty-five percent of the total workforce—more than eleven million people—were unemployed. The displacement of the American worker and the destruction of farming communities caused families such as the one in this story to split up or to leave their homes and communities in search of work. In 1935, the Social Security Act established public assistance, unemployment insurance, and social security, which offered economic relief to American workers and their families.

I Stand Here Ironing (1961)

I stand here ironing, and what you asked me moves tormented back and forth with the iron.

"I wish you would manage the time to come and talk with me about your daughter. I'm sure you can help me understand her. She's a youngster who needs help and whom I'm deeply interested in helping."

"Who needs help." ... Even if I came, what good would it do? You think because I am her mother I have a key, or that in some way you could use me as a key? She has lived for nineteen years. There is all that life that has happened outside of me, beyond me.

And when is there time to remember, to sift, to weigh, to estimate, to total? I will start and there will be an interruption and I will have to gather it all together again. Or I will become engulfed with all I did or did not do, with what should have been and what cannot be helped.

She was a beautiful baby. The first and only one of our five that was beautiful at birth. You do not guess how new and uneasy her tenancy in her now-loveliness. You did not know her all those years she was thought homely, or see her poring over her baby pictures, making me tell her over and over how beautiful she had been—and would be, I would tell her—and was now, to the seeing eye. But the seeing eyes were few or nonexistent. Including mine. 5

I nursed her. They feel that's important nowadays. I nursed all the children, but with her, with all the fierce rigidity of first motherhood, I did like the books then said. Though her cries battered me to trembling and my breasts ached with swollenness, I waited till the clock decreed.

Why do I put that first? I do not even know if it matters, or if it explains anything.

She was a beautiful baby. She blew shining bubbles of sound. She loved motion, loved light, loved color and music and textures. She would lie on the floor in her blue overalls patting the surface so hard in ecstasy her hands and feet would blur. She was a miracle to me, but when she was eight months old I had to leave her daytimes with the woman downstairs to whom she was no miracle at all, for I worked or looked for work and for Emily's father, who "could no longer endure" (he wrote in his good-bye note) "sharing want with us."

I was nineteen. It was the pre-relief, pre-WPA[1] world of the depression. I would start running as soon as I got off the streetcar, running up the stairs, the place smelling sour, and awake or asleep to startle awake, when she saw me she would break into a clogged weeping that could not be comforted, a weeping I can hear yet.

After a while I found a job hashing at night so I could be with her days, and it was better. But it came to where I had to bring her to his family and leave her. 10

It took a long time to raise the money for her fare back. Then she got chicken pox and I had to wait longer. When she finally came, I hardly knew her, walking quick and nervous like her father, looking like her father, thin, and dressed in a shoddy red that yellowed her skin and glared at the pockmarks. All the baby loveliness gone.

She was two. Old enough for nursery school they said, and I did not know then what I know now—the fatigue of the long day, and the lacerations of group life in the kinds of nurseries that are only parking places for children.

---

[1] *WPA:* The Works Progress Administration, created in 1935 as part of President Franklin D. Roosevelt's New Deal program. The purpose of the WPA (renamed the Works Projects Administration in 1939) was to provide jobs for the unemployed during the Great Depression.

Except that it would have made no difference if I had known. It was the only place there was. It was the only way we could be together, the only way I could hold a job.

And even without knowing, I knew. I knew the teacher that was evil because all these years it has curdled into my memory, the little boy hunched in the corner, her rasp, "why aren't you outside, because Alvin hits you? that's no reason, go out, scaredy." I knew Emily hated it even if she did not clutch and implore "don't go Mommy" like the other children, mornings.

She always had a reason why we should stay home. Momma, you look sick. Momma, I feel sick. Momma, the teachers aren't there today, they're sick. Momma, we can't go, there was a fire there last night. Momma, it's a holiday today, no school, they told me.

But never a direct protest, never rebellion. I think of our others in their three-, four-year-oldness—the explosions, the tempers, the denunciations, the demands—and I feel suddenly ill. I put the iron down. What in me demanded that goodness in her? And what was the cost, the cost to her of such goodness?

The old man living in the back once said in his gentle way: "You should smile at Emily more when you look at her." What *was* in my face when I looked at her? I loved her. There were all the acts of love.

It was only with the others I remembered what he said, and it was the face of joy, and not of care or tightness or worry I turned to them—too late for Emily. She does not smile easily, let alone almost always as her brothers and sisters do. Her face is closed and sombre, but when she wants, how fluid. You must have seen it in her pantomimes, you spoke of her rare gift for comedy on the stage that rouses laughter out of the audience so dear they applaud and applaud and do not want to let her go.

Where does it come from, that comedy? There was none of it in her when she came back to me that second time, after I had had to send her away again. She had a new daddy now to learn to love, and I think perhaps it was a better time.

Except when we left her alone nights, telling ourselves she was old enough.

"Can't you go some other time, Mommy, like tomorrow?" she would ask. "Will it be just a little while you'll be gone? Do you promise?"

The time we came back, the front door open, the clock on the floor in the hall. She rigid awake. "It wasn't just a little while. I didn't cry. Three times I called you, just three times, and then I ran downstairs to open the door so you could come faster. The clock talked loud. I threw it away, it scared me what it talked."

She said the clock talked loud again that night I went to the hospital to have Susan. She was delirious with the fever that comes before red measles, but she was fully conscious all the week I was gone and the week after we were home when she could not come near the new baby or me.

She did not get well. She stayed skeleton thin, not wanting to eat, and night after night she had nightmares. She would call for me, and I would rouse from exhaustion to sleepily call back: "You're all right, darling, go to sleep, it's just a dream," and if she still called, in a sterner voice, "now go to sleep, Emily, there's nothing to hurt you." Twice, only twice, when I had to get up for Susan anyhow, I went in to sit with her.

Now when it is too late (as if she would let me hold and comfort her like I do the others) I get up and go to her at once at her moan or restless stirring. "Are you awake, Emily? Can I get you something?" And the answer is always the same: "No, I'm all right, go back to sleep, Mother." 25

They persuaded me at the clinic to send her away to a convalescent home in the country where "she can have the kind of food and care you can't manage for her, and you'll be free to concentrate on the new baby." They still send children to that place. I see pictures on the society page of sleek young women planning affairs to raise money for it, or dancing at the affairs, or decorating Easter eggs or filling Christmas stockings for the children.

They never have a picture of the children so I do not know if the girls still wear those gigantic red bows and the ravaged looks on the every other Sunday when parents can come to visit "unless otherwise notified"—as we were notified the first six weeks.

Oh it is a handsome place, green lawns and tall trees and fluted flower beds. High up on the balconies of each cottage the children stand, the girls in their red bows and white dresses, the boys in white suits and giant red ties. The parents stand below shrieking up to be heard and the children shriek down to be heard, and between them the invisible wall: "Not to Be Contaminated by Parental Germs or Physical Affection."

There was a tiny girl who always stood hand in hand with Emily. Her parents never came. One visit she was gone. "They moved her to Rose Cottage," Emily shouted in explanation. "They don't like you to love anybody here."

She wrote once a week, the labored writing of a seven-year-old. "I am fine. How is the baby. If I write my leter nicly I will have a star. Love." There never was a star. We wrote every other day, letters she could never hold or keep but only hear read—once. "We simply do not have room for children to keep any personal possessions," they patiently explained when we pieced one Sunday's shrieking together to plead how much it would mean to Emily, who loved so to keep things, to be allowed to keep her letters and cards. 30

Each visit she looked frailer. "She isn't eating," they told us.

(They had runny eggs for breakfast or mush with lumps, Emily said later, I'd hold it in my mouth and not swallow. Nothing ever tasted good, just when they had chicken.)

It took us eight months to get her released home, and only the fact that she gained back so little of her seven lost pounds convinced the social worker.

I used to try to hold and love her after she came back, but her body would stay stiff, and after a while she'd push away. She ate little. Food sickened her, and I think much of life too. Oh she had physical lightness and brightness, twinkling by on skates, bouncing like a ball up and down up and down over the jump rope, skimming over the hill; but these were momentary.

She fretted about her appearance, thin and dark and foreign-looking at a time when every little girl was supposed to look or thought she should look a chubby blonde replica of Shirley Temple. The doorbell sometimes rang for her, but no one seemed to come and play in the house or be a best friend. Maybe because we moved so much. 35

There was a boy she loved painfully through two school semesters. Months later she told me how she had taken pennies from my purse to buy him candy. "Licorice was his favorite and I brought him some every day, but he still liked Jennifer better'n me. Why, Mommy?" The kind of question for which there is no answer.

School was a worry to her. She was not glib or quick in a world where glibness and quickness were easily confused with ability to learn. To her overworked and exasperated teachers she was an overconscientious "slow learner" who kept trying to catch up and was absent entirely too often.

I let her be absent, though sometimes the illness was imaginary. How different from my now-strictness about attendance with the others. I wasn't working. We had a new baby, I was home anyhow. Sometimes, after Susan grew old enough, I would keep her home from school, too, to have them all together.

Mostly Emily had asthma, and her breathing, harsh and labored, would fill the house with a curiously tranquil sound. I would bring the two old dresser mirrors and her boxes of collections to her bed. She would select beads and single earrings, bottle tops and shells, dried flowers and pebbles, old postcards and scraps, all sorts of oddments; then she and Susan would play Kingdom, setting up landscapes and furniture, peopling them with action.

Those were the only times of peaceful companionship between her and Susan. I have edged away from it, that poisonous feeling between them, that terrible balancing of hurts and needs I had to do between the two, and did so badly, those earlier years. 40

Oh there are conflicts between the others too, each one human, needing, demanding, hurting, taking—but only between Emily and Susan, no, Emily toward Susan that corroding resentment. It seems so obvious on the surface, yet it is not obvious. Susan, the second child, Susan, golden- and curly-haired and chubby, quick and articulate and assured, everything in appearance and manner Emily was not; Susan, not able to resist Emily's precious things, losing or sometimes clumsily breaking them; Susan telling jokes and riddles to company for applause while Emily sat silent (to say to me later: that was *my* riddle, Mother, I told it to Susan); Susan, who for all the five years' difference in age was just a year behind Emily in developing physically.

I am glad for that slow physical development that widened the difference between her and her contemporaries, though she suffered over it. She was too vulnerable for that terrible world of youthful competition, of preening and parading, of constant measuring of yourself against every other, of envy, "If I had that copper hair," "If I had that skin...." She tormented herself enough about not looking like the others, there was enough of the unsureness, the having to be conscious of words before you speak, the constant caring—what are they thinking of me? without having it all magnified by the merciless physical drives.

Ronnie is calling. He is wet and I change him. It is rare there is such a cry now. That time of motherhood is almost behind me when the ear is not one's own but must always be racked and listening for the child cry, the child call. We sit for a while and I hold him, looking out over the city spread in charcoal with its soft aisles of light. "*Shoogily*," he breathes and curls closer. I carry him back to bed, asleep. *Shoogily*. A funny word, a family word, inherited from Emily, invented by her to say: *comfort*.

In this and other ways she leaves her seal, I say aloud. And startle at my saying it. What do I mean? What did I start to gather together, to try and make coherent? I was at the terrible, growing years. War years. I do not remember them well. I was working, there were four smaller ones now, there was not time for her. She had to help be a mother, and housekeeper, and shopper. She had to set her seal. Mornings of crisis and near hysteria trying to get lunches packed, hair combed, coats and shoes found, everyone to school or Child Care on time, the baby ready for transportation. And always the paper scribbled on by a smaller one, the book looked at by Susan then mislaid, the homework not done. Running out to that huge school where she was one, she was lost, she was a drop; suffering over the unpreparedness, stammering and unsure in her classes.

There was so little time left at night after the kids were bedded down. She would struggle over books, always eating (it was in those years she developed her enormous appetite that is legendary in our family) and I would be ironing, or preparing food for the next day, or writing V-mail[2] to Bill, or tending the baby. Sometimes, to make me laugh, or out of her despair, she would imitate happenings or types at school. 45

I think I said once: "Why don't you do something like this in the school amateur show?" One morning she phoned me at work, hardly understandable through the weeping: "Mother, I did it. I won, I won; they gave me first prize; they clapped and clapped and wouldn't let me go."

Now suddenly she was Somebody, and as imprisoned in her difference as she had been in anonymity.

She began to be asked to perform at other high schools, even in colleges, then at city and statewide affairs. The first one we went to, I only recognized her that first moment when thin, shy, she almost drowned herself into the curtains. Then: Was this Emily? The control, the command, the convulsing and deadly clowning, the spell, then the roaring, stamping audience, unwilling to let this rare and precious laughter out of their lives.

Afterwards: You ought to do something about her with a gift like that—but without money or knowing how, what does one do? We have left it all to her,

---

[2]*V-mail:* Mail sent to or from members of the armed forces during World War II. Letters were reduced onto microfilm and enlarged and printed out at their destination.

and the gift has as often eddied inside, clogged and clotted, as been used and growing.

She is coming. She runs up the stairs two at a time with her light graceful step, and I know she is happy tonight. Whatever it was that occasioned your call did not happen today. 50

"Aren't you ever going to finish the ironing, Mother? Whistler painted his mother in a rocker. I'd have to paint mine standing over an ironing board." This is one of her communicative nights and she tells me everything and nothing as she fixes herself a plate of food out of the icebox.

She is so lovely. Why did you want me to come in at all? Why were you concerned? She will find her way.

She starts up the stairs to bed. "Don't get me up with the rest in the morning." "But I thought you were having midterms." "Oh, those," she comes back in, kisses me, and says quite lightly, "in a couple of years when we'll all be atom-dead they won't matter a bit."

She has said it before. She *believes* it. But because I have been dredging the past, and all that compounds a human being is so heavy and meaningful in me, I cannot endure it tonight.

I will never total it all. I will never come in to say: She was a child seldom smiled at. Her father left me before she was a year old. I had to work her first six years when there was work, or I sent her home and to his relatives. There were years she had care she hated. She was dark and thin and foreign-looking in a world where the prestige went to blondeness and curly hair and dimples, she was slow where glibness was prized. She was a child of anxious, not proud, love. We were poor and could not afford for her the soil of easy growth. I was a young mother, I was a distracted mother. There were other children pushing up, demanding. Her younger sister seemed all that she was not. There were years she did not want me to touch her. She kept too much in herself, her life was such she had to keep too much in herself. My wisdom came too late. She has much to her and probably little will come of it. She is a child of her age, of depression, of war, of fear. 55

Let her be. So all that is in her will not bloom—but in how many does it? There is still enough left to live by. Only help her to know—help make it so there is cause for her to know—that she is more than this dress on the ironing board, helpless before the iron.

Reading and Reacting

1. "I Stand Here Ironing" focuses on incidents that took place in the "pre-relief, pre-WPA world" of the Depression (par. 9). Considering social, political, and economic changes that have occurred since the 1930s, do you think the events the story presents could occur today? Explain.
2. In what sense is the image of a mother at an ironing board appropriate for this story?

3. The narrator is overwhelmed by guilt. What does she believe she has done wrong? What, if anything, do *you* think she has done wrong? Do you think she has been a good mother? Why or why not?
4. Who, or what, do you blame for the narrator's problems? For example, do you blame Emily's father? the Depression? the social institutions and "experts" to which the narrator turns?
5. Do you see the narrator as a victim limited by the times in which she lives? Do you agree with the narrator that Emily is "a child of her age, of depression, of war, of fear" (par. 55)? Or do you believe both women have some control over their own destinies, regardless of the story's historical setting?
6. What do you think the narrator wants for her daughter? Do you think her goals for Emily are realistic? Why or why not?
7. Paragraph 28 describes the physical setting of the convalescent home to which Emily was sent. What does this description add to the story?
8. To whom do you think the mother is speaking in this story?
9. **Journal Entry** Put yourself in Emily's position. What do you think she would like to tell her mother?
10. **Critical Perspective** Writing in *The Red Wheelbarrow*, psychologist Robert Coles discusses the complex family relationships depicted in "I Stand Here Ironing" and reaches an optimistic conclusion:

    > But the child did not grow to be a mere victim of the kind so many of us these days are rather eager to recognize—a hopeless tangle of psychopathology. The growing child, even in her troubled moments, revealed herself to be persistent, demanding, and observant. In the complaints we make, in the "symptoms" we develop, we reveal our strengths as well as our weaknesses. The hurt child could summon her intelligence, exercise her will, smile and make others smile.

    Do you agree with Coles's psychological evaluation of Emily? Do you find the story's ending as essentially uplifting, as he seems to? Why or why not?

Related Works: "Everyday Use" (p. 346), "Two Kinds" (p. 471), "Those Winter Sundays" (p. 672)

WRITING SUGGESTIONS: Setting

1. In "The Storm" and "I Stand Here Ironing," social constraints determined by the story's historical setting limit a woman's options. Explore the options each woman might reasonably exercise to break free of the limits that social institutions impose on her.
2. Write an essay in which you consider how "The Secret Lion" would be different if it took place not near the border between Mexico and the United States but in a different geographical and physical setting. In your essay, examine the changes (in plot development as well as in the story's conflicts, and the characters' reactions) that might occur as a result of the change in setting.

3. Select a story from another chapter, and write an essay in which you consider how setting affects its plot—for example, how it creates conflict or crisis, how it forces characters to act, or how it determines how the plot is resolved.
4. "The Storm" uses rich descriptive language to create a mood that dominates the story. This is also true of Charlotte Perkins Gilman's "The Yellow Wallpaper" (p. 315). Compare the use of such language in these two stories. Or, explicate a short passage from each story, and then compare the two passages, analyzing the two writers' use of language to create a mood.

Chapter

12

Point of View

Richard Wright
AP Images/Robert Kradin

Chitra Banerjee Divakruni
San Francisco Chronicle/Hearst Newspapers/Getty Images

Edgar Allan Poe
AP Images

Learning Objectives

After reading this chapter, you will be able to. . .

- Define point of view as it relates to fiction.
- Describe how a first-person point of view functions in fiction.
- Outline the types of irony represented in a work of fiction with first-person narrators.

- Recognize different points of view—including first-person, omniscient, limited omniscient, and objective—in a work of fiction.
- Describe how point of view affects the plot of a specific work of fiction.

One of the first choices writers make is who tells the story. This choice determines the story's **point of view**—the narrator's perspective in relation to the events in the story. The implications of this choice are far-reaching. Point of view colors everything, from readers' reactions to the characters to their understanding of the plot.

Consider the following scenario. Five people witness a crime and are questioned by the police. Their stories agree on certain points: a crime was committed, a body was found, and the crime occurred at noon. But in other ways their stories are different. The man who fled the scene was either tall or of average height; his hair was either dark or light; he either was carrying an object or was empty-handed. The events that led up to the crime and even the description of the crime itself are markedly different, depending on who tells the story. Thus, the **narrator**—the person telling the story—determines what details are included in the story and how they are arranged—in short, the plot. In addition, the perspective of the narrator affects the story's style, language, and themes.

The narrator of a work of fiction is not the same as the writer—even when a writer uses the first-person *I*. Writers create narrators to tell their stories. Often the personalities and opinions of narrators are far different from those of the author. The term **persona**—which literally means "mask"—is used for such narrators. By assuming this mask, a writer expands the creative possibilities of a work.

When deciding on a point of view for a work of fiction, a writer can choose to tell the story either in the **first person** or in the **third person**.

First-Person Narrators

Sometimes the narrator is a character who uses the **first person** (*I* or sometimes *we*) to tell the story. Often this narrator is a **major character**—Sammy in John Updike's "A&P" (p. 179) and the boy in James Joyce's "Araby" (p. 296), for example—who tells the story and is the focus of that story. Sometimes, however, a first-person narrator tells a story that is primarily about someone else. Such a narrator may be a **minor character** who plays a relatively small part in the story or simply an **observer** who reports events experienced or related by others. The narrator of William Faulkner's "A Rose for Emily" (p. 166), for example, is an unidentified witness to the story's events. By using *we* instead of *I*, this narrator speaks on behalf of all the town's residents, expressing their shared views of their neighbor, Emily Grierson, as the following excerpt illustrates:

> We did not say she was crazy then. We believed she had to do that. We remembered all the young men her father had driven away, and we knew that with nothing left, she would have to cling to that which had robbed her, as people will.

Writers gain several advantages when they use first-person narrators. First, they are able to present incidents convincingly. Readers are more willing to accept a statement like "My sister changed a lot after that day" than they are the impersonal observations of a third-person narrator. The first-person narrator also simplifies a writer's task of selecting details. Only the events and details that the narrator could have actually observed or experienced can be introduced into the story.

Another major advantage of first-person narrators is that their restricted view can create **irony**—a discrepancy between what is said and what readers believe to be true. Irony may be *dramatic*, *situational*, or *verbal*. **Dramatic irony** occurs when a narrator (or a character) perceives less than readers do; **situational irony** occurs when what happens is at odds with what readers are led to expect; **verbal irony** occurs when the narrator says one thing but actually means another.

"Gryphon," by Charles Baxter (p. 191), illustrates all three kinds of irony. Baxter creates **dramatic irony** when he has his main character see less than readers do. For example, at the end of the story, the young boy does not yet realize what readers already know—that he has learned more from Miss Ferenczi's way of teaching than from Mr. Hibler's. The setting of the story—a conventional school—creates **situational irony** because it contrasts with the unexpected events that unfold there. In addition, many of the narrator's comments create **verbal irony** because they convey the opposite of their literal meaning. At the end of the story, for example, after the substitute, Miss Ferenczi, has been fired, the narrator relates another teacher's comment that life will now return to "normal" and that their regular teacher will soon return to test them on their "knowledge." This comment is ironic considering all Miss Ferenczi has done to redefine the narrator's ideas about "normal" education and about "knowledge."

Unreliable Narrators

Sometimes first-person narrators are self-serving, mistaken, confused, unstable, or even insane. These **unreliable narrators**, whether intentionally or unintentionally, misrepresent events and misdirect readers. In Edgar Allan Poe's "The Cask of Amontillado" (p. 258), for example, the narrator, Montresor, tells his story to justify a crime he committed fifty years before. Montresor's version of what happened is not accurate, and perceptive readers know it: his obvious self-deception, his sadistic manipulation of Fortunato, his detached description of the cold-blooded murder, and his lack of remorse lead readers to question his sanity and, therefore, to distrust his version of events. This distrust creates an ironic distance between readers and narrator.

The narrator of Charlotte Perkins Gilman's "The Yellow Wallpaper" (p. 315) is also an unreliable narrator. Suffering from "nervous depression," she unintentionally distorts the facts when she says that the shapes in her bedroom wallpaper are changing and moving. Moreover, she does not realize what is wrong with her or why, or how her husband's "good intentions" are hurting her. Readers, however, see the disparity between the narrator's interpretation of events and their own, and this irony enriches their understanding of the story.

Some narrators are unreliable because they are naive. Because they are immature, sheltered, or innocent of evil, these narrators are not aware of the significance of the events they are relating. Having the benefit of experience, readers interpret events differently from the way these narrators do. When we read a passage by a child narrator—such as the following one from J. D. Salinger's classic 1951 novel *The Catcher in the Rye*—we are aware of the narrator's innocence, and we know his interpretation of events is flawed:

> Anyway, I keep picturing all these little kids playing some game in this big field of rye and all. Thousands of little kids, and nobody's around—nobody big, I mean—except me. And I'm standing on the edge of some crazy cliff. What I have to do, I have to catch everybody if they start to go over the cliff—I mean if they're running and they don't look where they're going I have to come out from somewhere and catch them. I'd just be the catcher in the rye...

The irony in the preceding passage comes from our knowledge that the naive narrator, Holden Caulfield, cannot stop children from growing up. Ultimately, they all fall off the "crazy cliff" and mature into adults. Although Holden is not aware of the futility of trying to protect children from the dangers of adulthood, readers know that his efforts are doomed from the start.

A naive narrator's background or social class can also limit the ability to understand a situation. The narrator in Sherwood Anderson's 1922 short story "I'm a Fool," for example, lies to impress a rich girl he meets at a racetrack. At the end of the story, the boy regrets the fact that he lied, believing that if he had told the truth, he could have seen the girl again. The reader knows, however, that the narrator (a laborer at the racetrack) is deceiving himself because the social gap that separates him and the girl could never be bridged.

Keep in mind that all first-person narrators are, in a sense, "unreliable" because they present a situation as only one person sees it. When you read, you should look for discrepancies between a narrator's view of events and your own. Discovering that a story has an unreliable narrator enables you not only to question the accuracy of the narrative but also to recognize the irony in the narrator's version of events. In this way, you gain insight into the story and learn something about the writer's purpose.

Third-Person Narrators

Sometimes a writer uses the **third person** (*he*, *she*, and *they*) to tell the story from the point of view of a narrator who is not a character. Third-person narrators fall into three categories: **omniscient**, **limited omniscient**, and **objective**.

Omniscient Narrators

Some third-person narrators are **omniscient** (all-knowing) narrators, moving at will from one character's mind to another's. One advantage of omniscient narrators is that they have none of the naïveté, dishonesty, gullibility, or mental instability that can characterize first-person narrators. In addition, because omniscient narrators are not characters in the story, their perception is not limited to what any one character can observe or comprehend. As a result, they can present a more inclusive view of events and characters than first-person narrators can.

Omniscient narrators can also convey their attitude toward their subject matter. For example, the omniscient narrator in the South African writer Nadine Gordimer's 1989 short story "Once upon a Time" uses sentence structure, word choice, repetition, and sarcasm to express disdain for the scene being described:

> In a house, in a suburb, in a city, there were a man and his wife who loved each other very much and were living happily ever after. They had a little boy, and they loved him very much. They had a cat and a dog that the little boy loved very much. They had a car and a caravan trailer for holidays, and a swimming-pool which was fenced so that the little boy and his playmates would not fall in and drown. They had a housemaid who was absolutely trustworthy and an itinerant gardener who was highly recommended by the neighbors. For when they began to live happily ever after they were warned, by that wise old witch, the husband's mother, not to take on anyone off the street.

Occasionally, omniscient narrators move not only in and out of the minds of the characters but also in and out of a **persona** (representing the voice of the author) who speaks directly to readers. This narrative technique was popular with writers during the eighteenth century, when the novel was a new literary form. It permitted writers to present themselves as masters of artifice, able to know and control all aspects of experience. Few contemporary writers would give themselves the license that Henry Fielding does in the following passage from *Tom Jones* (1749):

> And true it was that [Mr. Alworthy] did many of these things; but had he done nothing more I should have left him to have recorded his own merit on some fair freestone over the door of that hospital. Matters of a much more extraordinary kind are to be the subject of this history, or I should grossly misspend my time in writing so voluminous a work; and you my sagacious friend, might with equal profit and pleasure travel through some pages which certain droll authors have been facetiously pleased to call *The History of England.*

A contemporary example of this type of omniscient point of view occurs in Ursula K. LeGuin's "The Ones Who Walk Away from Omelas." This story presents a description of a city that in the narrator's words is "like a city in a fairy tale." As the story proceeds, however, the description of Omelas changes, and the narrator's tone changes as well: "Do you believe? Do you accept the festival, the city, the joy? No? Then let me describe one more thing." By undercutting her own narrative, the narrator underscores the ironic theme of the story, which suggests that it is impossible for human beings to ever achieve an ideal society.

Limited Omniscient Narrators

Third-person narrators can have **limited omniscience**, focusing on only what a single character experiences. In other words, nothing is revealed that the character does not see, hear, feel, or think.

Limited omniscient narrators, like all third-person narrators, have certain advantages over first-person narrators. When a writer uses a first-person narrator, the narrator's personality and speech color the story, creating a personal or even an idiosyncratic narrative. Also, the first-person narrator's character flaws or lack of knowledge may limit their awareness of the significance of events. Limited omniscient narrators are more flexible: they take readers into a particular character's mind just as a first-person narrator does, but without the first-person narrator's subjectivity, self-deception, or naïveté. In the following example from Anne Tyler's "Teenage Wasteland" (1984), the limited omniscient narrator presents the story from the point of view of a single character, Daisy:

> Daisy and Matt sat silent, shocked. Matt rubbed his forehead with his fingertips. Imagine, Daisy thought, how they must look to Mr. Lanham: an overweight housewife in a cotton dress and a too-tall, too-thin insurance agent in a baggy, frayed suit. Failures, both of them—the kind of people who are always hurrying to catch up, missing the point of things that everyone else grasps at once. She wished she'd worn nylons instead of knee socks.

Here the point of view gives readers the impression that they are standing off to the side watching Daisy and her husband Matt. However, while we have the advantage of this objective view, we are also able to see into the mind of one character.

Objective Narrators

Third-person **objective narrators**, who tell a story from an objective (or dramatic) point of view, remain entirely outside the characters' minds. With objective narrators, events unfold the way they would in a play or a movie: narrators tell the story by presenting dialogue and recounting events; they do not reveal the characters' (or their own) thoughts or attitudes. Thus, they allow readers to interpret the actions of the characters without any interference. Ernest Hemingway uses the objective point of view in his short story "A Clean, Well-Lighted Place" (1933):

> The waiter took the brandy bottle and another saucer from the counter inside the café and marched out to the old man's table. He put down the saucer and poured the glass full of brandy.
>
> "You should have killed yourself last week," he said to the deaf man. The old man motioned with his finger. "A little more," he said. The waiter poured on into the glass so that the brandy slopped over and ran down the stem into the top saucer of the pile. "Thank you," the old man said. The waiter took the bottle back inside the café. He sat down at the table with his colleague again.

The story's narrator is distant, seemingly emotionless, and this perspective is consistent with the author's purpose: for Hemingway, the attitude of the narrator reflects the stunned, almost anesthetized condition of people in the post–World War I world.

Selecting an Appropriate Point of View

The main criterion writers use when they decide on a point of view from which to tell a story is how the point of view they select will affect their narrative. The passages that follow illustrate the options available to writers.

Limited Omniscient Point of View

In the following passage from the short story "Doe Season" (p. 378), David Michael Kaplan uses a third-person limited omniscient narrator to tell the story of Andy, a nine-year-old girl who is going hunting with her father for the first time:

> They were always the same woods, she thought sleepily as they drove through the early morning darkness—deep and immense, covered with yesterday's snowfall, which had frozen overnight. They were the same woods that lay behind her house, *and they stretch all the way to here,* she thought, *for miles and miles, longer than I could walk in a day, or a week even, but they are still the same woods.* The thought made her feel good: it was like thinking of God; it was like thinking of the space between here and the moon; it was like thinking of all the foreign countries from her geography book where even now, Andy knew, people were going to bed, while they—she and her father and Charlie Spoon and Mac, Charlie's eleven-year-old son—were driving deeper into the Pennsylvania countryside, to go hunting.
>
> They had risen long before dawn. Her mother, yawning and not trying to hide her sleepiness, cooked them eggs and French toast. Her father smoked a cigarette and flicked ashes into his saucer while Andy listened, wondering *Why doesn't he come?* and *Won't he ever come?* until at last a car pulled into the graveled drive and honked. "That will be Charlie Spoon," her father said; he always said "Charlie Spoon," even though his real name was Spreun, because Charlie was, in a sense, shaped like a spoon, with a large head and a narrow waist and chest.

Here the limited omniscient point of view has the advantage of allowing the narrator to focus on the thoughts, fears, and reactions of the child while at the same time giving readers information about Andy that she herself is too immature or unsophisticated to know. Rather than simply presenting the thoughts of the child (represented in the story by italics), the third-person narrator makes connections between ideas and displays a level of language and a degree of insight that readers would not accept from Andy as a first-person narrator. In addition, the limited omniscient perspective enables the narrator to maintain some distance.

First-Person Point of View (Child)

Consider how different the passage would be if it were narrated by nine-year-old Andy:

> "I like the woods," I thought. "They're big and scary. I wonder if they're the same woods that are behind my house. They go on for miles. They're bigger than I could walk in a day, or a week even." It was neat to think that while we were driving into the woods people were going to bed in other countries.
>
> When I woke up this morning, I couldn't wait to go hunting. My mother was cooking breakfast, but all I could think of was, "When will he come?" and "Won't he ever come?" Finally, I heard a car honk. "That will be Charlie Spoon," my father said. I think he called him "Charlie Spoon" because he thought Charlie was shaped like a big spoon.

As a first-person narrator, nine-year-old Andy must have the voice of a child; moreover, she is restricted to only those observations that a nine-year-old could reasonably make. Because of these limitations, the passage lacks the level of vocabulary, syntax, and insight necessary to develop the central character and the themes of the story. This point of view could succeed only if Andy's words established an ironic contrast between her naive sensibility and the reality of the situation.

First-Person Point of View (Adult)

The writer could have avoided these problems and still gained the advantages of using a first-person narrator by having Andy tell her story as an adult looking back on a childhood experience. (This technique is used by James Joyce in "Araby" [p. 296], Charles Baxter in "Gryphon" [p. 191], and Alberto Alvaro Ríos in "The Secret Lion" [p. 222].)

> "They are always the same woods," I thought sleepily as we drove through the early morning darkness—deep and immense, covered with yesterday's snowfall, which had frozen overnight. "They're the same woods that lie behind my house, and they stretch all the way to here," I thought. I knew that they stretched for miles and miles, longer than I could walk in a day, or even in a week but that they were still the same woods. Knowing this made me feel good: I thought it was like thinking of God; it was like thinking of the space between that place and the moon; it was like thinking of all the foreign countries from my geography book where even then, I knew, people were going to bed, while we—my father and I and Charlie Spoon and Mac, Charlie's eleven-year-old son—were driving deeper into the Pennsylvania countryside, to go hunting.
>
> We had risen before dawn. My mother, who was yawning and not trying to hide her sleepiness, cooked us eggs and French toast. My father smoked a cigarette and flicked ashes into his saucer while I listened, wondering, "Why doesn't he come?" and "Won't he ever come?" until at last a car pulled into our driveway and honked. "That will be Charlie Spoon," my father said. He always said "Charlie Spoon," even though his real name was Spreun, because Charlie was, in a sense, shaped like a spoon, with a large head and a narrow waist and chest.

Although this passage presents the child's point of view, it does not use a child's voice; the language and scope of the passage are too sophisticated for a child. By using a mature style, the adult narrator considers ideas that a child could not possibly understand, such as the symbolic significance of the woods. In so doing, however, he sacrifices the objectivity and detachment that characterize the third-person limited omniscient narrator of the original story.

Omniscient Point of View

The writer could also have used an omniscient narrator to tell his story. In this case, the narrator would be free to reveal and comment not only on Andy's thoughts but also on those of her father, and possibly even on the thoughts of her mother and Charlie Spoon.

In the following passage, the omniscient narrator interprets the behaviour of the characters and tells what each one is thinking.

> They were always the same woods, she thought sleepily as they drove through the early morning darkness—deep and immense, covered with yesterday's snowfall, which had frozen overnight. They were the same woods that lay behind her house, and they stretch all the way to here, she thought, for miles and miles, longer than I could walk in a day, or a week even, but they are still the same woods.
>
> They had risen before dawn. The mother, yawning and not trying to hide her sleepiness, cooked them eggs and French toast. She looked at her husband and her daughter and wondered if she was doing the right thing by allowing them to go hunting together. "After all," she thought, "he's not the most careful person. Will he watch her? Make sure that no harm comes to her?"
>
> The father smoked a cigarette and flicked ashes into his saucer. He was listening to the sounds of the early morning. "I know everything will be all right," he thought. "It's about time Andy went hunting. When I was her age...." Andy listened, wondering Why doesn't he come? and Won't he ever come? until at last a car pulled into the graveled drive and honked. Suddenly the father cocked his head and said, "That will be Charlie Spoon."
>
> Andy thought it was funny that her father called Charlie "Spoon" even though his real name was Spreun, because Charlie was, in a sense, shaped like a spoon, with a large head and a narrow waist and chest.

Certainly this point of view has its advantages; for example, the wide scope of this perspective provides a great deal of information about the characters. However, the use of an omniscient point of view deprives the story of its focus on Andy and her unique perspective.

Objective Point of View

Finally, the writer could have used an objective narrator. This point of view would eliminate all interpretation by the narrator and force readers to make judgments solely based on what the characters say and do.

> Andy sat sleepily staring into her cereal. She played with the dry flakes of bran as they floated in the surface of the milk.
>
> Andy's mother, yawning, cooked them eggs and French toast. She looked at her husband and her daughter, paused for a second, and then went about what she was doing.

Andy's father smoked a cigarette and flicked ashes into his saucer. He looked out the window and said, "I wonder where Charlie Spoon is?"

Andy squirmed restlessly and repeatedly looked up at the clock that hung above the stove.

With an objective point of view, readers have to judge for themselves what motivates characters—much as they do in real life. The disadvantage of this point of view is that it creates a great deal of distance between the characters and the readers. Instead of gaining the intimate knowledge of Andy that the limited omniscient point of view provides—knowledge even greater than she herself has—readers must infer what she thinks and feels without any help from the narrator.

Checklist Selecting an Appropriate Point of View: Review

First-Person Narrators (use *I* or *WE*)

- *Major character telling their own story:* "Every morning I lay on the floor in the front parlour watching her door." (James Joyce, "Araby")
- *Minor character as witness:* "And so she died.... We did not even know she was sick; we had long since given up trying to get information...." (William Faulkner, "A Rose for Emily")

Third-Person Narrators (use *HE*, *SHE*, and *THEY*)

- *Omniscient—able to move at will from character to character and comment about them:* "In a house, in a suburb, in a city, there were a man and his wife who loved each other very much...." (Nadine Gordimer, "Once upon a Time")
- *Limited omniscient—restricts focus to a single character:* "The wagon went on. He did not know where they were going." (William Faulkner, "Barn Burning")
- *Objective (dramatic)—simply reports the dialogue and the actions of characters:* "'You'll be drunk,' the waiter said. The old man looked at him. The waiter went away." (Ernest Hemingway, "A Clean, Well-Lighted Place")

Checklist Writing about Point of View

- What is the dominant point of view from which the story is told?
- Is the narrator a character in the story? If so, is the narrator a participant in the story's events or just a witness?
- Does the story's point of view create irony?
- If the story has a first-person narrator, is the narrator reliable or unreliable?

- If the story has a third-person narrator, is the narrator omniscient? Does the narrator have limited omniscience? Is the narrator objective?
- What are the advantages of the story's point of view? What are the disadvantages?
- Does the point of view remain consistent throughout the story, or does it shift?
- How might a different point of view change the story?

Source: AP Photo/Robert Kradin

RICHARD WRIGHT (1908–1960) was born near Natchez, Mississippi, the son of sharecroppers. He had little formal schooling but as a young man was a voracious reader, especially of naturalistic fiction. Relocating to Chicago in the late 1920s, Wright worked as a postal clerk until 1935, when he joined the Federal Writers' Project. Deeply troubled by the economic and social oppression of Black Americans, Wright joined the Communist Party in 1932, and his early poems and stories reflect a Marxist perspective. In 1944, he broke with the party because of its stifling effect on his creativity.

Wright began to reach a mainstream audience when a group of four long stories on the theme of racial oppression and violence was judged best manuscript in a contest sponsored by *Story* magazine; these stories were published as *Uncle Tom's Children* in 1938. Two years later, Wright published his most famous work, *Native Son*, an angry and brutal novel exploring the moral devastation wrought by a racist society. The autobiographical *Black Boy* was published in 1945. Wright eventually left the United States for Paris in protest against the treatment of Black people in his native country. His later work was concerned with national independence movements in Africa and elsewhere in the developing world.

The following story, published in the posthumous collection *Eight Men* (1961), is uncharacteristic of Wright's work in many ways—not least of which is that it is told through the eyes of a white protagonist.

Cultural Context In 1957, the year "Big Black Good Man" was written, President Dwight D. Eisenhower sent paratroopers to Little Rock, Arkansas, to forestall violence over desegregation of the public schools. The crisis began on September 2, when Governor Orval Faubus ordered the Arkansas National Guard to blockade Central High School in Little Rock to prevent the entrance of nine black students. On September 20, NAACP lawyers Thurgood Marshall and Wiley Brandon obtained an injunction from the federal district court that ordered the troops removed. On September 25, the students entered the school, escorted by members of the 101st Airborne Division of the United States Army.

Big Black Good Man (1957)

Through the open window Olaf Jenson could smell the sea and hear the occasional foghorn of a freighter; outside, rain pelted down through an August night, drumming softly upon the pavements of Copenhagen,[1] inducing drowsiness, bringing dreamy memory, relaxing the tired muscles of his work-wracked body. He sat slumped in a swivel chair with his legs outstretched and his feet propped atop an edge of his desk. An inch of white ash tipped the end of his brown cigar and now and then he inserted the end of the stogie[2] into his mouth and drew gently upon it, letting wisps of blue smoke eddy from the corners of his wide, thin lips. The watery gray irises behind the thick lenses of his eyeglasses gave him a look of abstraction, of absentmindedness, of an almost genial idiocy. He sighed, reached for his half-empty bottle of beer, and drained it into his glass and downed it with a long slow gulp, then licked his lips. Replacing the cigar, he slapped his right palm against his thigh and said half aloud:

"Well, I'll be sixty tomorrow. I'm not rich, but I'm not poor either ... Really, I can't complain. Got good health. Traveled all over the world and had my share of girls when I was young ... And my Karen's a good wife. I own my home. Got no debts. And I love digging in my garden in the spring ... Grew the biggest carrots of anybody last year. Ain't saved much money, but what the hell ... Money ain't everything. Got a good job. Night portering ain't too bad." He shook his head and yawned. "Karen and I could of had some children, though. Would of been good company ... 'Specially for Karen. And I could of taught 'em languages ... English, French, German, Danish, Dutch, Swedish, Norwegian, and Spanish ..." He took the cigar out of his mouth and eyed the white ash critically. "Hell of a lot of good language learning did me ... Never got anything out of it. But those ten years in New York were fun ... Maybe I could of got rich if I'd stayed in America ... Maybe. But I'm satisfied. You can't have everything."

Behind him the office door opened and a young man, a medical student occupying room number nine, entered.

"Good evening," the student said.

"Good evening," Olaf said, turning. 5

The student went to the keyboard and took hold of the round, brown knob that anchored his key.

"Rain, rain, rain," the student said.

"That's Denmark for you," Olaf smiled at him.

"This dampness keeps me clogged up like a drainpipe," the student complained.

"That's Denmark for you," Olaf repeated with a smile. 10

"Good night," the student said.

"Good night, son," Olaf sighed, watching the door close.

Well, my tenants are my children, Olaf told himself. Almost all of his children were in their rooms now ... Only seventy-two and forty-four were

---

[1] *Copenhagen:* The capital of Denmark.

[2] *stogie:* A cheap cigar.

missing … Seventy-two might've gone to Sweden … And forty-four was maybe staying at his girl's place tonight, like he sometimes did … He studied the pear-shaped blobs of hard rubber, reddish brown like ripe fruit, that hung from the keyboard, then glanced at his watch. Only room thirty, eighty-one, and one hundred and one were empty … And it was almost midnight. In a few moments he could take a nap. Nobody hardly ever came looking for accommodations after midnight, unless a stray freighter came in, bringing thirsty, women-hungry sailors. Olaf chuckled softly. Why in hell was I ever a sailor? The whole time I was at sea I was thinking and dreaming about women. Then why didn't I stay on land where women could be had? Hunh? Sailors are crazy …

But he liked sailors. They reminded him of his youth, and there was something so direct, simple, and childlike about them. They always said straight out what they wanted, and what they wanted was almost always women and whisky … "Well, there's no harm in that … Nothing could be more natural," Olaf sighed, looking thirstily at his empty beer bottle. No; he'd not drink any more tonight; he'd had enough; he'd go to sleep …

He was bending forward and loosening his shoelaces when he heard the office door crack open. He lifted his eyes, then sucked in his breath. He did not straighten; he just stared up and around at the huge black thing that filled the doorway. His reflexes refused to function; it was not fear; it was just simple astonishment. He was staring at the biggest, strangest, and blackest man he'd ever seen in all his life. 15

"Good evening," the black giant said in a voice that filled the small office. "Say, you got a room?"

Olaf sat up slowly, not to answer but to look at this brooding black vision; it towered darkly some six and a half feet into the air, almost touching the ceiling, and its skin was so black that it had a bluish tint. And the sheer bulk of the man! … His chest bulged like a barrel; his rocklike and humped shoulders hinted of mountain ridges; the stomach ballooned like a threatening stone; and the legs were like telephone poles … The big black cloud of a man now lumbered into the office, bending to get its buffalolike head under the door frame, then advanced slowly upon Olaf, like a stormy sky descending.

"You got a room?" the big black man asked again in a resounding voice.

Olaf now noticed that the ebony giant was well dressed, carried a wonderful new suitcase, and wore black shoes that gleamed despite the raindrops that peppered their toes.

"You're American?" Olaf asked him. 20

"Yeah, man; sure," the black giant answered.

"Sailor?"

"Yeah. American Continental Lines."

Olaf had not answered the black man's question. It was not that the hotel did not admit men of color; Olaf took in all comers—blacks, yellows, whites, and browns … To Olaf, men were men, and, in his day, he'd worked and eaten and slept and fought with all kinds of men. But this particular black man ... Well, he didn't seem human. Too big, too black, too loud, too direct, and probably too violent to boot ... Olaf's five feet seven inches scarcely reached the black giant's shoulder and his frail body weighed less, perhaps, than one of the man's gigantic legs ... There was something about the man's intense blackness and ungainly bigness that frightened and insulted Olaf; he felt as though this man had come here expressly to remind him how puny, how tiny, and how weak and how white he was. Olaf knew, while registering his reactions, that he was being irrational and foolish; yet, for the first time in his life, he was emotionally determined to refuse a man a room solely on the basis of the man's size and color ... Olaf's lips parted as he groped for the right words in which to couch his refusal, but the black giant bent forward and boomed:

"I asked you if you got a room. I got to put up somewhere tonight, man."

"Yes, we got a room," Olaf murmured.

And at once he was ashamed and confused. Sheer fear had made him yield. And he seethed against himself for his involuntary weakness. Well, he'd look over his book and pretend that he'd made a mistake; he'd tell this hunk of blackness that there was really no free room in the hotel, and that he was so sorry ... Then, just as he took out the hotel register to make believe that he was poring over it, a thick roll of American bank notes, crisp and green, was thrust under his nose.

"Keep this for me, will you?" the black giant commanded. "Cause I'm gonna get drunk tonight and I don't wanna lose it."

Olaf stared at the roll; it was huge, in denominations of fifties and hundreds. Olaf's eyes widened.

"How much is there?" he asked.

"Two thousand six hundred," the giant said. "Just put it into an envelope and write 'Jim' on it and lock it in your safe, hunh?"

The black mass of man had spoken in a manner that indicated that it was taking it for granted that Olaf would obey. Olaf was licked. Resentment clogged the pores of his wrinkled white skin. His hands trembled as he picked up the money. No; he couldn't refuse this man ... The impulse to deny him was strong, but each time he was about to act upon it something thwarted him, made him shy off. He clutched about desperately for an idea. Oh yes, he could say that if he planned to stay for only one night, then he could not have the room, for it was against the policy of the hotel to rent rooms for only one night ...

"How long are you staying? Just tonight?" Olaf asked.

"Naw. I'll be here for five or six days, I reckon," the giant answered off handedly.

"You take room number thirty," Olaf heard himself saying. "It's forty kroner a day."

"That's all right with me," the giant said.

With slow, stiff movements, Olaf put the money in the safe and then turned and stared helplessly up into the living, breathing blackness looming above him. Suddenly he became conscious of the outstretched palm of the black giant; he was silently demanding the key to the room. His eyes downcast, Olaf surrendered the key, marveling at the black man's tremendous hands … He could kill me with one blow, Olaf told himself in fear.

Feeling himself beaten, Olaf reached for the suitcase, but the black hand of the giant whisked it out of his grasp.

"That's too heavy for you, big boy; I'll take it," the giant said.

Olaf let him. He thinks I'm nothing … He led the way down the corridor, sensing the giant's lumbering presence behind him. Olaf opened the door of number thirty and stood politely to one side, allowing the black giant to enter. At once the room seemed like a doll's house, so dwarfed and filled and tiny it was with a great living blackness … Flinging his suitcase upon a chair, the giant turned. The two men looked directly at each other now. Olaf saw that the giant's eyes were tiny and red, buried, it seemed, in muscle and fat. Black cheeks spread, flat and broad, topping the wide and flaring nostrils. The mouth was the biggest that Olaf had ever seen on a human face; the lips were thick, pursed, parted, showing snow-white teeth. The black neck was like a bull's … The giant advanced upon Olaf and stood over him.

"I want a bottle of whiskey and a woman," he said. "Can you fix me up?"

"Yes," Olaf whispered, wild with anger and insult.

But what was he angry about? He'd had requests like this every night from all sorts of men and he was used to fulfilling them; he was a night porter in a cheap, water-front Copenhagen hotel that catered to sailors and students. Yes, men needed women, but this man, Olaf felt, ought to have a special sort of woman. He felt a deep and strange reluctance to phone any of the women whom he habitually sent to men. Yet he had promised. Could he lie and say that none was available? No. That sounded too fishy. The black giant sat upon the bed, staring straight before him. Olaf moved about quickly, pulling down the window shades, taking the pink coverlet off the bed, nudging the giant with his elbow to make him move as he did so … That's the way to treat 'im … Show 'im I ain't scared of 'im … But he was still seeking for an excuse to refuse. And he could think of nothing. He felt hypnotized, mentally immobilized. He stood hesitantly at the door.

"You send the whiskey and the woman quick, pal?" the black giant asked, rousing himself from a brooding stare.

"Yes," Olaf grunted, shutting the door.

Goddamn, Olaf sighed. He sat in his office at his desk before the phone. Why did *he* have to come here? … I'm not prejudiced … No, not at all … But … He couldn't think any more. God oughtn't make men as big and black as that … But what the hell was he worrying about? He'd sent women of all races to men of all colors … So why not a woman to the black giant? Oh, only if the man were small, brown, and intelligent-looking … Olaf felt trapped.

With a reflex movement of his hand, he picked up the phone and dialed Lena. She was big and strong and always cut him in for fifteen per cent instead of the usual ten per cent. Lena had four small children to feed and clothe. Lena was willing; she was, she said, coming over right now. She didn't give a good goddamn about how big and black the man was ...

"Why you ask me that?" Lena wanted to know over the phone. "You never asked that before ..."

"But this one is *big*," Olaf found himself saying.

"He's just a man," Lena told him, her voice singing stridently, laughingly over the wire. "You just leave that to me. You don't have to do anything. *I'll* handle 'im."

Lena had a key to the hotel door downstairs, but tonight Olaf stayed awake. He wanted to see her. Why? He didn't know. He stretched out on the sofa in his office, but sleep was far from him. When Lena arrived, he told her again how big and black the man was.

"You told me that over the phone," Lena reminded him.

Olaf said nothing. Lena flounced off on her errand of mercy. Olaf shut the office door, then opened it and left it ajar. But why? He didn't know. He lay upon the sofa and stared at the ceiling. He glanced at his watch; it was almost two o'clock ... She's staying in there a long time ... Ah, God, but he could do with a drink ... Why was he so damned worked up and nervous about a nigger and a white whore? ... He'd never been so upset in all his life. Before he knew it, he had drifted off to sleep. Then he heard the office door swinging creakingly open on its rusty hinges. Lena stood in it, grim and businesslike, her face scrubbed free of powder and rouge. Olaf scrambled to his feet, adjusting his eyeglasses, blinking.

"How was it?" he asked her in a confidential whisper.

Lena's eyes blazed.

"What the hell's that to you?" she snapped. "There's your cut," she said, flinging him his money, tossing it upon the covers of the sofa. "You're sure nosy tonight. You wanna take over my work?"

Olaf's pasty cheeks burned red.

"You go to hell," he said, slamming the door.

"I'll meet you there!" Lena's shouting voice reached him dimly.

He was being a fool; there was no doubt about it. But, try as he might, he could not shake off a primitive hate for that black mountain of energy, of muscle, of bone; he envied the easy manner in which it moved with such a creeping and powerful motion; he winced at the booming and commanding voice that came to him when the tiny little eyes were not even looking at him; he shivered at the sight of those vast and clawlike hands that seemed always to hint of death ...

Olaf kept his counsel. He never spoke to Karen about the sordid doings at the hotel. Such things were not for women like Karen. He knew instinctively that Karen would have been amazed had he told her that he was worried sick about a nigger and a blonde whore ... No; he couldn't talk to anybody about it, not even the hard-bitten[3] old bitch who owned the hotel. She was concerned

[3] *hard-bitten:* Stubborn, tough.

only about money; she didn't give a damn about how big and how black a client was as long as he paid his room rent.

Next evening, when Olaf arrived for duty, there was no sight or sound of the black giant. A little later after one o'clock in the morning he appeared, left his key, and went out wordlessly. A few moments past two the giant returned, took his key from the board, and paused.

"I want that Lena again tonight. And another bottle of whiskey," he said boomingly.

"I'll call her and see if she's in," Olaf said.

"Do that," the black giant said and was gone. 65

He thinks he's God, Olaf fumed. He picked up the phone and ordered Lena and a bottle of whiskey, and there was a taste of ashes in his mouth. On the third night came the same request: Lena and whiskey. When the black giant appeared on the fifth night, Olaf was about to make a sarcastic remark to the effect that maybe he ought to marry Lena, but he checked it in time ... After all, he could kill me with one hand, he told himself.

Olaf was nervous and angry with himself for being nervous. Other black sailors came and asked for girls and Olaf sent them, but with none of the fear and loathing that he sent Lena and a bottle of whiskey to the giant ... All right, the black giant's stay was almost up. He'd said that he was staying for five or six nights; tomorrow night was the sixth night and that ought to be the end of this nameless terror.

On the sixth night Olaf sat in his swivel chair with his bottle of beer and waited, his teeth on edge, his fingers drumming the desk. But what the hell am I fretting for? ... The hell with 'im ... Olaf sat and dozed. Occasionally he'd awaken and listen to the foghorns of freighters sounding as ships came and went in the misty Copenhagen harbor. He was half asleep when he felt a rough hand on his shoulder. He blinked his eyes open. The giant, black and vast and powerful, all but blotted out his vision.

"What I owe you, man?" the giant demanded. "And I want my money."

"Sure," Olaf said, relieved, but filled as always with fear of this living wall of black flesh. 70

With fumbling hands, he made out the bill and received payment, then gave the giant his roll of money, laying it on the desk so as not to let his hands touch the flesh of the black mountain. Well, his ordeal was over. It was past two o'clock in the morning. Olaf even managed a wry smile and muttered a guttural "Thanks" for the generous tip that the giant tossed him.

Then a strange tension entered the office. The office door was shut and Olaf was alone with the black mass of power, yearning for it to leave. But the black mass of power stood still, immobile, looking down at Olaf. And Olaf could not, for the life of him, guess at what was transpiring in that mysterious black mind. The two of them simply stared at each other for a full two minutes, the giant's tiny little beady eyes blinking slowly as they seemed to measure and search Olaf's face. Olaf's vision dimmed for a second as terror seized him and he could feel a flush of heat overspread his body. Then Olaf sucked in his breath as the devil of blackness commanded:

"Stand up!"

Olaf was paralyzed. Sweat broke on his face. His worst premonitions about this black beast were coming true. This evil blackness was about to attack him, maybe kill him … Slowly Olaf shook his head, his terror permitting him to breathe:

"What're you talking about?" 75

"Stand up, I say!" the black giant bellowed.

As though hypnotized, Olaf tried to rise; then he felt the black paw of the beast helping him roughly to his feet.

They stood an inch apart. Olaf's pasty-white features were glued to the giant's swollen black face. The ebony ensemble of eyes and nose and mouth and cheeks looked down at Olaf, silently; then, with a slow and deliberate movement of his gorillalike arms, he lifted his mammoth hands to Olaf's throat. Olaf had long known and felt that this dreadful moment was coming; he felt trapped in a nightmare. He could not move. He wanted to scream, but could find no words. His lips refused to open; his tongue felt icy and inert. Then he knew that his end had come when the giant's black fingers slowly, softly encircled his throat while a horrible grin of delight broke out on the sooty face … Olaf lost control of the reflexes of his body and he felt a hot stickiness flooding his underwear … He stared without breathing, gazing into the grinning blackness of the face that was bent over him, feeling the black fingers caressing his throat and waiting to feel the sharp, stinging ache and pain of the bones in his neck being snapped, crushed … *He knew all along that I hated 'im … Yes, and now he's going to kill me for it,* Olaf told himself with despair.

The black fingers still circled Olaf's neck, not closing, but gently massaging it, as it were, moving to and fro, while the obscene face grinned into his. Olaf could feel the giant's warm breath blowing on his eyelashes and he felt like a chicken about to have its neck wrung and its body tossed to flip and flap dyingly in the dust of the barnyard … Then suddenly the black giant withdrew his fingers from Olaf's neck and stepped back a pace, still grinning. Olaf sighed, trembling, his body seeming to shrink; he waited. Shame sheeted him for the hot wetness that was in his trousers. *Oh, God, he's teasing me … He's showing me how easily he can kill me …* He swallowed, waiting, his eyes stones of gray.

The giant's barrel-like chest gave forth a low, rumbling chuckle of delight. 80

"You laugh?" Olaf asked whimperingly.

"Sure I laugh," the giant shouted.

"Please don't hurt me," Olaf managed to say.

"I wouldn't hurt you, boy," the giant said in a tone of mockery. "So long."

And he was gone. Olaf fell limply into the swivel chair and fought off losing consciousness. Then he wept. *He was showing me how easily he could kill* me … He made me shake with terror and then laughed and left … Slowly, Olaf recovered, stood, then gave vent to a string of curses: 85

"Goddamn 'im! My gun's right there in the desk drawer; I should of shot 'im. Jesus, I hope the ship he's on sinks … I hope he drowns and the sharks eat 'im …"

Later, he thought of going to the police, but sheer shame kept him back; and, anyway, the giant was probably on board his ship by now. And he had to get home and clean himself. Oh, Lord, what could he tell Karen? Yes, he would say that his stomach had been upset … He'd change clothes and return to work. He phoned the hotel owner that he was ill and wanted an hour off; the old bitch said that she was coming right over and that poor Olaf could have the evening off.

Olaf went home and lied to Karen. Then he lay awake the rest of the night dreaming of revenge. He saw that freighter on which the giant was sailing; he saw it springing a dangerous leak and saw a torrent of sea water flooding, gushing into all the compartments of the ship until it found the bunk in which the black giant slept. Ah, yes, the foamy, surging waters would surprise that sleeping black bastard of a giant and he would drown, gasping and choking like a trapped rat, his tiny eyes bulging until they glittered red, the bitter water of the sea pounding his lungs until they ached and finally burst … The ship would sink slowly to the bottom of the cold, black, silent depths of the sea and a shark, a *white* one, would glide aimlessly about the shut portholes until it found an open one and it would slither inside and nose about until it found that swollen, rotting, stinking carcass of the black beast and it would then begin to nibble at the decomposing mass of tarlike flesh, eating the bones clean … Olaf always pictured the giant's bones as being jet black and shining.

Once or twice, during these fantasies of cannibalistic revenge, Olaf felt a little guilty about all the many innocent people, women and children, all white and blonde, who would have to go down into watery graves in order that that white shark could devour the evil giant's black flesh … But, despite feelings of remorse, the fantasy lived persistently on, and when Olaf found himself alone, it would crowd and cloud his mind to the exclusion of all else, affording him the only revenge he knew. To make me suffer just for the pleasure of it, he fumed. Just to show me how strong he was … Olaf learned how to hate, and got pleasure out of it.

Summer fled on wings of rain. Autumn flooded Denmark with color. Winter made rain and snow fall on Copenhagen. Finally spring came, bringing violets and roses. Olaf kept to his job. For many months he feared the return of the black giant. But when a year had passed and the giant had not put in an appearance, Olaf allowed his revenge fantasy to peter out, indulging in it only when recalling the shame that the black monster had made him feel. 90

Then one rainy August night, a year later, Olaf sat drowsing at his desk, his bottle of beer before him, tilting back in his swivel chair, his feet resting atop a corner of his desk, his mind mulling over the more pleasant aspects of his life. The office door cracked open. Olaf glanced boredly up and around. His heart jumped and skipped a beat. The black nightmare of terror and shame that he had hoped that he had lost forever was again upon him … Resplendently dressed, suitcase in hand, the black looming mountain filled the doorway. Olaf's thin lips parted and a silent moan, half a curse, escaped them.

"Hi," the black giant boomed from the doorway.

Olaf could not reply. But a sudden resolve swept him: this time he would even the score. If this black beast came within so much as three feet of him, he would snatch his gun out of the drawer and shoot him dead, so help him God …

"No rooms tonight," Olaf heard himself announcing in a determined voice.

The black giant grinned; it was the same infernal grimace of delight and triumph that he had had when his damnable black fingers had been around his throat …

"Don't want no room tonight," the giant announced.

"Then what are you doing here?" Olaf asked in a loud but tremulous voice.

The giant swept toward Olaf and stood over him; and Olaf could not move, despite his oath to kill him …

"What do you want then?" Olaf demanded once more, ashamed that he could not lift his voice above a whisper.

The giant still grinned, then tossed what seemed the same suitcase upon Olaf's sofa and bent over it; he zippered it open with a sweep of his clawlike hand and rummaged in it, drawing forth a flat, gleaming white object done up in glowing cellophane. Olaf watched with lowered lids, wondering what trick was now being played on him. Then, before he could defend himself, the giant had whirled and again long, black, snakelike fingers were encircling Olaf's throat … Olaf stiffened, his right hand clawing blindly for the drawer where the gun was kept. But the giant was quick.

"Wait," he bellowed, pushing Olaf back from the desk.

The giant turned quickly to the sofa and, still holding his fingers in a wide circle that seemed a noose for Olaf's neck, he inserted the rounded fingers into the top of the flat, gleaming object. Olaf had the drawer open and his sweaty fingers were now touching the gun, but something made him freeze. The flat, gleaming object was a shirt and the black giant's circled fingers were fitting themselves into its neck …

"A perfect fit!" the giant shouted.

Olaf stared, trying to understand. His fingers loosened about the gun. A mixture of a laugh and a curse struggled in him. He watched the giant plunge his hands into the suitcase and pull out other flat, gleaming shirts.

"One, two, three, four, five, six," the black giant intoned, his voice crisp and businesslike. "Six nylon shirts. And they're all yours. One shirt for each time Lena came … See, Daddy-O?"

The black, cupped hands, filled with billowing nylon whiteness, were extended under Olaf's nose. Olaf eased his damp fingers from his gun and pushed the drawer closed, staring at the shirts and then at the black giant's grinning face.

"Don't you like 'em?" the giant asked.

Olaf began to laugh hysterically, then suddenly he was crying, his eyes so flooded with tears that the pile of dazzling nylon looked like snow in the dead of winter. Was this true? Could he believe it? Maybe this too was a trick? But, no. There were six shirts, all nylon, and the black giant had had Lena six nights.

"What's the matter with you, Daddy-O?" the giant asked. "You blowing your top? Laughing and crying …"

Olaf swallowed, dabbed his withered fists at his dimmed eyes; then he realized that he had his glasses on. He took them off and dried his eyes and sat up. He sighed, the tension and shame and fear and haunting dread of his fantasy went from him, and he leaned limply back in his chair …

"Try one on," the giant ordered.

Olaf fumbled with the buttons of his shirt, let down his suspenders, and pulled the shirt off. He donned a gleaming nylon one and the giant began buttoning it for him.

"Perfect, Daddy-O," the giant said.

His spectacled face framed in sparkling nylon, Olaf sat with trembling lips. So he'd not been trying to kill me after all.

"You want Lena, don't you?" he asked the giant in a soft whisper. "But I don't know where she is. She never came back here after you left—"

"I know where Lena is," the giant told him. "We been writing to each other. I'm going to her house. And, Daddy-O, I'm late." The giant zippered the suitcase shut and stood a moment gazing down at Olaf, his tiny little red eyes blinking slowly. Then Olaf realized that there was a compassion in that stare that he had never seen before.

"And I thought you wanted to kill me," Olaf told him. "I was scared of you …"

"Me? Kill you?" the giant blinked. "When?"

"That night when you put your fingers around my throat—"

"What?" the giant asked, then roared with laughter. "Daddy-O, you're a funny little man. I wouldn't hurt you. I like you. You a *good* man. You helped me."

Olaf smiled, clutching the pile of nylon shirts in his arms.

"You're a good man too," Olaf murmured. Then loudly, "You're a big black good man."

"Daddy-O, you're crazy," the giant said.

He swept his suitcase from the sofa, spun on his heel, and was at the door in one stride.

"Thanks!" Olaf cried after him.

The black giant paused, turned his vast black head, and flashed a grin.

"Daddy-O, drop dead," he said and was gone.

Reading and Reacting

1. Why do you suppose Wright presents events through Olaf's eyes? How would the story be different if Jim told it?
2. This story was published in 1957. What attitudes about race does Wright expect his American readers to have? Do these attitudes predispose readers to identify with Jim or with Olaf? Explain.

3. Why does Olaf dislike Jim? What does the narrator mean in paragraph 24 when he says that Jim's "intense blackness and ungainly bigness ... frightened and insulted Olaf"?
4. How do Jim's words and actions contribute to Olaf's fears? Are Olaf's reactions reasonable, or do you think he is overreacting?
5. The sailor's name is hardly mentioned in the story. Why not? List some words Wright uses to describe Jim. How do they affect your reaction to him?
6. Is the story's title ironic? In what other respects is the story ironic?
7. Why do you think Wright set the story in Copenhagen? Could it have been set in the United States in 1957?
8. What does Jim think of Olaf? Do you suppose he realizes the effect he has on him? How do you explain Jim's last comment?
9. **Journal Entry** What point does the story make about racial prejudice? Does Wright seem optimistic or pessimistic about race relations in the United States?
10. **Critical Perspective** In his article "The Short Stories: *Uncle Tom's Children, Eight Men*," Edward Margolies notes that "Big Black Good Man" was somewhat of a departure for Wright:

    "Big Black Good Man," which first appeared in *Esquire* in 1957, is the last short story Wright published in his lifetime. Possibly it is the last he ever wrote. In any event it represents a more traditional approach to storytelling in that Wright here avoids confining himself exclusively to dialogue. On the other hand, "Big Black Good Man" deviates from the usual Wright short story. For one thing, the narrative, by Wright's standards at least, is practically pointless. Scarcely anything "happens." There is no violence, practically no external narrative action, and no change of milieu.

    Do you agree that the story is "practically pointless"? If not, what point do you think the story makes?

Related Works: "The Cask of Amontillado" (p. 258), "The *Chicago Defender* Sends a Man to Little Rock" (p. 704), *Fences* (p. 1222)

Source: AP Images

EDGAR ALLAN POE (1809–1849) profoundly influenced many writers all over the world. His tales of psychological terror and the macabre, his hauntingly musical lyric poems, and his writings on the craft of poetry and short story writing affected the development of symbolic fiction, the modern detective story, and the gothic horror tale. In most of Poe's horror tales (as in "The Cask of Amontillado"), readers vicariously experience the story through the first-person narrator who tells the tale.

Poe was born in 1809, the son of a talented English-born actress who, deserted by her actor husband, died of tuberculosis before her son's third birthday. Although

Poe was raised in material comfort by foster parents, John and Frances Allan, in Richmond, Virginia, his life was increasingly uncertain: his foster mother loved him, but her husband became antagonistic. He kept the young Poe so short of money at the University of Virginia (and later at West Point) that Poe resorted to gambling to raise money for food and clothing. Finally, disgraced and debt-ridden, he left school.

Poe found work as a magazine editor, gaining recognition as a literary critic. In 1836, he married his frail thirteen-year-old cousin, Virginia Clemm. Poe produced many of his most famous stories and poems over the next few years, working feverishly to support his tubercular wife, but although his stories were widely admired, he never achieved financial success. His wife died in 1847. Less than two years after her death, Poe was found barely conscious on a Baltimore street; three days later, he was dead at age forty. To this day, the cause of Poe's death remains a mystery.

Cultural Context Throughout antiquity, catacombs, such as those in Poe's story, were used to bury the dead. Catacombs are underground cemeteries composed of passages with recesses for tombs. The early Christian catacombs of Rome, consisting of approximately forty known chambers located in a rough circle about three miles from the centre of the city, are the most extensive of all known catacombs. (Besides being used for burial, these catacombs were also used by early Christians as a refuge from persecution.) Funeral feasts were often celebrated in family vaults on the day of burial and on anniversary dates of the deaths of loved ones.

The Cask of Amontillado (1846)

The thousand injuries of Fortunato I had borne as I best could, but when he ventured upon insult I vowed revenge. You, who so well know the nature of my soul, will not suppose, however, that I gave utterance to a threat. *At length* I would be avenged; this was a point definitely settled—but the very definitiveness with which it was resolved precluded the idea of risk. I must not only punish but punish with impunity. A wrong is unredressed when retribution overtakes its redresser. It is equally unredressed when the avenger fails to make himself felt as such to him who has done the wrong.

It must be understood that neither by word nor deed had I given Fortunato cause to doubt my good will. I continued, as was my wont, to smile in his face, and he did not perceive that my smile *now* was at the thought of his immolation.

He had a weak point—this Fortunato—although in other regards he was a man to be respected and even feared. He prided himself on his connoisseurship in wine. Few Italians have the true virtuoso spirit. For the most part their enthusiasm is adopted to suit the time and opportunity, to practise imposture upon the British and Austrian *millionaires*. In painting and gemmary, Fortunato, like his countrymen, was a quack, but in the matter of old wines he was sincere. In this respect I did not differ from him materially;—I was skillful in the Italian vintages myself, and bought largely whenever I could.

It was about dusk, one evening during the supreme madness of the carnival season, that I encountered my friend. He accosted me with excessive warmth, for he had been drinking much. The man wore motley.[1] He had on a tight-fitting parti-striped dress, and his head was surmounted by the conical cap and bells. I was so pleased to see him that I thought I should never have done wringing his hand.

I said to him—"My dear Fortunato, you are luckily met. How remarkably well you are looking to-day. But I have received a pipe[2] of what passes for Amontillado,[3] and I have my doubts." 5

"How?" said he. "Amontillado? A pipe? Impossible! And in the middle of the carnival!"

"I have my doubts," I replied; "and I was silly enough to pay the full Amontillado price without consulting you in the matter. You were not to be found, and I was fearful of losing a bargain."

"Amontillado!"

"I have my doubts."

"Amontillado!" 10

"And I must satisfy them."

"Amontillado!"

"As you are engaged, I am on my way to Luchresi. If any one has a critical turn it is he. He will tell me—"

"Luchresi cannot tell Amontillado from Sherry."

"And yet some fools will have it that his taste is a match for your own."

"Come, let us go." 15

"Whither?"

"To your vaults."

"My friend, no; I will not impose upon your good nature. I perceive you have an engagement. Luchresi—"

"I have no engagement;—come." 20

"My friend, no. It is not the engagement, but the severe cold with which I perceive you are afflicted. The vaults are insufferably damp. They are encrusted with nitre."[4]

"Let us go, nevertheless. The cold is merely nothing. Amontillado! You have been imposed upon. And as for Luchresi, he cannot distinguish Sherry from Amontillado."

Thus speaking, Fortunato possessed himself of my arm; and putting on a mask of black silk and drawing a *roquelaire*[5] closely about my person, I suffered him to hurry me to my palazzo.

There were no attendants at home; they had absconded to make merry in honor of the time. I had told them that I should not return until the morning,

[1]*motley:* The many-colored attire of a court jester.

[2]*pipe:* In the United States and England, a cask containing a volume equal to 126 gallons.

[3]*Amontillado:* A pale, dry sherry; literally, a wine "from Montilla" (Spain).

[4]*nitre:* Mineral deposits.

[5]*roquelaire:* A short cloak.

and had given them explicit orders not to stir from the house. These orders were sufficient, I well knew, to insure their immediate disappearance, one and all, as soon as my back was turned.

I took from their sconces two flambeaux, and giving one to Fortunato, bowed him through several suites of rooms to the archway that led into the vaults. I passed down a long and winding staircase, requesting him to be cautious as he followed. We came at length to the foot of the descent, and stood together upon the damp ground of the catacombs of the Montresors.

The gait of my friend was unsteady, and the bells upon his cap jingled as he strode.

"The pipe," he said.

"It is farther on," said I; "but observe the white web-work which gleams from these cavern walls."

He turned towards me, and looked into my eyes with two filmy orbs that distilled the rheum of intoxication.

"Nitre?" he asked at length.

"Nitre," I replied. "How long have you had that cough?"

"Ugh! ugh! ugh!—ugh! ugh! ugh!—ugh! ugh! ugh!—ugh! ugh! ugh!—ugh! ugh! ugh!"

My poor friend found it impossible to reply for many minutes.

"It is nothing," he said at last.

"Come," I said, with decision, "we will go back; your health is precious. You are rich, respected, admired, beloved; you are happy, as once I was. You are a man to be missed. For me it is no matter. We will go back; you will be ill, and I cannot be responsible. Besides, there is Luchresi—"

"Enough," he said; "the cough is a mere nothing; it will not kill me. I shall not die of a cough."

"True—true," I replied; "and, indeed, I had no intention of alarming you unnecessarily—but you should use all proper caution. A draught of this Médoc[6] will defend us from the damps."

Here I knocked off the neck of a bottle which I drew from a long row of its fellows that lay upon the mould.

"Drink," I said, presenting him the wine.

He raised it to his lips with a leer. He paused and nodded to me familiarly, while his bells jingled.

"I drink," he said, "to the buried that repose around us."

"And I to your long life."

He again took my arm, and we proceeded.

"These vaults," he said, "are extensive."

"The Montresors," I replied, "were a great and numerous family."

"I forget your arms."

"A huge human foot d'or, in a field azure; the foot crushes a serpent rampant whose fangs are imbedded in the heel."

---

[6]*Médoc:* A red wine from the Médoc district, near Bordeaux, France.

"And the motto?"

"*Nemo me impune lacessit.*"[7]

"Good!" he said.

The wine sparkled in his eyes and the bells jingled. My own fancy grew warm with the Médoc. We had passed through long walls of piled skeletons, with casks and puncheons[8] intermingling, into the inmost recesses of the catacombs. I paused again, and this time I made bold to seize Fortunato by an arm above the elbow.

"The nitre!" I said; "see, it increases. It hangs like moss upon the vaults. We are below the river's bed. The drops of moisture trickle among the bones. Come, we will go back ere it is too late. Your cough—"

"It is nothing," he said; "let us go on. But first, another draught of the Médoc."

I broke and reached him a flagon of De Grâve.[9] He emptied it at a breath. His eyes flashed with a fierce light. He laughed and threw the bottle upwards with a gesticulation I did not understand.

I looked at him in surprise. He repeated the movement—a grotesque one.

"You do not comprehend?" he said.

"Not I," I replied.

"Then you are not of the brotherhood."

"How?"

"You are not of the masons."[10]

"Yes, yes," I said; "yes, yes."

"You? Impossible! A mason?"

"A mason," I replied.

"A sign," he said, "a sign."

"It is this," I answered, producing from beneath the folds of my *roquelaire* a trowel.

"You jest," he exclaimed, recoiling a few paces. "But let us proceed to the Amontillado."

"Be it so," I said, replacing the tool beneath the cloak and again offering him my arm. He leaned upon it heavily. We continued our route in search of the Amontillado. We passed through a range of low arches, descended, passed on, and descending again, arrived at a deep crypt, in which the foulness of the air caused our flambeaux rather to glow than flame.

At the most remote end of the crypt there appeared another less spacious. Its walls had been lined with human remains, piled to the vault overhead, in the fashion of the great catacombs of Paris. Three sides of this interior crypt

[7] *"Nemo me impune lacessit":* "No one insults me with impunity" (Latin); this is the legend on the royal coat of arms of Scotland.

[8] *puncheons:* Barrels.

[9] *De Grâve:* Correctly, "Graves," a light wine from the Bordeaux area.

[10] *masons:* Freemasons (members of a secret fraternity). The trowel is a symbol of their alleged origin as a guild of stonemasons.

were still ornamented in this manner. From the fourth side the bones had been thrown down, and lay promiscuously upon the earth, forming at one point a mound of some size. Within the wall thus exposed by the displacing of the bones, we perceived a still interior crypt or recess, in depth about four feet, in width three, in height six or seven. It seemed to have been constructed for no especial use within itself, but formed merely the interval between two of the colossal supports of the roof of the catacombs, and was backed by one of their circumscribing walls of solid granite.

It was in vain that Fortunato, uplifting his dull torch, endeavored to pry into the depth of the recess. Its termination the feeble light did not enable us to see.

"Proceed," I said; "herein is the Amontillado. As for Luchresi—" 70

"He is an ignoramus," interrupted my friend, as he stepped unsteadily forward, while I followed immediately at his heels. In an instant he had reached the extremity of the niche, and finding his progress arrested by the rock, stood stupidly bewildered. A moment more and I had fettered him to the granite. In its surface were two iron staples, distant from each other about two feet, horizontally. From one of these depended a short chain, from the other a padlock. Throwing the links about his waist, it was but the work of a few seconds to secure it. He was too much astounded to resist. Withdrawing the key I stepped back from the recess.

"Pass your hand," I said, "over the wall; you cannot help feeling the nitre. Indeed, it is *very* damp. Once more let me *implore* you to return. No? Then I must positively leave you. But I must first render you all the little attentions in my power."

"The Amontillado!" ejaculated my friend, not yet recovered from his astonishment.

"True," I replied; "the Amontillado."

As I said these words I busied myself among the pile of bones of which I have before spoken. Throwing them aside, I soon uncovered a quantity of building stone and mortar. With these materials and with the aid of my trowel,
I began vigorously to wall up the entrance of the niche. 75

I had scarcely laid the first tier of the masonry when I discovered that the intoxication of Fortunato had in a great measure worn off. The earliest indication I had of this was a low moaning cry from the depth of the recess. It was *not* the cry of a drunken man. There was a long and obstinate silence. I laid the second tier, and the third, and the fourth; and then I heard the furious vibrations of the chain. The noise lasted for several minutes, during which, that I might hearken to it with the more satisfaction, I ceased my labors and sat down upon the bones. When at last the clanking subsided, I resumed the trowel, and finished without interruption the fifth, the sixth, and the seventh tier. The wall was now nearly upon a level with my breast. I again paused, and holding the flambeaux over the mason-work, threw a few feeble rays upon the figure within.

A succession of loud and shrill screams, bursting suddenly from the throat of the chained form, seemed to thrust me violently back. For a brief moment

I hesitated, I trembled. Unsheathing my rapier, I began to grope with it about the recess; but the thought of an instant reassured me. I placed my hand upon the solid fabric of the catacombs, and felt satisfied. I reapproached the wall; I replied to the yells of him who clamoured. I re-echoed, I aided, I surpassed them in volume and in strength. I did this, and the clamourer grew still.

It was now midnight, and my task was drawing to a close. I had completed the eighth, the ninth and the tenth tier. I had finished a portion of the last and the eleventh; there remained but a single stone to be fitted and plastered in. I struggled with its weight; I placed it partially in its destined position. But now there came from out the niche a low laugh that erected the hairs upon my head. It was succeeded by a sad voice, which I had difficulty in recognizing as that of the noble Fortunato. The voice said—

"Ha! ha! ha!—he! he! he!—a very good joke, indeed—an excellent jest. We will have many a rich laugh about it at the palazzo—he! he! he!—over our wine—he! he! he!"

"The Amontillado!" I said.

"He! he! he!—he! he! he!—yes, the Amontillado. But is it not getting late? Will not they be awaiting us at the palazzo, the Lady Fortunato and the rest? Let us be gone."

"Yes," I said, "let us be gone."

"For the love of God, Montresor!"

"Yes," I said, "for the love of God."

But to these words I hearkened in vain for a reply. I grew impatient. I called aloud—

"Fortunato!"

No answer. I called again—

"Fortunato!"

No answer still. I thrust a torch through the remaining aperture and let it fall within. There came forth in return only a jingling of the bells. My heart grew sick on account of the dampness of the catacombs. I hastened to make an end of my labour. I forced the last stone into its position; I plastered it up. Against the new masonry I re-erected the old rampart of bones. For the half of a century no mortal has disturbed them. *In pace requiescat!*[11]

Reading and Reacting

1. Montresor cites a "thousand injuries" and an "insult" as his motives for murdering Fortunato. Given what you learn about the two men during the course of the story, what do you suppose the "injuries" and "insult" might be?
2. Is Montresor a reliable narrator? If not, what makes you question his version of events?

[11] *In pace requiescat:* "May he rest in peace" (Latin).

3. What is Montresor's concept of personal honour? Is it consistent or inconsistent with the values of contemporary American society? How relevant are the story's ideas about revenge and guilt to present-day society? Explain.
4. Does Fortunato ever understand why Montresor hates him? What is Fortunato's attitude toward Montresor?
5. What is the significance of Montresor's family coat of arms and motto? What is the significance of Fortunato's costume?
6. In what ways does Montresor manipulate Fortunato? What weaknesses does Montresor exploit?
7. Why does Montresor wait fifty years to tell his story? How might the story be different if he had told it the morning after the murder?
8. Why does Montresor wait for a reply before he puts the last stone in position? What do you think he wants Fortunato to say?
9. **Journal Entry** Does Poe's use of a first-person narrator make you more sympathetic toward Montresor than you would be if his story were told by a third-person narrator? Explain.
10. **Critical Perspective** In his discussion of this story in *Edgar Allan Poe: A Study of the Short Fiction*, Charles E. May says, "We can legitimately hypothesize that the listener is a priest and that Montresor is an old man who is dying and making final confession...."

    Do you agree or disagree with May's hypothesis? Do you think that Montresor has atoned for his sin? Who else could be listening to Montresor's story?

Related Works: "A Rose for Emily" (p. 166), "Porphyria's Lover" (p. 514), "The Wolf's Postscript to 'Little Red Riding Hood'" (p. 518)

WILLIAM FAULKNER (1897–1962) (picture and biography on p. 165) "Barn Burning" (1939) marks the first appearance of the Snopes clan in Faulkner's fiction. These ruthless, conniving, and unappealing poor white tenant farmers run roughshod over the aristocratic families of Yoknapatawpha County in three Faulkner novels: *The Hamlet* (1940), *The Town* (1957), and *The Mansion* (1959). According to Ben Wasson in *Count No Count*, Faulkner once told a friend that "somebody said I was a genius writer. The only thing I'd claim genius for is thinking up that name *Snopes*." In Southern literary circles, at least, the name "Snopes" still serves as a shorthand term for the graceless and greedy (but frequently successful) opportunists of the "New South."

Cultural Context Tenant farming is a system of agriculture in which workers (tenants) live on a landowner's property while providing labor. One form of tenant farming, which developed in the post–Civil War South, was known as *sharecropping*. Although white men, such as Ab Snopes, worked as sharecroppers, many of these workers were freed slaves. Sharecropping required a landowner to furnish land and housing, while a tenant supplied labor. In theory, sharecropping was supposed to benefit both the owners of the land and the people who farmed it. In practice, however, sharecropping was little better than slavery. At the end of the year, the sharecropper often owed so much money to the landowner for seeds, tools, and other supplies that he and his family would be tied to the land in a never-ending cycle of debt.

Barn Burning (1939)

The store in which the Justice of the Peace's court was sitting smelled of cheese. The boy, crouched on his nail keg at the back of the crowded room, knew he smelled cheese, and more: from where he sat he could see the ranked shelves close-packed with the solid, squat, dynamic shapes of tin cans whose labels his stomach read, not from the lettering which meant nothing to his mind but from the scarlet devils and the silver curve of fish—this, the cheese which he knew he smelled and the hermetic[1] meat which his intestines believed he smelled coming in intermittent gusts momentary and brief between the other constant one, the smell and sense just a little of fear because mostly of despair and grief, the old fierce pull of blood. He could not see the table where the Justice sat and before which his father and his father's enemy (*our enemy* he thought in that despair; *ourn! mine and hisn both! He's my father!*) stood, but he could hear them, the two of them that is, because his father had said no word yet:

"But what proof have you, Mr. Harris?"

"I told you. The hog got into my corn. I caught it up and sent it back to him. He had no fence that would hold it. I told him so, warned him. The next time I put the hog in my pen. When he came to get it I gave him enough wire to patch up his pen. The next time I put the hog up and kept it. I rode down to his house and saw the wire I gave him still rolled on to the spool in his yard. I told him he could have the hog when he paid me a dollar pound fee. That evening a nigger came with the dollar and got the hog. He was a strange nigger. He said, 'He say to tell you wood and hay kin burn.' I said, 'What?' 'That whut he say to tell you,' the nigger said. 'Wood and hay kin burn.' That night my barn burned. I got the stock out but I lost the barn."

"Where is the nigger? Have you got him?"

"He was a strange nigger, I tell you. I don't know what became of him." 5

"But that's not proof. Don't you see that's not proof?"

"Get that boy up here. He knows." For a moment the boy thought too that the man meant his older brother until Harris said, "Not him. The little one. The boy," and, crouching, small for his age, small and wiry like his father, in patched and faded jeans even too small for him, with straight, uncombed, brown hair and eyes gray and wild as storm scud, he saw the men between himself and the table part and become a lane of grim faces, at the end of which he saw the Justice, a shabby, collarless, graying man in spectacles, beckoning him. He felt no floor under his bare feet; he seemed to walk beneath the palpable weight of the grim turning faces. His father, stiff in his black Sunday coat donned not for the trial but for the moving, did not even look at him.

---

[1] *hermetic:* Canned.

He aims for me to lie, he thought, again with that frantic grief and despair. *And I will have to do hit.*

"What's your name, boy?" the Justice said.

"Colonel Sartoris Snopes," the boy whispered.

"Hey?" the Justice said. "Talk louder. Colonel Sartoris? I reckon anybody named for Colonel Sartoris in this country can't help but tell the truth, can they?" The boy said nothing. *Enemy! Enemy!* he thought; for a moment he could not even see, could not see that the Justice's face was kindly nor discern that his voice was troubled when he spoke to the man named Harris: "Do you want me to question this boy?" But he could hear, and during those subsequent long seconds while there was absolutely no sound in the crowded little room save that of quiet and intent breathing it was as if he had swung outward at the end of a grape vine, over a ravine, and at the top of the swing had been caught
in a prolonged instant of mesmerized gravity, weightless in time. 10

"No!" Harris said violently, explosively. "Damnation! Send him out of here!" Now time, the fluid world, rushed beneath him again, the voices coming to him again through the smell of cheese and sealed meat, the fear and despair and the old grief of blood:

"This case is closed. I can't find against you, Snopes, but I can give you advice. Leave this country and don't come back to it."

His father spoke for the first time, his voice cold and harsh, level, without emphasis: "I aim to. I don't figure to stay in a country among people who …" he said something unprintable and vile, addressed to no one.

"That'll do," the Justice said. "Take your wagon and get out of this country before dark. Case dismissed."

His father turned, and he followed the stiff black coat, the wiry figure walking a little stiffly from where a Confederate provost's man's[2] musket ball had taken him in the heel on a stolen horse thirty years ago, followed the two backs now, since his older brother had appeared from somewhere in the crowd, no taller than the father but thicker, chewing tobacco steadily, between the two lines of grim-faced men and out of the store and across the worn gallery and down the sagging steps and among the dogs and half-grown boys in the mild
May dust, where as he passed a voice hissed: 15

"Barn burner!"

Again he could not see, whirling; there was a face in a red haze, moonlike, bigger than the full moon, the owner of it half again his size, he leaping in the red haze toward the face, feeling no blow, feeling no shock when his head struck the earth, scrabbling up and leaping again, feeling no blow this time either and tasting no blood, scrabbling up to see the other boy in full flight and himself already leaping into pursuit as his father's hand jerked him back, the harsh, cold voice speaking above him: "Go get in the wagon."

It stood in a grove of locusts and mulberries across the road. His two hulking sisters in their Sunday dresses and his mother and her sister in calico and

[2]*provost's man's:* Military policeman's.

sunbonnets were already in it, sitting on and among the sorry residue of the dozen and more movings which even the boy could remember—the battered stove, the broken beds and chairs, the clock inlaid with mother-of-pearl, which would not run, stopped at some fourteen minutes past two o'clock of a dead and forgotten day and time, which had been his mother's dowry. She was crying, though when she saw him she drew her sleeve across her face and began to descend from the wagon. "Get back," the father said.

"He's hurt. I got to get some water and wash his …"

"Get back in the wagon," his father said. He got in too, over the tail-gate. His father mounted to the seat where the older brother already sat and struck the gaunt mules two savage blows with the peeled willow, but without heat. It was not even sadistic; it was exactly that same quality which in later years would cause his descendants to overrun the engine before putting a motor car into motion, striking and reining back in the same movement. The wagon went on, the store with its quiet crowd of grimly watching men dropped behind; a curve in the road hid it. *Forever* he thought. *Maybe he's done satisfied now, now that he has* … stopping himself, not to say it aloud even to himself. His mother's hand touched his shoulder.

"Does hit hurt?" she said.

"Naw," he said. "Hit don't hurt. Lemme be."

"Can't you wipe some of the blood off before hit dries?"

"I'll wash to-night," he said. "Lemme be, I tell you."

The wagon went on. He did not know where they were going. None of them ever did or ever asked, because it was always somewhere, always a house of sorts waiting for them a day or two days or even three days away. Likely his father had already arranged to make a crop on another farm before he … Again he had to stop himself. He (the father) always did. There was something about his wolf-like independence and even courage when the advantage was at least neutral which impressed strangers, as if they got from his latent ravening ferocity not so much a sense of dependability as a feeling that his ferocious conviction in the rightness of his own actions would be of advantage to all whose interest lay with his.

That night they camped, in a grove of oaks and beeches where a spring ran. The nights were still cool and they had a fire against it, of a rail lifted from a nearby fence and cut into lengths—a small fire, neat, niggard almost, a shrewd fire; such fires were his father's habit and custom always, even in freezing weather. Older, the boy might have remarked this and wondered why not a big one; why should not a man who had not only seen the waste and extravagance of war, but who had in his blood an inherent voracious prodigality with material not his own, have burned everything in sight? Then he might have gone a step farther and thought that that was the reason: that niggard blaze was the living fruit of nights passed during those four years in the woods hiding from all men, blue or gray, with his strings of horses (captured horses, he called them). And older still, he might have divined the true reason: that the element of fire spoke to some deep mainspring of his father's being, as the element of steel or of powder spoke to other men, as the one weapon for the preservation of integrity, else breath were not worth the breathing, and hence to be regarded with respect and used with discretion.

But he did not think this now and he had seen those same niggard blazes all his life. He merely ate his supper beside it and was already half asleep over his iron plate when his father called him, and once more he followed the stiff back, the stiff and ruthless limp, up the slope and on to the starlit road where, turning, he could see his father against the stars but without face or depth—a shape black, flat, and bloodless as though cut from tin in the iron folds of the frockcoat which had not been made for him, the voice harsh like tin and without heat like tin:

"You were fixing to tell them. You would have told him." He didn't answer. His father struck him with the flat of his hand on the side of the head, hard but without heat, exactly as he had struck the two mules at the store, exactly as he would strike either of them with any stick in order to kill a horse fly, his voice still without fear or anger: "You're getting to be a man. You got to learn. You got to learn to stick to your own blood or you ain't going to have any blood to stick to you. Do you think either of them, any man there this morning, would? Don't you know all they wanted was a chance to get at me because they knew I had them beat? Eh?" Later, twenty years later, he was to tell himself, "If I had said they wanted only truth, justice, he would have hit me again." But now he said nothing. He was not crying. He just stood there. "Answer me," his father said.

"Yes," he whispered. His father turned.

"Get on to bed. We'll be there tomorrow."

Tomorrow they were there. In the early afternoon the wagon stopped before a paintless two-room house identical almost with the dozen others it had stopped before even in the boy's ten years, and again, as on the other dozen occasions, his mother and aunt got down and began to unload the wagon, although his two sisters and his father and brother had not moved.

"Likely hit ain't fitten for hawgs," one of the sisters said.

"Nevertheless, fit it will and you'll hog it and like it," his father said. "Get out of them chairs and help your Ma unload."

The two sisters got down, big, bovine, in a flutter of cheap ribbons; one of them drew from the jumbled wagon bed a battered lantern, the other a worn broom. His father handed the reins to the older son and began to climb stiffly over the wheel. "When they get unloaded, take the team to the barn and feed them." Then he said, and at first the boy thought he was still speaking to his brother: "Come with me."

"Me?" he said.

"Yes," his father said. "You."

"Abner," his mother said. His father paused and looked back—the harsh level stare beneath the shaggy, graying, irascible brows.

"I reckon I'll have a word with the man that aims to begin tomorrow owning me body and soul for the next eight months."

They went back up the road. A week ago—or before last night, that is—he would have asked where they were going, but not now. His father had struck him before last night but never before had he paused afterward to explain why; it was as if the blow and the following calm, outrageous voice still rang, repercussed, divulging nothing to him save the terrible handicap of being young, the light weight of his few years, just heavy enough to prevent his soaring free of the world as it seemed to be ordered but not heavy enough to keep him footed solid in it, to resist it and try to change the course of its events.

Presently he could see the grove of oaks and cedars and the other flowering trees and shrubs, where the house would be, though not the house yet. They walked beside a fence massed with honeysuckle and Cherokee roses and came to a gate swinging open between two brick pillars, and now, beyond a sweep of drive, he saw the house for the first time and at that instant he forgot his father and the terror and despair both, and even when he remembered his father again (who had not stopped) the terror and despair did not return. Because, for all the twelve movings, they had sojourned until now in a poor country, a land of small farms and fields and houses, and he had never seen a house like this before. *Hit's big as a courthouse* he thought quietly, with a surge of peace and joy whose reason he could not have thought into words, being too young for that: *They are safe from him. People whose lives are a part of this peace and dignity are beyond his touch, he no more to them than a buzzing wasp: capable of stinging for a little moment but that's all; the spell of this peace and dignity rendering even the barns and stable and cribs which belong to it impervious to the puny flames he might contrive* ... this, the peace and joy, ebbing for an instant as he looked again at the stiff black back, the stiff and implacable limp of the figure which was not dwarfed by the house, for the reason that it had never looked big anywhere and which now, against the serene columned backdrop, had more than ever that impervious quality of something cut ruthlessly from tin, depthless, as though, sidewise to the sun, it would cast no shadow. Watching him, the boy remarked the absolutely undeviating course which his father held and saw the stiff foot come squarely down in a pile of fresh droppings where a horse had stood in the drive and which his father could have avoided by a simple change of stride. But it ebbed only for a moment, though he could not have thought this into words either, walking on in the spell of the house, which he could even want but without envy, without sorrow, certainly never with that ravening and jealous rage which unknown to him walked in the ironlike black coat before him: *Maybe he will feel it too. Maybe it will even change him now from what maybe he couldn't help but be.* 40

They crossed the portico. Now he could hear his father's stiff foot as it came down on the boards with clocklike finality, a sound out of all proportion to the displacement of the body it bore and which was not dwarfed either by the white door before it, as though it had attained to a sort of vicious and ravening minimum not to be dwarfed by anything—the flat, wide, black hat, the formal coat of broadcloth which had once been black but which had now that friction-glazed greenish cast of the bodies of old house flies, the lifted sleeve which was too large, the lifted hand like a curled claw. The door opened so promptly that the boy knew the Negro must have been watching them all the time, an old man with neat grizzled hair, in a linen jacket, who stood barring the door with his body, saying, "Wipe yo foots, white man, fo you come in here. Major ain't home nohow."

"Get out of my way, nigger," his father said, without heat too, flinging the door back and the Negro also and entering, his hat still on his head. And now the boy saw the prints of the stiff foot on the doorjamb and saw them appear on the pale rug behind the machinelike deliberation of the foot which seemed to bear (or transmit) twice the weight which the body compassed. The Negro was shouting "Miss Lula! Miss Lula!" somewhere behind them, then the boy, deluged as though by a warm wave by a suave turn of carpeted stair and a pendant glitter of chandeliers and a mute gleam of gold frames, heard the swift feet and saw her too, a lady—perhaps he had never seen her like before either—in a gray, smooth gown with lace at the throat and an apron tied at the waist and the sleeves turned back, wiping cake or biscuit dough from her hands with a towel as she came up the hall, looking not at his father at all but at the tracks on the blond rug with an expression of incredulous amazement.

"I tried," the Negro cried, "I tole him to ..."

"Will you please go away?" she said in a shaking voice. "Major de Spain is not at home. Will you please go away?"

His father had not spoken again. He did not speak again. He did not even look at her. He just stood stiff in the center of the rug, in his hat, the shaggy iron-gray brows twitching slightly above the pebble-colored eyes as he appeared to examine the house with brief deliberation. Then with the same deliberation he turned; the boy watched him pivot on the good leg and saw the stiff foot drag round the arc of the turning, leaving a final long and fading smear. His father never looked at it, he never once looked down at the rug. The Negro held the door. It closed behind them, upon the hysteric and indistinguishable woman-wail. His father stopped at the top of the steps and scraped his boot clean on the edge of it. At the gate he stopped again. He stood for a moment, planted stiffly on the stiff foot, looking back at the house. "Pretty and white, ain't it?" he said. "That's sweat. Nigger sweat. Maybe it ain't white enough yet to suit him. Maybe he wants to mix some white sweat with it." 45

Two hours later the boy was chopping wood behind the house within which his mother and aunt and the two sisters (the mother and aunt, not the two girls, he knew that; even at this distance and muffled by walls the flat loud voices of the two girls emanated an incorrigible idle inertia) were setting up the stove to prepare a meal, when he heard the hooves and saw the linen-clad man on a fine sorrel mare, whom he recognized even before he saw the rolled rug in front of the Negro youth following on a fat bay carriage horse—a suffused, angry face vanishing, still at full gallop, beyond the corner of the house where his father and brother were sitting in the two tilted chairs; and a moment later, almost before he could have put the axe down, he heard the hooves again and watched the sorrel mare go back out of the yard, already galloping again. Then his father began to shout one of the sisters' names, who presently emerged backward from the kitchen door dragging the rolled rug along the ground by one end while the other sister walked behind it.

"If you ain't going to tote, go on and set up the wash pot," the first said.

"You, Sarty!" the second shouted. "Set up the wash pot!" His father appeared at the door, framed against that shabbiness, as he had been against that other bland perfection, impervious to either, the mother's anxious face at his shoulder.

"Go on," the father said. "Pick it up." The two sisters stooped, broad, lethargic; stooping, they presented an incredible expanse of pale cloth and a flutter of tawdry ribbons.

"If I thought enough of a rug to have to git hit all the way from France I wouldn't keep hit where folks coming in would have to tromp on hit," the first said. They raised the rug.

"Abner," the mother said. "Let me do it."

"You go back and git dinner," his father said. "I'll tend to this."

From the woodpile through the rest of the afternoon the boy watched them, the rug spread flat in the dust beside the bubbling wash-pot, the two sisters stooping over it with that profound and lethargic reluctance, while the father stood over them in turn, implacable and grim, driving them though never raising his voice again. He could smell the harsh homemade lye[3] they were using; he saw his mother come to the door once and look toward them with an expression not anxious now but very like despair; he saw his father turn, and he fell to with the axe and saw from the corner of his eye his father raise from the ground a flattish fragment of field stone and examine it and return to the pot, and this time his mother actually spoke: "Abner. Abner. Please don't. Please, Abner."

Then he was done too. It was dusk; the whippoorwills had already begun. He could smell coffee from the room where they would presently eat the cold food remaining from the mid-afternoon meal, though when he entered the house he realized they were having coffee again probably because there was a fire on the hearth, before which the rug now lay spread over the backs of the two chairs. The tracks of his father's foot were gone. Where they had been were now long, water-cloudy scoriations resembling the sporadic course of a Lilliputian mowing machine.

It still hung there while they ate the cold food and then went to bed, scattered without order or claim up and down the two rooms, his mother in one bed, where his father would later lie, the older brother in the other, himself, the aunt, and the two sisters on pallets on the floor. But his father was not in bed yet. The last thing the boy remembered was the depthless, harsh silhouette of the hat and coat bending over the rug and it seemed to him that he had not even closed his eyes when the silhouette was standing over him, the fire almost dead behind it, the stiff foot prodding him awake. "Catch up the mule," his father said.

---

[3] *lye:* A soap made from wood ashes and water, unsuitable for washing fine fabrics.

When he returned with the mule his father was standing in the black door, the rolled rug over his shoulder. "Ain't you going to ride?" he said.

"No. Give me your foot."

He bent his knee into his father's hand, the wiry, surprising power flowed smoothly, rising, he rising with it, on to the mule's bare back (they had owned a saddle once; the boy could remember it though not when or where) and with the same effortlessness his father swung the rug up in front of him. Now in the starlight they retraced the afternoon's path, up the dusty road rife with honeysuckle, through the gate and up the black tunnel to the drive to the lightless house, where he sat on the mule and felt the rough warp of the rug drag across his thighs and vanish.

"Don't you want me to help?" he whispered. His father did not answer and now he heard again that stiff foot striking the hollow portico with that wooden and clocklike deliberation, that outrageous overstatement of the weight it carried. The rug, hunched, not flung (the boy could tell that even in the darkness) from his father's shoulder struck the angle of wall and floor with a sound unbelievably loud, thunderous, then the foot again, unhurried and enormous; a light came on in the house and the boy sat, tense, breathing steadily and quietly and just a little fast, though the foot itself did not increase its beat at all, descending the steps now; now the boy could see him.

"Don't you want to ride now?" he whispered. "We kin both ride now," the light within the house altering now, flaring up and sinking. *He's coming down the stairs now*, he thought. He had already ridden the mule up beside the horse block; presently his father was up behind him and he doubled the reins over and slashed the mule across the neck, but before the animal could begin to trot the hard, thin arm came round him, the hard, knotted hand jerking the mule back to a walk. 60

In the first red rays of the sun they were in the lot, putting plow gear on the mules. This time the sorrel mare was in the lot before he heard it at all, the rider collarless and even bareheaded, trembling, speaking in a shaking voice as the woman in the house had done, his father merely looking up once before stooping again to the hame[4] he was buckling, so that the man on the mare spoke to his stooping back:

"You must realize you have ruined that rug. Wasn't there anybody here, any of your women . . ." he ceased, shaking, the boy watching him, the older brother leaning now in the stable door, chewing, blinking slowly and steadily at nothing apparently. "It cost a hundred dollars. But you never had a hundred dollars. You never will. So I'm going to charge you twenty bushels of corn against your crop. I'll add it in your contract and when you come to the commissary you can sign it. That won't keep Mrs. de Spain quiet but maybe it will teach you to wipe your feet off before you enter her house again."

Then he was gone. The boy looked at his father, who still had not spoken or even looked up again, who was now adjusting the loggerhead in the hame.

---

[4]*hame:* Harness.

"Pap," he said. His father looked at him—the inscrutable face, the shaggy brows beneath which the gray eyes glinted coldly. Suddenly the boy went toward him, fast, stopping as suddenly. "You done the best you could!" he cried. "If he wanted hit done different why didn't he wait and tell you how? He won't git no twenty bushels! He won't git none! We'll gether hit and hide hit! I kin watch ..."

"Did you put the cutter back in that straight stock like I told you?" 65

"No, sir," he said.

"Then go do it."

That was Wednesday. During the rest of that week he worked steadily, at what was within his scope and some which was beyond it, with an industry that did not need to be driven nor even commanded twice; he had this from his mother, with the difference that some at least of what he did he liked to do, such as splitting wood with the half-size axe which his mother and aunt had earned, or saved money somehow, to present him with at Christmas. In company with the two older women (and on one afternoon, even one of the sisters), he built pens for the shoat and the cow which were a part of his father's contract with the landlord, and one afternoon, his father being absent, gone somewhere on one of the mules, he went to the field.

They were running a middle buster now, his brother holding the plow straight while he handled the reins, and walking beside the straining mule, the rich black soil shearing cool and damp against his bare ankles, he thought *Maybe this is the end of it. Maybe even that twenty bushels that seems hard to have to pay for just a rug will be a cheap price for him to stop forever and always from being what he used to be;* thinking, dreaming now, so that his brother had to speak sharply to him to mind the mule: *Maybe he even won't collect the twenty bushels. Maybe it will all add up and balance and vanish—corn, rug, fire; the terror and grief, the being pulled two ways like between two teams of horses—gone, done with for ever and ever.*

Then it was Saturday; he looked up from beneath the mule he was harnessing and saw his father in the black coat and hat. "Not that," his father said. "The wagon gear." And then, two hours later, sitting in the wagon bed behind his father and brother on the seat, the wagon accomplished a final curve, and he saw the weathered paintless store with its tattered tobacco- and patent-medicine posters and the tethered wagons and saddle animals below the gallery. He mounted the gnawed steps behind his father and brother, and there again was the lane of quiet, watching faces for the three of them to walk through. He saw the man in spectacles sitting at the plank table and he did not need to be told this was a Justice of the Peace; he sent one glare of fierce, exultant, partisan defiance at the man in collar and cravat now, whom he had seen but twice before in his life, and that on a galloping horse, who now wore on his face an expression not of rage but of amazed unbelief which the boy could not have known was at the incredible circumstance of being sued by one of his own tenants, and came and stood against his father and cried at the Justice: "He ain't done it! He ain't burnt ..." 70

"Go back to the wagon," his father said.

"Burnt?" the Justice said. "Do I understand this rug was burned too?"

"Does anybody here claim it was?" his father said. "Go back to the wagon." But he did not, he merely retreated to the rear of the room, crowded as that other had been, but not to sit down this time, instead, to stand pressing among the motionless bodies, listening to the voices:

"And you claim twenty bushels of corn is too high for the damage you did to the rug?"

"He brought the rug to me and said he wanted the tracks washed out of it. I washed the tracks out and took the rug back to him." 75

"But you didn't carry the rug back to him in the same condition it was in before you made the tracks on it."

His father did not answer, and now for perhaps half a minute there was no sound at all save that of breathing, the faint, steady suspiration of complete and intent listening.

"You decline to answer that, Mr. Snopes?" Again his father did not answer. "I'm going to find against you, Mr. Snopes. I'm going to find that you were responsible for the injury to Major de Spain's rug and hold you liable for it. But twenty bushels of corn seems a little high for a man in your circumstances to have to pay. Major de Spain claims it cost a hundred dollars. October corn will be worth about fifty cents. I figure that if Major de Spain can stand a ninety-five dollar loss on something he paid cash for, you can stand a five-dollar loss you haven't earned yet. I hold you in damages to Major de Spain to the amount of ten bushels of corn over and above your contract with him, to be paid to him out of your crop at gathering time. Court adjourned."

It had taken no time hardly, the morning was but half begun. He thought they would return home and perhaps back to the field, since they were late, far behind all other farmers. But instead his father passed on behind the wagon, merely indicating with his hand for the older brother to follow with it, and crossed the road toward the blacksmith shop opposite, pressing on after his father, overtaking him, speaking, whispering up at the harsh, calm face beneath the weathered hat: "He won't git no ten bushels neither. He won't git one. We'll . . ." until his father glanced for an instant down at him, the face absolutely calm, the grizzled eyebrows tangled above the cold eyes, the voice almost pleasant, almost gentle:

"You think so? Well, we'll wait till October anyway." 80

The matter of the wagon—the setting of a spoke or two and the tightening of the tires—did not take long either, the business of the tires accomplished by driving the wagon into the spring branch behind the shop and letting it stand there, the mules nuzzling into the water from time to time, and the boy on the seat with the idle reins, looking up the slope and through the sooty tunnel of the shed where the slow hammer rang and where his father sat on an upended cypress bolt, easily, either talking or listening, still sitting there when the boy brought the dripping wagon up out of the branch and halted it before the door.

"Take them on to the shade and hitch," his father said. He did so and returned. His father and the smith and a third man squatting on his heels inside the door were talking, about crops and animals; the boy, squatting too in the ammoniac dust and hoof-parings and scales of rust, heard his father tell a long and unhurried story out of the time before the birth of the older brother even when he had been a professional horsetrader. And then his father came up beside him where he stood before a tattered last year's circus poster on the other side of the store, gazing rapt and quiet at the scarlet horses, the incredible poisings and convolutions of tulle and tights and the painted leers of comedians, and said, "It's time to eat."

But not at home. Squatting beside his brother against the front wall, he watched his father emerge from the store and produce from a paper sack a segment of cheese and divide it carefully and deliberately into three with his pocket knife and produce crackers from the same sack. They all three squatted on the gallery and ate, slowly, without talking; then in the store again, they drank from a tin dipper tepid water smelling of the cedar bucket and of living beech trees. And still they did not go home. It was a horse lot this time, a tall rail fence upon and along which men stood and sat and out of which one by one horses were led, to be walked and trotted and then cantered back and forth along the road while the slow swapping and buying went on and the sun began to slant westward, they—the three of them—watching and listening, the older brother with his muddy eyes and his steady, inevitable tobacco, the father commenting now and then on certain of the animals, to no one in particular.

It was after sundown when they reached home. They ate supper by lamplight, then, sitting on the doorstep, the boy watched the night fully accomplish, listening to the whippoorwills and the frogs, when he heard his mother's voice: "Abner! No! No! Oh, God. Oh, God. Abner!" and he rose, whirled, and saw the altered light through the door where a candle stub now burned in a bottle neck on the table and his father, still in the hat and coat, at once formal and burlesque as though dressed carefully for some shabby and ceremonial violence, emptying the reservoir of the lamp back into the five-gallon kerosene can from which it had been filled, while the mother tugged at his arm until he shifted the lamp to the other hand and flung her back, not savagely or viciously, just hard, into the wall, her hands flung out against the wall for balance, her mouth open and in her face the same quality of hopeless despair as had been in her voice. Then his father saw him standing in the door.

"Go to the barn and get that can of oil we were oiling the wagon with," he said. The boy did not move. Then he could speak. 85

"What ..." he cried. "What are you ..."

"Go get that oil," his father said. "Go."

Then he was moving, running, outside the house, toward the stable: this the old habit, the old blood which he had not been permitted to choose for himself, which had been bequeathed him willy nilly and which had run for so long (and who knew where, battening on what of outrage and savagery and lust) before it came to him. *I could keep on*, he thought. *I could run on and on and never look back, never need to see his face again. Only I can't. I can't,* the rusted can in his hand now, the liquid sploshing in it as he ran back to the house and into it, into the sound of his mother's weeping in the next room, and handed the can to his father.

"Ain't you going to even send a nigger?" he cried. "At least you sent a nigger before!"

This time his father didn't strike him. The hand came even faster than the blow had, the same hand which had set the can on the table with almost excruciating care flashing from the can toward him too quick for him to follow it, gripping him by the back of his shirt and on to tiptoe before he had seen it quit the can, the face stooping at him in breathless and frozen ferocity, the cold, dead voice speaking over him to the older brother who leaned against the table, chewing with that steady, curious, sidewise motion of cows: 90

"Empty the can into the big one and go on. I'll catch up with you."

"Better tie him to the bedpost," the brother said.

"Do like I told you," the father said. Then the boy was moving, his bunched shirt and the hard, bony hand between his shoulderblades, his toes just touching the floor, across the room and into the other one, past the sisters sitting with spread heavy thighs in the two chairs over the cold hearth, and to where his mother and aunt sat side by side on the bed, the aunt's arms about his mother's shoulders.

"Hold him," the father said. The aunt made a startled movement. "Not you," the father said. "Lennie. Take hold of him. I want to see you do it." His mother took him by the wrist. "You'll hold him better than that. If he gets loose don't you know what he is going to do? He will go up yonder." He jerked his head toward the road. "Maybe I'd better tie him."

I'll hold him," his mother whispered. 95

"See you do then." Then his father was gone, the stiff foot heavy and measured upon the boards, ceasing at last.

Then he began to struggle. His mother caught him in both arms, he jerking and wrenching at them. He would be stronger in the end, he knew that. But he had no time to wait for it. "Lemme go!" he cried. "I don't want to have to hit you!"

"Let him go!" the aunt said. "If he don't go, before God, I am going up there myself!"

"Don't you see I can't?" his mother cried. "Sarty! Sarty! No! No! Help me, Lizzie!"

Then he was free. His aunt grasped at him but it was too late. He whirled, running, his mother stumbled forward on to her knees behind him, crying to the nearest sister: "Catch him, Net! Catch him!" But that was too late too, the sister (the sisters were twins, born at the same time, yet either of them now gave the impression of being, encompassing as much living meat and volume and weight as any other two of the family) not yet having begun to rise from the chair, her head, face, alone merely turned, presenting to him in the flying instant an astonishing expanse of young female features untroubled by any surprise even, wearing only an expression of bovine interest. Then he was out of the room, out of the house, in the mild dust of the starlit road and the heavy rifeness of honeysuckle, the pale ribbon unspooling with terrific slowness under his running feet, reaching the gate at last and turning in, running, his heart and lungs drumming, on up the drive toward the lighted house, the lighted door. He did not knock, he burst in, sobbing for breath, incapable for the moment of speech; he saw the astonished face of the Negro in the linen jacket without knowing when the Negro had appeared.

"De Spain!" he cried, panted. "Where's . . ." then he saw the white man too emerging from a white door down the hall. "Barn!" he cried. "Barn!"

"What?" the white man said. "Barn?"

"Yes!" the boy cried. "Barn!"

"Catch him!" the white man shouted.

But it was too late this time too. The Negro grasped his shirt, but the entire sleeve, rotten with washing, carried away, and he was out that door too and in the drive again, and had actually never ceased to run even while he was screaming into the white man's face.

Behind him the white man was shouting, "My horse! Fetch my horse!" and he thought for an instant of cutting across the park and climbing the fence into the road, but he did not know the park nor how high the vine-massed fence might be and he dared not risk it. So he ran on down the drive, blood and breath roaring; presently he was in the road again though he could not see it. He could not hear either: the galloping mare was almost upon him before he heard her, and even then he held his course, as if the very urgency of his wild grief and need must in a moment more find him wings, waiting until the ultimate instant to hurl himself aside and into the weed-choked roadside ditch as the horse thundered past and on, for an instant in furious silhouette against the stars, the tranquil early summer night sky which, even before the shape of the horse and rider vanished, stained abruptly and violently upward: a long, swirling roar incredible and soundless, blotting the stars, and he springing up and into the road again, running again, knowing it was too late yet still running even after he heard the shot and, an instant later, two shots, pausing now without knowing he had ceased to run, crying "Pap! Pap!", running again before he knew he had begun to run, stumbling, tripping over something and scrabbling up again without ceasing to run, looking backward over his shoulder at the glare as he got up, running on among the invisible trees, panting, sobbing, "Father! Father!"

At midnight he was sitting on the crest of a hill. He did not know it was midnight and he did not know how far he had come. But there was no glare behind him now and he sat now, his back toward what he had called home for four days anyhow, his face toward the dark woods which he would enter when breath was strong again, small, shaking steadily in the chill darkness, hugging himself into the remainder of his thin, rotten shirt, the grief and despair now no longer terror and fear but just grief and despair. *Father. My father*, he thought. "He was brave!" he cried suddenly, aloud but not loud, no more than a whisper:

"He was! He was in the war! He was in Colonel Sartoris' cav'ry!" not knowing that his father had gone to that war a private in the fine old European sense, wearing no uniform, admitting the authority of and giving fidelity to no man or army or flag, going to war as Malbrouck[5] himself did: for booty—it meant nothing and less than nothing to him if it were enemy booty or his own.

The slow constellations wheeled on. It would be dawn and then sunup after a while and he would be hungry. But that would be tomorrow and now he was only cold, and walking would cure that. His breathing was easier now and he decided to get up and go on, and then he found that he had been asleep because he knew it was almost dawn, the night almost over. He could tell that from the whippoorwills. They were everywhere now among the dark trees below him, constant and inflectioned and ceaseless, so that, as the instant for giving over to the day birds drew nearer and nearer, there was no interval at all between them. He got up. He was a little stiff, but walking would cure that too as it would the cold, and soon there would be the sun. He went on down the hill, toward the dark woods within which the liquid silver voices of the birds called unceasing—the rapid and urgent beating of the urgent and quiring heart of the late spring night. He did not look back.

Reading and Reacting

1. Is the third-person narrator of "Barn Burning" omniscient or is his omniscience limited? Explain.
2. What is the point of view of the story's italicized passages? What do readers learn from them? Do they create irony? How would the story have been different without these passages?
3. "Barn Burning" includes a great deal of dialogue. How would you characterize the level of diction of this dialogue? What information about various characters does it provide?
4. What conflicts are presented in "Barn Burning"? Are any of these conflicts avoidable? Which, if any, are resolved in the story? Explain.
5. Why does Ab Snopes burn barns? Are his actions are justified? Explain your reasoning.
6. What role does the Civil War play in "Barn Burning"? What does Ab Snopes's behavior during the war tell readers about him?
7. In the First and Second books of Samuel in the Old Testament, Abner was a relative of King Saul and commander in chief of his armies. Abner supported King Saul against David and was killed because of his own jealousy and rage. Why does Faulkner name Ab Snopes—loyal to no man, fighter "for booty, and father of the Snopes clan"—after this mighty biblical leader?
8. Why does Sarty Snopes insist that his father was brave? How does your knowledge of events unknown to the boy create irony?

[5]*Malbrouck:* A character in a popular eighteenth-century nursery rhyme about a famous warrior.

9. **Journal Entry** How would the story be different if it were told from Ab's point of view? From Sarty's? From the point of view of Ab's wife? From the point of view of a member of a community in which the Snopeses have lived?
10. **Critical Perspective** Critic Edmond L. Volpe argues in his article "'Barn Burning': A Definition of Evil" that "Barn Burning" is not really about the class conflict between the sharecropping Snopeses and landowners like the de Spains but rather about Sarty:

    > The story is centered upon Sarty's emotional dilemma. His conflict would not have been altered in any way if the person whose barn Ab burns had been a simple poor farmer, rather than an aristocratic plantation owner.... Sarty's struggle is against the repressive and divisive force his father represents. The boy's anxiety is created by his awakening sense of his own individuality. Torn between strong emotional attachment to the parent and his growing need to assert his own identity, Sarty's crisis is psychological and his battle is being waged far below the level of his intellectual and moral awareness.

    Do you believe "Barn Burning" is, as Volpe suggests, essentially a coming-of-age story, or do you believe it is about something else—class conflict, for example?

Related Works: "A Worn Path" (p. 370), "Baca Grande" (p. 532), "Daddy" (p. 571), "Digging" (p. 673), *Fences* (p. 1222)

San Francisco Chronicle/Hearst Newspapers/Getty Images

CHITRA BANERJEE DIVAKARUNI (1956–)

An internationally bestselling author, Divakaruni was born in Kolkata, India, but moved to the United States to attend graduate school. She currently teaches creative writing at the University of Houston. She has written books of short stories and poetry as well as novels for adult and younger readers. Her short story collections include *Arranged Marriage* (1994), which won the American Book Award and which includes "The Disappearance", and *The Unknown Errors of Our Lives* (2001). Most recently, Divakaruni published the novels *The Forest of Enchantments* (2019) and *The Last Queen* (2021). In addition to the American Book Award, Divakaruni has won multiple awards including Pushcart Prizes and the Light of India award, which recognizes the contributions of Indians around the world.

Cultural Context Arranged marriages, where family members seek matches for their children, are common across cultures throughout history. It is estimated that currently, over half the marriages worldwide are arranged. In some situations, an arranged marriage simply means that the families of the prospective couple do all the work of finding prospective mates for their children, but the young people have the power of veto. In other situations, particularly in some traditional cultures, the couple have no choice at all. Social and financial status, religious affiliation, age, and a sense of duty can determine whether a person has the ability to refuse an arranged marriage. Interestingly, divorce rates for arranged marriages are estimated to be about 4 percent, while in the United States, divorce rates are around 40 percent. Although some use this statistic to show that arranged marriages work, others say that it is simply a sign that those

who are in arranged marriages are disinclined to file for divorce. Or, as some critics point out, the women who lack money, education, and career skills simply have no options and are, for all intents, trapped in these relationships.

The Disappearance (1995)

At first when they heard about the disappearance, people didn't believe it.

Why, we saw her just yesterday at the Ram Ratan Indian Grocery, friends said, picking out radishes for pickling. And wasn't she at the Mountain View park with her little boy last week, remember, we waved from our car and she waved back, she was in that blue *salwaar-kameez*,[1] yes, she never did wear American clothes. And the boy waved too, he must be, what, two and a half? Looks just like her with those big black eyes, that dimple. What a shame, they said, it's getting so that you aren't safe anywhere in this country nowadays.

Because that's what everyone suspected, including the husband. Crime. Otherwise, he said to the investigating policeman (he had called the police that very night), how could a young Indian woman wearing a yellow-flowered *kurta*[2] and Nike walking shoes just *disappear?* She'd been out for her evening walk, she took one every day after he got back from the office. Yes, yes, always alone, she said that was her time for herself. (He didn't quite understand that, but he was happy to watch his little boy, play ball with him, perhaps, until she returned to serve them dinner.)

Did you folks have a quarrel, asked the policeman, looking up from his notepad with a frown, and the husband looked directly back into his eyes and said, No, of course we didn't.

Later he would think about what the policeman had asked, while he sat in front of his computer in his office, or while he lay in the bed which still seemed to smell of her. (But surely that was his imagination—the linen had been washed already.) He *had* told the truth about them not having a quarrel, hadn't he? (He prided himself on being an honest man, he often told his son how important it was not to lie, see what happened to Pinocchio's nose. And even now when the boy asked him where Mama was, he didn't say she had gone on a trip, as some of his friends' wives had advised him. I don't know, he said. And when the boy's thin face would crumple, want Mama, when she coming back, he held him in his lap awkwardly and tried to stroke his hair, like he had seen his wife do, but he couldn't bring himself to say what the boy needed to hear, *soon-soon*. I don't know, he said over and over.) 5

They hadn't really had a fight. She wasn't, thank God, the quarrelsome type, like some of his friends' wives. Quiet. That's how she was, at least around

---

[1] *salwaar-kameez:* Form of dress consisting of pajama-like pants, gathered at the waist and ankles; usually worn under a long, loose tunic.

[2] *kurta:* A long shirt, usually knee length, worn over drawstring trousers.

him, although sometimes when he came home unexpectedly he would hear her singing to her son, her voice slightly off-key but full and confident. Or laughing as she chased him around the family room, Mama's going to get you, get you, both of them shrieking with delight until they saw him. Hush now, she would tell the boy, settle down, and they would walk over sedately to give him his welcome-home kiss.

He couldn't complain, though. Wasn't that what he had specified when his mother started asking, When are you getting married, I'm getting old, I want to see a grandson before I die.

If you can find me a quiet, pretty girl, he wrote, not brash, like Calcutta girls are nowadays, not with too many western ideas. Someone who would be relieved to have her husband make the major decisions. But she had to be smart, at least a year of college, someone he could introduce to his friends with pride.

He'd flown to Calcutta to view several suitable girls that his mother had picked out. But now, thinking back, he can only remember her. She had sat, head bowed, jasmine plaited into her hair, silk sari draped modestly over her shoulders, just like all the other prospective brides he'd seen. Nervous, he'd thought, yearning to be chosen. But when she'd glanced up there had been a cool, considering look in her eyes. Almost disinterested, almost as though *she* were wondering if he would make a suitable spouse. He had wanted her then, had married her within the week in spite of his mother's protests (had she caught that same look?) that something about the girl just didn't feel *right*.

He was a good husband. No one could deny it. He let her have her way, indulged her, even. When the kitchen was remodeled, for example, and she wanted pink and gray tiles even though he preferred white. Or when she wanted to go to Yosemite Park instead of Reno, although he knew he would be dreadfully bored among all those bearshit-filled trails and dried-up waterfalls. Once in a while, of course, he had to put his foot down, like when she wanted to get a job or go back to school or buy American clothes. But he always softened his no's with a remark like, What for, I'm here to take care of you, or, You look so much prettier in your Indian clothes, so much more feminine. He would pull her onto his lap and give her a kiss and a cuddle which usually ended with him taking her to the bedroom. 10

That was another area where he'd had to be firm. Sex. She was always saying, Please, not tonight, I don't feel up to it. He didn't mind that. She was, after all, a well-bred Indian girl. He didn't expect her to behave like those American women he sometimes watched on X-rated videos, screaming and biting and doing other things he grew hot just thinking about. But her reluctance went beyond womanly modesty. After dinner for instance she would start on the most elaborate household projects, soaping down the floors, changing the liners in cabinets. The night before she disappeared she'd started cleaning windows, taken out the Windex and the rags as soon as she'd put the boy to bed, even though he said, Let's go. Surely he couldn't be blamed for raising his voice at those times (though never so much as to wake his son), or for grabbing her by the elbow and pulling her to the bed, like he did that last night. He was always careful not to hurt her, he prided himself on that. Not even a little slap, not like some of the men he'd known growing up, or even some of his friends now. And he always told himself he'd stop if she really begged him, if she cried. After some time, though, she would quit struggling and let him do what he wanted. But that was nothing new. That could have nothing to do with the disappearance.

Two weeks passed and there was no news of the woman, even though the husband had put a notice in the *San Jose Mercury* as well as a half-page ad in *India West*, which he photocopied and taped to neighborhood lampposts. The ad had a photo of her, a close-up taken in too-bright sunlight where she gazed gravely at something beyond the camera. WOMAN MISSING, read the ad. REWARD $100,000. (How on earth would he come up with that kind of money, asked his friends. The husband confessed that it would be difficult, but he'd manage somehow. His wife was more important to him, after all, than all the money in the world. And to prove it he went to the bank the very same day and brought home a sheaf of forms to fill so that he could take out a second mortgage on the house.) He kept calling the police station, too, but the police weren't much help. They were working on it, they said. They'd checked the local hospitals and morgues, the shelters. They'd even sent her description to other states. But there were no leads. It didn't look very hopeful.

So finally he called India and over a faulty long-distance connection that made his voice echo eerily in his ear told his mother what had happened. My poor boy, she cried, left all alone (the word flickered unpleasantly across his brain, *left, left*), how can you possibly cope with the household and a child as well. And when he admitted that yes, it was very difficult, could she perhaps come and help out for a while if it wasn't too much trouble, she had replied that of course she would come right away and stay as long as he needed her, and what was all this American nonsense about too much trouble, he was her only son, wasn't he. She would contact the wife's family too, she ended, so he wouldn't have to deal with that awkwardness.

Within a week she had closed up the little flat she had lived in since her husband's death, got hold of a special family emergency visa, and was on her way. Almost as though she'd been waiting for something like this to happen, said some of the women spitefully. (These were his wife's friends, though maybe acquaintances would be a more accurate word. His wife had liked to keep to herself, which had been just fine with him. He was glad, he'd told her several times, that she didn't spend hours chattering on the phone like the other Indian wives.)

He was angry when this gossip reached him (perhaps because he'd had the same insidious thought for a moment when, at the airport, he noticed how happy his mother looked, her flushed excited face appearing suddenly young).

Really, he said to his friends, some people see only what they *want* to see. Didn't *they* think it was a good thing she'd come over? Oh yes, said his friends. Look how well the household was running now, the furniture dusted daily, laundry folded and put into drawers (his mother, a smart woman, had figured out the washing machine in no time at all). She cooked all his favorite dishes, which his wife had never managed to learn quite right, and she took *such* good care of the little boy, walking him to the park each afternoon, bringing him into her bed when he woke up crying at night. (He'd told her once or twice that his wife had never done that, she had this idea about the boy needing to be independent. What nonsense, said his mother.) Lucky man, a couple of his friends added and he silently agreed, although later he thought it was ironic that they would say that about a man whose wife had disappeared. 15

As the year went on, the husband stopped thinking as much about the wife. It wasn't that he loved her any less, or that the shock of her disappearance was less acute. It was just that it wasn't on his mind all the time. There would be stretches of time—when he was on the phone with an important client, or when he was watching after-dinner TV or driving his son to kiddie gym class—when he would forget that his wife was gone, that he had had a wife at all. And even when he remembered that he had forgotten, he would experience only a slight twinge, similar to what he felt in his teeth when he drank something too cold too fast. The boy, too, didn't ask as often about his mother. He was sleeping through the nights again, he had put on a few pounds (because he was finally being fed right, said the grandmother), and he had started calling her "Ma," just like his father did.

So it seemed quite natural for the husband to, one day, remove the photographs of his wife from the frames that sat on the mantelpiece and replace them with pictures of himself and his little boy that friends had taken on a recent trip to Great America, and also one of the boy on his grandma's lap, holding a red birthday balloon, smiling (she said) exactly like his father used to at that age. He put the old pictures into a manila envelope and slid them to the back of a drawer, intending to show them to his son when he grew up. The next time his mother asked (as she had been doing ever since she got there), shall I put away all those saris and *81ameezzes*, it'll give you more space in the closet, he said, if you like. When she said, it's now over a year since the tragedy, shouldn't we have a prayer service done at the temple, he said OK. And when she told him, you really should think about getting married again, you're still young, and besides, the boy needs a mother, shall I contact second aunt back home, he remained silent but didn't disagree.

Then one night while cooking cauliflower curry, her specialty, his mother ran out of *hing*,[3] which was, she insisted, essential to the recipe. The Indian grocery was closed, but the husband remembered that sometimes his wife used to keep extra spices on the top shelf. So he climbed on a chair to look. There were no extra spices, but he did find something he had forgotten about, an old

[3] *hing:* An Indian spice.

tea tin in which he'd asked her to hide her jewelry in case the house ever got burgled. Nothing major was ever kept there. The expensive wedding items were all stored in a vault. Still, the husband thought it would be a good idea to take them into the bank in the morning.

But when he picked up the tin it felt surprisingly light, and when he opened it, there were only empty pink nests of tissue inside.

He stood there holding the tin for a moment, not breathing. Then he reminded himself that his wife had been a careless woman. He'd often had to speak to her about leaving things lying around. The pieces could be anywhere—pushed to the back of her makeup drawer or forgotten under a pile of books in the spare room where she used to spend inordinate amounts of time reading. Nevertheless he was not himself the rest of the evening, so much so that his mother said, What happened, you're awfully quiet, are you all right, your face looks funny. He told her he was fine, just a little pain in the chest area. Yes, he would make an appointment with the doctor tomorrow, no, he wouldn't forget, now could she please leave him alone for a while. 20

The next day he took the afternoon off from work, but he didn't go to the doctor. He went to the bank. In a small stuffy cubicle that smelled faintly of mold, he opened his safety deposit box to find that all her jewelry was gone. She hadn't taken any of the other valuables.

The edges of the cubicle seemed to fade and darken at the same time, as though the husband had stared at a lightbulb for too long. He ground his fists into his eyes and tried to imagine her on that last morning, putting the boy in his stroller and walking the twenty minutes to the bank (they only had one car, which he took to work; they could have afforded another, but why, he said to his friends, when she didn't even know how to drive). Maybe she had sat in this very cubicle and lifted out the emerald earrings, the pearl choker, the long gold chain. He imagined her wrapping the pieces carefully in plastic bags, the thin, clear kind one got at the grocery for vegetables, then slipping them into her purse. Or did she just throw them in anyhow, the strands of the necklace tangling, the brilliant green stones clicking against each other in the darkness inside the handbag, the boy laughing and clapping his hands at this new game.

At home that night he couldn't eat any dinner, and before he went to bed he did thirty minutes on the dusty exercise bike that sat in the corner of the family room. Have you gone crazy, asked his mother. He didn't answer. When he finally lay down, the tiredness did not put him to sleep as he had hoped. His calves ached from the unaccustomed strain, his head throbbed from the images that would not stop coming, and the bedclothes, when he pulled them up to his neck, smelled again of his wife's hair.

Where was she now? And with whom? Because surely she couldn't manage on her own. He'd always thought her to be like the delicate purple passion-flower vines that they'd put up on trellises along their back fence, and once, early in the marriage, had presented her with a poem he'd written about this. He remembered how, when he held out the sheet to her, she'd stared at him for a long moment and a look he couldn't quite read had flickered in her eyes.

Then she'd taken the poem with a small smile. He went over and over all the men she might have known, but they (mostly his Indian friends) were safely married and still at home, every one.

The bed felt hot and lumpy. He tossed his feverish body around like a caught animal, punched the pillow, threw the blanket to the floor. Even thought, for a wild moment, of shaking the boy awake and asking him, *Who did your mama see?* And as though he had an inbuilt antenna that picked up his father's agitation, in the next room the boy started crying (which he hadn't done for months), shrill screams that left him breathless. And when his father and grandmother rushed to see what the problem was, he pushed them from him with all the strength in his small arms, saying, Go way, don't want you, want Mama, want Mama. 25

After the boy had been dosed with gripe water[4] and settled in bed again, the husband sat alone in the family room with a glass of brandy. He wasn't a drinker. He believed that alcohol was for weak men. But somehow he couldn't face the rumpled bed just yet, the pillows wrested onto the floor. The unknown areas of his wife's existence yawning blackly around him like chasms. Should he tell the police, he wondered, would it do any good? What if somehow his friends came to know? *Didn't I tell you, right from the first*, his mother would say. And anyway it was possible she was already dead, killed by a stranger from whom she'd hitched a ride, or by a violent, jealous lover. He felt a small, bitter pleasure at the thought, and then a pang of shame.

Nevertheless he made his way to the dark bedroom (a trifle unsteadily; the drink had made him light-headed) and groped in the bottom drawer beneath his underwear until he felt the coarse manila envelope with her photos. He drew it out and, without looking at them, tore the pictures into tiny pieces. Then he took them over to the kitchen, where the trash compactor was.

The roar of the compactor seemed to shake the entire house. He stiffened, afraid his mother would wake and ask what was going on, but she didn't. When the machine ground to a halt, he took a long breath. Finished, he thought. Finished. Tomorrow he would contact a lawyer, find out the legal procedure for remarriage. Over dinner he would mention to his mother, casually, that it was OK with him if she wanted to contact second aunt. Only this time he didn't want a college-educated woman. Even good looks weren't that important. A simple girl, maybe from their ancestral village. Someone whose family wasn't well off, who would be suitably appreciative of the comforts he could provide. Someone who would be a real mother to his boy.

He didn't know then that it wasn't finished. That even as he made love to his new wife (a plump, cheerful girl, good-hearted, if slightly unimaginative), or helped his daughters with their homework, or disciplined his increasingly rebellious son, he would wonder about *her*. Was she alive? Was she happy? With a sudden anger that he knew to be irrational, he would try to imagine her body tangled in swaying kelp at the bottom of the ocean where it had been flung.

---

[4]*gripe water:* A traditional European remedy for colic.

Bloated. Eaten by fish. But all he could conjure up was the intent look on her face when she rocked her son back and forth, singing a children's rhyme in Bengali, *Khoka jabe biye korte, shonge chhasho dhol, my little boy is going to be married, six hundred drummers*. Years later, when he was an old man living in a home for seniors (his second wife dead, his daughters moved away to distant towns, his son not on speaking terms with him), he would continue to be dazzled by that brief unguarded joy in her face, would say to himself, again, how much she must have hated me to choose to give *that* up.

But he had no inkling of any of this yet. So he switched off the trash compactor with a satisfied click, the sense of a job well done and, after taking a shower (long and very hot, the way he liked it, the hard jets of water turning the skin of his chest a dull red), went to bed and fell immediately into a deep, dreamless sleep. 30

Reading and Reacting

1. Who is the narrator of "The Disappearance"? How does the narrative point of affect the description of events and characters in the story?
2. What is it about his wife that attracted the husband? What kind of bride was he seeking before he met her? What is the significance of the wife's "cool, considering look" (par. 9) when they first meet?
3. In paragraph 10, the narrator says, "He was a good husband. No one could deny it." Is this statement accurate? Is it ironic in any way? Explain.
4. How does the narrator suggest that the wife was unhappy? Why doesn't the husband see what the reader sees about his wife's state of mind? Does he ever realize why she left him?
5. How would you characterize the husband's relationship with his mother? What, if anything, did she have to do with the wife's disappearance?
6. The narrator never gives the characters' names. Why not?
7. What is the significance of the husband's discovery that his wife took all her jewelry when she left?
8. Do you think the wife was justified in leaving her son? Why do you think the son eventually stopped speaking to his father?
9. What aspects of the couple's troubled marriage strike you as culture-specific? What aspects strike you as universal?
10. How would the story be different without the last two paragraphs?
11. **Journal Entry** Assume that you are the wife in "The Disappearance." Write a letter to your husband explaining why you are leaving. Make sure you refer to events that are suggested by the story's narrator.
12. **Critical Perspective** Discussing "The Disappearance," Nilu N. Patel says that Divakaruni writes about the immigrant experience, specifically about women from India who are caught between two worlds. According to Patel, much of Divakaruni's writing is autobiographical. After she emigrated to the United States, Divakaruni started volunteering to help women who

were victims of domestic violence and other abusive situations. How does "The Disappearance" express the challenges facing women from India and other South Asian countries who come to the United States?

Related Works: "Girl" (p. 116), "I Stand Here Ironing" (p. 227), "Two Kinds" (p. 471), "Patterns" (p. 506), *Trifles* (p. 820), *The Cuban Swimmer* (p. 1122)

WRITING SUGGESTIONS: Point of View

1. How would Poe's "The Cask of Amontillado" be different if it were told by a minor character who observed the events? Rewrite the story from this point of view—or tell the story that precedes the story, explaining the "thousand injuries" and the "insult."
2. Assume that you are Jim, the sailor in "Big Black Good Man," and that you are keeping a journal of your travels. Write the journal entries for the time you spent in Copenhagen. Include your impressions of Olaf, Lena, the hotel, and anything else that caught your attention. Make sure you present your version of the key events described in the story—especially Olaf's reaction to you.
3. Both "The Cask of Amontillado" and "Barn Burning" deal with crimes that essentially go unpunished and with the emotions that accompany these crimes. In what sense does each story's use of point of view shape its treatment of the crime in question? For instance, how does point of view determine how much readers know about the motives for the crime, the crime's basic circumstances, and the extent to which the crime is justified?
4. Write a story in which you retell "The Disappearance" from the wife's point of view. Be true to the original story. Be sure to use the same narrative point of view as the story.

Chapter

13

Style, Tone, and Language

(Mary) Flannery O'Connor
AP Images

Charlotte Perkins Gilman
Historic Images/Alamy Stock Photo

James Joyce
AP Images

Learning Objectives

After reading this chapter, you will be able to...

- Identify how style, tone, and language function in a work of fiction.
- Identify and compare the characteristics of formal and informal diction.
- Identify the use of imagery and figures of speech in a work of fiction.
- Examine the tone of a specific work of fiction.
- Compare the styles and levels of different characters' speech in a work of fiction.

Style and Tone

One of the qualities that gives a work of literature its individuality is its **style**, the way writers use language, selecting and arranging words to say what they want to say. Style encompasses elements such as word choice, syntax, and sentence length. Style is also influenced by the presence, frequency, and prominence of imagery and figures of speech.

Closely related to style is **tone**, the attitude of a narrator or author toward the subject matter, characters, or audience. Word choice and sentence structure help to create a work's tone, which may be intimate or distant; bitter or affectionate; straightforward or cautious; supportive or critical; or respectful or condescending. (Tone may also be **ironic**; see Chapter 12, "Point of View," for a discussion of irony.)

The Uses of Language

Language offers writers almost limitless possibilities. Creative use of language, such as unusual word choice, word order, or sentence structure, can enrich a story and add to its overall effect. Sometimes, in fact, a writer's use of language can expand a story's possibilities through its very inventiveness. For example, James Joyce's innovative **stream-of-consciousness** style mimics thought, allowing ideas to run into one another as random associations are made so that readers may follow and participate in the thought processes of the narrator. Here is a stream-of-consciousness passage from Joyce's experimental 1922 novel *Ulysses*:

> frseeeeeeeefronnnng train somewhere whistling the strength those engines have in them like big giants and the water rolling all over and out of them all sides like the end of Loves old sweet sonnnng the poor men that have to be out all the night from their wives and families in those roasting engines stifling it was today. . . .

Skillfully used, language can enhance a story's other elements. It may, for example, help to create an atmosphere that is important to the story's plot or theme, as Kate Chopin's lush, rhythmic sentences help to create the sexually charged atmosphere of "The Storm" (p. 216)—an atmosphere that overpowers the characters and thus drives the plot.

Language may also help to delineate character, perhaps by conveying a character's mental state to readers. For example, the breathless, disjointed style of Edgar Allan Poe's "The Tell-Tale Heart" (p. 459) suggests the narrator's increasing emotional instability: "Was it possible they heard not? Almighty God!—no, no! They heard!—they suspected!—they *knew!*—they were making a mockery of my horror!" Similarly, in his 1925 short story "Big Two-Hearted River," Ernest Hemingway uses short, unconnected sentences to create a flat, emotionless prose style that reveals his character's alienation and fragility as he struggles to maintain control: "Now things were done. There had been this to do. Now it was done. It had been a hard trip. He was very tired. That was done. He had made his camp. He was settled. Nothing could touch him."

Language that places emphasis on the sounds and rhythm of words and sentences can also enrich a work of fiction. Consider the use of such language in the following sentence from James Joyce's "Araby" (p. 296):

> The light from the lamp opposite our door caught the white curve of her neck, lit up her hair that rested there and, falling, lit up the hand upon the railing.

Here the narrator is describing his first conversation with a girl who fascinates him, and the lyrical, almost musical language reflects his enchantment. Note in particular the **alliteration** (*l*ight/*l*amp; *c*aught/*c*urve; *h*air/*h*and), the repetition (lit up/lit up), and the rhyme (lit up her *hair*/that rested *there*) and **near rhyme** (falling/railing); these poetic devices weave the words of the sentence into a smooth, rhythmic whole.

Another example of this emphasis on sound may be found in the measured **parallelism** of this sentence from Nathaniel Hawthorne's 1843 story "The Birthmark":

> He had left his laboratory to the care of an assistant, cleared his fine countenance from the furnace smoke, washed the stain of acids from his fingers, and persuaded a beautiful woman to become his wife.

The style of this sentence, conveying methodical precision and order, reflects the compulsive personality of the character being described.

The following passage from Alberto Álvaro Ríos's story "The Secret Lion" (p. 222) illustrates the power of language to enrich a story:

> We had read the books, after all; we knew about bridges and castles and wildtreacherousraging alligatormouth rivers. We wanted them. So we were going to go out and get them. We went back that morning into that kitchen and we said, "We're going out there, we're going into the hills, we're going away for three days, don't worry." She said, "All right."
>
> "You know," I said to Sergio, "if we're going to go away for three days, well, we ought to at least pack a lunch."
>
> But we were two young boys with no patience for what we thought at the time was mom-stuff: making sa-and-wiches. My mother didn't offer. So we got out little kid knapsacks that my mother had sewn for us, and into them we put the jar of mustard. A loaf of bread. Knivesforksplates, bottles of Coke, a can opener. This was lunch for the two of us. And we were weighed down, humped over to be strong enough to carry this stuff. But we started walking anyway, into the hills. We were going to eat berries and stuff otherwise. "Goodbye." My mom said that.

Through language, the adult narrator of the preceding paragraphs recaptures the bravado of the boys in search of "wildtreacherousraging alligatormouth rivers" even as he suggests to readers that the boys are not going far. The story's use of language is original and inventive: words are blended together ("getridofit," "knivesforksplates"), linked to form new words ("mom-stuff"), and drawn out to mimic speech ("sa-and-wiches"). These experiments with language show the narrator's willingness to move back into a child's frame of reference while maintaining the advantage of distance. The adult narrator uses sentence fragments ("A loaf of bread."), colloquialisms ("kid," "mom," "stuff"), and contractions. He also includes conversational elements such as *you know* and *well* in the story's dialogue, accurately recreating the childhood scene even as he sees its folly and remains aware of the disillusionment that awaits him. Thus, the unique style permits the narrator to bring readers with him into the child's world while he maintains his adult stance: "But we were two young boys with no patience for what we thought at the time was mom-stuff. . . ."

Although many stylistic options are available to writers, a story's language must be consistent with their purpose and with the effect they hope to create. Just as writers may experiment with point of view or manipulate events to create a complex plot, so they can adjust language to suit a particular narrator or character or to convey a particular theme. In addition to the creative uses of language described above, writers also frequently experiment with *formal and informal diction*, *imagery*, and *figures of speech*.

Formal and Informal Diction

The level of diction—how formal or informal a story's language is—can reveal a good deal about a story's narrator and characters.

Formal diction is characterized by elaborate, complex sentences; a learned vocabulary; and a serious, objective, detached tone. It does not generally include contractions, shortened word forms (such as *phone*), regional expressions, or slang, and it may substitute *one* or *we* for *I*. At its most extreme, formal language is stiff and stilted, far removed from everyday speech.

When formal diction is used by a narrator or by a character, it may indicate erudition, a high educational level, a superior social or professional position, or emotional detachment. When one character's language is significantly more formal than others', that character may seem old-fashioned or stuffy; when language is inappropriately elevated or complex, it may reveal a character to be pompous or ridiculous; when a narrator's language is noticeably more formal than that of the story's characters, the narrator may seem superior or even condescending. Thus, the choice of a particular level (or levels) of diction in a story can convey information about characters and about the narrator's attitude toward them.

The following passage from Nathaniel Hawthorne's "The Birthmark" (1843) illustrates formal style:

> In the latter part of the last century there lived a man of science, an eminent proficient in every branch of natural philosophy, who not long before our story opens had made experience of a spiritual affinity more attractive than any chemical one. He had left his laboratory to the care of an assistant, cleared his fine countenance from the furnace smoke, washed the stain of acids from his fingers, and persuaded a beautiful woman to become his wife. In those days when the comparatively recent discovery of electricity and other kindred mysteries of Nature seemed to open paths into the region of miracle, it was not unusual for the love of science to rival the love of woman in its depth and absorbing

> energy. The higher intellect, the imagination, the spirit, and even the heart might all find their congenial ailment in pursuits which, as some of their ardent votaries believed, would ascend from one step of powerful intelligence to another, until the philosopher should lay his hand on the secret of creative force and perhaps make new worlds for himself.

The long and complex sentences, learned vocabulary ("countenance," "ailment," "votaries"), and absence of colloquialisms suit Hawthorne's purpose well, recreating the formal language of the earlier era in which his story is set. The narrator is aloof and controlled, and his diction makes this clear to readers.

Informal diction, consistent with everyday speech, is characterized by slang, contractions, colloquial expressions like *you know* and *I mean*, shortened word forms, incomplete sentences, and a casual, conversational tone. A first-person narrator may use an informal style, or characters may speak informally. In either case, informal diction tends to narrow the distance between readers and text.

Joyce Carol Oates's "Where Are You Going, Where Have You Been?" (p. 447) uses informal language through the casual, slangy style of the dialogue between the teenager Connie and her older stalker, Arnold Friend:

> "I ain't late, am I?" he said.
>
> "Who the hell do you think you are?" Connie said.
>
> "Toldja I'd be out, didn't I?"
>
> "I don't even know who you are."

Here, the level of the characters' diction is a key element of the story: because Arnold seems to speak Connie's language, she lets down her guard and becomes vulnerable to his advances.

Another kind of informal language is seen in the regionalisms and dialect used in Flannery O'Connor's "A Good Man Is Hard to Find" (p. 302), where speech patterns and individual words ("aloose"; "you all"; "britches") help to identify the region where the characters live and their social class.

Informal diction may also include language readers find offensive. In such cases, a character's use of obscenities may suggest anything from crudeness to adolescent bravado, and the use of racial or ethnic slurs indicates that a character is insensitive or bigoted.

The following passage from John Updike's "A&P" (p. 179) illustrates informal style:

> She had sort of oaky hair that the sun and salt had bleached, done up in a bun that was unravelling, and a kind of prim face. Walking into the A&P with your straps down, I suppose it's the only kind of face you *can* have. She held her head so high her neck, coming out of those white shoulders, looked kind of stretched, but I didn't mind. The longer her neck was, the more of her there was.

Here, the first-person narrator, a nineteen-year-old supermarket checkout clerk, uses a conversational style, including colloquialisms ("sort of," "I suppose," "kind of"), contractions ("it's," "didn't"), and the imprecise, informal *you* ("Walking into the A&P with *your* straps down . . ."). The narrator uses neither elaborate syntax nor a learned vocabulary.

Imagery

Imagery—words and phrases that describe what is seen, heard, smelled, tasted, or touched—can have a significant impact in a story. A writer may use a pattern of repeated imagery to convey a particular impression about a character or situation, or to communicate or reinforce a story's theme. For example, a character's newly discovered sense of freedom or sexuality can be conveyed through repeated use of words and phrases suggesting blooming or ripening (as in the two stories in this text by Kate Chopin).

In a more contemporary story, T. Coraghessan Boyle's "Greasy Lake" (p. 419), the narrator's vivid description of Greasy Lake uses rich visual imagery to evoke a scene:

> Through the center of town, up the strip, past the housing developments and shopping malls, street lights giving way to the thin streaming illumination of the headlights, trees crowding the asphalt in a black unbroken wall: that was the way out to Greasy Lake. The Indians had called it Wakan, a reference to the clarity of its waters. Now it was fetid and murky, the mud banks glittering with broken glass and strewn with beer cans and the charred remains of bonfires. There was a single ravaged island a hundred yards from shore, so stripped of vegetation it looked as if the air force had strafed it. We went up to the lake because everyone went there, because we wanted to snuff the rich scent of possibility on the breeze, watch a girl take off her clothes and plunge into the festering murk, drink beer, smoke pot, howl at the stars, savor the incongruous full-throated roar of rock and roll against the primeval susurrus of frogs and crickets. This was nature.

By characterizing a bucolic natural setting with surprising words like "fetid," "murky," and "greasy" and unpleasant images such as the "glittering of broken glass," the "ravaged island," and the "charred remains of bonfires," Boyle creates a picture that is completely at odds with the traditional view of nature. The incongruous images are nevertheless perfectly consistent with the sordid events that take place at Greasy Lake.

Figures of Speech

Figures of speech—such as *similes*, *metaphors*, and *personification*—can enrich a story, subtly revealing information about characters and themes.

By using **metaphors** and **similes**—figures of speech that compare two dissimilar items—writers can indicate a particular attitude toward characters and events. Thus, Flannery O'Connor's many grotesque similes in "A Good Man Is Hard to Find" help to dehumanize her characters; the children's mother, for example, has a face "as broad and innocent as a cabbage." In Tillie Olsen's "I Stand Here Ironing" (p. 227), an extended metaphor in which a mother compares her daughter to a dress waiting to be ironed expresses the mother's attitude toward her child, effectively suggesting the daughter's vulnerability. Similes and metaphors are used throughout in Kate Chopin's "The Storm" (p. 216). For example, in a scene of sexual awakening, Calixta's skin is "like a creamy lily," her passion is "like a white flame," and her mouth is "a fountain of delight"; these figures of speech add a lushness and sensuality to the story.

Personification—a figure of speech, closely related to metaphor, that endows inanimate objects or abstract ideas with life or with human characteristics—is used in "Araby" (p. 296), where houses, "conscious of decent lives within them, gazed at one another with brown imperturbable faces." This use of figurative language expands readers' vision of the story's setting and gives a dreamlike quality to the passage. (Other figures of speech, such as **hyperbole** and **understatement**, can also enrich works of fiction. See Chapter 21, "Figures of Speech," for further information.)

Allusions—references to familiar historical, cultural, literary, or biblical texts, figures, or events—may also expand readers' understanding and appreciation of a work. An allusion widens a work's context by bringing it into the context of a related subject or idea. For example, in Charles Baxter's short story "Gryphon" (p. 191), the narrator's allusions to *Pinocchio* and Betty Crocker enable readers who recognize the references to gain a deeper understanding of what certain characters are really like. (For information on the use of allusion in poetry, see Chapter 24.)

Note In analyzing the use of language in a work of fiction, you may occasionally encounter unfamiliar allusions (or foreign words and phrases or regional expressions), particularly in works treating cultures and historical periods other than your own. Frequently, such language will be clarified by the context or by explanatory notes in your text. If it is not, always look up the meaning.

Checklist Writing about Style, Tone, and Language

- Does the writer make any unusual or creative use of word choice, word order, or sentence structure?
- Is the story's tone intimate? distant? ironic? How does the tone support the writer's purpose?
- Does the style emphasize the sound and rhythm of language? For example, does the writer use alliteration and assonance? repetition and parallelism? What do such techniques add to the story?
- Is the level of diction generally formal, informal, or somewhere in between?
- Is there a difference between the diction used by the narrator and the diction used in the characters' speech? If so, what is the effect of this difference?

- Do any of the story's characters use regionalisms, colloquial language, slang, or nonstandard speech? If so, what effect does this language have?
- What do different characters' levels of diction reveal about them?
- What kind of imagery predominates? Where, and why, is imagery used?
- Does the story develop a pattern of imagery? How does this pattern of imagery help to convey the story's themes?
- Does the story use simile and metaphor? personification? What impact do these figures of speech have?
- Do figures of speech reinforce the story's themes? reveal information about characters?
- Does the story make any historical, literary, or biblical allusions? What do these allusions contribute to the story?
- Are any unfamiliar, obscure, or foreign words, phrases, or images used in the story? What do these words or expressions contribute to the story?

Source: AP Images

JAMES JOYCE (1882–1941) was born in Dublin but lived his entire adult life in self-imposed exile from his native Ireland. Though his parents sent him to schools that trained young men for the priesthood, Joyce saw himself as a religious and artistic rebel and fled to Paris soon after graduation in 1902. Recalled briefly to Dublin by his mother's fatal illness, Joyce returned to the Continent in 1904, taking with him an uneducated Irish country woman named Nora Barnacle, who became his wife in 1931. In dreary quarters in Trieste, Zurich, and Paris, Joyce struggled to support a growing family, sometimes teaching classes at Berlitz language schools.

Though Joyce never again lived in Ireland, he continued to write about Dublin. In fact, the publication of *Dubliners* (1914), a collection of short stories that included "Araby," was delayed for seven years because the Irish publisher feared libel suits from local citizens who were thinly disguised as characters in the stories. Joyce's autobiographical *Portrait of the Artist as a Young Man* (1916) tells of a young writer's rejection of family, church, and country. *Ulysses* (1922), the comic tale of eighteen hours in the life of a wandering Dublin advertising salesman, was banned when the United States Post Office brought charges of obscenity against the book, and it remained banned in the United States and England for more than a decade. With *Ulysses*, Joyce began a revolutionary journey away from traditional techniques of plot and characterization to the interior monologues and stream-of-consciousness style that mark his last great novel, *Finnegans Wake* (1939).

Cultural Context In the early twentieth century, as world travel and the shipment of goods around the globe expanded at a dizzying pace, the West experienced a fascination with the "Orient," an outdated term referring to a land of Eastern peoples and traditions. To peddle their wares, immigrants from the East established bazaars reminiscent of the ones in their homelands, displaying a dazzling array of spices, foods, and material goods. This appeal to the senses, representing the allure of the distant and unknown, became a highlight of many towns and cities. In this story, the bazaar represents the attraction of the strange and exotic for the young narrator.

Araby (1914)

North Richmond Street, being blind,[1] was a quiet street except at the hour when the Christian Brothers' School set the boys free. An uninhabited house of two storeys stood at the blind end, detached from its neighbours in a square ground. The other houses of the street, conscious of decent lives within them, gazed at one another with brown imperturbable faces.

The former tenant of our house, a priest, had died in the back drawing-room. Air, musty from having been long enclosed, hung in all the rooms, and the waste room behind the kitchen was littered with old useless papers. Among these I found a few paper-covered books, the pages of which were curled and damp: *The Abbot*, by Walter Scott, *The Devout Communicant* and *The Memoirs of Vidocq*.[2] I liked the last best because its leaves were yellow. The wild garden behind the house contained a central apple-tree and a few straggling bushes under one of which I found the late tenant's rusty bicycle-pump. He had been a very charitable priest; in his will he had left all his money to institutions and the furniture of his house to his sister.

When the short days of winter came dusk fell before we had well eaten our dinners. When we met in the street the houses had grown sombre. The space of sky above us was the colour of ever-changing violet and towards it the lamps of the street lifted their feeble lanterns. The cold air stung us and we played till our bodies glowed. Our shouts echoed in the silent street. The career of our play brought us through the dark muddy lanes behind the houses where we ran the gauntlet of the rough tribes from the cottages, to the back doors of the dark dripping gardens where odours arose from the ashpits, to the dark odorous stables where a coach-man smoothed and combed the horse or shook music from the buckled harness. When we returned to the street light from the kitchen windows had filled the areas. If my uncle was seen turning the corner we hid in the shadow until we had seen him safely housed. Or if Mangan's sister came out on the doorstep to call her brother in to his tea we watched her from

[1] *blind:* Dead-end.

[2] *The Abbot . . . Vidocq: The Abbot*—a historical novel by Sir Walter Scott (1771–1832)—an English Romantic novelist; *The Devout Communicant*—a variant title for *Pious Meditations*, written by an eighteenth-century English Franciscan friar, Pacifus Baker; *The Memoirs of Vidocq*—an autobiography of François-Jules Vidocq (1775–1857), a French criminal turned police agent.

our shadow peer up and down the street. We waited to see whether she would remain or go in and, if she remained, we left our shadow and walked up to Mangan's steps resignedly. She was waiting for us, her figure defined by the light from the half-opened door. Her brother always teased her before he obeyed and I stood by the railings looking at her. Her dress swung as she moved her body and the soft rope of her hair tossed from side to side.

Every morning I lay on the floor in the front parlour watching her door. The blind was pulled down to within an inch of the sash so that I could not be seen. When she came out on the doorstep my heart leaped. I ran to the hall, seized my books and followed her. I kept her brown figure always in my eye and, when we came near the point at which our ways diverged, I quickened my pace and passed her. This happened morning after morning. I had never spoken to her, except for a few casual words, and yet her name was like a summons to all my foolish blood.

Her image accompanied me even in places the most hostile to romance. On Saturday evenings when my aunt went marketing I had to go to carry some of the parcels. We walked through the flaring streets, jostled by drunken men and bargaining women, amid the curses of labourers, the shrill litanies of shop-boys who stood on guard by the barrels of pigs' cheeks, the nasal chanting of street-singers, who sang a *come-all-you* about O'Donovan Rossa,[3] or a ballad about the troubles in our native land. These noises converged in a single sensation of life for me: I imagined that I bore my chalice safely through a throng of foes. Her name sprang to my lips at moments in strange prayers and praises which I myself did not understand. My eyes were often full of tears (I could not tell why) and at times a flood from my heart seemed to pour itself out into my bosom. I thought little of the future. I did not know whether I would ever speak to her or not or, if I spoke to her, how I could tell her of my confused adoration. But my body was like a harp and her words and gestures were like fingers running upon the wires. 5

One evening I went into the back drawing-room in which the priest had died. It was a dark rainy evening and there was no sound in the house. Through one of the broken panes I heard the rain impinge upon the earth, the fine incessant needles of water playing in the sodden beds. Some distant lamp or lighted window gleamed below me. I was thankful that I could see so little. All my senses seemed to desire to veil themselves and, feeling that I was about to slip from them, I pressed the palms of my hands together until they trembled, murmuring: "O *love!* O *love!*" many times.

At last she spoke to me. When she addressed the first words to me I was so confused that I did not know what to answer. She asked me was I going to *Araby*. I forgot whether I answered yes or no. It would be a splendid bazaar, she said she would love to go.

---

[3]*O'Donovan Rossa:* Any popular song beginning "Come all you gallant Irishmen . . ."; O'Donovan Rossa was an Irish nationalist who was banished in 1870 for advocating violent rebellion against the British.

"And why can't you?" I asked.

While she spoke she turned a silver bracelet round and round her wrist. She could not go, she said, because there would be a retreat that week in her convent.[4] Her brother and two other boys were fighting for their caps and I was alone at the railings. She held one of the spikes, bowing her head towards me. The light from the lamp opposite our door caught the white curve of her neck, lit up her hair that rested there and, falling, lit up the hand upon the railing. It fell over one side of her dress and caught the white border of a petticoat, just visible as she stood at ease.

"It's well for you," she said.

"If I go," I said, "I will bring you something."

What innumerable follies laid waste my waking and sleeping thoughts after that evening! I wished to annihilate the tedious intervening days. I chafed against the work of school. At night in my bedroom and by day in the classroom her image came between me and the page I strove to read. The syllables of the word *Araby* were called to me through the silence in which my soul luxuriated and cast an Eastern enchantment over me. I asked for leave to go to the bazaar on Saturday night. My aunt was surprised and hoped it was not some Freemason[5] affair. I answered few questions in class. I watched my master's face pass from amiability to sternness; he hoped I was not beginning to idle. I could not call my wandering thoughts together. I had hardly any patience with the serious work of life which, now that it stood between me and my desire, seemed to me child's play, ugly monotonous child's play.

On Saturday morning I reminded my uncle that I wished to go to the bazaar in the evening. He was fussing at the hallstand, looking for the hatbrush, and answered me curtly:

"Yes, boy, I know."

As he was in the hall I could not go into the front parlour and lie at the window. I left the house in bad humour and walked slowly towards the school. The air was pitilessly raw and already my heart misgave me.

When I came home to dinner my uncle had not yet been home. Still it was early. I sat staring at the clock for some time and, when its ticking began to irritate me, I left the room. I mounted the staircase and gained the upper part of the house. The high cold empty gloomy rooms liberated me and I went from room to room singing. From the front window I saw my companions playing below in the street. Their cries reached me weakened and indistinct and, leaning my forehead against the cool glass, I looked over at the dark house where she lived. I may have stood there for an hour, seeing nothing but the brown-clad figure cast by my imagination, touched discreetly by the lamplight at the curved neck, at the hand upon the railings and at the border below the dress.

---

[4]*convent:* Her convent school.

[5]*Freemason:* At the time the story takes place, many Catholics in Ireland thought the Masonic Order was a threat to the church.

When I came downstairs again I found Mrs. Mercer sitting at the fire. She was an old garrulous woman, a pawnbroker's widow, who collected used stamps for some pious purpose. I had to endure the gossip of the tea-table. The meal was prolonged beyond an hour and still my uncle did not come. Mrs. Mercer stood up to go: she was sorry she couldn't wait any longer, but it was after eight o'clock and she did not like to be out late, as the night air was bad for her. When she had gone I began to walk up and down the room, clenching my fists. My aunt said:

"I'm afraid you may put off your bazaar for this night of Our Lord."

At nine o'clock I heard my uncle's latchkey in the halldoor. I heard him talking to himself and heard the hallstand rocking when it had received the weight of his overcoat. I could interpret these signs. When he was midway through his dinner I asked him to give me the money to go to the bazaar. He had forgotten.

"The people are in bed and after their first sleep now," he said. 20

I did not smile. My aunt said to him energetically:

"Can't you give him the money and let him go? You've kept him late enough as it is."

My uncle said he was very sorry he had forgotten. He said he believed in the old saying: "All work and no play makes Jack a dull boy." He asked me where I was going and, when I had told him a second time he asked me did I know *The Arab's Farewell to his Steed.*[6] When I left the kitchen he was about to recite the opening lines of the piece to my aunt.

I held a florin tightly in my hand as I strode down Buckingham Street towards the station. The sight of the streets thronged with buyers and glaring with gas recalled to me the purpose of my journey. I took my seat in a third-class carriage of a deserted train. After an intolerable delay the train moved out of the station slowly. It crept onward among ruinous houses and over the twinkling river. At Westland Row Station a crowd of people pressed to the carriage doors; but the porters moved them back, saying that it was a special train for the bazaar. I remained alone in the bare carriage. In a few minutes the train drew up beside an improvised wooden platform. I passed out on to the road and saw by the lighted dial of a clock that it was ten minutes to ten. In front of me was a large building which displayed the magical name.

I could not find any sixpenny entrance and, fearing that the bazaar would be closed, I passed in quickly through a turnstile, handing a shilling to a weary-looking man. I found myself in a big hall girdled at half its height by a gallery. Nearly all the stalls were closed and the greater part of the hall was in darkness. I recognised a silence like that which pervades a church after a service. I walked into the centre of the bazaar timidly. A few people were gathered about the stalls which were still open. Before a curtain, over which the words *Café*

---

[6]*The Arab's Farewell to his Steed:* A sentimental poem by Caroline Norton (1808–1877) that tells the story of a nomad's heartbreak after selling his much-loved horse.

Chantant[7] were written in coloured lamps, two men were counting money on a salver. I listened to the fall of the coins.

Remembering with difficulty why I had come I went over to one of the stalls and examined porcelain vases and flowered tea-sets. At the door of the stall a young lady was talking and laughing with two young gentlemen. I remarked their English accents and listened vaguely to their conversation.

"O, I never said such a thing!"

"O, but you did!"

"O, but I didn't!"

"Didn't she say that?"

"Yes. I heard her."

"O, there's a . . . fib!"

Observing me the young lady came over and asked me did I wish to buy anything. The tone of her voice was not encouraging; she seemed to have spoken to me out of a sense of duty. I looked humbly at the great jars that stood like eastern guards at either side of the dark entrance to the stall and murmured:

"No, thank you."

The young lady changed the position of one of the vases and went back to the two young men. They began to talk of the same subject. Once or twice the young lady glanced at me over her shoulder.

I lingered before her stall, though I knew my stay was useless, to make my interest in her wares seem the more real. Then I turned away slowly and walked down the middle of the bazaar. I allowed the two pennies to fall against the sixpence in my pocket. I heard a voice call from one end of the gallery that the light was out. The upper part of the hall was now completely dark.

Gazing up into the darkness I saw myself as a creature driven and derided by vanity; and my eyes burned with anguish and anger.

Reading and Reacting

1. How would you characterize the story's level of diction? Is this level appropriate for a story about a young boy's experiences? Explain.
2. Identify several figures of speech in the story. Where is Joyce most likely to use this kind of language? Why?
3. What words and phrases express the boy's extreme idealism and romantic view of the world? How does such language help to communicate the story's major theme?
4. In paragraph 4, the narrator says, "her name was like a summons to all my foolish blood." In the story's last sentence, he sees himself as "a creature driven and derided by vanity." What other expressions does the narrator use to describe his feelings? How would you characterize these feelings?
5. How does the narrator's choice of words illustrate the contrast between his day-to-day life and the exotic promise of the bazaar?

[7] *Café Chantant:* A Paris café featuring musical entertainment.

6. What does each of the italicized words suggest: "We walked through the *flaring* streets" (par. 5); "I heard the rain *impinge* upon the earth" (par. 6); "I *chafed* against the work of school" (par. 12); "I found myself in a big hall *girdled* at half its height by a gallery" (par. 25)? What other examples of unexpected word choice can you identify in the story?
7. What is it about the events described in this story that causes the narrator to remember them years later?
8. Identify words and phrases in the story that are associated with religion. What purpose do these references to religion serve? Do you think this pattern of words and phrases is intentional?
9. **Journal Entry** Rewrite a brief passage from this story in the voice of the young boy. Use informal style, simple figures of speech, and vocabulary appropriate for a child.
10. **Critical Perspective** In *Notes on the American Short Story Today*, Richard Kostelanetz discusses the **epiphany**, one of Joyce's most significant contributions to literature:

    > In Joyce's pervasively influential theory of the short story we remember, the fiction turned upon an epiphany, a moment of revelation in which, in [critic] Harry Levin's words, "amid the most encumbered circumstances it suddenly happens that the veil is lifted, the . . . mystery laid bare, and the ultimate secret of things made manifest." The epiphany, then, became a technique for jelling the narrative and locking the story's import into place. . . . What made this method revolutionary was the shifting of the focal point of the story from its end . . . to a spot within the body of the text, usually near (but not at) the end.

    Where in "Araby" does the story's epiphany occur? Does it do all that Kostelanetz believes an epiphany should do? Do you think that—at least in the case of "Araby"—the epiphany may not be as significant a force as Kostelanetz suggests?

Related Works: "A&P" (p. 179), "Gryphon" (p. 191), "The Girl with Bangs" (p. 204), "The Secret Lion" (p. 222), "Doe Season" (p. 378), "Shall I compare thee to a summer's day?" (p. 560), "How Do I Love Thee?" (p. 684), *Beauty* (p. 785)

Source: AP Images

(MARY) FLANNERY O'CONNOR (1925–1964) was born to a prosperous Catholic family in Savannah, Georgia, and spent most of her adult life on a farm near the town of Milledgeville. She left the South to study writing at the University of Iowa, moving to New York to work on her first novel, *Wise Blood* (1952). On a train going south for Christmas, O'Connor became seriously ill. She was diagnosed as having lupus, the immune system disease that had killed her father and would cause O'Connor's death when she was only thirty-nine years old.

While her mother ran the farm, O'Connor spent mornings writing and afternoons wandering the fields with a cane or on crutches. Her short story collection *A Good Man Is Hard to Find* (1955) and an excellent French translation of *Wise Blood* established her international reputation, which was solidified with the publication of a second novel, *The Violent Bear It Away* (1960), and a posthumously published book of short stories, *Everything That Rises Must Converge* (1965).

O'Connor, said a friend, believed that an artist "should face all the truth down to the worst of it." Yet however dark, her stories are infused with grim humor and a fierce belief in the possibility of spiritual redemption, even for her most tortured characters. A line from her short story "A Good Man Is Hard to Find" says much about what O'Connor perceived about both natural things and her characters: "The trees were full of silver-white sunlight and the meanest of them sparkled." In O'Connor's work, the "meanest" things and people can sparkle, touched by a kind of holy madness and beauty.

Cultural Context O'Connor is most often read and analysed as a Catholic author in the Protestant South, and concepts of free will, original sin, and the need for spiritual redemption appear throughout her work. According to Christian theology, humanity was created with free will—the freedom to choose to obey or to disobey God, the freedom to follow right or wrong. Human beings fell from their original state of innocence, however, and this fall allowed sin and corruption to enter the world. Thus, a "good man"—one who is perfectly upright—is not simply "hard to find" but *impossible* to find: *all* have sinned and fall short of the glory of God, says the Bible (Romans 3.23). Because of that first disobedience (original sin), humanity stands in need of redemption—a reuniting with God—which, according to Christian theology, comes through Jesus Christ.

A Good Man Is Hard to Find (1955)

The grandmother didn't want to go to Florida. She wanted to visit some of her connections in east Tennessee and she was seizing at every chance to change Bailey's mind. Bailey was the son she lived with, her only boy. He was sitting on the edge of his chair at the table, bent over the orange sports section of the *Journal*. "Now look here, Bailey," she said, "see here, read this," and she stood with one hand on her thin hip and the other rattling the newspaper at his bald head. "Here this fellow that calls himself The Misfit is aloose from the Federal Pen and headed toward Florida and you read here what it says he did to these people. Just you read it. I wouldn't take my children in any direction with a criminal like that aloose in it. I couldn't answer to my conscience if I did."

Bailey didn't look up from his reading so she wheeled around then and faced the children's mother, a young woman in slacks, whose face was as broad and innocent as a cabbage and was tied around with a green headkerchief that had two points on the top like a rabbit's ears. She was sitting on the sofa, feeding the baby his apricots out of a ja r. "The children have been to Florida before," the old lady said. "You all ought to take them somewhere else for a change so they would see different parts of the world and be broad. They never have been to east Tennessee."

The children's mother didn't seem to hear her but the eight-year-old boy, John Wesley, a stocky child with glasses, said, "If you don't want to go to Florida, why dontcha stay at home?" He and the little girl, June Star, were reading the funny papers on the floor.

"She wouldn't stay at home to be queen for a day," June Star said without raising her yellow head.

"Yes and what would you do if this fellow, the Misfit, caught you?" the grandmother asked. 5

"I'd smack his face," John Wesley said.

"She wouldn't stay at home for a million bucks," June Star said. "Afraid she'd miss something. She has to go everywhere we go."

"All right, Miss," the grandmother said. "Just remember that the next time you want me to curl your hair."

June Star said her hair was naturally curly.

The next morning the grandmother was the first one in the car, ready to go. She had her big black valise that looked like the head of a hippopotamus in one corner, and underneath it she was hiding a basket with Pitty Sing, the cat, in it. She didn't intend for the cat to be left alone in the house for three days because he would miss her too much and she was afraid he might brush against one of the gas burners and accidentally asphyxiate himself. Her son, Bailey, didn't like to arrive at a motel with a cat. 10

She sat in the middle of the back seat with John Wesley and June Star on either side of her. Bailey and the children's mother and the baby sat in front and they left Atlanta at eight forty-five with the mileage on the car at 55890. The grandmother wrote this down because she thought it would be interesting to say how many miles they had been when they got back. It took them twenty minutes to reach the outskirts of the city.

The old lady settled herself comfortably, removing her white cotton gloves and putting them up with her purse on the shelf in front of the back window. The children's mother still had on slacks and still had her head tied up in a green kerchief, but the grandmother had on a navy blue straw sailor hat with a bunch of white violets on the brim and a navy blue dress with a small white dot in the print. Her collars and cuffs were white organdy trimmed with lace and at her neckline she had pinned a purple spray of cloth violets containing a sachet. In case of an accident, anyone seeing her dead on the highway would know at once that she was a lady.

She said she thought it was going to be a good day for driving, neither too hot nor too cold, and she cautioned Bailey that the speed limit was fifty-five miles an hour and that the patrolmen hid themselves behind billboards and small clumps of trees and sped out after you before you had a chance to slow down. She pointed out interesting details of the scenery: Stone Mountain; the blue granite that in some places came up to both sides of the highway; the brilliant red clay banks slightly streaked with purple; and the various crops that made rows of green lace-work on the ground. The trees were full of silver-white sunlight and the meanest of them sparkled. The children were reading comic magazines and their mother had gone back to sleep.

"Let's go through Georgia fast so we won't have to look at it much," John Wesley said.

"If I were a little boy," said the grandmother, "I wouldn't talk about my native state that way. Tennessee has the mountains and Georgia has the
hills." 15

"Tennessee is just a hillbilly dumping ground," John Wesley said, "and Georgia is a lousy state too."

"You said it," June Star said.

"In my time," said the grandmother, folding her thin veined fingers, "children were more respectful of their native states and their parents and everything else. People did right then. Oh look at the cute little pickaninny!" she said and pointed to a Negro child standing in the door of a shack. "Wouldn't that make a picture, now?" she asked and they all turned and looked at the little Negro out of the back window. He waved.

"He didn't have any britches on," June Star said.

"He probably didn't have any," the grandmother explained. "Little niggers in the country don't have things like we do. If I could paint, I'd paint that
picture," she said. 20

The children exchanged comic books.

The grandmother offered to hold the baby and the children's mother passed him over the front seat to her. She set him on her knee and bounced him and told him about the things they were passing. She rolled her eyes and screwed up her mouth and stuck her leathery thin face into his smooth bland one. Occasionally he gave her a faraway smile. They passed a large cotton field with five or six graves fenced in the middle of it, like a small island. "Look at the graveyard!" the grandmother said, pointing it out. "That was the old family burying ground. That belonged to the plantation."

"Where's the plantation?" John Wesley asked.

"Gone with the Wind,"[1] said the grandmother. "Ha. Ha."

When the children finished all the comic books they had brought, they opened the lunch and ate it. The grandmother ate a peanut butter sandwich and an olive and would not let the children throw the box and the paper napkins out the window. When there was nothing else to do they played a game by choosing a cloud and making the other two guess what shape it suggested. John Wesley took one the shape of a cow and June Star guessed a cow and John Wesley said, no, an automobile, and June Star said he didn't play fair, and they
began to slap each other over the grandmother. 25

The grandmother said she would tell them a story if they would keep quiet. When she told a story, she rolled her eyes and waved her head and was very dramatic. She said once when she was a maiden lady she had been courted by a Mr. Edgar Atkins Teagarden from Jasper, Georgia. She said he was a very good-looking man and a gentleman and that he brought her a watermelon every Saturday afternoon with his initials cut in it, E. A. T. Well, one Saturday, she said, Mr. Teagarden brought the watermelon and there was nobody at home and he left it on the front porch and returned in his buggy to Jasper, but she

---

[1] *Gone with the Wind: Gone with the Wind* is a 1936 novel by Margaret Mitchell about the Civil War.

never got the watermelon, she said, because a nigger boy ate it when he saw the initials, E. A. T.! This story tickled John Wesley's funny bone and he giggled and giggled but June Star didn't think it was any good. She said she wouldn't marry a man that just brought her a watermelon on Saturday. The grandmother said she would have done well to marry Mr. Teagarden because he was a gentleman and had bought Coca-Cola stock when it first came out and that he died only a few years ago, a very wealthy man.

They stopped at The Tower for barbecued sandwiches. The Tower was a part stucco and part wood filling station and dance hall set in a clearing outside of Timothy. A fat man named Red Sammy Butts ran it and there were signs stuck here and there on the building and for miles up and down the highway saying, TRY RED SAMMY'S FAMOUS BARBECUE. NONE LIKE FAMOUS RED SAMMY'S! RED SAM! THE FAT BOY WITH THE HAPPY LAUGH. A VETERAN! RED SAMMY'S YOUR MAN!

Red Sammy was lying on the bare ground outside The Tower with his head under a truck while a gray monkey about a foot high, chained to a small chinaberry tree, chattered nearby. The monkey sprang back into the tree and got on the highest limb as soon as he saw the children jump out of the car and run toward him.

Inside, The Tower was a long dark room with a counter at one end and tables at the other and dancing space in the middle. They all sat down at a board table next to the nickelodeon and Red Sam's wife, a tall burnt-brown woman with hair and eyes lighter than her skin, came and took their order. The children's mother put a dime in the machine and played "The Tennessee Waltz," and the grandmother said that tune always made her want to dance. She asked Bailey if he would like to dance but he only glared at her. He didn't have a naturally sweet disposition like she did and trips made him nervous. The grandmother's brown eyes were very bright. She swayed her head from side to side and pretended she was dancing in her chair. June Star said play something she could tap to so the children's mother put in another dime and played a fast number and June Star stepped out onto the dance floor and did her tap routine.

"Ain't she cute?" Red Sam's wife said, leaning over the counter. "Would you like to come be my little girl?" 30

"No I certainly wouldn't," June Star said. "I wouldn't live in a broken-down place like this for a million bucks!" and she ran back to the table.

"Ain't she cute?" the woman repeated, stretching her mouth politely.

"Aren't you ashamed?" hissed the grandmother.

Red Sam came in and told his wife to quit lounging on the counter and hurry up with these people's order. His khaki trousers reached just to his hip bones and his stomach hung over them like a sack of meal swaying under his shirt. He came over and sat down at a table nearby and let out a combination sigh and yodel. "You can't win," he said. "You can't win," and he wiped his sweating red face off with a gray handkerchief. "These days you don't know who to trust," he said. "Ain't that the truth?"

"People are certainly not nice like they used to be," said the grandmother. 35

"Two fellers come in here last week," Red Sammy said, "driving a Chrysler. It was a old beat-up car but it was a good one and these boys looked all right to me. Said they worked at the mill and you know I let them fellers charge the gas they bought? Now why did I do that?"

"Because you're a good man!" the grandmother said at once.

"Yes'm, I suppose so," Red Sam said as if he were struck with this answer.

His wife brought the orders, carrying the five plates all at once without a tray, two in each hand and one balanced on her arm. "It isn't a soul in this green world of God's that you can trust," she said. "And I don't count nobody out of that, not nobody," she repeated, looking at Red Sammy.

"Did you read about that criminal, The Misfit, that's escaped?" asked the grandmother. 40

"I wouldn't be a bit surprised if he didn't attack this place right here," said the woman. "If he hears about it being here, I wouldn't be none surprised to see him. If he hears it's two cent in the cash register, I wouldn't be at all surprised if he . . ."

"That'll do," Red Sam said. "Go bring these people their Co'-Colas," and the woman went off to get the rest of the order.

"A good man is hard to find," Red Sammy said. "Everything is getting terrible. I remember the day you could go off and leave your screen door unlatched. Not no more."

He and the grandmother discussed better times. The old lady said that in her opinion Europe was entirely to blame for the way things were now. She said the way Europe acted you would think we were made of money and Red Sam said it was no use talking about it, she was exactly right. The children ran outside into the white sunlight and looked at the monkey in the lacy chinaberry tree. He was busy catching fleas on himself and biting each one carefully between his teeth as if it were a delicacy.

They drove off again into the hot afternoon. The grandmother took cat naps and woke up every few minutes with her own snoring. Outside of Toombsboro she woke up and recalled an old plantation that she had visited in this neighborhood once when she was a young lady. She said the house had six white columns across the front and that there was an avenue of oaks leading up to it and two little wooden trellis arbors on either side in front where you sat down with your suitor after a stroll in the garden. She recalled exactly which road to turn off to get to it. She knew that Bailey would not be willing to lose any time looking at an old house, but the more she talked about it, the more she wanted to see it once again and find out if the little twin arbors were still standing. "There was a secret panel in this house," she said craftily, not telling the truth but wishing that she were, "and the story went that all the family silver was hidden in it when Sherman came through but it was never found . . ." 45

"Hey!" John Wesley said. "Let's go see it! We'll find it! We'll poke all the woodwork and find it! Who lives there? Where do you turn off at? Hey Pop, can't we turn off there?"

"We never have seen a house with a secret panel!" June Star shrieked. "Let's go to the house with the secret panel! Hey Pop, can't we go see the house with the secret panel!"

"It's not far from here, I know," the grandmother said. "It wouldn't take over twenty minutes."

Bailey was looking straight ahead. His jaw was as rigid as a horseshoe. "No," he said.

The children began to yell and scream that they wanted to see the house with the secret panel. John Wesley kicked the back of the front seat and June Star hung over her mother's shoulder and whined desperately into her ear that they never had any fun even on their vacation, that they could never do what THEY wanted to do. The baby began to scream and John Wesley kicked the back of the seat so hard that his father could feel the blows in his kidney.

"All right!" he shouted and drew the car to a stop at the side of the road. "Will you all shut up? Will you all just shut up for one second? If you don't shut up, we won't go anywhere."

"It would be very educational for them," the grandmother murmured.

"All right," Bailey said, "but get this: this is the only time we're going to stop for anything like this. This is the one and only time."

"The dirt road that you have to turn down is about a mile back," the grandmother directed. "I marked it when we passed."

"A dirt road," Bailey groaned.

After they had turned around and were headed toward the dirt road, the grandmother recalled other points about the house, the beautiful glass over the front doorway and the candle-lamp in the hall. John Wesley said that the secret panel was probably in the fireplace.

"You can't go inside this house," Bailey said. "You don't know who lives there."

"While you all talk to the people in front, I'll run around behind and get in a window," John Wesley suggested.

"We'll all stay in the car," his mother said.

They turned onto the dirt road and the car raced roughly along in a swirl of pink dust. The grandmother recalled the times when there were no paved roads and thirty miles was a day's journey. The dirt road was hilly and there were sudden washes in it and sharp curves on dangerous embankments. All at once they would be on a hill, looking down over the blue tops of trees for miles around, then the next minute, they would be in a red depression with the dust-coated trees looking down on them.

"This place had better turn up in a minute," Bailey said, "or I'm going to turn around."

The road looked as if no one had traveled on it in months.

"It's not much farther," the grandmother said and just as she said it, a horrible thought came to her. The thought was so embarrassing that she turned red in the face and her eyes dilated and her feet jumped up, upsetting her valise in the corner. The instant the valise moved, the newspaper top she had over the basket under it rose with a snarl and Pitty Sing, the cat, sprang onto Bailey's shoulder.

The children were thrown to the floor and their mother, clutching the baby, was thrown out the door onto the ground; the old lady was thrown into the front seat. The car turned over once and landed right-side-up in a gulch off the side of the road. Bailey remained in the driver's seat with the cat—gray-striped with a broad white face and an orange nose—clinging to his neck like a caterpillar.

As soon as the children saw they could move their arms and legs, they scrambled out of the car, shouting, "We've had an ACCIDENT!" The grandmother was curled up under the dashboard, hoping she was injured so that Bailey's wrath would not come down on her all at once. The horrible thought she had had before the accident was that the house she had remembered so vividly was not in Georgia but in Tennessee. 65

Bailey removed the cat from his neck with both hands and flung it out the window against the side of a pine tree. Then he got out of the car and started looking for the children's mother. She was sitting against the side of the red gutted ditch, holding the screaming baby, but she only had a cut down her face and a broken shoulder. "We've had an ACCIDENT!" the children screamed in a frenzy of delight.

"But nobody's killed," June Star said with disappointment as the grandmother limped out of the car, her hat still pinned to her head but the broken front brim standing up at a jaunty angle and the violet spray hanging off the side. They all sat down in the ditch, except the children, to recover from the shock. They were all shaking.

"Maybe a car will come along," said the children's mother hoarsely.

"I believe I have injured an organ," said the grandmother, pressing her side, but no one answered her. Bailey's teeth were clattering. He had on a yellow sport shirt with bright blue parrots designed in it and his face was as yellow as the shirt. The grandmother decided that she would not mention that the house was in Tennessee.

The road was about ten feet above and they could see only the tops of the trees on the other side of it. Behind the ditch they were sitting in there were more woods, tall and dark and deep. In a few minutes they saw a car some distance away on top of a hill, coming slowly as if the occupants were watching them. The grandmother stood up and waved both arms dramatically to attract their attention. The car continued to come on slowly, disappeared around a bend and appeared again, moving even slower, on top of the hill they had gone over. It was a big black battered hearse-like automobile. There were three men in it. 70

It came to a stop just over them and for some minutes, the driver looked down with a steady expressionless gaze to where they were sitting, and didn't speak. Then he turned his head and muttered something to the other two and they got out. One was a fat boy in black trousers and a red sweat shirt with a silver stallion embossed on the front of it. He moved around on the right side of them and stood staring, his mouth partly open in a kind of loose grin. The other had on khaki pants and a blue striped coat and a gray hat pulled down very low, hiding most of his face. He came around slowly on the left side. Neither spoke.

The driver got out of the car and stood by the side of it, looking down at them. He was an older man than the other two. His hair was just beginning to gray and he wore silver-rimmed spectacles that gave him a scholarly look. He had a long creased face and didn't have on any shirt or undershirt. He had on blue jeans that were too tight for him and was holding a black hat and a gun. The two boys also had guns.

"We've had an ACCIDENT!" the children screamed.

The grandmother had the peculiar feeling that the bespectacled man was someone she knew. His face was as familiar to her as if she had known him all her life but she could not recall who he was. He moved away from the car and began to come down the embankment, placing his feet carefully so that he wouldn't slip. He had on tan and white shoes and no socks, and his ankles were red and thin. "Good afternoon," he said. "I see you all had you a little spill."

"We turned over twice!" said the grandmother. 75

"Oncet," he corrected. "We seen it happen. Try their car and see will it run, Hiram," he said quietly to the boy with the gray hat.

"What you got that gun for?" John Wesley asked. "Watcha gonna do with that gun?"

"Lady," the man said to the children's mother, "would you mind calling them children to sit down by you? Children make me nervous. I want all you all to sit down right together there where you're at."

"What are you telling US what to do for?" June Star asked.

Behind them the line of woods gaped like a dark open mouth. "Come here," said their mother. 80

"Look here now," Bailey began suddenly, "we're in a predicament! We're in . . ."

The grandmother shrieked. She scrambled to her feet and stood staring. "You're The Misfit!" she said. "I recognized you at once!"

"Yes'm," the man said, smiling slightly as if he were pleased in spite of himself to be known, "but it would have been better for all of you, lady, if you hadn't of reckernized me."

Bailey turned his head sharply and said something to his mother that shocked even the children. The old lady began to cry and The Misfit reddened.

"Lady," he said, "don't you get upset. Sometimes a man says things he don't mean. I don't reckon he meant to talk to you thataway." 85

"You wouldn't shoot a lady, would you?" the grandmother said and removed a clean handkerchief from her cuff and began to slap at her eyes with it.

The Misfit pointed the toe of his shoe into the ground and made a little hole and then covered it up again. "I would hate to have to," he said.

"Listen," the grandmother almost screamed, "I know you're a good man. You don't look a bit like you have common blood. I know you must come from nice people!"

"Yes mam," he said, "finest people in the world." When he smiled he showed a row of strong white teeth. "God never made a finer woman than my mother and my daddy's heart was pure gold," he said. The boy with the red sweat shirt had come around behind them and was standing with his gun at his hip. The Misfit squatted down on the ground. "Watch them children, Bobby Lee," he said. "You know they make me nervous." He looked at the six of them huddled together in front of him and he seemed to be embarrassed as if he couldn't think of anything to say. "Ain't a cloud in the sky," he remarked, looking up at it. "Don't see no sun but don't see no cloud neither."

"Yes, it's a beautiful day," said the grandmother. "Listen," she said, "you shouldn't call yourself The Misfit because I know you're a good man at heart. I can just look at you and tell." 90

"Hush!" Bailey yelled. "Hush! Everybody shut up and let me handle this!" He was squatting in the position of a runner about to sprint forward but he didn't move.

"I pre-chate that, lady," The Misfit said and drew a little circle in the ground with the butt of his gun.

"It'll take a half a hour to fix this here car," Hiram called, looking over the raised hood of it.

"Well, first you and Bobby Lee get him and that little boy to step over yonder with you," The Misfit said, pointing to Bailey and John Wesley. "The boys want to ast you something," he said to Bailey. "Would you mind stepping back in them woods there with them?"

"Listen," Bailey began, "we're in a terrible predicament! Nobody realizes what this is," and his voice cracked. His eyes were as blue and intense as the parrots in his shirt and he remained perfectly still. 95

The grandmother reached up to adjust her hat brim as if she were going to the woods with him but it came off in her hand. She stood staring at it and after a second she let it fall on the ground. Hiram pulled Bailey up by the arm as if he were assisting an old man. John Wesley caught hold of his father's hand and Bobby Lee followed. They went off toward the woods and just as they reached the dark edge, Bailey turned and supporting himself against a gray naked pine trunk, he shouted, "I'll be back in a minute, Mamma, wait on me!"

"Come back this instant!" his mother shrilled but they all disappeared into the woods.

"Bailey Boy!" the grandmother called in a tragic voice but she found she was looking at The Misfit squatting on the ground in front of her. "I just know you're a good man," she said desperately. "You're not a bit common!"

"Nome, I ain't a good man," The Misfit said after a second as if he had considered her statement carefully, "but I ain't the worst in the world neither. My daddy said I was a different breed of dog from my brothers and sisters. 'You know,' Daddy said, 'it's some that can live their whole life out without asking about it and it's others has to know why it is, and this boy is one of the latters. He's going to be into everything!'" He put on his black hat and looked up suddenly and then away deep into the woods as if he were embarrassed again. "I'm sorry I don't have on a shirt before you ladies," he said, hunching his shoulders slightly. "We buried our clothes that we had on when we escaped and we're just making do until we can get better. We borrowed these from some folks we met," he explained.

"That's perfectly all right," the grandmother said. "Maybe Bailey has an extra shirt in his suitcase." 100

"I'll look and see terrectly," The Misfit said.

"Where are they taking him?" the children's mother screamed.

"Daddy was a card himself," The Misfit said. "You couldn't put anything over on him. He never got in trouble with the Authorities though. Just had the knack of handling them."

"You could be honest too if you'd only try," said the grandmother. "Think how wonderful it would be to settle down and live a comfortable life and not have to think about somebody chasing you all the time."

The Misfit kept scratching in the ground with the butt of his gun as if he were thinking about it. "Yes'm, somebody is always after you," he murmured. 105

The grandmother noticed how thin his shoulder blades were just behind his hat because she was standing up looking down on him. "Do you ever pray?" she asked.

He shook his head. All she saw was the black hat wiggle between his shoulder blades. "Nome," he said.

There was a pistol shot from the woods, followed closely by another. Then silence. The old lady's head jerked around. She could hear the wind move through the tree tops like a long satisfied insuck of breath. "Bailey Boy!" she called.

"I was a gospel singer for a while," The Misfit said. "I been most everything. Been in the arm service, both land and sea, at home and abroad, been twict married, been an undertaker, been with the railroads, plowed Mother Earth, been in a tornado, seen a man burnt alive oncet," and he looked up at the children's mother and the little girl who were sitting close together, their faces white and their eyes glassy; "I even seen a woman flogged," he said.

"Pray, pray," the grandmother began, "pray, pray . . ." 110

"I never was a bad boy that I remember of," The Misfit said in an almost dreamy voice, "but somewheres along the line I done something wrong and got sent to the penitentiary. I was buried alive," and he looked up and held her attention to him by a steady stare.

"That's when you should have started to pray," she said. "What did you do to get sent to the penitentiary that first time?"

"Turn to the right, it was a wall," The Misfit said, looking up again at the cloudless sky. "Turn to the left, it was a wall. Look up it was a ceiling, look down it was a floor. I forget what I done, lady. I set there and set there, trying to remember what it was I done and I ain't recalled it to this day. Oncet in a while, I would think it was coming to me, but it never come."

"Maybe they put you in by mistake," the old lady said vaguely.

"Nome," he said. "It wasn't no mistake. They had the papers on me." 115

"You must have stolen something," she said.

The Misfit sneered slightly. "Nobody had nothing I wanted," he said. "It was a head-doctor at the penitentiary said what I had done was kill my daddy but I known that for a lie. My daddy died in nineteen ought nineteen of the epidemic flu and I never had a thing to do with it. He was buried in the Mount Hopewell Baptist churchyard and you can go there and see for yourself."

"If you would pray," the old lady said, "Jesus would help you."

"That's right," The Misfit said.

"Well then, why don't you pray?" she asked trembling with delight suddenly. 120

"I don't want no hep," he said. "I'm doing all right by myself."

Bobby Lee and Hiram came ambling back from the woods. Bobby Lee was dragging a yellow shirt with bright blue parrots in it.

"Thow me that shirt, Bobby Lee," The Misfit said. The shirt came flying at him and landed on his shoulder and he put it on. The grandmother couldn't name what the shirt reminded her of. "No, lady," The Misfit said while he was buttoning it up, "I found out the crime don't matter. You can do one thing or you can do another, kill a man or take a tire off his car, because sooner or later you're going to forget what it was you done and just be punished for it."

The children's mother had begun to make heaving noises as if she couldn't get her breath. "Lady," he asked, "would you and that little girl like to step off yonder with Bobby Lee and Hiram and join your husband?"

"Yes, thank you," the mother said faintly. Her left arm dangled helplessly and she was holding the baby, who had gone to sleep, in the other. "Hep that lady up, Hiram," The Misfit said as she struggled to climb out of the ditch, "and Bobby Lee, you hold onto that little girl's hand." 125

"I don't want to hold hands with him," June Star said. "He reminds me of a pig."

The fat boy blushed and laughed and caught her by the arm and pulled her off into the woods after Hiram and her mother.

Alone with The Misfit, the grandmother found that she had lost her voice. There was not a cloud in the sky nor any sun. There was nothing around her but woods. She wanted to tell him that he must pray. She opened and closed her mouth several times before anything came out. Finally she found herself saying, "Jesus, Jesus," meaning, Jesus will help you, but the way she was saying it, it sounded as if she might be cursing.

"Yes'm," The Misfit said as if he agreed. "Jesus thown everything off balance. It was the same case with Him as with me except He hadn't committed any crime and they could prove I had committed one because they had the papers on me. Of course," he said, "they never shown me my papers. That's why I sign myself now. I said long ago, you get you a signature and sign everything you do and keep a copy of it. Then you'll know what you done and you can hold up the crime to the punishment and see do they match and in the end you'll have something to prove you ain't been treated right. I call myself The Misfit," he said, "because I can't make what all I done wrong fit what all I gone through in punishment."

There was a piercing scream from the woods, followed closely by a pistol report. "Does it seem right to you, lady, that one is punished a heap and another ain't punished at all?" 130

"Jesus!" the old lady cried. "You've got good blood! I know you wouldn't shoot a lady! I know you come from nice people! Pray! Jesus, you ought not to shoot a lady. I'll give you all the money I've got!"

"Lady," The Misfit said, looking beyond her far into the woods, "there never was a body that give the undertaker a tip."

There were two more pistol reports and the grandmother raised her head like a parched old turkey hen crying for water and called, "Bailey Boy, Bailey Boy!" as if her heart would break.

"Jesus was the only One that ever raised the dead," The Misfit continued, "and He shouldn't have done it. He thown everything off balance. If He did what He said, then it's nothing for you to do but thow away everything and follow Him, and if He didn't, then it's nothing for you to do but enjoy the few minutes you got left the best way you can—by killing somebody or burning down his house or doing some other meanness to him. No pleasure but meanness," he said and his voice became almost a snarl.

"Maybe He didn't raise the dead," the old lady mumbled, not knowing what she was saying and feeling so dizzy that she sank down in the ditch with her legs twisted under her. 135

"I wasn't there so I can't say He didn't," The Misfit said. "I wisht I had of been there," he said, hitting the ground with his fist. "It ain't right I wasn't there because if I had of been there I would of known. Listen, lady," he said in a high voice, "if I had of been there I would of known and I wouldn't be like I am now." His voice seemed about to crack and the grandmother's head cleared for an instant. She saw the man's face twisted close to her own as if he were going to cry and she murmured, "Why you're one of my babies. You're one of my own children!" She reached out and touched him on the shoulder. The Misfit sprang back as if a snake had bitten him and shot her three times through the chest. Then he put his gun down on the ground and took off his glasses and began to clean them.

Hiram and Bobby Lee returned from the woods and stood over the ditch, looking down at the grandmother who half sat and half lay in a puddle of blood with her legs crossed under her like a child's and her face smiling up at the cloudless sky.

Without his glasses, The Misfit's eyes were red-rimmed and pale and defenseless-looking. "Take her off and thow her where you thown the others," he said, picking up the cat that was rubbing itself against his leg.

"She was a talker, wasn't she?" Bobby Lee said, sliding down the ditch with a yodel.

"She would of been a good woman," The Misfit said, "if it had been somebody there to shoot her every minute of her life." 140

"Some fun!" Bobby Lee said.

"Shut up, Bobby Lee," The Misfit said. "It's no real pleasure in life."

Reading and Reacting

1. How are the style and tone of the narrator's voice different from those of the characters? What, if anything, is the significance of this difference?
2. The figures of speech used in this story sometimes create unflattering, even grotesque, pictures of the characters. Find several examples of such negative figures of speech. Why do you think O'Connor uses them?
3. What does the grandmother's use of racial slurs reveal about her? How are readers expected to reconcile this language with her very proper appearance and her preoccupation with manners? How does her use of these words affect your reaction to her?
4. Explain the **irony** in this statement: "In case of an accident, anyone seeing her dead on the highway would know at once that she was a lady" (par. 12).
5. How does The Misfit's dialect characterize him?
6. What does the **allusion** to *Gone with the Wind* (par. 24) contribute to the story?
7. How do the style and tone of the two-paragraph description of the three men in the car (pars. 71–72) help to prepare readers for the events that follow?
8. When The Misfit tells the grandmother about his life, his language takes on a measured, rhythmic quality: "Been in the arm service, both land and sea, at home and abroad, been twict married, been an undertaker, been with the railroads, plowed Mother Earth, been in a tornado, seen a man burnt alive oncet . . ." (par. 109). Find other examples of rhythmic repetition and parallelism in this character's speech. How does this style help to develop The Misfit's character?
9. **Journal Entry** Why do you think the grandmother tells The Misfit that she recognizes him? Why does she fail to realize the danger of her remark?
10. **Critical Perspective** In his essay "Light and Shadow: Religious Grace in Two Stories by Flannery O'Connor," David Allen Cook writes:

    > The literary works of Flannery O'Connor often contend that religious belief can only be consummated by direct confrontation with evil, and for those uncommitted and unprepared, tragedy seems inevitable. For O'Connor's religious "pretenders," a moment of religious grace—a revelation of Truth—often does come, but at a devastating price. In . . . "A Good Man Is Hard to Find," we are presented with main characters that experience a deep epiphany after being spiritually challenged by the darker side of human nature.

    In this story, who are the religious "pretenders," and who has true faith? What is the price of achieving a moment of religious grace? What role does violence play in this equation?

Related Works: "Slide to Unlock" (p. 117), "The Cask of Amontillado (p. 258), "The Lottery" (p. 337), "Where Are You Going, Where Have You Been?" (p. 447), "Hitler's First Photograph" (p. 519)

Historic Images/Alamy Stock Photo

CHARLOTTE PERKINS GILMAN (1860–1935) was a prominent feminist and social thinker at the turn of the century. Her essays, lectures, and nonfiction works—such as *Women and Economics* (1898), *Concerning Children* (1900), and *The Man-Made World* (1911)—are forceful statements of Gilman's opinions on women's need for economic independence and social equality. Gilman is probably best known for three utopian feminist novels: *Moving the Mountain* (1911), *Herland* (1915; unpublished until 1978), and *With Her in Ourland* (1916). Her works are full of humor and satire. In *Herland*, for example, a male sociologist (wandering in by accident from the outside world) is chagrined to find that the women of "Herland" want him as a friend, not a lover.

Although "The Yellow Wallpaper" (1892) is not typical of Gilman's other fiction, it is considered her artistic masterpiece. The terse, clinical precision of the writing, conveying the tightly wound and distraught mental state of the narrator, is particularly chilling when it is read with a knowledge of Gilman's personal history. In the 1880s, she met and married a young artist, Charles Walter Stetson. Following the birth of their daughter, she grew increasingly depressed and turned to a noted Philadelphia neurologist for help. Following the traditions of the time, he prescribed complete bed rest and mental inactivity—a treatment that, Gilman said later, drove her "so near the borderline of utter mental ruin that I could see over." "The Yellow Wallpaper" is not simply a psychological study. Like most of Gilman's work, it makes a point—in this case, about the dangers of women's utter dependence on a male interpretation of their needs.

Cultural Context Recent research indicates that one out of every ten new mothers becomes seriously depressed within six months after childbirth. This condition is known as postpartum depression, and its symptoms include severe feelings of sadness or emptiness, withdrawal from family and friends, a strong sense of failure or inadequacy, intense concern (or lack of concern) about the baby, and, in more serious cases, thoughts about suicide or fears of harming the baby. Today's treatments include medication and psychotherapy, but at the time of this story, the standard treatment was a "rest cure," in which the patient was placed in isolation and kept from distractions that were believed to be dangerous. For many patients (as for the narrator of this story), this "cure" was worse than the condition itself.

The Yellow Wallpaper (1892)

It is very seldom that mere ordinary people like John and myself secure ancestral halls for the summer.

A colonial mansion, a hereditary estate, I would say a haunted house, and reach the height of romantic felicity—but that would be asking too much of fate!

Still I will proudly declare that there is something queer about it.

Else, why should it be let so cheaply? And why have stood so long untenanted?

John laughs at me, of course, but one expects that in marriage.

John is practical in the extreme. He has no patience with faith, an intense horror of superstition, and he scoffs openly at any talk of things not to be felt and seen and put down in figures.

John is a physician, and *perhaps*—(I would not say it to a living soul, of course, but this is dead paper and a great relief to my mind—) *perhaps* that is one reason I do not get well faster.

You see he does not believe I am sick!

And what can one do?

If a physician of high standing, and one's own husband, assures friends and relatives that there is really nothing the matter with one but temporary nervous depression—a slight hysterical tendency—what is one to do?

My brother is also a physician, and also of high standing, and he says the same thing.

So I take phosphates or phosphites[1]—whichever it is, and tonics, and journeys, and air, and exercise, and am absolutely forbidden to "work" until I am well again.

Personally, I disagree with their ideas.

Personally, I believe that congenial work, with excitement and change, would do me good.

But what is one to do?

I did write for a while in spite of them; but it *does* exhaust me a good deal—having to be so sly about it, or else meet with heavy opposition.

I sometimes fancy that in my condition if I had less opposition and more society and stimulus—but John says the very worst thing I can do is to think about my condition, and I confess it always makes me feel bad.

So I will let it alone and talk about the house.

The most beautiful place! It is quite alone, standing well back from the road, quite three miles from the village. It makes me think of English places that you read about, for there are hedges and walls and gates that lock, and lots of separate little houses for the gardeners and people.

There is a *delicious* garden! I never saw such a garden—large and shady, full of box-bordered paths, and lined with long grape-covered arbors with seats under them.

There were greenhouses, too, but they are all broken now.

There was some legal trouble, I believe, something about the heirs and co-heirs; anyhow, the place has been empty for years.

That spoils my ghostliness, I am afraid, but I don't care—there is something strange about the house—I can feel it.

---

[1] *phosphates or phosphites:* Both terms refer to salts of phosphorous acid. The narrator, however, means "phosphate," a carbonated beverage of water, flavoring, and a small amount of phosphoric acid.

I even said so to John one moonlight evening, but he said what I felt was a *draught*, and shut the window.

I get unreasonably angry with John sometimes. I'm sure I never used to be so sensitive. I think it is due to this nervous condition.

But John says if I feel so, I shall neglect proper self-control; so I take pains to control myself—before him, at least, and that makes me very tired.

I don't like our room a bit. I wanted one downstairs that opened on the piazza and had roses all over the window, and such pretty old-fashioned chintz hangings! But John would not hear of it.

He said there was only one window and not room for two beds, and no near room for him if he took another.

He is very careful and loving, and hardly lets me stir without special direction.

I have a schedule prescription for each hour in the day; he takes all care from me, and so I feel basely ungrateful not to value it more.

He said we came here solely on my account, that I was to have perfect rest and all the air I could get. "Your exercise depends on your strength, my dear," said he, "and your food somewhat on your appetite; but air you can absorb all the time." So we took the nursery at the top of the house.

It is a big, airy room, the whole floor nearly, with windows that look all ways, and air and sunshine galore. It was nursery first and then playroom and gymnasium, I should judge; for the windows are barred for little children, and there are rings and things in the walls.

The paint and paper look as if a boys' school had used it. It is stripped off—the paper—in great patches all around the head of my bed, about as far as I can reach, and in a great place on the other side of the room low down. I never saw a worse paper in my life.

One of those sprawling flamboyant patterns committing every artistic sin.

It is dull enough to confuse the eye in following, pronounced enough to constantly irritate and provoke study, and when you follow the lame uncertain curves for a little distance they suddenly commit suicide—plunge off at outrageous angles, destroy themselves in unheard of contradictions.

The color is repellent, almost revolting; a smouldering unclean yellow, strangely faded by the slow-turning sunlight.

It is a dull yet lurid orange in some places, a sickly sulphur tint in others.

No wonder the children hated it! I should hate it myself if I had to live in this room long.

There comes John, and I must put this away,—he hates to have me write a word.

* * *

We have been here two weeks, and I haven't felt like writing before, since that first day.

I am sitting by the window now, up in this atrocious nursery, and there is nothing to hinder my writing as much as I please, save lack of strength.

John is away all day, and even some nights when his cases are serious.

I am glad my case is not serious!

But these nervous troubles are dreadfully depressing.

John does not know how much I really suffer. He knows there is no *reason* to suffer, and that satisfies him.

Of course it is only nervousness. It does weigh on me so not to do my duty in any way!

I meant to be such a help to John, such a real rest and comfort, and here I am a comparative burden already!

Nobody would believe what an effort it is to do what little I am able,—to dress and entertain, and order things.

It is fortunate Mary is so good with the baby. Such a dear baby!

And yet I *cannot* be with him, it makes me so nervous.

I suppose John never was nervous in his life. He laughs at me so about this wallpaper!

At first he meant to repaper the room, but afterwards he said that I was letting it get the better of me, and that nothing was worse for a nervous patient than to give way to such fancies.

He said that after the wallpaper was changed it would be the heavy bedstead, and then the barred windows, and then that gate at the head of the stairs, and so on.

"You know the place is doing you good," he said, "and really, dear, I don't care to renovate the house just for a three months' rental."

"Then do let us go downstairs," I said, "there are such pretty rooms there."

Then he took me in his arms and called me a blessed little goose, and said he would go down cellar, if I wished, and have it whitewashed into the bargain.

But he is right enough about the beds and windows and things.

It is an airy and comfortable room as any one need wish, and, of course, I would not be so silly as to make him uncomfortable just for a whim.

I'm really getting quite fond of the big room, all but that horrid paper.

Out of one window I can see the garden, those mysterious deep-shaded arbors, the riotous old-fashioned flowers, and bushes and gnarly trees.

Out of another I get a lovely view of the bay and a little private wharf belonging to the estate. There is a beautiful shaded lane that runs down there from the house. I always fancy I see people walking in these numerous paths and arbors, but John has cautioned me not to give way to fancy in the least. He says that with my imaginative power and habit of story-making, a nervous weakness like mine is sure to lead to all manner of excited fancies, and that I ought to use my will and good sense to check the tendency. So I try.

I think sometimes that if I were only well enough to write a little it would relieve the press of ideas and rest me.

But I find I get pretty tired when I try.

It is so discouraging not to have any advice and companionship about my work. When I get really well, John says we will ask Cousin Henry and Julia down for a long visit; but he says he would as soon put fireworks in my pillow-case as to let me have those stimulating people about now.

I wish I could get well faster.

But I must not think about that. This paper looks to me as if it *knew* what a vicious influence it had!

There is a recurrent spot where the pattern lolls like a broken neck and two bulbous eyes stare at you upside down.

I get positively angry with the impertinence of it and the everlastingness. Up and down and sideways they crawl, and those absurd, unblinking eyes are everywhere. There is one place where two breadths didn't match, and the eyes go all up and down the line, one a little higher than the other.

I never saw so much expression in an inanimate thing before, and we all know how much expression they have! I used to lie awake as a child and get more entertainment and terror out of blank walls and plain furniture than most children could find in a toy-store.

I remember what a kindly wink the knobs of our big, old bureau used to have, and there was one chair that always seemed like a strong friend.

I used to feel that if any of the other things looked too fierce I could always hop into that chair and be safe.

The furniture in this room is no worse than inharmonious, however, for we had to bring it all from downstairs. I suppose when this was used as a playroom they had to take the nursery things out, and no wonder! I never saw such ravages as the children have made here.

The wallpaper, as I said before, is torn off in spots, and it sticketh closer than a brother—they must have had perseverance as well as hatred.

Then the floor is scratched and gouged and splintered, the plaster itself is dug out here and there, and this great heavy bed which is all we found in the room, looks as if it had been through the wars.

But I don't mind it a bit—only the paper.

There comes John's sister. Such a dear girl as she is, and so careful of me! I must not let her find me writing.

She is a perfect and enthusiastic housekeeper, and hopes for no better profession. I verily believe she thinks it is the writing which made me sick!

But I can write when she is out, and see her a long way off from these windows.

There is one that commands the road, a lovely shaded winding road, and one that just looks off over the country. A lovely country, too, full of great elms and velvet meadows.

This wallpaper has a kind of sub-pattern in a different shade, a particularly irritating one, for you can only see it in certain lights, and not clearly then.

But in the places where it isn't faded and where the sun is just so—I can see a strange, provoking, formless sort of figure, that seems to skulk about behind that silly and conspicuous front design.

There's sister on the stairs!

* * *

Well, the Fourth of July is over! The people are all gone and I am tired out. John thought it might do me good to see a little company, so we just had mother and Nellie and the children down for a week.

Of course I didn't do a thing. Jennie sees to everything now.

But it tired me all the same. 85

John says if I don't pick up faster he shall send me to Weir Mitchell[2] in the fall.

But I don't want to go there at all. I had a friend who was in his hands once, and she says he is just like John and my brother, only more so!

Besides, it is such an undertaking to go so far.

I don't feel as if it was worth while to turn my hand over for anything, and I'm getting dreadfully fretful and querulous.

I cry at nothing, and cry most of the time. 90

Of course I don't when John is here, or anybody else, but when I am alone.

And I am alone a good deal just now. John is kept in town very often by serious cases, and Jennie is good and lets me alone when I want her to.

So I walk a little in the garden or down that lovely lane, sit on the porch under the roses, and lie down up here a good deal.

I'm getting really fond of the room in spite of the wallpaper. Perhaps *because* of the wallpaper.

It dwells in my mind so! 95

I lie here on this great immovable bed—it is nailed down, I believe—and follow that pattern about by the hour. It is as good as gymnastics, I assure you. I start, we'll say, at the bottom, down in the corner over there where it has not been touched, and I determine for the thousandth time that I *will* follow that pointless pattern to some sort of a conclusion.

I know a little of the principle of design, and I know this thing was not arranged on any laws of radiation, or alternation, or repetition, or symmetry, or anything else that I ever heard of.

It is repeated, of course, by the breadths, but not otherwise.

Looked at in one way each breadth stands alone, the bloated curves and flourishes—a kind of "debased Romanesque" with *delirium tremens*[3] go waddling up and down in isolated columns of fatuity.

But, on the other hand, they connect diagonally, and the sprawling outlines run off in great slanting waves of optic horror, like a lot of wallowing seaweeds in full chase. 100

---

[2] *Weir Mitchell:* Silas Weir Mitchell (1829–1914), a Philadelphia neurologist-psychologist who introduced the "rest cure" for nervous diseases.

[3] *delirium tremens:* Mental confusion caused by alcohol poisoning and characterized by physical tremors and hallucinations.

The whole thing goes horizontally, too, at least it seems so, and I exhaust myself in trying to distinguish the order of its going in that direction.

They have used a horizontal breadth for a frieze, and that adds wonderfully to the confusion.

There is one end of the room where it is almost intact, and there, when the crosslights fade and the low sun shines directly upon it, I can almost fancy radiation after all,—the interminable grotesques seems to form around a common center and rush off in headlong plunges of equal distraction.

It makes me tired to follow it. I will take a nap I guess.

I don't know why I should write this. 105

I don't want to.

I don't feel able.

And I know John would think it absurd. But I *must* say what I feel and think in some way—it is such a relief!

But the effort is getting to be greater than the relief.

Half the time now I am awfully lazy, and lie down ever so much. 110

John says I mustn't lose my strength, and has me take cod liver oil and lots of tonics and things, to say nothing of ale and wine and rare meat.

Dear John! He loves me very dearly, and hates to have me sick. I tried to have a real earnest reasonable talk with him the other day, and tell him how I wish he would let me go and make a visit to Cousin Henry and Julia.

But he said I wasn't able to go, nor able to stand it after I got there; and I did not make out a very good case for myself, for I was crying before I had finished.

It is getting to be a great effort for me to think straight. Just this nervous weakness I suppose.

And dear John gathered me up in his arms, and just carried me upstairs and laid me on the bed, and sat by me and read to me till it tired my head. 115

He said I was his darling and his comfort and all he had, and that I must take care of myself for his sake, and keep well.

He says no one but myself can help me out of it, that I must use my will and self-control and not let any silly fancies run away with me.

There's one comfort, the baby is well and happy, and does not have to occupy this nursery with the horrid wallpaper.

If we had not used it, that blessed child would have! What a fortunate escape! Why, I wouldn't have a child of mine, an impressionable little thing, live in such a room for worlds.

I never thought of it before, but it is lucky that John kept me here after all, I can stand it so much easier than a baby, you see. 120

Of course I never mention it to them any more—I am too wise,—but I keep watch of it all the same.

There are things in that paper that nobody knows but me, or ever will.

Behind that outside pattern the dim shapes get clearer every day.

It is always the same shape, only very numerous.

And it is like a woman stooping down and creeping about behind that pattern. I don't like it a bit. I wonder—I begin to think—I wish John would take me away from here! 125

It is so hard to talk with John about my case, because he is so wise, and because he loves me so.

But I tried it last night.

It was moonlight. The moon shines in all around just as the sun does.

I hate to see it sometimes, it creeps so slowly, and always comes in by one window or another.

John was asleep and I hated to waken him, so I kept still and watched the moonlight on that undulating wallpaper till I felt creepy.

The faint figure behind seemed to shake the pattern, just as if she wanted to get out.

I got up softly and went to feel and see if the paper *did* move, and when I came back John was awake.

"What is it, little girl?" he said. "Don't go walking about like that—you'll get cold."

I thought it was a good time to talk, so I told him that I really was not gaining here, and that I wished he would take me away.

"Why, darling!" said he, "our lease will be up in three weeks, and I can't see how to leave before.

"The repairs are not done at home, and I cannot possibly leave town just now. Of course if you were in any danger, I could and would, but you really are better, dear, whether you can see it or not. I am a doctor, dear, and I know. You are gaining flesh and color, your appetite is better, I feel really much easier about you."

"I don't weigh a bit more," said I, "nor as much; and my appetite may be better in the evening when you are here, but it is worse in the morning when you are away!"

"Bless her little heart!" said he with a big hug, "she shall be as sick as she pleases! But now let's improve the shining hours by going to sleep, and talk about it in the morning!"

"And you won't go away?" I asked gloomily.

"Why, how can I, dear? It is only three weeks more and then we will take a nice little trip of a few days while Jennie is getting the house ready. Really dear you are better!"

"Better in body perhaps—" I began, and stopped short, for he sat up straight and looked at me with such a stern, reproachful look that I could not say another word.

"My darling," said he, "I beg of you, for my sake and for our child's sake, as well as for your own, that you will never for one instant let that idea enter your mind! There is nothing so dangerous, so fascinating, to a temperament like yours. It is a false and foolish fancy. Can you not trust me as a physician when I tell you so?"

So of course I said no more on that score, and we went to sleep before long. He thought I was asleep first, but I wasn't, and lay there for hours trying to decide whether that front pattern and the back pattern really did move together or separately.

On a pattern like this, by daylight, there is a lack of sequence, a defiance of law, that is a constant irritant to a normal mind.

The color is hideous enough, and unreliable enough, and infuriating enough, but the pattern is torturing.

You think you have mastered it, but just as you get well underway in following, it turns back-somersault and there you are. It slaps you in the face, knocks you down, and tramples upon you. It is like a bad dream.

The outside pattern is a florid arabesque, reminding one of a fungus. If you can imagine a toadstool in joints, an interminable string of toadstools, budding and sprouting in endless convolutions—why, that is something like it.

That is, sometimes!

There is one marked peculiarity about this paper, a thing nobody seems to notice but myself, and that is that it changes as the light changes.

When the sun shoots in through the east window—I always watch for that first long, straight ray—it changes so quickly that I never can quite believe it.

That is why I watch it always.

By moonlight—the moon shines in all night when there is a moon—I wouldn't know it was the same paper.

At night in any kind of light, in twilight, candlelight, lamplight, and worst of all by moonlight, it becomes bars! The outside pattern I mean, and the woman behind it is as plain as can be.

I didn't realize for a long time what the thing was that showed behind, that dim sub-pattern, but now I am quite sure it is a woman.

By daylight she is subdued, quiet. I fancy it is the pattern that keeps her so still. It is so puzzling. It keeps me quiet by the hour.

I lie down ever so much now. John says it is good for me, and to sleep all I can.

Indeed he started the habit by making me lie down for an hour after each meal.

It is a very bad habit I am convinced, for you see I don't sleep.

And that cultivates deceit, for I don't tell them I'm awake—O no!

The fact is I am getting a little afraid of John.

He seems very queer sometimes, and even Jennie has an inexplicable look.

It strikes me occasionally, just as a scientific hypothesis,—that perhaps it is the paper!

I have watched John when he did not know I was looking, and come into the room suddenly on the most innocent excuses, and I've caught him several times *looking at the paper!* And Jennie too. I caught Jennie with her hand on it once.

She didn't know I was in the room, and when I asked her in a quiet, a very quiet voice, with the most restrained manner possible, what she was doing with the paper—she turned around as if she had been caught stealing, and looked quite angry—asked me why I should frighten her so!

Then she said that the paper stained everything it touched, that she had found yellow smooches on all my clothes and John's, and she wished we would be more careful! 165

Did not that sound innocent? But I know she was studying that pattern, and I am determined that nobody shall find it out but myself!

Life is very much more exciting now than it used to be. You see I have something more to expect, to look forward to, to watch. I really do eat better, and am more quiet than I was.

John is so pleased to see me improve! He laughed a little the other day, and said I seemed to be flourishing in spite of my wallpaper.

I turned it off with a laugh. I had no intention of telling him it was *because* of the wallpaper—he would make fun of me. He might even want to take me away.

I don't want to leave now until I have found it out. There is a week more, and I think that will be enough. 170

I'm feeling ever so much better! I don't sleep much at night, for it is so interesting to watch developments; but I sleep a good deal in the daytime.

In the daytime it is tiresome and perplexing.

There are always new shoots on the fungus, and new shades of yellow all over it. I cannot keep count of them, though I have tried conscientiously.

It is the strangest yellow, that wallpaper! It makes me think of all the yellow things I ever saw—not beautiful ones like buttercups, but old foul, bad yellow things.

But there is something else about that paper—the smell! I noticed it the moment we came into the room, but with so much air and sun it was not bad. Now we have had a week of fog and rain, and whether the windows are open or not, the smell is here. 175

It creeps all over the house.

I find it hovering in the dining-room, skulking in the parlor, hiding in the hall, lying in wait for me on the stairs.

It gets into my hair.

Even when I go to ride, if I turn my head suddenly and surprise it—there is that smell!

Such a peculiar odor, too! I have spent hours in trying to analyze it, to find what it smelled like. 180

It is not bad—at first, and very gentle, but quite the subtlest, most enduring odor I ever met.

In this damp weather it is awful, I wake up in the night and find it hanging over me.

It used to disturb me at first. I thought seriously of burning the house—to reach the smell.

But now I am used to it. The only thing I can think of that it is like is the *color* of the paper! A yellow smell.

There is a very funny mark on this wall, low down, near the mop-board. A streak that runs round the room. It goes behind every piece of furniture, except the bed, a long, straight, even *smooch*, as if it had been rubbed over and over.

I wonder how it was done and who did it, and what they did it for. Round and round and round—round and round and round!—it makes me dizzy!

I really have discovered something at last.

Through watching so much at night, when it changes so, I have finally found out.

The front pattern *does* move—and no wonder! The woman behind shakes it!

Sometimes I think there are a great many women behind, and sometimes only one, and she crawls around fast, and her crawling shakes it all over.

Then in the very bright spots she keeps still, and in the very shady spots she just takes hold of the bars and shakes them hard.

And she is all the time trying to climb through. But nobody could climb through that pattern—it strangles so; I think that is why it has so many heads.

They get through, and then the pattern strangles them off and turns them upside down, and makes their eyes white!

If those heads were covered or taken off it would not be half so bad.

I think that woman gets out in the daytime!

And I'll tell you why—privately—I've seen her!

I can see her out of every one of my windows!

It is the same woman, I know, for she is always creeping, and most women do not creep by daylight.

I see her in that long shaded lane, creeping up and down. I see her in those dark grape arbors, creeping all around the garden.

I see her on that long road under the trees, creeping along, and when a carriage comes she hides under the blackberry vines.

I don't blame her a bit. It must be very humiliating to be caught creeping by daylight!

I always lock the door when I creep by daylight. I can't do it at night, for I know John would suspect something at once.

And John is so queer now, that I don't want to irritate him. I wish he would take another room! Besides, I don't want anybody to get that woman out at night but myself.

I often wonder if I could see her out of all the windows at once.

But, turn as fast as I can, I can only see out of one at one time.

And though I always see her, she *may* be able to creep faster than I can turn!

I have watched her sometimes away off in the open country, creeping as fast as a cloud shadow in a high wind.

If only that top pattern could be gotten off from the under one! I mean to try it, little by little.

I have found out another funny thing, but I shan't tell it this time! It does not do to trust people too much.

There are only two more days to get this paper off, and I believe John is beginning to notice. I don't like the look in his eyes.

And I heard him ask Jennie a lot of professional questions about me. She had a very good report to give.

She said I slept a good deal in the daytime.

John knows I don't sleep very well at night, for all I'm so quiet!

He asked me all sorts of questions, too, and pretended to be very loving and kind.

As if I couldn't see through him!

Still, I don't wonder he acts so, sleeping under this paper for three months.

It only interests me, but I feel sure John and Jennie are secretly affected by it.

* * *

Hurrah! This is the last day, but it is enough. John is to stay in town over night, and won't be out until this evening.

Jennie wanted to sleep with me—the sly thing! But I told her I should undoubtedly rest better for a night all alone.

That was clever, for really I wasn't alone a bit! As soon as it was moon-light and that poor thing began to crawl and shake the pattern, I got up and ran to help her.

I pulled and she shook, I shook and she pulled, and before morning we had peeled off yards of that paper.

A strip about as high as my head and half around the room.

And then when the sun came and that awful pattern began to laugh at me, I declared I would finish it to-day!

We go away to-morrow, and they are moving all my furniture down again to leave things as they were before.

Jennie looked at the wall in amazement, but I told her merrily that I did it out of pure spite at the vicious thing.

She laughed and said she wouldn't mind doing it herself, but I must not get tired.

How she betrayed herself that time!

But I am here, and no person touches this paper but me,—not *alive!*

She tried to get me out of the room—it was too patent! But I said it was so quiet and empty and clean now that I believed I would lie down again and sleep all I could; and not to wake me even for dinner—I would call when I woke.

So now she is gone, and the servants are gone, and the things are gone, and there is nothing left but that great bedstead nailed down, with the canvas mattress we found on it.

We shall sleep downstairs to-night, and take the boat home tomorrow.

I quite enjoy the room, now it is bare again.

How those children did tear about here!

This bedstead is fairly gnawed!

But I must get to work.

I have locked the door and thrown the key down into the front path.

I don't want to go out, and I don't want to have anybody come in, till John comes.

I want to astonish him.

I've got a rope up here that even Jennie did not find. If that woman does get out, and tries to get away, I can tie her!

But I forgot I could not reach far without anything to stand on!

This bed will *not* move!

I tried to lift and push it until I was lame, and then I got so angry I bit off a little piece at one corner—but it hurt my teeth.

Then I peeled off all the paper I could reach standing on the floor. It sticks horribly and the pattern just enjoys it! All those strangled heads and bulbous eyes and waddling fungus growths just shriek with derision!

I am getting angry enough to do something desperate. To jump out of the window would be admirable exercise, but the bars are too strong even to try.

Besides I wouldn't do it. Of course not. I know well enough that a step like that is improper and might be misconstrued.

I don't like to *look* out of the windows even—there are so many of those creeping women, and they creep so fast.

I wonder if they come out of that wallpaper as I did?

But I am securely fastened now by my well-hidden rope—you don't get *me* out in the road there!

I suppose I shall have to get back behind the pattern when it comes night, and that is hard!

It is so pleasant to be out in this great room and creep around as I please!

I don't want to go outside. I won't, even if Jennie asks me to.

For outside you have to creep on the ground, and everything is green instead of yellow.

But here I can creep smoothly on the floor, and my shoulder just fits in that long smooch around the wall, so I cannot lose my way.

Why there's John at the door!

It is no use, young man, you can't open it!

How he does call and pound!

Now he's crying for an axe.

It would be a shame to break down that beautiful door!

"John dear!" said I in the gentlest voice, "the key is down by the front steps, under a plantain leaf!"

That silenced him for a few moments.

Then he said—very quietly indeed, "Open the door, my darling!"

"I can't," said I. "The key is down by the front door under a plantain leaf!"

And then I said it again, several times, very gently and slowly, and said it so often that he had to go and see, and he got it of course, and came in. He stopped short by the door.

"What is the matter?" he cried. "For God's sake, what are you doing!"

I kept on creeping just the same, but I looked at him over my shoulder.

"I've got out at last," said I, "in spite of you and Jane. And I've pulled off most of the paper, so you can't put me back!"

Now why should that man have fainted? But he did, and right across my path by the wall, so that I had to creep over him every time!

Reading and Reacting

1. The story's narrator, who has recently had a baby, is suffering from what her husband, a doctor, calls "temporary nervous depression—a slight hysterical tendency" (par. 10). How accurate is his diagnosis? Explain.
2. What do the following comments reveal about the narrator's situation: "John laughs at me, of course, but one expects that in marriage" (par. 5); "I must put this away,—he hates to have me write a word" (par. 39); "He laughs at me so about this wallpaper" (par. 51); "Then he took me in his arms and called me a blessed little goose" (par. 56)?
3. What is it about the house, the grounds, and her room that upsets the narrator?
4. What images and figures of speech does the narrator use to describe the wallpaper? To what extent do you think her descriptions are accurate? Which images do you think she sees, and which ones do you think she imagines?
5. How does the narrator's mood change as the story progresses? How does her language change?
6. How would you characterize the narrator's tone? does she sound depressed? delusional? hysterical?
7. How do you explain the story's very short paragraphs? How do these short paragraphs help you to understand the narrator's mental state?
8. Study the story's punctuation—in particular, its use of dashes, question marks, and exclamation points. What does this use of punctuation contribute to the story?
9. **Journal Entry** Do you think a present-day woman would respond differently to such advice from her husband or doctor? Explain.
10. **Critical Perspective** "The Yellow Wallpaper" was originally seen by some readers as a ghost story and was anthologized as such. More recently, critics have tended to interpret the story from a feminist perspective, focusing on the way in which the nameless narrator is victimized by the men around her and by the values of the Victorian society they uphold. In the essay "An Unnecessary Maze of Sign-Reading," Mary Jacobus concludes that the overwhelmingly feminist perspective of recent criticism, though certainly valuable and enlightening, has overlooked other promising critical possibilities—for example, "the Gothic and uncanny elements present in the text."

If you were teaching "The Yellow Wallpaper," would you present it as a feminist story or as a chilling gothic ghost story? Do you think interpreting the story as a gothic horror tale precludes a feminist reading, or do you see the two interpretations as compatible?

Related Works: "The Story of an Hour" (p. 151), "The Disappearance" (p. 280), "Daddy" (p. 571), *Trifles* (p. 820), A *Doll's House* (p. 834)

WRITING SUGGESTIONS: Style, Tone, and Language

1. In the classic 1986 Vietnam War story "The Things They Carried," author Tim O'Brien considers the soldiers' emotional and psychological burdens as well as the physical "things they carry." Applying O'Brien's idea to "The Yellow Wallpaper" (p. 315), write an essay in which you consider what the narrator of this story "carries" (and what her husband "carries") and why.
2. In all three of this chapter's stories, characters are trapped. Whether trapped by social roles, by circumstance, or by their own limitations, they are unable to escape their destinies. Explain what factors imprison each character; then, consider whether—and how—each might escape.
3. Imagine The Misfit in a prison cell, relating the violent incident at the end of "A Good Man Is Hard to Find" to another prisoner—or to a member of the clergy. Would his tone be boastful? regretful? apologetic? defiant? Would he use the elaborate poetic style he sometimes uses in the story or more straightforward language? Tell his version of the incident in his own words.
4. John Updike's "A&P (p. 179), like "Araby," revolves around the central character's infatuation with an unattainable woman. Compare and contrast the infatuations described in these two stories. How does the language used by the narrators in the two stories communicate the two characters' fascination and subsequent disillusionment?

Chapter

14

Symbol, Allegory, and Myth

Alice Walker

Monica Morgan/Getty Images

Shirley Jackson

Pictorial Press Ltd/Alamy Stock Photo

Nathaniel Hawthorne

Mathew B. Brady/Bettmann/Getty Images

Learning Objectives

After reading this chapter, you will be able to...

- Define symbolism.
- Describe universal and conventional symbols.
- Explain literary symbols.

- Discuss allegory and allegorical figures in works of fiction.
- Discuss the significance of symbols in a work of fiction.
- Interpret the use of myths in fiction.

Symbol

A **symbol** is a person, object, action, place, or event that, in addition to its literal meaning, suggests a more complex meaning or range of meanings. **Universal** or **archetypal symbols**, such as the Hero, the Mother, the Outcast, or the Tempter, are so much a part of human experience that they suggest the same thing to most people, regardless of culture. **Conventional symbols** are also likely to suggest the same thing to most people (a rose suggests love, a skull and crossbones denotes poison), provided the people share cultural and social assumptions. For this reason, conventional symbols are often used as a kind of shorthand in films and advertising, where they elicit predictable responses.

A conventional symbol, such as the stars and stripes of the American flag, can evoke powerful feelings of pride and patriotism in a group of people who share certain cultural assumptions, just as the maple leaf and the Union Jack can. Symbols used in works of literature can function in much the same way, enabling writers to convey particular emotions or messages with a high degree of predictability. Thus, spring can be expected to suggest rebirth and promise; autumn, declining years and power; summer, youth and beauty. Because writers expect a dark forest to evoke fear or a rainbow to communicate hope, they can be quite confident in using such images to convey a particular idea or mood (provided the audience shares the writer's frame of reference).

Many symbols, however, suggest different things to different people, and different cultures may react differently to the same symbols. (In the United States, for example, an owl suggests wisdom; in India, it suggests the opposite.) Thus, symbols enhance meaning, expanding the possibilities for interpretation and for readers' interaction with the text. Because they are so potentially rich, symbols have the power to give added meaning to a work of literature by creating nuance and complexity.

Literary Symbols

Both universal and conventional symbols can function as **literary symbols**—symbols that take on additional meanings in particular works. For example, a watch or clock denotes time; as a conventional symbol, it suggests the passing of time; as a literary symbol in a particular work, it might also convey anything from a character's inability to recapture the past to the idea of time running out—or it might suggest something else.

Considering an object's symbolic significance can suggest a variety of ways to interpret a text. For example, William Faulkner focuses attention on an unseen watch in a pivotal scene in "A Rose for Emily" (p. 166). The narrator first describes Emily Grierson as "a small, fat woman in black, with a thin gold chain descending to her waist and vanishing into her belt." Several sentences later, the narrator notes that Emily's visitors "could hear the invisible watch ticking at the end of the gold chain." Like these visitors, readers are drawn to the unseen watch as it ticks away. Because Emily is portrayed as a woman living in the past, readers can assume that the watch is intended to reinforce the impression that she cannot see that time (the watch) has moved on. The vivid picture of the pale, plump woman in the musty room with the watch invisibly ticking does indeed suggest that she is frozen in time and remains unaware of the progress around her. Thus, the symbol of the watch enriches both the depiction of character and the story's theme.

In "Barn Burning" (p. 265), another Faulkner story, the clock is a more complex symbol. The itinerant Snopes family is without financial security and apparently without a future. The clock the mother carries from shack to shack—"The clock inlaid with mother-of-pearl, which would not run, stopped at some fourteen minutes past two o'clock of a dead and forgotten day and time, which had been [Sarty's] mother's dowry"—is their only valuable possession. The fact that the clock no longer works seems at first to suggest that time has run out for the family. On another level, the clock stands in stark contrast to Major de Spain's grand home, with its gold and glitter and Oriental rugs. Knowing that the clock was part of the mother's dowry and that a dowry suggests a promise, readers may conclude that the broken clock symbolizes lost hope. The fact that the mother still clings to the clock, however, could suggest just the opposite: her refusal to give up.

As you read, you should not try to find one exact equivalent for each symbol; that kind of search is reductive and unrewarding. Instead, consider the different meanings a symbol might suggest. Then consider how these various interpretations enrich other elements of the story and the work as a whole.

Recognizing Symbols

When is a clock just a clock, and when is it also a symbol with a meaning (or meanings) beyond its literal significance? If a character waiting for a friend glances once at a watch to check the time, there is probably nothing symbolic about the watch or about the act of looking at it. If, however, the watch keeps appearing again and again in the story, at key moments; if the narrator devotes a good deal of time to describing it; if it is placed in a conspicuous physical location; if characters keep noticing it and commenting on its presence; if it is lost (or found) at a critical moment; if its function in some way parallels the development of plot or character (for example, if it stops as a relationship ends or when a character dies); if the story's opening or closing paragraph focuses on the timepiece; or if the story is called "The Watch"—the watch most likely has symbolic significance. In other words, considering how an image is used, how often it is used, and when it appears will help you to determine whether or not it functions as a symbol.

Symbols expand the possible meanings of a story, thereby heightening interest and actively involving readers in the text. In "The Lottery" (p. 337) for example, the mysterious black box has symbolic significance. It is mentioned prominently and repeatedly, and it plays a pivotal role in the story's action. Of course, the black box is important on a purely literal level: it is the container from which the villagers draw slips of paper for the lottery. But the box has other associations as well, and it is these associations that suggest what its symbolic significance might be.

The black wooden box is very old, a relic of many past lotteries; the narrator observes that it represents tradition. It is also closed and closely guarded, suggesting mystery and uncertainty. It is shabby, "splintered badly along one side ... and in places faded or stained," and this state of disrepair could suggest that the ritual it is part of has also deteriorated or that tradition itself has deteriorated. The box is also simple in construction and design, suggesting the primitive (and therefore perhaps outdated) nature of the ritual. Thus, this symbol encourages readers to probe the story for values and ideas, to consider and weigh the suitability of a variety of interpretations. It serves as a "hot spot" that invites questions, and the answers to these questions reinforce and enrich the story's theme.

Allegory

An **allegory** communicates a doctrine, message, or moral principle by making it into a narrative in which the characters represent ideas, concepts, qualities, or other abstractions. Thus, an allegory is a story with two parallel and consistent levels of meaning—one literal and one figurative. The figurative level, which offers some moral or political lesson, is the story's main concern.

Whereas a symbol has multiple symbolic associations as well as a literal meaning, an **allegorical figure**—a character, object, place, or event in the allegory—has just one meaning within an **allegorical framework**, the set of ideas that conveys the allegory's message. (At the simplest level, for example, one character can stand for good, and another can stand for evil.) For this reason, allegorical figures do not open up a text to various interpretations the way symbols do. The allegorical figures are significant only because they represent something beyond their literal meaning in a fixed system. Because the purpose of allegory is to communicate a particular lesson, readers are not encouraged to speculate about the allegory's possible meanings; each element has only one equivalent, which readers must discover if they are to make sense of the story.

Naturally, the better a reader understands the political, religious, and literary assumptions of a writer (as well as the context of the work itself), the easier it will be to recognize the allegorical significance of the work. John Bunyan's *The Pilgrim's Progress*, for example, is a famous seventeenth-century allegory based on the Christian doctrine of salvation. In order to appreciate the complexity of Bunyan's work, readers would have to familiarize themselves with this doctrine.

One type of allegory, called a **beast fable**, is a short tale, usually including a moral, in which animals assume human characteristics. Aesop's *Fables* are the best-known examples of beast fables. More recently, contemporary writers have used beast fables to satirize the political and social conditions of our time. In one such tale, "The Gentlemen of the Jungle" by the Kenyan writer Jomo Kenyatta, an elephant is allowed to put his trunk inside a man's hut during a rainstorm. Not content with keeping his trunk dry, the elephant pushes his entire body inside the hut, displacing the man. When the man protests, the elephant takes the matter to the lion, who appoints a Commission of Enquiry to settle the matter. Eventually, the man is forced not only to abandon his hut to the elephant but also to build new huts for all the animals on the Commission. Even so, the jealous animals occupy the man's new hut and begin fighting for space; while they are arguing, the man burns down the hut, animals and all. Like the tales told by Aesop, "The Gentlemen of the Jungle" has a moral: "Peace is costly," says the man as he walks away happily, "but it's worth the expense."

The following passage from Kenyatta's tale reveals how the allegorical figures work within the framework of the allegory:

> The elephant, obeying the command of his master (the lion), got busy with the other ministers to appoint a Commission of Enquiry. The following elders of the jungle were appointed to sit in the Commission: (1) Mr. Rhinoceros; (2) Mr. Buffalo; (3) Mr. Alligator; (4) The Rt. Hon. Mr. Fox to act as chairman; and (5) Mr. Leopard to act as Secretary of the Commission. On seeing the personnel, the man protested and asked if it was not necessary to include in this Commission a member from his side. But he was told that it was impossible, since no one from his side was well enough educated to understand the intricacy of jungle law.

From this excerpt, we can see that each character represents a particular idea. For example, the members of the Commission stand for bureaucratic smugness and inequity, and the man stands for the citizens who are victimized by the government. In order to fully understand the allegorical significance of each figure in this story, of course, readers would have to know something about government bureaucracies, colonialism in Africa, and possibly a specific historical event in Kenya.

Some works contain both symbolic elements *and* allegorical elements, as Nathaniel Hawthorne's "Young Goodman Brown" (p. 354) does. The names of the story's two main characters, "Goodman" and "Faith," suggest that they fit within an allegorical system of some sort: Young Goodman Brown represents a good person who, despite his best efforts, strays from the path of righteousness; his wife, Faith, represents the quality he must hold on to in order to avoid temptation. As characters, they have no significance outside of their allegorical functions. Other elements of the story, however, are not so clear-cut. The older man whom Young Goodman Brown meets in the woods carries a staff that has carved on it "the likeness of a great black snake, so curiously wrought, that it might almost be seen to twist and wriggle itself like a living serpent." This staff, carried by a Satanic figure who represents evil and temptation, suggests the snake in the Garden of Eden, an association that neatly fits into the allegorical framework of the story. Alternatively, however, the staff could also suggest the "slippery," ever-changing nature of sin, the difficulty people have in perceiving sin, or even sexuality (which may explain Young Goodman Brown's susceptibility to temptation). This range of possible meanings suggests that the staff functions as a symbol (not an allegorical figure) that enriches Hawthorne's story.

Other stories work entirely on a symbolic level and contain no allegorical figures. "The Lottery," despite its moral overtones, is not an allegory because its characters, events, and objects are not arranged to serve one rigid, didactic purpose. In fact, many different interpretations have been suggested for this story. When it was first published in June 1948 in the *New Yorker*, some readers believed it to be a story about an actual custom or ritual. As author Shirley Jackson reports in her essay "Biography of a Story," even those who recognized it as fiction speculated about its meaning, seeing it as (among other things) an attack on prejudice; a criticism of society's need for a scapegoat; or a treatise on witchcraft, Christian martyrdom, or village gossip. The fact is that an allegorical interpretation will not account for every major character, object, and event in the story.

Myth

Throughout history, human beings have been makers of myths. For the purpose of this discussion, a **myth** is a story that is central to a culture; it embodies the values on which a culture or society is built. Thus, myths are not synonymous with falsehoods or fairy tales. Rather, they are stories that contain ideas that inform a culture and that give that culture meaning. In this sense, then, both an ancient epic and a contemporary religious text can be considered myths.

Although many myths have to do with religion, myths are not limited to the theological. Myths explain everything from natural phenomena—such as the creation of the world—to the existence of human beings and the beginnings of agriculture. The importance of myths rests on their ability to embody a set of beliefs that unifies both individuals and the society in which they live. By examining myths, we can learn much about our own origins and about our most deeply held beliefs.

One of the most prevalent types of myth is the **creation myth**. Almost every culture has an explanation for how the earth, sun, and stars—not to mention people—came into being. According to the ancient Greeks, for example, the world began as an empty void from which Nyx, a bird with black wings, emerged. She laid a golden egg, and out of it arose Eros, the god of love. The two halves of the eggshell became the earth and the sky, who fell in love with each other and had many children and grandchildren. These offspring became the gods of the Greek pantheon, who eventually created human beings in their own likeness. Each of these gods had a role to play in the creation and maintenance of the world, and their actions—in particular, their constant meddling in the lives of people—comprise the myths of ancient Greece.

In various cultures all over the world, creation myths take different forms. According to the ancient Japanese, for example, the world emerged from a single seed, which grew to form a god who, in turn, created other gods and eventually the islands of Japan and their inhabitants. Several Native American tribes share common beliefs about sky ancestors, who created the people on the planet.

In Western culture, the most recognizable creation myth appears in Genesis, the first book of the Old Testament. According to Genesis, God created the heavens and the earth as well as all living creatures—including Adam and Eve. Other stories are part of the oral tradition of Judaism and do not appear in Genesis. An example of such a story is the tale of Lilith, which emerged sometime between the eighth and eleventh centuries. According to this Hebrew myth, Lilith, who was created before Eve, was Adam's first wife. However, she refused to be subservient to Adam, and so she left Eden, eventually to be replaced by Eve. Talmudic tradition holds that she later consorted with demons and gave birth to a legion of demonic offspring who inhabit the dark places of the earth.

The influence of mythology on literature is profound, and our contemporary understanding of narrative fiction owes a great deal to mythology. In fact, many of the short stories in this anthology contain allusions to myth. Consider, for example, the role of myth in "The Lottery" and "Young Goodman Brown." In both of these short stories, myth is central to the characters' behavior, sensibility, and understanding of the world in which they live.

Checklist Writing about Symbol, Allegory, and Myth

- Are any universal symbols used in the work? any conventional symbols? What is their function?
- Is any character, place, action, event, or object given unusual prominence or emphasis in the story? If so, does this element seem to have symbolic as well as literal significance?
- What possible meanings does each symbol suggest?
- How do symbols help to depict the story's characters?
- How do symbols help to characterize the story's setting?
- How do symbols help to advance the story's plot?
- Does the story have a moral or didactic purpose? What is the message, idea, or moral principle the story seeks to convey? Is the story an allegory?

- What equivalent may be assigned to each allegorical figure in the story?
- What is the allegorical framework of the story?
- Does the story combine allegorical figures and symbols? How do they work together in the story?
- Does the story have any references to myth? If so, what do these references contribute to the story's plot or theme?

Pictorial Press Ltd/Alamy Stock Photo

SHIRLEY JACKSON (1916–1965) is best known for her restrained tales of horror and the supernatural, most notably her novel *The Haunting of Hill House* (1959) and the short story "The Lottery" (1948). Among her other works are two novels dealing with multiple personalities—*The Bird's Nest* (1954) and *We Have Always Lived in the Castle* (1962)—and two collections of comic tales about her children and family life, *Life among the Savages* (1953) and *Raising Demons* (1957). A posthumous collection of stories, *Just an Ordinary Day* (1997), was published after the discovery of a box of some of Jackson's unpublished papers in a Vermont barn and her heirs' subsequent search for her other uncollected works.

With her husband, literary critic Stanley Edgar Hyman, Jackson settled in the small town of Bennington, Vermont, but was never accepted by the townspeople. "The Lottery" is set in much the same kind of small, parochial town. Despite the story's matter-of-fact tone and familiar setting, its publication in the *New Yorker* provoked a torrent of letters from enraged and shocked readers. In her quiet way, Jackson presented the underside of village life and revealed to readers the dark side of human nature. Future writers of gothic tales recognized their great debt to Jackson. Horror master Stephen King dedicated his book *Firestarter* "to Shirley Jackson, who never had to raise her voice."

Cultural Context "The Lottery" is sometimes seen as a protest against totalitarianism, a form of authoritarian government that permits no individual freedom. In *Eichmann in Jerusalem* (1963), political scientist Hannah Arendt (1906–1975) wrote about totalitarianism as it pertained to Nazi Germany and the Holocaust. Here, she introduced the concept of "the banality of evil," the potential in ordinary people to do evil things. Americans of the post–World War II era saw themselves as "good guys" defending the world against foreign evils. Jackson's story, written scarcely three years after the liberation of Auschwitz, told Americans something they did not want to hear—that the face of human evil could look just like their next-door neighbor.

The Lottery (1948)

The morning of June 27th was clear and sunny, with the fresh warmth of a full-summer day; the flowers were blossoming profusely and the grass was richly green. The people of the village began to gather in the square, between the post office and the bank, around ten o'clock; in some towns there were so many people that the lottery took two days and had to be started on June 26th, but in this village, where there were only about three hundred people, the whole lottery took less than two hours, so it could begin at ten o'clock in the morning and still be through in time to allow the villagers to get home for noon dinner.

The children assembled first, of course. School was recently over for the summer, and the feeling of liberty sat uneasily on most of them; they tended to gather together quietly for a while before they broke into boisterous play, and their talk was still of the classroom and the teacher, of books and reprimands. Bobby Martin had already stuffed his pockets full of stones, and the other boys soon followed his example, selecting the smoothest and roundest stones; Bobby and Harry Jones and Dickie Delacroix—the villagers pronounced this name "Dellacroy"—eventually made a great pile of stones in one corner of the square and guarded it against the raids of the other boys. The girls stood aside, talking among themselves, looking over their shoulders at the boys, and the very small children rolled in the dust or clung to the hands of their older brothers or sisters.

Soon the men began to gather, surveying their own children, speaking of planting and rain, tractors and taxes. They stood together, away from the pile of stones in the corner, and their jokes were quiet and they smiled rather than laughed. The women, wearing faded house dresses and sweaters, came shortly after their menfolk. They greeted one another and exchanged bits of gossip as they went to join their husbands. Soon the women, standing by their husbands, began to call to their children, and the children came reluctantly, having to be called four or five times. Bobby Martin ducked under his mother's grasping hand and ran, laughing, back to the pile of stones. His father spoke up sharply, and Bobby came quickly and took his place between his father and his oldest brother.

The lottery was conducted—as were the square dances, the teen-age club, the Halloween program—by Mr. Summers, who had time and energy to devote to civic activities. He was a round-faced, jovial man and he ran the coal business, and people were sorry for him, because he had no children and his wife was a scold. When he arrived in the square, carrying the black wooden box, there was a murmur of conversation among the villagers, and he waved and called, "Little late today, folks." The postmaster, Mr. Graves, followed him, carrying a three-legged stool, and the stool was put in the center of the square and Mr. Summers set the black box down on it. The villagers kept their distance, leaving a space between themselves and the stool, and when Mr. Summers said, "Some of you fellows want to give me a hand?" there was a hesitation before two men, Mr. Martin and his oldest son, Baxter, came forward to hold the box steady on the stool while Mr. Summers stirred up the papers inside it.

The original paraphernalia for the lottery had been lost long ago, and the black box now resting on the stool had been put into use even before Old Man Warner, the oldest man in town, was born. Mr. Summers spoke frequently to the villagers about making a new box, but no one liked to upset even as much tradition as was represented by the black box. There was a story that the present box had been made with some pieces of the box that had preceded it, the one that had been constructed when the first people settled down to make a village here. Every year, after the lottery, Mr. Summers began talking again about a new box, but every year the subject was allowed to fade off without anything's being done. The black box grew shabbier each year; by now it was no longer completely black but splintered badly along one side to show the original wood color, and in some places faded or stained. 5

Mr. Martin and his oldest son, Baxter, held the black box securely on the stool until Mr. Summers had stirred the papers thoroughly with his hand. Because so much of the ritual had been forgotten or discarded, Mr. Summers had been successful in having slips of paper substituted for the chips of wood that had been used for generations. Chips of wood, Mr. Summers had argued, had been all very well when the village was tiny, but now that the population was more than three hundred and likely to keep on growing, it was necessary to use something that would fit more easily into the black box. The night before the lottery, Mr. Summers and Mr. Graves made up the slips of paper and put them in the box, and it was then taken to the safe of Mr. Summers's coal company and locked up until Mr. Summers was ready to take it to the square next morning. The rest of the year, the box was put away, sometimes one place, sometimes another; it had spent one year in Mr. Graves's barn and another year underfoot in the post office, and sometimes it was set on a shelf in the Martin grocery and left there.

There was a great deal of fussing to be done before Mr. Summers declared the lottery open. There were the lists to make up—of heads of families, heads of households in each family, members of each household in each family. There was the proper swearing-in of Mr. Summers by the postmaster, as the official of the lottery; at one time, some people remembered, there had been a recital of some sort, performed by the official of the lottery, a perfunctory, tuneless chant that had been rattled off duly each year; some people believed that the official of the lottery used to stand just so when he said or sang it, others believed that he was supposed to walk among the people, but years and years ago this part of the ritual had been allowed to lapse. There had been, also, a ritual salute, which the official of the lottery had had to use in addressing each person who came up to draw from the box, but this also had changed with time, until now it was felt necessary only for the official to speak to each person approaching. Mr. Summers was very good at all this; in his clean white shirt and blue jeans, with one hand resting carelessly on the black box, he seemed very proper and important as he talked interminably to Mr. Graves and the Martins.

Just as Mr. Summers finally left off talking and turned to the assembled villagers, Mrs. Hutchinson came hurriedly along the path to the square, her sweater thrown over her shoulders, and slid into place in the back of the crowd. "Clean forgot what day it was," she said to Mrs. Delacroix, who stood next to her, and they both laughed softly. "Thought my old man was out back stacking wood," Mrs. Hutchinson went on, "and then I looked out the window and the kids was gone, and then I remembered it was the twenty-seventh and came a-running." She dried her hands on her apron, and Mrs. Delacroix said, "You're in time, though. They're still talking away up there."

Mrs. Hutchinson craned her neck to see through the crowd and found her husband and children standing near the front. She tapped Mrs. Delacroix on the arm as a farewell and began to make her way through the crowd. The people separated good-humoredly to let her through; two or three people said, in voices just loud enough to be heard across the crowd, "Here comes your Missus, Hutchinson," and "Bill, she made it after all." Mrs. Hutchinson reached her husband, and Mr. Summers, who had been waiting, said cheerfully, "Thought we were going to have to get on without you, Tessie." Mrs. Hutchinson said, grinning, "Wouldn't have me leave m'dishes in the sink, now, would you, Joe?," and soft laughter ran through the crowd as the people stirred back into position after Mrs. Hutchinson's arrival.

"Well, now," Mr. Summers said soberly, "guess we better get started, get this over with, so's we can go back to work. Anybody ain't here?" 10

"Dunbar," several people said. "Dunbar, Dunbar."

Mr. Summers consulted his list. "Clyde Dunbar," he said. "That's right. He's broke his leg, hasn't he? Who's drawing for him?"

"Me, I guess," a woman said, and Mr. Summers turned to look at her. "Wife draws for her husband," Mr. Summers said. "Don't you have a grown boy to do it for you, Janey?" Although Mr. Summers and everyone else in the village knew the answer perfectly well, it was the business of the official of the lottery to ask such questions formally. Mr. Summers waited with an expression of polite interest while Mrs. Dunbar answered.

"Horace's not but sixteen yet," Mrs. Dunbar said regretfully. "Guess I gotta fill in for the old man this year."

"Right," Mr. Summers said. He made a note on the list he was holding. Then he asked, "Watson boy drawing this year?" 15

A tall boy in the crowd raised his hand. "Here," he said. "I'm drawing for m'mother and me." He blinked his eyes nervously and ducked his head as several voices in the crowd said things like "Good fellow, Jack," and "Glad to see your mother's got a man to do it."

"Well," Mr. Summers said, "guess that's everyone. Old Man Warner make it?"

"Here," a voice said, and Mr. Summers nodded.

A sudden hush fell on the crowd as Mr. Summers cleared his throat and looked at the list. "All ready?" he called. "Now, I'll read the names—heads of families first—and the men come up and take a paper out of the box. Keep the paper folded in your hand without looking at it until everyone has had a turn. Everything clear?"

The people had done it so many times that they only half listened to the directions; most of them were quiet, wetting their lips, not looking around.

Then Mr. Summers raised one hand high and said, "Adams." A man disengaged himself from the crowd and came forward. "Hi, Steve," Mr. Summers said, and Mr. Adams said, "Hi, Joe." They grinned at one another humorlessly and nervously. Then Mr. Adams reached into the black box and took out a folded paper. He held it firmly by one corner as he turned and went hastily back to his place in the crowd, where he stood a little apart from his family, not looking down at his hand. 20

"Allen," Mr. Summers said. "Anderson.... Bentham."

"Seems like there's no time at all between lotteries any more," Mrs. Delacroix said to Mrs. Graves in the back row. "Seems like we got through with the last one only last week."

"Time sure goes fast," Mrs. Graves said.

"Clark.... Delacroix."

"There goes my old man," Mrs. Delacroix said. She held her breath while her husband went forward. 25

"Dunbar," Mr. Summers said, and Mrs. Dunbar went steadily to the box while one of the women said, "Go on, Janey," and another said, "There she goes."

"We're next," Mrs. Graves said. She watched while Mr. Graves came around from the side of the box, greeted Mr. Summers gravely, and selected a slip of paper from the box. By now, all through the crowd there were men holding the small folded papers in their large hands, turning them over and over nervously. Mrs. Dunbar and her two sons stood together, Mrs. Dunbar holding the slip of paper.

"Harburt.... Hutchinson."

"Get up there, Bill," Mrs. Hutchinson said, and the people near her laughed.

"Jones." 30

"They do say," Mr. Adams said to Old Man Warner, who stood next to him, "that over in the north village they're talking of giving up the lottery."

Old Man Warner snorted. "Pack of crazy fools," he said. "Listening to the young folks, nothing's good enough for *them*. Next thing you know, they'll be wanting to go back to living in caves, nobody work any more, live *that* way for a while. Used to be a saying about 'Lottery in June, corn be heavy soon.' First thing you know, we'd all be eating stewed chickweed and acorns. There's *always* been a lottery," he added petulantly. "Bad enough to see young Joe Summers up there joking with everybody."

"Some places have already quit lotteries," Mrs. Adams said.

"Nothing but trouble in *that*," Old Man Warner said stoutly. "Pack of young fools."

"Martin." And Bobby Martin watched his father go forward. "Overdyke.... Percy." 35

"I wish they'd hurry," Mrs. Dunbar said to her older son. "I wish they'd hurry."

"They're almost through," her son said.

"You get ready to run tell Dad," Mrs. Dunbar said.

Mr. Summers called his own name and then stepped forward precisely and selected a slip from the box. Then he called, "Warner."

"Seventy-seventh year I been in the lottery," Old Man Warner said as he went through the crowd. "Seventy-seventh time." 40

"Watson." The tall boy came awkwardly through the crowd. Someone said, "Don't be nervous, Jack," and Mr. Summers said, "Take your time, son."

"Zanini."

After that, there was a long pause, a breathless pause, until Mr. Summers, holding his slip of paper in the air, said, "All right, fellows." For a minute, no one moved, and then all the slips of paper were opened. Suddenly, all the women began to speak at once, saying, "Who is it?," "Who's got it?," "Is it the Dunbars?," "Is it the Watsons?" Then the voices began to say, "It's Hutchinson. It's Bill," "Bill Hutchinson's got it."

"Go tell your father," Mrs. Dunbar said to her older son.

People began to look around to see the Hutchinsons. Bill Hutchinson was standing quiet, staring down at the paper in his hand. Suddenly, Tessie Hutchinson shouted to Mr. Summers, "You didn't give him time enough to take any paper he wanted. I saw you. It wasn't fair!" 45

"Be a good sport, Tessie," Mrs. Delacroix called, and Mrs. Graves said, "All of us took the same chance."

"Shut up, Tessie," Bill Hutchinson said.

"Well, everyone," Mr. Summers said, "that was done pretty fast, and now we've got to be hurrying a little more to get done in time." He consulted his next list. "Bill," he said, "you draw for the Hutchinson family. You got any other households in the Hutchinsons?"

"There's Don and Eva," Mrs. Hutchinson yelled, "Make *them* take their chance!"

"Daughters draw with their husbands' families, Tessie," Mr. Summers said gently. "You know that as well as anyone else." 50

"It wasn't *fair*," Tessie said.

"I guess not, Joe," Bill Hutchinson said regretfully. "My daughter draws with her husband's family, that's only fair. And I've got no other family except the kids."

"Then, as far as drawing for families is concerned, it's you," Mr. Summers said in explanation, "and as far as drawing for households is concerned, that's you, too. Right?"

"Right," Bill Hutchinson said.

"How many kids, Bill?" Mr. Summers asked formally. 55

"Three," Bill Hutchinson said. "There's Bill, Jr., and Nancy, and little Dave. And Tessie and me."

"All right, then," Mr. Summers said. "Harry, you got their tickets back?"

Mr. Graves nodded and held up the slips of paper. "Put them in the box, then," Mr. Summers directed. "Take Bill's and put it in."

"I think we ought to start over," Mrs. Hutchinson said, as quietly as she could. "I tell you it wasn't *fair*. You didn't give him time enough to choose. *Every*body saw that."

Mr. Graves had selected the five slips and put them in the box, and he dropped all the papers but those onto the ground, where the breeze caught them and lifted them off.

"Listen, everybody," Mrs. Hutchinson was saying to the people around her.

"Ready, Bill?" Mr. Summers asked, and Bill Hutchinson, with one quick glance around at his wife and children, nodded.

"Remember," Mr. Summers said, "take the slips and keep them folded until each person has taken one. Harry, you help little Dave." Mr. Graves took the hand of the little boy, who came willingly with him up to the box. "Take a paper out of the box, Davy," Mr. Summers said. Davy put his hand into the box and laughed. "Take just *one* paper," Mr. Summers said. "Harry, you hold it for him." Mr. Graves took the child's hand and removed the folded paper from the tight fist and held it while little Dave stood next to him and looked at him wonderingly.

"Nancy next," Mr. Summers said. Nancy was twelve, and her school friends breathed heavily as she went forward, switching her skirt, and took a slip daintily from the box. "Bill, Jr.," Mr. Summers said, and Billy, his face red and his feet overlarge, nearly knocked the box over as he got a paper out. "Tessie," Mr. Summers said. She hesitated for a minute, looking around defiantly, and then set her lips and went up to the box. She snatched a paper out and held it behind her.

"Bill," Mr. Summers said, and Bill Hutchinson reached into the box and felt around, bringing his hand out at last with the slip of paper in it.

The crowd was quiet. A girl whispered, "I hope it's not Nancy," and the sound of the whisper reached the edges of the crowd.

"It's not the way it used to be," Old Man Warner said clearly. "People ain't the way they used to be."

"All right," Mr. Summers said. "Open the papers. Harry, you open little Dave's."

Mr. Graves opened the slip of paper and there was a general sigh through the crowd as he held it up and everyone could see that it was blank. Nancy and Bill, Jr., opened theirs at the same time, and both beamed and laughed, turning around to the crowd and holding their slips of paper above their heads.

"Tessie," Mr. Summers said. There was a pause, and then Mr. Summers looked at Bill Hutchinson, and Bill unfolded his paper and showed it. It was blank.

"It's Tessie," Mr. Summers said, and his voice was hushed. "Show us her paper, Bill."

Bill Hutchinson went over to his wife and forced the slip of paper out of her hand. It had a black spot on it, the black spot Mr. Summers had made the night before with the heavy pencil in the coal-company office. Bill Hutchinson held it up, and there was a stir in the crowd.

"All right, folks," Mr. Summers said. "Let's finish quickly."

Although the villagers had forgotten the ritual and lost the original black box, they still remembered to use stones. The pile of stones the boys had made earlier was ready; there were stones on the ground with the blowing scraps of paper that had come out of the box. Mrs. Delacroix selected a stone so large she had to pick it up with both hands and turned to Mrs. Dunbar. "Come on," she said. "Hurry up."

Mrs. Dunbar had small stones in both hands, and she said, gasping for breath, "I can't run at all. You'll have to go ahead and I'll catch up with you."

The children had stones already, and someone gave little Davy Hutchinson a few pebbles.

Tessie Hutchinson was in the center of a cleared space by now, and she held her hands out desperately as the villagers moved in on her. "It isn't fair," she said. A stone hit her on the side of the head.

Old Man Warner was saying, "Come on, come on, everyone." Steve Adams was in the front of the crowd of villagers, with Mrs. Graves beside him.

"It isn't fair, it isn't right," Mrs. Hutchinson screamed, and then they were upon her.

Reading and Reacting

1. What possible significance, beyond their literal meaning, might each of the following have:
   - The village square
   - Mrs. Hutchinson's apron
   - Old Man Warner
   - The slips of paper
   - The stones
   - The black spot
2. "The Lottery" takes place in summer, a conventional symbol that has a positive connotation. What does this setting contribute to the story's plot? to its atmosphere?
3. What, if anything, might the names *Graves*, *Adams*, *Summers*, and *Delacroix* signify in the context of this story? Do you think these names are intended to have any special significance? Why or why not?
4. What role do the children play in the ritual? How can you explain their presence in the story? Do they have any symbolic role?
5. What symbolic significance might be found in the way the characters are dressed? in their conversation?
6. In what sense is the story's title ironic?
7. Throughout the story, there is a general atmosphere of excitement. What indication is there of nervousness or apprehension?
8. Early in the story, the boys stuff their pockets with stones, foreshadowing the attack in the story's conclusion. What other examples of foreshadowing can you identify?
9. **Journal Entry** How can a ritual like the lottery continue to be held year after year? Why does no one move to end it? Can you think of a modern-day counterpart to this lottery—a situation in which people continue to act

in ways they know to be wrong rather than challenge the status quo? How can you account for such behavior?

10. **Critical Perspective** When "The Lottery" was published in the June 26, 1948, issue of the *New Yorker*, its effect was immediate. The story, as the critic Judy Oppenheimer notes in her book *Private Demons: The Life of Shirley Jackson*, "provoked an unprecedented outpouring of fury, horror, rage, disgust, and intense fascination." As a result, Jackson received hundreds of letters, which included (among others) the following interpretations of the story:
    - The story is an attack on small-town America.
    - The story is a parable about the perversion of democracy.
    - The story is a criticism of prejudice, particularly anti-Semitism and the Holocaust.
    - The story has no point at all.

    How plausible do you think each of these interpretations is? Which comes closest to your interpretation of the story? Why?

Related Works: "The Cask of Amontillado" (p. 258), "Young Goodman Brown" (p. 354), "Where Are You Going, Where Have You Been?" (p. 447), "My Last Duchess" (p. 499), "Patterns" (p. 506), *Antigone* (p. 1191)

Monica Morgan/Getty Images

ALICE WALKER (1944–) was the youngest of eight children born to Willie Lee and Minnie Tallulah Grant Walker, sharecroppers who raised cotton. She left the rural South to attend Spelman College in Atlanta (1961–1963) and Sarah Lawrence College in Bronxville, New York (1963–1965).

In 1967, Walker moved to Mississippi, where she was supported in the writing of her first novel, *The Third Life of Grange Copeland* (1970), by a National Endowment for the Arts grant. Her short story "Everyday Use" was included in *Best American Short Stories 1973* and has been widely anthologized and studied. Other novels and collections of short stories followed, including *In Love & Trouble: Stories of Black Women* (1973), *Meridian* (1976), *You Can't Keep a Good Woman Down* (1981), *The Temple of My Familiar* (1989), *Possessing the Secret of Joy* (1993), *The Complete Stories* (1994), *By the Light of My Father's Smile* (1998), and *Now Is the Time to Open Your Heart* (2004). Walker has also published many works of poetry and nonfiction. Her latest books include the essay collection *The Cushion in the Road* (2013) as well as the poetry collections *The World Will Follow Joy* (2013) and *Taking the Arrow out of the Heart* (2018). Her third novel, *The Color Purple* (1982), won the American Book Award and a Pulitzer Prize and was made into an award-winning movie and a long-running Broadway play. Throughout her career, Alice Walker has been lauded for her commitment to using storytelling in service of racial and gender equality.

In the third year of her marriage, Walker took back her maiden name because she wanted to honor her great-great-great-grandmother who had walked, carrying her two children, from Virginia to Georgia. Walker's renaming is consistent with one of her goals in writing, which is to further the process of reconnecting people to their ancestors. She has said that "it is fatal to see yourself as separate" and that if people can reaffirm the past, they can "make a different future."

Cultural Context Quilting attained the status of art in Europe in the fourteenth century but reached its fullest development later in North America. By the end of the eighteenth century, the American quilt had taken on unique and distinctive features that separated it from quilts made in other parts of the world. For African Americans, quilting has particular significance. Some scholars think that during slavery, members of the Underground Railroad used quilts to send messages. One design, the Log Cabin, was hung outside to mark a house of refuge for fugitive slaves. Other quilts mapped escape routes out of a plantation or county, often by marking the stars that would act as a guide to freedom for those escaping at night. After the emancipation of slaves, quilts retained their cultural and historical significance, as the quilt in this story does.

Everyday Use (1973)

For Your Grandmama

I will wait for her in the yard that Maggie and I made so clean and wavy yesterday afternoon. A yard like this is more comfortable than most people know. It is not just a yard. It is like an extended living room. When the hard clay is swept clean as a floor and the fine sand around the edges lined with tiny, irregular grooves, anyone can come and sit and look up into the elm tree and wait for the breezes that never come inside the house.

Maggie will be nervous until after her sister goes: she will stand hopelessly in corners, homely and ashamed of the burn scars down her arms and legs, eying her sister with a mixture of envy and awe. She thinks her sister has held life always in the palm of one hand, that "no" is a word the world never learned to say to her.

You've no doubt seen those TV shows where the child who has "made it" is confronted, as a surprise, by her own mother and father, tottering in weakly from backstage. (A pleasant surprise, of course: What would they do if parent and child came on the show only to curse out and insult each other?) On TV mother and child embrace and smile into each other's faces. Sometimes the mother and father weep, the child wraps them in her arms and leans across the table to tell how she would not have made it without their help. I have seen these programs.

Sometimes I dream a dream in which Dee and I are suddenly brought together on a TV program of this sort. Out of a dark and soft-seated limousine I am ushered into a bright room filled with many people. There I meet a smiling, gray, sporty man like Johnny Carson who shakes my hand and tells me what a fine girl I have. Then we are on the stage and Dee is embracing me with tears in her eyes. She pins on my dress a large orchid, even though she has told me once that she thinks orchids are tacky flowers.

In real life I am a large, big-boned woman with rough, man-working hands. In the winter I wear flannel nightgowns to bed and overalls during the day.

I can kill and clean a hog as mercilessly as a man. My fat keeps me hot in zero weather. I can work outside all day, breaking ice to get water for washing; I can eat pork liver cooked over the open fire minutes after it comes steaming from the hog. One winter I knocked a bull calf straight in the brain between the eyes with a sledge hammer and had the meat hung up to chill before nightfall. But of course all this does not show on television. I am the way my daughter would want me to be: a hundred pounds lighter, my skin like an uncooked barley pancake. My hair glistens in the hot bright lights. Johnny Carson has much to do to keep up with my quick and witty tongue. 5

But that is a mistake. I know even before I wake up. Who ever knew a Johnson with a quick tongue? Who can even imagine me looking a strange white man in the eye? It seems to me I have talked to them always with one foot raised in flight, with my head turned in whichever way is farthest from them. Dee, though. She would always look anyone in the eye. Hesitation was no part of her nature.

"How do I look, Mama?" Maggie says, showing just enough of her thin body enveloped in pink skirt and red blouse for me to know she's there, almost hidden by the door.

"Come out into the yard," I say.

Have you ever seen a lame animal, perhaps a dog run over by some careless person rich enough to own a car, sidle up to someone who is ignorant enough to be kind to him? That is the way my Maggie walks. She has been like this, chin on chest, eyes on ground, feet in shuffle, ever since the fire that burned the other house to the ground.

Dee is lighter than Maggie, with nicer hair and a fuller figure. She's a woman now, though sometimes I forget. How long ago was it that the other house burned? Ten, twelve years? Sometimes I can still hear the flames and feel Maggie's arms sticking to me, her hair smoking and her dress falling off her in little black papery flakes. Her eyes seemed stretched open, blazed open by the flames reflected in them. And Dee. I see her standing off under the sweet gum tree she used to dig gum out of; a look of concentration on her face as she watched the last dingy gray board of the house fall in toward the red-hot brick chimney. Why don't you do a dance around the ashes? I'd wanted to ask her. She had hated the house that much. 10

I used to think she hated Maggie, too. But that was before we raised the money, the church and me, to send her to Augusta to school. She used to read to us without pity; forcing words, lies, other folks' habits, whole lives upon us two, sitting trapped and ignorant underneath her voice. She washed us in a river of make-believe, burned us with a lot of knowledge we didn't necessarily need to know. Pressed us to her with the serious way she read, to shove us away at just the moment, like dimwits, we seemed about to understand.

Dee wanted nice things. A yellow organdy dress to wear to her graduation from high school; black pumps to match a green suit she'd made from an old suit somebody gave me. She was determined to stare down any disaster in her efforts. Her eyelids would not flicker for minutes at a time. Often I fought off the temptation to shake her. At sixteen she had a style of her own, and knew what style was.

I never had an education myself. After second grade the school was closed down. Don't ask me why: in 1927 colored asked fewer questions than they do now. Sometimes Maggie reads to me. She stumbles along good-naturedly but can't see well. She knows she is not bright. Like good looks and money, quickness passed her by. She will marry John Thomas (who has mossy teeth in an earnest face) and then I'll be free to sit here and I guess just sing church songs to myself. Although I never was a good singer. Never could carry a tune. I was always better at a man's job. I used to love to milk till I was hooked in the side in '49. Cows are soothing and slow and don't bother you, unless you try to milk them the wrong way.

I have deliberately turned my back on the house. It is three rooms, just like the one that burned, except the roof is tin; they don't make shingle roofs any more. There are no real windows, just some holes cut in the sides, like the portholes in a ship, but not round and not square, with rawhide holding the shutters up on the outside. This house is in a pasture, too, like the other one. No doubt when Dee sees it she will want to tear it down. She wrote me once that no matter where we "choose" to live, she will manage to come see us. But she will never bring her friends. Maggie and I thought about this and Maggie asked me, "Mama, when did Dee ever *have* any friends?"

She had a few. Furtive boys in pink shirts hanging about on washday after school. Nervous girls who never laughed. Impressed with her they worshiped the well-turned phrase, the cute shape, the scalding humor that erupted like bubbles in lye. She read to them. 15

When she was courting Jimmy T she didn't have much time to pay to us, but turned all her faultfinding power on him. He *flew* to marry a cheap city girl from a family of ignorant flashy people. She hardly had time to recompose herself.

When she comes I will meet—but there they are!

Maggie attempts to make a dash for the house, in her shuffling way, but I stay her with my hand. "Come back here," I say. And she stops and tries to dig a well in the sand with her toe.

It is hard to see them clearly through the strong sun. But even the first glimpse of leg out of the car tells me it is Dee. Her feet were always neat-looking, as if God himself had shaped them with a certain style. From the other side of the car comes a short, stocky man. Hair is all over his head a foot long and hanging from his chin like a kinky mule tail. I hear Maggie suck in her breath. "Uhnnnh," is what it sounds like. Like when you see the wriggling end of a snake just in front of your foot on the road. "Uhnnnh."

Dee next. A dress down to the ground, in this hot weather. A dress so loud it hurts my eyes. There are yellows and oranges enough to throw back the light of the sun. I feel my whole face warming from the heat waves it throws out.

Earrings gold, too, and hanging down to her shoulders. Bracelets dangling and making noises when she moves her arm up to shake the folds of the dress out of her armpits. The dress is loose and flows, and as she walks closer, I like it. I hear Maggie go "Uhnnnh" again. It is her sister's hair. It stands straight up like the wool on a sheep. It is black as night and around the edges are two long pigtails that rope about like small lizards disappearing behind her ears. 20

"Wa-su-zo-Tean-o!"[1] she says, coming on in that gliding way the dress makes her move. The short stocky fellow with the hair to his navel is all grinning and he follows up with "Asalamalakim,[2] my mother and sister!" He moves to hug Maggie but she falls back, right up against the back of my chair. I feel her trembling there and when I look up I see the perspiration falling off her chin.

"Don't get up," says Dee. Since I am stout it takes something of a push. You can see me trying to move a second or two before I make it. She turns, showing white heels through her sandals, and goes back to the car. Out she peeks next with a Polaroid.[3] She stoops down quickly and lines up picture after picture of me sitting there in front of the house with Maggie cowering behind me. She never takes a shot without making sure the house is included. When a cow comes nibbling around the edge of the yard she snaps it and me and Maggie *and* the house. Then she puts the Polaroid in the back seat of the car, and comes up and kisses me on the forehead.

Meanwhile Asalamalakim is going through motions with Maggie's hand. Maggie's hand is as limp as a fish, and probably as cold, despite the sweat, and she keeps trying to pull it back. It looks like Asalamalakim wants to shake hands but wants to do it fancy. Or maybe he don't know how people shake hands. Anyhow, he soon gives up on Maggie.

"Well," I say. "Dee."

"No, Mama," she says. "Not 'Dee,' Wangero Leewanika Kemanjo!" 25

"What happened to 'Dee'?" I wanted to know.

"She's dead," Wangero said. "I couldn't bear it any longer, being named after the people who oppress me."

"You know as well as me you was named after your aunt Dicie," I said. Dicie is my sister. She named Dee. We called her "Big Dee" after Dee was born.

"But who was *she* named after?" asked Wangero.

"I guess after Grandma Dee," I said. 30

"And who was she named after?" asked Wangero.

"Her mother," I said, and saw Wangero was getting tired. "That's about as far back as I can trace it," I said. Though, in fact, I probably could have carried it back beyond the Civil War through the branches.

"Well," said Asalamalakim, "there you are."

"Uhnnnh," I heard Maggie say.

---

[1]*Wa-su-zo-Tean-o:* A greeting in Swahili; Dee sounds it out one syllable at a time.

[2]*Asalamalakim:* A greeting in Arabic: "Peace be upon you."

[3]*Polaroid:* A type of camera with self-developing film.

"There I was not," I said, "before 'Dicie' cropped up in our family, so why should I try to trace it that far back?" 35

He just stood there grinning, looking down on me like somebody inspecting a Model A car. Every once in a while he and Wangero sent eye signals over my head.

"How do you pronounce this name?" I asked.

"You don't have to call me by it if you don't want to," said Wangero.

"Why shouldn't I?" I asked. "If that's what you want us to call you, we'll call you."

"I know it might sound awkward at first," said Wangero. 40

"I'll get used to it," I said. "Ream it out again."

Well, soon we got the name out of the way. Asalamalakim had a name twice as long and three times as hard. After I tripped over it two or three times he told me to just call him Hakim-a-barber. I wanted to ask him was he a barber, but I didn't really think he was, so I didn't ask.

"You must belong to those beef-cattle peoples down the road," I said. They said "Asalamalakim" when they met you, too, but they didn't shake hands. Always too busy: feeding the cattle, fixing the fences, putting up salt-lick shelters, throwing down hay. When the white folks poisoned some of the herd the men stayed up all night with rifles in their hands. I walked a mile and a half just to see the sight.

Hakim-a-barber said, "I accept some of their doctrines, but farming and raising cattle is not my style." (They didn't tell me, and I didn't ask, whether Wangero [Dee] had really gone and married him.)

We sat down to eat and right away he said he didn't eat collards and pork was unclean. Wangero, though, went on through the chitlins and corn bread, the greens and everything else. She talked a blue streak over the sweet potatoes. Everything delighted her. Even the fact that we still used the benches her daddy made for the table when we couldn't afford to buy chairs. 45

"Oh, Mama!" she cried. Then turned to Hakim-a-barber. "I never knew how lovely these benches are. You can feel the rump prints," she said, running her hands underneath her and along the bench. Then she gave a sigh and her hand closed over Grandma Dee's butter dish. "That's it!" she said. "I knew there was something I wanted to ask you if I could have." She jumped up from the table and went over in the corner where the churn stood, the milk in it clabber by now. She looked at the churn and looked at it.

"This churn top is what I need," she said. "Didn't Uncle Buddy whittle it out of a tree you all used to have?"

"Yes," I said.

"Uh huh," she said happily. "And I want the dasher, too."

"Uncle Buddy whittle that, too?" asked the barber.

Dee (Wangero) looked up at me. 50

"Aunt Dee's first husband whittled the dash," said Maggie so low you almost couldn't hear her. "His name was Henry, but they called him Stash."

"Maggie's brain is like an elephant's," Wangero said, laughing. "I can use the churn top as a centerpiece for the alcove table," she said, sliding a plate over the churn, "and I'll think of something artistic to do with the dasher."

When she finished wrapping the dasher the handle stuck out. I took it for a moment in my hands. You didn't even have to look close to see where hands pushing the dasher up and down to make butter had left a kind of sink in the wood. In fact, there were a lot of small sinks; you could see where thumb and fingers had sunk into the wood. It was beautiful light yellow wood, from a tree that grew in the yard where Big Dee and Stash had lived.

After dinner Dee (Wangero) went to the trunk at the foot of my bed and started rifling through it. Maggie hung back in the kitchen over the dishpan. Out came Wangero with two quilts. They had been pieced by Grandma Dee and then Big Dee and me had hung them on the quilt frames on the front porch and quilted them. One was in the Lone Star pattern. The other was Walk Around the Mountain. In both of them were scraps of dresses Grandma Dee had worn fifty and more years ago. Bits and pieces of Grandpa Jarrell's Paisley shirts. And one teeny faded blue piece, about the size of a penny matchbox, that was from Great Grandpa Ezra's uniform that he wore in the Civil War. 55

"Mama," Wangero said sweet as a bird. "Can I have these old quilts?"

I heard something fall in the kitchen, and a minute later the kitchen door slammed.

"Why don't you take one or two of the others?" I asked. "These old things was just done by me and Big Dee from some tops your grandma pieced before she died."

"No," said Wangero. "I don't want those. They are stitched around the borders by machine."

"That'll make them last better," I said. 60

"That's not the point," said Wangero. "These are all pieces of dresses Grandma used to wear. She did all this stitching by hand. Imagine!" She held the quilts securely in her arms, stroking them.

"Some of the pieces, like those lavender ones, come from old clothes her mother handed down to her," I said, moving up to touch the quilts. Dee (Wangero) moved back just enough so that I couldn't reach the quilts. They already belonged to her.

"Imagine!" she breathed again, clutching them closely to her bosom.

"The truth is," I said, "I promised to give them quilts to Maggie, for when she marries John Thomas."

She gasped like a bee had stung her. "Maggie can't appreciate these quilts!" she said. "She'd probably be backward enough to put them to everyday use." 65

"I reckon she would," I said. "God knows I been saving 'em for long enough with nobody using 'em. I hope she will!" I didn't want to bring up how I had offered Dee (Wangero) a quilt when she went away to college. Then she had told me they were old-fashioned, out of style.

"But, they're *priceless!*" she was saying now, furiously; for she has a temper. "Maggie would put them on the bed and in five years they'd be in rags. Less than that!"

"She can always make some more," I said. "Maggie knows how to quilt."

Dee (Wangero) looked at me with hatred. "You just will not understand. The point is these quilts, *these* quilts!"

"Well," I said, stumped. "What would *you* do with them?"

"Hang them," she said. As if that was the only thing you *could* do with quilts.

Maggie by now was standing in the door. I could almost hear the sound her feet made as they scraped over each other.

"She can have them, Mama," she said, like somebody used to never winning anything, or having anything reserved for her. "I can 'member Grandma Dee without the quilts."

I looked at her hard. She had filled her bottom lip with checkerberry snuff and it gave her face a kind of dopey, hangdog look. It was Grandma Dee and Big Dee who taught her how to quilt herself. She stood there with her scarred hands hidden in the folds of her skirt. She looked at her sister with something like fear but she wasn't mad at her. This was Maggie's portion. This was the way she knew God to work.

When I looked at her like that something hit me in the top of my head and ran down to the soles of my feet. Just like when I'm in church and the spirit of God touches me and I get happy and shout. I did something I never had done before: hugged Maggie to me, then dragged her on into the room, snatched the quilts out of Miss Wangero's hands and dumped them into Maggie's lap. Maggie just sat there on my bed with her mouth open.

"Take one or two of the others," I said to Dee.

But she turned without a word and went out to Hakim-a-barber.

"You just don't understand," she said, as Maggie and I came out to the car.

"What don't I understand?" I wanted to know.

"Your heritage," she said. And then she turned to Maggie, kissed her, and said, "You ought to try to make something of yourself, too, Maggie. It's really a new day for us. But from the way you and Mama still live you'd never know it."

She put on some sunglasses that hid everything above the tip of her nose and her chin.

Maggie smiled; maybe at the sunglasses. But a real smile, not scared. After we watched the car dust settle I asked Maggie to bring me a dip of snuff. And then the two of us sat there just enjoying, until it was time to go in the house and go to bed.

Reading and Reacting

1. In American culture, what does a patchwork quilt symbolize?
2. What is the literal meaning of the two quilts to Maggie and her mother? to Dee? What symbolic meaning, if any, do they have to Maggie and her mother? Do the quilts have any symbolic meaning to Dee?

3. How does the contrast between the two sisters' appearances, personalities, lifestyles, and feelings about the quilts help to convey the story's theme?
4. What does the name *Wangero* signify to Dee? to her mother and sister? Could the name be considered a symbol? Why or why not?
5. Why do you think Maggie gives the quilts to her sister?
6. What is Dee's opinion of her mother and sister? Do you agree with her assessment?
7. What does the story's title suggest to you? Is it ironic? What other titles would be effective?
8. Discuss the possible meanings, aside from their literal meanings, that each of the following suggest:
    - The family's yard
    - Maggie's burn scars
    - The trunk in which the quilts are kept
    - Dee's Polaroid camera

    What symbolic functions, if any, do these items serve in the story?
9. **Journal Entry** What objects have the kind of symbolic value to you that the quilts have to Maggie? What gives these objects this value?
10. **Critical Perspective** In her article "The Black Woman Artist as Wayward," critic Barbara Christian characterizes "Everyday Use" as a story in which Alice Walker examines the "creative legacy" of ordinary African American women. According to Christian, the story "is about the use and misuse of the concept of heritage. The mother of two daughters, one selfish and stylish, the other scarred and caring, passes on to us its true definition."

    What definition of *heritage* does the mother attempt to pass on to her children? How is this definition like or unlike Dee's definition?

Related Works: "Discovering America" (p. 114), "Two Kinds" (p. 471), "Aunt Jennifer's Tigers" (p. 598), "Digging" (p. 673), *Beauty* (p. 785), *Trifles* (p. 820), *Fences* (p. 1222)

Mathew B. Brady/Bettmann/Getty Images

NATHANIEL HAWTHORNE (1804–1864) was born in Salem, Massachusetts, the great-great-grandson of a judge who presided over the infamous Salem witch trials. After his sea captain father was killed on a voyage when Hawthorne was four years old, his childhood was one of genteel poverty. An uncle paid for his education at Bowdoin College in Maine, where Hawthorne's friends included a future president of the United States, Franklin Pierce, who in 1853 appointed him U.S. consul in Liverpool, England. Hawthorne published four novels—*The Scarlet Letter* (1850), *The House of the Seven Gables* (1851), *The Blithedale Romance* (1852), and *The Marble Faun* (1860)—and more than one hundred short stories and sketches.

Hawthorne referred to his own work as *romance*. He used this term to mean not an escape from reality but rather a method of confronting "the depths of our common nature" and "the truth of the heart." His stories probe the dark side of human nature and frequently paint a world that is virtuous on the surface but which has, as Young Goodman Brown comes to believe, "one stain of guilt, one mighty blood spot" beneath. Hawthorne's stories often emphasize the ambiguity of human experience. For example, the reader is left to wonder whether Goodman Brown actually saw a witch's coven or dreamed about the event. For Hawthorne, what is important is Brown's recognition that evil may be found everywhere. "Young Goodman Brown," as Hawthorne's neighbor and friend Herman Melville once said, is a tale "as deep as Dante."

Cultural Context During the five months of the Salem witch trials of 1692, nineteen women and men accused of being witches were executed by hanging. The accusations began when a few young girls claimed they were possessed by the devil and accused three Salem women of witchcraft. As the hysteria grew throughout Massachusetts, the list of the accused grew as well. Eventually, 150 people were imprisoned before the governor dismissed the special witchcraft court and released the remaining twenty-two prisoners. It is in this historical setting that "Young Goodman Brown" takes place.

Young Goodman[1] Brown (1835)

Young Goodman Brown came forth at sunset, into the street of Salem village, but put his head back, after crossing the threshold, to exchange a parting kiss with his young wife. And Faith, as the wife was aptly named, thrust her own pretty head into the street, letting the wind play with the pink ribbons of her cap, while she called to Goodman Brown.

"Dearest heart," whispered she, softly and rather sadly, when her lips were close to his ear, "prithee, put off your journey until sunrise, and sleep in your own bed to-night. A lone woman is troubled with such dreams and such thoughts, that she's afeard of herself, sometimes. Pray, tarry with me this night, dear husband, of all nights in the year!"

"My love and my Faith," replied young Goodman Brown, "of all nights in the year, this one night must I tarry away from thee. My journey, as thou callest it, forth and back again, must needs be done 'twixt now and sunrise. What, my sweet, pretty wife, dost thou doubt me already, and we but three months married!"

"Then God bless you!" said Faith with the pink ribbons, "and may you find all well, when you come back."

"Amen!" cried Goodman Brown. "Say thy prayers, dear Faith, and go to bed
at dusk, and no harm will come to thee." 5

So they parted; and the young man pursued his way, until, being about to turn the corner by the meeting-house, he looked back and saw the head of Faith still peeping after him, with a melancholy air, in spite of her pink ribbons.

"Poor little Faith!" thought he, for his heart smote him. "What a wretch am I, to leave her on such an errand! She talks of dreams, too. Methought, as she spoke, there was trouble in her face, as if a dream had warned her what work is to be done to-night. But no, no! 't would kill her to think it. Well; she's a blessed angel on earth; and after this one night, I'll cling to her skirts and follow her to Heaven."

[1]*Goodman:* A form of address, similar to *Mr.*, meaning "husband."

With this excellent resolve for the future, Goodman Brown felt himself justified in making more haste on his present evil purpose. He had taken a dreary road, darkened by all the gloomiest trees of the forest, which barely stood aside to let the narrow path creep through, and closed immediately behind. It was as lonely as could be; and there is this peculiarity in such a solitude, that the traveller knows not who may be concealed by the innumerable trunks and the thick boughs overhead; so that, with lonely footsteps, he may yet be passing through an unseen multitude.

"There may be a devilish Indian behind every tree," said Goodman Brown to himself; and he glanced fearfully behind him, as he added, "What if the devil himself should be at my very elbow!"

His head being turned back, he passed a crook of the road, and looking forward again, beheld the figure of a man, in grave and decent attire, seated at the foot of an old tree. He arose at Goodman Brown's approach, and walked onward, side by side with him. 10

"You are late, Goodman Brown," said he. "The clock of the Old South[2] was striking, as I came through Boston; and that is full fifteen minutes agone."

"Faith kept me back awhile," replied the young man, with a tremor in his voice, caused by the sudden appearance of his companion, though not wholly unexpected.

It was now deep dusk in the forest, and deepest in that part of it where these two were journeying. As nearly as could be discerned, the second traveller was about fifty years old, apparently in the same rank of life as Goodman Brown, and bearing a considerable resemblance to him, though perhaps more in expression than features. Still, they might have been taken for father and son. And yet, though the elder person was as simply clad as the younger, and as simple in manner too, he had an indescribable air of one who knew the world, and would not have felt abashed at the governor's dinner-table, or in King William's[3] court, were it possible that his affairs should call him thither. But the only thing about him that could be fixed upon as remarkable, was his staff, which bore the likeness of a great black snake, so curiously wrought, that it might almost be seen to twist and wriggle itself like a living serpent. This, of course, must have been an ocular deception, assisted by the uncertain light.

"Come, Goodman Brown!" cried his fellow-traveller, "this is a dull pace for the beginning of a journey. Take my staff, if you are so soon weary."

"Friend," said the other, exchanging his slow pace for a full stop, "having kept covenant by meeting thee here, it is my purpose now to return whence I came. I have scruples, touching the matter thou wot'st[4] of." 15

"Sayest thou so?" replied he of the serpent, smiling apart. "Let us walk on, nevertheless, reasoning as we go, and if I convince thee not, thou shalt turn back. We are but a little way in the forest, yet."

---

[2]*Old South:* Old South Church in Boston, renowned meeting place for American patriots during the Revolution.

[3]*King William:* William III, king of England from 1689 to 1702.

[4]*wot'st of:* Know of.

"Too far, too far!" exclaimed the goodman, unconsciously resuming his walk. "My father never went into the woods on such an errand, nor his father before him. We have been a race of honest men and good Christians, since the days of the martyrs. And shall I be the first of the name of Brown that ever took this path and kept—"

"Such company, thou wouldst say," observed the elder person, interrupting his pause. "Well said, Goodman Brown! I have been as well acquainted with your family as with ever a one among the Puritans; and that's no trifle to say. I helped your grandfather, the constable, when he lashed the Quaker woman so smartly through the streets of Salem. And it was I that brought your father a pitch-pine knot, kindled at my own hearth, to set fire to an Indian village, in King Philip's war.[5] They were my good friends, both; and many a pleasant walk have we had along this path, and returned merrily after midnight. I would fain be friends with you, for their sake."

"If it be as thou sayest," replied Goodman Brown, "I marvel they never spoke of these matters. Or, verily, I marvel not, seeing that the least rumor of the sort would have driven them from New England. We are a people of prayer, and good works to boot, and abide no such wickedness."

"Wickedness or not," said the traveller with the twisted staff, "I have a very general acquaintance here in New England. The deacons of many a church have drunk the communion wine with me; the selectmen, of divers towns, make me their chairman; and a majority of the Great and General Court are firm supporters of my interest. The governor and I, too—but these are state secrets." 20

"Can this be so!" cried Goodman Brown, with a stare of amazement at his undisturbed companion. "Howbeit, I have nothing to do with the governor and council; they have their own ways, and are no rule for a simple husbandman like me. But, were I to go on with thee, how should I meet the eye of that good old man, our minister, at Salem village? Oh, his voice would make me tremble, both Sabbath-day and lecture-day!"[6]

Thus far, the elder traveller had listened with due gravity, but now burst into a fit of irrepressible mirth, shaking himself so violently, that his snakelike staff actually seemed to wriggle in sympathy.

"Ha, ha, ha!" shouted he, again and again; then composing himself, "Well, go on, Goodman Brown, go on; but, prithee, don't kill me with laughing!"

"Well, then, to end the matter at once," said Goodman Brown, considerably nettled, "there is my wife, Faith. It would break her dear little heart; and I'd rather break my own!"

"Nay, if that be the case," answered the other, "e'en go thy ways, Goodman Brown. I would not, for twenty old women like the one hobbling before us, that Faith should come to any harm." 25

---

[5] *King Philip's war:* A war of Indian resistance led by Metacomet of the Wampanoags, known to the English as "King Philip." The war, intended to halt expansion of English settlers in Massachusetts, collapsed after Metacomet's death in August 1676.

[6] *lecture-day:* The day of the midweek sermon, usually Thursday.

As he spoke, he pointed his staff at a female figure on the path, in whom Goodman Brown recognized a very pious and exemplary dame, who had taught him his catechism in youth, and was still his moral and spiritual adviser, jointly with the minister and Deacon Gookin.

"A marvel, truly, that Goody[7] Cloyse should be so far in the wilderness, at nightfall!" said he. "But, with your leave, friend, I shall take a cut through the woods, until we have left this Christian woman behind. Being a stranger to you, she might ask whom I was consorting with, and whither I was going."

"Be it so," said his fellow-traveller. "Betake you to the woods, and let me keep the path."

Accordingly, the young man turned aside, but took care to watch his companion, who advanced softly along the road, until he had come within a staff's length of the old dame. She, meanwhile, was making the best of her way, with singular speed for so aged a woman, and mumbling some indistinct words, a prayer, doubtless, as she went. The traveller put forth his staff, and touched her withered neck with what seemed the serpent's tail.

"The devil!" screamed the pious old lady. 30

"Then Goody Cloyse knows her old friend?" observed the traveller, confronting her, and leaning on his writhing stick.

"Ah, forsooth, and is it your worship, indeed?" cried the good dame. "Yea, truly is it, and in the very image of my old gossip, Goodman Brown, the grandfather of the silly fellow that now is. But, would your worship believe it? My broomstick hath strangely disappeared, stolen, as I suspect, by that unhanged witch, Goody Cory, and that, too, when I was all anointed with the juice of smallage and cinque-foil and wolf's bane[8]—"

"Mingled with fine wheat and the fat of a new-born babe," said the shape of old Goodman Brown.

"Ah, your worship knows the recipe," cried the old lady, cackling aloud. "So, as I was saying, being all ready for the meeting, and no horse to ride on, I made up my mind to foot it; for they tell me there is a nice young man to be taken into communion to-night. But now your good worship will lend me your arm, and we shall be there in a twinkling."

"That can hardly be," answered her friend. "I may not spare you my arm, Goody Cloyse, but here is my staff, if you will." 35

So saying, he threw it down at her feet, where, perhaps, it assumed life, being one of the rods which its owner had formerly lent to the Egyptian Magi. Of this fact, however, Goodman Brown could not take cognizance. He had cast his eyes in astonishment, and looking down again, beheld neither Goody Cloyse nor the serpentine staff, but his fellow-traveller alone, who waited for him as calmly as if nothing had happened.

---

[7] *Goody:* A contraction of "Goodwife," a term of politeness used in addressing a woman of humble station. Goody Cloyse, like Goody Cory and Martha Carrier, who appear later in the story, was one of the Salem "witches" sentenced in 1692.

[8] *smallage . . . wolf's bane:* Plants believed to have magical powers. Smallage is wild celery.

"That old woman taught me my catechism!" said the young man; and there was a world of meaning in this simple comment.

They continued to walk onward, while the elder traveller exhorted his companion to make good speed and persevere in the path, discoursing so aptly, that his arguments seemed rather to spring up in the bosom of his auditor, than to be suggested by himself. As they went he plucked a branch of maple, to serve for a walking-stick, and began to strip it of the twigs and little boughs, which were wet with evening dew. The moment his fingers touched them, they became strangely withered and dried up, as with a week's sunshine. Thus the pair proceeded, at a good free pace, until suddenly, in a gloomy hollow of the road, Goodman Brown sat himself down on the stump of a tree, and refused to go any farther.

"Friend," said he, stubbornly, "my mind is made up. Not another step will I budge on this errand. What if a wretched old woman do choose to go to the devil, when I thought she was going to Heaven! Is that any reason why I should quit my dear Faith, and go after her?"

"You will think better of this by and by," said his acquaintance, composedly. "Sit here and rest yourself awhile; and when you feel like moving again, there is my staff to help you along." 40

Without more words, he threw his companion the maple stick, and was as speedily out of sight as if he had vanished into the deepening gloom. The young man sat a few moments by the roadside, applauding himself greatly, and thinking with how clear a conscience he should meet the minister, in his morning walk, nor shrink from the eye of good old Deacon Gookin. And what calm sleep would be his, that very night, which was to have been spent so wickedly, but purely and sweetly now, in the arms of Faith! Amidst these pleasant and praiseworthy meditations, Goodman Brown heard the tramp of horses along the road, and deemed it advisable to conceal himself within the verge of the forest, conscious of the guilty purpose that had brought him thither, though now so happily turned from it.

On came the hoof-tramps and the voices of the riders, two grave old voices, conversing soberly as they drew near. These mingled sounds appeared to pass along the road, within a few yards of the young man's hiding-place; but owing, doubtless, to the depth of the gloom, at that particular spot, neither the travellers nor their steeds were visible. Though their figures brushed the small boughs by the wayside, it could not be seen that they intercepted, even for a moment, the faint gleam from the strip of bright sky, athwart which they must have passed. Goodman Brown alternately crouched and stood on tiptoe, pulling aside the branches, and thrusting forth his head as far as he durst, without discerning so much as a shadow. It vexed him the more, because he could have sworn, were such a thing possible, that he recognized the voices of the minister and Deacon Gookin, jogging along quietly, as they were wont to do, when bound to some ordination or ecclesiastical council. While yet within hearing, one of the riders stopped to pluck a switch.

"Of the two, reverend Sir," said the voice like the deacon's, "I had rather miss an ordination dinner than to-night's meeting. They tell me that some of our community are to be here from Falmouth and beyond, and others from

Connecticut and Rhode Island; besides several of the Indian powwows, who, after their fashion, know almost as much deviltry as the best of us. Moreover, there is a goodly young woman to be taken into communion."

"Mighty well, Deacon Gookin!" replied the solemn old tones of the minister. "Spur up, or we shall be late. Nothing can be done, you know, until I get on the ground."

The hoofs clattered again, and the voices, talking so strangely in the empty air, passed on through the forest, where no church had ever been gathered, nor solitary Christian prayed. Whither, then, could these holy men be journeying, so deep into the heathen wilderness? Young Goodman Brown caught hold of a tree, for support, being ready to sink down on the ground, faint and over-burthened with the heavy sickness of his heart. He looked up to the sky, doubting whether there really was a Heaven above him. Yet, there was the blue arch, and the stars brightening in it. 45

"With Heaven above, and Faith below, I will yet stand firm against the devil!" cried Goodman Brown.

While he still gazed upward, into the deep arch of the firmament, and had lifted his hands to pray, a cloud, though no wind was stirring, hurried across the zenith, and hid the brightening stars. The blue sky was still visible, except directly overhead, where this black mass of cloud was sweeping swiftly northward. Aloft in the air, as if from the depths of the cloud, came a confused and doubtful sound of voices. Once, the listener fancied that he could distinguish the accents of townspeople of his own, men and women, both pious and ungodly, many of whom he had met at the communion-table, and had seen others rioting at the tavern. The next moment, so indistinct were the sounds, he doubted whether he had heard aught but the murmur of the old forest, whispering without a wind. Then came a stronger swell of those familiar tones, heard daily in the sunshine, at Salem village, but never, until now, from a cloud at night. There was one voice, of a young woman, uttering lamentations, yet with an uncertain sorrow, and entreating for some favor, which, perhaps, it would grieve her to obtain. And all the unseen multitude, both saints and sinners, seemed to encourage her onward.

"Faith!" shouted Goodman Brown, in a voice of agony and desperation; and the echoes of the forest mocked him, crying—"Faith! Faith!" as if bewildered wretches were seeking her, all through the wilderness.

The cry of grief, rage, and terror was yet piercing the night, when the unhappy husband held his breath for a response. There was a scream, drowned immediately in a louder murmur of voices fading into far-off laughter, as the dark cloud swept away, leaving the clear and silent sky above Goodman Brown. But something fluttered lightly down through the air, and caught on the branch of a tree. The young man seized it and beheld a pink ribbon.

"My Faith is gone!" cried he, after one stupefied moment. "There is no good on earth, and sin is but a name. Come, devil! For to thee is this world given." 50

And maddened with despair, so that he laughed loud and long, did Goodman Brown grasp his staff and set forth again, at such a rate, that he seemed to fly along the forest path, rather than to walk or run. The road grew wilder and drearier, and more faintly traced, and vanished at length, leaving him in the heart of the dark wilderness, still rushing onward, with the instinct that guides mortal man to evil. The whole forest was peopled with frightful sounds: the creaking of the trees, the howling of wild beasts, and the yell of Indians; while, sometimes, the wind tolled like a distant church bell, and sometimes gave a broad roar around the traveller, as if all Nature was laughing him to scorn. But he was himself the chief horror of the scene, and shrank not from its other horrors.

"Ha! Ha! Ha!" roared Goodman Brown, when the wind laughed at him. "Let us hear which will laugh loudest! Think not to frighten me with your deviltry! Come witch, come wizard, come Indian powwow, come devil himself! And here comes Goodman Brown. You may as well fear him as he fear you!"

In truth, all through the haunted forest, there could be nothing more frightful than the figure of Goodman Brown. On he flew, among the black pines, brandishing his staff with frenzied gestures, now giving vent to an inspiration of horrid blasphemy, and now shouting forth such laughter, as set all the echoes of the forest laughing like demons around him. The fiend in his own shape is less hideous, than when he rages in the breast of man. Thus sped the demoniac on his course, until, quivering among the trees, he saw a red light before him, as when the felled trunks and branches of a clearing have been set on fire, and throw up their lurid blaze against the sky, at the hour of midnight. He paused, in a lull of the tempest that had driven him onward, and heard the swell of what seemed a hymn, rolling solemnly from a distance, with the weight of many voices. He knew the tune. It was a familiar one in the choir of the village meeting-house. The verse died heavily away, and was lengthened by a chorus, not of human voices, but of all the sounds of the benighted wilderness, pealing in awful harmony together. Goodman Brown cried out; and his cry was lost to his own ear, by its unison with the cry of the desert.

In the interval of silence, he stole forward, until the light glared full upon his eyes. At one extremity of an open space, hemmed in by the dark wall of the forest, arose a rock, bearing some rude, natural resemblance either to an altar or a pulpit, and surrounded by four blazing pines, their tops aflame, their stems untouched, like candles at an evening meeting. The mass of foliage, that had overgrown the summit of the rock, was all on fire, blazing high into the night, and fitfully illuminating the whole field. Each pendent twig and leafy festoon was in a blaze. As the red light arose and fell, a numerous congregation alternately shone forth, then disappeared in shadow, and again grew, as it were, out of the darkness, peopling the heart of the solitary woods at once.

"A grave and dark-clad company!" quoth Goodman Brown. 55

In truth, they were such. Among them, quivering to-and-fro, between gloom and splendor, appeared faces that would be seen, next day, at the council-board of the province, and others which, Sabbath after Sabbath, looked devoutly heavenward, and benignantly over the crowded pews, from the holiest pulpits in the land. Some affirm, that the lady of the governor was there. At least, there were high dames well known to her, and wives of honored husbands, and widows a great multitude, and ancient maidens, all of excellent repute, and fair young girls, who trembled lest their mothers should espy them. Either the sudden gleams of light, flashing over the obscure field, bedazzled Goodman Brown, or he recognized a score of the church members of Salem village, famous for their especial sanctity. Good old Deacon Gookin had arrived, and waited at the skirts of that venerable saint, his reverend pastor. But, irreverently consorting with these grave, reputable, and pious people, these elders of the church, these chaste dames and dewy virgins, there were men of dissolute lives and women of spotted fame, wretches given over to all mean and filthy vice, and suspected even of horrid crimes. It was strange to see, that the good shrank not from the wicked, nor were the sinners abashed by the saints. Scattered, also, among their pale-faced enemies, were the Indian priests, or powwows, who had often scared their native forest with more hideous incantations than any known to English witchcraft.

"But, where is Faith?" thought Goodman Brown; and, as hope came into his heart, he trembled.

Another verse of the hymn arose, a slow and mournful strain, such as the pious love, but joined to words which expressed all that our nature can conceive of sin, and darkly hinted at far more. Unfathomable to mere mortals is the lore of fiends. Verse after verse was sung, and still the chorus of the desert swelled between, like the deepest tone of a mighty organ. And, with the final peal of that dreadful anthem, there came a sound, as if the roaring wind, the rushing streams, the howling beasts, and every other voice of the unconverted wilderness were mingling and according with the voice of guilty man, in homage to the prince of all. The four blazing pines threw up a loftier flame, and obscurely discovered shapes and visages of horror on the smoke-wreaths, above the impious assembly. At the same moment, the fire on the rock shot redly forth, and formed a glowing arch above its base, where now appeared a figure. With reverence be it spoken, the apparition bore no slight similitude, both in garb and manner, to some grave divine of the New England churches.

"Bring forth the converts!" cried a voice, that echoed through the field and rolled into the forest.

At the word, Goodman Brown stepped forth from the shadow of the trees, and approached the congregation, with whom he felt a loathful brotherhood, by the sympathy of all that was wicked in his heart. He could have well-nigh sworn, that the shape of his own dead father beckoned him to advance, looking downward from a smoke-wreath, while a woman, with dim features of despair, threw out her hand to warn him back. Was it his mother? But he had no power to retreat one step, nor to resist, even in thought, when the minister and good old Deacon Gookin seized his arms, and led him to the blazing rock. Thither came also the slender form of a veiled female, led between Goody Cloyse, that pious teacher of the catechism, and Martha Carrier, who had received the devil's promise to be queen of hell. A rampant hag was she! And there stood the proselytes, beneath the canopy of fire. 60

"Welcome, my children," said the dark figure, "to the communion of your race! Ye have found, thus young, your nature and your destiny. My children, look behind you!"

They turned; and flashing forth, as it were, in a sheet of flame, the fiend-worshippers were seen; the smile of welcome gleamed darkly on every visage.

"There," resumed the sable form, "are all whom ye have reverenced from youth. Ye deemed them holier than yourselves, and shrank from your own sin, contrasting it with their lives of righteousness and prayerful aspirations heavenward. Yet, here are they all, in my worshipping assembly! This night it shall be granted you to know their secret deeds; how hoary-bearded elders of the church have whispered wanton words to the young maids of their households; how many a woman, eager for widow's weeds, has given her husband a drink at bedtime, and let him sleep his last sleep in her bosom; how beardless youths have made haste to inherit their father's wealth; and how fair damsels—blush not, sweet ones!—have dug little graves in the garden, and bidden me, the sole guest, to an infant's funeral. By the sympathy of your human hearts for sin, ye shall scent out all the places—whether in church, bedchamber, street, field, or forest—where crime has been committed, and shall exult to behold the whole earth one stain of guilt, one mighty blood-spot. Far more than this! It shall be yours to penetrate, in every bosom, the deep mystery of sin, the fountain of all wicked arts, and which inexhaustibly supplies more evil impulses than human power—than my power, at its utmost!—can make manifest in deeds. And now, my children, look upon each other."

They did so; and, by the blaze of the hell-kindled torches, the wretched man beheld his Faith, and the wife her husband, trembling before that unhallowed altar.

"Lo! There ye stand, my children," said the figure, in a deep and solemn tone, almost sad, with its despairing awfulness, as if his once angelic nature could yet mourn for our miserable race. "Depending upon one another's hearts, ye had still hoped that virtue were not all a dream! Now are ye undeceived!—Evil is the nature of mankind. Evil must be your only happiness. Welcome,
again, my children, to the communion of your race!" 65

"Welcome!" repeated the fiend-worshippers, in one cry of despair and triumph.

And there they stood, the only pair, as it seemed, who were yet hesitating on the verge of wickedness, in this dark world. A basin was hollowed, naturally, in the rock. Did it contain water, reddened by the lurid light? Or was it blood? Or, perchance, a liquid flame? Herein did the Shape of Evil dip his hand, and prepare to lay the mark of baptism upon their foreheads, that they might be partakers of the mystery of sin, more conscious of the secret guilt of others, both in deed and thought, than they could now be of their own. The husband cast one look at his pale wife, and Faith at him. What polluted wretches would the next glance show them to each other, shuddering alike at what they disclosed and what they saw!

"Faith! Faith!" cried the husband. "Look up to Heaven, and resist the Wicked One!"

Whether Faith obeyed, he knew not. Hardly had he spoken, when he found himself amid calm night and solitude, listening to a roar of the wind, which died heavily away through the forest. He staggered against the rock, and felt it chill and damp, while a hanging twig, that had been all on fire, besprinkled his cheek with the coldest dew.

The next morning, young Goodman Brown came slowly into the street of Salem village staring around him like a bewildered man. The good old minister was taking a walk along the grave-yard, to get an appetite for breakfast and meditate his sermon, and bestowed a blessing, as he passed, on Goodman Brown. He shrank from the venerable saint, as if to avoid an anathema. Old Deacon Gookin was at domestic worship, and the holy words of his prayer were heard through the open window. "What God doth the wizard pray to?" quoth Goodman Brown. Goody Cloyse, that excellent old Christian, stood in the early sunshine, at her own lattice, catechizing a little girl, who had brought her a pint of morning's milk. Goodman Brown snatched away the child, as from the grasp of the fiend himself. Turning the corner by the meeting-house, he spied the head of Faith, with the pink ribbons, gazing anxiously forth, and bursting into such joy at sight of him that she skipt along the street, and almost kissed her husband before the whole village. But Goodman Brown looked sternly and sadly into her face, and passed on without a greeting. 70

Had Goodman Brown fallen asleep in the forest, and only dreamed a wild dream of a witch-meeting?

Be it so, if you will. But, alas! It was a dream of evil omen for young Goodman Brown. A stern, a sad, a darkly meditative, a distrustful, if not a desperate man did he become, from the night of that fearful dream. On the Sabbath day, when the congregation were singing a holy psalm, he could not listen, because an anthem of sin rushed loudly upon his ear, and drowned all the blessed strain. When the minister spoke from the pulpit, with power and fervid eloquence, and with his hand on the open Bible, of the sacred truths of our religion, and of saint-like lives and triumphant deaths, and of future bliss or misery unutterable, then did Goodman Brown turn pale, dreading lest the roof should thunder down upon the gray blasphemer and his hearers. Often, awaking suddenly at midnight, he shrank from the bosom of Faith, and at morning or eventide, when the family knelt down at prayer, he scowled, and muttered to himself, and gazed sternly at his wife, and turned away. And when he had lived long, and was borne to his grave, a hoary corpse, followed by Faith, an aged woman, and children and grand-children, a goodly procession, besides neighbors not a few, they carved no hopeful verse upon his tombstone; for his dying hour was gloom.

Reading and Reacting

1. Who is the narrator of "Young Goodman Brown"? What advantages does the narrative point of view give the author?
2. What does young Goodman Brown mean when he says, "of all nights in the year, this one night must I tarry away from thee" (par. 3)? What is important about *this* night, and why does Goodman Brown believe he must journey "'twixt now and sunrise"?
3. Is Goodman Brown surprised to encounter the second traveler on the road, or does he seem to expect him? What is the significance of their encounter? What do you make of the fact that the stranger bears a strong resemblance to young Goodman Brown?
4. What sins are the various characters Goodman Brown meets in the woods guilty of committing?

5. "Young Goodman Brown" has two distinct settings: Salem and the woods. What are the differences between these settings? What significance does each setting have in the story?
6. Which figures in the story are allegorical, and which are symbols? On what evidence do you base your conclusions?
7. Why do the people gather in the woods? Why do they attend the ceremony?
8. Explain the change that takes place in young Goodman Brown at the end of the story. Why can he not listen to the singing of holy psalms or to the minister's sermons? What causes him to turn away from Faith and die in gloom?
9. **Journal Entry** At the end of the story, the narrator suggests that Goodman Brown might have fallen asleep and imagined his encounter with the witches. Do you agree? Why or why not?
10. **Critical Perspective** In *The Power of Blackness*, his classic study of nineteenth-century American writers, Harry Levin observes that Hawthorne had doubts about conventional religion. This, Levin believes, is why all efforts to read an enlightening theological message into Hawthorne's works are "doomed to failure."

    What comment do you think Hawthorne is making in "Young Goodman Brown" about religious faith?

Related Works: "Greasy Lake" (p. 419), "Where Are You Going, Where Have You Been?" (p. 447), *Trifles* (p. 820), *Hamlet* (p. 1012)

WRITING SUGGESTIONS: Symbol, Allegory, and Myth

1. In literature, a journey can often have symbolic significance. Write an essay in which you discuss the symbolic significance of the journey that takes place in "Young Goodman Brown." What is the purpose of the journey that the main character takes? How does this journey change him? If you wish, you can also examine the symbolic significance of Phoenix Jackson's journey in "A Worn Path" (p. 370).
2. A stranger figures prominently in "Young Goodman Brown." Write an essay in which you discuss the possible significance of this stranger. As you do so, examine the significance of the stranger's staff, the pink ribbons, Young Goodman Brown's wife's name, and the forest.
3. Write an essay in which you discuss the symbols in another reading in this anthology, for example, the road in "The Road Not Taken" (p. 605), The Misfit in "A Good Man Is Hard to Find" (p. 302), or the fair in "Araby" (p. 296).
4. If Shirley Jackson had wished to write "The Lottery" as an allegory whose purpose was to expose the evils of Nazi Germany, what revisions would she have had to make to convey the dangers of blind obedience to authority? Consider the story's symbols, the characters (and their names), and the setting.
5. In literary works, objects can function as symbols. In this chapter, for example, the quilt in "Everyday Use" and the box in "The Lottery" take on symbolic significance. Write an essay in which you analyze objects that have symbolic significance in two or three of the stories in this text and discuss how these objects help to convey the main themes of the stories in which they appear.

Chapter

15

Theme

Eudora Welty
Bettmann/Getty Images

David Michael Kaplan
Photograph by Joyce Winer. Courtesy of David Michael Kaplan.

Stephen Crane
Archivio GBB/Alamy Stock Photo

Learning Objectives

After reading this chapter, you will be able to...

- Define theme in a work of fiction.
- Differentiate between plot, subject, and theme in fiction.
- Identify the theme of a specific work of fiction.
- Consider how the title suggests the theme of a work of fiction.
- Explain how characters suggest the theme of a work of fiction.
- Describe how the plot suggests the theme of a work of fiction.
- Explain how point of view suggests the theme of a work of fiction.
- Detail how language and tone suggest the theme of a work of fiction.

The **theme** of a work of literature is its central or dominant idea. *Theme* is not the same as *plot* or *subject*, two terms with which it is sometimes confused. A summary of the **plot** of Tadeusz Borowski's "Silence," a story about survivors of the Holocaust, could be, "Prisoners are liberated from a concentration camp, and, despite the warnings of the American officer, they kill a captured German guard." The statement "'Silence' is about freed prisoners and a guard" could define the **subject** of the story. A statement of the theme of "Silence," however, has to do more than summarize its plot or define its subject; it has to convey the values and ideas expressed by the story.

Many effective stories are complex, expressing more than one theme, and "Silence" is no exception. You could say that "Silence" suggests that human beings have a need for vengeance. You could also say the story demonstrates that silence is sometimes the only response possible when people confront unspeakable horrors. Both these themes—and others—are expressed in the story, yet one theme seems to dominate: the idea that, under extreme conditions, the oppressed can have the same capacity for evil as their oppressors.

When you write about theme, you need to do more than tell what happens in the story. The theme you identify should be a general idea that extends beyond the story and applies to the world outside. Compare these two statements that a student wrote about Edgar Allan Poe's "The Cask of Amontillado" (p. 258):

> Poe's "The Cask of Amontillado" is about a man who has an obsessive desire for revenge.
>
> Poe's "The Cask of Amontillado" suggests that when the desire for revenge becomes obsessive, it can deprive individuals of all that makes them human.

The first statement merely tells what the story is about; the second statement identifies the story's theme, a general observation about humanity.

Granted, some short works (fairy tales or fables, for example) have themes that can only be expressed as **clichés**—overused phrases or expressions—or as **morals**—lessons dramatized by the work. The fairy tale "Cinderella," for example, expresses the clichéd theme that a virtuous girl who endures misfortune will eventually achieve her just reward; the fable "The Tortoise and the Hare" illustrates the moral "Slow and steady wins the race." Like "The Cask of Amontillado," however, the stories in this anthology have themes that are much more complex than clichés or morals.

Interpreting Themes

Contemporary critical theory holds that the theme of a work of fiction is as much a creation of readers as it is of the writer. Readers' backgrounds, knowledge, values, and beliefs all play a part in determining the theme (or themes) they will identify in a work. Many readers, for example, will realize that David Michael Kaplan's story "Doe Season" (p. 378)—in which the main character, Andy, goes hunting, kills her first deer, and is forced to confront suffering and death—expresses a conventional **initiation theme**, revealing the transition into adulthood to be a disillusioning and painful process. Still, different readers bring different perspectives to the story and, in some cases, see different themes.

During a classroom discussion of "Doe Season," a student familiar with hunting saw more than his classmates did in the story's conventional initiation theme. He knew that in many states there really is a doe season. Shorter than the ten-day buck season, it allows hunters to control the size of the deer herd by killing females. This knowledge enabled the student to conclude that, by the end of the story, the female child's innocence is destroyed, just as the doe is.

Another student pointed out that the participation of Andy—a female who uses a traditionally masculine name—in hunting, a traditional male rite of passage, leads to her killing the deer and to her subsequent disillusionment. It also leads to her decision to abandon her nickname. By contrasting "Andrea" with "Andy," the story reveals the conflict between aspects of her "feminine" nature (her compassion, for example) and her desire to emulate the men to whom killing is a sport. This interpretation led the student to conclude that the theme of "Doe Season" is that men and women, by their natures, have very different outlooks on life.

Other students rejected the negative portrayal of the story's male characters that the preceding interpretation implies. They pointed out that the father is a sympathetic figure who is extremely supportive; he encourages and defends his daughter. He takes her hunting because he loves her, not because he wants to initiate her into life or to hurt her. One student mentioned that Andy's reaction (called *buck fever*) when she sees the doe is common in children who kill their first deer. In light of this information, several students concluded that far from being about irreconcilable differences between men and women, "Doe Season" makes a statement about a young girl who is hunting for her own identity and who in the process discovers her own mortality. Her father is therefore the agent who enables her to confront the inevitability of death, a fact she must accept if she is going to take her place in the adult world. In this sense, the theme of the story is the idea that to mature, a child must come to terms with the reality of death.

Different readers may see different themes in a story, but any interpretation of a theme must make sense in light of what is actually in the story. Evidence from the work, not just your own feelings or assumptions, must support your interpretation, and a single statement by a character is not usually enough in itself to reveal a story's theme. Therefore, you must present a cross-section of examples from the text to support your interpretation of the story's theme. If you say that the theme of James Joyce's "Araby" (p. 296) is that an innocent idealist is inevitably doomed to disillusionment, you have to find examples from the text to support this statement. You could begin with the title, concluding that the word *Araby* suggests idealistic dreams of exotic beauty that the boy tries to find when he goes to a bazaar. You could reinforce this interpretation by pointing out that the unattainable woman is a symbol of all that the boy wants so desperately to find. Finally, you could show how idealism is ultimately crushed by society: at the end of the story, the boy stands alone in the darkness and realizes that his dreams are childish fantasies. Although other readers may have different responses to "Araby," they will find your interpretation reasonable if you support it with persuasive examples.

Identifying Themes

Every element of a story can shed light on its themes. As you analyze a short story, look for features that reveal and reinforce what you perceive to be the story's most important ideas.

- *The title can often provide insight into the theme or themes of a story.* The title of an F. Scott Fitzgerald story, "Babylon Revisited," emphasizes a major idea in the story—that Paris of the 1920s is like Babylon, the ancient city the Bible singles out as the epitome of evil and corruption. The story's protagonist, Charlie Wales, comes to realize that no matter how much money he lost after the 1929 stock market crash, he lost more—his wife and his daughter—during the boom, when he was in Paris. Charlie's search through his past—his return to "Babylon"—provides new meaning to his life and offers him at least a small bit of hope for the future.
- *Sometimes a narrator's or character's statement can reveal a theme.* For example, at the beginning of Alberto Álvaro Ríos's "The Secret Lion" (p. 222), the first-person narrator says, "I was twelve and in junior high school and something happened that we didn't have a name for, but it was there nonetheless like a lion, and roaring, roaring that way the biggest things do. Everything changed." Although the narrator does not directly announce the story's theme, he suggests that the story will convey the idea that the price children pay for growing up is realizing that everything changes and nothing stays the way it is.
- *The arrangement of events can suggest a story's theme*, as it does in an Ernest Hemingway story, "The Short Happy Life of Francis Macomber." At the beginning of the story, the title character is a coward who is stuck in an unhappy marriage. As the story progresses, he gradually learns the nature of courage and, finally, finds it in himself. At the moment of his triumph, however, Francis is shot by his wife; his "happy life" is short indeed. The way the events of the story are presented, through foreshadowing and flashbacks, reveals the connection between Macomber's marriage and his behavior as a hunter, and this connection in turn helps to reveal a possible theme: that sometimes courage can be more important than life itself.
- *A story's central conflict can offer clues to its theme.* For example, the main character in "The Yellow Wallpaper" (p. 315), a woman who has recently had a baby, is in conflict with the nineteenth-century society in which she lives. She is suffering from "temporary nervous depression," what doctors today recognize as postpartum depression. Following the

practice of the time, her physician has ordered complete bed rest and instructed her husband to deprive her of all mental and physical stimulation. This harsh treatment leads the narrator to lose her grasp on reality; eventually, she begins to hallucinate. The main conflict of the story is clearly between the woman and her society, which is controlled by men. This conflict communicates the central theme: that in nineteenth-century America, women are controlled not just by their husbands and the male medical establishment but also by the society men have created.

- *The point of view of a story can shed light on its theme*. For example, a writer's use of an unreliable first-person narrator can help to communicate the theme of a story. Thus, Montresor's self-serving first-person account of his crime in "The Cask of Amontillado"—along with his attempts to justify these actions—enables readers to understand the dangers of irrational anger and misplaced ideas about honor. The voice of a third-person narrator can also help to convey a story's theme. For example, the detachment of the narrator in Stephen Crane's Civil War novel *The Red Badge of Courage* reinforces the theme of the novel: that bravery, cowardice, war, and even life itself are insignificant when set beside the indifference of the universe.
- *Quite often a story's symbols—names, places, and objects—can suggest its theme*. For example, a rocking horse in D. H. Lawrence's "The Rocking-Horse Winner" can be seen as a symbol of a boy's desperate desire to remain a child. Interpreted in this way, it reinforces the theme that innocence cannot survive when it confronts adult greed and selfishness. Similarly, Hawthorne's "Young Goodman Brown" (p. 354) uses symbols such as the walking stick, the woods, sunset and night, and the vague shadows to develop one of its central themes: that once a person strays from the path of faith, evil is everywhere.
- *Finally, changes in a character can shed light on the theme or themes of the story*. The main character in Charles Baxter's "Gryphon" (p. 191), for example, eventually comes to realize that the "lies" his substitute teacher tells may be closer to the truth than the "facts" his other teachers present, and his changing attitude toward her helps to communicate the story's central theme about the nature of truth.

Checklist Writing about Theme

- What is the central theme of the story?
- What other themes can you identify?
- Does the title of the story suggest a theme?
- Does the narrator, or any character, make statements that express or imply a theme?

- In what way does the arrangement of events in the story suggest a theme?
- In what way does the central conflict of the story suggest a theme?
- How does the point of view shed light on the story's central theme?
- Do any symbols suggest a theme?
- Do any characters in the story change in any significant way? Do these changes convey a particular theme?

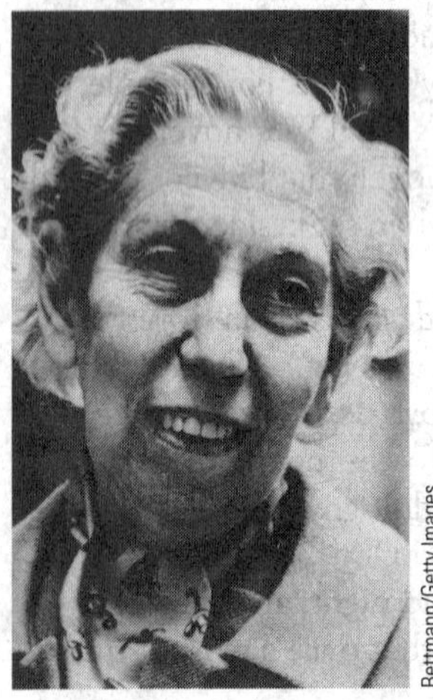
Bettmann/Getty Images

EUDORA WELTY (1909–2001) was born and raised in Jackson, Mississippi. After attending the Mississippi College for Women, the University of Wisconsin, and Columbia University (where she studied advertising), she returned to Jackson to pursue her long career as a writer, beginning as a journalist. In 1936, she wrote the first of her many short stories, which are gathered in *Collected Stories* (1980). Welty also wrote several novels, including *Delta Wedding* (1946), *Losing Battles* (1970), and the Pulitzer Prize–winning *The Optimist's Daughter* (1972). Her volume of memoirs, *One Writer's Beginnings* (1984), was a best-seller.

One of America's most accomplished writers, Welty focused much of her fiction on life in southern towns peopled with dreamers, eccentrics, and close-knit families. Her sharply observed characters are sometimes presented with great humor, sometimes with poignant lyricism, but always with clarity and sympathy. "Of course any writer is in part all of his characters," she observed. "How otherwise would they be known to him, occur to him, become what they are?" In "A Worn Path," Welty creates a particularly memorable character in the tenacious Phoenix Jackson, and through her she explores a theme that transcends race and region.

Cultural Context During the Great Depression of the 1930s, poverty and unemployment were widespread but were especially severe in isolated rural areas of the South. For the Black population living in this poor and undeveloped region, difficult economic conditions were made worse by the system of segregation that prevented them from voting, receiving a good education, or enjoying the same rights and privileges as their white counterparts. Hoping to improve their situation, many Black families left the South and moved into northern and midwestern cities where there were better opportunities for education and employment. Others, like the protagonist of this story, remained in the South despite the atmosphere of residual racism and oppression.

A Worn Path (1940)

It was December—a bright frozen day in the early morning. Far out in the country there was an old Negro woman with her head tied in a red rag, coming along a path through the pinewoods. Her name was Phoenix Jackson. She was very old and small and she walked slowly in the dark pine shadows, moving a little from side to side in her steps, with the balanced heaviness and lightness of a pendulum in a grandfather clock. She carried a thin, small cane made from an umbrella, and with this she kept tapping the frozen earth in front of her. This made a grave and persistent noise in the still air, that seemed meditative like the chirping of a solitary little bird.

She wore a dark striped dress reaching down to her shoe tops, and an equally long apron of bleached sugar sacks, with a full pocket: all neat and tidy, but every time she took a step she might have fallen over her shoelaces, which dragged from her unlaced shoes. She looked straight ahead. Her eyes were blue with age. Her skin had a pattern all its own of numberless branching wrinkles and as though a whole little tree stood in the middle of her forehead, but a golden color ran underneath, and the two knobs of her cheeks were illumined by a yellow burning under the dark. Under the red rag her hair came down on her neck in the frailest of ringlets, still black, and with an odor like copper.

Now and then there was a quivering in the thicket. Old Phoenix said, "Out of my way, all you foxes, owls, beetles, jack rabbits, coons and wild animals! . . . Keep out from under these feet, little bob-whites. . . . Keep the big wild hogs out of my path. Don't let none of those come running my direction. I got a long way." Under her small black-freckled hand her cane, limber as a buggy whip, would switch at the brush as if to rouse up any hiding things.

On she went. The woods were deep and still. The sun made the pine needles almost too bright to look at, up where the wind rocked. The cones dropped as light as feathers. Down in the hollow was the mourning dove—it was not too late for him.

The path ran up a hill. "Seem like there is chains about my feet, time I get this far," she said, in the voice of argument old people keep to use with themselves. "Something always take a hold of me on this hill—pleads I should stay." 5

After she got to the top she turned and gave a full, severe look behind her where she had come. "Up through pines," she said at length. "Now down through oaks."

Her eyes opened their widest, and she started down gently. But before she got to the bottom of the hill a bush caught her dress.

Her fingers were busy and intent, but her skirts were full and long, so that before she could pull them free in one place they were caught in another. It was not possible to allow the dress to tear. "I in the thorny bush," she said. "Thorns, you doing your appointed work. Never want to let folks pass, no sir. Old eyes thought you was a pretty little *green* bush."

Finally, trembling all over, she stood free, and after a moment dared to stoop for her cane.

"Sun so high!" she cried, leaning back and looking, while the thick tears went over her eyes. "The time getting all gone here." 10

At the foot of this hill was a place where a log was laid across the creek.

"Now comes the trial," said Phoenix.

Putting her right foot out, she mounted the log and shut her eyes. Lifting her skirt, leveling her cane fiercely before her, like a festival figure in some parade, she began to march across. Then she opened her eyes and she was safe on the other side.

"I wasn't as old as I thought," she said.

But she sat down to rest. She spread her skirts on the bank around her and folded her hands over her knees. Up above her was a tree in a pearly cloud of mistletoe. She did not dare to close her eyes, and when a little boy brought her a plate with a slice of marble-cake on it she spoke to him. "That would be acceptable," she said. But when she went to take it there was just her own hand in the air. 15

So she left that tree, and had to go through a barbed-wire fence. There she had to creep and crawl, spreading her knees and stretching her fingers like a baby trying to climb the steps. But she talked loudly to herself: she could not let her dress be torn now, so late in the day, and she could not pay for having her arm or her leg sawed off if she got caught fast where she was.

At last she was safe through the fence and risen up out in the clearing. Big dead trees, like black men with one arm, were standing in the purple stalks of the withered cotton field. There sat a buzzard.

"Who you watching?"

In the furrow she made her way along.

"Glad this not the season for bulls," she said, looking sideways, "and the good Lord made his snakes to curl up and sleep in the winter. A pleasure I don't see no two-headed snake coming around that tree, where it come once. It took a while to get by him, back in the summer." 20

She passed through the old cotton and went into a field of dead corn. It whispered and shook and was taller than her head. "Through the maze now," she said, for there was no path.

Then there was something tall, black, and skinny there, moving before her.

At first she took it for a man. It could have been a man dancing in the field. But she stood still and listened, and it did not make a sound. It was as silent as a ghost.

"Ghost," she said sharply, "who be you the ghost of? For I have heard of nary death close by."

But there was no answer—only the ragged dancing in the wind. 25

She shut her eyes, reached out her hand, and touched a sleeve. She found a coat and inside that an emptiness, cold as ice.

"You scarecrow," she said. Her face lighted. "I ought to be shut up for good," she said with laughter. "My senses is gone. I too old. I the oldest people I ever know. Dance, old scarecrow," she said, "while I dancing with you."

She kicked her foot over the furrow, and with mouth drawn down, shook her head once or twice in a little strutting way. Some husks blew down and whirled in streamers about her skirts.

Then she went on, parting her way from side to side with the cane, through the whispering field. At last she came to the end, to a wagon track where the silver grass blew between the red ruts. The quail were walking around like pullets, seeming all dainty and unseen.

"Walk pretty," she said. "This is the easy place. This the easy going." 30

She followed the track, swaying through the quiet bare fields, through the little strings of trees silver in their dead leaves, past cabins silver from weather, with the doors and windows boarded shut, all like old women under a spell sitting there. "I walking in their sleep," she said, nodding her head vigorously.

In a ravine she went where a spring was silently flowing through a hollow log. Old Phoenix bent and drank. "Sweet-gum makes the water sweet," she said, and drank more. "Nobody know who made this well, for it was here when I was born."

The track crossed a swampy part where the moss hung as white as lace from every limb. "Sleep on, alligators, and blow your bubbles." Then the track went into the road.

Deep, deep the road went down between the high green-colored banks. Overhead the live-oaks met, and it was as dark as a cave.

A black dog with a lolling tongue came up out of the weeds by the ditch. She was meditating, and not ready, and when he came at her she only hit him a little with her cane. Over she went in the ditch, like a little puff of milkweed. 35

Down there, her senses drifted away. A dream visited her, and she reached her hand up, but nothing reached down and gave her a pull. So she lay there and presently went to talking. "Old woman," she said to herself, "that black dog come up out of the weeds to stall you off, and now there he sitting on his fine tail, smiling at you."

A white man finally came along and found her—a hunter, a young man, with his dog on a chain.

"Well, Granny!" he laughed. "What are you doing there?"

"Lying on my back like a June-bug waiting to be turned over, mister," she said, reaching up her hand.

He lifted her up, gave her a swing in the air, and set her down. "Anything broken, Granny?" 40

"No sir, them old dead weeds is springy enough," said Phoenix, when she had got her breath. "I thank you for your trouble."

"Where do you live, Granny?" he asked, while the two dogs were growling at each other.

"Away back yonder, sir, behind the ridge. You can't even see it from here."

"On your way home?"

"No sir, I going to town." 45

"Why, that's too far! That's as far as I walk when I come out myself, and I get something for my trouble." He patted the stuffed bag he carried, and there hung down a little closed claw. It was one of the bob-whites, with its beak hooked bitterly to show it was dead. "Now you go on home, Granny!"

"I bound to go to town, mister," said Phoenix. "The time come around."

He gave another laugh, filling the whole landscape. "I know you old colored people! Wouldn't miss going to town to see Santa Claus!"

But something held old Phoenix very still. The deep lines in her face went into a fierce and different radiation. Without warning, she had seen with her own eyes a flashing nickel fall out of the man's pocket onto the ground.

"How old are you, Granny?" he was saying. 50

"There is no telling, mister," she said, "no telling."

Then she gave a little cry and clapped her hands and said, "Git on away from here, dog! Look! Look at that dog!" She laughed as if in admiration. "He ain't scared of nobody. He a big black dog." She whispered, "Sic him!"

"Watch me get rid of that cur," said the man. "Sic him, Pete! Sic him!"

Phoenix heard the dogs fighting, and heard the man running and throwing sticks. She even heard a gunshot. But she was slowly bending forward by that time, further and further forward, the lid stretched down over her eyes, as if she were doing this in her sleep. Her chin was lowered almost to her knees. The yellow palm of her hand came out from the fold of her apron. Her fingers slid down and along the ground under the piece of money with the grace and care they would have in lifting an egg from under a setting hen. Then she slowly straightened up, she stood erect, and the nickel was in her apron pocket. A bird flew by. Her lips moved. "God watching me the whole time. I come to stealing."

The man came back, and his own dog panted about them. "Well, I scared him off that time," he said, and then he laughed and lifted his gun and pointed it at Phoenix. 55

She stood straight and faced him.

"Doesn't the gun scare you?" he said, still pointing it.

"No, sir, I seen plenty go off closer by, in my day, and for less than what I done," she said, holding utterly still.

He smiled, and shouldered the gun. "Well, Granny," he said, "you must be a hundred years old, and scared of nothing. I'd give you a dime if I had any money with me. But you take my advice and stay home, and nothing will happen to you."

"I bound to go on my way, mister," said Phoenix. She inclined her head in the red rag. Then they went in different directions, but she could hear the gun shooting again and again over the hill. 60

She walked on. The shadows hung from the oak trees to the road like curtains. Then she smelled wood-smoke, and smelled the river, and she saw a steeple and the cabins on their steep steps. Dozens of little black children whirled around her. There ahead was Natchez shining. Bells were ringing. She walked on.

In the paved city it was Christmas time. There were red and green electric lights strung and crisscrossed everywhere, and all turned on in the daytime. Old Phoenix would have been lost if she had not distrusted her eyesight and depended on her feet to know where to take her.

She paused quietly on the sidewalk where people were passing by. A lady came along in the crowd, carrying an armful of red-, green- and silver-wrapped presents; she gave off perfume like the red roses in hot summer, and Phoenix stopped her.

"Please, missy, will you lace up my shoe?" She held up her foot.

"What do you want, Grandma?"

"See my shoe," said Phoenix. "Do all right for out in the country, but wouldn't look right to go in a big building."

"Stand still then, Grandma," said the lady. She put her packages down on the sidewalk beside her and laced and tied both shoes tightly.

"Can't lace 'em with a cane," said Phoenix. "Thank you, missy. I doesn't mind asking a nice lady to tie up my shoe, when I gets out on the street."

Moving slowly and from side to side, she went into the big building, and into a tower of steps, where she walked up and around and around until her feet knew to stop.

She entered a door, and there she saw nailed up on the wall the document that had been stamped with the gold seal and framed in the gold frame, which matched the dream that was hung up in her head.

"Here I be," she said. There was a fixed and ceremonial stiffness over her body.

"A charity case, I suppose," said an attendant who sat at the desk before her.

But Phoenix only looked above her head. There was sweat on her face, the wrinkles in her face shone like a bright net.

"Speak up, Grandma," the woman said. "What's your name? We must have your history, you know. Have you been here before? What seems to be the trouble with you?"

Old Phoenix only gave a twitch to her face as if a fly were bothering her.

"Are you deaf?" cried the attendant.

But then the nurse came in.

"Oh, that's just old Aunt Phoenix," she said. "She doesn't come for herself—she has a little grandson. She makes these trips just as regular as clockwork. She lives away back off the Old Natchez Trace." She bent down. "Well, Aunt Phoenix, why don't you just take a seat? We won't keep you standing after your long trip." She pointed.

The old woman sat down, bolt upright in the chair.

"Now, how is the boy?" asked the nurse.

Old Phoenix did not speak.

"I said, how is the boy?"

But Phoenix only waited and stared straight ahead, her face very solemn and withdrawn into rigidity.

"Is his throat any better?" asked the nurse. "Aunt Phoenix, don't you hear me? Is your grandson's throat any better since the last time you came for the medicine?"

With her hands on her knees, the old woman waited, silent, erect and motionless, just as if she were in armor.

"You mustn't take up our time this way, Aunt Phoenix," the nurse said. "Tell us quickly about your grandson, and get it over. He isn't dead, is he?"

At last there came a flicker and then a flame of comprehension across her face, and she spoke.

"My grandson. It was my memory had left me. There I sat and forgot why I made my long trip."

"Forgot?" The nurse frowned. "After you came so far?"

Then Phoenix was like an old woman begging a dignified forgiveness for waking up frightened in the night. "I never did go to school, I was too old at the Surrender,"[1] she said in a soft voice. "I'm an old woman without an education. It was my memory fail me. My little grandson, he is just the same, and I forgot it in the coming."

"Throat never heals, does it?" said the nurse, speaking in a loud, sure voice to old Phoenix. By now she had a card with something written on it, a little list. "Yes. Swallowed lye. When was it?—January—two-three years ago—"

Phoenix spoke unasked now. "No, missy, he not dead, he just the same. Every little while his throat begin to close up again, and he not able to swallow. He not get his breath. He not able to help himself. So the time come around, and I go on another trip for the soothing medicine."

"All right. The doctor said as long as you came to get it, you could have it," said the nurse. "But it's an obstinate case."

"My little grandson, he sit up there in the house all wrapped up, waiting by himself," Phoenix went on. "We is the only two left in the world. He suffer and it don't seem to put him back at all. He got a sweet look. He going to last. He wear a little patch quilt and peep out holding his mouth open like a little bird. I remembers so plain now. I not going to forget him again, no, the whole enduring time. I could tell him from all the others in creation."

"All right." The nurse was trying to hush her now. She brought her a bottle of medicine. "Charity," she said, making a check mark in a book.

Old Phoenix held the bottle close to her eyes, and then carefully put it into her pocket.

"I thank you," she said.

"It's Christmas time, Grandma," said the attendant. "Could I give you a few pennies out of my purse?"

"Five pennies is a nickel," said Phoenix stiffly.

"Here's a nickel," said the attendant.

Phoenix rose carefully and held out her hand. She received the nickel and then fished the other nickel out of her pocket and laid it beside the new one. She stared at her palm closely, with her head on one side.

Then she gave a tap with her cane on the floor.

"This is what come to me to do," she said. "I going to the store and buy my child a little windmill they sells, made out of paper. He going to find it hard to

[1] *the Surrender:* The surrender of General Robert E. Lee to General Ulysses S. Grant at the end of the Civil War, April 9, 1865.

believe there such a thing in the world. I'll march myself back where he waiting, holding it straight up in this hand."

She lifted her free hand, gave a little nod, turned around, and walked out of the doctor's office. Then her slow step began on the stairs, going down.

Reading and Reacting

1. How does the first paragraph set the scene for the rest of the story? How does it foreshadow the events that will take place later?
2. Traditionally, a **quest** is a journey in which a knight overcomes a series of obstacles in order to perform a prescribed feat. In what way is Phoenix's journey a quest? What obstacles does she face? What feat must she perform?
3. Because Phoenix is old, she has trouble seeing. What things does she have difficulty seeing? How do her mistakes shed light on her character? How do they contribute to the impact of the story?
4. What is the major theme of this story? What other themes are expressed?
5. A **phoenix** is a mythical bird that would live for five hundred years, be consumed by fire, and then rise from its own ashes. Why is the name of this creature appropriate for the main character of this story?
6. Phoenix is not intimidated by the man with the gun and has no difficulty asking a white woman to tie her shoe. In spite of her pride and her strength of character, Phoenix has no qualms about stealing a nickel or taking charity from the doctor. How do you account for this apparent contradiction?
7. How do the various people Phoenix encounters react to her? Do they treat her with respect? with disdain? Why do you think they react the way they do?
8. In paragraph 90, Phoenix says that she is an old woman without an education. Even so, what knowledge does she seem to have that the other characters lack?
9. **Journal Entry** Could "A Worn Path" be seen as an **allegory**? If so, what qualities or ideas might each of the characters represent?
10. **Critical Perspective** Writing about "A Worn Path," Eudora Welty said that the question she was asked most frequently by both students and teachers was whether Phoenix Jackson's grandson was actually dead. Here she attempts to answer this question:

    > I had not meant to mystify readers by withholding any fact; it is not a writer's business to tease. The story is told through Phoenix's mind and she undertakes her errand. As the author at one with the character as I tell it, I must assume that the boy is alive. As the reader, you are free to think as you like, of course; the story invites you to believe that no matter what happens, Phoenix for as long as she is able to walk and can hold to her purpose will make her journey.

    Do you think Phoenix's grandson is alive or dead? Why?

Related Works: "Miss Brill" (p. 185), "Araby" (p. 296), "Everyday Use" (p. 346), "The Negro Speaks of Rivers" (p. 725)

Photograph by Joyce Winer. Courtesy of David Michael Kaplan.

DAVID MICHAEL KAPLAN (1946–) is one of a group of American writers who, along with South American writers such as Gabriel García Márquez of Columbia, are called "magic realists." Magic realists work outside of the borders of traditional fantasy writing, seamlessly interweaving magical elements with detailed, realistically drawn "everyday" settings. These elements, says a reviewer of Kaplan's work, are invoked "to illuminate and underscore heightened moments of reality." The story "Doe Season," which appeared in Kaplan's debut collection, *Comfort* (1987), was included in *Best American Short Stories 1985.* Kaplan's first novel, *Skating in the Dark,* was published in 1991, and his writing text, *Revision: A Creative Approach to Writing and Re-writing Fiction,* was published in 1997. Kaplan teaches fiction writing at Loyola University Chicago.

Interestingly, the stories in *Comfort* break from classic "first-time author" tradition by sidestepping the autobiographical, young-man-comes-of-age theme. Instead, these stories are about young girls—or young women—coming to grips with parents (present or absent) and with loss and searching for ways to resolve their ambivalence about becoming women. In "Doe Season," Andy's surreal encounter with the doe may be a dream, but the beauty and horror of their meeting will stay with her for rest of her life.

Cultural Context When European settlers first came to America, deer roamed freely from coast to coast, and the settlers hunted them to put meat on the table. Today, deer are hunted in a regulated fashion to control their numbers and maintain a balance in their population. Deer hunting has long been viewed as a coming-of-age ritual for young men—and, more recently, for young women first entering adulthood, like the protagonist in this story. It used to be the tradition that a young hunter who missed his first deer had his shirttail cut off; if he succeeded, his face was smeared with the blood of his first kill. Some hunters still observe these initiation rites.

Doe Season (1985)

They were always the same woods, she thought sleepily as they drove through the early morning darkness—deep and immense, covered with yesterday's snowfall, which had frozen overnight. They were the same woods that lay behind her house, *and they stretch all the way to here*, she thought, *for miles and miles, longer than I could walk in a day, or a week even, but they are still the same woods*. The thought made her feel good: it was like thinking of God; it was like thinking of the space between here and the moon; it was like thinking of all the foreign countries from her geography book where even now, Andy knew, people were going to bed, while they—she and her father and Charlie Spoon and Mac, Charlie's eleven-year-old son—were driving deeper into the Pennsylvania countryside, to go hunting.

They had risen long before dawn. Her mother, yawning and not trying to hide her sleepiness, cooked them eggs and French toast. Her father smoked a cigarette and flicked ashes into his saucer while Andy listened, wondering *Why doesn't he come?* and *Won't he ever come?* until at last a car pulled into the graveled drive and honked. "That will be Charlie Spoon," her father said; he always said "Charlie Spoon," even though his real name was Spreun, because Charlie was, in a sense, shaped like a spoon, with a large head and a narrow waist and chest.

Andy's mother kissed her and her father and said, "Well, have a good time" and "Be careful." Soon they were outside in the bitter dark, loading gear by the back-porch light, their breath steaming. The woods behind the house were then only a black streak against the wash of night.

Andy dozed in the car and woke to find that it was half light. Mac—also sleeping—had slid against her. She pushed him away and looked out the window. Her breath clouded the glass, and she was cold; the car's heater didn't work right. They were riding over gentle hills, the woods on both sides now—the same woods, she knew, because she had been watching the whole way, even while she slept. They had been in her dreams, and she had never lost sight of them.

Charlie Spoon was driving. "I don't understand why she's coming," he said to her father. "How old is she anyway—eight?"

"Nine," her father replied. "She's small for her age."

"So—nine. What's the difference? She'll just add to the noise and get tired besides."

"No, she won't," her father said. "She can walk me to death. And she'll bring good luck, you'll see. Animals—I don't know how she does it, but they come right up to her. We go walking in the woods, and we'll spot more raccoons and possums and such than I ever see when I'm alone."

Charlie grunted.

"Besides, she's not a bad little shot, even if she doesn't hunt yet. She shoots the .22 real good."

"Popgun," Charlie said, and snorted. "And target shooting ain't deer hunting."

"Well, she's not gonna be shooting anyway, Charlie," her father said. "Don't worry. She'll be no bother."

"I still don't know why she's coming," Charlie said.

"Because she wants to, and I want her to. Just like you and Mac. No difference."

Charlie turned onto a side road and after a mile or so slowed down. "That's it!" he cried. He stopped, backed up, and entered a narrow dirt road almost hidden by trees. Five hundred yards down, the road ran parallel to a fenced-in field. Charlie parked in a cleared area deeply rutted by frozen tractor tracks. The gate was locked. *In the spring*, Andy thought, *there will be cows here, and a dog that chases them*, but now the field was unmarked and bare.

"This is it," Charlie Spoon declared. "Me and Mac was up here just two weeks ago, scouting it out, and there's deer. Mac saw the tracks."

"That's right," Mac said.

"Well, we'll just see about that," her father said, putting on his gloves. He turned to Andy. "How you doing, honeybun?"

"Just fine," she said.

Andy shivered and stamped as they unloaded: first the rifles, which they unsheathed and checked, sliding the bolts, sighting through scopes, adjusting the slings; then the gear, their food and tents and sleeping bags and stove stored in four backpacks—three big ones for Charlie Spoon and her father and Mac, and a day pack for her. 20

"That's about your size," Mac said, to tease her.

She reddened and said, "Mac, I can carry a pack big as yours any day." He laughed and pressed his knee against the back of hers, so that her leg buckled. "Cut it out," she said. She wanted to make an iceball and throw it at him, but she knew that her father and Charlie were anxious to get going, and she didn't want to displease them.

Mac slid under the gate, and they handed the packs over to him. Then they slid under and began walking across the field toward the same woods that ran all the way back to her home, where even now her mother was probably rising again to wash their breakfast dishes and make herself a fresh pot of coffee. *She is there, and we are here:* the thought satisfied Andy. There was no place else she would rather be.

Mac came up beside her. "Over there's Canada," he said, nodding toward the woods.

"Huh!" she said. "Not likely." 25

"I don't mean *right* over there. I mean farther up north. You think I'm dumb?"

Dumb as your father, she thought.

"Look at that," Mac said, pointing to a piece of cow dung lying on a spot scraped bare of snow. "A frozen meadow muffin." He picked it up and sailed it at her. "Catch!"

"Mac!" she yelled. His laugh was as gawky as he was. She walked faster. He seemed different today somehow, bundled in his yellow-and-black-checkered coat, a rifle in hand, his silly floppy hat not quite covering his ears. They all seemed different as she watched them trudge through the snow—Mac and her father and Charlie Spoon—bigger, maybe, as if the cold landscape enlarged rather than diminished them, so that they, the only figures in that landscape, took on size and meaning just by being there. If they weren't there, everything would be quieter, and the woods would be the same as before. *But they are here*, Andy thought, looking behind her at the boot prints in the snow, *and I am too, and so it's all different.*

"We'll go down to the cut where we found those deer tracks," Charlie said as they entered the woods. "Maybe we'll get lucky and get a late one coming through." 30

The woods descended into a gully. The snow was softer and deeper here, so that often Andy sank to her knees. Charlie and Mac worked the top of the gully while she and her father walked along the base some thirty yards behind them. "If they miss the first shot, we'll get the second," her father said, and she nodded as if she had known this all the time. She listened to the crunch of their boots, their breathing, and the drumming of a distant woodpecker. And the crackling. In winter the woods crackled as if everything were straining, ready to snap like dried chicken bones.

We are hunting, Andy thought. The cold air burned her nostrils.

They stopped to make lunch by a rock outcropping that protected them from the wind. Her father heated the bean soup her mother had made for them, and they ate it with bread already stiff from the cold. He and Charlie took a few pulls from a flask of Jim Beam while she scoured the plates with snow and repacked them. Then they all had coffee with sugar and powdered milk, and her father poured her a cup too. "We won't tell your momma," he said, and Mac laughed. Andy held the cup the way her father did, not by the handle but around the rim. The coffee tasted smoky. She felt a little queasy, but she drank it all.

Charlie Spoon picked his teeth with a fingernail. "Now, you might've noticed one thing," he said.

"What's that?" her father asked.

"You might've noticed you don't hear no rifles. That's because there ain't no other hunters here. We've got the whole damn woods to ourselves. Now, I ask you—do I know how to find 'em?"

"We haven't seen deer yet, neither."

"Oh, we will," Charlie said, "but not for a while now." He leaned back against the rock. "Deer're sleeping, resting up for the evening feed."

"I seen a deer behind our house once, and it was afternoon," Andy said.

"Yeah, honey, but that was *before* deer season," Charlie said, grinning. "They know something now. They're smart that way."

"That's right," Mac said.

Andy looked at her father—had she said something stupid?

"Well, Charlie," he said, "if they know so much, how come so many get themselves shot?"

"Them's the ones that don't *believe* what they know," Charlie replied. The men laughed. Andy hesitated, and then laughed with them.

They moved on, as much to keep warm as to find a deer. The wind became even stronger. Blowing through the treetops, it sounded like the ocean, and once Andy thought she could smell salt air. But that was impossible; the ocean was *hundreds* of miles away, farther than Canada even. She and her parents had gone last summer to stay for a week at a motel on the New Jersey shore. That was the first time she'd seen the ocean, and it frightened her. It was huge and empty, yet always moving. Everything lay hidden. If you walked in it, you couldn't see how deep it was or what might be below; if you swam, something could pull you under and you'd never be seen again. Its musky, rank smell made her think of things dying. Her mother had floated beyond the breakers, calling to her to come in, but Andy wouldn't go farther than a few feet into the surf. Her mother swam and splashed with animal-like delight while her father, smiling shyly, held his white arms above the waist-deep water as if afraid to get them wet. Once a comber rolled over and sent them both tossing, and when her mother tried to stand up, the surf receding behind, Andy saw that her mother's swimsuit top had come off, so that her breasts swayed free, her nipples like two dark eyes. Embarrassed, Andy looked around: except for two women under a yellow umbrella farther up, the beach was empty. Her mother stood up unsteadily, regained her footing. Taking what seemed the longest time, she calmly refixed her top. Andy lay on the beach towel and closed her eyes. The sound of the surf made her head ache.

And now it was winter; the sky was already dimming, not just with the absence of light but with a mist that clung to the hunters' faces like cobwebs. They made camp early. Andy was chilled. When she stood still, she kept wiggling her toes to make sure they were there. Her father rubbed her arms and held her to him briefly, and that felt better. She unpacked the food while the others put up the tents.

"How about rounding us up some firewood, Mac?" Charlie asked.

"I'll do it," Andy said. Charlie looked at her thoughtfully and then handed her the canvas carrier.

There wasn't much wood on the ground, so it took her a while to get a good load. She was about a hundred yards from camp, near a cluster of high, lichen-covered boulders, when she saw through a crack in the rock a buck and two does walking gingerly, almost daintily, through the alder trees. She tried to hush her breathing as they passed not more than twenty yards away. There was nothing she could do. If she yelled, they'd be gone; by the time she got back to camp, they'd be gone. The buck stopped, nostrils quivering, tail up and alert. He looked directly at her. Still she didn't move, not one muscle. He was a beautiful buck, the color of late-turned maple leaves. Unafraid, he lowered his tail, and he and his does silently merged into the trees. Andy walked back to camp and dropped the firewood.

"I saw three deer," she said. "A buck and two does."

"Where?" Charlie Spoon cried, looking behind her as if they might have followed her into camp.

"In the woods yonder. They're gone now."

"Well, hell!" Charlie banged his coffee cup against his knee.

"Didn't I say she could find animals?" her father said, grinning.

"Too late to go after them," Charlie muttered. "It'll be dark in a quarter hour. Damn!"

"Damn," Mac echoed.

"They just walk right up to her," her father said.

"Well, leastwise this proves there's deer here." Charlie began snapping long branches into shorter ones. "You know, I think I'll stick with you," he told Andy, "since you're so good at finding deer and all. How'd that be?"

"Okay, I guess," Andy murmured. She hoped he was kidding; no way did she want to hunt with Charlie Spoon. Still, she was pleased he had said it.

Her father and Charlie took one tent, she and Mac the other. When they were in their sleeping bags, Mac said in the darkness, "I bet you really didn't see no deer, did you?"

She sighed. "I did, Mac. Why would I lie?"

"How big was the buck?"

"Four point. I counted."

Mac snorted.

"You just believe what you want, Mac," she said testily.

"Too bad it ain't buck season," he said. "Well, I got to go pee."

"So pee."

She heard him turn in his bag. "You ever see it?" he asked.

"It? What's 'it'?"

"It. A pecker."

"Sure," she lied.

"Whose? Your father's?"

She was uncomfortable. "No," she said.

"Well, whose then?"

"Oh I don't know! Leave me be, why don't you?"

"Didn't see a deer, didn't see a pecker," Mac said teasingly.

She didn't answer right away. Then she said, "My cousin Lewis. I saw his."

"Well, how old's he?"

"One and a half."

"Ha! A baby! A baby's is like a little worm. It ain't a real one at all."

If he says he'll show me his, she thought, *I'll kick him. I'll just get out of my bag and kick him.*

"I went hunting with my daddy and Versh and Danny Simmons last year in buck season," Mac said, "and we got ourselves one. And we hog-dressed the thing. You know what that is, don't you?"

"No," she said. She was confused. What was he talking about now?

"That's when you cut him open and take out all his guts, so the meat don't spoil. Makes him lighter to pack out, too."

She tried to imagine what the deer's guts might look like, pulled from the gaping hole. "What do you do with them?" she said. "The guts?"

"Oh, just leave 'em for the bears."

She ran her finger like a knife blade along her belly.

"When we left them on the ground," Mac said, "they smoked. Like they were cooking."

"Huh," she said.

"They cut off the deer's pecker, too, you know."

Andy imagined Lewis's pecker and shuddered. "Mac, you're disgusting."

He laughed. "Well, I gotta go pee." She heard him rustle out of his bag. "Broo!" he cried, flapping his arms. "It's cold!"

He makes so much noise, she thought, *just noise and more noise.*

Her father woke them before first light. He warned them to talk softly and said that they were going to the place where Andy had seen the deer, to try to cut them off on their way back from their night feeding. Andy couldn't shake off her sleep. Stuffing her sleeping bag into its sack seemed to take an hour, and tying her boots was the strangest thing she'd ever done. Charlie Spoon made hot chocolate and oatmeal with raisins. Andy closed her eyes and, between beats of her heart, listened to the breathing of the forest. *When I open my eyes, it will be lighter*, she decided. But when she did, it was still just as dark, except for the swaths of their flashlights and the hissing blue flame of the stove. *There has to be just one moment when it all changes from dark to light*, Andy thought. She had missed it yesterday, in the car; today she would watch more closely.

But when she remembered again, it was already first light and they had moved to the rocks by the deer trail and had set up shooting positions—Mac and Charlie Spoon on the up-trail side, she and her father behind them, some six feet up on a ledge. The day became brighter, the sun piercing the tall pines, raking the hunters, yet providing little warmth. Andy now smelled alder and pine and the slightly rotten odor of rock lichen. She rubbed her hand over the stone and considered that it must be very old, had probably been here before the giant pines, *before anyone was in these woods at all*. A chipmunk sniffed on a nearby branch. She aimed an imaginary rifle and pressed the trigger. The chipmunk froze, then scurried away. Her legs were cramping on the narrow ledge. Her father seemed to doze, one hand in his parka, the other cupped lightly around the rifle. She could smell his scent of old wool and leather. His cheeks were speckled with gray-black whiskers, and he worked his jaws slightly, as if chewing a small piece of gum.

Please let us get a deer, she prayed.

A branch snapped on the other side of the rock face. Her father's hand stiffened on the rifle, startling her—*He hasn't been sleeping at all*, she marveled—and then his jaw relaxed, as did the lines around his eyes, and she heard Charlie Spoon call, "Yo, don't shoot, it's us." He and Mac appeared from around the rock. They stopped beneath the ledge. Charlie solemnly crossed his arms.

"I don't believe we're gonna get any deer here," he said drily.

Andy's father lowered his rifle to Charlie and jumped down from the ledge. Then he reached up for Andy. She dropped into his arms and he set her gently on the ground.

Mac sidled up to her. "I knew you didn't see no deer," he said.

"Just because they don't come when you want 'em to don't mean she didn't see them," her father said.

Still, she felt bad. Her telling about the deer had caused them to spend the morning there, cold and expectant, with nothing to show for it.

They tramped through the woods for another two hours, not caring much about noise. Mac found some deer tracks, and they argued about how old they were. They split up for a while and then rejoined at an old logging road that deer might use, and followed it. The road crossed a stream, which had mostly frozen over but in a few spots still caught leaves and twigs in an icy swirl. They forded it by jumping from rock to rock. The road narrowed after that, and the woods thickened.

They stopped for lunch, heating up Charlie's wife's corn chowder. Andy's father cut squares of applesauce cake with his hunting knife and handed them to her and Mac, who ate his almost daintily. Andy could faintly taste knife oil on the cake. She was tired. She stretched her leg; the muscle that had cramped on the rock still ached.

"Might as well relax," her father said, as if reading her thoughts. "We won't find deer till suppertime."

Charlie Spoon leaned back against his pack and folded his hands across his stomach. "Well, even if we don't get a deer," he said expansively, "it's still great to be out here, breathe some fresh air, clomp around a bit. Get away from the house and the old lady." He winked at Mac, who looked away.

"That's what the woods are all about, anyway," Charlie said. "It's where the women don't want to go." He bowed his head toward Andy. "With your exception, of course, little lady." He helped himself to another piece of applesauce cake.

"She ain't a woman," Mac said.

"Well, she damn well's gonna be," Charlie said. He grinned at her. "Or will you? You're half a boy anyway. You go by a boy's name. What's your real name? Andrea, ain't it?"

"That's right," she said. She hoped that if she didn't look at him, Charlie would stop.

"Well, which do you like? Andy or Andrea?"

"Don't matter," she mumbled. "Either."

"She's always been Andy to me," her father said.

Charlie Spoon was still grinning. "So what are you gonna be, Andrea? A boy or a girl?"

"I'm a girl," she said.

"But you want to go hunting and fishing and everything, huh?"

"She can do whatever she likes," her father said.

"Hell, you might as well have just had a boy and be done with it!" Charlie exclaimed.

"That's funny," her father said, and chuckled. "That's just what her momma tells me."

They were looking at her, and she wanted to get away from them all, even from her father, who chose to joke with them.

"I'm going to walk a bit," she said.

She heard them laughing as she walked down the logging trail. She flapped her arms; she whistled. *I don't care how much noise I make*, she thought. Two grouse flew from the underbrush, startling her. A little farther down, the trail ended in a clearing that enlarged into a frozen meadow; beyond it the woods began again. A few moldering posts were all that was left of a fence that had once enclosed the field. The low afternoon sunlight reflected brightly off the snow, so that Andy's eyes hurt. She squinted hard. A gust of wind blew across the field, stinging her face. And then, as if it had been waiting for her, the doe emerged from the trees opposite and stepped cautiously into the field. Andy watched: it stopped and stood quietly for what seemed a long time and then ambled across. It stopped again about seventy yards away and began to browse in a patch of sugar grass uncovered by the wind. Carefully, slowly, never taking her eyes from the doe, Andy walked backward, trying to step into the boot prints she'd already made. When she was far enough back into the woods, she turned and walked faster, her heart racing. *Please let it stay*, she prayed.

“There’s doe in the field yonder,” she told them.

They got their rifles and hurried down the trail.

“No use,” her father said. “We’re making too much noise any way you look at it.” 125

“At least we got us the wind in our favor,” Charlie Spoon said, breathing heavily.

But the doe was still there, grazing.

“Good Lord,” Charlie whispered. He looked at her father. “Well, whose shot?”

“Andy spotted it,” her father said in a low voice. “Let her shoot it.”

“What!” Charlie’s eyes widened. 130

Andy couldn’t believe what her father had just said. She’d only shot tin cans and targets; she’d never even fired her father’s .30-.30, and she’d never killed anything.

“I can’t,” she whispered.

“That’s right, she can’t,” Charlie Spoon insisted. “She’s not old enough and she don’t have a license even if she was!”

“Well, who’s to tell?” her father said in a low voice. “Nobody’s going to know but us.” He looked at her. “Do you want to shoot it, punkin?”

Why doesn’t it hear us? she wondered. *Why doesn’t it run away?* “I don’t know,” she said. 135

“Well, I’m sure as hell gonna shoot it,” Charlie said. Her father grasped Charlie’s rifle barrel and held it. His voice was steady.

“Andy’s a good shot. It’s her deer. She found it, not you. You’d still be sitting on your ass back in camp.” He turned to her again. “Now—do you want to shoot it, Andy? Yes or no.”

He was looking at her; they were all looking at her. Suddenly she was angry at the deer, who refused to hear them, who wouldn’t run away even when it could. “I’ll shoot it,” she said. Charlie turned away in disgust.

She lay on the ground and pressed the rifle stock against her shoulder bone. The snow was cold through her parka; she smelled oil and wax and damp earth. She pulled off one glove with her teeth. “It sights just like the .22,” her father said gently. “Cartridge’s already chambered.” As she had done so many times before, she sighted down the scope; now the doe was in the reticle. She moved the barrel until the cross hairs lined up. Her father was breathing beside her.

“Aim where the chest and legs meet, or a little above, punkin,” he was saying calmly. “That’s the killing shot.” 140

But now, seeing it in the scope, Andy was hesitant. Her finger weakened on the trigger. Still, she nodded at what her father said and sighted again, the cross hairs lining up in exactly the same spot—the doe had hardly moved, its brownish-gray body outlined starkly against the blue-backed snow. *It doesn’t know,* Andy thought. *It just doesn’t know.* And as she looked, deer and snow and faraway trees flattened within the circular frame to become like a picture on a calendar, not real, and she felt calm, as if she had been dreaming everything—the day, the deer, the hunt itself. And she, finger on trigger, was only a part of that dream.

“Shoot!” Charlie hissed.

Through the scope she saw the deer look up, ears high and straining.

Charlie groaned, and just as he did, and just at the moment when Andy knew—*knew*—the doe would bound away, as if she could feel its haunches tensing and gathering power, she pulled the trigger. Later she would think, *I felt the recoil, I smelled the smoke, but I don't remember pulling the trigger*. Through the scope the deer seemed to shrink into itself, and then slowly knelt, hind legs first, head raised as if to cry out. It trembled, still straining to keep its head high, as if that alone would save it; failing, it collapsed, shuddered, and lay still.

"Whoee!" Mac cried. 145

"One shot! One shot!" her father yelled, clapping her on the back. Charlie Spoon was shaking his head and smiling dumbly.

"I told you she was a great little shot!" her father said. "I told you!" Mac danced and clapped his hands. She was dazed, not quite understanding what had happened. And then they were crossing the field toward the fallen doe, she walking dreamlike, the men laughing and joking, released now from the tension of silence and anticipation. Suddenly Mac pointed and cried out, "Look at that!"

The doe was rising, legs unsteady. They stared at it, unable to comprehend, and in that moment the doe regained its feet and looked at them, as if it too were trying to understand. Her father whistled softly. Charlie Spoon unslung his rifle and raised it to his shoulder, but the doe was already bounding away. His hurried shot missed, and the deer disappeared into the woods.

"Damn, damn, damn," he moaned.

"I don't believe it," her father said. "That deer was dead." 150

"Dead, hell!" Charlie yelled. "It was gutshot, that's all. Stunned and gutshot. Clean shot, my ass!"

What have I done? Andy thought.

Her father slung his rifle over his shoulder. "Well, let's go. It can't get too far."

"Hell, I've seen deer run ten miles gutshot," Charlie said. He waved his arms. "We may never find her!"

As they crossed the field, Mac came up to her and said in a low voice, "Gutshoot a deer, you'll go to hell." 155

"Shut up, Mac," she said, her voice cracking. It was a terrible thing she had done, she knew. She couldn't bear to think of the doe in pain and frightened. *Please let it die*, she prayed.

But though they searched all the last hour of daylight, so that they had to recross the field and go up the logging trail in a twilight made even deeper by thick, smoky clouds, they didn't find the doe. They lost its trail almost immediately in the dense stands of alderberry and larch.

"I am cold, and I am tired," Charlie Spoon declared. "And if you ask me, that deer's in another county already."

"No one's asking you, Charlie," her father said.

They had a supper of hard salami and ham, bread, and the rest of the applesauce cake. It seemed a bother to heat the coffee, so they had cold chocolate instead. Everyone turned in early. 160

"We'll find it in the morning, honeybun," her father said, as she went to her tent.

"I don't like to think of it suffering." She was almost in tears.

"It's dead already, punkin. Don't even think about it." He kissed her, his breath sour and his beard rough against her cheek.

Andy was sure she wouldn't get to sleep; the image of the doe falling, falling, then rising again, repeated itself whenever she closed her eyes. Then she heard an owl hoot and realized that it had awakened her, so she must have been asleep after all. She hoped the owl would hush, but instead it hooted louder. She wished her father or Charlie Spoon would wake up and do something about it, but no one moved in the other tent, and suddenly she was afraid that they had all decamped, wanting nothing more to do with her. She whispered, "Mac, Mac," to the sleeping bag where he should be, but no one answered. She tried to find the flashlight she always kept by her side, but couldn't, and she cried in panic, "Mac, are you there?" He mumbled something, and immediately she felt foolish and hoped he wouldn't reply.

When she awoke again, everything had changed. The owl was gone, the woods were still, and she sensed light, blue and pale, light where before there had been none. *The moon must have come out*, she thought. And it was warm, too, warmer than it should have been. She got out of her sleeping bag and took off her parka—it was that warm. Mac was asleep, wheezing like an old man. She unzipped the tent and stepped outside.

The woods were more beautiful than she had ever seen them. The moon made everything ice-rimmed glimmer with a crystallized, immanent light, while underneath that ice the branches of trees were as stark as skeletons. She heard a crunching in the snow, the one sound in all that silence, and there, walking down the logging trail into their camp, was the doe. Its body, like everything around her, was silvered with frost and moonlight. It walked past the tent where her father and Charlie Spoon were sleeping and stopped no more than six feet from her. Andy saw that she had shot it, yes, had shot it cleanly, just where she thought she had, the wound a jagged, bloody hole in the doe's chest.

A heart shot, she thought.

The doe stepped closer, so that Andy, if she wished, could have reached out and touched it. It looked at her as if expecting her to do this, and so she did, running her hand, slowly at first, along the rough, matted fur, then down to the edge of the wound, where she stopped. The doe stood still. Hesitantly, Andy felt the edge of the wound. The torn flesh was sticky and warm. The wound parted under her touch. And then, almost without her knowing it, her fingers were within, probing, yet still the doe didn't move. Andy pressed deeper, through flesh and muscle and sinew, until her whole hand and more was inside the wound and she had found the doe's heart, warm and beating. She cupped it gently in her hand. *Alive*, she marveled. *Alive*.

The heart quickened under her touch, becoming warmer and warmer until it was hot enough to burn. In pain, Andy tried to remove her hand, but the wound closed about it and held her fast. Her hand was burning. She cried out in agony, sure they would all hear and come help, but they didn't. And then her hand pulled free, followed by a steaming rush of blood, more blood than she ever could have imagined—it covered her hand and arm, and she saw to her horror that her hand was steaming. She moaned and fell to her knees and plunged her hand into the snow. The doe looked at her gently and then turned and walked back up the trail.

In the morning, when she woke, Andy could still smell the blood, but she felt no pain. She looked at her hand. Even though it appeared unscathed, it felt weak and withered. She couldn't move it freely and was afraid the others would notice. *I will hide it in my jacket pocket*, she decided, *so nobody can see*. She ate the oatmeal that her father cooked and stayed apart from them all. No one spoke to her, and that suited her. A light snow began to fall. It was the last day of their hunting trip. She wanted to be home. 170

Her father dumped the dregs of his coffee. "Well, let's go look for her," he said.

Again they crossed the field. Andy lagged behind. She averted her eyes from the spot where the doe had fallen, already filling up with snow. Mac and Charlie entered the woods first, followed by her father. Andy remained in the field and considered the smear of gray sky, the nearby flock of crows pecking at unyielding stubble. *I will stay here*, she thought, *and not move for a long while*. But now someone—Mac—was yelling. Her father appeared at the woods' edge and waved for her to come. She ran and pushed through a brake of alderberry and larch. The thick underbrush scratched her face. For a moment she felt lost and looked wildly about. Then, where the brush thinned, she saw them standing quietly in the falling snow. They were staring down at the dead doe. A film covered its upturned eye, and its body was lightly dusted with snow.

"I told you she wouldn't get too far," Andy's father said triumphantly. "We must've just missed her yesterday. Too blind to see."

"We're just damn lucky no animal got to her last night," Charlie muttered.

Her father lifted the doe's foreleg. The wound was blood-clotted, brown, and caked like frozen mud. "Clean shot," he said to Charlie. He grinned. "My little girl." 175

Then he pulled out his knife, the blade gray as the morning. Mac whispered to Andy, "Now watch this," while Charlie Spoon lifted the doe from behind by its forelegs so that its head rested between his knees, its underside exposed. Her father's knife sliced thickly from chest to belly to crotch, and Andy was running from them, back to the field and across, scattering the crows who cawed and circled angrily. And now they were all calling to her—Charlie Spoon and Mac and her father—crying *Andy, Andy* (but that wasn't her name, she would no longer be called that); yet louder than any of them was the wind blowing through the treetops, like the ocean where her mother floated in green water, also calling *Come in, come in*, while all around her roared the mocking of the terrible, now inevitable, sea.

Reading and Reacting

1. The initiation of a child into adulthood is a common literary theme. In this story, hunting is presented as an **initiation rite**, a ritual that marks the transition into adulthood. In what way is hunting an appropriate coming-of-age ritual?
2. Which characters are in conflict in this story? Which ideas are in conflict? How do these conflicts help to communicate the story's initiation theme?
3. In the story's opening paragraph and elsewhere, Andy finds comfort and reassurance in the idea that the woods are "always the same"; later in the story, she remembers the ocean, "huge and empty, yet always moving. Everything lay hidden …" (par. 45). How does the contrast between the woods and the ocean suggest the transition she must make from childhood to adulthood?
4. How do the references to blood support the story's initiation theme? Do they suggest other themes as well?
5. Throughout the story, references are made to Andy's ability to inspire the trust of animals. As her father says, "Animals—I don't know how she does it, but they come right up to her" (par. 8). How does his comment foreshadow later events?
6. Why does Andy pray that she and the others will get a deer? What makes her change her mind? How does the change in Andy's character convey the story's theme?
7. Andy's mother is not an active participant in the story's events. Still, she is central to the story. Why is her role important? How does paragraph 45 reveal the significance of the mother's role?
8. What has Andy learned as a result of her experience? What do you think she still has to learn?
9. **Journal Entry** How would the story be different if Andy were a boy? What would be the same?
10. **Critical Perspective** In a review of *Comfort*, the book in which "Doe Season" appears, Susan Wood makes the following observation:

    > The dozen or so stories in David Michael Kaplan's affecting first collection share a common focus on the extraordinary moments of recognition in ordinary lives. He is at his best suggesting how such moments may alter, for better or for worse, our relationships with those to whom we are most deeply bound—children, parents, lovers—in love and guilt.

    At what point does "the extraordinary moment of recognition" occur in "Doe Season"? How does this moment alter Andy's relationship with both her parents?

Related Works: "A&P" (p. 179), "The Girl with Bangs" (p. 204), "The Secret Lion" (p. 222), "Greasy Lake" (p. 419), "The Lamb" (p. 700), *What Are You Going to Be?* (p. 790)

Archivio GBB/Alamy Stock Photo

STEPHEN CRANE (1871–1900), the youngest of fourteen children, was born in 1871 in New Jersey to Mary Crane, a writer of religious articles, and Johnathan Crane, a Methodist minister. Throughout his life, Crane traveled the world as a novelist, poet, short story writer, and war correspondent. An American by birth, he spent considerable time abroad as an expatriate coming into contact with such literary greats as Joseph Conrad and Henry James. He self-published his first book, *Maggie: A Girl of the Streets* (1893), under a pseudonym after publishers rejected the work because of its graphic depictions of slums, poverty, and prostitution. Crane achieved international acclaim for *The Red Badge of Courage* (1895), which is seen as a prime example of literary Realism and Naturalism. Although he died at just twenty-eight from tuberculosis, his published works include novels, story collections, and books of poetry. Due to his literary renown, Crane lived a highly public life and was known for his prodigious spending and public scandal. Among his most famous stories is "The Open Boat" (1897), which is based on a shipwreck he experienced. He left behind a body of work that scholars have recognized as highly influential on subsequent generations of writers.

Cultural Context Stephen Crane experienced a shipwreck on the morning of January 2, 1896, on his way to Cuba. Stranded at sea in a small lifeboat for over thirty hours, Crane and three crew members finally came ashore near Daytona Beach, Florida. Eventually, Crane turned his experience into "The Open Boat." Although relatively rare today, shipwrecks occurred with greater frequency during the nineteenth and early twentieth centuries, some resulting in great loss of life. For example, in 1896, the *Evening Star* left New York for New Orleans with 278 passengers and became trapped in a hurricane. Of the twenty-four passengers who were able to get into lifeboats, only ten survived. In January of 1840, the *Lexington*, a steamship, sailed from New York to Stonington, Connecticut. During the evening of January 13th, a cotton bale caught fire, causing the crew to lose control of the ship as it drifted helplessly. The situation descended into chaos, and when the ordeal was over, only four of the 158 crew and passengers survived before reaching shore on Long Island. And of course, one of the worst maritime disasters occurred in 1912 in the North Atlantic when the *Titanic* sank after hitting an iceberg, resulting in the deaths of more than 1500 people. This catastrophe caused an uproar and led to major changes in maritime regulations that resulted in increased safety.

The Open Boat (1898)

A Tale intended to be after the Fact.
Being the Experience of Four Men from the Sunk Steamer 'Commodore'

I

None of them knew the colour of the sky. Their eyes glanced level, and were fastened upon the waves that swept toward them. These waves were of the hue of slate, save for the tops, which were of foaming white, and all of the men knew the colours of the sea. The horizon narrowed and widened, and dipped and rose, and at all times its edge was jagged with waves that seemed thrust up in points like rocks.

Many a man ought to have a bath-tub larger than the boat which here rode upon the sea. These waves were most wrongfully and barbarously abrupt and tall, and each froth-top was a problem in small boat navigation.

The cook squatted in the bottom and looked with both eyes at the six inches of gunwale which separated him from the ocean. His sleeves were rolled over his fat forearms, and the two flaps of his unbuttoned vest dangled as he bent to bail out the boat. Often he said: "Gawd! That was a narrow clip." As he remarked it he invariably gazed eastward over the broken sea.

The oiler, steering with one of the two oars in the boat, sometimes raised himself suddenly to keep clear of water that swirled in over the stern. It was a thin little oar and it seemed often ready to snap.

The correspondent, pulling at the other oar, watched the waves and wondered why he was there. 5

The injured captain, lying in the bow, was at this time buried in that profound dejection and indifference which comes, temporarily at least, to even the bravest and most enduring when, willy nilly, the firm fails, the army loses, the ship goes down. The mind of the master of a vessel is rooted deep in the timbers of her, though he commanded for a day or a decade, and this captain had on him the stern impression of a scene in the greys of dawn of seven turned faces, and later a stump of a top-mast with a white ball on it that slashed to and fro at the waves, went low and lower, and down. Thereafter there was something strange in his voice. Although steady, it was deep with mourning, and of a quality beyond oration or tears.

"Keep 'er a little more south, Billie," said he.

"'A little more south,' sir," said the oiler in the stern.

A seat in this boat was not unlike a seat upon a bucking broncho, and, by the same token, a broncho is not much smaller. The craft pranced and reared, and plunged like an animal. As each wave came, and she rose for it, she seemed like a horse making at a fence outrageously high. The manner of her scramble over these walls of water is a mystic thing, and, moreover, at the top of them were ordinarily these problems in white water, the foam racing down from the summit of each wave, requiring a new leap, and a leap from the air. Then, after scornfully bumping a crest, she would slide, and race, and splash down a long incline, and arrive bobbing and nodding in front of the next menace.

A singular disadvantage of the sea lies in the fact that after successfully surmounting one wave you discover that there is another behind it just as important and just as nervously anxious to do something effective in the way of swamping boats. In a ten-foot dingey one can get an idea of the resources of the sea in the line of waves that is not probable to the average experience which is never at sea in a dingey. As each slaty wall of water approached, it shut all else from the view of the men in the boat, and it was not difficult to imagine that this particular wave was the final outburst of the ocean, the last effort of the grim water. There was a terrible grace in the move of the waves, and they came in silence, save for the snarling of the crests. 10

In the wan light, the faces of the men must have been grey. Their eyes must have glinted in strange ways as they gazed steadily astern. Viewed from a balcony, the whole thing would doubtlessly have been weirdly picturesque. But the men in the boat had no time to see it, and if they had had leisure there were other things to occupy their minds. The sun swung steadily up the sky, and they knew it was broad day because the colour of the sea changed from slate to emerald-green, streaked with amber lights, and the foam was like tumbling snow. The process of the breaking day was unknown to them. They were aware only of this effect upon the colour of the waves that rolled toward them.

In disjointed sentences the cook and the correspondent argued as to the difference between a life-saving station[1] and a house of refuge. The cook had said: "There's a house of refuge just north of the Mosquito Inlet Light, and as soon as they see us, they'll come off in their boat and pick us up."

"As soon as who see us?" said the correspondent.

"The crew," said the cook.

"Houses of refuge don't have crews," said the correspondent. "As I understand them, they are only places where clothes and grub are stored for the benefit of shipwrecked people. They don't carry crews."

"Oh, yes, they do," said the cook.

"No, they don't," said the correspondent.

"Well, we're not there yet, anyhow," said the oiler, in the stern.

"Well," said the cook, "perhaps it's not a house of refuge that I'm thinking of as being near Mosquito Inlet Light. Perhaps it's a life-saving station."

"We're not there yet," said the oiler, in the stern.

II

As the boat bounced from the top of each wave, the wind tore through the hair of the hatless men, and as the craft plopped her stern down again the spray slashed past them. The crest of each of these waves was a hill, from the top of which the men surveyed, for a moment, a broad tumultuous expanse, shining and wind-riven. It was probably splendid. It was probably glorious, this play of the free sea, wild with lights of emerald and white and amber.

"Bully good thing it's an on-shore wind," said the cook. "If not, where would we be? Wouldn't have a show."

"That's right," said the correspondent.

The busy oiler nodded his assent.

Then the captain, in the bow, chuckled in a way that expressed humour, contempt, tragedy, all in one. "Do you think we've got much of a show now, boys?" said he.

[1]*Life-Saving Station:* The United States Life-Saving Service (USLSS) operated from 1878 to 1915 and was the predecessor to the United States Coast Guard. The USLSS developed a network of resources to rescue people stranded at sea, including live-saving stations where those in need could find shelter.

Whereupon the three were silent, save for a trifle of hemming and hawing. To express any particular optimism at this time they felt to be childish and stupid, but they all doubtless possessed this sense of the situation in their mind. A young man thinks doggedly at such times. On the other hand, the ethics of their condition was decidedly against any open suggestion of hopelessness. So they were silent.

"Oh, well," said the captain, soothing his children, "we'll get ashore all right."

But there was that in his tone which made them think, so the oiler quoth: "Yes! If this wind holds!"

The cook was bailing: "Yes! If we don't catch hell in the surf."

Canton flannel gulls flew near and far. Sometimes they sat down on the sea, near patches of brown sea-weed that rolled over the waves with a movement like carpets on a line in a gale. The birds sat comfortably in groups, and they were envied by some in the dingey, for the wrath of the sea was no more to them than it was to a covey of prairie chickens a thousand miles inland. Often they came very close and stared at the men with black bead-like eyes. At these times they were uncanny and sinister in their unblinking scrutiny, and the men hooted angrily at them, telling them to be gone. One came, and evidently decided to alight on the top of the captain's head. The bird flew parallel to the boat and did not circle, but made short sidelong jumps in the air in chicken-fashion. His black eyes were wistfully fixed upon the captain's head. "Ugly brute," said the oiler to the bird. "You look as if you were made with a jack-knife." The cook and the correspondent swore darkly at the creature. The captain naturally wished to knock it away with the end of the heavy painter; but he did not dare do it, because anything resembling an emphatic gesture would have capsized this freighted boat, and so with his open hand, the captain gently and carefully waved the gull away. After it had been discouraged from the pursuit the captain breathed easier on account of his hair, and others breathed easier because the bird struck their minds at this time as being somehow grewsome and ominous. 30

In the meantime the oiler and the correspondent rowed. And also they rowed.

They sat together in the same seat, and each rowed an oar. Then the oiler took both oars; then the correspondent took both oars; then the oiler; then the correspondent. They rowed and they rowed. The very ticklish part of the business was when the time came for the reclining one in the stern to take his turn at the oars. By the very last star of truth, it is easier to steal eggs from under a hen than it was to change seats in the dingey. First the man in the stern slid his hand along the thwart and moved with care, as if he were of Sèvres. Then the man in the rowing seat slid his hand along the other thwart. It was all done with the most extraordinary care. As the two sidled past each other, the whole party kept watchful eyes on the coming wave, and the captain cried: "Look out now! Steady there!"

The brown mats of sea-weed that appeared from time to time were like islands, bits of earth. They were travelling, apparently, neither one way nor the other. They were, to all intents, stationary. They informed the men in the boat that it was making progress slowly toward the land.

The captain, rearing cautiously in the bow, after the dingey soared on a great swell, said that he had seen the lighthouse at Mosquito Inlet. Presently the cook remarked that he had seen it. The correspondent was at the oars then, and for some reason he too wished to look at the lighthouse, but his back was toward the far shore and the waves were important, and for some time he could not seize an opportunity to turn his head. But at last there came a wave more gentle than the others, and when at the crest of it he swiftly scoured the western horizon.

"See it?" said the captain.

"No," said the correspondent slowly, "I didn't see anything."

"Look again," said the captain. He pointed. "It's exactly in that direction."

At the top of another wave, the correspondent did as he was bid, and this time his eyes chanced on a small still thing on the edge of the swaying horizon. It was precisely like the point of a pin. It took an anxious eye to find a lighthouse so tiny.

"Think we'll make it, captain?"

"If this wind holds and the boat don't swamp, we can't do much else," said the captain.

The little boat, lifted by each towering sea, and splashed viciously by the crests, made progress that in the absence of sea-weed was not apparent to those in her. She seemed just a wee thing wallowing, miraculously top-up, at the mercy of five oceans. Occasionally, a great spread of water, like white flames, swarmed into her.

"Bail her, cook," said the captain serenely.

"All right, captain," said the cheerful cook.

III

It would be difficult to describe the subtle brotherhood of men that was here established on the seas. No one said that it was so. No one mentioned it. But it dwelt in the boat, and each man felt it warm him. They were a captain, an oiler, a cook, and a correspondent, and they were friends, friends in a more curiously iron-bound degree than may be common. The hurt captain, lying against the water-jar in the bow, spoke always in a low voice and calmly, but he could never command a more ready and swiftly obedient crew than the motley three of the dingey. It was more than a mere recognition of what was best for the common safety. There was surely in it a quality that was personal and heartfelt. And after this devotion to the commander of the boat there was this comradeship that the correspondent, for instance, who had been taught to be cynical of men, knew even at the time was the best experience of his life. But no one said that it was so. No one mentioned it.

"I wish we had a sail," remarked the captain. "We might try my overcoat on the end of an oar and give you two boys a chance to rest." So the cook and the correspondent held the mast and spread wide the overcoat. The oiler steered, and the little boat made good way with her new rig. Sometimes the oiler had to scull sharply to keep a sea from breaking into the boat, but otherwise sailing was a success. 45

Meanwhile the lighthouse had been growing slowly larger. It had now almost assumed colour, and appeared like a little grey shadow on the sky. The man at the oars could not be prevented from turning his head rather often to try for a glimpse of this little grey shadow.

At last, from the top of each wave the men in the tossing boat could see land. Even as the lighthouse was an upright shadow on the sky, this land seemed but a long black shadow on the sea. It certainly was thinner than paper. "We must be about opposite New Smyrna," said the cook, who had coasted this shore often in schooners. "Captain, by the way, I believe they abandoned that life-saving station there about a year ago."

"Did they?" said the captain.

The wind slowly died away. The cook and the correspondent were not now obliged to slave in order to hold high the oar. But the waves continued their old impetuous swooping at the dingey, and the little craft, no longer under way, struggled woundily over them. The oiler or the correspondent took the oars again.

Shipwrecks are *à propos* of nothing.[2] If men could only train for them and have them occur when the men had reached pink condition, there would be less drowning at sea. Of the four in the dingey none had slept any time worth mentioning for two days and two nights previous to embarking in the dingey, and in the excitement of clambering about the deck of a foundering ship they had also forgotten to eat heartily. 50

For these reasons, and for others, neither the oiler nor the correspondent was fond of rowing at this time. The correspondent wondered ingenuously how in the name of all that was sane could there be people who thought it amusing to row a boat. It was not an amusement; it was a diabolical punishment, and even a genius of mental aberrations could never conclude that it was anything but a horror to the muscles and a crime against the back. He mentioned to the boat in general how the amusement of rowing struck him, and the weary-faced oiler smiled in full sympathy. Previously to the foundering, by the way, the oiler had worked double-watch in the engine-room of the ship.

"Take her easy, now, boys," said the captain. "Don't spend yourselves. If we have to run a surf you'll need all your strength, because we'll sure have to swim for it. Take your time."

Slowly the land arose from the sea. From a black line it became a line of black and a line of white, trees and sand. Finally, the captain said that he could

---

[2] *à propos of nothing:* Unrelated to a matter nearer at hand.

make out a house on the shore. "That's the house of refuge, sure," said the cook. "They'll see us before long, and come out after us."

The distant lighthouse reared high. "The keeper ought to be able to make us out now, if he's looking through a glass," said the captain. "He'll notify the life-saving people."

"None of those other boats could have got ashore to give word of the wreck," said the oiler, in a low voice. "Else the life-boat would be out hunting us." 55

Slowly and beautifully the land loomed out of the sea. The wind came again. It had veered from the north-east to the south-east. Finally, a new sound struck the ears of the men in the boat. It was the low thunder of the surf on the shore. "We'll never be able to make the lighthouse now," said the captain. "Swing her head a little more north, Billie," said he.

"'A little more north,' sir," said the oiler.

Whereupon the little boat turned her nose once more down the wind, and all but the oarsman watched the shore grow. Under the influence of this expansion doubt and direful apprehension was leaving the minds of the men. The management of the boat was still most absorbing, but it could not prevent a quiet cheerfulness. In an hour, perhaps, they would be ashore.

Their backbones had become thoroughly used to balancing in the boat, and they now rode this wild colt of a dingey like circus men. The correspondent thought that he had been drenched to the skin, but happening to feel in the top pocket of his coat, he found therein eight cigars. Four of them were soaked with sea-water; four were perfectly scatheless. After a search, somebody produced three dry matches, and thereupon the four waifs rode impudently in their little boat, and with an assurance of an impending rescue shining in their eyes, puffed at the big cigars and judged well and ill of all men. Everybody took a drink of water.

IV

"Cook," remarked the captain, "there don't seem to be any signs of life about your house of refuge." 60

"No," replied the cook. "Funny they don't see us!"

A broad stretch of lowly coast lay before the eyes of the men. It was of dunes topped with dark vegetation. The roar of the surf was plain, and sometimes they could see the white lip of a wave as it spun up the beach. A tiny house was blocked out black upon the sky. Southward, the slim lighthouse lifted its little grey length.

Tide, wind, and waves were swinging the dingey northward. "Funny they don't see us," said the men.

The surf's roar was here dulled, but its tone was, nevertheless, thunderous and mighty. As the boat swam over the great rollers, the men sat listening to this roar. "We'll swamp sure," said everybody.

It is fair to say here that there was not a life-saving station within twenty miles in either direction, but the men did not know this fact, and in consequence they made dark and opprobrious remarks concerning the eyesight of the nation's life-savers. Four scowling men sat in the dingey and surpassed records in the invention of epithets.

"Funny they don't see us."

The light-heartedness of a former time had completely faded. To their sharpened minds it was easy to conjure pictures of all kinds of incompetency and blindness and, indeed, cowardice. There was the shore of the populous land, and it was bitter and bitter to them that from it came no sign.

"Well," said the captain, ultimately, "I suppose we'll have to make a try for ourselves. If we stay out here too long, we'll none of us have strength left to swim after the boat swamps."

And so the oiler, who was at the oars, turned the boat straight for the shore. There was a sudden tightening of muscles. There was some thinking.

"If we don't all get ashore—" said the captain. "If we don't all get ashore, I suppose you fellows know where to send news of my finish?"

They then briefly exchanged some addresses and admonitions. As for the reflections of the men, there was a great deal of rage in them. Perchance they might be formulated thus: "If I am going to be drowned—if I am going to be drowned—if I am going to be drowned, why, in the name of the seven mad gods who rule the sea, was I allowed to come thus far and contemplate sand and trees? Was I brought here merely to have my nose dragged away as I was about to nibble the sacred cheese of life? It is preposterous. If this old ninny-woman, Fate, cannot do better than this, she should be deprived of the management of men's fortunes. She is an old hen who knows not her intention. If she has decided to drown me, why did she not do it in the beginning and save me all this trouble? The whole affair is absurd.... But no, she cannot mean to drown me. She dare not drown me. She cannot drown me. Not after all this work." Afterward the man might have had an impulse to shake his fist at the clouds: "Just you drown me, now, and then hear what I call you!"

The billows that came at this time were more formidable. They seemed always just about to break and roll over the little boat in a turmoil of foam. There was a preparatory and long growl in the speech of them. No mind unused to the sea would have concluded that the dingey could ascend these sheer heights in time. The shore was still afar. The oiler was a wily surfman. "Boys," he said swiftly, "she won't live three minutes more, and we're too far out to swim. Shall I take her to sea again, captain?"

"Yes! Go ahead!" said the captain.

This oiler, by a series of quick miracles, and fast and steady oarsmanship, turned the boat in the middle of the surf and took her safely to sea again.

There was a considerable silence as the boat bumped over the furrowed sea to deeper water. Then somebody in gloom spoke. "Well, anyhow, they must have seen us from the shore by now."

The gulls went in slanting flight up the wind toward the grey desolate east. A squall, marked by dingy clouds, and clouds brick-red, like smoke from a burning building, appeared from the south-east.

"What do you think of those life-saving people? Ain't they peaches?"

"Funny they haven't seen us."

"Maybe they think we're out here for sport! Maybe they think we're fishin'. Maybe they think we're damned fools."

It was a long afternoon. A changed tide tried to force them southward, but wind and wave said northward. Far ahead, where coast-line, sea, and sky formed their mighty angle, there were little dots which seemed to indicate a city on the shore.

"St. Augustine?"

The captain shook his head. "Too near Mosquito Inlet."

And the oiler rowed, and then the correspondent rowed. Then the oiler rowed. It was a weary business. The human back can become the seat of more aches and pains than are registered in books for the composite anatomy of a regiment. It is a limited area, but it can become the theatre of innumerable muscular conflicts, tangles, wrenches, knots, and other comforts.

"Did you ever like to row, Billie?" asked the correspondent.

"No," said the oiler. "Hang it."

When one exchanged the rowing-seat for a place in the bottom of the boat, he suffered a bodily depression that caused him to be careless of everything save an obligation to wiggle one finger. There was cold sea-water swashing to and fro in the boat, and he lay in it. His head, pillowed on a thwart, was within an inch of the swirl of a wave crest, and sometimes a particularly obstreperous sea came in-board and drenched him once more. But these matters did not annoy him. It is almost certain that if the boat had capsized he would have tumbled comfortably out upon the ocean as if he felt sure that it was a great soft mattress.

"Look! There's a man on the shore!"

"Where?"

"There! See 'im? See 'im?"

"Yes, sure! He's walking along."

"Now he's stopped. Look! He's facing us!"

"He's waving at us!"

"So he is! By thunder!"

"Ah, now we're all right! Now we're all right! There'll be a boat out here for us in half-an-hour."

"He's going on. He's running. He's going up to that house there."

The remote beach seemed lower than the sea, and it required a searching glance to discern the little black figure. The captain saw a floating stick and they rowed to it. A bath-towel was by some weird chance in the boat, and, tying this on the stick, the captain waved it. The oarsman did not dare turn his head, so he was obliged to ask questions.

"What's he doing now?"

"He's standing still again. He's looking, I think.... There he goes again. Towards the house.... Now he's stopped again."

"Is he waving at us?"

"No, not now! he was, though."

"Look! There comes another man!"

"He's running."

"Look at him go, would you."

"Why, he's on a bicycle. Now he's met the other man. They're both waving at us. Look!"

"There comes something up the beach."

"What the devil is that thing?"

"Why, it looks like a boat."

"Why, certainly it's a boat."

"No, it's on wheels."

"Yes, so it is. Well, that must be the life-boat. They drag them along shore on a wagon."

"That's the life-boat, sure."

"No, by ——, it's—it's an omnibus."

"I tell you it's a life-boat."

"It is not! It's an omnibus. I can see it plain. See? One of these big hotel omnibuses."

"By thunder, you're right. It's an omnibus, sure as fate. What do you suppose they are doing with an omnibus? Maybe they are going around collecting the life-crew, hey?"

"That's it, likely. Look! There's a fellow waving a little black flag. He's standing on the steps of the omnibus. There come those other two fellows. Now they're all talking together. Look at the fellow with the flag. Maybe he ain't waving it."

"That ain't a flag, is it? That's his coat. Why certainly, that's his coat."

"So it is. It's his coat. He's taken it off and is waving it around his head. But would you look at him swing it."

"Oh, say, there isn't any life-saving station there. That's just a winter resort hotel omnibus that has brought over some of the boarders to see us drown."

"What's that idiot with the coat mean? What's he signaling, anyhow?"

"It looks as if he were trying to tell us to go north. There must be a life-saving station up there."

"No! He thinks we're fishing. Just giving us a merry hand. See? Ah, there, Willie."

"Well, I wish I could make something out of those signals. What do you suppose he means?"

"He don't mean anything. He's just playing."

"Well, if he'd just signal us to try the surf again, or to go to sea and wait, or go north, or go south, or go to hell—there would be some reason in it. But look at him. He just stands there and keeps his coat revolving like a wheel. The ass!"

"There come more people."

"Now there's quite a mob. Look! Isn't that a boat?"

"Where? Oh, I see where you mean. No, that's no boat."

"That fellow is still waving his coat."

"He must think we like to see him do that. Why don't he quit it? It don't mean anything."

"I don't know. I think he is trying to make us go north. It must be that there's a life-saving station there somewhere."

"Say, he ain't tired yet. Look at 'im wave."

"Wonder how long he can keep that up. He's been revolving his coat ever since he caught sight of us. He's an idiot. Why aren't they getting men to bring a boat out? A fishing boat—one of those big yawls—could come out here all right. Why don't he do something?"

"Oh, it's all right, now."

"They'll have a boat out here for us in less than no time, now that they've seen us."

A faint yellow tone came into the sky over the low land. The shadows on the sea slowly deepened. The wind bore coldness with it, and the men began to shiver.

"Holy smoke!" said one, allowing his voice to express his impious mood, "if we keep on monkeying out here! If we've got to flounder out here all night!"

"Oh, we'll never have to stay here all night! Don't you worry. They've seen us now, and it won't be long before they'll come chasing out after us."

The shore grew dusky. The man waving a coat blended gradually into this gloom, and it swallowed in the same manner the omnibus and the group of people. The spray, when it dashed uproariously over the side, made the voyagers shrink and swear like men who were being branded.

"I'd like to catch the chump who waved the coat. I feel like soaking him one, just for luck."

"Why? What did he do?"

"Oh, nothing, but then he seemed so damned cheerful."

In the meantime the oiler rowed, and then the correspondent rowed, and then the oiler rowed. Grey-faced and bowed forward, they mechanically, turn by turn, plied the leaden oars. The form of the lighthouse had vanished from the southern horizon, but finally a pale star appeared, just lifting from the sea. The streaked saffron in the west passed before the all-merging darkness, and the sea to the east was black. The land had vanished, and was expressed only by the low and drear thunder of the surf.

"If I am going to be drowned—if I am going to be drowned—if I am going to be drowned, why, in the name of the seven mad gods who rule the sea, was I allowed to come thus far and contemplate sand and trees? Was I brought here merely to have my nose dragged away as I was about to nibble the sacred cheese of life?"

The patient captain, drooped over the water-jar, was sometimes obliged to speak to the oarsman.

"Keep her head up! Keep her head up!"

"'Keep her head up,' sir." The voices were weary and low.

This was surely a quiet evening. All save the oarsman lay heavily and listlessly in the boat's bottom. As for him, his eyes were just capable of noting the tall black waves that swept forward in a most sinister silence, save for an occasional subdued growl of a crest.

The cook's head was on a thwart, and he looked without interest at the water under his nose. He was deep in other scenes. Finally he spoke. "Billie," he murmured, dreamfully, "what kind of pie do you like best?"

V

"Pie," said the oiler and the correspondent, agitatedly. "Don't talk about those things, blast you!"

"Well," said the cook, "I was just thinking about ham sandwiches, and—"

A night on the sea in an open boat is a long night. As darkness settled finally, the shine of the light, lifting from the sea in the south, changed to full gold. On the northern horizon a new light appeared, a small bluish gleam on the edge of the waters. These two lights were the furniture of the world. Otherwise there was nothing but waves.

Two men huddled in the stern, and distances were so magnificent in the dingey that the rower was enabled to keep his feet partly warmed by thrusting them under his companions. Their legs indeed extended far under the rowing-seat until they touched the feet of the captain forward. Sometimes, despite the efforts of the tired oarsman, a wave came piling into the boat, an icy wave of the night, and the chilling water soaked them anew. They would twist their bodies for a moment and groan, and sleep the dead sleep once more, while the water in the boat gurgled about them as the craft rocked.

The plan of the oiler and the correspondent was for one to row until he lost the ability, and then arouse the other from his sea-water couch in the bottom of the boat.

The oiler plied the oars until his head drooped forward, and the overpowering sleep blinded him. And he rowed yet afterward. Then he touched a man in the bottom of the boat, and called his name. "Will you spell me[3] for a little while?" he said, meekly.

"Sure, Billie," said the correspondent, awakening and dragging himself to a sitting position. They exchanged places carefully, and the oiler, cuddling down in the sea-water at the cook's side, seemed to go to sleep instantly.

The particular violence of the sea had ceased. The waves came without snarling. The obligation of the man at the oars was to keep the boat headed so that the tilt of the rollers would not capsize her, and to preserve her from filling when the crests rushed past. The black waves were silent and hard to be seen in the darkness. Often one was almost upon the boat before the oarsman was aware.

[3] *"Will you spell me"*: An expression used to request that someone take over a task.

In a low voice the correspondent addressed the captain. He was not sure that the captain was awake, although this iron man seemed to be always awake. "Captain, shall I keep her making for that light north, sir?"

The same steady voice answered him. "Yes. Keep it about two points off the port bow."

The cook had tied a life-belt around himself in order to get even the warmth which this clumsy cork contrivance could donate, and he seemed almost stove-like when a rower, whose teeth invariably chattered wildly as soon as he ceased his labour, dropped down to sleep. 160

The correspondent, as he rowed, looked down at the two men sleeping under-foot. The cook's arm was around the oiler's shoulders, and, with their fragmentary clothing and haggard faces, they were the babes of the sea, a grotesque rendering of the old babes in the wood.

Later he must have grown stupid at his work, for suddenly there was a growling of water, and a crest came with a roar and a swash into the boat, and it was a wonder that it did not set the cook afloat in his life-belt. The cook continued to sleep, but the oiler sat up, blinking his eyes and shaking with the new cold.

"Oh, I'm awful sorry, Billie," said the correspondent contritely.

"That's all right, old boy," said the oiler, and lay down again and was asleep.

Presently it seemed that even the captain dozed, and the correspondent thought that he was the one man afloat on all the oceans. The wind had a voice as it came over the waves, and it was sadder than the end. 165

There was a long, loud swishing astern of the boat, and a gleaming trail of phosphorescence, like blue flame, was furrowed on the black waters. It might have been made by a monstrous knife.

Then there came a stillness, while the correspondent breathed with the open mouth and looked at the sea.

Suddenly there was another swish and another long flash of bluish light, and this time it was alongside the boat, and might almost have been reached with an oar. The correspondent saw an enormous fin speed like a shadow through the water, hurling the crystalline spray and leaving the long glowing trail.

The correspondent looked over his shoulder at the captain. His face was hidden, and he seemed to be asleep. He looked at the babes of the sea. They certainly were asleep. So, being bereft of sympathy, he leaned a little way to one side and swore softly into the sea.

But the thing did not then leave the vicinity of the boat. Ahead or astern, on one side or the other, at intervals long or short, fled the long sparkling streak, and there was to be heard the whiroo of the dark fin. The speed and power of the thing was greatly to be admired. It cut the water like a gigantic and keen projectile. 170

The presence of this biding thing did not affect the man with the same horror that it would if he had been a picnicker. He simply looked at the sea dully and swore in an undertone.

Nevertheless, it is true that he did not wish to be alone. He wished one of his companions to awaken by chance and keep him company with it. But the captain hung motionless over the water-jar, and the oiler and the cook in the bottom of the boat were plunged in slumber.

VI

"If I am going to be drowned—if I am going to be drowned—if I am going to be drowned, why, in the name of the seven mad gods who rule the sea, was I allowed to come thus far and contemplate sand and trees?"

During this dismal night, it may be remarked that a man would conclude that it was really the intention of the seven mad gods to drown him, despite the abominable injustice of it. For it was certainly an abominable injustice to drown a man who had worked so hard, so hard. The man felt it would be a crime most unnatural. Other people had drowned at sea since galleys swarmed with painted sails, but still—

When it occurs to a man that nature does not regard him as important, and that she feels she would not maim the universe by disposing of him, he at first wishes to throw bricks at the temple, and he hates deeply the fact that there are no bricks and no temples. Any visible expression of nature would surely be pelleted with his jeers. 175

Then, if there be no tangible thing to hoot he feels, perhaps, the desire to confront a personification and indulge in pleas, bowed to one knee, and with hands supplicant, saying: "Yes, but I love myself."

A high cold star on a winter's night is the word he feels that she says to him. Thereafter he knows the pathos of his situation.

The men in the dingey had not discussed these matters, but each had, no doubt, reflected upon them in silence and according to his mind. There was seldom any expression upon their faces save the general one of complete weariness. Speech was devoted to the business of the boat.

To chime the notes of his emotion, a verse mysteriously entered the correspondent's head. He had even forgotten that he had forgotten this verse, but it suddenly was in his mind.

> *"A soldier of the Legion*[4] *lay dying in Algiers,*
> *There was lack of woman's nursing, there was dearth of woman's tears;*
> *But a comrade stood beside him, and he took that comrade's hand,*
> *And he said: 'I shall never see my own, my native land.'"*

In his childhood, the correspondent had been made acquainted with the fact that a soldier of the Legion lay dying in Algiers, but he had never regarded the fact as important. Myriads of his school-fellows had informed him of the soldier's plight, but the dinning had naturally ended by making him perfectly indifferent. He had never considered it his affair that a soldier of the Legion lay

---

[4]*the Legion:* The French Foreign Legion is a military body formed in the 1830s originally to support France's colonial efforts in Algeria.

dying in Algiers, nor had it appeared to him as a matter for sorrow. It was less to him than the breaking of a pencil's point. 180

Now, however, it quaintly came to him as a human, living thing. It was no longer merely a picture of a few throes in the breast of a poet, meanwhile drinking tea and warming his feet at the grate; it was an actuality—stern, mournful, and fine.

The correspondent plainly saw the soldier. He lay on the sand with his feet out straight and still. While his pale left hand was upon his chest in an attempt to thwart the going of his life, the blood came between his fingers. In the far Algerian distance, a city of low square forms was set against a sky that was faint with the last sunset hues. The correspondent, plying the oars and dreaming of the slow and slower movements of the lips of the soldier, was moved by a profound and perfectly impersonal comprehension. He was sorry for the soldier of the Legion who lay dying in Algiers.

The thing which had followed the boat and waited, had evidently grown bored at the delay. There was no longer to be heard the slash of the cut-water, and there was no longer the flame of the long trail. The light in the north still glimmered, but it was apparently no nearer to the boat. Sometimes the boom of the surf rang in the correspondent's ears, and he turned the craft seaward then and rowed harder. Southward, some one had evidently built a watch-fire on the beach. It was too low and too far to be seen, but it made a shimmering, roseate reflection upon the bluff back of it, and this could be discerned from the boat. The wind came stronger, and sometimes a wave suddenly raged out like a mountain-cat, and there was to be seen the sheen and sparkle of a broken crest.

The captain, in the bow, moved on his water-jar and sat erect. "Pretty long night," he observed to the correspondent. He looked at the shore. "Those life-saving people take their time."

"Did you see that shark playing around?" 185

"Yes, I saw him. He was a big fellow, all right."

"Wish I had known you were awake."

Later the correspondent spoke into the bottom of the boat.

"Billie!" There was a slow and gradual disentanglement. "Billie, will you spell me?"

"Sure," said the oiler. 190

As soon as the correspondent touched the cold comfortable sea-water in the bottom of the boat, and had huddled close to the cook's life-belt he was deep in sleep, despite the fact that his teeth played all the popular airs. This sleep was so good to him that it was but a moment before he heard a voice call his name in a tone that demonstrated the last stages of exhaustion. "Will you spell me?"

"Sure, Billie."

The light in the north had mysteriously vanished, but the correspondent took his course from the wide-awake captain.

Later in the night they took the boat farther out to sea, and the captain directed the cook to take one oar at the stern and keep the boat facing the seas. He was to call out if he should hear the thunder of the surf. This plan enabled the oiler and the correspondent to get respite together. "We'll give those boys a chance to get into shape again," said the captain. They curled down and, after a few preliminary chatterings and trembles, slept once more the dead sleep. Neither knew they had bequeathed to the cook the company of another shark, or perhaps the same shark.

As the boat caroused on the waves, spray occasionally bumped over the side and gave them a fresh soaking, but this had no power to break their repose. The ominous slash of the wind and the water affected them as it would have affected mummies.

"Boys," said the cook, with the notes of every reluctance in his voice, "she's drifted in pretty close. I guess one of you had better take her to sea again." The correspondent, aroused, heard the crash of the toppled crests.

As he was rowing, the captain gave him some whisky-and-water, and this steadied the chills out of him. "If I ever get ashore and anybody shows me even a photograph of an oar—"

At last there was a short conversation.

"Billie.... Billie, will you spell me?"

"Sure," said the oiler.

VII

When the correspondent again opened his eyes, the sea and the sky were each of the grey hue of the dawning. Later, carmine and gold was painted upon the waters. The morning appeared finally, in its splendour, with a sky of pure blue, and the sunlight flamed on the tips of the waves.

On the distant dunes were set many little black cottages, and a tall white windmill reared above them. No man, nor dog, nor bicycle appeared on the beach. The cottages might have formed a deserted village.

The voyagers scanned the shore. A conference was held in the boat. "Well," said the captain, "if no help is coming we might better try a run through the surf right away. If we stay out here much longer we will be too weak to do anything for ourselves at all." The others silently acquiesced in this reasoning. The boat was headed for the beach. The correspondent wondered if none ever ascended the tall wind-tower, and if then they never looked seaward. This tower was a giant, standing with its back to the plight of the ants. It represented in a degree, to the correspondent, the serenity of nature amid the struggles of the individual—nature in the wind, and nature in the vision of men. She did not seem cruel to him then, nor beneficent, nor treacherous, nor wise. But she was indifferent, flatly indifferent. It is, perhaps, plausible that a man in this situation, impressed with the unconcern of the universe, should see the innumerable flaws of his life, and have them taste wickedly in his mind and wish for another chance. A distinction between right and wrong seems absurdly clear to him, then, in this new ignorance of the grave-edge, and he understands that if he were given another opportunity he would mend his conduct and his words, and be better and brighter during an introduction or at a tea.

"Now, boys," said the captain, "she is going to swamp, sure. All we can do is to work her in as far as possible, and then when she swamps, pile out and scramble for the beach. Keep cool now, and don't jump until she swamps sure."

The oiler took the oars. Over his shoulders he scanned the surf. "Captain," he said, "I think I'd better bring her about, and keep her head-on to the seas and back her in." 205

"All right, Billie," said the captain. "Back her in." The oiler swung the boat then and, seated in the stern, the cook and the correspondent were obliged to look over their shoulders to contemplate the lonely and indifferent shore.

The monstrous in-shore rollers heaved the boat high until the men were again enabled to see the white sheets of water scudding up the slanted beach. "We won't get in very close," said the captain. Each time a man could wrest his attention from the rollers, he turned his glance toward the shore, and in the expression of the eyes during this contemplation there was a singular quality. The correspondent, observing the others, knew that they were not afraid, but the full meaning of their glances was shrouded.

As for himself, he was too tired to grapple fundamentally with the fact. He tried to coerce his mind into thinking of it, but the mind was dominated at this time by the muscles, and the muscles said they did not care. It merely occurred to him that if he should drown it would be a shame.

There were no hurried words, no pallor, no plain agitation. The men simply looked at the shore. "Now, remember to get well clear of the boat when you jump," said the captain.

Seaward the crest of a roller suddenly fell with a thunderous crash, and the long white comber came roaring down upon the boat. 210

"Steady now," said the captain. The men were silent. They turned their eyes from the shore to the comber and waited. The boat slid up the incline, leaped at the furious top, bounced over it, and swung down the long back of the wave. Some water had been shipped and the cook bailed it out.

But the next crest crashed also. The tumbling boiling flood of white water caught the boat and whirled it almost perpendicular. Water swarmed in from all sides. The correspondent had his hands on the gunwale at this time, and when the water entered at that place he swiftly withdrew his fingers, as if he objected to wetting them.

The little boat, drunken with this weight of water, reeled and snuggled deeper into the sea.

"Bail her out, cook! Bail her out," said the captain.

"All right, captain," said the cook. 215

"Now, boys, the next one will do for us, sure," said the oiler. "Mind to jump clear of the boat."

The third wave moved forward, huge, furious, implacable. It fairly swallowed the dingey, and almost simultaneously the men tumbled into the sea. A piece of life-belt had lain in the bottom of the boat, and as the correspondent went overboard he held this to his chest with his left hand.

The January water was icy, and he reflected immediately that it was colder than he had expected to find it off the coast of Florida. This appeared to his dazed mind as a fact important enough to be noted at the time. The coldness of the water was sad; it was tragic. This fact was somehow so mixed and confused with his opinion of his own situation that it seemed almost a proper reason for tears. The water was cold.

When he came to the surface he was conscious of little but the noisy water. Afterward he saw his companions in the sea. The oiler was ahead in the race. He was swimming strongly and rapidly. Off to the correspondent's left, the cook's great white and corked back bulged out of the water, and in the rear the captain was hanging with his one good hand to the keel of the overturned dingey.

There is a certain immovable quality to a shore, and the correspondent wondered at it amid the confusion of the sea. 220

It seemed also very attractive, but the correspondent knew that it was a long journey, and he paddled leisurely. The piece of life-preserver lay under him, and sometimes he whirled down the incline of a wave as if he were on a hand-sled.

But finally he arrived at a place in the sea where travel was beset with difficulty. He did not pause swimming to inquire what manner of current had caught him, but there his progress ceased. The shore was set before him like a bit of scenery on a stage, and he looked at it and understood with his eyes each detail of it.

As the cook passed, much farther to the left, the captain was calling to him, "Turn over on your back, cook! Turn over on your back and use the oar."

"All right, sir." The cook turned on his back, and, paddling with an oar, went ahead as if he were a canoe.

Presently the boat also passed to the left of the correspondent with the captain clinging with one hand to the keel. He would have appeared like a man raising himself to look over a board fence, if it were not for the extraordinary gymnastics of the boat. The correspondent marvelled that the captain could still hold to it. 225

They passed on, nearer to shore—the oiler, the cook, the captain—and following them went the water-jar, bouncing gaily over the seas.

The correspondent remained in the grip of this strange new enemy—a current. The shore, with its white slope of sand and its green bluff, topped with little silent cottages, was spread like a picture before him. It was very near to him then, but he was impressed as one who in a gallery looks at a scene from Brittany or Holland.

He thought: "I am going to drown? Can it be possible? Can it be possible? Can it be possible?" Perhaps an individual must consider his own death to be the final phenomenon of nature.

But later a wave perhaps whirled him out of this small deadly current, for he found suddenly that he could again make progress toward the shore. Later still, he was aware that the captain, clinging with one hand to the keel of the dingey, had his face turned away from the shore and toward him, and was calling his name. "Come to the boat! Come to the boat!"

In his struggle to reach the captain and the boat, he reflected that when one gets properly wearied, drowning must really be a comfortable arrangement, a cessation of hostilities accompanied by a large degree of relief, and he was glad of it, for the main thing in his mind for some moments had been horror of the temporary agony. He did not wish to be hurt.

Presently he saw a man running along the shore. He was undressing with most remarkable speed. Coat, trousers, shirt, everything flew magically off him.

"Come to the boat," called the captain.

"All right, captain." As the correspondent paddled, he saw the captain let himself down to bottom and leave the boat. Then the correspondent performed his one little marvel of the voyage. A large wave caught him and flung him with ease and supreme speed completely over the boat and far beyond it. It struck him even then as an event in gymnastics, and a true miracle of the sea. An overturned boat in the surf is not a plaything to a swimming man.

The correspondent arrived in water that reached only to his waist, but his condition did not enable him to stand for more than a moment. Each wave knocked him into a heap, and the under-tow pulled at him.

Then he saw the man who had been running and undressing, and undressing and running, come bounding into the water. He dragged ashore the cook, and then waded towards the captain, but the captain waved him away, and sent him to the correspondent. He was naked, naked as a tree in winter, but a halo was about his head, and he shone like a saint. He gave a strong pull, and a long drag, and a bully heave at the correspondent's hand. The correspondent, schooled in the minor formulæ, said: "Thanks, old man." But suddenly the man cried: "What's that?" He pointed a swift finger. The correspondent said: "Go."

In the shallows, face downward, lay the oiler. His forehead touched sand that was periodically, between each wave, clear of the sea.

The correspondent did not know all that transpired afterward. When he achieved safe ground he fell, striking the sand with each particular part of his body. It was as if he had dropped from a roof, but the thud was grateful to him.

It seems that instantly the beach was populated with men with blankets, clothes, and flasks, and women with coffee-pots and all the remedies sacred to their minds. The welcome of the land to the men from the sea was warm and generous, but a still and dripping shape was carried slowly up the beach, and the land's welcome for it could only be the different and sinister hospitality of the grave.

When it came night, the white waves paced to and fro in the moonlight, and the wind brought the sound of the great sea's voice to the men on shore, and they felt that they could then be interpreters.

Reading and Reacting

1. What challenges do the men in the boat face? What is each character responsible for? What does each character represent?
2. What are the major themes of "The Open Boat?" How do the following elements reinforce these themes?
    - The color of the sea
    - The description of the waves
    - The size of the lifeboat
    - The faces of the men
3. Except for the Oiler, Billie, all the men in the boat are referred to by their jobs. Why? How would the story be different if the men were referred to by their names?
4. How does the correspondent's attitude toward nature change as the story progresses?
5. What is the narrative point of view of the story? How does this point of view reinforce the story's themes?
6. In Section VI, the following verse "mysteriously entered the correspondent's head."

    "A soldier of the Legion lay dying in Algiers,
    There was a lack of woman's nursing, there was dearth of
    woman's tears;
    But a comrade stood beside him, and he took that comrade's hand,
    And he said: 'I shall never see my own, my native land.'"

    What is the significance of this verse? What realization does it lead correspondent to?

7. "The Open Boat" includes a number of symbols—for example, the wet cigars, the soldier the correspondent remembers from his youth, the wind tower, the sea, the open lifeboat, and the shark. What significance does each of these symbols have in the story?
8. In what sense is the death of the Oiler ironic?
9. Find Winslow Homer's painting *The Gulf Stream* online. How does this painting reflect the major themes of "The Open Boat?"
10. **Journal Entry** "The Open Boat" is an example of the literary movement known as *naturalism*. Look up this term and write a paragraph in which you discuss how Crane's depiction of nature and people's place in it is naturalistic.
11. **Critical Perspective** In her analysis of "The Open Boat," Donna Gerstenberger says, "With his opening sentence, 'None of them knew the color of the sky,' Crane makes clear a major concern of 'The Open Boat.' The word *knew* in this famous sentence is the key word, for the story that follows is about man's limited capacities for knowing reality." In what respects is man's limited capacity to know reality a major theme in the story?

WRITING SUGGESTIONS: Theme

1. One of the major themes of Stephen Crane's story "The Open Boat" is the inability of human beings to prevail over nature. How does Crane use the relationship of the reporter and the others in the lifeboat to develop this theme?
2. Both "Doe Season" and "A Worn Path" deal with characters who make journeys. What is the significance of each journey? How do the protagonists of these two stories overcome the obstacles they encounter? In what sense are these journeys symbolic as well as actual?
3. Like "Doe Season," the following poem focuses on a child's experience with hunting. Write an essay in which you contrast its central theme with the central theme of "Doe Season."

Robert Huff (1924–1993)

Rainbow[1]

After the shot the driven feathers rock
In the air and are by sunlight trapped.
Their moment of descent is eloquent.
It is the rainbow echo of a bird
Whose thunder, stopped, puts in my daughter's eyes
A question mark. She does not see the rainbow,
And the folding bird-fall was for her too quick.
It is about the stillness of the bird
Her eyes are asking. She is three years old;
Has cut her fingers; found blood tastes of salt;
But she has never witnessed quiet blood,
Nor ever seen before the peace of death.
I say: "The feathers—Look!" but she is torn
And wretched and draws back. And I am glad
That I have wounded her, have winged her heart,
And that she goes beyond my fathering.

[1]Publication date is not available.

Chapter

16

Fiction for Further Reading

Ambrose Bierce (1842-1914)

An Occurrence at Owl Creek Bridge (1988)

I

A man stood upon a railroad bridge in northern Alabama, looking down into the swift water twenty feet below. The man's hands were behind his back, the wrists bound with a cord. A rope closely encircled his neck. It was attached to a stout cross-timber above his head and the slack fell to the level of his knees. Some loose boards laid upon the ties supporting the rails of the railway supplied a footing for him and his executioners—two private soldiers of the Federal army, directed by a sergeant who in civil life may have been a deputy sheriff. At a short remove upon the same temporary platform was an officer in the uniform of his rank, armed. He was a captain. A sentinel at each end of the bridge stood with his rifle in the position known as "support," that is to say, vertical in front of the left shoulder, the hammer resting on the forearm thrown straight across the chest—a formal and unnatural position, enforcing an erect carriage of the body. It did not appear to be the duty of these two men to know what was occurring at the center of the bridge; they merely blockaded the two ends of the foot planking that traversed it.

Beyond one of the sentinels nobody was in sight; the railroad ran straight away into a forest for a hundred yards, then, curving, was lost to view. Doubtless there was an outpost farther along. The other bank of the stream was open ground—a gentle slope topped with a stockade of vertical tree trunks, loopholed for rifles, with a single embrasure through which protruded the muzzle of a brass cannon commanding the bridge. Midway up the slope between the bridge and fort were the spectators—a single company of infantry in line, at "parade rest," the butts of their rifles on the ground, the barrels inclining slightly backward against the right shoulder, the hands crossed upon the stock. A lieutenant stood at the right of the line, the point of his sword upon the ground, his left hand resting upon his right. Excepting the group of four at the center of the bridge, not a man moved. The company faced the bridge, staring stonily, motionless. The sentinels, facing the banks of the stream, might have been statues to adorn the bridge. The captain stood with folded arms, silent, observing the work of his subordinates, but making no sign. Death is a dignitary who when he comes announced is to be received with formal manifestations of respect, even by those most familiar with him. In the code of military etiquette silence and fixity are forms of deference.

The man who was engaged in being hanged was apparently about thirty-five years of age. He was a civilian, if one might judge from his habit, which was that of a planter. His features were good—a straight nose, firm mouth, broad forehead, from which his long, dark hair was combed straight back, falling behind his ears to the collar of his well fitting frock coat. He wore a moustache and pointed beard, but no whiskers; his eyes were large and dark gray, and had a kindly expression which one would hardly have expected in one whose neck was in the hemp. Evidently this was no vulgar assassin. The liberal military code makes provision for hanging many kinds of persons, and gentlemen are not excluded.

The preparations being complete, the two private soldiers stepped aside and each drew away the plank upon which he had been standing. The sergeant turned to the captain, saluted and placed himself immediately behind that officer, who in turn moved apart one pace. These movements left the condemned man and the sergeant standing on the two ends of the same plank, which spanned three of the cross-ties of the bridge. The end upon which the civilian stood almost, but not quite, reached a fourth. This plank had been held in place by the weight of the captain; it was now held by that of the sergeant. At a signal from the former the latter would step aside, the plank would tilt and the condemned man go down between two ties. The arrangement commended itself to his judgement as simple and effective. His face had not been covered nor his eyes bandaged. He looked a moment at his "unsteadfast footing," then let his gaze wander to the swirling water of the stream racing madly beneath his feet. A piece of dancing driftwood caught his attention and his eyes followed it down the current. How slowly it appeared to move! What a sluggish stream!

He closed his eyes in order to fix his last thoughts upon his wife and children. The water, touched to gold by the early sun, the brooding mists under the banks at some distance down the stream, the fort, the soldiers, the piece of drift—all had distracted him. And now he became conscious of a new disturbance. Striking through the thought of his dear ones was sound which he could neither ignore nor understand, a sharp, distinct, metallic percussion like the stroke of a blacksmith's hammer upon the anvil; it had the same ringing quality. He wondered what it was, and whether immeasurably distant or near by—it seemed both. Its recurrence was regular, but as slow as the tolling of a death knell. He awaited each new stroke with impatience and—he knew not why—apprehension. The intervals of silence grew progressively longer; the delays became maddening. With their greater infrequency the sounds increased in strength and sharpness. They hurt his ear like the thrust of a knife; he feared he would shriek. What he heard was the ticking of his watch. 5

He unclosed his eyes and saw again the water below him. "If I could free my hands," he thought, "I might throw off the noose and spring into the stream. By diving I could evade the bullets and, swimming vigorously, reach the bank, take to the woods and get away home. My home, thank God, is as yet outside their lines; my wife and little ones are still beyond the invader's farthest advance."

As these thoughts, which have here to be set down in words, were flashed into the doomed man's brain rather than evolved from it the captain nodded to the sergeant. The sergeant stepped aside.

II

Peyton Farquhar was a well to do planter, of an old and highly respected Alabama family. Being a slave owner and like other slave owners a politician, he was naturally an original secessionist and ardently devoted to the Southern cause. Circumstances of an imperious nature, which it is unnecessary to relate here, had prevented him from taking service with that gallant army which had fought the disastrous campaigns ending with the fall of Corinth, and he chafed under the inglorious restraint, longing for the release of his energies, the larger life of the soldier, the opportunity for distinction. That opportunity, he felt, would come, as it comes to all in wartime. Meanwhile he did what he could. No service was too humble for him to perform in the aid of the South, no adventure too perilous for him to undertake if consistent with the character of a civilian who was at heart a soldier, and who in good faith and without too much qualification assented to at least a part of the frankly villainous dictum that all is fair in love and war.

One evening while Farquhar and his wife were sitting on a rustic bench near the entrance to his grounds, a gray-clad soldier rode up to the gate and asked for a drink of water. Mrs. Farquhar was only too happy to serve him with her own white hands. While she was fetching the water her husband approached the dusty horseman and inquired eagerly for news from the front.

"The Yanks are repairing the railroads," said the man, "and are getting ready for another advance. They have reached the Owl Creek bridge, put it in order and built a stockade on the north bank. The commandant has issued an order, which is posted everywhere, declaring that any civilian caught interfering with the railroad, its bridges, tunnels, or trains will be summarily hanged. I saw the order." 10

"How far is it to the Owl Creek bridge?" Farquhar asked.

"About thirty miles."

"Is there no force on this side of the creek?"

"Only a picket post half a mile out, on the railroad, and a single sentinel at this end of the bridge."

"Suppose a man—a civilian and student of hanging—should elude the picket post and perhaps get the better of the sentinel," said Farquhar, smiling, "what could he accomplish?" 15

The soldier reflected. "I was there a month ago," he replied. "I observed that the flood of last winter had lodged a great quantity of driftwood against the wooden pier at this end of the bridge. It is now dry and would burn like tinder."

The lady had now brought the water, which the soldier drank. He thanked her ceremoniously, bowed to her husband and rode away. An hour later, after nightfall, he repassed the plantation, going northward in the direction from which he had come. He was a Federal scout.

III

As Peyton Farquhar fell straight downward through the bridge he lost consciousness and was as one already dead. From this state he was awakened—ages later, it seemed to him—by the pain of a sharp pressure upon his throat, followed by a sense of suffocation. Keen, poignant agonies seemed to shoot from his neck downward through every fiber of his body and limbs. These pains appeared to flash along well defined lines of ramification and to beat with an inconceivably rapid periodicity. They seemed like streams of pulsating fire heating him to an intolerable temperature. As to his head, he was conscious of nothing but a feeling of fullness—of congestion. These sensations were unaccompanied by thought. The intellectual part of his nature was already effaced; he had power only to feel, and feeling was torment. He was conscious of motion. Encompassed in a luminous cloud, of which he was now merely the fiery heart, without material substance, he swung through unthinkable arcs of oscillation, like a vast pendulum. Then all at once, with terrible suddenness, the light about him shot upward with the noise of a loud splash; a frightful roaring was in his ears, and all was cold and dark. The power of thought was restored; he knew that the rope had broken and he had fallen into the stream. There was no additional strangulation; the noose about his neck was already suffocating him and kept the water from his lungs. To die of hanging at the bottom of a river!—the idea seemed to him ludicrous. He opened his eyes in the darkness and saw above him a gleam of light, but how distant, how inaccessible! He was still sinking, for the light became fainter and fainter until it was a mere glimmer. Then it began to grow and brighten, and he knew that he was rising toward the surface—knew it with reluctance, for he was now very comfortable. "To be hanged and drowned," he thought, "that is not so bad; but I do not wish to be shot. No; I will not be shot; that is not fair."

He was not conscious of an effort, but a sharp pain in his wrist apprised him that he was trying to free his hands. He gave the struggle his attention, as an idler might observe the feat of a juggler, without interest in the outcome. What splendid effort!—what magnificent, what superhuman strength! Ah, that was a fine endeavor! Bravo! The cord fell away; his arms parted and floated upward, the hands dimly seen on each side in the growing light. He watched them with a new interest as first one and then the other pounced upon the noose at his neck. They tore it away and thrust it fiercely aside, its undulations resembling those of a water snake. "Put it back, put it back!" He thought he shouted these words to his hands, for the undoing of the noose had been succeeded by the direst pang that he had yet experienced. His neck ached horribly; his brain was on fire, his heart, which had been fluttering faintly, gave a great leap, trying to force itself out at his mouth. His whole body was racked and wrenched with an insupportable anguish! But his disobedient hands gave no heed to the command. They beat the water vigorously with quick, downward strokes, forcing him to the surface. He felt his head emerge; his eyes were blinded by the sunlight; his chest expanded convulsively, and with a supreme and crowning agony his lungs engulfed a great draught of air, which instantly he expelled in a shriek!

He was now in full possession of his physical senses. They were, indeed, preternaturally keen and alert. Something in the awful disturbance of his organic system had so exalted and refined them that they made record of things never before perceived. He felt the ripples upon his face and heard their separate sounds as they struck. He looked at the forest on the bank of the stream, saw the individual trees, the leaves and the veining of each leaf—he saw the very insects upon them: the locusts, the brilliant bodied flies, the gray spiders stretching their webs from twig to twig. He noted the prismatic colors in all the dewdrops upon a million blades of grass. The humming of the gnats that danced above the eddies of the stream, the beating of the dragon flies' wings, the strokes of the water spiders' legs, like oars which had lifted their boat—all these made audible music. A fish slid along beneath his eyes and he heard the
rush of its body parting the water. 20

He had come to the surface facing down the stream; in a moment the visible world seemed to wheel slowly round, himself the pivotal point, and he saw the bridge, the fort, the soldiers upon the bridge, the captain, the sergeant, the two privates, his executioners. They were in silhouette against the blue sky. They shouted and gesticulated, pointing at him. The captain had drawn his pistol, but did not fire; the others were unarmed. Their movements were grotesque and horrible, their forms gigantic.

Suddenly he heard a sharp report and something struck the water smartly within a few inches of his head, spattering his face with spray. He heard a second report, and saw one of the sentinels with his rifle at his shoulder, a light cloud of blue smoke rising from the muzzle. The man in the water saw the eye of the man on the bridge gazing into his own through the sights of the rifle. He observed that it was a gray eye and remembered having read that gray eyes were keenest, and that all famous marksmen had them. Nevertheless, this one had missed.

A counter-swirl had caught Farquhar and turned him half round; he was again looking at the forest on the bank opposite the fort. The sound of a clear, high voice in a monotonous singsong now rang out behind him and came across the water with a distinctness that pierced and subdued all other sounds, even the beating of the ripples in his ears. Although no soldier, he had frequented camps enough to know the dread significance of that deliberate, drawling, aspirated chant; the lieutenant on shore was taking a part in the morning's work.

How coldly and pitilessly—with what an even, calm intonation, presaging, and enforcing tranquility in the men—with what accurately measured interval fell those cruel words:

"Company!... Attention!... Shoulder arms!... Ready!... Aim!... Fire!"

Farquhar dived—dived as deeply as he could. The water roared in his ears like the voice of Niagara, yet he heard the dull thunder of the volley and, rising again toward the surface, met shining bits of metal, singularly flattened, oscillating slowly downward. Some of them touched him on the face and hands, then fell away, continuing their descent. One lodged between his collar and neck; it was uncomfortably warm and he snatched it out.

As he rose to the surface, gasping for breath, he saw that he had been a long time under water; he was perceptibly farther downstream—nearer to safety. The soldiers had almost finished reloading; the metal ramrods flashed all at once in the sunshine as they were drawn from the barrels, turned in the air, and thrust into their sockets. The two sentinels fired again, independently and ineffectually.

The hunted man saw all this over his shoulder; he was now swimming vigorously with the current. His brain was as energetic as his arms and legs; he thought with the rapidity of lightning:

"The officer," he reasoned, "will not make that martinet's error a second time. It is as easy to dodge a volley as a single shot. He has probably already given the command to fire at will. God help me, I cannot dodge them all!"

An appalling splash within two yards of him was followed by a loud, rushing sound, DIMINUENDO, which seemed to travel back through the air to the fort and died in an explosion which stirred the very river to its deeps! A rising sheet of water curved over him, fell down upon him, blinded him, strangled him! The cannon had taken an hand in the game. As he shook his head free from the commotion of the smitten water he heard the deflected shot humming through the air ahead, and in an instant it was cracking and smashing the branches in the forest beyond.

"They will not do that again," he thought; "the next time they will use a charge of grape. I must keep my eye upon the gun; the smoke will apprise me—the report arrives too late; it lags behind the missile. That is a good gun."

Suddenly he felt himself whirled round and round—spinning like a top. The water, the banks, the forests, the now distant bridge, fort and men, all were commingled and blurred. Objects were represented by their colors only; circular horizontal streaks of color—that was all he saw. He had been caught in a vortex and was being whirled on with a velocity of advance and gyration that made him giddy and sick. In few moments he was flung upon the gravel at the foot of the left bank of the stream—the southern bank—and behind a projecting point which concealed him from his enemies. The sudden arrest of his motion, the abrasion of one of his hands on the gravel, restored him, and he wept with delight. He dug his fingers into the sand, threw it over himself in handfuls and audibly blessed it. It looked like diamonds, rubies, emeralds; he could think of nothing beautiful which it did not resemble. The trees upon the bank were giant garden plants; he noted a definite order in their arrangement, inhaled the fragrance of their blooms. A strange roseate light shone through the spaces among their trunks and the wind made in their branches the music of Aeolian harps. He had not wish to perfect his escape—he was content to remain in that enchanting spot until retaken. 30

A whiz and a rattle of grapeshot among the branches high above his head roused him from his dream. The baffled cannoneer had fired him a random farewell. He sprang to his feet, rushed up the sloping bank, and plunged into the forest.

All that day he traveled, laying his course by the rounding sun. The forest seemed interminable; nowhere did he discover a break in it, not even a woodman's road. He had not known that he lived in so wild a region. There was something uncanny in the revelation.

By nightfall he was fatigued, footsore, famished. The thought of his wife and children urged him on. At last he found a road which led him in what he knew to be the right direction. It was as wide and straight as a city street, yet it seemed untraveled. No fields bordered it, no dwelling anywhere. Not so much as the barking of a dog suggested human habitation. The black bodies of the trees formed a straight wall on both sides, terminating on the horizon in a point, like a diagram in a lesson in perspective. Overhead, as he looked up through this rift in the wood, shone great golden stars looking unfamiliar and grouped in strange constellations. He was sure they were arranged in some order which had a secret and malign significance. The wood on either side was full of singular noises, among which—once, twice, and again—he distinctly heard whispers in an unknown tongue.

His neck was in pain and lifting his hand to it found it horribly swollen. He knew that it had a circle of black where the rope had bruised it. His eyes felt congested; he could no longer close them. His tongue was swollen with thirst; he relieved its fever by thrusting it forward from between his teeth into the cold air. How softly the turf had carpeted the untraveled avenue—he could no longer feel the roadway beneath his feet!

Doubtless, despite his suffering, he had fallen asleep while walking, for now he sees another scene—perhaps he has merely recovered from a delirium. He stands at the gate of his own home. All is as he left it, and all bright and beautiful in the morning sunshine. He must have traveled the entire night. As he pushes open the gate and passes up the wide white walk, he sees a flutter of female garments; his wife, looking fresh and cool and sweet, steps down from the veranda to meet him. At the bottom of the steps she stands waiting, with a smile of ineffable joy, an attitude of matchless grace and dignity. Ah, how beautiful she is! He springs forwards with extended arms. As he is about to clasp her he feels a stunning blow upon the back of the neck; a blinding white light blazes all about him with a sound like the shock of a cannon—then all is darkness and silence! 35

Peyton Farquhar was dead; his body, with a broken neck, swung gently from side to side beneath the timbers of the Owl Creek bridge.

* * *

T. Coraghessan Boyle (1948–)

Greasy Lake (1985)

It's about a mile down on the dark side of Route 88.
—Bruce Springsteen

There was a time when courtesy and winning ways went out of style, when it was good to be bad, when you cultivated decadence like a taste. We were all dangerous characters then. We wore torn-up leather jackets, slouched around with toothpicks in our mouths, sniffed glue and ether and what somebody claimed was cocaine. When we wheeled our parents' whining station wagons out into the street we left a patch of rubber half a block long. We drank gin and grape juice, Tango, Thunderbird, and Bali Hai. We were nineteen. We were bad. We read André Gide[1] and struck elaborate poses to show that we didn't give a shit about anything. At night, we went up to Greasy Lake.

Through the center of town, up the strip, past the housing developments and shopping malls, street lights giving way to the thin streaming illumination of the headlights, trees crowding the asphalt in a black unbroken wall: that was the way out to Greasy Lake. The Indians had called it Wakan, a reference to the clarity of its waters. Now it was fetid and murky, the mud banks glittering with broken glass and strewn with beer cans and the charred remains of bonfires. There was a single ravaged island a hundred yards from shore, so stripped of vegetation it looked as if the air force had strafed it. We went up to the lake because everyone went there, because we wanted to snuff the rich scent of possibility on the breeze, watch a girl take off her clothes and plunge into the festering murk, drink beer, smoke pot, howl at the stars, savor the incongruous full-throated roar of rock and roll against the primeval susurrus[2] of frogs and crickets. This was nature.

I was there one night, late, in the company of two dangerous characters. Digby wore a gold star in his right ear and allowed his father to pay his tuition at Cornell; Jeff was thinking of quitting school to become a painter/musician/head-shop proprietor. They were both expert in the social graces, quick with a sneer, able to manage a Ford with lousy shocks over a rutted and gutted blacktop road at eighty-five while rolling a joint as compact as a Tootsie Roll Pop stick. They could lounge against a bank of booming speakers and trade "man"s with the best of them or roll out across the dance floor as if their joints worked on bearings. They were slick and quick and they wore their mirror shades at breakfast and dinner, in the shower, in closets and caves. In short, they were bad.

---

[1]*André Gide:* French novelist and critic (1869–1951) whose work—much of it semiautobiographical—examines the conflict between desire and discipline and shows individuals battling conventional morality.
[2]*susurrus:* A whispering or rustling sound.

I drove. Digby pounded the dashboard and shouted along with Toots & the Maytals while Jeff hung his head out the window and streaked the side of my mother's Bel Air with vomit. It was early June, the air soft as a hand on your cheek, the third night of summer vacation. The first two nights we'd been out till dawn, looking for something we never found. On this, the third night, we'd cruised the strip sixty-seven times, been in and out of every bar and club we could think of in a twenty-mile radius, stopped twice for bucket chicken and forty-cent hamburgers, debated going to a party at the house of a girl Jeff's sister knew, and chucked two dozen raw eggs at mailboxes and hitchhikers. It was 2:00 A.M.; the bars were closing. There was nothing to do but take a bottle of lemon-flavored gin up to Greasy Lake.

The taillights of a single car winked at us as we swung into the dirt lot with its tufts of weed and washboard corrugations; '57 Chevy, mint, metallic blue. On the far side of the lot, like the exoskeleton of some gaunt chrome insect, a chopper leaned against its kickstand. And that was it for excitement: some junkie half-wit biker and a car freak pumping his girlfriend. Whatever it was we were looking for, we weren't about to find it at Greasy Lake. Not that night. 5

But then all of a sudden Digby was fighting for the wheel. "Hey, that's Tony Lovett's car! Hey!" he shouted, while I stabbed at the brake pedal and the Bel Air nosed up to the gleaming bumper of the parked Chevy. Digby leaned on the horn, laughing, and instructed me to put my brights on. I flicked on the brights. This was hilarious. A joke. Tony would experience premature withdrawal and expect to be confronted by grim-looking state troopers with flashlights. We hit the horn, strobed the lights, and then jumped out of the car to press our witty faces to Tony's windows; for all we knew we might even catch a glimpse of some little fox's tit, and then we could slap backs with red-faced Tony, roughhouse a little, and go on to new heights of adventure and daring.

The first mistake, the one that opened the whole floodgate, was losing my grip on the keys. In the excitement, leaping from the car with the gin in one hand and a roach clip in the other, I spilled them in the grass—in the dark, rank, mysterious nighttime grass of Greasy Lake. This was a tactical error, as damaging and irreversible in its way as Westmoreland's decision to dig in at Khe Sanh.[3] I felt it like a jab of intuition, and I stopped there by the open door, peering vaguely into the night that puddled up round my feet.

The second mistake—and this was inextricably bound up with the first—was identifying the car as Tony Lovett's. Even before the very bad character in greasy jeans and engineer boots ripped out of the driver's door, I began to realize that this chrome blue was much lighter than the robin's-egg of Tony's car, and that Tony's car didn't have rear-mounted speakers. Judging from their

---

[3]*Khe Sanh:* In late 1967, North Vietnamese and Viet Cong forces mounted a strong attack against American troops at Khe Sanh, leading General William C. Westmoreland, commander of United States forces in Vietnam, to "dig in" to defend an area of relatively little tactical importance.

expressions, Digby and Jeff were privately groping toward the same inevitable and unsettling conclusion as I was.

In any case, there was no reasoning with this bad greasy character—clearly he was a man of action. The first lusty Rockette[4] kick of his steel-toed boot caught me under the chin, chipped my favorite tooth, and left me sprawled in the dirt. Like a fool, I'd gone down on one knee to comb the stiff hacked grass for the keys, my mind making connections in the most dragged-out, testudineous[5] way, knowing that things had gone wrong, that I was in a lot of trouble, and that the lost ignition key was my grail and my salvation. The three or four succeeding blows were mainly absorbed by my right buttock and the tough piece of bone at the base of my spine.

Meanwhile, Digby vaulted the kissing bumpers and delivered a savage kung-fu blow to the greasy character's collarbone. Digby had just finished a course in martial arts for phys-ed credit and had spent the better part of the past two nights telling us apocryphal tales of Bruce Lee types and of the raw power invested in lightning blows shot from coiled wrists, ankles, and elbows. The greasy character was unimpressed. He merely backed off a step, his face like a Toltec mask, and laid Digby out with a single whistling roundhouse blow . . . but by now Jeff had got into the act, and I was beginning to extricate myself from the dirt, a tinny compound of shock, rage, and impotence wadded in my throat. 10

Jeff was on the guy's back, biting at his ear. Digby was on the ground, cursing. I went for the tire iron I kept under the driver's seat. I kept it there because bad characters always keep tire irons under the driver's seat, for just such an occasion as this. Never mind that I hadn't been involved in a fight since sixth grade, when a kid with a sleepy eye and two streams of mucus depending from his nostrils hit me in the knee with a Louisville slugger,[6] never mind that I'd touched the tire iron exactly twice before, to change tires: it was there. And I went for it.

I was terrified. Blood was beating in my ears, my hands were shaking, my heart turning over like a dirtbike in the wrong gear. My antagonist was shirtless, and a single cord of muscle flashed across his chest as he bent forward to peel Jeff from his back like a wet overcoat. "Motherfucker," he spat, over and over, and I was aware in that instant that all four of us—Digby, Jeff, and myself included—were chanting "motherfucker, motherfucker," as if it were a battle cry. (What happened next? the detective asks the murderer from beneath the turned-down brim of his porkpie hat. I don't know, the murderer says, something came over me. Exactly.)

---

[4]*Rockette:* The reference is to the Rockettes, a dance troupe at New York's Radio City Music Hall noted for precision and cancan-like high kicks.

[5]*testudineous:* Slow, like the pace of a tortoise.

[6]*Louisville slugger:* A popular brand of baseball bat.

Digby poked the flat of his hand in the bad character's face and I came at him like a kamikaze, mindless, raging, stung with humiliation—the whole thing, from the initial boot in the chin to this murderous primal instant involving no more than sixty hyperventilating, gland-flooding seconds—I came at him and brought the tire iron down across his ear. The effect was instantaneous, astonishing. He was a stunt man and this was Hollywood, he was a big grimacing toothy balloon and I was a man with a straight pin. He collapsed. Wet his pants. Went loose in his boots.

A single second, big as a zeppelin, floated by. We were standing over him in a circle, gritting our teeth, jerking our necks, our limbs and hands and feet twitching with glandular discharges. No one said anything. We just stared down at the guy, the car freak, the lover, the bad greasy character laid low. Digby looked at me; so did Jeff. I was still holding the tire iron, a tuft of hair clinging to the crook like dandelion fluff, like down. Rattled, I dropped it in the dirt, already envisioning the headlines, the pitted faces of the police inquisitors, the gleam of handcuffs, clank of bars, the big black shadows rising from the back of the cell . . . when suddenly a raw torn shriek cut through me like all the juice in all the electric chairs in the country.

It was the fox. She was short, barefoot, dressed in panties and a man's shirt. "Animals!" she screamed, running at us with her fists clenched and wisps of blow-dried hair in her face. There was a silver chain round her ankle, and her toenails flashed in the glare of the headlights. I think it was the toenails that did it. Sure, the gin and the cannabis and even the Kentucky Fried may have had a hand in it, but it was the sight of those flaming toes that set us off—the toad emerging from the loaf in *Virgin Spring*,[7] lipstick smeared on a child: she was already tainted. We were on her like Bergman's deranged brothers—see no evil, hear none, speak none—panting, wheezing, tearing at her clothes, grabbing for flesh. We were bad characters, and we were scared and hot and three steps over the line—anything could have happened. 15

It didn't.

Before we could pin her to the hood of the car, our eyes masked with lust and greed and the purest primal badness, a pair of headlights swung into the lot. There we were, dirty, bloody, guilty, dissociated from humanity and civilization, the first of the Ur-crimes[8] behind us, the second in progress, shreds of nylon panty and spandex brassiere dangling from our fingers, our flies open, lips licked—there we were, caught in the spotlight. Nailed.

We bolted. First for the car, and then, realizing we had no way of starting it, for the woods. I thought nothing. I thought escape. The headlights came at me like accusing fingers. I was gone.

Ram-bam-bam, across the parking lot, past the chopper and into the feculent undergrowth at the lake's edge, insects flying up in my face, weeds whipping, frogs and snakes and red-eyed turtles splashing off into the night: I was

[7] *Virgin Spring:* A film by Swedish director Ingmar Bergman.

[8] *Ur-crimes:* Primitive crimes.

already ankle-deep in muck and tepid water and still going strong. Behind me, the girl's screams rose in intensity, disconsolate, incriminating, the screams of the Sabine women,[9] the Christian martyrs, Anne Frank[10] dragged from the garret. I kept going, pursued by those cries, imagining cops and bloodhounds. The water was up to my knees when I realized what I was doing: I was going to swim for it. Swim the breadth of Greasy Lake and hide myself in the thick clot of woods on the far side. They'd never find me there.

I was breathing in sobs, in gasps. The water lapped at my waist as I looked out over the moon-burnished ripples, the mats of algae that clung to the surface like scabs. Digby and Jeff had vanished. I paused. Listened. The girl was quieter now, screams tapering to sobs, but there were male voices, angry, excited, and the high-pitched ticking of the second car's engine. I waded deeper, stealthy, hunted, the ooze sucking at my sneakers. As I was about to take the plunge—at the very instant I dropped my shoulder for the first slashing stroke—I blundered into something. Something unspeakable, obscene, something soft, wet, moss-grown. A patch of weed? A log? When I reached out to touch it, it gave like a rubber duck, it gave like flesh. 20

In one of those nasty little epiphanies for which we are prepared by films and TV and childhood visits to the funeral home to ponder the shrunken painted forms of dead grandparents, I understood what it was that bobbed there so inadmissibly in the dark. Understood, and stumbled back in horror and revulsion, my mind yanked in six different directions (I was nineteen, a mere child, an infant, and here in the space of five minutes I'd struck down one greasy character and blundered into the waterlogged carcass of a second), thinking, The keys, the keys, why did I have to go and lose the keys? I stumbled back, but the muck took hold of my feet—a sneaker snagged, balance lost—and suddenly I was pitching face forward into the buoyant black mass, throwing out my hands in desperation while simultaneously conjuring the image of reeking frogs and muskrats revolving in slicks of their own deliquescing[11] juices. AAAAArrrgh! I shot from the water like a torpedo, the dead man rotating to expose a mossy beard and eyes cold as the moon. I must have shouted out, thrashing around in the weeds, because the voices behind me suddenly became animated.

"What was that?"

"It's them, it's them: they tried to, tried to . . . *rape* me!" Sobs.

A man's voice, flat Midwestern accent. "You sons a bitches, we'll kill you!"

Frogs, crickets. 25

---

[9]*Sabine women:* According to legend, members of an ancient Italian tribe abducted by Romans who took the women for wives. The "Rape of the Sabine Women" has been depicted by various artists, most notably by seventeenth-century French painter Nicolas Poussin.

[10]*Anne Frank:* German Jewish girl (1929–1945) whose family hid in an attic in Amsterdam during the Nazi occupation of the Netherlands. Frank, who along with her family was discovered by storm troopers and sent to die at the concentration camp at Belsen, is famous for her diary, which recounts her days in hiding. A new version of the diary containing five missing pages surfaced in 1998.

[11]*deliquescing:* Melting.

Then another voice, harsh, *r*-less, Lower East Side: "Motherfucker!" I recognized the verbal virtuosity of the bad greasy character in the engineer boots. Tooth chipped, sneakers gone, coated in mud and slime and worse, crouching breathless in the weeds waiting to have my ass thoroughly and definitively kicked and fresh from the hideous stinking embrace of a three-days-dead-corpse, I suddenly felt a rush of joy and vindication: the son of a bitch was alive! Just as quickly, my bowels turned to ice. "Come on out of there, you pansy mothers!" the bad greasy character was screaming. He shouted curses till he was out of breath.

The crickets started up again, then the frogs. I held my breath. All at once there was a sound in the reeds, a swishing, a splash: thunk-a-thunk. They were throwing rocks. The frogs fell silent. I cradled my head. Swish, swish, thunk-a-thunk. A wedge of feldspar the size of a cue ball glanced off my knee. I bit my finger.

It was then that they turned to the car. I heard a door slam, a curse, and then the sound of the headlights shattering—almost a good-natured sound, celebratory, like corks popping from the necks of bottles. This was succeeded by the dull booming of the fenders, metal on metal, and then the icy crash of the windshield. I inched forward, elbows and knees, my belly pressed to the muck, thinking of guerrillas and commandos and *The Naked and the Dead*.[12] I parted the weeds and squinted the length of the parking lot.

The second car—it was a Trans-Am—was still running, its high beams washing the scene in a lurid stagy light. Tire iron flailing, the greasy bad character was laying into the side of my mother's Bel Air like an avenging demon, his shadow riding up the trunks of the trees. Whomp. Whomp. Whomp-whomp. The other two guys—blond types, in fraternity jackets—were helping out with tree branches and skull-sized boulders. One of them was gathering up bottles, rocks, muck, candy wrappers, used condoms, pop-tops, and other refuse and pitching it through the window on the driver's side. I could see the fox, a white bulb behind the windshield of the '57 Chevy. "Bobbie," she whined over the thumping, "come *on*." The greasy character paused a moment, took one good swipe at the left taillight, and then heaved the tire iron halfway across the lake. Then he fired up the '57 and was gone.

Blond head nodded at blond head. One said something to the other, too low for me to catch. They were no doubt thinking that in helping to annihilate my mother's car they'd committed a fairly rash act, and thinking too that there were three bad characters connected with that very car watching them from the woods. Perhaps other possibilities occurred to them as well—police, jail cells, justices of the peace, reparations, lawyers, irate parents, fraternal censure. Whatever they were thinking, they suddenly dropped branches, bottles, and rocks and sprang for their car in unison, as if they'd choreographed it. Five seconds. That's all it took. The engine shrieked, the tires squealed, a cloud of dust rose from the rutted lot and then settled back on darkness. 30

[12] *The Naked and the Dead:* A popular and critically praised 1948 novel by Norman Mailer depicting Army life among U.S. soldiers during World War II.

I don't know how long I lay there, the bad breath of decay all around me, my jacket heavy as a bear, the primordial ooze subtly reconstituting itself to accommodate my upper thighs and testicles. My jaws ached, my knee throbbed, my coccyx[13] was on fire. I contemplated suicide, wondered if I'd need bridgework, scraped the recesses of my brain for some sort of excuse to give my parents—a tree had fallen on the car, I was blindsided by a bread truck, hit and run, vandals had got to it while we were playing chess at Digby's. Then I thought of the dead man. He was probably the only person on the planet worse off than I was. I thought about him, fog on the lake, insects chirring eerily, and felt the tug of fear, felt the darkness opening up inside me like a set of jaws. Who was he, I wondered, this victim of time and circumstance bobbing sorrowfully in the lake at my back. The owner of the chopper, no doubt, a bad older character come to this. Shot during a murky drug deal, drowned while drunkenly frolicking in the lake. Another headline. My car was wrecked; he was dead.

When the eastern half of the sky went from black to cobalt and the trees began to separate themselves from the shadows, I pushed myself up from the mud and stepped out into the open. By now the birds had begun to take over for the crickets, and dew lay slick on the leaves. There was a smell in the air, raw and sweet at the same time, the smell of the sun firing buds and opening blossoms. I contemplated the car. It lay there like a wreck along the highway, like a steel sculpture left over from a vanished civilization. Everything was still. This was nature.

I was circling the car, as dazed and bedraggled as the sole survivor of an air blitz, when Digby and Jeff emerged from the trees behind me. Digby's face was crosshatched with smears of dirt; Jeff's jacket was gone and his shirt was torn across the shoulder. They slouched across the lot, looking sheepish, and silently came up beside me to gape at the ravaged automobile. No one said a word. After a while Jeff swung open the driver's door and began to scoop the broken glass and garbage off the seat. I looked at Digby. He shrugged. "At least they didn't slash the tires," he said.

It was true: the tires were intact. There was no windshield, the headlights were staved in, and the body looked as if it had been sledgehammered for a quarter a shot at the county fair, but the tires were inflated to regulation pressure. The car was drivable. In silence, all three of us bent to scrape the mud and shattered glass from the interior. I said nothing about the biker. When we were finished, I reached in my pocket for the keys, experienced a nasty stab of recollection, cursed myself, and turned to search the grass. I spotted them almost immediately, no more than five feet from the open door, glinting like jewels in the first tapering shaft of sunlight. There was no reason to get philosophical about it: I eased into the seat and turned the engine over.

It was at that precise moment that the silver Mustang with the flame decals rumbled into the lot. All three of us froze; then Digby and Jeff slid into the car and slammed the door. We watched as the Mustang rocked and bobbed

---

[13]*coccyx:* Tailbone.

across the ruts and finally jerked to a halt beside the forlorn chopper at the far end of the lot. "Let's go," Digby said. I hesitated, the Bel Air wheezing beneath me. 35

Two girls emerged from the Mustang. Tight jeans, stiletto heels, hair like frozen fur. They bent over the motorcycle, paced back and forth aimlessly, glanced once or twice at us, and then ambled over to where the reeds sprang up in a green fence round the perimeter of the lake. One of them cupped her hands to her mouth. "Al," she called, "Hey, Al!"

"Come on," Digby hissed. "Let's get out of here."

But it was too late. The second girl was picking her way across the lot, unsteady on her heels, looking up at us and then away. She was older—twenty-five or six—and as she came closer we could see there was something wrong with her: she was stoned or drunk, lurching now and waving her arms for balance. I gripped the steering wheel as if it were the ejection lever of a flaming jet, and Digby spat out my name, twice, terse and impatient.

"Hi," the girl said.

We looked at her like zombies, like war veterans, like deaf-and-dumb pencil peddlers. 40

She smiled, her lips cracked and dry. "Listen," she said, bending from the waist to look in the window, "you guys seen Al?" Her pupils were pinpoints, her eyes glass. She jerked her neck. "That's his bike over there—Al's. You seen him?"

Al. I didn't know what to say. I wanted to get out of the car and retch, I wanted to go home to my parents' house and crawl into bed. Digby poked me in the ribs. "We haven't seen anybody," I said.

The girl seemed to consider this, reaching out a slim veiny arm to brace herself against the car. "No matter," she said, slurring the *t*'s, "he'll turn up." And then, as if she'd just taken stock of the whole scene—the ravaged car and our battered faces, the desolation of the place—she said: "Hey, you guys look like some pretty bad characters—been fightin', huh?" We stared straight ahead, rigid as catatonics. She was fumbling in her pocket and muttering something. Finally she held out a handful of tablets in glassine wrappers: "Hey, you want to party, you want to do some of these with me and Sarah?"

I just looked at her. I thought I was going to cry. Digby broke the silence. "No, thanks," he said, leaning over me. "Some other time."

I put the car in gear and it inched forward with a groan, shaking off pellets of glass like an old dog shedding water after a bath, heaving over the ruts on its worn springs, creeping toward the highway. There was a sheen of sun on the lake. I looked back. The girl was still standing there, watching us, her shoulders slumped, hand outstretched. 45

* * *

Junot Díaz (1968–)

No Face (1996)

In the morning he pulls on his mask and grinds his fist into his palm. He goes to the guanábana tree and does his pull-ups, nearly fifty now, and then he picks up the café dehuller and holds it to his chest for a forty count. His arms, chest and neck bulge and the skin around his temple draws tight, about to split. But no! He's unbeatable and drops the dehuller with a fat Yes. He knows that he should go but the morning fog covers everything and he listens to the roosters for a while. Then he hears his family stirring. Hurry up, he says to himself. He runs past his tío's land and with a glance he knows how many beans of café his tío has growing red, black and green on his conucos. He runs past the water hose and the pasture, and then he says FLIGHT and jumps up and his shadow knifes over the tops of the trees and he can see his family's fence and his mother washing his little brother, scrubbing his face and his feet.

* * *

The storekeepers toss water on the road to keep the dust down; he sweeps past them. No Face! a few yell out but he has no time for them. First he goes to the bars, searches the nearby ground for dropped change. Drunks sometimes sleep in the alleys so he moves quietly. He steps over the piss-holes and the vomit, wrinkles his nose at the stink. Today he finds enough coins in the tall crackling weeds to buy a bottle of soda or a johnnycake. He holds the coins tightly in his hands and under his mask he smiles.

At the hottest part of the day Lou lets him into the church with its bad roof and poor wiring and gives him café con leche and two hours of reading and writing. The books, the pen, the paper all come from the nearby school, donated by the teacher. Father Lou has small hands and bad eyes and twice he's gone to Canada for operations. Lou teaches him the English he'll need up north. I'm hungry. Where's the bathroom? I come from the Dominican Republic. Don't be scared.

After his lessons he buys Chiclets and goes to the house across from the church. The house has a gate and orange trees and a cobblestone path. A TV trills somewhere inside. He waits for the girl but she doesn't come out. Normally she'd peek out and see him. She'd make a TV with her hands. They both speak with their hands.

Do you want to watch? 5

He'd shake his head, put his hands out in front of him. He never went into casas ajenas. *No. I like being outside.*

I'd rather be inside where it's cool.

He'd stay until the cleaning woman, who also lived in the mountains, yelled from the kitchen, Stay away from here. Don't you have any shame? Then he'd grip the bars of the gate and pull them a bit apart, grunting, to show her who she was messing with.

Each week Padre Lou lets him buy a comic book. The priest takes him to the bookseller and stands in the street, guarding him, while he peruses the shelves.

Today he buys Kaliman, who takes no shit and wears a turban. If his face were covered he'd be perfect. 10

* * *

He watches for opportunities from corners, away from people. He has his power of INVISIBILITY and no one can touch him. Even his tío, the one who guards the dams, strolls past and says nothing. Dogs can smell him though and a couple nuzzle his feet. He pushes them away since they can betray his location to his enemies. So many wish him to fall. So many wish him gone.

A viejo[1] needs help pushing his cart. A cat needs to be brought across the street.

Hey No Face! a motor driver yells. What the hell are you doing? You haven't started eating cats, have you?

He'll be eating kids next, another joins in.

Leave that cat alone, it's not yours. 15

He runs. It's late in the day and the shops are closing and even the motorbikes at each corner have dispersed, leaving oil stains and ruts in the dirt.

* * *

The ambush comes when he's trying to figure out if he can buy another johnnycake. Four boys tackle him and the coins jump out of his hand like grasshoppers. The fat boy with the single eyebrow sits on his chest and his breath flies out of him. The others stand over him and he's scared.

We're going to make you a girl, the fat one says and he can hear the words echoing through the meat of the fat boy's body. He wants to breathe but his lungs are as tight as pockets.

You ever been a girl before?

I betcha he hasn't. It ain't a lot of fun. 20

He says STRENGTH and the fat boy flies off him and he's running down the street and the others are following. You better leave him alone, the owner of the beauty shop says but no one ever listens to her, not since her husband left her for a Haitian. He makes it back to the church and slips inside and hides. The boys throw rocks against the door of the church but then Eliseo, the groundskeeper says, Boys, prepare for hell, and runs his machete on the sidewalk. Everything outside goes quiet. He sits down under a pew and waits for nighttime, when he can go back home to the smokehouse to sleep. He rubs the blood on his shorts, spits on the cut to get the dirt out.

Are you okay? Padre Lou asks.

I've been running out of energy.

Padre Lou sits down. He looks like one of those Cuban shopkeepers in his shorts and guayabera. He pats his hands together. I've been thinking about you up north. I'm trying to imagine you in the snow.

Snow won't bother me. 25

Snow bothers everybody.

---

[1]*viejo:* Spanish for "old man."

Do they like wrestling?

Padre Lou laughs. Almost as much as we do. Except nobody gets cut up, not anymore.

He comes out from under the pew then and shows the priest his elbow. The priest sighs, Let's go take care of that, OK?

Just don't use the red stuff.

We don't use the red stuff anymore. We have the white stuff now and it doesn't hurt.

I'll believe that when I see it.

* * *

No one has ever hidden it from him. They tell him the story over and over again, as though afraid that he might forget.

On some nights he opens his eyes and the pig has come back. Always huge and pale. Its hooves peg his chest down and he can smell the curdled bananas on its breath. Blunt teeth rip a strip from under his eye and the muscle revealed is delicious, like lechosa. He turns his head to save one side of his face; in some dreams he saves his right side and in some his left but in the worst ones he cannot turn his head, its mouth is like a pothole and nothing can escape it. When he awakens he's screaming and blood braids down his neck; he's bitten his tongue and it swells and he cannot sleep again until he tells himself to be a man.

* * *

Padre Lou borrows a Honda motorcycle and the two set out early in the morning. He leans into the turns and Lou says, Don't do that too much. You'll tip us.

Nothing will happen to us! he yells.

The road to Ocoa is empty and the fincas[2] are dry and many of the farmsteads have been abandoned. On a bluff he sees a single black horse. It's eating a shrub and a garza[3] is perched on its back.

The clinic is crowded with bleeding people but a nurse with bleached hair brings them through to the front.

How are we today? the doctor says.

I'm fine, he says. When are you sending me away?

The doctor smiles and makes him remove his mask and then massages his face with his thumbs. The doctor has colorless food in his teeth. Have you had trouble swallowing?

No.

Breathing?

No.

Have you had any headaches? Does your throat ever hurt? Are you ever dizzy?

Never.

---

[2] *fincas:* Spanish for farms.

[3] *garza:* Spanish for heron.

The doctor checks his eyes, his ears, and then listens to his breathing. Everything looks good, Lou.

I'm glad to hear that. Do you have a ballpark figure?

Well, the doctor says. We'll get him there eventually.

Padre Lou smiles and puts a hand on his shoulder. What do you think about that?

He nods but doesn't know what he should think. He's scared of the operations and scared that nothing will change, that the Canadian doctors will fail like the santeras his mother hired, who called every spirit in the celestial directory for help. The room he's in is hot and dim and dusty and he's sweating and wishes he could lie under a table where no one can see. In the next room he met a boy whose skull plates had not closed all the way and a girl who didn't have arms and a baby whose face was huge and swollen and whose eyes were dripping pus. 50

You can see my brain, the boy said. All I have is this membrane thing and you can see right into it.

* * *

In the morning he wakes up hurting. From the doctor, from a fight he had outside the church. He goes outside, dizzy, and leans against the guanabana tree. His little brother Pesao is awake, flicking beans at the chickens, his little body bowed and perfect and when he rubs the four-year-old's head he feels the sores that have healed into yellow crusts. He aches to pick at them but the last time the blood had *gushed* and Pesao had *screamed.*

Where have you been? Pesao asks.

I've been fighting evil.

I want to do that. 55

You won't like it, he says.

Pesao looks at his face, giggles and flings another pebble at the hens, who scatter indignantly.

He watches the sun burn the mists from the fields and despite the heat the beans are thick and green and flexible in the breeze. His mother sees him on the way back from the outhouse. She goes to fetch his mask.

He's tired and aching but he looks out over the valley, and the way the land curves away to hide itself reminds him of the way Lou hides his dominos when they play. Go, she says. Before your father comes out.

He knows what happens when his father comes out. He pulls on his mask and feels the fleas stirring in the cloth. When she turns her back, he hides, blending into the weeds. He watches his mother hold Pesao's head gently under the faucet and when the water finally urges out from the pipe Pesao yells as if he's been given a present or a wish come true. 60

He runs, down towards town, never slipping or stumbling. Nobody's faster.

* * *

Louise Erdrich (1954–)

The Red Convertible (1984)

I was the first one to drive a convertible on my reservation. And of course it was red, a red Olds. I owned that car along with my brother Henry Junior. We owned it together until his boots filled with water on a windy night and he bought out my share. Now Henry owns the whole car, and his younger brother Lyman (that's myself), Lyman walks everywhere he goes.

How did I earn enough money to buy my share in the first place? My one talent was I could always make money. I had a touch for it, unusual in a Chippewa. From the first I was different that way, and everyone recognized it. I was the only kid they let in the American Legion Hall to shine shoes, for example, and one Christmas I sold spiritual bouquets for the mission door to door. The nuns let me keep a percentage. Once I started, it seemed the more money I made the easier the money came. Everyone encouraged it. When I was fifteen I got a job washing dishes at the Joliet Cafe, and that was where my first big break happened.

It wasn't long before I was promoted to busing tables, and then the short-order cook quit and I was hired to take her place. No sooner than you know it I was managing the Joliet. The rest is history. I went on managing. I soon became part owner, and of course there was no stopping me then. It wasn't long before the whole thing was mine.

After I'd owned the Joliet for one year, it blew over in the worst tornado ever seen around here. The whole operation was smashed to bits. A total loss. The fryalator[1] was up in a tree, the grill torn in half like it was paper. I was only sixteen. I had it all in my mother's name, and I lost it quick, but before I lost it I had every one of my relatives, and their relatives, to dinner, and I also bought that red Olds I mentioned, along with Henry.

* * *

The first time we saw it! I'll tell you when we first saw it. We had gotten a ride up to Winnipeg, and both of us had money. Don't ask me why, because we never mentioned a car or anything, we just had all our money. Mine was cash, a big bankroll from the Joliet's insurance. Henry had two checks – a week's extra pay for being laid off, and his regular check from the Jewel Bearing Plant. 5

We were walking down Portage anyway, seeing the sights, when we saw it. There it was, parked, large as life. Really as *if* it was alive. I thought of the word *repose*, because the car wasn't simply stopped, parked, or whatever. That car reposed, calm and gleaming, a FOR SALE sign in its left front window. Then, before we had thought it over at all, the car belonged to us and our pockets were empty. We had just enough money for gas back home.

We went places in that car, me and Henry. We took off driving all one whole summer. We started off toward the Little Knife River and Mandaree in Fort Berthold and then we found ourselves down in Wakpala somehow, and

[1] *fryalator:* Often spelled "frialator," a kitchen appliance used for deep-frying food.

then suddenly we were over in Montana on the Rocky Boy, and yet the summer was not even half over. Some people hang on to details when they travel, but we didn't let them bother us and just lived our everyday lives here to there.

I do remember this one place with willows. I remember I lay under those trees and it was comfortable. So comfortable. The branches bent down all around me like a tent or a stable. And quiet, it was quiet, even though there was a powwow close enough so I could see it going on. The air was not too still, not too windy either. When the dust rises up and hangs in the air around the dancers like that, I feel good. Henry was asleep with his arms thrown wide. Later on, he woke up and we started driving again. We were somewhere in Montana, or maybe on the Blood Reserve—it could have been anywhere. Anyway it was where we met the girl.

* * *

All her hair was in buns around her ears, that's the first thing I noticed about her. She was posed alongside the road with her arm out, so we stopped. That girl was short, so short her lumber shirt looked comical on her, like a nightgown. She had jeans on and fancy moccasins and she carried a little suitcase.

"Hop on in," says Henry. So she climbs in between us. 10

"We'll take you home," I says. "Where do you live?"

"Chicken," she says.

"Where the hell's that?" I ask her.

"Alaska."

"Okay," says Henry, and we drive. 15

We got up there and never wanted to leave. The sun doesn't truly set there in summer, and the night is more a soft dusk. You might doze off, sometimes, but before you know it you're up again, like an animal in nature. You never feel like you have to sleep hard or put away the world. And things would grow up there. One day just dirt or moss, the next day flowers and long grass. The girl's name was Susy. Her family really took to us. They fed us and put us up. We had our own tent to live in by their house, and the kids would be in and out of there all day and night. They couldn't get over me and Henry being brothers, we looked so different. We told them we knew we had the same mother, anyway.

One night Susy came in to visit us. We sat around in the tent talking of this and that. The season was changing. It was getting darker by that time, and the cold was even getting just a little mean. I told her it was time for us to go. She stood up on a chair.

"You never seen my hair," Susy said.

That was true. She was standing on a chair, but still, when she unclipped her buns the hair reached all the way to the ground. Our eyes opened. You couldn't tell how much hair she had when it was rolled up so neatly. Then my brother Henry did something funny. He went up to the chair and said, "Jump on my shoulders." So she did that, and her hair reached down past his waist, and he started twirling, this way and that, so her hair was flung out from side to side.

"I always wondered what it was like to have long pretty hair," Henry says. Well we laughed. It was a funny sight, the way he did it. The next morning we got up and took leave of those people. 20

On to greener pastures, as they say. It was down through Spokane and across Idaho then Montana and very soon we were racing the weather right along under the Canadian border through Columbus, Des Lacs, and then we were in Bottineau County and soon home. We'd made most of the trip, that summer, without putting up the car hood at all. We got home just in time, it turned out, for the army to remember Henry had signed up to join it.

I don't wonder that the army was so glad to get my brother that they turned him into a Marine. He was built like a brick outhouse anyway. We liked to tease him that they really wanted him for his Indian nose. He had a nose big and sharp as a hatchet, like the nose on Red Tomahawk, the Indian who killed Sitting Bull, whose profile is on signs all along the North Dakota highways. Henry went off to training camp, came home once during Christmas, then the next thing you know we got an overseas letter from him. It was 1970, and he said he was stationed up in the northern hill country. Whereabouts I did not know. He wasn't such a hot letter writer, and only got off two before the enemy caught him. I could never keep it straight, which direction those good Vietnam soldiers were from.

I wrote him back several times, even though I didn't know if those letters would get through. I kept him informed all about the car. Most of the time I had it up on blocks in the yard or half taken apart, because that long trip did a hard job on it under the hood.

I always had good luck with numbers, and never worried about the draft myself. I never even had to think about what my number was. But Henry was never lucky in the same way as me. It was at least three years before Henry came home. By then I guess the whole war was solved in the government's mind, but for him it would keep on going. In those years I'd put his car into almost perfect shape. I always thought of it as his car while he was gone, even though when he left he said, "Now it's yours," and threw me his key.

"Thanks for the extra key," I'd said. "I'll put it up in your drawer just in case
I need it." He laughed. 25

* * *

When he came home, though, Henry was very different, and I'll say this: the change was no good. You could hardly expect him to change for the better, I know. But he was quiet, so quiet, and never comfortable sitting still anywhere but always up and moving around. I thought back to times we'd sat still for whole afternoons, never moving a muscle, just shifting our weight along the ground, talking to whoever sat with us, watching things. He'd always had a joke, then, too, and now you couldn't get him to laugh, or when he did it was more the sound of a man choking, a sound that stopped up the throats of other people around him. They got to leaving him alone most of the time, and I didn't blame them. It was a fact: Henry was jumpy and mean.

I'd bought a color TV set for my mom and the rest of us while Henry was away. Money still came very easy. I was sorry I'd ever fought it though, because of Henry. I was also sorry I'd bought color, because with black-and-white the pictures seem older and farther away. But what are you going to do? He sat in front of it, watching it, and that was the only time he was completely still.

But it was the kind of stillness that you see in a rabbit when it freezes and before it will bolt. He was not easy. He sat in his chair gripping the armrests with all his might, as if the chair itself was moving at a high speed and if he let go at all he would rocket forward and maybe crash right through the set.

Once I was in the room watching TV with Henry and I heard his teeth click at something. I looked over, and he'd bitten through his lip. Blood was going down his chin. I tell you right then I wanted to smash that tube to pieces. I went over to it but Henry must have known what I was up to. He rushed from his chair and shoved me out of the way, against the wall. I told myself he didn't know what he was doing.

My mom came in, turned the set off real quiet, and told us she had made something for supper. So we went and sat down. There was still blood going down Henry's chin, but he didn't notice it and no one said anything even though every time he took a bite of his bread his blood fell onto it until he was eating his own blood mixed in with the food.

* * *

While Henry was not around we talked about what was going to happen to him. There were no Indian doctors on the reservation, and my mom couldn't come around to trusting the old man, Moses Pillager, because he courted her long ago and was jealous of her husbands. He might take revenge through her son. We were afraid that if we brought Henry to a regular hospital they would keep him. 30

"They don't "fix them in those places," Mom said; "they just give them drugs."

"We wouldn't get him there in the first place," I agreed, "so let's just forget about it."

Then I thought about the car.

Henry had not even looked at the car since he'd gotten home, though like I said, it was in tip-top condition and ready to drive. I thought the car might bring the old Henry back somehow. So I bided my time and waited for my chance to interest him in the vehicle.

One night Henry was off somewhere. I took myself a hammer. I went out to that car and I did a number on its underside. Whacked it up. Bent the tail pipe double. Ripped the muffler loose. By the time I was done with the car it looked worse than any typical Indian car that has been driven all its life on reservation roads, which they always say are like government promises—full of holes. It just about hurt me, I'll tell you that! I threw dirt in the carburetor and I ripped all the electric tape off the seats. I made it look just as beat up as I could. Then I sat back and waited for Henry to find it. 35

Still, it took him over a month. That was all right, because it was just getting warm enough; not melting, but warm enough to work outside.

"Lyman," he says, walking in one day, "that red car looks like shit."

"Well it's old," I says. "You got to expect that."

"No way!" says Henry. "That car's a classic! But you went and ran the piss right put of it, Lyman, and you know it don't deserve that. I kept that car in A-one shape. You don't remember. You're too young. But when I left, that car was running like a watch. Now I don't even know if I can get it to start again, let alone get it anywhere near its old condition."

"Well you try," I said, like I was getting mad, "but I say it's a piece of junk." 40

Then I walked out before he could realize I knew he'd strung together more than six words at once.

* * *

After that I thought he'd freeze himself to death working on that car. He was out there all day, and at night he rigged up a little lamp, ran a cord out the window, and had himself some light to see by while he worked. He was better than he had been before, but that's still not saying much. It was easier for him to do the things the rest of us did. He ate more slowly and didn't jump up and down during the meal to get this or that or look out the window. I put my hand in the back of the TV set, I admit, and fiddled around with it good, so that it was almost impossible now to get a clear picture. He didn't look at it very often anyway. He was always out with that car or going off to get parts for it. By the time it was really melting outside, he had it fixed.

I had been feeling down in the dumps about Henry around this time. We had always been together before. Henry and Lyman. But he was such a loner now that I didn't know how to take it. So I jumped at the chance one day when Henry seemed friendly. It's not that he smiled or any- thing. He just said, "Let's take that old shitbox for a spin." Just the way he said it made me think he could be coming around.

We went out to the car. It was spring. The sun was shining very bright. My only sister, Bonita, who was just eleven years old, came out and made us stand together for a picture. Henry leaned his elbow on the red car's windshield, and he took his other arm and put it over my shoulder, very carefully, as though it was heavy for him to lift and he didn't want to bring the weight down all at once.

"Smile," Bonita said, and he did. 45

* * *

That picture. I never look at it anymore. A few months ago, I don't know why, I got his picture out and tacked it on the wall. I felt good about Henry at the time, close to him. I felt good having his picture on the wall, until one night when I was looking at television. I was a little drunk and stoned. I looked up at the wall and Henry was staring at me. I don't know what it was, but his smile had changed, or maybe it was gone. All I know is I couldn't stay in the same room with that picture. I was shaking. I got up, closed the door, and went into the kitchen. A little later my friend Ray came over and we both went back into that room. We put the picture in a brown bag, folded the bag over and over tightly, then put it way back in a closet.

I still see that picture now, as if it tugs at me, whenever I pass that closet door. The picture is very clear in my mind. It was so sunny that day Henry had to squint against the glare. Or maybe the camera Bonita held flashed like a mirror, blinding him, before she snapped the picture. My face is right out in the sun, big and round. But he might have drawn back, because the shadows on his face are deep as holes. There are two shadows curved like little hooks around the ends of his smile, as if to frame it and try to keep it there— that one, first smile that looked like it might have hurt his face. He has his field jacket on and the worn-in clothes he'd come back in and kept wearing ever since. After Bonita took the picture, she went into the house and we got into the car. There was a full cooler in the trunk. We started off, east, toward Pembina and the Red River because Henry said he wanted to see the high water.

* * *

The trip over there was beautiful. When everything starts changing, drying up, clearing off, you feel like your whole life is starting. Henry felt it, too. The top was down and the car hummed like a top. He'd really put it back in shape, even the tape on the seats was very carefully put down and glued back in layers. It's not that he smiled again or even joked, but his face looked to me as if it was clear, more peaceful. It looked as though he wasn't thinking of anything in particular except the bare fields and windbreaks and houses we were passing.

The river was high and full of winter trash when we got there. The sun was still out, but it was colder by the river. There were still little clumps of dirty snow here and there on the banks. The water hadn't gone over the banks yet, but it would, you could tell. It was just at its limit, hard swollen, glossy like an old gray scar. We made ourselves a fire, and we sat down and watched the current go. As I watched it I felt something squeezing inside me and tightening and trying to let go all at the same time. I knew I was not just feeling it myself; I knew I was feeling what Henry was going through at that moment. Except that I couldn't stand it, the closing and opening. I jumped to my feet. I took Henry by the shoulders, and I started shaking him. "Wake up," I says, "wake up, wake up, wake up!" I didn't know what had come over me. I sat down beside him again.

His face was totally white and hard. Then it broke, like stones break all of
a sudden when water boils up inside them. 50

"I know it," he says. "I know it. I can't help it. It's no use."

We start talking. He said he knew what I'd done with the car. It was obvious it had been whacked out of shape and not just neglected. He said he wanted to give the car to me for good now, it was no use. He said he'd fixed it just to give it back and I should take it.

"No way," I says, "I don't want it." "That's okay," he says, "you take it."

"I don't want it, though," I says back to him, and then to emphasize, just to emphasize, you understand, I touch his shoulder. He slaps my hand off.

"Take that car," he says. 55

"No," I say. "Make me," I say, and then he grabs my jacket and rips the arm loose. That jacket is a class act, suede with tags and zippers. I push Henry backwards, off the log. He jumps up and bowls me over. We go down in a clinch and come up swinging hard, for all we're worth, with our fists. He socks my jaw so hard I feel like it swings loose. Then. I'm at his rib cage and. land a good one under his chin so his head snaps back. He's dazzled. He looks at me and I look at him and then his eyes are full of tears and blood and at first I think he's crying. But no, he's laughing. "Ha! Ha!" he says. "Ha! Ha! Take good care of it."

"Okay," I says. "Okay, no problem; Ha! Ha!"

I can't help it, and I start laughing, too. My face feels fat and strange, and after a while I get a beer from the cooler in the trunk, and when I hand it to Henry he takes his shirt and wipes my germs off. "Hoof-and-mouth disease," he says. For some reason this cracks me up, and so we're really laughing for a while, and then we drink all the rest of the beers one by one and throw them in the river and see how far, how fast, the current takes them before they fill up and sink.

"You want to go on back?" I ask after a while. "Maybe we could snag a couple nice Kashpaw girls."

He says nothing. But I can his mood is turning again.

"They're all crazy, the girls up here, every damn one of them."

"You're crazy too," I say, to jolly him up. "Crazy Lamartine boys!"

He looks as though he will take this wrong at first. His face twists, then clears, and he jumps up on his feet. "That's right!" he says. "Crazier 'n hell. Crazy Indians!"

I think it's the old Henry again. He throws off his jacket and starts springing his legs up from the knees like a fancy dancer. He's down doing something between a grass dance and a bunny hop, no kind of dance I ever saw before, but neither has anyone else on all this green growing earth. He's wild. He wants to pitch whoopee![2] He's up and at me and all over. All this time I'm laughing so hard, so hard my belly is getting tied up in a knot.

"Got to cool me off!" he shouts all of a sudden. Then he runs over to the river and jumps in.

There's boards and other things in the current. It's so high. No sound comes from the river after the splash he makes, so I run right over. I look around. It's getting dark. I see he's halfway across the water already, and I know he didn't swim there but the current took him. It's far. I hear his voice, though, very clearly across it.

"My boots are filling," he says.

He says this in a normal voice, like he just noticed and he doesn't know what to think of it. Then he's gone. A branch comes by. Another branch. And I go in.

* * *

By the time I get out of the river, off the snag I pulled myself onto, the sun is down. I walk back to the car, turn on the high beams, and drive it up the bank. I put it in first gear and then I take my foot off the clutch. I get out, close the door, and watch it plow softly into the water. The headlights reach in as they go down, searching, still lighted even after the water swirls over the back end. I wait. The wires short out. It is all finally dark. And then there is only the water, the sound of it going and running and going and running and running.

* * *

[2]*pitch whoopee:* An expression denoting wild celebration; sometimes has a sexual connotation, as in the song, "Makin' whoopee."

Zora Neale Hurston (1891–1960)

Sweat (1926)

It was eleven o'clock of a Spring night in Florida. It was Sunday. Any other night, Delia Jones would have been in bed for two hours by this time. But she was a wash-woman, and Monday morning meant a great deal to her. So she collected the soiled clothes on Saturday when she returned the clean things. Sunday night after church, she sorted them and put the white things to soak. It saved her almost a half day's start. A great hamper in the bedroom held the clothes that she brought home. It was so much neater than a number of bundles lying around.

She squatted in the kitchen floor beside the great pile of clothes, sorting them into small heaps according to color, and humming a song in a mournful key, but wondering through it all where Sykes, her husband, had gone with her horse and buckboard.[1]

Just then something long, round, limp and black fell upon her shoulders and slithered to the floor beside her. A great terror took hold of her. It softened her knees and dried her mouth so that it was a full minute before she could cry out or move. Then she saw that it was the big bull whip her husband liked to carry when he drove.

She lifted her eyes to the door and saw him standing there bent over with laughter at her fright. She screamed at him.

"Sykes, what you throw dat whip on me like dat? You know it would skeer me–looks just like a snake, an' you knows how skeered Ah is of snakes." 5

"Course Ah knowed it! That's how come Ah done it." He slapped his leg with his hand and almost rolled on the ground in his mirth. "If you such a big fool dat you got to have a fit over a earth worm or a string, Ah don't keer how bad Ah skeer you."

"You aint got no business doing it. Gawd knows it's a sin. Some day Ah'm goin' tuh drop dead from some of yo' foolishness. 'Nother thing, where you been wid mah rig? Ah feeds dat pony. He aint fuh you to be drivin' wid no bull whip."

"You sho is one aggravatin' nigger woman!" he declared and stepped into the room. She resumed her work and did not answer him at once. "Ah done tole you time and again to keep them white folks' clothes outa dis house."

He picked up the whip and glared down at her. Delia went on with her work. She went out into the yard and returned with a galvanized tub and set it on the washbench. She saw that Sykes had kicked all of the clothes together again, and now stood in her way truculently, his whole manner hoping, praying, for an argument. But she walked calmly around him and commenced to re-sort the things.

"Next time, Ah'm gointer kick 'em outdoors," he threatened as he struck a match along the leg of his corduroy breeches. 10

---

[1] *buckboard:* A horse-drawn, four-wheeled carriage with a frontal board attached to the axle instead of springs.

Delia never looked up from her work, and her thin, stooped shoulders sagged further. "Ah aint for no fuss t'night Sykes. Ah just come from taking sacrament at the church house."

He snorted scornfully. "Yeah, you just come from de church house on a Sunday night, but heah you is gone to work on them clothes. You ain't nothing but a hypocrite. One of them amen-corner Christians[2]–sing, whoop, and shout, then come home and wash white folks clothes on the Sabbath."

He stepped roughly upon the whitest pile of things, kicking them helter-skelter as he crossed the room. His wife gave a little scream of dismay, and quickly gathered them together again.

"Sykes, you quit grindin' dirt into these clothes! How can Ah git through by Sat'day if Ah don't start on Sunday?"

"Ah don't keer if you never git through. Anyhow, Ah done promised Gawd and a couple of other men, Ah aint gointer have it in mah house. Don't gimme no lip neither, else Ah'll throw 'em out and put mah fist up side yo' head to
boot." 15

Delia's habitual meekness seemed to slip from her shoulders like a blown scarf. She was on her feet; her poor little body, her bare knuckly hands bravely defying the strapping hulk before her.

"Looka heah, Sykes, you done gone too fur. Ah been married to you fur fifteen years, and Ah been takin' in washin' for fifteen years. Sweat, sweat, sweat! Work and sweat, cry and sweat, pray and sweat!"

"What's that got to do with me?" he asked brutally.

"What's it got to do with you, Sykes? Mah tub of suds is filled yo' belly with vittles more times than yo' hands is filled it. Mah sweat is done paid for this house and Ah reckon Ah kin keep on sweatin' in it."

She seized the iron skillet from the stove and struck a defensive pose, which act surprised him greatly, coming from her. It cowed him and he did not strike
her as he usually did. 20

"Naw you won't," she panted, "that ole snaggle-toothed black woman you runnin' with aint comin' heah to pile up on mah sweat and blood. You aint paid for nothin' on this place, and Ah'm gointer stay right heah till Ah'm toted out foot foremost."

"Well, you better quit gittin' me riled up, else they'll be totin' you out sooner than you expect. Ah'm so tired of you Ah don't know whut to do. Gawd! how Ah hates skinny wimmen!"

A little awed by this new Delia, he sidled out of the door and slammed the back gate after him. He did not say where he had gone, but she knew too well. She knew very well that he would not return until nearly daybreak also. Her work over, she went on to bed but not to sleep at once. Things had come to a pretty pass![3]

---

[2]*amen-corner Christians:* A term describing the worshippers who congregated in a specific section of the church close to the pulpit and who were known to engage most vocally in the service (by shouting "Amen!," for example).

[3]*a pretty pass:* A difficult situation.

She lay awake, gazing upon the debris that cluttered their matrimonial trail. Not an image left standing along the way. Anything like flowers had long ago been drowned in the salty stream that had been pressed from her heart. Her tears, her sweat, her blood. She had brought love to the union and he had brought a longing after the flesh. Two months after the wedding, he had given her the first brutal beating. She had the memory of his numerous trips to Orlando with all of his wages when he had returned to her penniless, even before the first year had passed. She was young and soft then, but now she thought of her knotty, muscled limbs, her harsh knuckly hands, and drew herself up into an unhappy little ball in the middle of the big feather bed. Too late now to hope for love, even if it were not Bertha it would be someone else. This case differed from the others only in that she was bolder than the others. Too late for everything except her little home. She had built it for her old days, and planted one by one the trees and flowers there. It was lovely to her, lovely.

Somehow, before sleep came, she found herself saying aloud: "Oh well, whatever goes over the Devil's back, is got to come under his belly.[4] Sometime or ruther, Sykes, like everybody else, is gointer reap his sowing." After that she was able to build a spiritual earthworks against her husband. His shells could no longer reach her. Amen. She went to sleep and slept until he announced his presence in bed by kicking her feet and rudely snatching the covers away. 25

"Gimme some kivah heah, an' git yo' damn foots over on yo' own side! Ah oughter mash you in yo' mouf fuh drawing dat skillet on me."

Delia went clear to the rail without answering him. A triumphant indifference to all that he was or did.

* * *

The week was as full of work for Delia as all other weeks, and Saturday found her behind her little pony, collecting and delivering clothes.

It was a hot, hot day near the end of July. The village men on Joe Clarke's porch even chewed cane listlessly. They did not hurl the cane-knots as usual. They let them dribble over the edge of the porch. Even conversation had collapsed under the heat.

"Heah come Delia Jones," Jim Merchant said, as the shaggy pony came 'round the bend of the road toward them. The rusty buckboard was heaped with baskets of crisp, clean laundry. 30

"Yep," Joe Lindsay agreed. "Hot or col', rain or shine, jes ez reg'lar ez de weeks roll roun' Delia carries 'em an' fetches 'em on Sat'day."

"She better if she wanter eat," said Moss. "Syke Jones aint wuth de shot an' powder hit would tek tuh kill 'em. Not to huh he aint."

---

[4] *". . . whatever goes over the Devil's back, is got to come under his belly":* Expression meaning that people become victims of the harm they do to others.

"He sho' aint," Walter Thomas chimed in. "It's too bad, too, cause she wuz a right pritty lil trick when he got huh. Ah'd uh mah'ied huh mahseff if he hadnter beat me to it."

Delia nodded briefly at the men as she drove past.

"Too much knockin' will ruin any 'oman. He done beat huh 'nough tuh kill three women, let 'lone change they looks," said Elijah Moseley. "How Syke kin stommuck dat big black greasy Mogul he's layin' roun wid, gits me. Ah swear dat eight-rock couldn't kiss a sardine can Ah done throwed out de back do' 'way las' yeah."

"Aw, she's fat, thass how come. He's allus been crazy 'bout fat women," put in Merchant. "He'd a' been tied up wid one long time ago if he could a' found one tuh have him. Did Ah tell yuh 'bout him come sidlin' roun' mah wife–bringin' her a basket uh pecans outa his yard fuh a present? Yessir, mah wife! She tol' him tuh take 'em right straight back home, cause Delia works so hard ovah dat washtub she reckon everything on de place taste lak sweat an' soapsuds. Ah jus' wisht Ah'd a' caught 'im 'dere! Ah'd a' made his hips ketch on fiah down dat shell road."

"Ah know he done it, too. Ah sees 'im grinnin' at every 'oman dat passes," Walter Thomas said. "But even so, he useter eat some mighty big hunks uh humble pie tuh git dat lil 'oman he got. She wuz ez pritty ez a speckled pup! Dat wuz fifteen yeahs ago. He useter be so skeered uh losin' huh, she could make him do some parts of a husband's duty. Dey never wuz de same in de mind."

"There oughter be a law about him," said Lindsay. "He aint fit tuh carry guts tuh a bear."

Clarke spoke for the first time. "Taint no law on earth dat kin make a man be decent if it aint in 'im. There's plenty men dat takes a wife lak dey do a joint uh sugar-cane. It's round, juicy an' sweet when dey gits it. But dey squeeze an' grind, squeeze an' grind an' wring tell dey wring every drop uh pleasure dat's in 'em out. When dey's satisfied dat dey is wrung dry, dey treats 'em jes lak dey do a cane-chew. Dey throws em away. Dey knows whut dey is doin' while dey is at it, an' hates theirselves fuh it but they keeps on hangin' after huh tell she's empty. Den dey hates huh fuh bein' a cane-chew an' in de way."

"We oughter take Syke an' dat stray 'oman uh his'n down in Lake Howell swamp an' lay on de rawhide[5] till they cain't say Lawd a' mussy.' He allus wuz uh ovahbearin' niggah, but since dat white 'oman from up north done teached 'im how to run a automobile, he done got too biggety to live–an' we oughter kill 'im," Old Man Anderson advised.

A grunt of approval went around the porch. But the heat was melting their civic virtue, and Elijah Moseley began to bait Joe Clarke.

"Come on, Joe, git a melon outa dere an' slice it up for yo' customers. We'se all sufferin' wid de heat. De bear's done got me!"

"Thass right, Joe, a watermelon is jes' whut Ah needs tuh cure de eppizudicks," Walter Thomas joined forces with Moseley. "Come on dere, Joe. We all

---

[5] *"lay on de rawhide"*: to whip; a reference to a whip made from raw animal skin (hide).

is steady customers an' you aint set us up in a long time. Ah chooses dat long, bowlegged Floridy favorite."

"A god, an' be dough. You all gimme twenty cents and slice way," Clarke retorted. "Ah needs a col' slice m'self. Heah, everybody chip in. Ah'll lend y'll mah meat knife."

The money was quickly subscribed and the huge melon brought forth. At that moment, Sykes and Bertha arrived. A determined silence fell on the porch and the melon was put away again.

Merchant snapped down the blade of his jackknife and moved toward the store door.

"Come on in, Joe, an' gimme a slab uh sow belly an' uh pound uh coffee–almost fuhgot 'twas Sat'day. Got to git on home." Most of the men left also.

Just then Delia drove past on her way home, as Sykes was ordering magnificently for Bertha. It pleased him for Delia to see.

"Git whutsoever yo' heart desires, Honey. Wait a minute, Joe. Give huh two bottles uh strawberry soda-water, uh quart uh parched ground-peas, an' a block uh chewin' gum."

With all this they left the store, with Sykes reminding Bertha that this was his town and she could have it if she wanted it.

The men returned soon after they left, and held their watermelon feast.

"Where did Syke Jones git da 'oman from nohow?" Lindsay asked.

"Ovah Apopka. Guess dey musta been cleanin' out de town when she lef'. She don't look lak a thing but a hunk uh liver wid hair on it."

"Well, she sho' kin squall," Dave Carter contributed. "When she gits ready tuh laff, she jes' opens huh mouf an' latches it back tuh de las' notch. No ole grandpa alligator down in Lake Bell ain't got nothin' on huh."

* * *

Bertha had been in town three months now. Sykes was still paying her room rent at Della Lewis'–the only house in town that would have taken her in. Sykes took her frequently to Winter Park to "stomps." He still assured her that he was the swellest man in the state.

"Sho' you kin have dat lil' ole house soon's Ah kin git dat 'oman outa dere. Everything b'longs tuh me an' you sho' kin have it. Ah sho' 'bominates uh skinny 'oman. Lawdy, you sho' is got one portly shape on you! You kin git anything you wants. Dis is mah town an' you sho' kin have it."

Delia's work-worn knees crawled over the earth in Gethsemane and up the rocks of Calvary many, many times during these months. She avoided the villagers and meeting places in her efforts to be blind and deaf. But Bertha nullified this to a degree, by coming to Delia's house to call Sykes out to her at the gate.

Delia and Sykes fought all the time now with no peaceful interludes. They slept and ate in silence. Two or three times Delia had attempted a timid friendliness, but she was repulsed each time. It was plain that the breaches must remain agape.

The sun had burned July to August. The heat streamed down like a million hot arrows, smiting all things living upon the earth. Grass withered, leaves browned, snakes went blind in shedding and men and dogs went mad. Dog days!

Delia came home one day and found Sykes there before her. She wondered, but started to go on into the house without speaking, even though he was standing in the kitchen door and she must either stoop under his arm or ask him to move. He made no room for her. She noticed a soap box beside the steps, but paid no particular attention to it, knowing that he must have brought it there. As she was stooping to pass under his outstretched arm, he suddenly pushed her backward, laughingly.

"Look in de box dere Delia, Ah done brung yuh somethin'!"

She nearly fell upon the box in her stumbling, and when she saw what it held, she all but fainted outright.

"Syke! Syke, mah Gawd! You take dat rattlesnake 'way from heah! You gottuh. Oh, Jesus, have mussy!"

"Ah aint gut tuh do nuthin' uh de kin'–fact is Ah aint got tuh do nothin' but die. Taint no use uh you puttin' on airs makin' out lak you skeered uh dat snake–he's gointer stay right heah tell he die. He wouldn't bite me cause Ah knows how tuh handle 'im. Nohow he wouldn't risk breakin' out his fangs 'gin yo' skinny laigs."

"Naw, now Syke, don't keep dat thing 'roun' heah tuh skeer me tuh death. You knows Ah'm even feared uh earth worms. Thass de biggest snake Ah evah did see. Kill 'im Syke, please."

"Doan ast me tuh do nothin' fuh yuh. Goin' roun' trying' tuh be so damn asterperious.[6] Naw, Ah aint gonna kill it. Ah think uh damn sight mo' uh him dan you! Dat's a nice snake an' anybody doan lak 'im kin jes' hit de grit."

The village soon heard that Sykes had the snake, and came to see and ask questions.

"How de hen-fire did you ketch dat six-foot rattler, Syke?" Thomas asked.

"He's full uh frogs so he caint hardly move, thass how. Ah eased up on 'm. But Ah'm a snake charmer an' knows how tuh handle 'em. Shux, dat aint nothin'. Ah could ketch one eve'y day if Ah so wanted tuh."

"Whut he needs is a heavy hick'ry club leaned real heavy on his head. Dat's de bes 'way tuh charm a rattlesnake."

"Naw, Walt, y'll jes' don't understand dese diamon' backs lak Ah do," said Sykes in a superior tone of voice.

The village agreed with Walter, but the snake stayed on. His box remained by the kitchen door with its screen wire covering. Two or three days later it had digested its meal of frogs and literally came to life. It rattled at every movement in the kitchen or the yard. One day as Delia came down the kitchen steps she saw his chalky-white fangs curved like scimitars hung in the wire meshes. This time she did not run away with averted eyes as usual. She stood for a long

[6]*asterperious:* slang for *conceited.*

time in the doorway in a red fury that grew bloodier for every second that she regarded the creature that was her torment.

That night she broached the subject as soon as Sykes sat down to the table.

"Syke, Ah wants you tuh take dat snake 'way fum heah. You done starved me an' Ah put up widcher, you done beat me an Ah took dat, but you done kilt all mah insides bringin' dat varmint heah."

Sykes poured out a saucer full of coffee and drank it deliberately before he answered her. 75

"A whole lot Ah keer 'bout how you feels inside uh out. Dat snake aint goin' no damn wheah till Ah gits ready fuh 'im tuh go. So fur as beatin' is concerned, yuh aint took near all dat you gointer take ef yuh stay 'roun' me."

Delia pushed back her plate and got up from the table. "Ah hates you, Sykes," she said calmly. "Ah hates you tuh de same degree dat Ah useter love yuh. Ah done took an' took till mah belly is full up tuh mah neck. Dat's de reason Ah got mah letter fum de church an' moved mah membership tuh Woodbridge—so Ah don't haf tuh take no sacrament wid yuh. Ah don't wantuh see yuh 'roun' me atall. Lay 'roun' wid dat 'oman all yuh wants tuh, but gwan 'way fum me an' mah house. Ah hates yuh lak uh suck-egg dog."

Sykes almost let the huge wad of corn bread and collard greens he was chewing fall out of his mouth in amazement. He had a hard time whipping himself up to the proper fury to try to answer Delia.

"Well, Ah'm glad you does hate me. Ah'm sho' tiahed uh you hangin' ontuh me. Ah don't want yuh. Look at yuh stringey ole neck! Yo' rawbony laigs an' arms is enough tuh cut uh man tuh death. You looks jes' lak de devvul's doll-baby tuh me. You cain't hate me no worse dan Ah hates you. Ah been hatin' you fuh years."

"Yo' ole black hide don't look lak nothin' tuh me, but uh passle uh wrinkled up rubber, wid yo' big ole yeahs flappin' on each side lak uh paih uh buzzard wings. Don't think Ah'm gointuh be run 'way fum mah house neither. Ah'm goin' tuh de white folks bout you, mah young man, de very nex' time you lay yo' han's on me. Mah cup is done run ovah."[7] Delia said this with no signs of fear and Sykes departed from the house, threatening her, but made not the slightest move to carry out any of them. 80

That night he did not return at all, and the next day being Sunday, Delia was glad she did not have to quarrel before she hitched up her pony and drove the four miles to Woodbridge.

She stayed to the night service—"love feast"—which was very warm and full of spirit. In the emotional winds her domestic trials were borne far and wide so that she sang as she drove homeward.

"Jurden water, black an' col'

---

[7] *"Mah cup is done run ovah"*: a reference to the Hebrew psalm, "My cup runneth over," usually meaning the speaker feels overwhelmed by having too much of life's blessings. Here, Delia is referencing those blessings with sarcasm.

Chills de body, not de soul
An' Ah wantah cross Jurden in uh calm time."

She came from the barn to the kitchen door and stopped.

"Whut's de mattah, ol' satan, you aint kickin' up yo' racket?" She addressed the snake's box. Complete silence. She went on into the house with a new hope in its birth struggles. Perhaps her threat to go to the white folks had frightened Sykes! Perhaps he was sorry! Fifteen years of misery and suppression had brought Delia to the place where she would hope anything that looked towards a way over or through her wall of inhibitions.

She felt in the match safe behind the stove at once for a match. There was only one there.

"Dat niggah wouldn't fetch nothin' heah tuh save his rotten neck, but he kin run thew whut Ah brings quick enough. Now he done toted off nigh on tuh haff uh box uh matches. He done had dat 'oman heah in mah house, too."

Nobody but a woman could tell how she knew this even before she struck the match. But she did and it put her into a new fury.

Presently she brought in the tubs to put the white things to soak. This time she decided she need not bring the hamper out of the bedroom; she would go in there and do the sorting. She picked up the pot-bellied lamp and went in. The room was small and the hamper stood hard by the foot of the white iron bed. She could sit and reach through the bedposts–resting as she worked.

"Ah wantah cross Jurden in uh calm time," she was singing again. The mood of the "love feast" had returned. She threw back the lid of the basket almost gaily. Then, moved by both horror and terror, she sprang back toward the door. There lay the snake in the basket! He moved sluggishly at first, but even as she turned round and round, jumped up and down in an insanity of fear, he began to stir vigorously. She saw him pouring his awful beauty from the basket upon the bed, then she seized the lamp and ran as fast as she could to the kitchen. The wind from the open door blew out the light and the darkness added to her terror. She sped to the darkness of the yard, slamming the door after her before she thought to set down the lamp. She did not feel safe even on the ground, so she climbed up in the hay barn.

There for an hour or more she lay sprawled upon the hay a gibbering wreck.

Finally, she grew quiet, and after that, coherent thought. With this, stalked through her a cold, bloody rage. Hours of this. A period of introspection, a space of retrospection, then a mixture of both. Out of this an awful calm.

"Well, Ah done de bes' Ah could. If things aint right, Gawd knows taint mah fault."

She went to sleep–a twitch sleep–and woke up to a faint gray sky. There was a loud hollow sound below. She peered out. Sykes was at the wood-pile, demolishing a wire-covered box.

He hurried to the kitchen door, but hung outside there some minutes before he entered, and stood some minutes more inside before he closed it after him.

The gray in the sky was spreading. Delia descended without fear now, and crouched beneath the low bedroom window. The drawn shade shut out the dawn, shut in the night. But the thin walls held back no sound.

"Dat ol' scratch[8] is woke up now!" She mused at the tremendous whirr inside, which every woodsman knows, is one of the sound illusions. The rattler is a ventriloquist. His whirr sounds to the right, to the left, straight ahead, behind, close under foot–everywhere but where it is. Woe to him who guesses wrong unless he is prepared to hold up his end of the argument! Sometimes he strikes without rattling at all.

Inside, Sykes heard nothing until he knocked a pot lid off the stove while trying to reach the match safe in the dark. He had emptied his pockets at Bertha's.

The snake seemed to wake up under the stove and Sykes made a quick leap into the bedroom. In spite of the gin he had had, his head was clearing now.

"'Mah Gawd!" he chattered, "ef Ah could on'y strack uh light!"

The rattling ceased for a moment as he stood paralyzed. He waited. It seemed that the snake waited also.

"Oh, fuh de light! Ah thought he'd be too sick"–Sykes was muttering to himself when the whirr began again, closer, right underfoot this time. Long before this, Sykes' ability to think had been flattened down to primitive instinct and he leaped–onto the bed.

Outside Delia heard a cry that might have come from a maddened chimpanzee, a stricken gorilla. All the terror, all the horror, all the rage that man possibly could express, without a recognizable human sound.

A tremendous stir inside there, another series of animal screams, the intermittent whirr of the reptile. The shade torn violently down from the window, letting in the red dawn, a huge brown hand seizing the window stick, great dull blows upon the wooden floor punctuating the gibberish of sound long after the rattle of the snake had abruptly subsided. All this Delia could see and hear from her place beneath the window, and it made her ill. She crept over to the four-o'clocks and stretched herself on the cool earth to recover.

She lay there. "Delia. Delia!" She could hear Sykes calling in a most despairing tone as one who expected no answer. The sun crept on up, and he called. Delia could not move–her legs were gone flabby. She never moved, he called, and the sun kept rising.

"Mah Gawd!" She heard him moan, "Mah Gawd fum Heben!" She heard him stumbling about and got up from her flower-bed. The sun was growing warm. As she approached the door she heard him call out hopefully, "Delia, is dat you Ah heah?"

She saw him on his hands and knees as soon as she reached the door. He crept an inch or two toward her–all that he was able, and she saw his horribly swollen neck and his one open eye shining with hope. A surge of pity too strong to support bore her away from that eye that must, could not, fail to see the tubs.

[8]*ol' scratch:* the devil.

He would see the lamp. Orlando with its doctors was too far. She could scarcely reach the Chinaberry tree, where she waited in the growing heat while inside she knew the cold river was creeping up and up to extinguish that eye which must know by now that she knew.

* * *

Joyce Carol Oates (1938–)

Where Are You Going, Where Have You Been? (1966)

For Bob Dylan

Her name was Connie. She was fifteen and she had a quick nervous giggling habit of craning her neck to glance into mirrors, or checking other people's faces to make sure her own was all right. Her mother, who noticed everything and knew everything and who hadn't much reason any longer to look at her own face, always scolded Connie about it. "Stop gawking at yourself, who are you? You think you're so pretty?" she would say. Connie would raise her eyebrows at these familiar complaints and look right through her mother, into a shadowy vision of herself as she was right at that moment: she knew she was pretty and that was everything. Her mother had been pretty once too, if you could believe those old snapshots in the album, but now her looks were gone and that was why she was always after Connie.

"Why don't you keep your room clean like your sister? How've you got your hair fixed—what the hell stinks? Hair spray? You don't see your sister using that junk."

Her sister June was twenty-four and still lived at home. She was a secretary in the high school Connie attended, and if that wasn't bad enough—with her in the same building—she was so plain and chunky and steady that Connie had to hear her praised all the time by her mother and her mother's sisters. June did this, June did that, she saved money and helped clean the house and cooked and Connie couldn't do a thing, her mind was all filled with trashy daydreams. Their father was away at work most of the time and when he came home he wanted supper and he read the newspaper at supper and after supper he went to bed. He didn't bother talking much to them, but around his bent head Connie's mother kept picking at her until Connie wished her mother was dead and she herself was dead and it was all over. "She makes me want to throw up sometimes," she complained to her friends. She had a high, breathless, amused voice which made everything she said sound a little forced, whether it was sincere or not.

There was one good thing: June went places with girl friends of hers, girls who were just as plain and steady as she, and so when Connie wanted to do that her mother had no objections. The father of Connie's best girl friend drove the girls the three miles to town and left them off at a shopping plaza, so that they could walk through the stores or go to a movie, and when he came to pick them up again at eleven he never bothered to ask what they had done.

They must have been familiar sights, walking around that shopping plaza in their shorts and flat ballerina slippers that always scuffed the sidewalk, with charm bracelets jingling on their thin wrists; they would lean together to whisper and laugh secretly if someone passed by who amused or interested them. Connie had long dark blond hair that drew anyone's eye to it, and she wore part of it pulled up on her head and puffed out and the rest of it she let fall down her back. She wore a pull-over jersey blouse that looked one way when she was at home and another way when she was away from home. Everything about her had two sides to it, one for home and one for anywhere that was not home: her walk that could be childlike and bobbing, or languid enough to make anyone think she was hearing music in her head, her mouth which was pale and smirking most of the time, but bright and pink on these evenings out, her laugh which was cynical and drawling at home—"Ha, ha, very funny"—but high-pitched and nervous anywhere else, like the jingling of the charms on her bracelet. 5

Sometimes they did go shopping or to a movie, but sometimes they went across the highway, ducking fast across the busy road, to a drive-in restaurant where older kids hung out. The restaurant was shaped like a big bottle, though squatter than a real bottle, and on its cap was a revolving figure of a grinning boy who held a hamburger aloft. One night in mid-summer they ran across, breathless with daring, and right away someone leaned out a car window and invited them over, but it was just a boy from high school they didn't like. It made them feel good to be able to ignore him. They went up through the maze of parked and cruising cars to the bright-lit, fly-infested restaurant, their faces pleased and expectant as if they were entering a sacred building that loomed out of the night to give them what haven and what blessing they yearned for. They sat at the counter and crossed their legs at the ankles, their thin shoulders rigid with excitement, and listened to the music that made everything so good: the music was always in the background like music at a church service, it was something to depend upon.

A boy named Eddie came in to talk with them. He sat backwards on his stool, turning himself jerkily around in semi-circles and then stopping and turning again, and after a while he asked Connie if she would like something to eat. She said she did and so she tapped her friend's arm on her way out—her friend pulled her face up into a brave droll look—and Connie said she would meet her at eleven, across the way. "I just hate to leave her like that," Connie said earnestly, but the boy said that she wouldn't be alone for long. So they went out to his car and on the way Connie couldn't help but let her eyes wander over the windshields and faces all around her, her face gleaming with a joy that had nothing to do with Eddie or even this place; it might have been the music. She drew her shoulders up and sucked in her breath with the pure pleasure of being alive, and just at that moment she happened to glance at a face just a few feet from hers. It was a boy with shaggy black hair, in a convertible jalopy painted gold. He stared at her and then his lips widened into a grin. Connie slit her eyes at him and turned away, but she couldn't help glancing back and there he was still watching her. He wagged a finger and laughed and said, "Gonna get you, baby," and Connie turned away again without Eddie noticing anything.

She spent three hours with him, at the restaurant where they ate hamburgers and drank Cokes in wax cups that were always sweating, and then down an alley a mile or so away, and when he left her off at five to eleven only the movie house was still open at the plaza. Her girl friend was there, talking with a boy. When Connie came up the two girls smiled at each other and Connie said, "How was the movie?" and the girl said, "*You* should know." They rode off with the girl's father, sleepy and pleased, and Connie couldn't help but look at the darkened shopping plaza with its big empty parking lot and its signs that were faded and ghostly now, and over at the drive-in restaurant where cars were still circling tirelessly. She couldn't hear the music at this distance.

Next morning June asked her how the movie was and Connie said, "So-so."

She and that girl and occasionally another girl went out several times a week that way, and the rest of the time Connie spent around the house—it was summer vacation—getting in her mother's way and thinking, dreaming, about the boys she met. But all the boys fell back and dissolved into a single face that was not even a face, but an idea, a feeling, mixed up with the urgent insistent pounding of the music and the humid night air of July. Connie's mother kept dragging her back to the daylight by finding things for her to do or saying, suddenly, "What's this about the Pettinger girl?" 10

And Connie would say nervously, "Oh, her. That dope." She always drew thick clear lines between herself and such girls, and her mother was simple and kindly enough to believe her. Her mother was so simple, Connie thought, that it was maybe cruel to fool her so much. Her mother went scuffling around the house in old bedroom slippers and complained over the telephone to one sister about the other, then the other called up and the two of them complained about the third one. If June's name was mentioned her mother's tone was approving, and if Connie's name was mentioned it was disapproving. This did not really mean she disliked Connie and actually Connie thought that her mother preferred her to June because she was prettier, but the two of them kept up a pretense of exasperation, a sense that they were tugging and struggling over something of little value to either of them. Sometimes, over coffee, they were almost friends, but something would come up—some vexation that was like a fly buzzing suddenly around their heads—and their faces went hard with contempt.

One Sunday Connie got up at eleven—none of them bothered with church—and washed her hair so that it could dry all day long, in the sun. Her parents and sister were going to a barbecue at an aunt's house and Connie said no, she wasn't interested, rolling her eyes to let her mother know just what she thought of it. "Stay home alone then," her mother said sharply. Connie sat out back in a lawn chair and watched them drive away, her father quiet and bald, hunched around so that he could back the car out, her mother with a look that was still angry and not at all softened through the windshield, and in the back seat poor old June all dressed up as if she didn't know what a barbecue was, with all the running yelling kids and the flies. Connie sat with her eyes closed in the sun, dreaming and dazed with the warmth about her as if this were a kind of love, the caresses of love, and her mind slipped over onto thoughts of the boy she had been with the night before and how nice he had been, how sweet it always was, not the way someone like June would suppose but sweet, gentle, the way it was in movies and promised in songs; and when she opened her eyes she hardly knew where she was, the back yard ran off into weeds and a fence-line of trees and behind it the sky was perfectly blue and still. The asbestos "ranch house" that was now three years old startled her—it looked small. She shook her head as if to get awake.

It was too hot. She went inside the house and turned on the radio to drown out the quiet. She sat on the edge of her bed, barefoot, and listened for an hour and a half to a program called *XYZ Sunday Jamboree*, record after record of hard, fast, shrieking songs she sang along with, interspersed by exclamations from "Bobby King": "An' look here you girls at Napoleon's—Son and Charley want you to pay real close attention to this song coming up!"

And Connie paid close attention herself, bathed in a glow of slow-pulsed joy that seemed to rise mysteriously out of the music itself and lay languidly about the airless little room, breathed in and breathed out with each gentle rise and fall of her chest.

After a while she heard a car coming up the drive. She sat up at once, startled, because it couldn't be her father so soon. The gravel kept crunching all the way in from the road—the driveway was long—and Connie ran to the window. It was a car she didn't know. It was an open jalopy, painted a bright gold that caught the sunlight opaquely. Her heart began to pound and her fingers snatched at her hair, checking it, and she whispered "Christ. Christ," wondering how bad she looked. The car came to a stop at the side door and the horn sounded four short taps as if this were a signal Connie knew. 15

She went into the kitchen and approached the door slowly, then hung out the screen door, her bare toes curling down off the step. There were two boys in the car and now she recognized the driver: he had shaggy, shabby black hair that looked crazy as a wig and he was grinning at her.

"I ain't late, am I?" he said.

"Who the hell do you think you are?" Connie said.

"Toldja I'd be out, didn't I?"

"I don't even know who you are." 20

She spoke sullenly, careful to show no interest or pleasure, and he spoke in a fast bright monotone. Connie looked past him to the other boy, taking her time. He had fair brown hair, with a lock that fell onto his forehead. His sideburns gave him a fierce, embarrassed look, but so far he hadn't even bothered to glance at her. Both boys wore sunglasses. The driver's glasses were metallic and mirrored everything in miniature.

"You wanta come for a ride?" he said.

Connie smirked and let her hair fall loose over one shoulder.

"Don'tcha like my car? New paint job," he said. "Hey."

"What?" 25

"You're cute."

She pretended to fidget, chasing flies away from the door.

"Don'tcha believe me, or what?" he said.

"Look, I don't even know who you are," Connie said in disgust.

"Hey, Ellie's got a radio, see. Mine's broke down." He lifted his friend's arm and showed her the little transistor the boy was holding, and now Connie began to hear the music. It was the same program that was playing inside the
house. 30

"Bobby King?" she said.

"I listen to him all the time. I think he's great."

"He's kind of great," Connie said reluctantly.

"Listen, that guy's *great*. He knows where the action is."

Connie blushed a little, because the glasses made it impossible for her to see just what this boy was looking at. She couldn't decide if she liked him or if he was just a jerk, and so she dawdled in the doorway and wouldn't come down or
go back inside. She said, "What's all that stuff painted on your car?" 35

"Can'tcha read it?" He opened the door very carefully, as if he was afraid it might fall off. He slid out just as carefully, planting his feet firmly on the ground, the tiny metallic world in his glasses slowing down like gelatine hardening and in the midst of it Connie's bright green blouse. "This here is my name, to begin with," he said. ARNOLD FRIEND was written in tarlike black letters on the side, with a drawing of a round grinning face that reminded Connie of a pumpkin, except it wore sunglasses. "I wanta introduce myself, I'm Arnold Friend and that's my real name and I'm gonna be your friend, honey, and inside the car's Ellie Oscar, he's kinda shy." Ellie brought his transistor radio up to his shoulder and balanced it there. "Now these numbers are a secret code, honey," Arnold Friend explained. He read off the numbers 33, 19, 17 and raised his eyebrows at her to see what she thought of that, but she didn't think much of it. The left rear fender had been smashed and around it was written, on the gleaming gold background: DONE BY CRAZY WOMAN DRIVER. Connie had to laugh at that. Arnold Friend was pleased at her laughter and looked up at her. "Around the other side's a lot more—you wanta come and see them?"

"No."

"Why not?"

"Why should I?"

"Don'tcha wanta see what's on the car? Don'tcha wanta go for a ride?" 40

"I don't know."

"Why not?"

"I got things to do."

"Like what?"

"Things." 45

He laughed as if she had said something funny. He slapped his thighs. He was standing in a strange way, leaning back against the car as if he were balancing himself. He wasn't tall, only an inch or so taller than she would be if she came down to him. Connie liked the way he was dressed, which was the way all of them dressed: tight faded jeans stuffed into black, scuffed boots, a belt that pulled his waist in and showed how lean he was, and a white pull-over shirt that was a little soiled and showed the hard small muscles of his arms and shoulders. He looked as if he probably did hard work, lifting and carrying things. Even his neck looked muscular. And his face was a familiar face, somehow: the jaw and chin and cheeks slightly darkened, because he hadn't shaved for a day or two, and the nose long and hawk-like, sniffing as if she were a treat he was going to gobble up and it was all a joke.

"Connie, you ain't telling the truth. This is your day set aside for a ride with me and you know it," he said, still laughing. The way he straightened and recovered from his fit of laughing showed that it had been all fake.

"How do you know what my name is?" she said suspiciously.

"It's Connie."

"Maybe and maybe not." 50

"I know my Connie," he said, wagging his finger. Now she remembered him even better, back at the restaurant, and her cheeks warmed at the thought of how she sucked in her breath just at the moment she passed him—how she must have looked to him. And he had remembered her. "Ellie and I come out here especially for you," he said. "Ellie can sit in back. How about it?"

"Where?"

"Where what?"

"Where're we going?"

He looked at her. He took off the sunglasses and she saw how pale the skin around his eyes was, like holes that were not in shadow but instead in light. His eyes were chips of broken glass that catch the light in an amiable way. He smiled. It was as if the idea of going for a ride somewhere, to some place, was a new idea to him. 55

"Just for a ride, Connie sweetheart."

"I never said my name was Connie," she said.

"But I know what it is. I know your name and all about you, lots of things," Arnold Friend said. He had not moved yet but stood still leaning back against the side of his jalopy. "I took a special interest in you, such a pretty girl, and found out all about you like I know your parents and sister are gone somewheres and I know where and how long they're going to be gone, and I know who you were with last night, and your best girl friend's name is Betty. Right?"

He spoke in a simple lilting voice, exactly as if he were reciting the words to a song. His smile assured her that everything was fine. In the car Ellie turned up the volume on his radio and did not bother to look around at them.

"Ellie can sit in the back seat," Arnold Friend said. He indicated his friend with a casual jerk of his chin, as if Ellie did not count and she should not bother with him. 60

"How'd you find out all that stuff?" Connie said.

"Listen: Betty Schultz and Tony Fitch and Jimmy Pettinger and Nancy Pettinger," he said, in a chant. "Raymond Stanley and Bob Hutter—"

"Do you know all those kids?"

"I know everybody."

"Look, you're kidding. You're not from around here." 65

"Sure."

"But—how come we never saw you before?"

"Sure you saw me before," he said. He looked down at his boots, as if he were a little offended. "You just don't remember."

"I guess I'd remember you," Connie said.

"Yeah?" He looked up at this, beaming. He was pleased. He began to mark time with the music from Ellie's radio, tapping his fists lightly together. Connie looked away from his smile to the car, which was painted so bright it almost hurt her eyes to look at it. She looked at that name, ARNOLD FRIEND. And up at the front fender was an expression that was familiar—MAN THE FLYING SAUCERS. It was an expression kids had used the year before, but didn't use this year. She looked at it for a while as if the words meant something to her that she did not yet know. 70

"What're you thinking about? Huh?" Arnold Friend demanded. "Not worried about your hair blowing around in the car, are you?"

"No."

"Think I maybe can't drive good?"

"How do I know?"

"You're a hard girl to handle. How come?" he said. "Don't you know I'm your friend? Didn't you see me put my sign in the air when you walked by?" 75

"What sign?"

"My sign." And he drew an X in the air, leaning out toward her. They were maybe ten feet apart. After his hand fell back to his side the X was still in the air, almost visible. Connie let the screen door close and stood perfectly still inside it, listening to the music from her radio and the boy's blend together. She stared at Arnold Friend. He stood there so stiffly relaxed, pretending to be relaxed, with one hand idly on the door handle as if he were keeping himself up that way and had no intention of ever moving again. She recognized most things about him, the tight jeans that showed his thighs and buttocks and the greasy leather boots and the tight shirt, and even that slippery friendly smile of his, that sleepy dreamy smile that all the boys used to get across ideas they didn't want to put into words. She recognized all this and also the singsong way he talked, slightly mocking, kidding, but serious and a little melancholy, and she recognized the way he tapped one fist against the other in homage to the perpetual music behind him. But all these things did not come together.

She said suddenly, "Hey, how old are you?"

His smile faded. She could see then that he wasn't a kid, he was much older—thirty, maybe more. At this knowledge her heart began to pound faster.

"That's a crazy thing to ask. Can'tcha see I'm your own age?" 80

"Like hell you are."

"Or maybe a coupla years older, I'm eighteen."

"Eighteen?" she said doubtfully.

He grinned to reassure her and lines appeared at the corners of his mouth. His teeth were big and white. He grinned so broadly his eyes became slits and she saw how thick the lashes were, thick and black as if painted with a black tarlike material. Then he seemed to become embarrassed, abruptly, and looked over his shoulder at Ellie. "*Him*, he's crazy," he said. "Ain't he a riot, he's a nut, a real character." Ellie was still listening to the music. His sunglasses told nothing about what he was thinking. He wore a bright orange shirt unbuttoned halfway to show his chest, which was a pale, bluish chest and not muscular like Arnold Friend's. His shirt collar was turned up all around and the very tips of the collar pointed out past his chin as if they were protecting him. He was pressing the transistor radio up against his ear and sat there in a kind of daze, right in the sun.

"He's kinda strange," Connie said. 85

"Hey, she says you're kinda strange! Kinda strange!" Arnold Friend cried. He pounded on the car to get Ellie's attention. Ellie turned for the first time and Connie saw with shock that he wasn't a kid either—he had a fair, hairless face, cheeks reddened slightly as if the veins grew too close to the surface of his skin, the face of a forty-year-old baby. Connie felt a wave of dizziness rise in her at this sight and she stared at him as if waiting for something to change the shock of the moment, make it all right again. Ellie's lips kept shaping words, mumbling along with the words blasting in his ear.

"Maybe you two better go away," Connie said faintly.

"What? How come?" Arnold Friend cried. "We come out here to take you for a ride. It's Sunday." He had the voice of the man on the radio now. It was the same voice, Connie thought. "Don'tcha know it's Sunday all day and honey, no matter who you were with last night today you're with Arnold Friend and don't you forget it!—Maybe you better step out here," he said, and this last was in a different voice. It was a little flatter, as if the heat was finally getting to him.

"No. I got things to do."

"Hey." 90

"You two better leave."

"We ain't leaving until you come with us."

"Like hell I am—"

"Connie, don't fool around with me. I mean, I mean, don't fool *around*," he said, shaking his head. He laughed incredulously. He placed his sunglasses on top of his head, carefully, as if he were indeed wearing a wig, and brought the stems down behind his ears. Connie stared at him, another wave of dizziness and fear rising in her so that for a moment he wasn't even in focus but was just a blur, standing there against his gold car, and she had the idea that he had driven up the driveway all right but had come from nowhere before that and belonged nowhere and that everything about him and even about the music that was so familiar to her was only half real.

"If my father comes and sees you—" 95

"He ain't coming. He's at a barbecue."

"How do you know that?"

"Aunt Tillie's. Right now they're—uh—they're drinking. Sitting around," he said vaguely, squinting as if he were staring all the way to town and over to Aunt Tillie's backyard. Then the vision seemed to get clear and he nodded energetically. "Yeah. Sitting around. There's your sister in a blue dress, huh? And high heels, the poor sad bitch—nothing like you sweetheart! And your mother's helping some fat woman with the corn, they're cleaning the corn—husking the corn—"

"What fat woman?" Connie cried.

"How do I know what fat woman. I don't know every goddam fat woman in the world!" Arnold Friend laughed. 100

"Oh, that's Mrs. Hornby. . . . Who invited her?" Connie said. She felt a little light-headed. Her breath was coming quickly.

"She's too fat. I don't like them fat. I like them the way you are, honey," he said, smiling sleepily at her. They stared at each other for a while, through the screen door. He said softly, "Now what you're going to do is this: you're going to come out that door. You're going to sit up front with me and Ellie's going to sit in the back, the hell with Ellie, right? This isn't Ellie's date. You're my date. I'm your lover, honey."

"What? You're crazy—"

"Yes, I'm your lover. You don't know what that is but you will," he said. "I know that too. I know all about you. But look: it's real nice and you couldn't ask for nobody better than me, or more polite. I always keep my word. I'll tell you how it is, I'm always nice at first, the first time. I'll hold you so tight you won't think you have to try to get away or pretend anything because you'll know you can't. And I'll come inside you where it's all secret and you'll give in to me and you'll love me—"

"Shut up! You're crazy!" Connie said. She backed away from the door. She put her hands against her ears as if she'd heard something terrible, something not meant for her. "People don't talk like that, you're crazy," she muttered. Her heart was almost too big now for her chest and its pumping made sweat break out all over her. She looked out to see Arnold Friend pause and then take a step toward the porch lurching. He almost fell. But, like a clever drunken man, he managed to catch his balance. He wobbled in his high boots and grabbed hold of one of the porch posts. 105

"Honey?" he said. "You still listening?"

"Get the hell out of here!"

"Be nice, honey. Listen."

"I'm going to call the police—"

He wobbled again and out of the side of his mouth came a fast spat curse, an aside not meant for her to hear. But even this "Christ!" sounded forced. Then he began to smile again. She watched this smile come, awkward as if he were smiling from inside a mask. His whole face was a mask, she thought wildly, tanned down onto his throat but then running out as if he had plastered makeup on his face but had forgotten about his throat. 110

"Honey—? Listen, here's how it is. I always tell the truth and I promise you this: I ain't coming in that house after you."

"You better not! I'm going to call the police if you—if you don't—"

"Honey," he said, talking right through her voice, "honey, I'm not coming in there but you are coming out here. You know why?"

She was panting. The kitchen looked like a place she had never seen before, some room she had run inside but which wasn't good enough, wasn't going to help her. The kitchen window had never had a curtain, after three years, and there were dishes in the sink for her to do—probably—and if you ran your hand across the table you'd probably feel something sticky there.

"You listening, honey? Hey?" 115

"—going to call the police—"

"Soon as you touch the phone I don't need to keep my promise and can come inside. You won't want that."

She rushed forward and tried to lock the door. Her fingers were shaking. "But why lock it," Arnold Friend said gently, talking right into her face. "It's just a screen door. It's just nothing." One of his boots was at a strange angle, as if his foot wasn't in it. It pointed out to the left, bent at the ankle. "I mean, anybody can break through a screen door and glass and wood and iron or anything else if he needs to, anybody at all and specially Arnold Friend. If the place got lit up with a fire honey you'd come running out into my arms, right into my arms and safe at home—like you knew I was your lover and'd stopped fooling around. I don't mind a nice shy girl but I don't like no fooling around." Part of those words were spoken with a slight rhythmic lilt, and Connie somehow recognized them—the echo of a song from last year, about a girl rushing into her boy friend's arms and coming home again—

Connie stood barefoot on the linoleum floor, staring at him. "What do you want?" she whispered.

"I want you," he said. 120

"What?"

"Seen you that night and thought, that's the one, yes sir. I never needed to look any more."

"But my father's coming back. He's coming to get me. I had to wash my hair first—" She spoke in a dry, rapid voice, hardly raising it for him to hear.

"No, your daddy is not coming and yes, you had to wash your hair and you washed it for me. It's nice and shining and all for me, I thank you, sweetheart," he said, with a mock bow, but again he almost lost his balance. He had to bend and adjust his boots. Evidently his feet did not go all the way down; the boots must have been stuffed with something so that he would seem taller. Connie stared out at him and behind him Ellie in the car, who seemed to be looking off toward Connie's right, into nothing. This Ellie said, pulling the words out of the air one after another as if he were just discovering them, "You want me to pull out the phone?"

"Shut your mouth and keep it shut," Arnold Friend said, his face red from bending over or maybe from embarrassment because Connie had seen his boots. "This ain't none of your business." 125

"What—what are you doing? What do you want?" Connie said. "If I call the police they'll get you, they'll arrest you—"

"Promise was not to come in unless you touch that phone, and I'll keep that promise," he said. He resumed his erect position and tried to force his shoulders back. He sounded like a hero in a movie, declaring something important. He spoke too loudly and it was as if he were speaking to someone behind Connie. "I ain't made plans for coming in that house where I don't belong but just for you to come out to me, the way you should. Don't you know who I am?"

"You're crazy," she whispered. She backed away from the door but did not want to go into another part of the house, as if this would give him permission to come through the door. "What do you. . . . You're crazy, you . . ."

"Huh? What're you saying, honey?"

Her eyes darted everywhere in the kitchen. She could not remember what it was, this room. 130

"This is how it is, honey: you come out and we'll drive away, have a nice ride. But if you don't come out we're gonna wait till your people come home and then they're all going to get it."

"You want that telephone pulled out?" Ellie said. He held the radio away from his ear and grimaced, as if without the radio the air was too much for him.

"I toldja shut up, Ellie," Arnold Friend said, "you're deaf, get a hearing aid, right? Fix yourself up. This little girl's no trouble and's gonna be nice to me, so Ellie keep to yourself, this ain't your date—right? Don't hem in on me. Don't hog. Don't crush. Don't bird dog. Don't trail me," he said in a rapid meaningless voice, as if he were running through all the expressions he'd learned but was no longer sure which one of them was in style, then rushing on to new ones, making them up with his eyes closed, "Don't crawl under my fence, don't squeeze in my chipmunk hole, don't sniff my glue, suck my popsicle, keep your own greasy fingers on yourself!" He shaded his eyes and peered in at Connie, who was backed against the kitchen table. "Don't mind him honey he's just a creep. He's a dope. Right? I'm the boy for you and like I said you come out here nice like a lady and give me your hand, and nobody else gets hurt, I mean, your nice old bald-headed daddy and your mummy and your sister in her high heels. Because listen: why bring them in this?"

"Leave me alone," Connie whispered.

"Hey, you know that old woman down the road, the one with the chickens and stuff—you know her?" 135

"She's dead!"

"Dead? What? You know her?" Arnold Friend said.

"She's dead—"

"Don't you like her?"

"She's dead—she's—she isn't here any more—" 140

"But don't you like her, I mean, you got something against her? Some grudge or something?" Then his voice dipped as if he were conscious of a rudeness. He touched the sunglasses perched on top of his head as if to make sure they were still there. "Now you be a good girl."

"What are you going to do?"

"Just two things, or maybe three," Arnold Friend said. "But I promise it won't last long and you'll like me that way you get to like people you're close to. You will. It's all over for you here, so come on out. You don't want your people in any trouble, do you?"

She turned and bumped against a chair or something, hurting her leg, but she ran into the back room and picked up the telephone. Something roared in her ear, a tiny roaring, and she was so sick with fear that she could do nothing but listen to it—the telephone was clammy and very heavy and her fingers groped down to the dial but were too weak to touch it. She began to scream into the phone, into the roaring. She cried out, she cried for her mother, she felt her breath start jerking back and forth in her lungs as if it were something Arnold Friend were stabbing her with again and again with no tenderness. A noisy sorrowful wailing rose all about her and she was locked inside it the way she was locked inside the house.

After a while she could hear again. She was sitting on the floor with her wet back against the wall. 145

Arnold Friend was saying from the door, "That's a good girl. Put the phone back."

She kicked the phone away from her.

"No, honey. Pick it up. Put it back right."

She picked it up and put it back. The dial tone stopped.

"That's a good girl. Now you come outside." 150

She was hollow with what had been fear, but what was now just an emptiness. All that screaming had blasted it out of her. She sat, one leg cramped under her, and deep inside her brain was something like a pinpoint of light that kept going and would not let her relax. She thought, I'm not going to see my mother again. She thought, I'm not going to sleep in my bed again. Her bright green blouse was all wet.

Arnold Friend said, in a gentle-loud voice that was like a stage voice, "The place where you came from ain't there any more, and where you had in mind to go is cancelled out. This place you are now—inside your daddy's house—is nothing but a cardboard box I can knock down any time. You know that and always did know it. You hear me?"

She thought, I have got to think. I have to know what to do.

"We'll go out to a nice field, out in the country here where it smells so nice and it's sunny," Arnold Friend said. "I'll have my arms around you so you won't need to try to get away and I'll show you what love is like, what it does. The hell with this house! It looks solid all right," he said. He ran a fingernail down the screen and the noise did not make Connie shiver, as it would have the day before. "Now put your hand on your heart, honey. Feel that? That feels solid too but we know better, be nice to me, be sweet like you can because what else is there for a girl like you but to be sweet and pretty and give in?—and get away before her people come back?"

She felt her pounding heart. Her hand seemed to enclose it. She thought for the first time in her life that it was nothing that was hers, that belonged to her, but just a pounding, living thing inside this body that wasn't really hers either. 155

"You don't want them to get hurt," Arnold Friend went on. "Now get up, honey. Get up all by yourself."

She stood.

"Now turn this way. That's right. Come over here to me—Ellie, put that away, didn't I tell you? You dope. You miserable creepy dope," Arnold Friend said. His words were not angry but only part of an incantation. The incantation was kindly. "Now come out through the kitchen to me honey and let's see a smile, try it, you're a brave sweet little girl and now they're eating corn and hotdogs cooked to bursting over an outdoor fire, and they don't know one thing about you and never did and honey you're better than them because not a one of them would have done this for you."

Connie felt the linoleum under her feet; it was cool. She brushed her hair back out of her eyes. Arnold Friend let go of the post tentatively and opened his arms for her, his elbows pointing in toward each other and his wrists limp, to show that this was an embarrassed embrace and a little mocking, he didn't want to make her self-conscious.

She put out her hand against the screen. She watched herself push the door slowly open as if she were safe back somewhere in the other doorway, watching this body and this head of long hair moving out into the sunlight where Arnold Friend waited. 160

"My sweet little blue-eyed girl," he said, in a half-sung sigh that had nothing to do with her brown eyes but was taken up just the same by the vast sunlit reaches of the land behind him and on all sides of him, so much land that Connie had never seen before and did not recognize except to know that she was going to it.

* * *

Edgar Allan Poe (1809–1849)

The Tell-Tale Heart (1843)

True!—nervous—very, very dreadfully nervous I had been and am; but why *will* you say that I am mad? The disease had sharpened my senses—not destroyed—not dulled them. Above all was the sense of hearing acute. I heard all things in the heaven and in the earth. I heard many things in hell. How, then, am

I mad? Hearken! and observe how healthily—how calmly I can tell you the whole story.

It is impossible to say how first the idea entered my brain; but once conceived, it haunted me day and night. Object there was none. Passion there was none. I loved the old man. He had never wronged me. He had never given me insult. For his gold I had no desire. I think it was his eye! yes, it was this! One of his eyes resembled that of a vulture—a pale eye, with a film over it. Whenever it fell upon me, my blood ran cold; and so by degrees—very gradually—I made up my mind to take the life of the old man, and thus rid myself of the eye forever.

Now this is the point. You fancy me mad. Madmen know nothing. But you should have seen *me*. You should have seen how wisely I proceeded—with what caution—with what foresight—with what dissimulation I went to work! I was never kinder to the old man than during the whole week before I killed him. And every night, about midnight, I turned the latch of his door and opened it—oh, so gently! And then, when I had made an opening sufficient for my head, I put in a dark lantern, all closed, closed, so that no light shone out, and then I thrust in my head. Oh, you would have laughed to see how cunningly I thrust it in! I moved it slowly—very, very slowly, so that I might not disturb the old man's sleep. It took me an hour to place my whole head within the opening so far that I could see him as he lay upon his bed. Ha!—would a madman have been so wise as this? And then, when my head was well in the room, I undid the lantern cautiously—oh, so cautiously—cautiously (for the hinges creaked)—I undid it just so much that a single thin ray fell upon the vulture eye. And this I did for seven long nights—every night just at midnight—but I found the eye always closed; and so it was impossible to do the work; for it was not the old man who vexed me, but his Evil Eye. And every morning, when the day broke, I went boldly into the chamber, and spoke courageously to him, calling him by name in a hearty tone, and inquiring how he had passed the night. So you see he would have been a very profound old man, indeed, to suspect that every night, just at twelve, I looked in upon him while he slept.

Upon the eighth night I was more than usually cautious in opening the door. A watch's minute hand moves more quickly than did mine. Never before that night had I *felt* the extent of my own powers—of my sagacity. I could scarcely contain my feelings of triumph. To think that there I was, opening the door little by little, and he not even to dream of my secret deeds or thoughts. I fairly chuckled at the idea; and perhaps he heard me; for he moved on the bed suddenly, as if startled. Now you may think that I drew back—but no. His room was as black as pitch with the thick darkness (for the shutters were close fastened through fear of robbers), and so I knew that he could not see the opening of the door, and I kept pushing it on steadily, steadily.

I had my head in, and was about to open the lantern, when my thumb slipped upon the tin fastening, and the old man sprang up in the bed, crying out—"Who's there?" 5

I kept quite still and said nothing. For a whole hour I did not move a muscle, and in the meantime I did not hear him lie down. He was still sitting up in the bed listening;—just as I have done, night after night, hearkening to the death watches[1] in the wall.

Presently I heard a slight groan, and I knew it was the groan of mortal terror. It was not a groan of pain or of grief—oh, no!—it was the low stifled sound that arises from the bottom of the soul when overcharged with awe. I knew the sound very well. Many a night, just at midnight, when all the world slept, it has welled up from my own bosom, deepening, with its dreadful echo, the terrors that distracted me. I say I knew it well. I knew what the old man felt, and pitied him, although I chuckled at heart. I knew that he had been lying awake ever since the first slight noise, when he had turned in the bed. His fears had been ever since growing upon him. He had been trying to fancy them causeless, but could not. He had been saying to himself—"It is nothing but the wind in the chimney—it is only a mouse crossing the floor," or "it is merely a cricket which has made a single chirp." Yes, he had been trying to comfort himself with these suppositions; but he had found all in vain. *All in vain*; because Death, in approaching him, had stalked with his black shadow before him, and enveloped the victim. And it was the mournful influence of the unperceived shadow that caused him to feel—although he neither saw nor heard—to *feel* the presence of my head within the room.

When I had waited a long time, very patiently, without hearing him lie down, I resolved to open a little—a very, very little crevice in the lantern. So I opened it—you cannot imagine how stealthily, stealthily—until, at length, a single dim ray, like the thread of the spider, shot from out of the crevice and fell upon the vulture eye.

It was open—wide, wide open—and I grew furious as I gazed upon it. I saw it with perfect distinctness—all a dull blue, with a hideous veil over it that chilled the very marrow in my bones; but I could see nothing else of the old man's face or person: for I had directed the ray as if by instinct, precisely upon the damned spot.

And now have I not told you that what you mistake for madness is but over-acuteness of the senses?—now, I say, there came to my ears a low, dull, quick sound, such as a watch makes when enveloped in cotton. I knew *that* sound well, too. It was the beating of the old man's heart. It increased my fury, as the beating of a drum stimulates the soldier into courage. 10

But even yet I refrained and kept still. I scarcely breathed. I held the lantern motionless. I tried how steadily I could maintain the ray upon the eye. Meantime the hellish tattoo of the heart increased. It grew quicker and quicker, and louder and louder every instant. The old man's terror *must* have been extreme! It grew louder, I say, louder every moment!—do you mark me well? I have told you that I am nervous: so I am. And now at the dead hour of

[1] *death watches:* Wood-burrowing beetles. Their clicking sound was superstitiously thought of as an omen of death.

the night, amid the dreadful silence of that old house, so strange a noise as this excited me to uncontrollable terror. Yet, for some minutes longer I refrained and stood still. But the beating grew louder, louder! I thought the heart must burst. And now a new anxiety seized me—the sound would be heard by a neighbor! The old man's hour had come! With a loud yell, I threw open the lantern and leaped into the room. He shrieked once—once only. In an instant I dragged him to the floor, and pulled the heavy bed over him. I then smiled gaily, to find the deed so far done. But, for many minutes, the heart beat on with a muffled sound. This, however, did not vex me; it would not be heard through the wall. At length it ceased. The old man was dead. I removed the bed and examined the corpse. Yes, he was stone, stone dead. I placed my hand upon the heart and held it there many minutes.

If still you think me mad, you will think so no longer when I describe the wise precautions I took for the concealment of the body. The night waned, and I worked hastily, but in silence. First of all I dismembered the corpse. I cut off the head and the arms and the legs.

I then took up three planks from the flooring of the chamber, and deposited all between the scantlings. I then replaced the boards so cleverly, so cunningly, that no human eye—not even *his*—could have detected anything wrong. There was nothing to wash out—no stain of any kind—no bloodspot whatever. I had been too wary for that. A tub had caught all—ha! ha!

When I had made an end of these labors, it was four o'clock—still dark as midnight. As the bell sounded the hour, there came a knocking at the street door. I went down to open it with a light heart,—for what had I *now* to fear? There entered three men, who introduced themselves, with perfect suavity, as officers of the police. A shriek had been heard by a neighbor during the night; suspicion of foul play had been aroused, information had been lodged at the police office, and they (the officers) had been deputed to search the premises.

I smiled,—for *what* had I to fear? I bade the gentlemen welcome. The shriek, I said, was my own in a dream. The old man, I mentioned, was absent in the country. I took my visitors all over the house. I bade them search—search *well*. I led them, at length, to *his* chamber. I showed them his treasures, secure, undisturbed. In the enthusiasm of my confidence, I brought chairs into the room, and desired them *here* to rest from their fatigues, while I myself, in the wild audacity of my perfect triumph, placed my own seat upon the very spot beneath which reposed the corpse of the victim. 15

The officers were satisfied. My *manner* had convinced them. I was singularly at ease. They sat, and while I answered cheerily, they chatted of familiar things. But, ere long, I felt myself getting pale and wished them gone. My head ached, and I fancied a ringing in my ears: but still they sat and still chatted. The ringing became more distinct:—it continued and became more distinct: I talked more freely to get rid of the feeling: but it continued and gained definitiveness—until, at length, I found that the noise was *not* within my ears.

No doubt I now grew *very* pale:—but I talked more fluently, and with a heightened voice. Yet the sound increased—and what could I do? It was a *low, dull, quick sound—much such a sound as a watch makes when enveloped in cotton.* I gasped for breath—and yet the officers heard it not. I talked more quickly—more vehemently; but the noise steadily increased. I arose and argued about trifles, in a high key and with violent gesticulations; but the noise steadily increased. Why *would* they not be gone? I paced the floor to and fro with heavy strides, as if excited to fury by the observations of the men—but the noise steadily increased. Oh God! what *could* I do? I foamed—I raved—I swore! I swung the chair upon which I had been sitting, and grated it upon the boards, but the noise arose over all and continually increased. It grew louder—louder—*louder!* And still the men chatted pleasantly, and smiled. Was it possible they heard not? Almighty God!—no, no! They heard!—they suspected!—they *knew!*—they were making a mockery of my horror!—this I thought, and this I think. But anything was better than this agony! Anything was more tolerable than this derision! I could bear those hypocritical smiles no longer! I felt that I must scream or die!—and now—again!—hark! louder! louder! louder! *louder!*—

"Villains!" I shrieked, "dissemble no more! I admit the deed!—tear up the planks!—here, here!—it is the beating of his hideous heart!"

* * *

John Steinbeck (1902–1968)

The Chrysanthemums (1937)

The high grey-flannel fog of winter closed off the Salinas Valley from the sky and from all the rest of the world. On every side it sat like a lid on the mountains and made of the great valley a closed pot. On the broad, level land floor the gang plows bit deep and left the black earth shining like metal where the shares had cut. On the foothill ranches across the Salinas River, the yellow stubble fields seemed to be bathed in pale cold sunshine, but there was no sunshine in the valley now in December. The thick willow scrub along the river flamed with sharp and positive yellow leaves.

It was a game of quiet and of waiting. The air was cold and tender. A light wind blew up from the southwest so that the farmers were mildly hopeful of a good rain before long; but fog and rain do not go together.

Across the river, on Henry Allen's foothill ranch there was little work to be done, for the hay was cut and stored and the orchards were plowed up to receive the rain deeply when it should come. The cattle on the higher slopes were becoming shaggy and rough-coated.

Elisa Allen, working in her flower garden, looked down across the yard and saw Henry, her husband, talking to two men in business suits. The three of them stood by the tractor shed, each man with one foot on the side of the little Fordson. They smoked cigarettes and studied the machine as they talked.

Elisa watched them for a moment and then went back to her work. She was thirty-five. Her face was lean and strong and her eyes were as clear as water. Her figure looked blocked and heavy in her gardening costume, a man's black hat pulled low down over her eyes, clod-hopper shoes, a figured print dress almost completely covered by a big corduroy apron with four big pockets to hold the snips, the trowel and scratcher, the seeds and the knife she worked with. She wore heavy leather gloves to protect her hands while she worked. 5

She was cutting down the old year's chrysanthemum stalks with a pair of short and powerful scissors. She looked down toward the men by the tractor shed now and then. Her face was eager and mature and handsome; even her work with the scissors was over-eager, over-powerful. The chrysanthemum stems seemed too small and easy for her energy.

She brushed a cloud of hair out of her eyes with the back of her glove, and left a smudge of earth on her cheek in doing it. Behind her stood the neat white farm house with red geraniums close-banked around it as high as the windows. It was a hard-swept looking little house with hard-polished windows, and a clean mud-mat on the front steps.

Elisa cast another glance toward the tractor shed. The strangers were getting into their Ford coupe. She took off a glove and put her strong fingers down into the forest of new green chrysanthemum sprouts that were growing around the old roots. She spread the leaves and looked down among the close-growing stems. No aphids were there, no sowbugs or snails or cutworms. Her terrier fingers destroyed such pests before they could get started.

Elisa started at the sound of her husband's voice. He had come near quietly, and he leaned over the wire fence that protected her flower garden from cattle and dogs and chickens.

"At it again," he said. "You've got a strong new crop coming." 10

Elisa straightened her back and pulled on the gardening glove again. "Yes. They'll be strong this coming year." In her tone and on her face there was a little smugness.

"You've got a gift with things," Henry observed. "Some of those yellow chrysanthemums you had this year were ten inches across. I wish you'd work out in the orchard and raise some apples that big."

Her eyes sharpened. "Maybe I could do it, too. I've a gift with things, all right. My mother had it. She could stick anything in the ground and make it grow. She said it was having planters' hands that knew how to do it."

"Well, it sure works with flowers," he said.

"Henry, who were those men you were talking to?" 15

"Why, sure, that's what I came to tell you. They were from the Western Meat Company. I sold those thirty head of three-year-old steers. Got nearly my own price, too."

"Good," she said. "Good for you."

"And I thought," he continued, "I thought how it's Saturday afternoon, and we might go into Salinas for dinner at a restaurant, and then to a picture show—to celebrate, you see."

"Good," she repeated. "Oh, yes. That will be good."

Henry put on his joking tone. "There's fights tonight. How'd you like to go to the fights?"

"Oh, no," she said breathlessly. "No, I wouldn't like fights."

"Just fooling, Elisa. We'll go to a movie. Let's see. It's two now. I'm going to take Scotty and bring down those steers from the hill. It'll take us maybe two hours. We'll go in town about five and have dinner at the Cominos Hotel. Like that?"

"Of course I'll like it. It's good to eat away from home."

"All right, then. I'll go get up a couple of horses."

She said, "I'll have plenty of time to transplant some of these sets, I guess."

She heard her husband calling Scotty down by the barn. And a little later she saw the two men ride up the pale yellow hillside in search of the steers.

There was a little square sandy bed kept for rooting the chrysanthemums. With her trowel she turned the soil over and over, and smoothed it and patted it firm. Then she dug ten parallel trenches to receive the sets. Back at the chrysanthemum bed she pulled out the little crisp shoots, trimmed off the leaves of each one with her scissors and laid it on a small orderly pile.

A squeak of wheels and plod of hoofs came from the road. Elisa looked up. The country road ran along the dense bank of willows and cottonwoods that bordered the river, and up this road came a curious vehicle, curiously drawn. It was an old spring-wagon, with a round canvas top on it like the cover of a prairie schooner.[1] It was drawn by an old bay horse and a little grey-and-white burro. A big stubble-bearded man sat between the cover flaps and drove the crawling team. Underneath the wagon, between the hind wheels, a lean and rangy mongrel dog walked sedately. Words were printed on the canvas, in clumsy, crooked letters. "Pots, pans, knives, sisors, lawn mores, Fixed." Two rows of articles, and the triumphantly definitive "Fixed" below. The black paint had run down in little sharp points beneath each letter.

Elisa, squatting on the ground, watched to see the crazy, loose-jointed wagon pass by. But it didn't pass. It turned into the farm road in front of her house, crooked old wheels skirling and squeaking. The rangy dog darted from between the wheels and ran ahead. Instantly the two ranch shepherds flew out at him. Then all three stopped, and with stiff and quivering tails, with taut straight legs, with ambassadorial dignity, they slowly circled, sniffing daintily. The caravan pulled up to Elisa's wire fence and stopped. Now the newcomer dog, feeling outnumbered, lowered his tail and retired under the wagon with raised hackles and bared teeth.

---

[1] *prairie schooner:* Covered wagon used by American pioneers.

The man on the wagon seat called out, "That's a bad dog in a fight when he gets started." 30

Elisa laughed. "I see he is. How soon does he generally get started?"

The man caught up her laughter and echoed it heartily. "Sometimes not for weeks and weeks," he said. He climbed stiffly down, over the wheel. The horse and the donkey drooped like unwatered flowers.

Elisa saw that he was a very big man. Although his hair and beard were greying, he did not look old. His worn black suit was wrinkled and spotted with grease. The laughter had disappeared from his face and eyes the moment his laughing voice ceased. His eyes were dark, and they were full of the brooding that gets in the eyes of teamsters and of sailors. The calloused hands he rested on the wire fence were cracked, and every crack was a black line. He took off his battered hat.

"I'm off my general road, ma'am," he said. "Does this dirt road cut over across the river to the Los Angeles highway?"

Elisa stood up and shoved the thick scissors in her apron pocket. "Well, yes, it does, but it winds around and then fords the river. I don't think your team could pull through the sand." 35

He replied with some asperity. "It might surprise you what them beasts can pull through."

"When they get started?" she asked.

He smiled for a second. "Yes. When they get started."

"Well," said Elisa, "I think you'll save time if you go back to the Salinas road and pick up the highway there."

He drew a big finger down the chicken wire and made it sing. "I ain't in any hurry, ma'am. I go from Seattle to San Diego and back every year. Takes all my time. About six months each way. I aim to follow nice weather." 40

Elisa took off her gloves and stuffed them in the apron pocket with the scissors. She touched the under edge of her man's hat, searching for fugitive hairs. "That sounds like a nice kind of a way to live," she said.

He leaned confidentially over the fence. "Maybe you noticed the writing on my wagon. I mend pots and sharpen knives and scissors. You got any of them things to do?"

"Oh, no," she said quickly. "Nothing like that." Her eyes hardened with resistance.

"Scissors is the worst thing," he explained. "Most people just ruin scissors trying to sharpen 'em, but I know how. I got a special tool. It's a little bobbit kind of thing, and patented. But it sure does the trick."

"No. My scissors are all sharp." 45

"All right, then. Take a pot," he continued earnestly, "a bent pot, or a pot with a hole. I can make it like new so you don't have to buy no new ones. That's a saving for you."

"No," she said shortly. "I tell you I have nothing like that for you to do."

His face fell to an exaggerated sadness. His voice took on a whining undertone. "I ain't had a thing to do today. Maybe I won't have no supper tonight.

You see I'm off my regular road. I know folks on the highway clear from Seattle to San Diego. They save their things for me to sharpen up because they know I do it so good and save them money."

"I'm sorry," Elisa said irritably. "I haven't anything for you to do."

His eyes left her face and fell to searching the ground. They roamed about until they came to the chrysanthemum bed where she had been working. "What's them plants, ma'am?"

The irritation and resistance melted from Elisa's face. "Oh, those are chrysanthemums, giant whites and yellows. I raise them every year, bigger than anybody around here."

"Kind of a long-stemmed flower? Looks like a quick puff of colored smoke?" he asked.

"That's it. What a nice way to describe them."

"They smell kind of nasty till you get used to them," he said.

"It's a good bitter smell," she retorted, "not nasty at all."

He changed his tone quickly. "I like the smell myself."

"I had ten-inch blooms this year," she said.

The man leaned farther over the fence. "Look. I know a lady down the road a piece, has got the nicest garden you ever seen. Got nearly every kind of flower but no chrysanthemums. Last time I was mending a copper-bottom washtub for her (that's a hard job but I do it good), she said to me, 'If you ever run acrost some nice chrysanthemums I wish you'd try to get me a few seeds.' That's what she told me."

Elisa's eyes grew alert and eager. "She couldn't have known much about chrysanthemums. You *can* raise them from seed, but it's much easier to root the little sprouts you see there."

"Oh," he said. "I s'pose I can't take none to her, then."

"Why yes you can," Elisa cried. "I can put some in damp sand, and you can carry them right along with you. They'll take root in the pot if you keep them damp. And then she can transplant them."

"She'd sure like to have some, ma'am. You say they're nice ones?"

"Beautiful," she said. "Oh, beautiful." Her eyes shone. She tore off the battered hat and shook out her dark pretty hair. "I'll put them in a flower pot, and you can take them right with you. Come into the yard."

While the man came through the picket gate Elisa ran excitedly along the geranium-bordered path to the back of the house. And she returned carrying a big red flower pot. The gloves were forgotten now. She kneeled on the ground by the starting bed and dug up the sandy soil with her fingers and scooped it into the bright new flower pot. Then she picked up the little pile of shoots she had prepared. With her strong fingers she pressed them into the sand and tamped around them with her knuckles. The man stood over her. "I'll tell you what to do," she said. "You remember so you can tell the lady."

"Yes, I'll try to remember."

"Well, look. These will take root in about a month. Then she must set them out, about a foot apart in good rich earth like this, see?" She lifted a handful of dark soil for him to look at. "They'll grow fast and tall. Now remember this: In July tell her to cut them down, about eight inches from the ground."

"Before they bloom?" he asked.

"Yes, before they bloom." Her face was tight with eagerness. "They'll grow right up again. About the last of September the buds will start."

She stopped and seemed perplexed. "It's the budding that takes the most care," she said hesitantly. "I don't know how to tell you." She looked deep into his eyes, searchingly. Her mouth opened a little, and she seemed to be listening. "I'll try to tell you," she said. "Did you ever hear of planting hands?"

"Can't say I have, ma'am." 70

"Well, I can only tell you what it feels like. It's when you're picking off the buds you don't want. Everything goes right down into your fingertips. You watch your fingers work. They do it themselves. You can feel how it is. They pick and pick the buds. They never make a mistake. They're with the plant. Do you see? Your fingers and the plant. You can feel that, right up your arm. They know. They never make a mistake. You can feel it. When you're like that you can't do anything wrong. Do you see that? Can you understand that?"

She was kneeling on the ground looking up at him. Her breast swelled passionately.

The man's eyes narrowed. He looked away self-consciously. "Maybe I know," he said. "Sometimes in the night in the wagon there—"

Elisa's voice grew husky. She broke in on him, "I've never lived as you do, but I know what you mean. When the night is dark—why, the stars are sharp-pointed, and there's quiet. Why, you rise up and up! Every pointed star gets driven into your body. It's like that. Hot and sharp and—lovely."

Kneeling there, her hand went out toward his legs in the greasy black trousers. Her hesitant fingers almost touched the cloth. Then her hand dropped to the ground. She crouched low like a fawning dog. 75

He said, "It's nice, just like you say. Only when you don't have no dinner, it ain't."

She stood up then, very straight, and her face was ashamed. She held the flower pot out to him and placed it gently in his arms. "Here. Put it in your wagon, on the seat, where you can watch it. Maybe I can find something for you to do."

At the back of the house she dug in the can pile and found two old and battered aluminum saucepans. She carried them back and gave them to him. "Here, maybe you can fix these."

His manner changed. He became professional. "Good as new I can fix them." At the back of his wagon he sat a little anvil, and out of an oily tool box dug a small machine hammer. Elisa came through the gate to watch him while he pounded out the dents in the kettles. His mouth grew sure and knowing. At a difficult part of the work he sucked his under-lip.

"You sleep right in the wagon?" Elisa asked. 80

"Right in the wagon, ma'am. Rain or shine I'm dry as a cow in there."

"It must be nice," she said. "It must be very nice. I wish women could do such things."

"It ain't the right kind of a life for a woman."

Her upper lip raised a little, showing her teeth. "How do you know? How can you tell?" she said.

"I don't know, ma'am," he protested. "Of course I don't know. Now here's your kettles, done. You don't have to buy no new ones."

"How much?"

"Oh, fifty cents'll do. I keep my prices down and my work good. That's why I have all them satisfied customers up and down the highway."

Elisa brought him a fifty-cent piece from the house and dropped it in his hand. "You might be surprised to have a rival some time. I can sharpen scissors, too. And I can beat the dents out of little pots. I could show you what a woman might do."

He put his hammer back in the oily box and shoved the little anvil out of sight. "It would be a lonely life for a woman, ma'am, and a scarey life, too, with animals creeping under the wagon all night." He climbed over the singletree,[2] steadying himself with a hand on the burro's white rump. He settled himself in the seat, picked up the lines. "Thank you kindly, ma'am," he said. "I'll do like you told me; I'll go back and catch the Salinas road."

"Mind," she called, "if you're long in getting there, keep the sand damp."

"Sand, ma'am? . . . Sand? Oh, sure. You mean around the chrysanthemums. Sure I will." He clucked his tongue. The beasts leaned luxuriously into their collars. The mongrel dog took his place between the back wheels. The wagon turned and crawled out the entrance road and back the way it had come, along the river.

Elisa stood in front of her wire fence watching the slow progress of the caravan. Her shoulders were straight, her head thrown back, her eyes half-closed, so that the scene came vaguely into them. Her lips moved silently, forming the words "Good-bye—good-bye." Then she whispered, "That's a bright direction. There's a glowing there." The sound of her whisper startled her. She shook herself free and looked about to see whether anyone had been listening. Only the dogs had heard. They lifted their heads toward her from their sleeping in the dust, and then stretched out their chins and settled asleep again. Elisa turned and ran hurriedly into the house.

In the kitchen she reached behind the stove and felt the water tank. It was full of hot water from the noonday cooking. In the bathroom she tore off her soiled clothes and flung them into the corner. And then she scrubbed herself with a little block of pumice, legs and thighs, loins and chest and arms, until her skin was scratched and red. When she had dried herself she stood in front of a mirror in her bedroom and looked at her body. She tightened her stomach and threw out her chest. She turned and looked over her shoulder at her back.

[2] *singletree:* A wooden bar that connects a wagon to the horses' harnesses.

After a while she began to dress, slowly. She put on her newest underclothing and her nicest stockings and the dress which was the symbol of her prettiness. She worked carefully on her hair, penciled her eyebrows and rouged her lips.

Before she was finished she heard the little thunder of hoofs and the shouts of Henry and his helper as they drove the red steers into the corral. She heard the gate bang shut and set herself for Henry's arrival. 95

His step sounded on the porch. He entered the house calling, "Elisa, where are you?"

"In my room, dressing. I'm not ready. There's hot water for your bath. Hurry up. It's getting late."

When she heard him splashing in the tub, Elisa laid his dark suit on the bed, and shirt and socks and tie beside it. She stood his polished shoes on the floor beside the bed. Then she went to the porch and sat primly and stiffly down. She looked toward the river road where the willow-line was still yellow with frosted leaves so that under the high grey fog they seemed a thin band of sunshine. This was the only color in the grey afternoon. She sat unmoving for a long time. Her eyes blinked rarely.

Henry came banging out of the door, shoving his tie inside his vest as he came. Elisa stiffened and her face grew tight. Henry stopped short and looked at her. "Why—why, Elisa. You look so nice!"

"Nice? You think I look nice? What do you mean by 'nice'?" 100

Henry blundered on. "I don't know. I mean you look different, strong and happy."

"I am strong? Yes, strong. What do you mean 'strong'?"

He looked bewildered. "You're playing some kind of a game," he said helplessly. "It's a kind of a play. You look strong enough to break a calf over your knee, happy enough to eat it like a watermelon."

For a second she lost her rigidity. "Henry! Don't talk like that. You didn't know what you said." She grew complete again. "I'm strong," she boasted. "I never knew before how strong."

Henry looked down toward the tractor shed, and when he brought his eyes back to her, they were his own again. "I'll get out the car. You can put on your coat while I'm starting." 105

Elisa went into the house. She heard him drive to the gate and idle down his motor, and then she took a long time to put on her hat. She pulled it here and pressed it there. When Henry turned the motor off she slipped into her coat and went out.

The little roadster[3] bounced along on the dirt road by the river, raising the birds and driving the rabbits into the brush. Two cranes flapped heavily over the willow-line and dropped into the river-bed.

Far ahead on the road Elisa saw a dark speck. She knew.

---

[3]*roadster:* An early roofless automobile, with a single seat for two or three passengers.

She tried not to look as they passed it, but her eyes would not obey. She whispered to herself sadly, "He might have thrown them off the road. That wouldn't have been much trouble, not very much. But he kept the pot," she explained. "He had to keep the pot. That's why he couldn't get them off the road."

The roadster turned a bend and she saw the caravan ahead. She swung full around toward her husband so she could not see the little covered wagon and the mismatched team as the car passed them. 110

In a moment it was over. The thing was done. She did not look back.

She said loudly, to be heard above the motor, "It will be good, tonight, a good dinner."

"Now you're changed again," Henry complained. He took one hand from the wheel and patted her knee. "I ought to take you in to dinner oftener. It would be good for both of us. We get so heavy out on the ranch."

"Henry," she asked, "could we have wine at dinner?"

"Sure we could. Say! That will be fine." 115

She was silent for a while; then she said, "Henry, at those prize fights, do the men hurt each other very much?"

"Sometimes a little, not often. Why?"

"Well, I've read how they break noses, and blood runs down their chests. I've read how the fighting gloves get heavy and soggy with blood."

He looked around at her. "What's the matter, Elisa? I didn't know you read things like that." He brought the car to a stop, then turned to the right over the Salinas River bridge.

"Do any women ever go to the fights?" she asked. 120

"Oh, sure, some. What's the matter, Elisa? Do you want to go? I don't think you'd like it, but I'll take you if you really want to go."

She relaxed limply in the seat. "Oh, no. No. I don't want to go. I'm sure I don't." Her face was turned away from him. "It will be enough if we can have wine. It will be plenty." She turned up her coat collar so he could not see that she was crying weakly—like an old woman.

* * *

Amy Tan (1952–)

Two Kinds (1989)

My mother believed you could be anything you wanted to be in America. You could open a restaurant. You could work for the government and get good retirement. You could buy a house with almost no money down. You could become rich. You could become instantly famous.

"Of course you can be prodigy, too," my mother told me when I was nine. "You can be best anything. What does Auntie Lindo know? Her daughter, she is only best tricky."

America was where all my mother's hopes lay. She had come here in 1949 after losing everything in China: her mother and father, her family home, her first husband, and two daughters, twin baby girls. But she never looked back with regret. There were so many ways for things to get better.

We didn't immediately pick the right kind of prodigy. At first my mother thought I could be a Chinese Shirley Temple. We'd watch Shirley's old movies on TV as though they were training films. My mother would poke my arm and say, "*Ni kan*"—You watch. And I would see Shirley tapping her feet, or singing a sailor song, or pursing her lips into a very round O while saying, "Oh my goodness."

"*Ni kan,*" said my mother as Shirley's eyes flooded with tears. "You already know how. Don't need talent for crying!" 5

Soon after my mother got this idea about Shirley Temple, she took me to a beauty training school in the Mission district and put me in the hands of a student who could barely hold the scissors without shaking. Instead of getting big fat curls, I emerged with an uneven mass of crinkly black fuzz. My mother dragged me off to the bathroom and tried to wet down my hair.

"You look like Negro Chinese," she lamented, as if I had done this on purpose.

The instructor of the beauty training school had to lop off these soggy clumps to make my hair even again. "Peter Pan is very popular these days," the instructor assured my mother. I now had hair the length of a boy's, with straight-across bangs that hung at a slant two inches above my eyebrows. I liked the haircut and it made me actually look forward to my future fame.

In fact, in the beginning, I was just as excited as my mother, maybe even more so. I pictured this prodigy part of me as many different images, trying each one on for size. I was a dainty ballerina girl standing by the curtains, waiting to hear the right music that would send me floating on my tiptoes. I was like the Christ child lifted out of the straw manger, crying with holy indignity. I was Cinderella stepping from her pumpkin carriage with sparkly cartoon music filling the air.

In all of my imaginings, I was filled with a sense that I would soon become *perfect*. My mother and father would adore me. I would be beyond reproach. I would never feel the need to sulk for anything. 10

But sometimes the prodigy in me became impatient. "If you don't hurry up and get me out of here, I'm disappearing for good," it warned. "And then you'll always be nothing."

Every night after dinner, my mother and I would sit at the Formica kitchen table. She would present new tests, taking her examples from stories of amazing children she had read in *Ripley's Believe It or Not*, or *Good Housekeeping*, *Reader's Digest*, and a dozen other magazines she kept in a pile in our bathroom. My mother got these magazines from people whose houses she cleaned. And since she cleaned many houses each week, we had a great assortment. She would look through them all, searching for stories about remarkable children.

The first night she brought out a story about a three-year-old boy who knew the capitals of all the states and even most of the European countries. A teacher was quoted as saying the little boy could also pronounce the names of the foreign cities correctly.

"What's the capital of Finland?" my mother asked me, looking at the magazine story.

All I knew was the capital of California, because Sacramento was the name of the street we lived on in Chinatown. "Nairobi!" I guessed, saying the most foreign word I could think of. She checked to see if that was possibly one way to pronounce "Helsinki" before showing me the answer. 15

The tests got harder—multiplying numbers in my head, finding the queen of hearts in a deck of cards, trying to stand on my head without using my hands, predicting the daily temperatures in Los Angeles, New York, and London.

One night I had to look at a page from the Bible for three minutes and then report everything I could remember. "Now Jehoshaphat had riches and honor in abundance and . . . that's all I remember, Ma," I said.

And after seeing my mother's disappointed face once again, something inside of me began to die. I hated the tests, the raised hopes and failed expectations. Before going to bed that night, I looked in the mirror above the bathroom sink and when I saw only my face staring back—and that it would always be this ordinary face—I began to cry. Such a sad, ugly girl! I made high-pitched noises like a crazed animal, trying to scratch out the face in the mirror.

And then I saw what seemed to be the prodigy side of me—because I had never seen that face before. I looked at my reflection, blinking so I could see more clearly. The girl staring back at me was angry, powerful. This girl and I were the same. I had new thoughts, willful thoughts, or rather thoughts filled with lots of won'ts. I won't let her change me, I promised myself. I won't be what I'm not.

So now on nights when my mother presented her tests, I performed listlessly, my head propped on one arm. I pretended to be bored. And I was. I got so bored I started counting the bellows of the foghorns out on the bay while my mother drilled me in other areas. The sound was comforting and reminded me of the cow jumping over the moon. And the next day, I played a game with myself, seeing if my mother would give up on me before eight bellows. After a while I usually counted only one, maybe two bellows at most. At last she was beginning to give up hope. 20

Two or three months had gone by without any mention of my being a prodigy again. And then one day my mother was watching *The Ed Sullivan Show* on TV. The TV was old and the sound kept shorting out. Every time my mother got halfway up from the sofa to adjust the set, the sound would go back on and Ed would be talking. As soon as she sat down, Ed would go silent again. She got up, the TV broke into loud piano music. She sat down. Silence. Up and down, back and forth, quiet and loud. It was like a stiff embraceless dance between her and the TV set. Finally she stood by the set with her hand on the sound dial.

She seemed entranced by the music, a little frenzied piano piece with this mesmerizing quality, sort of quick passages and then teasing lilting ones before it returned to the quick playful parts.

"*Ni kan*," my mother said, calling me over with hurried hand gestures, "Look here."

I could see why my mother was fascinated by the music. It was being pounded out by a little Chinese girl, about nine years old, with a Peter Pan haircut. The girl had the sauciness of a Shirley Temple. She was proudly modest like a proper Chinese child. And she also did this fancy sweep of a curtsy, so that the fluffy skirt of her white dress cascaded slowly to the floor like the petals of a large carnation.

In spite of these warning signs, I wasn't worried. Our family had no piano and we couldn't afford to buy one, let alone reams of sheet music and piano lessons. So I could be generous in my comments when my mother bad-mouthed the little girl on TV. 25

"Play note right, but doesn't sound good! No singing sound," complained my mother.

"What are you picking on her for?" I said carelessly. "She's pretty good. Maybe she's not the best, but she's trying hard." I knew almost immediately I would be sorry I said that.

"Just like you," she said. "Not the best. Because you not trying." She gave a little huff as she let go of the sound dial and sat down on the sofa.

The little Chinese girl sat down also to play an encore of "Anitra's Dance" by Grieg. I remember the song, because later on I had to learn how to play it.

Three days after watching *The Ed Sullivan Show*, my mother told me what my schedule would be for piano lessons and piano practice. She had talked to Mr. Chong, who lived on the first floor of our apartment building. Mr. Chong was a retired piano teacher and my mother had traded housecleaning services for weekly lessons and a piano for me to practice on every day, two hours a day, from four until six. 30

When my mother told me this, I felt as though I had been sent to hell. I whined and then kicked my foot a little when I couldn't stand it anymore.

"Why don't you like me the way I am? I'm *not* a genius! I can't play the piano. And even if I could, I wouldn't go on TV if you paid me a million dollars!" I cried.

My mother slapped me. "Who ask you be genius?" she shouted. "Only ask you be your best. For you sake. You think I want you be genius? Hnnh! What for! Who ask you!"

"So ungrateful," I heard her mutter in Chinese. "If she had as much talent as she has temper, she would be famous now."

Mr. Chong, whom I secretly nicknamed Old Chong, was very strange, always tapping his fingers to the silent music of an invisible orchestra. He looked ancient in my eyes. He had lost most of the hair on top of his head and he wore thick glasses and had eyes that always looked tired and sleepy. But he must have been younger than I thought, since he lived with his mother and was not yet married. 35

I met Old Lady Chong once and that was enough. She had this peculiar smell like a baby that had done something in its pants. And her fingers felt like a dead person's, like an old peach I once found in the back of the refrigerator; the skin just slid off the meat when I picked it up.

I soon found out why Old Chong had retired from teaching piano. He was deaf. "Like Beethoven!" he shouted to me. "We're both listening only in our head!" And he would start to conduct his frantic silent sonatas.

Our lessons went like this. He would open the book and point to different things, explaining their purpose: "Key! Treble! Bass! No sharps or flats! So this is C major! Listen now and play after me!"

And then he would play the C scale a few times, a simple chord, and then, as if inspired by an old, unreachable itch, he gradually added more notes and running trills and a pounding bass until the music was really something quite grand.

I would play after him, the simple scale, the simple chord, and then I just played some nonsense that sounded like a cat running up and down on top of garbage cans. Old Chong smiled and applauded and then said, "Very good! But now you must learn to keep time!" 40

So that's how I discovered that Old Chong's eyes were too slow to keep up with the wrong notes I was playing. He went through the motions in half-time. To help me keep rhythm, he stood behind me, pushing down on my right shoulder for every beat. He balanced pennies on top of my wrists so I would keep them still as I slowly played scales and arpeggios. He had me curve my hand around an apple and keep that shape when playing chords. He marched stiffly to show me how to make each finger dance up and down, staccato like an obedient little soldier.

He taught me all these things, and that was how I also learned I could be lazy and get away with mistakes, lots of mistakes. If I hit the wrong notes because I hadn't practiced enough, I never corrected myself. I just kept playing in rhythm. And Old Chong kept conducting his own private reverie.

So maybe I never really gave myself a fair chance. I did pick up the basics pretty quickly, and I might have become a good pianist at that young age. But I was so determined not to try, not to be anybody different that I learned to play only the most ear-splitting preludes, the most discordant hymns.

Over the next year, I practiced like this, dutifully in my own way. And then one day I heard my mother and her friend Lindo Jong both talking in a loud bragging tone of voice so others could hear. It was after church, and I was leaning against the brick wall wearing a dress with stiff white petticoats. Auntie Lindo's daughter, Waverly, who was about my age, was standing farther down the wall about five feet away. We had grown up together and shared all the closeness of two sisters squabbling over crayons and dolls. In other words, for the most part, we hated each other. I thought she was snotty. Waverly Jong had gained a certain amount of fame as "Chinatown's Littlest Chinese Chess Champion."

"She bring home too many trophy," lamented Auntie Lindo that Sunday. "All day she play chess. All day I have no time do nothing but dust off her winnings." She threw a scolding look at Waverly, who pretended not to see her.

"You lucky you don't have this problem," said Auntie Lindo with a sigh to my mother.

And my mother squared her shoulders and bragged: "Our problem worser than yours. If we ask Jing-mei wash dish, she hear nothing but music. It's like you can't stop this natural talent."

And right then, I was determined to put a stop to her foolish pride.

A few weeks later, Old Chong and my mother conspired to have me play in a talent show which would be held in the church hall. By then, my parents had saved up enough to buy me a secondhand piano, a black Wurlitzer spinet with a scarred bench. It was the showpiece of our living room.

For the talent show, I was to play a piece called "Pleading Child" from Schumann's *Scenes from Childhood.* It was a simple, moody piece that sounded more difficult than it was. I was supposed to memorize the whole thing, playing the repeat parts twice to make the piece sound longer. But I dawdled over it, playing a few bars and then cheating, looking up to see what notes followed. I never really listened to what I was playing. I daydreamed about being somewhere else, about being someone else.

The part I liked to practice best was the fancy curtsy: right foot out, touch the rose on the carpet with a pointed foot, sweep to the side, left leg bends, look up and smile.

My parents invited all the couples from the Joy Luck Club[1] to witness my debut. Auntie Lindo and Uncle Tin were there. Waverly and her two older brothers had also come. The first two rows were filled with children both younger and older than I was. The littlest ones got to go first. They recited simple nursery rhymes, squawked out tunes on miniature violins, twirled Hula Hoops, pranced in pink ballet tutus, and when they bowed or curtsied, the audience would sigh in unison, "Awww," and then clap enthusiastically.

When my turn came, I was very confident. I remember my childish excitement. It was as if I knew, without a doubt, that the prodigy side of me really did exist. I had no fear whatsoever, no nervousness. I remember thinking to myself, This is it! This is it! I looked out over the audience, at my mother's blank face, my father's yawn, Auntie Lindo's stiff-lipped smile, Waverly's sulky expression. I had on a white dress layered with sheets of lace, and a pink bow in my Peter Pan haircut. As I sat down I envisioned people jumping to their feet and Ed Sullivan rushing up to introduce me to everyone on TV.

---

[1]*Joy Luck Club:* A name denoting the mother's circle of friends, all of whom were Chinese immigrants to the United States.

And I started to play. It was so beautiful. I was so caught up in how lovely I looked that at first I didn't worry how I would sound. So it was a surprise to me when I hit the first wrong note and I realized something didn't sound quite right. And then I hit another and another followed that. A chill started at the top of my head and began to trickle down. Yet I couldn't stop playing, as though my hands were bewitched. I kept thinking my fingers would adjust themselves back, like a train switching to the right track. I played this strange jumble through two repeats, the sour notes staying with me all the way to the end.

When I stood up, I discovered my legs were shaking. Maybe I had just been nervous and the audience, like Old Chong, had seen me go through the right motions and had not heard anything wrong at all. I swept my right foot out, went down on my knee, looked up and smiled. The room was quiet, except for Old Chong, who was beaming and shouting, "Bravo! Bravo! Well done!" But then I saw my mother's face, her stricken face. The audience clapped weakly, and as I walked back to my chair, with my whole face quivering as I tried not to cry, I heard a little boy whisper loudly to his mother, "That was awful," and the mother whispered back, "Well, she certainly tried." 55

And now I realized how many people were in the audience, the whole world it seemed. I was aware of eyes burning into my back. I felt the shame of my mother and father as they sat stiffly throughout the rest of the show.

We could have escaped during intermission. Pride and some strange sense of honor must have anchored my parents to their chairs. And so we watched it all: the eighteen-year-old boy with a fake mustache who did a magic show and juggled flaming hoops while riding a unicycle. The breasted girl with white makeup who sang from *Madama Butterfly* and got honorable mention. And the eleven-year-old boy who won first prize playing a tricky violin song that sounded like a busy bee.

After the show, the Hsus, the Jongs, and the St. Clairs from the Joy Luck Club came up to my mother and father.

"Lots of talented kids," Auntie Lindo said vaguely, smiling broadly.

"That was somethin' else," said my father, and I wondered if he was referring to me in a humorous way, or whether he even remembered what I had done. 60

Waverly looked at me and shrugged her shoulders. "You aren't a genius like me," she said matter-of-factly. And if I hadn't felt so bad, I would have pulled her braids and punched her stomach.

But my mother's expression was what devastated me: a quiet, blank look that said she had lost everything. I felt the same way, and it seemed as if everybody were now coming up, like gawkers at the scene of an accident, to see what parts were actually missing. When we got on the bus to go home, my father was humming the busy-bee tune and my mother was silent. I kept thinking she wanted to wait until we got home before shouting at me. But when my father unlocked the door to our apartment, my mother walked in and then went to the back, into the bedroom. No accusations. No blame. And in a way, I felt disappointed. I had been waiting for her to start shouting, so I could shout back and cry and blame her for all my misery.

I assumed my talent-show fiasco meant I never had to play the piano again. But two days later, after school, my mother came out of the kitchen and saw me watching TV.

"Four clock," she reminded me as if it were any other day. I was stunned, as though she were asking me to go through the talent-show torture again. I wedged myself more tightly in front of the TV.

"Turn off TV," she called from the kitchen five minutes later.

I didn't budge. And then I decided. I didn't have to do what my mother said anymore. I wasn't her slave. This wasn't China. I had listened to her before and look what happened. She was the stupid one.

She came out from the kitchen and stood in the arched entryway of the living room. "Four clock," she said once again, louder.

"I'm not going to play anymore," I said nonchalantly. "Why should I? I'm not a genius."

She walked over and stood in front of the TV. I saw her chest was heaving up and down in an angry way.

"No!" I said, and I now felt stronger, as if my true self had finally emerged. So this was what had been inside me all along.

"No! I won't!" I screamed.

She yanked me by the arm, pulled me off the floor, snapped off the TV. She was frighteningly strong, half pulling, half carrying me toward the piano as I kicked the throw rugs under my feet. She lifted me up and onto the hard bench. I was sobbing by now, looking at her bitterly. Her chest was heaving even more and her mouth was open, smiling crazily as if she were pleased I was crying.

"You want me to be someone that I'm not!" I sobbed. "I'll never be the kind of daughter you want me to be!"

"Only two kinds of daughters," she shouted in Chinese. "Those who are obedient and those who follow their own mind! Only one kind of daughter can live in this house. Obedient daughter!"

"Then I wish I wasn't your daughter. I wish you weren't my mother," I shouted. As I said these things I got scared. It felt like worms and toads and slimy things crawling out of my chest, but it also felt good, as if this awful side of me had surfaced, at last.

"Too late change this," said my mother shrilly.

And I could sense her anger rising to its breaking point. I wanted to see it spill over. And that's when I remembered the babies she had lost in China, the ones we never talked about. "Then I wish I'd never been born!" I shouted. "I wish I were dead! Like them."

It was as if I had said the magic words. Alakazam!—and her face went blank, her mouth closed, her arms went slack, and she backed out of the room, stunned, as if she were blowing away like a small brown leaf, thin, brittle, lifeless.

It was not the only disappointment my mother felt in me. In the years that followed, I failed her so many times, each time asserting my own will, my right to fall short of expectations. I didn't get straight As. I didn't become class president. I didn't get into Stanford. I dropped out of college.

For unlike my mother, I did not believe I could be anything I wanted to be. I could only be me. 80

And for all those years, we never talked about the disaster at the recital or my terrible accusations afterward at the piano bench. All that remained unchecked, like a betrayal that was now unspeakable. So I never found a way to ask her why she had hoped for something so large that failure was inevitable.

And even worse, I never asked her what frightened me the most: Why had she given up hope?

For after our struggle at the piano, she never mentioned my playing again. The lessons stopped. The lid to the piano was closed, shutting out the dust, my misery, and her dreams.

So she surprised me. A few years ago, she offered to give me the piano, for my thirtieth birthday. I had not played in all those years. I saw the offer as a sign of forgiveness, a tremendous burden removed.

"Are you sure?" I asked shyly. "I mean, won't you and Dad miss it?" 85

"No, this your piano," she said firmly. "Always your piano. You only one can play."

"Well, I probably can't play anymore," I said. "It's been years."

"You pick up fast," said my mother, as if she knew this was certain. "You have natural talent. You could been genius if you want to."

"No I couldn't."

"You just not trying," said my mother. And she was neither angry nor sad. She said it as if to announce a fact that could never be disproved. "Take it," she said. 90

But I didn't at first. It was enough that she had offered it to me. And after that, every time I saw it in my parents' living room, standing in front of the bay windows, it made me feel proud, as if it were a shiny trophy I had won back.

Last week I sent a tuner over to my parents' apartment and had the piano reconditioned, for purely sentimental reasons. My mother had died a few months before and I had been getting things in order for my father, a little bit at a time. I put the jewelry in special silk pouches. The sweaters she had knitted in yellow, pink, bright orange—all the colors I hated—I put those in moth-proof boxes. I found some old Chinese silk dresses, the kind with little slits up the sides. I rubbed the old silk against my skin, then wrapped them in tissue and decided to take them home with me.

After I had the piano tuned, I opened the lid and touched the keys. It sounded even richer than I remembered. Really, it was a very good piano. Inside the bench were the same exercise notes with handwritten scales, the same secondhand music books with their covers held together with yellow tape.

I opened up the Schumann book to the dark little piece I had played at the recital. It was on the left-hand side of the page, "Pleading Child." It looked more difficult than I remembered. I played a few bars, surprised at how easily the notes came back to me.

And for the first time, or so it seemed, I noticed the piece on the right-hand side. It was called "Perfectly Contented." I tried to play this one as well. It had a lighter melody but the same flowing rhythm and turned out to be quite easy. "Pleading Child" was shorter but slower; "Perfectly Contented" was longer, but faster. And after I played them both a few times, I realized they were two halves
of the same song. 95

* * *

Part 3

Poetry

Chapter

17

Understanding Poetry

Learning Objectives

After reading this chapter, you will be able to...

- Outline the history of poetry.
- Describe major poetic movements.
- Summarize the historical, cultural, and national origins of poetic movements.
- Describe how poetry is different from other forms of literature.
- Identify figurative language in poems.
- Recognize lyric and narrative poems.

Archibald MacLeish (1892–1982)

Ars Poetica (1926)

A poem should be palpable and mute
As a globed fruit,

Dumb
As old medallions to the thumb,

Silent as the sleeve-worn stone
Of casement ledges where the moss has grown—

A poem should be wordless
As the flight of birds.

*

A poem should be motionless in time
As the moon climbs,

Leaving, as the moon releases
Twig by twig the night-entangled trees,

Leaving, as the moon behind the winter leaves,
Memory by memory the mind—

A poem should be motionless in time
As the moon climbs.

*

A poem should be equal to:
Not true.

For all the history of grief
An empty doorway and a maple leaf.

For love
The leaning grasses and two lights above the sea—

A poem should not mean
But be.

AP Images/Beth A. Keiser

Billy Collins (1941–)

Introduction to Poetry (1988)

I ask them to take a poem
and hold it up to the light
like a color slide

or press an ear against its hive.

I say drop a mouse into a poem
and watch him probe his way out,

or walk inside the poem's room
and feel the walls for a light switch.

I want them to waterski
across the surface of a poem
waving at the author's name on the shore.

But all they want to do
is tie the poem to a chair with rope
and torture a confession out of it.

They begin beating it with a hose
to find out what it really means.

Origins of Modern Poetry

The history of poetry begins where the history of all literature begins—with the **oral tradition,** information passed down from one generation to another by word of mouth. For thousands of years, in a time before literacy and the printing press, the oral tradition was relied on as a way of preserving stories, histories, values, and beliefs. These stories were usually put into the form of rhyming poems with repeated words and sounds used to make the poems easier to memorize and remember.

These extended narratives were eventually transcribed as **epics**—long poems depicting the actions of heroic figures who determine the fate of a nation or an entire race. Early epics include Homer's *Iliad* and *Odyssey*, the *Epic of Gilgamesh*, the *Bhagavad Gita*, and Virgil's *Aeneid*. Early poetry can also be found in various religious texts, including ancient Hindu holy books like the Upanishads; sections of the Bible, including the Song of Solomon; and the Koran.

During the **Anglo-Saxon era** (late-sixth to mid-eleventh centuries), poetry flourished as a literary form. Unfortunately, only about 30,000 lines of poetry survive from this period. Those poems that did survive are marked by violence, carnage, and heroic deeds as well as Pagan and Christian themes. The major texts of this time include *Beowulf*, *The Battle of Maldon*, and *The Dream of the Rood*, which is one of the earliest Christian poems. The theme of Christian morality in poetry continued into the Middle Ages with poems such as William Langland's *Piers Plowman*, which consists of three religious dream visions, and Chaucer's *Canterbury Tales*, a collection of narrative poems told by pilgrims as they travel to Canterbury, England. Using a slightly different approach to similar subject matter, Dante Alighieri wrote the Italian epic poem *The Divine Comedy*, which depicts an imaginary journey through hell, purgatory, and heaven. In the South of France, poets of the Provençal region, the **troubadours,** wrote complex lyric poems. Composed for singing and not recitation, these poems focused mainly on secular themes such as chivalry and courtly love.

The next major literary period, the **Renaissance** (late-fourteenth to mid-sixteenth centuries), witnessed the rebirth of science, philosophy, and the classical arts. Perhaps the most important writer of this period was William Shakespeare. A prolific poet, Shakespeare also wrote plays in verse, continuing in the tradition of the ancient Greek tragedian Sophocles and the ancient Roman playwright Seneca. Other notable writers of the Renaissance included Sir Philip Sidney, Christopher Marlowe, and Edmund Spenser.

Illustration of Trojan horse from Virgil's *Aenied*
Bettmann/Getty Images

During the seventeenth century, several literary movements emerged that contributed to poetry's growing prevalence and influence. John Milton continued the tradition of Christian poetry with his epic *Paradise Lost*, which told the tale of Adam and Eve's exile from the Garden of Eden. The **metaphysical poets** (John Donne, Andrew Marvell, and George Herbert) used elaborate figures of speech and favored intellect over emotions in their writing. Their poems were characterized by reason, complex comparisons and allusions, and paradoxes, and they introduced the **meditative poem** (a poem that abstractly ponders a concept or idea) into the literary world.

Image depicting the pilgrims from Geoffrey Chaucer's *The Canterbury Tales*

Roy 18 D II f.148 Lydgate and the Canterbury Pilgrims Leaving Canterbury from the 'Troy Book and the Siege of Thebes' by John Lydgate (c.1370–c.1451) 1412–22 (vellum) (detail of 8063), English School (15th century)/British Library, London, UK/

From the middle of the seventeenth century until almost the end of the eighteenth century, a movement know as **neoclassicism** appeared. This movement rejected the frills of Renaissance poetry and advocated a return to the order and discipline of classical Greek and Roman poetry. British poets such as John Dryden, Alexander Pope, and Samuel Johnson are among the best-known of the neoclassical poets.

Toward the end of the eighteenth century, the movement known as **Romanticism** began. Where neoclassic poetry emphasized the past, formality, and stylistic rigidity, the Romantic poetry stressed individualism. It was marked by heightened emotion and sentiment; a strong sense of individualism; a fascination with nature, the Middle Ages, and mysticism; a rebellion against social and political norms; and a return to first-person lyric poems. The early British Romantics included Samuel Taylor Coleridge, William Wordsworth, and William Blake. This generation was followed by the later Romantics, including Percy Bysshe Shelley, John Keats, George Gordon, and Lord Byron. American Romantics (called **transcendentalists**) included Henry David Thoreau, Ralph Waldo Emerson, and Walt Whitman.

The nineteenth century was marked by yet another shift in poetic consciousness that corresponded with the reign of Queen Victoria in England. This time, poets moved away from the contemplation of the self within nature that characterized Romanticism and focused on themes such as social injustice, patriotism, religious faith, and romantic love.

Illuminated manuscript (fifteenth century) from Dante's *Divine Comedy* depicting Dante and Virgil in Hell
Alfredo Dagli Orti/Shutterstock.com

John Martin's painting *The Bard* (1817) illustrating the mystical view of nature characteristic of Romanticism
The Bard, c.1817 (oil on canvas), Martin, John (1789–1854)/Yale Center for British Art, Paul Mellon Collection, USA/Paul Mellon Collection/Bridgeman Images

Illuminated manuscript from William Blake's "The Tyger"
©Fitzwilliam Museum, University of Cambridge, UK/Bridgeman Art Library

Undated engraving illustrating Edgar Allan Poe's "The Raven"
Bettmann/Getty Images

Notable British poets of the **Victorian Age** included Matthew Arnold, Robert Browning, Elizabeth Barrett Browning, and Alfred Lord Tennyson. American poets of this period included Edgar Allan Poe, Henry Wadsworth Longfellow, Emily Dickinson, and Phillis Wheatley, an enslaved person who became the first Black poet.

The twentieth century had perhaps the largest number of literary movements to date with each one reflecting its predecessors and influencing future generations of poets. In the early twentieth century, a literary movement that became known as **modernism** developed. As writers responded to the increasing complexity of a changing world, the overarching sentiment of modernism was that the "old ways" would no longer suffice in a world that had changed almost overnight as a result of the rise of industrialization and urbanization, as well as the devastation of World War I. Key modernist poets included W. H. Auden, William Butler Yeats, Ezra Pound, and T. S. Eliot, whose epic poem *The Waste Land* expressed the fragmentation of consciousness in the modern world.

After World War I, poets began to challenge the prevailing ideas of subject matter and form. Ezra Pound, along with Amy Lowell and other poets, founded **imagism**, a poetic movement that emphasized free verse and the writer's response to a visual scene or an object. William Carlos Williams wrote poems that were often deceptively simple, while the poetry of Wallace Stevens was often opaque and difficult to grasp. Dylan Thomas and E. E. Cummings also experimented with form with Cummings intentionally manipulating the accepted constructs of grammar, syntax, and punctuation.

In the 1920s, the United States experienced the **Harlem Renaissance**. This rebirth of arts and culture was centered in Harlem, an area in New York City where, by the mid-1920s, the Black population had reached 150,000. At that time, Harlem was teeming with creativity, especially in music (jazz and blues), literature, art, and drama. The poets who were part of the Harlem Renaissance—including Langston Hughes, Countee Cullen, James Weldon Johnson, Claude McKay, and Jean Toomer—chose diverse subject matter and styles, but they were united in their celebration of African American culture.

In the early 1930s, a group of poets gathered at an experimental college in Black Mountain, North Carolina, with the aim of teaching and writing about poetry in a new way. These **Black Mountain Poets** called for an "open field" poetry that was based on natural patterns of breath rather than fixed poetic forms. Notable poets in this group included Robert Creeley, Denise Levertov, and Charles Olson. Meanwhile, in Latin America, poets such as Pablo Neruda were experimenting with subject matter, language, form, and imagery.

In the late 1940s, in the aftermath of World War II, a group of disillusioned American poets turned to eastern mysticism, especially Buddhism, and newly available hallucinogenic drugs to achieve higher consciousness. They became known as the **Beat poets**, and their work was known for social and political criticism that challenged the social norms of the time. These poets included Lawrence Ferlinghetti and Allen Ginsberg, whose long poem *Howl*, which initially was deemed obscene, became an unofficial anthem of the revolutionary 1960s.

Up until the late 1950s, subject matter in American poetry was largely impersonal, concentrating chiefly on symbols, ideas, and politics. This changed when a group of poets—including Robert Lowell, Anne Sexton, W. D. Snodgrass, and Sylvia Plath—began to write **confessional poems** about their own personal experiences, emotions, triumphs, and tragedies (including

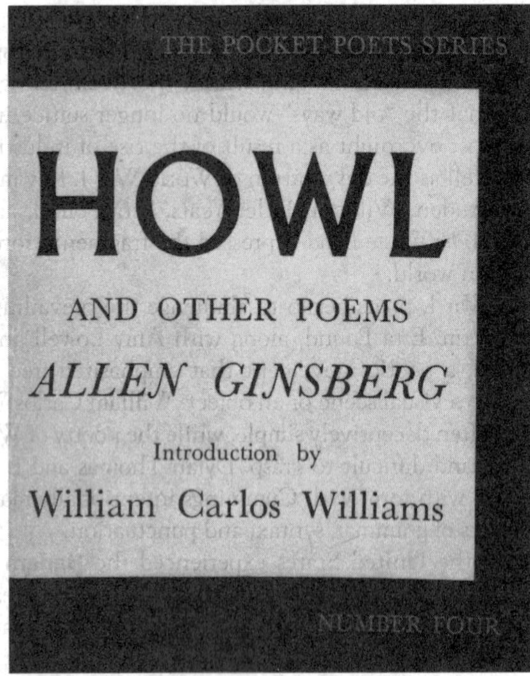

Cover of the first edition of *Howl*, published by City Lights Books in 1956

Source: 1956 by City Lights Books

mental illness and attempted suicide). Although there was considerable backlash against these poets from writers who thought that such highly personal subjects were not suitable for poetry, contemporary poets such as Sharon Olds continue to write confessional poetry.

The early 1960s witnessed the rise of the **Black Arts Movement**, which had its roots in the ideas of the civil rights struggle, Malcolm X and the Nation of Islam, and the Black Power Movement. The Black Arts poets wrote political works that addressed the sociopolitical and cultural context of Black life in the United States. Notable authors in this group included Amiri Baraka, Gwendolyn Brooks, Jayne Cortez, and Etheridge Knight.

The next major literary movement in poetry had its beginnings in the mid- to late-1980s with slam poetry. **Slam poetry**, with origins in the oral tradition, was influenced by the Beat poets, who stressed the live performance of poems. In a **slam**, poets compete either individually or in teams before an audience, which serves as the judge. (The structure of a traditional poetry slam was created by Marc Smith, a poet and construction worker, in 1986.) Slam poetry is concerned with current events and social and political themes, and often the winning poet is the one who best combines enthusiasm, presentation, and attitude with contemporary subject matter. A home base for slam poetry is the

Staceyann Chin, acclaimed slam poet and the star of *Def Poetry Jam on Broadway*
Richard Termine/The New York Times/Redux

Nyuorican Poets Café in New York City, which has become a forum for poetry, music, video, and theater. Notable slam poets past and present include Miguel Piñero, Maggie Estep, Jeffrey McDaniel, and Bob Holman.

A spinoff of slam poetry is the **spoken word** movement, which, unlike slam poetry, is a rehearsed performance. Spoken word performances have captivated a broad audience due in part to television shows such as HBO's *Def Poetry Jam* (2002–2007). **Hip-hop** and **rap**, musical forms whose lyrics rely heavily on rhyme, alliteration, assonance, consonance, and other poetic devices, also owe a debt to slam poetry and the spoken word movement.

Contemporary poetry is an extremely diverse genre whose practitioners have been influenced by many of the literary movements discussed earlier. Some contemporary poets embrace narrative poetry; others favor the lyric. Some write free verse; others experiment with traditional forms like the **sonnet** or the **villanelle**. Still others write **concrete poetry**, which uses words as well as varying type sizes and type fonts to form pictures on a page, or other forms of **visual poetry**.

With the advent of digital media, new forms of poetry have emerged that use multimedia elements to create texts. Not just words, but also sound, images, and video combine to create new poetic forms and new levels of aesthetic experience. For example, **hypertext poetry** has links to other texts (or visuals) that are available electronically. These links can appear all at once on the screen or they can be revealed gradually, creating multiple levels of meaning. **Kinetic poetry** is a form in which letters (or words) drift around the screen, gradually coalescing to form phrases, lines, and possibly entire poems. **Interactive poetry** depends on readers contributing content that enhances and possibly determines the meaning of the poem. **Code poetry** is programming code expressed as poetry. The most famous code poem is "Black Perl," which is written in Perl programming language. These and other forms of digital poetry use digital technology to challenge and expand the notion of what poetry is and should be.

Defining Poetry

Throughout history and across national and cultural boundaries, poetry has occupied an important place. In ancient China and Japan, for example, poetry was prized above all else. One story tells of a samurai warrior who, when defeated and awaiting execution, asked for a pen and paper. Thinking that he wanted to write a will before being executed, his captor granted his wish. Instead of writing a will, however, the warrior wrote a farewell poem that so moved his captor that he immediately released him.

To the ancient Greeks and Romans, poetry was the highest medium of spiritual and philosophical expression. Today, throughout the world, poetry continues to delight and to inspire. For many people in countless places, poetry is the language of the emotions, the medium of expression they use when they speak from the heart.

But what exactly *is* poetry? Is it, as Seamus Heaney says, "language in orbit"? Is it as, Rita Dove observes, "language at its most distilled and most powerful"? Is it, as Billy Collins laments, something that must be beaten with a hose "to find out what it really means" (p. 483)? Or is a poem simply what Marianne Moore calls "all this fiddle"?

One way of defining poetry is to examine how it is different from other forms of literature, such as fiction or drama. The first and most important element of poetry that distinguishes it from other genres is its **form**. Unlike prose, which is written from margin to margin, poetry is made up of individual **lines**. A poetic line begins and ends where the poet chooses: it can start at the left margin or halfway across the page, and it can end at the right margin or after only a word or two. Poets choose when to stop, or break, the line according to their sense of rhythm and meter.

Poets also use the **sound** of the words themselves, alone and in conjunction with the other words of the poem, to create a sense of rhythm and melody. **Alliteration** (the repetition of initial consonant sounds in consecutive or neighboring words), **assonance** (the repetition of vowel sounds), and **consonance** (the repetition of consonant sounds within words) are three devices commonly used by poets to help create the music of a poem. Poets can also use **rhyme** (either at the ends of lines or within the lines themselves), which contributes to the pattern of sounds in a poem.

In addition, poets are more likely than writers of other kinds of literature to rely on **imagery**, words or phrases that describe the senses. These vivid descriptions or details help the reader to connect with the poet's ideas in a tangible way. Poets also make extensive use of **figurative language**, including metaphors and similes, to convey their ideas and to help their readers access these ideas.

Another way of defining poetry is to examine our assumptions about it. Different readers, different poets, different generations of readers and poets, and different cultures often have different expectations about poetry. As a result, they have varying assumptions about what poetry should be, and these assumptions raise questions. Must poetry be written to delight or inspire, or can a poem have a political or social message? Must a poem's theme be conveyed subtly, embellished with imaginatively chosen sounds and words, or can it be explicit and straightforward? Must a poem rhyme and have a definite structure? Such questions, which have been debated by literary critics as well as by poets for many years, have no easy answers—and perhaps no answers at all. For example, most readers would agree that the following lines qualify as poetry.

William Shakespeare (1564–1616)

That time of year thou mayst in me behold (1609)

That time of year thou mayst in me behold
When yellow leaves, or none, or few, do hang
Upon those boughs which shake against the cold,
Bare ruined choirs, where late the sweet birds sang.
In me thou see'st the twilight of such day
As after sunset fadeth in the West,
Which by and by black night doth take away,
Death's second self that seals up all in rest.
In me thou see'st the glowing of such fire,
That on the ashes of his youth doth lie,
As the deathbed whereon it must expire,
Consumed with that which it was nourished by.
 This thou perceiv'st, which makes thy love more strong,
 To love that well which thou must leave ere long.

This poem includes many of the characteristics that Western readers commonly associate with poetry. For instance, its lines have a regular pattern of rhyme and meter that identifies it as a **sonnet**. The poem also develops a complex network of related images and figures of speech that compare the lost youth of the aging speaker to the sunset and to autumn. Finally, the pair of rhyming lines at the end of the poem expresses a familiar poetic theme: the lovers' realization that they must eventually die makes their love stronger.

Although most readers would classify Shakespeare's sonnet as a poem, they might be less certain about the following lines.

E. E. Cummings (1894–1962)

l(a (1923)

l(a
le
af
fa
ll
s)
one
l
iness

Unlike Shakespeare's poem, "l(a" does not seem to have any of the characteristics normally associated with poetry. It has no meter, rhyme, or imagery. It has no repeated sounds and no figures of speech. It cannot even be read aloud because its "lines" are fragments of words. In spite of its odd appearance, however, "l(a" does communicate a conventional poetic theme.

When reconstructed, the words Cummings broke apart have the following appearance: "l (a leaf falls) one l iness." In a sense, this poem is a complex visual and verbal pun. If the parenthetical insertion "(a leaf falls)" is removed, the remaining letters spell "loneliness." Moreover, the form of the letter *l* in loneliness suggests the number *1*—which, in turn, suggests the loneliness and isolation of the individual, as reflected in nature (the single leaf). Like Shakespeare, Cummings uses an image of a leaf to express his ideas about life and human experience. At the same time, by breaking words into bits and pieces, Cummings suggests the flexibility of language and conveys the need to break out of customary ways of using words to define experience.

As these two poems illustrate, defining what a poem is (and what it is not) can be difficult. Poems can rhyme or not rhyme. They can be divided into stanzas and have a distinct form, or they can flow freely and have no discernable form. These and other choices are what many poets find alluring about the process of writing poetry. As a form, poetry is compact and concise, and choosing the right words to convey ideas is a challenge. As a literary genre, it offers room for experimentation while at the same time remaining firmly grounded in a literary tradition that stretches back through time to antiquity.

Recognizing Kinds of Poetry

Most poems are either **narrative** poems, which recount a story, or **lyric** poems, which communicate a speaker's mood, feelings, or state of mind.

Narrative Poetry

Although any brief poem that tells a story, such as Edwin Arlington Robinson's "Richard Cory" (p. 734), may be considered a narrative poem, the two most familiar forms of narrative poetry are the *epic* and the *ballad.*

Epics are narrative poems that recount the accomplishments of heroic figures, typically including expansive settings, superhuman feats, and gods and supernatural beings. The language of epic poems tends to be formal, even elevated, and often quite elaborate. In ancient times, epics were handed down orally; more recently, poets have written literary epics, such as John Milton's *Paradise Lost* (1667), Ezra Pound's *The Cantos* (1915–1969), and Nobel Prize–winning poet Derek Walcott's *Omeros* (1990), that follow many of the same conventions.

The **ballad** is another type of narrative poetry with roots in an oral tradition. Originally intended to be sung, a ballad uses repeated words and phrases, including a refrain, to advance its story. Some—but not all—ballads use the **ballad stanza**. For an example of a traditional ballad in this book, see "Bonny Barbara Allan" (p. 696).

Lyric Poetry

Like narrative poems, lyric poems take various forms.

An **elegy** is a poem in which a poet mourns the death of a specific person (or persons), as in "To an Athlete Dying Young" (p. 540).

An **ode** is a long lyric poem, formal and serious in style, tone, and subject matter. An ode typically has a fairly complex stanzaic pattern, such as the **terza rima** used by Percy Bysshe Shelley in "Ode to the West Wind" (p. 736). Another ode in this text is John Keats's "Ode on a Grecian Urn" (p. 727).

An **occasional poem** is written to celebrate a particular event or occasion. An example is Billy Collins's 2002 poem "The Names," read before a joint session of Congress to commemorate the first anniversary of the terrorist attacks on the World Trade Center.

A **meditation** is a lyric poem that focuses on a physical object, using this object as a vehicle for considering larger issues. Edmund Waller's seventeenth-century poem "Go, lovely rose" is a meditation.

A **pastoral**—for example, Christopher Marlowe's "The Passionate Shepherd to His Love" (p. 730)—is a lyric poem that celebrates the simple, idyllic pleasures of country life.

A **dramatic monologue** is a poem where the speaker addresses one or more silent listeners and often reveals much more than intended. Robert Browning's "My Last Duchess" (p. 499) and "Porphyria's Lover" (p. 514) and Alfred Lord Tennyson's "Ulysses" (p. 739) are dramatic monologues.

As you read the poems in this text, you will encounter works with a wide variety of forms, styles, and themes. Some you will find appealing, amusing, uplifting, or moving; others may strike you as puzzling, intimidating, or depressing. But regardless of your critical reaction to the poems, one thing is certain: if you take the time to connect with the lines you are reading, you will come away from them thinking not just about the images and ideas they express but also about yourself and your world.

Chapter

18

Voice

Langston Hughes
Library of Congress Prints and Photographs Division [LC-USZ62-43605]

Robert Browning
AP Images

Loüise Glück
Robin Marchant/Getty Images

Rafael Campo
© Estate of Robert Giard

Learning Objectives

After reading this chapter, you will be able to...

- Define the role of the speaker in poems.
- Identify the relation between the speaker and the author in poems.
- Describe the tone of poems.
- Outline the methods poets use to indicate tone.
- Interpret the speaker's attitude based on the poem's tone.
- Evaluate the use of irony in poems.

Bettmann/Getty Images

Emily Dickinson (1830–1886)

I'm nobody! Who are you? (1891)

I'm nobody! Who are you?
Are you—Nobody—Too?
Then there's a pair of us?
Don't tell! They'd advertise—you know!
How dreary—to be—Somebody!
How public—like a Frog—
To tell one's name—the livelong June—
To an admiring Bog!

The Speaker in the Poem

When they read a work of fiction, readers must decide whether the narrator is sophisticated or unsophisticated, trustworthy or untrustworthy, innocent or experienced. Just as fiction depends on a narrator, poetry depends on a **speaker** who describes events, feelings, and ideas to readers. Finding out as much as possible about this speaker can help readers to interpret a poem. For example, the speaker in Emily Dickinson's "I'm nobody! Who are you?" seems at first to be not just self-effacing but also playful, even flirtatious. As the poem continues, however, the speaker becomes more complex. In the first stanza, she reveals her private self—internal, isolated, with little desire to be well known; in the second stanza, she expresses disdain for those who seek to become "somebody," whom she sees as self-centered, self-promoting, and inevitably superficial. Far from being defeated by her isolation, the speaker rejects fame and celebrates her status as a "nobody."

One question readers might ask about "I'm nobody! Who are you?" is how close the speaker's voice is to the poet's. Readers who conclude that the poem is about the conflict between a poet's public and private selves may be tempted to see the speaker and the poet as one. But this is not necessarily the case. Like the narrator of a short story, the speaker of a poem is a **persona**, or mask, that the poet puts on. Granted, in some poems, little distance exists between the poet and the speaker. Without hard evidence to support a link between speaker and poet, however, readers should not simply assume they are one and the same.

In many cases, the speaker is quite different from the poet—even when the speaker's voice conveys the attitude of the poet, either directly or indirectly. In the 1789 poem "The Chimney Sweeper" (p. 700), for example, William Blake assumes the voice of a child to criticize the system of child labor that existed in eighteenth-century England. Even though the child speaker does not understand the economic and social forces that cause his misery, readers sense the poet's anger as the trusting speaker describes the appalling conditions under which he works. The poet's indignation is especially apparent in the biting irony of the last line, in which the victimized speaker echoes the moral precepts of the time by innocently assuring readers that if all people do their duty, "they need not fear harm."

Sometimes the poem's speaker is anonymous. In such cases—as in William Carlos Williams's "Red Wheelbarrow" (p. 547), for example—the first-person voice is absent, and the speaker remains outside the poem. At other times, the speaker has a set identity—a king, a beggar, a highwayman, a sheriff, a husband, a wife, a rich man, a murderer, a child, a mythical figure, an explorer, a teacher, a faithless lover, a saint—or even a flower, an animal, or a clod of earth. Whatever the case, the speaker is not the poet but rather a creation that the poet uses to convey ideas. (For this reason, poems by a single poet may have very different voices. Compare Sylvia Plath's bitter and sardonic poem "Daddy" [p. 571] with her nurturing and celebratory work "Morning Song" [p. 511], for example.)

Sometimes a poem's title tells readers that the poet is assuming a particular persona. In the following poem, for example, the title identifies the speaker as a fictional character, Gretel from the fairy tale "Hansel and Gretel."

Robin Marchant/Getty Images

Louise Glück (1943–)

Gretel in Darkness (1971)

This is the world we wanted.
All who would have seen us dead
are dead. I hear the witch's cry
break in the moonlight through a sheet
of sugar: God rewards.
Her tongue shrivels into gas....
Now, far from women's arms
And memory of women, in our father's hut
we sleep, are never hungry.
Why do I not forget?
My father bars the door, bars harm
from this house, and it is years.

No one remembers. Even you, my brother,
summer afternoons you look at me as though
you meant to leave,
as though it never happened.
But I killed for you. I see armed firs,
the spires of that gleaming kiln—

Nights I turn to you to hold me
but you are not there.
Am I alone? Spies
hiss in the stillness, Hansel
we are there still, and it is real, real,
that black forest, and the fire in earnest.

Illustration of "Hansel and Gretel" (1930)
VTR/Alamy Stock Photo

The speaker in this poem comments on her life after her encounter with the witch in the forest. Speaking to her brother, Hansel, Gretel observes that they now live in the world they wanted: they live with their father in his hut, and the witch and the wicked stepmother are dead. Even so, the memory of the events in the forest haunts Gretel making it impossible for her to live "happily ever after."

By assuming the persona of Gretel, the poet is able to convey some interesting and complex ideas. On one level, Gretel represents any person who has lived through a traumatic experience. Memories of the event keep breaking through into the present, frustrating her attempts to reestablish her belief in the goodness of the world. The voice we hear is sad, alone, and frightened: "Nights I turn to you to hold me," she says, "but you are not there." Although the murder Gretel committed for her brother was justified, it seems to haunt her. "No one remembers," laments Gretel, not even her brother. At some level, she realizes that, by killing the witch, she has killed a part of herself, perhaps the part of women that men fear and consequently transform into witches and wicked stepmothers. The world that is left after the killing is her father's and her brother's, not her own, and she is now alone haunted by the memories of the black forest. In this sense, Gretel—"Now, far from women's arms / And memory of women"—may be the voice of all victimized women who, because of men, act against their own best interests—and ultimately regretting it.

As "Gretel in Darkness" illustrates, a title can identify a poem's speaker, but the speaker's words can provide even more information. In the next poem, the first line of each stanza establishes the identity of the speaker—and defines his perspective.

Library of Congress Prints and Photographs Division [LC-USZ62-43605]

Langston Hughes (1902–1967)

Negro (1926)

I am a Negro:
   Black as the night is black,
   Black like the depths of my Africa.

I've been a slave:
   Caesar told me to keep his door-steps clean.
   I brushed the boots of Washington.

I've been a worker:
Under my hand the pyramids arose.
I made mortar for the Woolworth Building.

I've been a singer:
All the way from Africa to Georgia
I carried my sorrow songs.
I made ragtime.

I've been a victim:
The Belgians cut off my hands in the Congo.
They lynch me still in Mississippi.

I am a Negro:
Black as the night is black,
Black like the depths of my Africa.

Here the speaker, identifying himself as "a Negro," assumes the roles Black Americans have historically played in Western society—slave, worker, singer, and victim. By so doing, he gives voice to his ancestors who, by being forced to serve others, were deprived of their identities. By presenting not only their suffering but also their accomplishments, the speaker asserts his pride in being Black. The speaker also implies that the suffering of Black people has been caused by economic exploitation: Romans, Egyptians, Belgians, and Americans all used Black labor to help build their societies. In this context, the speaker's implied warning is clear: except for the United States, all the societies that have exploited Blacks have declined, and long after the fall of those empires, Black people still endure.

In each of the preceding poems, the speaker is alone. The following poem, a **dramatic monologue**, presents a more complex situation in which the poet creates a complete dramatic scene. The speaker is developed as a character whose distinctive personality is revealed through his words as he addresses a silent listener.

AP Images

Robert Browning (1812–1889)

My Last Duchess (1842)

Ferrara

That's my last Duchess painted on the wall,
Looking as if she were alive. I call
That piece a wonder, now: Frà Pandolf's[1] hands
Worked busily a day, and there she stands.
Will't please you sit and look at her? I said

[1] *Frà Pandolf:* "Brother" Pandolf, a fictive painter.

"Frà Pandolf" by design, for never read
Strangers like you that pictured countenance,
The depth and passion of its earnest glance,
But to myself they turned (since none puts by
The curtain I have drawn for you, but I)
And seemed as they would ask me, if they durst,
How such a glance came there; so, not the first
Are you to turn and ask thus. Sir, 'twas not
Her husband's presence only, called that spot
Of joy into the Duchess' cheek: perhaps
Frà Pandolf chanced to say "Her mantle laps
Over my lady's wrist too much," or "Paint
Must never hope to reproduce the faint
Half-flush that dies along her throat": such stuff
Was courtesy, she thought, and cause enough
For calling up that spot of joy. She had
A heart—how shall I say?—too soon made glad,
Too easily impressed; she liked whate'er
She looked on, and her looks went everywhere.
Sir, 'twas all one! My favor at her breast,
The dropping of the daylight in the West,
The bough of cherries some officious fool
Broke in the orchard for her, the white mule
She rode with round the terrace—all and each
Would draw from her alike the approving speech,
Or blush, at least. She thanked men—good! but thanked
Somehow—I know not how—as if she ranked
My gift of a nine-hundred-years-old name
With anybody's gift. Who'd stoop to blame
This sort of trifling? Even had you skill
In speech—(which I have not)—to make your will
Quite clear to such an one, and say, "Just this
Or that in you disgusts me; here you miss,
Or there exceed the mark"—and if she let
Herself be lessoned so, nor plainly set
Her wits to yours, forsooth, and made excuse
—E'en then would be some stooping; and I choose
Never to stoop. Oh sir, she smiled, no doubt,
Whene'er I passed her; but who passed without
Much the same smile? This grew; I gave commands;
Then all smiles stopped together. There she stands
As if alive. Will't please you rise? We'll meet
The company below, then. I repeat,
The Count your master's known munificence
Is ample warrant that no just pretense
Of mine for dowry will be disallowed;

Though his fair daughter's self, as I avowed
At starting, is my object. Nay, we'll go
Together down, sir. Notice Neptune,[2] though,
Taming a sea horse, thought a rarity,
Which Claus of Innsbruck[3] cast in bronze for me!

Art gallery similar to setting of "My Last Duchess"
The King's Closet, Windsor Castle, from "Royal Residences", engraved by William James Bennett (1769–1844), published by William Henry Pyne (1769–1843), 1816, Wild, Charles (1781–1835) (after)/Private Collection/The Stapleton Collection/Bridgeman Images

The speaker in "My Last Duchess" is most likely Alfonso II, Duke of Ferrara, Italy, whose young wife, Lucrezia, died in 1561 after only three years of marriage. Shortly after her death, the duke began negotiations to marry again. When the poem opens, the duke is showing a portrait of his late wife to an emissary of an unnamed count who is there to arrange a marriage between the duke and the count's daughter. The duke remarks that the artist, Frà Pandolf, has caught a certain look on the duchess's face. This look aroused the jealousy of the duke, who thought that it should have been reserved for him alone. Eventually, the duke could tolerate the situation no longer; he "gave commands," and "all smiles stopped together."

Though silent, the listener plays a subtle but important role in the poem: his presence establishes the dramatic situation that allows the character of the duke to be revealed. The duke tells his story to communicate to the emissary exactly what he expects from his prospective bride and from her father. As he speaks, the duke provides only the information that he wants the emissary to take back to his master, the count. Although the duke appears vain and superficial, he is actually extraordinarily shrewd. Throughout the poem, he turns the conversation to his own ends and gains the advantage through flattery and false modesty. The success of the poem lies in the poet's ability to develop the

[2] *Neptune:* In Roman mythology, the god of the sea.
[3] *Claus of Innsbruck:* A fictive—or unidentified—sculptor. The count of Tyrol's capital was at Innsbrück, Austria.

voice of this complex character, who embodies both superficial elegance and shocking cruelty.

FURTHER READING: The Speaker in the Poem

Leslie Marmon Silko (1948–)

Where Mountain Lion Lay Down with Deer (1973)

I climb the black rock mountain
  stepping from day to day
        silently.
I smell the wind for my ancestors
    pale blue leaves
    crushed wild mountain smell.
Returning
  up the gray stone cliff
  where I descended
      a thousand years ago.
Returning to faded black stone.
  where mountain lion lay down with deer.
It is better to stay up here
          watching wind's reflection
          in tall yellow flowers.
The old ones who remember me are gone
      the old songs are all forgotten
and the story of my birth.
How I danced in snow-frost moonlight
        distant stars to the end of the Earth,
How I swam away
        in freezing mountain water
        narrow mossy canyon tumbling down
          out of the mountain
          out of the deep canyon stone
        down
         the memory
          spilling out
          into the world.

Reading and Reacting

1. Who is speaking in line 4? in line 9? Can you explain this shift?
2. From where is the speaker returning? What is the speaker trying to recover?
3. **Journal Entry** Is it important to know that the poet is Native American? How does this information affect your interpretation of the poem?

4. **Critical Perspective** In her 1983 essay "Answering the Deer," poet and critic Paula Gunn Allen observes that the possibility of cultural extinction is a reality Native Americans must face. Native American women writers, says Allen, face this fact directly but with a kind of hope:

   > The sense of hope . . . comes about when one has faced ultimate disaster time and time again over the ages and has emerged . . . stronger and more certain of the endurance of the people, the spirits, and the land from which they both arise and which informs both with life. Transformation, or more directly, metamorphosis, is the oldest tribal ceremonial theme. . . . And it comes once again into use within American Indian poetry of extinction and regeneration that is ultimately the only poetry any contemporary Indian woman can write.

   Does Silko's poem address the issue of cultural extinction and the possibility of regeneration or metamorphosis? How?

Related Works: "Two Kinds" (p. 471), "We Wear the Mask" (p. 535), "Simile" (p. 565), *The Cuban Swimmer* (p. 1122)

© Estate of Robert Giard

Rafael Campo (1964–   )

My Voice (1996)

To cure myself of wanting Cuban songs,
I wrote a Cuban song about the need
For people to suppress their fantasies,
Especially unhealthy ones. The song
Began by making reference to the sea,
Because the sea is like a need so great
And deep it never can be swallowed. Then
The song explores some common myths
About the Cuban people and their folklore:
The story of a little Carib[1] boy
Mistakenly abandoned to the sea;
The legend of a bird who wanted song
So desperately he gave up flight; a queen
Whose strength was greater than a rival king's.
The song goes on about morality,
And then there is a line about the sea,
How deep it is, how many creatures need
Its nourishment, how beautiful it is
To need. The song is ending now, because
I cannot bear to hear it any longer.
I call this song of needful love my voice.

[1] *Carib:* A member of the native people of the Caribbean islands.

Reading and Reacting

1. Why does the speaker want to cure himself "of wanting Cuban songs" (line 1)? To what songs is he referring? Why, at the end of the poem, can he no longer "bear to hear" his own Cuban song?
2. At one point in the poem, Campo refers to "the Cuban people and their folklore" (9). What examples of folklore does he give? Why are these stories important to Campo?
3. **Journal Entry** Campo is a practicing physician. In what way does "My Voice" reflect his need to heal? What is the difference between *healing* and *curing*?

Related Works: "Araby" (p. 296), "9773 Comanche Avenue" (p. 552), *The Cuban Swimmer* (p. 1122)

The Tone of the Poem

The **tone** of a poem conveys the speaker's attitude toward the subject or audience. In speech, this attitude can be conveyed easily: stressing a word in a sentence can modify or color a statement. For example, the statement "Of course, you would want to go to that restaurant" is quite straightforward, but changing the emphasis to "Of course *you* would want to go to *that* restaurant" transforms a neutral statement into a sarcastic one. For poets, however, conveying a particular tone to readers poses a challenge because readers rarely hear poets' spoken voices. Instead, poets indicate tone by using rhyme, meter, word choice, sentence structure, figures of speech, and imagery.

The range of possible tones is wide. For example, a poem's speaker may be joyful, sad, playful, serious, comic, intimate, formal, relaxed, condescending, or ironic. In the following poem, notice the speaker's detached, almost irreverent attitude toward his subject.

Robert Frost (1874–1963)

Fire and Ice (1923)

Some say the world will end in fire,
Some say in ice.
From what I've tasted of desire
I hold with those who favor fire.
But if it had to perish twice,
I think I know enough of hate
To say that for destruction ice
Is also great
And would suffice.

Here the speaker uses word choice, rhyme, and especially **understatement** to comment on the human condition. The conciseness as well as the simple, regular meter and rhyme suggest an **epigram**—a short poem that makes a pointed comment in an unusually clear, and often witty, manner. This pointedness is consistent with the speaker's glib, unemotional tone, as is the last line's wry understatement that ice "would suffice." The contrast between the poem's serious message—that hatred and indifference are equally destructive—and its informal style and offhand tone complement the speaker's detached, almost smug, posture.

Sometimes shifts in tone reveal changes in the speaker's attitude. In the next poem, subtle shifts in tone reveal a change in the speaker's attitude toward war.

Underwood And Underwood/The LIFE Images Collection/Getty Images

Thomas Hardy (1840–1928)

The Man He Killed (1902)

"Had he and I but met
By some old ancient inn,
We should have sat us down to wet
Right many a nipperkin![1]

"But ranged as infantry,
And staring face to face,
I shot at him as he at me,
And killed him in his place.

"I shot him dead because—
Because he was my foe,
Just so: my foe of course he was;
That's clear enough; although

"He thought he'd 'list,[2] perhaps,
Off-hand-like—just as I—
Was out of work—had sold his traps—
No other reason why.

"Yes; quaint and curious war is!
You shoot a fellow down
You'd treat if met where any bar is,
Or help to half-a crown."[3]

---

[1]*nipperkin:* A small container of liquor.
[2]*'list:* Enlist.
[3]*crown:* A unit of British currency.

British infantry fighting in South Africa during the Boer War
Library of Congress Prints and Photographs Division [LC-USZ62-42613]

The speaker in this poem is a soldier relating a wartime experience. Quotation marks indicate that he is engaged in conversation—perhaps in a pub—and his dialect indicates that he is a member of the English working class. For him, at least at first, the object of war is simple: kill or be killed. To Hardy, this speaker represents all men who are thrust into a war without understanding its underlying social, economic, or ideological causes. In this sense, the speaker and his enemy are both victims of forces beyond their comprehension or control.

The tone of "The Man He Killed" changes as the speaker tells his story. In the first two stanzas, sentences are smooth and unbroken, establishing the speaker's matter-of-fact tone and reflecting his confidence that he has done what he had to do. In the third and fourth stanzas, broken syntax reflects the narrator's increasingly disturbed state of mind as he tells about the man he killed. The poem's singsong meter and regular rhyme scheme *(met/wet, inn/nipperkin)* suggest that the speaker is struggling to maintain his composure; the smooth sentence structure of the last stanza and the use of a cliché ("Yes; quaint and curious war is!") indicate that the speaker is trying to trivialize an incident that has seriously traumatized him.

Sometimes a poem's tone can establish an ironic contrast between the speaker and the subject. The speaker's abrupt change of tone at the end of the next poem establishes such a contrast.

Amy Lowell (1874–1925)

Patterns (1915)

I walk down the garden-paths,
And all the daffodils

Are blowing, and the bright blue squills.
I walk down the patterned garden-paths
In my stiff, brocaded gown.
With my powdered hair and jewelled fan,
I too am a rare
Pattern. As I wander down
The garden-paths.

My dress is richly figured,
And the train
Makes a pink and silver stain
On the gravel, and the thrift
Of the borders.
Just a plate of current fashion
Tripping by in high-heeled, ribboned shoes.
Not a softness anywhere about me,
Only whalebone[1] and brocade.
And I sink on a seat in the shade
Of a lime tree. For my passion
Wars against the stiff brocade.
The daffodils and squills
Flutter in the breeze
As they please.
And I weep;
For the lime-tree is in blossom
And one small flower has dropped upon my bosom.

And the splashing of waterdrops
In the marble fountain
Comes down the garden-paths.
The dripping never stops.
Underneath my stiffened gown
Is the softness of a woman bathing in a marble basin,
A basin in the midst of hedges grown
So thick, she cannot see her lover hiding,
But she guesses he is near,
And the sliding of the water
Seems the stroking of a dear
Hand upon her.
What is Summer in a fine brocaded gown!
I should like to see it lying in a heap upon the ground.
All the pink and silver crumpled up on the ground.

I would be the pink and silver as I ran along the paths,
And he would stumble after,

[1] *whalebone:* The type of bone used to stiffen corsets.

Bewildered by my laughter.
I should see the sun flashing from his sword-hilt and buckles
on his shoes.
I would choose
To lead him in a maze along the patterned paths,
A bright and laughing maze for my heavy-booted lover.
Till he caught me in the shade,
And the buttons of his waistcoat bruised my body as
he clasped me,
Aching, melting, unafraid.
With the shadows of the leaves and the sundrops,
And the plopping of the waterdrops,
All about us in the open afternoon—
I am very like to swoon
With the weight of this brocade,
For the sun sifts through the shade.

Underneath the fallen blossom
In my bosom,
Is a letter I have hid.
It was brought to me this morning by a rider from the Duke.
Madam, we regret to inform you that Lord Hartwell
Died in action Thursday se'nnight.[2]
As I read it in the white, morning sunlight,
The letters squirmed like snakes.
"Any answer, Madam," said my footman.
"No," I told him.
"See that the messenger takes some refreshment.
No, no answer."
And I walked into the garden,
Up and down the patterned paths,
In my stiff, correct brocade.
The blue and yellow flowers stood up proudly in the sun,
Each one.
I stood upright too,
Held rigid to the pattern
By the stiffness of my gown.
Up and down I walked.
Up and down.
In a month he would have been my husband.
In a month, here, underneath this lime,

[2]*se'nnight:* "Seven night," or a week ago Thursday.

We would have broken the pattern;
He for me, and I for him,
He as Colonel, I as Lady,
On this shady seat.
He had a whim
That sunlight carried blessing.
And I answered, "It shall be as you have said."
Now he is dead.
In Summer and in Winter I shall walk
Up and down
The patterned garden-paths
In my stiff, brocaded gown.
The squills and daffodils
Will give place to pillared roses, and to asters, and to snow.
I shall go
Up and down,
In my gown,
Gorgeously arrayed,
Boned and stayed.
And the softness of my body will be guarded from embrace
By each button, hook, and lace.
For the man who should loose me is dead,
Fighting with the Duke in Flanders,[3]
In a pattern called a war.
Christ! What are patterns for?

The speaker begins by describing herself walking down garden paths. She wears a stiff brocaded gown, has powdered hair, and carries a jeweled fan. By her own admission, she is "a plate of current fashion." Although her tone is controlled, she is preoccupied by sensual thoughts. Beneath her "stiffened gown / Is the softness of a woman bathing in a marble basin," and the "sliding of the water" in a fountain reminds the speaker of the stroking of her lover's hand. She imagines herself shedding her brocaded gown and running with her lover along the maze of "patterned paths." The sensuality of the speaker's thoughts stands in ironic contrast to the images of stiffness and control that dominate the poem: her passion "Wars against the stiff brocade." She is also full of repressed rage. She knows that her lover has been killed, and she realizes the meaninglessness of the patterns of her life, patterns to which she has conformed, just as her lover conformed by going to war. Throughout the poem, the speaker's tone reflects her barely contained anger and frustration. In the last line, when she finally lets out her rage, the poem's point about the senselessness of conformity and war becomes apparent.

---

[3]*Flanders:* A region in northwestern Europe, including part of northern France and western Belgium. Flanders was a site of prolonged fighting during World War I.

FURTHER READING: The Tone of the Poem

Triton blowing his horn (detail from Trevi fountain, Rome)
sootra/Shutterstock.com

William Wordsworth (1770–1850)

The World Is Too Much with Us (1807)

The world is too much with us; late and soon,
Getting and spending, we lay waste our powers;
Little we see in Nature that is ours;
We have given our hearts away, a sordid boon!
This Sea that bares her bosom to the moon;
The winds that will be howling at all hours,
And are up-gathered now like sleeping flowers;
For this, for everything, we are out of tune;
It moves us not. Great God! I'd rather be
A Pagan suckled in a creed outworn;
So might I, standing on this pleasant lea,
Have glimpses that would make me less forlorn;
Have sight of Proteus[1] rising from the sea;
Or hear old Triton[2] blow his wreathed horn.

Reading and Reacting

1. What is the speaker's attitude toward the contemporary world? How is this attitude revealed through the poem's tone?
2. This poem is a **sonnet,** a highly structured traditional form. How do the regular meter and rhyme scheme reinforce the poem's tone?
3. **Journal Entry** Imagine that you are a modern-day environmentalist, labor organizer, or corporate executive. Write a response to the sentiments expressed in this poem.
4. **Critical Perspective** In his 1972 essay "Two Roads to Wordsworth," M. H. Abrams notes that critics have tended to view Wordsworth in one of two ways:

   > One Wordsworth is simple, elemental, forthright, the other is complex, paradoxical, problematic; one is an affirmative poet of life, love, and joy, the other is an equivocal or self-divided poet whose affirmations are implicitly qualified . . . by a pervasive sense of morality and an ever-incipient despair of life; . . . one is the Wordsworth of light, the other the Wordsworth of [shadow], or even darkness.

---

[1] *Proteus:* Sometimes said to be Poseidon's son, this Greek sea-god had the ability to change shape at will and to tell the future.

[2] *Triton:* The trumpeter of the sea, this sea-god is usually pictured blowing on a conch shell. Triton was the son of Poseidon, ruler of the sea.

Does your reading of "The World Is Too Much with Us" support one of these versions of Wordsworth over the other? Which one? Why?

Related Works: "Araby" (p. 296), "The Road Not Taken" (p. 605), "Dover Beach" (p. 699), "The Lake Isle of Innisfree" (p. 745)

Everett Collection Historical/Alamy Stock Photo

Sylvia Plath (1932–1963)

Morning Song (1962)

Love set you going like a fat gold watch.
The midwife slapped your footsoles, and your bald cry
Took its place among the elements.

Our voices echo, magnifying your arrival. New statue.
In a drafty museum, your nakedness
Shadows our safety. We stand round blankly as walls.

I'm no more your mother
Than the cloud that distills a mirror to reflect its own slow
Effacement at the wind's hand.

All night your moth-breath
Flickers among the flat pink roses. I wake to listen:
A far sea moves in my ear.

One cry, and I stumble from bed, cow-heavy and floral
In my Victorian nightgown.
Your mouth opens clean as a cat's. The window square

Whitens and swallows its dull stars. And now you try
Your handful of notes;
The clear vowels rise like balloons.

Reading and Reacting

1. Who is the speaker? To whom is she speaking? What does the poem reveal about her?
2. What is the poem's subject? What attitudes about this subject do you suppose the poet expects her readers to have?
3. How is the tone of the first stanza different from that of the third? How does the tone of each stanza reflect its content?
4. **Journal Entry** In what sense does this poem reinforce traditional ideas about motherhood? How does it challenge them?
5. **Critical Perspective** Sylvia Plath's life, which ended in suicide, was marked by emotional turbulence and instability. As Anne Stevenson observes in *Bitter Fame*, her 1988 biography of Plath, in the weeks immediately

preceding the composition of "Morning Song" a fit of rage over her husband's supposed infidelity caused Plath to destroy many of his books and poetic works in progress. Then, only a few days later, she suffered a miscarriage. According to Stevenson, "Morning Song" is about sleepless nights and surely reflects Plath's depression. However, in a 1991 biography, *Rough Magic*, Paul Alexander says, "Beautiful, simple, touching, 'Morning Song' was Plath's—then—definitive statement of motherhood."

Which biographer's assessment of the poem do you think makes more sense? Why?

Related Works: "The Yellow Wallpaper" (p. 315), "Metaphors" (p. 566), "Daddy" (p. 571), "Those Winter Sundays" (p. 672)

Everett Collection Historical/Alamy Stock Photo

Claude McKay (1890–1948)

The White City (1922)

I will not toy with it nor bend an inch.
Deep in the secret chambers of my heart
I muse my life-long hate, and without flinch
I bear it nobly as I live my part.
My being would be a skeleton, a shell,
If this dark Passion that fills my every mood,
And makes my heaven in the white world's hell,
Did not forever feed me vital blood.
I see the mighty city through a mist—
The strident trains that speed the goaded mass,
The poles and spires and towers vapor-kissed,
The fortressed port through which the great ships pass,
The tides, the wharves, the dens I contemplate,
Are sweet like wanton loves because I hate.

Reading and Reacting

1. How would you characterize the tone of this sonnet?
2. How is the speaker's description of the city in the third quatrain consistent with the emotions expressed in lines 1–8?
3. The closing couplet of a Shakespearean sonnet traditionally sums up the poem's concerns. Is this the case here? Explain.
4. **Journal Entry** What possible meanings does the phrase "the white world's hell" (line 7) have? How does it express the poem's central theme?
5. **Critical Perspective** According to Cary Nelson in *Modern American Poetry*, "'The White City' is not an attack on white people but rather a critique of race-based economic and political power." Which parts of the poem support this assessment? Which do not?

Related Works: "Discovering America" (p. 114), "Big, Black Good Man" (p. 246), "Sweat" (p. 438), "Negro" (p. 498), "Harlem" (p. 561), "Incident" (p. 579), *Fences* (p. 1222)

Gather Ye Rosebuds While Ye May (1909 oil painting)

Robert Herrick (1591–1674)

To the Virgins, to Make Much of Time (1646)

Gather ye rosebuds while ye may,
Old Time is still a-flying;
And this same flower that smiles
  today,
Tomorrow will be dying.

The glorious lamp of heaven,
  the sun,
The higher he's a-getting,
The sooner will his race be run,
And nearer he's to setting.

That age is best which is the first,
When youth and blood are warmer;
But being spent, the worse, and worst
Times still succeed the former.

Then be not coy, but use your time,
And while ye may, go marry;
For having lost but once your prime,
You may forever tarry.

Reading and Reacting

1. How would you characterize the speaker? Do you think he expects his listeners to share his views? How might his expectations affect his tone?
2. This poem is developed like an argument. What is the speaker's main point? How does he support it?
3. What effect does the poem's use of rhyme have on its tone?
4. **Journal Entry** Whose side are you on—the speaker's or those he addresses?
5. **Critical Perspective** Critic Roger Rollin offers the following reading of the final stanza of "To the Virgins, to Make Much of Time":

   > This last stanza makes it clear enough that to the speaker young women are coy by [custom or choice] rather than by nature. Their receptivity to love is under their control. The delaying tactics that social custom prescribes for them are self-defeating, threatening to waste life's most precious commodities—time, youth, and love.

Does Rollin's interpretation seem plausible to you? What evidence do you find in the final stanza, or elsewhere in the poem, that the virgins addressed are not naturally "coy" but rather are constrained by social convention?

Related Works: "The Passionate Shepherd to His Love" (p. 730), *The Brute* (p. 769), *Beauty* (p. 785)

Irony

Just as in fiction and drama, **irony** occurs in poetry when a discrepancy exists between two levels of meaning or experience. Consider the tone of the following lines by Stephen Crane:

Do not weep, maiden, for war is kind.
Because your lover threw wild hands toward the sky
And the afrightened steed ran on alone,
Do not weep.
War is kind.

Surely the speaker in this poem does not intend his words to be taken literally. How can war be "kind"? Isn't war exactly the opposite of "kind"? By making this ironic statement, the speaker actually conveys the opposite idea: war is a cruel, mindless exercise of violence.

Skillfully used, irony enables a poet to make a pointed comment about a situation or to manipulate a reader's emotions. Implicit in irony is the writer's assumption that readers will not be misled by the literal meaning of a statement. For irony to work, readers must recognize the disparity between what is said and what is meant, or between what a speaker thinks is occurring and what readers know to be occurring.

One kind of irony that appears in poetry is **dramatic irony**, which occurs when a speaker believes one thing and readers realize something else. In the following poem, the poet uses a deranged speaker to tell a story that is filled with irony.

Robert Browning (1812–1889)

Porphyria's Lover (1836)

The rain set early in to-night,
  The sullen wind was soon awake,
It tore the elm-tops down for spite,
  And did its worst to vex the lake:
  I listened with heart fit to break.
When glided in Porphyria; straight
  She shut the cold out and the storm,

And kneeled and made the cheerless grate
  Blaze up, and all the cottage warm;
  Which done, she rose, and from her form
Withdrew the dripping cloak and shawl,
  And laid her soiled gloves by, untied
Her hat and let the damp hair fall,
  And, last, she sat down by my side
  And called me. When no voice replied,
She put my arm about her waist,
  And made her smooth white shoulder bare,
And all her yellow hair displaced,
  And, stooping, made my cheek lie there,
  And spread, o'er all, her yellow hair,
Murmuring how she loved me—she
  Too weak, for all her heart's endeavour,
To set its struggling passion free
  From pride, and vainer ties dissever,
  And give herself to me for ever.
But passion sometimes would prevail,
  Nor could to-night's gay feast restrain
A sudden thought of one so pale
  For love of her, and all in vain:
So, she was come through wind and rain.
Be sure I looked up at her eyes
  Happy and proud; at last I knew
Porphyria worshipped me; surprise
  Made my heart swell, and still it grew
  While I debated what to do.
That moment she was mine, mine, fair,
  Perfectly pure and good: I found
A thing to do, and all her hair
  In one long yellow string I wound
  Three times her little throat around,
And strangled her. No pain felt she;
  I am quite sure she felt no pain.
As a shut bud that holds a bee,
  I warily oped her lids: again
  Laughed the blue eyes without a stain.
And I untightened next the tress
  About her neck; her cheek once more
Blushed bright beneath my burning kiss:
  I propped her head up as before,
  Only, this time my shoulder bore
Her head, which droops upon it still:
  The smiling rosy little head,

So glad it has its utmost will,
  That all it scorned at once is fled,
  And I, its love, am gained instead!
Porphyria's love: she guessed not how
  Her darling one wish would be heard.
And thus we sit together now,
  And all night long we have not stirred,
  And yet God has not said a word!

Like Browning's "My Last Duchess" (p. 499), this poem is a **dramatic monologue**, a poem that assumes an implied listener as well as a speaker. The speaker recounts his story in a straightforward manner, seemingly unaware of the horror of his tale. In fact, much of the effect of this poem comes from the speaker's telling his tale of murder in a flat, unemotional tone—and from readers' gradual realization that the speaker is insane.

The irony of the poem, as well as its title, becomes apparent as the monologue progresses. At first, the speaker fears that Porphyria is too weak to free herself from pride and vanity to love him. As he looks into her eyes, however, he comes to believe that she worships him. The moment the speaker realizes that Porphyria loves him, he feels compelled to kill her and keep her his forever. According to him, she is at this point "mine, mine, fair, / Perfectly pure and good," and he believes that by murdering her, he actually fulfills "Her darling one wish"—to stay with him forever. As he attempts to justify his actions, the speaker reveals himself to be a deluded psychopathic killer.

Another kind of irony is **situational irony**, which occurs when the situation itself contradicts readers' expectations. For example, in "Porphyria's Lover" the meeting of two lovers ironically results not in joy and passion but in murder.

In the next poem, the situation also creates irony.

Sueddeutsche Zeitung Photo/Alamy Stock Photo

Percy Bysshe Shelley (1792–1822)

Ozymandias[1] (1818)

I met a traveler from an antique land
Who said: Two vast and trunkless legs of stone
Stand in the desert. Near them, on the sand,
Half sunk, a shattered visage lies, whose frown,
And wrinkled lip, and sneer of cold command,
Tell that its sculptor well those passions read
Which yet survive, stamped on these lifeless things,
The hand that mocked them, and the heart that fed;
And on the pedestal these words appear:

[1] *Ozymandias:* The Greek name for Ramses II, ruler of Egypt in the thirteenth century B.C.

"My name is Ozymandias, king of kings:
Look on my works, ye Mighty, and despair!"
Nothing beside remains. Round the decay
Of that colossal wreck, boundless and bare
The lone and level sands stretch far away.

The speaker in "Ozymandias" recounts a tale about a colossal statue that lies shattered in the desert. Its head lies separated from the trunk, and the face has a wrinkled lip and a "sneer of cold command." On the pedestal of the monument are words exhorting all those who pass: "Look on my works, ye Mighty, and despair!" The situational irony of the poem has its source in the contrast between the "colossal wreck" and the boastful inscription on its base: Ozymandias is a monument to the vanity of those who mistakenly think they can withstand the ravages of time.

Perhaps the most common kind of irony found in poetry is **verbal irony**, which is created when words say one thing but mean another, often exactly the opposite. When verbal irony is particularly biting, it is called **sarcasm**—for example, Stephen Crane's use of the word *kind* in his antiwar poem "War Is Kind." In speech, verbal irony is easy to detect through the speaker's change in tone or emphasis. In writing, when these signals are absent, verbal irony becomes more difficult to convey. Poets must depend on the context of a remark or on the contrast between a word and other images in the poem to create irony.

Head of Ramses II, possible inspiration for "Ozymandias"
Nick Brundle Photography/Moment/Getty Images

FURTHER READING: Irony

An 1870 engraving by Gustav Doré depicting a scene from "Little Red Riding Hood"
Bettmann/Getty Images

Agha Shahid Ali (1949–2001)

The Wolf's Postscript to "Little Red Riding Hood"*

First, grant me my sense of history:
I did it for posterity,
for kindergarten teachers
and a clear moral:
Little girls shouldn't wander off
in search of strange flowers,
and they mustn't speak to strangers.

And then grant me my generous sense of plot:
Couldn't I have gobbled her up
right there in the jungle?
Why did I ask her where her grandma lived?
As if I, a forest-dweller,
didn't know of the cottage
under the three oak trees
and the old woman lived there
all alone?
As if I couldn't have swallowed her years before?

And you may call me the Big Bad Wolf,
now my only reputation.
But I was no child-molester
though you'll agree she was pretty.

And the huntsman:
Was I sleeping while he snipped
my thick black fur
and filled me with garbage and stones?
I ran with that weight and fell down,
simply so children could laugh
at the noise of the stones
cutting through my belly,
at the garbage spilling out
with a perfect sense of timing,
just when the tale
should have come to an end.

*Publication date unavailable.

Reading and Reacting

1. How does Ali portray the Big Bad Wolf? How is this characterization different from the one in the classic fairy tale "Little Red Riding Hood"?
2. How would you describe the tone of this poem? How does Ali create this tone?
3. The wolf says that he "did it for posterity" and "for kindergarten teachers." What does he mean?
4. Why does the wolf think that he needs to add a postscript to "Little Red Riding Hood"?
5. **Journal Entry** What "clear moral" does the poem have? In what sense is this moral ironic?

Related Works: "Gretel in Darkness" (p. 497), "Porphyria's Lover" (p. 514), "The Chimney Sweeper" (p. 700), *Beauty* (p. 785)

Adolph Hitler as a baby
Photo 12/Getty Images

Wislawa Szymborska (1923–2012)

Hitler's First Photograph (1986)

And who's this little fellow in his itty-bitty robe?
That's tiny baby Adolf, the Hitler's little boy!
Will he grow up to be an LL.D.?[1]
Or a tenor in Vienna's Opera House?
Whose teensy hand is this, whose little ear and eye and nose?
Whose tummy full of milk, we just don't know:
printer's, doctor's, merchant's, priest's?
Where will those tootsy-wootsies finally wander?
To garden, to school, to an office, to a bride,
maybe to the Burgermeister's[2] daughter?

Precious little angel, mommy's sunshine, honeybun,
while he was being born a year ago,
there was no dearth of signs on the earth and in the sky:
spring sun, geraniums in windows,
the organ-grinder's music in the yard,
a lucky fortune wrapped in rosy paper,
then just before the labor his mother's fateful dream:
a dove seen in dream means joyful news,
if it is caught, a long-awaited guest will come.
Knock knock, who's there, it's Adolf's heartchen[3] knocking.

---

[1] *LL.D.: Legum Doctor,* or Doctor of Law.
[2] *Burgermeister:* An executive of a town in Germany.
[3] *heartchen:* A partial translation of a German word meaning "little heart."

A little pacifier, diaper, rattle, bib,
our bouncing boy, thank God and knock on wood, is well,
looks just like his folks, like a kitten in a basket,
like the tots in every other family album.
Shush, let's not start crying, sugar,
the camera will click from under that black hood.

The Klinger Atelier,[4] Grabenstrasse,[5] Braunau,[6]
and Braunau is small but worthy town,
honest businesses, obliging neighbors,
smell of yeast dough, of gray soap.
No one hears howling dogs, or fate's footsteps.
A history teacher loosens his collar
and yawns over homework.

Reading and Reacting

1. What attitude toward the subject does the speaker expect readers to have? How do you know? How much information about Hitler does the speaker expect readers to know?
2. How do words like "angel," sunshine," "honeybun," and "sugar" create irony in the poem?
3. What does the speaker mean in line 31 of the poem by saying, "No one hears howling dogs, or fate's footsteps"?
4. Why does the poem end with the image of a history teacher loosening his tie and yawning? What effect does this image have on you?
5. **Journal Entry** What point do you think Szymborska is making in this poem? How does irony help her make this point?
6. **Critical Perspective** Speaking of "Hitler's First Photograph," critic Alan Reid makes this observation:

> "Hitler's First Photograph" is one of the most chilling poetic inspections of the psychopathological phenomena associated with its namesake and Nazism ever written. By describing Hitler in his first year of life from the perspective of his parents (any parents), [Szymborska] jolts us out of our complacency around the question of how this could have happened.... She prods us to question whether the signs were there and, if they were not, to ask what gives rise to such abominations and to recognize the need to be vigilant.

Do you agree with Reid's assessment of the poem? Why or why not?

Related Works: "I Stand Here Ironing" (p. 227), "Young Goodman Brown" (p. 354), "What Shall I Give My Children?" (p. 538), "Daddy" (p. 571), "Those Winter Sundays" (p. 672), "The Lamb" (p. 700)

[4]*Klinger Atelier:* Painting of Max Klinger's artist's studio.
[5]*Grabenstrasse:* Street in Austria.
[6]*Braunau:* Birthplace of Hitler in Austria-Hungary.

Checklist Writing about Voice

The Speaker in the Poem

- What do we know about the speaker?
- Is the speaker anonymous, or do they have a particular identity?
- How does assuming a particular persona help the poet to convey their ideas?
- Does the title give readers any information about the speaker's identity?
- How does word choice provide information about the speaker?
- Does the speaker make any direct statements to readers that help establish their identity or character?
- Does the speaker address anyone? How can you tell? How does the presence of a listener affect the speaker?

The Tone of the Poem

- What is the speaker's attitude toward their subject?
- How do word choice, rhyme, meter, sentence structure, figures of speech, and imagery help to convey the attitude of the speaker?
- Is the poem's tone consistent? How do shifts in tone reveal the changing mood or attitude of the speaker?

Irony

- Does the poem include dramatic irony? situational irony? verbal irony?

WRITING SUGGESTIONS: Voice

1. The poet Robert Frost once said that he wanted to write "poetry that talked." According to Frost, "whenever I write a line it is because that line has already been spoken clearly by a voice within my mind, an audible voice." Choose some poems in this chapter (or from elsewhere in the book) that you consider "poetry that talks." Then, write an essay about how successful they are in communicating "an audible voice."
2. Compare the speakers' voices in "Patterns" (p. 506), and "Gretel in Darkness" (p. 497). How are their attitudes toward men similar? How are they different?
3. The theme of Herrick's poem "To the Virgins, to Make Much of Time" (p. 513) is known as **carpe diem**, or "seize the day." Read Andrew Marvell's

"To His Coy Mistress" (p. 575), which has the same theme, and compare its tone with that of "To the Virgins, to Make Much of Time."

4. Because the speaker and the poet are not the same, poems by the same author can have different voices. Compare the voices of several poems by one poet—for example, Sylvia Plath, W. H. Auden, Robert Frost, or William Blake—whose works are included in this anthology.

Chapter

19

Word Choice, Word Order

Adrienne Rich
AP Images/Chuck Knoblock

Margaret Atwood
AP Images/Dave Thomson

Gwendolyn Brooks
©Bill Tague

Learning Objectives

After reading this chapter, you will be able to...

- Analyze how word choice affects the meaning of a poem.
- Identify abstract and concrete words in a poem.
- Identify specific and general words in a poem.
- Interpret a poem based on the connotations of the words the poet has chosen.
- Identify formal and informal diction in a poem.
- Analyze how word order affects the meaning of a poem.

Duffy-Marie Arnoult/WireImage/Getty Images

Bob Holman (1948–)

Beautiful[1] (2002)

January 3, 2002

Dear Bob,
You are not allowed to use
the word "beautiful" in a poem
this year.
Signed,
The Rest of the World
Except for You

Words identify and name, characterize and distinguish, compare and contrast. Words describe, limit, and embellish; words locate and measure. Even though words may be elusive and uncertain and changeable, a single word—such as Holman's "beautiful" in the poem above—can also be meaningful. In poetry, as in love and politics, words matter.

Beyond the quantitative—how many words, how many letters and syllables—is a much more important consideration: the *quality* of words. Which words are chosen and why? Why are certain words placed next to others? What does a word suggest in a particular context? How are the words arranged? What exactly constitutes the "right word"?

Word Choice

In poetry, even more than in fiction or drama, words are the focus—sometimes even the true subject—of a work. For this reason, the choice of one word over another can be crucial. Because poems are brief, they must compress many ideas into just a few lines; poets know how much weight each individual word carries, so they choose with great care, trying to select words that imply more than they state.

In general, poets (like prose writers) select words because they communicate particular ideas. However, poets may also choose words for their sound. For example, a word may echo another word's sound, and such repetition may place emphasis on both words; a word may rhyme with another word and therefore be chosen to preserve the poem's rhyme scheme; or a word may have a particular combination of stressed and unstressed syllables needed to maintain

[1] *Beautiful:* Of this poem, the author wrote to us, "With a poem this short, every word counts. Take note of the date: January 3. So this is an actual New Year's Resolution. But also take note of the year, and where I live. This is 2002, just four months after the 9-11 Attacks. At the time I was living just 5 blocks from the World Trade Towers. It was like being in a war zone. This poem is how a poet tries to cope with an event of this magnitude and sorrow."

the poem's metrical pattern. Occasionally, a poet may even choose a word because of how it looks on the page.

At the same time, poets may choose words for their degree of concreteness or abstraction, specificity or generality. A **concrete** word refers to an item that is a perceivable, tangible entity—for example, a kiss or a flag. An **abstract** word refers to an intangible idea, condition, or quality, something that cannot be perceived by the senses—love or patriotism, for example. **Specific** words refer to particular items; **general** words refer to entire classes or groups of items. The following sequence illustrates the movement from general to specific.

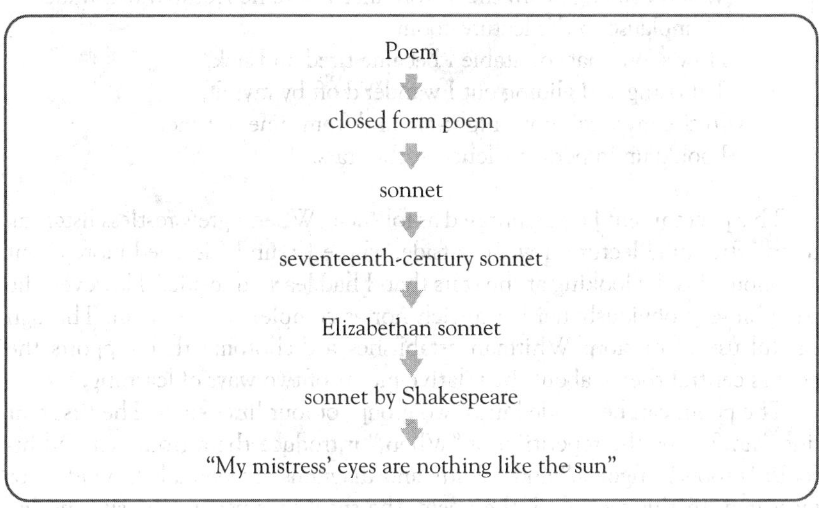

Sometimes a poet wants a precise word, one that is both specific and concrete. At other times, a poet might prefer general or abstract language, which may allow for more subtlety—or even for intentional ambiguity.

Finally, a word may be chosen for its **connotation**—what it suggests. Every word has one or more **denotations**—what it signifies without emotional associations, judgments, or opinions. The word *family*, for example, denotes "a group of related things or people." Connotation is a more complex matter; after all, a single word may have many different associations. In general terms, a word may have a connotation that is positive, neutral, or negative. Thus, *family* may have a positive connotation when it describes a group of loving relatives, a neutral connotation when it describes a biological category, and an ironically negative connotation when it describes an organized crime family. Beyond this distinction, *family*, like any other word, may have a variety of emotional and social associations, suggesting loyalty, warmth, home, security, or duty. In fact, many words have somewhat different meanings in different contexts. When poets choose words, then, they must consider what a particular word may suggest to readers as well as what it denotes.

In the poem that follows, the poet chooses words for their sounds and for their relationships to other words as well as for their connotations.

Walt Whitman (1819–1892)

When I Heard the Learn'd Astronomer (1865)

When I heard the learn'd astronomer,
When the proofs, the figures, were ranged in columns before me,
When I was shown the charts and diagrams, to add, divide, and measure them,
When I sitting heard the astronomer where he lectured with much applause in the lecture-room,
How soon unaccountable I became tired and sick,
Till rising and gliding out I wander'd off by myself,
In the mystical moist night-air, and from time to time,
Look'd up in perfect silence at the stars.

This poem might be paraphrased as follows: "When I grew restless listening to an astronomy lecture, I went outside, where I found I learned more about astronomy just by looking at the stars than I had learned inside." However, the paraphrase is obviously neither as rich nor as complex as the poem. Through careful use of diction, Whitman establishes a dichotomy that supports the poem's central theme about the relative merits of two ways of learning.

The poem can be divided into two groups of four lines each. The first four lines, unified by the repetition of "When," introduce the astronomer and his tools: "proofs," "figures," and "charts and diagrams" to be added, divided, or measured. In this section of the poem, the speaker is passive: he sits and listens ("I heard"; "I was shown"; "I sitting heard"). The repetition of "When" reinforces the dry monotony of the lecture. In the next four lines, the choice of words signals the change in the speaker's actions and reactions. The confined lecture hall is replaced by "the mystical moist night-air," and the dry lecture and the applause give way to "perfect silence"; instead of sitting passively, the speaker becomes active (he rises, glides, wanders); instead of listening, he looks. The mood of the first half of the poem is restrained: the language is concrete and physical, and the speaker is passively receiving information from a "learn'd" authority. The rest of the poem, celebrating intuitive knowledge and feelings, is more abstract, freer. Throughout the poem, the lecture hall is set in sharp contrast to the natural world outside its walls.

After considering the poem as a whole, readers should not find it hard to understand why the poet selected certain words. Whitman's use of "lectured" in line 4 rather than a more neutral word like "spoke" is appropriate both because it suggests formality and distance and because it echoes "lecture-room" in the same line. The word "sick" in line 5 is striking because it connotes physical as well as emotional distress, more effectively conveying the extent of the speaker's discomfort than "bored" or "restless" would. "Rising" and "gliding" (line 6) are used rather than "standing up" and "walking out" both because of the way their stressed vowel sounds echo each other (and echo "time to time" in the next line) and because of their connotation of dreaminess, which is consistent with "wander'd" (line 6) and "mystical" (line 7). The word "moist" (line 7) is chosen not only because its consonant sounds echo the *m* and *st* sounds in "mystical," but also because it establishes a contrast with the dry, airless lecture hall. Finally, line 8's "perfect silence" is a better choice than a reasonable substitute like "complete silence" or "total silence," either of which would suggest the degree of the silence but not its quality.

FURTHER READING: Word Choice

Rhina Espaillat (1932–)

Bilingual/Bilingüe (1998)

My father liked them separate, one there,
one here (allá y aquí), as if aware

that words might cut in two his daughter's heart
(el corazón) and lock the alien part
to what he was—his memory, his name
(su nombre)—with a key he could not claim.
"English outside this door, Spanish inside,"
he said, "y basta."[1] But who can divide

the world, the word (mundo y palabra) from
any child? I knew how to be dumb

and stubborn (testaruda); late, in bed,
I hoarded secret syllables I read

until my tongue (mi lengua) learned to run
where his stumbled. And still the heart was one.

I like to think he knew that, even when,
proud (orgulloso) of his daughter's pen,

he stood outside mis versos,[2] half in fear
of words he loved but wanted not to hear.

Reading and Reacting

1. Why do you think the poet includes parenthetical Spanish translations in this poem? Are they necessary? Why do you think the Spanish words "y basta" (line 8) and "mis versos" (line 17) are not translated as the others are?

[1] *"y basta.":* and enough.
[2] *mis versos:* my poems.

2. Some of the words in this poem might be seen as having more than one connotation. Consider, for example, "alien" (line 4), "word" (line 9), "dumb" (line 10), and "syllables" (line 12). What meanings could each of these words have? Which meaning do you think the poet intended them to have?
3. What is the relationship between "the word" and "the world" in this poem?
4. **Journal Entry** What is the father's fear? Do you think this fear is justified? Why do you think he doesn't want to hear his daughter's words?

Related Works: "The Secret Lion" (p. 222), "Two Kinds" (p. 471), "Baca Grande" (p. 532)

AP Images/Chuck Knoblock

Adrienne Rich (1929–2012)

Living in Sin (1955)

She had thought the studio would keep itself,
no dust upon the furniture of love.
Half heresy, to wish the taps less vocal,
the panes relieved of grime. A plate of pears,
a piano with a Persian shawl, a cat
stalking the picturesque amusing mouse
had risen at his urging.
Not that at five each separate stair would writhe
under the milkman's tramp; that morning light
so coldly would delineate the scraps
of last night's cheese and three sepulchral bottles;
that on the kitchen shelf among the saucers
a pair of beetle-eyes would fix her own—
envoy from some black village in the mouldings …
Meanwhile, he, with a yawn,
sounded a dozen notes upon the keyboard,
declared it out of tune, shrugged at the mirror,
rubbed at his beard, went out for cigarettes;
while she, jeered by the minor demons,
pulled back the sheets and made the bed and found
a towel to dust the table-top,
and let the coffee-pot boil over on the stove.
By evening she was back in love again,
though not so wholly but throughout the night
she woke sometimes to feel the daylight coming
like a relentless milkman up the stairs.

1950s milkman making delivery
Bettmann/Getty Images

Reading and Reacting

1. How might this poem's impact change if each of these words were deleted: "Persian" (line 5), "picturesque" (line 6), "sepulchral" (line 11), "minor" (line 19), "sometimes" (line 25)?
2. What words in the poem have strongly negative connotations? What do these words suggest about the relationship the poem describes? How does the image of the "relentless milkman" (line 26) sum up this relationship?
3. This poem, about a woman in love, uses very few words conventionally associated with love poems. Instead, many of its words denote the everyday routine of housekeeping. Give examples of such words. Why do you think they are used?
4. **Journal Entry** What connotations does the title have? What other phrases have similar denotative meanings? How do their connotations differ? Why do you think Rich chose the title "Living in Sin"?
5. **Critical Perspective** In "Her Cargo: Adrienne Rich and the Common Language," an essay examining the poet's work over almost thirty years,

Alicia Ostriker offers the following analysis of Rich's early poems, including "Living in Sin":

> They seem about to state explicitly . . . a connection between feminine subordination in male-dominated middle-class relationships, and emotionally lethal inarticulateness for both sexes. But the poetry . . . is minor because it is polite. It illustrates symptoms but does not probe sources. There is no disputing the ideas of the predecessors, and Adrienne Rich at this point is a cautious good poet in the sense of being a good girl, a quality noted with approval by her reviewers.

Does your reading of "Living in Sin" support Ostriker's characterization of the poem as "polite" and "cautious"? Do you think Rich is "being a good girl"?

Related Works: "Hills Like White Elephants" (p. 101), "The Storm" (p. 216), "What lips my lips have kissed" (p. 684)

Levels of Diction

The diction of a poem may be formal or informal or fall anywhere in between, depending on the identity of the speaker and on the speaker's attitude toward the reader and toward the poem's subject. At one extreme, very formal poems can seem lofty and dignified, far removed in style and vocabulary from everyday speech. At the other extreme, highly informal poems can be full of jargon, regionalisms, and slang. Many poems, of course, use language that falls somewhere between formal and informal diction.

Formal diction is characterized by a learned vocabulary and grammatically correct forms. In general, formal diction does not include colloquialisms, such as contractions and shortened word forms (*phone* for *telephone*). As the following poem illustrates, a speaker who uses formal diction can sound aloof and impersonal.

AP Images/Dave Thomson

Margaret Atwood (1939–   )

The City Planners (1966)

Cruising these residential Sunday
streets in dry August sunlight:
what offends us is
the sanities:
the houses in pedantic rows, the planted
sanitary trees, assert
levelness of surface like a rebuke
to the dent in our car door.
No shouting here, or
shatter of glass; nothing more abrupt
than the rational whine of a power mower

cutting a straight swath in the discouraged grass.

But though the driveways neatly
sidestep hysteria
by being even, the roofs all display
the same slant of avoidance to the hot sky,
certain things:
the smell of spilled oil a faint

sickness lingering in the garages,
a splash of paint on brick surprising as a bruise,
a plastic hose poised in a vicious

coil; even the too-fixed stare of the wide windows
give momentary access to
the landscape behind or under
the future cracks in the plaster

when the houses, capsized, will slide
obliquely into the clay seas, gradual as glaciers
that right now nobody notices.

That is where the City Planners
with the insane faces of political conspirators
are scattered over unsurveyed
territories, concealed from each other,
each in his own private blizzard;

guessing directions, they sketch
transitory lines rigid as wooden borders
on a wall in the white vanishing air

tracing the panic of suburb
order in a bland madness of snows.

1950s suburban housing development
Masterfile

Atwood's speaker is clearly concerned about the poem's central issue, but rather than use *I*, the poem uses the first-person plural (*us*) to convey some degree of emotional detachment. Although phrases such as "sickness lingering in the garages" and "insane faces of political conspirators" clearly communicate the speaker's disapproval, formal words—"pedantic," "rebuke," "display," "poised," "obliquely," "conspirators," "transitory"—help her to maintain her distance. Both the speaker herself and her attack on the misguided city planners gain credibility through her balanced, measured tone and through her use of language that is as formal and "professional" as theirs.

Informal diction is the language closest to everyday conversation. It includes **colloquialisms**—contractions, shortened word forms, and the like—and may also include slang, regional expressions, and even nonstandard words.

In the poem that follows, the speaker uses informal diction to highlight the contrast between James Baca, a law student speaking to the graduating class of his old high school, and the graduating seniors.

Jim Sagel (1947–1998)

Baca Grande[1] (1982)

Una vaca se topó con un ratón y le dice:
"Tú—¿tan chiquito y con bigote?" Y le responde el ratón:
"Y tú tan grandota—¿y sin brassiere?"[2]

It was nearly a miracle
James Baca remembered anyone at all
from the old hometown gang
having been two years at Yale
no less
and halfway through law school
at the University of California at Irvine
They hardly recognized him either
in his three-piece grey business suit
and surfer-swirl haircut
with just the menacing hint
of a tightly trimmed Zapata moustache
for cultural balance
and relevance

He had come to deliver the keynote address
to the graduating class of 80
at his old alma mater

[1]*Baca Grande: Baca* is both a phonetic spelling of the Spanish word *vaca* (cow) and the last name of one of the poem's characters. *Grande* means "large."
[2]*Una … brassiere?:* A cow ran into a rat and said: "You—so small and with a moustache?" The rat responded: "And you—so big and without a bra?"

and show off his well-trained lips
which laboriously parted
    each Kennedyish "R"
and drilled the first person pronoun
through the microphone
like an oil bit
with the slick, elegantly honed phrases
that slid so smoothly
off his meticulously bleached
    tongue
He talked Big Bucks
with astronautish fervor and if he
    the former bootstrapless James A. Baca
could dazzle the ass
off the universe
then even you
    yes you

Joey Martinez toying with your yellow
    tassle
and staring dumbly into space
could emulate Mr. Baca someday
    possibly
well
there was of course
such a thing
as being an outrageously successful
gas station attendant too
    let us never forget
it doesn't really matter what you do
so long as you excel
    James said
never believing a word
of it
for he had already risen
        as high as they go

Wasn't nobody else
from this deprived environment
who'd ever jumped
        straight out of college
into the Governor's office
and maybe one day
he'd sit in that big chair
    himself
and when he did
he'd forget this damned town

and all the petty little people
in it
once and for all

That much he promised himself

"Baca Grande" uses numerous colloquialisms, including contractions; conversational placeholders, such as "no less" and "well"; shortened word forms, such as "gas"; slang terms, such as "Big Bucks"; whimsical coinages ("Kennedyish," "astronautish," "bootstrapless"); nonstandard grammatical constructions, such as "Wasn't nobody else"; and even profanity. The level of language is perfectly appropriate for the poem's speaker, one of the students Baca addresses—suspicious, streetwise, and unimpressed by Baca's "three-piece grey business suit" and "surfer-swirl haircut." In fact, the informal diction is a key element of the poem, highlighting the gap between the slick James Baca, with "his well-trained lips / which laboriously parted / each Kennedyish 'R'" and members of his audience, with their unpretentious, forthright speech—and also the gap between Baca as he is today and the student he once was. In this sense, "Baca Grande" is as much a linguistic commentary as a social one.

FURTHER READING: Levels of Diction

Adrienne Su (1967–)

The English Canon[1] (2000)

It's not that the first speakers left out women
Unless they were goddesses, harlots, or impossible loves
Seen from afar, often while bathing,

And it's not that the only parts my grandfathers
could have played
Were as extras in Xanadu[2]
Nor that it gives no instructions for shopping or cooking.

The trouble is, I've spent my life
Getting over the lyrics
That taught me to brush my hair till it's gleaming,

Stay slim, dress tastefully, and not speak of sex,
Death, violence, or the desire for any of them,
And to let men do the talking and warring

[1] *English Canon:* Those works in English traditionally thought worthy of study.
[2] *Xanadu:* The summer capital of the emperor Kublai Kahn; also the setting for the poem "Kubla Khan" (p. 707) by the English poet Samuel Taylor Coleridge.

And bringing of the news. I know a girl's got to protest
These days, but she also has to make money
And do her share of journalism and combat,

And she has to know from the gut whom to trust,
Because what do her teachers know, living in books,
And what does she know, starting from scratch?

Reading and Reacting

1. What criticisms does the speaker have of the traditional English literary canon?
2. List the words and expressions that identify this poem's diction as informal. Given the poem's subject and theme, do you think this informal language (and the speaker's use of contractions) is a strength or a weakness?
3. What does the speaker mean when she says, "The trouble is, I've spent my life / Getting over the lyrics" (7–8)?
4. **Journal Entry** Reread the poem's last two lines. What does the speaker know that her teachers do not know? What do her teachers know that she does not know?
5. **Critical Perspective** In her essay "Teaching Literature: Canon, Controversy, and the Literary Anthology," Barbara Mujica discusses the way in which literary anthologies (like this one) naturally tend to create lists of works, known as **canons**, that are of especially high quality:

   > "Anthology".... is from the Greek word for "collection of flowers," a term implying selection. The very format of an anthology prompts canon formation ... Anthologies convey the notion of evolution (the succession of literary movements) and hierarchy (the recognition of masterpieces). They create and reform canons, establish literary reputations, and help institutionalize the national culture, which they reflect.

   How would you characterize the attitude of the speaker in "The English Canon" toward the process that Mujica describes? What is your own attitude toward the idea of canons in literature? Do you think some works can be said to be indisputably better than others?

Related Works: "Gryphon" (p. 191), "The Disappearance" (p. 280), "Shakespearean Sonnet" (p. 660), "Theme for English B" (p. 726)

Paul Laurence Dunbar (1872–1906)

We Wear the Mask (1896)

We wear the mask that grins and lies,
It hides our cheeks and shades our eyes—
This debt we pay to human guile;
With torn and bleeding hearts we smile,
And mouth with myriad subtleties.

Why should the world be over-wise,
In counting all our tears and sighs?
Nay, let them only see us, while
We wear the mask.

We smile, but, O great Christ, our cries
To thee from tortured souls arise.
We sing, but oh the clay is vile
Beneath our feet, and long the mile;
But let the world dream otherwise,
We wear the mask!

Reading and Reacting

1. Which of the following words and phrases do you see as formal? Why?
   - "human guile" (line 3)
   - "torn and bleeding hearts" (4)
   - "myriad subtleties" (5)
   - "over-wise" (6)
   - "tortured souls" (11)
   - "vile" (12)
2. Some words and phrases listed in question 1 were chosen at least in part to conform to the poem's rhyme scheme and metrical pattern. If rhyme and meter were not an issue, what other words and phrases could you substitute for those listed? How would your substitutions change the poem?
3. Do you think the poem's meter and rhyme make it seem more or less formal? Explain.
4. Given the poem's subject matter, is its relatively formal level of diction appropriate? Why or why not?
5. **Journal Entry** What exactly is the mask to which the speaker refers? Who is the "we" who wears this mask? (Note that Dunbar is an African American poet writing in the late nineteenth century.)
6. **Critical Perspective** In his book *Paul Laurence Dunbar*, Peter Revell explains that "'We Wear the Mask' itself is 'masked'" in its hidden references to race. How does the poem's diction help to mask its message?

Related Works: "Big Black Good Man" (p. 246), "Negro" (p. 498), "Yet Do I Marvel" (p. 662)

Source: ©Bill Tague

Gwendolyn Brooks (1917–2000)

We Real Cool (1959)

The Pool Players.
Seven at the Golden Shovel.

We real cool. We
Left School. We

Lurk late. We
Strike straight. We

Sing sin. We
Thin gin. We

Jazz June. We
Die soon.

Reading and Reacting

1. What elements of nonstandard English grammar appear in this poem? How does the use of such language affect your attitude toward the speaker?
2. Every word in this poem is a single syllable. Why?
3. Why do you think the poet begins with "We" only in the first line instead of isolating each complete sentence on its own line? How does this strategy change the poem's impact?
4. **Journal Entry** Write a prose version of this poem, adding words, phrases, and sentences to expand the poem into a paragraph.
5. **Critical Perspective** In *Gwendolyn Brooks: Poetry and the Heroic Voice*, critic D. H. Malhem writes of "We Real Cool," "Despite presentation in the voice of the gang, this is a maternal poem, gently scolding yet deeply sorrowing for the hopelessness of the boys."

   Do you agree with Malhem that the speaker's attitude is "maternal"?

Related Works: "Greasy Lake" (p. 419), "Where Are You Going, Where Have You Been?" (p. 447), "Why I Went to College" (p. 632)

Players in a pool hall (1950s)
Mac Gramlich/Hulton Archive/Getty Images

Gwendolyn Brooks (1917–2000)

What Shall I Give My Children? (1949)

What shall I give my children? who are poor,
Who are adjudged the leastwise of the land,
Who are my sweetest lepers, who demand
No velvet and no velvety velour;
But who have begged me for a brisk contour,
Crying that they are quasi, contraband
Because unfinished, graven by a hand
Less than angelic, admirable or sure.
My hand is stuffed with mode, design, device.
But I lack access to my proper stone.
And plenitude of plan shall not suffice
Nor grief nor love shall be enough alone
To ratify my little halves who bear
Across an autumn freezing everywhere.

Reading and Reacting

1. Unlike "We Real Cool" (p. 536), also by Gwendolyn Brooks, this sonnet's diction is quite formal. Given the subject of each poem, do the poet's decisions about level of diction make sense to you?
2. Which words in this poem do you see as unlikely to be used in conversation?
3. Apart from individual words, what else strikes you as formal about this poem?
4. **Journal Entry** Consulting a dictionary if necessary, suggest a synonym for each of the formal words you identified in question 2. Then, write out three or four lines of this poem in more conversational language.

Related Work: "We Real Cool" (p. 536)

Word Order

The order in which words are arranged in a poem is as important as the choice of words. Because English sentences nearly always have a subject-verb-object sequence, with adjectives preceding the nouns they modify, a departure from this order calls attention to itself. Thus, poets can use readers' expectations about word order to their advantage.

For example, poets often manipulate word order to place emphasis on a word. Sometimes they achieve this emphasis by using a very unconventional sequence; sometimes they simply place the word first or last in a line or place it in a stressed position in the line. Poets may also choose a particular word order to make two related—or startlingly unrelated—words fall in adjacent or parallel positions, calling attention to the similarity (or the difference) between them. In other cases, poets may manipulate syntax to preserve a poem's rhyme or meter or to highlight sound correspondences that might otherwise not be noticeable. Finally, irregular syntax may be used throughout a poem to reveal a speaker's mood—for example, to give a playful quality to a poem or to suggest a speaker's disoriented state.

In the poem that follows, word order frequently departs from conventional English syntax.

Edmund Spenser (1552–1599)

One day I wrote her name upon the strand (1595)

One day I wrote her name upon the strand,[1]
But came the waves and washed it away:
Again I wrote it with a second hand,
But came the tide and made my pains his prey.
"Vain man," said she, "that doest in vain assay,
A mortal thing so to immortalize,
For I myself shall like to this decay,
And eek[2] my name be wiped out likewise."
"Not so," quod[3] I, "let baser things devise,
To die in dust, but you shall live by fame:
My verse your virtues rare shall eternize,
And in the heavens write your glorious name.
Where whenas death shall all the world subdue,
Our love shall live, and later life renew."

"One day I wrote her name upon the strand," a sonnet, has a fixed metrical pattern and rhyme scheme. To accommodate the sonnet's rhyme and meter, Spenser makes a number of adjustments in syntax. For example, to make sure certain rhyming words fall at the ends of lines, the poet sometimes moves words out of their conventional order, as the following three comparisons illustrate.

---

[1] *strand:* Beach.
[2] *eek:* Also, indeed.
[3] *quod:* Said.

Conventional Word Order	Inverted Sequence
"'Vain man,' she said, 'that doest *assay in vain*.'"	"'Vain man,' said she, 'that doest *in vain assay*.'" ("Assay" appears at end of line 5, to rhyme with line 7's "decay.")
"My verse shall *eternize your rare virtues*."	"My verse *your virtues rare shall eternize*." ("Eternize" appears at end of line 11 to rhyme with line 9's "devise.")
"Where whenas death shall *subdue all the world*, / Our love shall live, and later renew life."	"Where whenas death shall *all the world subdue*, / Our love shall live, and *later life renew*." (Rhyming words "subdue" and "renew" are placed at ends of lines.)

To make sure the metrical pattern stresses certain words, the poet occasionally moves a word out of conventional order and places it in a stressed position. The following comparison illustrates this technique.

Conventional Word Order	Inverted Sequence
"But *the waves came* and washed it away."	"But *came the waves* and washed it away." (Stress in line 2 falls on "waves" rather than on "the.")

As the previous comparisons show, Spenser's adjustments in syntax are motivated at least in part by a desire to preserve his sonnet's rhyme and meter.

FURTHER READING: Word Order

A. E. Housman (1859–1936)

To an Athlete Dying Young (1896)

The time you won your town the race
We chaired you through the market-place;
Man and boy stood cheering by,
And home we brought you shoulder-high.

Today, the road all runners come,
Shoulder-high we bring you home,
And set you at your threshold down,
Townsman of a stiller town.

Smart lad, to slip betimes away
From fields where glory does not stay,

And early though the laurel grows
It withers quicker than the rose.

Eyes the shady night has shut
Cannot see the record cut,
And silence sounds no worse than cheers
After earth has stopped the ears.

Now you will not swell the rout
Of lads that wore their honors out,
Runners whom renown outran
And the name died before the man.

So set, before its echoes fade,
The fleet foot on the sill of shade,
And hold to the low lintel up
The still-defended challenge-cup.

And round that early-laureled head
Will flock to gaze the strengthless dead,
And find unwithered on its curls
The garland briefer than a girl's.

Reading and Reacting

1. Where does the poem's meter or rhyme scheme require the poet to depart from conventional syntax?
2. Edit the poem so its word order is more conventional. Do your changes improve the poem? Why or why not?
3. **Journal Entry** Whom do you think the speaker might be? What might the speaker's relationship to the athlete be?

Related Works: "To the Virgins, to Make Much of Time" (p. 513), "Nothing Gold Can Stay" (p. 553)

Charles Jensen (1977–)

Poem in Which Words Have Been Left Out (2012)

—The "Miranda Rights," established 1966

You have the right to remain
anything you can and will be.
An attorney you cannot afford
will be provided to you.
You have silent will.
You can be against law.

You cannot afford one.
You remain silent. Anything you say
will be provided to you.
The right can and will be
against you. The right provided you.
Have anything you say be
right. Anything you say can be right.
Say you have the right attorney.
The right remain silent.
Be held. Court the one. Be provided.
You cannot be you.

Reading and Reacting

1. In the 1966 case of *Miranda v. Arizona*, the Supreme Court ruled that all suspects be advised of their rights. Look up the wording of the Miranda warning as it is used today. Then, identify specific lines of the poem that conform to and depart from this wording.
2. How is the word *right* used in this poem? What meanings does it have in different contexts?
3. What "words have been left out" of this poem?
4. How do you interpret the poem's last line? Does it contradict the first two lines? Explain.
5. **Journal Entry** What commentary do you think this poem is making about the American judicial system?

Related Works: "Accident" (p. 110), "A Good Man is Hard to Find" (p. 302), "The Community College Revises Its Curriculum in Response to Changing Demographics" (p. 720), *Trifles* (p. 820)

Checklist Writing about Word Choice and Word Order

Word Choice

- Which words are of key importance in the poem? What is the denotative meaning of each of these key words?
- Which key words have neutral connotations? Which have negative connotations? Which have positive connotations? Beyond its literal meaning, what does each word suggest?
- Why is each word chosen instead of a synonym? (For example, is the word chosen for its sound? its connotation? its relationship to other words in the poem? its contribution to the poem's metrical pattern?)
- What other words could be effectively used in place of words now in the poem? How would these substitutions change the poem's meaning?

- Are any words or phrases repeated? Why?

Levels of Diction

- How would you characterize the poem's level of diction? Why is this level of diction used? Is it appropriate?
- Does the poem mix different levels of diction? If so, why?

Word Order

- Is the poem's word order conventional, or are words arranged in unexpected order?
- What is the purpose of the unusual word order? (For example, does it preserve the poem's meter or rhyme scheme? Does it highlight particular sound correspondences? Does it place emphasis on a particular word or phrase? Does it reflect the speaker's mood?)
- How would the poem's impact change if conventional syntax were used?

WRITING SUGGESTIONS: Word Choice, Word Order

1. Reread the poems in this book by E. E. Cummings: "l'a" (p. 492), "the sky was can dy" (p. 636), and "next to god of course America" (p. 708). Do you believe Cummings chose the words in these poems primarily for their sound? for their appearance on the page? What other factors might have influenced his choices?
2. The tone of "We Real Cool" (p. 536) is flat and unemotional; the problem on which it focuses, however, is serious. Expand this concise poem into a few paragraphs that retain the poem's informal, colloquial tone but use more detailed, more emotional language to communicate the hopeless situation of the speaker and his friends. Include dialogue as well as narrative.
3. Reread "Living in Sin" (p. 528) and "The English Canon" (p. 534), and choose one or two other poems in this book whose speaker is a woman. Compare the speakers' levels of diction and choice of words. What does their language reveal about their lives?
4. Analyze the choice of words and the level of diction in several poems in this book that express social or political criticism. Poems that might work well include Claude McKay's "If We Must Die" (p. 731) and Louise Erdrich's "Indian Boarding School: The Runaways" (p. 719).

Chapter 20

Imagery

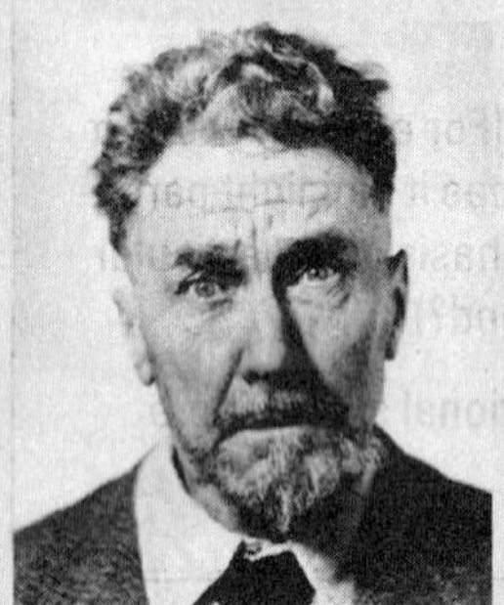

Ezra Pound
AP Images

Lola Ridge
Historic Collection/Alamy Stock Photo

William Carlos Williams
Bettmann/Getty Images

Learning Objectives

After reading this chapter, you will be able to...

- Describe how imagery functions in poems.
- Describe the relationship between imagery and mood in poems.
- Examine how a poet creates a scene with the use of imagery.
- Examine how imagery enables a poet to convey ideas.
- Identify the types of imagery in poems.

Steven Flanders

Jane Flanders (1940–2001)

Cloud Painter (1984)

Suggested by the life and art of John Constable[1]

At first, as you know, the sky is incidental—
a drape, a backdrop for trees and steeples.

[1]*John Constable:* British painter (1776–1837) noted for his landscapes.

Here an oak clutches a rock (already he works outdoors),
a wall buckles but does not break,
water pearls through a lock, a haywain[2] trembles.

The pleasures of landscape are endless. What we see
around us should be enough.
Horizons are typically high and far away.
Still, clouds let us drift and remember. He is, after all,
a miller's son, used to trying
to read the future in the sky, seeing instead
ships, horses, instruments of flight.
Is that his mother's wash flapping on the line?
His schoolbook, smudged, illegible?

In this period the sky becomes significant.
Cloud forms are technically correct—mares' tails,
sheep-in-the-meadow, thunderheads.
You can almost tell which scenes have been interrupted
by summer showers.

Now his young wife dies.
His landscapes achieve belated success.
He is invited to join the Academy. I forget
whether he accepts or not.

In any case, the literal forms give way
to something spectral, nameless. His palette shrinks
to gray, blue, white—the colors of charity.

Horizons sink and fade,
trees draw back till they are little more than frames,
then they too disappear.

Finally the canvas itself begins to vibrate
with waning light,
as if the wind could paint.
And we too, at last, stare into a space
which tells us nothing,
except that the world can vanish along with our need for it.

Because the purpose of poetry—and, for that matter, of all literature—is to expand the perception of readers, poets appeal to the senses. In "Cloud Painter," Jane Flanders uses **images**, such as the mother's wash on the line and the smudged schoolbook, to enable readers to visualize particular scenes in

[2]*haywain:* An open horse-drawn wagon for carrying hay.

John Constable (1776–1837). Landscape, Noon, *The Haywain.* 1821. Oil on canvas, 130½ × 185½ cm. London, National Gallery.

John Constable's early paintings. Clouds are described so readers can picture them—"mares' tails, / sheep-in-the-meadow, thunderheads." Thus, "Cloud Painter" is not only about the work of John Constable but also about the ability of an artist—poet or painter—to call up images in the minds of an audience. To achieve this end, a poet uses **imagery**, language that evokes a physical sensation produced by one or more of the five senses—sight, hearing, taste, touch, and smell.

Although the effect can be complex, the way images work is simple: when you read the word *red*, your memory of the various red things that you have seen determines how you picture the image. In addition, the word *red* may have **connotations**—emotional associations that define your response. A red sunset, for example, can have a positive connotation or a negative one, depending on whether it is associated with the end of a perfect day or with air pollution. By choosing images carefully, poets not only create pictures in a reader's mind but also create a great number of imaginative associations. These associations help poets to establish the **atmosphere** or **mood** of the poem. The image of softly falling snow in "Stopping by Woods on a Snowy Evening" (p. 10), for example, creates a quiet, almost mystical mood.

Readers come to a poem with their own experiences, so an image in a poem does not suggest exactly the same thing to all readers. In "Cloud Painter," for example, the poet presents the image of an oak tree clutching a rock. Although most readers will probably see a picture that is generally consistent with the one the poet sees, no two images will be identical. Every reader will have a unique mental image of a tree clinging to a rock; some images will be remembered experiences, whereas others will be imaginative creations. Some readers may even be familiar enough with the work of the painter John Constable to visualize a particular tree clinging to a particular rock in one of his paintings. By conveying what the poet imagines, images open readers' minds to perceptions and associations different from—and possibly more original and complex than—their own.

One advantage of imagery is its extreme economy. A few carefully chosen words enable poets to evoke a range of emotions and reactions. In the following poem, William Carlos Williams uses simple visual images to create a rich and compelling picture.

Bettmann/Getty Images

William Carlos Williams (1883–1963)

Red Wheelbarrow (1923)

so much depends
upon

a red wheel
barrow

glazed with rain
water

beside the white
chickens

What is immediately apparent in this poem is its verbal economy. The poet does not tell readers what the barnyard smells like or what sounds the animals make. In fact, he does not even present a detailed picture of the scene. How large is the wheelbarrow? What is its condition? How many chickens are in the barnyard? In this poem, the answers to these questions are not important.

Even without answering these questions, the poet is able to use simple imagery to create a scene on which, he says, "so much depends." The wheelbarrow establishes a momentary connection between the poet and his world. Like a still-life painting, the red wheelbarrow beside the white chickens gives order to a world that is full of seemingly unrelated objects. In this poem, the poet suggests that our ability to perceive the objects of this world gives our lives meaning and that our ability to convey our perceptions to others is central to our lives as well as to poetry.

Images enable poets to present ideas that would be difficult to convey in any other way. One look at a dictionary will illustrate that concepts such as *beauty* and *mystery* are so abstract that they are difficult to define, let alone to discuss in specific terms. However, by choosing an image or a series of images to embody these ideas, poets can effectively make their feelings known, as Ezra Pound does in the two-line poem that follows.

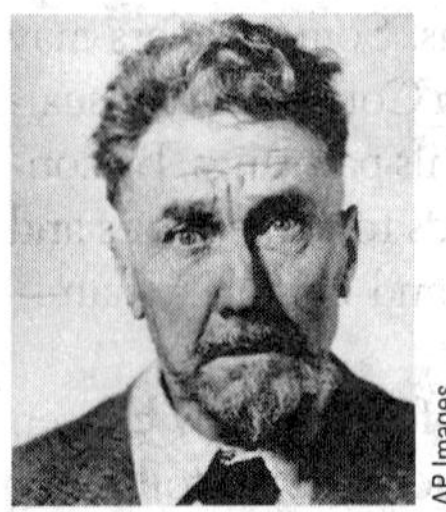
AP Images

Ezra Pound (1885–1972)

In a Station of the Metro (1916)

The apparition of these faces in the crowd;
Petals on a wet, black bough.

This poem is almost impossible to paraphrase because the information it communicates is less important than the feelings associated with this information. The poem's title indicates that the first line is meant to suggest a group of people standing in a station of the Paris subway. The scene, however, is presented not as a clear picture but as an "apparition," suggesting that it is unexpected or even dreamlike. In contrast with the image of the subway platform is the image of the people's faces as flower petals on the dark branch of a tree. Thus, the subway platform—dark, cold, wet, subterranean (associated with baseness, death, and hell)—is juxtaposed with flower petals—delicate, pale, radiant, lovely (associated with the ideal, life, and heaven). These contrasting images, presented without comment, bear the entire weight of the poem.

Although images can be strikingly visual, they can also appeal to the senses of hearing, smell, taste, and touch. The following poem uses images of sound and taste as well as sight.

Paris Metro station platform
Hulton Archive/ Archive Photos/Getty Images

Gary Snyder (1930–)

Some Good Things to Be Said for the Iron Age (1970)

A ringing tire iron
    dropped on the pavement
Whang of a saw
brusht on limbs
the taste
of rust

Here, Snyder presents two commonplace aural images: the ringing of a tire iron and the sound of a saw. These somewhat ordinary images gain power, however, through their visual isolation on separate lines in the poem. Together they produce a harsh and jarring chord that creates a sense of uneasiness in the reader. This poem does more than present sensory images, though; it also conveys the speaker's interpretations of these images. The last two lines imply not only that the time in which we live (the Iron Age) is base and mundane, but also that it is declining, decaying into an age of rust. The title of the poem makes an ironic comment, suggesting that compared to the time that is approaching, the age of iron may be "good." Thus, in the mind of the poet, ordinary events gain added significance, and images that spring from everyday experience become sources of insight.

Much visual imagery is **static**, freezing the moment and thereby giving it the timeless quality of painting or sculpture. ("Red Wheelbarrow" presents such a tableau, and so does "In a Station of the Metro.") In contrast, some imagery is **kinetic**, conveying a sense of motion or change.

William Carlos Williams (1883–1963)

The Great Figure (1938)

Among the rain
and lights
I saw the figure 5
in gold
on a red
firetruck
moving
tense
unheeded
to gong clangs

siren howls
and wheels rumbling
through the dark city.

Commenting on "The Great Figure" in his autobiography, Williams explained that while walking in New York, he heard the sound of a fire engine. As he turned the corner, he saw a golden figure 5 on a red background speed by. The impression was so forceful that he immediately jotted down a poem about it. In the poem, Williams attempts to recreate the sensation the figure 5 made as it moved into his consciousness. The poet presents images in the order in which he perceived them: first the 5, and then the red fire truck howling and clanging into the darkness. Thus, "The Great Figure" uses images of sight, sound, and movement to convey the poet's experience. The American painter Charles Demuth was fascinated by the poem. Working closely with Williams, he attempted to capture the poem's kinetic energy in a painting.

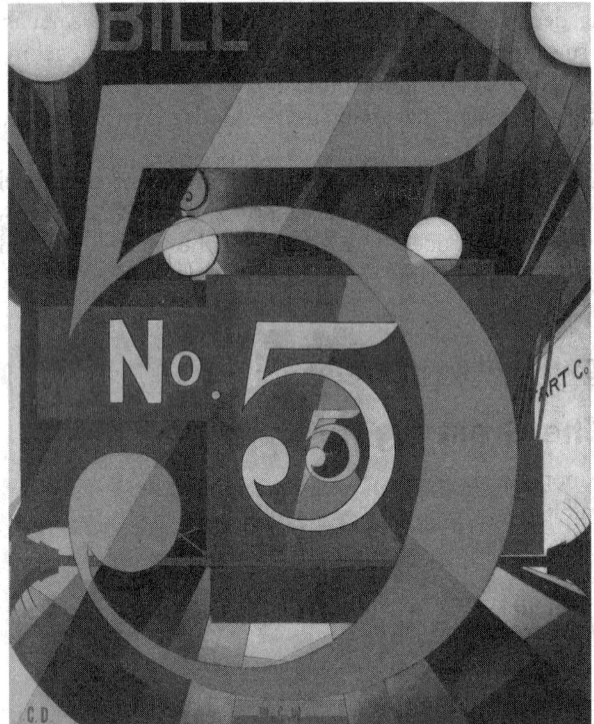

Charles Henry Demuth (1883–1935). *The Figure 5 in Gold.* Oil on composition board, 36 × 29¾ in.

Everett Collection/Shutterstock.com

Note A special use of imagery, called **synesthesia**, occurs when one sense is described in terms of another sense—for example, when a sound is described with color. When people say they are feeling *blue* or describe music as *hot* or *smooth*, they are using synesthesia.

FURTHER READING: Imagery

F. J. Bergmann (1954–)

An Apology (2003)

Forgive me
for backing over
and smashing
your red wheelbarrow.

It was raining
and the rear wiper
does not work on
my new plum-colored SUV.

I am also sorry
about the white
chickens.

Reading and Reacting

1. A **parody** is a literary work that imitates the style of another work for comic effect or ridicule. Bergmann's "An Apology" is a parody of William Carlos Williams's "Red Wheelbarrow" (p. 547). Why do you think Bergmann chose this poem to parody?
2. What aspects of "Red Wheelbarrow" does Bergmann parody? Do these elements deserve to be parodied, or do you think Bergmann's parody is unjustified or unfair?
3. Is Bergmann's purpose to ridicule "Red Wheelbarrow" or does he have some other purpose? Explain.
4. **Journal Entry** Write a parody of another poem in this book. Make sure you decide in advance what elements of the poem you want to parody.
5. **Critical Perspective** Blogger and critic Kerry Michael Wood observes that some readers think that critics have read too much into "The Red Wheelbarrow." According to him, however, "The Red Wheelbarrow" is a "sparkling gem" of the Imagist school of poetry that "insisted on 'no ideas but in things.'"

   Do you agree or disagree with Wood's assessment? Explain.

Related Works: "Red Wheelbarrow" (p. 547), "My mistress' eyes are nothing like the sun" (p. 557)

David Trinidad (1953–)

9773 Comanche Ave. (2010)

In color photographs, my childhood house looks
fresh as an uncut sheet cake—
pale yellow buttercream, ribbons of white trim
squeezed from the grooved tip of a pastry tube.
Whose dream was this confection?
This suburb of identical, pillow-mint homes?
The sky, too, is pastel. Children roller skate
down the new sidewalk. Fathers stake young trees.
Mothers plan baby showers and Tupperware parties.
The Avon Lady treks door to door.
Six or seven years old, I stand on the front porch,
hand on the decorative cast-iron trellis that frames it,
squinting in California sunlight,
striped short-sleeved shirt buttoned at the neck.
I sit in the backyard (this picture's black-and-white),
my Flintstones playset spread out on the grass.
I arrange each plastic character, each dinosaur,
each palm tree and round "granite" house.
Half a century later, I barely recognize it
when I search the address on Google Maps
and, via "Street view," find myself face to face—
foliage overgrown, facade remodeled and painted
a drab brown. I click to zoom: light hits
one of the windows. I can almost see what's inside.

Reading and Reacting

1. What two scenes is the poem describing? How are they different?
2. What is the main theme of this poem?
3. What different kinds of images does the poem present? How do they reinforce the central theme of the poem?
4. To what senses do the images of the poem appeal?
5. **Journal Entry** Search an address on Google Maps. How would you describe what you see?

Related Works: "The Secret Lion" (p. 222), "Evolution of My Block" (p. 608), "Spring and All" (p. 638)

Lola Ridge (1873–1941)

Wall Street at Night (1920)

Long vast shapes ... cooled and flushed through with darkness ...
Lidless windows
Glazed with a flashy luster
From some little pert café chirping up like a sparrow.
And down among iron guts
Piled silver
Throwing gray spatter of light ... pale without heat ...
Like the pallor[1] of dead bodies.

Reading and Reacting

1. What are the "long vast shapes" that the speaker mentions in line 1?
2. Find examples of similes, metaphors, and personification. How do these figures of speech reinforce the poem's theme?
3. Wall Street, an eight-block long street in the Financial District of New York City, is the financial center of the United States. What is Ridge's opinion of Wall Street and all it represents? How do you know?
4. **Journal Entry** This poem was written in 1893, a year when there was a serious economic depression in the United States. What images in "Wall Street at Night" suggest this economic turmoil?

Related Works: "Discovering America" (p. 114), "A Worn Path" (p. 370), "The World Is Too Much with Us" (p. 510), "The City Planners" (p. 530)

Robert Frost (1874–1963)

Nothing Gold Can Stay (1923)

Nature's first green is gold,
Her hardest hue to hold.
Her early leaf's a flower;
But only so an hour.
Then leaf subsides to leaf.
So Eden sank to grief.
So dawn goes down to day.
Nothing gold can stay.

---

[1] *pallor:* Paleness.

Painting of the Garden of Eden

Reading and Reacting

1. What is this poem's central idea?
2. What does the first line of the poem mean? In what sense is this line ironic?
3. What is the significance of the colors green and gold in this poem? What do these colors have to do with "Eden" and "dawn"?
4. **Journal Entry** How do the various images in the poem prepare readers for the last line? Do you think the title spoils the impact of the last line?
5. **Critical Perspective** In "The Figure a Poem Means," the introduction to the first edition of his *Collected Poems* (1930), Frost laid out a theory of poetry:

> It begins in delight, it inclines to the impulse, it assumes direction with the first line laid down, it runs a course of lucky events, and ends in a clarification of life—not necessarily a great clarification … but a momentary stay against confusion. . . . Like a piece of ice on a hot stove the poem must ride on its own melting. . . . Read it a hundred times: it will forever keep its freshness as a metal keeps its fragrance. It can never lose its sense of a meaning that once unfolded by surprise as it went.

Explain how Frost's remarks apply to "Nothing Gold Can Stay."

Related Works: "The Secret Lion" (p. 222), "Araby" (p. 296), "Greasy Lake" (p. 419), "Shall I compare thee to a summer's day?" (p. 560), "God's Grandeur" (p. 724)

Jean Toomer (1894–1967)

Reapers (1923)

Black reapers with the sound of steel on stones
Are sharpening scythes. I see them place the hones[1]
In their hip-pockets as a thing that's done,
And start their silent swinging, one by one.
Black horses drive a mower through the weeds,
And there, a field rat, startled, squealing bleeds,
His belly close to ground. I see the blade,
Blood-stained, continue cutting weeds and shade.

Reading and Reacting

1. What determines the order of the images in this poem? At what point does the speaker comment on these images?
2. The first four lines of the poem seem to suggest that the workers are content. What image contradicts this impression? How does it do so?
3. What ideas are traditionally associated with the image of the reaper? the scythe? the harvest? (To answer these questions, you may want to consult a reference source, such as <www.symbols.com>.) In what way does the speaker rely on these conventional associations to help convey ideas? Can you appreciate the poem without understanding these associations?
4. **Journal Entry** Who do you think the speaker might be? Why?
5. **Critical Perspective** As Brian Joseph Benson and Mabel Mayle Dillard point out in their 1980 study *Jean Toomer*, the poet disagreed with some other artists of the Harlem Renaissance, choosing not to focus on "Negro" themes for a primarily Black audience but rather to try to make his work universal in scope.

   Do you think he has achieved this goal in "Reapers"?

Related Works: "A Worn Path" (p. 370), "The White City" (p. 512), "Because I could not stop for Death—" (p. 709), "The Negro Speaks of Rivers" (p. 725)

Kobayashi Issa (1763–1827)

Haiku[1]

Not yet Buddha—
The mindless old
pine

---

[1] *hones:* Stones used to sharpen cutting instruments.

[1] *Haiku:* Translated by David G. Lanoue. The original publication date of this poem is unavailable.

Reading and Reacting

1. Buddhists believe that every person goes through cycles of death and rebirth until reaching the state of nirvana. A key element in achieving this state is the extinction of all desire. In line 1 of the poem, who (or what) has not yet achieved nirvana and become a Buddha?
2. What two images are compared in the poem? What insight or spiritual message is suggested by this comparison?
3. What is the tone of this poem? Do you think the speaker intends to be taken literally?
4. **Journal Entry** Read the definition of *haiku* on page 632. In what respects is this poem a haiku? How is it unlike traditional haiku?
5. **Critical Perspective** In his essay series *Confessions of a Translator*, David G. Lanoue writes the following about Kobayashi Issa's haiku:

    > Though Japanese children are made to memorize it, this haiku is no mere child's poem. It not only vocalizes Issa's Buddhist compassion for, and sense of karmic connection with, sentient life, it hints of a political meaning.

    In what sense is this poem "political"? How does it express the Buddhist idea of "compassion for all life"?

Related Works: "Gryphon" (p. 191), "A Worn Path" (p. 370), "Four Haiku" (p. 633)

Frederick Morgan (1922–2004)

The Busses (1995)

From our corner window
rainy winter mornings
nudging their way down Park
moistly glowing, puddled by the rain.
Stopping at doorways here and there
where children climb aboard
they merge into the traffic's flow
and dwindle from our sight.
We watch—then turn away,
and when in changing light
we look again, we see a stream
dark and serene in China,
down which sleek goldfish dart and gleam.

Reading and Reacting

1. Who is the speaker? Why do you think the speaker uses the first-person plural pronoun *we*?

2. What words in the poem rhyme? What ideas do these rhyming words emphasize?
3. In the first two stanzas of the poem, the speaker describes school busses picking up children—probably along Park Avenue in New York City. In the third stanza, the imagery abruptly changes. How does this change expand the poem's meaning?
4. **Journal Entry** What point is this poem making? How does the image in the last stanza help make this point?

Related Works: "How to Talk to Girls at Parties" (p. 155), "The Secret Lion" (p. 222), "Red Wheelbarrow" (p. 547), "In a Station of the Metro" (p. 548), "For Once, Then, Something" (p. 647)

Red and white damasked rose
The Natural History Museum/Alamy Stock Photo

William Shakespeare (1564–1616)

My mistress' eyes are nothing like the sun (1609)

My mistress' eyes are nothing like the sun;
Coral is far more red than her lips' red;
If snow be white, why then her breasts are dun;
If hairs be wires, black wires grow on her head.
I have seen roses damasked red and white,
But no such roses see I in her cheeks;
And in some perfumes is there more delight
Than in the breath that from my mistress reeks.
I love to hear her speak, yet well I know
That music hath a far more pleasing sound;
I grant I never saw a goddess go:
My mistress, when she walks, treads on the ground.
And yet, by heaven, I think my love as rare
As any she, belied with false compare.

Reading and Reacting

1. What point does Shakespeare make in the first twelve lines of his sonnet?
2. What point does the rhymed couplet at the end of the poem make?
3. How is Shakespeare's imagery like and unlike that of traditional love poems? For example, how is the imagery in this poem different from that in Elizabeth Barrett Browning's "How Do I Love Thee?" (p. 684).
4. **Journal Entry** How do you think the woman to whom the poem is addressed will react?
5. **Critical Perspective** During the Renaissance, poets commonly used the **Petrarchan conceit** to praise their lovers. In this type of metaphor, the author draws exaggerated comparisons between his beloved and a physical object—for example, the sun, a flower, or a precious jewel. According to

critic Felicia Jean Steele, "Traditional readings of Shakespeare's Sonnet 130 argue that Shakespeare cunningly employs Petrarchan imagery while deliberately undermining it."

How does this poem use the Petrarchan conceit? How does it undermine this convention?

Related Works: "A&P" (p. 179), "The Storm" (p. 216), "General Review of the Sex Situation" (p. 686), *The Brute* (p. 769)

Checklist Writing about Imagery

- Do the images in the poem appeal to the sense of sight? hearing? taste? touch? smell?
- Does the poem depend on a single image or on several different images?
- Does the poem depend on a group of related images?
- What details make the images memorable?
- What mood do the images create?
- Are the images static or kinetic?
- How do the poem's images help to convey its theme?
- How effective are the images? How do they enhance your enjoyment of the poem?

WRITING SUGGESTIONS: Imagery

1. Read the definition of **haiku** on page 632. How are short poems such as "Some Good Things to Be Said for the Iron Age" (p. 549) and "In a Station of the Metro" (p. 548) like and unlike haiku?
2. After rereading "Cloud Painter" (p. 544) and "The Great Figure" (p. 549), read "Musée des Beaux Arts" (p. 665), and study the corresponding paintings *Landscape, Noon, the Haywain* (p. 546), *The Figure 5 in Gold* (p. 550), and *Landscape with the Fall of Icarus* (p. 666). Then, write an essay in which you draw some conclusions about the differences between artistic and poetic images.
3. Analyze the role of imagery in the depiction of the parent/child relationships in "My Papa's Waltz" (p. 672) and "Digging" (p. 673). How does each poem's imagery convey the nature of the relationship it describes?
4. Write an essay in which you discuss the color imagery in "Nothing Gold Can Stay" (p. 553). In what way does color reinforce the theme of the poems?

Chapter

21

Figures of Speech

N. Scott Momaday
AP Images/Jacques Brinon

Audre Lorde
Jack Mitchell/Archive Photos/Getty Images

Nancy Mercado
Ricardo Muniz

Sylvia Plath
Everett Collection Historical/Alamy Stock Photo

Langston Hughes
Library of Congress Prints and Photographs Division [LC-USZ62-43605]

Learning Objectives

After reading this chapter, you will be able to...

- Explain how figures of speech function in poetry.
- Define simile and metaphor and explain how they function in a poem.
- Define personification as it is used in poetry.
- Compare hyperbole and understatement as they are used in poetry.
- Define metonymy and synecdoche as they are used in poetry.
- Define apostrophe as it is used in poetry.
- Identify examples of figures of speech within a poem.
- Analyze how figures of speech help to convey a poem's meaning.

Bettmann/Getty Images

William Shakespeare (1564–1616)

Shall I compare thee to a summer's day? (1609)

Shall I compare thee to a summer's day?
Thou art more lovely and more temperate.
Rough winds do shake the darling buds of May,
And summer's lease hath all too short a date.
Sometime too hot the eye of heaven shines,
And often is his gold complexion dimmed;
And every fair from fair sometimes declines,
By chance, or nature's changing course, untrimmed.
But thy eternal summer shall not fade,
Nor lose possession of that fair thou ow'st;[1]
Nor shall death brag thou wand'rest in his shade,
When in eternal lines to time thou grow'st.
So long as men can breathe or eyes can see,
So long lives this, and this gives life to thee.

Although writers experiment with language in all kinds of literary works, poets in particular recognize the power of a figure of speech to take readers beyond the literal meaning of a word. For this reason, **figures of speech**—expressions that use words to achieve effects beyond the power of ordinary language—are more prominent in poetry than in other kinds of writing. For example, the previous sonnet compares a loved one to a summer's day to make the point that, unlike the fleeting summer, the loved one will—within the poem—remain forever young. But this sonnet goes beyond the obvious equation (loved one = summer's day): the speaker's assertion that his loved one will live forever in his poem actually says more about his confidence in his own talent and reputation (and about the power of language) than about the loved one's beauty.

Simile, Metaphor, and Personification

When William Wordsworth opens a poem with "I wandered lonely as a cloud" (p. 678), he conveys a good deal more than he would if he simply began, "I wandered, lonely." By comparing himself in his loneliness to a cloud, the speaker suggests that he, like the cloud, is a part of nature and that he too is drifting, passive, blown by winds, and lacking will or substance. Thus, by using a figure of speech, the poet can suggest a wide variety of feelings and associations in very few words.

[1] *that fair thou ow'st:* That beauty you possess.

The phrase "I wandered lonely as a cloud" is a **simile**, a comparison between two unlike items that uses *like* or *as*. When an imaginative comparison between two unlike items does not use *like* or *as*—that is, when it says "a *is* b" rather than "a is *like* b"—it is a **metaphor**.

Accordingly, when the speaker in Adrienne Rich's "Living in Sin" (p. 528) speaks of "daylight coming / like a relentless milkman up the stairs," she is using a strikingly original simile to suggest that daylight brings not the conventional associations of promise and awakening but rather a stale, never-ending routine that is greeted without enthusiasm. This idea is consistent with the rest of the poem, an account of an unfulfilling relationship. However, when the speaker in the Audre Lorde poem on page 563 says, "Rooming houses are old women," she uses a metaphor, equating two elements to stress their common associations with emptiness, transience, and hopelessness. At the same time, by identifying rooming houses as old women, Lorde is using **personification**, a special kind of comparison, closely related to metaphor, that gives life or human characteristics to inanimate objects or abstract ideas.

Sometimes, as in Wordsworth's "I wandered lonely as a cloud," a single brief simile or metaphor can be appreciated for what it communicates on its own. At other times, however, a simile or metaphor may be one of several related figures of speech that work together to convey a poem's meaning. The following poem, for example, presents a series of related similes. Together, they suggest the depth of the problem the poem explores in a manner that each individual simile could not do on its own.

Harlem street scene, 1957
AP Images/Robert Kradin

Langston Hughes (1902–1967)

Harlem (1951)

What happens to a dream deferred?

Does it dry up
like a raisin in the sun?
Or fester like a sore—
And then run?
Does it stink like rotten meat?
Or crust and sugar over—
like a syrupy sweet?

Maybe it just sags
like a heavy load.

Or does it explode?

The dream to which Hughes alludes in this poem is the dream vof racial equality. It is also the American Dream—and, by extension, any important unrealized dream. The speaker offers six tentative answers to the question asked in the poem's first line, and five of the six are presented as similes. As the poem unfolds, the speaker considers different alternatives: the dream can shrivel up and die, fester, decay, crust over—or sag under the weight of the burden those who hold the dream must carry. In each case, the speaker transforms an abstract entity—a dream—into a concrete item—a raisin in the sun, a sore, rotten meat, syrupy candy, a heavy load. The final line, italicized for emphasis, gains power less from what it says than from what it leaves unsaid. Unlike the other alternatives explored in the poem, "*Or does it explode?*" is not presented as a simile. Nevertheless, because of the pattern of figurative language the poem has established, readers can supply the other, unspoken half of the comparison: ". . . like a bomb."

Sometimes a single extended simile or extended metaphor is developed throughout a poem. The following poem develops an **extended simile**, comparing a poet to an acrobat.

Lawrence Ferlinghetti (1919–2021)

Constantly Risking Absurdity (1958)

Constantly risking absurdity
                                        and death
            whenever he performs
                                        above the heads
                                                            of his audience
the poet like an acrobat
                                        climbs on rime
                                              to a high wire of his own making
and balancing on eyebeams
                                              above a sea of faces
                  paces his way
                                        to the other side of day
        performing entrechats
                                        and sleight-of-foot tricks
and other high theatrics
                                        and all without mistaking
                        any thing
                                        for what it may not be

                  For he's the super realist
                                                  who must perforce perceive
                        taut truth
                                        before the taking of each stance or step
in his supposed advance
                                        toward that still higher perch
where Beauty stands and waits
                                        with gravity
                                                  to start her death-defying leap

And he
a little charleychaplin man
who may or may not catch
her fair eternal form
spreadeagled in the empty air
of existence

In his extended comparison of a poet and an acrobat, Ferlinghetti characterizes the poet as a circus performer, at once swinging recklessly on a trapeze and balancing carefully on a tightrope.

What the poem suggests is that the poet, like an acrobat, works hard at his craft but manages to make it all look easy. Something of an exhibitionist, the poet is innovative and creative, taking impossible chances yet also building on traditional skills in his quest for truth and beauty. Moreover, like an acrobat, the poet is balanced "on eyebeams / above a sea of faces," for he too depends on audience reaction to help him keep his performance focused. The poet may be "the super realist," but he also has plenty of playful tricks up his sleeve: "entrechats / and sleight-of-foot tricks / and other high theatrics," including puns ("above the heads / of his audience"), unexpected rhyme ("climbs on rime"), alliteration ("taut truth"), coinages ("a little charleychaplin man"), and all the other linguistic acrobatics available to poets. (Even the arrangement of the poem's lines on the page suggests the acrobatics its words describe.) Like these tricks, the poem's central simile is a whimsical one, perhaps suggesting that Ferlinghetti is poking fun at poets who take their craft too seriously. In any case, the simile helps him to illustrate the acrobatic possibilities of language in a fresh and original manner.

The following poem develops an **extended metaphor**, personifying rooming houses as old women.

Jack Mitchell/Archive Photos/Getty Images

Audre Lorde (1934–1992)

Rooming houses are old women (1968)

Rooming houses are old women
rocking dark windows into their whens
waiting incomplete circles
rocking
rent office to stoop to
community bathrooms to gas rings and
under-bed boxes of once useful garbage
city issued with a twice monthly check
and the young men next door
with their loud midnight parties
and fishy rings left in the bathtub
no longer arouse them

from midnight to mealtime no stops inbetween
light breaking to pass through jumbled up windows
and who was it who married the widow that Buzzie's
son messed with?
To Welfare and insult form the slow shuffle
from dayswork to shopping bags
heavy with leftovers
Rooming houses
are old women waiting
searching
through darkening windows
the end or beginning of agony
old women seen through half-ajar doors
hoping
they are not waiting
but being
the entrance to somewhere
unknown and desired
but not new.

So closely does Lorde equate rooming houses and old women in this poem that at times it is difficult to tell which of the two is actually the poem's subject. Despite the poem's assertion, rooming houses are *not* old women; however, they are *comparable to* the old women who live there because their walls enclose a lifetime of disappointments as well as the physical detritus of life. Like the old women, rooming houses are in decline, rocking away their remaining years. And, like the houses they inhabit, these women's boundaries are fixed—"rent office to stoop to / community bathrooms to gas rings"—and their hopes and expectations are few. They are surrounded by other people's loud parties, but their own lives have been reduced to a "slow shuffle" to nowhere, a hopeless, frightened—and perhaps pointless—"waiting / searching." Over time, these women and the places in which they live have become one. By using an unexpected comparison between two seemingly unrelated entities, the poem illuminates both the essence of the rooming houses and the essence of their elderly occupants.

FURTHER READING: Simile, Metaphor, and Personification

Robert Burns (1759–1796)

Oh, my love is like a red, red rose (1796)

Oh, my love is like a red, red rose
That's newly sprung in June;
My love is like the melody
That's sweetly played in tune.

So fair art thou, my bonny lass,
So deep in love am I;
And I will love thee still, my dear,
Till a' the seas gang[1] dry.

Till a' the seas gang dry, my dear,
And the rocks melt wi' the sun;
And I will love thee still, my dear,
While the sands o' life shall run.

And fare thee weel, my only love!
And fare thee weel awhile!
And I will come again, my love
Though it were ten thousand mile.

Reading and Reacting

1. Why does the speaker compare his love to a rose? What other simile is used in the poem? For what purpose is it used?
2. Why do you suppose Burns begins his poem with similes? Would moving them to the end change the poem's impact?
3. Where does the speaker seem to exaggerate the extent of his love? Why does he exaggerate? Do you think this exaggeration weakens the poem? Explain.
4. **Journal Entry** Create ten original similes that begin with, "My love is like __________."

Related Works: "The Girl with Bangs" (p. 204), "Araby" (p. 296), "My mistress' eyes are nothing like the sun" (p. 557), "To His Coy Mistress" (p. 575), "How Do I Love Thee?" (p. 684), *The Brute* (p. 769)

AP Images/Jacques Brinon

N. Scott Momaday (1934–)

Simile (1974)

What did we say to each other
that now we are as the deer
who walk in single file
with heads high
with ears forward
with eyes watchful
with hooves always placed on firm ground
in whose limbs there is latent flight

[1] *gang:* Go.

Reading and Reacting

1. In what sense are the speaker and the person he is speaking to like the deer he describes in this extended simile? In what sense are their limbs in "latent flight" (line 8)?
2. Without using similes or metaphors, paraphrase this poem.
3. This entire poem consists of a single sentence, but it has no punctuation. Do you see this as a problem? What punctuation marks, if any, would you add? Why?
4. **Journal Entry** What do you suppose the speaker and the person he addresses might have said to each other to inspire the feelings described in this poem?

Related Work: "Let me not to the marriage of true minds" (p. 735)

Sylvia Plath (1932–1963)

Metaphors (1960)

I'm a riddle in nine syllables,
An elephant, a ponderous house,
A melon strolling on two tendrils.
O red fruit, ivory, fine timbers!
This loaf's big with its yeasty rising.
Money's new-minted in this fat purse.
I'm a means, a stage, a cow in calf.
I've eaten a bag of green apples,
Boarded the train there's no getting off.

Reading and Reacting

1. The speaker in this poem is a pregnant woman. Do all the metaphors she uses to characterize herself seem appropriate? For example, in what sense is the speaker "a means, a stage" (line 7)?
2. If you were going to expand this poem, what other metaphors (or similes) would you add?
3. What are the "nine syllables" to which the speaker refers in the poem's first line? What significance does the number *nine* have in terms of the poem's subject? in terms of its form?
4. **Journal Entry** Would you say the speaker has a positive, negative, or neutral attitude toward her pregnancy? Which metaphors give you this impression?

Related Work: "I Stand Here Ironing" (p. 227)

Randall Jarrell (1914–1965)

The Death of the Ball Turret Gunner[1] (1945)

From my mother's sleep I fell into the State
And I hunched in its belly till my wet fur froze.
Six miles from earth, loosed from its dream of life,
I woke to black flak and the nightmare fighters.
When I died they washed me out of the turret with a hose.

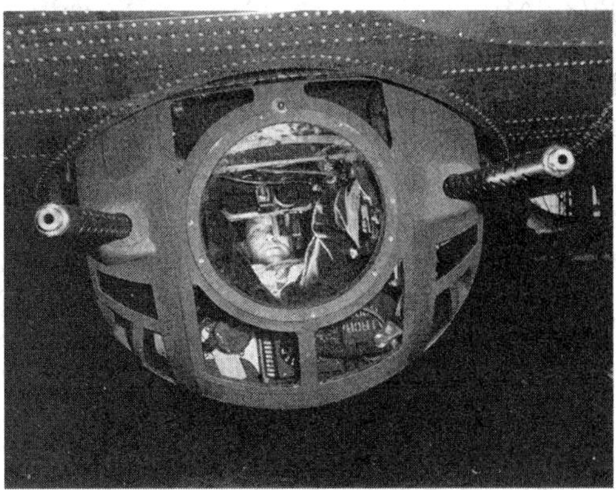

Gunner in ball turret
Source: ©Cape Canaveral Hangar, United States Air Force

Reading and Reacting

1. Who is the speaker? To what does he compare himself in the poem's first two lines? What words establish this comparison?
2. Contrast the speaker's actual identity with the one he creates for himself in lines 1 and 2. What elements of his actual situation do you think lead him to characterize himself as he does in these lines?
3. **Journal Entry** Both this poem and "Dulce et Decorum Est" (p. 687) use figures of speech to describe the horrors of war. Which poem has a greater impact on you? How does the poem's figurative language contribute to this impact?
4. **Critical Perspective** Critic Frances Ferguson has argued that "The Death of the Ball Turret Gunner" "thoroughly manifests the lack of a middle between the gunner's birth and his death. . . . Because the poem presents a man who seems to have lived in order to die, we forget the fiction that he must have

---

[1] *Ball turret gunner:* World War II machine gunner positioned upside-down in a plexiglass sphere in the belly of a bomber.

lived." However, in a later explication, Patrick J. Horner writes that the "manipulation of time reveals the stunning brevity of the gunner's waking life and the State's total disregard for that phenomenon. . . . Because of the telescoping of time, [the poem] resonates with powerful feeling."

With which critic do you agree? Do you see the "lack of a middle" as a positive or negative quality of this poem?

Related Works: "The Soldier" (p. 689), from *In Time of War* (p. 689)

John Donne (1572–1631)

A Valediction: Forbidding Mourning (1611)

As virtuous men pass mildly away,
And whisper to their souls to go,
Whilst some of their sad friends do say
The breath goes now, and some say no:

So let us melt, and make no noise,
No tear-floods, nor sigh-tempests move;
'Twere profanation of our joys
To tell the laity[1] our love.

Moving of th' earth brings harms and fears;
Men reckon what it did and meant;
But trepidation of the spheres,
Though greater far, is innocent.

Dull sublunary lovers' love
(Whose soul is sense) cannot admit
Absence, because it doth remove
Those things which elemented it.

But we, by a love so much refined
That ourselves know not what it is,
Inter-assurèd of the mind,
Care less, eyes, lips, and hands to miss.

Our two souls, therefore, which are one,
Though I must go, endure not yet
A breach, but an expansion,
Like gold to airy thinness beat.

If they be two, they are two so
As stiff twin compasses[2] are two:

---

[1] *laity:* Here, "common people."

[2] *compasses:* V-shaped instruments used for drawing circles.

Thy soul, the fixed foot, makes no show
To move, but doth, if th' other do.

And though it in the center sit,
Yet when the other far doth roam,
It leans and harkens after it,
And grows erect as that comes home.

Such wilt thou be to me, who must,
Like th' other foot, obliquely run;
Thy firmness makes my circle just,[3]
And makes me end where I begun.

Engraving of compass
iStock.com/Benoitb

Reading and Reacting

1. Beginning with line 25, the poem develops an extended metaphor that compares the speaker and his loved one to "twin compasses" (line 26), attached yet separate. Why is the compass (pictured earlier) an especially apt metaphor? What physical characteristics of the compass does the poet emphasize?

[3] *just:* Perfect.

2. The poem uses other figures of speech to characterize both the lovers' union and their separation. To what other events does the speaker compare his separation from his loved one? To what other elements does he compare their attachment? Do you think these comparisons make sense? Why or why not?
3. **Journal Entry** To what other object could Donne have compared his loved one and himself? Explain the logic of the extended metaphor you suggest.
4. **Critical Perspective** In *John Donne and the Metaphysical Poets*, Judah Stampfer writes of this poem's "thin, dry texture, its stanzas of pinched music," noting that its form "has too clipped a brevity to qualify as a song" and that its "music wobbles on a dry, measured beat." Yet, he argues, "the poem comes choked with emotional power" because "the speaker reads as a naturally reticent man, leaving his beloved in uncertainty and deep trouble." Stampfer concludes, "Easy self-expression here would be self-indulgent, if not reprehensible. . . . For all his careful dignity, we feel a heart is breaking here."

   Do you find such emotional power in this highly intellectual poem?

Related Works: "To My Dear and Loving Husband" (p. 575), "How Do I Love Thee?" (p. 684), *A Doll's House* (p. 834)

Hyperbole and Understatement

Two additional kinds of figurative language, *hyperbole* and *understatement*, also give poets opportunities to suggest meaning beyond the literal level of language.

Hyperbole is intentional exaggeration—saying more than is actually meant. In the poem "Oh, my love is like a red, red rose" (p. 564), when the speaker says that he will love his lady until all the seas go dry, he is using hyperbole.

Understatement is the opposite—saying less than is meant. When the speaker in the poem "Fire and Ice" (p. 504), weighing two equally grim alternatives for the end of the world, says that "for destruction ice / Is also great / And would suffice," he is using understatement. In both cases, the poets expect their readers to understand that their words are not to be taken literally.

By using hyperbole and understatement, poets enhance the impact of their poems. For example, poets can use hyperbole to convey exaggerated anger or graphic images of horror—and to ridicule and satirize as well as to inflame and shock. With understatement, poets can convey the same kind of powerful emotions subtly, without artifice or embellishment, thereby leading readers to read more closely than they might otherwise.

The emotionally charged poem that follows uses hyperbole to convey anger and bitterness that seem almost beyond the power of words.

Everett Collection Historical/Alamy Stock Photo

Sylvia Plath (1932–1963)

Daddy (1965)

You do not do, you do not do
Any more, black shoe
In which I have lived like a foot
For thirty years, poor and white,
Barely daring to breathe or Achoo.

Daddy, I have had to kill you.
You died before I had time—
Marble-heavy, a bag full of God,
Ghastly statue with one grey toe
Big as a Frisco seal

And a head in the freakish Atlantic
Where it pours bean green over blue
In the waters off beautiful Nauset.
I used to pray to recover you.
Ach, du.[1]

In the German tongue, in the Polish town[2]
Scraped flat by the roller
Of wars, wars, wars.
But the name of the town is common.
My Polack friend

Says there are a dozen or two.
So I never could tell where you
Put your foot, your root,
I never could talk to you.
The tongue stuck in my jaw.

It stuck in a barb wire snare.
Ich, ich, ich, ich,[3]
I could hardly speak.
I thought every German was you.
And the language obscene

An engine, an engine
Chuffing me off like a Jew.
A Jew to Dachau, Auschwitz, Belsen.[4]

---

[1] *Ach, du:* "Ah, you" (German).
[2] *Polish town:* Grabôw, where Plath's father was born.
[3] *ich:* "I" (German).
[4] *Dachau, Auschwitz, Belsen:* Nazi concentration camps.

I began to talk like a Jew.
I think I may well be a Jew.

The snows of the Tyrol, the clear beer of Vienna
Are not very pure or true.
With my gypsy ancestress and my weird luck
And my Taroc pack and my Taroc pack
I may be a bit of a Jew.

I have always been scared of *you*,
With your Luftwaffe,[5] your gobbledygoo.
And your neat moustache
And yousr Aryan eye, bright blue.
Panzer[6]-man, panzer-man, O You—

Not God but a swastika
So black no sky could squeak through.
Every woman adores a Fascist,
The boot in the face, the brute
Brute heart of a brute like you.

You stand at the blackboard, daddy,
In the picture I have of you,
A cleft in your chin instead of your foot
But no less a devil for that, no not
Any less the black man who

Bit my pretty red heart in two.
I was ten when they buried you.
At twenty I tried to die
And get back, back, back to you.
I thought even the bones would do.

But they pulled me out of the sack,
And they stuck me together with glue.
And then I knew what to do.
I made a model of you,
A man in black with a Meinkampf[7] look

And a love of the rack and the screw.
And I said I do, I do.
So daddy, I'm finally through.
The black telephone's off at the root,
The voices just can't worm through.

---

[5]*Luftwaffe:* The German air force.

[6]*Panzer:* Protected by armor. The Panzer division was the German armored division.

[7]*Meinkampf: Mein Kampf* (My Struggle) is Adolf Hitler's autobiography.

If I've killed one man, I've killed two—
The vampire who said he was you
And drank my blood for a year,
Seven years, if you want to know.
Daddy, you can lie back now.

There's a stake in your fat black heart
And the villagers never liked you.
They are dancing and stamping on you.
They always *knew* it was you.
Daddy, daddy, you bastard, I'm through.

Nazi poster, 1941
Hulton Archive/Archive Photos/Getty Images

In her anger and frustration, the speaker sees herself as a helpless victim—a foot entrapped in a shoe, a Jew in a concentration camp—of her father's (and, later, her husband's) absolute tyranny. Thus, her hated father is characterized as a "black shoe," "a bag full of God," a "Ghastly statue," and, eventually, a Nazi, a torturer, the devil, a vampire. The poem "Daddy" is widely accepted by scholars as autobiographical, and the fact that Plath's own father was actually neither a Nazi nor a sadist (nor, obviously, the devil or a vampire) makes it clear that the figures of speech in the poem are wildly exaggerated. Even so, they may convey the poet's true feelings toward her father—and, perhaps, toward the patriarchal society in which she lived.

Plath uses hyperbole to communicate these emotions to readers who she knows cannot possibly feel the way she does. Her purpose, therefore, is not only to shock but also to enlighten, to persuade, and perhaps even to empower her readers. Throughout the poem, the inflammatory language is set in ironic opposition to the childish, affectionate term "Daddy"—most strikingly in the last line's choked out "Daddy, daddy, you bastard, I'm through." The result of the exaggerated rhetoric is a poem that is vivid and shocking. And, although some might believe that Plath's almost wild exaggeration undermines the poem's impact, others would argue that the powerful language is necessary to convey the extent of the speaker's rage.

Like "Daddy," the following poem describes a situation whose emotional impact is devastating. In this case, however, the poet does not use highly charged language; instead, she uses understatement, presenting her imagined scenario without embellishment.

Edna St. Vincent Millay (1892–1950)

If I should learn, in some quite casual way (1931)

If I should learn, in some quite casual way,
That you were gone, not to return again—
Read from the back-page of a paper, say,
Held by a neighbor in a subway train,
How at a corner of this avenue
And such a street (so are the papers filled)
A hurrying man—who happened to be you—
At noon today had happened to be killed,
I should not cry aloud—could not cry
Aloud, or wring my hands in such a place—
I should but watch the station lights rush by
With a more careful interest on my face,
Or raise my eyes and read with greater care
Where to store furs and how to treat the hair.

Although this poem's speaker imagines a tragic scenario—receiving the news of her lover's death—her language is restrained. In the poem's first eight lines, words and expressions like "quite casual" (1), "say" (3), "this avenue / And such a street" (5–6), and "happened to be" (7, 8) convey a sense of randomness. The speaker's voice is detached and passive. In the remaining six lines, which describe her reaction to the news, she calmly explains her unwillingness to make a scene, telling what she will not do—"cry / Aloud, or wring my hands . . ." (9–10)—and expressing her determination to adopt an air of studied interest in the subway car's trivial advertisements. The poem's language and tone are consistently flat and unemotional, conveying a sense of detachment and resignation.

FURTHER READING: Hyperbole and Understatement

Anne Bradstreet (1612–1672)

To My Dear and Loving Husband (1678)

If ever two were one, then surely we.
If ever man were lov'd by wife, then thee;
If ever wife was happy in a man,
Compare with me ye women if you can.
I prize thy love more than whole Mines of gold,
Or all the riches that the East doth hold.
My love is such that Rivers cannot quench,
Nor ought but love from thee, give recompense.
Thy love is such I can no way repay,
The heavens reward thee manifold I pray.
Then while we live, in love let's so persever,
That when we live no more, we may live ever.

Reading and Reacting

1. Review the claims the poem's speaker makes about her husband in lines 5–8. Are such exaggerated declarations of love necessary or would the rest of the poem be sufficient to convey the extent of her devotion to her husband?
2. **Journal Entry** Compare this poem's declarations of love to those of John Donne's speaker in "A Valediction: Forbidding Mourning" (p. 586). Which speaker do you find more convincing? Why?

Related Works: "A Rose for Emily" (p. 166), "How Do I Love Thee?" (p. 684), "Let me not to the marriage of true minds" (p. 735)

Andrew Marvell (1621–1678)

To His Coy Mistress (1681)

Had we but world enough and time,
This coyness, lady, were no crime.
We would sit down and think which way
To walk, and pass our long love's day.
Thou by the Indian Ganges' side
Should'st rubies find; I by the tide
Of Humber[1] would complain. I would

[1] *Humber:* An estuary on the east coast of England.

Love you ten years before the Flood,
And you should, if you please, refuse
Till the conversion of the Jews.
My vegetable love should grow
Vaster than empires, and more slow.
An hundred years should go to praise
Thine eyes, and on thy forehead gaze,
Two hundred to adore each breast,
But thirty thousand to the rest.
An age at least to every part,
And the last age should show your heart.
For, lady, you deserve this state,
Nor would I love at lower rate.
    But at my back I always hear
Time's wingèd chariot hurrying near,
And yonder all before us lie
Deserts of vast eternity.
Thy beauty shall no more be found,
Nor in thy marble vault shall sound
My echoing song; then worms shall try
That long preserved virginity,
And your quaint honor turn to dust,
And into ashes all my lust.
The grave's a fine and private place,
But none, I think, do there embrace.
    Now therefore, while the youthful hue
Sits on thy skin like morning glew[2]
And while thy willing soul transpires
At every pore with instant fires,
Now let us sport us while we may;
And now, like amorous birds of prey,
Rather at once our time devour
Than languish in his slow-chapped[3] power.
Let us roll all our strength and all
Our sweetness up into one ball
And tear our pleasures with rough strife
Thorough the iron gates of life.
Thus, though we cannot make our sun
Stand still, yet we will make him run.

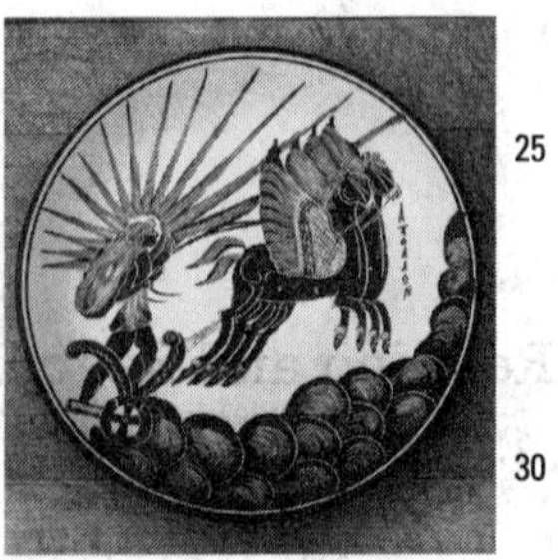

Winged horses pulling chariot
Art Directors & TRIP/Alamy Stock Photo

[2]*glew:* Dew.
[3]*slow-chapped:* Slowly crushing.

Reading and Reacting

1. In this poem, Marvell's speaker sets out to convince a reluctant woman to become his lover. To make his case more persuasive, he uses hyperbole, exaggerating time periods, sizes, spaces, and the possible fate of the woman if she refuses him. Identify as many examples of hyperbole as you can.
2. The tone of "To His Coy Mistress" is more whimsical than serious. Given this tone, what do you see as the purpose of Marvell's use of hyperbole?
3. **Journal Entry** Using contemporary prose, paraphrase the first four lines of the poem. Then, beginning with the word *However*, compose a few new sentences of prose, continuing the argument Marvell's speaker makes.
4. **Critical Perspective** In her essay "Andrew Marvell's 'To His Coy Mistress': A Feminist Reading," critic Margaret Wald presents the following analysis of the poem:

   > Andrew Marvell's speaker in "To His Coy Mistress" invokes Petrarchan convention, a poetic mode originating in the fourteenth century in which a male lover uses exaggerated metaphors to appeal to his female beloved. Yet Marvell alludes to such excessive—and disempowering—pining only to defy this tradition of unrequited love. Instead of respectful adulation, he offers lustful invitation; rather than anticipating rejection, he assumes sexual dominion over the eponymous "mistress." The poem is as much a celebration of his rhetorical mastery as it is of his physical conquest.

   In what sense is the speaker in this poem celebrating his beloved? In what sense is he celebrating himself? Is his portrayal of his loved one entirely positive? Which elements, if any, are negative?

Related Works: "Where Are You Going, Where Have You Been?" (p. 447), "To the Virgins, to Make Much of Time" (p. 513), "The Passionate Shepherd to His Love" (p. 730), *The Brute* (p. 769)

Robert Frost (1874–1963)

"Out, Out—" (1916)

The buzz saw snarled and rattled in the yard
And made dust and dropped stove-length sticks of wood,
Sweet-scented stuff when the breeze drew across it.
And from there those that lifted eyes could count
Five mountain ranges one behind the other
Under the sunset far into Vermont.
And the saw snarled and rattled, snarled and rattled,
As it ran light, or had to bear a load.
And nothing happened: day was all but done.
Call it a day, I wish they might have said

To please the boy by giving him the half hour
That a boy counts so much when saved from work.
His sister stood beside them in her apron
To tell them "Supper." At the word, the saw,
As if to prove saws knew what supper meant,
Leaped out at the boy's hand, or seemed to leap—
He must have given the hand. However it was,
Neither refused the meeting. But the hand!
The boy's first outcry was a rueful laugh,
As he swung toward them holding up the hand
Half in appeal, but half as if to keep
The life from spilling. Then the boy saw all—
Since he was old enough to know, big boy
Doing a man's work, though a child at heart—
He saw all spoiled. "Don't let him cut my hand off—
The doctor, when he comes. Don't let him, sister!"
So. But the hand was gone already.
The doctor put him in the dark of ether.
He lay and puffed his lips out with his breath.
And then—the watcher at his pulse took fright.
No one believed. They listened at his heart.
Little—less—nothing!—and that ended it.
No more to build on there. And they, since they
Were not the one dead, turned to their affairs.

Reading and Reacting

1. The poem's title is an **allusion** to a passage in Shakespeare's *Macbeth* (5.5.23–28) that addresses the brevity and meaninglessness of life in very emotional terms:

> Out, out brief candle!
> Life's but a walking shadow, a poor player,
> That struts and frets his hour upon the stage
> And then is heard no more. It is a tale
> Told by an idiot, full of sound and fury,
> Signifying nothing.

What idea do you think Frost wants to convey through the title "Out, Out—"?

2. Explain why each of the following qualifies as understatement:

- "Neither refused the meeting." (line 18)
- "He saw all spoiled." (line 25)
- "—and that ended it." (line 32)
- "No more to build on there." (line 33)

Can you identify any other examples of understatement in the poem?

3. **Journal Entry** Do you think the poem's impact is strengthened or weakened by its understated tone?
4. **Critical Perspective** In an essay on Frost in his book *Affirming Limits*, poet and critic Robert Pack focuses on the single word "So" in line 27 of "Out, Out—":

   > For a moment, his narration is reduced to the impotent word "So," and in that minimal word all his restrained grief is held.... That "So" is the narrator's cry of bearing witness to a story that must be what it is in a scene he cannot enter. He cannot rescue or protect the boy.... In the poem's sense of human helplessness in an indifferent universe, we are all "watchers," and what we see is death without redemption, "signifying nothing." So. So? So! How shall we read that enigmatic word?

   How do you read this "enigmatic word"? Why?

Related Works: "The Lottery" (p. 337), "To an Athlete Dying Young" (p. 540), "The Death of the Ball Turret Gunner" (p. 567), "Death Be Not Proud" (p. 713)

Countee Cullen (1903–1946)

Incident (1925)

Once riding in old Baltimore,
Heart-filled, head-filled with glee;
I saw a Baltimorean
Keep looking straight at me.
Now I was eight and very small,
And he was no whit bigger,
And so I smiled, but he poked out
His tongue, and called me, "Nigger."
I saw the whole of Baltimore
From May until December;
Of all the things that happened there
That's all that I remember.

Reading and Reacting

1. This poem's last two lines are extremely understated. What words or lines in the poem are *not* understated? Does this use of both direct and understated language make sense? Explain.
2. What do you think the speaker might be referring to by "all the things that happened" in Baltimore (11)? Why?
3. **Journal Entry** Retell the events of this poem in a paragraph, paraphrasing lines 1–10 but quoting the last two lines exactly. Include a few sentences that reveal the speaker's emotions.

4. **Critical Perspective** According to critic Jervis Anderson, Countee Cullen, although one of the most prominent African American poets of his time, placed relatively little emphasis in his work on race and racial politics:

> Cullen did not, could not, avoid entirely the question of race. But his view of himself as a poet did not permit him to make that question his main subject.... Usually, Cullen engaged the race problem obliquely—at times with deft jabs and glancing blows... at times with understated amusement, as in "Incident."

Do you agree with Anderson that, in "Incident," Cullen deals with race with "understated amusement"? What evidence for or against this interpretation do you see in the poem?

Related Works: "Big Black Good Man" (p. 302), "Negro" (p. 498), "Ethel's Sestina" (p. 626), "Yet Do I Marvel" (p. 662), "If We Must Die" (p. 731)

Metonymy and Synecdoche

Metonymy and synecdoche are two related figures of speech. **Metonymy** is the substitution of the name of one thing for the name of another thing that most readers associate with the first—for example, using *hired gun* to mean "paid assassin" or *suits* to mean "business executives." A specific kind of metonymy, called **synecdoche**, is the substitution of a part for the whole (for example, using *wheels* to refer to an automobile or *bread*—as in "Give us this day our daily bread"—to mean "food") or the whole for a part (for example, using *the law* to refer to a police officer).

With metonymy and synecdoche, instead of describing something by saying it is like something else (as in simile) or by equating it with something else (as in metaphor), writers can characterize an object or concept by using a term that evokes it. The following poem illustrates the use of synecdoche.

Richard Lovelace (1618–1658)

To Lucasta Going to the Wars (1649)

Tell me not, Sweet, I am unkind
That from the nunnery
Of thy chaste breast and quiet mind,
To war and arms I fly.

True, a new mistress now I chase,
The first foe in the field;
And with a stronger faith embrace
A sword, a horse, a shield.

Yet this inconstancy is such
As you too shall adore;
I could not love thee, Dear, so much,
Loved I not Honor more.

Prince Rupert's cavalry charging at Edgehill, 1642
Chronicle/Alamy Stock Photo

Here, Lovelace's use of synecdoche allows him to condense a number of complex ideas into a very few words. In line 3, when the speaker says that he is flying from his loved one's "chaste breast and quiet mind," he is using "breast" and "mind" to stand for all his loved one's physical and intellectual attributes. In line 8, when he says that he is embracing "A sword, a horse, a shield," he is using these three items to represent the trappings of war—and, thus, to represent war itself.

Apostrophe

With **apostrophe**, a poem's speaker addresses an absent person or thing—for example, a historical or literary figure or even an inanimate object or an abstract concept.

In the following poem, the speaker addresses the Twin Towers of the World Trade Center, destroyed in the terrorist attacks of September 11, 2001.

Nancy Mercado (1959–)

Going to Work (2001)

On their daily trips
Commuters shed tears now
Use American flags
Like veiled women
To hide their sorrows
Rush to buy throwaway cameras
To capture your twin ghosts

Frantically I too
Purchase your memory
On postcards & coffee mugs
In New York City souvenir shops
Afraid I'll forget your facade
Forget my hallowed Sunday
Morning PATH Train rides
My subway travels through
The center of your belly
Day after day

Afraid I'll forget your powers
To transform helicopters
Into ladybugs gliding in the air
To turn New York City
Into a breathing map
To display the curvature
Of our world

In "Going to Work," the poem's speaker describes her reactions in the aftermath of the September 11th attacks and remembers how, before the towers were destroyed, she traveled to work on the PATH (Port Authority Trans-Hudson) train that ran beneath them. Now, she says, commuters "Rush to buy throwaway cameras / To capture your twin ghosts." She continues, "Frantically I too / Purchase your memory" in the form of souvenirs. In the speaker's mind, the towers loom large; despite her fears, there is little danger of her forgetting them. In their remembered size and power, they still "display the curvature / Of our world."

FURTHER READING: Apostrophe

John Keats (1795–1821)

Ode to a Nightingale (1819)

I

My heart aches, and a drowsy numbness pains
My sense, as though of hemlock[1] I had drunk,
Or emptied some dull opiate[2] to the drains
One minute past, and Lethe[3]-wards had sunk:
'Tis not through envy of thy happy lot.
But being too happy in thine happiness,—
That thou, light-wingèd Dryad[4] of the trees,
In some melodious plot
Of beechen[5] green, and shadows numberless,
Singest of summer in full-throated ease.

II

O for a draught[6] of vintage! that hath been
Cool'd a long age in the deep-delvèd[7] earth,
Tasting of Flora[8] and the country-green,
Dance, and Provençal[9] song, and sunburnt mirth!
O for a beaker full of the warm South!
Full of the true, the blushful Hippocrene,[10]
With beaded bubbles winking at the brim,
And purple-stainèd mouth;
That I might drink, and leave the world unseen,
And with thee fade away into the forest dim:

III

Fade far away, dissolve, and quite forget
What thou among the leaves hast never known,
The weariness, the fever, and the fret
Here, where men sit and hear each other groan;
Where palsy shakes a few, sad, last grey hairs,

---

[1] *hemlock:* A medicinal plant used as a sedative or, in higher doses, a deadly poison.
[2] *opiate:* A medicine containing opium, a substance derived from poppies, which aids sleep and relieves pain.
[3] *Lethe:* In Greek mythology, a river in Hades, the land of the dead. Those who drank its water lost all memory of the past.
[4] *Dryad:* A spirit believed to inhabit trees.
[5] *beechen:* Of or relating to a beech tree.
[6] *draught:* A large sip of liquid.
[7] *deep-delvèd:* Excavated.
[8] *Flora:* In Roman mythology, the goddess of flowers.
[9] *Provençal:* From Provence, a region of southern France.
[10] *Hippocrene:* A fountain on Mt. Helicon, in Greece, considered sacred to the Muses.

Where youth grows pale, and spectre-thin, and dies;
Where but to think is to be full of sorrow
And leaden-eyed despairs,
Where beauty cannot keep her lustrous eyes,
Or new Love pine at them beyond to-morrow.

IV

Away! away! for I will fly to thee,
Not charioted by Bacchus[11] and his pards,[12]
But on the viewless wings of Poesy,
Though the dull brain perplexes and retards:
Already with thee! tender is the night,
And haply the Queen-Moon is on her throne,
Cluster'd around by all her starry Fays;[13]
But here there is no light,
Save what from heaven is with the breezes blown
Through verdurous[14] glooms and winding mossy ways.

V

I cannot see what flowers are at my feet,
Nor what soft incense hangs upon the boughs,
But, in embalmèd darkness, guess each sweet
Wherewith the seasonable month endows
The grass, the thicket, and the fruit-tree wild;
White hawthorn, and the pastoral eglantine;[15]
Fast-fading violets cover'd up in leaves;
And mid-May's eldest child,
The coming musk-rose, full of dewy wine,
The murmurous haunt of flies on summer eves.

VI

Darkling I listen; and, for many a time
I have been half in love with easeful Death,
Call'd him soft names in many a musèd rhyme,
To take into the air my quiet breath;
Now more than ever seems it rich to die,
To cease upon the midnight with no pain,
While thou art pouring forth the soul abroad
In such an ecstasy!
Still wouldst thou sing, and I have ears in vain—
To thy high requiem become a sod.

[11] *Bacchus:* The god of wine.
[12] *pards:* Leopards or panthers.
[13] *Fays:* Fairies.
[14] *verdurous:* Green with vegetation.
[15] *eglantine:* A plant also known as the sweet-briar.

VII

Thou wast not born for death, immortal Bird!
No hungry generations tread thee down;
The voice I hear this passing night was heard
In ancient days by emperor and clown:
Perhaps the self-same song that found a path
Through the sad heart of Ruth, when, sick for home,
She stood in tears amid the alien corn;[16]
The same that ofttimes hath
Charm'd magic casements,[17] opening on the foam
Of perilous seas, in faery lands forlorn.[18]

VIII

Forlorn! the very word is like a bell
To toll me back from thee to my sole self!
Adieu! the fancy cannot cheat so well
As she is famed to do, deceiving elf.
Adieu![19] adieu! the plaintive anthem fades
Past the near meadows, over the still stream,
Up the hill-side; and now 'tis buried deep
In the next valley-glades:
Was it a vision, or a waking dream?
Fled is that music:—Do I wake or sleep?

Lithograph of nightingale, c. 1830

The Nightingale of France, c.1830 (colour litho), Oudart, Paul Louis (b.1796) (after)/Bibliotheque des Arts Decoratifs, Paris, France/Archives Charmet/Bridgeman Images

[16] *corn:* Grain.
[17] *casements:* Windows.
[18] *forlorn:* Lost.
[19] *Adieu:* Farewell.

Reading and Reacting

1. Where does the speaker first address the nightingale? Where else does he speak directly to the nightingale?
2. In lines 19–20, the speaker expresses his desire to "leave the world unseen, / And with thee fade away into the forest dim. . . ." Why does he want to "fade away"? What is it about the "forest dim" that attracts him? Give some examples from the poem to contrast the speaker's world with the world of the nightingale.
3. What is it that the speaker admires about the nightingale? In what sense does he see the nightingale as superior to human beings?
4. **Journal Entry** If you were to write an **ode**—a long, serious, and formal poem—to a creature or an object, what would you choose as your subject? Why? How do you see your own world as different from (and inferior to) the world of your subject?

Related Works: "Young Goodman Brown" (p. 354), "The World Is Too Much with Us" (p. 510), "Death Be Not Proud" (p. 713), "Ode on a Grecian Urn" (p. 727), "Ode to the West Wind" (p. 736)

Allen Ginsberg (1926–1997)

A Supermarket in California (1956)

What thoughts I have of you tonight, Walt Whitman,[1] for I walked down the sidestreets under the trees with a headache self-conscious looking at the full moon.
In my hungry fatigue, and shopping for images, I went into the neon fruit supermarket, dreaming of your enumerations!
What peaches and what penumbras! Whole families shopping at night! Aisles full of husbands! Wives in the avocados, babies in the tomatoes!—and you, Garcia Lorca,[2] what were you doing down by the watermelons?

I saw you, Walt Whitman, childless, lonely old grubber, poking among the meats in the refrigerator and eyeing the grocery boys.[3]
I heard you asking questions of each: Who killed the pork chops? What price bananas? Are you my Angel?
I wandered in and out of the brilliant stacks of cans following you, and followed in my imagination by the store detective.

---

[1] *Walt Whitman:* American poet (1819–1892) whose poems frequently praise the commonplace and often contain lengthy "enumerations."

[2] *Federico Garcia Lorca:* Spanish poet and dramatist (1899–1936).

[3] *eyeing the grocery boys:* Whitman's sexual orientation is the subject of much debate. Ginsberg is suggesting here that Whitman was homosexual.

We strode down the open corridors together in our solitary fancy tasting artichokes, possessing every frozen delicacy, and never passing the cashier.

Where are we going, Walt Whitman? The doors close in an hour. Which way does your beard point tonight?

(I touch your book[4] and dream of our odyssey in the supermarket and feel absurd.)

Will we walk all night through solitary streets? The trees add shade to shade, lights out in the houses, we'll both be lonely.

Will we stroll dreaming of the lost America of love past blue automobiles in driveways, home to our silent cottage?

Ah, dear father, graybeard, lonely old courage-teacher, what America did you have when Charon[5] quit poling his ferry and you got out on a smoking bank and stood watching the boat disappear on the black waters of Lethe?[6]

Reading and Reacting

1. In this poem, Ginsberg's speaker wanders through the aisles of a supermarket, speaking to the nineteenth-century American poet Walt Whitman and asking Whitman a series of questions. Why do you think the speaker addresses Whitman? What kind of answers do you think he is looking for?
2. In paragraph 2, the speaker says he is "shopping for images." What does he mean? Why does he look for these images in a supermarket? Does he find them?
3. Is this poem about supermarkets? about Walt Whitman? about poetry? about love? about America? What do you see as its primary subject? Why?
4. **Journal Entry** Does the incongruous image of the respected poet "poking / among the meats" (paragraph 4) in the supermarket strengthen the poem's impact, or does it undercut any serious "message" the poem might have? Explain.
5. **Critical Perspective** The critic Leslie Fiedler discusses some of the ways in which Ginsberg's style resembles that of Walt Whitman:

   > Everything about Ginsberg is . . . blatantly Whitmanian: his meter is resolutely anti-iambic, his line groupings stubbornly anti-stanzaic, his diction aggressively colloquial and American, his voice public.

   Does this characterization apply to "A Supermarket in California"? If so, how?

Related Works: "A&P" (p. 179), "Chicago" (p. 634), *from* "Out of the Cradle Endlessly Rocking" (p. 637), "I Hear America Singing" (p. 741), *from* "Song of Myself" (p. 742), *The Cuban Swimmer* (p. 1122)

---

[4] *your book: Leaves of Grass.*

[5] *Charon:* In Greek mythology, the ferryman who transported the dead over the river Styx to Hades.

[6] *Lethe:* In Greek mythology, the river of forgetfulness (one of five rivers in Hades).

Checklist Writing about Figures of Speech

- What figures of speech are used in the poem? Identify any examples of simile, metaphor, personification, hyperbole, understatement, metonymy, synecdoche, and apostrophe.
- What two elements are being compared in each use of simile, metaphor, and personification? What characteristics are shared by the two items being compared?
- Does the poet use hyperbole? Why? For example, is it used to move or to shock readers, or is its use intended to produce a humorous or satirical effect? Would more understated language be more effective?
- Does the poet use understatement? For what purpose? Would more emotionally charged language be more effective?
- If the poem includes metonymy or synecdoche, what term is being substituted for another? To what object or concept does the term refer?
- If the poem includes apostrophe, whom or what does the speaker address? What does the use of apostrophe accomplish?
- How do figures of speech contribute to the impact of the poem as a whole?

WRITING SUGGESTIONS: Figures of Speech

1. Figures of speech are often used to describe characters in literary works. Choose two or three works that focus on a single character—for example, "A Rose for Emily" (p. 166), "Miss Brill" (p. 185), "Gryphon" (p. 191), or "Richard Cory" (p. 734)—and explain how figures of speech are used to characterize each work's central figure. If you like, you may write about works that focus on real (rather than fictional) people, such as "Dreams of Suicide" (p. 659) or "Emmett Till" (p. 719).
2. Write an essay in which you discuss the different ways poets use figures of speech to examine the nature of poetry itself. What kinds of figures of speech do poets use to describe their craft? (You might begin by reading the two poems about poetry that open Chapter 17.)
3. Write a letter (or a poem) replying to the speaker in the poem by Marvell, Bradstreet, Donne, or Burns that appears in this chapter. Use figures of speech to express the depth of your love and the extent of your devotion.

4. Choose three or four poems that have a common subject—for example, love or nature—and write an essay in which you draw some general conclusions about the relative effectiveness of the poems' use of figures of speech to examine that subject. (If you like, you may focus on the poems clustered under the heads "Poems about Parents," "Poems about Nature," "Poems about Love," and "Poems about War" in Chapter 25.)
5. Select a poem and a short story that deal with the same subject, and write an essay in which you compare their use of figures of speech.

Chapter

22

Sound

Jacob Saenz

Walt Whitman

Emily Dickinson

Learning Objectives

After reading this chapter, you will be able to. . .

- Describe how rhythm functions in a poem.
- Explain how meter functions in a poem.
- Identify commonly used metric feet and metric lines.
- Identify the metrical pattern of a poem.
- Describe how sound functions in a poem.
- Explain how rhyme functions in a poem.
- Analyze a poem based on its rhythm, rhyme, and meter.

Detail of vase showing Achilles killing Hector

The Trustees of the British Museum / Art Resource, NY

Walt Whitman (1819–1892)

Had I the Choice*

Had I the choice to tally greatest bards,
To limn[1] their portraits, stately, beautiful, and
emulate at will,
Homer with all his wars and warriors—Hector,
Achilles, Ajax,
Or Shakespeare's woe-entangled Hamlet, Lear,
Othello—Tennyson's fair ladies,
Meter or wit the best, or choice conceit to wield
in perfect
rhyme, delight of singers;
These, these, O sea, all these I'd gladly barter,
Would you the undulation of one wave, its trick
to me transfer,
Or breathe one breath of yours upon my verse,
And leave its odor there.

Rhythm

Rhythm—the regular recurrence of sounds—is at the center of all natural phenomena: the beating of a heart, the lapping of waves against the shore, the croaking of frogs on a summer's night, the whispering of wheat swaying in the wind. Even mechanical phenomena, such as the movement of rush-hour traffic through a city's streets, have a kind of rhythm. Poetry, which explores these phenomena, often tries to reflect the same rhythms. Walt Whitman expresses this idea in "Had I the Choice" when he says that he would gladly trade the "perfect rhyme" of Shakespeare for the ability to reproduce "the undulation of one wave" in his verse.

Public speakers frequently repeat key words and phrases to create rhythm. Martin Luther King Jr. uses this technique (called **anaphora**) in his "I Have a Dream" speech when he repeats the phrase "I have a dream" to create a rhythm that ties the central section of the speech together:

> I say to you today, my friends, even though we face the difficulties of today and tomorrow, I still have a dream. It is a dream deeply rooted in the American dream. I have a dream that one day this nation will rise up and live out the true meaning of its creed: "We hold these truths to be self-evident, that all men are created equal." I have a dream that one day, on the red hills of Georgia, sons of former slaves and the

*Publication date is not available.

[1] *limn:* To draw, depict.

> sons of former slave owners will be able to sit down together at the table of brotherhood. I have a dream that one day even the state of Mississippi, a state sweltering with the heat of injustice, sweltering with the heat of oppression, will be transformed into an oasis of freedom and justice. I have a dream that my four little children will one day live in a nation where they will not be judged by the color of their skin, but by the content of their character.

Poets too create rhythm by using repeated words and phrases, as Gwendolyn Brooks does in the poem that follows.

Gwendolyn Brooks (1917–2000)

Sadie and Maud (1945)

Maud went to college.
Sadie stayed at home.
Sadie scraped life
With a fine-tooth comb.

She didn't leave a tangle in.
Her comb found every strand.
Sadie was one of the livingest chits
In all the land.

Sadie bore two babies
Under her maiden name.
Maud and Ma and Papa
Nearly died of shame.

When Sadie said her last so-long
Her girls struck out from home.
(Sadie had left as heritage
Her fine-tooth comb.)

Maud, who went to college,
Is a thin brown mouse.
She is living all alone
In this old house.

Much of the force of this poem comes from the repeated words "Sadie" and "Maud," which shift the focus from one subject to the other and back again ("Maud went to college / Sadie stayed home"). The poem's singsong rhythm recalls the rhymes children recite when jumping rope. This evocation of carefree childhood is ironically contrasted with the adult realities that both Sadie and Maud face as they grow up: Sadie stays at home and has two children out of wedlock; Maud goes to college and ends up "a thin brown mouse." The speaker implies that the alternatives Sadie and Maud represent are both undesirable. Although Sadie "scraped life / with a fine-tooth comb," she dies young and leaves nothing to her girls but her desire to experience life. Maud, who graduated from college, shuts out life and cuts herself off from her roots.

Just as the repetition of words and phrases can create rhythm, so can the appearance of words on the printed page. How a poem looks is especially important in **open form poetry** (see p. 634), which dispenses with traditional patterns of versification. In the following excerpt from "The Moon Is Hiding In" by E. E. Cummings, for example, an unusual arrangement of words forces readers to slow down and then to speed up, creating a rhythm that emphasizes a key phrase—"The / lily":

> the moon is hiding
> in her hair.
> The
> lily
> of heaven
> full of all dreams,
> draws down.

Meter

Although rhythm can be affected by the regular repetition of words and phrases or by the arrangement of words into lines, poetic rhythm is largely created by **meter**, the recurrence of regular units of stressed and unstressed syllables. A **stress** (or accent) occurs when one syllable is emphasized more than another, unstressed, syllable: *fór • ceps, bá • sic, il • lú • sion, ma • lár • i • a.* In a poem, even one-syllable words can be stressed to create a particular effect. For example, in Elizabeth Barrett Browning's line "How do I love thee? Let me count the ways," the metrical pattern that places stress on "love" creates one meaning; stressing "I" would create another.

Scansion is the analysis of patterns of stressed and unstressed syllables within a ʹ line. The most common method of poetic notation indicates stressed syllables with a ʹ and unstressed syllables with a ˘. Although scanning lines gives readers the "beat" of the poem, scansion only generally suggests the sound of spoken language, which contains an infinite variety of stresses. By providing a graphic representation of the stressed and unstressed syllables of a poem, scansion aids understanding, but it is no substitute for reading the poem aloud and experimenting with various patterns of emphasis.

The basic unit of meter is a **foot**—a group of syllables with a fixed pattern of stressed and unstressed syllables. The chart that follows illustrates the most common types of metrical feet in English and American verse.

Foot	Stress Pattern	Example
Iamb	˘ ´	They pace | in sleek | chi val | ric cer | tain ty (Adrienne Rich)
Trochee	´ ˘	Thou, when | thou re | turn'st, wilt | tell me (John Donne)
Anapest	˘ ˘ ´	With a hey, | and a ho, | and a hey | no ni no (William Shakespeare)
Dactyl	´ ˘ ˘	Constantly | risking ab | surdity (Lawrence Ferlinghetti)

Iambic and *anapestic* meters are called **rising meters** because they progress from unstressed to stressed syllables. *Trochaic* and *dactylic* meters are called **falling meters** because they progress from stressed to unstressed syllables.

The following types of metrical feet, less common than those previously listed, are used to add emphasis or to provide variety rather than to create the dominant meter of a poem.

Foot	Stress Pattern	Example
Spondee	´ ´	Pomp, pride | and circumstance of glorious war! (William Shakespeare)
Pyrrhic	˘ ˘	A horse! a horse! My king | dom for | a horse! (William Shakespeare)

A metric line of poetry is measured by the number of feet it contains.

Monometer	one foot	**Pentameter**	five feet
Dimeter	two feet	**Hexameter**	six feet
Trimeter	three feet	**Heptameter**	seven feet
Tetrameter	four feet	**Octameter**	eight feet

The name for a metrical pattern of a line of verse identifies the name of the foot used and the number of feet the line contains. For example, the most common foot in English poetry is the **iamb**, consisting of an unstressed syllable followed by a stressed syllable, most often occurring in lines of three or five feet.

Metrical Pattern	Example
Iambic trimeter	˘ ´ ˘ ´ ˘ ´ Eight hun | dred of | the brave (William Cowper)
Iambic pentameter	˘ ´ ˘ ´ ˘ O, how | much more | doth ´ ˘ ´ ˘ ´ beau | ty beau | teous seem (William Shakespeare)

Because **iambic pentameter** is so well suited to the rhythms of English speech, writers frequently use it in plays and poems. Shakespeare's plays, for example, are written in unrhymed lines of iambic pentameter called **blank verse** (see pp. 615).

Many other metrical combinations are also possible; a few are illustrated here.

Metrical Pattern	Example
Trochaic trimeter	´ ˘ ´ ˘ ´ ˘ Like a | high-born | maiden (Percy Bysshe Shelley)
Anapestic tetrameter	˘ ˘ ´ ˘ ˘ ´ The As sy | rian came down | ˘ ˘ ´ ˘ ˘ ´ like the wolf | on the fold (Lord Byron)
Dactylic hexameter	´ ˘ ˘ ´ ˘ ˘ Maid en most | beau ti ful | ´ ˘ ˘ ´ ˘ ˘ ´ moth er most | boun ti ful, | la ˘ ˘ ´ dy of | lands, (A. C. Swinburne)
Iambic heptameter	˘ ´ ˘ ´ ˘ ´ ˘ The yel | low fog | that rubs | its ´ ˘ ´ ˘ ´ back | up on | the win | ˘ ´ dow-panes (T. S. Eliot)

Scansion can be an extremely technical process, and when readers become bogged down with anapests and dactyls, they can easily forget that poetic scansion is not an end in itself. Meter should be appropriate for the ideas expressed by the poem, and it should help to create a suitable tone. A light, skipping rhythm, for example, would be inappropriate for an **elegy**, and a slow, heavy rhythm would surely be out of place in an **epigram** or a limerick. The following lines of a poem by Samuel Taylor Coleridge illustrate the uses of different types of metrical feet:

> Trochee trips from long to short;
> From long to long in solemn sort
> Slow Spondee stalks; strong foot! yet ill able
> Ever to come up with Dactyl trisyllable.
> Iambics march from short to long—
> With a leap and a bound the swift Anapests throng;
> One syllable long, with one short at each side,
> Amphibrachys hastes with a stately stride—
> First and last being long, middle short, Amphimacer
> Strikes his thundering hoofs like a proud high-bred Racer.

A poet may use one kind of meter—iambic meter, for example—throughout a poem but may occasionally vary line length to relieve monotony or to call attention to a word or idea. In the following poem, the poet uses iambic lines of different lengths.

Bettmann/Getty Images

Emily Dickinson (1830–1886)

I like to see it lap the Miles— (1891)

I like to see it lap the Miles—
And lick the Valleys up—
And stop to feed itself at Tanks—
And then—prodigious step

Around a Pile of Mountains—
And supercilious peer
In Shanties—by the sides of Roads—
And then a Quarry pare

To fit its Ribs
And crawl between

Complaining all the while
In horrid—hooting stanza—
Then chase itself down Hill—

And neigh like Boanerges[1]—
Then—punctual as a Star
Stop—docile and omnipotent
At its own stable door—

Dickinson's poem is a single sentence that, except for some pauses, stretches unbroken from beginning to end. Iambic lines of varying lengths actually suggest the movements of the train that the poet describes. Lines of iambic tetrameter, such as the first, give readers a sense of the train's steady, rhythmic movement across a flat landscape, and shorter lines ("To fit its Ribs / And crawl between") suggest the train's slowing motion. Beginning with two iambic dimeter lines and progressing to iambic trimeter lines, the third stanza increases in speed just like the train that is racing downhill "In horrid—hooting stanza—."

When a poet uses more than one type of metrical foot, any variation in a metrical pattern—the substitution of a trochee for an iamb, for instance—immediately calls attention to itself. For example, in line 16 of "I like to see it lap the Miles," the poet departs from iambic meter by placing unexpected stress on the first word, *stop*. By emphasizing this word, the poet brings the flow of the poem to an abrupt halt, suggesting the jolt riders experience when a train comes to a stop.

Another way of varying the meter of a poem is to introduce a pause known as a **caesura**—a Latin word meaning "a cutting"—within a line. When scanning a poem, you indicate a caesura with two parallel lines: | |. Unless a line of poetry is extremely short, it probably will contain a caesura.

A caesura occurs after a punctuation mark or at a natural break in phrasing:

How do I love thee? || Let me count the ways.
Elizabeth Barrett Browning

Two loves I have || of comfort and despair.
William Shakespeare

High on a throne of royal state, || which far
Outshone the wealth of Ormus || and of Ind
John Milton

Sometimes more than one caesura occurs in a single line:

'Tis good. || Go to the gate. || Somebody knocks.
William Shakespeare

[1]*Boanerges:* A vociferous preacher and orator. Also, the name, meaning "son of thunder," Jesus gave to apostles John and James because of their fiery zeal.

Although the end of a line may mark the end of a metrical unit, it does not always coincide with the end of a sentence. Lines that have distinct pauses at the end—usually signaled by punctuation—are called **end-stopped lines**. Lines that do not end with strong pauses are called **run-on lines**. (Sometimes the term **enjambment** is used to describe run-on lines.) End-stopped lines can sometimes seem formal, or even forced, because their length is rigidly dictated by the poem's meter, rhythm, and rhyme scheme. In the following excerpt from John Keats's "La Belle Dame sans Merci," for example, rhythm, meter, and rhyme dictate the pauses that occur at the ends of the lines:

> O, what can ail thee, knight-at-arms,
> Alone and palely loitering?
> The sedge has wither'd from the lake,
> And no birds sing.

In contrast to end-stopped lines, run-on lines often seem more natural. Because their ending points are determined by the rhythms of speech and by the meaning and emphasis the poet wishes to convey rather than by meter and rhyme, run-on lines are suited to the open form of much modern poetry. In the following lines from the poem "We Have Come Home," by Lenrie Peters, run-on lines give readers the sense of spoken language:

> We have come home
> From the bloodless war
> With sunken hearts
> Our boots full of pride—
> From the true massacre of the soul
> When we have asked
> "What does it cost
> To be loved and left alone?"

Rather than relying exclusively on end-stopped or run-on lines, poets often use a combination of the two to produce the effects they want.

FURTHER READING: Rhythm and Meter

Adrienne Rich (1929–2012)

Aunt Jennifer's Tigers (1951)

Aunt Jennifer's tigers prance across a screen,
Bright topaz denizens of a world of green.
They do not fear the men beneath the tree;
They pace in sleek chivalric certainty.[1]

[1] *chivalric certainty:* With pride and honor.

Aunt Jennifer's fingers fluttering through her wool
Find even the ivory needle hard to pull.
The massive weight of Uncle's wedding band
Sits heavily upon Aunt Jennifer's hand.

When Aunt is dead, her terrified hands will lie
Still ringed with ordeals she was mastered by.
The tigers in the panel that she made
Will go on prancing, proud and unafraid.

Reading and Reacting

1. What is the dominant metrical pattern of the poem? How does the meter enhance the contrast the poem develops?
2. The lines in the first stanza are end-stopped, and those in the second and third stanzas combine end-stopped and run-on lines. What does the poet achieve by varying the rhythm?
3. What ideas do the caesuras in the first and fourth lines of the last stanza emphasize?
4. **Journal Entry** What is the speaker's opinion of Aunt Jennifer's marriage? Do you think the speaker is commenting on this marriage or on marriage in general?
5. **Critical Perspective** In *The Aesthetics of Power*, Claire Keyes writes of this poem that although it is formally beautiful, almost perfect, its voice creates problems:

    [T]he tone seldom approaches intimacy, the speaker seeming fairly detached from the fate of Aunt Jennifer. . . . The dominant voice of the poem asserts the traditional theme that art outlives the person who produces it. . . . The speaker is almost callous in her disregard for Aunt's death. . . . Who cares that Aunt Jennifer dies? The speaker does not seem to; she gets caught up in those gorgeous tigers. . . . Here lies the dominant voice: Aunt is not compelling; her creation is.

    Do you agree with Keyes's interpretation of the poem?

Related Works: "A Rose for Emily" (p. 166), "Miss Brill" (p. 185), "Everyday Use" (p. 346), "Rooming houses are old women" (p. 563)

Thomas Lux (1946–2017)

A Little Tooth (1989)

Your baby grows a tooth, then two,
and four, and five, then she wants some meat
directly from bone. It's all
over: she'll learn some words she'll fall
in love with cretins, dolts, a sweet
talker on his way to jail. And you,

your wife, get old, flyblown, and rue
nothing. You did, you loved, your feet
are sore. It's dusk. Your daughter's tall.

Reading and Reacting

1. This poem was selected to be featured in the New York City's "Poetry in Motion" program, which posts poems in public busses and trains. What qualities make "A Little Tooth" suitable for this program?
2. What is the dominant metrical pattern of this poem? Do you think this meter is an appropriate choice here? Explain.
3. Where in the poem does Lux use caesuras? What effect do these pauses have?
4. **Journal Entry** "A Little Tooth" is characterized by its extreme compression. What ideas does the poem express? Does the poem effectively communicate these ideas, or does it try to do too much in too few lines?
5. **Critical Perspective** Writing about Thomas Lux's work in the journal *Poetry*, Peter Campion makes the following observation:

   > The problem is not simply that Lux knows the course his poems will take before he begins, though this probably contributes. It's that he writes from above his material. Reading Lux you rarely sense a consciousness moving down in the lines themselves. The poems are set speeches: their odd images or turns of phrase glimmer for moments then disappear as Lux glides on toward his desired effect.

   Do you feel that Campion's criticisms apply to "A Little Tooth"? Why or why not?

Related Works: "Everyday Use" (p. 346), "Doe Season" (p. 378), "Where Are You Going, Where Have You Been?" (p. 447), "Sadie and Maud" (p. 592)

Lewis Carroll (1832–1898)

A Boat Beneath a Sunny Sky (1872)

A boat beneath a sunny sky,
Lingering onward dreamily
In an evening of July—

Children three that nestle near,
Eager eye and willing ear,
Pleased a simple tale to hear—

Long has paled that sunny sky:
Echoes fade and memories die:
Autumn frosts have slain July.

Still she haunts me, phantomwise,
Alice moving under skies
Never seen by waking eyes.

Children yet, the tale to hear,
Eager eye and willing ear,
Lovingly shall nestle near.

In a Wonderland they lie,
Dreaming as the days go by,
Dreaming as the summers die:

Ever drifting down the stream—
Lingering in the golden gleam—
Life, what is it but a dream?

Reading and Reacting

1. Lewis Carroll (whose real name was Charles Lutwidge Dodgson) took three young sisters (including Alice Pleasance Liddell) on a boat trip in 1862. As he rowed, he told them a story of a girl named Alice, who follows a rabbit down a rabbit hole to Wonderland. The girls—especially Alice—were so enchanted by the story, that they asked Carroll to write it down. Eventually, this story became *Alice's Adventures in Wonderland*. What specific references to this boat trip are in the poem?
2. What is the poem's primary metrical pattern? How does this pattern help establish the poem's mood?
3. Where in the poem does Carroll use caesuras? What effect does each of these pauses have?
4. What point is Carroll making about childhood? about Wonderland? What do you think Carroll means in the poem's last line: "Life, what is it but a dream?"
5. **Journal Entry** "A Boat Beneath a Sunny Sky" is an **acrostic poem**; that is, the first letter of each line spells out a word—in this case, *Alice Pleasance Liddell*. Is this technique just a clever device, or does it somehow add to the poem? Explain.

Related Works: "Encounters with Unexpected Animals" (p. 111), "A&P" (p. 179), "Gretel in Darkness" (p. 497), "What Shall I Give My Children?" (p. 538), "One day I wrote her name upon the strand" (p. 539), "Where the Sidewalk Ends" (p. 607), "Jabberwocky" (p. 609)

Alliteration and Assonance

Just as poetry depends on rhythm, it also depends on the sounds of individual words. An effect pleasing to the ear, such as "Did he who made the Lamb make thee?" from William Blake's "The Tyger" (p. 702), is called **euphony**. A jarring or discordant effect, such as "The vorpal blade went snicker-snack!" from Lewis Carroll's "Jabberwocky" (p. 609), is called **cacophony**.

One of the earliest, and perhaps the most primitive, methods of enhancing sound is **onomatopoeia**, which occurs when the sound of a word echoes its meaning, as it does in common words such as *bang, crash,* and *hiss*. Poets make broad application of this technique by using combinations of words that suggest a correspondence between sound and meaning, as Edgar Allan Poe does in these lines from his poem "The Bells":

> Yet the ear, it fully knows,
> By the twanging
> And the clanging,
> How the danger ebbs and flows;
> Yet the ear distinctly tells,
> In the jangling
> And the wrangling
> How the danger sinks and swells
> By the sinking or the swelling in the anger of the bells—
> Of the bells,—
> Of the bells, bells, bells, bells. . . .

Poe's primary objective in this poem is to re-create the sound of ringing bells. Although he succeeds, the aural effect throughout the 113-line poem is extremely tedious. A more subtle use of onomatopoetic words appears in the following passage from *An Essay on Criticism* by Alexander Pope:

> Soft is the strain when Zephyr gently blows,
> And the smooth stream in smoother numbers flows;
> But when the loud surges lash the sounding shore,
> The hoarse, rough verse should like the torrent roar:
> When Ajax strives some rock's vast weight to throw,
> The line too Labors, and the words move slow.

After earlier admonishing readers that sound must echo sense, Pope uses onomatopoetic words such as *lash* and *roar* to convey the fury of the sea, and he uses repeated consonants to echo the sounds these words suggest. Notice, for example, how the *s* and *m* sounds suggest the gently blowing Zephyr and the flowing of the smooth stream and how the series of *r* sounds echoes the torrent's roar.

Alliteration—the repetition of consonant sounds in consecutive or neighboring words, usually at the beginning of words—is another device used to enhance sound in a poem. Both Poe ("sinks and swells") and Pope ("smooth stream") make use of alliteration in the preceding excerpts.

Assonance—the repetition of the same or similar vowel sounds, especially in stressed syllables—can also enrich a poem. When used effectively, assonance can create both mood and tone in a subtle, musical way. Consider, for example, the use of assonance in the following lines from Dylan Thomas's "Do not go gentle into that good night": "Old age should burn and rave at close of day; / Rage, rage, against the dying of the light."

Sometimes assonance unifies an entire poem. In the following poem, assonance emphasizes the thematic connections among words and thus links the poem's ideas.

Robert Herrick (1591–1674)

Delight in Disorder (1648)

A sweet disorder in the dress
Kindles in clothes a wantonness.
A lawn[1] about the shoulders thrown
Into a fine distractión;
An erring lace, which here and there
Enthralls the crimson stomacher;[2]
A cuff neglectful, and thereby
Ribbons to flow confusedly;
A winning wave, deserving note,
In the tempestuous petticoat;
A careless shoestring, in whose tie
I see a wild civility;
Do more bewitch me than when art
Is too precise in every part.

Repeated vowel sounds extend throughout this poem—for example, "shoulders" and "thrown" in line 3; and "tie," "wild," and "precise" in lines 11, 12, and 14. Using alliteration as well as assonance, Herrick subtly links certain words—"tempestuous petticoat," for example. By connecting these words, he calls attention to the pattern of imagery that helps to convey the poem's theme.

Rhyme

In addition to alliteration and assonance, poets create sound patterns with **rhyme**—the use of matching sounds in two or more words: "tight" and "might"; "born" and "horn"; "sleep" and "deep." For a rhyme to be **perfect**, final vowel and consonant sounds must be the same, as they are in each of the preceding examples. **Imperfect rhyme** (also called *near rhyme*, *slant rhyme*, *approximate rhyme*, or **consonance**) occurs when the final consonant sounds in two words are the same but the preceding vowel sounds are different—"learn"

[1] *lawn:* A shawl made of fine fabric.
[2] *stomacher:* A heavily embroidered garment worn by females over the chest and stomach.

/ "barn" or "pads" / "lids," for example. Finally, **eye rhyme** occurs when two words look as if they should rhyme but do not—for example, "watch" and "catch or "move" and "love."

Rhyme can also be classified according to the position of the rhyming syllables in a line of verse. The most common type of rhyme is **end rhyme**, which occurs at the end of a line:

Tyger! Tyger! burning bright
In the forests of the night
William Blake, "The Tyger"

Internal rhyme occurs within a line:

The Sun came up upon the left,
Out of the sea came he!
And he shone bright and on the right
Went down into the sea.
Samuel Taylor Coleridge, "The Rime of the Ancient Mariner"

Beginning rhyme occurs at the beginning of a line:

Red river, red river,
Slow flow heat is silence
No will is still as a river
T. S. Eliot, "Virginia"

Rhyme can also be classified according to the number of syllables that correspond. **Masculine rhyme** (also called **rising rhyme**) occurs when single syllables correspond ("can" / "ran"; "descend" / "contend"). **Feminine rhyme** (also called **double rhyme** or **falling rhyme**) occurs when two syllables, a stressed one followed by an unstressed one, correspond ("ocean" / "motion"; "leaping" / "sleeping"). **Triple rhyme** occurs when three syllables correspond. Less common than the other two, triple rhyme is often used for humorous or satiric purposes, as in the following lines from the long poem *Don Juan* by Lord Byron:

Sagest of women, even of widows, she
  Resolved that Juan should be quite a paragon,
And worthy of the noblest pedigree:
  (His sire of Castile, his dam from Aragon).

The conventional way to describe a poem's rhyme scheme is to chart rhyming sounds that appear at the ends of lines. The sound that ends the first line is designated *a*, and all subsequent lines that end in that sound are also labeled *a*. The next sound to appear at the end of a line is designated *b*, and all other lines whose last sounds rhyme with it are also designated *b*—and so on through the alphabet. The lines of the poem that follows are labeled in this manner.

Robert Frost (1874–1963)

The Road Not Taken (1915)

Two roads diverged in a yellow wood, a
And sorry I could not travel both b
And be one traveler, long I stood a
And looked down one as far as I could a
To where it bent in the undergrowth; b

Then took the other, as just as fair c
And having perhaps the better claim, d
Because it was grassy and wanted wear; c
Though as for that, the passing there c
Had worn them really about the same, d

And both that morning equally lay e
In leaves no step had trodden black f
Oh, I kept the first for another day! e
Yet knowing how way leads on to way, e
I doubted if I should ever come back. f

I shall be telling this with a sigh g
Somewhere ages and ages hence: h
two roads diverged in a wood, and I— g
I took the one less traveled by, g
And that has made all the difference. h

The rhyme scheme of the four five-line stanzas in "The Road Not Taken" is the same in each stanza: *abaab*, *cdccd*, and so on. Except for the last line of the poem, all the rhymes are masculine. Despite its regular rhyme scheme, the poem sounds conversational, as if someone is speaking it without any effort or planning. The beauty of this poem comes from Frost's subtle use of rhyme, which makes the lines flow together, and from the alternating rhymes, which suggest the divergent roads that confront the speaker.

FURTHER READING: Alliteration, Assonance, and Rhyme

Gerard Manley Hopkins (1844–1889)

Pied Beauty (1918)

Glory be to God for dappled things—
For skies of couple-color as a brinded[1] cow;
For rose-moles all in stipple upon trout that swim;

[1] *brinded:* Brindled (streaked).

Fresh-firecoal chestnut-falls; finches' wings;
Landscape plotted and pieced—fold, fallow, and plow;
And áll trádes, their gear and tackle and trim.[2]
All things counter, original, spare, strange;
Whatever is fickle, freckled (who knows how?)
With swift, slow; sweet, sour; adazzle, dim;
He fathers-forth whose beauty is past change:
Praise him.

John Constable, Summer Evening Near East Bergholt, Suffolk (1806–1809)
V&A Images, London / Art Resource, NY

Reading and Reacting

1. Identify examples of onomatopoeia, alliteration, assonance, imperfect rhyme, and perfect rhyme. Do you think all these techniques are essential to the poem? Are any of them annoying or distracting?
2. What is the central idea of this poem? How do the sounds of the poem help to communicate this idea?
3. Identify examples of masculine and feminine rhyme.
4. **Journal Entry** Hopkins uses both pleasing and discordant sounds in his poem. Identify uses of euphony and cacophony, and explain how these techniques affect your reactions to the poem.
5. **Critical Perspective** In her essay "The Allegory of Form in Hopkins's Religious Sonnets," Jennifer A. Wagner discusses the ways in which Gerard Manley Hopkins saw relationships between what his poems were saying and how they expressed it:

   > Hopkins's most profound perception with regard to the form lies precisely in his demand for the conventional integrity of the sonnet, in his "dogmatic" (his word) insistence on the division of the octave and sestet—and in his recognition of the revisionary movement in the sonnet structure. . . . For Hopkins the play

[2] *trim:* Equipment.

> between octave and sestet is not incidental; it creates a "turn" that becomes a trope of limitation or reduction.

Since "Pied Beauty" is what is known as a "curtal," or shortened, sonnet, it is not divided into sections of eight and six lines (the "octet" and "sestet" that Wagner mentions). Still, there is a turn, or change of emphasis, between the poem's two parts. How does the poem change after that turn occurs?

Related Works: "I wandered lonely as a cloud" (p. 678), "Loveliest of Trees" (p. 680), *Beauty* (p. 785)

Shel Silverstein (1930–1999)

Where the Sidewalk Ends (1974)

There is a place where the sidewalk ends
And before the street begins,
And there the grass grows soft and white,
And there the sun burns crimson bright,
And there the moon-bird rests from his flight,
To cool in the peppermint wind.

Let us leave this place where the smoke blows black
And the dark street winds and bends.
Past the pits where the asphalt flowers grow
We shall walk with a walk that is measured and slow,
And watch where the chalk-white arrows go
To the place where the sidewalk ends.

Yes we'll walk with a walk that is measured and slow,
And we'll go where the chalk-white arrows go,
For the children, they mark, and the children, they know
The place where the sidewalk ends.

Reading and Reacting

1. Describe the rhyme scheme of this poem. How does the rhyme scheme contribute to the poem's overall effect?
2. What words does the poem repeat? What ideas does this repetition emphasize?
3. Where does the poem use alliteration and assonance? Do the alliteration and assonance contribute something vital to the poem or are they just a distraction?
4. **Journal Entry** Silverstein is primarily known as a children's poet. What message does "Where the Sidewalk Ends" have for children? What message might it have for adults?

Related Works: "Gryphon" (p. 191), "A Boat Beneath a Sunny Sky" (p. 600), "The Lamb" (p. 700)

Maryam Fakouris

Jacob Saenz

Evolution of My Block (2010)

As a boy I bicycled the block
w/a brown mop top falling
into a tail bleached blond,

gold-like under golden light,
like colors of Noble Knights
'banging on corners, unconcerned

w/the colors I bore—a shorty
too small to war with, too brown
to be down for the block.

White Knights became brown
Kings still showing black & gold
on corners now crowned,

the block a branch branded
w/la corona graffitied on
garage doors by the pawns.

As a teen, I could've beamed
the crown, walked in w/out
the beat down custom,

warred w/my cousin
who claimed Two-Six,
the set on the next block

decked in black & beige.
But I preferred games to gangs,
books to crooks wearing hats

crooked to the left or right
fighting for a plot, a block
to spot & mark w/blood

of boys who knew no better
way to grow up than throw up
the crown & be down for whatever.

Reading and Reacting

1. Identify several different kinds of rhyme in this poem. Then find examples of alliteration and assonance.
2. What image does the poem create? How do rhyme, alliteration, and assonance help Saenz convey this image?
3. What words are repeated throughout the poem? What is the purpose of this repetition?

4. Explain the poem's title. How has the speaker's block "evolved"? Has the speaker also evolved? Explain.
5. **Journal Entry** How is the speaker different from the other boys on his block? How do you account for these differences?

Related Works: "The Secret Lion" (p. 222), "Greasy Lake" (p. 419), "The United Fruit Co." (p. 732), *The Cuban Swimmer* (p. 1122)

Illustration of Jabberwock from *Alice in Wonderland*
Chronicle/Alamy Stock Photo

Lewis Carroll (1832–1898)

Jabberwocky (1871)

'Twas brillig, and the slithy toves
Did gyre and gimble in the wabe:
All mimsy were the borogoves,
And the mome raths outgrabe.

"Beware the Jabberwock, my son!
The jaws that bite, the claws that catch!
Beware the Jubjub bird, and shun
The frumious Bandersnatch!"

He took his vorpal sword in hand;
Long time the manxome foe he sought—
So rested he by the Tumtum tree
And stood awhile in thought.

And, as in uffish thought he stood,
The Jabberwock, with eyes of flame,
Came whiffling through the tulgey wood,
And burbled as it came!

One, two! One, two! And through and through
The vorpal blade went snicker-snack!
He left it dead, and with its head
He went galumphing back.

"And hast thou slain the Jabberwock?
Come to my arms, my beamish boy!
O frabjous day! Callooh, Callay!"
He chortled in his joy.

'Twas brillig, and the slithy toves
Did gyre and gimble in the wabe:
All mimsy were the borogoves,
And the mome raths outgrabe.

Reading and Reacting

1. Many words in this poem may be unfamiliar to you. Are they actual words? Use a dictionary to check before you dismiss any. Do some words that do not appear in the dictionary nevertheless seem to have meaning in the context of the poem? Explain.
2. This poem contains many examples of onomatopoeia. What meanings does the sound of each of these words suggest?
3. **Journal Entry** Summarize the story the poem tells. In what sense is this poem a story of a young man's initiation into adulthood?
4. **Critical Perspective** According to Humpty Dumpty in Carroll's *Alice in Wonderland*, the nonsense words in the poem are **portmanteau words** (i.e., words whose form and meaning are derived from two other distinct words—as *smog* is a portmanteau of *smoke* and *fog*). Critic Elizabeth Sewell, however, rejects this explanation: "*[F]rumious*, for instance, is not a word, and does not have two meanings packed up in it; it is a group of letters without any meaning at all.... [I]t looks like other words, and almost certainly more than two."

   Which nonsense words in the poem seem to you to be portmanteau words, and which do not? Can you suggest possible sources for the words that are not portmanteau words?

Related Works: "A&P" (p. 179), "Gryphon" (p. 191), "The Secret Lion" (p. 222), "To Lucasta Going to the Wars" (p. 580), "A Boat Beneath a Sunny Sky" (p. 600), "Ulysses" (p. 739)

Checklist Writing about Sound

Rhythm and Meter

- Does the poem contain repeated words and phrases? If so, how do they help to create rhythm?
- Does the poem use one kind of meter throughout, or does the meter vary from line to line?
- How does the meter contribute to the overall effect of the poem?
- Where do caesuras appear? What effect do they have?
- Are the lines of the poem end-stopped, run-on, or a combination of the two? What effects are created by the presence or absence of pauses at the ends of lines?

Alliteration, Assonance, and Rhyme

- Does the poem include alliteration or assonance?
- Does the poem have a regular rhyme scheme?

- Does the poem use internal rhyme? beginning rhyme?
- Does the poem include examples of masculine, feminine, or triple rhyme?
- How does rhyme unify the poem?
- How does rhyme reinforce the poem's ideas?

WRITING SUGGESTIONS: Sound

1. William Blake's "The Tyger" appeared in a collection entitled *Songs of Experience*. Compare this poem (p. 702) to "The Lamb" (p. 700), which appeared in a collection called *Songs of Innocence*. In what sense are the speakers in these two poems either "innocent" or "experienced"? How does sound help to convey the voice of the speakers in these two poems?
2. "Sadie and Maud" (p. 592), like "My Papa's Waltz" (p. 672) and "Daddy" (p. 571), communicates the speaker's attitude toward home and family. How does the presence or absence of rhyme in these poems help to convey the speakers' attitudes?
3. Robert Frost once said that writing **free verse** poems, which have no fixed metrical pattern, is like playing tennis without a net. What do you think he meant? Do you agree? After reading "Out, Out—" (p. 577), "Stopping by Woods on a Snowy Evening" (p. 10), and "The Road Not Taken" (p. 605), write an essay in which you discuss Frost's use of meter.
4. Select two or three contemporary poems that have no end rhyme. Write an essay in which you discuss what these poets gain and lose by not using end rhyme.
5. Prose writers as well as poets use assonance, alliteration, and repetition. Choose two or three a passages of prose—from "Araby" (p. 296), "Barn Burning" (p. 265), or "The Tell-Tale Heart" (p. 459), for example—and discuss their use of assonance, alliteration, and repetition. Where are these techniques used? How do they help the writer create a mood?

Chapter 23

Form

Alberto Álvaro Ríos

Courtesy of Alberto Álvaro Ríos

Yusef Komunyakaa

© Chris Felver/Bridgeman Images

Elizabeth Bishop

Everett Collection Historical/Alamy Stock Photo

Martín Espada

AP Images/Daily Hampshire Gazette, Kevin Gutting

Learning Objectives

After reading this chapter, you will be able to. . .

- Define form as it relates to poetry.
- Identify the general characteristics of open- and closed-form poems and their historical origins.
- Identify different stanzaic forms.
- Describe the features that characterize blank verse, the sonnet, the sestina, the villanelle, the epigram, the haiku, and the concrete poem.
- Distinguish between Shakespearean and Petrarchan sonnets.

GL Archive/Alamy Stock Photo

John Keats (1795–1821)

On the Sonnet (1819)

If by dull rhymes our English must be chained,
And like Andromeda,[1] the sonnet sweet
Fettered, in spite of painéd loveliness,
Let us find, if we must be constrained,
Sandals more interwoven and complete
To fit the naked foot of Poesy:
Let us inspect the lyre, and weigh the stress
Of every chord, and see what may be gained
By ear industrious, and attention meet;
Misers of sound and syllable, no less
Than Midas[2] of his coinage, let us be
Jealous of dead leaves in the bay-wreath crown;
So, if we may not let the Muse be free,
She will be bound with garlands of her own.

Andromeda in Chains
Giorgio Vasari/Alinari Archives/Fine Art/Corbis

[1]*Andromeda:* In Greek mythology, an Ethiopian princess chained to a rock to appease a sea monster.
[2]*Midas:* A legendary king of Phrygia whose wish that everything he touched would turn to gold was granted by the god Dionysus.

The **form** of a literary work is its structure or shape, the way its elements fit together to form a whole; **poetic form** is the design of a poem described in terms of rhyme, meter, and stanzaic pattern.

Until the twentieth century, most poetry was written in **closed form** (sometimes called **fixed form**), characterized by regular patterns of meter, rhyme, line length, and stanzaic divisions. Early poems that were passed down orally—epics and ballads, for example—relied on regular form to facilitate memorization. Even after poems began to be written down, poets tended to favor regular patterns. In fact, until relatively recently, regular form was what distinguished poetry from prose. Of course, strict adherence to regular patterns sometimes produced poems that were, in John Keats's words, "chained" by "dull rhymes" and "fettered" by the rules governing a particular form (p. 613). But rather than feeling "constrained" by form, many poets have experimented with imagery, figures of speech, allusion, and other techniques, moving away from rigid patterns of rhyme and meter and thus stretching closed form to its limits.

As they sought new ways in which to express themselves, poets also borrowed forms from other cultures, adapting them to the demands of their own languages. English and American poets, for example, adopted (and still use) early French forms, such as the **villanelle** and the **sestina**, and early Italian forms, such as the **Petrarchan sonnet** and **terza rima**. The nineteenth-century American poet Henry Wadsworth Longfellow studied Icelandic epics; the twentieth-century poet Ezra Pound studied the works of French troubadours; and Pound and other twentieth-century American poets, such as Richard Wright and Carolyn Kizer, were inspired by Japanese haiku. Other American poets, such as Vachel Lindsay, Langston Hughes, and Maya Angelou, looked closer to home—to the rhythms of blues, jazz, and spirituals—for inspiration.

As time went on, more and more poets moved away from closed form to experiment with **open form** poetry (sometimes called **free verse** or *vers libre*), varying line length within a poem, dispensing with meter and stanzaic divisions, breaking lines in unexpected places, and even abandoning any semblance of formal structure. In English, nineteenth-century poets—such as William Blake and Matthew Arnold—experimented with lines of irregular meter and length, and Walt Whitman wrote **prose poems**, poems whose lines extend from the left to the right margin, with no line breaks, so that they look like prose. (Well before this time, Asian poetry and some biblical passages had used a type of free verse.) In nineteenth-century France, symbolist poets, such as Baudelaire, Rimbaud, Verlaine, and Mallarmé, also used free verse. In the early twentieth century, a group of American poets—including Ezra Pound, William Carlos Williams, and Amy Lowell—who were associated with a movement known as **imagism** wrote poetry that dispensed with traditional principles of English versification, creating new rhythms and meters.

Although much contemporary English and American poetry is composed in open form, many poets also continue to write in closed form—even in very traditional, highly structured patterns. Still, new forms, and new variations of old forms, are being created all the time. And because contemporary poets do not necessarily feel bound by rules or restrictions about what constitutes "acceptable" poetic form, they experiment freely, trying to discover the form that best suits the poem's purpose, subject, language, and theme.

Closed Form

A **closed form** poem has an identifiable, repeated pattern, with lines of similar length arranged in groups of two, three, four, or more. A closed form poem also tends to rely on a regular metrical pattern and rhyme scheme.

Despite what its name suggests, closed form poetry does not have to be confining or conservative. In fact, contemporary poets often experiment with closed form—for example, by using characteristics of open form poetry (such as lines of varying length) within a closed form. Sometimes poets move back and forth within a single poem from open to closed to open form; sometimes (like their eighteenth-century counterparts) they combine different stanzaic forms (stanzas of two and three lines, for example) within a single poem.

Even when poets work within a traditional closed form, such as a sonnet, sestina, or villanelle, they can break new ground. For example, they can write a sonnet with an unexpected meter or rhyme scheme (or with no consistent pattern of rhyme or meter at all), add an extra line or even extra stanzas to a traditional sonnet, combine two different traditional sonnet forms in a single poem, or write an abbreviated version of a sestina or villanelle. In other words, poets can use traditional forms as building blocks, combining them in innovative ways to create new patterns and new forms.

Sometimes a pattern (such as **blank verse**) simply determines the meter of a poem's individual lines. At other times, the pattern extends to the level of the **stanza**, with lines arranged into groups (**couplets**, **quatrains**, and so on). At still other times, as in the case of traditional closed forms like sonnets, a poetic pattern gives shape to an entire poem.

Blank Verse

Blank verse is unrhymed poetry with each line written in a pattern of five stressed and five unstressed syllables called **iambic pentameter** (see p. 595). Many passages from Shakespeare's plays, such as the following lines from *Hamlet*, are written in blank verse:

To sleep! perchance to dream:—ay, there's the rub;
For in that sleep of death what dreams may come,
When we have shuffled off this mortal coil,
Must give us pause: there's the respect
That makes calamity of so long life

Stanza

A **stanza** is a group of two or more lines with the same metrical pattern—and often with a regular rhyme scheme as well—separated by blank space from other such groups of lines. Stanzas in poetry are like paragraphs in prose: they group related ideas into units.

A two-line stanza with rhyming lines of similar length and meter is called a **couplet**. The **heroic couplet**, first used by Chaucer and later very popular throughout the eighteenth century, consists of two rhymed lines of iambic pentameter, with a weak pause after the first line and a strong pause after the second. The following example, from Alexander Pope's *An Essay on Criticism*, is a heroic couplet:

> True ease in writing comes from art, not chance,
> As those move easiest who have learned to dance.

A three-line stanza with lines of similar length and a set rhyme scheme is called a **tercet**. Percy Bysshe Shelley's "Ode to the West Wind" (p. 736) is built largely of tercets:

> O wild West Wind, thou breath of Autumn's being,
> Thou, from whose unseen presence the leaves dead
> Are driven, like ghosts from an enchanter fleeing,
>
> Yellow, and black, and pale, and hectic red,
> Pestilence-stricken multitudes: O Thou,
> Who chariotest to their dark wintry bed

Although in many tercets all three lines rhyme, "Ode to the West Wind" uses a special rhyme scheme, also used by Dante, called **terza rima**. This rhyme scheme (*aba*, *bcb*, *cdc*, *ded*, and so on) creates an interlocking series of stanzas: line 2's *dead* looks ahead to the rhyming words *red* and *bed*, which close lines 4 and 6, and the pattern continues throughout the poem. Robert Frost's 1928 poem "Acquainted with the Night" is a contemporary example of terza rima.

A four-line stanza with lines of similar length and a set rhyme scheme is called a **quatrain**. The quatrain, the most widely used and versatile unit in English and American poetry, is used by William Wordsworth in the following excerpt from "She dwelt among the untrodden ways":

> A violet by a mossy stone
>   Half hidden from the eye!
> —Fair as a star, when only one
>   Is shining in the sky.

Quatrains are frequently used by contemporary poets as well—for example, in Theodore Roethke's "My Papa's Waltz" (p. 672) and Adrienne Rich's "Aunt Jennifer's Tigers" (p. 598).

One special kind of quatrain, called the **ballad stanza**, alternates lines of eight and six syllables; typically, only the second and fourth lines rhyme. The following lines from the traditional Scottish ballad "Sir Patrick Spence" illustrate the ballad stanza:

> The king sits in Dumferling toune,
>   Drinking the blude-reid wine:
> "O whar will I get guid sailor
>   To sail this schip of mine?"

Common measure, a four-line stanzaic pattern closely related to the ballad stanza, is used in hymns as well as in poetry. It differs from the ballad stanza in that its rhyme scheme is *abab* rather than *abcb*.

Other stanzaic forms include **rhyme royal**, a seven-line stanza *(ababbcc)* set in iambic pentameter, used in Sir Thomas Wyatt's sixteenth-century poem "They Flee from Me" as well as in Theodore Roethke's twentieth-century "I Knew a Woman"; **ottava rima**, an eight-line stanza *(abababcc)* set in iambic pentameter; and the **Spenserian stanza**, a nine-line form *(ababbcbcc)* whose first eight lines are set in iambic pentameter and whose last line is in iambic hexameter. The Romantic poets John Keats and Percy Bysshe Shelley were among those who used the Spenserian stanza. (See Chapter 22 for definitions and examples of various metrical patterns.)

The Sonnet

Perhaps the most familiar kind of traditional closed form poem written in English is the **sonnet**, a fourteen-line poem with a distinctive rhyme scheme and metrical pattern. The English or **Shakespearean sonnet**, which consists of fourteen lines divided into three quatrains and a concluding couplet, is written in iambic pentameter and follows the rhyme scheme *abab cdcd efef gg*. The **Petrarchan sonnet**, popularized in the fourteenth century by the Italian poet Francesco Petrarch, also consists of fourteen lines of iambic pentameter, but these lines are divided into an eight-line unit called an **octave** and a six-line unit (composed of two tercets) called a **sestet**. The rhyme scheme of the octave is *abba abba*; the rhyme scheme of the sestet is *cde cde*.

The conventional structures of these sonnet forms reflect the arrangement of ideas within the poem. In the Shakespearean sonnet, the poet typically presents three "paragraphs" of related thoughts, introducing an idea in the first quatrain, developing it in the two remaining quatrains, and summing up in a succinct closing couplet. In the Petrarchan sonnet, the octave introduces a problem that is resolved in the sestet. (Many Shakespearean sonnets also have a problem-solution structure.) Some poets vary the traditional patterns somewhat to suit the poem's language or ideas. For example, they may depart from the pattern to sidestep a forced rhyme or unnatural stress on a syllable, or they may shift from problem to solution in a place other than between octave and sestet.

The following poem is a traditional English sonnet.

William Shakespeare (1564–1616)

When, in disgrace with Fortune and men's eyes (1609)

When, in disgrace with Fortune and men's eyes,
I all alone beweep my outcast state,
And trouble deaf heaven with my bootless[1] cries,
And look upon myself and curse my fate,
Wishing me like to one more rich in hope,
Featured like him, like him with friends possessed,
Desiring this man's art, and that man's scope,
With what I most enjoy contented least,
Yet in these thoughts myself almost despising,
Haply[2] I think on thee, and then my state,
Like to the lark at break of day arising
From sullen earth, sings hymns at heaven's gate;
For thy sweet love rememb'red such wealth brings
That then I scorn to change my state with kings.

Goddess of Fortune turning wheel
Charles Walker Collection/Alamy Stock Photo

[1] *bootless:* Futile.
[2] *Haply:* Luckily.

Shakespeare's sonnet is written in iambic pentameter and has a conventional rhyme scheme: *abab* (eyes-state-cries-fate), *cdcd* (hope-possessed-scope-least), *efef* (despising-state-arising-gate), *gg* (brings-kings). In this poem, in which the speaker explains how thoughts of his loved one can rescue him from despair, each quatrain is unified by subject matter as well as by rhyme.

In the first quatrain, the speaker presents his problem: he is down on his luck and out of favor with his peers, isolated in self-pity and cursing his fate. In the second quatrain, he develops this idea further: he is envious of others and dissatisfied with things that usually please him. In the third quatrain, the focus shifts. The first two quatrains have developed a dependent clause ("When …") that introduces a problem, and now line 9 begins to present the solution. In the third quatrain, the speaker explains how, in the midst of his despair and self-hatred, he thinks of his loved one, and his spirits soar. The closing couplet sums up the mood transformation the poem describes and explains its significance: when the speaker realizes the emotional riches his loved one gives him, he is no longer envious of others.

FURTHER READING: The Sonnet

Bust of Homer

Portrait bust of Homer (marble), Greek, (9th century BC)
Private Collection/Photo © Boltin Picture Library/ Bridgeman Images

John Keats (1795–1821)

On First Looking into Chapman's Homer[1] (1816)

Much have I traveled in the realms of gold,
And many goodly states and kingdoms seen;
Round many western islands have I been
Which bards in fealty to Apollo[2] hold.
Oft of one wide expanse had I been told
That deep-browed Homer ruled as his demesne,[3]
Yet did I never breathe its pure serene[4]
Till I heard Chapman speak out loud and bold.
Then felt I like some watcher of the skies
When a new planet swims into his ken;
Or like stout Cortez[5] when with eagle eyes
He stared at the Pacific—and all his men
Looked at each other with a wild surmise—
Silent, upon a peak in Darien.[6]

---

[1] *Chapman's Homer:* The translation of Homer's works by Elizabethan poet George Chapman.
[2] *Apollo:* Greek god of light, truth, reason, male beauty; associated with music and poetry.
[3] *demesne:* Realm, domain.
[4] *serene:* Air, atmosphere.
[5] *Cortez:* It was Vasco de Balboa (not Hernando Cortez as Keats suggests) who first saw the Pacific Ocean, from "a peak in Darien."
[6] *Darien:* Former name of the Isthmus of Panama.

Reading and Reacting

1. Is this a Petrarchan or a Shakespearean sonnet? How can you tell?
2. **Journal Entry** The sestet's change of focus is introduced with the word *Then* in line 9. How does the mood of the sestet differ from the mood of the octave? How does the language differ?
3. **Critical Perspective** As Keats's biographer Aileen Ward observes, Homer's epic tales of gods and heroes were known to most readers of Keats's day only in a very formal eighteenth-century translation by Alexander Pope. Here is Pope's description of Ulysses escaping from a shipwreck:

    his knees no more
Perform'd their office, or his weight upheld:
His swoln heart heav'd, his bloated body swell'd:
From mouth to nose the briny torrent ran,
And lost in lassitude lay all the man,
Deprived of voice, of motion, and of breath,
The soul scarce waking in the arms of death ...

In a rare 1616 edition of Chapman's translation, Keats discovered a very different poem:

    both knees falt'ring, both
His strong hands hanging down, and all with froth
His cheeks and nostrils flowing, voice and breath
Spent to all use, and down he sank to death.
The sea had soak'd his heart through. . . .

This, as Ward notes, was "poetry of a kind that had not been written in England for two hundred years."

Can you understand why Keats was so moved by Chapman's translation? Do you think Keats's own poem seems closer in its form and language to Pope or to Chapman?

Related Works: "Gryphon" (p. 191), "Araby" (p. 296), "When I Heard the Learn'd Astronomer" (p. 526), *Trifles* (p. 820)

Edna St. Vincent Millay (1892–1950)

Love is not all (1931)

Love is not all: it is not meat nor drink
Nor slumber nor a roof against the rain;

Nor yet a floating spar to men that sink
And rise and sink and rise and sink again;
Love can not fill the thickened lung with breath,
Nor clean the blood, nor set the fractured bone;
Yet many a man is making friends with death
Even as I speak, for lack of love alone.
It well may be that in a difficult hour,
Pinned down by pain and moaning for release,
Or nagged by want past resolution's power,
I might be driven to sell your love for peace,
Or trade the memory of this night for food.
It well may be. I do not think I would.

Reading and Reacting

1. Describe the poem's rhyme scheme. Is it a Petrarchan or a Shakespearean sonnet?
2. Does this poem have a problem–solution structure, or is there some other thematic distinction between its octave and its sestet?
3. Why are the words "It well may be" repeated in lines 9 and 14?
4. **Journal Entry** The poem's first six lines list all the things that love is *not* and what it *cannot* do. Why do you think the poet chose not to enumerate what love *is* and what it *can* do?
5. **Critical Perspective** In an essay on Edna St. Vincent Millay's love sonnets, poet and critic Anna Evans notes the ways in which Millay's unconventional lifestyle provided material for her poetry:

    > Some of Millay's finest sonnets written during her marriage are presumed to be addressed to her younger poet lover George Dillon, who became part of a ménage a trois in the Millay household … The narrator of "Love is not all: it is not meat or drink" demonstrates Millay's newest philosophy of romantic love. There is no doubt that the speaker is expressing love for the object of the poem, yet there is no commitment, the love is spoken of already almost as of something in the past, and the poem lacks an absolute conviction of permanence.

    What evidence can you find in the poem to support Evans's claims that there is no romantic "commitment," and that the speaker "lacks an absolute conviction of permanence"?

Related Works: "If I should learn, in some quite casual way" (p. 574), "When, in disgrace with Fortune and men's eyes" (p. 618), "How Do I Love Thee?" (p. 684), "What lips my lips have kissed" (p. 684), "General Review of the Sex Situation" (p. 686)

Lynn Aarti Chandhok (1963–)

The Carpet Factory (2001)

A wood shack on the riverbank. Inside,
through dust-filled shafts of light, bright colors rise
and drown the warps, transforming their brown threads
to poppy fields, the Tree of Life, a wide
sun hemmed by cartwheeled tulips, fountainheads
that spew blue waterfalls of peacock eyes.

With furious fingers mothlike at the weft,
the children tie and cut and tie and cut
and tamp the knots down, turning blade to gavel.
Each pull's a dust-cloud *plink*—bereft
of music. Toothless men spit betelnut
in blood-red stains. Everywhere, reds unravel.

The bended limbs of saplings twist and part
and weave into the prayer rug's pale silk heart.

Reading and Reacting

1. Look carefully at this poem's rhyme scheme and at the way its lines are divided into stanzas. Is it more like a Shakespearean or a Petrarchan sonnet? Explain.
2. This poem uses color imagery to describe a prayer rug. Identify the references to color. Do all these references describe the rug?
3. What point does this poem make about the carpet factory? How does the closing couplet sum up this point?
4. **Journal Entry** How are the descriptions of the factory—and of its child laborers—different from the descriptions of the carpets produced there?
5. **Critical Perspective** Reviewing Lynn Aarti Chandhok's book *The View from Zero Bridge*, Patty Paine focuses on the poem "The Carpet Factory":

> This poem itself is meticulously crafted and beautifully realized. The form and the content merge seamless ... One can see the slants of light, the children's fingers darting at the weft, hear the plink and watch the blood-red spittle seep into the ground. By taking such care with her images, the poet has created an intimacy and familiarity that transports the reader into a world that is fully formed ... The specter of child labor hovers over "The Carpet Factory," and Chandhok confronts the issue through imagery rather than polemics.

Given its focus on the issue of child labor, do you see this poem as social protest? Or, do you see the poem's content as less important than its form and imagery? Do you agree with Paine that the poem's "form and content merge seamlessly"?

Related Works: "Girl" (p. 116), "Gretel in Darkness" (p. 497), "Aunt Jennifer's Tigers" (p. 598), "Indian Boarding School: The Runaways" (p. 719), *Trifles* (p. 820)

The Sestina

The **sestina**, introduced in thirteenth-century France, is composed of six six-line stanzas and a three-line conclusion called an **envoi**. The sestina form does not require end rhyme; however, it requires that each line end with one of six key words, which are repeated throughout the poem in a fixed order. The alternation of these six words in different positions—but always at the ends of lines—in each of the poem's six stanzas creates a rhythmic verbal pattern that unifies the poem, as the key words do in the poem that follows.

Courtesy of Alberto Alvaro Rios

Alberto Álvaro Ríos (1952–)

Nani (1982)

Sitting at her table, she serves
the sopa de arroz[1] to me
instinctively, and I watch her,
the absolute mamá, and eat words
I might have had to say more
out of embarrassment. To speak,
now-foreign words I used to speak,
too, dribble down her mouth as she serves
me albóndigas.[2] No more
than a third are easy to me.
By the stove she does something with words
and looks at me only with her
back. I am full. I tell her
I taste the mint, and watch her speak
smiles at the stove. All my words
make her smile. Nani never serves

[1] *sopa de arroz:* Rice soup.
[2] *albóndigas:* Meatballs.

herself, she only watches me
with her skin, her hair. I ask for more.

I watch the mamá warming more
tortillas for me. I watch her
fingers in the flame for me.
Near her mouth, I see a wrinkle speak
of a man whose body serves
the ants like she serves me, then more words
from more wrinkles about children, words
about this and that, flowing more
easily from these other mouths. Each serves
as a tremendous string around her,
holding her together. They speak
nani was this and that to me
and I wonder just how much of me
will die with her, what were the words
I could have been, was. Her insides speak
through a hundred wrinkles, now, more
than she can bear, steel around her,
shouting, then, What is this thing she serves?

She asks me if I want more.
I own no words to stop her.
Even before I speak, she serves.

In many respects, Ríos's poem closely follows the form of the traditional sestina. For example, it interweaves six key words—"serves," "me," "her," "words," "more," and "speak"—through six groups of six lines each, rearranging the order in which the words appear so that the first line of each group of six lines ends with the same key word that also ended the preceding group of lines. The poem repeats the key words in exactly the order prescribed: *abcdef*, *faebdc*, *cfdabe*, and so on. In addition, the sestina closes with a three-line envoi that includes all six of the poem's key words, three at the ends of lines and three within the lines. Despite this generally strict adherence to the sestina form, Ríos departs from the form by grouping his six sets of six lines not into six separate stanzas but rather into two eighteen-line stanzas.

The sestina form suits Ríos's subject matter. The focus of the poem, on the verbal and nonverbal interaction between the poem's "me" and "her," is reinforced by each of the related words. "Nani" is a poem about communication, and the key words return to probe this theme again and again. Throughout the poem, these repeated words help to create a fluid, melodic, and tightly woven work.

FURTHER READING: The Sestina

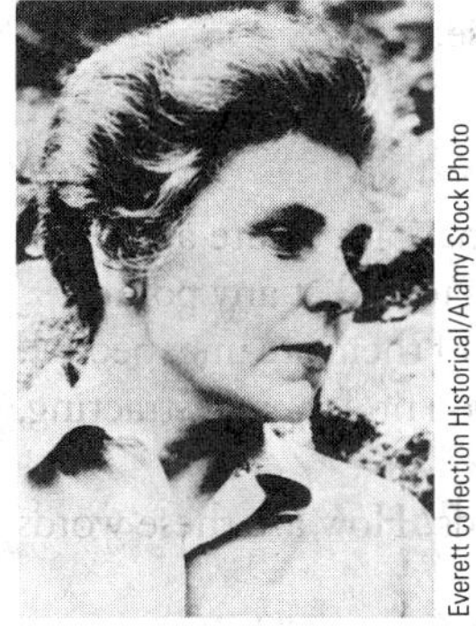
Everett Collection Historical/Alamy Stock Photo

Elizabeth Bishop (1911–1979)

Sestina (1965)

September rain falls on the house.
In the failing light, the old grandmother
sits in the kitchen with the child
beside the Little Marvel Stove,
reading the jokes from the almanac,
laughing and talking to hide her tears.

She thinks that her equinoctial tears
and the rain that beats on the roof of the house
were both foretold by the almanac,
but only known to a grandmother.
The iron kettle sings on the stove.
She cuts some bread and says to the child,

It's time for tea now; but the child
is watching the teakettle's small hard tears
dance like mad on the hot black stove,
the way the rain must dance on the house.
Tidying up, the old grandmother
hangs up the clever almanac

on its string. Birdlike, the almanac
hovers half open above the child,
hovers above the old grandmother
and her teacup full of dark brown tears.
She shivers and says she thinks the house
feels chilly, and puts more wood in the stove.

It was to be, says the Marvel Stove.
I know what I know, says the almanac.
With crayons the child draws a rigid house
and a winding pathway. Then the child
puts in a man with buttons like tears
and shows it proudly to the grandmother.

But secretly, while the grandmother
busies herself about the stove,
the little moons fall down like tears
from between the pages of the almanac
into the flower bed the child
has carefully placed in the front of the house.

Time to plant tears, says the almanac.
The grandmother sings to the marvellous stove
and the child draws another inscrutable house.

Reading and Reacting

1. Does the poet's adherence to the traditional sestina form create any problems? For example, do you think word order seems forced at any point?
2. Consider the adjectives used in this poem. Which of them are unexpected? What is the effect of these surprising choices? Do you find them distracting, or do you think they strengthen the poem?
3. **Journal Entry** What are this sestina's six key words? How are these words related to the poem's theme?
4. **Critical Perspective** In his essay "Elizabeth Bishop's Surrealist Inheritance," Richard Mullen writes the following:

   > Some of the enchanted mystery which permeates Elizabeth Bishop's poetry arises from her preoccupation with dreams, sleep, and the borders between sleeping and waking. Her poems contain much of the magic, uncanniness and displacement associated with the works of the surrealists, for she too explores the workings of the unconscious and the interplay between conscious perception and dream.

   What examples can you find in "Sestina" of "the enchanted mystery" to which Mullen refers? In what ways is the poem dreamlike?

Related Works: "Nani" (p. 623), "My Papa's Waltz" (p. 672)

Patricia Smith (1955–)

Ethel's Sestina (2006)

Ethel Freeman's body sat for days in her wheelchair outside the New Orleans Convention Center. Her son Herbert, who has assured his mother that help was on the way, was forced to leave her there once she died.

Gon' be obedient in this there chair,
gon's bide my time, fanning against this sun.
I ask my boy, and all he says is *Wait.*
He wipes my brow with steam, says I should sleep.
I trust his every word. Herbert my son.
I believe him when he says help gon' come

Been so long since all these suffrin' folks come
to this place. Now on the ground 'round my chair,

they sweat in my shade, keep asking my son
could that be a bus they see. It's the sun
foolin' them, shining much too loud for sleep,
making us hear engines, wheels. Not yet. Wait.

Lawd, some folks prayin' for rain while they wait,
forgetting what rain can do. When it come,
it smashes living flat, wakes you from sleep,
eats streets, washes you clean out of the chair
you be sittin' in. Best to praise this sun,
shinin' its dry shine *Lawd have mercy, son.*

Is it coming? Such a strong man, my son.
Can't help but believe when he tells us, *Wait.*
Wait some more. Wish some trees would block this sun.
We wait. Ain't no white men or buses come,
but look—see that there? Get me out this chair,
help me stand on up. No time for sleepin',

cause look what's rumbling this way. If you sleep
you gon' miss it. *Look there*, I tell my son.
He don't hear. I'm 'bout to get out this chair,
but the ghost in my legs tells me to wait,
wait for the salvation that's sho to come.
I see my savior's face 'longside that sun.

Nobody sees me running toward the sun.
Lawd, they think I done gone and fell asleep.
They don't hear *Come.*

Come.
Come.
Come.
Come.
Come.
Come.

Ain't but one power make me leave my son.
I can't wait, Herbert. Lawd knows I can't wait.
Don't cry, boy, I ain't in that chair no more.

Wish you coulda come on this journey, son,
seen that ol' sweet sun lift me out of sleep.
Didn't have to wait. And see my golden chair?

People waiting for help outside the New Orleans Convention Center after Hurricane Katrina in 2005
Mario Tama/Getty Images

Reading and Reacting

1. What six key words are repeated in this poem? What other words are repeated? Why?
2. Where does this sestina depart from its required form? Is this departure justified by the poem's theme or subject matter? Does it strengthen or weaken the poem's impact?
3. **Journal Entry** Write a few sentences—or a few lines of poetry—from Herbert's point of view, expressing what you think he would like to tell his mother.
4. **Critical Perspective** In an interview with Cherryl Floyd-Miller for the Webzine *Torch*, Patricia Smith talked about the qualities of a good "persona poem":

   > I think the persona poem moves us out of our space, moves us out of our comfort zone where we're almost forced to take a really hard look at another life. Whether it be something you're just doing for the fun of it, like, you know, wow, what's it like to be Little Richard for a day, or you're sitting next to some woman who is clutching like twenty bags or something on the subway, you know that her whole life is in those bags, and you realize just how close everyone's life is to your own.

   Does "Ethel's Sestina" take you "out of [your] comfort zone"? Does it make you "realize just how close everyone's life is to your own"?

Related Works: "Girl" (p. 116), "Everyday Use" (p. 346), "Incident" (p. 579), "Do not go gentle into that good night" (p. 676), *Fences* (p. 1222)

The Villanelle

The **villanelle**, first introduced in France during the Middle Ages, is a nineteen-line poem composed of five tercets and a concluding quatrain; its rhyme scheme is *aba aba aba aba aba abaa*. Two different lines are systematically repeated in the poem: line 1 appears again in lines 6, 12, and 18, and line 3 reappears as lines 9, 15, and 19. Thus, each tercet concludes with an exact (or close) duplication of either line 1 or line 3, and the final quatrain concludes by repeating both line 1 and line 3.

Earth Mother, painting of Mother Nature by Sir Edward Burne-Jones, 1882

Earth Mother, 1882 (encaustic on panel), Burne-Jones, Sir Edward Coley (1833-98) / Worcester Art Museum, Massachusetts, USA / Bridgeman Images

Theodore Roethke (1908–1963)

The Waking (1953)

I wake to sleep, and take my waking slow.
I feel my fate in what I cannot fear.
I learn by going where I have to go.

We think by feeling. What is there to know?
I hear my being dance from ear to ear.
I wake to sleep, and take my waking slow.

Of those so close beside me, which are you?
God bless the Ground! I shall walk softly there,
And learn by going where I have to go.

Light takes the Tree; but who can tell us how?
The lowly worm climbs up a winding stair;
I wake to sleep, and take my waking slow.

Great Nature has another thing to do
To you and me; so take the lively air,
And, lovely, learn by going where to go.

This shaking keeps me steady. I should know.
What falls away is always. And is near.
I wake to sleep, and take my waking slow.
I learn by going where I have to go.

"The Waking," like all villanelles, closely intertwines threads of sounds and words. The repeated lines and the very regular rhyme and meter give the poem a monotonous, almost hypnotic, rhythm. This poem uses end rhyme and repeats entire lines. It also makes extensive use of alliteration ("I feel my fate in what I cannot fear") and internal rhyme ("I hear my being dance from ear to ear"; "I wake to sleep and take my waking slow"). The result is a tightly constructed poem of overlapping sounds and images.

Deborah Paredez (1970–)

Wife's Disaster Manual (2012)

When the forsaken city starts to burn,
after the men and children have fled,
stand still, silent as prey, and slowly turn

back. Behold the curse. Stay and mourn
the collapsing doorways, the unbroken bread
in the forsaken city starting to burn.

Don't flinch. Don't join in.
Resist the righteous scurry and instead
stand still, silent as prey. Slowly turn

your thoughts away from escape: the iron
gates unlatched, the responsibilities shed.
When the forsaken city starts to burn,

surrender to your calling, show concern
for those who remain. Come to a dead
standstill. Silent as prey, slowly turn

into something essential. Learn
the names of the fallen. Refuse to run ahead
when the forsaken city starts to burn.
Stand still and silent. Pray. Return.

Reading and Reacting

1. This poem is a series of commands. To whom are these commands addressed? What reaction do you think the speaker expects?
2. What does the word *forsaken* mean? What is the "forsaken city"?
3. What two lines are repeated in this villanelle? What is the poem's rhyme scheme? Does it depart from the traditional structure of the villanelle in any respects? Explain.
4. **Journal Entry** What do you think this poem is about? What makes you think so?

Related Works: "Fire and Ice" (p. 504), "The World Is Too Much with Us" (p. 510), "Going to Work" (p. 582), "The End and the Beginning" (p. 693)

The Epigram

Originally, an epigram was an inscription carved in stone on a monument or statue. As a literary form, an **epigram** is a very brief poem that makes a pointed, often sarcastic, comment in a surprising twist at the end. In a sense, it is a poem with a punch line. Although some epigrams rhyme, others do not. Many are only two lines long, but others are somewhat longer. What they have in common is their economy of language and their tone.

FURTHER READING: The Epigram

Samuel Taylor Coleridge (1772–1834)

What Is an Epigram? (1802)

What is an epigram? a dwarfish whole,
Its body brevity, and wit its soul.

Dorothy Parker (1893–1967)

News Item (1937)

Men seldom make passes
At girls who wear glasses.

Reading and Reacting

1. Explain the point made in each of the epigrams above.
2. Evaluate each poem. What qualities do you conclude make an epigram effective?
3. **Journal Entry** In what respects are short-short stories (see Chapter 7) and ten-minute plays (see Chapter 28) like epigrams?
4. **Critical Perspective** In "Making Love Modern: Dorothy Parker and Her Public," Nina Miller explains why Dorothy Parker's poetry achieved its considerable popularity during the 1920s:

    > Sophistication—that highly prized commodity which was to define the Jazz Age—meant cynicism and a barbed wit, and women like Parker were perfectly situated to dominate this discourse. In the twenties, as a wisecracking member of the celebrated Algonquin Round Table, Parker would be at the cutting edge of a mannered and satirical wittiness, one which determined the shape of her poetry in important ways.

    What is it that makes "News Item" witty? If it is satirical, what attitudes in society does it satirize?

Related Works: "Fire and Ice" (p. 504), "Shakespearean Sonnet" (p. 660), "General Review of the Sex Situation" (p. 686)

AP Images/Daily Hampshire Gazette, Kevin Gutting

Martín Espada (1957–)

Why I Went to College (2000)

If you don't,
my father said,
you better learn
to eat soup
through a straw,
'cause I'm gonna
break your jaw

Reading and Reacting

1. How is "Why I Went to College" different from the epigrams on page 632? How is it similar to them?
2. What function does the poem's title serve? Is it the epigram's "punch line" or does it serve another purpose?
3. What can you infer about the speaker's father from this poem? Why, for example, do you think he wants his son to go to college?
4. **Journal Entry** Exactly why did the speaker go to college? Expand this short poem into a paragraph written from the speaker's point of view.

Related Works: "Baca Grande" (p. 532), "My Papa's Waltz" (p. 672), "'Faith' is a fine invention" (p. 710)

Haiku

Like an epigram, a haiku compresses words into a very small package. Unlike an epigram, however, a haiku focuses on an image, not an idea. A traditional Japanese form, the **haiku** is a brief unrhymed poem that presents the essence of some aspect of nature, concentrating a vivid image in three lines. Although in the strictest sense, a haiku consists of seventeen syllables divided into three lines of five, seven, and five syllables, respectively, not all poets conform to this rigid structure.

The following poem is a translation of a classic Japanese haiku by Matsuo Bashō:

> Silent and still: then
> Even sinking into the rocks,
> The cicada's screech.

Notice that this poem conforms to the haiku's three-line structure and traditional subject matter, vividly depicting a natural scene without comment or analysis.

FURTHER READING: Haiku

Matsuo Bashō (1644–1694)

Four Haiku*

Translated by Geoffrey Bownas and Anthony Thwaite

Spring:
A hill without a name
Veiled in morning mist.

The beginning of autumn:
Sea and emerald paddy
Both the same green.

The winds of autumn
Blow: yet still green
The chestnut husks.

A flash of lightning:
Into the gloom
Goes the heron's cry.

Reading and Reacting

1. Haiku are admired for their extreme economy and their striking images. What are the central images in each of Bashō's haiku? To what senses do these images appeal?
2. In another poem, Bashō says that art begins with "The depths of the country / and a rice-planting song." What do you think he means? How do these four haiku exemplify this idea?
3. Do you think the conciseness of these poems increases or decreases the impact of their images? Explain.
4. **Journal Entry** "In a Station of the Metro" (p. 548) is Ezra Pound's version of a haiku. How successful do you think his poem is as a haiku? Do you think a longer poem could have conveyed the images more effectively?

Related Works: "Where Mountain Lion Lay Down with Deer" (p. 502), "Some Good Things to Be Said for the Iron Age" (p. 549), "the sky was can dy" (p. 636), "Fog" (p. 680), "Birches" (p. 680), "Meeting at Night" (p. 683)

---

*Publication date is not available.

Open Form

Although an **open form** poem may make occasional use of rhyme and meter, it has no familiar pattern or design: no conventional stanzaic divisions, no consistent metrical pattern or line length, no repeated rhyme scheme. Still, open form poetry is not necessarily shapeless, untidy, or randomly ordered. All poems have form, and the form of a poem may be determined by factors such as repeated sounds, the appearance of words on the printed page, or pauses in natural speech as well as by a conventional metrical pattern or rhyme scheme.

Open form poetry invites readers to participate in the creative process, to discover the relationship between form and meaning. In fact, some modern poets believe that only open form offers them freedom to express their ideas or that the subject matter or mood of their poetry demands a relaxed, experimental approach to form. For example, when Lawrence Ferlinghetti portrays the poet as an acrobat who "climbs on rime" (p. 562), he constructs his poem in a way that is consistent with the poet/acrobat's willingness to take risks. Thus, the poem's idiosyncratic form supports its ideas about the limitless possibilities of poetry and the poet as experimenter.

Without a conventional pattern, however, poets must create forms that suit their needs, and they must continue to shape and reshape the look of the poem on the page as they revise its words. Thus, open form is a challenge, but it is also a way for poets to experiment with fresh arrangements of words and new juxtapositions of ideas, as Carl Sandburg does in the following poem.

Bettmann/Getty Images

Carl Sandburg (1878–1967)

Chicago (1914)

Hog Butcher for the World,
Tool Maker, Stacker of Wheat,
Player with Railroads and the Nation's Freight
Handler;
Stormy, husky, brawling,
City of the Big Shoulders:
They tell me you are wicked and I believe them, for
I have seen your painted women under the gas
lamps
luring the farm boys.
And they tell me you are crooked and I answer: Yes,
it is true
I have seen the gunman kill and go free to kill again.
And they tell me you are brutal and my reply is: On the
faces of
women and children I have seen the marks of wanton
hunger.

And having answered so I turn once more to those who sneer at
 this my city, and I give them back the sneer and say to them:
Come and show me another city with lifted head singing so
 proud to be alive and coarse and strong and cunning.
Flinging magnetic curses amid the toil of piling job on job,
 here is a tall bold slugger set vivid against the little soft cities;
Fierce as a dog with tongue lapping for action, cunning as a
 savage pitted against the wilderness,
 Bareheaded,
  Shoveling,
  Wrecking,
  Planning,
  Building, breaking, rebuilding,
Under the smoke, dust all over his mouth, laughing with white
 teeth,
Under the terrible burden of destiny laughing as a young man
 laughs,
Laughing even as an ignorant fighter laughs who has never
 lost a battle,
Bragging and laughing that under his wrist is the pulse,
 and under his ribs the heart of the people,
    Laughing!
Laughing the stormy, husky, brawling laughter of Youth,
 half-naked, sweating, proud to be Hog Butcher, Tool Maker,
 Stacker of Wheat, Player with Railroads and Freight Handler to
 the Nation.

Chicago street scene, 1925
Hulton Deutsch/Corbis Historical/Getty Images

"Chicago" uses capitalization and punctuation conventionally, and it generally (though not always) arranges words in lines in a way that is consistent with the natural divisions of phrases and sentences. However, the poem is not divided into stanzas, and its lines vary widely in length—from a single word isolated on a line to a line crowded with words—and follow no particular metrical pattern. Instead, its form is created through its pattern of alternating sections of long and short lines; through its repeated words and phrases ("They tell me" in lines 6–8, "under" in lines 18–19, and "laughing" in lines 18–23, for example); through **alliteration** (for example, "slugger set vivid against the little soft cities" in line 11); and, most of all, through the piling up of words and images into catalogs in lines 1–5, 13–17, and 22.

To understand Sandburg's reasons for choosing such a form, readers need to consider the poem's subject matter and theme. "Chicago" celebrates the scope and power of a "Stormy, husky, brawling" city, one that is exuberant and outgoing, not sedate and civilized. Chicago is a city that does not follow anyone else's rules; it is, after all, "Bareheaded, / Shoveling, / Wrecking, / Planning, / Building, breaking, rebuilding," constantly active, in flux, on the move, "proud to be alive." "Fierce as a dog ... cunning as a savage," the city is characterized as, among other things, a worker, a fighter, and a harborer of "painted women" and killers and hungry women and children. Just as Chicago itself does not conform to the rules, the poem departs from the orderly confines of stanzaic form and measured rhyme and meter, a kind of form that is, after all, better suited to "the little soft cities" than to the "tall bold slugger" that is Chicago.

Of course, open form poetry does not have to look like Sandburg's poem. The following poem, an extreme example of open form, looks almost as if it has spilled out of a box of words.

E. E. Cummings (1894–1962)

the sky was can dy (1925)

the
        sky
                was
can dy lu
minous
                edible
spry
        pinks shy
lemons
greens coo l choc
olate
s.

    un der,
    a lo
co
mo
    tive   s pout
                    ing
                        vi
                    o
                    lets

Like many of Cummings's poems, this one seems ready to skip off the page. Its irregular line length and its unconventional capitalization, punctuation, and word divisions immediately draw readers' attention to its form. Despite these oddities, and despite the absence of orderly rhyme and meter, the poem does have its conventional elements.

A closer examination reveals that the poem's theme—the beauty of the sky—is quite conventional; that the poem is divided, though somewhat crudely, into two sections; and that the poet does use some rhyme—"spry" and "shy," for example. However, Cummings's sky is described not in traditional terms but rather as something "edible." The breaks within words ("can dy lu / minous"; "coo l choc / olate / s") seem to expand the words' possibilities, visually stretching them to the limit, extending their taste and visual image over several lines and, in the case of the poem's last two words, visually reinforcing the picture the words describe. In addition, the isolation of syllables exposes hidden rhyme, as in "lo / co / mo" and "lu" / "coo." Thus, by using open form, Cummings illustrates the capacity of a poem to move beyond the traditional boundaries set by words and lines.

FURTHER READING: Open Form

Walt Whitman (1819–1892)

from "Out of the Cradle Endlessly Rocking" (1881)

Out of the cradle endlessly rocking,
Out of the mocking-bird's throat, the musical shuttle,
Out of the Ninth-month[1] midnight,
Over the sterile sands and the fields beyond, where the child
    leaving his bed wander'd alone, bareheaded, barefoot,

[1] *Ninth-month:* The Quaker designation for September; in context, an allusion to the human birth cycle.

Down from the shower'd halo,
Up from the mystic play of shadows twining and twisting as if
they were alive,
Out from the patches of briers and blackberries,
From the memories of the bird that chanted to me,
From your memories sad brother, from the fitful risings and
fallings I heard,
From under that yellow half-moon late-risen and swollen as if
with tears,
From those beginning notes of yearning and love there in the
mist,
From the thousand responses of my heart never to cease,
From the myriad thence-arous'd words,
From the word stronger and more delicious than any,
From such as now they start the scene revisiting,
As a flock, twittering, rising, or overhead passing,
Borne hither, ere all eludes me, hurriedly,
A man, yet by these tears a little boy again,
Throwing myself on the sand, confronting the waves,
I, chanter of pains and joys, uniter of here and hereafter,
Taking all hints to use them, but swiftly leaping beyond them,
A reminiscence sing.

Reading and Reacting

1. This excerpt, the first twenty-two lines of a poem nearly two hundred lines long, has no regular metrical pattern or rhyme scheme. What gives it its form?
2. How might you explain why the poem's lines vary in length?
3. **Journal Entry** Compare this excerpt with the excerpt from Whitman's "Song of Myself" (p. 742). In what respects are the forms of the two poems similar?

Related Works: "Chicago" (p. 634), "I Hear America Singing" (p. 741)

William Carlos Williams (1883–1963)

Spring and All (1923)

By the road to the contagious hospital
under the surge of the blue

mottled clouds driven from the
northeast—a cold wind. Beyond, the

waste of broad, muddy fields
brown with dried weeds, standing and fallen

patches of standing water
the scattering of tall trees

All along the road the reddish
purplish, forked, upstanding, twiggy
stuff of bushes and small trees
with dead, brown leaves under them
leafless vines—

Lifeless in appearance, sluggish
dazed spring approaches—

They enter the new world naked,
cold, uncertain of all
save that they enter. All about them
the cold, familiar wind—

Now the grass, tomorrow
the stiff curl of wildcarrot leaf
One by one objects are defined—
It quickens: clarity, outline of leaf

But now the stark dignity of
entrance—Still, the profound change
has come upon them: rooted, they
grip down and begin to awaken

Contagious Hospital, Brookline, MA, 1909
Library of Congress, Prints & Photographs Division, Reproduction number HABS NY-6086-L-1

Reading and Reacting

1. Although this poem is written in free verse and lacks a definite pattern of meter or rhyme, it includes some characteristics of closed form poetry. Give some examples.
2. What does Williams accomplish by visually isolating lines 7–8 and lines 14–15?
3. "Spring and All" includes assonance, alliteration, and repetition. Give several examples of each technique, and explain what each adds to the poem.
4. **Journal Entry** What do you think the word *All* means in the poem's title?
5. **Critical Perspective** According to critic Bonnie Costello, "Williams thought about the creative process in painters' terms, and he asks us to experience the work as we might experience a modern painting. His great achievement was to bring some of its qualities into poetry."

   Consider the images Williams uses in this poem. In what ways is this poem like a painting? Which images are conveyed in "painters' terms"? How does he use these images to create meaning in the poem?

Related Works: "l(a" (p. 492), "Pied Beauty" (p. 605), "I wandered lonely as a cloud" (p. 678)

Yusef Komunyakaa (1947–)

Nude Interrogation (1998)

Did you kill anyone over there? Angelica shifts
her gaze from the Janis Joplin poster to the Jimi
Hendrix, lifting the pale muslin blouse over her
head. The blacklight deepens the blues when
the needle drops into the first groove of "All
Along the Watchtower." I don't want to look
at the floor. Did you kill anyone? Did you dig
a hole, crawl inside, and wait for your target?
Her miniskirt drops into a rainbow at her feet.
Sandalwood incense hangs a slow comet of
perfume over the room. I shake my head. She
unhooks her bra and flings it against a bookcase
made of plywood and cinderblocks. Did you use
an M-16, a hand-grenade, a bayonet, or your
own two strong hands, both thumbs pressed
against that little bird in the throat? She stands
with her left thumb hooked into the elastic of
her sky-blue panties. When she flicks off the

blacklight, snowy hills rush up to the windows. Did you kill anyone
over there? Are you right-handed or left-handed? Did you drop your
gun afterwards? Did you kneel beside the corpse and turn it over?
She's nude against the falling snow. Yes. The record spins like a
bull's-eye on the far wall of Xanadu.[1] Yes, I say. I was scared of the
silence. The night was too big. And afterwards, I couldn't stop looking up at the sky.

Reading and Reacting

1. Who is the speaker? Why is Angelica interrogating him? How is the fact that she is undressing during this interrogation related to the questions she asks?
2. What do you think is going through the speaker's mind as he watches Angelica undress? Is he thinking about her, or is he thinking about Vietnam? How can you tell?
3. **Journal Entry** Retype this poem so it looks like a story, adding paragraph breaks and quotation marks as necessary. Do you think its impact is greater in this format? Why or why not?
4. **Critical Perspective** Writing in the *New York Times Book Review*, critic Katha Pollitt focuses on "poetic clichés," which, she says, are "attempts to energize the poem by annexing a subject that is guaranteed to produce a knee-jerk response in the reader. This saves a lot of bother all around, and enables poet and reader to drowse together in a warm bath of mutual admiration for each other's capacity for deep feeling and right thinking." Among the poetic clichés Pollitt discusses is something she calls "the CNN poem, which retells in overheated free verse a prominent news story involving war, famine, torture, child abuse or murder."

   Do you think Komunyakaa's poem is a "CNN poem," or do you see it as something more than just "poetic cliché"? Explain.

Related Works: "Atrocities" (p. 688), "Facing It" (p. 690), *Applicant* (p. 807)

Concrete Poetry

With roots in the ancient Greek pattern poems and the sixteenth- and seventeenth-century **emblem poems**, contemporary **concrete poetry** uses words—sometimes, different fonts and type sizes—to shape a picture on the page.

[1]*Xanadu*: A mythical location and image of other worldly beauty in the poem "Kubla Khan" by Samuel Taylor Coleridge.

May Swenson (1913–1989)

Women (1970)

Women   Or they
  should be   should be
    pedestals   little horses
      moving   those wooden
        pedestals   sweet
          moving   oldfashioned
            to the   painted
              motions   rocking
                of men   horses
                the gladdest things in the toyroom
                  The   feelingly
                pegs   and then
              of their   unfeelingly
            ears   To be
          so familiar   joyfully
        and dear   ridden
      to the trusting   rockingly
    fists   ridden until
  To be chafed   the restored
egos dismount and the legs stride away
Immobile   willing
  sweetlipped   to be set
  sturdy   into motion
    and smiling   Women
      women   should be
        should always   pedestals
          be waiting   to men

The form of a concrete poem is not something that emerges from the poem's words and images; it is something predetermined by the visual image the poet has decided to create. Although some concrete poems are little more than novelties, others—like the previous poem—can be original and enlightening.

The curved shape of Swenson's poem immediately reinforces its title, and the arrangement of words on the page suggests a variety of visual directions readers might follow. The two columns seem at first to suggest two alternatives: "Women should be . . ." / "Or they should be. . . ." A closer look, however, reveals that the poem's central figures of speech, such as woman as rocking horse and woman as pedestal, move back and forth between the two columns of images. This exchange of positions might suggest that the two possibilities are really just two ways of looking at one limited role. Thus, the experimental form of the poem visually challenges the apparent complacency of its words, suggesting that women, like words, need not fall into traditional roles or satisfy conventional expectations.

FURTHER READING: Concrete Poetry

Michael Nicholson/Corbis Historical/ Getty Images

George Herbert (1593–1633)

Easter Wings (1633)

Lord, who createdst man in wealth and store,
Though foolishly he lost the same,
Decaying more and more
Till he became
Most poor,
With thee
Oh, let me rise
As larks, harmoniously,
And sing this day thy victories;
Then shall the fall further the flight in me.
My tender age in sorrow did begin;
And still with sicknesses and shame
Thou didst so punish sin,
That I became
Most thin.
With thee
Let me combine,
And feel this day thy victory;
For if I imp my wing on thine,
Affliction shall advance the flight in me.

Reading and Reacting

1. In this example of a seventeenth-century emblem poem, lines are arranged so that shape and subject matter reinforce each other. Explain how this is accomplished. (For example, how does line length support the poem's images and ideas?)
2. This poem has a definite rhyme scheme. How would you describe it? What relationship do you see between the rhyme scheme and the poem's visual divisions?

Related Works: "l(a" (p. 492), "A Valediction: Forbidding Mourning" (p. 568), "When I Have Fears" (p. 729)

Checklist Writing about Form

- Is the poem written in open or closed form? On what characteristics do you base your conclusion?
- Why did the poet choose open or closed form? For example, is the poem's form consistent with its subject matter, tone, or theme? Is it determined by the conventions of the historical period in which it was written?
- If the poem is arranged in closed form, does the pattern apply to single lines, to groups of lines, or to the entire poem? What factors determine the breaks between groups of lines?
- Is the poem a sonnet? a sestina? a villanelle? an epigram? a haiku? How do the traditional form's conventions suit the poet's language and theme? Does the poem follow the rules of the form at all times, or does it break any new ground?
- If the poem is arranged in open form, what determines the breaks at the ends of lines?
- Are certain words or phrases isolated on lines? Why?
- How do elements such as assonance, alliteration, rhyme, and repetition of words give the poem form?
- What use does the poet make of punctuation and capitalization? of white space on the page?
- Is the poem a prose poem? How does this form support the poem's subject matter?
- Is the poem a concrete poem? How does the poet use the visual shape of the poem to convey meaning?

WRITING SUGGESTIONS: Form

1. Reread the definitions of closed form and open form in this chapter. Based on these definitions, do you think concrete poems are "open" or "closed"? Explain your position in a short essay, supporting your thesis with specific references to the concrete poems in this chapter.
2. Some poets—for example, Emily Dickinson and Robert Frost—write both open and closed form poems. Choose one open and one closed form poem by a single poet, and analyze the two poems, explaining the poet's possible reasons for choosing each type of form.

3. Do you see complex forms, such as the villanelle and the sestina, as exercises or even merely as opportunities for poets to show off their skills—or do you believe the special demands of the forms add something valuable to a poem? To help you answer this question, read Dylan Thomas's "Do not go gentle into that good night" (p. 676) and Elizabeth Bishop's "Sestina" (p. 625).
4. Like "Nude Interrogation" (p. 640), Joy Harjo's "Invisible Fish" (p. 682) is a **prose poem**, a poem that looks more like prose than poetry. Find some additional prose poems online, and write an essay in which you consider why the form seems suitable for Kumunkakaa's and Harjo's poems and two or three of those you have found. Is there a particular kind of subject matter that seems especially appropriate for a prose poem?

Chapter

24

Symbol, Allegory, Allusion, Myth

Christina Rossetti
Chronicle/Alamy Stock Photo

William Butler Yeats
Bettmann/Getty Images

W. H. Auden
Chronicle/Alamy Stock Photo

Virgil Suarez
© Virgil Suárez

Learning Objectives

After reading this chapter, you will be able to. . .

- Explain how symbolism is used in a poem.
- Recognize conventional or universal symbols in a poem.
- Analyze the use of a symbol in a poem.
- Define allegory as it relates to poetry.
- Recognize allegorical figures in a poem.
- Define allusion as it relates to poetry.
- Define myth as it relates to poetry.

Bettmann/Getty Images

William Blake (1757–1827)

The Sick Rose (1794)

O Rose thou art sick.
The invisible worm
That flies in the night,
In the howling storm:
Has found out thy bed
Of crimson joy:
And his dark secret love
Does thy life destroy.

Symbol

A **symbol** is an idea or image that suggests something else—but not in the simple way that a dollar sign stands for money or a flag represents a country. A symbol is an image that transcends its literal, or denotative, meaning in a complex way. For example, if someone gives a rose to a loved one, it could simply be a sign of love. But in the poem "The Sick Rose," the rose has a range of contradictory and complementary meanings. What does the rose represent? Beauty? Perfection? Passion? Something else? Blake further complicates the matter by saying that the rose is "sick," infected by a worm that could symbolize death, decay, or sexuality. As this poem illustrates, the distinctive trait of a symbol is that its meaning cannot easily be pinned down or defined.

Such ambiguity can be frustrating, but it is precisely this characteristic of a symbol that enriches a poem by giving it multiple layers of meaning. As Robert Frost said, a symbol is a little thing that touches a larger thing. In the poem of his that follows, the central symbol does just this.

Robert Frost (1874–1963)

For Once, Then, Something (1923)

Others taunt me with having knelt at well-curbs
Always wrong to the light, so never seeing
Deeper down in the well than where the water
Gives me back in a shining surface picture
Me myself in the summer heaven, godlike,
Looking out of a wreath of fern and cloud puffs.
Once, when trying with chin against a well-curb,
I discerned, as I thought, beyond the picture,
Through the picture, a something white, uncertain,
Something more of the depths—and then I lost it.

Water came to rebuke the too clear water.
One drop fell from a fern, and lo, a ripple
Shook whatever it was lay there at bottom,
Blurred it, blotted it out. What was that whiteness?
Truth? A pebble of quartz? For once, then, something.

The central symbol in this poem is the "something" that the speaker thinks he sees at the bottom of a well. Traditionally, the act of looking down a well suggests a search for truth. In this poem, the speaker says that he always seems to look down the well at the wrong angle, so that all he can see is his own reflection—the surface, not the depths. Once, however, the speaker thought he saw something "beyond the picture," something "white, uncertain," but the image remained indistinct, disappearing when a drop of water from a fern caused the water to ripple. The poem ends with the speaker questioning the significance of what he saw. Like a reader encountering a symbol, the speaker is left trying to come to terms with images that cannot be clearly perceived and associations that cannot be readily understood. In light of the elusive nature of truth, all the speaker can do is ask questions that have no definite answers.

Symbols that appear in poetic works can be *conventional* or *universal*. **Conventional symbols** are those recognized by people who share certain cultural and social assumptions. For example, national flags evoke a general and agreed-upon response in most people of a particular country, and—for better or for worse—American children have for years perceived the golden arches of McDonald's as a symbol of food and fun. **Universal symbols** are those likely to be recognized by people regardless of their culture. In 1890, the noted Scottish anthropologist Sir James George Frazer wrote the first version of his work *The Golden Bough* in which he identified parallels between the rites and beliefs of early pagan cultures and those of Christianity. Fascinated by Frazer's work, the psychologist Carl Jung sought to explain these parallels by formulating a theory of **archetypes**, which held that certain images or ideas reside in the subconscious of all people. According to Jung, archetypal symbols include water, symbolizing rebirth; spring, symbolizing growth; and winter, symbolizing death.

Sometimes symbols that appear in poems can be obscure or highly idiosyncratic. William Blake is one of many poets (William Butler Yeats is another) whose works combine symbols from different cultural, theological, and philosophical sources to form complex networks of personal symbolic associations. To Blake, for example, the scientist Isaac Newton represents the tendency of scientists to quantify experience while ignoring the beauty and mystery of nature. Readers cannot begin to understand his use of Newton as a symbol until they have read a number of Blake's more difficult poems.

How do you know when an idea or image in a poem is a symbol? At what point do you decide that a particular object or idea goes beyond the literal level and takes on symbolic significance? When is a rose more than a rose or a well more than a well? Frequently you can recognize a symbol by its prominence or repetition. In "For Once, Then, Something," for example, the well is introduced in the first line of the poem, and it is the poem's focal point; in "The Sick Rose," the importance of the rose is emphasized by the title.

It is not enough, however, to identify an image or idea that seems to suggest something else. Your decision that a particular item has symbolic significance must be supported by the details of the poem and make sense in light of the ideas the poem develops. In the following poem, the symbolic significance of the volcano helps readers to understand the poem's central theme.

Eruption of Mt. Etna (Sicily), 2001
TONY GENTILE/Reuters

<u>Emily Dickinson</u> (1830–1886)

Volcanoes be in Sicily (1914)

Volcanoes be in Sicily
And South America
I judge from my Geography—
Volcanoes nearer here
A Lava step at any time
Am I inclined to climb—
A Crater I may contemplate
Vesuvius at Home.

This poem opens with a statement of fact: volcanoes are in Sicily and South America. In line 3, however, the speaker introduces the improbable idea that volcanoes are located near where she is now. Readers familiar with Dickinson know that her poems are highly autobiographical and that she lived in Amherst, Massachusetts, where there are no volcanoes. This information leads readers to suspect that they should not take the speaker's observation literally and that, in the context of the poem, volcanoes may have symbolic significance. But what do volcanoes suggest here?

On the one hand, volcanoes represent the awesome creative power of nature; on the other hand, they suggest its destructiveness. The speaker's contemplation of the crater of Vesuvius—the volcano that buried the ancient Roman city of Pompeii in A.D. 79—is therefore filled with contradictory associations. Because Dickinson was a recluse, volcanoes—active, destructive, unpredictable, and dangerous—may be seen as symbolic of everything she fears in the outside world—and, perhaps, within herself. Volcanoes may also suggest her own creative power, which, like a volcano, is something to be feared as well as contemplated. Dickinson seems to have a voyeur's attraction to danger and power, but she also fears them. For this reason, Dickinson keeps real volcanoes at a distance but uses her imagination to visit a symbolic, but no less terrifying, "Vesuvius at Home."

FURTHER READING: Symbol

AP Images

Edgar Allan Poe (1809–1849)

The Raven (1844)

Once upon a midnight dreary, while I pondered, weak and weary,
Over many a quaint and curious volume of forgotten lore,
While I nodded, nearly napping, suddenly there came a tapping,
As of some one gently rapping, rapping at my chamber door.
"'Tis some visitor," I muttered, "tapping at my chamber door—
Only this, and nothing more."

Ah, distinctly I remember it was in the bleak December,
And each separate dying ember wrought its ghost upon the floor.
Eagerly I wished the morrow;—vainly I had sought to borrow
From my books surcease of sorrow—sorrow for the lost Lenore—
For the rare and radiant maiden whom the angels name Lenore—
Nameless here for evermore.

And the silken sad uncertain rustling of each purple curtain
Thrilled me—filled me with fantastic terrors never felt before;
so that now, to still the beating of my heart, I stood repeating
"'Tis some visitor entreating entrance at my chamber door;—
Some late visitor entreating entrance at my chamber door;
This it is, and nothing more."

Presently my soul grew stronger; hesitating then no longer,
"Sir," said I, "or Madam, truly your forgiveness I implore;
But the fact is I was napping, and so gently you came rapping,
And so faintly you came tapping, tapping at my chamber door,
That I scarce was sure I heard you"—here I opened wide the door;—
Darkness there, and nothing more.

Deep into that darkness peering, long I stood there wondering, fearing,
Doubting, dreaming dreams no mortal ever dared to dream before;
But the silence was unbroken, and the darkness gave no token,

And the only word there spoken was the whispered word,
"Lenore!"
This I whispered, and an echo murmured back the word,
"Lenore!"—
Merely this, and nothing more.

Back into the chamber turning, all my soul within me burning,
Soon I heard again a tapping somewhat louder than before.
"Surely," said I, "surely that is something at my window lattice;
Let me see, then, what thereat is, and this mystery explore—
Let my heart be still a moment and this mystery explore;—
'Tis the wind and nothing more!"

Open here I flung the shutter, when, with many a flirt and flutter,
In there stepped a stately raven of the saintly days of yore;
Not the least obeisance made he; not an instant stopped or stayed he;
But, with mien of lord or lady, perched above my chamber door—
Perched upon a bust of Pallas[1] just above my chamber door—
Perched, and sat, and nothing more.

Then this ebony bird beguiling my sad fancy into smiling,
By the grave and stern decorum of the countenance it wore,
"Though thy crest be shorn and shaven, thou," I said, "art sure no
craven,
Ghastly grim and ancient raven wandering from the Nightly shore—
Tell me what thy lordly name is on the Night's Plutonian[2] shore!"
Quoth the raven, "Nevermore."

Much I marvelled this ungainly fowl to hear discourse so plainly,
Though its answer little meaning—little relevancy bore,
For we cannot help agreeing that no living human being
Ever yet was blessed with seeing bird above his chamber door—
Bird or beat upon the sculptured bust above his chamber door,
With such name as "Nevermore."

But the raven, sitting lonely on the placid bust, spoke only
That one word, as if his soul in that one word he did outpour.
Nothing farther then he uttered—not a feather then he fluttered—
Till I scarcely more than muttered "Other friends have flown
before—
On the morrow *he* will leave me, as my hopes have flown before."
Then the bird said "Nevermore."

Startled at the stillness broken by reply so aptly spoken,
"Doubtless," said I, "what it utters is its only stock and store

---

[1]*Pallas:* Athena, Greek goddess of wisdom.
[2]*Plutonian:* Dark; Pluto was the Greek god of the dead and ruler of the underworld.

Caught from some unhappy master whom unmerciful Disaster
Followed fast and followed faster till his songs one burden bore—
Till the dirges of his Hope that melancholy burden bore
Of 'Never—nevermore.'"

But the raven still beguiling all my sad soul into smiling,
Straight I wheeled a cushioned seat in front of bird and bust and door;
Then, upon the velvet sinking, I betook myself to linking
Fancy unto fancy, thinking what this ominous bird of yore—
What this grim, ungainly, ghastly, gaunt, and ominous bird of yore
Meant in croaking "Nevermore."

This I sat engaged in guessing, but no syllable expressing
To the fowl whose fiery eyes now burned into my bosom's core;
This and more I sat divining, with my head at ease reclining
On the cushion's velvet lining that the lamplight gloated o'er,
But whose velvet violet lining with the lamplight gloating o'er,
She shall press, ah, nevermore!

Then, methought, the air grew denser, perfumed from an unseen censer
Swung by angels whose faint foot-falls tinkled on the tufted floor.
"Wretch," I cried, "thy God hath lent thee—by these angels he hath sent thee
Respite—respite and nepenthe[3] from thy memories of Lenore!
Quaff, oh quaff this kind nepenthe and forget this lost Lenore!"
Quoth the raven, "Nevermore."

"Prophet!" said I, "thing of evil!—prophet still, if bird or devil!—
Whether Tempter sent, or whether tempest tossed thee here ashore,
Desolate, yet all undaunted, on this desert land enchanted—
On this home by Horror haunted—tell me truly, I implore—
Is there—*is* there balm in Gilead?[4]—tell me—tell me, I implore!"
Quoth the raven, "Nevermore."

"Prophet!" said I, "thing of evil—prophet still, if bird or devil!
By that Heaven that bends above us—by that God we both adore—
Tell this soul with sorrow laden if, within the distant Aidenn,[5]
It shall clasp a sainted maiden whom the angels name Lenore—
Clasp a rare and radiant maiden whom the angels name Lenore."
Quoth the raven, "Nevermore."

[3]*nepenthe:* A drug mentioned in the *Odyssey* as a remedy for grief.
[4]*Gilead:* A region mentioned in the Bible; noted for its soothing ointments.
[5]*Aidenn:* A variation of Eden, the home of Adam and Eve.

"Be that word our sign of parting, bird or fiend!" I shrieked upstarting—
"Get thee back into the tempest and the Night's Plutonian shore!
Leave no black plume as a token of that lie thy soul hath spoken!
Leave my loneliness unbroken!—quit the bust above my door!
Take thy beak from out my heart, and take thy form from off my door!"
Quoth the raven, "Nevermore."

And the raven, never flitting, still is sitting, still is sitting
On the pallid bust of Pallas just above my chamber door;
And his eyes have all the seeming of a demon's that is dreaming,
And the lamp-light o'er him streaming throws his shadow on the floor;
And my soul from out that shadow that lies floating on the floor
Shall be lifted—nevermore!

Raven
iStock.com/D-Keine

Reading and Reacting

1. Who is the speaker in the poem? What is his state of mind? How does the raven mirror the speaker's mental state?
2. "The Raven" contains a good deal of alliteration. Identify some examples. How does this use of repeated initial consonant sounds help to convey the mood of the poem?
3. The speaker refers to the raven in a number of different ways. At one point, it is simply "an ebony bird" (line 42); at another, it is a "prophet" and "a thing of evil" (85). How else does the speaker characterize the raven?
4. **Journal Entry** What is the symbolic significance of the raven? of the repeated word "nevermore"? of the bust of Pallas, the ancient Greek god of wisdom?
5. **Critical Perspective** According to Christoffer Nilsson, who maintains a website dedicated to the works of Poe, "The Raven" was composed with almost mathematical precision. When writing the stanza in which the

interrogation of the raven reaches its climax (third stanza from the end), Poe wanted to make certain that no preceding stanza would "surpass this in rhythmical effect":

> Poe then worked backwards from this stanza and used the word "Nevermore" in many different ways, so that even with the repetition of this word, it would not prove to be monotonous. Poe builds the tension in this poem up, stanza by stanza, but after the climaxing stanza he tears the whole thing down, and lets the narrator know that there is no meaning in searching for a moral in the raven's "nevermore."

Do you agree with Nilsson that it makes no sense to look for a moral in the raven's "nevermore"? What kind of moral, if any, do you think "Nevermore" implies for the speaker?

Related Works: "Rooming houses are old women" (p. 563), "Ode to a Nightingale" (p. 583), "The Tyger" (p. 702), *Hamlet* (p. 1012)

Virgil Suárez (1962–)

Isla (2000)

In Los Angeles I grew up watching *The Three Stooges*,
The Little Rascals, *Speed Racer*, and the Godzilla movies,

those my mother called "*Los monstruos*," and though I didn't
yet speak English, I understood why such a creature would,

upon being woken up from its centuries-long slumber, rise
and destroy Tokyo's buildings, cars, people—I understood

by the age of twelve what it meant to be unwanted, exiled,
how you move from one country to another where nobody

wants you, nobody knows you, and I sat in front of the TV,
transfixed by the snow-fizz on our old black and white,

and when Godzilla bellows his eardrum-crushing growl,
I screamed back, this victory-holler from one so rejected

and cursed to another. When the monster whipped its tail
and destroyed, I threw a pillow across my room; each time

my mother stormed into the room and asked me what,
what I thought I was doing throwing things at the walls.

"*!Ese monstruo, esa isla!*" she'd say. That monster, that island,
and I knew she wasn't talking about the movie. She meant

her country, mine, that island in the Caribbean we left behind,
itself a reptile-looking mass on each map, on my globe,

a crocodile-like creature rising again, eating us so completely.
—for Jarret Keene

Reading and Reacting

1. What specific elements in the poem make you think that the island is a symbol?
2. Why does the speaker discuss Godzilla? What relation does Godzilla have to Cuba—the island the speaker "left behind"?
3. What does the island symbolize to the speaker? to the speaker's mother? to you?
4. **Journal Entry** The speaker uses Spanish in two places (as well as the title) in the poem. Why? What would be lost if these phrases were written in English?

Related Works: "Geraldo No Last Name" (p. 109), "Sticks" (p. 120), "Metaphors" (p. 566), "I Hear America Singing" (p. 741), *The Cuban Swimmer* (p. 1122)

Allegory

Allegory is a form of narrative that conveys a message or doctrine (usually moral or political) by using people, places, or things to stand for abstract ideas. **Allegorical figures**, each with a strict equivalent, form an **allegorical framework**, a set of ideas that conveys the allegory's message or lesson. Thus, the allegory takes place on two levels: a **literal level** that tells a story and a **figurative level** on which the allegorical figures in the story stand for ideas, concepts, and other qualities.

Like symbols, allegorical figures suggest other things. But unlike symbols, which have a range of possible meanings, allegorical figures can always be assigned specific meanings. (Because writers use allegory to instruct, they gain nothing by hiding its significance.) Thus, symbols open up possibilities for interpretation, whereas allegories tend to restrict possibilities.

Quite often an allegory involves a journey or an adventure, as in the case of Dante's *Divine Comedy*, which traces a journey through Hell, Purgatory, and Heaven. Within an allegory, everything can have meaning: the road on which the characters walk, the people they encounter, or a phrase that one of them repeats throughout the journey. Once you understand the allegorical framework, your main task is to see how the various elements fit within this system. Some allegorical poems can be relatively straightforward, but others can be so complicated that it takes a great deal of effort to unlock their meaning. In the following poem, a journey is central to the allegory.

Chronicle/Alamy Stock Photo

Christina Rossetti (1830–1894)

Uphill (1861)

Does the road wind up-hill all the way?
  Yes, to the very end.
Will the day's journey take the whole long day?
  From morn to night, my friend.

But is there for the night a resting-place?
  A roof for when the slow dark hours begin.
May not the darkness hide it from my face?
  You cannot miss that inn.

Shall I meet other wayfarers at night?
  Those who have gone before.
Then must I knock, or call when just in sight?
  They will not keep you standing at that door.

Shall I find comfort, travel-sore and weak?
  Of labor you shall find the sum.
Will there be beds for me and all who seek?
  Yea, beds for all who come.

The Pilgrims going up the hill Difficulty.

Illustration from 1776 printing of *The Pilgrim's Progress*

Lebrecht Music & Arts/Alamy Stock Photo

"Uphill" uses a question-and-answer structure to describe a journey along an uphill road. Like the one described in John Bunyan's seventeenth-century allegory *The Pilgrim's Progress*, this is a spiritual journey, one that suggests the challenges a person faces throughout life. The day-and-night duration of the journey stands for life and death, and the inn at the end of the road stands for the grave, the final resting place.

FURTHER READING: Allegory

May Swenson (1913–1989)

The Watch (1965)

When I
took my
watch to the watchfixer I
felt privileged but also pained to watch the operation. He
had long fingernails and a voluntary squint. He
fixed a magnifying cup over his
squint eye. He
undressed my
watch. I
watched him
split her
in three layers and lay her
middle—a quivering viscera—in a circle on a little plinth. He
shoved shirtsleeves up and leaned like an ogre over my
naked watch. With critical pincers he
poked and stirred. He
lifted out little private things with a magnet too tiny for me
to watch almost. "Watch out!" I
almost said. His
eye watched, enlarged, the secrets of my
watch, and I
watched anxiously. Because what if he
touched her
ticker too rough, and she
gave up the ghost out of pure fright? Or put her
things back backwards so she'd
run backwards after this? Or he
might lose a minuscule part, connected to her
exquisite heart, and mix her
up, instead of fix her.

And all the time,
all the time-
pieces on the walls, on the shelves, told the time,
told the time
in swishes and ticks,
swishes and ticks,
and seemed to be gloating, as they watched and told. I
felt faint, I
was about to lose my
breath—my
ticker going lickety-split—when watchfixer clipped her
three slices together with a gleam and two flicks of his
tools like chopsticks. He
spat out his
eye, lifted her
high, gave her
a twist, set her
hands right, and laid her
little face, quite as usual, in its place on my
wrist.

Reading and Reacting

1. On one level, this poem describes what happens when the speaker takes a watch in for repair. What details suggest that the poem is about something more?
2. In what sense do the figures in this poem create an allegorical framework?
3. What comment does the poem make on men? on the condition of women?
4. **Journal Entry** What is the moral lesson of this poem?
5. **Critical Perspective** Discussing May Swenson's work, the poet Grace Schulman observed, "Questions are the wellspring of May Swenson's art… In her speculations and her close observations, she fulfills Marianne Moore's formula for the working artist: 'Curiosity, observation, and a great deal of joy in the thing'." Do you agree that "The Watch" fulfills Marianne Moore's formula?

Related Works: "Girl" (p. 116), "The Story of an Hour" (p. 151), "A&P" (p. 179), "My Last Duchess" (p. 499), "Daddy" (p. 571), *Trifles* (p. 820)

Allusion

An **allusion** is a brief reference to a person, place, or event (fictional or actual) that readers are expected to recognize. Like symbols and allegories, allusions enrich a work by introducing associations from another context.

Although most poets expect readers to recognize their references, some use allusions to exclude certain readers from their work. In his 1922 poem "The Waste Land," for example, T. S. Eliot alludes to historical events, ancient languages, and obscure literary works. He even includes a set of notes to accompany his poem, but they do little more than complicate an already difficult text. (As you might expect, initial critical response to this poem was mixed: some critics said that it was a work of genius, while others thought that it was arcane and pretentious.)

In a sense, allusions favor those readers who have the background or knowledge to recognize them and excludes those who do not. At one time, writers could expect educated readers to recognize allusions to the Bible and to Greek and Roman classics. For example, when Christopher Marlowe referred to "Olympus' top" in his sixteenth-century play *Doctor Faustus*, he expected his readers to know that he was alluding to Mount Olympus, the home of the gods in Greek mythology. Today, this assumption is not valid, but with the advent of search engines such as *Google*, interpreting an allusion requires nothing more than entering a keyword (or keywords) into a web browser. If, when reading a poem, you come across a reference to which you are not familiar, take the time to look it up. Your understanding and appreciation of a poem will be enhanced by your ability to interpret an unfamiliar reference.

Allusions can come from any source: history, the arts, other works of literature, the Bible, current events, or even the personal life of the poet. Notice how the following poem uses allusions to prominent literary figures as well as to myth to develop its theme.

William Meredith (1919–2007)

Dreams of Suicide (1980)

(in sorrowful memory of Ernest Hemingway, Sylvia Plath, and John Berryman)

I

I reach for the awkward shotgun not to disarm
you, but to feel the metal horn,
furred with the downy membrane of dream.
More surely than the unicorn,
you are the mythical beast.

II

Or I am sniffing an oven. On all fours
I am imitating a totemic animal
but she is not my totem or the totem
of my people, this is not my magic oven.

III

If I hold you tight by the ankles,
still you fly upward from the iron railing.
Your father made these wings,
after he made his own, and now from beyond
he tells you *fly down*, in the voice
my own father might say *walk, boy*.

This poem is dedicated to the memory of three writers who died by suicide. In each stanza, the speaker envisions in a dream the death of one of the writers. In the first stanza, he dreams of Ernest Hemingway, who died by a self-inflicted gunshot wound. The speaker grasps the "metal horn" of Hemingway's shotgun and transforms Hemingway into a mythical beast who, like a unicorn, represents the rare, unique talent of the artist. In the second stanza, the speaker dreams of Sylvia Plath, who died by asphyxiation in a gas oven. He sees himself, like Plath, on his knees imitating an animal sniffing an oven. In the third stanza, the speaker dreams of John Berryman, who leaped to his death. Berryman is characterized as Icarus, a mythological figure who, along with his father Daedalus, fled Crete by building wings made of feathers and wax. Together they flew away; however, ignoring his father's warning, Icarus flew so close to the sun that the wax melted, and he fell to his death in the sea. In this poem, then, the speaker uses allusions to make a point about the difficult lives of writers—and, perhaps, to convey his own empathy for those who could not survive the struggle to reconcile art and life.

FURTHER READING: Allusion

R. S. Gwynn (1948–)

Shakespearean Sonnet (2005)

(With a first line taken from the TV listings)

A man is haunted by his father's ghost.
A boy and girl love while their families fight.
A Scottish king is murdered by his host.
Two couples get lost on a summer night.
A hunchback murders all who block his way.
A ruler's rivals plot against his life.
A fat man and a prince make rebels pay.
A noble Moor has doubts about his wife.
An English king decides to conquer France.
A duke learns that his best friend is a she,
A forest sets the scene for this romance.

An old man and his daughters disagree.
A Roman leader makes a big mistake.
A sexy queen is bitten by a snake.

Reading and Reacting

1. Why does Gwynn write his poem in the form of a Shakespearean sonnet?
2. Each line of the poem summarizes the plot of a Shakespeare play in the form of a TV listing. What do you think Gwynn hopes to accomplish with these summaries?
3. Where does Gwynn use alliteration? At what point does he use irony?
4. **Journal Entry** Try to identify all the Shakespearean plays Gwynn alludes to in his poem.
5. **Critical Perspective** According to critic Bruce Bawer, R. S. Gwynn's recurrent theme is "the decay of Western civilization—trash culture, fashionable politics, education made E-Z—and the enduring faults, frailties, fallacies, foibles, and fraudulencies of the human comedy." In what sense, if any, do you think "Shakespearean Sonnet" is about "the decay of Western civilization"?

Related Works: "The English Canon" (p. 534), "An Apology" (p. 551), "Shall I compare thee to a summer's day?" (p. 560), "When, in disgrace with Fortune and men's eyes" (p. 618), *Hamlet* (p. 1012)

Myth

A **myth** is a narrative that embodies—and in some cases helps to explain—the religious, philosophical, moral, and political values of a culture. Using gods and supernatural beings, myths try to make sense of occurrences in the natural world. (The term *myth* can also refer to a private belief system devised by an individual poet as well as to any fully realized fictitious setting in which a literary work takes place, such as the myths of William Faulkner's Yoknapatawpha County or of novelist Lawrence Durrell's Alexandria.) Contrary to popular usage, *myth* does not mean "falsehood." In the broadest sense, myths are stories—usually whole groups of stories—that can be true or partly true as well as false; regardless of their degree of accuracy, however, myths frequently express the deepest beliefs of a culture. According to this definition, the *Iliad* and the *Odyssey*, the Koran, and the Old and New Testaments can all be referred to as myths.

The mythologist Joseph Campbell observed that myths contain truths that link people together, whether they live today or lived 2,500 years ago. Myths attempt to explain phenomena that human beings care about, regardless of when and where they live. It is not surprising, then, that myths frequently contain **archetypal images**—images that cut across cultural and racial boundaries and touch us at a very deep level. Many Greek myths illustrate this power. For example, when Orpheus descends into Hades to rescue his wife, Eurydice, he acts out the universal human desire to transcend death; and when Telemachus sets out in search of his father, Odysseus, he reminds readers that we are all lost children searching for parents. When Icarus ignores his father and flies too near the sun and when Pandora cannot resist looking into a box that she has been told not to open, we are reminded of the human weaknesses we all share.

When poets use myths, they are actually making allusions. They expect readers to bring to the poem the cultural, emotional, and ethical context of the myths to which they are alluding. At one time, when all educated individuals studied the Greek and Latin classics as well as the Bible and other religious texts, poets could safely assume that readers would recognize the mythological allusions they made. Today, many readers are unable to understand the full significance of an allusion or its application within a poem. Many of the poems in this anthology are accompanied by notes, but these may not provide all the information you will need to understand the full significance of each mythological allusion. For this reason, you may have to look elsewhere for answers, turning to dictionaries, encyclopedias, or online information sites such as *The World Encyclopedia of Mythology* <www.mythopedia.com>.

Sometimes a poet alludes to a myth in a title; sometimes references to various myths appear throughout a poem; at other times, an entire poem focuses on a single myth. In each case, as in the following poem, the use of myth helps to develop the poem's theme.

Countee Cullen (1903–1946)

Yet Do I Marvel (1925)

I doubt not God is good, well-meaning, kind,
And did He stoop to quibble could tell why
The little buried mole continues blind,
Why flesh that mirrors Him must some day die,
Make plain the reason tortured Tantalus
Is baited by the fickle fruit, declare
If merely brute caprice dooms Sisyphus
To struggle up a never-ending stair.
Inscrutable His ways are, and immune
To catechism by a mind too strewn
With petty cares to slightly understand
What awful brain compels His awful hand.
Yet do I marvel at this curious thing:
To make a poet black, and bid him sing!

Engraving of Tantalus reaching for fruit
Print Collector/Hulton Archieves/Getty Images

The speaker begins by affirming his belief in the benevolence of God but then questions why God engages in what appear to be capricious acts. As part of his catalog of questions, the speaker alludes to Tantalus and Sisyphus, two figures from Greek mythology. Tantalus was a king who was condemned to Hades for his crimes. There, he was forced to stand in a pool of water up to his chin. Overhead hung a tree branch laden with fruit. When Tantalus got thirsty and tried to drink, the level of the water dropped, and when he got hungry and reached for fruit, it moved just out of reach. Thus, Tantalus was doomed to be near what he most desired but forever unable to obtain it. Sisyphus also was condemned to Hades. For his disrespect of Zeus, he was sentenced to endless toil. Every day, Sisyphus pushed a boulder up a steep hill. Every time he neared the top, the boulder rolled back down the hill, and Sisyphus had to begin again. Like Tantalus, the speaker in "Yet Do I Marvel" cannot have what he wants; like Sisyphus, he is forced to toil in vain. He wonders why a well-meaning God would "make a poet black, and bid him sing" in a racist society that does not listen to his voice. Thus, the poet's two allusions to Greek mythology enrich the poem by connecting the suffering of the speaker as a Black poet to a universal drama that has been acted out again and again.

FURTHER READING: Myth

Bettmann/Getty Images

William Butler Yeats (1865–1939)

Leda and the Swan (1924)

A sudden blow: the great wings beating still
Above the staggering girl, her thighs caressed
By the dark webs, her nape caught in his bill,
He holds her helpless breast upon his breast.

How can those terrified vague fingers push
The feathered glory from her loosening thighs?
And how can body, laid in that white rush,
But feel the strange heart beating where it lies?

A shudder in the loins engenders there
The broken wall, the burning roof and tower
And Agamemnon dead.
Being so caught up,
So mastered by the brute blood of the air,
Did she put on his knowledge with his power
Before the indifferent beak could let her drop?

Peter Paul Rubens, *Leda and the Swan*, 1598
bpk, Berlin / Art Resource, NY

Reading and Reacting

1. According to the classic Greek myth, Zeus, in the form of a swan, impregnated a human woman, Leda, who as a result, gave birth to Helen of Troy. What is the significance of this event?

2. How is Leda portrayed? Why is the swan described as a "feathered glory" (line 6)? Why in the poem's last line is Leda dropped by his "indifferent beak"?
3. The third stanza refers to the Trojan War, which was indirectly caused by the event described in the poem. How does the allusion to the Trojan War help develop the theme of the poem?
4. **Journal Entry** Does the poem answer the question asked in its last two lines? Explain.
5. **Critical Perspective** According to Richard Ellmann, this poem deals with "transcendence of opposites." The bird's "rape of the human, the coupling of god and woman, the moment at which one epoch ended and another began ... in the act which included all these Yeats had the violent symbol for the transcendence of opposites which he needed."

   What opposite or contrary forces exist in the myth of Leda and the swan? Do you think the poem implies that these forces can be reconciled?

Related Works: "Greasy Lake" (p. 419), "Where Are You Going, Where Have You Been?" (p. 447), "The Second Coming" (p. 746)

Chronicle/Alamy Stock Photo

W. H. Auden (1907–1973)

Musée des Beaux Arts (1940)

About suffering they were never wrong,
The Old Masters: how well they understood
Its human position; how it takes place
While someone else is eating or opening a
  window or just walking dully along
How, when the aged are reverently, passionately
  waiting
For the miraculous birth, there always must be
Children who did not specially want it to
  happen, skating
On a pond at the edge of the wood:
They never forgot
That even the dreadful martyrdom must run its
  course
Anyhow in a corner, some untidy spot
Where the dogs go on with their doggy life
  and the torturer's horse
Scratches its innocent behind on a tree.
In Brueghel's *Icarus*, for instance: how everything
  turns away
Quite leisurely from the disaster; the ploughman may
Have heard the splash, the forsaken cry,

But for him it was not an important failure; the sun shone
As it had to on the white legs disappearing into the green
Water; and the expensive delicate ship that must have seen
Something amazing, a boy falling out of the sky,
Had somewhere to get to and sailed calmly on.

Bruegel, Pieter the Elder (1525–1569). *Landscape with the Fall of Icarus*
Dea/A. Dagli Ortti/De Agostini/Getty Images

Reading and Reacting

1. Reread the summary of the myth of Icarus on page 660. What does Auden's interpretation of this myth contribute to the poem?
2. What point does the poet make by referring to the "Old Masters" (line 2)?
3. **Journal Entry** Bruegel's painting *Landscape with the Fall of Icarus* is shown earlier. How does looking at this painting help you to understand the poem? To what specific details in the painting does the poet refer?

Related Works: "The Lottery" (p. 337), "One day I wrote her name upon the strand" (p. 554), "Shall I compare thee to a summer's day?" (p. 560), "Not Waving but Drowning" (p. 738), "The Second Coming" (p. 746)

Checklist Writing about Symbol, Allegory, Allusion, Myth

Symbol

- Are there any symbols in the poem? What leads you to believe they are symbols?
- Are these symbols conventional?

- Are they universal or archetypal?
- Are any symbols obscure or highly idiosyncratic?
- What is the literal meaning of each symbol in the context of the poem?
- Beyond its literal meaning, what else could each symbol suggest?
- How does your interpretation of each symbol enhance your understanding of the poem?

Allegory

- Is the poem an allegory?
- Are there any allegorical figures within the poem? How can you tell?
- What do the allegorical figures signify on a literal level?
- What lesson does the allegory illustrate?

Allusion

- Are there any allusions in the poem?
- Do you recognize the names, places, historical events, or literary works to which the poet alludes?
- In what way does each allusion deepen the poem's meaning? Does any allusion interfere with your understanding or enjoyment of the poem? If so, how?
- Would the poem be more effective without a particular allusion?

Myth

- What myths or mythological figures are alluded to?
- How does the poem use myth to convey its meaning?
- How faithful is the poem to the myth? Does the poet add material to the myth? Are any details from the original myth omitted? Is any information distorted? Why?

WRITING SUGGESTIONS: Symbol, Allegory, Allusion, Myth

1. Read "Aunt Jennifer's Tigers" (p. 598), and "Living in Sin" (p. 528) by Adrienne Rich. Then write an essay in which you discuss the similarities and differences in Rich's use of symbols in these poems.

2. Many popular songs make use of allusion. Choose one or two popular songs that you know well, and analyze their use of allusion, paying particular attention to whether the allusions expand the impact and meaning of the song or create barriers to listeners' understanding.
3. Read the Emily Dickinson poem "Because I could not stop for Death—" (p. 709), and then write an interpretation of the poem, identifying its allegorical figures.
4. What applications do the lessons of myth have for life today? Analyze a poem in which myth is central, and then discuss how you might use myth to make generalizations about your own life.

Chapter

25

Discovering Themes in Poetry

Joy Harjo

Paul Abdoo/Archive Photos/Getty Images

Robert Hayden

Oscar White/Corbis Historical/Getty Images

Edna St. Vincent Millay

Library of Congress Prints and Photographs Division[LC-USZ62-42479]

Learning Objectives

After reading this chapter, you will be able to. . .

- Define theme as it relates to poetry.
- Explain how form can suggest a poem's central theme.
- Identify the themes that are developed in a particular poem.
- Compare poems that develop similar themes.

Hulton Deutsch/Corbis Historical/Getty Images

Robert Herrick (1591–1674)

The Argument of His Book (1648)

I sing of brooks, of blossoms, birds, and bowers,
Of April, May, of June, and July-flowers;
I sing of May-poles, hock-carts, wassails, wakes,
Of bridegrooms, brides and of their bridal-cakes;
I write of youth, of love, and have access
By these to sing of cleanly wantonness;
I sing of dews, of rains, and piece by piece
Of balm, of oil, of spice and ambergris;
I sing of times trans-shifting, and I write
How roses first came red and lilies white;
I write of groves, of twilights, and I sing
The court of Mab,[1] and of the fairy king;
I write of Hell; I sing (and ever shall)
Of Heaven, and hope to have it after all.

Dance around Maypole
Hulton Archive/Getty Images

As the prior poem makes clear, a poem can be about anything, from the mysteries of the universe to poetry itself. Although no subject is really inappropriate for poetic treatment, certain conventional subjects—family, nature, love, war, death, the folly of human desires, and the inevitability of growing old—recur frequently.

[1] *Mab:* Queen of the fairies.

A poem's theme, however, is more than its subject. In general terms, *theme* refers to the ideas that the poet explores, the concerns that the poem examines. More specifically, a poem's **theme** is its main point or idea. Poems "about death," for example, may examine the difficulty of facing one's own mortality, eulogize a friend, assert the need for the acceptance of life's cycles, or cry out against death's inevitability. Such poems may also explore the **carpe diem** theme—the belief that life is brief, so we must "seize the day."

To understand the theme of a poem, readers should consider its form, voice, tone, language, images, allusions, and sound—all of its individual elements. Together, these elements communicate the ideas that are important in the poem. Keep in mind, however, that a poem may not mean the same thing to every reader. Different readers will bring different backgrounds, attitudes, and experiences to a poem and will therefore see things in various ways. Moreover, various poets may approach the same subject in drastically different ways, emphasizing different elements as they view the subject matter from their own unique perspectives. Ultimately, there are as many different themes, and ways to approach these themes, as there are writers (and readers) of poetry.

Poems about Parents

Although poets' individual experiences may be vastly different from the experiences of their readers, certain ideas seem universal in poems about parents. On the one hand, such poems can express positive sentiments: love, joy, wistfulness, nostalgia, and gratitude for childhood's happy memories and a parent's unconditional love. On the other hand, they may express negative emotions: detachment, frustration, resentment, regret, or even anger. When they write about parents, poets may create speakers who are emotionally engaged or distant, curious or apathetic, remorseful or grateful; they may idealize parents or attack them. Regardless of the particulars of the poem's specific theme, however, virtually all poems about parents address one basic concept: the influence parents have over their children.

For as long as poets have been writing poetry, their personal experiences (and childhoods) have influenced their subject matter and their poems. In American poetry, poems about parents became more common with the advent of **confessionalism**, a movement in the mid-1950s in which poets began to write subjective verse about their personal experiences. Poems in Robert Lowell's *Life Studies* and W. D. Snodgrass's *Heart's Needle* both addressed the positive and negative aspects of the poets' families (including their parents and children), thus opening the door for an influx of poems about similar themes. Poems by Sylvia Plath and Anne Sexton dealt with previously taboo subjects such as abortion, suicide, and mental illness. Though confessional poets often adapted or fictionalized their experiences when putting them into verse, the line between art and life could be thin: both Plath and Sexton died by suicide.

The poems in this section all deal with issues related to parents and family, but their styles, voices, and focuses are very different. Sometimes the speakers' voices express ambivalence, communicating conventional sentiments of love and admiration alongside perplexity, frustration, and even anger. This ambivalence is apparent in Theodore Roethke's "My Papa's Waltz" (p. 672) and Robert Hayden's "Those Winter Sundays" (p. 672) as adult speakers struggle to make peace with their parents' long-ago behavior. In Seamus Heaney's "Digging" (p. 673), the speaker is more positive, finding traits in his father (and grandfather) that he would like to emulate. Judith Ortiz Cofer's "My Father in the Navy: A Childhood Memory" (p. 674) is a meditation on a visual image of the speaker's father, and Mitsuye Yamada's "The Night Before Goodbye" (p. 674) considers a mother's quiet sacrifice. Finally, Andrew Hudgins's "Elegy for My Father, Who Is Not Dead" (p. 676) and Dylan Thomas's "Do not go gentle into that good night" (p. 676) examine the speakers' emotional reactions to the idea of their parents' deaths.

Bettmann/Getty Images

Theodore Roethke (1908–1963)

My Papa's Waltz (1948)

The whiskey on your breath
Could make a small boy dizzy;
But I hung on like death:
Such waltzing was not easy.

We romped until the pans
Slid from the kitchen shelf;
My mother's countenance
Could not unfrown itself.

The hand that held my wrist
Was battered on one knuckle;
At every step you missed
My right ear scraped a buckle.

You beat time on my head
With a palm caked hard by dirt,
Then waltzed me off to bed
Still clinging to your shirt.

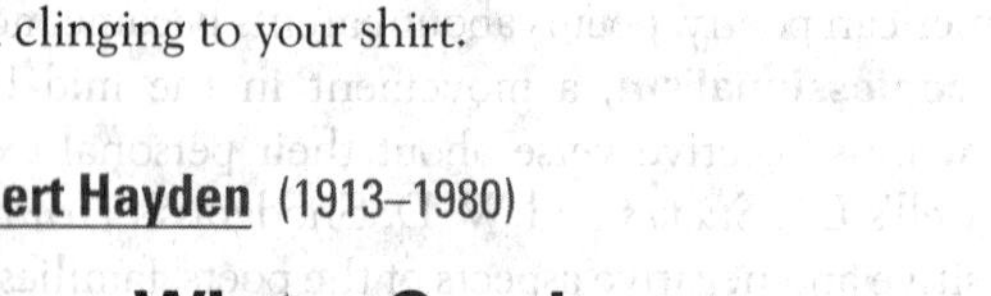

Oscar White/Corbis Historical/Getty Images

Robert Hayden (1913–1980)

Those Winter Sundays (1962)

Sundays too my father got up early
and put his clothes on in the blueblack cold,
then with cracked hands that ached
from labor in the weekday weather made

banked fires blaze. No one ever thanked him.
I'd wake and hear the cold splintering,
breaking.
When the rooms were warm, he'd call,
and slowly I would rise and dress,
fearing the chronic angers of that house,

Speaking indifferently to him,
who had driven out the cold
and polished my good shoes as well.
What did I know, what did I know
of love's austere and lonely offices?

Jeff Morgan 12/Alamy Stock Photo

Seamus Heaney (1939–2013)

Digging (1966)

Between my finger and my thumb
The squat pen rests; snug as a gun.

Under my window, a clean rasping sound
When the spade sinks into gravelly ground:
My father, digging. I look down

Till his straining rump among the flowerbeds
Bends low, comes up twenty years away
Stooping in rhythm through potato drills
Where he was digging.

The coarse boot nestled on the lug, the shaft
Against the inside knee was levered firmly.
He rooted out tall tops, buried the bright edge deep
To scatter new potatoes that we picked
Loving their cool hardness in our hands.

By God, the old man could handle a spade.
Just like his old man.

My grandfather cut more turf in a day
Than any other man on Toner's bog.
Once I carried him milk in a bottle
Corked sloppily with paper. He straightened up
To drink it, then fell to right away

Nicking and slicing neatly, heaving sods
Over his shoulder, going down and down
For the good turf. Digging.

The cold smell of potato mould, the squelch and slap
Of soggy peat, the curt cuts of an edge
Through living roots awaken in my head.
But I've no spade to follow men like them.

Between my finger and my thumb
The squat pen rests.
I'll dig with it.

Judith Ortiz Cofer (1952–2016)

My Father in the Navy: A Childhood Memory (1982)

Stiff and immaculate
in the white cloth of his uniform
and a round cap on his head like a halo,
he was an apparition on leave from a shadow-world
and only flesh and blood when he rose from below
the waterline where he kept watch over the engines
and dials making sure the ship parted the waters
on a straight course.
Mother, brother and I kept vigil
on the nights and dawns of his arrivals,
watching the corner beyond the neon sign of a quasar
for the flash of white our father like an angel
heralding a new day.
His homecomings were the verses
we composed over the years making up
the siren's song that kept him coming back
from the bellies of iron whales
and into our nights
like the evening prayer.

Mitsuye Yamada (1923–)

The Night Before Goodbye (1976)

Mama is mending
my underwear
while my brothers sleep.
Her husband taken away by the FBI
one son lured away by the Army

now another son and daughter
lusting for the free world outside.
She must let go.
The war goes on.
She will take one still small son
and join Papa in internment[1]
to make a family.
Still sewing
squinting in the dim light
in room C barrack 4 block 4
she whispers
Remember
keep your underwear
in good repair
in case of accident
don't bring shame
on us.

Manzanar Relocation Center, 1943
Library of Congress Prints and Photographs Division[LC-DIG-ppprs-00284]

[1] *internment:* Shortly after the attack on Pearl Harbor, President Roosevelt ordered that all people of Japanese ancestry—even American citizens—be removed from the West Coast. About 112,000 people were relocated to "internment camps," where they remained until after the war's end.

Andrew Hudgins (1951–)

Elegy for My Father, Who Is Not Dead (1987)

One day I'll lift the telephone
and be told my father's dead. He's ready.
In the sureness of his faith, he talks
about the world beyond this world
as though his reservations have
been made. I think he wants to go,
a little bit – a new desire
to travel building up, an itch
to see fresh worlds. Or older ones.
He thinks that when I follow him
he'll wrap me in his arms and laugh,
they way he did when I arrived
on earth. I do not think he's right.
He's ready. I am not. I can't
just say goodbye as cheerfully
as if he were embarking on a trip
to make my later trip go well.
I see myself on deck, convinced
his ship's gone down, while he's convinced
I'll see him standing on the dock
and waving, shouting, Welcome back.

AP Images

Dylan Thomas (1914–1953)

Do not go gentle into that good night* (1952)

Do not go gentle into that good night,
Old age should burn and rave at close of day;
Rage, rage against the dying of the light.

Though wise men at their end know dark is right,
Because their words had forked no lightning they
Do not go gentle into that good night.

Good men, the last wave by, crying how bright
Their frail deeds might have danced in a green bay,
Rage, rage against the dying of the light.

*This poem was written during the last illness of the poet's father.

Wild men who caught and sang the sun in flight,
And learn, too late, they grieved it on its way,
Do not go gentle into that good night.

Grave men, near death, who see with blinding sight
Blind eyes could blaze like meteors and be gay,
Rage, rage against the dying of the light.

And you, my father, there on the sad height,
Curse, bless, me now with your fierce tears, I pray,
Do not go gentle into that good night.
Rage, rage against the dying of the light.

Reading and Reacting: Poems about Parents

1. What is each speaker's attitude toward the parent who is the poem's focus?
2. Which words, images, and figures of speech in each poem have positive associations? Which create a negative impression?
3. How would you characterize each poem's tone? For example, is the tone sentimental? playful? angry? resentful? regretful? admiring?
4. What conflicts are explored in each poem?
5. What does each poem say about the parent? What does each poem reveal about the child?
6. What is each poem's central theme?

Related Works: "I Stand Here Ironing" (p. 227), "Two Kinds" (p. 471), "Daddy" (p. 571), *All My Sons* (p. 891), *The Glass Menagerie* (p. 958), *Fences* (p. 1222)

Poems about Nature

In his 1913 poem "Trees," the American poet Joyce Kilmer neatly summarized the symbiotic relationship that exists between poetry and nature: "I think that I shall never see / A poem lovely as a tree." Poets have always found inspiration in the beauty, majesty, and grandeur of the natural world; in fact, some forms of poetry are dedicated solely to the subject of nature. For example, a **pastoral** is a literary form that deals nostalgically with a simple rural life. Many of the early Greek and Roman pastorals were about shepherds who passed the time writing about love while watching their flocks. In these poems, the shepherd's life is idealized; thus, the pastoral tradition celebrates simple times and the beauty of the rural life. Similarly, an **idyll**, a short work in verse or prose (or a painting or a piece of music), depicts simple pastoral or rural scenes, often in idealized terms.

Some literary movements also focused on the subject of nature. For the **romantic poets**, nature was a source of inspiration, authenticity, and spiritual refreshment, qualities they by and large saw as lacking in the lives of Europeans—both the educated classes and those working in the mills and factories that came with industrialization. Later, the American **transcendentalists**, including Ralph Waldo Emerson and Henry David Thoreau, examined the relationships between philosophy, religion, and nature. In *Walden*, for example, Thoreau wrote about the pleasures and rewards of withdrawing from mainstream life to live a simple life in the woods.

Although all poems about nature deal with the same general subject, their approaches and focuses can differ greatly. Poems "about nature" may focus on the seasons, the weather, mountains or the sea, birds or animals, or trees and flowers. They may praise the beauty of nature, assert the superiority of its simplest creatures, consider nature's evanescence, or mourn its destruction. In this section, romantic poet William Wordsworth's "I wandered lonely as a cloud" extols the virtue of nature and the value of immersing oneself in its beauty, while in "The Windhover" (p. 679), Gerard Manley Hopkins celebrates the divinity of God's natural kingdom, and in "Loveliest of Trees" (p. 680), A. E. Housman's speaker acknowledges the importance of appreciating nature's simple beauty while he still has time. Some poems about nature focus on a single image. For example, in Carl Sandburg's "Fog" (p. 680), the speaker focuses on the image of fog hanging over the city. Other nature poems convey the pull of memory, as in Robert Frost's "Birches" (p. 680), where the speaker recalls the childhood pleasure of climbing trees and longs for the simplicity of those times. Finally, other poems, particularly those by contemporary poets, expose the fragility of nature and warn of the approaching destruction of the natural world, as Joy Harjo's "Invisible Fish" (p. 682) does.

Georgios Kollidas/Alamy Stock Photo

William Wordsworth (1770–1850)

I wandered lonely as a cloud (1807)

I wandered lonely as a cloud
    That floats on high o'er vales and hills,
When all at once I saw a crowd,
    A host, of golden daffodils,
Beside the lake, beneath the trees,
Fluttering and dancing in the breeze.

Continuous as the stars that shine
    And twinkle on the milky way,
They stretched in never-ending line
    Along the margin of a bay:
Ten thousand saw I at a glance,
Tossing their heads in sprightly dance.

The waves beside them danced; but they
    Out-did the sparkling waves in glee;

A poet could not but be gay,
In such a jocund company;
I gazed—and gazed—but little thought
What wealth the show to me had brought:

For oft, when on my couch I lie
In vacant or in pensive mood,
They flash upon that inward eye
Which is the bliss of solitude;
And then my heart with pleasure fills,
And dances with the daffodils.

Photo 12/Alamy Stock Photo

Gerard Manley Hopkins (1844–1889)

The Windhover[1] (1877)

To Christ Our Lord

I caught this morning morning's minion,[2] kingdom
of daylight's dauphin, dapple-dawn-drawn
Falcon, in his riding
Of the rolling level underneath him steady air,
and striding
High there, how he rung upon the rein[3] of a
wimpling[4] wing
In his ecstasy! then off, off forth on swing,
As a skate's heel sweeps smooth on a bow-bend:
the hurl and gliding
Rebuffed the big wind. My heart in hiding
Stirred for a bird,—the achieve of, the mastery of
the thing!

Brute beauty and valor and act, oh, air, pride,
plume, here
Buckle! and the fire that breaks from thee
then, a billion
Times told lovelier, more dangerous, O my chevalier!

No wonder of it: shéer plód, makes plow down
sillion[5]
Shine, and blue-bleak embers, ah my dear,
Fall, gall themselves, and gash gold-vermilion.

---

[1] *Windhover:* A kestrel, a European falcon able to hover in the air with its head to the wind.
[2] *minion:* Favorite.
[3] *rung upon the rein:* A horse is "rung upon the rein" when it circles at the end of a long rein held by a trainer.
[4] *wimpling:* Rippling.
[5] *sillion:* The ridge between two furrows.

A. E. Housman (1859–1936)

Loveliest of Trees (1896)

Loveliest of trees, the cherry now
Is hung with bloom along the bough,
And stands about the woodland ride
Wearing white for Eastertide.

Now, of my threescore years and ten,
Twenty will not come again,
And take from seventy springs a score,
It only leaves me fifty more.

And since to look at things in bloom
Fifty springs are little room,
About the woodlands I will go
To see the cherry hung with snow.

Carl Sandburg (1878–1967)

Fog (1961)

The fog comes
on little cat feet.

It sits looking
over harbor and city
on silent haunches
and then moves on.

Bettmann/Getty Images

Robert Frost (1874–1963)

Birches (1915)

When I see birches bend to left and right
Across the lines of straighter darker trees,
I like to think some boy's been swinging them.
But swinging doesn't bend them down to stay
As ice-storms do. Often you must have seen them
Loaded with ice a sunny winter morning
After a rain. They click upon themselves
As the breeze rises, and turn many-colored
As the stir cracks and crazes their enamel.
Soon the sun's warmth makes them shed crystal shells

Shattering and avalanching on the snow-crust—
Such heaps of broken glass to sweep away
You'd think the inner dome of heaven had fallen.
They are dragged to the withered bracken by the load,
And they seem not to break; though once they are bowed
So low for long, they never right themselves:
You may see their trunks arching in the woods
Years afterwards, trailing their leaves on the ground
Like girls on hands and knees that throw their hair
Before them over their heads to dry in the sun.
But I was going to say when Truth broke in
With all her matter-of-fact about the ice-storm
I should prefer to have some boy bend them
As he went out and in to fetch the cows—
Some boy too far from town to learn baseball,
Whose only play was what he found himself,
Summer or winter, and could play alone.
One by one he subdued his father's trees
By riding them down over and over again
Until he took the stiffness out of them,
And not one but hung limp, not one was left
For him to conquer. He learned all there was
To learn about not launching out too soon
And so not carrying the tree away
Clear to the ground. He always kept his poise
To the top branches, climbing carefully
With the same pains you use to fill a cup
Up to the brim, and even above the brim.
Then he flung outward, feet first, with a swish,
Kicking his way down through the air to the ground.
So was I once myself a swinger of birches.
And so I dream of going back to be.
It's when I'm weary of considerations,
And life is too much like a pathless wood
Where your face burns and tickles with the cobwebs
Broken across it, and one eye is weeping
From a twig's having lashed across it open.
I'd like to get away from earth awhile
And then come back to it and begin over.
May no fate willfully misunderstand me
And half grant what I wish and snatch me away
Not to return. Earth's the right place for love:
I don't know where it's likely to go better.

I'd like to go by climbing a birch tree,
And climb black branches up a snow-white trunk
Toward Heaven, till the tree could bear no more,
But dipped its top and set me down again.
That would be good both going and coming back.
One could do worse than be a swinger of birches.

Joy Harjo (1951–)

Invisible Fish (1989)

Invisible fish swim this ghost ocean now described by waves of sand, by water-worn rock. Soon the fish will learn to walk. Then humans will come ashore and paint dreams on the dying stone. Then later, much later, the ocean floor will be punctuated by Chevy trucks, carrying the dreamers' descendants, who are going to the store.

Reading and Reacting: Poems about Nature

1. What aspect of nature does the poem focus on?
2. What is the speaker's attitude toward nature? For example, is nature seen as a benevolent, comforting, threatening, awe-inspiring, or overwhelming force?
3. Which words, images, and figures of speech in the poem have positive associations? Which create a negative impression of nature?
4. How would you characterize each poem's tone? For example, is the speaker hopeful? thoughtful? humbled? frightened?
5. Is the natural world the poem's true subject or is it just the poem's setting? Explain.
6. What is each poem's central theme?

Related Works: "Doe Season" (p. 378), "Greasy Lake" (p. 419), "Nothing Gold Can Stay" (p. 553), "Four Haiku" (p. 633)

Poems about Love

Since the earliest times, romantic love has been one of the great themes of poetry. In the European tradition, Sappho, whose works exist today largely in fragments, is one of the early classic Greek poets. Even more influential, in part because most of their works survived over time, were the Romans Catullus and Ovid. Although the Bible may strike some as an unlikely place to find love poetry, the *Song of Songs* is just that (although it is also commonly interpreted as an allegory of the love between God and his people). In *La Vita Nuova*

(*The New Life*), Dante wrote about the life-changing effect of his meeting with Beatrice, a beautiful young woman who was to die young. It is this same Beatrice with whose help Dante embarks on his journey from Hell to Heaven in *The Divine Comedy*.

Love has played an equally important part in English poetry. During the Middle Ages, poems such as *Sir Gawain and the Green Knight* and *Le Morte d'Arthur* employed the conventions of "courtly love," in which a protagonist performs gallant deeds to win the hand of a fair maiden. Examples of Renaissance love poems include many of the sonnets of William Shakespeare and Edmund Spenser as well as Christopher Marlowe's "The Passionate Shepherd to His Love" (p. 730), which was answered by Sir Walter Raleigh's "The Nymph's Reply to the Shepherd" (p. 734).

Although the Renaissance may arguably be considered the high point of love poetry in English, the tradition has continued to the present day. Increased opportunities for women to read, write, and publish poetry have brought new perspectives to what was once a male-dominated field. **Confessional poetry** has allowed a more direct, frank discussion of love. And, of course, love songs today are as much in fashion as they were in the time of Shakespeare, Dante, or Sappho—and heard by more people than ever.

In each of the poems in this section, the poets address the subject of love in their own unique ways. Husband and wife Robert Browning and Elizabeth Barrett Browning are represented by the traditional love poems "Meeting at Night" (p. 683), "Parting at Morning" (p. 684), and "How Do I Love Thee?" (p. 684), which is one of the most frequently quoted poems in the English language.

In Edna St. Vincent Millay's "What lips my lips have kissed" (p. 684), the speaker reminisces about her past lovers with a mixture of nostalgia and wistfulness, and the speaker in Jehanne Dubrow's "Before the Deployment" (p. 685) relives her soldier–lover's departure. On a lighter note, Leigh Hunt's "Jenny Kissed Me" (p. 685) expresses the joy a kiss can bring, and Dorothy Parker's "General Review of the Sex Situation" (p. 686) is a tongue-in-cheek comment on the perceived differences between women and men.

Robert Browning (1812–1889)

Meeting at Night (1845)

The gray sea and the long black land;
And the yellow half-moon large and low;
And the startled little waves that leap
In fiery ringlets from their sleep,
As I gain the cove with pushing prow,
And quench its speed i' the slushy sand.

Then a mile of warm sea-scented beach;
Three fields to cross till a farm appears;
A tap at the pane, the quick sharp scratch
And blue spurt of a lighted match,
And a voice less loud, through its joys and fears,
Than the two hearts beating each to each!

Parting at Morning (1845)

Round the cape of a sudden came the sea,
And the sun looked over the mountain's rim:
And straight was a path of gold for him,
And the need of a world of men for me.

Elizabeth Barrett Browning (1806–1861)

How Do I Love Thee? (1850)

How do I love thee? Let me count the ways.
I love thee to the depth and breadth and height
My soul can reach, when feeling out of sight
For the ends of being and ideal grace.
I love thee to the level of every day's
Most quiet need, by sun and candle-light.
I love thee freely, as men strive for right.
I love thee purely, as they turn from praise.
I love thee with the passion put to use
In my old griefs, and with my childhood's faith.
I love thee with a love I seemed to lose
With my lost saints. I love thee with the breath,
Smiles, tears, of all my life; and, if God choose,
I shall but love thee better after death.

Library of Congress Prints and Photographs Division[LC-USZ62-42479]

Edna St. Vincent Millay (1892–1950)

What lips my lips have kissed (1923)

What lips my lips have kissed, and where, and why,
I have forgotten, and what arms have lain
Under my head till morning; but the rain
Is full of ghosts tonight, that tap and sigh
Upon the glass and listen for reply,

And in my heart there stirs a quiet pain
For unremembered lads that not again
Will turn to me at midnight with a cry.
Thus in the winter stands the lonely tree,
Nor knows what birds have vanished one by one,
Yet knows its boughs more silent than before:
I cannot say what loves have come and gone,
I only know that summer sang in me
A little while, that in me sings no more.

Jehanne Dubrow (1975–)

Before the Deployment (2010)

He kisses me before he goes. While I,
still dozing, half-asleep, laugh and rub my face

against the sueded surface of the sheets,
thinking it's him I touch, his skin beneath

my hands, my body curving in to meet
his body there. I never hear him leave.

But I believe he shuts the bedroom door,
as though unsure if he should change his mind,

pull off his boots, crawl beneath the blankets
left behind, his hand a heat against my breast,

our heart rates slowing into rest. Perhaps
all good-byes should whisper like a piece of silk—

and then the quick surprise of waking, alone
except for the citrus ghost of his cologne.

Leigh Hunt (1784–1859)

Jenny Kissed Me (1838)

Jenny kissed me when we met,
Jumping from the chair she sat in.
Time, you thief! who love to get
Sweets into your list, put that in.
Say I'm weary, say I'm sad;
Say that health and wealth have missed me;
Say I'm growing old, but add—
Jenny kissed me!

Dorothy Parker (1893–1967)

General Review of the Sex Situation (1933)

Woman wants monogamy;
Man delights in novelty.
Love is woman's moon and sun;
Man has other forms of fun.

Woman lives but in her lord;
Count to ten, and man is bored.
With this the gist and sum of it,
What earthly good can come of it?

Reading and Reacting: Poems about Love

1. What general ideas about love are expressed in each poem?
2. What conventional images and figures of speech are used to express feelings of love?
3. Does any poem include any unexpected (or even shocking) images or figures of speech?
4. How would you characterize the tone of each poem? For example, is the tone happy? sad? celebratory? regretful? ambivalent?
5. What does each poem reveal about the speaker? about the person to whom the poem is addressed?
6. What is each poem's central theme?

Related Works: "Hills Like White Elephants" (p. 101), "The Storm" (p. 216), "Living in Sin" (p. 528), "My mistress' eyes are nothing like the sun" (p. 557), "Shall I compare thee to a summer's day?" (p. 560), "A Valediction: Forbidding Mourning" (p. 568), "To My Dear and Loving Husband" (p. 575), *The Brute* (p. 769)

Poems about War

In poetry, war is as ancient a theme as love and nature. In fact, the earliest poems, including Homer's *Iliad* and *Odyssey* and Virgil's *Aeneid*, have at their centers epic battles and struggles. These poems were created in metered verse so they could be remembered and passed down from one generation to the next. Portions of them would be recited at public gatherings and festivals, making them analogous to today's war movies. Epic poems reflected the belief that war could be a noble and glorious endeavor, and they often glorified the heroes of the wars and battles they described. Even in the earliest of these poems, however, there is a sense of the futility and devastation that war brings with it; for example, in the *Iliad*, many of the Greeks laying siege to the city of Troy are sick of the war and want to go home. In the *Aeneid*, the scene where Aeneas witnesses the destruction of his native Troy by the Greeks, and by the gods aiding them, is one of the most moving in literature.

In modern times, poets have tended to concentrate on the horrors of war, no doubt in part because technology has allowed armies to do more damage more quickly than ever before. World War I, which saw the first widespread use of aircraft, poison gas, and machine guns in warfare, marked a turning point in war and in poetic responses to it. One of the best-known poems to come out of that war is "Dulce et Decorum Est" (p. 687), written toward the end of the war by Wilfred Owen, a soldier who was killed on the Western Front in 1918. The poem, which was not published until after Owen's death, includes graphic images and ends with a bitterly ironic quotation that summarizes the mentality that fuels war: "It is sweet and fitting to die for one's country." In "Atrocities" (p. 688), Siegfried Sassoon, a contemporary of Owen's, offers a similarly cynical look at war (and warriors).

Of course, not all poems about war are poems of protest. For example, "The Soldier," by Rupert Brooke (p. 689), a contemporary of both Owen's and Sassoon's, celebrates the nobility of fighting for the sake of one's beloved country.

Unlike these poems, modern poems about war do not always focus on soldiers. For example, W. H. Auden's poem from "In Time of War" (p. 689) examines the evils of the Nanking Massacre and the Dachau concentration camp.

In the post–World War II years, enemies were not as clearly defined as they had been in the past. The war in Vietnam unfolded before the American people on their television screens, and, as a result, many Americans (including American soldiers) came to question the war and its goals. This attempt to come to terms with the war and its aftermath carried over into poems about that war, as seen in Yusef Komunyakaa's "Facing It" (p. 690), in which a Vietnam veteran visits the Vietnam War Memorial in Washington D.C.

The post-Vietnam years have seen troops from various nations take part in conflicts around the globe—conflicts whose costs have been high and whose goals have not always been as clear-cut as they were in past conflicts. Writing about the Iraq war in "Mosul" (p. 690), David Hernandez focuses on setting, considering the physical realities of war, and in "All Things Not Considered" (p. 691), Naomi Shihab Nye writes about the civilian victims of the continuing Israeli-Palestinian conflict. Finally, Wislawa Szymborska's "The End and the Beginning" (p. 693) addresses the problem of cleaning up the damage left behind.

Wilfred Owen (1893–1918)

Dulce et Decorum Est[1] (1920)

Bent double, like old beggars under sacks,
Knock-kneed, coughing like hags, we cursed through sludge,

---

[1] *Dulce et Decorum Est:* The title and last two lines are from Horace, *Odes* 3.2: "Sweet and fitting it is to die for one's country."

Till on the haunting flares we turned our backs
And towards our distant rest began to trudge.
Men marched asleep. Many had lost their boots
But limped on, blood-shod. All went lame; all blind;
Drunk with fatigue; deaf even to the hoots
Of tired, outstripped Five-Nines[2] that dropped behind.

Gas! GAS Quick, boys!—An ecstasy of fumbling,
Fitting the clumsy helmets just in time;
But someone still was yelling out and stumbling
And flound'ring like a man in fire or lime . . .
Dim, through the misty panes and thick green light,
As under a green sea, I saw him drowning.
In all my dreams, before my helpless sight,
He plunges at me, guttering, choking, drowning.
If in some smothering dreams you too could pace
Behind the wagon that we flung him in,
And watch the white eyes writhing in his face,
His hanging face, like a devil's sick of sin;
If you could hear, at every jolt, the blood
Come gargling from the froth-corrupted lungs,
Obscene as cancer, bitter as the cud
Of vile, incurable sores on innocent tongues,—
My friend, you would not tell with such high zest
To children ardent for some desperate glory,
The old Lie: Dulce et decorum est
Pro patria mori.

Siegfried Sassoon (1886–1967)

Atrocities (1919)

You told me, in your drunken-boasting mood,
How once you butchered prisoners. That was good!
I'm sure you felt no pity while they stood
Patient and cowed and scared, as prisoners should.

How did you do them in? Come, don't be shy:
You know I love to hear how Germans die,
Downstairs in dug-outs. 'Camerad! they cry;
Then squeal like stoats when bombs begin to fly.

And you? I know your record. You went sick
When orders looked unwholesome: then, with trick
And lie, you wangled home. And here you are,
Still talking big and boozing in a bar.

[2]*Five-Nines:* Shells that explode on impact and release poison gas.

British soldier, WWI

Science & Society Picture Library/Getty Images

Rupert Brooke (1887–1915)

The Soldier (1915)

If I should die, think only this of me;
That there's some corner of a foreign field
That is forever England. There shall be
In that rich earth a richer dust concealed;
A dust whom England bore, shaped, made aware,
Gave, once, her flowers to love, her ways to roam,
A body of England's breathing English air,
Washed by the rivers, blest by suns of home.

And think, this heart, all evil shed away,
A pulse in the eternal mind, no less
Gives somewhere back the thoughts by England given;
Her sights and sounds; dreams happy as her day;
And laughter, learnt of friends; and gentleness,
In hearts at peace, under an English heaven.

W. H. Auden (1907–1973)

from "In Time of War" (1939)

XVI

Here war is simple like a monument:
A telephone is speaking to a man;
Flags on a map assert that troops were sent;
A boy brings milk in bowls. There is a plan

For living men in terror of their lives,
Who thirst at nine who were to thirst at noon,
And can be lost and are, and miss their wives,
And, unlike an idea, can die too soon.

But ideas can be true although men die,
And we can watch a thousand faces
Made active by one lie:

And maps can really point to places
Where life is evil now:
Nanking[1] Dachau.[2]

[1] *Nanking:* A city in China where, in 1937, massacres and rapes were committed on a massive scale by the Japanese Imperial Army.

[2] *Dachau:* A concentration camp in Germany, opened in 1933 and liberated by American forces in 1945.

Yusef Komunyakaa (1947–)

Facing It (1988)

My black face fades,
hiding inside the black granite.
I said I wouldn't,
dammit: No tears.
I'm stone. I'm flesh.
My clouded reflection eyes me
like a bird of prey, the profile of night
slanted against morning. I turn
this way—the stone lets me go.
I turn that way—I'm inside
the Vietnam Veterans Memorial
again, depending on the light
to make a difference.
I go down the 58,022 names,
half-expecting to find
my own in letters like smoke.
I touch the name Andrew Johnson;
I see the booby trap's white flash.
Names shimmer on a woman's blouse
but when she walks away
the names stay on the wall.
Brushstrokes flash, a red bird's
wings cutting across my stare.
The sky. A plane in the sky.
A white vet's image floats
closer to me, then his pale eyes
look through mine. I'm a window.
He's lost his right arm
inside the stone. In the black mirror
a woman's trying to erase names:
No, she's brushing a boy's hair.

Hand tracing names of the dead on the Vietnam War Memorial.
AP Images/Dennis Cook

David Hernandez (1971–)

Mosul[1] (2011)

The donkey. The donkey pulling the cart.
The caravan of dust. The cart made of plywood,
of crossbeam and junkyard tires. The donkey

[1] *Mosul:* The second largest city in Iraq.

made of donkey. The long face. The long ears.
The curled lashes. The obsidian eyes blinking
in the dust. The cart rolling, cracking the knuckles
of pebbles. The dust. The blanket over the cart.
The hidden mortar shells. The veins of wires.
The remote device. The red light. The donkey
trotting. The blue sky. The rolling cart. The dust
smudging the blue sky. The silent bell of the sun.
The Humvee. The soldiers. The dust-colored
uniforms. The boy from Montgomery, the boy
from Little Falls. The donkey cart approaching.
The dust. The laughter on their lips. The dust
on their lips. The moment before the moment.
The shockwave. The dust. The dust. The dust.

Naomi Shihab Nye (1952–)

All Things Not Considered*

You cannot stitch the breath
back into this boy.

A brother and sister were playing with toys
when their room exploded.

In what language
is this holy?

The Jewish boys killed in the cave
were skipping school, having an adventure.

Asel Asleh, Palestinian, age 17, believed in the field
beyond right and wrong where people came together

to talk. He kneeled to help someone else
stand up before he was shot.

If this is holy,
could we have some new religions please?

Mohammed al-Durra huddled against his father
in the street, terrified. The whole world saw him die.

An Arab father on crutches burying his 4 month girl weeps,
"I spit in the face of this ugly world."

*

*Publication date not available.

Most of us would take our children over land.
We would walk in the fields forever homeless
with our children,
huddle under cliffs, eat crumbs and berries,
to keep our children.
This is what we say from a distance
because we can say whatever we want.

*

No one was right.
Everyone was wrong.
What if they'd get together
and say that?
At a certain point
the flawed narrator wins.

People made mistakes for decades.
Everyone hurt in similar ways
at different times.
Some picked up guns because guns were given.
If they were holy it was okay to use guns.
Some picked up stones because they had them.
They had millions of them.
They might have picked up turnip roots
or olive pits.
Picking up things to throw and shoot:
at the same time people were studying history,
going to school.

*

The curl of a baby's graceful ear.
The calm of a bucket

waiting for water.
Orchards of the old Arab men

who knew each tree.
Jewish and Arab women

standing silently together.
Generations of black.

Are people the only holy land?

Alberto Cristofari A3/Contrasto/Redux

Wislawa Szymborska (1923–2012)

The End and the Beginning (1993)

After every war
someone has to clean up.
Things won't
straighten themselves up, after all.

Someone has to push the rubble
to the side of the road.
so the corpse-filled wagons
can pass.

Someone has to get mired
in scum and ashes,
sofa springs,
splintered glass,
and bloody rags.

Someone has to drag in a girder
to prop up a wall,
Someone has to glaze a window,
rehang a door.

Photogenic it's not,
and takes years.
All the cameras have left
for another war.

We'll need the bridges back,
and new railway stations.
Sleeves will go ragged
from rolling them up.
Someone, broom in hand,
still recalls the way it was.

Someone else listens
and nods with unsevered head.
But already there are those nearby
starting to mill about
who will find it dull.

From out of the bushes
sometimes someone still unearths
rusted-out arguments
and carries them to the garbage pile.

Those who knew
what was going on here
must make way for
those who know little.
And less than little.
And finally as little as nothing.

In the grass that has overgrown
causes and effects,
someone must be stretched out
blade of grass in his mouth
gazing at the clouds.

Reading and Reacting: Poems about War

1. What is each speaker's attitude toward war? Does the speaker seem to be focusing on a particular war or on war in general?
2. What conventional images and figures of speech does each poem use to express its ideas about war?
3. Do any of the poems use unusual, unexpected, or shocking images or figures of speech?
4. How would you describe each poem's tone? For example, is the tone angry? cynical? sad? disillusioned? resigned?
5. How does each poem's form help to communicate the speaker's attitude toward war?
6. What is each poem's central theme?

Related Works: "The Man He Killed" (p. 505), "Patterns" (p. 506), "The Death of the Ball Turret Gunner" (p. 567)

WRITING SUGGESTIONS: Discovering Themes in Poetry

1. Compare any two poems in this chapter about parents, nature, love, or war. Or, identify some poems in this book that focus on the subject of work and compare two of those poems.
2. Write an **explication** of one of the poems in this chapter.
3. Write an essay in which you compare one of the poems in this chapter to a short story or play on the same general subject. (For possible topics, consult the Related Works list that follows each group of poems.)

4. Some poets write multiple poems on the same general subject. For example, Shakespeare wrote many love poems, and Robert Frost wrote a number of poems about nature. Choose two poems by a single poet that explore the same subject, and compare and contrast the two poems' treatment of this subject.
5. A number of poems in this book focus on the theme of poetry itself. Choose three poems that explore this theme and write an essay that compares the poems' ideas about reading and writing poetry.

Chapter 26

Poetry for Further Reading

Wallace Stevens
AP Images/Hartford Courant

Louise Erdrich
Agence Opale/Alamy Stock Photo

Edwin Arlington Robinson
Bettmann/Getty Images

James Emanuel
The New York Times

Anonymous

Bonny Barbara Allan

(Traditional Scottish ballad)

It was in and about the Martinmas[1] time,
When the green leaves were afalling,
That Sir John Graeme, in the West Country,

[1] *Martinmas:* Saint Martin's Day, November 11.

Fell in love with Barbara Allan.
He sent his men down through the town,
To the place where she was dwelling;
"O haste and come to my master dear,
Gin[2] ye be Barbara Allan."

O hooly,[3] hooly rose she up,
To the place where he was lying,
And when she drew the curtain by:
"Young man, I think you're dying."

"O it's I'm sick, and very, very sick,
And 'tis a' for Barbara Allan."—
"O the better for me ye's never be,
Tho your heart's blood were aspilling.

"O dinna ye mind,[4] young man," said she,
"When ye was in the tavern adrinking,
That ye made the health gae round and round,
And slighted Barbara Allan?"

He turned his face unto the wall,
And death was with him dealing:
"Adieu, adieu, my dear friends all,
And be kind to Barbara Allan."

And slowly, slowly raise she up,
And slowly, slowly left him,
And sighing said she could not stay,
Since death of life had reft him.

She had not gane a mile but twa,[5]
When she heard the dead-bell ringing,
And every jow[6] that the dead-bell geid,
It cried, "Woe to Barbara Allan!"

"O mother, mother, make my bed!
O make it saft and narrow!
Since my love died for me today,
I'll die for him tomorrow."

---

[2] *Gin:* If.
[3] *hooly:* Slowly.
[4] *O dinna ye mind:* Don't you remember?
[5] *twa:* Two.
[6] *jow:* Stroke.

Anonymous

Go Down, Moses*

Go down, Moses,
Way down in Egypt's land
Tell old Pharaoh
To let my people go.

When Israel was in Egypt's land
Let my people go
Oppressed so hard they could not stand
Let my people go.

Go down, Moses,
Way down in Egyptland
Tell old Pharaoh
"Let my people go."

"Thus saith the Lord," bold Moses said,
"Let my people go;
If not I'll smite your first-born dead
Let my people go.

"No more shall they in bondage toil,
Let my people go;
Let them come out with Egypt's spoil,
Let my people go."

The Lord told Moses what to do
Let my people go;
To lead the children of Israel through,
Let my people go.

Go down, Moses,
Way down in Egyptland,
Tell old Pharaoh,
"Let my people go!"

*Music, especially religious songs, or "spirituals," was one of the few means of expression permitted for slaves. Many of these spirituals contained coded messages conveying antislavery sentiments or even directions on how to use the Underground Railroad. For example, the spiritual "Wade in the Water" seemed, on the surface, to be about crossing the River Jordan to reach the Promised Land. But its lyrics contained vital information, including the idea that crossing streams was a good way for runaway slaves to cover their scent and thus to lose the bloodhounds used to track them.

Matthew Arnold (1822–1888)

Dover Beach (1867)

The sea is calm tonight.
The tide is full, the moon lies fair
Upon the straits;—on the French coast the light
Gleams and is gone; the cliffs of England stand,
Glimmering and vast, out in the tranquil bay.
Come to the window, sweet is the night-air!
Only, from the long line of spray
Where the sea meets the moon-blanched[1] land,
Listen! you hear the grating roar
Of pebbles which the waves draw back, and fling,
At their return, up the high strand,[2]
Begin, and cease, and then again begin,
With tremulous cadence slow, and bring
The eternal note of sadness in.

Sophocles[3] long ago
Heard it on the Aegean,[4] and it brought
Into his mind the turbid ebb and flow
Of human misery; we
Find also in the sound a thought,
Hearing it by this distant northern sea.

The Sea of Faith
Was once, too, at the full, and round earth's shore
Lay like the folds of a bright girdle furled.
But now I only hear
Its melancholy, long, withdrawing roar,
Retreating, to the breath
Of the night-wind, down the vast edges drear
And naked shingles[5] of the world.
Ah, love, let us be true
To one another! for the world, which seems
To lie before us like a land of dreams,
So various, so beautiful, so new,
Hath really neither joy, nor love, nor light,
Nor certitude, nor peace, nor help for pain;
And we are here as on a darkling[6] plain

---

[1] *moon-blanched:* Whitened by moonlight.
[2] *strand:* Beach.
[3] *Sophocles:* Greek playwright (496–406 b.c.), author of tragedies such as *Oedipus the King* and *Antigone*.
[4] *Aegean:* Sea between Greece and Turkey.
[5] *shingles:* Gravel beaches.
[6] *darkling:* Darkening.

Swept with confused alarms of struggle and flight,
Where ignorant armies clash by night.

William Blake (1757–1827)

The Chimney Sweeper[1] (1789)

When my mother died I was very young,
And my father sold me while yet my tongue
Could scarcely cry " 'weep! 'weep! 'weep! 'weep!"
So your chimneys I sweep, and in soot I sleep.

There's little Tom Dacre, who cried when his head,
That curled like a lamb's back, was shaved: so I said
"Hush, Tom! never mind it, for when your head's bare
You know that the soot cannot spoil your white hair."

And so he was quiet, and that very night,
As Tom was a-sleeping, he had such a sight!
That thousands of sweepers, Dick, Joe, Ned, and Jack,
Were all of them locked up in coffins of black.

And by came an Angel who had a bright key,
And he opened the coffins and set them all free;
Then down a green plain leaping, laughing, they run,
And wash in a river, and shine in the sun.

Then naked and white, all their bags left behind,
They rise upon clouds and sport in the wind;
And the Angel told Tom, if he'd be a good boy,
He'd have God for his father, and never want joy.

And so Tom awoke; and we rose in the dark,
And got with our bags and our brushes to work.
Though the morning was cold, Tom was happy and warm;
So if all do their duty they need not fear harm.

William Blake (1757–1827)

The Lamb (1789)

Little Lamb, who made thee?
Dost thou know who made thee?

[1] *The Chimney Sweeper:* During the eighteenth and early nineteenth centuries, orphans as young as four years old were apprenticed to chimney sweepers.

Gave thee life & bid thee feed,
By the stream & o'er the mead;
Gave thee clothing of delight,
Softest clothing wooly bright;
Gave thee such a tender voice,
Making all the vales rejoice!
  Little Lamb who made thee?
  Dost thou know who made thee?

  Little Lamb I'll tell thee,
  Little Lamb I'll tell thee!
He is callèd by thy name,
For he calls himself a Lamb:
He is meek & he is mild,
He became a little child:
I a child & thou a lamb,
We are callèd by his name.
  Little Lamb God bless thee.
  Little Lamb God bless thee.

William Blake (1757–1827)

London (1794)

I wander through each chartered street,
Near where the chartered Thames does flow,
And mark in every face I meet
Marks of weakness, marks of woe.

In every cry of every man,
In every infant's cry of fear,
In every voice, in every ban,
The mind-forged manacles I hear.

How the chimney-sweeper's cry
Every black'ning church appalls;
And the hapless soldier's sigh
Runs in blood down palace walls.

But most through midnight streets I hear
How the youthful harlot's curse
Blasts the new born infant's tear,
And blights with plagues the marriage hearse.

William Blake (1757–1827)

To see a World in a Grain of Sand (1803)

To see a World in a Grain of Sand
And a Heaven in a Wild Flower,
Hold Infinity in the palm of your hand
And Eternity in an hour.

William Blake (1757–1827)

The Tyger (1794)

Tyger! Tyger! burning bright
In the forests of the night,
What immortal hand or eye
Could frame thy fearful symmetry?

In what distant deeps or skies
Burnt the fire of thine eyes?
On what wings dare he aspire?
What the hand dare seize the fire?

And what shoulder, and what art,
Could twist the sinews of thy heart?
And when thy heart began to beat,
What dread hand? and what dread feet?

What the hammer? what the chain?
In what furnace was thy brain?
What the anvil? what dread grasp
Dare its deadly terrors clasp?

When the stars threw down their spears,
And watered heaven with their tears,
Did he smile his work to see?
Did he who made the Lamb make thee?

Tyger! Tyger! burning bright
In the forests of the night,
What immortal hand or eye
Dare frame thy fearful symmetry?

Anne Bradstreet (1612–1672)

The Author to Her Book[1] (1678)

Thou ill-formed offspring of my feeble brain,
Who after birth did'st by my side remain,
Till snatched from thence by friends, less wise than true,
Who thee abroad exposed to public view;
Made thee in rags, halting, to the press to trudge,
Where errors were not lessened, all may judge.
At thy return my blushing was not small,
My rambling brat (in print) should mother call;
I cast thee by as one unfit for light,
Thy visage was so irksome in my sight
Yet being mine own, at length affection would
Thy blemishes amend, if so I could:
I washed thy face, but more defects I saw,
And rubbing off a spot, still made a flaw.
I stretched thy joints to make thee even feet,[2]
Yet still thou run'st more hobbling than is meet;[3]
In better dress to trim thee was my mind,
But nought save homespun cloth in the house I find.
In this array, 'mongst vulgars[4] may'st thou roam;
In critics' hands beware thou dost not come;
And take thy way where yet thou are not known.
If for thy Father asked, say thou had'st none;
And for thy Mother, she alas is poor,
Which caused her thus to send thee out of door.

---

[1] *Her Book:* Bradstreet addresses *The Tenth Muse,* a collection of her poetry published without her consent in 1650.
[2] *even feet:* Metrical feet.
[3] *meet:* Appropriate or decorous.
[4] *vulgars:* Common people.

Gwendolyn Brooks (1917–2000)

The *Chicago Defender*[1] Sends a Man to Little Rock (1960)

Fall, 1957[2]

In Little Rock the people bear
Babes, and comb and part their hair

And watch the want ads, put repair
To roof and latch. While wheat toast burns
A woman waters multiferns.

Time upholds or overturns
The many, tight, and small concerns.

In Little Rock the people sing
Sunday hymns like anything,
Through Sunday pomp and polishing.

And after testament and tunes,
Some soften Sunday afternoons
With lemon tea and Lorna Doones.

I forecast
And I believe
Come Christmas Little Rock will cleave
To Christmas tree and trifle, weave,
From laugh and tinsel, texture fast.

In Little Rock is baseball; Barcarolle.[3]
That hotness in July . . . the uniformed figures raw and
implacable
And not intellectual,
Batting the hotness or clawing the suffering dust.
The Open Air Concert, on the special twilight green. . . .
When Beethoven is brutal or whispers to lady-like air.
Blanket-sitters are solemn, as Johann troubles to lean
To tell them what to mean. . . .

---

[1] *Chicago Defender:* A weekly newspaper for African American readers.

[2] *Fall, 1957:* When black students first entered the public high school in Little Rock, Arkansas, in 1957, the city erupted in race riots protesting desegregation.

[3] *Barcarolle:* A Venetian gondolier's song, or a song suggesting the rhythm of rowing.

There is love, too, in Little Rock. Soft women softly
Opening themselves in kindness,
Or, pitying one's blindness,
Awaiting one's pleasure
In azure
Glory with anguished rose at the root. . . .
To wash away old semi-discomfitures.
They re-teach purple and unsullen blue.
The wispy soils go. And uncertain
Half-havings have they clarified to sures.

In Little Rock they know
Not answering the telephone is a way of rejecting life,

That it is our business to be bothered, is our business
To cherish bores or boredom, be polite
To lies and love and many-faceted fuzziness.

I scratch my head, massage the hate-I-had.
I blink across my prim and pencilled pad.
The saga I was sent for is not down.
Because there is a puzzle in this town.
The biggest News I do not dare
Telegraph to the Editor's chair:
"They are like people everywhere."

The angry Editor would reply
In hundred harryings of Why.

And true, they are hurling spittle, rock,
Garbage and fruit in Little Rock.
And I saw coiling storm a-writhe
On bright madonnas. And a scythe
Of men harassing brownish girls.
(The bows and barrettes in the curls
And braids declined away from joy.)

I saw a bleeding brownish boy. . . .

The lariat lynch-wish I deplored.

The loveliest lynchee was our Lord.

Gwendolyn Brooks (1917–2000)

Medgar Evers[1] (1964)

For Charles Evers[2]

The man whose height his fear improved he
arranged to fear no further. The raw
intoxicated time was time for better birth or a final death.

Old styles, old tempos, all the engagement of
the day—the sedate, the regulated fray—

the antique light, the Moral rose, old gusts,
tight whistlings from the past, the mothballs
in the Love at last our man forswore.

Medgar Evers annoyed confetti and assorted
brands of businessmen's eyes.

The shows came down: to maxims and surprise.
And palsy.

Roaring no rapt arise-ye to the dead, he
leaned across tomorrow. People said that
he was holding clean globes in his hands.

George Gordon, Lord Byron (1788–1824)

She Walks in Beauty (1815)

I

She walks in beauty, like the night
  Of cloudless climes and starry skies;
And all that's best of dark and bright
  Meet in her aspect and her eyes:
Thus mellowed to that tender light
  Which heaven to gaudy day denies.

II

One shade the more, one ray the less,
  Had half impaired the nameless grace
Which waves in every raven tress,
  Or softly lightens o'er her face;

---

[1] *Medgar Evers:* African American civil rights leader who was killed by a sniper in 1963.
[2] *Charles Evers:* Medgar Evers's brother.

Where thoughts serenely sweet express
How pure, how dear their dwelling place.

III

And on that cheek, and o'er that brow,
So soft, so calm, yet eloquent,
The smiles that win, the tints that glow,
But tell of days in goodness spent,
A mind at peace with all below,
A heart whose love is innocent!

Glasshouse Images/Alamy Stock Photo

Samuel Taylor Coleridge (1772–1834)

Kubla Khan[1] (1797, 1798)

Or, a Vision in a Dream. A Fragment.

In Xanadu did Kubla Khan
A stately pleasure-dome decree:
Where Alph,[2] the sacred river, ran
Through caverns measureless to man
Down to a sunless sea.
So twice five miles of fertile ground
With walls and towers were girdled round;
And there were gardens bright with sinuous rills,
Where blossomed many an incense-bearing tree;
And here were forests ancient as the hills,
Enfolding sunny spots of greenery.

But oh! that deep romantic chasm which slanted
Down the green hill athwart a cedarn cover!
A savage place! as holy and enchanted
As e'er beneath a waning moon was haunted
By woman wailing for her demon-lover!
And from this chasm, with ceaseless turmoil seething,
As if this earth in fast thick pants were breathing,
A mighty fountain momently was forced:
Amid whose swift half-intermitted burst
Huge fragments vaulted like rebounding hail,
Or chaffy grain beneath the thresher's flail:
And 'mid these dancing rocks at once and ever

---

[1] *Kubla Khan:* Coleridge mythologizes the actual Kublai Khan, a thirteenth-century Mongol emperor, as well as the Chinese city of Xanadu.

[2] *Alph:* Probably derived from the Greek river Alpheus, whose waters, according to legend, rose from the Ionian Sea in Sicily as the fountain of Arethusa.

It flung up momently the sacred river.
Five miles meandering with a mazy motion
Through wood and dale the sacred river ran,
Then reached the caverns measureless to man,
And sank in tumult to a lifeless ocean:
And 'mid this tumult Kubla heard from far
Ancestral voices prophesying war!

The shadow of the dome of pleasure
Floated midway on the waves;
Where was heard the mingled measure
From the fountain and the caves.
It was a miracle of rare device,
A sunny pleasure-dome with caves of ice!

A damsel with a dulcimer
In a vision once I saw:
It was an Abyssinian maid,
And on her dulcimer she played,
Singing of Mount Abora.[3]
Could I revive within me
Her symphony and song,
To such a deep delight 'twould win me,
That with music loud and long,
I would build that dome in air,
That sunny dome! those caves of ice!
And all who heard should see them there,
And all should cry, Beware! Beware!
His flashing eyes, his floating hair
Weave a circle round him thrice,[4]
And close your eyes with holy dread,
For he on honey-dew hath fed,
And drunk the milk of Paradise.

E. E. Cummings (1894–1962)

next to of course god america i (1926)

"next to of course god america i
love you land of the pilgrims' and so forth oh
say can you see by the dawn's early my
country 'tis of centuries come and go

---

[3] *Mount Abora:* Some scholars see a reminiscence here of John Milton's *Paradise Lost* 4.280–82: "where Abassin kings their issue guard / Mount Amara, though this by some supposed / True Paradise under the Ethiop Line."

[4] *Weave ... thrice:* A magic ritual to keep away intruding spirits.

and are no more what of it we should worry
in every language even deafanddumb
thy sons acclaim your glorious name by gorry
by jingo by gee by gosh by gum
why talk of beauty what could be more beautiful than these heroic happy dead
who rushed like lions to the roaring slaughter
they did not stop to think they died instead
then shall the voice of liberty be mute?"

He spoke. And drank rapidly a glass of water

Emily Dickinson (1830–1886)

Because I could not stop for Death— (1863)

Because I could not stop for Death—
He kindly stopped for me—
The Carriage held but just Ourselves—
And Immortality.

We slowly drove—He knew no haste
And I had put away
My labor and my leisure too,
For His Civility—

We passed the School, where Children strove
At Recess—in the Ring—
We passed the Fields of Gazing Grain—
We passed the Setting Sun—

Or rather—He passed Us—
The Dews drew quivering and chill—
For only Gossamer, my Gown—
My Tippet[1]—only Tulle—

We passed before a House that seemed
A Swelling of the Ground—
The Roof was scarcely visible—
The Cornice—in the Ground—

Since then—'tis Centuries—and yet
Feels shorter than the Day
I first surmised the Horses' Heads
Were toward Eternity—

[1] *Tippet:* A short cape or scarf.

Emily Dickinson (1830–1886)

"Faith" is a fine invention (1860)

"Faith" is a fine invention
When Gentlemen can *see*—
But *Microscopes* are prudent
In an Emergency.

Emily Dickinson (1830–1886)

"Hope" is the thing with feathers— (1861)

"Hope" is the thing with feathers—
That perches in the soul—
And sings the tune without the words—
And never stops—at all—

And sweetest—in the Gale—is heard—
And sore must be the storm—
That could abash the little Bird—
That kept so many warm—

I've heard it in the chillest land—
And on the strangest Sea—
Yet, never, in Extremity,
It asked a crumb—of Me.

Emily Dickinson (1830–1886)

I heard a Fly buzz—when I died— (1862)

I heard a Fly buzz—when I died—
The Stillness in the Room
Was like the Stillness in the Air—
Between the Heaves of Storm—

The Eyes around—had wrung them dry—
And Breaths were gathering firm
For that last Onset—when the King
Be witnessed—in the Room—

I willed my Keepsakes—Signed away
What portion of me be
Assignable—and then it was
There interposed a Fly—

With Blue—uncertain stumbling Buzz—
Between the light—and me—
And then the Windows failed—and then
I could not see to see—

Emily Dickinson (1830–1886)

Much Madness is divinest Sense— (1862)

Much Madness is divinest Sense—
To a discerning Eye—
Much Sense—the starkest Madness—
'Tis the Majority
In this, as All, prevail—

Assent—and you are sane—
Demur—you're straightway dangerous—
And handled with a Chain—

Emily Dickinson (1830–1886)

My Life had stood—a Loaded Gun (c. 1863)

My Life had stood—a Loaded Gun—
In Corners—till a Day
The Owner passed—identified—
And carried Me away—

And now We roam in Sovereign Woods—
And now We hunt the Doe—
And every time I speak for Him—
The Mountains straight reply—

And do I smile, such cordial light
Upon the Valley glow—
It is as a Vesuvian[1] face
Had let its pleasure through—

And when at Night—Our good Day done—
I guard My Master's Head—
'Tis better than the Eider-Duck's[2]
Deep Pillow—to have shared—

---

[1] *Vesuvian:* The volcano Mount Vesuvius erupted in a.d. 79, destroying the city of Pompeii.
[2] *Eider-Duck's:* Eider ducks produce a soft down (eiderdown) used as pillow stuffing.

To foe of His—I'm deadly foe—
None stir the second time—
On whom I lay a Yellow Eye—
Or an emphatic Thumb—

Though I than He—may longer live
He longer must—than I—
For I have but the power to kill,
Without—the power to die—

Emily Dickinson (1830–1886)

The Soul selects her own Society— (1862)

The Soul selects her own Society—
Then—shuts the Door—
To her divine Majority—
Present no more—

Unmoved—she notes the Chariots—pausing—
At her low Gate—
Unmoved—an Emperor be kneeling
Upon her Mat—

I've known her—from an ample nation—
Choose One—
Then—close the Valves of her attention—
Like Stone—

Emily Dickinson (1830–1886)

There is no Frigate like a Book (1873)

There is no Frigate like a Book
To take us Lands away
Nor any Coursers like a Page
Of prancing Poetry—
This Traverse may the poorest take
Without oppress of Toll—
How frugal is the Chariot
That bears the Human soul.

Emily Dickinson (1830–1886)

There's a certain Slant of light (c. 1861)

There's a certain Slant of light,
Winter Afternoons—
That oppresses, like the Heft
Of Cathedral Tunes—

Heavenly Hurt, it gives us—
We can find no scar,
But internal difference,
Where the Meanings, are—

None may teach it—Any—
'Tis the Seal Despair—
An imperial affliction
Sent us of the Air—

When it comes, the landscape listens—
Shadows—hold their breath—
When it goes, 'tis like the Distance
On the look of Death—

Emily Dickinson (1830–1886)

This is my letter to the World (1862)

This is my letter to the World
That never wrote to Me—
The simple News that Nature told—
With tender Majesty

Her Message is committed
To Hands I cannot see
For love of Her—Sweet—countrymen—
Judge tenderly—of Me

Lifestyle pictures/Alamy Stock Photo

John Donne (1572–1631)

Death Be Not Proud (c. 1610)

Death be not proud, though some have callèd thee
Mighty and dreadful, for thou art not so;
For those whom thou think'st thou dost overthrow
Die not, poor death, nor yet canst thou kill me.
From rest and sleep, which but thy pictures be,

Much pleasure, then from thee much more must flow,
And soonest our best men with thee do go,
Rest of their bones, and soul's delivery.
Thou art slave to fate, chance, kings, and desperate men,
And dost with poison, war, and sickness dwell,
And poppy, or charms can make us sleep as well,
And better than thy stroke; why swell'st thou then?
One short sleep past, we wake eternally,
And death shall be no more; death, thou shalt die.

John Donne (1572–1631)

The Flea (1633)

Mark but this flea, and mark in this[1]
How little that which thou deny'st me is;
It sucked me first, and now sucks thee,
And in this flea our two bloods mingled be;
Thou know'st that this cannot be said
A sin, nor shame, nor loss of maidenhead,
   Yet this enjoys before it woo,
   And pampered swells with one blood made of two,
   And this, alas, is more than we would do.[2]

Oh stay, three lives in one flea spare,
Where we almost, yea more than, married are.
This flea is you and I, and this
Our marriage bed, and marriage temple is;
Though parents grudge, and you, we're met
And cloistered in these living walls of jet.
   Though use make you apt to kill me,
   Let not to that, self-murder added be,
   And sacrilege, three sins in killing three.

Cruel and sudden, hast thou since
Purpled thy nail in blood of innocence?
Wherein could this flea guilty be,
Except in that drop which it sucked from thee?
Yet thou triumph'st, and say'st that thou
Find'st not thyself, nor me, the weaker now;

[1] *mark in this:* Note the moral lesson in it.
[2] *more than we would do:* If we do not join our blood.

'Tis true; then learn how false, fears be;
Just so much honor, when thou yield'st to me,
Will waste, as this flea's death took life from thee.

T. S. Eliot (1888–1965)

The Love Song of J. Alfred Prufrock (1917)

S'io credessi che mia risposta fosse
A persona che mai tornasse al mondo,
Questa fiamma staria senza piu scosse.
Ma perciocche giammai di questo fondo
Non torno vivo alcun, s'i'odo il vero,
Senza tema d'infamia ti rispondo.[1]

Let us go then, you and I,
When the evening is spread out against the sky
Like a patient etherized upon a table;
Let us go, through certain half-deserted streets,
The muttering retreats
Of restless nights in one-night cheap hotels
And sawdust restaurants with oyster-shells:
Streets that follow like a tedious argument
Of insidious intent
To lead you to an overwhelming question …
Oh, do not ask, "What is it?"
Let us go and make our visit.

In the room the women come and go
Talking of Michelangelo.

The yellow fog that rubs its back upon the window-panes,
The yellow smoke that rubs its muzzle on the window-panes
Licked its tongue into the corners of the evening,
Lingered upon the pools that stand in drains,
Let fall upon its back the soot that falls from chimneys,
Slipped by the terrace, made a sudden leap,
And seeing that it was a soft October night,
Curled once about the house, and fell asleep.

---

[1]*S'io … rispondo:* The epigraph is from Dante's *Inferno*, Canto 27. In response to the poet's question about his identity, Guido da Montefelto, who for his sin of fraud must spend eternity wrapped in flames, replies: "If I thought that I was speaking to someone who could go back to the world, this flame would shake me no more. But since from this place nobody ever returns alive, if what I hear is true, I answer you without fear of infamy."

And indeed there will be time
For the yellow smoke that slides along the street,
Rubbing its back upon the window-panes;
There will be time, there will be time
To prepare a face to meet the faces that you meet;
There will be time to murder and create,
And time for all the works and days[2] of hands
That lift and drop a question on your plate;
Time for you and time for me,
And time yet for a hundred indecisions,
And for a hundred visions and revisions,
Before the taking of a toast and tea.

In the room the women come and go
Talking of Michelangelo.

And indeed there will be time
To wonder, "Do I dare?" and, "Do I dare?"
Time to turn back and descend the stair,
With a bald spot in the middle of my hair—
(They will say: "How his hair is growing thin!")
My morning coat, my collar mounting firmly to the chin,
My necktie rich and modest, but asserted by a simple pin—
(They will say: "But how his arms and legs are thin!")
Do I dare
Disturb the universe?
In a minute there is time
For decisions and revisions which a minute will reverse.

For I have known them all already, known them all—
Have known the evenings, mornings, afternoons,
I have measured out my life with coffee spoons;
I know the voices dying with a dying fall[3]
Beneath the music from a farther room.
So how should I presume?

And I have known the eyes already, known them all—
The eyes that fix you in a formulated phrase,
And when I am formulated, sprawling on a pin,
When I am pinned and wriggling on the wall,
Then how should I begin
To spit out all the butt-ends of my days and ways?
And how should I presume?

---

[2]*works and days: Works and Days*, by the eighth-century b.c. Greek poet Hesiod, is a poem that celebrates farm life.

[3]*dying fall:* An allusion to Orsino's speech in *Twelfth Night* (1.1): "That strain again! It had a dying fall."

And I have known the arms already, known them all—
Arms that are braceleted and white and bare
(But in the lamplight, downed with light brown hair!)
Is it perfume from a dress
That makes me so digress?
Arms that lie along a table, or wrap about a shawl.
And should I then presume?
And how should I begin?

* * *

Shall I say, I have gone at dusk through narrow streets
And watched the smoke that rises from the pipes
Of lonely men in shirt-sleeves, leaning out of windows? . . .

I should have been a pair of ragged claws
Scuttling across the floors of silent seas.

* * *

And the afternoon, the evening, sleeps so peacefully!
Smoothed by long fingers,
Asleep . . . tired . . . or it malingers,
Stretched on the floor, here beside you and me.
Should I, after tea and cakes and ices,
Have the strength to force the moment to its crisis?
But though I have wept and fasted, wept and prayed,
Though I have seen my head (grown slightly bald) brought in upon a platter,[4]
I am no prophet—and here's no great matter;
I have seen the moment of my greatness flicker,
And I have seen the eternal Footman[5] hold my coat, and snicker,
And in short, I was afraid.
And would it have been worth it, after all,
After the cups, the marmalade, the tea,

Among the porcelain, among some talk of you and me,
Would it have been worth while,
To have bitten off the matter with a smile,
To have squeezed the universe into a ball
To roll it toward some overwhelming question,

---

[4]*head . . . platter:* Like John the Baptist, who was beheaded by King Herod (see Matthew 14.3–11).
[5]*eternal Footman:* Perhaps death or fate.

To say: "I am Lazarus,[6] come from the dead,
Come back to tell you all, I shall tell you all"—
If one, settling a pillow by her head,
Should say: "That is not what I meant at all.
That is not it, at all."

And would it have been worth it, after all,
Would it have been worth while,
After the sunsets and the dooryards and the sprinkled streets,
After the novels, after the teacups, after the skirts that trail along the floor—
And this, and so much more?—
It is impossible to say just what I mean!
But as if a magic lantern threw the nerves in patterns on a screen:
Would it have been worth while
If one, settling a pillow or throwing off a shawl,
And turning toward the window, should say:
"That is not it at all,
That is not what I meant, at all."

* * *

No! I am not Prince Hamlet, nor was meant to be;
Am an attendant lord, one that will do
To swell a progress,[7] start a scene or two,
Advise the prince; no doubt, an easy tool,
Deferential, glad to be of use,
Politic, cautious, and meticulous;
Full of high sentence,[8] but a bit obtuse;
At times, indeed, almost ridiculous—
Almost, at times, the Fool.

I grow old … I grow old …
I shall wear the bottoms of my trousers rolled.

Shall I part my hair behind? Do I dare to eat a peach?
I shall wear white flannel trousers, and walk upon the beach.
I have heard the mermaids singing, each to each.

I do not think that they will sing to me.

I have seen them riding seaward on the waves
Combing the white hair of the waves blown back
When the wind blows the water white and black.

[6] *Lazarus:* A man whom Christ raised from the dead (see John 11.1–44).
[7] *a progress:* Here, in the Elizabethan sense of a royal journey.
[8] *sentence:* Opinions.

We have lingered in the chambers of the sea
By sea-girls wreathed with seaweed red and brown
Till human voices wake us, and we drown.

The New York Times

James A. Emanuel (1921–2013)

Emmett Till[1] (1968)

I hear a whistling
Through the water.
Little Emmett
Won't be still.
He keeps floating
Round the darkness,
Edging through
The silent chill.
Tell me, please,
That bedtime story
Of the fairy
River Boy
Who swims forever,
Deep in treasures,
Necklaced in
A coral toy.

Agence Opale/Alamy Stock Photo

Louise Erdrich (1954–)

Indian Boarding School: The Runaways (1984)

Home's the place we head for in our sleep.
Boxcars stumbling north in dreams
don't wait for us. We catch them on the run.
The rails, old lacerations that we love,
shoot parallel across the face and break

[1]*Emmett Till:* Emmett Till, a fourteen-year-old African American boy from Chicago, was visiting relatives in Mississippi when he allegedly whistled at a white woman who ran a local store. Unfamiliar with the racial climate of the South, he did not realize that his actions would generate a savage response. Several days later, he was kidnapped, and his severely beaten and mutilated body was later found in the river with a heavy cotton gin fan tied around his neck with barbed wire. His death prompted a new chapter in the Civil Rights struggle; the investigation into his murder was reopened in 2004.

just under Turtle Mountains.[1] Riding scars
you can't get lost. Home is the place they cross.

The lame guard strikes a match and makes the dark
less tolerant. We watch through cracks in boards
as the land starts rolling, rolling till it hurts
to be here, cold in regulation clothes.
We know the sheriff's waiting at midrun
to take us back. His car is dumb and warm.
The highway doesn't rock, it only hums
like a wing of long insults. The worn-down welts
of ancient punishments lead back and forth.

All runaways wear dresses, long green ones,
the color you would think shame was. We scrub
the sidewalks down because it's shameful work.
Our brushes cut the stone in watered arcs
and in the soak frail outlines shiver clear
a moment, things us kids pressed on the dark
face before it hardened, pale, remembering
delicate old injuries, the spines of names and leaves.

Martín Espada (1957–)

The Community College Revises Its Curriculum in Response to Changing Demographics (2000)

SPA 100 Conversational Spanish
2 credits

The course
is especially concerned
with giving police
the ability
to express themselves
tersely
in matters of interest
to them

Robert Frost (1874–1963)

Mending Wall (1914)

Something there is that doesn't love a wall,
That sends the frozen-ground-swell under it,

[1] *Turtle Mountains:* Erdrich is a descendant of the Turtle Mountain band of the Chippewa.

And spills the upper boulders in the sun;
And makes gaps even two can pass abreast.
The work of hunters is another thing:
I have come after them and made repair
Where they have left not one stone on a stone,
But they would have the rabbit out of hiding,
To please the yelping dogs. The gaps I mean,
No one has seen them made or heard them made,
But at spring mending-time we find them there.
I let my neighbor know beyond the hill;
And on a day we meet to walk the line
And set the wall between us once again.
We keep the wall between us as we go.
To each the boulders that have fallen to each.
And some are loaves and some so nearly balls
We have to use a spell to make them balance:
"Stay where you are until our backs are turned!"
We wear our fingers rough with handling them.
Oh, just another kind of outdoor game,
One on a side. It comes to little more:
There where it is we do not need the wall:
He is all pine and I am apple orchard.
My apple trees will never get across
And eat the cones under his pines, I tell him.
He only says, "Good fences make good neighbors."
Spring is the mischief in me, and I wonder
If I could put a notion in his head:
"*Why* do they make good neighbors? Isn't it
Where there are cows? But here there are no cows.
Before I built a wall I'd ask to know
What I was walling in or walling out,
And to whom I was like to give offense.
Something there is that doesn't love a wall,
That wants it down." I could say "Elves" to him,
But it's not elves exactly, and I'd rather
He said it for himself. I see him there
Bringing a stone grasped firmly by the top
In each hand, like an old-stone savage armed.
He moves in darkness as it seems to me,
Not of woods only and the shade of trees.
He will not go behind his father's saying,
And he likes having thought of it so well
He says again, "Good fences make good neighbors."

Thomas Hardy (1840–1928)

The Convergence of the Twain (1912)

(Lines on the loss of the "Titanic")

I

In a solitude of the sea
Deep from human vanity,
And the Pride of Life that planned her, stilly couches she.

II

Steel chambers, late the pyres[1]
Of her salamandrine fires,[2]
Cold currents thrid,[3] and turn to rhythmic tidal lyres.

III

Over the mirrors meant
To glass the opulent
The sea-worm crawls—grotesque, slimed, dumb, indifferent.

IV

Jewels in joy designed
To ravish the sensuous mind
Lie lightless, all their sparkles bleared and black and blind.

V

Dim moon-eyed fishes near
Gaze at the gilded gear
And query: "What does this vaingloriousness down here?" . . .

VI

Well: while was fashioning
This creature of cleaving wing,
The Immanent[4] Will that stirs and urges everything

---

[1]*pyres:* Funeral pyres; piles of wood on which corpses were burned in ancient rites.
[2]*salamandrine fires:* An allusion to the old belief that salamanders could live in fire.
[3]*thrid:* Thread (archaic verb form).
[4]*Immanent:* Inherent, dwelling within.

VII

Prepared a sinister mate
For her—so gaily great—
A Shape of Ice, for the time far and dissociate.

VIII

And as the smart ship grew
In stature, grace, and hue,
In shadowy silent distance grew the Iceberg too.

IX

Alien they seemed to be:
No mortal eye could see
The intimate welding of their later history,

X

Or sign that they were bent
By paths coincident
On being anon[5] twin halves of one august[6] event,

XI

Till the Spinner of the Years
Said "Now!" And each one hears,
And consummation comes, and jars two hemispheres.

William Ernest Henley (1849–1903)

Invictus (1888)

Out of the night that covers me,
Black as the Pit from pole to pole,
I thank whatever gods may be
For my unconquerable soul.

In the fell clutch of circumstance
I have not winced nor cried aloud.
Under the bludgeonings of chance
My head is bloody, but unbowed.

---

[5]*anon:* Soon.
[6]*august:* Awe-inspiring, majestic.

Beyond this place of wrath and tears
Looms but the Horror of the shade,
And yet the menace of the years
Finds, and shall find, me unafraid.

It matters not how strait the gate,
How charged with punishments the scroll.
I am the master of my fate:
I am the captain of my soul.

Gerard Manley Hopkins (1844–1889)

God's Grandeur (1877)

The world is charged with the grandeur of God.
    It will flame out, like shining from shook foil;
    It gathers to a greatness, like the ooze of oil
Crushed. Why do men then now not reck his rod?
Generations have trod, have trod, have trod;
    And all is seared with trade; bleared, smeared with toil;
    And wears man's smudge and shares man's smell: the soil
Is bare now, nor can foot feel, being shod.

And for all this, nature is never spent;
    There lives the dearest freshness deep down things;
And though the last lights off the black West went
    Oh, morning, at the brown brink eastward, springs—
Because the Holy Ghost over the bent
    World broods with warm breast and with ah! bright wings.

Langston Hughes (1902–1967)

Birmingham Sunday (September 15, 1963)[1] (1967)

Four little girls
Who went to Sunday School that day
And never came back home at all
But left instead
Their blood upon the wall

[1]*September 15, 1963:* On this date, only weeks after Martin Luther King Jr.'s historic March on Washington, four young African American girls were killed at their Sunday school in Birmingham, Alabama, by a bomb, likely in response to recent civil rights activities in the area.

With spattered flesh
And bloodied Sunday dresses
Torn to shreds by dynamite
That China made aeons ago—
Did not know
That what China made
Before China was ever Red at all
Would redden with their blood
This Birmingham-on-Sunday wall.
  Four tiny girls
Who left their blood upon that wall,
In little graves today await
The dynamite that might ignite
The fuse of centuries of Dragon Kings[2]
Whose tomorrow sings a hymn
The missionaries never taught Chinese
In Christian Sunday School
To implement the Golden Rule.
  Four little girls
Might be awakened someday soon
By songs upon the breeze
As yet unfelt among magnolia trees.

Langston Hughes (1902–1967)

The Negro Speaks of Rivers (1921)

I've known rivers:
I've known rivers ancient as the world and old as the flow of
  human blood in human veins.

My soul has grown deep like the rivers.

I bathed in the Euphrates[1] when dawns were young.
I built my hut near the Congo[2] and it lulled me to sleep.
I looked upon the Nile and raised the pyramids above it.
I heard the singing of the Mississippi when Abe Lincoln went
  down to New Orleans, and I've seen its muddy bosom turn
  all golden in the sunset.

---

[2] *Dragon Kings:* In Chinese myth and lore, the dragon is a beneficent force that dispenses blessings in both the natural and supernatural worlds. Eventually, the dragon became a symbol of imperial China. The dragon has also been used in the mythology of white supremacist groups like the Ku Klux Klan.

---

[1] *Euphrates:* Major river of southwest Asia; with the Tigris, the Euphrates forms a valley sometimes referred to as the "cradle of civilization."

[2] *Congo:* River in equatorial Africa, the continent's second longest.

I've known rivers:
Ancient, dusky rivers.

My soul has grown deep like the rivers.

Langston Hughes (1902–1967)

Theme for English B (1949)

The instructor said,

Go home and write
a page tonight.
And let that page come out of you—
Then, it will be true.

I wonder if it's that simple?
I am twenty-two, colored, born in Winston-Salem.
I went to school there, then Durham, then here
to this college on the hill above Harlem.
I am the only colored student in my class.
The steps from the hill lead down into Harlem,
through a park, then I cross St. Nicholas,
Eighth Avenue, Seventh, and I come to the Y,
the Harlem Branch Y, where I take the elevator
up to my room, sit down and write this page:

It's not easy to know what is true for you or me
at twenty-two, my age. But I guess I'm what
I feel and see and hear, Harlem, I hear you:
hear you, hear me—we two—you, me, talk on this page.

(I hear New York, too) Me—who?
Well, I like to eat, sleep, drink, and be in love.
I like to work, read, learn, and understand life.
I like a pipe for a Christmas present,
or records—Bessie,[1] bop,[2] or Bach.
I guess being colored doesn't make me *not* like
the same things other folks like who are other races.
So will my page be colored that I write?
Being me, it will not be white.
But it will be
a part of you, instructor.
You are white—

---

[1] *Bessie:* Bessie Smith (1894–1937), blues singer.

[2] *bop:* Short for "bebop," a jazz style developed in the early 1940s by Charlie Parker, Dizzy Gillespie, and others.

yet a part of me, as I am a part of you.
That's American.
Sometimes perhaps you don't want to be a part of me.
Nor do I often want to be a part of you.
But we are, that's true!
As I learn from you,
I guess you learn from me—
although you're older—and white—
and somewhat more free.

This is my page for English B.

Sketch by John Keats of the Sosibios Vase that may have inspired "Ode on a Grecian Urn."
The Picture Art Collection/Alamy Stock Photo

John Keats (1795–1821)

Ode on a Grecian Urn (1819)

I

Thou still unravish'd bride of quietness,
  Thou foster-child of silence and slow time,
Sylvan[1] historian, who canst thus express
A flowery tale more sweetly than our rhyme:
What leaf-fring'd legend haunts about thy shape
  Of deities or mortals, or of both,
In Tempe[2] or the dales of Arcady?[3]
  What men or gods are these? What maidens loth?
What mad pursuit? What struggle to escape?
What pipes and timbrels? What wild ecstasy?

II

Heard melodies are sweet, but those unheard
  Are sweeter; therefore, ye soft pipes, play on;
Not to the sensual ear, but, more endear'd,
  Pipe to the spirit ditties of no tone:
Fair youth, beneath the trees, thou canst not leave
  Thy song, nor ever can those trees be bare;
    Bold lover, never, never canst thou kiss,
Though winning near the goal—yet, do not grieve;
  She cannot fade, though thou hast not thy bliss,
For ever wilt thou love, and she be fair!

[1] *Sylvan:* Pertaining to woods or forests.
[2] *Tempe:* A beautiful valley in Greece.
[3] *Arcady:* The valleys of Arcadia, a mountainous region on the Greek peninsula. Like Tempe, they represent a rustic pastoral ideal.

III

Ah, happy, happy boughs! that cannot shed
  Your leaves, nor ever bid the spring adieu;
And, happy melodist, unwearied,
  For ever piping songs for ever new;
More happy love! more happy, happy love!
  For ever warm and still to be enjoy'd,
    For ever panting, and for ever young;
All breathing human passion far above,
  That leaves a heart high-sorrowful and cloy'd,
A burning forehead, and a parching tongue.

IV

Who are these coming to the sacrifice?
  To what green altar, O mysterious priest,
Lead'st thou that heifer lowing at the skies,
  And all her silken flanks with garlands drest?
What little town by river or sea shore,
  Or mountain-built with peaceful citadel,
    Is emptied of this folk, this pious morn?
And, little town, thy streets for evermore
  Will silent be; and not a soul to tell
    Why thou art desolate, can e'er return.

V

O Attic[4] shape! Fair attitude! with brede[5]
  Of marble men and maidens overwrought,[6]
With forest branches and the trodden weed;
  Thou, silent form, dost tease us out of thought
As doth eternity: Cold Pastoral!
  When old age shall this generation waste,
    Thou shalt remain, in midst of other woe
Than ours, a friend to man, to whom thou say'st,
  "Beauty is truth, truth beauty,"—that is all
    Ye know on earth, and all ye need to know.

[4]*Attic:* Characteristic of Athens or Athenians.
[5]*brede:* Braid.
[6]*overwrought:* Elaborately ornamented.

John Keats (1795–1821)

When I Have Fears (1818)

When I have fears that I may cease to be
Before my pen has gleaned my teeming brain,
Before high-pilèd books, in charact'ry,[1]
Hold like rich garners the full-ripened grain;
When I behold, upon the night's starred face,
Huge cloudy symbols of a high romance,
And think that I may never live to trace
Their shadows, with the magic hand of chance;
And when I feel, fair creature of an hour,
That I shall never look upon thee more,
Never have relish in the faery power
Of unreflecting love!—then on the shore
Of the wide world I stand alone, and think
Till Love and Fame to nothingness do sink.

Ada Limón (1976–)

The Contract Says: We'd Like the Conversation to be Bilingual (2018)

When you come, bring your brown-
ness so we can be sure to please
the funders. Will you check this
box; we're applying for a grant.
Do you have any poems that speak
to troubled teens? Bilingual is best.
Would you like to come to dinner
with the patrons and sip Patrón?
Will you tell us the stories that make
us uncomfortable, but not complicit?
Don't read the one where you
are just like us. Born to a green house,
garden, don't tell us how you picked
tomatoes and ate them in the dirt
watching vultures pick apart another
bird's bones in the road. Tell us the one
about your father stealing hubcaps

[1] *charact'ry:* Print.

after a colleague said that's what his
kind did. Tell us how he came
to the meeting wearing a poncho
and tried to sell the man his hubcaps
back. Don't mention your father
was a teacher, spoke English, loved
making beer, loved baseball, tell us
again about the poncho, the hubcaps,
how he stole them, how he did the thing
he was trying to prove he didn't do.

Christopher Marlowe (1564–1593)

The Passionate Shepherd to His Love (1600)

Come live with me and be my love,
And we will all the pleasures prove
That valleys, groves, hills, and fields,
Woods, or steepy mountain yields.

And we will sit upon the rocks,
Seeing the shepherds feed their flocks
By shallow rivers, to whose falls
Melodious birds sing madrigals.

And I will make thee beds of roses
And a thousand fragrant posies,
A cap of flowers and a kirtle[1]
Embroidered all with leaves of myrtle;

A gown made of the finest wool
Which from our pretty lambs we pull;
Fair-linèd slippers for the cold,
With buckles of the purest gold;

A belt of straw and ivy buds,
With coral clasps and amber studs.
And if these pleasures may thee move,
Come live with me and be my love.

The shepherds' swains shall dance and sing
For thy delight each May morning.
If these delights thy mind may move,
Then live with me and be my love.

[1] *kirtle:* Skirt.

Claude McKay (1890–1948)

If We Must Die (1922)

If we must die, let it not be like hogs
Hunted and penned in an inglorious spot,
While round us bark the mad and hungry dogs,
Making their mock at our accursed lot.
If we must die, O let us nobly die,
So that our precious blood may not be shed
In vain; then even the monsters we defy
Shall be constrained to honor us though dead!
O kinsmen! we must meet the common foe!
Though far outnumbered let us show us brave,
And for their thousand blows deal one deathblow!
What though before us lies the open grave?
Like men we'll face the murderous, cowardly pack,
Pressed to the wall, dying, but fighting back!

© Harriet Levin Millan

Harriet Levin Millan (1956–)

Bucharest 1918 (2021)

An uncle was killed during the war
for wearing the wrong color hat.
He wasn't a soldier. He didn't see the rifle barrel
aimed at his neck. He was standing by the side

of the road watching a bird, a red-tailed woodpecker,
listening for its home. Death is a home
unseen by the side of the road,
the rifle barrel aimed. A bird listens with its neck.

During the war many uncles were killed.
They were not soldiers. They were wearing colorful hats.
During the war many uncles stood at the sides of roads
watching the wrong birds, the wrong homes,

not seeing the roadside clearing. During a war,
wearing the wrong color is to stand on your neck,
not as a soldier, not as a woodpecker. Aimed at
from the bottom of a tree, killed

by the side of the road while watching a bird.
My uncle was wrongly killed on the wrong side

of the road. Red war for his neck.
During a war, no uncles are home.

They are red-tailed, barreling from their homes,
slung, as a rifle is slung across someone's shoulders.
Seeing is to peck like a woodpecker, a red-necked
lengthy death, right here in front of me.

John Milton (1608–1674)

When I consider how my light is spent[1] (1655?)

When I consider how my light is spent,
   Ere half my days in this dark world and wide,
   And that one talent[2] which is death to hide
Lodged with me useless, though my soul more bent
To serve therewith my Maker, and present
   My true account, lest He returning chide;
   "Doth God exact day-labor, light denied?"
I fondly[3] ask. But Patience, to prevent
That murmur, soon replies, "God doth not need
   Either man's work or His own gifts. Who best
   Bear His mild yoke, they serve Him best. His state
Is kingly: thousands at His bidding speed,
And post o'er land and ocean without rest;
They also serve who only stand and wait."

Pablo Neruda (1904–1973)

The United Fruit Co.[1] (1950)

Translated by Robert Bly

When the trumpet sounded, it was
all prepared on the earth,
and Jehovah parceled out the earth

[1] *how my light is spent:* A meditation on his blindness.
[2] *one talent:* See Jesus' parable of the talents in Matthew 25.14–30.
[3] *fondly:* Foolishly.

[1] *United Fruit Co.:* Incorporated in New Jersey in 1899 by Andrew Preston and Minor C. Keith, United Fruit became a major force in growing, transporting, and merchandising Latin American produce, especially bananas. The company is notorious for its involvement in politics, and as a result, its name came to represent "Yankee" imperialism and oppression.

to Coca-Cola, Inc., Anaconda,
Ford Motors, and other entities:
The Fruit Company, Inc.
reserved for itself the most succulent,
the central coast of my own land,
the delicate waist of America.
It rechristened its territories
as the "Banana Republics"
and over the sleeping dead,
over the restless heroes
who brought about the greatness,
the liberty and the flags,
it established the comic opera:
abolished the independencies,
presented crowns of Caesar,
unsheathed envy, attracted
the dictatorship of the flies,
Trujillo flies, Tacho flies,
Carias flies, Martinez flies,
Ubico flies,[2] damp flies
of modest blood and marmalade,
drunken flies who zoom
over the ordinary graves,
circus flies, wise flies
well trained in tyranny.

Among the bloodthirsty flies
the Fruit Company lands its ships,
taking off the coffee and the fruit;
the treasure of our submerged
territories flows as though
on plates into the ships.

Meanwhile Indians are falling
into the sugared chasms
of the harbors, wrapped
for burial in the mist of the dawn:
a body rolls, a thing
that has no name, a fallen cipher,
a cluster of dead fruit
thrown down on the dump.

[2] *Trujillo, Tacho, Carias, Martinez, Ubico:* Political dictators.

Sir Walter Raleigh (1552–1618)

The Nymph's Reply to the Shepherd (1600)

If all the world and love were young,
And truth in every shepherd's tongue,
These pretty pleasures might me move
To live with thee and be thy love.

Time drives the flocks from field to fold,
When rivers rage and rocks grow cold;
And Philomel[1] becometh dumb;
The rest complains of cares to come.

The flowers do fade, and wanton fields
To wayward winter reckoning yields:
A honey tongue, a heart of gall,
Is fancy's spring, but sorrow's fall.

Thy gowns, thy shoes, thy beds of roses,
Thy cap, thy kirtle, and thy posies
Soon break, soon wither, soon forgotten,
In folly ripe, in reason rotten.

Thy belt of straw and ivy buds,
Thy coral clasps and amber studs.
All these in me no means can move
To come to thee and be thy love.

But could youth last, and love still breed,
Had joys no date, nor age no need,
Then these delights my mind might move
To live with thee and be thy love.

Bettmann/Getty Images

Edwin Arlington Robinson (1869–1935)

Richard Cory (1897)

Whenever Richard Cory went down town,
We people on the pavement looked at him:
He was a gentleman from sole to crown,
Clean favored, and imperially slim.

And he was always quietly arrayed,
And he was always human when he talked;
But still he fluttered pulses when he said,
"Good-morning," and he glittered when he walked.

And he was rich—yes, richer than a king—
And admirably schooled in every grace:

[1] *Philomel:* The nightingale.

In fine, we thought that he was everything
To make us wish that we were in his place.

So on we worked, and waited for the light,
And went without the meat, and cursed the bread;
And Richard Cory, one calm summer night,
Went home and put a bullet through his head.

William Shakespeare (1564–1616)

Let me not to the marriage of true minds (1609)

Let me not to the marriage of true minds
Admit impediments.[1] Love is not love
Which alters when it alteration finds,
Or bends with the remover to remove:
Oh, no! it is an ever-fixéd mark,
That looks on tempests and is never shaken;
It is the star to every wandering bark,
Whose worth's unknown, although his height be taken.[2]
Love's not Time's fool,[3] though rosy lips and cheeks
Within his bending sickle's compass come;
Love alters not with his brief hours and weeks,
But bears it out even to the edge of doom.[4]
    If this be error and upon me proved,
    I never writ, nor no man ever loved.

William Shakespeare (1564–1616)

Not marble, nor the gilded monuments (1609)

Not marble, nor the gilded monuments
Of princes, shall outlive this powerful rhyme;
But you shall shine more bright in these contents
Than unswept stone, besmeared with sluttish time.
When wasteful war shall statues overturn,
And broils root out the work of masonry,

---

[1] *Admit impediments:* A reference to "The Order of Solemnization of Matrimony" in the Anglican Book of Common Prayer: "I require that if either of you know any impediments why ye may not be lawfully joined together in Matrimony, ye do now confess it."
[2] *Whose worth's . . . taken:* Although the altitude of a star may be measured, its worth is unknowable.
[3] *Love's not Time's fool:* Love is not mocked by Time.
[4] *doom:* Doomsday.

Nor Mars[1] his sword nor war's quick fire shall burn
The living record of your memory.
'Gainst death and all-oblivious enmity
Shall you pace forth; your praise shall still find room
Even in the eyes of all posterity
That wear this world out to the ending doom.
So, till the judgment that yourself arise,
You live in this, and dwell in lovers' eyes.

Percy Bysshe Shelley (1792–1822)

Ode to the West Wind (1820)

I

O wild West Wind, thou breath of Autumn's being,
Thou, from whose unseen presence the leaves dead
Are driven, like ghosts from an enchanter fleeing,

Yellow, and black, and pale, and hectic red,[1]
Pestilence-stricken multitudes: O Thou,
Who chariotest to their dark wintry bed

The winged seeds, where they lie cold and low,
Each like a corpse within its grave, until
Thine azure sister of the Spring[2] shall blow

Her clarion o'er the dreaming earth, and fill
(Driving sweet buds like flocks to feed in air)
With living hues and odours plain and hill:
Wild Spirit, which art moving everywhere;
Destroyer and Preserver; hear, O hear!

II

Thou on whose stream, mid the steep sky's commotion,
Loose clouds like Earth's decaying leaves are shed,
Shook from the tangled boughs of Heaven and Ocean,

Angels of rain and lightning: there are spread
On the blue surface of thine aery surge,
Like the bright hair uplifted from the head

---

[1] *Mars:* The Roman god of war.

---

[1] *Yellow . . . hectic red:* A reference to a tubercular fever that produces flushed cheeks.
[2] *azure . . . Spring:* The west wind of the spring.

Of some fierce Maenad,[3] even from the dim verge
Of the horizon to the zenith's height,
The locks of the approaching storm. Thou Dirge

Of the dying year, to which this closing night
Will be the dome of a vast sepulchre,
Vaulted with all thy congregated might

Of vapours, from whose solid atmosphere
Black rain and fire and hail will burst: O hear!

III

Thou who didst waken from his summer dreams
The blue Mediterranean, where he lay,
Lulled by the coil of his crystalline streams,

Beside a pumice isle in Baiae's bay,[4]
And saw in sleep old palaces and towers
Quivering within the wave's intenser day,

All overgrown with azure moss and flowers
So sweet, the sense faints picturing them! Thou
For whose path the Atlantic's level powers

Cleave themselves into chasms, while far below
The sea-blooms and the oozy woods which wear
The sapless foliage of the ocean, know

Thy voice, and suddenly grow grey with fear,
And tremble and despoil themselves: O hear!

IV

If I were a dead leaf thou mightest bear;
If I were a swift cloud to fly with thee;
A wave to pant beneath thy power, and share

The impulse of thy strength, only less free
Than thou, O Uncontrollable! If even
I were as in my boyhood, and could be

The comrade of thy wanderings over Heaven,
As then, when to outstrip thy skiey speed
Scarce seemed a vision; I would ne'er have striven

---

[3]*Maenad:* A female votary who danced wildly in ceremonies for Dionysus (or Bacchus), Greek god of wine and vegetation, who according to legend died in the fall and was reborn in the spring.

[4]*Baiae's bay:* A bay in the Mediterranean Sea, west of Naples. It was known for the opulent villas built by Roman emperors along its shores.

As thus with thee in prayer in my sore need,
Oh! lift me as a wave, a leaf, a cloud!
I fall upon the thorns of life! I bleed!

A heavy weight of hours has chained and bowed
One too like thee: tameless, and swift, and proud.

V

Make me thy lyre,[5] even as the forest is:
What if my leaves are falling like its own!
The tumult of thy mighty harmonies

Will take from both a deep, autumnal tone,
Sweet though in sadness. Be thou, Spirit fierce,
My spirit! Be thou me, impetuous one!

Drive my dead thoughts over the universe
Like withered leaves to quicken a new birth!
And, by the incantation of this verse,

Scatter, as from an unextinguished hearth
Ashes and sparks, my words among mankind!
Be through my lips to unawakened Earth

The trumpet of a prophecy! O Wind,
If Winter comes, can Spring be far behind?

Stevie Smith (1902–1971)

Not Waving but Drowning (1957)

Nobody heard him, the dead man,
But still he lay moaning:
I was much further out than you thought
And not waving but drowning.

Poor chap, he always loved larking
And now he's dead
It must have been too cold for him his heart gave way,
They said.

Oh, no no no, it was too cold always
(Still the dead one lay moaning)
I was much too far out all my life
And not waving but drowning.

---

[5] *lyre:* An Aeolian harp, a stringed instrument that produces musical sounds when exposed to the wind.

AP Images/Hartford Courant

Wallace Stevens (1879–1955)

Anecdote of the Jar (1923)

I placed a jar in Tennessee,
And round it was, upon a hill.
It made the slovenly wilderness
Surround that hill.

The wilderness rose up to it,
And sprawled around, no longer wild.
The jar was round upon the ground
And tall and of a port in air.

It took dominion everywhere.
The jar was gray and bare.
It did not give of bird or bush,
Like nothing else in Tennessee.

AP Images

Alfred, Lord Tennyson (1809–1892)

Ulysses[1] (1833)

It little profits that an idle king,
By this still hearth, among these barren crags,
Matched with an agèd wife, I mete and dole
Unequal laws unto a savage race
That hoard, and sleep, and feed, and know not me.
I cannot rest from travel; I will drink
Life to the lees. All times I have enjoyed
Greatly, have suffered greatly, both with those
That loved me, and alone; on shore, and when
Through scudding drifts the rainy Hyades[2]
Vexed the dim sea. I am become a name;
For always roaming with a hungry heart
Much have I seen and known—cities of men
And manners, climates, councils, governments,
Myself not least, but honored of them all—
And drunk delight of battle with my peers,

---

[1] *Ulysses:* A legendary Greek king of Ithaca and hero of Homer's *Odyssey*, Ulysses (or Odysseus) is noted for his daring and cunning. After his many adventures—including encounters with the Cyclops, the cannibalistic Laestrygones, and the enchantress Circe—Ulysses returned home to his faithful wife, Penelope. Tennyson portrays an older Ulysses pondering his situation.

[2] *Hyades:* A group of stars whose rising was supposedly followed by rain and thus stormy seas.

Far on the ringing plains of windy Troy.[3]
I am a part of all that I have met;
Yet all experience is an arch wherethrough
Gleams that untraveled world whose margin fades
Forever and forever when I move.
How dull it is to pause, to make an end,
To rust unburnished, not to shine in use!
As though to breathe were life! Life piled on life
Were all too little, and of one to me
Little remains; but every hour is saved
From that eternal silence, something more,
A bringer of new things; and vile it were
For some three suns to store and hoard myself,
And this grey spirit yearning in desire
To follow knowledge like a sinking star,
Beyond the utmost bound of human thought.
    This is my son, mine own Telemachus,
To whom I leave the scepter and the isle—
Well-loved of me, discerning to fulfill
This labor, by slow prudence to make mild
A rugged people, and through soft degrees
Subdue them to the useful and the good.
Most blameless is he, centered in the sphere
Of common duties, decent not to fail
In offices of tenderness, and pay
Meet adoration to my household gods,
When I am gone. He works his work, I mine.
    There lies the port; the vessel puffs her sail;
There gloom the dark, broad seas. My mariners,
Souls that have toiled, and wrought, and thought with me—
That ever with a frolic welcome took
The thunder and the sunshine, and opposed
Free hearts, free foreheads—you and I are old;
Old age hath yet his honor and his toil.
Death closes all; but something ere the end,
Some work of noble note, may yet be done,
Not unbecoming men that strove with Gods.
The lights begin to twinkle from the rocks;
The long day wanes; the low moon climbs; the deep
Moans round with many voices. Come, my friends,
'Tis not too late to seek a newer world.
Push off, and sitting well in order smite

[3] *Troy:* An ancient city in Asia Minor. According to legend, Paris, king of Troy, abducted Helen, the beautiful wife of Menelaus, king of Sparta, initiating the Trojan War, in which numerous Greek heroes, including Ulysses, fought.

The sounding furrows; for my purpose holds
To sail beyond the sunset, and the baths
Of all the western stars, until I die.
It may be that the gulfs will wash us down;
It may be we shall touch the Happy Isles,[4]
And see the great Achilles,[5] whom we knew.
Though much is taken, much abides; and though
We are not now that strength which in old days
Moved earth and heaven, that which we are, we are—
One equal temper of heroic hearts,
Made weak by time and fate, but strong in will
To strive, to seek, to find, and not to yield.

Phillis Wheatley (1753–1784)

On Being Brought from Africa to America (1773)

'Twas mercy brought me from my *Pagan* land,
Taught my benighted soul to understand
That there's a God, that there's a *Saviour* too:
Once I redemption neither sought nor knew.
Some view our sable race with scornful eye,
"Their colour is a diabolic die."
Remember, *Christians*, *Negroes*, black as *Cain*,
May be refin'd, and join th' angelic train.

Walt Whitman (1819–1892)

I Hear America Singing (1867)

I hear America singing, the varied carols I hear,
Those of mechanics, each one singing his as it should be blithe and strong,
The carpenter singing his as he measures his plank or beam,
The mason singing his as he makes ready for work, or leaves off work,
The boatman singing what belongs to him in his boat, the deckhand singing on the steamboat deck,
The shoemaker singing as he sits on his bench, the hatter singing as he stands,

[4]*Happy Isles:* Elysium, or Paradise, believed to be in the far western ocean.
[5]*Achilles:* Greek hero of the Trojan War.

The wood-cutter's song, the ploughboy's on his way in the morning, or at noon intermission or at sundown,
The delicious singing of the mother, or of the young wife at work, or of the girl sewing or washing,
Each singing what belongs to him or her and to none else,
The day what belongs to the day—at night the party of young fellows, robust, friendly,
Singing with open mouths their strong melodious songs.

Walt Whitman (1819–1892)

A Noiseless Patient Spider (1881)

A noiseless patient spider,
I mark'd where on a little promontory it stood isolated,
Mark'd how to explore the vacant vast surrounding,
It launch'd forth filament, filament, filament, out of itself,
Ever unreeling them, ever tirelessly speeding them.

And you O my soul where you stand,
Surrounded, detached, in measureless oceans of space,
Ceaselessly musing, venturing, throwing, seeking the spheres to connect them,
Till the bridge you will need be form'd, till the ductile anchor hold,
Till the gossamer thread you fling catch somewhere, O my soul.

Walt Whitman (1819–1892)

from "Song of Myself" (1855)

I

I celebrate myself, and sing myself,
And what I assume you shall assume,
For every atom belonging to me as good belongs to you.

I loafe and invite my soul,
I lean and loafe at my ease observing a spear of summer grass.

My tongue, every atom of my blood, form'd from this soil, this air,
Born here of parents born here from parents the same, and their parents the same,
I, now thirty-seven years old in perfect health begin,
Hoping to cease not till death.

Creeds and schools in abeyance,
Retiring back a while sufficed at what they are, but never forgotten,
I harbor for good or bad, I permit to speak at every hazard,
Nature without check with original energy.

II

Houses and rooms are full of perfumes, the shelves are crowded
with perfumes,
I breathe the fragrance myself and know it and like it,
The distillation would intoxicate me also, but I shall not let it.

The atmosphere is not a perfume, it has no taste of the distillation,
it is odorless,
It is for my mouth forever, I am in love with it,
I will go to the bank by the wood and become undisguised
and naked,
I am mad for it to be in contact with me.

The smoke of my own breath,
Echoes, ripples, buzz'd whispers, love-root, silk-thread, crotch
and vine,
My respiration and inspiration, the beating of my heart, the
passing of blood and air through my lungs,
The sniff of green leaves and dry leaves, and of the shore and
dark-color'd sea-rocks, and of hay in the barn,

The sound of the belch'd words of my voice loos'd to the eddies
of the wind,
A few light kisses, a few embraces, a reaching around of arms,
The play of shine and shade on the trees as the supple boughs wag,
The delight alone or in the rush of the streets, or along the fields
and hill-sides,
The feeling of health, the full-noon trill, the song of me rising
from bed and meeting the sun.

Have you reckon'd a thousand acres much? have you
reckon'd the
earth much?
Have you practis'd so long to learn to read?
Have you felt so proud to get at the meaning of poems?

Stop this day and night with me and you shall possess the origin
of all poems,
You shall possess the good of the earth and sun,
(there are millions
of suns left,)

You shall no longer take things at second or third hand, nor look
through the eyes of the dead, nor feed on the
spectres in books,
You shall not look through my eyes either, nor take things
from me,
You shall listen to all sides and filter them from your self.

William Wordsworth (1770–1850)

Composed upon Westminster Bridge, September 3 1802 (1802)

Earth has not any thing to show more fair:
Dull would he be of soul who could pass by
A sight so touching in its majesty:
This City now doth, like a garment, wear
The beauty of the morning; silent, bare,
Ships, towers, domes, theatres, and temples lie
Open unto the fields, and to the sky;
All bright and glittering in the smokeless air.
Never did sun more beautifully steep
In his first splendour, valley, rock, or hill;
Ne'er saw I, never felt, a calm so deep!
The river glideth at his own sweet will:
Dear God! the very houses seem asleep;
And all that mighty heart is lying still!

William Wordsworth (1770–1850)

London, 1802 (1802)

Milton![1] thou should'st be living at this hour:
England hath need of thee: she is a fen
Of stagnant waters: altar, sword and pen,
Fireside, the heroic wealth of hall and bower,
Have forfeited their ancient English dower
Of inward happiness. We are selfish men;
Oh! raise us up, return to us again;
And give us manners, virtue, freedom, power.

[1] *Milton:* John Milton (1608–1674), poet, best known for *Paradise Lost.*

Thy soul was like a star, and dwelt apart:
Thou hadst a voice whose sound was like the sea:
Pure as the naked heavens, majestic, free,
So didst thou travel on life's common way,
In cheerful godliness; and yet thy heart
The lowliest duties on herself did lay.

William Wordsworth (1770–1850)

My heart leaps up when I behold (1807)

My heart leaps up when I behold
  A rainbow in the sky:
So was it when my life began;
So is it now I am a man;
So be it when I shall grow old,
  Or let me die!
The Child is father of the Man;
And I could wish my days to be
Bound each to each by natural piety.

William Butler Yeats (1865–1939)

The Lake Isle of Innisfree (1892)

I will arise and go now, and go to Innisfree,[1]
And a small cabin build there, of clay and wattles[2] made:
Nine bean-rows will I have there, a hive for the honey-bee,
And live alone in the bee-loud glade.

And I shall have some peace there, for peace comes dropping slow,
Dropping from the veils of the morning to where the cricket sings;
There midnight's all a glimmer, and noon a purple glow,
And evening full of the linnet's wings.

I will arise and go now, for always night and day
I hear lake water lapping with low sounds by the shore;
While I stand on the roadway, or on the pavements grey,
I hear it in the deep heart's core.

---

[1] *Innisfree:* An island in Lough (Lake) Gill, County Sligo, in Ireland.
[2] *wattles:* Stakes interwoven with twigs or branches, used for walls and roofing.

William Butler Yeats (1865–1939)

The Second Coming[1] (1921)

Turning and turning in the widening gyre[2]
The falcon cannot hear the falconer;
Things fall apart; the center cannot hold;
Mere anarchy is loosed upon the world,
The blood-dimmed tide is loosed, and everywhere
The ceremony of innocence is drowned;
The best lack all conviction, while the worst
Are full of passionate intensity.[3]

Surely some revelation is at hand;
Surely the Second Coming is at hand;
The Second Coming! Hardly are those words out
When a vast image out of *Spiritus Mundi*[4]
Troubles my sight: somewhere in sands of the desert
A shape with lion body and the head of a man,
A gaze blank and pitiless as the sun,
Is moving its slow thighs, while all about it
Reel shadows of the indignant desert birds.
The darkness drops again; but now I know
That twenty centuries[5] of stony sleep
Were vexed to nightmare by a rocking cradle,
And what rough beast, its hour come round at last,
Slouches towards Bethlehem to be born?

---

[1] *The Second Coming:* The phrase usually refers to the return of Christ. Yeats theorized cycles of history, much like the turning of a wheel. Here he offers a poetic comment on his view of the dissolution of civilization at the end of one such cycle.
[2] *gyre:* Spiral.
[3] *Mere.... intensity:* Lines 4–8 refer to the Russian Revolution of 1917.
[4] *Spiritus Mundi:* Literally, "Spirit of the World" (Latin). Yeats believed all souls to be connected by a "Great Memory."
[5] *twenty centuries:* The centuries between the birth of Christ and the twentieth century, in which Yeats was writing.

Part 4

Drama

Chapter

27

Understanding Drama

Learning Objectives

After reading this chapter, you will be able to. . .

- Summarize the historical and cultural origins of modern drama.
- Analyze the staging and performance history of drama.
- Define tragedy as it pertains to drama.
- Define comedy as it pertains to drama.
- Identify the distinctive characteristics of works of drama.

Dramatic Literature

The distinctive appearance of a script, with its divisions into acts and scenes, identifies **drama** as a unique form of literature. A play is written to be performed in front of an audience by actors who take on the roles of the characters and who present the story through dialogue and action. (An exception is a **closet drama**, which is meant to be read, not performed.) In fact, the term *theater* comes from the Greek word *theasthai*, which means "to view" or "to see." Thus, drama is different from novels and short stories, which are meant to be read.

Origins of Modern Drama

The Ancient Greek Theater

The dramatic presentations of ancient Greece evolved from the religious rites performed to honor the god Dionysus to mark the coming of spring. Playwrights such as Aeschylus (525–456 B.C.), Sophocles (496–406 B.C.), and Euripides (480?–406 B.C.) wrote plays to be performed and judged at competitions held during the yearly Dionysian festivals. Works were chosen by a selection board and evaluated by a panel of judges. The first plays were tragedies, and out of these developed the genres of comedy and satire. Unfortunately, very few of these ancient Greek plays survive. According to tradition, the first actor

Grand Theater at Ephesus (3rd century B.C.), a Greek settlement in what is now Turkey
Dave G. Houser/Corbis Documentary/Getty Images

in a Greek drama was Thespis, from whose name we derive the word *thespian*, which means *actor*.

The open-air, semicircular ancient Greek theater, built into the side of a hill, looked much like a primitive version of a modern sports stadium. Some Greek theaters, such as the Athenian theater, could seat almost seventeen thousand spectators. Sitting in tiered seats, the audience would look down on the **orchestra**, or "dancing place," occupied by the **chorus**—originally a group of men (led by an individual called the **choragos**) who danced and chanted. The chorus later evolved into a group of onlookers who commented on the drama.

Raised a few steps above the orchestra was a platform on which the actors performed. Behind this platform was a **skene**, or building, that originally served as a resting place or dressing room. (The modern word *scene* is derived from the Greek *skene*.) Behind the skene was a line of pillars called a **colonnade**, which was covered by a roof. Actors used the skene for entrances and exits; beginning with the plays of Sophocles, painted backdrops were hung there. These backdrops, however, were most likely more decorative than realistic. Historians believe that realistic props and scenery were probably absent from the ancient Greek theater. Instead, the setting was suggested by the play's dialogue, and the audience had to imagine the physical details of a scene.

Two mechanical devices were used. One, a rolling cart or platform, was sometimes employed to introduce action that had occurred offstage. For example, actors frozen in position could be rolled onto the roof of the skene to illustrate an event such as the killing of Oedipus's father, which occurred before the play began. Another mechanical device, a small crane, was used to show gods ascending to or descending from heaven. Such devices enabled playwrights to dramatize the myths that were celebrated at the Dionysian festivals.

The ancient Greek theater was designed to enhance acoustics. The flat stone wall of the skene reflected the sound from the orchestra and the stage, and the curved shape of the amphitheater captured the sound, enabling the audience to hear the lines spoken by the actors. Each actor wore a stylized mask, or **persona**, to convey to the audience the personality traits of the particular character being portrayed—a king, a soldier, a wise old man, a young girl (female roles were played by men). The mouths of these masks were probably constructed so they amplified the voice and projected it into the audience. In addition, the actors wore *kothorni*, high shoes that elevated them above the stage, perhaps also helping to project their voices. Due to the excellent acoustics, audiences who see plays performed in these ancient theaters today can hear clearly without the aid of microphones or speaker systems.

Because actors wore masks and males played the parts of women and gods as well as men, acting methods in the ancient Greek theater were probably not realistic. In their masks, high shoes, and full-length tunics (called *chiton*), actors could not hope to appear natural or to mimic the attitudes of everyday life. Instead, they probably recited their lines while standing in stylized poses, with emotions conveyed more by gesture and tone than by action. Typically, three actors had all the speaking roles. One actor—the **protagonist**—would play the central role and have the largest speaking part. Two other actors would divide the remaining lines between them. Although other characters would come on and off the stage, they would usually not have speaking roles.

Ancient Greek tragedies were typically divided into five parts. The first part was the **prologos**, or prologue, in which an actor gave the background or explanations that the audience needed to follow the rest of the drama. Then came the **párodos**, in which the chorus entered and commented on the events presented in the prologue. Following this were several **episodia**, or episodes, in which characters spoke to one another on the stage and developed the central conflict of the play. Alternating with episodes were **stasimon** (choral odes), in which the chorus commented on the exchanges that had taken place during the preceding episode. Frequently, the choral odes were divided into *strophes*, or stanzas, which were recited or sung as the chorus moved across the orchestra in one direction, and *antistrophes*, which were recited as it moved in the opposite direction. (Interestingly, the chorus stood between the audience and the actors, often functioning as an additional audience, expressing the political, social, and moral views of the community.) The fifth part was the **exodos**, the last scene of the play, during which the conflict was resolved and the actors left the stage.

Using music, dance, and verse—as well as a variety of architectural and technical innovations—the ancient Greek theater was able to convey the traditional themes of tragedy. Thus, the Greek theater powerfully expressed ideas that were central to the religious festivals in which they first appeared: the reverence for the cycles of life and death, the unavoidable dictates of the gods, and the inscrutable and irresistible workings of fate.

The Elizabethan Theater

The Elizabethan theater, influenced by the classical traditions of Roman and Greek dramatists, traces its roots back to local religious pageants performed at medieval festivals during the twelfth and thirteenth centuries. Town **guilds**—organizations of craftsmen who worked in the same profession—reenacted Old and New Testament stories: the fall of man, Noah and the flood, David and Goliath, and the crucifixion of Christ, for example. Church fathers encouraged these plays because they brought the Bible to a largely illiterate audience. Sometimes these spectacles, called **mystery plays**, were presented in the market square or on the church steps, and at other times actors appeared on movable stages or wagons called **pageants**, which could be wheeled to a given location. (Some of these wagons were quite elaborate, with trapdoors and pulleys and an upper tier that simulated heaven.) As mystery plays became more popular,

Performance of a mystery play
Lebrecht Music & Arts/Alamy Stock Photo

they were performed in series over several days, presenting an entire cycle of a holiday—the crucifixion and resurrection of Christ during Easter, for example.

Related to mystery plays are **morality plays**, which developed in the fourteenth and fifteenth centuries. Unlike mystery plays, which depict scenes from the Bible, morality plays allegorize the Christian way of life. Typically, characters representing various virtues and vices struggle or debate over the soul of man. *Everyman* (1500), the best known of these plays, dramatizes the good and bad qualities of Everyman and shows his struggle to determine what is of value to him as he journeys toward death.

By the middle of the sixteenth century, mystery and morality plays had lost ground to a new secular drama. One reason for this decline was that mystery and morality plays were associated with Catholicism and, after Henry VIII broke with the Catholic Church in 1533, the Anglican clergy actively discouraged them. In addition, newly discovered plays of ancient Greece and Rome introduced a dramatic tradition that supplanted the traditions of religious drama. English plays that followed the classic model were sensational and bombastic, often dealing with murder, revenge, and blood retribution. Appealing to privileged classes and commoners alike, these plays were extremely popular. (One source estimates that, in London, between 20,000 and 25,000 people attended performances each week.)

In spite of the popularity of the theater, actors and playwrights encountered a number of difficulties. First, they faced opposition from city officials who were averse to theatrical presentations because they thought that the crowds attending these performances spread disease. Puritans also opposed the theater because they thought plays were immoral and sinful. Finally, some people attached to the royal court opposed the theater because they thought that the playwrights undermined the authority of Queen Elizabeth by spreading seditious ideas. As a result, during Elizabeth's reign (1558–1603), performances were placed under the strict control of the **Master of Revels**, a public official who had the power to censor plays (and did so with great regularity) and to grant licenses for performances.

Acting companies that wanted to put on a performance had to obtain a license—possible only with the patronage of a powerful nobleman—and to perform the play in an area designated by the queen. Despite these difficulties, a number of actors and playwrights gained a measure of financial independence by joining together and forming acting companies. These companies of professional actors performed works such as Christopher Marlowe's *Tamburlaine* and Thomas Kyd's *The Spanish Tragedy* in tavern courtyards and then eventually in permanent theaters. According to scholars, the structures of the Elizabethan theater evolved from these tavern courtyards.

William Shakespeare's plays were performed at the Globe Theatre (a corner of which was unearthed in December 1988). Although scholars do not know the exact design of the original Globe, drawings from the period provide a good idea of its physical features. The major difference between the Globe and today's theaters is the multiple stages on which action could be performed. The Globe consisted of a large main **stage** that extended out into the open-air **yard** where the **groundlings**, or common people, stood. Spectators who paid more sat on small stools in two or three levels of galleries that extended in front of and around the stage. (The theater could probably seat almost two thousand people at a performance.) Most of the play's action occurred on the stage, which had no curtain and could be seen from three sides. Beneath the stage was a space called the **hell**, which could be reached when the floorboards were removed. This space enabled actors to "disappear" or descend into a hole or grave when the play called for such action. Above the stage was a roof called the **heavens**, which protected the actors from the weather and contained ropes and pulleys used to lower props or to create special effects.

At the rear of the stage was a narrow **alcove** covered by a curtain that could be open or closed. This curtain, often painted, functioned as a decorative rather than a realistic backdrop. The main function of this alcove was to enable actors to hide or disappear when the script called for them to do so. Some Elizabethan theaters contained a **rear stage** instead of an alcove. Because the rear stage was concealed by a curtain, props could be arranged on it ahead of time. When the action on the rear stage was finished, the curtain would be closed, and the action would continue on the front stage.

On either side of the rear stage was a door through which the actors could enter and exit the front stage. Above the rear stage was a curtained stage called the **chamber**, which functioned as a balcony or as any other setting located above the action taking place on the stage below. On either side of the chamber were casement windows, which actors could use when a play called for a conversation with someone leaning out a window or standing on a balcony. Above the chamber was the **music gallery**, a balcony that housed the musicians who provided musical interludes throughout the play (and that doubled as a stage if the play required it). The **huts**, windows located above the music gallery, could be used by characters playing lookouts or sentries. Because of the many acting sites, more than one action could take place simultaneously. For example, lookouts could stand in the towers of Hamlet's castle while Hamlet and Horatio walked the walls below.

During Shakespeare's time, the theater had many limitations that challenged the audience's imagination. First, young boys—usually between the ages of ten and twelve—played all the women's parts. In addition, there was no artificial lighting, so plays had to be performed in daylight. Rain, wind, or clouds could disrupt a performance or ruin an image—such as "the morn in russet mantle clad"—that the audience was asked to imagine. Finally, because few sets and props were used, the audience often had to visualize the high walls of a castle or the trees of a forest. The plays were performed without intermission, except for musical interludes that occurred at various points. Thus, the experience of seeing one of Shakespeare's plays staged in the Elizabethan theater was different from seeing it staged in a modern theater.

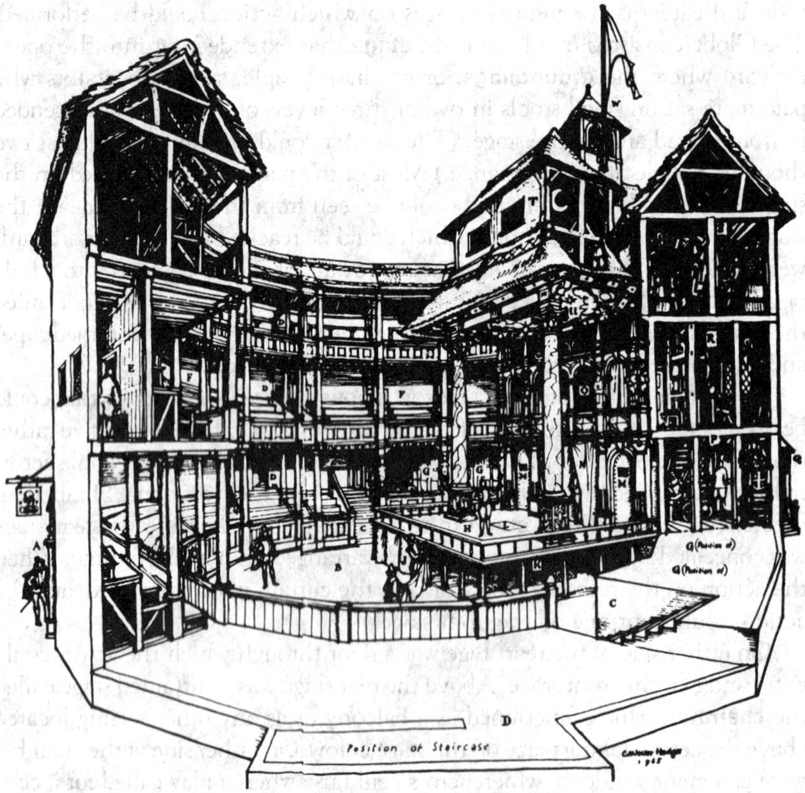

The Globe Playhouse,

1599-1613

A CONJECTURAL

RECONSTRUCTION

KEY

AA Main entrance
B The Yard
CC Entrances to lowest gallery
D Entrances to staircase and upper galleries
E Corridor serving the different sections of the middle gallery
F Middle gallery ('Twopenny Rooms')
G 'Gentlemen's Rooms' or 'Lords' Rooms'
H The stage
J The hanging being put up round the stage
K The 'Hell' under the stage
L The stage trap, leading down to the Hell
MM Stage doors
N Curtained 'place behind the stage'
O Gallery above the stage, used as required sometimes by musicians, sometimes by spectators, and often as part of the play
P Back-stage area (the tiring-house)
Q Tiring-house door
R Dressing-rooms
S Wardrobe and storage
T The hut housing the machine for lowering enthroned gods, etc., to the stage
U The 'Heavens'
W Hoisting the playhouse flag

The Globe Playhouse, 1599–1613; a Conjectural Reconstruction. From C. Walter Hodges *The Globe Restored: A Study of the Elizabethan Theatre.* New York: Norton, 1973.

C.W. Hodges. Conjectural Reconstruction of the Globe Playhouse, 1965. Pen & ink.

Aerial view of the reconstructed Globe Theatre in London
Fiona Hanson/PA Images/Getty Images

Today, a reconstruction of the Globe Theatre (above) stands on the south bank of the Thames River in London. In the 1940s, American actor Sam Wanamaker who moved to London and was shocked to find nothing that commemorated the site of the original Globe. He eventually decided to try to raise enough money to reconstruct the Globe in its original location. The Globe Playhouse Trust was founded in the 1970s, but the actual construction of the new theater did not begin until the 1980s. After a number of setbacks—for example, the Trust ran out of funds after the construction of a large underground "diaphragm" wall needed to keep out the river water—the project was finally completed. The first performance at the reconstructed Globe was given on June 14, 1996, which would have been the late Sam Wanamaker's 77th birthday.

The Modern Theater

Unlike the theaters of ancient Greece and Elizabethan England, seventeenth- and eighteenth-century theaters—such as the Palais Royal, where the great French playwright Molière presented many of his plays—were covered by a roof, beautifully decorated, and illuminated by candles so that plays could be performed at night. The theater remained brightly lit even during performances, partly because there was no easy way to extinguish hundreds of candles and partly because people went to the theater as much to see each other as to see the play.

A curtain opened and closed between acts, and the audience of about five hundred spectators sat in a long room and viewed the play on a **picture-frame stage**. This type of stage, which resembles the stages on which plays are performed today, contained the action within a **proscenium arch** that surrounded the opening through which the audience viewed the performance. Thus, the action seemed to take place in an adjoining room with one of its walls cut away. Painted scenery (some of it quite elaborate), intricately detailed costumes, and stage makeup were commonplace, and for the first time women performed female roles. In addition, a complicated series of ropes, pulleys, and cranks enabled stagehands to change scenery quickly, and sound-effects machines could give audiences the impression that they were hearing a galloping horse or a raging thunderstorm. Because the theaters were small, audiences were relatively close to the stage, so actors could use subtle movements and facial expressions to enhance their performances.

Many of the first innovations in the theater were quite basic. For example, the first stage lighting was produced by candles lining the front of the stage. This method of lighting was not only ineffective—actors were lit from below and had to step forward to be fully illuminated—but also dangerous. Costumes and even entire theaters could (and did) catch fire. Later, covered lanterns with reflectors provided better and safer lighting. In the nineteenth century, a device that used an oxyhydrogen flame directed on a cylinder of lime created extremely bright illumination that could, with the aid of a lens, be concentrated into a spotlight. (It is from this method of stage lighting that we get the expression *to be in the limelight*.)

Eventually, in the twentieth century, electric lights provided a dependable and safe way of lighting the stage. Electric spotlights, footlights, and ceiling light bars made the actors clearly visible and enabled playwrights to create special effects. In Tennessee Williams's *The Glass Menagerie* (p. 958), for example, shafts of light focus attention on action in certain areas of the stage while other areas are dimly lit.

Along with electric lighting came other innovations, such as electronic amplification. Microphones made it possible for actors to speak conversationally and to avoid using unnaturally loud "stage diction" to project their voices to the rear of the theater. Microphones placed at various points around the stage enabled actors and actresses to interact naturally and to deliver their lines audibly even without facing the audience. More recently, small wireless microphones have eliminated the unwieldy wires and the "dead spaces" left between upright or hanging microphones, allowing characters to move freely around the stage.

The true revolutions in staging came with the advent of **realism** in the middle of the nineteenth century. Until this time, scenery had been painted on canvas backdrops that trembled visibly, especially when they were intersected by doors through which actors and actresses entered. With realism came settings that were accurate down to the smallest detail. (Improved lighting, which revealed the inadequacies of painted backdrops, made such realistic stage settings necessary.) Backdrops were replaced by the **box set**, three flat panels arranged to form connected walls, with the fourth wall removed to give the audience the illusion of looking into a room. The room itself was decorated with real furniture, plants, and pictures on the walls; the door of one room might connect to another completely furnished room, or a window might open to a garden filled with realistic foliage. In addition, new methods of changing scenery were employed. Elevator stages, hydraulic lifts, and moving platforms enabled directors to make complicated changes in scenery out of the audience's view.

During the late nineteenth and early twentieth centuries, however, some playwrights reacted against what they saw as the excesses of realism. They introduced **surrealistic stage settings**, in which color and scenery mirrored the uncontrolled images of dreams, and **expressionistic stage settings**, in which costumes and scenery were exaggerated and distorted to reflect the workings of a troubled, even unbalanced mind. In addition, playwrights used lighting to create areas of light, shadow, and color that reinforced the themes of the play or reflected the emotions of the protagonist. Eugene O'Neill's 1920 play *The Emperor Jones*, for example, used a series of expressionistic scenes to show the deteriorating mental state of the terrified protagonist.

Sets in contemporary plays run the gamut from realistic to fantastic, from a detailed re-creation of a room in a production of Tennessee Williams's *The Glass Menagerie* (1945) to dreamlike sets for Eugene O'Neill's *The Emperor*

Thrust-Stage Theater. Rendering of the thrust stage at the Guthrie Theatre in Minneapolis. With seats on three sides of the stage area, the thrust stage and its background can assume many forms. Entrances can be made from the aisles, from the sides, through the stage floor, and from the back.

Alvis Upitis/Getty Images

Jones (1920) and Edward Albee's *The Sandbox* (1959). Motorized devices, such as revolving turntables, and *wagons*—scenery mounted on wheels—make rapid changes of scenery possible. The Broadway musical *Les Misérables*, for example, required scores of elaborate sets—Parisian slums, barricades, walled gardens—to be shifted as the audience watched. A gigantic barricade constructed on stage at one point in the play was later rotated to show the carnage that had taken place on both sides of a battle. Light, sound, and smoke were used to heighten the impact of the scene.

Today, as dramatists attempt to break down the barriers that separate audiences from the action they are viewing, plays are not limited to the picture-frame stage; in fact, they are performed on many different kinds of stages. Some plays take place on a **thrust stage** (pictured on the previous page), which has an area that projects out into the audience. Other plays are performed on an **arena stage**, with the audience surrounding the actors. (This kind of performance is often called **theater in the round**.) In addition, experiments have been done with **environmental staging**, in which the stage surrounds the audience or several stages are situated at various locations throughout the audience. Plays may also be performed outdoors, in settings ranging from parks to city streets.

Some playwrights even try to blur the line that divides the audience from the stage by having actors move through or sit in the audience—or even by eliminating the stage entirely. For example, *Tony 'n Tina's Wedding*, a **participatory**

Arena-Stage Theater. In an arena-stage theater, the audience surrounds the stage area, which may or may not be raised. Use of scenery is limited—perhaps to a single piece of scenery standing alone in the middle of the stage.

Danvpro/iStock/Getty Images

Scene from the participatory drama *Sleep No More*
Lucas Jackson/Reuters/Corbis

drama created in 1988 by the theater group Artificial Intelligence, takes place not in a theater but at a church where a wedding is performed and then at a catering hall where the wedding reception is held. Throughout the play, the members of the audience function as guests, joining in the wedding celebration and mingling with the actors, who improvise freely.

A more recent example of participatory drama is *Sleep No More*, which takes place in a block of warehouses (which has been transformed into the McKittrick Hotel) in the Chelsea neighborhood of New York City. The play is a wordless production of Shakespeare's *Macbeth*. Audience members, who must wear white Venetian carnival masks and remain silent at all times, are taken by elevator to various floors of the "hotel." Once deposited, they are free to follow any of the actors, who appear and disappear at will, or to explore the hotel's many rooms. The action can be intense, with audience members chasing actors down dark, narrow hallways or up and down stairs to other floors of the hotel, and at times, being pulled into the action of the play.

Today, no single architectural form defines the theater. The modern stage is a flexible space suited to the many varieties of contemporary theatrical production.

Tragedy and Comedy

Tragedy

In his *Poetics*, Aristotle (384–322 B.C.E.) sums up ancient Greek thinking about drama when he defines a **tragedy**—a drama treating a serious subject and involving persons of significance. According to Aristotle, when the members of an audience see a tragedy, they should feel both pity (and thus closeness to the protagonist) and fear (and thus revulsion) because they recognize in themselves the potential for similar reactions. The purging of these emotions that audience members experience as they see the dramatic action unfold is called **catharsis**. For catharsis to occur, the protagonist of a tragedy must be worthy of the audience's attention and sympathy.

Sergey Tarasov/Shutterstock.com

Because of the character's exalted position, the fall of a tragic protagonist is greater than that of an average person; therefore, it arouses more pity and fear in the audience. Often, society suffers as a result of the actions of the protagonist. Before the action of Sophocles' *Oedipus the King* (p. 1137), for example, Oedipus has freed Thebes from the deadly grasp of the Sphinx by answering her riddle and, as a result, has been welcomed as king. But because of his sins, Oedipus is an affront to the gods and brings famine and pestilence to the city. When his fall finally comes, it is sudden and absolute.

According to Aristotle, the protagonist of a tragedy is neither all good nor all evil but a mixture of the two. The protagonist is like the rest of us—only more exalted and possessing some weakness or flaw **(hamartia)**. This tragic flaw—perhaps narrowness of vision or overwhelming pride **(hubris)**—is typically the element that creates the conditions for tragedy. Shakespeare's Romeo

Claire Danes is surprised as Leonardo DiCaprio takes her hand to kiss in scene from the film *Romeo + Juliet*, 1996.

20th Century-Fox/Getty Images

and Juliet, for example, are so much in love they think they can ignore the blood feud that rages between their two families. However, their naive efforts to sustain their love despite the feud lead them to their tragic deaths. Similarly, Richard III's blind ambition to gain the throne causes him to murder all those who stand in his way. His unscrupulousness sets into motion the forces that eventually cause his death.

Irony—a discrepancy between what characters say and what the audience believes to be true—is central to tragedy. **Dramatic irony** (also called **tragic irony**) emerges from a situation in which the audience knows more about the dramatic situation than a character does. As a result, the protagonist's words and actions may be consistent with what that character expects but at odds with what the audience knows will happen. Thus, a character may say or do something that causes the audience to infer a meaning beyond what the character intends or realizes. The dramatic irony is clear, for example, when Oedipus announces that whoever has disobeyed the dictates of the gods will be exiled. The audience knows, although Oedipus does not, that he has just condemned himself. **Cosmic irony**, also called **irony of fate**, occurs when God, fate, or some larger, uncontrollable force seems to be intentionally deceiving characters into believing they can escape their fate. Too late, they realize that trying to avoid their destiny is futile. Years before Oedipus was born, for example, the oracle of Apollo foretold that Oedipus would kill his parents. Naturally, his parents attempted to thwart the prophecy, but ironically, their actions ensured that the prophecy would be fulfilled.

At some point in a tragedy—after the climax—protagonists begin to recognize and understand the reasons for their downfall. This moment of recognition (called the **catastrophe**) elevates tragic protagonists to grandeur and gives their suffering meaning. Without this recognition, there would be no tragedy, just **pathos**—suffering that exists simply to satisfy the sentimental or morbid sensibilities of the audience. In spite of the death of the protagonist, then, tragedy enables the audience to see the nobility of the character and thus to experience a sense of elation. In Shakespeare's *King Lear*, for example, a king at the height of his powers decides to divide his kingdom among his three daughters. Too late he realizes that, without his power, he is just a bothersome old man to his ambitious children. Only after going mad does he understand the vanity of his former existence; he dies a humbled but enlightened man.

According to Aristotle, a tragedy achieves the illusion of reality when it has **unity of action**—that is, when the play contains only those actions that lead to its tragic outcome. Later critics interpreted this constraint to mean that including subplots or mixing tragic and comic elements would destroy this unity. To the concept of unity of action, these later critics added two other requirements: **unity of place**—the requirement that the play have a single setting—and **unity of time**—the requirement that the events depicted by the play take no longer than the actual duration of the play (or, at most, a single day).

The **three unities** have had a long and rather uneven history. For example, although Shakespeare observed the unities in some of his plays—such as *The Tempest* and *The Comedy of Errors*—he had no compunctions about writing plays with subplots and frequent changes of location. He also wrote **tragicomedies**, such as *The Merchant of Venice*, which have a serious theme appropriate for tragedy but end happily, usually because of a sudden turn of events. During the eighteenth century, with its emphasis on classic form, the unities were adhered to quite strictly. In the late eighteenth and early nineteenth centuries, with the onset of romanticism and its emphasis on the natural, interest in the unities of place and time waned. Even though some modern plays (particularly one-act plays) do observe the unities—*Trifles* (p. 820), for example, has a single setting and takes place during a period of time that corresponds to the length of the play—few modern dramatists strictly adhere to them.

Ideas about appropriate subjects for tragedy have also changed. For Aristotle, the protagonist of a tragedy had to be exceptional—a king, for example. The protagonists of Greek tragedies were usually historical or mythical figures. Shakespeare often used kings and princes as protagonists—Richard II and Hamlet, for example—but he also used people of lesser rank, as in *Romeo and Juliet* and *A Midsummer Night's Dream*. In our times, interest in the lives of monarchs has been overshadowed by involvement in the lives of ordinary people. Modern tragedies—*Death of a Salesman*, for example—are more likely to focus on a traveling salesman than on a king.

With the rise of the middle class in the nineteenth century, ideas about the nature of tragedy changed. Responding to the age's desire for sentimentality, playwrights produced **melodramas**, sensational plays that appealed mainly to the emotions. Melodramas include many of the elements of tragedy but end happily and often rely on conventional plots and stock characters. Because the protagonists in melodramas—often totally virtuous heroines suffering at the hands of impossibly wicked villains—helplessly endure their tribulations without ever gaining insight or enlightenment, they never achieve tragic status. As a result, they remain cardboard cutouts who exist only to exploit the emotions of the audience. Melodrama survives today in many films and in television soap operas.

Ian McKellen (Dr. Tomas Stockmann) in *An Enemy of the People* by Henrik Ibsen in London, 1997.
Donald Cooper/Alamy Stock Photo

Realism, which arose in the late nineteenth century as a response to the artificiality of melodrama, presented serious (and sometimes tragic) themes and believable characters in the context of everyday contemporary life. Writers of realistic drama used their plays to educate their audiences about the problems of the society in which they lived. For this reason, realistic drama focuses on the commonplace and eliminates the unlikely coincidences and excessive sentimentality of melodrama.

Dramatists such as Henrik Ibsen scrutinize the lives of ordinary people, not larger-than-life characters. After great suffering, these characters rise above the limitations of their mediocre lives and exhibit courage or emotional strength. The insight they gain often focuses attention on a social problem—the restrictive social conventions that define the behavior of women in nineteenth-century marriages, for example. Realistic drama also features settings and props similar to those used in people's daily lives and includes dialogue that reflects the way people actually speak.

Developing alongside realism was a literary movement called **naturalism**. Like realism, naturalism rejected the unrealistic plots and sentimentality of melodrama, but unlike realism, naturalism sought to explore the depths of the human condition. Influenced by Charles Darwin's ideas about evolution and natural selection and Karl Marx's ideas about economic forces that shape people's lives, naturalism is a pessimistic philosophy that presents a world that is at worst hostile and at best indifferent to human concerns. It portrays human beings as higher-order animals who are driven by basic instincts—especially hunger, fear, greed, and sexuality—and who are subject to economic, social, and biological forces beyond their understanding or control. For these reasons, it is well suited to tragic themes.

The nineteenth-century French writer Émile Zola did much to develop the theory of naturalism, as did the American writers Stephen Crane, Frank Norris, and Theodore Dreiser. Elements of naturalism also find their way into the work of contemporary dramatists, such as Tennessee Williams. Unlike other tragic characters, the protagonists of naturalist works are crushed not by the gods or by fate but by poverty, animal drives, or social class. Willy Loman in *Death of a Salesman*, for example, is subject to the economic forces of a society that does not value its workers and discards those it no longer finds useful.

Comedy

A **comedy** treats themes and characters with humor and typically has a happy ending. Whereas tragedy focuses on the hidden dimensions of the tragic hero's character, comedy focuses on the public persona, the protagonist as a social being. Tragic figures are typically seen in isolation, questioning the meaning of their lives and trying to comprehend their suffering. Hamlet—draped in sable, longing for death, and self-consciously contemplating his duty—epitomizes the isolation of the tragic hero.

Unlike tragic heroes, comic figures exist in the public arena, where people intentionally assume the masks of pretension and self-importance. The purpose of comedy is to strip away these masks and expose human beings for what they are. Whereas tragedy reveals the nobility of the human condition, comedy reveals its inherent folly, portraying human beings as selfish, hypocritical, vain, weak, irrational, and capable of self-delusion. Thus, the basic function of comedy is critical—to tell people that things are not what they seem and

A Midsummer Night's Dream at Glyndebourne Festival Opera, East Sussex, England in 2001.
Donald Cooper/Alamy Stock Photo

that appearances are not necessarily reality. In the comic world, nothing is solid or predictable, and accidents and coincidences are more important to the plot than reason. Many of Shakespeare's comedies, for example, depend on exchanged or confused identities. The wordplay and verbal nonsense of comedy add to this general confusion.

Comedies typically rely on certain familiar plot devices. Many comedies begin with a startling or unusual situation that attracts the audience's attention. In Shakespeare's *A Midsummer Night's Dream*, for example, Theseus, the duke of Athens, rules that Hermia will either marry the man her father has chosen for her or be put to death. Such an event could lead to tragedy if comedy did not intervene to save the day.

Comedy often depends on obstacles and hindrances to further its plot: the more difficult the problems the lovers face, the more satisfying their eventual triumph will be. For this reason, the plot of a comedy is usually more complex than the plot of a tragedy. Compare the rather straightforward plot of *Hamlet* (p. 1012)—a prince ordered to avenge his murdered father's death is driven mad with indecision and, after finally acting decisively, is killed himself—with the mix-ups, mistaken identities, and general confusion of *A Midsummer Night's Dream*.

Finally, comedies have happy endings. Whereas tragedy ends with death, comedy ends with an affirmation of life. Eventually, the confusion and misunderstandings reach a point where some resolution must be achieved: the difficulties of the lovers are overcome, the villains are banished, and the lovers marry—or at least express their intention to do so. In this way, the lovers establish their connection with the rest of society, and its values are affirmed.

The first comedies, written in Greece in the fifth century B.C., heavily satirized the religious and social issues of the day and were characterized by bawdy humor. In the fourth and third centuries B.C., this **Old Comedy** gave way to **New Comedy**, a comedy of romance with stock characters—lovers and untrustworthy servants, for example—and conventional settings. Lacking the bitter satire and bawdiness of Old Comedy, New Comedy depends on outrageous plots, mistaken identities, young lovers, interfering parents, and conniving servants. Ultimately, the young lovers outwit all those who stand between them and, in so doing, affirm the primacy of youth and love over old age and death.

Old and New Comedy represent two distinct lines of humor that extend to modern times. Old Comedy depends on **satire**—biting humor that diminishes a person, idea, or institution by ridiculing it or holding it up to scorn. Unlike most comedy, which exists simply to make people laugh, satire is social criticism, deriding hypocrisy, pretension, and vanity or condemning vice. At its best, satire appeals to the intellect, has a serious purpose, and arouses thoughtful laughter. New Comedy may also be satiric, but the satire is often tempered by elements of **farce**, comedy in which stereotypical characters engage in boisterous horseplay and slapstick humor, all the while making jokes and sexual innuendoes—as they do in Anton Chekhov's *The Brute* (p. 769).

English comedy got its start in the sixteenth century in the form of farcical episodes that appeared in morality plays. During the Renaissance, comedy developed rapidly, beginning in 1533 with Nicholas Udall's *Ralph Roister Doister* and eventually evolving into Shakespeare's **romantic comedy**—such as *A Midsummer Night's Dream*—in which love is the main subject, and idealized heroines and lovers endure great difficulties until the inevitable happy ending is reached.

Also during the Renaissance, particularly in the seventeenth century, writers such as Ben Jonson experimented with a different type of comedy—the **comedy of humours**, which focused on characters whose behavior was controlled by a characteristic trait, or *humour*. During the Renaissance, a person's temperament was thought to be determined by the mix of fluids, or humours, in the body. When one humour dominated, a certain type of disposition resulted. Playwrights capitalized on this belief, writing comedies in which characters are motivated by stereotypical behaviors that result from the imbalance of the humours. In comedies such as Jonson's *Volpone* and *The Alchemist*, characters such as the suspicious husband and the miser can be manipulated by others because of their predictable dispositions.

Closely related to the comedy of humours is the satiric **comedy of manners**, which developed during the sixteenth and seventeenth centuries and achieved great popularity in the nineteenth century. This form focused on the manners and customs of society and directed its satire against characters who violated social conventions and rules of behavior. The comedy comes from players striving to maintain appearances while at the same time revealing the truth behind artificial codes of conduct. These plays tend to be memorable more for their witty dialogue than for their development of characters or setting. Oliver Goldsmith's *She Stoops to Conquer*, George Bernard Shaw's *Pygmalion*, and even some of the television sitcoms of today are examples of this type of comedy.

In the eighteenth century, a reaction against the perceived immorality of the comedy of manners led to **sentimental comedy**, which eventually achieved great popularity. This kind of comedy relied on sentimental emotion rather than on wit or humor to move an audience. It also dwelled on the virtues rather than on the vices of life. The heroes of sentimental comedy are unimpeachably noble, moral, and honorable; the pure, virtuous, middle-class heroines suffer trials and tribulations calculated to move the audience to tears rather than to laughter. Eventually, the distress of the hero and heroine is resolved in a sometimes contrived (but always happy) ending. Sir Richard Steele's *The Conscious Lovers* (1722) is an example of sentimental comedy.

In his 1877 essay *The Idea of Comedy*, novelist and critic George Meredith suggests that comedy that appeals to the intellect should be called **high comedy**. Thus, Shakespeare's *As You Like It* and George Bernard Shaw's *Pygmalion* can be characterized as high comedy. When comedy has little or no intellectual appeal, according to Meredith, it is **low comedy**. Low comedy appears in parts of Shakespeare's *The Taming of the Shrew* and as comic relief in *Macbeth*.

The twentieth century developed its own characteristic comic forms, reflecting the uncertainty and pessimism of a period marked by two world wars, the Holocaust, and nuclear destruction, as well as threats posed by environmental pollution and ethnic and racial conflict—and, in this century, the terrorist attacks of September 11, 2001, and the onset of the COVID pandemic in 2019. Combining laughter and hints of tragedy, these modern tragicomedies feature **antiheroes**, characters who, instead of manifesting dignity and power, are ineffectual or petty. Their plight frequently elicits laughter, not pity and fear, from the audience. **Black or dark comedies**, for example, rely on the morbid and the absurd. These works are usually so satiric and bitter that they threaten to slip over into tragedy. The screenplay of Joseph Heller's novel *Catch-22*, which ends with a character dropping bombs on his own men, is a classic example of such comedy. **Theater of the absurd**, which includes comedies such as Samuel Beckett's *Waiting for Godot* and Tom Stoppard's *Rosencrantz and Guildenstern Are Dead*, begins with the assumption that the human condition is irrational. Typically, this type of drama does not have a conventional plot; instead, it presents a series of apparently unrelated images and illogical exchanges of dialogue meant to reinforce the idea that human beings live in a remote, confusing, and often incomprehensible universe. Absurdist dramas seem to go in circles, never progressing to a climax or achieving a resolution, thus reinforcing the theme of the endless and meaningless repetition that characterizes modern life.

Defining Drama

Traditionally, plays are divided into **acts** and **scenes**. Between acts, there is sometimes an **intermission**, a pause in the action that can be used to heighten the dramatic tension created at the end of the previous scene (as well as to represent the passage of time between one act and the next). The number of acts in a play can range from one to five, depending on the length and scope of the play itself. Shakespeare's *Hamlet* and *A Midsummer Night's Dream* both have five acts, but most full-length contemporary plays have just two or three.

Some shorter plays have only one act. In a **one-act play** such as Chekov's *The Brute*, the playwright is faced with the challenge of creating a dramatic work that includes all the elements that are part of longer plays—exposition, conflict, climax, and resolution. Because these plays are shorter, their imagery and dialogue are often more concise. In fact, because there is less time to devote to character development, subtext, or the consequences of events, one-act plays differ from full-length plays in the same way that short stories differ from novels.

An even more recent development in drama is the **ten-minute play**—a play in which all the actors are on stage and all events take place within a ten-minute time period (see Chapter 28). On an even smaller scale, a **monologue**—an extended speech delivered by one character—can stand alone as a complete dramatic work, as in Joyce Carol Oates's *When I Was a Little Girl and My Mother Didn't Want Me* (1997). Some contemporary plays—including Eve Ensler's *The Vagina Monologues* (1996) and Claudia Shear's *Blown Sideways Through Life* (1994)—are composed entirely of a series of interrelated dramatic monologues.

Some contemporary drama is **improvisational**, which means that it is either partially or completely unscripted. This dramatic tradition is a descendant of **commedia dell'arte**, an Italian form of improvisational theater that began in the sixteenth century and was popular until the eighteenth century. Today, many theater actors are trained in "improv" work, which challenges them to sharpen their concentration and to trust in their own instincts rather than relying solely on a script. Some improvisational plays rely on audience participation, requiring actors to improvise in response to audience members' spontaneous contributions to the play.

Dramatic works differ from other prose works in a number of fairly obvious ways. In addition to being divided into **acts** and **scenes**, they include **stage directions** that specify characters' entrances and exits and describe what settings look like and how characters look and act; and they consist primarily of **dialogue**, lines spoken by the characters. And, of course, plays are different from other prose works in that they are written not to be read but to be performed in front of an audience.

Unlike novels and short stories, plays do not usually have narrators to tell the audience what a character is thinking or what happened in the past; for the most part, the audience knows only what characters reveal. To compensate for the absence of a narrator, playwrights can use **monologues** (extended speeches by one character), **soliloquies** (monologues in which a character expresses private thoughts while alone on stage), or **asides** (brief comments by a character who reveals thoughts by speaking directly to the audience without being heard by the other characters). Some plays, however, do have narrators. For example, Tom in *The Glass Menagerie* functions as a narrator, speaking directly to the audience, commenting on the action, and providing information about himself and his sister Laura. In addition to these dramatic techniques, a play can also use costumes, scenery, props, music, lighting, and other techniques to enhance its impact on the audience.

The play that follows, Anton Chekhov's *The Brute* (1888), is typical of modern drama in many respects. A one-act play translated from Russian, it is essentially a struggle of wills between two headstrong characters, a man and a woman, with action escalating through the characters' increasingly heated exchanges of dialogue. Stage directions describe the setting—"the drawing room of a country house"—and announce the appearance of various props. They also describe the major characters' appearances as well as their actions, gestures, and emotions. Because the play is a **farce**, it features broad physical comedy, asides, wild dramatic gestures, and elaborate figures of speech, all designed to enhance its comic effect.

Bettmann/Getty Images

ANTON CHEKHOV (1860–1904) is an important nineteenth-century Russian playwright and short story writer. He became a doctor and, as a young adult, supported the rest of his family after his father's bankruptcy. After his early adult years in Moscow, Chekhov spent the rest of his life in the country, moving to Yalta, a resort town in Crimea, for his health (he suffered from tuberculosis). He continued to write plays, mostly for the Moscow Art Theatre, although he could not supervise their production as he would have wished. His plays include *The Seagull* (1896), *Uncle Vanya* (1898), *The Three Sisters* (1901), and *The Cherry Orchard* (1904).

The Brute, or *The Bear* (1888), is one of a number of one-act farces Chekhov wrote just before his major plays. It is based on a French farce (*Les Jurons de Cadillac* by Pierre Breton) about a man who cannot refrain from swearing. The woman he loves offers to marry him if he can avoid swearing for one hour; he is unable to do it, but he fails so charmingly that she agrees to marry him anyway.

Cultural Context The custom of dueling has been popular throughout history in many countries. Generally speaking, as in *The Brute*, duels are fought as a matter of honor—in response to an insult, an offense to one's character, or an affront to one's dignity. Once a challenge to a duel has been issued, negotiators (called *seconds*) agree on the time, place, and weaponry involved, as well as the point of surrender (first blood drawn or death). In a pistol duel, the participants stand back to back, count off a predetermined number of paces, turn, and fire. Today, dueling is illegal in most countries, and killing someone during a duel is considered murder.

The Brute

A Joke in One Act (1888)

Translated by Eric Bentley

CHARACTERS

Mrs. Popov, *widow and landowner, small, with dimpled cheeks*
Mr. Grigory S. Smirnov, *gentleman farmer, middle-aged*
Luka, *Mrs. Popov's footman, an old man*
Gardener
Coachman
Hired Men

SCENE

The drawing room of a country house. Mrs. Popov, in deep mourning, is staring hard at a photograph. Luka is with her.

Luka: It's not right, ma'am, you're killing yourself. The cook has gone off with the maid to pick berries. The cat's having a high old time in the yard catching birds. Every living thing is happy. But you stay moping here in the house like it was a convent, taking no pleasure in nothing. I mean it, ma'am! It must be a full year since you set foot out of doors.

Mrs. Popov: I must never set foot out of doors again, Luka. Never! I have nothing to set foot out of doors *for*. My life is done. *He* is in his grave. I have buried myself alive in this house. We are *both* in our graves.

Luka: You're off again, ma'am. I just won't listen to you no more. Mr. Popov is dead, but what can we do about that? It's God's doing. God's will be done. You've cried over him, you've done your share of mourning, haven't you? There's a limit to everything. You can't go on weeping and wailing forever. My old lady died, for that matter, and I wept and wailed over her a whole month long. Well, that was it. I couldn't weep and wail all my life. She just wasn't worth it. *(He sighs.)* As for the neighbors, you've forgotten all about them, ma'am. You don't visit them and you don't let them visit you. You and I are like a pair of spiders—excuse the expression, ma'am—here we are in this house like a pair of spiders, we never see the light of day. And it isn't like there was no nice people around either. The whole county's swarming with 'em. There's a regiment quartered at Riblov, and the officers are so good-looking! The girls can't take their eyes off them—There's a ball at the camp every Friday—The military band plays most every day of the week—What do you say, ma'am? You're young, you're pretty, you could enjoy yourself! Ten years from now you may want to strut and show your feathers to the officers, and it'll be too late.

Mrs. Popov: *(firmly)* You must never bring this subject up again, Luka. Since Popov died, life has been an empty dream to me, you know that. *You* may think I am alive. Poor ignorant Luka! You are wrong. I am dead. I'm in my grave. Never more shall I see the light of day, never strip from my body this … raiment of death! Are you listening, Luka? Let his ghost learn how I love him! Yes, *I* know, and *you* know, he was often unfair to me, he was cruel to me, and he was unfaithful to me. What of it? *I* shall be faithful to *him*, that's all. I will show him how *I* can love. Hereafter, in a better world than this, he will welcome me back, the same loyal girl I always was—

Luka: Instead of carrying on this way, ma'am, you should go out in the garden and take a bit of a walk, ma'am. Or why not harness Toby and take a drive? Call on a couple of the neighbours, ma'am?

Mrs. Popov: *(breaking down)* Oh, Luka!

Luka: Yes, ma'am? What have I said, ma'am? Oh, dear!

Mrs. Popov: Toby! You said Toby! He adored that horse. When he drove me out to the Korchagins and the Vlasovs, it was always with Toby! He was a wonderful driver, do you remember, Luka? So graceful! So strong! I can see him now, pulling at those reins with all his might and main! Toby! Luka, tell them to give Toby an extra portion of oats today.

Luka: Yes, ma'am.

A bell rings.

Mrs. Popov: Who is that? Tell them I'm not at home.

Luka: Very good, ma'am. *(Exit.)*

Mrs. Popov: *(gazing again at the photograph)* You shall see, my Popov, how a wife can love and forgive. Till death do us part. Longer than that. Till death re-unite us forever! *(Suddenly a titter breaks through her tears.)* Aren't you ashamed of yourself, Popov? Here's your little wife, being good, being faithful, so faithful she's locked up here waiting for her own funeral, while you—doesn't it make you ashamed, you naughty boy? You were terrible, you know. You were unfaithful, and you made those awful scenes about it, you stormed out and left me alone for weeks—

Enter Luka.

Luka: *(upset)* There's someone asking for you, ma'am. Says he must—

Mrs. Popov: I suppose you told him that since my husband's death I see no one?

Luka: Yes, ma'am. I did, ma'am. But he wouldn't listen, ma'am. He says it's urgent.

Mrs. Popov: *(shrilly)* I see no one!!

Luka: He won't take no for an answer, ma'am. He just curses and swears and comes in anyway. He's a perfect monster, ma'am. He's in the dining room right now.

Mrs. Popov: In the dining room, is he? I'll give him his come-uppance. Bring him in here this minute.

Exit Luka.

(Suddenly sad again.) Why do they do this to me? Why? Insulting my grief, intruding on my solitude? *(She sighs.)* I'm afraid I'll have to enter a convent. I will, I must enter a convent!

Enter Mr. Smirnov and Luka.

Smirnov: *(to Luka)* Dolt! Idiot! You talk too much! *(Seeing Mrs. Popov. With dignity.)* May I have the honor of introducing myself, madam? Grigory S. Smirnov, landowner and lieutenant of artillery, retired. Forgive me, madam, if I disturb your peace and quiet, but my business is both urgent and weighty.

Mrs. Popov: *(declining to offer him her hand)* What is it you wish, sir?

Smirnov: At the time of his death, your late husband—with whom I had the honor to be acquainted, ma'am—was in my debt to the tune of twelve hundred rubles. I have two notes to prove it. Tomorrow, ma'am, I must pay the interest on a bank loan. I have therefore no alternative, ma'am, but to ask you to pay me the money today.

Mrs. Popov: Twelve hundred rubles? But what did my husband owe it to you for?

Smirnov: He used to buy his oats from me, madam.

Mrs. Popov: *(to Luka, with a sigh)* Remember what I said, Luka: tell them to give Toby an extra portion of oats today!

Exit Luka.

My dear Mr.—what was the name again?

Smirnov: Smirnov, ma'am.

Mrs. Popov: My dear Mr. Smirnov, if Mr. Popov owed you money, you shall be paid—to the last ruble, to the last kopeck. But today—you must excuse me, Mr.—what was it?

Smirnov: Smirnov, ma'am.

Mrs. Popov: Today, Mr. Smirnov, I have no ready cash in the house. *(Smirnov starts to speak.)* Tomorrow, Mr. Smirnov, no, the day after tomorrow, all will be well. My steward will be back from town. I shall see that he pays what is owing. Today, no. In any case, today is exactly seven months from Mr. Popov's death. On such a day you will understand that I am in no mood to think of money.

Smirnov: Madam, if you don't pay up now, you can carry me out feet foremost. They'll seize my estate.

Mrs. Popov: You can have your money. *(He starts to thank her.)* Tomorrow. *(He again starts to speak.)* That is: the day after tomorrow.

Smirnov: I don't need the money the day after tomorrow. I need it today.

Mrs. Popov: I'm sorry, Mr.—

Smirnov: *(shouting)* Smirnov!

Mrs. Popov: *(sweetly)* Yes, of course. But you can't have it today.

Smirnov: But I can't wait for it any longer!

Mrs. Popov: Be sensible, Mr. Smirnov. How can I pay you if I don't have it?

Smirnov: You don't have it?

Mrs. Popov: I don't have it.

Smirnov: Sure?

Mrs. Popov: Positive.

Smirnov: Very well. I'll make a note to that effect. *(Shrugging.)* And then they want me to keep cool. I meet the tax commissioner on the street, and he says, "Why are you always in such a bad humor, Smirnov?" Bad humor! How can I help it, in God's name? I need money, I need it desperately. Take yesterday: I leave home at the crack of dawn, I call on all my debtors. Not a one of them pays up. Footsore and weary, I creep at midnight into some little dive, and try to snatch a few winks of sleep on the floor by the vodka barrel. Then today, I come here, fifty miles from home, saying to myself, "At last, at last, I can be sure of something," and you're not in the mood! You give me a mood! Christ, how can I help getting all worked up?

Mrs. Popov: I thought I'd made it clear, Mr. Smirnov, that you'll get your money the minute my steward is back from town.

Smirnov: What the hell do I care about your steward? Pardon the expression, ma'am. But it was you I came to see.

Mrs. Popov: What language! What a tone to take to a lady! I refuse to hear another word. *(Quickly, exit.)*

Smirnov: Not in the mood, huh? "Exactly seven months since Popov's death," huh? How about me? *(Shouting after her.)* Is there this interest to pay, or isn't there? I'm asking you a question: is there this interest to pay, or isn't there? So your husband died, and you're not in the mood, and your steward's gone off some place, and so forth and so on, but what can *I* do about all that, huh? What do *you* think I should do? Take a running jump and shove my head through the wall? Take off in a balloon? You don't know my *other* debtors. I call on Gruzdeff. Not at home. I look for Yaroshevitch. He's hiding out. I find Kooritsin. He kicks up a row, and I have to throw him through the window. I work my way right down the list. Not a kopeck. Then I come to you, and God damn it to hell, if you'll pardon the expression, you're not in the mood! *(Quietly, as he realizes he's talking to air.)* I've spoiled them all, that's what, I've let them play me for a sucker. Well, I'll show them. I'll show this one. I'll stay right here till she pays up. Ugh! *(He shudders with rage.)* I'm in a rage! I'm in a positively towering rage! Every nerve in my body is trembling at forty to the dozen! I can't breathe, I feel ill, I think I'm going to faint, hey, you there!

Enter Luka.

Luka: Yes, sir? Is there anything you wish, sir?

Smirnov: Water! Water! No, make it vodka.

Exit Luka.

Consider the logic of it. A fellow creature is desperately in need of cash, so desperately in need that he has to seriously contemplate hanging himself, and this woman, this mere chit of a girl, won't pay up, and why not? Because, forsooth, she isn't in the mood! Oh, the logic of women! Come to that, I never have liked them, I could do without the whole sex. Talk to a woman? I'd rather sit on a barrel of dynamite, the very thought gives me gooseflesh. Women! Creatures of poetry and romance! Just to see one in the distance gets me mad. My legs start twitching with rage. I feel like yelling for help.

Enter Luka, handing Smirnov a glass of water.

Luka: Mrs. Popov is indisposed, sir. She is seeing no one.

Smirnov: Get out.

Exit Luka.

Indisposed, is she? Seeing no one, huh? Well, she can see me or not, but I'll be here, I'll be right here till she pays up. If you're sick for a week, I'll be here for a week. If you're sick for a year, I'll be here for a year. You won't get around *me* with your widow's weeds and your schoolgirl dimples. I know all about dimples. *(Shouting through the window.)* Semyon, let the horses out of those shafts, we're not leaving, we're staying, and tell them to give the horses some oats, yes, oats, you fool, what do you think? *(Walking away from the window.)* What a mess, what an unholy mess! I didn't sleep last night, the heat is terrific today, not a damn one of 'em has paid up, and here's this—this skirt in mourning that's not in the mood! My head aches, where's that—*(He drinks from the glass.)* Water, ugh! You there!

Enter Luka.

Luka: Yes, sir. You wish for something, sir?

Smirnov: Where's that confounded vodka I asked for?

Exit Luka.

(Smirnov sits and looks himself over.) Oof! A fine figure of a man *I* am! Unwashed, uncombed, unshaven, straw on my vest, dust all over me. The little woman must've taken me for a highwayman. *(Yawns.)* I suppose it wouldn't be considered polite to barge into a drawing room in this state, but who cares? I'm not a visitor, I'm a creditor—most unwelcome of guests, second only to Death.

Enter Luka.

Luka: *(handing him the vodka)* If I may say so, sir, you take too many liberties, sir.

Smirnov: What?!

Luka: Oh, nothing, sir, nothing.

Smirnov: Who in hell do you think you're talking to? Shut your mouth!

Luka: *(aside)* There's an evil spirit abroad. The Devil must have sent him. Oh! *(Exit Luka.)*

Smirnov: What a rage I'm in! I'll grind the whole world to powder. Oh, I feel ill again. You there!

Enter Mrs. Popov.

Mrs. Popov: *(looking at the floor)* In the solitude of my rural retreat, Mr. Smirnov, I've long since grown unaccustomed to the sound of the human voice. Above all, I cannot bear shouting. I must beg you not to break the silence.

Smirnov: Very well. Pay me my money and I'll go.

Mrs. Popov: I told you before, and I tell you again, Mr. Smirnov. I have no cash, you'll have to wait till the day after tomorrow. Can I express myself more plainly?

Smirnov: And *I* told *you* before, and *I* tell *you* again, that I need the money today, that the day after tomorrow is too late, and that if you don't pay, and pay now, I'll have to hang myself in the morning!

Mrs. Popov: But I have no cash. This is quite a puzzle.

Smirnov: You won't pay, huh?

Mrs. Popov: I *can't* pay, Mr. Smirnov.

Smirnov: In that case, I'm going to sit here and wait. *(Sits down.)* You'll pay up the day after tomorrow? Very good. Till the day after tomorrow, here I sit. *(Pause. He jumps up.)* Now look, do I have to pay that interest tomorrow, or don't I? Or do you think I'm joking?

Mrs. Popov: I must ask you not to raise your voice, Mr. Smirnov. This is not a stable.

Smirnov: Who said it was? Do I have to pay the interest tomorrow or not?

Mrs. Popov: Mr. Smirnov, do you know how to behave in the presence of a lady?

Smirnov: No, madam, I do not know how to behave in the presence of a lady.

Mrs. Popov: Just what I thought. I look at you, and I say: ugh! I hear you talk, and I say to myself: "That man doesn't know how to talk to a lady."

Smirnov: You'd like me to come simpering to you in French, I suppose. "*Enchanté, madame! Merci beaucoup* for not paying zee money, *madame*! *Pardonnez-moi* if I 'ave disturbed you, *madame*! How *charmante* you look in mourning, *madame*!"

Mrs. Popov: Now you're being silly, Mr. Smirnov.

Smirnov: *(mimicking)* "Now you're being silly, Mr. Smirnov." "You don't know how to talk to a lady, Mr. Smirnov." Look here, Mrs. Popov, I've known more women than you've known pussy cats. I've fought three duels on their account. I've jilted twelve, and been jilted by nine others. Oh, yes, Mrs. Popov, I've played the fool in my time, whispered sweet nothings, bowed and scraped and endeavored to please. Don't tell me I don't know what it is to love, to pine away with longing, to have the blues, to melt like butter, to be weak as water. I was full of tender emotion. I was carried away with passion. I squandered half my fortune on the sex. I chattered about women's emancipation. But there's an end to everything, dear madam. Burning eyes, dark eyelashes, ripe, red lips, dimpled cheeks, heaving bosoms, soft whisperings, the moon above; the lake below—I don't give a rap for that sort of nonsense any more, Mrs. Popov. I've found out about women. Present company excepted, they're liars. Their behavior is mere play acting; their conversation is sheer gossip. Yes, dear lady, women, young or old, are false, petty, vain, cruel, malicious, unreasonable. As for intelligence, any sparrow could give them points. Appearances, I admit, can be deceptive. In appearance, a woman may be all poetry and romance, goddess and angel, muslin and fluff. To look at her exterior is to be transported to heaven. But I have looked at her interior, Mrs. Popov, and what did I find there—in her very soul? A crocodile. *(He has gripped the back of the chair so firmly that it snaps.)* And, what is more revolting, a crocodile with an illusion, a crocodile that imagines tender sentiments are its own special province, a crocodile that thinks itself queen of the realm of love! Whereas, in sober fact, dear madam, if a woman can love anything except a lapdog you can hang me by the feet on that nail. For a man, love is suffering, love is sacrifice. A woman just swishes her train around and tightens her grip on your nose. Now, you're a woman, aren't you, Mrs. Popov? You must be an expert on some of this. Tell me, quite frankly, did you ever know a woman to be—faithful, for instance? Or even sincere? Only old hags, huh? Though some women are old hags from birth. But as for the others? You're right: a faithful woman is a freak of nature—like a cat with horns.

Mrs. Popov: Who *is* faithful, then? Who *have* you cast for the faithful lover? Not man?

Smirnov: Right first time, Mrs. Popov: man.

Mrs. Popov: *(going off into a peal of bitter laughter)* Man! Man is faithful! That's a new one! *(Fiercely.)* What right do you have to say this, Mr. Smirnov? Men faithful? Let me tell you something. Of all the men I have ever known my late husband Popov was the best. I loved him, and there are women who know how to love, Mr. Smirnov. I gave him my youth, my happiness, my life, my fortune. I worshipped the ground he trod on—and what happened? The best of men was unfaithful to me, Mr. Smirnov. Not once in a while. All the time. After he died, I found his desk drawer full of love letters. While he was alive, he was always going away for the week-end. He squandered my money. He made love to other women before my very eyes. But, in spite of all, Mr. Smirnov, *I* was faithful. Unto death. And beyond. I am *still* faithful, Mr. Smirnov! Buried alive in this house, I shall wear mourning till the day I, too, am called to my eternal rest.

Smirnov: *(laughing scornfully)* Expect me to believe that? As if I couldn't see through all this hocus-pocus. Buried alive! Till you're called to your eternal rest! Till when? Till some little poet—or some little subaltern with his first moustache—comes riding by and asks: "Can that be the house of the mysterious Tamara who for love of her late husband has buried herself alive, vowing to see no man?" Ha!

Mrs. Popov: *(flaring up)* How dare you? How dare you insinuate—?

Smirnov: You may have buried yourself alive, Mrs. Popov, but you haven't forgotten to powder your nose.

Mrs. Popov: *(incoherent)* How dare you? How—?

Smirnov: Who's raising his voice now? Just because I call a spade a spade. Because I shoot straight from the shoulder. Well, don't shout at me, I'm not your steward.

Mrs. Popov: I'm not shouting, you're shouting! Oh, leave me alone!

Smirnov: Pay me the money, and I will.

Mrs. Popov: You'll get no money out of me!

Smirnov: Oh, so that's it!

Mrs. Popov: Not a ruble, not a kopeck. Get out! Leave me alone!

Smirnov: Not being your husband, I must ask you not to make scenes with me. *(He sits.)* I don't like scenes.

Mrs. Popov: *(choking with rage)* You're sitting down?

Smirnov: Correct, I'm sitting down.

Mrs. Popov: I asked you to leave!

Smirnov: Then give me the money. *(Aside.)* Oh, what a rage I'm in, what a rage!

Mrs. Popov: The impudence of the man! I won't talk to you a moment longer. Get out. *(Pause.)* Are you going?

Smirnov: No.

Mrs. Popov: No?!

Smirnov: No.

Mrs. Popov: On your head be it. Luka!

Enter Luka.

Show the gentleman out, Luka.

Luka: *(approaching)* I'm afraid, sir, I'll have to ask you, um, to leave, sir, now, um—

Smirnov: *(jumping up)* Shut your mouth, you old idiot! Who do you think you're talking to? I'll make mincemeat of you.

Luka: *(clutching his heart)* Mercy on us! Holy saints above! *(He falls into an armchair.)* I'm taken sick! I can't breathe!!

Mrs. Popov: Then where's Dasha? Dasha! Dasha! Come here at once! *(She rings.)*

Luka: They gone picking berries, ma'am, I'm alone here—Water, water, I'm taken sick!

Mrs. Popov: *(to Smirnov)* Get out, you!

Smirnov: Can't you even be polite with me, Mrs. Popov?

Mrs. Popov: *(clenching her fists and stamping her feet)* With you? You're a wild animal, you were never house-broken!

Smirnov: What? What did you say?

Mrs. Popov: I said you were a wild animal, you were never house-broken.

Smirnov: *(advancing upon her)* And what right do you have to talk to me like that?

Mrs. Popov: Like what?

Smirnov: You have insulted me, madam.

Mrs. Popov: What of it? Do you think I'm scared of you?

Smirnov: So you think you can get away with it because you're a woman. A creature of poetry and romance, huh? Well, it doesn't go down with me. I hereby challenge you to a duel.

Luka: Mercy on us! Holy saints alive! Water!

Smirnov: I propose we shoot it out.

Mrs. Popov: Trying to scare me again? Just because you have big fists and a voice like a bull? You're a brute.

Smirnov: No one insults Grigory S. Smirnov with impunity! And I don't care if you *are* a female.

Mrs. Popov: *(trying to outshout him)* Brute, brute, brute!

Smirnov: The sexes are equal, are they? Fine: then it's just prejudice to expect men alone to pay for insults. I hereby challenge—

Mrs. Popov: *(screaming)* All right! You want to shoot it out? All right! Let's shoot it out!

Smirnov: And let it be here and now!

Mrs. Popov: Here and now! All right! I'll have Popov's pistols here in one minute! *(Walks away, then turns.)* Putting one of Popov's bullets through your silly head will be a pleasure! Au revoir. *(Exit.)*

Smirnov: I'll bring her down like a duck, a sitting duck. I'm not one of your little poets, I'm no little subaltern with his first moustache. No, sir, there's no weaker sex where I'm concerned!

Luka: Sir! Master! *(He goes down on his knees.)* Take pity on a poor old man, and do me a favor: go away. It was bad enough before, you nearly scared me to death. But a duel—!

Smirnov: *(ignoring him)* A duel! That's equality of the sexes for you! That's women's emancipation! Just as a matter of principle I'll bring her down like a duck. But what a woman! "Putting one of Popov's bullets through your silly head . . ." Her cheeks were flushed, her eyes were gleaming! And, by God, she's accepted the challenge! I never knew a woman like this before!

Luka: Sir! Master! Please go away! I'll always pray for you!

Smirnov: *(again ignoring him)* What a woman! Phew!! *She's* no sour puss, *she's* no cry baby. She's fire and brimstone. She's a human cannon ball. What a shame I have to kill her!

Luka: *(weeping)* Please, kind sir, please, go away!

Smirnov: *(as before)* I like her, isn't that funny? With those dimples and all? I like her. I'm even prepared to consider letting her off that debt. And where's my rage? It's gone. I never knew a woman like this before.

Enter Mrs. Popov with pistols.

Mrs. Popov: *(boldly)* Pistols, Mr. Smirnov! *(Matter of fact.)* But before we start, you'd better show me how it's done. I'm not too familiar with these things. In fact I never gave a pistol a second look.

Luka: Lord, have mercy on us, I must go hunt up the gardener and the coachman. Why has this catastrophe fallen upon us, O Lord? *(Exit.)*

Smirnov: *(examining the pistols)* Well, it's like this. There are several makes: one is the Mortimer, with capsules, especially constructed for dueling. What you have here are Smith and Wesson triple-action revolvers, with extractor, first-rate job, worth ninety rubles at the very least. You hold it this way. *(Aside.)* My God, what eyes she has! They're setting me on fire.

Mrs. Popov: This way?

Smirnov: Yes, that's right. You cock the trigger, take aim like this, head up, arm out like this. Then you just press with this finger here, and it's all over. The main thing is, keep cool, take slow aim, and don't let your arm jump.

Mrs. Popov: I see. And if it's inconvenient to do the job here, we can go out in the garden.

Smirnov: Very good. Of course, I should warn you: I'll be firing in the air.

Mrs. Popov: What? This is the end. Why?

Smirnov: Oh, well—because—for private reasons.

Mrs. Popov: Scared, huh? *(She laughs heartily.)* Now don't you try to get out of it, Mr. Smirnov. My blood is up. I won't be happy till I've drilled a hole through that skull of yours. Follow me. What's the matter? Scared?

Smirnov: That's right. I'm scared.

Mrs. Popov: Oh, come on, what's the matter with you?

Smirnov: Well, um, Mrs. Popov, I, um, I like you.

Mrs. Popov: *(laughing bitterly)* Good God! He likes me, does he? The gall of the man. *(Showing him the door.)* You may leave, Mr. Smirnov.

Smirnov: *(Quietly puts the gun down, takes his hat, and walks to the door. Then he stops and the pair look at each other without a word. Then, approaching gingerly.)* Listen, Mrs. Popov. Are you still mad at me? I'm in the devil of a temper myself, of course. But then, you see—what I mean is—it's this way—the fact is—*(Roaring.)* Well, is it my fault, damn it, if I like you? *(Clutches the back of a chair. It breaks.)* Christ, what fragile furniture you have here. I like you. Know what I mean? I could fall in love with you.

Mrs. Popov: I hate you. Get out!

Smirnov: What a woman! I never saw anything like it. Oh, I'm lost, I'm done for, I'm a mouse in a trap.

Mrs. Popov: Leave this house, or I shoot!

Smirnov: Shoot away! What bliss to die of a shot that was fired by that little velvet hand! To die gazing into those enchanting eyes. I'm out of my mind. I know: you must decide at once. Think for one second, then decide. Because if I leave now, I'll never be back. Decide! I'm a pretty decent chap. Landed gentleman, I should say. Ten thousand a year. Good stable. Throw a kopeck up in the air, and I'll put a bullet through it. Will you marry me?

Mrs. Popov: *(indignant, brandishing the gun)* We'll shoot it out! Get going! Take your pistol!

Smirnov: I'm out of my mind. I don't understand anything any more. *(Shouting.)* You there! That vodka!

Mrs. Popov: No excuses! No delays! We'll shoot it out!

Smirnov: I'm out of my mind. I'm falling in love. I *have* fallen in love. *(He takes her hand vigorously; she squeals.)* I love you. *(He goes down on his knees.)* I love you as I've never loved before. I jilted twelve, and was jilted by nine others. But I didn't love a one of them as I love you. I'm full of tender emotion. I'm melting like butter. I'm weak as water. I'm on my knees like a fool, and I offer you my hand. It's a shame, it's a disgrace. I haven't been in love in five years. I took a vow against it. And now, all of a sudden, to be swept off my feet, it's a scandal. I offer you my hand, dear lady. Will you or won't you? You won't? Then don't! *(He rises and walks toward the door.)*

Mrs. Popov: I didn't say anything.

Smirnov: *(stopping)* What?

Mrs. Popov: Oh, nothing, you can go. Well, no, just a minute. No, you can go. Go! I detest you! But, just a moment. Oh, if you knew how furious I feel! *(Throws the gun on the table.)* My fingers have gone to sleep holding that horrid thing. *(She is tearing her handkerchief to shreds.)* And what are you standing around for? Get out of here!

Smirnov: Goodbye.

Mrs. Popov: Go, go, go! *(Shouting.)* Where are you going? Wait a minute! No, no, it's all right, just go. I'm fighting mad. Don't come near me, don't come near me!

Smirnov: *(who is coming near her)* I'm pretty disgusted with myself—falling in love like a kid, going down on my knees like some moongazing whippersnapper, the very thought gives me gooseflesh. *(Rudely.)* I love you. But it doesn't make sense. Tomorrow, I have to pay that interest, and we've already started mowing. *(He puts his arm about her waist.)* I shall never forgive myself for this.

Mrs. Popov: Take your hands off me, I hate you! Let's shoot it out!

A long kiss. Enter Luka with an axe, the Gardener with a rake, the coachman with a pitchfork, hired men with sticks.

Luka: *(seeing the kiss)* Mercy on us! Holy saints above!

Mrs. Popov: *(dropping her eyes)* Luka, tell them in the stable that Toby is *not* to have any oats today.

* * *

Reading and Reacting

1. Chekhov only briefly describes the play's setting. What other information could he have provided? Why do you think he chose not to?
2. Note that there are few stage directions provided for *The Brute*. Do you think Chekhov should have given more information? Explain.
3. Consider the dialogue of *The Brute*. Does each character have a distinctive voice? If so, what do these different voices reveal about the characters?
4. *The Brute*, like most plays, does not have a narrator, so everything you find out about the characters comes from what they reveal about themselves as they speak. What techniques does Chekhov use to convey this information to the audience? For example, does he use soliloquies, monologues, or asides?
5. Chekhov called *The Brute* "a joke in one act." In what sense is this play a "joke"?
6. How do Mrs. Popov and Mr. Smirnov change during the play? What do they discover about themselves?
7. What is the significance of the play's title? Is it ironic in any way?
8. **Journal Entry** How would *The Brute* be different if it were presented as a short story?
9. **Critical Perspective** Reacting to the charge that he was a depressing writer, Chekhov said that he had "never wanted tears."

> I wanted to tell people honestly: "Look at yourselves. See how badly you live and how tiresome you are." The main thing is that people should understand this. When they do, they will surely create a new and better life for themselves.

10. How does this statement apply to *The Brute*? Does Chekhov force Mrs. Popov and Mr. Smirnov to look at themselves? Do they "create a new and better life for themselves"? Explain.

Related Works: "The Girl with Bangs" (p. 204), "My Last Duchess" (p. 499), "The Wolf's Postscript to 'Little Red Riding Hood'" (p. 518), "Oh, my love is like a red, red rose" (p. 564)

A Note on Translations

Many dramatic works that we read or see are translations from other languages. For example, Ibsen wrote in Norwegian, Sophocles in Greek, Molière in French, and Chekhov in Russian. Before English-speaking viewers or readers can evaluate the language of a translated play, they must understand that the language they hear or read is the translator's interpretation of what the playwright intended to communicate. For example, certain words do not have corresponding words in English. In addition, some phrases are idiomatic and cannot be understood outside their original cultural contexts. Finally, some words have specific **connotations**—emotional associations—that the equivalent words in English do not have. For this reason, a translation is an interpretation, not a search for literal equivalents; this means that a translation is always different from the original. Moreover, because different translators make different choices when they try to convey a sense of the original, two translations of the same work can vary considerably.

Compare these two versions of an exchange of dialogue from two translations of the same Chekhov play, called *The Brute* in the translation that begins on page 769 and *The Bear* in the alternate version.

From *The Brute*

Smirnov: You'd like me to come simpering to you in French, I suppose. "*Enchanté, madame! Merci beaucoup* for not paying zee money, *madame! Pardonnez-moi* if I 'ave disturbed you, *madame!* How *charmante* you look in mourning, *madame!*"

Mrs. Popov: Now you're being silly, Mr. Smirnov.

Smirnov: *(mimicking)* "Now you're being silly, Mr. Smirnov." "You don't know how to talk to a lady, Mr. Smirnov." Look here, Mrs. Popov. I've known more women than you've known pussy cats. I've fought three duels on their account. I've jilted twelve, and been jilted by nine others. Oh, yes, Mrs. Popov, I've played the fool in my time, whispered sweet nothings, bowed and scraped and endeavored to please. Don't tell me I don't know what it is to love, to pine away with longing, to have the blues, to melt like butter, to be weak as water. I was full of tender emotion. I was carried away with passion. I squandered half my fortune on the sex. I chattered about women's emancipation. But there's an end to everything, dear madam . . . . (1.71–73)

From *The Bear*

Smirnov: Ach, it's astonishing! How would you like me to talk to you? In French, perhaps? *(Lisps in anger.) Madame, je vous prie* . . . . How happy I am that you're not paying me the money . . . . Ah, pardon, I've made you uneasy! Such lovely weather we're having today! And you look so becoming in your mourning dress. *(Bows and scrapes.)*

Mrs. Popov: That's rude and not very clever!

Smirnov: *(teasing)* Rude and not very clever! I don't know how to behave in the company of ladies. Madam, in my time I've seen far more women than you've seen sparrows. Three times I've fought duels over women; I've jilted twelve women, nine have jilted me! Yes! There was a time when I played the fool; I became sentimental over women, used honeyed words, fawned on them, bowed and scraped . . . . I loved, suffered, sighed at the moon; I became limp, melted, shivered ... I loved passionately, madly, every which way, devil take me, I chattered away like a magpie about the emancipation of women, ran through half my fortune as a result of my tender feelings; but now, if you will excuse me, I'm on to your ways! I've had enough!

Although both translations convey Smirnov's anger and frustration, they use different words (with different connotations), different phrasing, and even different stage directions. In *The Bear*, for example, only one French phrase is used, whereas *The Brute* uses several and specifies a French accent as well; other differences between the two translations include *The Bear*'s use of "teasing," "sparrows," and "I've had enough!" where *The Brute* uses "mimicking," "pussy cats," and "But there's an end to everything, dear madam." (Elsewhere in the play, *The Bear* uses profanity while *The Brute* uses more polite language.)

Chapter 28

Drama Sampler: Ten-Minute Plays

José Rivera
REUTERS/Alamy Stock Photo

Jeni Mahoney
Courtesy of Sarah Jessup

James McLindon
Courtesy of James McLindon

Steven Korbar
Courtesy of Steven Korbar

Harold Pinter
UPPA/ZUMAPRESS.com/Newscom

Learning Objectives

After reading this chapter, you will be able to...

- Identify a ten-minute play.
- Describe the elements of a ten-minute play.
- Analyze character development within a ten-minute play.
- Examine the central conflict within a ten-minute play.

Throughout the long history of playwriting, many types and forms of drama have emerged. In recent years, theater has become more experimental, as evidenced by the proliferation of one-act and ten-minute plays, which strive to convey complex ideas in a short amount of time. While traditional one-act plays such as Anton Chekhov's *The Brute* (p. 769) and Susan Glaspell's *Trifles* (p. 820) may have the luxury of unfolding in a more extended period, the **ten-minute play**, which must be performed in ten minutes or less, offers a very small window of opportunity in which the playwright can create meaning. In fact, as director Jon Jory has noted, the ten-minute play is, in a sense, the dramatic equivalent of the **haiku** in that it is intended to be taken in all at once and thus to have a particularly intense effect on the audience. According to Jory, considered to be the father of the ten-minute play genre, these plays "must, by nature, imply rather than explain. They often depend on metaphor to extend their reach. They stick like glue in the mind because the viewer remembers the *whole* play."

Since a page of script roughly translates into a minute of time onstage, a ten-minute play is generally limited to about ten pages. Despite its brevity, however, a ten-minute play is more than just a scene or an excerpt from a longer play: it is written to stand alone as a complete dramatic work. Although its brief length means it has little or no room for **exposition**, it must introduce a **conflict** (usually relatively early in the play), and it must provide a **resolution**, just as any other play does.

Ten-minute plays are generally staged in groups, allowing the audience to watch several plays in sequence. Casts are usually small; often, the same actors appear in a number of different plays. For this reason, elaborate costumes and staging are impractical (and therefore rare). The most popular venue for a ten-minute play is a drama festival, and numerous competitions offer prizes that include the staging of the winning play. The most prominent contest is sponsored by the Actors Theatre of Louisville, which stages the annual Humana Festival of New American Plays.

The ten-minute plays in this sampler, despite their brief length, manage to treat a variety of provocative subjects. In Jane Martin's *Beauty* (p. 785), the two protagonists trade lives, with unexpected consequences, while Steven Korbar's "*What Are You Going to Be?*" explores parents' reactions to their daughter's choice of a burka as a Halloween costume. In James McLindon's *Choices*, a graduate student faces a financial dilemma; in Jeni Mahoney's *Come Rain or Come Shine*, a misunderstanding between a mother and her son tests the limits of tolerance; and in Harold Pinter's *Applicant* (p. 807), a job interview does not go as planned. Finally, José Rivera's *Tape* features a protagonist forced to confront his entire life.

JANE MARTIN, a prize-winning playwright, has never made a public appearance or spoken about any of her works. In fact, she has never given an interview, and no picture of her has ever been published. As one critic wryly observed, Martin is "America's best known, unknown playwright." Martin first came to the attention of American theater audiences with her collection of monologues, *Talking With ...*, a work that premiered at the 1981 Humana Festival of New

American Plays at the Actors Theatre of Louisville, Kentucky. Her other works include *Vital Signs; What Mama Don't Know; Cementville;* the Pulitzer Prize–nominated *Keely and Du* (winner of the 1994 American Theatre Critics Association New Play Award); *Criminal Hearts; Middle Aged White Guys; Jack and Jill; Mr. Bundy; Flaming Guns of the Purple Sage; Good Boys; Flags;* and *Sez She.* Martin's name is widely believed to be a pseudonym. Jon Jory, former artistic director of the Actors Theatre of Louisville—and director of the premieres of all of Martin's plays—is spokesperson for the playwright and, according to some people, may actually be the playwright behind the pen name. Jory has repeatedly denied this; in a 1994 interview, he said that Martin "feels she could not write plays if people knew who she was, regardless of her identity or gender." In Jory's opinion, "The point in the end is the plays themselves.... But if Jane's anonymity is a P. T. Barnum publicity stunt, it's one of the longest circus acts going."

Beauty (2000)

CHARACTERS

Carla

Bethany

An apartment. Minimalist set. A young woman, Carla, on the phone.

Carla: In love with me? You're in love with me? Could you describe yourself again? Uh-huh. Uh-huh. And you spoke to me? *(A knock at the door.)* Listen, I always hate to interrupt a marriage proposal, but ... could you possibly hold that thought? *(Puts phone down and goes to door. Bethany, the same age as Carla and a friend, is there. She carries the sort of Mideastern lamp we know of from* Aladdin.*)*

Bethany: Thank God you were home. I mean, you're not going to believe this!

Carla: Somebody on the phone. *(Goes back to it.)*

Bethany: I mean, I just had a beach urge, so I told them at work my uncle was dying ...

Carla: *(motions to Bethany for quiet)* And you were the one in the leather jacket with the tattoo? What was the tattoo? *(Carla again asks Bethany, who is gesturing wildly that she should hang up, to cool it.)* Look, a screaming eagle from shoulder to shoulder, maybe. There were a lot of people in the bar.

Bethany: *(gesturing and mouthing)* I have to get back to work.

Carla: *(on phone)* See, the thing is, I'm probably not going to marry someone I can't remember ... particularly when I don't drink. Sorry. Sorry. Sorry. *(She hangs up.)* Madness.

Bethany: So I ran out to the beach ...

Carla: This was some guy I never met who apparently offered me a beer ...

Bethany: ... low tide and this ... *(The lamp.)* ... was just sitting there, lying there ...

Carla: ... and he tracks me down ...

Bethany: ... on the beach, and I lift this lid thing ...

Carla: ... and seriously proposes marriage.

Bethany: ... and a genie comes out.

Carla: I mean, that's twice in a ... what?

Bethany: A genie comes out of this thing.

Carla: A genie?

Bethany: I'm not kidding, the whole Disney kind of thing, swirling smoke, and then this twenty-foot-high, see-through guy in like an Arabian outfit.

Carla: Very funny.

Bethany: Yes, funny, but twenty feet high! I look up and down the beach, I'm alone. I don't have my pepper spray or my hand alarm. You know me, when I'm petrified I joke. I say his voice is too high for Robin Williams, and he says he's a castrati. Naturally. Who else would I meet?

Carla: What's a castrati?

Bethany: You know ...

The appropriate gesture.

Carla: Bethany, dear one, I have three modeling calls. I am meeting Ralph Lauren!

Bethany: Okay, good. Ralph Lauren. Look, I am not kidding!

Carla: You're not kidding what?!

Bethany: There is a genie in this thingamajig.

Carla: Uh-huh. I'll be back around eight.

Bethany: And he offered me *wishes!*

Carla: Is this some elaborate practical joke because it's my birthday?

Bethany: No, happy birthday, but I'm like crazed because I'm on this deserted beach with a twenty-foot-high, see-through genie, so like sarcastically ... you know how I need a new car ... I said fine, gimme 25,000 dollars ...

Carla: On the beach with the genie?

Bethany: Yeah, right, exactly, and it rains down out of the sky.

Carla: Oh sure.

Bethany: *(pulling a wad out of her purse)* Count it, those are thousands. I lost one in the surf.

Carla sees the top bill. Looks at Bethany, who nods encouragement. Carla thumbs through them.

Carla: These look real.

Bethany: Yeah.

Carla: And they rained down out of the sky?

Bethany: Yeah.

Carla: You've been really strange lately, are you dealing?

Bethany: Dealing what, I've even given up chocolate.

Carla: Let me see the genie.

Bethany: Wait, wait.

Carla: Bethany, I don't have time to screw around. Let me see the genie or let me go on my appointments.

Bethany: Wait! So I pick up the money ... see, there's sand on the money ... and I'm like nuts so I say, you know, "Okay, look, ummm, big guy, my uncle is in the hospital" ... because as you know when I said to the people at work my uncle was dying, I was on one level telling the truth although it had nothing to do with the beach, but he was in Intensive Care after the accident, and that's on my mind, so I say, okay, Genie, heal my uncle ... which is like impossible given he was hit by two trucks, and the genie says, "Yes, Master" ... like they're supposed to say, and he goes into this like kind of whirlwind, kicking up sand and stuff, and I'm like, "Oh my God!" and the air clears, and he bows, you know, and says, "It is done, Master," and I say, "Okay, whatever-you-are, I'm calling on my cell phone," and I get it out and I get this doctor who is like dumbstruck who says my uncle came to, walked out of Intensive Care and left the hospital! I'm not kidding, Carla.

Carla: On your mother's grave?

Bethany: On my mother's grave.

They look at each other.

Carla: Let me see the genie.

Bethany: No, no, look, that's the whole thing ... I was just, like, reacting, you know, responding, and that's already two wishes ... although I'm really pleased about my uncle, the $25,000 thing, I could have asked for $10 million, and there is only one wish left.

Carla: So ask for $10 million.

Bethany: I don't think so. I don't think so. I mean, I gotta focus in here. Do you have a sparkling water?

Carla: No. Bethany, I'm missing Ralph Lauren now. Very possibly my one chance to go from catalogue model to the very, very big time, so, if you are joking, stop joking.

Bethany: Not joking. See, see, the thing is, I know what I want. In my guts. Yes. Underneath my entire bitch of a life is this unspoken, ferocious, all-consuming urge ...

Carla: *(trying to get her to move this along)* Ferocious, all-consuming urge ...

Bethany: I want to be like you.

Carla: Me?

Bethany: Yes.

Carla: Half the time you don't even like me.

Bethany: Jealous. The ogre of jealousy.

Carla: You're the one with the $40,000 job straight out of school. You're the one who has published short stories. I'm the one hanging on by her fingernails in modeling. The one who has creeps calling her on the phone. The one who had to have a nose job.

Bethany: I want to be beautiful.

Carla: You are beautiful.

Bethany: Carla, I'm not beautiful.

Carla: You have charm. You have personality. You know perfectly well you're pretty.

Bethany: "Pretty," see, that's it. Pretty is the minor leagues of beautiful. Pretty is what people discover about you after they know you. Beautiful is what knocks them out across the room. Pretty, you get called a couple of times a year; *beautiful* is twenty-four hours a day.

Carla: Yeah? So?

Bethany: So?! We're talking *beauty* here. Don't say "So?" Beauty is the real deal. You are the center of any moment of your life. People stare. Men flock. I've seen you get offered discounts on makeup for no reason. Parents treat beautiful children better. Studies show your income goes up. You can have sex anytime you want it. Men have to know me. That takes up to a year. I'm continually horny.

Carla: Bethany, I don't even like sex. I can't have a conversation without men coming on to me. I have no privacy. I get hassled on the street. They start pressuring me from the beginning. Half the time, it never occurs to them to start with a conversation. Smart guys like you. You've had three long-term relationships, and you're only twenty-three. I haven't had one. The good guys, the smart guys are scared to death of me. I'm surrounded by male bimbos who think a preposition is when you go to school away from home. I have no woman friends except you. I don't even want to talk about this!

Bethany: I knew you'd say something like this. See, you're "in the club" so you can say this. It's the way beauty functions as an elite. You're trying to keep it all for yourself.

Carla: I'm trying to tell you it's no picnic.

Bethany: But it's what everybody wants. It's the nasty secret at large in the world. It's the unspoken tidal desire in every room and on every street. It's the unspoken, the soundless whisper ... millions upon millions of people longing hopelessly and forever to stop being whatever they are and be beautiful, but the difference between those ardent multitudes and me is that I have a goddamn genie and one more wish!

Carla: Well, it's not what I want. This is me, Carla. I have never read a whole book. Page six, I can't remember page four. The last thing I read was *The Complete Idiot's Guide to WordPerfect.* I leave dinner parties right after the dessert because I'm out of conversation. You know the dumb blond joke about the application where it says, "Sign here," she put Sagittarius? I've done that. Only beautiful guys approach me, and that's because they want to borrow my eye shadow. I barely exist outside a mirror! You don't want to *be me.*

Bethany: None of you tell the truth. That's why you have no friends. We can all see you're just trying to make us feel better because we aren't in your league. This only proves to me it should be my third wish. Money can only buy things. Beauty makes you the center of the universe.

Bethany picks up the lamp.

Carla: Don't do it. Bethany, don't wish it! I am telling you you'll regret it.

Bethany lifts the lid. There is a tremendous crash, and the lights go out. Then they flicker and come back up, revealing Bethany and Carla on the floor where they have been thrown by the explosion. We don't realize it at first, but they have exchanged places.

Carla/Bethany: Oh God.
Bethany/Carla: Oh God.
Carla/Bethany: Am I bleeding? Am I dying?
Bethany/Carla: I'm so dizzy. You're not bleeding.
Carla/Bethany: Neither are you.
Bethany/Carla: I feel so weird.
Carla/Bethany: Me too. I feel ... *(Looking at her hands.)* Oh, my God, I'm wearing your jewelry. I'm wearing your nail polish.
Bethany/Carla: I know I'm over here, but I can see myself over there.
Carla/Bethany: I'm wearing your dress. I have your legs!!
Bethany/Carla: These aren't my shoes. I can't meet Ralph Lauren wearing these shoes!
Carla/Bethany: I wanted to be beautiful, but I didn't want to be you.
Bethany/Carla: Thanks a lot!!
Carla/Bethany: I've got to go. I want to pick someone out and get laid.
Bethany/Carla: You can't just walk out of here in my body!
Carla/Bethany: Wait a minute. Wait a minute. What's eleven eighteenths of 1,726?
Bethany/Carla: Why?
Carla/Bethany: I'm a public accountant. I want to know if you have my brain.
Bethany/Carla: One hundred thirty-two and a half.
Carla/Bethany: You have my brain.
Bethany/Carla: What shade of Rubenstein lipstick does Cindy Crawford wear with teal blue?
Carla/Bethany: Raging Storm.
Bethany/Carla: You have my brain. You poor bastard.
Carla/Bethany: I don't care. Don't you see?
Bethany/Carla: See what?
Carla/Bethany: We both have the one thing, the one and only thing everybody wants.
Bethany/Carla: What is that?
Carla/Bethany: It's better than beauty for me; it's better than brains for you.
Bethany/Carla: What? What?!
Carla/Bethany: Different problems.

Blackout.

* * *

Courtesy of Steven Korbar

STEVEN KORBAR (1967–) is an actor and playwright whose plays have been produced across the United States and Canada. His plays *Mrs. Jansen Isn't Here Now* and *Table for Four* appeared in the collection *The Best Ten-Minute Plays 2010*, and his work was featured in the 2013 Queer Theatre Festival in Washington D.C. Published in the collection *The Best Ten-Minute Plays 2013*, the following play won the Merce award at the Secret Rose Theatre's 2011 10-Minute Play Festival in Los Angeles. Korbar's recent plays include *I Saw What You Said* (2017), *Old Aquatics* (2018), and *In Her Golden Years* (2019).

"What Are You Going to Be?" (2011)

CHARACTERS

Greg: thirties to forties

Carol: thirties to forties

Natalie: an adolescent girl

SETTING:

An upper middle class home—decorated for Halloween.

TIME:

Early evening

Lights come up to find CAROL *seated in a living room setting. She is very still and appears rather stunned. After a moment* GREG *enters. He is carrying a grocery bag and is in high spirits.*

Greg: Okay, don't get mad at me, but I broke my promise —I bought more Halloween candy! I know we already have a ton but A) they were having an incredible sale and B) and most importantly . . . they're "Junior Mints"! I figure we can just put them in the back of the cupboard and conveniently forget them till Trick or Treating is over tomorrow night. Oh don't be all angry. "Junior Mints"! . . . What's the matter?

Carol: *(A choked voice)* . . . Natalie . . .

Greg: *(Stricken)* What? . . . What!? *(Quickly becoming hysterical. Dropping the bag)* Oh God! Natalie. NATALIE! Where is she, where . . .

Carol: No. No, she's fine. She's not hurt or sick or anything.

Greg: Then why did you . . . Oh my God! What is wrong with you!? Why did you say "Natalie" like something horrible happened?

Carol: *(Flatly)* I'm sorry.

Greg: You scared the living . . . you don't joke around like that—you took ten years off my life, you, you made me drop my "Junior Mints."

Carol: I'm very sorry, I should have phrased what I had to say differently.

Greg: What could you have to say that was worth giving me a cardiac infarction?

Carol: Natalie . . . finally decided what she's going to be for Halloween.

Greg: *(A beat)* Her Halloween costume. Carol, what is the point of all this family therapy if you're just going to keep overreacting to every little thing? You know what Dr. Penelope told you; perspective is what we have to strive for. If you just take a step back and a deep cleansing breath, pretty soon you're going to see that what seemed so dire really wasn't such a terrible . . .

NATALIE enters. We assume she is a normal adolescent girl, though it is hard to tell as she is dressed in the burka[1] *of a Muslim woman from the Middle East. Her costume is heavy, black and very constricting. GREG stares at her for a long moment. He looks at CAROL and then back to NATALIE, trying desperately not to overreact.*

. . . Hey princess.

Natalie: Hi Dad.

Greg: What'cha doing?

Natalie: Just trying on my Halloween costume.

Greg: So you decided against the ballerina?

Natalie: Yeah. I'm going to be a Muslim woman from the Middle East instead.

Greg: Why . . . did you decide to be that?

Natalie: Cause I wanted a costume not a lot of other girls would have.

Greg: . . . Good job.

Natalie: There isn't any reason you don't want me wearing this . . . is there?

Greg: I . . . can't think of any.

Natalie: Good. Well, I'm going to go back to my room, figure out which way is Mecca[2] and practice lying face down on the floor.

NATALIE exits.

Greg: *(A long beat. Trying desperately to sound reasonable)* Well . . . we said no Lady Gaga.

Carol: This is not my fault. I am a good mother—there are no preservatives in anything I feed that girl.

Greg: This is not about fault. This can be an opportunity; to learn more about our daughter and try to understand her thought process.

Natalie: *(Off stage)* I can hear every word you're saying.

Greg: *(Yelling towards the direction of her room)* Well then shut your door Missy!

(To CAROL. More quietly)

Let's just try to discuss this quietly. Now, where did she get the . . .

Carol: Burka is the word you're trying to sound casual saying. And I don't know where she got it—I was too terrified to look through her browsing history.

Greg: There is no reason to be terrified. There is nothing wrong with being Middle Eastern. We cannot let her feel we have a problem with that. Muslims are human beings just like you and me—we see them every day on "Anderson Cooper." We just have to figure out why Natalie wants to dress like one.

---

[1] *burka:* A full-body garment worn by some Muslim women when they are out in public.

[2] *Mecca:* Islamic holy city in Saudi Arabia.

Carol: I know why—to destroy me. She's rejecting everything I've ever taught her about being a modern, post-feminist woman and chosen the most subservient, oppressed female role model she could find. My God, she might as well just be dressing up as my mother for Halloween!

Greg: Those are a completely different set of issues. What matters now is that if we decide it's better for her not to wear this costume, she doesn't think it's because we have any sort of discriminatory . . .

NATALIE enters.

Natalie: Hey mom, can I have a needle and thread to fix my costume; I think too much of my face is showing.

Greg: You know sweetie, we actually wanted to talk to you about your costume and what you'll be wearing tomorrow night.

Natalie: I'll be wearing this.

Greg: Maybe . . . but your mom and I would like you to be aware of all your options. For instance, you could reexamine the whole line of Disney princesses—there's Jasmine from *Aladdin*. All the same ethnicity and you could look so pretty.

Natalie: No. Nobody my age is going to wear a princess costume. And even if I did it sure wouldn't be Jasmine—she's a total infidel. Anyway, who cares what I wear, it's just a costume and the costumes we wear shouldn't matter . . . right Dad?

Greg: Right! . . . right.

Carol: Natalie, it's just that we feel it might seem disrespectful to people of the Muslim faith for you to be wearing this as a costume for Halloween.

Greg: *(Impressed with* CAROL'S *ruse)* Good! *(Immediately to NATALIE. Earnestly)* Right. Halloween is more of a secular holiday and it's just better to keep religion out of it.

Carol: Remember how the Davis's passed out bible quotes instead of candy last Halloween; their house got TP'd for four straight nights.

Natalie: *(Suspiciously)* Tell me the truth; this really isn't because the two of you have got some weird thing against Islam, is it?

Greg: No!

Carol: No!

Greg: No!

Carol: No!

Greg: It's just; you don't want to belittle anyone's faith sweetie. I mean, you wouldn't run around asking for candy dressed as a Catholic nun, would you?

Carol: Well honey, some people do go out dressed as nuns. It's a costume; they go out dressed as slutty nuns.

Greg: . . . Those are slutty nurses.

Natalie: No, she's right. Some are nurses but a lot of them are slutty nuns too.

Greg: Okay, fine. There are slutty nun costumes; but you wouldn't go out dressed in one would you?

Natalie: No. I already know two girls who are going as that.

Greg: *(More frustrated)* I think it is just culturally insensitive to these people as a group. And by these people I do not mean . . . *(Catching himself and making air quotes)* "These People." I just, I don't feel comfortable with you dressing this way.

Natalie: When Lauren Nakamura went dressed as a geisha last year, the two of you wouldn't stop gushing about how adorable she looked.

Greg: That is completely different.

Natalie: Why, because Arabs frighten you but you find Asians all cute and non-threatening?

Greg: Absolutely not!

Carol: No!

Greg: Do not put words in my mouth! The image of the passive Asian is nothing but a ridiculous, antiquated racial stereotype!

Carol: Of course it is.

Greg: Just look at Pearl Harbor. *(After realizing what he's said, putting a discrete hand over his mouth)*

Carol: What your father means is he would like you to find another costume to wear.

Natalie: What would he like me to be; a white, male, Protestant who can prove he's straight?

GREG instinctively moves to attack NATALIE, muttering something like "You miserable little . . . ." CAROL restrains him.

Carol: This is not a judgment on anyone's religion or race.

Natalie: Then why is Dad getting all freaked out?

Greg: I am not getting freaked out: nobody ever even mentioned terrorism.

Natalie: What!?

Greg: I mean; it is wrong to ascribe the worst in human nature to any one particular people. And anybody who does that is ignorant and we should just feel sorry for them.

Natalie: Then I can go like this?

Greg: I will lock you in the crawl space first.

Natalie: Well my friend Lele really is Muslim and she likes this costume and she's totally cool with me wearing it.

Greg: I don't care what your friend thinks. You are not wearing that costume. It is inappropriate; it's thoughtless and wearing it would just be plain insulting to the people and culture of Islam!

Natalie: Is that what all of your Muslim friends say Dad?

GREG tries to answer but is left with his mouth open. NATALIE stares at him for a beat, turns and exits in triumphant silence.

Greg: *(A beat, then erupting in frustration)* What is going on here! I don't understand, why is she doing this to us!

Natalie: *(Off stage)* I can still hear you!

Greg: I am going to remove that door from its hinges!

Natalie: *(Off stage)* That doesn't even make sense—I could hear you better then!

Greg: I know that! *(Moving to CAROL. Whispering)* She used to be so sweet when she was little.

Carol: I told you we shouldn't have let her have all those inoculations.

Greg: We could just cram her into a stuffed pumpkin and that was her costume.

Carol: Polio and Rubella; fine. But she was never right again after that Smallpox vaccine.

Greg: *(Humiliated)* I said terrorist.

Carol: And Pearl Harbor.

Greg: Since the day she was born I've tried to teach her to respect diversity. She has been to every church, heard every philosophy; we introduced her to that school friend of yours who's a Wiccan[3] and a lesbian. I've taken that girl to so many Bat mitzvahs[4] in the last year I could practically poach a salmon all by myself. I paid $125.00 for a dress so she could look right at her friend's quinceañera[5] and another $15.00 to the gardener to learn how to pronounce *quinceañera*! What in the hell more do I have to do—she wouldn't go with me to the Tyler Perry movie!

Carol: If you ask me this whole place is just crawling with Radon.

Greg: Will you stop blaming everything on hazardous materials.

Carol: Well I told you; it's not me. I breast fed that kid for fourteen months and stayed gluten free the whole time—I did my part.

Greg: Well all I know is I left a peaceful home this morning, worked hard all day for my family and when I walked back through the front door this evening suddenly it's a Jihad![6] Where did that come from?

Carol: Well not my side of the family—she didn't inherit any of that gamy, exotic blood from me.

Greg: . . . And what in the hell is that supposed to mean?

CAROL *does not respond.*

I'm part Dutch, part Scots/Irish and 1/8th Armenian.

CAROL *points at him as if to say "Bingo."*

Armenia is in Europe.

Carol: Oh no it's not. Not real Europe. Not *Sound of Music* Europe. You've always had a little smudge of the Third World on you; I knew it the first time I saw that dusky little mother of yours—I mean, no offence, but the woman's always looked like she just finished carrying a jug of water on her head.

---

[3]*Wiccan:* A follower of Wicca, a religion rooted in magic and nature.

[4]*Bat mitzvah:* A rite of passage for Jewish girls passing into womanhood.

[5]*quinceañera:* A rite of passage for Hispanic girls passing into womanhood.

[6]*Jihad:* Islamic holy war.

Greg: Are you out of your mind?

Carol: And there's another trait that's straight out of the Casbah[7]—your condescending manner towards women. So archaic and primitive—it's downright patriarchal.

Greg: Oh really, is that what your Wiccan friend would call it?

Carol: And a homophobe to boot.

Greg: You are making me very angry!

Carol: Oh boy, start gathering up your stones everybody: I feel an honor killing coming on!

Greg: Do you even understand the sociopolitical implications of what you're saying? This is the kind of thinking that fostered colonialism for the last two centuries.

NATALIE enters no longer wearing the burka.

Natalie: Okay, okay, okay—just stop the arguing, alright! If this is what it's going to do to you, fine; I won't wear the stupid costume. If my parents can't handle somebody dressing a little different then I guess I was just expecting too much! Everyone has their secret little hates and prejudices, even my own mother and father. That's just how it is. So I'll just do what you want. I'll go back to wearing my original Lady Gaga costume . . . unless you have something against her religion too?

CAROL and GREG simultaneously shake their heads.

Okay then. That's how it's going to be and we won't even talk about it anymore.

I'm not a baby—it's not like I can't stand disappointment. I guess I have to start getting used to it sometime, don't I?

Greg: *(Earnestly)* Natalie . . . I want you to know I think you've shown a lot of maturity tonight. And maturity is a rare thing at any age.

Natalie: Thanks Dad—I bet that's just how Anderson Cooper would have put it.

NATALIE exits. There is a silence.

Greg: Well, I think it all worked out for the best.

Carol: In the long run I think so.

Greg: It's good she made the decision by herself.

Carol: It wouldn't have been right if we'd had to force her.

Greg: These are volatile times; it's just better not to broach certain subjects.

Greg: *(Suddenly aware)* . . . Did she just play us?

Carol: Played us like a violin.

Greg: She was never going to wear that as a costume, was she?

Carol: She was going as Lady Gaga if she'd had to slit our throats.

Greg: We really did kind of raise a terrorist, didn't we?

Carol: Utterly remorseless.

---

[7] *Casbah:* North African fortress or walled quarter of a city.

Greg: It's just stunning. How she manipulated us. The way she preyed on our irrational fears and exploited our ingrained prejudices. And for no other reason but to get what she wanted from us.

Carol: I always did tell her she could be the first woman president of the United States.

Greg: Well, she sure had my number. If anyone asks me, I guess I know what I'm going to be for Halloween.

Carol: Your own adolescent daughter's little bitch?

Greg: I was going to say a hypocrite. How can I ever look another Arab American in the eye again?

Carol: Well, since I don't think there are any in our "Emotional Eating" class, I doubt it will be a problem. Anyway, Halloween will be over and done with tomorrow night, and if we're lucky we can just put the whole horrible thing behind us.

Greg: Can we? Christmas is only two months away.

Carol: *(Remembering a horrible fact)* . . . . Oh my God.

Greg: She's still got her heart set on that puppy.

Carol: Oh no! The dander . . . the dander. We can't have it in the house!

Greg: *(Low and fatalistic)* We may not have a choice Carol. We may not have a choice. *(A distraught beat. Then yelling in the direction of* NATALIE'S *bedroom)*

I know you can hear me!

NATALIE *is heard laughing off stage.* CAROL *and* GREG *cower together.*

* * *

Courtesy of James McLindon

JAMES MCLINDON has won the Heideman Award for ten-minute plays five times, among many other awards. A Harvard Law School graduate, he is a member of the Nylon Theater Company in New York and has been a Fellow with the Dramatists Guild and twice a Next Voices Playwriting Fellow. His many residencies have included time with the O'Neill National Playwrights Conference. McLindon's plays include *Salvation* (2008); *Comes a Faery* (2010), which was a finalist for the Humana Festival of New American Plays; *When We Get Good Again* (2012); *Pooka* (2014); *Broken* (2015); and *I Don't Know* (2016).

Choices (2019)

CHARACTERS

PROSPECTIVE CLIENT . . . . . . MID-20s to 30s, ANY GENDER OR AGE

DEBT COUNSELOR. . . . . MID-20s to 40s, ANY GENDER OR AGE

SETTING:

A modest living room (think poor graduate student), the present.

PROSPECTIVE CLIENT, mid-20s to 30s, sits at her/his coffee (or dining room) table across from DEBT COUNSELOR, mid-20s to 30s. DEBT COUNSELOR has the calmness and patience of a funeral home director for the most part, there to help and alert to steer clear of any heaviness with a ready euphemism. All of that is underlaid with an enthusiastic love of his product. PROSPECTIVE CLIENT is a little anxious, really needing this to work. DEBT COUNSELOR has been waiting for PROSPECTIVE CLIENT to finish reading a pamphlet. PROSPECTIVE CLIENT now looks up, perplexed.

PROSPECTIVE CLIENT: I'm sorry, I just don't get it.

DEBT COUNSELOR: It's pretty simple. It's just … disruptive.

PROSPECTIVE CLIENT: No, I know, it sounds simple ….

DEBT COUNSELOR: Think of it as a choice. We're all about choices. You can choose this. Or not.

PROSPECTIVE CLIENT: No, no, I want to choose this, believe me. I feel like I'm on a hamster wheel just trying to keep up with the payments, but … this just seems too good to be true.

DEBT COUNSELOR: That's often what disruption looks like. Remember all the things you used to have to pay to read, like newspapers, magazines? Now you get them on-line for free. We're disrupting the entire debt consolidation industry, sort of like that.

PROSPECTIVE CLIENT: Okay, but … I still don't get it.

DEBT COUNSELOR: Tell me what you don't get.

PROSPECTIVE CLIENT: So, you pay off my student loans—

DEBT COUNSELOR: Your crushing student loans.

PROSPECTIVE CLIENT: Yes, thank you, my 247,000 dollars in student loans, and all I have to do is pay you 72 dollars a month?

DEBT COUNSELOR: Yes.

PROSPECTIVE CLIENT: For 20 years.

DEBT COUNSELOR: Yes.

PROSPECTIVE CLIENT: And that's it. That's all I ever have to pay you.

DEBT COUNSELOR: That's all you ever have to pay us.

PROSPECTIVE CLIENT calculates in her/his head.

PROSPECTIVE CLIENT: Okay, so I'm not really great at math, but I think that's only, like, $170,000?

DEBT COUNSELOR: It's actually about $17,000.

PROSPECTIVE CLIENT: Only 17,000 dollars!? Okay, now I don't get this even more.

DEBT COUNSELOR: Tell me what you don't get.

PROSPECTIVE CLIENT: What don't I—? You give me 247,000 dollars to pay off my debt today and all I have to give you is 17,000 dollars over 20 years?

DEBT COUNSELOR: Right. Mainly to keep you focused.

PROSPECTIVE CLIENT: So you lose money.

DEBT COUNSELOR: No—

PROSPECTIVE CLIENT: Yeah, you lose money. Nobody sets up a business to lose money, unless they're, like, money laundering or something. Wait, are you guys money laundering?

DEBT COUNSELOR: No.

PROSPECTIVE CLIENT: What are you doing?

DEBT COUNSELOR: We're providing choices. *(Pause)* I think maybe you skipped footnote seven.

PROSPECTIVE CLIENT: I didn't read the footnotes.

DEBT COUNSELOR: You should read the footnotes.

PROSPECTIVE CLIENT: I never do.

DEBT COUNSELOR: You always should.

PROSPECTIVE CLIENT: Okay, fine, what does footnote seven say?

DEBT COUNSELOR: It answers this question.

PROSPECTIVE CLIENT: About whether you're money-laundering?

DEBT COUNSELOR: About how we get paid. *(A pause.)*

PROSPECTIVE CLIENT: So how do you? I mean, after I finish my payments you'll be short about 230,000 dollars. Not to mention any interest. So where do you get the rest (from)—? Oh, there're a bunch of hidden fees, aren't there?

DEBT COUNSELOR: There are no fees at all.

PROSPECTIVE CLIENT: Then c'mon, how do you get your money back from me?

DEBT COUNSELOR: We don't get it back from you.

PROSPECTIVE CLIENT: You don't?

DEBT COUNSELOR: We don't. *(Pause)* From you.

PROSPECTIVE CLIENT: Who do you get it back from?

DEBT COUNSELOR: The insurance company.

PROSPECTIVE CLIENT: What insurance company?

DEBT COUNSELOR: You should really read footnote seven—

PROSPECTIVE CLIENT: Just tell me, what insurance company!?

DEBT COUNSELOR: Your insurance company.

PROSPECTIVE CLIENT: Why would my car insurance company pay you?

DEBT COUNSELOR: Not your car insurance company.

PROSPECTIVE CLIENT: Well, that's the only insurance I have. I sure don't have homeowners because you can't afford to buy a house when you owe 247,000—

DEBT COUNSELOR: Your life insurance company. *(A pause.)*

PROSPECTIVE CLIENT: I don't have life insurance.

DEBT COUNSELOR: Footnote seven.

PROSPECTIVE CLIENT: I have to get life insurance?

DEBT COUNSELOR: We pay for it.

PROSPECTIVE CLIENT: What good does life insurance do anyone?

DEBT COUNSELOR: It depends.

PROSPECTIVE CLIENT: Unless I die.

DEBT COUNSELOR: Read footnote seven.

PROSPECTIVE CLIENT: Oh my god. You've looked at my DNA! You have, you totally have! That DNA company that said I was 2.3% Neanderthal sold you my data and you looked at it and you know I have a genetic abnormality and I'm going to die young, so that's how you— What are you writing down?

DEBT COUNSELOR: No, please, go on, that's a really interesting business model.

PROSPECTIVE CLIENT: Stop it! That's not your business model?

DEBT COUNSELOR: No, but it's pretty good though. Way disruptive.

PROSPECTIVE CLIENT: So I'm not going to die in the next 20 years?

DEBT COUNSELOR: Well, how would I know that?

PROSPECTIVE CLIENT: There's no DNA stuff in your file on me?

DEBT COUNSELOR: All we have is what you gave us.

PROSPECTIVE CLIENT: *(Exhaling)* I'm not going to die young.

DEBT COUNSELOR: Well, not in the next 20 years. As far as I know.

PROSPECTIVE CLIENT: Do you qualify everything you say.

DEBT COUNSELOR: When it needs to be. Because we're totally honest. With our clients.

PROSPECTIVE CLIENT: So how do you make money from my life insurance?

DEBT COUNSELOR: How does anyone make money from life insurance?

PROSPECTIVE CLIENT: Somebody has to die. *(Pause)* But you just said I wouldn't!

DEBT COUNSELOR: I said I don't know anything about your DNA. Or your health at all for that matter. We don't worry about that. Please. Read footnote seven.

PROSPECTIVE CLIENT stares at DEBT COUNSELOR, who stares back. A beat.

DEBT COUNSELOR: Please.

PROSPECTIVE CLIENT: Okay, fine.

PROSPECTIVE CLIENT returns to reading the pamphlet. Then PROSPECTIVE CLIENT looks up at DEBT COUNSELOR, stunned.

PROSPECTIVE CLIENT: Oh my god!

DEBT COUNSELOR: *(Excited for the first time)* I know, right!? The first time I read it, I was like, Whaaaaat!? But the more you think about it, the more genius it is. Dis! Effing! Ruption! Amiright!? *(Catching himself, quieting)* Sorry. I just love this product so much.

PROSPECTIVE CLIENT: I'm not going to agree to this! Does anyone ever agree to this?

DEBT COUNSELOR: No. *(Pause)* Not at first. But then they think about it. And they think, well, when I took out my crushing student loans, I knew that they would impact my life. Severely impact my life. For a whole lot of my life. Decades and decades. And see, that's all this is really. You just assumed that the impact would be frontloaded. And all we do is ... backload it for you.

PROSPECTIVE CLIENT: Me dying at *(whatever age is about 20 years older than actor)* in 20 years, that's what you call "severely impacting" my life?

DEBT COUNSELOR: Well, it seems severe to me.

PROSPECTIVE CLIENT: No, it's severe, it's very severe!

DEBT COUNSELOR: Yes. But. What a much better life it will have been. These next 20 years anyway. Which, after all, is your prime.

PROSPECTIVE CLIENT: How do you ... you know ... do it?

DEBT COUNSELOR: Do what?

PROSPECTIVE CLIENT: Make it so you get to, you know, collect.

DEBT COUNSELOR: *(Pause)* Before we get into the details, I think it's best that you get comfortable with the concept (first)—

PROSPECTIVE CLIENT: How!?

DEBT COUNSELOR: Well, it's up to you. See? Choices. Most people opt to handle matters themselves. We'll give you some recommendations and howtos in the next brochure— it's under "Self-Termination." A lot of people, though, find they're too ... squeamish? for Self-Term when push comes to shove and for them we offer Appointment Service. You know how you can schedule a caesarian these days? Well, this is sort of ...

PROSPECTIVE CLIENT: The exact opposite.

DEBT COUNSELOR: Yes. The App Serv team is excellent, guaranteed painless and they can make anything look like an accident. And finally, there are some people who are squeamish, but who also find that having an actual appointment makes them ...

PROSPECTIVE CLIENT: Freaking terrified?

DEBT COUNSELOR: Mmm, anxious. For them we offer a third approach, a service where you just go about your business and we ... take it from there. That one's called Dealer's Choice. *(Pause)* You don't have to decide that now.

PROSPECTIVE CLIENT: A lot of people must just run when their time is up.

DEBT COUNSELOR: Oh, people are surprisingly ethical about it. Also, we implant a chip that sends us your GPS coordinates.

PROSPECTIVE CLIENT: What if you dig the chip out?

DEBT COUNSELOR: We don't put it anywhere too ... accessible? And if you did get it out, we always have the Recovery Team.

PROSPECTIVE CLIENT: The chips are that valuable?

DEBT COUNSELOR: You're that valuable. You know how the Coast Guard has rescue and recovery units. This is more recovery and ... not rescue.

A long pause.

DEBT COUNSELOR: You can always say no. We're all about choices.

Suddenly, DEBT COLLECTOR has an edge, a subtle darkness. Maybe there's a lighting change for her next speech.

DEBT COUNSELOR: Quantity or quality. You can live in your run-down studio apartment if you want. With a roommate. And drive a 15-year-old beater. And eat ramen noodles. And never take a decent vacation. And waste a lot of your life living on the shoulder of poverty.

PROSPECTIVE CLIENT: Or I can have only 20 years left.

DEBT COUNSELOR: Twenty debt-free years to keep and spend your money. To travel, buy a house, have a life, whatever that means to you. And do you really want to live longer than that?

PROSPECTIVE CLIENT: My parents got to.

DEBT COUNSELOR: But do you want to? With the rising tides of climate change lapping at your ankles and blowing down your little garret. With the last shreds of our democracy fraying before your eyes, while the old world order collapses. I don't think it's too much to say that the ones who choose to go with us are in many ways the lucky ones. *(Pause; brighter again)* Hey, it's a big decision, so you take your time, talk to your friends, your family. And if you do choose to go with us, just give me a call.

DEBT COUNSELOR hands PROSPECTIVE CLIENT a card, shakes hands, and begins to leave.

PROSPECTIVE CLIENT: Wait. Are ... are you a client?

DEBT COUNSELOR turns back. He smiles and pulls up his shirt. He points to his back.

DEBT COUNSELOR: There's my GPS scar. Take a look around on the beach this summer. You'll be surprised. *(As he smiles)* Call me.

He EXITS. PROSPECTIVE CLIENT looks at his card, snorts in derision, then throws it in the waste can. PROSPECTIVE CLIENT looks around the small apartment, then sits down and thinks for a few moments. S/he picks the trash can up, starts to reach in to remove the card, and then stops. Still holding the can, s/he looks up, uneasy, thinking. Lights down slowly. Curtain.

Courtesy of Sarah Jessup

JENI MAHONEY (1964–) has published many plays as well as a feature-length screenplay. She directed the BFA in Playwriting program at Playwrights Horizons Theater School at New York University's Tisch School of the Arts for a decade. She is also the founding artistic director of Seven Devils Playwrights Conference and co-artistic director of id Theatre Company. Mahoney is the recipient of the Field's Independent Artist Challenge Program Grant and Columbia University's Woolrich Postgraduate Fellowship. In 2014, Mahoney was inducted into the Indie Theatre Hall of Fame. Today, Mahoney teaches for the Stonecoast MFA program at the University of Southern Maine. Her recent plays include *Fata Morgana* (2015) and *Mercy Falls* (2019).

Come Rain or Come Shine (2005)

CHARACTERS

Mom, *40s*

Luke, *her son, 20s*

Chris, *Luke's friend, 20s*

PLACE

Mom's house

Mom, a 40-ish woman, urban hippie comfy in her casual clothes and middle-aged body, cleans (bides the mess) and talks on the phone. Liza Minelli sings "Come Rain or Come Shine" in the background. She is on the phone.

Mom: No, you're right. No, I don't know what I was thinking.

Mom reaches for a stack of new CDs still in the plastic wrap and sorts through them.

Um ... Sara Brightman, *Best of Broadway*, *Les Mis*. Too much, right? No, I'll return 'em. Hey, what about *Rent*—that's something I might actually be listening to, right?

She makes a face, obviously not the response she wanted. Mom opens a nearby drawer and drops the CDs in.

I know. I just want to be supportive. As long as he's happy, right? That's all any mother can ask for.

Mom spots someone walking up to the driveway.

Oh! There they are! What? Yeah, nice-looking, in a sort of corporate way. Okay. Bye.

She hangs up the phone, puts it down—any old place, not in the charger, and sits on the couch and picks up a magazine—trying to look casual. The door opens slightly. Luke, 20s, young, impeccably neat, much more conservative than his mother, peeks in. Shy by nature, he hesitates at the door before entering.

Luke: Mom—?
Mom: (*Pretending casual surprise.*) Boo-key!

She goes to him warmly and hugs him. A second figure lingers behind Luke.

Lukey, Boo-key. My gosh, is it three already?

Luke: We're a little early.
Mom: Of course you are. Always punctual. Oh, I missed you so much!
Luke: Good to see you too, Mom.
Mom: Well, come in already, you big goof!

Luke indicates his friend.

Luke: Mom, this Chris. Chris, my Mom.

Chris leans into the room. Like Luke, he is dressed conservatively, obviously particular about his appearance and more well-practiced socially than Luke. Chris reaches out a hand to Mom.

Chris: Pleased to meet you, Mrs. Wilson.
Mom: Chris.

She stares at him meaningfully, then confides playfully—

Mom: It's Ms., actually—but you can just call me Mom.
Chris: Thanks, that's very … friendly, Ms. Wilson.
Mom: Yes. Well. Come in. Sit down. Tell me all about the drive!

The two men sit on the couch.

Luke: Are you alright. Mom?
Mom: No, I'm not "alright," I'm thrilled! My long-lost Lukey Boo-key is here with his friend. Chris. See? Isn't this nice?
Luke: 'Cause you might want to cut down on the caffeine. . . .
Mom: Drinks! You boys must be parched. What can I get you? Would you like a Cosmopolitan?
Luke: A what???
Mom: I hear they're all the rage.
Luke: When did you start drinking?
Mom: Me? No. I just thought you and Chris might want a drink.
Chris: No thanks, Ms. Wilson. I don't drink.

Mom smiles warmly.

Mom: Good for you, Chris. I can't tell you how glad I am to hear that. Really. Knowing that you respect your body, makes me respect you that much more.
Chris: Thank you, Ms. Wilson.
Mom: Oh, Luke. I like your friend very much.
Luke: You know, I think I'll take that drink—Como, Commic, whatever-you-call-it.
Chris: Luke, do you think that's a good idea?
Luke: Oh … yes.
Mom: Okay, then.

Mom flits—as best she can—to the kitchen. As soon as she is gone, Luke makes a bee line for the front door.

Chris: Hey!
Luke: I can't do this.
Chris: It's just cold feet.

Chris goes to Luke and puts his arm around him and turns him back toward the room. Luke hyperventilates.

Luke: … can't … breathe… .
Chris: That's totally normal. Luke, your mom seems very sweet.

Luke: You don't understand. THAT is not my mom! I don't know who that charming lady is. I've never, EVER heard my mom offer anybody a mixed drink that didn't include wheat germ and flax seed oil.

Chris: She's nervous, Luke, just like you. It's clear she misses you. She wants to be a part of your life. That's a great start. Hey, maybe offering you a drink is just her way of treating you like a grown-up.

Luke: You think?

Chris nods. A loud crash and a curse from the kitchen—Luke smiles: of course Chris is right.

Luke: Everything okay—

Mom: Fine, fine! Just … ah, why don't you put on some music! There are some CDs in the junk drawer!

Before Luke can get to the CD drawer, Chris stops him.

Chris: Remember what we talked about, Luke: you gotta be who you are and be proud of it.

Luke nods in agreement.

How many of us there are, hiding the shadows—afraid to tell our parents, our bosses, our friends? Afraid of what? This is America. We have as much right to be here as they do. More! And it's about time we stood up and got counted.

Mom enters proudly with a pink Cosmo in a martini glass. She hands it to Luke. He puts it down without drinking it.

Mom: Aren't you going to try it?

Luke: Mom, look.

Luke is stuck. Chris jumps in.

Chris: Why don't you have a seat, Mrs. Wilson. I think Luke has something he wants to say.

Mom sits.

Mom: Of course. What did you want to say, Luke?

Luke: Mom, I …

Mom: I love you, Luke. You can tell me anything. Don't you know that by now?

Luke: It's just that … I've been afraid that—

Mom: Afraid? Of me?

Luke: You gotta admit you're acting a bit … strange.

Mom: Maybe I did go a bit overboard. I just wanted you to know that I support you—whatever choices you make for your self and your life. Haven't I always lived a life of tolerance and acceptance—why should my son be any different?

Chris: I know that is a comfort for Luke. He was a little nervous about coming here today.

Mom: And seeing you here with Chris ... well, I just couldn't be happier. You're a lovely man, Chris—just the kind of partner I would pick for my son.

Luke: What?

Mom: He obviously loves you, Luke.

Chris: Well, I—

Luke: Mom! Chris is not my lover!

Chris: Your what???

Mom: It's alright, Luke—

Luke: I can't believe you—

Chris: Are you implying that I'm—?

Luke: You think I'm gay!

Mom: I love you no matter what you are.

Luke: I'm not gay! Why would you—I can't believe—That's why you told Chris to call you Mom, isn't it? Isn't it! You think he's your new son-in-law!

Mom: Well, then who the hell is he??

Luke: He's my roommate, Mom.

Chris: Housemate—we're not—we don't—we don't share a *room*.

Mom: So ... then ... what's this all about?

Luke: Have a seat, Mom.

Mom: Are you okay, Lukey?

Luke: Just sit, Mom.

Mom sits nervously.

Mom: Now you're scaring me.

Chris: You'll be laughing in few minutes. Trust me. We all will.

Luke: Don't you get it? She wants me to be gay. *That* she could accept. She could be the proud "out" mother of her "I'm queer, I'm here" son—she could buy T-shirts, and join parent groups and march on Washington ...

To Mom.

But I'm not gay, Mom. I'm not. I'm sorry. I'm ... a Republican.

Beat. Mom laughs, but her laughter quickly shifts from disbelief to shock. She searches Luke's eyes for any sign.

Mom: You're—

Luke: Republican. Come on, Mom. John Kerry? I just couldn't do it any more. He was ... a weasel, Mom. I'm sorry.

Mom: A ... a ... weasel?? John Kerry is a weasel? Compared to Bush?

Luke: He's a leader, Mom. And that's the long and short of it. He's got convictions, he knows what they are and he's not afraid to stand up for what he believes in.

Mom: I—can't believe what I'm hearing.

Chris: We're at war, Mrs. Wilson, in case you hadn't noticed. You don't change doctors in the middle of an operation.

Mom: You do if the doctor is killing you.

Luke: But you don't replace the doctor with a philosophy professor.

Mom: You're both …

Chris: … Republican …

She looks at Luke. He is a stranger to her. She gets up and crosses to the kitchen as if to leave.

Luke: Mom—

Chris goes to Mom. Takes her arm to stop her. Mom looks at Chris pointedly—he releases her. She spots the Cosmo on the table and decides to take it.

Mom: Okay, I'm going to need some time to sit with this.

She is about to exit when—

Chris: Hold up—

Mom turns to face Chris and Luke. Luke stares dejectedly at his feet.

Let me get this straight—you would accept Luke being gay, but you can't accept him being a Republican?

Mom: You're not born Republican. Luke was raised with solid LIBERAL values. He was raised to have a complex and nuanced understanding of national and international policy. We took him on Peace Corp vacations, spent holidays working soup kitchens! I poured my life and soul into this boy—what did I do wrong, Luke? Is it me? Is it my fault?

Luke: It's nobody's fault, Mom. It's just what I am.

Mom: It is not "what you are." It's a choice—a choice, I might add, that is going to kill your father, Luke, KILL HIM—

Chris: Now, Ms. Wilson, we all know that's an exaggeration—

Mom: Do you know where your father is right now, Luke? Do you know where he is? He is out protesting the reclassification of farmed salmon to inflate the administration's so-called environmental policy!

Chris: Why should farmed salmon be prejudiced against?

Mom looks at Chris as if he's an idiot.

Mom: And to think, just moments ago you looked so smart.

Luke: Mom, lay off him.

Mom: Tell me, Luke, is this the kind of thinking you aspire to? Is this what you think? Is global warming a myth? Is Alaskan oil going to save the SUV? I knew we never should have let you go to college in the Midwest!

Luke: Mom! Did you ever stop to think that maybe … just maybe … if everyone disagrees with you, you might be wrong?

Mom: Everybody does not disagree with me.

Luke: Okay. Let's say 4 million more people agree with me.

Mom: Luke, those people are—

Luke: What? Stupid? Is that what you were going to call "those people"? Is that what you're calling me?

Mom: I was going to say … reactionaries.

Chris: Do you know why people voted in droves this year, Mrs. Wilson? To put an end once and for all to this nonsense about the Democratic Party being the "silent majority." It's not. THAT is the lesson here. THAT is why people like Luke and myself have to come out of the shadows and make our voices heard. Welcome to the real America, Mrs. Wilson. This is it.

Mom: You don't know me. How dare you come into my house and lecture me about the "real" America.

Chris: So much for tolerance, right?

Mom: I think you should go now.

Chris: I was just leaving anyway, can't stand the smell of hypocrisy. Come on—

Chris nods to Luke and heads out the door, but Luke holds his ground.

Luke: Well, what about it, Mom? Should I go too?

Mom stands frozen. Miserable. There is nothing more to say. Luke turns to Chris, who disappears out the door, leaving it open. Luke goes to the door and takes the handle as if to shut the door behind Chris. He turns to Mom. She smiles: maybe he'll stay.

Luke: I'm not stupid, Mom.

Luke exits, leaving the door open behind him. Mom remains frozen, Cosmo untouched in her hand.

"Come Rain or Come Shine" plays as the lights fade to black.

* * *

UPPA/ZUMA Press/Newscom

HAROLD PINTER (1930–2008) was an English playwright, screenwriter, director, actor, and poet. He won numerous awards, including the 2005 Nobel Prize in Literature, and held several honorary university degrees. His work has appeared in numerous collections, including *Various Voices: Sixty Years of Prose, Poetry, Politics, 1948–2008* (2009). A vocal political activist, Pinter often explored absurd and dark subjects in his work.

Applicant (1961)

An office. Lamb, a young man, eager, cheerful, enthusiastic, is striding nervously, alone. The door opens. Miss Piffs comes in. She is the essence of efficiency.

Piffs: Ah, good morning.

Lamb: Oh, good morning, miss.

Piffs: Are you Mr. Lamb?

Lamb: That's right.

Piffs (*studying a sheet of paper*): Yes. You're applying for this vacant post, aren't you?

Lamb: I am actually, yes.

Piffs: Are you a physicist?

Lamb: Oh yes, indeed. It's my whole life.

Piffs (languidly): Good, Now our procedure is, that before we discuss the applicant's qualifications we like to subject him to a little test to determine his psychological suitability. You've no objection?

Lamb: Oh, good heavens, no.

Piffs: Jolly good.

Miss Piffs has taken some objects out of a drawer and goes to Lamb. She places a chair for him.

Piffs: Please sit down. (*He sits*) Can I fit these to your palms?

Lamb (affably): What are they?

Piffs: Electrodes.

Lamb: Oh yes, of course. Funny little things.

She attaches them to his palms.

Piffs: Now the earphones.

She attaches earphones to his head.

Lamb: I say, how amusing.

Piffs: Now I plug in.

She plugs in to the wall.

Lamb (*a trifle nervously*): Plug in, do you? Oh yes, of course. Yes, you'd have to, wouldn't you?

Miss Piffs perches on a high stool and looks down on Lamb.

This helps to determine my… my *suitability* does it?

Piffs: Unquestionably. Now relax. Just relax. Don't think about a thing.

Lamb: No.

Piffs: Relax completely. Rela-a-a-x. Quite relaxed?

Lamb nods. Miss Piffs presses a button on the side of her stool. A piercing high pitched buzz-hum is heard. Lamb jolts rigid. His hands go to his earphones. He is propelled from the chair. He tries to crawl under the chair. Miss Piffs watches, impassive. The noise stops. Lamb peeps out from under the chair, crawls out, stands, twitches, emits a short chuckle and collapses in the chair.

Piffs: Would you say you were an excitable person?

Lamb: Not—not unduly, no. Of course, I—

Piffs: Would you say you were a moody person?

Lamb: Moody? No, I wouldn't say I was moody—well, sometimes occasionally—

Piffs: Do you ever get fits of depression?

Lamb: Well, I wouldn't call them depression exactly—

Piffs: Do you often do things you regret in the morning?

Lamb: Regret? Things I regret? Well, it depends what you mean by often, really—I mean when you say often—

Piffs: Are you often puzzled by women?

Lamb: Women?

Piffs: Men.

Lamb: Men? Well, I was just going to answer the question about women—

Piffs: Do you often feel puzzled?

Lamb: Puzzled?

Piffs: By women.

Lamb: Women?

Piffs: Men.

Lamb: Oh, now just a minute, I.... Look, do you want separate answers or a joint answer?

Piffs: After your day's work do you ever feel tired? Edgy? Fretty? Irritable? At a loose end? Morose? Frustrated? Morbid? Unable to concentrate? Unable to sleep? Unable to eat? Unable to remain seated? Unable to remain upright? Lustful? Indolent? On heat? Randy? Full of desire? Full of energy? Full of dread? Drained? of energy, of dread? of desire?

Pause.

Lamb (*thinking*): Well, it's difficult to say really...

Piffs: Are you a good mixer?

Lamb: Well, you've touched on quite an interesting point there—

Piffs: Do you suffer from eczema, listlessness, or falling coat?

Lamb: Er ...

Piffs: Are you virgo intacta?[1]

Lamb: I beg your pardon?

Piffs: Are you virgo intacta?

Lamb: Oh, I say, that's rather embarrassing. I mean—in front of a lady—

Piffs: Are you virgo intacta?

Lamb: Yes, I am, actually. I'll make no secret of it.

Piffs: Have you always been virgo intacta?

Lamb: Oh yes, always. Always.

Piffs: From the word go?

Lamb: Go? Oh yes, from the word go.

Piffs: Do women frighten you?

She presses a button on the other side of her stool. The stage is plunged into redness, which flashes on and off in time with her questions.

---

[1] *Virgo intacta:* A virgin.

Piffs (*building*): Their clothes? Their shoes? Their voices? Their laughter? Their stares? Their way of walking? Their way of sitting? Their way of smiling? Their way of talking? Their mouths? Their hands? Their feet? Their shins? Their thighs? Their knees? Their eyes? Their (*Drumbeat*). Their (*Drumbeat*). Their (*Cymbal bang*). Their (*Trombone chord*). Their (*Bass note*).

Lamb (*in a high voice*): Well it depends what you mean really—

The light still flashes. She presses the other button and the piercing buzz-hum is heard again. Lamb's hands go to his earphones. He is propelled from the chair, falls, rolls, crawls, totters, and collapses.

Silence.

He lies face upwards. Miss Piffs looks at him then walks to Lamb and bends over him.

Piffs: Thank you very much, Mr. Lamb. We'll let you know.

* * *

REUTERS/Alamy Stock Photo

JOSÉ RIVERA (1955–) was born in San Juan, Puerto Rico, and grew up in a household where the only book was a Bible. When he was four years old, his family moved to New York. Early in his life, he saw a staged version of the play *Rumpelstiltskin* and decided to become a playwright. He has written numerous plays and won several awards, including two Obie Awards, a Fulbright Fellowship, and the Whiting Foundation Writing Award. In 2002, Rivera wrote the screenplay for *The Motorcycle Diaries,* a movie based on a motorcycle trip that Cuban revolutionary Che Guevara took as a young man. In 2005, Rivera became the first Puerto Rican to be nominated for an Academy Award for best adapted screenplay. Rivera's most recent plays are *The Garden of Tears and Kisses, Sermon for the Senses,* and *Charlotte,* all published in 2014. He remains active in writing for film and television. In addition to writing numerous short films, in 2020, Rivera wrote an episode for the television series *Penny Dreadful: City of Angels.*

Tape (1993)

CHARACTERS

Person
Attendant

A small dark room. No windows. One door. A Person is being led in by an Attendant. In the room is a simple wooden table and chair. On the table is a large reel-to-reel tape recorder, a glass of water, and a pitcher of water.

Person: Dark in here.
Attendant: I'm sorry.
Person: No, I know it's not your fault.
Attendant: I'm afraid of those lights …
Person: I guess, what does it matter now?

Attendant: … not very bright.
Person: Who cares, really?
Attendant: We don't want to cause you any undue suffering. If it's too dark in here, I'll make sure one of the other attendants replaces the light bulb.

(The Person looks at the Attendant.)

Person: Any "undue suffering"?
Attendant: That's right. *(The Person looks at the room.)*
Person: Is this where I'll be?
Attendant: That's right.
Person: Will you be outside?
Attendant: Yes.
Person: The entire time?
Attendant: The entire time.
Person: Is it boring?
Attendant: I'm sorry?
Person: Is it boring? You know. Waiting outside all the time.
Attendant: *(Soft smile.)* It's my job. It's what I do.
Person: Of course. *(Beat.)* Will I get anything to eat or drink?
Attendant: Well, we're not really set up for that. We don't have what you'd call a kitchen. But we can send out for things. Little things. Cold food.
Person: I understand.
Attendant: Soft drinks.
Person: *(Hopefully.)* Beer?
Attendant: I'm afraid not.
Person: Not even on special occasions like my birthdays?
Attendant: *(Thinking.)* I guess maybe on your birthday.
Person: *(Truly appreciative.)* Great, thanks. *(Beat.)*
Attendant: Do you have any more questions before we start? Because if you do, that's okay. It's okay to ask as many questions as you want. I'm sure you're very curious. I'm sure you'd like to know as much as possible, so you can figure out how it all fits together and what it all means. So please ask. That's why I'm here. Don't worry about the time. We have a lot of time. *(Beat.)*
Person: I don't have any questions.
Attendant: *(Disappointed.)* Are you sure?
Person: There's not much I really have to know is there? Really?
Attendant: No, I guess not. I just thought …
Person: It's okay. I appreciate it. I guess I really want to sit.
Attendant: Sit. *(The person sits on the chair and faces the tape recorder.)*
Person: Okay, I'm sitting.
Attendant: Is it … comfortable?
Person: Does it matter? Does it really fucking matter?
Attendant: No. I suppose not. *(The Attendant looks sad. The Person looks at the Attendant and feels bad.)*
Person: Hey I'm sorry. I know it's not your fault. I know you didn't mean it. I'm sorry.

Attendant: It's all right.

Person: What's your name anyway? Do you have a name?

Attendant: Not really. It's not allowed.

Person: Really? Not allowed? Who says?

Attendant: The rules say.

Person: Have you actually seen these rules? Are they in writing?

Attendant: Oh yes. There's a long and extensive training course.

Person: *(Surprised.)* There is?

Attendant: Oh yes. It's quite rigorous.

Person: Imagine that.

Attendant: You have to be a little bit of everything. Confidant, confessor, friend, stern taskmaster. Guide.

Person: I guess that would take time.

Attendant: My teachers were all quite strong and capable. They really pushed me. I was grateful. I knew I had been chosen for something unique and exciting. Something significant. Didn't mind the hard work and sleepless nights.

Person: *(Surprised.)* Oh? You sleep?

Attendant: *(Smiles.)* When I can. *(Beat.)*

Person: Do you dream? *(Beat.)*

Attendant: No. *(Beat.)* That's not allowed. *(Beat.)*

Person: I'm sorry.

Attendant: No. It's something you get used to.

Person: *(Trying to be chummy.)* I know. I went years and years without being able to remember one single dream I had. It really scared the shit out of me when I was ten and …

Attendant: I know.

Person: I'm sorry.

Attendant: I said I know. I know that story. When you were ten.

Person: Oh. Yeah. I guess you would know everything. Every story.

Attendant: *(Apologetic.)* It's part of the training.

Person: I figured. *(A long uncomfortable silence.)*

Attendant: *(Softly.)* Have you ever operated a reel-to-reel tape recorder before?

Person: No I haven't. I mean—no.

Attendant: It's not hard.

Person: I, uhm, these things were pretty obsolete by the time I was old enough to afford stereo equipment, you know, I got into cassettes, and, later, CDs, but never one of these jobbies.

Attendant: It's not hard. *(Demonstrates.)* On here. Off here. Play. Pause. Rewind.

Person: *(Surprised.)* Rewind?

Attendant: In some cases the quality of the recording is so poor … you'll want torewind it until you understand.

Person: No fast forward?

Attendant: No.

Person: It looks like a pretty good one. Sturdy. Very strong.

Attendant: They get a lot of use.

Person: I bet. *(Beat.)* Is this the only tape? *(The Attendant laughs out loud—then quickly stops.)*

Attendant: No.
Person: I didn't think so.
Attendant: There are many more.
Person: How many? A lot?
Attendant: There are ten thousand boxes.
Person: *Ten* thousand?
Attendant: I'm afraid so.
Person: Did I really ...
Attendant: I'm afraid you did.
Person: So ... everyone goes into a room like this?
Attendant: Exactly like this. There's no differentiation. Everyone's equal.
Person: For once.
Attendant: What isn't equal, of course, is the ... amount of time you spend here listening.
Person: Oh God.
Attendant: *(Part of the training.)* Listening, just to yourself. To your voice.
Person: I know.
Attendant: Listening, word by word, to every lie you ever told while you were alive.
Person: Oh God!
Attendant: Every ugly lie to every person, every single time, every betrayal, every lying thought, every time you lied to yourself, deep in your mind, we were listening, we were recording, and it's all in these tapes, ten thousand boxes of them, in your own words, one lie after the next, over and over, until we're finished. So the amount of time varies. The amount of time you spend here all depends on how many lies you told. How many boxes of tape we have to get through together.
Person: *(Almost in tears.)* I'm sorry ...
Attendant: Too late.
Person: I said I'm sorry! I said I'm sorry! I said it a million times! What happened to forgiveness? I don't want to be here! I don't want this! I don't want to listen! I don't want to hear myself! I didn't mean to say the things that I said! I don't want to listen!
Attendant: Yes, well. Neither did we. Neither did we. *(The Attendant looks sadly at the Person. The Attendant turns on the tape recorder. The Attendant hits the Play button, the reels spin slowly, and the tape starts snaking its way through the machine. Silence. The Attendant leaves the room, leaving the Person all alone. The Person nervously pours a glass of water, accidentally spilling water on the floor. From the depths of the machine comes a long-forgotten voice.)*
Woman's Voice: "Where have you been? Do you know I've been looking all over? Jesus Christ! I went to Manny's! I went to the pharmacy! The school! I even called the police! Look at me, Jesus Christ, I'm shaking! Now look at me—look at me and tell me where the hell you were! Tell me right now!" *(Silence. As the Person waits for the lying response, the lights fade to black.)*

* * *

Reading and Reacting

1. Do you think any of the characters in the six plays in this chapter are fully developed, or do you see most (or all) of them as flat characters, or even stereotypes? Given the limits of its form, do you think a ten-minute play can ever really develop a character? Why or why not?
2. Each of the plays in this chapter has only two or three characters. Should any additional parts have been written for these plays? Explain.
3. Could the roles in this chapter's plays be portrayed by actors of any gender? of any age? of any race? Why or why not?
4. Identify the central conflict in each play. What do you see as the **climax**, or highest point of tension, in each? Where does the climax generally occur in these plays?
5. Each play in this chapter has a single setting, and each of these settings is described only minimally. Do any settings seem to require more detailed descriptions? If you were going to expand each play, what additional settings might you show?
6. Considering the subject matter of each of the plays in this chapter, what kinds of topics seem to be most appropriate for ten-minute plays? Why do you think this is so? What kinds of topics would *not* be suitable for ten-minute plays?
7. **Critical Perspective** The Web site *10-Minute-Plays.com*, whose slogan is "High-octane drama for a fast-food nation," summarizes the structure of a ten-minute play as follows:

   Pages 1 to 2: Set up the world of your main character.
   Pages 2 to 3: Something happens to throw your character's world out of balance.
   Pages 4 to 7: Your character struggles to restore order to his world.
   Page 8: Just when your character is about to restore order, something happens to complicate matters.
   Pages 9 to 10: Your character either succeeds or fails in his attempt to restore order.

Although not every play in this chapter is exactly ten pages long, do they all nevertheless conform to the general structure outlined above?

WRITING SUGGESTIONS: Ten-Minute Plays

1. Write a response expressing your reactions to *Choices*, *Come Rain or Come Shine*, or *What Are You Going to Be?*
2. Write an explication of *Applicant* or *Tape*.
3. Assume you are a director providing background for an actor who is to play the role of Carla or Bethany in *Beauty*. Write a character analysis of one of these characters, outlining her background and explaining her emotions, actions, conflicts, and motivation.
4. Write an essay about the cultural context of one of the plays in this chapter.
5. Choose a scene from one of the longer plays in this text that has a definite beginning, middle, and end. Then, rewrite this scene as a self-contained ten-minute play. (If you like, you can update the scene to the present time, change the characters' names or genders, and make other changes you see as necessary.)
6. Write an original ten-minute play for two characters.

Chapter

29

Plot

Henrik Ibsen

Hulton Archive/Stringer/Getty Images

Susan Glaspell

AP Images

Arthur Miller

New York Times Co./Archive Photos/Getty Images

Learning Objectives

After reading this chapter, you will be able to. . .

- Identify how plot functions in dramatic works.
- Describe the relationship between plot and structure.
- Identify how the structure shapes a play's plot.
- Outline how plot is developed in a play.
- Analyze the plot of a specific play.
- Identify a play's climax.
- Identify a subplot in a play and explain its relationship to the main plot.

Plot denotes the way events are arranged in a work of literature. Although the conventions of drama require that the plot of a play be presented somewhat differently from the plot of a short story, the same components of plot are present in both. Plot in a dramatic work, like plot in a short story, is shaped by conflicts that are revealed, intensified, and resolved through the characters' actions. (See Chapter 9 for a discussion of conflict.)

Plot Structure

In 1863, the German novelist and playwright Gustav Freytag devised a pyramid to represent a prototype for the plot of a dramatic work. According to Freytag, a play typically begins with **exposition**, which presents characters and setting and introduces the basic situation in which the characters are involved. Then, during the **rising action**, complications develop, conflicts emerge, suspense builds, and crises occur. The rising action culminates in a **climax**, a point at which the plot's tension peaks. Finally, during the **falling action**, the intensity subsides, eventually winding down to a **resolution**, or **denouement**, in which all loose ends are tied up.

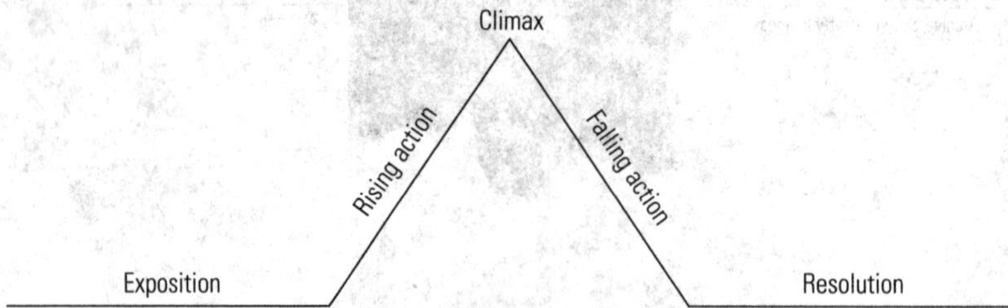

The familiar plot of a detective story follows Freytag's concept of plot: the exposition section includes the introduction of the detective and the explanation of the crime; the rising action develops as the investigation of the crime proceeds, with suspense increasing as the solution approaches; the high point of the action, the climax, comes with the revelation of the crime's solution; and the falling action presents the detective's explanation of the solution. The story concludes with a resolution that typically includes the capture of the criminal and the restoration of order.

The action of Susan Glaspell's one-act play *Trifles* (p. 820), which in many ways resembles a detective story, can be diagrammed like this:

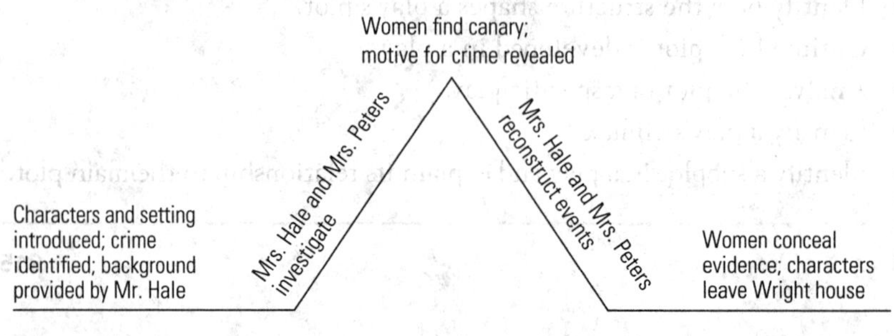

Of course, the plot of a complex dramatic work rarely conforms to the neat pattern represented by Freytag's pyramid. For example, a play can lack exposition entirely. Because long stretches of exposition can be dull, a playwright may decide to arouse audience interest by moving directly into conflict, as Sophocles does in *Oedipus the King* (p. 1137) and as Milcha Sanchez-Scott does in *The Cuban Swimmer* (p. 1122). Similarly, because audiences tend to lose interest after the play's climax is reached, a playwright may choose to dispense with extended falling action. Thus, after Hamlet's death, the play ends quite abruptly, with no apparent resolution.

Plot and Subplot

While the main plot is developing, a parallel plot, called a **subplot**, may be developing alongside it. This structural device is common in the works of Shakespeare and in many other plays as well. The subplot's function may not immediately be clear, so at first it may seem to draw attention away from the main plot. Ultimately, however, the subplot reinforces elements of the primary plot. In Henrik Ibsen's *A Doll's House* (p. 834), for example, the threat of Dr. Rank's impending death parallels the threat of Nora's approaching exposure; for both of them, time is running out.

In Shakespeare's *King Lear*, a more elaborate subplot involves the Earl of Gloucester, who, like Lear, misjudges his children, favoring a deceitful son who does not deserve his support and overlooking a more deserving one. Both families suffer greatly as a result of the fathers' misplaced loyalties. Thus, the parallel plot places additional emphasis on Lear's poor judgment and magnifies the consequences of his misguided acts: both fathers, and all but one of the five children, are dead by the play's end. A subplot can also set up a contrast with the main plot—as it does in *Hamlet* (p. 1012), where Fortinbras acts decisively to avenge his father, an action that underscores Hamlet's hesitation and procrastination when faced with a similar challenge.

Plot Development

In a dramatic work, plot unfolds through **action**: what characters say and do. Generally, a play does not include a narrator. Instead, dialogue, stage directions, and various staging techniques work together to move the play's action along.

Exchanges of **dialogue** reveal what is happening and, sometimes, indicate what happened in the past or suggest what will happen in the future. Characters can recount past events to other characters, announce an intention to take some action in the future, or summarize events that are occurring offstage. Thus, dialogue takes the place of formal narrative.

On the printed page, **stage directions** efficiently move readers from one location and time period to another by specifying entrances and exits and identifying the play's structural divisions—acts and scenes—and their accompanying changes of setting.

Staging techniques can also advance a play's action. For example, a change in lighting can shift the focus to another part of the stage—and thus to another place and time. An adjustment of scenery or props—for example, a breakfast table, complete with morning paper, replacing a bedtime setting—can indicate that the action has moved forward in time, as can a change of costumes. Music can also move a play's action along, predicting excitement or doom or a romantic interlude—or signaling a particular character's entrance.

Occasionally, a play does have a formal narrator to move the plot along. For example, in Thornton Wilder's play *Our Town* (1938), a character known as the Stage Manager functions as a narrator, not only describing the play's setting and introducing the characters to the audience but also soliciting questions from characters scattered around the audience, prompting characters, and interrupting dialogue. Tennessee Williams's *The Glass Menagerie* (p. 958) also features a character who serves as the play's narrator.

Flashbacks

Many plays—such as Arthur Miller's well-known 1949 play *Death of a Salesman*—include **flashbacks**, which depict events that occurred before the play's main action. Dialogue can also summarize events that occurred earlier, thereby overcoming the limitations set by the time frame in which the play's action unfolds. Thus, Mr. Hale in *Trifles* tells the other characters how he discovered John Wright's murder, and Nora in *A Doll's House* confides her secret past to her friend Kristine. As characters on stage are brought up to date, the audience is also given necessary information—facts that are essential to an understanding of the characters' motivation. (In less realistic dramas, characters can interrupt the action to deliver long monologues or soliloquies that fill in background details—or even address the audience directly, as Tom does in *The Glass Menagerie*.)

Foreshadowing

In addition to revealing past events, dialogue can **foreshadow**, or look ahead to, future action. In many cases, seemingly unimportant comments have significance that becomes clear as the play develops. For example, in Act 3 of *A Doll's House*, Torvald Helmer says to Kristine, "An exit always ought to be perfectly timed, Mrs. Linde. But I can't make Nora understand that!" At the end of the play, Nora's exit is not only effective but also memorable.

Elements of staging—such as props, scenery, lighting, music, and sound effects—can also foreshadow events to come. Finally, various bits of **stage business**—gestures or movements designed to attract the audience's attention—may also foreshadow future events. In *A Doll's House*, for example, Nora's habit of sneaking forbidden macaroons seems at first to suggest her fear of her husband, but her actions actually foreshadow her eventual defiance of his authority.

Checklist Writing about Plot

- What happens in the play?
- What is the play's central conflict? How is it resolved? What other conflicts are present?
- What section of the play constitutes its rising action?
- Where does the play's climax occur?
- What crises can you identify?
- How is suspense created?
- What section of the play constitutes its falling action?
- Does the play contain a subplot? What is its purpose? How is it related to the main plot?
- How do characters' actions advance the play's plot?
- How does dialogue advance the play's plot?
- How do stage directions advance the play's plot?
- How do staging techniques advance the play's plot?
- Does the play include a narrator?
- Does the play include flashbacks? foreshadowing? Does the play's dialogue contain summaries of past events or references to events in the future? How does the use of flashbacks or foreshadowing advance the play's plot?

AP Images

SUSAN GLASPELL (1882–1948) was born in Davenport, Iowa, and graduated from Drake University in 1899. First a reporter and then a freelance writer, she lived in Chicago (where she was part of the Chicago literary renaissance that included poet Carl Sandburg and novelist Theodore Dreiser) and later in Greenwich Village. In addition to *Trifles,* her works include two other plays, *The Verge* (1921) and *Alison's House* (1930), and several novels, including *Fidelity* (1915) and *The Morning Is Near Us* (1939). With her husband, George Cram Cook, she founded the Provincetown Players, which became the staging ground for innovative plays by Eugene O'Neill, among others.

Glaspell herself wrote plays for the Provincetown Players, beginning with *Trifles,* which she created for the 1916 season although she had never previously written a drama. The play opened on August 8, 1916, with Glaspell and her husband in the cast. Glaspell said she wrote *Trifles* in one afternoon, sitting in the empty theater and looking at the bare stage: "After a time, the stage became a kitchen—a kitchen there all by itself." She remembered a murder trial she had covered in Iowa in her days as a reporter, and the story began to play itself out on the stage as she gazed. Throughout her revisions, she said, she returned to look at the stage to see whether the events she was recording came to life on it. Although Glaspell later rewrote *Trifles* as a short story called "A Jury of Her Peers," the play remains her most successful and memorable work.

Cultural Context One of the main themes of this play is the contrast between women and men in terms of their roles, rights, and responsibilities. In 1916, when *Trifles* was first produced, women were not allowed to serve on juries in most states. This circumstance was in accordance with other rights denied to women, including the right to vote, which was not ratified in all states until 1920. Unable to participate in the most basic civic functions, women largely discussed politics only among themselves and were relegated to positions of lesser status in their personal and professional lives.

Trifles (1916)

CHARACTERS

George Henderson, *county attorney*
Henry Peters, *sheriff*
Lewis Hale, *a neighboring farmer*
Mrs. Peters
Mrs. Hale

SCENE

The kitchen in the now abandoned farmhouse of John Wright, a gloomy kitchen, and left without having been put in order—unwashed pans under the sink, a loaf of bread outside the breadbox, a dish towel on the table—other signs of incompleted work. At the rear the outer door opens and the Sheriff comes in followed by the County Attorney and Hale. The Sheriff and Hale are men in middle life, the County Attorney is a young man; all are much bundled up and go at once to the stove. They are followed by two women—the Sheriff's wife first; she is a slight wiry woman, a thin nervous face. Mrs. Hale is larger and would ordinarily be called more comfortable looking, but she is disturbed now and looks fearfully about as she enters. The women have come in slowly, and stand close together near the door.

County Attorney: *(rubbing his hands)* This feels good. Come up to the fire, ladies.

Mrs. Peters: *(after taking a step forward)* I'm not—cold.

Sheriff: *(unbuttoning his overcoat and stepping away from the stove as if to mark the beginning of official business)* Now, Mr. Hale, before we move things about, you explain to Mr. Henderson just what you saw when you came here yesterday morning.

County Attorney: By the way, has anything been moved? Are things just as you left them yesterday?

Sheriff: *(looking about)* It's just the same. When it dropped below zero last night I thought I'd better send Frank out this morning to make a fire for us—no use getting pneumonia with a big case on, but I told him not to touch anything except the stove—and you know Frank.

County Attorney: Somebody should have been left here yesterday.

Sheriff: Oh—yesterday. When I had to send Frank to Morris Center for that man who went crazy—I want you to know I had my hands full yesterday. I knew you could get back from Omaha by today and as long as I went over everything here myself—

County Attorney: Well, Mr. Hale, tell just what happened when you came here yesterday morning.

Hale: Harry and I had started to town with a load of potatoes. We came along the road from my place and as I got here I said, "I'm going to see if I can't get John Wright to go in with me on a party telephone." I spoke to Wright about it once before and he put me off, saying folks talked too much anyway, and all he asked was peace and quiet—I guess you know about how much he talked himself; but I thought maybe if I went to the house and talked about it before his wife, though I said to Harry that I didn't know as what his wife wanted made much difference to John—

County Attorney: Let's talk about that later, Mr. Hale. I do want to talk about that, but tell now just what happened when you got to the house.

Hale: I didn't hear or see anything; I knocked at the door, and still it was all quiet inside. I knew they must be up, it was past eight o'clock. So I knocked again, and I thought I heard somebody say, "Come in." I wasn't sure, I'm not sure yet, but I opened the door—this door *(indicating the*

In this scene from the Provincetown Players' 1917 production of Susan Glaspell's *Trifles*, the three men discuss the crime while Mrs. Peters and Mrs. Hale look on.

Billy Rose Theatre Collection, New York Public Library for the Performing Arts. Astor, Lenox & Tilden Foundation *door by which the two women are still standing)* and there in that rocker—*(pointing to it)* sat Mrs. Wright.

They all look at the rocker.

County Attorney: What—was she doing?

Hale: She was rockin' back and forth. She had her apron in her hand and was kind of—pleating it.

County Attorney: And how did she—look?

Hale: Well, she looked queer.

County Attorney: How do you mean—queer?

Hale: Well, as if she didn't know what she was going to do next. And kind of done up.

County Attorney: How did she seem to feel about your coming?

Hale: Why, I don't think she minded—one way or other. She didn't pay much attention. I said, "How do, Mrs. Wright, it's cold, ain't it?" And she said, "Is it?"—and went on kind of pleating at her apron. Well, I was surprised; she didn't ask me to come up to the stove, or to set down, but just sat there, not even looking at me, so I said, "I want to see John." And then she—laughed. I guess you would call it a laugh. I thought of Harry and the team outside, so I said a little sharp: "Can't I see John?" "No," she says, kind o' dull like. "Ain't he home?" says I. "Yes," says she, "he's home." "Then why can't I see him?" I asked her, out of patience. "'Cause he's dead," says she. "*Dead?*" says I. She just nodded her head, not getting a bit excited, but rockin' back and forth. "Why—where is he?" says I, not knowing what to say. She just pointed upstairs—like that. *(Himself pointing to the room above.)* I got up, with the idea of going up there. I walked from there to here—then I says, "Why, what did he die of?" "He died of a rope round his neck," says she, and just went on pleatin' at her apron. Well, I went out and called Harry. I thought I might—need help. We went upstairs and there he was lyin'—

County Attorney: I think I'd rather have you go into that upstairs, where you can point it all out. Just go on now with the rest of the story.

Hale: Well, my first thought was to get that rope off. It looked … *(stops, his face twitches)* … but Harry, he went up to him, and he said, "No, he's dead all right, and we'd better not touch anything." So we went back down stairs. She was still sitting that same way. "Has anybody been notified?" I asked. "No," says she, unconcerned. "Who did this, Mrs. Wright?" said Harry. He said it businesslike—and she stopped pleatin' of her apron. "I don't know," she says. "You don't *know*?" says Harry. "No," says she. "Weren't you sleepin' in the bed with him?" says Harry. "Yes," says she, "but I was on the inside." "Somebody slipped a rope round his neck and strangled him and you didn't wake up?" says Harry. "I didn't wake up," she said after him. We must 'a looked as if we didn't see how that could be, for after a minute she said, "I sleep sound." Harry was going to ask her more questions but I said maybe we ought to let her tell her story first to the coroner, or the sheriff, so Harry went fast as he could to Rivers' place, where there's a telephone.

County Attorney: And what did Mrs. Wright do when she knew that you had gone for the coroner?

Hale: She moved from that chair to this one over here *(pointing to a small chair in the corner)* and just sat there with her hands held together and looking down. I got a feeling that I ought to make some conversation, so I said I had come in to see if John wanted to put in a telephone, and at that she started to laugh, and then she stopped and looked at me—scared. *(The County Attorney, who has had his notebook out, makes a note.)* I dunno, maybe it wasn't scared. I wouldn't like to say it was. Soon Harry got back, and then Dr. Lloyd came, and you, Mr. Peters, and so I guess that's all I know that you don't.

County Attorney: *(looking around)* I guess we'll go upstairs first—and then out to the barn and around there. *(To the Sheriff.)* You're convinced that there was nothing important here—nothing that would point to any motive.

Sheriff: Nothing here but kitchen things.

The County Attorney, after again looking around the kitchen, opens the door of a cupboard closet. He gets up on a chair and looks on a shelf. Pulls his hand away, sticky.

County Attorney: Here's a nice mess.

The women draw nearer.

Mrs. Peters: *(to the other woman)* Oh, her fruit; it did freeze. *(To the County Attorney.)* She worried about that when it turned so cold. She said the fire'd go out and her jars would break.

Sheriff: Well, can you beat the women! Held for murder and worryin' about her preserves.

County Attorney: I guess before we're through she may have something more serious than preserves to worry about.

Hale: Well, women are used to worrying over trifles.

The two women move a little closer together.

County Attorney: *(with the gallantry of a young politician)* And yet, for all their worries, what would we do without the ladies? *(The women do not unbend. He goes to the sink, takes a dipperful of water from the pail and pouring it into a basin, washes his hands. Starts to wipe them on the roller towel, turns it for a cleaner place.)* Dirty towels! *(Kicks his foot against the pans under the sink.)* Not much of a housekeeper, would you say, ladies?

Mrs. Hale: *(stiffly)* There's a great deal of work to be done on a farm.

County Attorney: To be sure. And yet *(with a little bow to her)* I know there are some Dickson county farmhouses which do not have such roller towels.

He gives it a pull to expose its full length again.

Mrs. Hale: Those towels get dirty awful quick. Men's hands aren't always as clean as they might be.

County Attorney: Ah, loyal to your sex, I see. But you and Mrs. Wright were neighbors. I suppose you were friends, too.

Mrs. Hale: *(shaking her head)* I've not seen much of her of late years. I've not been in this house—it's more than a year.

County Attorney: And why was that? You didn't like her?

Mrs. Hale: I liked her all well enough. Farmers' wives have their hands full, Mr. Henderson. And then—

County Attorney: Yes—?

Mrs. Hale: *(looking about)* It never seemed a very cheerful place.

County Attorney: No—it's not cheerful. I shouldn't say she had the home-making instinct.

Mrs. Hale: Well, I don't know as Wright had, either.

County Attorney: You mean that they didn't get on very well?

Mrs. Hale: No, I don't mean anything. But I don't think a place'd be any cheerfuller for John Wright's being in it.

County Attorney: I'd like to talk more of that a little later. I want to get the lay of things upstairs now.

He goes to the left, where three steps lead to a stair door.

Sheriff: I suppose anything Mrs. Peters does'll be all right. She was to take in some clothes for her, you know, and a few little things. We left in such a hurry yesterday.

County Attorney: Yes, but I would like to see what you take, Mrs. Peters, and keep an eye out for anything that might be of use to us.

Mrs. Peters: Yes, Mr. Henderson.

The women listen to the men's steps on the stairs, then look about the kitchen.

Mrs. Hale: I'd hate to have men coming into my kitchen, snooping around and criticizing.

She arranges the pans under sink which the County Attorney had shoved out of place.

Mrs. Peters: Of course it's no more than their duty.

Mrs. Hale: Duty's all right, but I guess that deputy sheriff that came out to make the fire might have got a little of this on. *(Gives the roller towel a pull.)* Wish I'd thought of that sooner. Seems mean to talk about her for not having things slicked up when she had to come away in such a hurry.

Mrs. Peters: *(who has gone to a small table in the left rear corner of the room, and lifted one end of a towel that covers a pan)* She had bread set.

Stands still.

Mrs. Hale: *(eyes fixed on a loaf of bread beside the breadbox, which is on a low shelf at the other side of the room. Moves slowly toward it.)* She was going to put this in there. *(Picks up loaf, then abruptly drops it. In a manner of returning to familiar things.)* It's a shame about her fruit. I wonder if it's all gone. *(Gets up on the chair and looks.)* I think there's some here that's all right, Mrs. Peters. Yes—here; *(holding it toward the window)* this is cherries, too. *(Looking again.)* I declare I believe that's the only one. *(Gets down, bottle in her hand. Goes to the sink and wipes it off on the outside.)* She'll feel awful bad after all her hard work in the hot weather. I remember the afternoon I put up my cherries last summer.

She puts the bottle on the big kitchen table, center of the room. With a sigh, is about to sit down in the rocking-chair. Before she is seated realizes what chair it is; with a slow look at it, steps back. The chair which she has touched rocks back and forth.

Mrs. Peters: Well, I must get those things from the front room closet. *(She goes to the door at the right, but after looking into the other room, steps back.)* You coming with me, Mrs. Hale? You could help me carry them.

They go in the other room; reappear, Mrs. Peters carrying a dress and skirt, Mrs. Hale following with a pair of shoes.

Mrs. Peters: My, it's cold in there. 55

She puts the clothes on the big table, and hurries to the stove.

Mrs. Hale: *(examining her skirt)* Wright was close. I think maybe that's why she kept so much to herself. She didn't even belong to the Ladies Aid. I suppose she felt she couldn't do her part, and then you don't enjoy things when you feel shabby. She used to wear pretty clothes and be lively, when she was Minnie Foster, one of the town girls singing in the choir. But that—oh, that was thirty years ago. This all you was to take in?

Mrs. Peters: She said she wanted an apron. Funny thing to want, for there isn't much to get you dirty in jail, goodness knows. But I suppose just to make her feel more natural. She said they was in the top drawer in this cupboard. Yes, here. And then her little shawl that always hung behind the door. *(Opens stair door and looks.)* Yes, here it is.

Quickly shuts door leading upstairs.

Mrs. Hale: *(abruptly moving toward her)* Mrs. Peters?

Mrs. Peters: Yes, Mrs. Hale?

Mrs. Hale: Do you think she did it? 60

Mrs. Peters: *(in a frightened voice)* Oh, I don't know.

Mrs. Hale: Well, I don't think she did. Asking for an apron and her little shawl. Worrying about her fruit.

Mrs. Peters: *(starts to speak, glances up, where footsteps are heard in the room above. In a low voice.)* Mr. Peters says it looks bad for her. Mr. Henderson is awful sarcastic in a speech and he'll make fun of her sayin' she didn't wake up.

Mrs. Hale: Well, I guess John Wright didn't wake when they was slipping that rope under his neck.

Mrs. Peters: No, it's strange. It must have been done awful crafty and still. They say it was such a—funny way to kill a man, rigging it all up like that.

Mrs. Hale: That's just what Mr. Hale said. There was a gun in the house. He says that's what he can't understand.

Mrs. Peters: Mr. Henderson said coming out that what was needed for the case was a motive; something to show anger, or—sudden feeling.

Mrs. Hale: *(who is standing by the table)* Well, I don't see any signs of anger around here. *(She puts her hand on the dish towel which lies on the table, stands looking down at table, one half of which is clean, the other half messy.)* It's wiped to here. *(Makes a move as if to finish work, then turns and looks at loaf of bread outside the breadbox. Drops towel. In that voice of coming back to familiar things.)* Wonder how they are finding things upstairs. I hope she had it a little more red-up[1] up there. You know, it seems kind of *sneaking.* Locking her up in town and then coming out here and trying to get her own house to turn against her!

Mrs. Peters: But Mrs. Hale, the law is the law.

Mrs. Hale: I s'pose 'tis. *(Unbuttoning her coat.)* Better loosen up your things, Mrs. Peters. You won't feel them when you go out.

Mrs. Peters takes off her fur tippet, goes to hang it on hook at back of room, stands looking at the under part of the small corner table.

Mrs. Peters: She was piecing a quilt.

She brings the large sewing basket and they look at the bright pieces.

Mrs. Hale: It's log cabin pattern. Pretty, isn't it? I wonder if she was goin' to quilt it or just knot it?

Footsteps have been heard coming down the stairs. The Sheriff enters followed by Hale and the County Attorney.

Sheriff: They wonder if she was going to quilt it or just knot it!

The men laugh; the women look abashed.

County Attorney: *(rubbing his hands over the stove)* Frank's fire didn't do much up there, did it? Well, let's go out to the barn and get that cleared up.

The men go outside.

Mrs. Hale: *(resentfully)* I don't know as there's anything so strange, our takin' up our time with little things while we're waiting for them to get the evidence. *(She sits down at the big table smoothing out a block with decision.)* I don't see as it's anything to laugh about.

Mrs. Peters: *(apologetically)* Of course they've got awful important things on their minds.

---

[1] *red-up:* Spruced-up (slang).

Pulls up a chair and joins Mrs. Hale at the table.

Mrs. Hale: *(examining another block)* Mrs. Peters, look at this one. Here, this is the one she was working on, and look at the sewing! All the rest of it has been so nice and even. And look at this! It's all over the place! Why, it looks as if she didn't know what she was about!

After she has said this they look at each other, then start to glance back at the door.

After an instant Mrs. Hale has pulled at a knot and ripped the sewing.

Mrs. Peters: Oh, what are you doing, Mrs. Hale?

Mrs. Hale: *(mildly)* Just pulling out a stitch or two that's not sewed very good. *(Threading a needle.)* Bad sewing always made me fidgety.

Mrs. Peters: *(nervously)* I don't think we ought to touch things.

Mrs. Hale: I'll just finish up this end. *(Suddenly stopping and leaning forward.)* Mrs. Peters?

Mrs. Peters: Yes, Mrs. Hale?

Mrs. Hale: What do you suppose she was so nervous about?

Mrs. Peters: Oh—I don't know. I don't know as she was nervous. I sometimes sew awful queer when I'm just tired. *(Mrs. Hale starts to say something, looks at Mrs. Peters, then goes on sewing.)* Well, I must get these things

In this scene from a 2010 production of Susan Glaspell's *Trifles*, Mrs. Peters and Mrs. Hale discuss the discovery of a birdcage.

Courtesy of Prudence Katze

wrapped up. They may be through sooner than we think. *(Putting apron and other things together.)* I wonder where I can find a piece of paper, and string.

Mrs. Hale: In that cupboard, maybe.

Mrs. Peters: *(looking in cupboard)* Why, here's a birdcage. *(Holds it up.)* Did she have a bird, Mrs. Hale?

Mrs. Hale: Why, I don't know whether she did or not—I've not been here for so long. There was a man around last year selling canaries cheap, but I don't know as she took one; maybe she did. She used to sing real pretty herself.

Mrs. Peters: *(glancing around)* Seems funny to think of a bird here. But she must have had one, or why would she have a cage? I wonder what happened to it.

Mrs. Hale: I s'pose maybe the cat got it.

Mrs. Peters: No, she didn't have a cat. She's got that feeling some people have about cats—being afraid of them. My cat got in her room and she was real upset and asked me to take it out.

Mrs. Hale: My sister Bessie was like that. Queer, ain't it?

Mrs. Peters: *(examining the cage)* Why, look at this door. It's broke. One hinge is pulled apart.

Mrs. Hale: *(looking too)* Looks as if someone must have been rough with it.

Mrs. Peters: Why, yes.

She brings the cage forward and puts it on the table.

Mrs. Hale: I wish if they're going to find any evidence they'd be about it. I don't like this place.

Mrs. Peters: But I'm awful glad you came with me, Mrs. Hale. It would be lonesome for me sitting here alone.

Mrs. Hale: It would, wouldn't it? *(Dropping her sewing.)* But I tell you what I do wish, Mrs. Peters. I wish I had come over sometimes when *she* was here. I—*(looking around the room)*—wish I had.

Mrs. Peters: But of course you were awful busy, Mrs. Hale—your house and your children.

Mrs. Hale: I could've come. I stayed away because it weren't cheerful—and that's why I ought to have come. I—I've never liked this place. Maybe because it's down in a hollow and you don't see the road. I dunno what it is but it's a lonesome place and always was. I wish I had come over to see Minnie Foster sometimes. I can see now—

Shakes her head.

Mrs. Peters: Well, you mustn't reproach yourself, Mrs. Hale. Somehow we just don't see how it is with other folks until—something comes up.

Mrs. Hale: Not having children makes less work—but it makes a quiet house, and Wright out to work all day, and no company when he did come in. Did you know John Wright, Mrs. Peters?

Mrs. Peters: Not to know him; I've seen him in town. They say he was a good man.

Mrs. Hale: Yes—good; he didn't drink, and kept his word as well as most, I guess, and paid his debts. But he was a hard man, Mrs. Peters. Just to pass the time of day with him—*(Shivers.)* Like a raw wind that gets to the bone. *(Pauses, her eye falling on the cage.)* I should think she would 'a wanted a bird. But what do you suppose went with it?

Mrs. Peters: I don't know, unless it got sick and died.

She reaches over and swings the broken door, swings it again. Both women watch it.

Mrs. Hale: You weren't raised round here, were you? *(Mrs. Peters shakes her head.)* You didn't know—her?

Mrs. Peters: Not till they brought her yesterday.

Mrs. Hale: She—come to think of it, she was kind of like a bird herself—real sweet and pretty, but kind of timid and—fluttery. How—she—did—change. *(Silence; then as if struck by a happy thought and relieved to get back to everyday things.)* Tell you what, Mrs. Peters, why don't you take the quilt in with you? It might take up her mind.

Mrs. Peters: Why, I think that's a real nice idea, Mrs. Hale. There couldn't possibly be any objection to it, could there? Now, just what would I take? I wonder if her patches are in here—and her things.

They look in the sewing basket.

Mrs. Hale: Here's some red. I expect this has got sewing things in it. *(Brings out a fancy box.)* What a pretty box. Looks like something somebody would give you. Maybe her scissors are in here. *(Opens box. Suddenly puts her hand to her nose.)* Why—*(Mrs. Peters bends nearer, then turns her face away.)* There's something wrapped up in this piece of silk.

Mrs. Peters: Why, this isn't her scissors.

Mrs. Hale: *(lifting the silk)* Oh, Mrs. Peters—it's—

Mrs. Peters bends closer.

Mrs. Peters: It's the bird.

Mrs. Hale: *(jumping up)* But, Mrs. Peters—look at it! Its neck! Look at its neck! It's all—other side *to.*

Mrs. Peters: Somebody—wrung—its—neck.

Their eyes meet. A look of growing comprehension, of horror. Steps are heard outside. Mrs. Hale slips the box under quilt pieces, and sinks into her chair. Enter Sheriff and County Attorney. Mrs. Peters rises.

County Attorney: *(as one turning from serious things to little pleasantries)* Well, ladies, have you decided whether she was going to quilt it or knot it?

Mrs. Peters: We think she was going to—knot it.

County Attorney: Well, that's interesting, I'm sure. *(Seeing the birdcage.)* Has the bird flown?

Mrs. Hale: *(putting more quilt pieces over the box)* We think the—cat got it.
County Attorney: *(preoccupied)* Is there a cat?

Mrs. Hale glances in a quick covert way at Mrs. Peters.

Mrs. Peters: Well, not *now*. They're superstitious, you know. They leave. 120
County Attorney: *(to Sheriff Peters, continuing an interrupted conversation)* No sign at all of anyone having come from the outside. Their own rope. Now let's go up again and go over it piece by piece. *(They start upstairs.)* It would have to have been someone who knew just the—

Mrs. Peters sits down. The two women sit there not looking at one another, but as if peering into something and at the same time holding back. When they talk now it is in the manner of feeling their way over strange ground, as if afraid of what they are saying, but as if they cannot help saying it.

Mrs. Hale: She liked the bird. She was going to bury it in that pretty box.
Mrs. Peters: *(in a whisper)* When I was a girl—my kitten—there was a boy took a hatchet, and before my eyes—and before I could get there—*(Covers her face an instant.)* If they hadn't held me back I would have—*(catches herself, looks upstairs where steps are heard, falters weakly)*—hurt him.
Mrs. Hale: *(with a slow look around her)* I wonder how it would seem never to have had any children around. *(Pause.)* No, Wright wouldn't like the bird—a thing that sang. She used to sing. He killed that, too.
Mrs. Peters: *(moving uneasily)* We don't know who killed the bird. 125
Mrs. Hale: I knew John Wright.
Mrs. Peters: It was an awful thing was done in this house that night, Mrs. Hale. Killing a man while he slept, slipping a rope around his neck that choked the life out of him.
Mrs. Hale: His neck. Choked the life out of him.

Her hand goes out and rests on the birdcage.

Mrs. Peters: *(with rising voice)* We don't know who killed him. We don't know.
Mrs. Hale: *(her own feeling not interrupted)* If there'd been years and years of 130
nothing, then a bird to sing to you, it would be awful—still, after the bird was still.
Mrs. Peters: *(something within her speaking)* I know what stillness is. When we homesteaded in Dakota, and my first baby died—after he was two years old, and me with no other then—
Mrs. Hale: *(moving)* How soon do you suppose they'll be through, looking for the evidence?
Mrs. Peters: I know what stillness is. *(Pulling herself back.)* The law has got to punish crime, Mrs. Hale.
Mrs. Hale: *(not as if answering that)* I wish you'd seen Minnie Foster when she wore a white dress with blue ribbons and stood up there in the choir and

sang. *(A look around the room.)* Oh, I *wish* I'd come over here once in a while! That was a crime! That was a crime! Who's going to punish that?

Mrs. Peters: *(looking upstairs)* We mustn't—take on.

Mrs. Hale: I might have known she needed help! I know how things can be—for women. I tell you, it's queer, Mrs. Peters. We live close together and we live far apart. We all go through the same things—it's all just a different kind of the same thing. *(Brushes her eyes; noticing the bottle of fruit, reaches out for it.)* If I was you I wouldn't tell her her fruit was gone. Tell her it *ain't*. Tell her it's all right. Take this in to prove it to her. She—she may never know whether it was broke or not.

Mrs. Peters: *(takes the bottle, looks about for something to wrap it in; takes petticoat from the clothes brought from the other room, very nervously begins winding this around the bottle. In a false voice)* My, it's a good thing the men couldn't hear us. Wouldn't they just laugh! Getting all stirred up over a little thing like a—dead canary. As if that could have anything to do with—with—wouldn't they *laugh!*

The men are heard coming downstairs.

Mrs. Hale: *(under her breath)* Maybe they would—maybe they wouldn't.

County Attorney: No, Peters, it's all perfectly clear except a reason for doing it. But you know juries when it comes to women. If there was some definite thing. Something to show—something to make a story about—a thing that would connect up with this strange way of doing it—

The women's eyes meet for an instant. Enter Hale from outer door.

Hale: Well, I've got the team around. Pretty cold out there.

County Attorney: I'm going to stay here a while by myself. *(To the Sheriff.)* You can send Frank out for me, can't you? I want to go over everything. I'm not satisfied that we can't do better.

Sheriff: Do you want to see what Mrs. Peters is going to take in?

The County Attorney goes to the table, picks up the apron, laughs.

County Attorney: Oh, I guess they're not very dangerous things the ladies have picked out. *(Moves a few things about, disturbing the quilt pieces which cover the box. Steps back.)* No, Mrs. Peters doesn't need supervising. For that matter, a sheriff's wife is married to the law. Ever think of it that way, Mrs. Peters?

Mrs. Peters: Not—just that way.

Sheriff: *(chuckling)* Married to the law. *(Moves toward the other room.)* I just want you to come in here a minute, George. We ought to take a look at these windows.

County Attorney: *(scoffingly)* Oh, windows!

Sheriff: We'll be right out, Mr. Hale.

Hale goes outside. The Sheriff follows the County Attorney into the other room. Then Mrs. Hale rises, hands tight together, looking intensely at Mrs. Peters, whose eyes make a slow turn, finally meeting Mrs. Hale's. A moment Mrs. Hale holds her, then her own eyes point the way to where the box is concealed. Suddenly Mrs. Peters throws back quilt pieces and tries to put the box in the bag she is wearing. It is too big. She opens box, starts to take bird out, cannot touch it, goes to pieces, stands there helpless. Sound of a knob turning in the other room. Mrs. Hale snatches the box and puts it in the pocket of her big coat. Enter County Attorney and Sheriff.

County Attorney: *(facetiously)* Well, Henry, at least we found out that she was not going to quilt it. She was going to—what is it you call it, ladies?

Mrs. Hale: *(her hand against her pocket)* We call it—knot it, Mr. Henderson.

* * *

Reading and Reacting

1. What key events have occurred before the start of the play? Why do you suppose these events are not presented in the play itself?
2. What are the "trifles" to which the title refers? How do these "trifles" advance the play's plot?
3. Glaspell's short story version of *Trifles* is called "A Jury of Her Peers." Who are Mrs. Wright's peers? What do you suppose the verdict would be if she were tried for her crime in 1916, when only men were permitted to serve on juries? If the trial were held today, do you think a jury might reach a different verdict? What would your own verdict be? Do you think Mrs. Hale and Mrs. Peters do the right thing by concealing the evidence?
4. *Trifles* is a one-act play, and all its action occurs in the Wrights' kitchen. What do you see as the advantages and disadvantages of this confined setting?
5. All the background information readers have about Mrs. Wright is provided by Mrs. Hale. Do you consider her to be a reliable source of information? Why or why not?
6. Mr. Hale's summary of his conversation with Mrs. Wright is the reader's only chance to hear her version of events. How might the play be different if Mrs. Wright appeared as a character?
7. How does each of the following events advance the play's action: the men's departure from the kitchen, the discovery of the quilt pieces, the discovery of the dead bird?
8. What assumptions about women do the male characters make? How do the female characters support or challenge these assumptions?
9. **Journal Entry** In what sense is the process of making a quilt an appropriate metaphor for the plot of *Trifles*?
10. **Critical Perspective** In *American Drama from the Colonial Period through World War I*, Gary A. Richardson says that in *Trifles*, Glaspell developed a new structure for her action:

> While action in the traditional sense is minimal, Glaspell is nevertheless able to rivet attention on the two women, wed the audience to their perspective,

> and make a compelling case for the fairness of their actions. Existing on the margins of their society, Mrs. Peters and Mrs. Hale become emotional surrogates for the jailed Minnie Wright, effectively exonerating her action as "justifiable homicide."
>
> *Trifles* is carefully crafted to match Glaspell's subject matter—the action meanders, without a clearly delineated beginning, middle, or end....

Exactly how does Glaspell "rivet attention on" Mrs. Hale and Mrs. Peters? In what sense is the play's "meandering" structure "carefully crafted to match Glaspell's subject matter"?

Related Works: "I Stand Here Ironing" (p. 227), "Everyday Use" (p. 346), "The Yellow Wallpaper" (p. 315), "Harlem" (p. 561), "Daddy" (p. 571), *A Doll's House* (p. 834)

Hulton Archive/Stringer/Getty Images

HENRIK IBSEN (1828–1906), Norway's foremost dramatist, was born into a prosperous family; however, his father lost his fortune when Ibsen was six. When Ibsen was fifteen, he was apprenticed to an apothecary away from home and was permanently estranged from his family. During his apprenticeship, he studied to enter the university and wrote plays. Although he did not pass the university entrance exam, his second play, *The Warrior's Barrow* (1850), was produced by the Christiania Theatre in 1850. He began a life in the theater, writing plays and serving as artistic director of a theatrical company. Disillusioned by the public's lack of interest in theater, he left Norway, living with his wife and son in Italy and Germany between 1864 and 1891. By the time he returned to Norway, he was famous and revered. Ibsen's most notable plays include *Brand* (1865), *Peer Gynt* (1867), *A Doll's House* (1879), *Ghosts* (1881), *An Enemy of the People* (1882), *The Wild Duck* (1884), *Hedda Gabler* (1890), and *When We Dead Awaken* (1899).

A Doll's House marks the beginning of Ibsen's successful realist period, during which he explored the ordinary lives of small-town people—in this case, writing what he called "a modern tragedy." Ibsen based the play on a true story, which closely paralleled the main events of the play: a wife borrows money to finance a trip for an ailing husband, repayment is demanded, she forges a check and is discovered. (In the real-life story, however, the husband demanded a divorce, and the wife had a nervous breakdown and was committed to a mental institution.) The issue in *A Doll's House,* he said, is that there are "two kinds of moral law,... one in man and a completely different one in woman. They do not understand each other...." Nora and Helmer's marriage is destroyed because they cannot comprehend or accept their differences. The play begins conventionally but does not fulfill the audience's expectations for a tidy resolution; as a result, it was not a success when it was first performed. Nevertheless, the publication of *A Doll's House* made Ibsen internationally famous.

Cultural Context During the nineteenth century, the law treated women only a little better than it treated children. Women could not vote, and they were not considered able to handle their own financial affairs. A woman could not borrow money in her own name, and when she married, her finances were placed under the control of her husband. Moreover, working outside the home was out of the question for a middle-class woman. So, if a woman were to leave her husband, she was not likely to have any way of supporting herself, and she would lose the custody of her children. At the time when *A Doll's House* was first performed, most viewers were offended by the way Nora spoke to her husband, and Ibsen was considered an anarchist for suggesting that a woman could leave her family in search of herself. However, Ibsen argued that he was merely asking people to look at, and think about, the social structure they supported.

A Doll's House (1879)

Translated by Nicholas Rudall

CHARACTERS

Nora Helmer

Torvald Helmer, a lawyer and Nora's husband

Dr. Rank

Mrs. Linde

Nils Krogstad, a bank clerk

The Helmers' Three Small Children

Anna Marie, the children's nurse

Helene, a maid

A Delivery Boy

ACT 1

A comfortable, tastefully but not expensively furnished room. There is a door in the back right wall that leads to the front hallway of the apartment. A doorway on the left leads to Torvald's study. Between the doors is a piano. Halfway down the stage left wall is another door and a window. Near the window is a round table, an armchair, and a sofa. Halfway down the stage right wall is a door and near it a porcelain stove, two armchairs, and a rocking chair. Between the stove and the door is a small table. There are engravings on the walls. There is an etagere with small china figures and objects d'art; a small bookcase with richly bound leather books. There is a carpet on the floor, a fire burning in the stove. It is a winter day.

A bell rings in the hallway. Shortly after, we hear the front door being opened. Nora enters. She is humming happily to herself. She is wearing street clothes and is carrying an armful of wrapped packages, which she puts down on the table. She leaves the hall door open. Through it we can see the delivery boy. He is holding a Christmas tree and a basket, which he hands to the maid who had let them in.

Nora: Hide the tree carefully, Helene. The children mustn't catch a glimpse of it until this evening. Not until we've decorated it. *(to the delivery boy)* How much do I owe you? *(taking out her purse)*

Delivery Boy: Fifty pence, ma'am.

Nora: There's a hundred. No, keep the change. *(The boy thanks her and leaves. Nora shuts the door and begins to take off her street clothes. She is laughing softly to herself. She takes a bag of macaroons from her pocket, eats a couple, then crosses quietly to Torvald's door and listens carefully.)* Mmm! He's home. *(hums as she crosses to the table)*

Torvald: *(from the study)* Is that my little lark twittering away out there?

Nora: *(opening packages)* Yes it is!

Torvald: Is that my little squirrel fussing about in there?

Nora: Yes.

Torvald: And when did she come home?

Nora: *(putting the bag of macaroons back in her pocket and wiping her mouth)* A minute ago. Do come in, Torvald. Come and see what I've bought.

Torvald: I'm busy. *(soon after, he opens the door and looks in, pen in hand)* Did you say bought? All that? Has Madam Extravagant been throwing money away again?

Nora: But Torvald. ... This year we should ... oh, let ourselves go a little. It's the first Christmas we haven't had to count the pennies.

Torvald: But we can't just go wasting money.

Nora: I know, Torvald. But we can waste just a little bit, can't we? Just a teeny bit? You've got a big salary now...you're going to make piles and piles of money.

Torvald: Yes. After New Year's. And even then it's a full three months before the whole raise comes through.

Nora: Pah! We can borrow money until then.

Torvald: Nora! *(taking her playfully by the ear)* There you go again! Scatterbrain! Look, what if I borrowed a thousand crowns today and you spent the lot over Christmas, and then on New Year's Eve a tile fell off the roof, hit me on the head, and I lay there ...

Nora: *(hand on her mouth)* Oh! Don't say such things!

Torvald: Yes, but what if it actually happened—then what?

Nora: If something so terrible happened, I wouldn't care if I had debts or not.

Torvald: But what about the people I'd borrowed from?

Nora: Them? Who cares about them? I don't know them.

Torvald: Nora, Nora! Just like a woman! I am serious. Nora, you know how I feel about all that. NO DEBTS. Never borrow! When a home has its foundations built upon borrowing, upon debt, then some part of its freedom, some part of its beauty is lost. Until now we have fought a brave battle, the two of us. And we will keep on fighting for the little while that we still have to.

Nora: Whatever you say, Torvald. *(at the stove)*

Torvald: *(following her)* My little songbird's wings must not droop. Come now. Don't be a sulky little squirrel. *(takes out his wallet)* Nora! Guess what I have here!

Nora: *(turning quickly)* Money!

Torvald: There, *(handing her some money)* you see? I know how expensive it is to run a house at Christmas.

Nora: Ten, twenty, thirty, forty. Oh thank you, Torvald. I can really take care of everything with this.

Torvald: Well, you'll have to.

Nora: I promise. I promise. But come and see all that I bought. It was so cheap! Look, some new clothes for Ivar—and a little sword. A horsie and a trumpet for Robert. And a doll with its own little bed for Emmy.

Scene from *A Doll's House* with Toby Stephens (as Torvald Helmer) and Gillian Anderson (as Nora) at The Donmar Warehouse, London, UK in May 2009

Robbie Jack/Corbis Historical/Getty Images

They're not very good, but she'll break them to bits in no time anyway. And I bought some dress material and some handkerchiefs for the maids. Old Anna Marie really deserves something better.

Torvald: And what's in that package there?

Nora: No, Torvald, no! Not until tonight!

Torvald: I see. But tell me, Little Miss Extravagant, what did you think of for yourself?

Nora: For me? Oh I don't want anything.

Torvald: Of course you do. Now tell me, what would you really really—within reason of course … like to have?

Nora: I honestly don't know. Although, Torvald …

Torvald: Yes?

Nora: *(playing with the buttons on his jacket—but not looking at him)* If you really want to give me something—then maybe—maybe you could …

Torvald: Out with it, come on.

Nora: *(speaking fast)* You could give me money, Torvald. No more than you think you can spare. … Then … one of these days I'll buy something with it.

Torvald: But Nora—

Nora: Oh please, Torvald my darling, please. Do that for me. And I could wrap the money in pretty gold paper and hang it on the tree. Wouldn't that be fun?

Torvald: What do we call those little birds that fly through their money?

Nora: I know. Spendthrifts! Yes, yes, I know. But do what I ask, Torvald, and then I'll have time to make up my mind about what I need most. Now that's sensible of me, isn't it?

Torvald: *(smiling)* Yes, very … if you could actually hang onto the money I gave you and then spend it on something for yourself. But it would go for the house—or something frivolous. And then I'd only have to give you some more.

Nora: Oh but Torvald—

Torvald: Don't contradict me, Nora. Sweet Nora.… Spendthrifts *are* sweet, but they spend an awful lot of money. You have no idea what it costs a man to feed these little birds.

Nora: How can you say that! I save everything I can!

Torvald: *(laughing)* I know, I know. Everything you can. But that adds up to nothing at all!

Nora: *(humming again and with a smile of satisfaction)* Mmmm. … If only you knew … if only you knew … songbirds and squirrels have a lot of expenses.

Torvald: You're so strange, so like your father. You can find money anywhere and everywhere. But the moment you have it, it runs right through your fingers. You have no idea what you've done with it. Ah well, one takes you as you are. It runs in the blood. It's ingrained—these things are hereditary, Nora.

Nora: I wish I'd inherited many of Papa's qualities.

Torvald: And I wish you to be only as you are, my songbird, my sweet little lark. Wait a minute … I have the feeling … no … how should I put it …? You look very guilty about … something …

Nora: I do?

Torvald: Yes, you do. Look me straight in the eye.

Nora: *(looking at him)* Well?

Torvald: *(shaking his finger)* Little Miss Sweet Tooth! Have you been running wild in town again today?

Nora: No. What gives you that idea?

Torvald: Little Miss Sweet Tooth didn't make a little detour down to the patisserie?

Nora: No. Honestly, Torvald.

Torvald: Not even a little nibble?

Nora: No. Not a bite.

Torvald: Not even a macaroon or two … ?

Nora: No, Torvald. Honestly, I prom—

Torvald: It's all right, it's all right … I'm only joking.

Nora: I could never deceive you.

Torvald: I know, I know and you *have* given me your word. *(crossing to her)* Well, keep your little Christmas secrets to yourself. Nora, my darling, I'm sure they'll all be revealed this evening when we light the tree.

Nora: Did you remember to ask Dr. Rank?

Torvald: No. But there is no need. It is assumed he will dine with us. All the same, I'll invite him when he stops by this morning. I've ordered some superb wine. Nora, you have no idea how much I'm looking forward to this evening.

Nora: Me too! And the children will be so happy, Torvald.

Torvald: It's such a gratifying feeling … to have a safe, secure job … a comfortable salary. It … it gives one such … satisfaction.

Nora: Oh it's wonderful.

Torvald: Remember last Christmas? For three whole weeks you locked yourself up in your room. Every night. Making flowers for the Christmas tree. Till well past midnight. And other decorations to surprise us. That was one of the most boring periods of my entire life.

Nora: I wasn't bored.

Torvald: But the results, Nora, were … well … pretty pathetic.

Nora: Don't bring all that up again. I couldn't help it that the cat tore everything to shreds.

Torvald: No, it wasn't your fault. You tried so hard to please us all. And that's what counts. But … I'm so glad the hard times are over.

Nora: Yes. It's really wonderful.

Torvald: This year I don't have to sit in my study alone, boring myself to death. And you don't have to tire your precious eyes and your beautiful, delicate hands.

Nora: *(clapping her hands)* No. It's true … it's true, Torvald. … I don't have to, do I? I love to hear you say that. *(taking his arm)* Now. Let me tell you what I think we should do. Right after Christmas— *(doorbell)* The doorbell! *(tidying the room)* Someone *would* have to come just now. What a bore!

Torvald: I'm not at home to visitors, don't forget.

Maid: *(from the hallway)* Ma'am, a lady to see you—

Nora: All right, show her in.

Maid: *(to Torvald)* And the doctor's just come too.

Torvald: Did he go to my study?

Maid: Yes sir, he did.

(Torvald goes back to his room. The maid ushers in Mrs. Linde, who is dressed in traveling clothes, then shuts the door.)

Mrs. Linde: *(hesitant and somewhat dejected)* Hello, Nora.

Nora: *(uncertainly)* Hello …

Mrs. Linde: You don't recognize me.

Nora: No. … I'm not sure. … Wait a minute. … It can't … Kristine! Is that you?

Mrs. Linde: Yes, it's me.

Nora: Kristine! To think I didn't recognize you! But then … how could … ? *(in a quieter voice)* You've changed so much. Kristine.

Mrs. Linde: Yes. No doubt I have. It's been nine— ten long years.

Nora: Has it been that long since we last met? Yes. Yes, it has. For me these last eight years have been so truly happy. And so you've come into town too now. Made the long trip in winter. That was brave of you.

Mrs. Linde: The ship got in this morning.

Nora: So you came to enjoy yourself here over Christmas. Of course. That's wonderful! And we *will* enjoy ourselves. But take your coat off. *(helps her)* There now, let's sit here and be warm and cozy by the stove. No, sit in the easy chair. I'll take the rocker. … *(takes her hands)* Yes, now you look like your old self again. It was just that first moment. But you look paler, Kristine … paler and maybe a little bit thinner.

Mrs. Linde: And much much older, Nora.

Nora: Yes … perhaps a bit older … a teeny weeny bit older. But not much. *(suddenly serious)* But how thoughtless of me to sit here chattering away. Sweet Kristine, I'm so sorry, so sorry.

Mrs. Linde: What do you mean?

Nora: You lost your husband.

Mrs. Linde: Yes. three years ago.

Nora: I knew about it, of course. I read it in the newspapers. Kristine, I meant to write. I really did … but I kept putting it off … there was always something …

Mrs. Linde: Nora, I understand completely.

Nora: No! … it was awful of me, Kristine. How much you must have suffered. And he left you nothing?

Mrs. Linde: Nothing.

Nora: And there were no children?

Mrs. Linde: No.

Nora: You have nothing then?

Mrs. Linde: Not even a sense of loss. Nothing to … touch me.

Nora: *(looking incredulously at her)* But Kristine, how could that be?

Mrs. Linde: *(smiling, tired, and smoothing her hair)* Oh, it happens sometimes.

Nora: So completely alone. That must be impossibly hard for you. I have three beautiful children. You can't see them at the moment—they're out with the maid. But you must talk to me, tell me everything—

Mrs. Linde: No! No no, tell me about you.

Nora: No, you first. Today I don't want to be selfish. Today it's all about you. But there *is* something I must tell you about. Did you hear about the extraordinary good luck we just had?

Mrs. Linde: No, tell me about it.

Nora: Torvald has been made manager of the bank. Isn't that extraordinary?

Mrs. Linde: Your husband? That's wonderful.

Nora: Isn't it? You can't always depend on an income if you're a lawyer … especially if you won't go near cases that aren't aboveboard and … and honorable. And of course Torvald would never do that … and I'm completely behind him on that … . Oh we are both absolutely thrilled! He'll start work at the bank right after New Year's, and he'll get a huge salary and lots of commissions. From now on we can live quite differently … we can live as we want. Oh Kristine, I feel so happy, so free. Won't it be wonderful to have piles of money and not a care in the world?

Mrs. Linde: Well, it would be wonderful to have enough to meet one's daily needs.

Nora: No! Not just daily needs. But piles and piles of money!

Mrs. Linde: *(smiling)* Nora! Nora! You still haven't come to your senses! Even at school you just loved to spend money.

Nora: *(with a quiet laugh)* Yes, that's what Torvald still says about me. *(wagging her finger)* But this "Nora! Nora!" isn't quite as silly as you all think. We were in no position for me to waste any money. We had to work. … Both of us.

Mrs. Linde: You too?

Nora: Yes. I did a few odd jobs—needlework, embroidery, crocheting—that sort of thing *(casually)* … and some other things too. You know that Torvald left his department when we got married? He had no chance of being promoted in his firm. And of course he needed to earn more money. That first year he drove himself so hard. He took on all kinds of extra work. He didn't stop from morning to night. It took its toll. He became deathly ill. His doctors said it was essential for him to go south and travel.

Mrs. Linde: Didn't you spend a whole year in Italy?

Nora: Yes. But it wasn't easy to get away. I'd just had the baby … Ivar. But we *had* to go. Oh, it was a wonderful trip—and it saved Torvald's life. But it was terrifyingly expensive, Kristine.

Mrs. Linde: I'm sure it was.

Nora: Four thousand eight hundred crowns. That is *so* much money!

Mrs. Linde: It's lucky you had it when you needed it.

Nora: Well, the fact is we got it from Papa.

Mrs. Linde: Oh, I see. That was about the time your father died.

Nora: Yes. Just about then. But I couldn't even go and see him. I couldn't look after him. I had to stay here. I was expecting Ivar, and I had to take care of my poor sick Torvald. Oh my dear Papa! I never saw him again, Kristine. That was the worst time in all my married life.

Mrs. Linde: I know how much you loved him. And then you went to Italy?

Nora: Yes. We could afford it now, and the doctors insisted. We left a month later.

Mrs. Linde: And your husband came home completely cured.

Nora: Fit as a fiddle.

Mrs. Linde: But … the doctor?

Nora: Who?

Mrs. Linde: The man who came in with me.... I thought the maid called him "doctor."

Nora: Oh! Yes, that's Dr. Rank. But he's not making a house call. He's our best friend. He stops by at least once a day. No, Torvald has been completely healthy since we got back, and the children are strong and fit. And so am I. *(she jumps up and claps her hands)* Oh dear God, Kristine, it's so wonderful to be alive and happy! But how awful of me—here I am talking only about myself. *(sitting on a stool next to Kristine and placing her arms across her knees)* Don't be angry with me. Tell me, is it true that you weren't in love with your husband? Why did you marry him then?

Mrs. Linde: Well, my mother was still alive, but she was an invalid confined to her bed—and I had my two younger brothers to look after. In all good conscience, I didn't think I could refuse his offer.

Nora: No. of course not. Was he a rich man?

Mrs. Linde: I think he was very well off. ... But the business was precarious, Nora, and when he died everything fell apart and there was nothing left.

Nora: And then—?

Mrs. Linde: Well, I had to scratch out a living somehow. I had a little shop. I did a little teaching and whatever else I could find. The last three years have been work work work without a moment's rest. But it's over now, Nora. My poor mother doesn't need me anymore. She's passed on. And my brothers—they've got jobs and are taking care of themselves.

Nora: You must feel so free. ...

Mrs. Linde: Oh no ... just unspeakably empty. I have nothing to live for. *(she gets up and is visibly anxious)* That's why I couldn't stand it any more in that godforsaken place. Perhaps it will be easier here to find something to do ... to occupy my mind. If only I were lucky enough to find a steady job, maybe some office work.

Nora: But Kristine, that would be exhausting. You already look so tired. You'd be far better off going to a health spa.

Mrs. Linde: *(moving to the window)* I have no father to give me money to go traveling, Nora.

Nora: *(getting up)* Oh, don't be angry with me.

Mrs. Linde: *(going to her)* Oh Nora, don't *you* be angry with me! The worst part of this whole situation is all the bitterness stored up inside me. You've got no one to work *for* ... and yet you've got to grab every opportunity. You have to live ... and you become selfish. You know when you told me about all your good luck I was happier for myself than for you.

Nora: What do you mean? Oh I see. You thought perhaps Torvald could do something for you.

Mrs. Linde: Yes. Exactly.

Nora: And he will, Kristine. Just leave it to me. I'll bring it up so ... delicately. I'll find something nice to humor him with. Oh, I can't wait to help you.

Mrs. Linde: You are so kind, Nora, to be thinking of me—more than kind when you know so little about the hardships of this life.

Nora: I—? I know so little?

Mrs. Linde: *(smiling)* Well, good heavens, a little bit of needlework and things like that. … Nora, you are still a child.

Nora: *(with a toss of her head, she begins to pace)* Well, you don't have to act so superior.

Mrs. Linde: Oh?

Nora: You're like everybody else. You all think I'm incapable of doing anything serious …

Mrs. Linde: Oh come …

Nora: … or of ever having to face the brutality of life …

Mrs. Linde: Nora, my dear. You've just been telling me what you've been through.

Nora: Oh, that was nothing. I haven't told you about the really important thing.

Mrs. Linde: The important thing? What was that?

Nora: I'm not surprised that you look down on me, Kristine. But you have no right to. You're proud of yourself because you worked so hard all those years looking after your mother.

Mrs. Linde: I'm not looking down on anyone. But I *am* proud … of course, and happy that I know I was able to make my mother's last days a little more comfortable.

Nora: And you're proud of what you did for your brothers.

Mrs. Linde: I think I have every right to be.

Nora: I think so too. But let me tell you something, Kristine. I have something to be proud of too.

Mrs. Linde: I'm sure you do. Tell me about it.

Nora: Keep your voice down … . Just think if Torvald were to hear us! He mustn't find out. Not for the world. No *one* must find out. … No one but you, Kristine.

Mrs. Linde: Find out what?

Nora: *(pulling her over to the sofa)* Come over here. Oh yes, I've got something to be proud of. It was I who saved Torvald's life.

Mrs. Linde: Saved his life? How?

Nora: I told you about our trip to Italy. Well, Torvald would never have recovered if we hadn't gone there.

Mrs. Linde: Yes. But your father gave you all the money. …

Nora: *(smiling)* That's what Torvald thinks, and so does everyone else, but …

Mrs. Linde: What?

Nora: Papa never gave us a penny. I raised all the money myself.

Mrs. Linde: You? All that money?

Nora: Four thousand eight hundred crowns. What do you think of that?

Mrs. Linde: Nora! How could you do that? Did you win the lottery?

Nora: *(with a touch of contempt)* The lottery! Pah! How could I be proud of that?

Mrs. Linde: Where did you get it then?

Nora: *(smiling and then humming a little tune)* Aha! Tum tee tum.

Mrs. Linde: Well, you couldn't have borrowed it.

Nora: Oh, why not?

Mrs. Linde: Because it's not possible for a wife to borrow money without her husband's consent.

Nora: *(tossing her head)* Oh, that's not true. … Not when a wife has a little talent for business. … A wife who knows how to get things done.

Mrs. Linde: But Nora, I don't see how …

Nora: No, there's no reason you should. Anyway, I never said anything about *borrowing* the money. There are all kinds or ways I could have got my hands on it. *(stretching back on the sofa)* I could have gotten it from some admirer—after all, I am rather attractive. …

Mrs. Linde: Please be serious.

Nora: You really are dying to find out, aren't you, Kristine?

Mrs. Linde: Nora, my dear, listen. You haven't done anything … that you might regret?

Nora: How could I regret saving my husband's life?

Mrs. Linde: You might regret that you did something behind his back.

Nora: But I couldn't possibly tell him. Good heavens! Can't you see? It would have been terrible if he had found out how sick he really was. The doctors came to *me* and told *me* that his life was in danger … he would only survive if I took him to the South. Well, of course I tried coaxing him to go at first. I told him it would be so nice for me to take a holiday abroad—like other young wives. I tried everything. I cried. I begged. I told him that he had a duty to think of my … condition. … That he had to be a sweetheart and do what I asked. I dropped hints … oh … that he could easily borrow the money. Kristine, he nearly exploded in anger. He accused me of being frivolous. He said it was his duty as a husband not to give in to what I think he called my "little whims and daydreams." So I thought to myself, "All right, but your life is going to be saved somehow." Then I thought of a way to do it.

Mrs. Linde: But … but your father must have told him that you didn't get the money from *him*.

Nora: No—it was just about then that Papa died. I had always intended to tell him and ask him to keep it a secret. But he was so sick … and in the end, well, unfortunately I didn't need to tell him.

Mrs. Linde: And you—you've never told your husband?

Nora: Good heavens, no! How could I? He has such strict rules about these sorts of things. And, well, like most men, Torvald has his pride. He'd feel humiliated—hurt, even—if he thought he was indebted to me in any way. It would spoil everything. This lovely, happy home would never be the same.

Mrs. Linde: Aren't you ever going to tell him?

Nora: *(smiling and thoughtful)* Well, maybe someday. But not for a long time. When I'm no longer pretty. No, don't laugh, what I mean is … when

Torvald doesn't love me as much as he does now. When he no longer enjoys watching me dancing and dressing up and reciting little poems. It might be a good idea to have that up my sleeve. … *(breaking off)* But that's all nonsense. That time will never come. So? Kristine, what do you think of my great secret? I'm not so useless after all? And it hasn't been easy, I can tell you. It's a huge worry to have to meet your obligations on time. In the business world there are things called quarterly payments and installments. They're always so terribly hard to pay on time. So whenever I could. I've scraped together a little bit here, a little bit there. There wasn't much I could save out of the housekeeping money. Torvald has to live a comfortable life, and the children have to look nice. I didn't think I should touch the money I'd set aside for my little sweethearts.

Mrs. Linde: So it all had to come out of your allowance? Oh poor Nora!

Nora: Of course it did. After all, this was my choice. So if Torvald gave me money for a new dress or something, I never spent more than half. I bought the simplest, cheapest things. Thank heavens I look good in almost anything. So … Torvald never even noticed. But, Kristine, it hasn't been easy. Isn't it nice to be beautifully dressed?

Mrs. Linde: Yes, it is.

Nora: And I found other ways of making money. Last winter I was very lucky. I got a lot of copying to do, and I locked myself away and sat there writing—often till after midnight. Oh, sometimes I got so tired. But, you know, it was so much fun sitting there, working, earning money. It almost felt like being a man.

Mrs. Linde: How much have you been able to pay off?

Nora: Well, I don't exactly know. It's difficult with something like that to know how much you owe. I know this much … every penny I've made, scraped together, I've paid. Oh God, sometimes I've been at my wit's end. *(she smiles)* I used to sit here and think of some rich old man who'd fallen in love with me … and …

Mrs. Linde: Who? Who was that?

Nora: Wait … and that be died and that in his will in huge letters it said, "All my money is to go to the beautiful Nora Helmer, cash in hand."

Mrs. Linde: But Nora … who is this man?

Nora: Oh good heavens, don't you understand? There's no "old man." I just sat here and imagined him … oh so many times. I had nowhere to go, nowhere to look for money. But that's all done with now. That stupid old man can stay where he is. I don't care. He's gone and the will is gone. My troubles are over. *(she jumps up)* Oh Kristine, just think … nothing to worry about anymore, no more! I can laugh and play with the children. I can buy all the new modern things for the house—which Torvald loves. And soon it will be spring. Blue skies will come back, maybe we'll go away for a little while, maybe we'll see the sea again. Oh, isn't it wonderful to be happy and full of life? *(doorbell rings in the hallway)*

Mrs. Linde: *(getting up)* That's the door—perhaps I should go. …

Nora: No, stay. It's for Torvald. They won't come in here.

Maid: *(at door)* Excuse me, there's someone to see the lawyer.

Nora: The bank manager.

Maid: Yes, the bank manager. But I didn't know … since the doctor's with him.

Nora: Who is it?

Krogstad: *(in doorway)* It's me, Mrs. Helmer.

(Mrs. Linde is startled, collects herself, turns to window)

Nora: *(very tense and in a low voice)* What is it? Why do you want to see my husband?

Krogstad: Bank business. In a way. I have a small job in savings at the bank, and I've heard that your husband is to be the new manager, so …

Nora: So it's only …

Krogstad: Only business, Mrs. Helmer, boring business. Nothing else whatsoever.

Nora: Well, he is in his study. *(She gives a brief bow and shuts the door. Then she tends to the stove.)*

Mrs. Linde: Nora, who was that?

Nora: His name is Krogstad. He's a lawyer.

Mrs. Linde: So, it *was* him. …

Nora: You know him?

Mrs. Linde: I used to … years ago. He worked in a lawyer's office in my hometown.

Nora: Yes, he did.

Mrs. Linde: He's changed.

Nora: He had a very unhappy marriage.

Mrs. Linde: Then he's a widower now?

Nora: Yes, with lots of children. *(she closes the door of the stove and shifts her rocking chair)* There, that should burn well now.

Mrs. Linde: I hear he's involved in all kinds of business deals.

Nora: Really? Well you may have heard right. I don't know anything about … But let's stop talking about business … it's so boring.

(Dr. Rank comes out of Torvald's study)

Dr. Rank: *(in doorway)* No no, my dear man. I don't want to be in your way. And anyway, I'd like to see your wife for a while. *(he shuts the door and notices Mrs. Linde)* Oh, I beg your pardon. I seem to be in the way here too.

Nora: Of course you're not! Dr. Rank—Mrs. Linde.

Dr. Rank: I keep on hearing that name in this house! Didn't I pass you on the stairs on the way up?

Mrs. Linde: Yes. I don't like stairs. I have to go very slowly.

Dr. Rank: You're not feeling well?

Mrs. Linde: Just tired, I think. I've been working too hard.

Dr. Rank: That's all? So you've come to town for a rest? Lots of parties, eh?

Mrs. Linde: I've come to look for work.

Dr. Rank: Not a very clever cure for exhaustion.

Mrs. Linde: One has to live, Doctor.

Dr. Rank: Yes, current opinion seems to be in favor of it.

Nora: Now, Dr. Rank, you want to live as much as anybody.

Dr. Rank: Indeed I do. However terrible I may actually feel, I want to prolong the agony. For as long as possible. My patients all seem to have the same idea. And it even applies to those whose sickness is moral. At this moment there is a man in there with Helmer who's a moral cripple.

Mrs. Linde: *(softly)* Ahhh.

Nora: Who do you mean?

Dr. Rank: Oh, you wouldn't know him … he's a lawyer by the name of Krogstad. He's a thoroughly rotten human being. But the first words out of his mouth—as if it were important—"Oh, but I have to live."

Nora: Oh, what did he want to see Torvald about?

Dr. Rank: I've no idea. I think he said something about the bank.

Nora: I didn't know that Krog … the lawyer had anything to do with the bank.

Dr. Rank: Yes. he has some sort of job there. *(to Mrs. Linde)* I don't know if the same thing happens in your town, but here there are people who go around sniffing out moral corruption, and when they've found it they *reward* the owner with a well-paid job—just so they can keep an eye on him. An honest man will find himself left out in the cold.

Mrs. Linde: Well, perhaps the sick do need looking after.

Dr. Rank: *(with a shrug of his shoulders)* There you are, you see. That's the sort of opinion that's turning society into a home for the diseased.

Nora: *(She has been deep in her own thoughts. She suddenly gives a quiet chuckle and claps her hands.)*

Dr. Rank: Why do you laugh at what I said? Do you really understand what society means?

Nora: Oh, what do I care about your boring old society? I was laughing about something else, something very funny. Tell me, Dr. Rank, do all the people who work at the bank have to report to Torvald now?

Dr. Rank: Do you find that so "very funny"?

Nora: *(smiling and humming)* Ah … that's my business. *(walking around the room)* Well, yes, it really is very funny to think that we—that Torvald has so much power over so many people. *(taking the paper bag from her pocket)* Dr. Rank, would you like a macaroon?

Dr. Rank: Macaroons? Well! I thought they were forbidden in this house.

Nora: They are. But Kristine gave these to me.

Mrs. Linde: *(somewhat frightened)* What? I … I …

Nora: Nothing to be frightened of. You didn't know that Torvald had forbidden them. The fact is, he's afraid they will ruin my teeth. But … pah … once in a while … that's all right, isn't it. Dr. Rank? *(putting one in his mouth)* Here!

Have one. And one for you, Kristine. And I'll have one too ... just a teeny one. No more than two! *(walking about again)* Oh I'm *so* happy! There's just one thing more that I would *love* to do.

Dr. Rank: And what is that?

Nora: Something I've been *longing* to say in front of Torvald.

Dr. Rank: Why can't you say it?

Nora: Oh. I couldn't ... it's very bad.

Mrs. Linde: Bad?

Dr. Rank: Then you'd better not ... though perhaps in front of *us*? What is it that you'd *love* to say in front of Torvald?

Nora: I'd love to say—Well, I'll be damned!

Dr. Rank: You must be mad!

Mrs. Linde: Nora! My dear ...

Dr. Rank: Well, go ahead! ... he's coming out.

Nora: *(hiding the macaroons)* Sh! Sh! Sh!

(Torvald comes out with his coat over his arm and his hat in his hand)

Nora: *(crossing to him)* So. Torvald, my dear, you got rid of him?

Torvald: Yes. He's just left.

Nora: Let me introduce you—this is Kristine. She just came into town.

Torvald: Kristine ... ? I beg your pardon. ... I don't remember ...

Nora: Mrs. Linde, dear. Kristine Linde.

Torvald: Oh yes. You and my wife were at school together, weren't you?

Mrs. Linde: Yes. That's when we met.

Nora: Just think, she came all this way to see you!

Torvald: To see me?

Nora: Kristine is extremely good at office work. And she really wants to work for a man who knows what he's doing so she can perfect her skills.

Torvald: That's a wise choice, Mrs. Linde.

Nora: So when she heard you'd been made manager of the bank—there was a telegram or something—she came here as quickly as she could. You'll be able to do something for Kristine, won't you, Torvald, for my sake?

Torvald: Well, it's not impossible. ... I presume you are a widow, Mrs. Linde?

Mrs. Linde: Yes.

Torvald: And you've had some experience in accountancy?

Mrs. Linde: Yes. A fair amount.

Torvald: Then it's more than likely I can find a position for you.

Nora: *(clapping her hands)* There you are. Didn't I tell you?

Torvald: You came at the right moment, Mrs. Linde.

Mrs. Linde: How can I ever thank you?

Torvald: There's no need ... *(putting on his overcoat)* But now you must excuse me...

Dr. Rank: Wait a moment. I'll come with you. *(getting his fur coat from the hall and warming it by the stove)*

Nora: Come back soon, Torvald my dear.

Torvald: I won't be more than an hour.

Nora: Are you going too, Kristine?

Mrs. Linde: *(putting on her coat)* Yes. I must go. I have to find a room.

Torvald: Then perhaps we can all walk down the street together.

Nora: *(helping her)* It's such a shame that we don't have more room … but we couldn't possibly—

Mrs. Linde: Don't even think of it! Goodbye, my dear Nora. And thank you.

Nora: Goodbye for now—you'll come back this evening, won't you? And you too, Dr. Rank. What? "If you feel up to it"? Of course you will. Wrap yourself up warmly.

(They all go out into the hallway still talking. Then the children's voices are heard on the stairs.)

Nora: Here they are. Here they are!! *(She runs to open the door. Anna Marie, the Nurse, comes in with the children.)* Come on in! Come in! *(she bends down and kisses them)* Oh, my little sweethearts! Look at them, Kristine, aren't they darling?

Dr. Rank: Let's not stand here in the draft.

Torvald: Come along. Mrs. Linde. Only a mother could stand to be here now!

(They go down the stairs. The children, the Nurse, and Nora come back into the room.)

Nora: Oh, you look so nice and healthy. Pink cheeks—like apples! … no, like roses! *(the children chatter through the following)* Did you have a good time? Oh that's good! You gave Emmy and Bob a ride on your sled? Both of them? At the same time? Oh my goodness! You're such a big boy, Ivar. Let me take her for a moment, Anna, my little baby doll! *(taking the baby from the Nurse and dancing with her)* Yes. Mummy will dance with Bobby too! What? You played snowballs? Oh, I wish I'd been there. Leave them, Nanny, I'll take their things off … let me do it … it's such fun. You go off now, Anna Marie, you look half frozen. There's some hot coffee on the stove in there. *(The Nurse goes into the room on the left. Nora takes off the children's outdoor clothes, throwing them on the floor. They keep talking to her all at once.)* What? A big doggie ran after you? But he didn't bite you. No, big doggies don't bite little doll babies … Ivar! No! Don't open the parcels. What's inside? Wouldn't you like to know! Oh no, it's nothing nice at all! You want to play a game? What do you want to play? Hide-and-seek? Yes. Let's play hide-and-seek. Bob, you hide first. Me? All right, I'll go first.

(The children and Nora play the game both in the living room and in the room next to it. They are screaming with laughter. Nora hides under the table. The children run about looking but can't find her. Then the sound of her muffled laughter makes them run to the table and lift the cloth and they see her. Lots of shouting. She comes out on all fours trying to mock-frighten them. More shouts. There has been a knocking at the front door. No one has noticed. The door half opens. Krogstad is standing there waiting as the game continues.)

Krogstad: Excuse me, Mrs. Helmer …

Nora: *(stifles a cry and starts to get up)* Oh! What do you want?

Krogstad: I'm sorry … but the front door was open. Perhaps someone forgot to shut it.

Nora: *(rising)* My husband is out, Mr. Krogstad.

Krogstad: I know.

Nora: What do you want then?

Krogstad: A word with you.

Nora: Me! *(to the children, gently)* Go in and see Nanny. What? No. The strange man won't hurt mummy … as soon as he's gone we'll finish our game. *(She takes the children into the other room and shuts the door. She is tense and wary.)* You want to see me?

Krogstad: Yes. I do.

Nora: Today? But it's not the first of the month yet. …

Krogstad: No. It's Christmas Eve. And it's up to you whether you have a merry Christmas or not.

Nora: What do you want? I can't spare anything today. …

Krogstad: We'll talk about that later. This is about something else. Perhaps you can spare me a moment?

Nora: Well … yes … I can … but …

Krogstad: Good. I was sitting in Olsen's restaurant and saw your husband going down the street …

Nora: Well?

Krogstad: With a lady.

Nora: So…?

Krogstad: May I be so bold as to ask if it was a Mrs. Linde?

Nora: It was.

Krogstad: She just arrived in town?

Nora: Yes. Today.

Krogstad: She's a good friend of yours?

Nora: Yes, she is. But I don't see …

Krogstad: I knew her too. Once upon a time.

Nora: Yes. I know.

Krogstad: Oh? You know about it? I thought so. In that case I can ask you straight out: Is Mrs. Linde going to get a job at the bank?

Nora: How dare you question me, Mr. Krogstad. … You, one of my husband's subordinates. But since you ask I will tell you. Yes, Mrs. Linde is going to work at the bank. And it was I who recommended her, Mr. Krogstad. Now you know.

Krogstad: Well, that's what I suspected.

Nora: *(pacing)* So. … It seems that I have a little influence. Just because one is a woman doesn't necessarily mean—and a subordinate, Mr. Krogstad, should be careful not to cross anyone who has … well …

Krogstad: Influence?

Nora: Exactly.

Krogstad: *(changing his tone of voice)* Mrs. Helmer, I expect you will be good enough to use your influence on my behalf.

Nora: What do you mean?

Krogstad: That you will be kind enough to see to it that I don't lose my subordinate position at the bank.

Nora: What do you mean? Who is proposing to take it away from you?

Krogstad: Oh, you don't have to pretend you don't know. I completely understand. ... Your friend is not particularly keen to come into contact with me again. And I quite understand whom I'd have to thank for being fired.

Nora: But I assure you ...

Krogstad: I'm sure you do. But to come to the point. I think it's time for you to use your influence to make sure that doesn't happen.

Nora: But. Mr. Krogstad! I have no influence!

Krogstad: You don't? I thought you just said ...

Nora: Well, naturally I didn't intend you to think *that's* what I meant. Me? Why would you think that I have any influence of that kind on my husband?

Krogstad: Oh, I've known your husband since we were students. I don't think he's less ... susceptible ... than other husbands.

Nora: If you continue to speak disrespectfully of my husband, I will turn you out of the house.

Krogstad: That's very brave, Mrs. Helmer.

Nora: I'm not afraid of you any more. After the New Year, I will be finished with the whole thing.

Krogstad: *(controlling himself)* Now you listen to me. Mrs. Helmer. If necessary I am ready to fight for my little job at the bank as if I were fighting for my life.

Nora: I can see that.

Krogstad: It's not just for the money. In fact that's the least important thing. It's something else—I might as well tell you. It's this. I'm sure you know, like everybody else, that some years ago I made an unfortunate mistake.

Nora: I've heard something about it.

Krogstad: It never went to trial. But after that, all doors were closed to me. So I turned to the business that brought us together. I had to make a living. And to tell the truth, I haven't been as bad as some others. But it's time for me to be done with all that. My sons are growing up. And for their sake I must regain my reputation in this town. The job at the bank was the first step up for me—and now your husband is going to kick me back down into the mud.

Nora: You must believe me, Mr. Krogstad. I have no power to help you.

Krogstad: But if you set your mind to it. ... You should be aware that I have the means to force you ...

Nora: Are you threatening to tell my husband that I owe you money?

Krogstad: Well, what if I did tell him?

Nora: That would be a totally contemptible thing to do. *(sobbing)* I have kept this from him with pride and with happiness. I could not bear lo have him find out like that—from *you*—in such an ugly, clumsy way. It would be terribly unpleasant for me.

Krogstad: Just unpleasant? …

Nora: *(impetuously)* All right, then—tell him. But it'll be all the worse for you. My husband will see for himself what a monster you are. And there is no way that you will keep your job.

Krogstad: I meant—do you think that it would be "unpleasant" for you only at home?

Nora: If my husband does find out, he will of course immediately pay you what is still owed. And then we will have nothing more to do with you.

Krogstad: *(moving toward her)* Listen, Mrs. Helmer. Either I have a bad memory or you don't know much about business. I think I have to remind you of a few details.

Nora: What do you mean?

Krogstad: When your husband was ill, you came to me to borrow four thousand eight hundred crowns.

Nora: I didn't know where else to go.

Krogstad: I promised to get you the money…

Nora: Yes. And you did.

Krogstad: … I promised to get you the money on certain conditions. You were so worried about your husband's health, so anxious to get the money for your trip, that I don't think you paid much attention to the details. So. I think it's appropriate that I remind you. I promised to get the money if you would sign a security bond, which I then drew up.

Nora: And I signed it.

Krogstad: Exactly. Underneath your signature was a clause naming your father as security. He was supposed to sign this clause.

Nora: Supposed to? He did.

Krogstad: I'd left the date blank. In other words, your father was to enter the date on the day he signed it. Do you remember that?

Nora: Yes. I think so.

Krogstad: Then I gave you the document for you to mail to your father? Is that correct?

Nora: Yes.

Krogstad: And obviously you mailed it immediately because—oh, just five or six days later—you brought it to me, duly signed by your father. And I gave you the money.

Nora: So? Haven't I been paying it off regularly?

Krogstad: Yes. Pretty regularly. But—to get back to my point—you were having a very hard time then, weren't you, Mrs. Helmer?

Nora: I certainly was.

Krogstad: Your father was very sick, I believe.

Nora: He was near the end.

Krogstad: And he died soon afterward?

Nora: Yes.

Krogstad: Tell me, Mrs. Helmer, do you by any chance remember the day he died? The date, I mean.

Nora: Papa died on the 29th of September.

Krogstad: That is correct. I've made sure of that for myself. And that's what's so strange, *(producing the paper)* I can't explain it.

Nora: What is strange?

Krogstad: What is strange, Mrs. Helmer, is that your father signed this contract three days after his death.

Nora: What? I don't understand.

Krogstad: Your father died on the 29th of September. But if you look here, you'll see that he dated his signature "October 2nd." Isn't that strange. Mrs. Helmer? *(Nora is silent)* Can you explain it? *(Nora is still silent)* It's also strange that "October 2nd" and the year aren't in your father's handwriting, though I do think I recognize the hand. Now, of course, that could be explained—your father might have forgotten to date his signature, and someone else might just have guessed the date *before* they knew of his death. Nothing wrong with that. It's the signature that's important. That *is* genuine, isn't it, Mrs. Helmer? Your father really did sign his own name, didn't he?

Nora: *(pauses, then looks him straight in the eye and with a toss of her head)* No, he did not. I signed Papa's name.

Krogstad: Mrs. Helmer! You realize that is a very dangerous confession?

Nora: Why? You'll get your money back soon enough.

Krogstad: Let me ask you something. Why didn't you mail the contract to your father?

Nora: I couldn't. He was much too sick. If I'd asked him for his signature. I'd have had to tell him what the money was for. And in his condition. I couldn't tell him my husband was deathly ill. I couldn't possibly.

Krogstad: It would have been better for you if you'd canceled the trip.

Nora: That was impossible! That trip was to save my husband's life. I couldn't cancel it.

Krogstad: But did it never occur to you that you were deceiving me?

Nora: Why should I worry about that? I wasn't thinking about you at all. I hated the way you handled everything—so coldhearted, making everything so difficult—even though you knew how desperately ill my husband was.

Krogstad: Mrs. Helmer. It's obvious that you don't understand what it is that you are guilty of. Just let me tell you about what *I* did—the thing that ruined my reputation. It was nothing more and nothing worse than what you did.

Nora: You? Are you trying to tell me that *you* would have had the courage to try to save your wife's life?

Krogstad: The law doesn't care about motives.

Nora: Then the law is stupid.

Krogstad: Stupid or not, it is the law that will judge you if I produce this paper in court.

Nora: I don't believe it. Is a daughter not allowed to protect her dying father from worry and care? Is a wife not allowed to save her husband's life? I don't know much about the law. But I'm sure that there must *be* laws that allow things like that. You are a lawyer. You must know about laws like that. You must be a very poor lawyer, Mr. Krogstad.

Krogstad: Perhaps. But when it comes to business—the kind of business you and I have engaged in—don't you think I know about that? All right. Do as you like. But I tell you this. If I lose my job again, I'll bring you down with me. *(he bows and exits)*

Nora: *(she seems buried in thought for a short time, then tosses her head)* That's nonsense! He's just trying to frighten me! I'm not so stupid as he thinks. *(she starts clearing up the children's things)* And yet—? No, it can't be true. I did it because I love my husband.

The Children: *(in the doorway, sharing the conversation)* Mother, the strange man has gone out through the front gate.

Nora: Yes, sweethearts, I know. But don't tell anyone about the strange man. Do you hear me? Not even Papa.

Children: No, Mother. Let's go play!

Nora: No, not now.

Children: But, Mama, you promised!

Nora: Yes, but I can't now. Run on in. … I've got such a lot to do. Off you go, my sweethearts! *(She shuttles them into the room one by one, then shuts the door. She sits on the sofa and starts doing some needlework, but soon stops.)* No! *(she throws down the needlework, gets up, goes to the hall door, and calls out)* Helene? Bring the tree in! *(goes to the table on the left, opens a drawer, and then stops)* No! No! It can't be true!

Maid: *(coming in with tree)* Where shall I put it, Madam?

Nora: Here. In the middle of the room.

Maid: Can I get you anything else?

Nora: No, thank you, I've got everything.

(Maid exits.)

Nora: *(starting to dress the tree)* I'll put a candle here—flowers there—oh, that awful man! Everything's fine. The tree will look beautiful. I'll do everything I can to please you, Torvald—I'll sing for you, dance for you. *(Torvald comes in with some papers under his arm)* Oh, are you back already?

Torvald: Yes. Was anyone here?

Nora: Here? No.

Torvald: That's strange. I saw Krogstad leaving by the front gate.

Nora: Oh, did you? Oh yes, I forgot. Krogstad was here for a short while.

Torvald: Nora … I can see from your face that he's been here, begging you to put in a good word for him.

Nora: Yes.

Torvald: And you were supposed to make it seem like it was your idea. You were to hide the fact that he'd been here. Isn't that what he asked you?

Nora: Yes, Torvald. But …

Torvald: Nora, Nora. And you would agree to something like that? Even to have a conversation with a man like that, to promise him anything? And on top of everything, to lie to me?

Nora: Lie?

Torvald: Didn't you just say that no one had been here? *(shaking his finger at her)* My little songbird must never do that again. A songbird must sing with a pure voice—no false notes, *(putting his arm around her waist)* Isn't that right? Yes, I know it is. *(letting her go)* We'll say no more about it. *(sitting down by the stove)* How warm and cozy it is in here. *(going through his papers)*

Nora: *(after a short pause, during which she dresses the tree)* Torvald?

Torvald: Yes?

Nora: I am *so* looking forward to the fancy dress ball at the Stenborgs the day after tomorrow.

Torvald: And I am "*so*" curious to see how you're going to surprise me.

Nora: Oh, I've been so very silly.

Torvald: What do you mean?

Nora: I can't think of anything to wear! Everything seems so silly and unimportant.

Torvald: Ah. Does my little Nora finally realize that?

Nora: *(standing behind his chair with her hands on the back of it)* Are you very busy, Torvald?

Torvald: Well—

Nora: What are all those papers?

Torvald: Bank business.

Nora: Already?

Torvald: I asked the retiring manager to give me the authority to make the necessary changes in staff and to reorganize the workload. I have to spend Christmas week doing that. Everything has to be ready for the new year.

Nora: Was that why this poor man, Krogstad—

Torvald: Hmm.

Nora: *(leaning against the back of the chair and stroking his hair)* If you weren't so busy, I'd ask you a really big favor, Torvald.

Torvald: What? Tell me.

Nora: You have the best taste of anyone I know. And I do want to look nice al the fancy dress ball. Torvald, couldn't you help me decide what I should go as, what sort of dress I should wear?

Torvald: Aha! So the stubborn little lady needs someone to come to her rescue?

Nora: Yes, Torvald. I can't do a thing without you.

Torvald: All right, I'll think it over. I'm sure we'll come up with something.

Nora: That's so sweet of you. *(Going to the Christmas tree. Short pause.)* The red flowers look really pretty. Tell me, did Krogstad do something very bad?

Torvald: He forged someone's name. Have you any idea what that means?

Nora: Isn't it possible that he had no choice?

Torvald: Yes. But in many cases like this, it was probably—indiscretion. I'm not without compassion. I won't condemn a man altogether just because of one mistake.

Nora: I know you wouldn't, Torvald.

Torvald: There have been many men who have been rehabilitated if they confess their faults and take their punishment.

Nora: Punishment?

Torvald: But Krogstad did nothing of the kind. He got himself out of it by trickery. And that is why he is now completely ruined.

Nora: Do you think it would—

Torvald: *(interrupting)* Just think how a guilty man like that has to lie and be a hypocrite with everyone, how he has to put on a false mask even in front of those he loves, even in front of his own wife and children. And the children—that's the worst thing of all, Nora.

Nora: How?

Torvald: Because an atmosphere of lies infects and poisons the entire household. Every breath the children take is filled with the germs of evil.

Nora: *(coming near to him)* How can you be sure of that?

Torvald: My dear, I've seen it many times in my career as a lawyer. Most of the people who get into trouble early in life have had a mother who lies and cheats.

Nora: Why do you only say the mother?

Torvald: It usually seems to come from the mother's influence, although of course a lying father would have the same effect. All lawyers are familiar with the scenario. This man Krogstad has been consistently poisoning his own children with his lies and deception. That is why I say that he is a moral degenerate. *(holding out his hands to her)* And that is why my sweet little Nora must promise not to speak on his behalf. Give me your hand on it. Come on, what's this? Give me your hand! There now, that's settled. I can assure you it would be quite impossible for me to work with him. I literally feel physically sick in the presence of such people.

Nora: *(taking her hand out of his and going to the other side of the Christmas tree)* It's so hot in here. And I have so much to do.

Torvald: *(getting up and putting his papers in order)* Yes. I must try to get through some of these before dinner. And I must think about your fancy dress too! Oh, and maybe I have a little something wrapped in gold paper to hang on the tree.... *(patting her on the head)* My sweet little songbird. *(he goes to his room and shuts the door)*

Nora: *(after a pause, whispering)* No. It can't be true. It can't be. It can't be.

(Nurse opens the door on the left.)

Nurse: The children are pestering me to let them come in and see their Mama.

Nora: No. No. Don't let them come in to me. Stay with them, Anna.

Nurse: Very well. Madam. *(she shuts the door)*

Nora: *(her face pale with fright)* Corrupt my little children? Poison my home? *(short pause, then, with a toss of her head)* It's not true. It can't possibly be true.

ACT 2

The same setting as Act 1. But the Christmas tree is now in the corner by the piano, stripped of its ornaments and with burned-down candles on its somewhat tattered branches. Nora's cloak and hat are lying on the sofa. She is pacing the room, visibly uncomfortable. She stops by the sofa and picks up her cloak.

Nora: *(dropping the cloak)* Is that someone coming? *(goes to the door and listens)* No—there's no one there. Nobody will come on Christmas day—or tomorrow either. But perhaps— *(opens the door nod looks out)* There's nothing in the mailbox. It's empty. *(reentering the room)* Nonsense! Of course he can't be serious. It just couldn't happen.... No! I have three small children.

(The Nurse enters from the room on the left with a big cardboard box.)

Nurse: I finally found the box with the fancy dress.

Nora: Thanks, put it on the table.

Nurse: It's badly in need of repair.

Nora: I'd love to tear it into thousands of little pieces.

Nurse: Good heavens! It can easily be put right with a little bit of patience.

Nora: Yes. Well, I'll go and get Mrs. Linde to give me a hand with it.

Nurse: Going out again? In this weather? You'll catch your death of cold, Madam.

Nora: Worse things could happen. How are the children?

Nurse: The poor little dears are playing with their Christmas presents, but—

Nora: Are they asking for me all the time?

Nurse: Well, they're so used to having their Mama with them....

Nora: Well, Anna, I won't be able to be with them as much anymore.

Nurse: Oh well, little children get used to everything.

Nora: Do you think so? Do you think they'd forget their mother if she went away for good?

Nurse: Good heavens. ... Went away for good?

Nora: I want you to tell me something I've often wondered about—how did you have the heart to give your child away to people you didn't know?

Nurse: I had no choice—if I was to be my little Nora's nanny.

Nora: Yes, but how could you be *willing* to do it?

Nurse: Well, I was going to get a good position, wasn't I? A poor girl who's got into trouble should count herself lucky. Besides, that terrible man wasn't going to do a thing to help.

Nora: I expect your daughter has forgotten all about you.

Nurse: No. Indeed she hasn't. She wrote to me when she got confirmed and when she got married.

Nora: *(putting her arms around her neck)* Dear old Anna Marie, you were such a good mother to me when I was a little girl.

Nurse: Well, my poor little Nora had no other mother but me.

Nora: And if my little ones had no other mother, I'm sure you'd—oh what nonsense I'm talking. *(opening the box)* Go in and see them—. Now I have to—you'll see tomorrow how beautiful I will look.

Nurse: I know there'll be no one more beautiful than you at the ball. *(goes into the room on the left)*

Nora: *(starts to unpack the box, then pushes it away)* I wish I were brave enough to go out. Oh, I hope nobody comes. I hope everything will be all right here at home. Oh what nonsense! Nobody'll come. I just mustn't think about it. Let me brush the muff. Oh what beautiful, beautiful gloves. Stop thinking about it. Stop! One, two, three, four, five, six ... *(she gives a little scream)* There's someone coming! *(starts for the door, then stands uncertainly)*

(Mrs. Linde enters from the hall, where she has taken off her cloak and hat.)

Nora: Oh it's you, Kristine! There's no one else outside, is there? How nice of you to come.

Mrs. Linde: They told me you were asking for me.

Nora: Yes, I was just passing by. As a matter of fact, there is something you could help me with. Sit down by me on the sofa. Look at this. Tomorrow night there's a fancy dress ball upstairs at the Stenborgs. Torvald wants me to go as a Neapolitan fishergirl. He wants me to dance the tarantella that I learned in Capri.

Mrs. Linde: I see. So you're going in character.

Nora: That's what Torvald wants. Here's the dress. Look. Torvald had it made for me there. But it's torn, and I have no idea—

Mrs. Linde: Well, we can easily fix that. Some of the trimming has come loose here and there, that's all. Needle and thread? Now then, that's all we need. *(starting to sew)* So. You're going to be all dressed up tomorrow, Nora. I'll tell you what—I'll pop in for a moment to see you in all your finery. Oh, I forgot to thank you for a wonderful evening yesterday.

Nora: *(gets up and crosses the room)* Well, I don't think yesterday was all that wonderful. You should have come to town a little bit sooner, Kristine. But Torvald really knows how to make a house look beautiful.

Mrs. Linde: And so do you. You're not your father's daughter for nothing. But tell me, is Dr. Rank always as depressed as he was last night?

Nora: No, last night it was very noticeable. I have to tell you—he's got a life-threatening disease. It's a form of consumption—and it affects his spine.

Oh the poor man. His father was a terrible creature who lived a life of excess—and his son was sickly from childhood—do you understand what I mean?

Mrs. Linde: *(putting down her sewing)* My dear Nora, how do you know about such things?

Nora: *(walking about)* Ah, when you've had three children as I have, well, people drop by, married women—and they know quite a bit about medical problems—and they talk—about one thing and another.

Mrs. Linde: *(Resumes her sewing. A short silence.)* Does Dr. Rank come here every day?

Nora: Every day. He's Torvald's best friend, and a good friend of mine too. He's just like one of the family.

Mrs. Linde: But tell me—can he be trusted? I mean, isn't he the sort of man who is always eager to please?

Nora: Not in the least. What makes you think that?

Mrs. Linde: Well. When you introduced me to him yesterday, he said that he had often heard my name mentioned in this house. But afterward I noticed that your husband hadn't the slightest idea who I was. So how could Dr. Rank … ?

Nora: You're quite right, Kristine. Torvald loves me so much that he wants me all to himself. That's what he says. Early on, he seemed, well, jealous if I even mentioned the people I was so fond of at home. So naturally I stopped doing that. But I often talk about things like that with Dr. Rank because he likes to listen to me.

Mrs. Linde: Now you listen to *me*, Nora. You're still almost a child in many ways. I'm a little bit more mature, a little bit more experienced. I must tell you this—you ought to put a stop to this with Dr. Rank.

Nora: Put a stop to what?

Mrs. Linde: Two things, I think. Yesterday there was some silly talk about a rich admirer who would leave you money—

Nora: An admirer who doesn't exist. Unfortunately. What else?

Mrs. Linde: Dr. Rank is a wealthy man?

Nora: Yes, he is.

Mrs. Linde: And he has no dependents?

Nora: No. No one, but…

Mrs. Linde: And he comes here every day?

Nora: That's what I said.

Mrs. Linde: How could a gentleman be so tactless?

Nora: I don't understand what you mean.

Mrs. Linde: Don't pretend, Nora. Do you think I can't guess who lent you the four thousand eight hundred crowns?

Nora: Are you out of your mind? How could you think that? A friend of both of us who comes here every day? Can't you see how terribly awkward that would be?

Mrs. Linde: It's really not him?

Nora: No. Absolutely not. It would never have entered my head for a moment. Besides, he had no money to lend at the time. He inherited it afterward.

Mrs. Linde: Well, Nora, that was lucky for you. I think.

Nora: No, it would never have entered my head to ask Dr. Rank. Although I'm quite sure that if I had asked him—

Mrs. Linde: But you wouldn't—?

Nora: Of course not. There's no need as far as I can see. ... But I'm quite sure that if I told Dr. Rank—

Mrs. Linde: Behind your husband's back?

Nora: Well, I have to put a stop to things with the other person—and *that* will be behind his back. I *must* put a stop to it with him.

Mrs. Linde: Yes. That's what I told you yesterday, but—

Nora: *(pacing)* It's so much easier for a *man* to put things like that right—

Mrs. Linde: One's husband, yes.

Nora: Nonsense. *(stops pacing)* When you pay off a debt you get your contract back, don't you?

Mrs. Linde: Yes. That's the normal procedure.

Nora: And you can tear it up into thousands of pieces, and throw it on the fire—nasty filthy piece of paper.

Mrs. Linde: *(puts down her sewing and, looking Nora straight in the eye, gets up slowly)* Nora, you're hiding something from me, aren't you?

Nora: Do I look as if I were?

Mrs. Linde: Something has happened since yesterday morning. Nora, what is it?

Nora: *(crossing to her)* Kristine— *(stops and listens)* Sh! Torvald just came back. Do you mind going into the children for a moment? Torvald hates to see sewing things in this room. Let Anna Marie give you a hand.

Mrs. Linde: *(gathering up some of the things)* Of course. But I'm not leaving here until we've had this out with each other. *(she goes into the room on the left just as Torvald comes in)*

Nora: *(crossing to him)* I've missed you so much, Torvald.

Torvald: Was that the dressmaker?

Nora: No, it was Kristine. She's helping me mend my dress. You'll see, I'll look really pretty.

Torvald: Wasn't that a good idea I had?

Nora: Wonderful. But don't you think it's nice of me to do what you want?

Torvald: Nice? To do as your husband wishes? You little scamp! But I'm sure you didn't mean it like that. But ... I mustn't disturb you. You'll want to be trying on your dress, I'm sure.

Nora: You're going to be working?

Torvald: *(showing her a bundle of papers)* Yes, look at this. I've just been to the bank. *(going into his room)*

Nora: Torvald!

Torvald: Yes?

Nora: If your little squirrel asked you for something, and she was very, very nice …

Torvald: What?

Nora: Would you do it?

Torvald: I'd want to hear what it was first.

Nora: Your little squirrel would run all over the place and do her little tricks. You just have to be nice and do what she wants.

Torvald: Tell me what you mean.

Nora: Your skylark would sing, warble in every room, singing loud, singing soft …

Torvald: Well, she does that anyway.

Nora: I'd be a fairy and dance for you in the moon-light, Torvald.

Torvald: Nora, you're not talking about—the thing you asked of me this morning.…

Nora: *(going toward him)* Yes. Torvald. I beg you, I beg you.

Torvald: How dare you bring up that business again?

Nora: You *must* do as I ask. You *must* let Krogstad keep his job at the bank.

Torvald: My dear Nora, I have arranged to give his position to Mrs. Linde.

Nora: Yes, I know you've been really kind about that. But you could just as easily fire someone other than Krogstad.

Torvald: You are being *incredibly* stubborn. Just because you chose to give him so thoughtless a promise—that you would speak on his behalf—I'm supposed to—

Nora: That's not the reason, Torvald. I'm doing this for you. This man writes for the most dreadful, slanderous newspapers. You told me so yourself. He can do you a terrible amount of harm. I'm scared to death of him—

Torvald: Oh, I understand. You're thinking about the past and you're afraid.

Nora: What do you mean?

Torvald: Well, of course you're thinking about your father.

Nora: Yes. Yes, that's it. Just remember what those malicious people wrote in the papers about Papa, how they slandered him. I'm sure they would have had him dismissed if the Department had not sent you over to look into the matter, and if you hadn't been so kind and helpful to him.

Torvald: My dear Nora. There's a very important difference between your father and me. Your father's reputation as a public official was not above suspicion. Mine *is*—and I hope it will remain so, as long as I hold my position.

Nora: But you can never tell what these people might do to you! We ought to have enough money to be comfortable, we ought to be cozy and happy in our quiet little home. We should have no cares. You and I and the children. That is why I'm begging you.

Torvald: And it's just because you *are* pleading on his behalf that you make it impossible for me to keep him on. Everyone at the bank already knows that I intend to dismiss Krogstad. Are people going to say now that the new manager has changed his mind just because his wife asked him?

Nora: And what if they did?

Torvald: Oh yes. Just so this stubborn little woman can get her own way. Do you think I'm going to make myself look like a fool in front of my whole staff? Do you think I'm going to let people think I'm a man who will change his mind because of outside pressures? I can assure you I'd feel the consequences of that pretty quickly. And in any case, there's one thing that makes it impossible for me to keep Krogstad at the bank as long as I am the manager.

Nora: What's that?

Torvald: I might perhaps have overlooked his moral failings if I had to—

Nora: Yes, you could, couldn't you?

Torvald: —and I hear that he's a hard worker. *But* I knew him when we were boys. It was one of those impulsive friendships that often haunt one in later life. I might as well tell you quite plainly that we were once on very intimate terms with one another. But this man has no tact when other people are around. On the contrary, he thinks our past friendship gives him the right to be on familiar terms with me. All the time it's "Hi there, Torvald, old pal!" That sort of thing. It is *extremely* difficult for me. He would make my position in the bank totally intolerable.

Nora: Torvald, I can't believe you mean that.

Torvald: Can't you? Why not?

Nora: Because it's such a narrow-minded way of looking at things.

Torvald: Narrow-minded? What do you mean? Do you think I'm narrow-minded?

Nora: No, just the opposite, my love. And that is why ...

Torvald: No. You said that I had a narrow-minded way of looking at things. Well then, *I* myself must be narrow-minded. All right, I'm going to put an end to this. *(he goes to the hall door and calls out)* Helene!

Nora: What are you going to do?

Torvald: *(rummaging through his papers)* Settle it once and for all. *(Maid enters)* Here. Take this letter, go downstairs, and find a messenger. Immediately. Tell him to deliver it right away. The address is on it. Here's the money.

Maid: Yes, sir. *(exits with the letter)*

Torvald: *(putting his papers together)* Now then, Madam Stubborn.

Nora: *(almost out of breath)* Torvald, what was that letter?

Torvald: Krogstad's dismissal.

Nora: Call her back, Torvald. There's still time. Torvald, call her back! Do it for me, do it for you, do it for the children. Do you hear me, Torvald, call her back! You don't know what this letter can do to us.

Torvald: It's too late.

Nora: Yes, it's too late.

Torvald: My dear Nora. I can forgive you for being so upset. But it really is an insult to me. Isn't it an insult to think that I should be afraid of a starving pen pusher? But I forgive you because, in its own way, it speaks so eloquently of your love for me. *(he takes her in his arms)* And that is how it should be, my darling Nora. You can be sure that whatever happens, I will be brave and strong. You'll see thatI am man enough to take everything upon myself.

Nora: *(her voice is horror-stricken)* What do you mean by that?

Torvald: Everything …

Nora: *(recovering)* You'll never have to do that.

Torvald: Well, well, we'll share the burden, Nora, as man and wife should. That's how it's going to be. *(putting his arms around her)* Are you happy now? There, there. No more frightened little dove's eyes. It's all in your imagination. So. You must go and rehearse the tarantella and practice on the tambourine. I'll go into the office and shut the door, and I will hear nothing. You can make as much noise as you like. *(turns back at the door)* And when Dr. Rank comes, tell him where he can find me. *(nods to her, takes his papers, goes into his room, and shuts the door)*

Nora: *(Nora is rooted to the spot, very bewildered, and whispers to herself)* He actually could do it. He *will* do it. He'll do it in spite of everything. No, no, no. Never, never. Anything rather than that. I need help … anything. *(the doorbell rings in a familiar pattern)* Dr. Rank! Anything! Anything other than that … *(She puts her hands over her face, pulls herself together, opens the door. Rank is standing in the hall, hanging up his coat. During the following conversation, it begins to grow dark.)*

Nora: Good day, Dr. Rank. I recognized your ring. But you mustn't go in to Torvald now. I think he's busy.

Dr. Rank: And you?

Nora: *(ushers him in and shuts the door)* Oh, you know that I always have time for you.

Dr. Rank: Thank you. I shall take advantage of that for as long as I can.

Nora: What do you mean by that? For as long as you can?

Dr. Rank: Does that alarm you?

Nora: It was such a strange way of putting it. Is something going to happen?

Dr. Rank: Nothing that I haven't been preparing for. But I didn't expect it to happen so soon.

Nora: *(holding him tightly by the arm)* What did they tell you? Dr. Rank, you must talk to me.

Dr. Rank: *(sitting down by the stove)* It's all over. Nothing can be done.

Nora: *(with a sigh of relief)* Are you talking about yourself?

Dr. Rank: Who else? You can't lie to yourself. I'm the worst of all my patients, Mrs. Helmer. Recently I've been assessing my internal net worth. And I'm bankrupt. Perhaps within a month I'll lie rotting in the graveyard.

Nora: What a disgusting thing to say!

Dr. Rank: Well, it *is* disgusting. And the fact is that I will have to endure so much more before the graveyard. I will make only one more examination of myself. When I've done that I will know— with some certainty— when the disintegration will begin. There's something I want to tell you. Torvald … is a very refined man. That makes him absolutely incapable of facing anything that is unpleasant. I won't have him visit me in my sick-room.

Nora: Oh but Dr. Rank …

Dr. Rank: I won't have him in there. Not under any circumstances. My door is locked to him. As soon as I am absolutely sure that the end is coming. I will send you my card with a black cross on it. And then you will know that the pain and suffering is coming to an end.

Nora: You are talking nonsense. I wanted you to be so happy today.

Dr. Rank: With death watching my every move? To have to suffer this because of another man's sin. There's no justice. In every single family, in one way or another, there is some inexorable curse which brings retribution.

Nora: *(putting her hands over her ears)* Nonsense. Talk about something happy!

Dr. Rank: Oh, we can laugh about the whole thing! My innocent spine has to suffer because my father, well, enjoyed himself when he was young.

Nora: *(sitting at the table on the left)* You mean that he loved asparagus and pâté de foie gras and that sort of thing, don't you?

Dr. Rank: Yes, and truffles.

Nora: Yes, truffles. And oysters too. I'm sure.

Dr. Rank: Oysters, yes of course.

Nora: And gallons of port and champagne. It's so sad that all these wonderful things should attack our bodies.

Dr. Rank: Especially sad that they should take revenge on the bodies of those who didn't have the chance to enjoy them.

Nora: Yes. That's the worst part.

Dr. Rank: *(looking at her carefully)* Hmm.

Nora: *(after a short pause)* Why did you smile?

Dr. Rank: No, it was you.

Nora: No, it was you, Dr. Rank.

Dr. Rank: *(getting up)* You're a much greater tease than I thought.

Nora: Well, I'm in a silly mood today.

Dr. Rank: So it seems.

Nora: *(putting her hands on his shoulders)* Dear, dear, Dr. Rank. Death cannot ever take you away from Torvald and me.

Dr. Rank: Oh, you'd easily recover from the loss. The departed are soon forgotten.

Nora: *(looking at him anxiously)* Do you believe that?

Dr. Rank: People form new friendships.

Nora: Who will form new friendships?

Dr. Rank: You and Torvald, when I'm gone. You're already well on the way, I think. What did Mrs. Linde want here last night?

Nora: Aha! You don't mean to say that you're jealous of Kristine?

Dr. Rank: Yes, I am. She will take over from me in this house. When I'm gone this woman will—

Nora: Shh! Keep your voice down. She's in the other room.

Dr. Rank: Today again. You see?

Nora: She's only come to sew my dress for me. Good heavens, you're totally unreasonable. *(sitting down on the sofa)* Now be nice, Dr. Rank. And tomorrow you'll see how beautifully I shall dance. And you can think that I'm dancing all for you—and for Torvald too, of course, *(taking various things out of the box)* Dr. Rank, come and sit down over here. I want to show you something.

Dr. Rank: *(sitting down)* What is it?

Nora: Just look at these.

Dr. Rank: Silk stockings.

Nora: Flesh-colored. Aren't they beautiful? It's so clark in here now, but tomorrow—no, no, no! You must only look at the feet! Oh well. You can have a little look at the legs too.

Dr. Rank: Hmm.

Nora: Why do you look so doubtful? Don't you think they'll fit me?

Dr. Rank: I have no way of forming an opinion on that.

Nora: *(looking at him for a moment)* Shame on you! *(hitting him lightly on the ear with the stockings)* That's to punish you. *(folding them up again)*

Dr. Rank: And what other nice little things am I going to be allowed to see?

Nora: Not a thing more. Nothing. You were so naughty. *(she looks among the things humming to herself)*

Dr. Rank: *(after a short silence)* When I'm sitting here, talking to you, so intimately, I can't imagine— even for a second—what would have happened to me if I'd never come into this house.

Nora: *(smiling)* I think you really do feel at home with us.

Dr. Rank: *(in a low voice, looking straight ahead)* And to have to leave it all.

Nora: Nonsense. You're not going to leave it all.

Dr. Rank: *(recovering)* And not to be able to leave behind even the slightest token of one's thanks, not even a fleeting regret—nothing but an empty place which the first person who comes will fill as well as anyone else.

Nora: And if I asked you now for a— no …

Dr. Rank: For what?

Nora: For something that really proves the depth of your friendship.

Dr. Rank: Yes, yes.

Nora: I mean a really big favor.

Dr. Rank: Would you honestly make me so happy, just for once?

Nora: But you don't know what it is yet.

Dr. Rank: No, but tell me.

Nora: I really can't, Dr. Rank. It's something that makes no sense. I need advice, I need help, I need a favor.

Dr. Rank: The bigger it is, the better. I've no idea what you mean. Tell me. Can't you trust me?

Nora: More than anyone else. I know you are my best, my truest friend. So I will tell you what it is. Dr. Rank, it is something you must help me stop from happening. You know how much Torvald loves me, how devoted he is, how inexpressibly deep his love for me is. He'd never, even for a second, hesitate to give his life for me.

Dr. Rank: *(leaning toward her)* Nora—do you think he's the only one? …

Nora: *(with a slight start)* The only one?

Dr. Rank: The only one who would give his life for you….

Nora: *(sadly)* Ah. Is that it?

Dr. Rank: I was determined that you should know that before I … went away. There will never be a better opportunity than now. So now you know, Nora. And now you know too that you can trust me in a way that you couldn't trust anyone else.

Nora: *(rising deliberately and quietly)* Let me get by you.

Dr. Rank: *(making room for her to pass by but sitting still)* Nora.

Nora: *(at the hall door)* Helene! Bring in the lamp! *(going over to the stove)* Dear Dr. Rank, that was really awful of you.

Dr. Rank: To have loved you as much as everybody else? Was that awful?

Nora: No. But to *tell* me! There was really no need.

Dr. Rank: What do you mean? Did you know? *(Maid enters with lamp, sets it down on the table, and exits)* Nora—Mrs. Helmer—tell me, did you have any idea of this?

Nora: Oh, how would I know whether I had any idea or not? I really can't tell you. But for you to be so clumsy, Dr. Rank! We were getting on so well.

Dr. Rank: In any case, now you know that you can have your way with me, body and soul. So, won't you tell me what's on your mind?

Nora: *(looking at him)* After what just happened?

Dr. Rank: I beg you. Tell me what it is.

Nora: I can't tell you anything now.

Dr. Rank: No, no, you mustn't punish me like that. Let me do for you whatever a man can do.

Nora: You can do nothing for me now. Anyway, I really don't need any help. You'll find that the whole thing is just … my imagination. It really is! Of course it is! *(sitting down in the rocking chair and smiling)* You're really a terrible man, aren't you. Dr. Rank? Aren't you ashamed of yourself now that the light is on?

Dr. Rank: Not at all. But perhaps I had better go—go for good.

Nora: No you will not. You must come here every day, just as before. You know very well that Torvald needs you.

Dr. Rank: Yes. And you?

Nora: Oh, I'm always wonderfully happy when you come.

Dr. Rank: That's exactly what confused me. You are an enigma to me. I have often thought that you would just as soon share my company as Torvald's.

Nora: Yes, you see there are those whom one loves and those whom one would choose to spend one's time with.

Dr. Rank: There's something in that.

Nora: When I was at home I loved Papa most of all. But I always had great fun sneaking off to the maids' quarters. They never passed judgment, and they always talked to each other about such amusing things.

Dr. Rank: Oh, I see—I've taken *their* place.

Nora: *(jumping up and going to him)* Oh dear, sweet Dr. Rank. That's not what I meant at all. But I'm sure you understand that being with Torvald is a little bit like being with Papa. …

(Maid enters from the hallway.)

Maid: Excuse me, ma'am. *(whispers and hands her a card)*

Nora: *(glancing at card)* Oh! *(puts card in her pocket)*

Dr. Rank: Is anything the matter?

Nora: No, no, nothing at all. It's just … just … it's my new dress. …

Dr. Rank: But your dress is over there.

Nora: Oh yes, that one. This is a new one. I ordered it. Torvald mustn't find out about it—

Dr. Rank: So that was your great secret!

Nora: Of course, of course. Just go in to him. He's sitting in the inner room. Keep him there as long as you—

Dr. Rank: You can rest assured I won't let him get away, *(goes into Torvald's study)*

Nora: *(to Maid)* He's waiting in the kitchen?

Maid: Yes, he came up the back stairs.

Nora: Didn't you tell him no one was home?

Maid: Yes, but that didn't do any good.

Nora: He won't go away?

Maid: No. He says he won't go till he sees you, ma'am.

Nora: Well, let him come in. But quietly! Helene, you mustn't say a word about this to anybody. It's a surprise—for my husband.

Maid: Yes, ma'am. I understand. *(exit)*

Nora: It's going to happen! This terrible, terrible thing. I can't do anything to stop it. No, no, no, it can't happen. It will not happen. *(She bolts the door of the study. The Maid opens the hall door for Krogstad and then closes it. He is wearing a fur coat and hat and high boots.)*

Nora: *(going toward him)* Keep your voice down—my husband is at home.

Krogstad: It doesn't matter about that.

Nora: What do you want from me?

Krogstad: I want you to explain something.

Nora: Hurry up, then. What is it?

Krogstad: I'm sure you know that I have been dismissed.

Nora: There was nothing I could do, Mr. Krogstad. I tried to interfere, I really, really did, but it was no use.

Krogstad: Does your husband have so little love for you? He knows what damage I can do to you, and yet he persists—

Nora: How could you think that he knows anything about this?

Krogstad: No. I suppose not. It would not be at all like our respected Torvald Helmer to have the courage—

Nora: Please, Mr. Krogstad, show my husband some respect.

Krogstad: All the respect he deserves. So. You've kept all this business to yourself. Then I guess you've got a clearer picture than you had yesterday of what it is that you have done.

Nora: More than you could ever show me.

Krogstad: Yes, I'm such a "poor lawyer."

Nora: What do you want from me?

Krogstad: I only wanted to see how you were, Mrs. Helmer. I've been thinking about you all day. I'm just a clerk, a pen-pusher, a—well, even a man like me has some feelings, you know.

Nora: Then why don't you show them? Think of my little children.

Krogstad: Did you or your husband ever think of mine? Never mind about that. I came to tell you that you mustn't worry too much. First of all, I am not going to bring any formal charges.

Nora: No, of course, I was sure you wouldn't.

Krogstad: The whole thing can be settled quite amicably. There's no reason why anyone should know anything about it. We'll keep it a secret between the three of us.

Nora: My husband must never find out anything about it.

Krogstad: And how will you stop that? Are you saying that you can pay off the balance?

Nora: No, not just at the moment.

Krogstad: Perhaps you have a plan for raising the money fairly soon?

Nora: No plan that I would put into practice.

Krogstad: Well, in any case it wouldn't have been any use. If you stood there with your hands full of money, I still wouldn't give you back the contract.

Nora: And what do you intend doing with it?

Krogstad: Nothing. I shall just hold on to it—keep it in my possession. No one who's not involved need know anything about it. So if you've been thinking of doing something desperate—

Nora: I have.

Krogstad: If you've been thinking of running away from home—

Nora: I have.

Krogstad: —or even worse—

Nora: How did you know?

Krogstad: —then give up the idea.

Nora: How did you know I had thought of *that*?

Krogstad: Most of us think of that at first. I did too. But I didn't have the courage.

Nora: *(faintly)* Neither did I.

Krogstad: *(sounding relieved)* No. That's it, isn't it?
You didn't have the courage.

Nora: No. I haven't, I haven't.

Krogstad: Besides, it would have been a very foolish thing to do. Once the first domestic storm has passed—. Well, I have a letter for your husband in my pocket.

Nora: Telling him everything?

Krogstad: As gently as possible.

Nora: *(quickly)* He mustn't get that letter. Tear it up. I'll get some money somehow.

Krogstad: But Mrs. Helmer, I think I told you just now—

Nora: I'm not talking about the money I owe you. Just tell me how much you're asking my husband for, and I'll get it for you.

Krogstad: I'm not asking your husband for a penny.

Nora: What do you want then?

Krogstad: Listen. I want to get my reputation back, Mrs. Helmer. And your husband is going to have to help me. For the past year and a half my life has been exemplary—even though it was a struggle and I had very little money. I was happy to make my way up step by step. But now I've been thrown back down again. And it's not going to be enough for me just to be taken back in again. I tell you—I want to get ahead. I want to get back into the bank but in a better job. Your husband must find a place for me—

Nora: He will never do that.

Krogstad: Oh yes he will. I know him. He won't utter a peep. And as soon as I'm back in there again, with him, you'll see! Within a year I'll be the manager's right-hand man. It'll be Nils Krogstad, not Torvald Helmer, who's running the bank.

Nora: You'll never see the day....

Krogstad: Do you mean that you will—?

Nora: Now I have the courage.

Krogstad: You don't frighten me. A fine, pampered lady like you—

Nora: You'll see, you'll see.

Krogstad: Under the ice, perhaps? Down, down into the black, icy water. And then in the spring you'll float up to the surface all bloated and unrecognizable, your hair fallen out.

Nora: You don't frighten me.

Krogstad: Nor you me. Mrs. Helmer, people don't do such things. In any case, what would be the use? He would still be completely in my power.

Nora: Even then? When I am no longer—

Krogstad: Don't forget that I am in complete control of your reputation. *(Nora is speechless and just stares at him)* So. Now I have warned you. Don't do anything foolish. When Torvald has gotten my letter, I expect a reply from him. And don't you forget that it is your husband who has forced me to do this sort of thing again. I can never forgive him for that. Goodbye, Mrs. Helmer *(exits through the hall)*

Nora: *(goes to the hall door, opens it slightly, and listens)* He's going. He's not putting the letter in the box. No. No. It couldn't happen! *(opens the door* *slowly)* What? He's standing outside and not going downstairs. Did he change his mind? Is he …? *(The letter is dropped in the box, and Krogstad's footsteps can be heard going drum the stairs. Nora stifles a cry, then runs across the room to the table by the sofa. A short pause.)* It's in the mailbox. *(crosses back to the door)* There it is. Oh Torvald, Torvald, there's no hope for us now!

(Mrs. Linde comes in from the room on the left with the dress.)

Mrs. Linde: There. I think it's all done. Would you like to try it on—?

Nora: *(in a hoarse whisper)* Kristine, come here.

Mrs. Linde: *(throwing the dress down on the sofa)* What's the matter? You look so upset!

Nora: Come here. Do you see that letter? There, look—you can see it through the glass in the mailbox.

Mrs. Linde: Yes, I can see it.

Nora: That letter is from Krogstad.

Mrs. Linde: Nora—Krogstad lent you the money!

Nora: Yes. And now Torvald will find out all about it.

Mrs. Linde: Believe me. Nora, that's the best thing that could happen—for both of you.

Nora: But there's something you don't know—I forged a signature.

Mrs. Linde: Good heavens—!

Nora: I'm telling this only to you, Kristine. I want you to be my witness.

Mrs. Linde: Your witness? What do you mean? What do you want me to—?

Nora: If I should lose my mind—no, it could easily happen—

Mrs. Linde: Nora!

Nora: Or if anything else should happen to me— anything … and I weren't to be here …

Mrs. Linde: Nora! Nora, you're out of your mind.

Nora: And if it turned out that someone wanted to take all the responsibility, all the blame … you understand? …

Mrs. Linde: Yes. Yes. But how could you think … ?

Nora: You must he my witness that *it is not true*. Kristine, I am not out of my mind. In fact I have come to my senses. And I repeat: no one else knows anything about this. I and I alone did it. Remember that.

Mrs. Linde: I promise you I will. But I don't understand all of this.

Nora: How could you? A miracle is about to happen….

Mrs. Linde: A miracle?

Nora: Yes. A miracle. But it's so devastating, Kristine. It mustn't happen—not for all the world.

Mrs. Linde: I will go and see Krogstad right away.

Nora: No. You mustn't. He might do you some harm.

Mrs. Linde: There was a time when he would have done anything for me.

Nora: Krogstad?

Mrs. Linde: Where does he live?

Nora: How would I know? Oh yes— *(feeling in her pocket)* here's his card. But the letter, the letter—!

Torvald: *(calling from his room, knocking on the door)* Nora!

Nora: *(anxiously)* What is it? What do you want?

Torvald: Don't be alarmed. We're not coming in. You've locked the door. Are you trying on your dress?

Nora: Yes, I am. I look so nice, Torvald.

Mrs. Linde: *(she has read the card)* He lives just round the corner.

Nora: But it's no use. It's hopeless. The letter is lying there in the box.

Mrs. Linde: And your husband has the key?

Nora: Yes. He always has it.

Mrs. Linde: Krogstad must ask for his letter back before your husband reads it. He must make up some excuse.

Nora: But Torvald always at this time of day—

Mrs. Linde: Find some way of stopping him. Go in and see him while I'm gone. I'll be back as soon as I can. *(she goes out quickly)*

Nora: *(goes to Torvald's door, opens it, and peeps in)* Torvald!

Torvald: *(from inside)* Well? Am I finally allowed into my own room? Come along, Rank, now you're going to see— *(stopping in the doorway)* What's this?

Nora: What's what, dear?

Torvald: Rank had led me to believe there would be a wonderful transformation.

Dr. Rank: *(in doorway)* That's what I thought. But evidently I was wrong.

Nora: Well, no one can admire me in my dress until tomorrow night.

Torvald: My dear Nora, you look exhausted. Have you been doing too much rehearsing?

Nora: No. I've not rehearsed at all.

Torvald: But you'll have to …

Nora: Yes, Torvald, I know I do. But I can't make any progress at all without you. I've totally forgotten the whole thing.

Torvald: Oh, we'll soon get it right again.

Nora: Yes, help me Torvald. Promise me. I'm so nervous about it. All those people. … You must give me all your time this evening. No more business—you mustn't even pick up a pen. Promise me, Torvald dear.

Torvald: I promise. This evening I will be totally at your service, you helpless little creature. Oh, but while I think of it, I'll just go and— *(goes toward the hall door)*

Nora: Where are you going?

Torvald: To see if there's any mail.

Nora: No. No, don't do that, Torvald.

Torvald: Why not?

Nora: Torvald, please don't. There's nothing there.

Torvald: Well, let me look. *(Turns to go to the mailbox. Nora goes to the piano and plays the first bars of the tarantella. Torvald stops in the doorway.)* Aha!

Nora: I can't dance tomorrow if I don't rehearse.

Torvald: *(going to her)* Are you really so nervous about it?

Nora: Yes, I really am. Let me rehearse right now. There's time before we go to dinner. Sit down and play for me. Torvald. You can make criticisms and correct me if I do the wrong steps.

Torvald: Well, if you want me to—with pleasure! *(sits at piano)*

Nora: *(Takes a tambourine out of the box along with a long, brightly colored shawl, which she drapes around her shoulders. She leaps to the front of the room and calls out.)* Now play for me. I'm going to dance.

(Torvald plays and Nora dances. Dr. Rank stands behind Torvald at the piano and watches.)

Torvald: *(playing)* Slower! Slower!

Nora: This is the only way I know how!

Torvald: Not so violently. Nora!

Nora: No, this is right!

Torvald: *(stopping playing)* No. No. That's all wrong.

Nora: Didn't I tell you?

Dr. Rank: Let me play for her.

Torvald: *(getting up)* Yes, do. It'll be easier for me to correct her.

(Dr. Rank sits down and plays. Nora dances more and more wildly. Torvald is standing by the stove and gives her frequent instructions. She seems oblivious. Her hair falls down over her shoulders. She pays no attention to it and goes on dancing. Enter Mrs. Linde.)

Mrs. Linde: *(standing in awe at the door)* Oh!!

Nora: *(dancing)* It's such fun, Kristine.

Torvald: Nora, my darling, you're dancing as if your life depended on it.

Nora: It does, it does.

Torvald: Stop, Rank, stop! This is sheer madness. Stop, I tell you. *(Dr. Rank stops playing. Nora suddenly stands still. Torvald goes up to her.)* I would never have believed it. You've forgotten everything I taught you.

Nora: *(tossing aside the tambourine)* There you are, you see?

Torvald: You need a lot of coaching.

Nora: Yes, I really do. You must teach me right up to the last minute. Promise me, Torvald!

Torvald: You can depend on me.

Nora: You must think only of me—nothing else. Not today or tomorrow. You mustn't, open a single letter, not even go near the mailbox—

Torvald: So, you're still afraid of that man—

Nora: Yes, I am.

Torvald: Nora, I can tell by your face that there's a letter from him out there.

Nora: I don't know. Perhaps there is. But you mustn't read anything like that right now. We mustn't let anything dreadful come between us until this is all over.

Dr. Rank: *(whispers to Torvald)* You mustn't contradict her.

Torvald: *(taking her in his arms)* My little one shall have her own way. But tomorrow night, after you've danced—

Nora: You will be free—

(The Maid appears in the doorway on the right.)

Maid: Dinner is served, ma'am.

Nora: We will have champagne, Helene.

Maid: Very good, ma'am.

Torvald: Well, well, well—we're having a banquet!

Nora: Yes. A champagne banquet till the wee small hours. *(calling out)* And—Helene—some macaroons! Lots. Just for once!

Torvald: Calm down! Don't be so nervous! Be my own little lark, as always.

Nora: Yes, dear, I will. But go in now. You too, Dr. Rank. Kristine, would you help me put my hair up?

Dr. Rank: *(whispering to Torvald as they go out)* There isn't, anything, um … She's not expecting …?

Torvald: Oh no, nothing like that…. It's just another instance of this childlike nervousness I was telling you about. *(they exit to the right)*

Nora: Well?

Mrs. Linde: Gone out of town.

Nora: I could tell from your face.

Mrs. Linde: He's coming back tomorrow evening. I left him a note.

Nora: You shouldn't have done anything. You must let everything take its course. In a way, it's wonderful to be waiting for a miracle.

Mrs. Linde: And what are you waiting for?

Nora: Oh, you wouldn't understand. Go in and join them. I'll be in in a moment.

(Mrs. Linde goes into the dining room. Nora stands still for a while, as if regaining her composure. Then she looks at her watch. Five o'clock. Seven hours till midnight. Then twenty-four hours till the next midnight. Then the tarantella will be finished. Twenty-four plus seven? Thirty-one hours to live.)

Torvald: *(from the doorway)* Where's my little lark?

Nora: *(going to him with her arms outstretched)* Here she is!

ACT 3

The same setting. The table has been placed in the center of the room, with chairs around it. A lamp is on the table. The hallway door is open. Music is heard from upstairs. Mrs. Linde is sitting at the table, slowly turning the pages of a book. She tries to concentrate but cannot. Every now and then she listens for a sound from the hallway.

Mrs. Linde: He's not here yet … *(looking at her watch)* … and the lime is nearly up. If he doesn't— *(Goes to the outer hall and opens the downstairs* *door carefully. Quiet footsteps are heard on the stairs. She whispers.)* Come in. There's no one here.

Krogstad: *(in the doorway)* I got the note from you at home. What is this all about?

Mrs. Linde: I *have* to talk to you.

Krogstad: Really? And do *I have* to be *here*?

Mrs. Linde: Look, I couldn't possibly meet with you where I live. There's no private entrance to my rooms. Come in. We are quite alone. The maid is asleep, and the Helmers are at the party upstairs.

Krogstad: Are the Helmers really going to a party tonight?

Mrs. Linde: Yes. Why not?

Krogstad: Of course, why not?

Mrs. Linde: Now, Nils, we must have a talk.

Krogstad: What can we two possibly have to talk about?

Mrs. Linde: A great deal, I think.

Krogstad: I wouldn't have thought so.

Mrs. Linde: No. I don't think you ever really understood me.

Krogstad: What was there to understand? The whole world saw exactly what was happening—a woman without any feelings was leaving her man when a more lucrative prospect showed up.

Mrs. Linde: Do you really believe that I have no feelings? And do you think it was so easy for me to do it?

Krogstad: Wasn't it?

Mrs. Linde: Nils, did you really think so?

Krogstad: If your version of events is right, then why did you write me that letter?

Mrs. Linde: What else could I do? I *had* to break up with you. And so it was my duty to kill any feelings you had for me.

Krogstad: *(flexing his hands)* So that was it. All that—all for money.

Mrs. Linde: Remember that I had an invalid mother and two little brothers to take care of. We couldn't wait for you, Nils. You didn't have any prospects at the time.

Krogstad: That may be true. But you had no right to leave me for another man.

Mrs. Linde: I don't know, I don't know. I've asked myself many times if I had that right.

Krogstad: *(in a gentler tone)* When I lost you, I felt as if the ground beneath my feet had given way. Look at me now—I'm like a shipwrecked man clinging to a piece of wreckage.

Mrs. Linde: But help may be near.

Krogstad: It *was* near. But then you came and got in my way.

Mrs. Linde: I didn't intend to, Nils. I only found out today that I was going to take your place at the bank.

Krogstad: If you say so, I believe you. But now that you know, aren't you going to let me keep it?

Mrs. Linde: No, because there would be no benefit for you at all.

Krogstad: "Benefit, benefit!"—that's what *I* would do.

Mrs. Linde: I have learned to think carefully before I act. Life and bitter necessity have taught me that.

Krogstad: And life has taught me not to trust fine speeches.

Mrs. Linde: Then life has taught you something very useful. But surely you must believe in actions?

Krogstad: What do you mean?

Mrs. Linde: You said you were like a shipwrecked man clinging to a piece of wreckage.

Krogstad: I had every reason to say that.

Mrs. Linde: Well, I'm like a shipwrecked woman clinging to a piece of wreckage—no one to mourn for, to care for.

Krogstad: You made that choice.

Mrs. Linde: At that time there was no other choice.

Krogstad: Well, what about now?

Mrs. Linde: Nils, what would you think of us two shipwrecked people joining together?

Krogstad: What do you mean?

Mrs. Linde: Two people on the same piece of wreckage would stand a better chance than on their own.

Krogstad: Kristine!

Mrs. Linde: Why do you think I came to town?

Krogstad: You mean that you were thinking of me?

Mrs. Linde: I couldn't bear to live without working. All my life, for as long as I can remember, I have worked. It has been my greatest, my only pleasure. But now I'm all alone in the world. My life is empty, and I feel lost. There is no pleasure at all in working for oneself. Nils, give me something, give me someone to work for.

Krogstad: How can I trust that? It's just a woman's overly exaggerated sense of decency that makes you suggest that.

Mrs. Linde: Have you ever noticed such a thing in me before?

Krogstad: Could you really do this? You know all about my past?

Mrs. Linde: Yes.

Krogstad: And you know my reputation in this town?

Mrs. Linde: Just now you seemed to imply that if you'd been with me, you might have been a different man.

Krogstad: I'm sure of it.

Mrs. Linde: Is it too late?

Krogstad: Have you thought about this carefully, Kristine? Yes, I'm sure you have. I can see it in your face. Do you really have the courage—?

Mrs. Linde: I want to be a mother to someone. Your children need a mother. And we two need each other. Nils, I have faith in the real you—I can face anything with you.

Krogstad: *(taking her hands)* Thank you, thank you, Kristine. Now I must find a way to regain my reputation in the world. Oh, but I forgot—

Mrs. Linde: *(listening)* Sh! The tarantella! Go, go now.

Krogstad: Why? What is it?

Mrs. Linde: Can't you hear them upstairs? When the dance is over, they'll be downstairs immediately.

Krogstad: Yes. I'll go. But none of this is any use. I'm sure you don't know what steps I've taken as regards the Helmers.

Mrs. Linde: Yes, I know all about that.

Krogstad: And you still can—?

Mrs. Linde: I can understand to what lengths a man like you might go when you have no hope.

Krogstad: If only I could undo what I have done.

Mrs. Linde: You can't. Your letter is out there in the mailbox.

Krogstad: Are you sure?

Mrs. Linde: Quite sure, but—

Krogstad: *(looking at her carefully)* Is that what all this is about? You want to save your friend no matter the cost? Tell me ... tell me honestly, is that it?

Mrs. Linde: Nils, a woman who has sold out once before to help someone else doesn't do it a second time.

Krogstad: I'll ask for my letter back.

Mrs. Linde: No.

Krogstad: Yes, of course I will. I'll wait here until Torvald comes down. I'll tell him he must give me my letter back—that it's only about my dismissal—that he mustn't read it.

Mrs. Linde: No, Nils, you mustn't ask for your letter back.

Krogstad: Tell me the truth. Isn't that why you asked me to meet you here?

Mrs. Linde: At first, yes. I was frightened. But twenty-four hours have passed since then, and in that time I have observed some incredible things happening in this house. Torvald must find out all about it. This painful secret must be revealed. They must come to a complete understanding between themselves. That is impossible with all this deception, this hiding of the truth.

Krogstad: All right. As long as you take full responsibility. But there is one thing I can do. And I will do it at once.

Mrs. Linde: *(listening)* You must go quickly. The dance is over, it's not safe for us here any longer.

Krogstad: I will wait for you down below.

Mrs. Linde: Yes, wait for me. You'll walk me home.

Krogstad: I've never had such an amazing piece of luck in my life. *(he goes out through the outer door, but the door between the living room and the hall remains open)*

Mrs. Linde: *(tidying up the room and getting her hat and cloak ready)* What a difference, what a difference! Someone to work for, someone to live for—a home to take care of. And I will do that. I wish they'd hurry up and come— *(listens)* There they are now. I'd better put on my things. *(takes up her hat and cloak)*

(Torvald and Nora can be heard talking outside. A key is turned. Torvald brings Nora almost forcibly into the hall. She is wearing her Italian costume and a large black shawl. Torvald is in evening dress with a black cloak open over his shoulders.)

Nora: *(struggling with Torvald in the doorway)* No, no, don't make me go in. I want to go back upstairs. I don't want to leave so early.

Torvald: But my dearest Nora …

Nora: Please, Torvald dear, *please*—just for an hour longer.

Torvald: Not for a minute, my sweet Nora. You know that's what we agreed. Come in here. You'll catch a cold out there. *(he brings her gently into the room even though she resists)*

Mrs. Linde: Good evening.

Nora: Kristine!

Torvald: You're here so late, Mrs. Linde?

Mrs. Linde: Yes. Please excuse me. I really wanted to see Nora in her dress.

Nora: And you've been sitting here waiting for me?

Mrs. Linde: Yes. Unfortunately, I came too late, you'd already gone upstairs. And I thought to myself that I couldn't leave without seeing you.

Torvald: *(taking off Nora's shawl)* Well? Have a good look at her. I think she's worth a look. Isn't she beautiful, Mrs. Linde?

Mrs. Linde: Yes, she really is.

Torvald: Doesn't she look remarkably lovely? Everyone thought so at the ball. But this sweet little thing is terribly stubborn. What are we going to do with her? It's hard to believe, but I almost had to drag her away.

Nora: Torvald, you will be very sorry for not letting me stay, even for just half an hour.

Torvald: Listen to her, Mrs. Linde! She danced the tarantella. She was an enormous success, and she deserved it. Although perhaps the performance was somewhat too realistic—a little more … I mean … than artistic conventions demanded. But never mind. The important thing is, she was a success. She was an enormous success. Do you think I'd let her stay after that, and spoil the effect? No indeed. I put my arm around the lovely little girl from Capri—my *Capri*cious little girl from Capri, I should say. We made one round of the room, we bowed to either side, and, as they say in romantic novels, the beautiful vision disappeared. An exit always ought to be perfectly timed, Mrs. Linde. But I can't make Nora understand that! Phew! This room is hot. *(throws his cloak on a chair and opens the door of his study)* Oh! It's all dark in here. Oh, of course—excuse me— *(he goes in and lights some candles)*

Nora: *(quickly and in a whisper)* Well?

Mrs. Linde: *(in a low voice)* I've talked with him.

Nora: Yes, and?

Mrs. Linde: Nora, you've got to tell your husband all about it.

Nora: *(without any expression)* I knew it.

Mrs. Linde: You have nothing to be afraid of from Krogstad. But you must tell your husband.

Nora: I won't tell him.

Mrs. Linde: Then the letter will.

Nora: Thank you, Kristine. Now I know what I have to do. Sh!

Torvald: *(coming in)* Well, Mrs. Linde, have you admired her?

Mrs. Linde: Yes, and now I must say good night.

Torvald: Already? Is this knitting yours?

Mrs. Linde: *(picking it up)* Yes, thank you. I'd almost forgotten it.

Torvald: So you knit?

Mrs. Linde: Of course.

Torvald: You know, you ought to take up embroidery.

Mrs. Linde: Really? Why?

Torvald: It's much more … becoming. Watch me. You hold the embroidery like this in your left hand, with the needle in your right—like this—making a long, graceful curve. Do you see?

Mrs. Linde: Yes. Perhaps—

Torvald: Yes, but knitting! Thai will always be *un*becoming. Watch—your arms are close together, the needles go up and down—it looks sort of Chinese. They had really excellent champagne.

Mrs. Linde: Well, good night, Nora. Don't be stubborn anymore.

Torvald: That's right, Mrs. Linde.

Mrs. Linde: Good night, Mr. Helmer.

Torvald: *(walking her to the door)* Good night, good night. I hope you'll get home all right. I'd be very happy to—but you don't have far to go. Good night, good night. *(she goes out, he shuts the door after her, and comes back in)* Ah! At last! At last we've gotten rid of her. She's such an old bore, that woman.

Nora: Aren't you tired, Torvald?

Torvald: Not in the least.

Nora: You're not sleepy?

Torvald: Not at all. On the contrary, I feel full of life. And you? You look tired and quite sleepy.

Nora: Yes, I am very tired. I want to go to sleep right away.

Torvald: There! I was right not to let you stay any longer.

Nora: Everything you do is right, Torvald.

Torvald: *(kissing her on the forehead)* Finally my little lark is speaking the truth. Did you notice that Dr. Rank was in really good spirits tonight?

Nora: Really? Was he? I didn't talk to him at all.

Torvald: I didn't say much to him. But I haven't seen him having such a good time for ages. *(looking at her for a while and then going nearer to her)* It's delicious to be home again, all by ourselves, to be alone with you—you fascinating, lovely little creature.

Nora: Don't look at me like that, Torvald.

Torvald: Why shouldn't I look at the thing I love most? All that beauty—and it's mine, all mine.

Nora: *(going to the other side of the table)* No, Torvald, you mustn't say things like that to me tonight.

Torvald: *(following her)* I can see you've still got the tarantella in your blood. It makes you more captivating than ever. Listen, the guests are beginning to leave. *(in a lower voice)* Nora, soon the whole house will be quiet.

Nora: Yes. I hope so.

Torvald: Yes, my own darling Nora. Do you know, when I'm out at a party with you, like tonight, do you know why I don't talk to you very much, stay away from you, and only occasionally cast a furtive glance in your direction? Do you know why? It's because I pretend to myself that we are secretly in love and you are my secret fiancée. And that no one knows there is anything at all between us.

Nora: Yes, yes. I know that you're thinking about me all the time.

Torvald: And then, when we're leaving and I'm putting the shawl over your lovely young shoulders, on your beautiful neck, then I pretend to myself that you are my young bride. And that we've just come from our wedding, and that I'm bringing you home for the first time—and that I'm going to be alone with you for the first time—all alone with my shy little darling. This whole evening I've been longing only for you. When I watched the sensual movements of the tarantella, my blood was on fire. I couldn't stand it any longer, and that's why I brought you down so early.

Nora: Go now, Torvald. You must let me go. I don't want—

Torvald: What? You must be joking! My little Nora, you don't want? I'm your husband, aren't I?

(A knock at the outer door.)

Nora: *(with a start)* Did you hear that?

Torvald: *(going into the hall)* Who is it?

Dr. Rank: *(outside)* It's me. May I come in for a moment?

Torvald: *(in an annoyed whisper)* Oh, what does he want now? *(aloud)* Can you wait a moment? *(unlocking the door)* Come in! It's kind of you not to just pass by.

Dr. Rank: I thought I heard your voice. I felt that I'd like to drop in. *(quickly looking around the room)* Ah yes—these dear rooms that I know so well. You're very happy and cozy in here, you two.

Torvald: I think you made yourself quite happy upstairs too.

Dr. Rank: Very much so. And why shouldn't I? Why shouldn't I enjoy all the world has to offer—at least as much as I can for as long as I can. The wine was superb.

Torvald: Especially the champagne.

Dr. Rank: You noticed that too? I can hardly believe how much I managed to put away.

Nora: Torvald drank a large amount of champagne tonight too.

Dr. Rank: Did he?

Nora: Yes. And he's always in such good spirits afterward.

Dr. Rank: Well, why shouldn't you enjoy a happy evening after a hard day's work?

Torvald: Hard day's work? I'm afraid I can't lay claim to that.

Dr. Rank: *(clapping him on the back)* But I can.

Nora: Dr. Rank, have you been working on some scientific experiments?

Dr. Rank: Exactly.

Torvald: Listen to that. Little Nora talking about scientific experiments.

Nora: May I congratulate you on the result?

Dr. Rank: Indeed you may.

Nora: It was favorable, then?

Dr. Rank: Best possible result for both doctor and patient. Certainty.

Nora: *(quickly and inquiringly)* Certainty?

Dr. Rank: Absolute certainty. So didn't I have the right to enjoy myself tonight?

Nora: Yes, you certainly did, Dr. Rank.

Torvald: I agree. As long as you don't have to pay for it in the morning.

Dr. Rank: Ah well, in this life nothing comes without a price.

Nora: Dr. Rank, do you enjoy these fancy dress balls?

Dr. Rank: Yes, if there are lots of pretty costumes.

Nora: Tell me, what shall we two wear next year?

Torvald: You little featherbrain! You're thinking about next year already?

Dr. Rank: We two? Well, I can tell you. You will go as a guardian angel.

Torvald: What do you think would be an appropriate costume for that?

Dr. Rank: Your wife should go dressed as she is in everyday life.

Torvald: That was a nice turn of phrase. But tell us what you would go as?

Dr. Rank: Well, my dear friend, I've already made up my mind about that.

Torvald: Well?

Dr. Rank: At the next fancy dress ball I will be invisible.

Torvald: That's very funny!

Dr. Rank: I'll have a big black hat—did you ever hear of hats that make you invisible? If you put one on, nobody can see you.

Torvald: *(suppressing a smile)* Yes, yes, quite right.

Dr. Rank: But I'm totally forgetting what I came for. Torvald, give me a cigar. One of the black Havanas.

Torvald: With the greatest of pleasure. *(offering him his case)*

Dr. Rank: *(taking a cigar and cutting off the end)* Thank you.

Nora: *(striking a match)* Let me give you a light.

Dr. Rank: Thank you. *(she holds the match for him to light the cigar)* And now, goodbye.

Torvald: Goodbye, goodbye, you dear old man.

Nora: Sleep well, Dr. Rank.

Dr. Rank: Thank you for the wish.

Nora: Wish me the same.

Dr. Rank: You? Well, if that's what you want—sleep well. And thank you for the light. *(he nods to both of them and goes out)*

Torvald: *(in a quiet voice)* He's drunk more than he should.

Nora: *(absently)* Perhaps. *(Torvald takes a bunch of keys out of his pocket and goes into the hall)* Torvald, what are you doing out there?

Torvald: Emptying the letterbox. It's full. There'll be no room for the newspaper in the morning.

Nora: Are you going to work tonight?

Torvald: You know very well that I'm not. What's this? Someone's been picking at the lock!

Nora: The lock?

Torvald: Yes, someone's been ... what's ... ? I'm sure the maid wouldn't— Here's a broken hairpin. Nora, it's one of yours.

Nora: *(quickly)* It must have been the children, then.

Torvald: You must teach them not to do things like that. There, I've got it open. *(taking out the letters and calling out to the kitchen)* Helene! Helene! Put the front door light out. *(Comes back in the room, shuts the hall door. His hands are full of letters.)* Look at this. Look at this pile of letters. *(sorting through them)* What on earth is this?

Nora: *(at the window)* The letter. No, Torvald, no!

Torvald: Two of Dr. Rank's cards.

Nora: Dr. Rank's?

Torvald: *(looking at them)* Yes, they were on top. He must have put them in on his way out.

Nora: Did he write anything on them?

Torvald: There's a black cross over his name. Look at that. That's so disturbing. It looks as if he were announcing his own death.

Nora: That's exactly what he's doing.

Torvald: What? Do you know anything about this? Has he spoken to you?

Nora: Yes. He told me that when the cards arrived it would be his way of saying goodbye. He's going to lock himself away and die.

Torvald: My poor old friend! Of course I knew we wouldn't have him with us for very long. But so soon! And he's hiding himself away like a wounded animal.

Nora: If it has to happen, it's best that it should be done without a word. Don't you think so, Torvald?

Torvald: *(walking up and down)* He'd become part of our lives. I can't think of him as having left us. He suffered and he was lonely. He was like a cloud, a dark background to our sunlit happiness. Well, perhaps it's for the best. For him anyway. *(standing still)* And perhaps it is for us too, Nora. We have only ourselves now. *(putting his arms around her)* My wife, my darling, I don't feel I can hold you tight enough. You know, Nora, I've often wished that you might be in some great danger, so that I could risk my life, everything, just for you.

Nora: *(disengaging herself and speaking in a firm, clear voice)* You must read your letters now, Torvald.

Torvald: No, not tonight. I want to be with you. I want to be with my darling wife.

Nora: When your best friend is dying?

Torvald: Yes, you're right. It's touched us both. Something ugly has come between us. The thought of mortality in all its horror. We must try to empty our minds of that. Until we do—we'll each go to our own room.

Nora: *(hanging on to his neck)* Good night, Torvald, good night.

Torvald: *(kissing her on the forehead)* Good night, my little songbird. Sleep well, Nora. I'm going to read my letters. *(he takes the mail and goes into his study, shutting the door)*

Nora: *(groping around the room, picks up Torvald's cloak, throws it around her, speaking in quick, broken whispers)* Never to see him again. Never, never. *(putting her shawl over her head)* Never to see my children again—never again. Never, never—the black icy water—deep, deep down. If only it were all over. He's got it now and he's reading it. Goodbye, Torvald. Goodbye, my children. *(she's about to rush out through the hall when Torvald opens his door quickly and stands with the letter in his hand)*

Torvald: Nora!

Nora: Ah.

Torvald: What's this? Do you know what's in this letter?

Nora: Yes, I know. Let me go. Let me get out of here.

Torvald: *(holding her back)* Where are you going?

Nora: *(trying to get free)* You can't save me, Torvald.

Torvald: *(staggering)* Is this true? Is this true? It's … horrible. No, no! It *can't* be true.

Nora: It is true. I have loved you more than anything else in the world.

Torvald: Oh, don't give me any silly excuses.

Nora: *(stepping toward him)* Torvald.

Torvald: You … miserable thing. What have you done?

Nora: Let me go. You're not going to suffer for my sake. You're not going to take this upon yourself.

Torvald: Let's have no melodrama here. *(locking the hall door)* You're going to stay here and give me an explanation. Do you understand what you've done? Answer me! Do you understand what you've done?

Nora: *(looking steadily at him, with her face hardening)* Yes. I'm beginning to understand everything.

Torvald: *(pacing around the room)* What a rude awakening. These eight years, she who was my pride and joy was a hypocrite. A liar. No, worse, worse—a criminal. It's so unspeakably awful. For shame, for shame! *(Nora is silent and looks steadily at him. He stands in front of her.)* I should have suspected that something like this would happen. I should've known. Your father's total lack of principle—don't interrupt—his total lack of principle has finally come out in you. No religion, no ethics, no sense of duty. I'm being punished now for turning a blind eye to all that he did. And I did that just for you. And this is how you repay me.

Nora: Yes. This is how.

Torvald: You've destroyed all my happiness. You've ruined my future. I can't bear to think of it. I'm in the hands of a man with no scruples. He can do what he likes with me. He can ask anything he wants, order me to do anything—and I dare not say no. And I have to sink to such depths of agony, all because of a thoughtless woman.

Nora: When I am gone, you will be free.

Torvald: Don't play with words, please. Your father was always very good at that. What good would it do me if you were "gone," as you say? None at all. He can tell the world about all this, and if he does, I may be suspected, falsely, of having been a partner in your crime. In fact, most people would probably think that I was behind it—that it was I who suggested it. And I have you to thank for all of this. You, the one I have loved throughout our married life. Do you understand what it is you have done to me?

Nora: *(coldly and quietly)* Yes.

Torvald: It's so hard to believe—I can't take it all in! But—you and I must come to some understanding. Take off that shawl. Take it off, I tell you! I must find a way of appeasing him. We've got to make sure that this business is hushed up, no matter the cost. As for you and me, we've got to make it look like everything between us is just as it was before. Naturally, that's only for the eyes of the world. You will still remain here in my house. That is taken for granted. But you will not be allowed to raise the children. I could not trust you with them. To think that I have to say that to someone I have loved so deeply—someone I still—no, that is all over. From this moment on, it's not a question of happiness. All there is now is saving what's left of our shattered lives, keeping up appearances. *(front doorbell rings, Torvald jumps)* What's that? At this time? It can't get any worse, he can't … Keep out of sight, Nora. Say you're ill. *(Nora does not move. Torvald goes and unlocks the hall door. The Maid, half dressed, comes to the door.)*

Maid: A letter for the mistress.

Torvald: Give it to me. *(he takes the letter and shuts the door)* It's from him. You can't have it—I'll read it myself.

Nora: Yes, read it.

Torvald: *(standing by the lamp)* I can hardly bring myself to do it. This could be the ruin of us both. No, I have to know. *(he tears open the letter, reads a few lines, looks at a piece of paper enclosed, and gives a shout)* Nora! *(she looks at him with questions in her eyes)* Nora! No, I've got to read it again. It's true! Yes, I'm saved. Nora, I'm saved!

Nora: And I?

Torvald: You too, of course. We're both saved. The two of us. Look! He's sent you the contract back. He says that he's sorry. He apologizes … there's a happy change of events in his life. Oh, never mind what he says … we're saved, Nora! No one can do anything to you. Oh, Nora, Nora—no, first I must destroy these terrible things. Let me see … *(looking at the contract)* No, no, I don't want to look at it. The whole thing will be nothing but a bad dream. *(tears up the contract and the letters, throws them into the stove, and watches them burn)* There. Now they're gone forever. He said that since Christmas Eve … you … these past three days must have been agonizing for you, Nora.

Nora: I've been fighting a hard battle.

Torvald: And you must have suffered. There was no way out except—but no, we mustn't think about all the horror you went through. All we must do is shout with joy and keep telling each other it's over, it's over! Listen to me, Nora, you don't seem to understand that it's all over. What's the matter?—such a cold, hard face. Oh my poor Nora, I quite understand. You can hardly believe that I have forgiven you. But it's true, Nora, I swear to you. I've forgiven you. Totally. I know that what you did you did because you love me.

Nora: That is true.

Torvald: You loved me as a wife should love her husband. You were just too naive to understand the implications of what you were doing. But do you think I love you the less because you didn't understand how to do things on your own? No, no. You must rely on me. I will advise you and give you directions. I wouldn't be a man if this female helplessness didn't make you twice as attractive to me. You must forget the harsh things I said when I was so upset at first. I thought my whole world was collapsing about me. I have forgiven you, Nora. I swear to you, I have forgiven you.

Nora: Thank you for forgiving me. *(she goes out through the door on the right)*

Torvald: No, don't go— *(looking in)* What are you doing in there?

Nora: *(inside)* Taking off my costume.

Torvald: *(standing by the open door)* Yes. Do that. Try to calm yourself down. Put your mind at ease, my frightened little songbird. You're safe now, and my big broad wings will protect you. *(walking to and fro by the door)* Nora, our home is so warm and cozy. Here you will always be safe. I will protect you—like a hunted dove that I've saved from the talons of a hawk. I will calm your poor beating heart. Little by little it will happen. Trust me, Nora. Tomorrow morning you'll think about it quite differently. Soon everything will be as it was before. In no time you won't need me to assure you that I have forgiven you. You will be absolutely sure that I have. Surely you can't imagine that I would reject you or even reproach you? You can't imagine what a real man's heart is like, Nora. It is so indescribably sweet and satisfying for a man to know that he has forgiven his wife—completely forgiven her and with all his heart. It's as if that simple act has made her doubly his own. It's as if he had given her a new life. And so, in a way she is now both wife and child to him. That is what you will be for me from now on, little frightened helpless darling. You mustn't worry about anything, Nora. All you have to do is be open, frank, and honest with me, and I will be the conscience and the will for you and … What's this? Not in bed? You've changed.

Nora: *(in her everyday clothes)* Yes, Torvald, I've changed.

Torvald: But why?— It's so late.

Nora: I won't go to sleep tonight.

Torvald: But my dear Nora—

Nora: *(looking at her watch)* It's not that late. Sit down, Torvald. You and I have a lot to say to each other. *(she sits down at one side of the table)*

Torvald: Nora—what's this?—your eyes are so cold!

Nora: Sit down. This will take some time; we have a lot to talk about.

Torvald: *(sits down at the opposite side of the table)* You're frightening me, Nora!—I don't understand you.

Nora: No, that's just it. You don't understand me, and I've never understood you either—until tonight. No, you mustn't interrupt me. I want you to just listen to what I have to say. Torvald, it's time we settled our accounts.

Torvald: What do you mean by that?

Nora: *(after a short silence)* Doesn't anything strike you as strange in our sitting here like this?

Torvald: What would that be?

Nora: We've been married now for eight years. Do you realize that this is the first time that we two, you and I, man and wife, have had a serious conversation?

Torvald: What do you mean serious?

Nora: In all these eight years—no, longer than that—from the moment we first met, we have never exchanged a *word* on any serious subject.

Torvald: Well, why would I keep on talking to you about my worries? There was nothing you could do to help.

Nora: I'm not talking about business. What I'm saying is that we have never really sat down together to try and get to the bottom of anything.

Torvald: But, my dear Nora, what good would that have done you?

Nora: That's just it. You have never understood me. I have been greatly wronged, Torvald—first by Papa and then by you.

Torvald: What! By your father and me?—the two men who loved you more than anyone else in the world?

Nora: *(shaking her head)* You have never loved me. You just thought it was pleasant to be *in* love with me.

Torvald: Nora, what are you saying?

Nora: It's perfectly true, Torvald. When I was at home with Papa, he gave me his opinions on everything. So I had the same opinions as he did. If I disagreed with him I concealed the fact, because he wouldn't have liked it.

He called me his doll-child, and he played with me just as I used to play with my dolls. And when I came to live in your house—

Torvald: What a way to talk about our marriage!

Nora: *(undisturbed)* I mean that I was simply handed over from Papa to you. You arranged everything to suit your own tastes, and so I had the same tastes as you—or else I pretended to. I'm really not sure which—I think sometimes the one and sometimes the other. When I look back on it, it seems to me that I was living here like a pauper—from hand to mouth. The whole reason for my existence was to perform tricks for you, Torvald. But that's what you wanted. You and Papa have committed a great sin against me. It is your fault that I have made nothing of my life.

Torvald: How unreasonable and how ungrateful, Nora! Haven't you been happy here?

Nora: No, I have never been happy. I thought I was, but I haven't been.

Torvald: Not—happy!

Nora: No. Just cheerful. You have always been so kind to me. But our home has been nothing but a playroom. I have been your doll-wife, just as at home I was Papa's doll-child; and in this house the children have been my dolls. I thought it was great fun when you played with me, and they thought it was great fun when I played with them. That is what our marriage has been, Torvald.

Torvald: There's some truth in what you say—though you've exaggerated and made too much of it. But in the future things will be different. Playtime is over, and it's time for lessons.

Nora: Whose lessons? Mine or the children's?

Torvald: Yours *and* the children's, Nora, my darling.

Nora: I'm sorry, Torvald, but you are not the man to teach me how to be a proper wife to you.

Torvald: How can you say that!

Nora: And how am I fit to bring up the children?

Torvald: Nora!

Nora: Didn't you say yourself a little while ago—that you dare not trust me to bring them up?

Torvald: That was in a moment of anger! Why do you pay any attention to that?

Nora: No, you were perfectly right. I am not fit to bring them up. There is something else I must do first. I must try to educate myself—and you are not the man to help me do that. I must do that by myself. That is why I am leaving you.

Torvald: *(springing up)* What did you say?

Nora: I must be by myself if I'm going to understand myself and the world around me. That is why I can't stay with you any longer.

Torvald: Nora, Nora!

Nora: I am leaving, right away. I'm sure Kristine will take me in for the night—

Torvald: You're out of your mind! I won't allow it! I forbid you!

Nora: There's no point in forbidding me anything any longer. I'll take with me only what belongs to me. I'll take nothing from you—now or later.

Torvald: What kind of mad behavior is this?

Nora: Tomorrow I will go home—to my old home, I mean. It will be easier for me to find something to do there.

Torvald: You foolish woman! You can't see what you're doing!

Nora: I must try and make some sense of all this, Torvald.

Torvald: You're deserting your home, your husband, and your children! Think what people will say!

Nora: I can't think about that at all. All I know is that I have no other option.

Torvald: I am deeply shocked. Is this how you neglect your most sacred duties?

Nora: What do you think are my most sacred duties?

Torvald: Do I need to tell you? Your duty to your husband and your children!

Nora: I have another duty just as sacred.

Torvald: No, you don't. What duty could that be?

Nora: My duty to myself.

Torvald: Before everything else, you are a wife and a mother.

Nora: I don't believe that any more. I believe that before everything I am a thinking human being, just as you are—or, at any rate, that I must try to become one. I know very well, Torvald, that most people would think you are right, and that your views would be supported in books. But I can no longer be satisfied with what most people say or what's written in books. I must think things over for myself and try to understand them.

Torvald: Why not try to understand your place in your own home? Haven't you got a dependable guide in things like—your religion?

Nora: I'm afraid, Torvald, I don't really know what religion is.

Torvald: What are you saying?

Nora: All I know is what my pastor told me when I was confirmed. He told us that religion was this, that, and the other. When I have left all this behind, when I am alone, I will look into that too. I will find out if what the pastor said is true, or at least if it is true for me.

Torvald: This is unheard of in a girl like you! But if religion can't put you on the right path, then let me try to prick your conscience. You have *some* moral sense, don't you? Or—now answer me—am I supposed to think that you don't?

Nora: Well, Torvald, that is not an easy question to answer. I really don't know. I am totally perplexed. All I know is that you and I look at it very differently. And I am finding out too that the law is very different from what I thought. I find it impossible to convince myself that the law is right. According to the law, a woman has no right to protect her old and dying father, or to save her husband's life. I can't believe that.

Torvald: You're talking like a child. You don't understand the world we live in.

Nora: No, I don't. But I intend to try. I'm going to find out which is right, the world or I.

Torvald: You are not well, Nora, you must have a fever. I almost think you may be out of your mind.

Nora: My mind has never been so clear and determined as tonight.

Torvald: And with this clear mind of yours you are determined to abandon your husband and your children?

Nora: Yes.

Torvald: Then there is only one possible explanation.

Nora: What?

Torvald: You do not love me anymore.

Nora: No, that is just it.

Torvald: Nora!—how can you say that?

Nora: It's very painful, Torvald. You have always been so kind to me, but I can't help it. I don't love you anymore.

Torvald: *(regaining his composure)* Are you clear and determined about that too?

Nora: Yes, absolutely clear and determined. That is why I won't stay here any longer.

Torvald: And can you tell me what I have done to lose your love?

Nora: Yes, I can. It was tonight, when the miracle didn't happen. It was then that I saw you were not the man I thought you were.

Torvald: Please explain yourself—I don't understand.

Nora: I had waited so patiently for eight years. Goodness knows, I didn't think that miracles happen every day. Then this … this … disaster fell upon me, and I felt quite sure that the miracle was finally going to happen. When Krogstad's letter was in the mailbox, never for a moment did I think you would accept his conditions. I was absolutely sure that you would say to him: Go ahead! Publish it. Let the whole world know! And after that—

Torvald: Yes, what then?—after I had exposed my wife to shame and disgrace?

Nora: After that—I was absolutely sure that you would step forward and assume all the blame and say, "I am the guilty one."

Torvald: Nora—!

Nora: What you are thinking is that I would never have accepted a sacrifice like that from you. No, of course I wouldn't. But what would my word have been against yours? That was the miracle I was hoping for. The miracle I was afraid of. It was to make sure that did not happen that I was ready to kill myself.

Torvald: I would slave night and day for you, Nora—I would endure sorrow and poverty for your sake. But no man would sacrifice his honor even for the one he loves.

Nora: Thousands of women have done that.

Torvald: You're thinking and talking like a stupid child.

Nora: Perhaps. But you don't think or talk like the man I could spend the rest of my life with. As soon as you stopped being frightened—and you weren't afraid of what was happening to me, you were afraid of what was happening to you—when it was over, as far as you were concerned it was just as if nothing had happened. Exactly as before, I was your little lark. I was your doll. Of course you would handle it twice as gently. It was so delicate and fragile. *(getting up)* Torvald—it was then it dawned on me that for eight years I've been living with a stranger and I had borne him three children—. Oh, I can't bear to think of it! I could tear myself to pieces!

Torvald: *(sadly)* Yes. I see, I see. A gulf has opened up between us—I see that now. But Nora, couldn't we bridge that gulf?

Nora: The woman I am now is no wife for you.

Torvald: I could change who I am—

Nora: Perhaps—if your doll is taken away from you.

Torvald: But to lose you!—to lose you forever! No, no, Nora, I can't accept that.

Nora: *(going out to the right)* That is why it must happen. *(she comes back with her cloak and hat and a small bag which she puts on a chair by the table)*

Torvald: Nora. Nora, not now! Wail until tomorrow.

Nora: *(putting on her cloak)* I can't spend the night in the house of a stranger.

Torvald: But we could live here like brother and sister—?

Nora: *(putting on her hat)* You know that that wouldn't last. *(puts the cloak round her)* Goodbye, Torvald. I won't see my children. I know they're in better hands than mine. The woman I am now would be no use to them.

Torvald: But someday, Nora—someday?

Nora: How can I answer that? I've no idea of what's going to become of me.

Torvald: But you are my wife, whatever happens to you.

Nora: Listen, Torvald. I have heard that when a wife leaves her husband's house, as I am doing now, he is legally freed from all obligations toward her. In any case, *I* am setting you free. You're not to feel like a prisoner in any way. I will not feel that way at all. There must be perfect freedom on both sides. Here is your ring back. Give me mine.

Torvald: That too?

Nora: That too.

Torvald: Here it is.

Nora: There. Now it's all over. I've put the keys here. The maids know all about running the house—much better than I do. Tomorrow, after I've left, Kristine will come and pack the things I brought with me from home. I'll have them sent on to me.

Torvald: It's all over! All over!—Nora, will you never think of me again?

Nora: I know that I will often think of you … and the children … and this house.

Torvald: May I write to you, Nora?

Nora: No—never. You must never do that.

Torvald: But at least let me send you—

Nora: Nothing—nothing—

Torvald: Just let me help you if you ever need it.

Nora: No, I can never accept anything from a stranger.

Torvald: Nora—can I never be anything more than a stranger to you?

Nora: *(taking her bag)* Oh, Torvald, the greatest miracle of all would have to happen.

Torvald: What would that be?

Nora: You and I would have to change so much that—. Oh, Torvald, I don't believe in miracles anymore.

Torvald: But I will. Tell me!—changed so much that—?

Nora: That our life together would be a real marriage. Goodbye. *(she goes out through the hall)*

Torvald: *(sinks down on a chair at the door and buries his face in his hands)* Nora! Nora! *(looks round and rises)* Empty. She's gone. *(a glimmer of hope flashes across his face)* The greatest miracle of all—?

(The sound of a door shutting is heard from below.)

* * *

Reading and Reacting

1. What is your attitude toward Nora at the beginning of the play? How does your attitude toward her change as the play progresses? What actions and lines of dialogue change your assessment of her?
2. List the key events that occurred before the start of the play. How do we learn of each event?
3. Explain the role of each of the following in advancing the play's action: the Christmas tree, the locked mailbox, the telegram Dr. Rank receives, Dr. Rank's calling cards.
4. In Act 2, Torvald says, "You can be sure that whatever happens, I will be brave and strong. You'll see I am man enough to take everything upon myself." How does this statement influence Nora's subsequent actions?
5. Explain how each of the following foreshadows events that will occur later in the play: Torvald's comments about Krogstad's children (Act 1); Torvald's attitude toward Nora's father (Act 2); Krogstad's suggestions about suicide (Act 2).
6. In addition to the play's main plot—which concerns the blackmail of Nora by Krogstad and her attempts to keep her crime secret from Torvald—the play contains several subplots. Some of them began to develop before the start of the play, and some unfold alongside the main plot. Identify these subplots. How do they advance the themes of survival, debt, sacrifice, and duty that run through the play?

7. Is Kristine Linde as much of a "modern woman" as Nora? Is she actually *more* of a modern woman? Is she essential to the play? How might the play be different without her?
8. **Journal Entry** Do you see *A Doll's House* as primarily about the struggle between the needs of the individual and the needs of society or about the conflict between women's roles in the family and in the larger society? Explain.
9. **Critical Perspective** Since its earliest performances, there has been much comment on the conclusion of *A Doll's House*. Many viewers have found the play's ending unrealistically harsh. In fact, a famous German actress refused to play the scene as written because she insisted she would never leave her children. (Ibsen reluctantly rewrote the ending for her; in this version, Helmer forces Nora to the doorway of the children's bedroom, and she sinks to the floor as the curtain falls.) Moreover, many critics have found it hard to accept Nora's sudden transformation from, in the words of Elizabeth Hardwick in her essay "Ibsen's Women," "the girlish, charming wife to the radical, courageous heroine setting out alone."

   What is your response to the play's ending? Do you think it makes sense in light of what we have learned about Nora and her marriage? Or do you agree with Hardwick that Nora's abandonment of her children is not only implausible but also a "rather casual" gesture that "drops a stain on our admiration of Nora"?

Related Works: "The Story of an Hour" (p. 151), "The Disappearance" (p. 280), "The Yellow Wallpaper" (p. 315), "Daddy" (p. 571)

New York Times Co./Archive Photos/Getty Images

ARTHUR MILLER (1915–2005) was born in New York City and graduated in 1938 from the University of Michigan, where he began to write plays. His first big success, which won the New York Drama Critics Circle Award, was *All My Sons* (1947). Other significant plays are *The Crucible* (1953), based on the Salem witch trials of 1692, which Miller saw as parallel to contemporary investigations of suspected Communists by the House Un-American Activities Committee; *A View from the Bridge* (1955); and *After the Fall* (1955). His most significant play is *Death of a* Salesman (1949), which quickly became an American classic, showing that a tragedy can also be also a realistic story of an ordinary person. Miller's play *The Last Yankee* opened off-Broadway in 1993, *Broken Glass* was both published and performed in 1994, and *Mr. Peter's Connection* was published in 1998. In 2001, Miller was awarded an NEH fellowship and the John H. Finney Award for Exemplary Service to New York City.

Cultural Context *All My Sons* is set in a very specific time and place (1947, suburban Ohio), featuring characters who are white and middle class. Despite the very specific context Miller chose, efforts have been made over the years to explore different staging and casting options that would enable the play to address the concerns of contemporary audiences. For example, in 2015, the Talawa Theatre Company, a prominent Black-led British theater group, staged a production of *All My Sons* with an all-Black cast. Considering the status of Black soldiers during World War II—in particular, the challenges they faced when trying to become pilots—this version of the play likely had an impact on its audience that was very different from that of the original play. A recent Broadway production used color-blind casting, with George played by a Black man—although all the other characters were white—and a 2022 Broadway production of Miller's *Death of a Salesman* featured an all-Black cast.

All My Sons (1947)

CHARACTERS

Joe Keller (Keller)	**Dr. Jim Bayliss (Jim)**
Kate Keller, mother	**Sue Bayliss**
Chris Keller	**Frank Lubey**
Ann Deever	**Lydia Lubey**
George Deever	**Bert**

ACT ONE

The back yard of the Keller home in the outskirts of an American town. August of our era.

The stage is hedged on right and left by tall, closely planted poplars which lend the yard a secluded atmosphere. Upstage is filled with the back of the house and its open, unroofed porch which extends into the yard some six feet. The house is two stories high and has seven rooms. It would have cost perhaps fifteen thousand in the early twenties when it was built. Now it is nicely painted, looks tight and comfortable, and the yard is green with sod, here and there plants whose season is gone. At the right, beside the house, the entrance of the driveway can be seen, but the poplars cut off view of its continuation downstage. In the left corner, downstage, stands the four-foot-high stump of a slender apple tree whose upper trunk and branches lie toppled beside it, fruit still clinging to its branches.

Downstage right is a small, trellised arbor, shaped like a sea-shell, with a decorative bulb hanging from its forward-curving roof. Garden chairs and a table are scattered about. A garbage pail on the ground next to the porch steps, a wire leaf-burner near it.

On the rise: It is early Sunday morning. Joe Keller is sitting in the sun reading the want ads of the Sunday paper, the other sections of which lie neatly on the ground beside him. Behind his back, inside the arbor, Doctor Jim Bayliss is reading part of the paper at the table.

Keller is nearing sixty. A heavy man of stolid mind and build, a business man these many years, but with the imprint of the machine-shop worker and boss still upon him. When he reads, when he speaks, when he listens, it is with the terrible concentration of the uneducated man for whom there is still wonder in many commonly known things, a man whose judgements must be dredged out of experience and a peasant-like common sense. A man among men.

Doctor Bayliss is nearly forty. A wry self-controlled man, an easy talker, but with a wisp of sadness that clings even to his self-effacing humor.

At curtain, Jim is standing at left, staring at the broken tree. He taps a pipe on it, blows through the pipe, feels in his pockets for tobacco, then speaks.

Jim: Where's your tobacco?

Keller: I think I left it on the table.

Jim goes slowly to table on the arbor at right, finds a pouch, and sits there on the bench, filling his pipe.

Keller: Gonna rain tonight.

Jim: Paper says so?

Keller: Yeah, right here.

Jim: Then it can't rain.

Frank Lubey enters, from right, through a small space between the poplars. Frank is thirty-two but balding. A pleasant, opinionated man, uncertain of himself, with a tendency toward peevishness when crossed, but always wanting it pleasantly and neighborly. He rather saunters in, leisurely, nothing to do. He does not notice Jim in the arbor. On his greeting, Jim does not bother looking up.

Frank: Hya.

Keller: Hello, Frank. What's doin'?

Frank: Nothin'. Walking off my breakfast. *(Looks up at the sky.)* That beautiful? Not a cloud.

Keller: *(Looks up.)* Yeah, nice.

Frank: Every Sunday ought to be like this.

Keller: *(Indicating the sections beside him.)* Want the paper?

Frank: What's the difference, it's all bad news. What's today's calamity?

Keller: I don't know, I don't read the news part anymore. It's more interesting in the want ads.

Frank: Why, you trying to buy something?

Keller: No, I'm just interested. To see what people want, y'know? For instance here's a guy is lookin' for two Newfoundland dogs. Now what's he want with two Newfoundland dogs?

Frank: That is funny.

Keller: Here's another one. Wanted—Old Dictionaries. High prices paid. Now what's a man going to do with an old dictionary?

Frank: Why not? Probably a book collector.

Keller: You mean he'll make a living out of that?

Frank: Sure, there's a lot of them.

Keller: *(Shakes his head.)* All the kind of business goin' on. In my day, either you were a lawyer, or a doctor, or you worked in a shop. Now...

Frank: Well, I was going to be a forester once.

Keller: Well, that shows you; in my day, there was no such thing. *(Scanning the page, sweeping it with his hand.)* You look at a page like this you realize how ignorant you are. *(Softly, with wonder, as he scans page.)* Psss!

Frank: *(Noticing tree.)* Hey, what happened to your tree?

Keller: Ain't that awful? The wind must've got it last night. You heard the wind, didn't you?

Frank: Yeah, I got a mess in my yard, too. *(Goes to tree.)* What a pity. *(Turns to Keller.)* What did Kate say?

Keller: They're all asleep yet. I'm just waiting for her to see it.

Frank: *(Struck.)* You know—it's funny.

Keller: What?

Frank: Larry was born in August. He'd been twenty-seven this month. And his tree blows down.

Keller: *(Touched.)* I'm surprised you remember his birthday, Frank. That's nice.

Frank: Well, I'm working on his horoscope.

Keller: How can you make him a horoscope? That's for the future, ain't it?

Frank: Well, what I'm doing is this, see. Larry was reported missing on November 25th, right?

Keller: Yeah?

Frank: Well, then, we assume that if he was killed it was on November 25th. Now, what Kate wants…

Keller: Oh, Kate asked you to make a horoscope?

Frank: Yeah, what she wants to find out is whether November 25th was a favorable day for Larry.

Keller: What is that, favorable day?

Frank: Well, a favorable day for a person is a fortunate day, according to his stars. In other words it would be practically impossible for him to have died on his favorable day.

Keller: Well, was that his favorable day?—November 25th?

Frank: That's what I'm working on to find out. It takes time! See, the point is, if November 25th was his favorable day, then it's completely possible he's alive somewhere, because…I mean, it's possible. *(He notices Jim now. Jim is looking at him as though at an idiot. To Jim—with an uncertain laugh.)* I didn't even see you.

Keller: *(To Jim.)* Is he talkin' sense?

Jim: He's all right. He's just completely out of his mind, that's all.

Frank: *(Peeved.)* The trouble with you is, you don't *believe* in anything.

Jim: And your trouble is that you believe in *anything*. *You* didn't see my kid this morning, did you?

Frank: No.

Keller: Imagine? He walked off with his thermometer. Right out of his bag.

Jim: *(Gets up.)* What a problem. One look at a girl and he takes her temperature.

(Goes to the driveway, looks upstage toward street.)

Frank: That boy's going to be a real doctor; he's smart.

Jim: Over my dead body he'll be a doctor. A good beginning, too.

Frank: Why? It's an honorable profession.

Jim: *(Looks at him tiredly.)* Frank, will you stop talking like a civics book? *(Keller laughs.)*

Frank: Why, I saw a movie a couple of weeks ago, reminded me of you. There was a doctor in that picture…

Keller: Don Ameche!

Frank: I think it was, yeah. And he worked in his basement discovering things. That's what you ought to do; you could help humanity, instead of…

Jim: I would love to help humanity on a Warner Brothers salary.

Keller: *(Points at him, laughing.)* That's very good, Jim.

Jim: *(Looks toward house.)* Well, where's the beautiful girl was supposed to be here?

Frank: *(Excited.)* Annie came?

Keller: Sure, sleepin' upstairs. We picked her up on the one o'clock train last night. Wonderful thing. Girl leaves here, a scrawny kid. Couple of years go by, she's a regular woman. Hardly recognized her, and she was running in and out of this yard all her life. That was a very happy family used to live in your house, Jim.

Jim: Like to meet her. The block can use a pretty girl. In the whole neighborhood there's not a damned thing to look at. *(Enter Sue, Jim's wife, from left. She is rounding forty, an overweight woman who fears it. On seeing her, Jim wryly adds:)*…Except my wife, of course.

Sue: *(In same spirit.)* Mrs. Adams is on the phone, you dog.

Jim: *(To Keller.)* Such is the condition which prevails. *(Going to his wife.)* my love, my light…

Sue: Don't sniff around me. *(Points to their house, left.)* And give her a nasty answer. I can smell her perfume over the phone.

Jim: What's the matter with her now?

Sue: I don't know, dear. She sounds like she's in terrible pain—unless her mouth is full of candy.

Jim: Why don't you just tell her to lay down?

Sue: She enjoys it more when you tell her to lay down. And when are you going to see Mr. Hubbard?

Jim: My dear; Mr. Hubbard is not sick, and I have better things to do than to sit there and hold his hand.

Sue: It seems to me that for ten dollars you could hold his hand.

Jim: *(To Keller.)* If your son wants to play golf tell him I'm ready. *(Going left.)* Or if he'd like to take a trip around the world for about thirty years. *(He exits left.)*

Keller: Why do you needle him? He's a doctor, women are supposed to call him up.

Sue: All I said was Mrs. Adams is on the phone. Can I have some of your parsley?

Keller: Yeah, sure. *(Sue goes left to parsley box and pulls some parsley.)* You were a nurse too long, Susie. You're too…too…realistic.

Sue: *(Laughing, points at him.)* Now you said it! *(Enter Lydia Lubey from right. She is a robust, laughing girl of twenty-seven.)*

Lydia: Frank, the toaster…*(Sees the others.)* Hya.

Keller: Hello!

Lydia: *(To Frank.)* The toaster is off again.

Frank: Well, plug it in, I just fixed it.

Lydia: *(Kindly, but insistently.)* Please, dear, fix it back like it was before.

Frank: I don't know why you can't learn to turn on a simple thing like a toaster!

(Frank exits right.)

Sue: *(Laughs.)* Thomas Edison.

Lydia: *(Apologetically.)* He's really very handy. *(She sees broken tree.)* Oh, did the wind get your tree?

Keller: Yeah, last night.

Lydia: Oh, what a pity. Annie get in?

Keller: She'll be down soon. Wait'll you meet her, Sue, she's a knockout.

Sue: I should've been a man. People are always introducing me to beautiful women. *(To Joe.)* Tell her to come over later: I imagine she'd like to see what we did with her house. And thanks. *(Sue exits left.)*

Lydia: Is she still unhappy, Joe?

Keller: Annie? I don't suppose she goes around dancing on her toes, but she seems to be over it.

Lydia: She going to get married? Is there anybody…?

Keller: I suppose…say, it's a couple of years already. She can't mourn a boy forever.

Lydia: It's so strange. Annie's here and not even married. And I've got three babies. I always thought it'd be the other way around.

Keller: Well, that's what a war does. I had two sons, now I got one. It changed all the tallies. In my day when you had sons it was an honor. Today, a doctor could make a million dollars if he could figure out a way to bring a boy into the world without a trigger finger.

Lydia: You know, I was just reading…*(Enter Chris Keller from house, stands in doorway.)*

Lydia: Hya, Chris. *(Frank shouts from off right)*.

Frank: Lydia, come in here! If you want the toaster to work don't plug in the malted mixer.

Lydia: *(Embarrassed, laughs.)* Did I…?

Frank: And the next time I fix something don't tell me I'm crazy! Now come in here!

Lydia: *(To Keller.)* I'll never hear the end of this one.

Keller: *(Calling to Frank.)* So what's the difference? Instead of toast have a malted!

Lydia: Sh! sh! *(She exits right, laughing.)*

(Chris watches her off. He is thirty-two; like his father, solidly built, a listener. A man capable of immense affection and loyalty. He has a cup of coffee in one hand, part of a doughnut in the other.)

Keller: You want the paper?

Chris: That's all right, just the book section. *(He bends down and pulls out part of the paper on porch floor.)*

Keller: You're always reading the book section and you never buy a book.

Chris: *(Coming down to settee.)* I like to keep abreast of my ignorance. *(He sits on settee.)*

Keller: What is that, every week a new book comes out?

Chris: Lots of new books.

Keller: All different.

Chris: All different.

Keller: *(Shakes his head, puts knife down on bench, takes oilstone up to the cabinet.)* Psss! Annie up yet?

Chris: Mother's giving her breakfast in the dining-room.

Keller: *(Crosses, downstage of stool, looking at broken tree.)* See what happened to the tree?

Chris: *(Without looking up.)* Yeah.

Keller: What's Mother going to say? *(Bert runs on from driveway. He is about eight. He jumps on stool, then on Keller's back.)*

Bert: You're finally up.

Keller: *(Swinging him around and putting him down.)* Ha! Bert's here! Where's Tommy? He's got his father's thermometer again.

Bert: He's taking a reading.

Chris: What!

Bert: But it's only oral.

Keller: Oh, well, there's no harm in oral. So what's new this morning, Bert?

Bert: Nothin'. *(He goes to broken tree, walks around it.)*

Keller: Then you couldn't've made a complete inspection of the block. In the beginning, when I first made you a policeman you used to come in every morning with something new. Now, nothin's ever new.

Bert: Except some kids from Thirtieth Street. They started kicking a can down the block, and I made them go away because you were sleeping.

Keller: Now you're talkin', Bert. Now you're on the ball. First thing you know I'm liable to make you a detective.

Bert: *(Pulls him down by the lapel and whispers in his ear.)* Can I see the jail now?

Keller: Seein' the jail ain't allowed, Bert. You know that.

Bert: Aw, I betcha there isn't even a jail. I don't see any bars on the cellar windows.

Keller: Bert, on my word of honor, there's a jail in the basement. I showed you my gun, didn't I?

Bert: But that's a hunting gun.

Keller: That's an arresting gun!

Bert: Then why don't you ever arrest anybody? Tommy said another dirty word to Doris yesterday, and you didn't even demote him.

Keller: *(He chuckles and winks at Chris, who is enjoying all this.)* Yeah, that's a dangerous character, that Tommy. *(Beckons him closer.)* What word does he say?

Bert: *(Backing away quickly in great embarrassment.)* Oh, I can't say that.

Keller: *(Grabs him by the shirt and pulls him back.)* Well, gimme an idea.

Bert: I can't. It's not a nice word.

Keller: Just whisper it in my ear. I'll close my eyes. Maybe I won't even hear it.

Bert: *(On tiptoe, puts his lips to Keller's ear, then in unbearable embarrassment steps back.)* I can't Mr. Keller.

Chris: *(Laughing.)* Don't make him do that.

Keller: Okay, Bert. I take your word. Now go out, and keep both eyes peeled.

Bert: *(Interested.)* For what?

Keller: For what! Bert, the whole neighborhood is depending on you. A policeman don't ask questions. Now peel them eyes!

Bert: *(Mystified, but willing.)* Okay. *(He runs off right back of arbor.)*

Keller: *(Calling after him.)* And mum's the word, Bert.

Bert: *(Stops and sticks his head thru the arbor.)* About what?

Keller: Just in general. Be v-e-r-y careful.

Bert: *(Nods in bewilderment.)* Okay. *(Bert exits down right.)*

Keller: *(Laughs.)* I got all the kids crazy!

Chris: One of these days, they'll all come in here and beat your brains out.

Keller: What's she going to say? Maybe we ought to tell her before she sees it.

Chris: She saw it.

Keller: How could she see it? I was the first one up. She was still in bed.

Chris: She was out here when it broke.

Keller: When?

Chris: About four this morning. *(Indicating window above them.)* I heard it cracking and I woke up and looked out. She was standing right here when it cracked.

Keller: What was she doing out here four in the morning?

Chris: I don't know. When it cracked she ran back into the house and cried in the kitchen.

Keller: Did you talk to her?

Chris: No, I… I figured the best thing was to leave her alone. *(Pause.)*

Keller: *(Deeply touched.)* She cried hard?

Chris: I could hear her right through the floor of my room.

Keller: *(Slight pause.)* What was she doing out here at that hour? *(Chris silent. An undertone of anger showing.)* She's dreaming about him again. She's walking around at night.

Chris: I guess she is.

Keller: She's getting just like after he died. *(Slight pause.)* What's the meaning of that?

Chris: I don't know the meaning of it. *(Slight pause.)* But I know one thing, Dad. We've made a terrible mistake with Mother.

Keller: What?

Chris: Being dishonest with her. That kind of thing always pays off, and now it's paying off.

Keller: What do you mean, dishonest?

Chris: You know Larry's not coming back and I know it. Why do we allow her to go on thinking that we believe with her?

Keller: What do you want to do, argue with her?

Chris: I don't want to argue with her, but it's time she realized that nobody believes Larry is alive any more. *(Keller simply moves away, thinking, looking at the ground.)* Why shouldn't she dream of him, walk the nights waiting for him? Do we contradict her? Do we say straight out that we have no hope any more? That we haven't had any hope for years now?

Keller: *(Frightened at the thought.)* You can't say that to her.

Chris: We've got to say it to her.

Keller: How're you going to prove it? Can you prove it?

Chris: For God's sake, three years! Nobody comes back after three years. It's insane.

Keller: To you it is, and to me. But not to her. You can talk yourself blue in the face, but there's no body and no grave, so where are you?

Chris: Sit down, Dad. I want to talk to you.

Keller: *(Looks at him searchingly a moment, and sitting…)* The trouble is the Goddam newspapers. Every month some boy turns up from nowhere, so the next one is going to be Larry, so…

Chris: All right, all right, listen to me. *(Slight pause. Keller sits on settee.)* You know why I asked Annie here, don't you?

Keller: *(He knows, but…)* Why?

Chris: You know.

Keller: Well, I got an idea, but…What's the story?

Chris: I'm going to ask her to marry me. *(Slight pause.)*

Keller: *(Nods.)* Well, that's only your business, Chris.

Chris: You know it's not only my business.

Keller: What do you want me to do? You're old enough to know your own mind.

Chris: *(Asking, annoyed.)* Then it's all right, I'll go ahead with it?

Keller: Well, you want to be sure Mother isn't going to…

Chris: Then it isn't just my business.

Keller: I'm just sayin'…

Chris: Sometimes you infuriate me, you know that? Isn't it your business, too, if I tell this to Mother and she throws a fit about it? You have such a talent for ignoring things.

Keller: I ignore what I gotta ignore. The girl is Larry's girl…

Chris: She's not Larry's girl.

Keller: From Mother's point of view he is not dead and you have no right to take his girl. *(Slight pause.)* Now you can go on from there if you know where to go, but I'm tellin' you I don't know where to go. See? I don't know. Now what can I do for you?

Chris: I don't know why it is, but every time I reach out for something I want, I have to pull back because other people will suffer. My whole bloody life, time after time after time.

Keller: You're a considerate fella, there's nothing wrong in that.

Chris: To hell with that.

Keller: Did you ask Annie yet?

Chris: I wanted to get this settled first.

Keller: How do you know she'll marry you? Maybe she feels the same way Mother does?

Chris: Well, if she does, then that's the end of it. From her letters I think she's forgotten him. I'll find out. And then we'll thrash it out with Mother? Right? Dad, don't avoid me.

Keller: The trouble is, you don't see enough women. You never did.

Chris: So what? I'm not fast with women.

Keller: I don't see why it has to be Annie...

Chris: Because it is.

Keller: That's a good answer, but it don't answer anything. You haven't seen her since you went to war. It's five years.

Chris: I can't help it. I know her best. I was brought up next door to her. These years when I think of someone for my wife, I think of Annie. What do you want, a diagram?

Keller: I don't want a diagram...I...I'm...She thinks he's coming back, Chris. You marry that girl and you're pronouncing him dead. Now what's going to happen to Mother? Do you know? I don't. *(Pause.)*

Chris: All right, then, Dad.

Keller: *(Thinking Chris has retreated.)* Give it some more thought.

Chris: I've given it three years of thought. I'd hoped that if I waited, Mother would forget Larry and then we'd have a regular wedding and everything happy. But if that can't happen here, then I'll have to get out.

Keller: What the hell is *this*?

Chris: I'll get out. I'll get married and live some place else. Maybe in New York.

Keller: Are you crazy?

Chris: I've been a good son too long, a good sucker. I'm through with it.

Keller: You've got a business here, what the hell is this?

Chris: The business! The business doesn't inspire me.

Keller: Must you be inspired?

Chris: Yes. I like it an hour a day. If I have to grub for money all day long at least at evening I want it beautiful. I want a family, I want some kids, I want to build something that I can give myself to. Annie is in the middle of that. Now...where do I find it?

Keller: You mean...*(Goes to him.)* Tell me something, you mean you'd leave the business?

Chris: Yes. On this I would.

Keller: *(Pause.)* Well…you don't want to think like that.

Chris: Then help me stay here.

Keller: All right, but…but don't think like that. Because what the hell did I work for? That's only for you, Chris, the whole shootin' match is for you!

Chris: I know that, Dad. Just you help me stay here.

Keller: *(Puts a fist up to Chris' jaw.)* But don't think that way, you hear me?

Chris: I am thinking that way.

Keller: *(Lowering his hand.)* I don't understand you, do I?

Chris: No, you don't. I'm a pretty tough guy.

Keller: Yeah, I can see that. *(Mother appears on porch. She is in her early fifties, a woman of uncontrolled inspirations, and an overwhelming capacity for love.)*

Mother: Joe?

Chris: *(Going toward porch.)* Hello, Mom.

Mother: *(Indicating house behind her. To Keller.)* Did you take a bag from under the sink?

Keller: Yeah, I put it in the pail.

Mother: Well, get it out of the pail. That's my potatoes. *(Chris bursts out laughing. Goes up into alley.)*

Keller: *(Laughing.)* I thought it was garbage.

Mother: Will you do me a favor, Joe? Don't be helpful.

Keller: I can afford another bag of potatoes.

Mother: Minnie scoured that pail in boiling water last night. It's cleaner than your teeth.

Keller: And I don't understand why, after I worked forty years and I got a maid, why I have to take out the garbage.

Mother: If you would make up your mind that every bag in the kitchen isn't full of garbage, you wouldn't be throwing out my vegetables. Last time it was the onions.

(Chris comes on, hands her bag.)

Keller: I don't like garbage in the house.

Mother: Then don't eat. *(She goes into the kitchen with bag.)*

Chris: That settles you for today.

Keller: Yeah, I'm in last place again. I don't know, once upon a time I used to think that when I got money again I would have a maid and my wife would take it easy. Now I got money, and I got a maid, and my wife is workin' for the maid. *(He sits in one of the chairs. Mother comes out on last line. She carries a pot of string beans.)*

Mother: It's her day off, what are you crabbing about?

Chris: *(To Mother.)* Isn't Annie finished eating?

Mother: *(Looking around preoccupiedly at yard.)* She'll be right out. *(Moves.)* That wind did some job on this place. *(Of the tree.)* So much for that, thank God.

Keller: *(Indicating chair beside him.)* Sit down, take it easy.

Mother: *(She presses her hand to top of her head.)* I've got such a funny pain on the top of my head.

Chris: Can I get you an aspirin?

Mother: *(Picks a few petals off ground, stands there smelling them in her hand, then sprinkles them over plants.)* No more roses. It's so funny…everything decides to happen at the same time. This month is his birthday; his tree blows down, Annie comes. Everything that happened seems to be coming back. I was just down the cellar, and what do I stumble over? His baseball glove. I haven't seen it in a century.

Chris: Don't you think Annie looks well?

Mother: Fine. There's no question about it. She's a beauty…I still don't know what brought her here. Not that I'm not glad to see her, but…

Chris: I just thought we'd all like to see each other again. *(Mother just looks at him, nodding ever so slightly—almost as though admitting something.)* And I wanted to see her myself.

Mother: *(Her nods halt. To Keller.)* The only thing is I think her nose got longer. But I'll always love that girl. She's one that didn't jump into bed with somebody else as soon as it happened with her fella.

Keller: *(As though that were impossible for Annie.)* Oh, what're you…?

Mother: Never mind. Most of them didn't wait till the telegrams were opened. I'm just glad she came, so you can see I'm not *completely* out of my mind. *(Sits, and rapidly breaks string beans in the pot.)*

Chris: Just because she isn't married doesn't mean she's been mourning Larry.

Mother: *(With an undercurrent of observation.)* Why then isn't she?

Chris: *(A little flustered.)* Well…it could have been any number of things.

Mother: *(Directly at him.)* Like what, for instance?

Chris: *(Embarrassed, but standing his ground.)* I don't know. Whatever it is. Can I get you an aspirin? *(Mother puts her hand to her head.)*

Mother: *(She gets up and goes aimlessly toward the trees on rising.)* It's not like a headache.

Keller: You don't sleep, that's why. She's wearing out more bedroom slippers than shoes.

Mother: I had a terrible night. *(She stops moving.)* I never had a night like that.

Chris: *(Looks at Keller.)* What was it, Mom? Did you dream?

Mother: More, more than a dream.

Chris: *(Hesitantly.)* About Larry?

Mother: I was fast asleep and…*(Raising her arm over the audience.)* Remember the way he used to fly low past the house when he was in training? When we used to see his face in the cockpit going by? That's the way I saw him. Only high up. Way, way up, where the clouds are. He was so real I could reach out and touch him. And suddenly he started to fall. And crying, crying to me… Mom, Mom! I could hear him like he was in the room. Mom!… it was his voice! If I could touch him I knew I could stop him, if

I could only... *(Breaks off, allowing her outstretched hand to fall.)* I woke up and it was so funny... The wind... it was like the roaring of his engine. I came out here... I must've still been half asleep. I could hear that roaring like he was going by. The tree snapped right in front of me... and I like... came awake. *(She is looking at tree. She suddenly realizes something, turns with a reprimanding finger shaking slightly at Keller.)* See? We should never have planted that tree. I said so in the first place; it was too soon to plant a tree for him.

Chris: *(Alarmed.)* Too soon!

Mother: *(Angering.)* We rushed into it. Everybody was in such a hurry to bury him. I *said* not to plant it yet. *(To Keller.)* I *told* you to...!

Chris: Mother, Mother! *(She looks into his face.)* The wind blew it down. What significance has that got? What are you talking about? Mother, please...Don't go through it all again, will you? It's no good, it doesn't accomplish anything. I've been thinking, y'know?—maybe we ought to put our minds to forgetting him?

Mother: That's the third time you've said that this week.

Chris: Because it's not right; we never took up our lives again. We're like at a railroad station waiting for a train that never comes in.

Mother: *(Presses top of her head.)* Get me an aspirin, heh?

Chris: Sure, and let's break out of this, heh, Mom? I thought the four of us might go out to dinner a couple of nights, maybe go dancing out at the shore.

Mother: Fine. *(To Keller.)* We can do it tonight.

Keller: Swell with me!

Chris: Sure, let's have some fun. *(To Mother.)* You'll start with this aspirin. *(He goes up and into the house with new spirit. Her smile vanishes.)*

Mother: *(With an accusing undertone.)* Why did he invite her here?

Keller: Why does that bother you?

Mother: She's been in New York three and a half years, why all of a sudden...?

Keller: Well, maybe...maybe he just wanted to see her...

Mother: Nobody comes seven hundred miles "just to see".

Keller: What do you mean? He lived next door to the girl all his life, why shouldn't he want to see her again? *(Mother looks at him critically.)* Don't look at me like that, he didn't tell me any more than he told you.

Mother: *(A warning and a question.)* He's not going to marry her.

Keller: How do you know he's even thinking about it?

Mother: It's got that about it.

Keller: *(Sharply watching her reaction.)* Well? So what?

Mother: *(Alarmed.)* What's going on here, Joe?

Keller: Now listen, kid...

Mother: *(Avoiding contact with him.)* She's not his girl, Joe; she knows she's not.

Keller: You can't read her mind.

Mother: Then why is she still single? New York is full of men, why isn't she married? *(Pause.)* Probably a hundred people told her she's foolish, but she's waited.

Keller: How do you know why she waited?

Mother: She knows what I know, that's why. She's faithful as a rock. In my worst moments, I think of her waiting, and I know again that I'm right.

Keller: Look, it's a nice day. What are we arguing for?

Mother: *(Warningly.)* Nobody in this house dast[1] take her faith away, Joe. Strangers might. But not his father, not his brother.

Keller: *(Exasperated.)* What do you want me to do? What do you want?

Mother: I want you to act like he's coming back. Both of you. Don't think I haven't noticed you since Chris invited her. I won't stand for any nonsense.

Keller: But, Kate…

Mother: Because if he's not coming back, then I'll kill myself! Laugh. Laugh at me. *(She points to tree.)* But why did that happen the very night she came back? Laugh, but there are meanings in such things. She goes to sleep in his room and his memorial breaks in pieces. Look at it; look. *(She sits on bench at his left.)* Joe…

Keller: Calm yourself.

Mother: Believe with me, Joe. I can't stand all alone.

Keller: Calm yourself.

Mother: Only last week a man turned up in Detroit, missing longer than Larry. You read it yourself.

Keller: All right, all right, calm yourself.

Mother: You above all have got to believe, you…

Keller: *(Rises.)* Why me above all?

Mother: …Just don't stop believing…

Keller: What does that mean, me above all? *(Bert comes rushing on from left.)*

Bert: Mr. Keller! Say, Mr. Keller…*(Pointing up driveway)* Tommy just said it again!

Keller: *(Not remembering any of it.)* Said what?… Who?…

Bert: The dirty word.

Keller: Oh. Well…

Bert: Gee, aren't you going to arrest him? I warned him.

Mother: *(With suddenness.)* Stop that, Bert. Go home. *(Bert backs up, as she advances.)* There's no jail here.

Keller: *(As though to say, "Oh-what-the-hell-let-him-believe-there-is.")* Kate…

Mother: *(Turning on Keller, furiously.)* There's no jail here! I want you to stop that jail business! *(He turns, shamed, but peeved.)*

Bert: *(Past her to Keller.)* He's right across the street…

---

[1] *dast*: Dare

Mother: Go home, Bert. *(Bert turns around and goes up driveway. She is shaken. Her speech is bitten off, extremely urgent.)* I want you to stop that, Joe. That whole jail business!

Keller: *(Alarmed, therefore angered.)* Look at you, look at you shaking.

Mother: *(Trying to control herself, moving about clasping her hands.)* I can't help it.

Keller: What have I got to hide? What the hell is the matter with you, Kate?

Mother: I didn't say you had anything to hide, I'm just telling you to stop it! Now stop it! *(As Ann and Chris appear on porch. Ann is twenty-six, gentle but despite herself capable of holding fast to what she knows. Chris opens door for her.)*

Ann: Hya, Joe! *(She leads off a general laugh that is not self-conscious because they know one another too well.)*

Chris: *(Bringing Ann down, with an outstretched, chivalric arm.)* Take a breath of that air, kid. You never get air like that in New York.

Mother: *(Genuinely overcome with it.)* Annie, where did you get that dress!

Ann: I couldn't resist. I'm taking it right off before I ruin it. *(Swings around.)* How's that for three weeks' salary?

Mother: *(To Keller.)* Isn't she the most...? *(To Ann.)* It's gorgeous, simply gor...

Chris: *(To Mother.)* No kidding, now, isn't she the prettiest gal you ever saw?

Mother: *(Caught short by his obvious admiration, she finds herself reaching out for a glass of water and aspirin in his hand, and...)* You gained a little weight, didn't you, darling? *(She gulps pill and drinks.)*

Ann: It comes and goes.

Keller: Look how nice her legs turned out!

Ann: *(She runs to fence, left.)* Boy, the poplars got thick, didn't they?

Keller: *(Moves up to settee and sits.)* Well, it's three years, Annie. We're gettin' old, kid.

Mother: How does Mom like New York? *(Ann keeps looking through trees.)*

Ann: *(A little hurt.)* Why'd they take our hammock away?

Keller: Oh, no, it broke. Couple of years ago.

Mother: What broke? He had one of his light lunches and flopped into it.

Ann: *(She laughs and turns back toward Jim's yard...)* Oh, excuse me! *(Jim has come to fence and is looking over it. He is smoking a cigar. As she cries out, he comes on around on stage.)*

Jim: How do you do? *(To Chris.)* She looks very intelligent!

Chris: Ann, this is Jim...Doctor Bayliss.

Ann: *(Shaking Jim's hand.)* Oh, sure, he writes a lot about you.

Jim: Don't believe it. He likes everybody. In the battalion he was known as Mother McKeller.

Ann: I can believe it...You know—? *(To Mother.)* It's so strange seeing him come out of that yard. *(To Chris.)* I guess I never grew up. It almost seems that Mom and Pop are in there now. And you and my brother are doing Algebra, and Larry trying to copy my homework. Gosh, those dear dead days beyond recall.

Jim: Well, I hope that doesn't mean you want me to move out?

Sue: *(Calling from off left.)* Jim, come in here! Mr. Hubbard is on the phone!

Jim: I told you I don't want …

Sue: *(Commandingly sweet.)* Please, dear! Please!!

Jim: *(Resigned.)* All right, Susie, *(Trailing off.)* all right, all right… *(To Ann.)* I've only met you, Ann, but if I may offer you a piece of advice—When you marry, never—even in your mind—never count your husband's money.

Sue: *(From off.)* Jim?!

Jim: At once! *(Turns and goes left.)* At once. *(He exits left.)*

Mother: *(Ann is looking at her. She speaks meaningfully.)* I told her to take up the guitar. It'd be a common interest for them. *(They laugh.)* Well, he loves the guitar!

Ann: *(As though to overcome Mother, she becomes suddenly lively, crosses to Keller on settee, sits on his lap.)* Let's eat at the shore tonight! Raise some hell around here, like we used to before Larry went!

Mother: *(Emotionally.)* You think of him! You see? *(Triumphantly.)* She thinks of him!

Ann: *(With an uncomprehending smile.)* What do you mean, Kate?

Mother: Nothing. Just that you…remember him, he's in your thoughts.

Ann: That's a funny thing to say; how could I help remembering him?

Mother: *(It is drawing to a head the wrong way for her; she starts anew. She rises and comes to Ann.)* Did you hang up your things?

Ann: Yeah…*(To Chris.)* Say, you've sure gone in for clothes. I could hardly find room in the closet.

Mother: No, don't you remember? That's Larry's room.

Ann: You mean…they're Larry's?

Mother: Didn't you recognize them?

Ann: *(Slowly rising, a little embarrassed.)* Well, it never occurred to me that you'd … I mean the shoes are all shined.

Mother: Yes, dear. *(Slight pause. Ann can't stop staring at her. Mother breaks it by speaking with the relish of gossip, putting her arm around Ann and walking stage left with her.)* For so long I've been aching for a nice conversation with you, Annie. Tell me something.

Ann: What?

Mother: I don't know. Something nice.

Chris: *(Wryly.)* She means do you go out much?

Mother: Oh, shut up.

Keller: And are any of them serious?

Mother: *(Laughing, sits in her chair.)* Why don't you both choke?

Keller: Annie, you can't go into a restaurant with that woman any more. In five minutes thirty-nine strange people are sitting at the table telling her their life story.

Mother: If I can't ask Annie a personal question…

Keller: Askin' is all right, but don't beat her over the head. You're beatin' her, you're beatin' her. *(They are laughing.)*

Ann: *(To Mother. Takes pan of beans off stool, puts them on floor under chair and sits.)* Don't let them bulldoze you. Ask me anything you like. What do you want to know, Kate? Come on, let's gossip.

Mother: *(To Chris and Keller.)* She's the only one is got any sense. *(To Ann.)* Your mother…she's not getting a divorce, heh?

Ann: No, she's calmed down about it now. I think when he gets out they'll probably live together. In New York, of course.

Mother: That's fine. Because your father is still…I mean he's a decent man after all is said and done.

Ann: I don't care. She can take him back if she likes.

Mother: And you? You…*(Shakes her head negatively.)*…go out much? *(Slight pause.)*

Ann: *(Delicately.)* You mean am I still waiting for him?

Mother: Well, no. I don't expect you to wait for him but…

Ann: *(Kindly.)* But that's what you meant, isn't it?

Mother: …Well…yes.

Ann: Well, I'm not, Kate.

Mother: *(Faintly.)* You're not?

Ann: Isn't it ridiculous? You don't really imagine he's…?

Mother: I know, dear, but don't say it's ridiculous, because the papers were full of it; I don't know about New York, but there was half a page about a man missing even longer than Larry, and he turned up from Burma.

Chris: *(Coming to Ann.)* He couldn't have wanted to come home very badly, Mom.

Mother: Don't be so smart.

Chris: You can have a helluva time in Burma.

Ann: *(Rises and swings around in back of Chris.)* So I've heard.

Chris: Mother, I'll bet you money that you're the only woman in the country who after three years is still…

Mother: You're sure?

Chris: Yes, I am.

Mother: Well, if you're sure then you're sure. *(She turns her head away an instant.)* They don't say it on the radio but I'm sure that in the dark at night they're still waiting for their sons.

Chris: Mother, you're absolutely—

Mother: *(Waving him off.)* Don't be so damned smart! Now stop it! *(Slight pause.)* There are just a few things you *don't* know. All of you. And I'll tell you one of them, Annie. Deep, deep in your heart you've always been waiting for him.

Ann: *(Resolutely.)* No, Kate.

Mother: *(With increasing demand.)* But deep in your heart, Annie!

Chris: She ought to know, shouldn't she?

Mother: Don't let them tell you what to think. Listen to your heart. Only your heart.

Ann: Why does your heart tell you he's alive?

Mother: Because he has to be.

Ann: But why, Kate?

Mother: *(Going to her.)* Because certain things have to be, and certain things can never be. Like the sun has to rise, it has to be. That's why there's God. Otherwise anything could happen. But there's God, so certain things can never happen. I would know, Annie—just like the day he *(Indicates Chris.)* went into that terrible battle. Did he write me? Was it in the papers? No, but that morning I couldn't raise my head off the pillow. Ask Joe. Suddenly, I knew. I knew! And he was nearly killed that day. Ann, you *know* I'm right!

Ann: *(She stands there in silence, then turns trembling, going upstage.)* No, Kate.

Mother: I have to have some tea. *(Frank appears from left, carrying ladder.)*

Frank: Annie! *(Coming down.)* How are you, gee whiz!

Ann: *(Taking his hand.)* Why, Frank, you're losing your hair.

Keller: He's got responsibility.

Frank: Gee whiz!

Keller: Without Frank the stars wouldn't know when to come out.

Frank: *(Laughs. To Ann.)* You look more womanly. You've matured. You…

Keller: Take it easy, Frank, you're a married man.

Ann: *(As they laugh.)* You still haberdashering?

Frank: Why not? Maybe I too can get to be president.[2] How's your brother? Got his degree, I hear.

Ann: Oh, George has his own office now!

Frank: Don't say! *(Funereally.)* And your dad? Is he…?

Ann: *(Abruptly.)* Fine. I'll be in to see Lydia.

Frank: *(Sympathetically.)* How about it, does Dad expect a parole soon?

Ann: *(With growing ill-ease.)* I really don't know, I…

Frank: *(Staunchly defending her father for her sake.)* I mean because I feel, y'know, that if an intelligent man like your father is put in prison, there ought to be a law that says either you execute him, or let him go after a year.

Chris: *(Interrupting.)* Want a hand with that ladder, Frank?

Frank: *(Taking cue.)* That's all right, I'll… *(Picks up ladder.)* I'll finish the horoscope tonight, Kate. *(Embarrassed.)* See you later, Ann, you look wonderful. *(He exits right. They look at Ann.)*

Ann: *(To Chris, sits slowly on stool.)* Haven't they stopped talking about Dad?

Chris: *(Comes down and sits on arm of chair.)* Nobody talks about him any more.

Keller: *(Rises and comes to her.)* Gone and forgotten, kid.

Ann: Tell me. Because I don't want to meet anybody on the block if they're going to…

Chris: I don't want you to worry about it.

Ann: *(To Keller.)* Do they still remember the case, Joe? Do they talk about you?

Keller: The only one still talks about it is my wife.

---

[2] *get to be president*: President Harry Truman was a haberdasher, someone who sells men's clothing.

Mother: That's because you keep on playing policeman with the kids. All their parents hear out of you is jail, jail, jail.

Keller: Actually what happened was that when I got home from the penitentiary the kids got very interested in me. You know kids. I was *(Laughs.)* like the expert on the jail situation. And as time passed they got it confused and...I ended up a detective. *(Laughs.)*

Mother: Except that *they* didn't get it confused. *(To Ann.)* He hands out police badges from the Post Toasties boxes. *(They laugh.)*

Ann: *(Wondrously at them, happily. She rises and comes to Keller, putting her arm around his shoulder.)* Gosh, it's wonderful to hear you laughing about it.

Chris: Why, what'd you expect?

Ann: The last thing I remember on this block was one word—"Murderers!" Remember that, Kate?...Mrs. Hammond standing in front of our house and yelling that word...She's still around, I suppose?

Mother: They're all still around.

Keller: Don't listen to her. Every Saturday night the whole gang is playin' poker in this arbor. All the ones who yelled murderer takin' my money now.

Mother: Don't, Joe, she's a sensitive girl, don't fool her. *(To Ann.)* They still remember about Dad. It's different with him—*(Indicates Joe.)*—he was exonerated, your father's still there. That's why I wasn't so enthusiastic about your coming. Honestly, I know how sensitive you are and I told Chris, I said...

Keller: Listen, you do like I did and you'll be all right. The day I come home, I got out of my car;—but not in front of the house...on the corner. You should've been here, Annie, and you too, Chris; you'd-a seen something. Everybody knew I was getting out that day; the porches were loaded. Picture it now; none of them believed I was innocent. The story was, I pulled a fast one getting myself exonerated. So I get out of my car, and I walk down the street. But very slow. And with a smile. The beast! I was the beast; the guy who sold cracked cylinder heads to the Army Air Force; the guy who made twenty-one P-40's crash in Australia. Kid, walkin' down the street that day I was guilty as hell. Except I wasn't, and there as a court paper in my pocket to prove I wasn't, and I walked... past...the porches. Result? Fourteen months later I had one of the best shops in the state again, a respected man again; bigger than ever.

Chris: *(With admiration.)* Joe McGuts.

Keller: *(Now with great force.)* That's the only way you lick 'em is guts! *(To Ann.)* The worst thing you did was to move away from here. You made it tough for your father when he gets out. That's why I tell you, I like to see him move back right on this block.

Mother: *(Pained.)* How could they move back?

Keller: It ain't gonna end *till* they move back! *(To Ann.)* Till people play cards with him again, and talk with him, and smile with him—you play cards with a man you know he can't be a murderer. And the next time you write him I like you to tell him just what I said. *(Ann simply stares at him.)* You hear me?

Ann: *(Surprised.)* Don't you hold anything against him?

Keller: Annie, I never believed in crucifying people.

Ann: *(Mystified.)* But he was your partner, he dragged you through the mud...

Keller: Well, he ain't my sweetheart, but you gotta forgive, don't you?

Ann: You, either, Kate? Don't you feel any...?

Keller: *(To Ann.)* The next time you write Dad...

Ann: I don't write him.

Keller: *(Struck.)* Well, every now and then you...

Ann: *(A little ashamed, but determined.)* No, I've *never* written to him. Neither has my brother. *(To Chris.)* Say, do you feel this way, too?

Chris: He murdered twenty-one pilots.

Keller: What the hell kinda talk is that?

Mother: That's not a thing to say about a man.

Ann: What else can you say? When they took him away I followed him, went to him every visiting day. I was crying all the time. Until the news came about Larry. Then I realized. It's wrong to pity a man like that. Father or no father, there's only one way to look at him. He knowingly shipped out parts what would crash an airplane. And how do you know Larry wasn't one of them?

Mother: I was waiting for that. *(Going to her.)* As long as you're here, Annie, I want to ask you never to say that again.

Ann: You surprise me. I thought you'd be mad at him.

Mother: What your father did had nothing to do with Larry. Nothing.

Ann: But we can't know that.

Mother: *(Striving for control.)* As long as you're here!

Ann: *(Perplexed.)* But, Kate...

Mother: Put that out of your head!

Keller: Because...

Mother: *(Quickly to Keller.)* That's all, that's enough. *(Places her hand on her head.)* Come inside now, and have some tea with me. *(She turns and goes up steps.)*

Keller: *(To Ann.)* The one thing you...

Mother: *(Sharply.)* He's not dead, so there's no argument! Now come!

Keller: *(Angrily.)* In a minute! *(Mother turns and goes into house.)* Now look, Annie...

Chris: All right, Dad, forget it.

Keller: No, she dasn't feel that way. Annie...

Chris: I'm sick of the whole subject, now cut it out.

Keller: You want her to go on like this? *(To Ann.)* Those cylinder heads when into P-40's only. What's the matter with you? You know Larry never flew a P-40.

Chris: So who flew those P-40s, pigs?

Keller: The man was a fool, but don't make a murderer out of him. You got no sense? Look what it does to her! *(To Ann.)* Listen, you gotta appreciate what was doin' in that shop in the war. The both of you! It was a madhouse. Every half hour the Major callin' for cylinder heads, they were whippin' us with the telephone. The trucks were hauling them away hot, damn near. I mean just try to see it human, see it human. All of a sudden a batch comes out with a crack. That happens, that's the business. A fine, hairline crack. All right, so...so he's a little man, your father, always scared of loud voices. What'll the Major say?—Half a day's production shot...What'll I say? You know what I mean? Human. *(He pauses.)* So he takes out his tools and he...covers over the cracks. All right...that's bad, it's wrong, but that's what a little man does. If I could have gone in that day I'd a told him—junk 'em, Steve, we can afford it. But alone he was afraid. But I know he meant no harm. He believed they'd hold up a hundred percent. That's a mistake, but it ain't murder. You mustn't feel that way about him. You understand me? It ain't right.

Ann: *(She regards him a moment.)* Joe, Let's forget it.

Keller: Annie, the day the news came out about Larry he was in the next cell to mine...Dad. And he cried, Annie...he cried half the night.

Ann: *(Touched.)* He shoulda cried all night. *(Slight pause.)*

Keller: *(Almost angered.)* Annie, I do not understand why you...!

Chris: *(Breaking in—with nervous urgency.)* Are you going to stop it?!

Ann: Don't yell at him. He just wants everybody happy.

Keller: *(Clasps her around the waist, smiling.)* That's my sentiments. Can you stand steak?

Chris: And champagne?

Keller: Now you're operatin'! I'll call Swanson's for a table! Big time tonight, Annie!

Ann: Can't scare me.

Keller: *(To Chris, pointing at Ann.)* I like that girl. Wrap her up. *(They laugh. Goes up porch.)* You got nice legs, Annie!...I want to see everybody drunk tonight. *(Pointing to Chris.)* Look at him, he's blushin'! *(He exits, laughing, into house.)*

Chris: *(Calling after him.)* Drink your tea, Casanova. *(He turns to Ann.)* Isn't he a great guy?

Ann: You're the only one I know who loves his parents!

Chris: I know. It went out of style, didn't it?

Ann: *(With a sudden touch of sadness.)* It's all right. It's a good thing. *(She looks about.)* You know? It's lovely here. The air is sweet.

Chris: *(Hopefully.)* You're not sorry you came?

Ann: Not sorry, no. But I'm...not going to stay...

Chris: Why?

Ann: In the first place, your mother as much as told me to go.

Chris: Well...

Ann: You saw that...and then you...you've been kind of...

Chris: What?

Ann: Well...kind of embarrassed ever since I got here.

Chris: The trouble is I planned on kind of sneaking up on you over a period of a week or so. But they take it for granted that we're all set.

Ann: I knew they would. Your mother anyway.

Chris: How did you know?

Ann: From *her* point of view, why else would I come?

Chris: Well...would you want to? *(Ann studies him.)* I guess you know this is why I asked you to come.

Ann: I guess this is why I came.

Chris: Ann, I love you. I love you a great deal. *(Finally.)* I love you. *(Pause. She waits.)* I have no imagination...that's all I know to tell you. *(Ann, waiting, ready.)* I'm embarrassing you. I didn't want to tell it to you here. I wanted some place we'd never been; a place where we'd be brand new to each other...You feel it's wrong here, don't you? This yard, this chair? I want you to be ready for me. I don't want to win you away from anything.

Ann: *(Putting her arms around him.)* Oh, Chris, I've been ready a long, long time!

Chris: Then he's gone forever. You're sure.

Ann: I almost got married two years ago.

Chris: ...why didn't you?

Ann: You started to write me... *(Slight pause.)*

Chris: You felt something that far back?

Ann: Every day since!

Chris: Ann, why didn't you let me know?

Ann: I was waiting for you, Chris. Till then you never wrote. And when you did, what did you say? You sure can be ambiguous, you know.

Chris: *(He looks toward house, then at her, trembling.)* Give me a kiss, Ann. Give me a... *(They kiss.)* God, I kissed you, Annie, I kissed Annie. How long, how long I've been waiting to kiss you!

Ann: I'll never forgive you. Why did you wait all these years? All I've done is sit and wonder if I was crazy for thinking of you.

Chris: Annie, we're going to live now! I'm going to make you so happy. *(He kisses her, but without their bodies touching.)*

Ann: *(A little embarrassed.)* Not like that you're not.

Chris: I kissed you...

Ann: Like Larry's brother. Do it like you, Chris. *(He breaks away from her abruptly.)* What is it, Chris?

Chris: Let's drive some place...I want to be alone with you.

Ann: No...what is it, Chris, your mother?

Chris: No...nothing like that...

Ann: Then what's wrong?...Even in your letters, there was something ashamed.

Chris: Yes. I suppose I have been. But it's going from me.

Ann: You've got to tell me—

Chris: I don't know how to start. *(He takes her hand. He speaks quietly, factually at first.)*

Ann: It wouldn't work this way. *(Slight pause.)*

Chris: It's all mixed up with so many other things...You remember, overseas, I was in command of a company?

Ann: Yeah, sure.

Chris: Well, I lost them.

Ann: How many?

Chris: Just about all.

Ann: Oh, gee!

Chris: It takes a little time to toss that off. Because they weren't just men. For instance, one time it'd been raining several days and this kid came to me, and gave me his last pair of dry socks. Put them in my pocket. That's only a little thing…but…that's the kind of guys I had. They didn't die; they killed themselves for each other. I mean that exactly; a little more selfish and they'd 've been here today. And I got an idea—watching them go down. Everything was being destroyed, see, but it seemed to me that one new thing was made. A kind of…responsibility. Man for man. You understand me?—To show that, to bring that on to the earth again like some kind of a monument and everyone would feel it standing there, behind him, and it would make a difference to him. *(Pause.)* And then I came home and it was incredible. I….there was no meaning in it here; the whole thing to them was a kind of a—bus accident. I went to work with Dad, and that rat-race again. I felt…what you said…ashamed somehow. Because nobody was changed at all. It seemed to make suckers out of a lot of guys. I felt wrong to be alive, to open the bank-book, to drive the new car, to see the new refrigerator. I mean you can take those things out of a war, but when you drive that car you've got to know that it came out of the love a man can have for a man, you've got to be a little better because of that. Otherwise what you have is really loot, and there's blood on it. I didn't want to take any of it. And I guess that included you.

Ann: And you still feel that way?

Chris: I want you now, Annie.

Ann: Because you mustn't feel that way any more. Because you have a right to whatever you have. Everything, Chris, understand that? To me, too… And the money, there's nothing wrong in your money. Your father put hundreds of planes in the air, you should be proud. A man should be paid for that…

Chris: Oh Annie, Annie…I'm going to make a fortune for you!

Keller: *(Offstage.)* Hello…Yes. Sure.

Ann: *(Laughing softly.)* What'll I do with a fortune…? *(They kiss. Keller enters from house.)*

Keller: *(Thumbing toward house.)* Hey, Ann, your brother… *(They step apart shyly. Keller comes down, and wryly…)* What is this, Labor Day[3]?

Chris: *(Waving him away, knowing the kidding will be endless.)* All right, all right…

Ann: You shouldn't burst out like that.

Keller: Well, nobody told me it was Labor Day. *(Looks around.)* Where's the hot dogs?

---

[3] *Labor Day.* Kissing booths were often featured at Labor Day celebrations.

Chris: *(Loving it.)* All right. You said it once.

Keller: Well, as long as I know it's Labor Day from now on, I'll wear a bell around my neck.

Ann: *(Affectionately.)* He's so subtle!

Chris: George Bernard Shaw[4] as an elephant.

Keller: George!—hey, you kissed it out of my head—your brother's on the phone.

Ann: *(Surprised.)* My brother?

Keller: Yeah, George. Long distance.

Ann: What's the matter, is anything wrong?

Keller: I don't know, Kate's talking to him. Hurry up, she'll cost him five dollars.

Ann: *(She takes a step upstage, then comes down toward Chris.)* I wonder if we ought to tell your mother yet? I mean I'm not very good in an argument.

Chris: We'll wait till tonight. After dinner. Now don't get tense, just leave it to me.

Keller: What're you telling her?

Chris: Go ahead, Ann. *(With misgivings, Ann goes up and into house.)* We're getting married, Dad. *(Keller nods indecisively.)* Well, don't you say anything?

Keller: *(Distracted.)* I'm glad, Chris, I'm just...George is calling from Columbus.

Chris: Columbus!

Keller: Did Annie tell you he was going to see his father today?

Chris: No, I don't think she knew anything about it.

Keller: *(Asking uncomfortably.)* Chris! You...you think you know her pretty good?

Chris: *(Hurt and apprehensive.)* What kind of question?

Keller: I'm just wondering. All these years George don't go to see his father. Suddenly he goes...and she comes here.

Chris: Well, what about it?

Keller: It's crazy, but it comes to my mind. She don't hold nothin' against me, does she?

Chris: *(Angry.)* I don't know what you're talking about.

Keller: *(A little more combatively.)* I'm just talkin'. To his last day in court the man blamed it all on me; and this is his daughter. I mean if she was sent here to find out something?

Chris: *(Angered.)* Why? What is there to find out?

Ann: *(On phone, offstage.)* Why are you so excited, George? What happened there?

Keller: I mean if they want to open up the case again, for the nuisance value[5], to hurt us?

---

[4]*George Bernard Shaw*: George Bernard Shaw (1856–1950) was an Irish playwright.

[5]*nuisance value*: The amount of money a defendant will pay to a plaintiff in exchange for the plaintiff to stop pursuing a case.

(Together.)

Chris: Dad...how could you think that of her?

Ann: *(Still on phone.)* But what did he say to you, for God's sake?

Keller: It couldn't be, heh. You know.

Chris: Dad, you amaze me...

Keller: *(Breaking in.)* All right, forget it, forget it. *(With great force, moving about.)* I want a clean start for you, Chris. I want a new sign over the plant—Christopher Keller, Incorporated.

Chris: *(A little uneasily.)* J. O. Keller is good enough.

Keller: We'll talk about it. I'm going to build you a house, stone, with a driveway from the road. I want you to spread out, Chris, I want you to use what I made for you...*(He is close to him now.)*...I mean, with joy, Chris, without shame...with joy.

Chris: *(Touched.)* I will, Dad.

Keller: *(With deep emotion.)* ...Say it to me.

Chris: Why?

Keller: Because sometimes I think you're...ashamed of the money.

Chris: No, don't feel that.

Keller: Because it's good money, there's nothing wrong with that money.

Chris: *(A little frightened.)* Dad, you don't have to tell me this.

Keller: *(With overriding affection and self-confidence now. He grips Chris by the back of the neck, and with laughter between his determined jaws.)* Look, Chris, I'll go to work on Mother for you. We'll get her so drunk tonight we'll all get married! *(Steps away, with a wide gesture of his arm.)* There's gonna be a wedding, kid, like there never was seen! Champagne, tuxedos...!

(He breaks off as Ann's voice comes out loud from the house where she is still talking on phone.)

Ann: Simply because when you get excited you don't control yourself... *(Mother comes out of house.)* Well, what did he tell you for God's sake? *(Pause.)* All right, come then. *(Pause.)* Yes, they'll all be here. Nobody's running away from you. And try to get hold of yourself, will you? *(Pause.)* All right, all right. Goodbye. *(There is a brief pause as Ann hangs up receiver, then comes out of kitchen.)*

Chris: Something happen?

Keller: He's coming here?

Ann: On the seven o'clock. He's in Columbus. *(To Mother.)* I told him it would be all right.

Keller: Sure, fine! Your father took sick?

Ann: *(Mystified.)* No, George didn't say he was sick. I... *(Shaking it off.)* I don't know, I suppose it's something stupid, you know my brother... *(She comes to Chris.)* Let's go for a drive, or something...

Chris: Sure. Give me the keys, Dad.

Mother: Drive through the park. It's beautiful now.

Chris: Come on, Ann. *(To them.)* Be back right away.

Ann: *(As she and Chris exit up driveway.)* See you. *(Mother comes down toward Keller, her eyes fixed on him.)*

Keller: Take your time. *(To Mother.)* What does George want?

Mother: He's been in Columbus since this morning with Steve. He's gotta see Annie right away, he says.

Keller: What for?

Mother: I don't know. *(She speaks with warning.)* He's a lawyer now, Joe. George is a lawyer. All these years he never even sent a postcard to Steve. Since he got back from the war, not a post-card.

Keller: So what?

Mother: *(Her tension breaking out.)* Suddenly he takes an airplane from New York to see him. An airplane!

Keller: Well? So?

Mother: *(Trembling.)* Why?

Keller: I don't read minds. Do you?

Mother: Why, Joe? What has Steve suddenly got to tell him that he takes an airplane to see him?

Keller: What do I care what Steve's got to tell him?

Mother: You're sure, Joe?

Keller: *(Frightened, but angry.)* Yes, I'm sure.

Mother: *(She sits stiffly in a chair.)* Be smart now, Joe. The boy is coming. Be smart.

Keller: *(Desperately.)* Once and for all, did you hear what I said? I said I'm sure!

Mother: *(She nods weakly.)* All right, Joe. *(He straightens up.)* Just...be smart. *(Keller, in hopeless fury, looks at her, turns around, goes up to porch and into house, slamming screen door violently behind him. Mother sits in chair downstage, stiffly, staring, seeing.)*

CURTAIN

ACT TWO

As twilight falls, that evening.

On the rise, Chris is discovered at right, sawing the broken-off tree, leaving stump standing alone. He is dressed in good pants, white shoes, but without a shirt. He disappears with tree up the alley when Mother appears on porch. She comes down and stands watching him. She has on a dressing-gown, carries a tray of grape-juice drink in a pitcher, and glasses with sprigs of mint in them.

Mother: *(Calling up alley)* Did you have to put on good pants to do that? *(She comes downstage and puts tray on table in the arbor. Then looks around uneasily, then feels pitcher for coolness. Chris enters from alley brushing off his hands.)* You notice there's more light with that thing gone?

Chris: Why aren't you dressing?

Mother: It's suffocating upstairs. I made a grape drink for Georgie. He always liked grape. Come and have some.

Chris: *(Impatiently.)* Well, come on, get dressed. And what's Dad sleeping so much for? *(He goes to table and pours a glass of juice.)*

Mother: He's worries. When he's worried he sleeps. *(Pauses. Looks into his eyes.)* We're dumb, Chris. Dad and I are stupid people. We don't know anything. You've got to protect us.

Chris: You're silly; what's there to be afraid of?

Mother: To his last day in court Steve never gave up the idea that Dad made him do it. If they're going to open the case again I won't live through it.

Chris: George is just a damn fool, Mother. How can you take him seriously?

Mother: That family hates us. Maybe even Annie...

Chris: Oh, now, Mother...

Mother: You think just because you like everybody, they like you!

Chris: All right, stop working yourself up. Just leave everything to me.

Mother: When George goes home tell her to go with him.

Chris: *(Non-committally.)* Don't worry about Annie.

Mother: Steve is her father, too.

Chris: Are you going to cut it out? Now, come.

Mother: *(Going upstage with him.)* You don't realize how people can hate, Chris, they can hate so much they'll tear the world to pieces... *(Ann, dressed up, appears on porch.)*

Chris: Look! She's dressed already. *(As he and Mother mount porch.)* I've just got to put on a shirt.

Ann: *(In a preoccupied way.)* Are you feeling well, Kate?

Mother: What's the difference, dear. There are certain people, y'know, the sicker they get the longer they live. *(She goes into house.)*

Chris: You look nice.

Ann: We're going to tell her tonight.

Chris: Absolutely, don't worry about it.

Ann: I wish we could tell her now. I can't stand scheming. My stomach gets hard.

Chris: It's not scheming, we'll just get her in a better mood.

Mother: *(Offstage, in the house.)* Joe, are you going to sleep all day!

Ann: *(Laughing.)* The only one who's relaxed is your father. He's fast asleep.

Chris: I'm relaxed.

Ann: Are you?

Chris: Look. *(He holds out his hand and makes it shake.)* Let me know when George gets here. *(He goes into the house. She moves aimlessly, and then is drawn toward tree stump. She goes to it, hesitantly touches broken top in the hush of her thoughts. Offstage Lydia calls, "Johnny! Come get your supper!" Sue enters from left, and halts, seeing Ann.)*

Sue: Is my husband...?

Ann: *(Turns, startled.)* Oh!

Sue: I'm terribly sorry.

Ann: It's all right, I...I'm just a little silly about the dark.

Sue: *(Looks about.)* It's getting dark.

Ann: Are you looking for your husband?

Sue: As usual. *(Laughs tiredly.)* He spends so much time here, they'll be charging him rent.

Ann: Nobody was dressed so he drove over to the depot to pick up my brother.

Sue: Oh, your brother's in?

Ann: Yeah, they ought to be here any minute now. Will you have a cold drink?

Sue: I will, thanks. *(Ann goes to table and pours.)* My husband. Too hot to drive me to beach.—Men are like little boys; for the neighbors they'll always cut the grass.

Ann: People like to do things for the Kellers. Been that way since I can remember.

Sue: It's amazing. I guess your brother's coming to give you away, heh?

Ann: *(Giving her drink.)* I don't know. I suppose

Sue: You must be all nerved up.

Ann: It's always a problem getting yourself married, isn't it?

Sue: That depends on your shape, of course. I don't see why you should have had a problem.

Ann: I've had chances—

Sue: I'll bet. It's romantic…it's very unusual to me, marrying the brother of your sweetheart.

Ann: I don't know. I think it's mostly that whenever I need somebody to tell me the truth I've always thought of Chris. When he tells you something you know it's so. He relaxes me.

Sue: And he's got money. That's important, you know.

Ann: It wouldn't matter to me.

Sue: You'd be surprised. It makes all the difference. I married an intern. On my salary. And that was bad, because as soon as a woman supports a man he owes her something. You can never owe somebody without resenting them. *(Ann laughs.)* That's true, you know.

Ann: Underneath, I think the doctor is very devoted.

Sue: Oh, certainly. But it's bad when a man always sees the bars in front of him. Jim thinks he's in jail all the time.

Ann: Oh…

Sue: That's why I've been intending to ask you a small favor, Ann…it's something very important to me.

Ann: Certainly, if I can do it.

Sue: You can. When you take up housekeeping, try to find a place away from here.

Ann: Are you fooling?

Sue: I'm very serious. My husband is unhappy with Chris around.

Ann: How is that?

Sue: Jim's a successful doctor. But he's got an idea he'd like to do medical research. Discover things. You see?

Ann: Well, isn't that good?

Sue: Research pays twenty-five dollars a week minus laundering the hair shirt. You've got to give up your life to go into it.

Ann: How does Chris?

Sue: *(With growing feeling.)* Chris makes people want to be better than it's possible to be. He does that to people.

Ann: Is that bad?

Sue: My husband has a family, dear. Every time he has a session with Chris he feels as though he's compromising by not giving up everything for research. As though Chris or anybody else isn't compromising. It happens with Jim every couple of years. He meets a man and makes a statue out of him.

Ann: Maybe he's right. I don't mean that Chris is a statue, but…

Sue: Now darling, you know he's not right.

Ann: I don't agree with you. Chris…

Sue: Let's face it, dear. Chris is working with his father, isn't he? He's taking money out of that business every week in the year.

Ann: What of it?

Sue: You ask me what of it?

Ann: I certainly do. *(She seems about to burst out.)* You oughtn't cast aspersions like that, I'm surprised at you.

Sue: You're surprised at me!

Ann: He'd never take five cents out of that plant if there was anything wrong in it.

Sue: You know that.

Ann: I know it. I resent everything you've said.

Sue: *(Moving toward her.)* You know what I resent, dear?

Ann: Please, I don't want to argue.

Sue: I resent living next to the Holy Family. It makes me look like a bum, you understand?

Ann: I can't do anything about that.

Sue: Who is he to ruin a man's life? Everybody knows Joe pulled a fast one to get out of jail.

Ann: That's not true!

Sue: Then why don't you go out and talk to people? Go on, talk to them. There's not a person on the block who doesn't know the truth.

Ann: That's a lie. People come here all the time for cards and…

Sue: So what? They give him credit for being smart. I do, too, I've got nothing against Joe. But if Chris wants people to put on the hair shirt let him take off his broadcloth. He's driving my husband crazy with that phony idealism of his, and I'm at the end of my rope on it! *(Chris enters on porch, wearing shirt and tie now. She turns quickly, hearing. With a smile.)* Hello, darling. How's Mother?

Chris: I thought George came.

Sue: No, it was just us.

Chris: *(Coming down to them.)* Susie, do me a favor, heh? Go up to Mother and see if you can calm her. She's all worked up.

Sue: She still doesn't know about you two?

Chris: *(Laughs a little.)* Well, she senses it, I guess. You know my mother.

Sue: *(Going up to porch.)* Oh, yeah, she's psychic.

Chris: Maybe there's something in the medicine chest.

Sue: I'll give her one of everything. *(On porch.)* Don't worry about Kate; couple of drinks, dance her around a little...she'll love Ann. *(To Ann.)* Because you're the female version of him. *(Chris laughs.)* Don't be alarmed, I said version. *(She goes into house.)*

Chris: Interesting woman, isn't she?

Ann: Yeah, she's very interesting.

Chris: She's a great nurse, you know, she...

Ann: *(In tension, but trying to control it.)* Are you still doing that?

Chris: *(Sensing something wrong, but still smiling.)* Doing what?

Ann: As soon as you get to know somebody you find a distinction for them. How do you know she's a great nurse?

Chris: What's the matter, Ann?

Ann: The woman hates you. She despises you!

Chris: Hey...what's hit you?

Ann: Gee, Chris...

Chris: What happened here?

Ann: You never...Why didn't you tell me?

Chris: Tell you what?

Ann: She says they think Joe is guilty.

Chris: What difference does it make what they think?

Ann: I don't care what they think, I just don't understand why you took the trouble to deny it. You said it was all forgotten.

Chris: I didn't want you to feel there was anything wrong in you coming here, that's all. I know a lot of people think my father was guilty, and I assumed there might be some question in your mind.

Ann: But I never once said I suspected him.

Chris: Nobody says it.

Ann: Chris, I know how much you love him, but it could never...

Chris: Do you think I could forgive him if he'd done that thing?

Ann: I'm not here out of a blue sky, Chris. I turned my back on my father, if there's anything wrong here now...

Chris: I know that, Ann.

Ann: George is coming from Dad, and I don't think it's with a blessing.

Chris: He's welcome here. You've got nothing to fear from George.

Ann: Tell me that...just tell me that.

Chris: The man is innocent, Ann. Remember he was falsely accused once and it put him through hell. How would you behave if you were faced with the same thing again? Annie, believe me, there's nothing wrong for you here, believe me, kid.

Ann: All right, Chris, all right. *(They embrace as Keller appears quietly on porch. Ann simply studies him.)*

Keller: Every time I come out here it looks like Playland! *(They break and laugh in embarrassment.)*

Chris: I thought you were going to shave?

Keller: *(Sitting on bench.)* In a minute. I just woke up, I can't see nothin'.

Ann: You look shaved.

Keller: Oh, no. *(Massages his jaw.)* Gotta be extra special tonight. Big night, Annie. So how's it feel to be a married woman?

Ann: *(Laughs.)* I don't know, yet.

Keller: *(To Chris.)* What's the matter, you slippin'? *(He takes a little box of apples from under the bench as they talk.)*

Chris: The great roué!

Keller: What is that, roué?

Chris: It's French.

Keller: Don't talk dirty. *(They laugh.)*

Chris: *(To Ann.)* You ever meet a bigger ignoramus?

Keller: Well, somebody's got to make a living.

Ann: *(As they laugh.)* That's telling him.

Keller: I don't know, everbody's gettin' so Goddam educated in this country there'll be nobody to take away the garbage. *(They laugh.)* It's gettin' so the only dumb ones left are the bosses.

Ann: You're not so dumb, Joe.

Keller: I know, but you go into our plant, for instance. I got so many lieutenants, majors and colonels that I'm ashamed to ask somebody to sweep the floor. I gotta be careful I'll insult somebody. No kiddin'. It's a tragedy: you stand on the street today and spit, you're gonna hit a college man.

Chris: Well, don't spit.

Keller: *(Breaks apple in half, passing it to Ann and Chris.)* I mean to say, it's comin' to a pass. *(He takes a breath.)* I been thinkin', Annie...your brother, George. I been thinkin' about your brother George. When he comes I like you to *brooch* something to him.

Chris: Broach.

Keller: What's the matter with brooch?

Chris: *(Smiling.)* It's not English.

Keller: When I went to night school it was brooch.

Ann: *(Laughing.)* Well, in day school it's broach.

Keller: Don't surround me, will you? Seriously, Ann...You say he's not well. George, I been thinkin', why should he knock himself out in New York with that cut-throat competition, when I got so many friends here; I'm very friendly with some big lawyers in town. I could set George up here.

Ann: That's awfully nice of you, Joe.

Keller: No, kid, it ain't nice of me. I want you to understand me. I'm thinking of Chris. *(Slight pause.)* See...this is what I mean. You get older, you want to feel that you...accomplished something. My only accomplishment is my son. I ain't brainy. That's all I accomplished. Now, a year, eighteen months, your father'll be a free man. Who is he going to come to, Annie? His baby. You. He'll come, old, mad, into your house.

Ann: That can't matter any more, Joe.

Keller: I don't want that hate to come between us. *(Gestures between Chris and himself.)*

Ann: I can only tell you that that could never happen.

Keller: You're in love now, Annie, but believe me, I'm older than you and I know—a daughter is a daughter, and a father is a father. And it could happen. *(He pauses.)* I like you and George to go to him in prison and tell him…"Dad, Joe wants to bring you into the business when you get out."

Ann: *(Surprised, even shocked.)* You'd have him as a partner?

Keller: No, no partner. A good job. *(Pause. He sees she is shocked, a little mystified. He gets up, speaks more nervously.)* I want him to know, Annie… while he's sitting there I want him to know that when he gets out he's got a place waitin' for him. It'll take his bitterness away. To know you got a place…it sweetens you.

Ann: Joe, you owe him nothing.

Keller: I owe him a good kick in the teeth, but he's your father…

Chris: Then kick him in the teeth! I don't want him in the plant, so that's that! You understand? And besides, don't talk about him like that. People misunderstand you!

Keller: And I don't understand why she has to crucify the man.

Chris: Well, it's her father, if she feels…

Keller: No, no…

Chris: *(Almost angrily.)* What's it to you? Why…?

Keller: *(A commanding outburst in his high nervousness.)* A father is a father! *(As though the outburst had revealed him, he looks about, wanting to retract it. His hand goes to his cheek.)* I better…I better shave. *(He turns and a smile is on his face. To Ann.)* I didn't mean to yell at you, Annie.

Ann: Let's forget the whole thing, Joe.

Keller: Right. *(To Chris.)* She's likeable.

Chris: *(A little peeved at the man's stupidity.)* Shave, will you?

Keller: Right again.

(As he turns to porch Lydia comes hurrying from her house, right.)

Lydia: I forgot all about it…*(Seeing Chris and Ann.)* Hya. *(To Joe.)* I promised to fix Kate's hair for tonight. Did she comb it yet?

Keller: Always a smile, hey, Lydia?

Lydia: Sure, why not?

Keller: *(Going up on porch.)* Come on up and comb my Katie's hair. *(Lydia goes up on porch.)* She's got a big night, make her beautiful.

Lydia: I will.

Keller: *(He holds door open for her and she goes into kitchen. To Chris and Ann.)* Hey, that could be a song. *(He sings softly.)*

"Come on up and comb my Katie's hair…

Oh, come on up, 'cause she's my lady fair—"

(To Ann.) How's that for one year of night school? *(He continues singing as he goes into kitchen.)* "Oh, come on up, come on up, and comb my lady's hair—"

(Jim Bayliss rounds corner of driveway, walking rapidly. Jim crosses to Chris, motions him up and pulls him down to stage left, excitedly. Keller stands just inside kitchen door, watching them.)

Chris: What's the matter? Where is he?

Jim: Where's your mother?

Chris: Upstairs, dressing.

Ann: *(Crossing to them rapidly.)* What happened to George?

Jim: I asked him to wait in the car. Listen to me now. Can you take some advice? *(They wait.)* Don't bring him in here.

Ann: Why?

Jim: Kate is in bad shape, you can't explode this in front of her.

Ann: Explode what?

Jim: You know why he's here, don't try to kid it away. There's blood in his eye; drive him somewhere and talk to him alone.

(Ann turns to go up drive, takes a couple of steps, sees Keller and stops. He goes quietly on into house.)

Chris: *(Shaken, and therefore angered.)* Don't be an old lady.

Jim: He's come to take her home. What does that mean? *(To Ann.)* You know what that means. Fight it out with him some place else.

Ann: *(She comes back down toward Chris.)* I'll drive...him somewhere.

Chris: *(Goes to her.)* No.

Jim: Will you stop being an idiot?

Chris: Nobody's afraid of him here. Cut that out! *(He starts for driveway, but is brought up short by George, who enters there. George is Chris's age, but a paler man, now on the edge of his self-restraint. He speaks quietly, as though afraid to find himself screaming. An instant's hesitation and Chris steps up to him, hand extended, smiling.)* Helluva way to do; what're you sitting out there for?

George: Doctor said your mother isn't well, I...

Chris: So what? She'd want to see you, wouldn't she? We've been waiting for you all afternoon. *(He puts his hand on George's arm, but George pulls away, coming across toward Ann.)*

Ann: *(Touching his collar.)* This is filthy, didn't you bring another shirt? *(George breaks away from her, and moves down and left, examining the yard. Door opens, and he turns rapidly, thinking it is Kate, but it's Sue. She looks at him; he turns away and moves on left, to fence. He looks over it at his former home. Sue comes downstage.)*

Sue: *(Annoyed.)* How about the beach, Jim?

Jim: Oh, it's too hot to drive.

Sue: How'd you get to the station—Zeppelin?

Chris: This is Mrs. Bayliss, George. *(Calling, as George pays no attention, staring at house off left.)* George! *(George turns.)* Mrs. Bayliss.

Sue: How do you do.

George: *(Removing his hat.)* You're the people who bought our house, aren't you?

Sue: That's right. Come and see what we did with it before you leave.

George: *(He walks down and away from her.)* I liked it the way it was.

Sue: *(After a brief pause.)* He's frank, isn't he?

Jim: *(Pulling her off left.)* See you later…Take it easy, fella. *(They exit, left.)*

Chris: *(Calling after them.)* Thanks for driving him! *(Turning to George.)* How about some grape juice? Mother made it especially for you.

George: *(With forced appreciation.)* Good old Kate, remembered my grape juice.

Chris: You drank enough of it in this house. How've you been, George?—Sit down.

George: *(He keeps moving.)* It takes me a minute. *(Looking around.)* It seems impossible.

Chris: What?

George: I'm back here.

Chris: Say, you've gotten a little nervous, haven't you?

George: Yeah, toward the end of the day. What're you, big executive now?

Chris: Just kind of medium. How's the law?

George: I don't know. When I was studying in the hospital it seemed sensible, but outside there doesn't seem to be much of a law. The trees got thick, didn't they? *(Points to stump.)* What's that?

Chris: Blew down last night. We had it there for Larry. You know.

George: Why, afraid you'll forget him?

Chris: *(Starts for George.)* Kind of remark is that?

Ann: *(Breaking in, putting a restraining hand on Chris.)* When did you start wearing a hat?

George: *(Discovers hat in his hand.)* Today. From now on I decided to look like a lawyer, anyway. *(He holds it up to her.)* Don't you recognize it?

Ann: Why? Where…?

George: Your father's…he asked me to wear it.

Ann: How is he?

George: He got smaller.

Ann: Smaller?

George: Yeah, little. *(Holds out his hand to measure.)* He's a little man. That's what happens to suckers, you know. It's good I went to him in time—another year there'd be nothing left but his smell.

Chris: What's the matter, George, what's the trouble?

George: The trouble? The trouble is when you make suckers out of people once, you shouldn't try to do it twice.

Chris: What does that mean?

George: *(To Ann.)* You're not married yet, are you?

Ann: George, will you sit down and stop—?

George: Are you married yet?

Ann: No, I'm not married yet.

George: You're not going to marry him.

Ann: Why am I not going to marry him?

George: Because his father destroyed your family.

Chris: Now look, George…

George: Cut it short, Chris. Tell her to come home with me. Let's not argue, you know what I've got to say.

Chris: George, you don't want to be the voice of God, do you?

George: I'm…

Chris: That's been your trouble all your life, George, you dive into things. What kind of a statement is that to make? You're a big boy now.

George: I'm a big boy now.

Chris: Don't come bulling in here. If you've got something to say, be civilized about it.

George: Don't civilize me!

Ann: Shhh!

Chris: *(Ready to hit him.)* Are you going to talk like a grown man or aren't you?

Ann: *(Quickly, to forestall an outburst.)* Sit down, dear. Don't be angry, what's the matter? *(He allows her to seat him, looking at her.)* Now what happened? You kissed me when I left, now you…

George: *(Breathlessly.)* My life turned upside down since then. I couldn't go back to work when you left. I wanted to go to Dad and tell him you were going to be married. It seemed impossible not to tell him. He loved you so much… *(He pauses.)* Annie…we did a terrible thing. We can never be forgiven. Not even to send him a card at Christmas. I didn't see him once since I got home from the war! Annie, you don't know what was done to that man. You don't know what happened.

Ann: *(Afraid.)* Of course I know.

George: You can't know, you wouldn't be here. Dad came to work that day. The night foreman came to him and showed him the cylinder heads… they were coming out of the process with defects. There was something wrong with the process. So Dad went directly to the phone and called here and told Joe to come down right away. But the morning passed. No sign of Joe. So Dad called again. By this time he had over a hundred defectives. The Army was screaming for stuff and Dad didn't have anything to ship. So Joe told him… on the phone he told him to weld, cover up the cracks in any way he could, and ship them out.

Chris: Are you through now?

George: *(Surging up at him.)* I'm not through now! *(Back to Ann.)* Dad was afraid. He wanted Joe there if he was going to do it. But Joe can't come down…he's sick. Sick! He suddenly gets the flu! Suddenly! But he promised to take responsibility. Do you understand what I'm saying? On the telephone you can't have responsibility! In a court you can always deny a phone call and that's exactly what he did. They knew he was a liar the first time, but in the appeal they believed that rotten lie and now Joe is a big shot and your father is the patsy. *(He gets up.)* Now what're you going to do? Eat his food, sleep in his bed? Answer me; what're you going to do?

Chris: What are you going to do, George?

George: He's too smart for me, I can't prove a phone call.

Chris: Then how dare you come in here with that rot?

Ann: George, the court…

George: The court didn't know your father! But you know him. You know in your heart Joe did it.

Chris: *(Whirling him around.)* Lower your voice or I'll throw you out of here!

George: She knows. She knows.

Chris: *(To Ann.)* Get him out of here, Ann. Get him out of here.

Ann: George, I know everything you've said. Dad told me that whole thing in court, and they…

George: *(Almost a scream.)* The court did not know him, Annie!

Ann: Shhh!… But he'll say anything, George. You know how quick he can lie.

George: *(Turning to Chris, with deliberation.)* I'll ask you something, and look me in the eye when you answer me.

Chris: I'll look you in the eye.

George: You know your father…

Chris: I know him well.

George: And he's the kind of boss to let a hundred and twenty-one cylinder heads be repaired and shipped out of his shop without even knowing it?

Chris: He's that kind of boss.

George: And that's the same Joe Keller who never left his shop without first going around to see that all the lights were out.

Chris: *(With growing anger.)* The same Joe Keller.

George: The same man who knows how many minutes a day his workers spend in the toilet.

Chris: The same man.

George: And my father, that frightened mouse who'd never buy a shirt without somebody along—that man would dare do such a thing on his own?

Chris: On his own. And because he's a frightened mouse this is another thing he'd do;—throw the blame on somebody else because he's not man enough to take it himself. He tried it in court but it didn't work, but with a fool like you it works!

George: Oh, Chris, you're a liar to yourself!

Ann: *(Deeply shaken.)* Don't talk like that!

Chris: *(Sits facing George.)* Tell me, George. What happened? The court record was good enough for you all these years, why isn't it good now? Why did you believe it all these years?

George: *(After a slight pause.)* Because you believed it…That's the truth, Chris. I believed everything, because I thought you did. But today I heard it from his mouth. From his mouth it's altogether different than the record. Anyone who knows him, and knows your father, will believe it from his mouth. Your Dad took everything we have. I can't beat that. But she's one item he's not going to grab. *(He turns to Ann.)* Get your things. Everything they have is covered with blood. You're not the kind of girl who can live with that. Get your things.

Chris: Ann…you're not going to believe that, are you?

Ann: *(She goes to him.)* You know it's not true, don't you?

George: How can he tell you? It's his father. *(To Chris.)* None of these things ever even cross your mind?

Chris: Yes, they crossed my mind. Anything can cross your mind!

George: He *knows*, Annie. He knows!

Chris: The Voice of God!

George: Then why isn't your name on the business? Explain that to her!

Chris: What the hell has that got to do with...?

George: Annie, why isn't his name on it?

Chris: Even when I don't own it!

George: Who're you kidding? Who gets it when he dies? *(To Ann.)* Open your eyes, you know the both of them, isn't that the first thing they'd do, the way they love each other?—J. O. Keller & Son? *(Pause. Ann looks from him to Chris.)* I'll settle it. Do you want to settle it, or are you afraid to?

Chris: ...What do you mean?

George: Let me go up and talk to your father. In ten minutes you'll have the answer. Or are you afraid of the answer?

Chris: I'm not afraid of the answer. I know the answer. But my mother isn't well and I don't want a fight here now.

George: Let me go to him.

Chris: You're not going to start a fight here now.

George: *(To Ann.)* What more do you want!!! *(There is a sound of footsteps in the house.)*

Ann: *(Turns her head suddenly toward house.)* Someone's coming.

Chris: *(To George, quietly.)* You won't say anything now.

Ann: You'll go soon. I'll call a cab.

George: You're coming with me.

Ann: And don't mention marriage, because we haven't told her yet.

George: You're coming with me.

Ann: You understand? Don't...George, you're not going to start anything now! *(She hears footsteps.)* Shsh! *(Mother enters on porch. She is dressed almost formally, her hair is fixed. They are all turned toward her. On seeing George she raises both hands, comes down toward him.)*

Mother: Georgie, Georgie.

George: *(He has always liked her.)* Hello, Kate.

Mother: *(She cups his face in her hands.)* They made an old man out of you. *(Touches his hair.)* Look, you're gray.

George: *(Her pity, open and unabashed, reaches into him, and he smiles sadly.)* I know, I...

Mother: I told you when you went away, don't try for medals.

George: *(He laughs, tiredly.)* I didn't try, Kate. They made it very easy for me.

Mother: *(Actually angry.)* Go on. You're all alike. *(To Ann.)* Look at him, why did you say he's fine? He looks like a ghost.

George: *(Relishing her solicitude.)* I feel all right.

Mother: I'm sick to look at you. What's the matter with your mother, why don't she feed you?

Ann: He just hasn't any appetite.

Mother: If he ate in my house he'd have an appetite. *(To Ann.)* I pity your husband! *(To George.)* Sit down. I'll make you a sandwich.

George: *(Sits with an embarrassed laugh.)* I'm really not hungry.

Mother: Honest to God, it breaks my heart to see what happened to all the children. How we worked and planned for you, and you end up no better than us.

George: *(With deep feeling for her.)* You…you haven't changed at all, you know that, Kate?

Mother: None of us changed, Georgie. We all love you. Joe was just talking about the day you were born and the water got shut off. People were carrying basins from a block away—a stranger would have thought the whole neighborhood was on fire! *(They laugh. She sees the juice. To Ann.)* Why didn't you give him some juice!

Ann: *(Defensively.)* I offered it to him.

Mother: *(Scoffingly.)* You offered it to him! *(Thrusting glass into George's hand.)* Give it to him! *(To George, who is laughing.)* And now you're going to sit here and drink some juice…and look like something!

George: *(Sitting.)* Kate, I feel hungry already.

Chris: *(Proudly.)* She could turn Mahatma Gandhi into a heavyweight!

Mother: *(To Chris, with great energy.)* Listen, to hell with the restaurant! I got a ham in the icebox, and frozen strawberries, and avocados, and…

Ann: Swell, I'll help you!

George: The train leaves at eight-thirty, Ann.

Mother: *(To Ann.)* You're leaving?

Chris: No, Mother, she's not…

Ann: *(Breaking through it, going to George.)* You hardly got here; give yourself a chance to get acquainted again.

Chris: Sure, you don't even know us anymore.

Mother: Well, Chris, if they can't stay, don't…

Chris: No, it's just a question of George, Mother, he planned on…

George: *(He gets up politely, nicely, for Kate's sake.)* Now wait a minute, Chris…

Chris: *(Smiling and full of command, cutting him off.)* If you want to go, I'll drive you to the station now, but if you're staying, no arguments while you're here.

Mother: *(At last confessing the tension.)* Why should he argue? *(She goes to him, and with desperation and compassion, stroking his hair.)* Georgie and us have no argument. How could we have an argument, Georgie? We all got hit by the same lightning, how can you…? Did you see what happened to Larry's tree, Georgie? *(She has taken his arm, and unwillingly he moves across stage with her.)* Imagine? While I was dreaming of him in the middle of the night, the wind came along and… *(Lydia enters on porch. As soon as she sees him.)*

Lydia: Hey, Georgie! Georgie! Georgie! Georgie! Georgie! *(She comes down to him eagerly. She has a flowered hat in her hand, which Kate takes from her as she goes to George.)*

George: *(They shake hands eagerly, warmly.)* Hello, Laughy. What'd you do, grow?

Lydia: I'm a big girl now.

Mother: Look what she can do to a hat!

Ann: *(To Lydia, admiring the hat.)* Did you make that?

Mother: In ten minutes! *(She puts it on.)*

Lydia: *(Fixing it on her head.)* I only rearranged it.

George: You still make your own clothes?

Chris: *(Of Mother.)* Ain't she classy! All she needs now is a Russian wolfhound.

Mother: *(Moving her head from left to right.)* It feels like somebody is sitting on my head.

Ann: No, it's beautiful, Kate.

Mother: *(Kisses Lydia—to George.)* She's a genius! You should've married her. *(They laugh.)* This one can feed you!

Lydia: *(Strangely embarrassed.)* Oh, stop that, Kate.

George: *(To Lydia.)* Didn't I hear you had a baby?

Mother: You don't hear so good. She's got three babies.

George: *(A little hurt by it—to Lydia.)* No kidding, three?

Lydia: Yeah, it was one, two, three—You've been away a long time, Georgie.

George: I'm beginning to realize.

Mother: *(To Chris and George.)* The trouble with you kids is you *think* too much.

Lydia: Well, we think, too.

Mother: Yes, but not all the time.

George: *(With almost obvious envy.)* They never took Frank, heh?

Lydia: *(A little apologetically.)* No, he was always one year ahead of the draft.

Mother: It's amazing. When they were calling boys twenty-seven Frank was just twenty-eight, when they made it twenty-eight, he was just twenty-nine. That's why he took up astrology. It's all in when you were born, it just goes to show.

Chris: What does it go to show?

Mother: *(To Chris.)* Don't be so intelligent. Some superstitions are very nice! *(To Lydia.)* Did he finish Larry's horoscope?

Lydia: I'll ask him now, I'm going in. *(To George, a little sadly, almost embarrassed.)* Would you like to see my babies? Come on.

George: I don't think so, Lydia.

Lydia: *(Understanding.)* All right. Good luck to you, George.

George: Thanks. And to you…And Frank. *(She smiles at him, turns and goes off right to her house. George stands staring after her.)*

Lydia: *(As she runs off.)* Oh, Frank!

Mother: *(Reading his thoughts.)* She got pretty, heh?

George: *(Sadly.)* Very pretty.

Mother: *(As a reprimand.)* She's beautiful, you damned fool!

George: *(Looks around longingly; and softly, with a catch in his throat.)* She makes it seem so nice around here.

Mother: *(Shaking her finger at him.)* Look what happened to you because you wouldn't listen to me! I told you to marry that girl and stay out of the war!

George: *(Laughs at himself.)* She used to laugh too much.

Mother: And you didn't laugh enough. While you were getting mad about Fascism Frank was getting into her bed.

George: *(To Chris.)* He won the war, Frank.

Chris: All the battles.

Mother: *(In pursuit of this mood.)* The day they started the draft, Georgie, I told you you loved that girl.

Chris: *(Laughs.)* And truer love hath no man!

Mother: I'm smarter than any of you.

George: *(Laughing.)* She's wonderful!

Mother: And now you're going to listen to me, George. You had big principles, Eagle Scouts the three of you; so now I got a tree, and this one, *(Indicating Chris.)* when the weather gets bad he can't stand on his feet; and that big dope *(Pointing to Lydia's house.)* next door who never reads anything but Andy Gump has three children and his house paid off. Stop being a philosopher, and look after yourself. Like Joe was just saying—you move back here, he'll help you get set, and I'll find you a girl and put a smile on your face.

George: Joe? Joe wants me here?

Ann: *(Eagerly.)* He asked me to tell you, and I think it's a good idea.

Mother: Certainly. Why must you make believe you hate us? Is that another principle?—that you have to hate us? You don't hate us, George, I know you, you can't fool me, I diapered you. *(Suddenly to Ann.)* You remember Mr. Marcy's daughter?

Ann: *(Laughing, to George.)* She's got you hooked already! *(George laughs, is excited.)*

Mother: You look her over, George; you'll see she's the most beautiful…

Chris: She's got warts, George.

Mother: *(To Chris.)* She hasn't got warts! *(To George.)* So the girl has a little beauty mark on her chin…

Chris: And two on her nose.

Mother: You remember. Her father's the retired police inspector.

Chris: Sergeant, George.

Mother: He's a very kind man!

Chris: He looks like a gorilla.

Mother: *(To George.)* He never shot anybody. *(They all burst out laughing, as Keller appears in doorway. George rises abruptly, stares at Keller, who comes rapidly down to him.)*

Keller: *(The laughter stops. With strained joviality.)* Well! Look who's here! *(Extending his hand.)* Georgie, good to see ya.

George: *(Shaking hands—somberly.)* How're you, Joe?

Keller: So-so. Gettin' old. You comin' out to dinner with us?

George: No, got to be back in New York.

Ann: I'll call a cab for you. *(She goes up into the house.)*

Keller: Too bad you can't stay, George. Sit down. *(To Mother.)* He looks fine.

Mother: He looks terrible.

Keller: That's what I said, you look terrible, George. *(They laugh.)* I wear the pants and she beats me with the belt.

George: I saw your factory on the way from the station. It looks like General Motors.

Keller: I wish it was General Motors, but it ain't. Sit down, George. Sit down. *(Takes cigar out of his pocket.)* So you finally went to see your father, I hear?

George: Yes, this morning. What kind of stuff do you make now?

Keller: Oh, little of everything. Pressure cookers, an assembly for washing machines. Got a nice, flexible plant now. So how'd you find Dad? Feel all right?

George: *(Searching Keller, he speaks indecisively.)* No, he's not well, Joe.

Keller: *(Lighting his cigar.)* Not his heart again, is it?

George: It's everything, Joe. It's his soul.

Keller: *(Blowing out smoke.)* Uh huh—

Chris: How about seeing what they did with your house?

Keller: Leave him be.

George: *(To Chris, indicating Keller.)* I'd like to talk to him.

Keller: Sure, he just got here. That's the way they do, George. A little man makes a mistake and they hang him by his thumbs; the big ones become ambassadors. I wish you'd-a told me you were going to see Dad.

George: *(Studying him.)* I didn't know you were interested.

Keller: In a way, I am. I would like him to know, George, that as far as I'm concerned, any time he wants, he's got a place with me. I would like him to know that.

George: He hates your guts, Joe. Don't you know that?

Keller: I imagined it. But that can change, too.

Mother: Steve was never like that.

George: He's like that now. He'd like to take every man who made money in the war and put him up against a wall.

Chris: He'll need a lot of bullets.

George: And he'd better not get any.

Keller: That's a sad thing to hear.

George: *(With bitterness dominant.)* Why? What'd you expect him to think of you?

Keller: *(The force of his nature rising, but under control.)* I'm sad to see he hasn't changed. As long as I know him, twenty-five years, the man never learned how to take the blame. You know that, George.

George: *(He does.)* Well, I…

Keller: But you do know it. Because the way you come in here you don't look like you remember it. I mean like in 1937 when we had the shop on Flood Street. And he damn near blew us all up with that heater he left burning for two days without water. He wouldn't admit that was his fault, either. I had to fire a mechanic to save his face. You remember that.

George: Yes, but…

Keller: I'm just mentioning it, George. Because this is just another one of a lot of things. Like when he gave Frank that money to invest in oil stock.

George: *(Distressed.)* I know that, I…

Keller: *(Driving in, but restrained.)* But it's good to remember those things, kid. The way he cursed Frank because the stock went down. Was that Frank's fault? To listen to him Frank was a swindler. And all the man did was to give him a bad tip.

George: *(Gets up, moves away.)* I know those things…

Keller: Then remember them, remember them. *(Ann comes out of house.)* There are certain men in the world who rather see everybody hung before they'll take blame. You understand me, George? *(They stand facing each other, George trying to judge him.)*

Ann: *(Coming downstage.)* The cab's on its way. Would you like to wash?

Mother: *(With the thrust of hope.)* Why must he go? Make the midnight, George.

Keller: Sure, you'll have dinner with us!

Ann: How about it? Why not? We're eating at the lake, we could have a swell time.

George: *(Long pause, as he looks at Ann, Chris, Keller, then back to her.)* All right.

Mother: Now you're talking.

Chris: I've got a shirt that'll go right with that suit.

Mother: Size fifteen and a half, right, George?

George: Is Lydia…? I mean—Frank and Lydia coming?

Mother: I'll get you a date that'll make her look like a… *(She starts upstage.)*

George: *(Laughs.)* No, I don't want a date.

Chris: I know somebody just for you! Charlotte Tanner! *(He starts for the house.)*

Keller: Call Charlotte, that's right.

Mother: Sure, call her up. *(Chris goes into house.)*

Ann: You go up and pick out a shirt and tie.

George: *(He stops, looks around at them and the place.)* I never felt at home anywhere but here. I feel so… *(He nearly laughs, and turns away from them.)* Kate, you look so young, you know? You didn't change at all. It… rings an old bell. *(Turns to Keller.)* You too, Joe, you're amazingly the same. The whole atmosphere is.

Keller: Say, I ain't got time to get sick.

Mother: He hasn't been laid up in fifteen years…

Keller: Except my flu during the war.

Mother: Huhh?

Keller: My flu, when I was sick during…the war.

Mother: Well, sure… *(To George.)* I mean except for that flu. *(George stands perfectly still.)* Well, it slipped my mind, don't look at me that way. He wanted to go to the shop but he couldn't lift himself off the bed. I thought he had pneumonia.

George: Why did you say he's never…?

Keller: I know how you feel, kid, I'll never forgive myself. If I could've gone in that day I'd never allow Dad to touch those heads.

George: She said you've never been sick.

Mother: I said he was sick, George.

George: *(Going to Ann.)* Ann, didn't you hear her say…?

Mother: Do you remember every time you were sick?

George: I'd remember pneumonia. Especially if I got it just the day my partner was going to patch up cylinder heads… What happened that day, Joe?

Frank: *(Enters briskly from driveway, holding Larry's horoscope in his hand. He comes to Kate.)* Kate! Kate!

Mother: Frank, did you see George?

Frank: *(Extending his hand.)* Lydia told me, I'm glad to… you'll have to pardon me. *(Pulling Mother over right.)* I've got something amazing for you, Kate, I finished Larry's horoscope.

Mother: You'd be interested in this, George. It's wonderful the way he can understand the…

Chris: *(Entering from house.)* George, the girl's on the phone…

Mother: *(Desperately.)* He finished Larry's horoscope!

Chris: Frank, can't you pick a better time than this?

Frank: The greatest men who ever lived believed in the stars!

Chris: Stop filling her head with that junk!

Frank: Is it junk to feel that there's a greater power than ourselves? I've studied the stars of his life! I won't argue with you, I'm telling you. Somewhere in this world your brother is alive!

Mother: *(Instantly to Chris.)* Why isn't it possible?

Chris: Because it's insane.

Frank: Just a minute now. I'll tell you something and you can do as you please. Just let me say it. He was supposed to have died on November twenty fifth. But November twenty fifth was his favorable day.

Chris: Mother!

Mother: Listen to him!

Frank: It was a day when everything good was shining on him, the kind of day he should've married on. You can laugh at a lot of it, I can understand you laughing. But the odds are a million to one that a man won't die on his favorable day. That's known, that's known, Chris!

Mother: Why isn't it possible, why isn't it possible, Chris!

George: *(To Ann.)* Don't you understand what she's saying? She just told you to go. What are you waiting for now?

Chris: Nobody can tell her to go. *(A car horn is heard.)*

Mother: *(To Frank.)* Thank you, darling, for your trouble. Will you tell him to wait, Frank?

Frank: *(As he goes.)* Sure thing.

Mother: *(Calling out.)* They'll be right out, driver!

Chris: She's not leaving, Mother.

George: You heard her say it, he's never been sick!

Mother: He misunderstood me, Chris! *(Chris, looks at her, struck.)*

George: *(To Ann.)* He simply told your father to kill pilots, and covered himself in bed!

Chris: You'd better answer him, Annie. Answer him.

Mother: I packed your bag, darling…

Chris: What?

Mother: I packed your bag. All you've got to do is close it.

Ann: I'm not closing anything. He asked me here and I'm staying till he tells me to go. *(To George.)* Till Chris tells me!

Chris: That's all! Now get out of here, George!

Mother: *(To Chris.)* But if that's how he feels…

Chris: That's all, nothing more till Christ comes, about the case or Larry as long as I'm here! *(To George.)* Now get out of here, George!

George: *(To Ann.)* You tell me. I want to hear you tell me.

Ann: Go, George! *(They disappear up the driveway, Ann saying, "Don't take it that way, Georgie! Please don't take it that way".)*

(Chris turns to his mother.)

Chris: What do you mean you packed her bag? How dare you pack her bag?

Mother: Chris…

Chris: How dare you pack her bag?

Mother: She doesn't belong here.

Chris: Then I don't belong here.

Mother: She's Larry's girl.

Chris: And I'm his brother and he's dead, and I'm marrying his girl.

Mother: Never, never in this world!

Keller: You lost your mind?

Mother: You have nothing to say!

Keller: *(Cruelly.)* I got plenty to say. Three and a half years you been talking like a maniac—

Mother: *(She smashes him across the face.)* Nothing. You have nothing to say. Now I say. He's coming back, and everybody has got to wait.

Chris: Mother, Mother…

Mother: Wait, wait…

Chris: How long? How long?

Mother: *(Rolling out of her.)* Till he comes; forever and ever till he comes!

Chris: *(As an ultimatum.)* Mother, I'm going ahead with it.

Mother: Chris, I've never said no to you in my life, now I say no!

Chris: You'll never let him go till I do it.

Mother: I'll never let him go and you'll never let him go…!

Chris: I've let him go. I've let him go a long…

Mother: *(With no less force, but turning from him.)* Then let your father go. *(Pause. Chris stands transfixed.)*

Keller: She's out of her mind.

Mother: Altogether! *(To Chris, but not facing them.)* Your brother's alive, darling, because if he's dead, your father killed him. Do you understand me now? As long as you live, that boy is alive. God does not let a son be killed by his father. Now you see, don't you? Now you see. *(Beyond control, she hurries up and into house.)*

Keller: *(Chris has not moved. He speaks insinuatingly, questioningly.)* She's out of her mind.

Chris: *(A broken whisper.)* Then… you did it?

Keller: *(The beginning of plea in his voice.)* He never flew a P-40—

Chris: *(Struck. Deadly.)* But the others.

Keller: *(Insistently.)* She's out of her mind. *(He takes a step toward Chris, pleadingly.)*

Chris: *(Unyielding.)* Dad… you did it?

Keller: He never flew a P-40, what's the matter with you?

Chris: *(Still asking, and saying.)* Then you did it. To the others.

(Both hold their voices down.)

Keller: *(Afraid of him, his deadly insistence.)* What's the matter with you? What the hell is the matter with you?

Chris: *(Quietly, incredibly.)* How could you do that? How?

Keller: What's the matter with you!

Chris: Dad… Dad, you killed twenty-one men!

Keller: What, killed?

Chris: You killed them, you murdered them.

Keller: *(As though throwing his whole nature open before Chris.)* How could I kill anybody?

Chris: Dad! Dad!

Keller: *(Trying to hush him.)* I didn't kill anybody!

Chris: Then explain it to me. What did you do? Explain it to me or I'll tear you to pieces!

Keller: *(Horrified at his overwhelming fury.)* Don't, Chris, don't…

Chris: I want to know what you did, now what did you do? You had a hundred and twenty cracked engine-heads, how what did you do?

Keller: If you're going to hang me then I…

Chris: I'm listening, God almighty, I'm listening!

Keller: *(Their movements now are those of subtle pursuit and escape. Keller keeps a step out of Chris' range as he talks.)* You're a boy, what could I do! I'm in business, a man is in business; a hundred and twenty cracked, you're out of business; you got a process, the process don't work you're out of business; you don't know how to operate, your stuff is no good; they close you up, they tear up your contracts, what the hell's it to them? You lay forty years into a business and they knock you out in five minutes, what could I do, let them take forty years, let them take my life away? *(His voice cracking.)* I never thought they'd install them. I swear to God. I thought they'd stop 'em before anybody took off.

Chris: Then why'd you ship them out?

Keller: By the time they could spot them I thought I'd have the process going again, and I could show them they needed me and they'd let it go by. But weeks passed and I got no kick-back, so I was going to tell them.

Chris: Then why didn't you tell them?

Keller: It was too late. The paper, it was all over the front page, twenty-one went down, it was too late. They came with handcuffs into the shop, what could I do? *(He sits on bench at center.)* Chris... Chris, I did it for you, it was a chance and I took it for you. I'm sixty-one years old, when would I have another chance to make something for you? Sixty-one years old you don't get another chance, do ya?

Chris: You even knew they wouldn't hold up in the air.

Keller: I didn't say that...

Chris: But you were going to warn them not to use them...

Keller: But that don't mean...

Chris: It means you knew they'd crash.

Keller: It don't mean that.

Chris: Then you *thought* they'd crash.

Keller: I was afraid maybe...

Chris: You were afraid maybe! God in heaven, what kind of a man are you? Kids were hanging in the air by those heads. You knew that!

Keller: For you, a business for you!

Chris: *(With burning fury.)* For me! Where do you live, where have you come from? For me!—I was dying every day and you were killing my boys and you did it for me? What the hell do you think I was thinking of, the Goddam business? Is that as far as your mind can see, the business? What is that, the world—the business? What the hell do you mean, you did it for me? Don't you have a country? Don't you live in the world? What the hell are you? You're not even an animal, no animal kills his own, what are you? What must I do to you? I ought to tear the tongue out of your mouth, what must I do? *(With his fist he pounds down upon his father's shoulder. He stumbles away, covering his face as he weeps.)* What must I do, Jesus God, what must I do?

Keller: Chris..., My Chris...

CURTAIN

ACT THREE

Two o'clock the following morning, Mother is discovered on the rise, rocking ceaselessly in a chair, staring at her thoughts. It is an intense, slight, sort of rocking. A light shows from upstairs bedroom, lower floor windows being dark. The moon is strong and casts its bluish light.

Presently Jim, dressed in jacket and hat, appears from the left, and seeing her, goes up beside her.

Jim: Any news?

Mother: No news.

Jim: *(Gently.)* You can't sit up all night, dear, why don't you go to bed?

Mother: I'm waiting for Chris. Don't worry about me, Jim, I'm perfectly all right.

Jim: But it's almost two o'clock.

Mother: I can't sleep. *(Slight pause.)* You had an emergency?

Jim: *(Tiredly.)* Somebody had a headache and thought he was dying. *(Slight pause.)* Half of my patients are quite mad. Nobody realizes how many people are walking around loose, and they're cracked as coconuts. Money. Money-money-money-money. You say it long enough it doesn't mean anything. *(She smiles, makes a silent laugh.)* Oh, how I'd love to be around when that happens!

Mother: *(Shakes her head.)* You're so childish, Jim! Sometimes you are.

Jim: *(Looks at her a moment.)* Kate. *(Pause.)* What happened?

Mother: I told you. He had an argument with Joe. Then he got in the car and drove away.

Jim: What kind of an argument?

Mother: An argument, Joe…he was crying like a child, before.

Jim: They argued about Ann?

Mother: *(Slight hesitation.)* No, not Ann. Imagine? *(Indicates lighted window above.)* She hasn't come out of that room since he left. All night in that room.

Jim: *(Looks at window, then at her.)* What'd Joe do, tell him?

Mother: *(She stops rocking.)* Tell him what?

Jim: Don't be afraid, Kate, I know. I've always known.

Mother: How?

Jim: It occurred to me a long time ago.

Mother: I always had the feeling that in the back of his head, Chris…almost knew. I didn't think it would be such a shock.

Jim: *(Gets up.)* Chris would never know how to live with a thing like that. It takes a certain talent…for lying. You have it, and I do. But not him.

Mother: What do you mean…he's not coming back?

Jim: Oh, no, he'll come back. We all come back, Kate. These private little revolutions always die. The compromise is always made. In a peculiar way. Frank is right—every man does have a star. The star of one's honesty. And you spend your life groping for it, but once it's out it never lights again. I don't think he went very far. He probably just wanted to be alone to watch his star go out.

Mother: Just as long as he comes back.

Jim: I wish he wouldn't, Kate. One year I simply took off, went to New Orleans; for two months I lived on bananas and milk, and studied a certain disease. It was beautiful. And then she came, and she cried. And I went back home with her. And now I live in the usual darkness; I can't find myself; it's even hard sometimes to remember the kind of man I wanted to be. I'm a good husband; Chris is a good son—he'll come back. *(Keller comes out on porch in dressing-gown and slippers. He goes upstage—to alley. Jim goes to him.)*

Jim: I have a feeling he's in the park. I'll look around for him. Put her to bed, Joe; this is no good for what she's got. *(Jim exits up driveway.)*

Keller: *(Coming down.)* What does he want here?

Mother: His friend is not home.

Keller: *(His voice is husky. Comes down to her.)* I don't like him mixing in so much.

Mother: It's too late, Joe. He knows.

Keller: *(Apprehensively.)* How does he know?

Mother: He guessed a long time ago.

Keller: I don't like that.

Mother: *(Laughs dangerously, quietly into the line.)* What you don't like…

Keller: Yeah, what I don't like.

Mother: You can't bull yourself through this one, Joe, you better be smart now. This thing—this thing is not over yet.

Keller: *(Indicating lighted window above.)* And what is she doing up there? She don't come out of the room.

Mother: I don't know, what is she doing? Sit down, stop being mad. You want to live? You better figure out your life.

Keller: She don't know, does she?

Mother: She saw Chris storming out of here. It's one and one—she knows how to add.

Keller: Maybe I ought to talk to her?

Mother: Don't ask me, Joe.

Keller: *(Almost an outburst.)* Then who do I ask? But I don't think she'll do anything about it.

Mother: You're asking me again.

Keller: I'm askin' you. What am I, a stranger? I thought I had a family here. What happened to my family?

Mother: You've got a family. I'm simply telling you that I have no strength to think any more.

Keller: You have no strength. The minute there's trouble you have no strength.

Mother: Joe, you're doing the same thing again; all your life whenever there's trouble you yell at me and you think that settles it.

Keller: Then what do I do? Tell me, talk to me, what do I do?

Mother: Joe… I've been thinking this way. If he comes back…

Keller: What do you mean "if"?… he's comin' back!

Mother: I think if you sit him down and you… explain yourself. I mean you ought to make it clear to him that you know you did a terrible thing. *(Not looking into his eyes.)* I mean if he saw that you realize what you did. You see?

Keller: What ice does that cut?

Mother: *(A little fearfully.)* I mean if you told him that you want to pay for what you did.

Keller: *(Sensing… quietly.)* How can I pay?

Mother: Tell him… you're willing to go to prison. *(Pause.)*

Keller: *(Struck, amazed.)* I'm willing to…?

Mother: *(Quickly.)* You wouldn't go, he wouldn't ask you to go. But if you told him you wanted to, if he could feel that you wanted to pay, maybe he would forgive you.

Keller: He would forgive me! For what?

Mother: Joe, you know what I mean.

Keller: I don't know what you mean! You wanted money, so I made money. What must I be forgiven? You wanted money, didn't you?

Mother: I didn't want it that way.

Keller: I didn't want it that way, either! What difference is it what you want? I spoiled the both of you. I should've put him out when he was ten like I was put out, and make him earn his keep. Then he'd know how a buck is made in this world. Forgiven! I could live on a quarter a day myself, but I got a family so I…

Mother: Joe, Joe… it don't excuse it that you did it for the family.

Keller: It's got to excuse it!

Mother: There's something bigger than the family to him.

Keller: Nothin' is bigger!

Mother: There is to him.

Keller: There's nothin' he could do that I wouldn't forgive. Because he's my son. Because I'm his father and he's my son.

Mother: Joe, I tell you…

Keller: Nothin's bigger than that. And you're goin' to tell him, you understand? I'm his father and he's my son, and if there's something bigger than that I'll put a bullet in my head!

Mother: You stop that!

Keller: You heard me. Now you know what to tell him. *(Pause. He moves from her—halts.)* But he wouldn't put me away though… He wouldn't do that… Would he?

Mother: He loved you, Joe, you broke his heart.

Keller: But to put me away…

Mother: I don't know. I'm beginning to think we don't really know him. They say in the war he was such a killer. Here he was always afraid of mice. I don't know him. I don't know what he'll do.

Keller: Goddam, if Larry was alive he wouldn't act like this. He understood the way the world is made. He listened to me. To him the world had a forty-foot front, it ended at the building line. This one, everything bothers him. You make a deal, overcharge two cents, and his hair falls out. He don't understand money. Too easy, it came too easy. Yes sir. Larry. That was a boy we lost. Larry. Larry. *(He slumps on chair in front of her.)* What am I gonna do, Kate…

Mother: Joe, Joe, please… you'll be all right, nothing is going to happen…

Keller: *(Desperately, lost.)* For you, Kate, for both of you, that's all I ever lived for…

Mother: I know, darling, I know… *(Ann enters from house. They say nothing, waiting for her to speak.)*

Ann: Why do you stay up? I'll tell you when he comes.

Keller: *(Rises, goes to her.)* You didn't eat supper, did you? *(To Mother.)* Why don't you make her something?

Mother: Sure, I'll…

Ann: Never mind, Kate, I'm all right. *(They are unable to speak to each other.)* There's something I want to tell you. *(She starts, then halts.)* I'm not going to do anything about it…

Mother: She's a good girl! *(To Keller.)* You see? She's a…

Ann: I'll do nothing about Joe, but you're going to do something for me. *(Directly to Mother.)* You made Chris feel guilty with me. Whether you wanted to or not, you've crippled him in front of me. I'd like you to tell him that Larry is dead and that you know it. You understand me? I'm not going out of here alone. There's no life for me that way. I want you to set him free. And then I promise you, everything will end, and we'll go away, and that's all.

Keller: You'll do that. You'll tell him.

Ann: I know what I'm asking, Kate. You had two sons. But you've only got one now.

Keller: You'll tell him…

Ann: And you've got to say it to him so he knows you mean it.

Mother: My dear, if the boy was dead, it wouldn't depend on my words to make Chris know it… The night he gets into your bed, his heart will dry up. Because he knows and you know. To his dying day he'll wait for his brother! No, my dear, no such thing. You're going in the morning, and you're going alone. That's your life, that's your lonely life. *(She goes to porch, and starts in.)*

Ann: Larry is dead, Kate.

Mother: *(She stops.)* Don't speak to me.

Ann: I said he's dead. I know! He crashed off the coast of China November twenty-fifth! His engine didn't fail him. But he died. I know…

Mother: How did he die? You're lying to me. If you know, how did he die?

Ann: I loved him. You know I loved him. Would I have looked at anyone else if I wasn't sure? That's enough for you.

Mother: *(Moving on her.)* What's enough for me? What're you talking about? *(She grasps Ann's wrists.)*

Ann: You're hurting my wrists.

Mother: What are you talking about! *(Pause. She stares at Ann a moment, then turns and goes to Keller.)*

Ann: Joe, go in the house…

Keller: Why should I…

Ann: Please go.

Keller: Lemme know when he comes. *(Keller goes into house.)*

Mother: *(She sees Ann take a letter from her pocket.)* What's that?

Ann: Sit down… *(Mother moves left to chair, but does not sit.)* First you've got to understand. When I came, I didn't have any idea that Joe… I had nothing against him or you. I came to get married. I hoped... So I didn't bring this to hurt you. I thought I'd show it to you only if there was no other way to settle Larry in your mind.

Mother: Larry? *(Snatches letter from Ann's hand.)*

Ann: He wrote to me just before he—*(Mother opens and begins to read letter.)* I'm not trying to hurt you, Kate. You're making me do this, now remember you're—Remember. I've been so lonely, Kate... I can't leave here alone again. *(A long, low moan comes from Mother's throat as she reads.)* You made me show it to you. You wouldn't believe me. I told you a hundred times, why wouldn't you believe me!

Mother: Oh, my God...

Ann: *(With pity and fear.)* Kate, please, please...

Mother: My God, my God...

Ann: Kate, dear, I'm so sorry... I'm so sorry. *(Chris enters from driveway. He seems exhausted.)*

Chris: What's the matter...?

Ann: Where were you?... you're all perspired. *(Mother doesn't move.)* Where were you?

Chris: Just drove around a little. I thought you'd be gone.

Ann: Where do I go? I have nowhere to go.

Chris: *(To Mother.)* Where's Dad?

Ann: Inside lying down.

Chris: Sit down, both of you. I'll say what there is to say.

Mother: I didn't hear the car...

Chris: I left it in the garage.

Mother: Jim is out looking for you.

Chris: Mother... I'm going away. There are a couple of firms in Cleveland, I think I can get a place. I mean, I'm going away for good. *(To Ann alone.)* I know what you're thinking, Annie. It's true. I'm yellow. I was made yellow in this house because I suspected my father and I did nothing about it, but if I knew that night when I came home what I know now, he'd be in the district attorney's office by this time, and I'd have brought him there. Now if I look at him, all I'm able to do is cry.

Mother: What are you talking about? What else can you do?

Chris: I could jail him! I could jail him, if I were human any more. But I'm like everybody else now. I'm practical now. You made me practical.

Mother: But you have to be.

Chris: The cats in that alley are practical, the bums who ran away when we were fighting were practical. Only the dead ones weren't practical. But now I'm practical, and I spit on myself. I'm going away. I'm going now.

Ann: *(Goes up to stop him.)* I'm coming with you...

Chris: No, Ann.

Ann: Chris, I don't ask you to do anything about Joe.

Chris: You do, you do...

Ann: I swear I never will.

Chris: In your heart you always will.

Ann: Then do what you have to do!

Chris: Do what? What is there to do? I've looked all night for a reason to make him suffer.

Ann: There's reason, there's reason!

Chris: What? Do I raise the dead when I put him behind bars? Then what'll I do it for? We used to shoot a man who acted like a dog, but honor was real there, you were protecting something. But here? This is the land of the great big dogs, you don't love a man here, you eat him! That's the principle; the only one we live by—it just happened to kill a few people this time, that's all. The world's that way, how can I take it out on him? What sense does that make? This is a zoo, a zoo!

Ann: *(To Mother.)* You know what he's got to do! Tell him!

Mother: Let him go.

Ann: I won't let him go. You'll tell him what he's got to do…

Mother: Annie!

Ann: Then I will! *(Keller enters from house. Chris sees him, goes down right near arbor.)*

Keller: What's the matter with you? I want to talk to you.

Chris: I've got nothing to say to you.

Keller: *(Taking his arm.)* I want to talk to you!

Chris: *(Pulling violently away from him.)* Don't do that, Dad. I'm going to hurt you if you do that. There's nothing to say, so say it quick.

Keller: Exactly what's the matter? What's the matter? You got too much money? Is that what bothers you?

Chris: *(With an edge of sarcasm.)* It bothers me.

Keller: If you can't get used to it, then throw it away. You hear me? Take every cent and give it to charity, throw it in the sewer. Does that settle it? In the sewer, that's all. You think I'm kidding? I'm tellin' you what to do, if it's dirty then burn it. It's your money, that's not my money. I'm a dead man, I'm an old dead man, nothing's mine. Well, talk to me!—what do you want to do!

Chris: It's not what I want to do. It's what you want to do.

Keller: What should I do? *(Chris is silent.)* Jail? You want me to go to jail? If you want me to go, say so! Is that where I belong?—then tell me so! *(Slight pause.)* What's the matter, what can't you tell me? *(Furiously.)* You say everything else to me, say that! *(Slight pause.)* I'll tell you why you can't say it. Because you know I don't belong there. Because you know! *(With growing emphasis and passion, and a persistent tone of desperation.)* Who worked for nothin' in that war? When they work for nothin', I'll work for nothin'. Did they ship a gun or a truck outa Detroit before they got their price? Is that clean? It's dollars and cents, nickels and dimes; war and peace, it's nickels and dimes, what's clean? Half the Goddam country is gotta go if I go! That's why you can't tell me.

Chris: That's exactly why.

Keller: Then…why am *I* bad?

Chris: *I* know you're no worse than most men but I thought you were better. I never saw you as a man. I saw you as my father. *(Almost breaking.)* I can't look at you this way, I can't look at myself! *(He turns away, unable to face Keller. Ann goes quickly to Mother, takes letter from her and starts for Chris. Mother instantly rushes to intercept her.)*

Mother: Give me that!

Ann: He's going to read it! *(She thrusts letter into Chris' hand.)* Larry. He wrote it to me the day he died…

Keller: Larry!

Mother: Chris, it's not for you. *(He starts to read.)* Joe… go away…

Keller: *(Mystified, frightened.)* Why'd she say, Larry, what…?

Mother: *(She desperately pushes him toward alley, glancing at Chris.)* Go to the street, Joe, go to the street! *(She comes down beside Keller.)* Don't, Chris… *(Pleading from her whole soul.)* Don't tell him…

Chris: *(Quietly)* Three and one half years… talking, talking. Now you tell me what you must do… This is how he died, now tell me where you belong.

Keller: *(Pleading.)* Chris, a man can't be a Jesus in this world!

Chris: I know all about the world. I know the whole crap story. Now listen to this, and tell me what a man's got to be! *(Reads.)* "My dear Ann:…" You listening? He wrote this the day he died. Listen, don't cry… listen! "My dear Ann: It is impossible to put down the things I feel. But I've got to tell you something. Yesterday they flew in a load of papers from the States and I read about Dad and your father being convicted. I can't express myself. I can't tell you how I feel—I can't bear to live any more. Last night I circled the base for twenty minutes before I could bring myself in. How could he have done that? Every day three or four men never come back and he sits back there doing business… I don't know how to tell you what I feel…. I can't face anybody. I'm going out on a mission in a few minutes. They'll probably report me missing. If they do, I want you to know that you mustn't wait for me. I tell you, Ann, if I had him here now I could kill him—" *(Keller grabs letter from Chris' hand and reads it. After a long pause.)* Now blame the world. Do you understand that letter?

Keller: *(He speaks almost inaudibly.)* I think I do. Get the car, I'll put on my jacket. *(He turns and starts slowly for the house. Mother rushes to intercept him.)*

Mother: Why are you going? You'll sleep, why are you going?

Keller: I can't sleep here. I'll feel better if I go.

Mother: You're so foolish. Larry was your son too, wasn't he? You know he'd never tell you to do this.

Keller: *(Looking at letter in his hand.)* Then what is this if it isn't telling me? Sure, he was my son. But I think to him they were all my sons. And I guess they were, I guess they were. I'll be right down. *(Exits into house.)*

Mother: *(To Chris, with determination.)* You're not going to take him!

Chris: I'm taking him.

Mother: It's up to you, if you tell him to stay he'll stay. Go and tell him!

Chris: Nobody could stop him now.

Mother: You'll stop him! How long will he live in prison?—are you trying to kill him?

Chris: *(Holding out letter.)* I thought you read this!

Mother: *(Of Larry, the letter.)* The war is over! Didn't you hear?—it's over!

Chris: Then what was Larry to you? A stone that fell into the water? It's not enough for him to be sorry. Larry didn't kill himself to make you and Dad sorry.

Mother: What more can we be!

Chris: You can be better! Once and for all you can know there's a universe of people outside and you're responsible to it, and unless you know that you threw away your son because that's why he died.

(A shot is heard in the house. They stand frozen for a brief second. Chris starts for porch, pauses at step, turns to Ann.)

Chris: Find Jim! *(He goes on into the house and Ann runs up driveway. Mother stands alone, transfixed.)*

Mother: *(Softly, almost moaning.)* Joe… Joe… Joe… Joe… *(Chris comes out of house, down to Mother's arms.)*

Chris: *(Almost crying.)* Mother, I didn't mean to…

Mother: Don't, dear. Don't take it on yourself. Forget now. Live. *(Chris stirs as if to answer.)* Shhh… *(She puts his arms down gently and moves toward porch.)* Shhh… *(As she reaches porch steps she begins sobbing, as*

THE CURTAIN FALLS

* * *

Reading and Reacting

1. Using Freytag's pyramid as a model, outline the plot of *All My Sons*. Does it include all five stages of plot? If not, why not?
2. Review the play's stage directions. What kind of information do they provide? Should readers be given more information about the characters and setting? Should they be given *less* information? Explain.
3. Which of the following do you consider to be foreshadowing, and why?
    - Kate Keller's headaches
    - The game Joe Keller plays with Bert
    - The horoscope Frank is preparing
4. *All My Sons* is set entirely outdoors, in a suburban backyard. Is this setting appropriate? What, if anything, does it add to the play? Should any of the action take place in a different setting? If so, where?
5. Throughout the play, Kate Keller's speeches are introduced not with her name (as the other characters' speeches are) but with the title "Mother." Why do you think Miller chose to do this? Do you think it was a good decision?
6. Why doesn't Kate want to admit that Larry is dead? Consider all possible reasons.

7. Evaluate the speech toward the end of Act II in which Joe Keller defends himself. What is his defense? Do you find it at all convincing? Why or why not?
8. In Act III, when Kate says, "There's something bigger than the family to him" who is the "him" to whom she refers? What is the "something"? What does this comment reveal about Kate? About Joe? About the play's other characters?
9. Among other things, this is a play about fathers (Joe Keller and Steve Deever) and sons (Chris and Larry Keller, George Deever). What comment about fathers and sons is Miller making with the play's title?
10. Does the play's ending seem justified? Surprising? Melodramatic? Explain.
11. What do you think might happen to the characters after the play ends? Why? Do you think this outcome is inevitable? Explain.
12. **Journal Entry** What is the significance of the fallen tree? Do you see it as a symbol? Why or why not?
13. **Critical Perspective** *All My Sons* is set in 1947, just after the end of World War II. In a 2019 review of a performance of the play, *New York Times* theater critic Jesse Green notes, "although the play has its serious problems, irrelevance will never be one of them."

    Do you agree with Green that the play remains (and will always remain) relevant? In answering this question, consider not just the ethical and moral issues that are raised but also the characters' actions and their relationships to one another.

Related Works: "The Lottery" (p. 337), "The Man He Killed" (p. 505), "Those Winter Sundays" (p. 672), *Fences* (p. 1222)

WRITING SUGGESTIONS: Plot

1. Central to the plots of both *Trifles* and *A Doll's House* is a woman who commits a crime. Compare and contrast the desperate situations that motivate the two women. Then, consider the reactions of other characters in the two plays to each woman's crime. (If you like, you may substitute *All My Sons*, which also focuses on a crime, for one of these two plays.)
2. Consider the male characters in *A Doll's House* and *Trifles*. How are their attitudes toward women, and their actions and reactions, similar? How are they different?
3. In *Trifles*, the action unfolds in a confined, isolated space. In *All My Sons*, conversely, the action takes place outdoors. How do these two different kinds of settings influence the plots of the two plays?
4. Write a monologue for Nora in *A Doll's House*, including everything you think she would like to tell her children.
5. The characters in *All My Sons* make frequent references to Larry Keller, a key character who does not actually appear in the play. Compare the treatment of this character to the treatment of the absent character (Mrs. Wright) in *Trifles*—or to the absent father in *The Glass Menagerie* (p. 958).

Chapter

30

Character

Tennessee Williams

Jack Mitchell/Archive Photos/Getty Images

William Shakespeare

Bettmann/Getty Images

Learning Objectives

After reading this chapter, you will be able to. . .

- Explain the role of character in a dramatic work.
- Identify characters in a play as round or flat, static or dynamic.
- Explain what language and tone reveal about characters within a dramatic work.
- Identify language in a play as formal or informal, plain or elaborate.
- Identify irony in a dramatic work, and explain how it is used.
- Explain how characters' actions influence a dramatic work.
- Describe how an actor might interpret a role in a dramatic work.
- Identify the major and minor characters in a dramatic work.
- Analyze the relationship between characters in a dramatic work.

In Tennessee Williams's play *The Glass Menagerie*, which appears later in this chapter, the protagonist, Tom Wingfield, functions as the play's narrator. Stepping out of his role as a character and speaking directly to the audience, he directs the play's action, music, lighting, and other elements. In addition, he summarizes characters' actions, explains what motivates them, and discusses the significance of their behavior in the context of the play—commenting on his own character's actions as well. As narrator, Tom also presents useful background information about the characters. For example, when he introduces his coworker, Jim, he prepares the audience for Jim's entrance and helps them to understand his subsequent actions:

> In high school Jim was a hero. He had tremendous Irish good nature and vitality with the scrubbed and polished look of white chinaware. He seemed to move in a continual spotlight. ... But Jim apparently ran into more interference after his graduation. ... His speed had definitely slowed. Six years after he left high school he was holding a job that wasn't much better than mine. (Scene 6)

Most plays, however, do not include narrators who present background. Instead, the audience learns about characters from their own words and from comments by others about them, as well as from the characters' actions. When reading a play, we learn about the characters from the playwright's stage directions; when watching a performance, we gain insight into characters from the way actors interpret them.

Characters in plays, like characters in novels and short stories, may be **round** or **flat**, **static** or **dynamic**. Generally speaking, major characters are likely to be round, whereas minor characters are likely to be flat. Through the language and the actions of the characters, audiences learn whether the characters are multidimensional, skimpily developed, or perhaps merely **foils**: players whose main purpose is to shed light on more important characters. Audiences also learn about the emotions, attitudes, and values that help to shape the characters—their hopes and fears, their strengths and weaknesses. In addition, by comparing characters' early words and actions with later ones, audiences learn whether characters grow and change emotionally.

Characters' Words

Characters' words reveal the most about their attitudes, feelings, beliefs, and values. Sometimes information is communicated (to other characters as well as to the audience) in a **monologue**—an extended speech by one character. A **soliloquy**—a monologue revealing a character's thoughts and feelings, directed at the audience and presumed not to be heard by other characters—can also convey information about a character. For example, Hamlet's well-known soliloquy that begins "To be or not to be" eloquently communicates his distraught mental state—his resentment of his mother and uncle, his confusion about what course of action to take, and his suicidal thoughts. Finally, **dialogue**—an exchange of words between two characters—can reveal misunderstanding or conflict between them, or it can show their agreement, mutual support, or similar beliefs.

In Henrik Ibsen's *A Doll's House* (p. 834), dialogue reveals a good deal about the characters. Nora Helmer, the spoiled young wife, has broken the law and kept her crime secret from her husband. Through her words, we learn about her motivation, her values, her emotions, and her reactions to other characters and to her potentially dangerous situation. We learn, for example, that she is flirtatious: "If your little squirrel asked you for something, and she was very, very nice ..." We also see that she is childishly unrealistic about the consequences of her actions. When her husband, Torvald, asks what she would do if he was seriously injured, leaving her in debt, she says, "If something so terrible happened, I wouldn't care if I had debts or not." When Torvald presses, "but what about the people I'd borrowed from?" she naively dismisses them: "Them? Who cares about them! I don't know them." As the play progresses, Nora's lack of understanding of the power of the law becomes more and more significant as she struggles with her moral and ethical dilemma.

The inability of both Nora and Torvald to confront ugly truths is also revealed through their words. When, in Act 1, Nora tells Krogstad, her blackmailer, that his revealing her secret "would be terribly unpleasant," he responds, "Just unpleasant?" Later on, in Act 3, Torvald echoes her sentiments, dismissing the horror with, "We must try to empty our minds of that."

The ease with which Torvald is able to dismiss his dying friend Dr. Rank in Act 3 ("He suffered and he was lonely. He was like a cloud, a dark background to our sunlit happiness. Well, perhaps it's for the best.") foreshadows the lack of support he will give Nora immediately thereafter. Especially revealing is his use of *I* and *my* and *me*, which convey his self-centeredness:

> You've destroyed all my happiness. You've ruined my future. I can't bear to think of it. I'm in the hands of a man with no scruples. He can do what he likes with me. He can ask anything he wants, order me to do anything—and I dare not say no. And I have to sink to such depths of agony, all because of a thoughtless woman.

Just as Torvald's words reveal that he has not been changed by the play's events, Nora's words show that she has changed significantly. Her dialogue near the end of Act 3 shows that she has become a responsible, determined woman—one who understands her situation and options and is no longer blithely oblivious to her duties. When she says, "My mind has never been so clear and determined as tonight," she is calm and decisive. When she says, "Our home has been nothing but a playroom. I have been your doll-wife, just as at home I was Papa's doll-child," she reveals a new self-awareness. And, when she confronts her husband, she displays—perhaps for the first time in their relationship—complete honesty.

Sometimes what other characters say to (or about) a character can reveal more to an audience than the character's own words. For example, in *A Doll's House*, when the dying Dr. Rank says, apparently without malice, "Torvald ... is a very refined man. That makes him absolutely incapable of facing anything that is unpleasant," the audience not only thinks ill of the man who is too "refined" to visit his sick friend but also questions his ability to withstand situations that may be emotionally or morally "unpleasant" as well.

When a character is offstage for much (or even all) of the action, the audience must rely on other characters' assessments of the absent character. In Susan Glaspell's *Trifles* (p. 820), the play's focus is on an absent character, Minnie Wright, who is described solely through other characters' comments. The evidence suggests that Mrs. Wright killed her husband, and only Mrs. Hale's and Mrs. Peters's comments about Mrs. Wright's dreary life can delineate her character and suggest a likely motive for the murder. Although Mrs. Wright never appears on stage, we learn essential information from the other women about her—for example, that as a young girl she liked to sing and that more recently she was so distraught about the lack of beauty in her life that even her sewing revealed her distress.

Whether a character's words are in the form of a monologue, a soliloquy, or dialogue—and whether they reveal information about the character who is speaking or about someone else—words are always revealing. Explicitly or implicitly, they convey a character's nature, attitudes, and relationships with other characters.

Keep in mind that the kind of language characters use can vary widely. A character may, for example, use learned words, foreign words, elaborate figures of speech, irony or sarcasm, regionalisms, slang, jargon, clichés, or profanity. Words can also be used to indicate tone—for example, to express irony. Any of these uses of language may communicate vital information to the audience about a character's background, attitudes, and motivation. And, of course, a character's language may change as a play progresses, and this too may be revealing.

Formal and Informal Language

The level of diction a character uses can give audiences a good deal of information. One character in a dramatic work may speak very formally, using absolutely correct grammar, a learned vocabulary, and long, complex sentences; another may speak in an informal style, using conversational speech, colloquialisms, and slang. At times, two characters with different levels of language may be set in opposition for dramatic effect, as they are in Irish playwright George Bernard Shaw's classic play *Pygmalion* (1912), which updates the ancient Greek myth of a sculptor who creates (and falls in love with) a statue of a woman. In Shaw's version, a linguistics professor sets out to teach "proper" speech and manners to a woman who sells flowers on the street. Throughout the play, the contrasting language of Henry Higgins, the professor, and Eliza Doolittle, the flower seller, reveals their differing social standing. The following exchange illustrates this contrast:

Liza: I ain't got no mother. Her that turned me out was my sixth stepmother. But I done without them. And I'm a good girl, I am.

Higgins: Very well, then, what on earth is all this fuss about?

A character's accent or dialect may also be significant. In **comedies of manners**, for example, rustic or provincial characters, identified by their speech, are often objects of humor. In *Pygmalion*, Eliza Doolittle uses cockney dialect, the dialect spoken in the East End of London. At first, her colorful, distinctive language (complete with expressions like *Nah-ow*, *garn*, and *ah-ah-ah-ow-ow-ow-oo*) and her nonstandard grammatical constructions make her an object of ridicule; later, the transformation of her speech reveals the dramatic changes in her character.

Plain and Elaborate Language

A character's speech may be simple and straightforward or complex and convoluted; it may be plain and unadorned or embellished with elaborate **figures of speech**. The relative complexity or lack of complexity of a character's speech may have different effects on the audience. For example, a character whose language is simple and unsophisticated may seem to be unintelligent, unenlightened, gullible, or naive—especially if that character also uses slang, dialect, or colloquial expressions. Conversely, a character's plain, down-to-earth language may convey common sense or intelligence. In fact, plain language may be quite emotionally powerful. For example, Willy Loman's speech in Arthur Miller's classic 1949 play *Death of a Salesman*, about an eighty-four-year-old fellow salesman named Dave Singleman, moves the audience with its sincerity and directness:

> Do you know? When he died—and by the way he died the death of a salesman, in his green velvet slippers in the smoker of the New York, New Haven and Hartford, going into Boston—when he died, hundreds of salesmen and buyers were at his funeral. Things were sad on a lotta trains for months after that.

Like plain speech, elaborate language may have different effects in different contexts. Sometimes, the use of figures of speech can make a character seem to have depth and insight and analytical skills absent in other characters. In the following excerpt from a soliloquy in Act 1 Scene 2 of *Hamlet*, for example, complex language reveals the depth of Hamlet's anguished self-analysis:

Hamlet: O, that this too too solid flesh would melt,
Thaw, and resolve itself into a dew!
Or that the Everlasting had not fix'd
His canon 'gainst self-slaughter! O God! O God!
How weary, stale, flat, and unprofitable
Seem to me all the uses of this world!
Fie on't, O fie, 'tis an unweeded garden,
That grows to seed. . . .

In these lines, Hamlet compares the world to a garden gone to seed. His use of imagery and figures of speech vividly communicates his feelings about the world and his internal struggle against the temptation to end his life.

Sometimes, however, elaborate language may make a character seem aloof, pompous, or even untrustworthy. In the following passages from Shakespeare's

King Lear, Goneril and Regan, the deceitful daughters, use complicated verbal constructions to conceal their true feelings from their father, King Lear. In contrast, Cordelia—the loyal, loving daughter—uses simple, straightforward language that suggests her sincerity and lack of artifice. Compare the three speeches:

Goneril: Sir, I love you more than words can wield the matter;
Dearer than eyesight, space, and liberty;
Beyond what can be valued, rich or rare;
No less than life, with grace, health, beauty, honour;
As much as child e'er lov'd, or father found;
A love that makes breath poor, and speech unable.
Beyond all manner of so much I love you. …

Regan: Sir, I am made
Of the selfsame metal that my sister is,
And prize me at her worth. In my true heart
I find she names my very deed of love;
Only she comes too short, that I profess
Myself an enemy to all other joys
Which the most precious square of sense possesses,
And find I am alone felicitate
In your dear Highness' love. …

Cordelia: Unhappy that I am, I cannot heave
My heart into my mouth. I love your Majesty
According to my bond; no more no less. …

Cordelia's unwillingness, even when she is prodded by Lear, to exaggerate her feelings or misrepresent her love through inflated language shows the audience her honesty and nobility. The contrast between her language and that of her sisters makes their very different motives clear.

Tone

Tone reveals a character's mood or attitude. Tone can be flat or emotional, bitter or accepting, affectionate or aloof, anxious or calm. Contrasts in tone can indicate differences in outlook or emotional state between two characters; changes in tone from one point in a play to another can suggest corresponding changes within a character. At the end of *A Doll's House*, for example, Nora is resigned to what she must do, and her language is appropriately controlled. Her husband, however, is desperate to change her mind, and his language reflects this desperation. The following exchanges of dialogue from the end of Act 3 illustrate the two characters' contrasting emotional states:

Torvald: But to lose you!—to lose you forever! No, no, Nora, I can't accept that.

Nora: *(going out to the right)* That is why it must happen.
Torvald: It's all over! All over!—Nora, will you never think of me again?
Nora: I know that I will often think of you ... and the children ... and this house.

In earlier scenes between the two characters, Nora is emotional—at times, hysterical—and her husband is considerably more controlled. As the exchanges above indicate, both Nora and Torvald Helmer have changed drastically during the course of the play.

Irony

Irony, a contradiction or discrepancy between two levels of meaning, can reveal a great deal about character. **Verbal irony**—a contradiction between what a character says and what he or she means—is very important in drama, where the verbal interplay between characters may carry the weight of the play. For example, when Nora and Dr. Rank discuss the latest news about his health in *A Doll's House*, there is deep irony in his use of the word "certainty" in light of his comment, "I am absolutely sure that the end is coming." Although the word might seem to suggest a reassuring confirmation, here it is actually meant to suggest death, and both Nora and Dr. Rank understand this.

Dramatic irony depends on the audience's knowing something that a character has not yet realized, or on one character's knowing something that other characters do not know. In some cases, dramatic irony is created by an audience's awareness of historical background or events of which characters are unaware. Familiar with the story of Oedipus, for example, the audience of *Oedipus the King* (p. 1137) knows that the man who has caused all the problems in Thebes—the man Oedipus vows to find and take revenge on—is Oedipus himself. In other cases, dramatic irony emerges when the audience learns something—something the characters do not yet know or comprehend—from a play's unfolding action. The central irony in *A Doll's House*, for example, is that the family's "happy home" rests on a foundation of secrets, lies, and deception. Torvald does not know about the secrets, and Nora does not understand how they have poisoned her marriage. The audience, however, quickly becomes aware of the atmosphere of deceit—and aware of how it threatens the family's happiness.

Dramatic irony may also be conveyed through dialogue. Typically, dramatic irony is revealed when a character says something that gives the audience information that other characters, offstage at the time, do not know. In *A Doll's House*, the audience knows—because Nora has explained her situation to Kristine—that Nora spent the previous Christmas season hard at work, earning money to pay her secret debt. Torvald, however, remains unaware of her activities and believes her story that she was using the time to make holiday decorations, which the cat destroyed. This belief is consistent with his impression of Nora as an irresponsible child, yet the audience has quite a different impression of her. This discrepancy, one of many contradictions between the audience's view of Nora and Torvald's view of her, helps to create dramatic tension in the play.

Finally, **asides** (comments to the audience that other characters do not hear) can create dramatic irony by undercutting dialogue, providing ironic contrast between what the characters on stage know and what the audience knows. In Anton Chekhov's *The Brute* (p. 769), for example, the audience knows that Mr. Smirnov is succumbing to Mrs. Popov's charms because he says, in an aside, "My God, what eyes she has! They're setting me on fire." Mrs. Popov, however, is not yet aware of his infatuation. The discrepancy between the audience's awareness and the character's adds to the play's humor.

Characters' Actions

Through their actions, characters convey their values and attitudes to the audience. Actions also reveal aspects of a character's personality. For example, when Nora in *A Doll's House* plays hide-and-seek with her children, eats forbidden macaroons, and takes childish joy in Christmas, her immaturity is apparent.

Audiences also learn about characters from what they do *not* do. Thus, Nora's failure to remain in touch with her friend Kristine, who has had a hard life, reveals her selfishness, and the decision by Mrs. Peters and Mrs. Hale in *Trifles* not to give their evidence to the sheriff indicates their defiant support for Mrs. Wright and their understanding of what motivated her to take such drastic action.

Finally, audiences learn a good deal about characters by observing how they interact with other characters. In William Shakespeare's *Othello*, Iago is the embodiment of evil, and as the play's action unfolds, we discover his true nature. He reveals the secret marriage of Othello and Desdemona to her father; he schemes to arouse Othello's jealousy, making him believe Desdemona has been unfaithful with his lieutenant, Cassio; he persuades Cassio to ask Desdemona to plead his case with Othello, knowing this act will further arouse Othello's suspicions; he encourages Othello to be suspicious of Desdemona's defense of Cassio; he plants Desdemona's handkerchief in Cassio's room; and, finally, he persuades Othello to kill Desdemona and then kills his own wife, Emilia, to prevent her from exposing his role in the intrigue. As the play progresses, then, Iago's dealings with others consistently reveal him to be evil and corrupt.

Stage Directions

When we read a play (rather than see it performed), we also read the playwright's italicized **stage directions**, the notes that concern **staging**—the scenery, props, lighting, music, sound effects, costumes, and other elements that contribute to the way the play looks and sounds to an audience (see Chapter 31). In addition to commenting on staging, stage directions may supply physical details about the characters, suggesting their age, appearance, movements, gestures, and facial expressions. These details may in turn convey additional information about characters: appearance may reveal social position or economic status, expressions may reveal attitudes, and so on. Stage directions may also indicate the manner in which a line of dialogue is to be delivered—*confidently* or *hesitantly*, for instance. Thus, the way a line is spoken may reveal a character to be excited, upset, angry, shy, or disappointed. Finally, stage directions may indicate changes in characters—for example, a character whose speech is described as timid in early scenes may deliver lines emphatically and forcefully later on in the play.

Some stage directions provide a good deal of detail about character; others do little more than list characters' names. Arthur Miller is one playwright who often provides detailed information about character through stage directions. In *Death of a Salesman*, for example, Miller's stage directions at the beginning of Act 1 characterize the salesman, Willy Loman, immediately and specifically:

> *He is past sixty years of age, dressed quietly. Even as he crosses the stage to the doorway of the house, his exhaustion is apparent. He unlocks the door, comes into the kitchen, and thankfully lets his burden down, feeling the soreness of his palms. A word-sigh escapes his lips ...*

Subsequent stage directions indicate how lines are to be spoken. For example, in the play's opening lines, Willy's wife Linda calls out to him "*with some trepidation*"; Linda speaks "*very carefully, delicately*," and Willy speaks "*with casual irritation*." These instructions to readers (and actors) are meant to suggest the strained relationship between the two characters.

George Bernard Shaw is well known for the full character description in his stage directions. In these directions—seen by readers of the play but of course not heard by audiences—he communicates complex information about characters' attitudes and values, motivation and reactions, and relationships with other characters. In doing so, Shaw himself functions as a kind of narrator, explicitly communicating his own attitudes toward various characters. (The voice in Shaw's stage directions is not the voice of a character in the play; it is the voice of the playwright.) Shaw's stage directions for *Pygmalion* initially describe Eliza Doolittle as follows:

> *She is not at all an attractive person. She is perhaps eighteen, perhaps twenty, hardly older. She wears a little sailor hat of black straw that has long been exposed to the dust and soot of London and has seldom if ever been brushed. Her hair needs washing rather badly; its mousy color can hardly be natural. She wears a shoddy black coat that reaches nearly to her knees and is shaped to her waist. She has a brown skirt with a coarse apron. Her boots are much the worse for wear. She is no doubt as clean as she can afford to be; but compared to the ladies she is very dirty. Her features are no worse than theirs; but their condition leaves something to be desired; and she needs the services of a dentist.*

Rather than providing an objective summary of the character's most notable physical attributes, Shaw injects subjective comments (*"seldom if ever brushed"*; *"color can hardly be natural"*; *"no doubt as clean as she can afford to be"*) that reveal his attitude toward Eliza. This initially supercilious attitude, which he has in common with Professor Higgins, is tempered considerably by the end of the play, helping to make Eliza's transformation more obvious to readers than it would be if measured by her words and actions alone. By Act 5, the tone of the stage directions characterizing Eliza has changed to admiration: "*Eliza enters, sunny, self-possessed, and giving a staggeringly convincing exhibition of ease of manner.*"

Stage directions in most other plays are not nearly as comprehensive. In *Hamlet*, for example, characters are introduced with only the barest identifying tags: "Claudius, *King of Denmark*"; "Hamlet, *Son to the former, and nephew to the present King*"; "*Gertrude, Queen of Denmark, mother to Hamlet.*" Most of the play's stage directions do little more than chronicle the various characters' entrances and exits or specify particular physical actions: "*Enter Ghost*"; "*Spreads his arms*"; "*Ghost beckons Hamlet*"; "*He kneels*"; "*Sheathes his sword*"; "*Leaps in the grave.*" Occasionally, stage directions specify a prop ("*Puts down the skull*"); a sound effect ("*A noise within*"); or a costume ("*Enter the ghost in his night-gown*"). Such brevity is typical of Shakespeare's plays, in which characters are delineated almost solely by their words—and, not incidentally, by the way actors have interpreted the characters over the years. In fact, because Shakespeare's stage directions only suggest characters' gestures, physical reactions, movements, and facial expressions, actors have been left quite free to experiment, reading various interpretations into Shakespeare's characters.

Actors' Interpretations

When we see a play performed, we gain insight into the characters not merely through what they say and do or how other characters react to them, but also through the way the actors interpret the roles. If a playwright does not specify characters' mannerisms, gestures, or movements, or does not indicate how a line is to be delivered, actors are free to interpret their roles as they believe they should be played. Even when a playwright *does* specify such actions, actors have a good deal of freedom to decide which gestures or expressions will convey a particular emotion.

In "Some Thoughts on Playwriting" (1941), American dramatist Thornton Wilder argues that "the theatre is an art which reposes upon the work of many collaborators" rather than on "one governing selecting will." Citing examples from Shakespeare and Ibsen, Wilder illustrates the great degree of "intervention" that may occur in dramatic productions. For example, Wilder observes, Shakespeare's Shylock (a character in *The Merchant of Venice*) has been portrayed by two different actors as "noble, wronged and indignant" and as "a vengeful and hysterical buffoon"—and both performances were considered plausible interpretations. As noted earlier, the absence of detailed stage directions in Shakespeare's plays makes possible (and perhaps even encourages) such widely divergent interpretations. However, as Wilder points out, even when playing roles created by a dramatist such as Ibsen, whose stage directions are typically quite specific, actors and directors have a good deal of leeway. Thus, actress Janet McTeer, who played the part of Ibsen's Nora in the 1997 London production of *A Doll's House*, saw Nora and Torvald, despite their many problems, as "the perfect couple," deeply in love and involved in a passionate marriage. "You have to make that marriage sexually credible," McTeer told the *New York Times*, "to imagine they have a wonderful time in bed, so there becomes something to lose. If you play them as already past it or no longer attracted to each other, then there is no play." This interpretation is not inconsistent with the play, but it does go beyond what Ibsen actually wrote.

Similarly, the role of Catherine in David Auburn's 2001 play *Proof* has been played by several actresses—among them Mary-Louise Parker, Jennifer Jason Leigh, Anne Heche, Gwyneth Paltrow, and Lea Salonga—and each actress has interpreted this complex character in a different way. As *New York Times* theater critic John Rockwell observes, "Catherine can be loopy-ethereal-sexy (Ms. Parker), earthy and even a little bitter (Ms. Leigh), or adorable-needy-fragile (Ms. Heche), and Mr. Auburn's structure and characters and ideas still work."

Irish playwright Samuel Beckett devotes a good deal of attention to indicating actors' movements and gestures and their physical reactions to one another. In his 1952 play *Waiting for Godot*, for example, Beckett's stage directions seem to choreograph every gesture, every emotion, every intention:

- *(he looks at them ostentatiously in turn to make it clear they are both meant)*
- *Vladimir seizes Lucky's hat. Silence of Lucky. He falls. Silence. Panting of the victors.*
- *Estragon hands him the boot. Vladimir inspects it, throws it down angrily.*
- *Estragon pulls, stumbles, falls. Long silence.*
- *He goes feverishly to and fro, halts finally at extreme left, broods.*

Beckett provides full and obviously carefully thought-out stage directions and, in so doing, attempts to retain a good deal of control over his characters. Still, in a 1988 production of *Godot*, director Mike Nichols and comic actors Robin Williams and Steve Martin felt free to improvise, adding gestures and movements not specified or even hinted at—and most critics believed that this production remained true to the tragicomic spirit of Beckett's existentialist play. In a sense, then, the playwright's words on the page are just the beginning of the characters' lives on the stage.

Checklist Writing about Character

- Does any character serve as a narrator? If so, what information does this narrator supply about the other characters? How reliable is the narrator?
- Who are the major characters? What do we know about them?
- Do the major characters change and grow during the play, or do they remain essentially unchanged?
- What do the minor characters contribute to the play?
- Does the play include monologues or soliloquies? What do these extended speeches reveal about the characters?
- What is revealed about the characters through dialogue?
- Do characters use foreign words, regionalisms, slang, jargon, clichés, or profanity? What does such use of language reveal about the characters? About the play's theme?
- Is the characters' language formal or informal?
- Is the characters' language plain or elaborate?
- Do different characters use different kinds of language? What is the significance of these differences?
- How does language reveal each character's emotional state?
- Does the tone of any character's language change significantly as the play progresses? What does this change reveal?
- Does the play include verbal irony? dramatic irony? How is irony conveyed? What purpose does irony achieve?
- What is revealed about the characters through what others say about them?
- What is revealed about characters through their actions?
- What is revealed about characters through the play's stage directions?
- How might different actors' interpretations change an audience's understanding of the characters?

Jack Mitchell/Archive Photos/Getty Images

TENNESSEE WILLIAMS (1911–1983) was born Thomas Lanier Williams in Columbus, Mississippi, on March 26, 1911. His father, who came from a well-to-do and well-connected Tennessee family, was a shoe salesman who was often on the road. His mother was the daughter of a minister, and her genteel ways left her ill-equipped to handle her three rowdy children.

Williams enrolled at the University of Missouri, but he found that college did not give him enough opportunity to write, so he left school and worked at his father's shoe company—and as a waiter, an elevator operator, and a theater usher—while he wrote. Hoping to learn playwriting, he eventually went back to college and graduated from the University of Iowa in 1938. A year later, he adopted his college nickname and began to publish as Tennessee Williams.

Williams's earliest staged play, *Cairo, Shanghai, Bombay,* was produced in Memphis in 1937, followed closely by *Candles to the Sun* and *The Fugitive Kind.* Williams's career took off, and he went on to write over fifty plays, ten works of fiction, several books of poetry, and other collections of writing, including his letters and memoirs. His most successful plays include *The Glass Menagerie* (1945), *A Streetcar Named Desire* (1947), *Cat on a Hot Tin Roof* (1955), *Night of the Iguana* (1961), and *Sweet Bird of Youth* (1959). A rediscovered early play, *Not about Nightingales,* was staged in New York City in 1999.

The Glass Menagerie, Williams's first major success, won the New York Drama Critics Circle Award, freeing Williams to write plays full-time. He saw his play as somewhat autobiographical: he said that his sister Rose had a collection of glass animals in her room in St. Louis, and he gave his own real first name to Tom, Laura's brother in the play. In the first movie version of the play, the story was altered to include a second, more promising Gentleman Caller at its conclusion, giving it a happy ending. To the end of his life, Williams strongly disliked this change.

Tennessee Williams found acclaim wherever he took his plays, from the age of thirty-four and the remarkable success of *The Glass Menagerie* until the end of his life. He received four New York Drama Critics Circle Awards, won a Pulitzer Prize for *Streetcar* in 1948, and saw both *Streetcar* and *The Glass Menagerie* made into successful Hollywood films. *Cat on a Hot Tin Roof* (for which he won his second Pulitzer), *Orpheus Descending,* and *Night of the Iguana* were also filmed.

Cultural Context Williams's work is largely autobiographical, often drawing comparisons between his family and his characters and using the backdrops with which he was most familiar. Williams moved around a good deal—from New Orleans, to Key West, to New York City, to Provincetown. Each locale had a significant gay population, where Williams, who was gay himself, felt comfortable. Through much of his life, Williams battled alcoholism, drug abuse, and mental illness. His older sister Rose, who was diagnosed as schizophrenic, underwent a prefrontal lobotomy in her late twenties and was institutionalized for the remainder of her life; Williams himself suffered a mental breakdown at a young age. In the end, he choked to death on a bottle cap in a New York City hotel room.

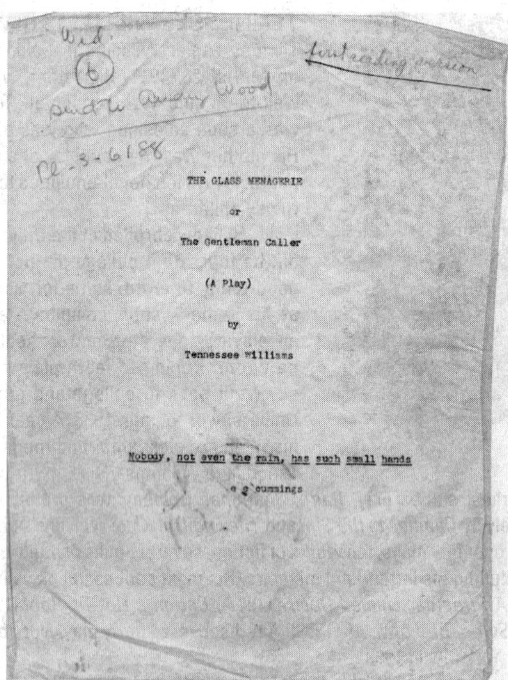

THE GLASS MENAGERIE

or

The Gentleman Caller

(A Play)

by

Tennessee Williams

Nobody, not even the rain, has such small hands

e e cummings

This title page, from a 1944 manuscript, includes as its epigraph the last line from the E. E. Cummings poem "somewhere i have never travelled, gladly beyond"

The Glass Menagerie (1945)

Nobody, not even the rain, has such small hands.
E. E. Cummings

CHARACTERS

Amanda Wingfield, *the mother. A little woman of great but confused vitality clinging frantically to another time and place. Her characterization must be carefully created, not copied from type. She is not paranoiac, but her life is paranoia. There is much to admire in Amanda, and as much to love and pity as there is to laugh at. Certainly she has endurance and a kind of heroism, and though her foolishness makes her unwittingly cruel at times, there is tenderness in her slight person.*

Laura Wingfield, *her daughter. Amanda, having failed to establish contact with reality, continues to live vitally in her illusions, but Laura's situation is even graver. A childhood illness has left her crippled, one leg slightly shorter than the other, and held in a brace. This defect need not be more than suggested on the stage. Stemming from this, Laura's separation increases till she is like a piece of her own glass collection, too exquisitely fragile to move from the shelf.*

Tom Wingfield, *her son. And the narrator of the play. A poet with a job in a warehouse. His nature is not remorseless, but to escape from a trap he has to act without pity.*

Jim O'Connor, *the gentleman caller. A nice, ordinary, young man.*

SCENE

An alley in St. Louis.

PART I

Preparation for a Gentleman Caller.

PART II

The Gentleman Calls.

TIME

Now and the Past.

SCENE 1

The Wingfield apartment is in the rear of the building, one of those vast hive-like conglomerations of cellular living-units that flower as warty growths in over-crowded urban centers of lower middle-class population and are symptomatic of the impulse of this largest and fundamentally enslaved section of American society to avoid fluidity and differentiation and to exist and function as one interfused mass of automatism.

The apartment faces an alley and is entered by a fire-escape, a structure whose name is a touch of accidental poetic truth, for all of these huge buildings are always burning with the slow and implacable fires of human desperation. The fire-escape is included in the set—that is, the landing of it and steps descending from it.

The scene is memory and is therefore nonrealistic. Memory takes a lot of poetic license. It omits some details; others are exaggerated, according to the emotional value of the articles it touches, for memory is seated predominantly in the heart. The interior is therefore rather dim and poetic.

At the rise of the curtain, the audience is faced with the dark, grim rear wall of the Wingfield tenement. This building, which runs parallel to the footlights, is flanked on both sides by dark, narrow alleys which run into murky canyons of tangled clotheslines, garbage cans and the sinister latticework of neighboring fire-escapes. It is up and down these side alleys that exterior entrances and exits are made, during the play. At the end of Tom's opening commentary, the dark tenement wall slowly reveals (by means of a transparency) the interior of the ground floor Wingfield apartment.

Downstage is the living room, which also serves as a sleeping room for Laura, the sofa unfolding to make her bed. Upstage, center, and divided by a wide arch or second proscenium with transparent faded portieres (or second curtain), is the dining room. In an old-fashioned what-not in the living room are seen scores of transparent glass animals. A blown-up photograph of the father hangs on the wall of the living room, facing the audience, to the left of the archway. It is the face of a very handsome young man in a doughboy's First World War cap. He is gallantly smiling, ineluctably smiling, as if to say, "I will be smiling forever."

The audience hears and sees the opening scene in the dining room through both the transparent fourth wall of the building and the transparent gauze portieres of the dining-room arch. It is during this revealing scene that the fourth wall slowly ascends, out of sight. This transparent exterior wall is not brought down again until the very end of the play, during Tom's final speech.

The narrator is an undisguised convention of the play. He takes whatever license with dramatic convention as is convenient to his purposes.

Tom enters dressed as a merchant sailor from the alley, stage left, and strolls across the front of the stage to the fire-escape. There he stops and lights a cigarette. He addresses the audience.

Tom: Yes, I have tricks in my pocket, I have things up my sleeve. But I am the opposite of a stage magician. He gives you illusion that has the appearance of truth. I give you truth in the pleasant disguise of illusion. To begin with, I turn back time. I reverse it to that quaint period, the thirties, when the huge middle class of America was matriculating in a school for the blind. Their eyes had failed them, or they had failed their eyes, and so they were having their fingers pressed forcibly down on the fiery Braille alphabet of a dissolving economy. In Spain there was revolution.[1] Here there was only shouting and confusion. In Spain there was Guernica.[2] Here there were disturbances of labor, sometimes pretty violent, in otherwise peaceful cities such as Chicago, Cleveland, Saint Louis. . . . This is the social background of the play.

Music.

The play is memory. Being a memory play, it is dimly lighted, it is sentimental, it is not realistic. In memory everything seems to happen to music. That explains the fiddle in the wings. I am the narrator of the play, and also a character in it. The other characters are my mother, Amanda, my sister, Laura, and a gentleman caller who appears in the final scenes. He is the most realistic character in the play, being an emissary from a world of reality that we were somehow set apart from.

---

[1] *revolution:* The Spanish Civil War (1936–1939).

[2] *Guernica:* A Basque town in northern Spain, bombed and practically destroyed on April 27, 1937, by German planes aiding fascist General Francisco Franco's Nationalists. The destruction is depicted in one of Pablo Picasso's most famous paintings, *Guernica* (1937).

But since I have a poet's weakness for symbols, I am using this character also as a symbol; he is the long delayed but always expected something that we live for. There is a fifth character in the play who doesn't appear except in this larger-than-life photograph over the mantel. This is our father who left us a long time ago. He was a telephone man who fell in love with long distances; he gave up his job with the telephone company and skipped the light fantastic out of town. . . . The last we heard of him was a picture post-card from Mazatlan, on the Pacific coast of Mexico, containing a message of two words—"Hello—Good-bye!" and an address. I think the rest of the play will explain itself. . . .

Amanda's voice becomes audible through the portieres.

Legend On Screen: "Où Sont Les Neiges."[3]

He divides the portieres and enters the upstage area.

Amanda and Laura are seated at a drop-leaf table. Eating is indicated by gestures without food or utensils. Amanda faces the audience. Tom and Laura are seated in profile.

The interior has lit up softly and through the scrim we see Amanda and Laura seated at the table in the upstage area.

Amanda: *(calling)* Tom?

Tom: Yes, Mother.

Amanda: We can't say grace until you come to the table!

Tom: Coming, Mother. *(He bows slightly and withdraws, reappearing a few moments later in his place at the table.)*

Amanda: *(to her son)* Honey, don't *push* with your *fingers*. If you have to push with something, the thing to push with is a crust of bread. And chew—chew! Animals have sections in their stomachs which enable them to digest food without mastication, but human beings are supposed to chew their food before they swallow it down. Eat food leisurely, son, and really enjoy it. A well-cooked meal has lots of delicate flavors that have to be held in the mouth for appreciation. So chew your food and give your salivary glands a chance to function!

Tom deliberately lays his imaginary fork down and pushes his chair back from the table.

Tom: I haven't enjoyed one bite of this dinner because of your constant directions on how to eat it. It's you that makes me rush through meals with your hawk-like attention to every bite I take. Sickening—spoils my appetite—all this discussion of animals' secretion—salivary glands—mastication!

---

[3] *"Où Sont Les Neiges"*: "Where the snows [of yesteryear]." A famous line by French poet François Villon (1431–1463?).

Amanda: *(lightly)* Temperament like a Metropolitan star! *(He rises and crosses downstage.)* You're not excused from the table.

Tom: I am getting a cigarette.

Amanda: You smoke too much.

Laura rises.

Laura: I'll bring in the blanc mange.

He remains standing with his cigarette by the portieres during the following.

Amanda: *(rising)* No, sister, no, sister—you be the lady this time and I'll be the darky.

Laura: I'm already up.

Amanda: Resume your seat, little sister—I want you to stay fresh and pretty—for gentlemen callers!

Laura: I'm not expecting any gentlemen callers.

Amanda: *(crossing out to kitchenette. Airily)* Sometimes they come when they are least expected! Why, I remember one Sunday afternoon in Blue Mountain— *(Enters kitchenette.)*

Tom: I know what's coming!

Laura: Yes. But let her tell it.

Tom: Again?

Laura: She loves to tell it.

Amanda returns with bowl of dessert.

Amanda: One Sunday afternoon in Blue Mountain—your mother received—*seventeen!*—gentlemen callers! Why, sometimes there weren't chairs enough to accommodate them all. We had to send the nigger over to bring in folding chairs from the parish house.

Tom: *(remaining at portieres)* How did you entertain those gentlemen callers?

Amanda: I understood the art of conversation!

Scene from the 2019 ballet premiere of *The Glass Menagerie*, with Alina Cojocaru (as Laura Rose Wingfield), performed at the Hamburg State Opera

Picture Alliance/Getty Images

Tom: I bet you could talk.
Amanda: Girls in those days *knew* how to talk, I can tell you.
Tom: Yes?

Image: Amanda As A Girl On A Porch Greeting Callers.

Amanda: They knew how to entertain their gentlemen callers. It wasn't enough for a girl to be possessed of a pretty face and a graceful figure—although I wasn't slighted in either respect. She also needed to have a nimble wit and a tongue to meet all occasions.
Tom: What did you talk about?
Amanda: Things of importance going on in the world! Never anything coarse or common or vulgar. *(She addresses Tom as though he were seated in the vacant chair at the table though he remains by portieres. He plays this scene as though he held the book.)* My callers were gentlemen—all! Among my callers were some of the most prominent young planters of the Mississippi Delta—planters and sons of planters!

Tom motions for music and a spot of light on Amanda. Her eyes lift, her face glows, her voice becomes rich and elegiac.

Screen Legend: "Où Sont Les Neiges."

There was young Champ Laughlin who later became vice-president of the Delta Planters Bank. Hadley Stevenson who was drowned in Moon Lake and left his widow one hundred and fifty thousand in Government bonds. There were the Cutrere brothers, Wesley and Bates. Bates was one of my bright particular beaux! He got in a quarrel with that wild Wainright boy. They shot it out on the floor of Moon Lake Casino. Bates was shot through the stomach. Died in the ambulance on his way to Memphis. His widow was also well-provided for, came into eight or ten thousand acres, that's all. She married him on the rebound—never loved her—carried my picture on him the night he died! And there was that boy that every girl in the Delta had set her cap for! That beautiful, brilliant young Fitzhugh boy from Green County!
Tom: What did he leave his widow?
Amanda: He never married! Gracious, you talk as though all of my old admirers had turned up their toes to the daisies!
Tom: Isn't this the first you mentioned that still survives?
Amanda: That Fitzhugh boy went North and made a fortune—came to be known as the Wolf of Wall Street! He had the Midas touch, whatever he touched turned to gold! And I could have been Mrs. Duncan J. Fitzhugh, mind you! But—I picked your *father!*
Laura: *(rising)* Mother, let me clear the table.
Amanda: No dear, you go in front and study your typewriter chart. Or practice your shorthand a little. Stay fresh and pretty!—It's almost time for our gentlemen callers to start arriving. *(She flounces girlishly toward the kitchenette.)* How many do you suppose we're going to entertain this afternoon?

Tom throws down the paper and jumps up with a groan.

Laura: *(alone in the dining room)* I don't believe we're going to receive any, Mother.

Amanda: *(reappearing, airily)* What? No one—not one? You must be joking! *(Laura nervously echoes her laugh. She slips in a fugitive manner through the half-open portieres and draws them gently behind her. A shaft of very clear light is thrown on her face against the faded tapestry of the curtains.) (Music: "The Glass Menagerie" under faintly.) (Lightly.)* Not one gentleman caller? It can't be true! There must be a flood, there must have been a tornado!

Laura: It isn't a flood, it's not a tornado, Mother. I'm just not popular like you were in Blue Mountain. . . . *(Tom utters another groan. Laura glances at him with a faint, apologetic smile. Her voice catching a little.)* Mother's afraid I'm going to be an old maid.

The Scene Dims Out With "Glass Menagerie" Music.

SCENE 2

"Laura, Haven't You Ever Liked Some Boy?"

On the dark stage the screen is lighted with the image of blue roses.

Gradually Laura's figure becomes apparent and the screen goes out.

The music subsides.

Laura is seated in the delicate ivory chair at the small clawfoot table.

She wears a dress of soft violet material for a kimono—her hair tied back from her forehead with a ribbon.

She is washing and polishing her collection of glass.

Amanda appears on the fire-escape steps. At the sound of her ascent, Laura catches her breath, thrusts the bowl of ornaments away and seats herself stiffly before the diagram of the typewriter keyboard as though it held her spellbound. Something has happened to Amanda. It is written in her face as she climbs to the landing: a look that is grim and hopeless and a little absurd.

She has on one of those cheap or imitation velvety-looking cloth coats with imitation fur collar. Her hat is five or six years old, one of those dreadful cloche hats that were worn in the late twenties, and she is clasping an enormous black patent-leather pocketbook with nickel clasp and initials. This is her fulldress outfit, the one she usually wears to the D.A.R.[1]

Before entering she looks through the door.

---

[1]*D.A.R.:* Daughters of the American Revolution, an organization for female descendants of participants in the American Revolution, founded in 1890. That Amanda is a member says much about her concern with the past, as well as about her pride and affectations.

She purses her lips, opens her eyes wide, rolls them upward and shakes her head.

Then she slowly lets herself in the door. Seeing her mother's expression Laura touches her lips with a nervous gesture.

Laura: Hello, Mother, I was— *(She makes a nervous gesture toward the chart on the wall. Amanda leans against the shut door and stares at Laura with a martyred look.)*

Amanda: Deception? Deception? *(She slowly removes her hat and gloves, continuing the swift suffering stare. She lets the hat and gloves fall on the floor—a bit of acting.)*

Laura: *(shakily)* How was the D.A.R. meeting? *(Amanda slowly opens her purse and removes a dainty white handkerchief which she shakes out delicately and delicately touches to her lips and nostrils.)* Didn't you go to the D.A.R. meeting, Mother?

Amanda: *(faintly, almost inaudibly)*—No.—No. *(Then more forcibly.)* I did not have the strength—to go the D.A.R. In fact, I did not have the courage! I wanted to find a hole in the ground and hide myself in it forever! *(She crosses slowly to the wall and removes the diagram of the typewriter keyboard. She holds it in front of her for a second, staring at it sweetly and sorrowfully—then bites her lips and tears it in two pieces.)*

Laura: *(faintly)* Why did you do that, Mother? *(Amanda repeats the same procedure with the chart of the Gregg Alphabet.)* Why are you—

Amanda: Why? Why? How old are you, Laura?

Laura: Mother, you know my age.

Amanda: I thought that you were an adult; it seems that I was mistaken. *(She crosses slowly to the sofa and sinks down and stares at Laura.)*

Laura: Please don't stare at me, Mother.

Amanda closes her eyes and lowers her head. Count ten.

Amanda: What are we going to do, what is going to become of us, what is the future?

Count ten.

Laura: Has something happened, Mother? *(Amanda draws a long breath and takes out the handkerchief again. Dabbing process.)* Mother, has—something happened?

Amanda: I'll be all right in a minute. I'm just bewildered—*(count five)*—by life. . . .

Laura: Mother, I wish that you would tell me what's happened.

Amanda: As you know, I was supposed to be inducted into my office at the D.A.R. this afternoon. *(Image: A Swarm Of Typewriters.)* But I stopped off at Rubicam's Business College to speak to your teachers about your having a cold and ask them what progress they thought you were making down there.

Laura: Oh. . . .

Amanda: I went to the typing instructor and introduced myself as your mother. She didn't know who you were. Wingfield, she said. We don't have any such student enrolled at the school! I assured her she did, that you had been going to classes since early in January. "I wonder," she said, "if you could be talking about that terribly shy little girl who dropped out of school after only a few days' attendance?" "No," I said, "Laura, my daughter, has been going to school every day for the past six weeks!" "Excuse me," she said. She took the attendance book out and there was your name, unmistakably printed, and all the dates you were absent until they decided that you had dropped out of school. I still said, "No, there must have been some mistake! There must have been some mix-up in the records!" And she said, "No—I remember her perfectly now. Her hand shook so that she couldn't hit the right keys! The first time we gave a speed-test, she broke down completely—was sick at the stomach and almost had to be carried into the wash-room! After that morning she never showed up any more. We phoned the house but never got any answer"—while I was working at Famous and Barr, I suppose, demonstrating those—Oh! I felt so weak I could barely keep on my feet. I had to sit down while they got me a glass of water! Fifty dollars' tuition, all of our plans—my hopes and ambitions for you—just gone up the spout, just gone up the spout like that. *(Laura draws a long breath and gets awkwardly to her feet. She crosses to the Victrola and winds it up.)* What are you doing?

Laura: Oh! *(She releases the handle and returns to her seat.)*

Amanda: Laura, where have you been going when you've gone out pretending that you were going to business college?

Laura: I've just been going out walking.

Amanda: That's not true.

Laura: It is. I just went walking.

Amanda: Walking? Walking? In winter? Deliberately courting pneumonia in that light coat? Where did you walk to, Laura?

Laura: It was the lesser of two evils, Mother. *(Image: Winter Scene In Park.)* I couldn't go back up. I—threw up—on the floor!

Amanda: From half past seven till after five every day you mean to tell me you walked around in the park, because you wanted to make me think that you were still going to Rubicam's Business College?

Laura: It wasn't as bad as it sounds. I went inside places to get warmed up.

Amanda: Inside where?

Laura: I went in the art museum and the bird-houses at the Zoo. I visited the penguins every day! Sometimes I did without lunch and went to the movies. Lately I've been spending most of my afternoons in the Jewel-box, that big glass house where they raise the tropical flowers.

Amanda: You did all this to deceive me, just for the deception? *(Laura looks down.)* Why?

Laura: Mother, when you're disappointed, you get that awful suffering look on your face, like the picture of Jesus' mother in the museum!

Amanda: Hush!
Laura: I couldn't face it.

Pause. A whisper of strings.

Legend: "The Crust Of Humility."

Amanda: *(hopelessly fingering the huge pocketbook)* So what are we going to do the rest of our lives? Stay home and watch the parades go by? Amuse ourselves with the glass menagerie, darling? Eternally play those worn-out phonograph records your father left as a painful reminder of him? We won't have a business career—we've given that up because it gave us nervous indigestion! *(Laughs wearily.)* What is there left but dependency all our lives? I know so well what becomes of unmarried women who aren't prepared to occupy a position. I've seen such pitiful cases in the South—barely tolerated spinsters living upon the grudging patronage of sister's husband or brother's wife!—stuck away in some little mouse-trap of a room—encouraged by one in-law to visit another—little birdlike women without any nest—eating the crust of humility all their life! Is that the future that we've mapped out for ourselves? I swear it's the only alternative I can think of! It isn't a very pleasant alternative, is it? Of course—some girls *do marry. (Laura twists her hands nervously.)* Haven't you ever liked some boy?
Laura: Yes I liked one once. *(Rises.)* I came across his picture a while ago.
Amanda: *(with some interest)* He gave you his picture?
Laura: No, it's in the year-book.
Amanda: *(disappointed)* Oh—a high-school boy.

Screen Image: Jim As A High-School Hero Bearing A Silver Cup.

Laura: Yes. His name was Jim. *(Laura lifts the heavy annual from the clawfoot table.)* Here he is in *The Pirates of Penzance.*[2]
Amanda: *(absently)* The what?
Laura: The operetta the senior class put on. He had a wonderful voice and we sat across the aisle from each other Mondays, Wednesdays and Fridays in the Aud. Here he is with the silver cup for debating! See his grin?
Amanda: *(absently)* He must have had a jolly disposition.
Laura: He used to call me—Blue Roses.

Image: Blue Roses.

Amanda: Why did he call you such a name as that?
Laura: When I had that attack of pleurosis—he asked me what was the matter when I came back. I said pleurosis—he thought that I said Blue Roses! So that's what he always called me after that. Whenever he saw

[2] *The Pirates of Penzance:* A musical by Gilbert and Sullivan.

me, he'd holler, "Hello, Blue Roses!" I didn't care for the girl that he went out with. Emily Meisenbach. Emily was the best-dressed girl at Soldan. She never struck me, though, as being sincere . . . It says in the Personal Section—they're engaged. That's—six years ago! They must be married by now.

Amanda: Girls that aren't cut out for business careers usually wind up married to some nice man. *(Gets up with a spark of revival.)* Sister, that's what you'll do!

Laura utters a startled, doubtful laugh. She reaches quickly for a piece of glass.

Laura: But, Mother—

Amanda: Yes? *(Crossing to photograph.)*

Laura: *(in a tone of frightened apology)* I'm—crippled!

Image: Screen.

Amanda: Nonsense! Laura, I've told you never, never to use that word. Why, you're not crippled, you just have a little defect—hardly noticeable, even! When people have some slight disadvantage like that, they cultivate other things to make up for it—develop charm—and vivacity—and—charm! That's all you have to do! *(She turns again to the photograph.)* One thing your father had *plenty* of—was *charm!*

Tom motions to the fiddle in the wings.

The Scene Fades Out With Music.

SCENE 3

Legend On The Screen: "After The Fiasco—"

Tom speaks from the fire-escape landing.

Tom: After the fiasco at Rubicam's Business College, the idea of getting a gentleman caller for Laura began to play a more important part in Mother's calculations. It became an obsession. Like some archetype of the universal unconscious, the image of the gentleman caller haunted our small apartment. . . . *(Image: Young Man At Door With Flowers.)* An evening at home rarely passed without some allusion to this image, this spectre, this hope. . . . Even when he wasn't mentioned, his presence hung in Mother's preoccupied look and in my sister's frightened, apologetic manner—hung like a sentence passed upon the Wingfields! Mother was a woman of action as well as words. She began to take logical steps in the planned direction. Late that winter and in the early spring—realizing that extra money would be needed to properly feather the nest and plume the bird—she conducted a vigorous campaign on the telephone, roping in subscribers to one of those magazines for matrons called *The*

Home-maker's Companion, the type of journal that features the serialized sublimations of ladies of letters who think in terms of delicate cup-like breasts, slim, tapering waists, rich, creamy thighs, eyes like wood-smoke in autumn, fingers that soothe and caress like strains of music, bodies as powerful as Etruscan sculpture.

Screen Image: A Glamour Magazine Cover.

Amanda enters with phone on long extension cord. She is spotted in the dim stage.

Amanda: Ida Scott? This is Amanda Wingfield! We *missed* you at the D.A.R. last Monday! I said to myself: She's probably suffering with that sinus condition! How is that sinus condition? Horrors! Heaven have mercy!—You're a Christian martyr, yes, that's what you are, a Christian martyr! Well, I just now happened to notice that your subscription to the *Companion's* about to expire! Yes, it expires with the next issue, honey!—just when that wonderful new serial by Bessie Mae Hopper is getting off to such an exciting start. Oh, honey, it's something that you can't miss! You remember how *Gone With the Wind* took everybody by storm? You simply couldn't go out if you hadn't read it. All everybody *talked* was Scarlett O'Hara. Well, this is a book that critics already compare to *Gone With the Wind*. It's the *Gone With the Wind* of the post–World War generation!—What?—Burning?—Oh, honey, don't let them burn, go take a look in the oven and I'll hold the wire! Heavens—I think she's hung up!

Dim Out.

Legend On Screen: "You Think I'm In Love With Continental Shoemakers?"

Before the stage is lighted, the violent voices of Tom and Amanda are heard. They are quarreling behind the portieres. In front of them stands Laura with clenched hands and panicky expression.

A clear pool of light on her figure throughout this scene.

Tom: What in Christ's name am I—
Amanda: *(shrilly)* Don't you use that—
Tom: Supposed to do!
Amanda: Expression! Not in my—
Tom: Ohhh!
Amanda: Presence! Have you gone out of your senses?
Tom: I have, that's true, *driven* out!
Amanda: What is the matter with you, you—big—big—IDIOT!
Tom: Look—I've got *no thing*, no single thing—
Amanda: Lower your voice!
Tom: In my life here that I can call my OWN! Everything is—
Amanda: Stop that shouting!

Tom: Yesterday you confiscated my books! You had the nerve to—

Amanda: I took that horrible novel back to the library—yes! That hideous book by that insane Mr. Lawrence.[1] *(Tom laughs wildly.)* I cannot control the output of diseased minds or people who cater to them—*(Tom laughs still more wildly.)* BUT I WON'T ALLOW SUCH FILTH BROUGHT INTO MY HOUSE! No, no, no, no, no!

Tom: House, house! Who pays rent on it, who makes a slave of himself to—

Amanda: *(fairly screeching)* Don't you DARE to—

Tom: No, no, *I* mustn't say things! *I've* got to just—

Amanda: Let me tell you—

Tom: I don't want to hear any more! *(He tears the portieres open. The upstage area is lit with a turgid smoky red glow.)*

Amanda's hair is in metal curlers and she wears a very old bathrobe, much too large for her slight figure, a relic of the faithless Mr. Wingfield.

An upright typewriter and a wild disarray of manuscripts are on the drop-leaf table. The quarrel was probably precipitated by Amanda's interruption of his creative labor. A chair lying overthrown on the floor.

Their gesticulating shadows are cast on the ceiling by the fiery glow.

Amanda: You *will* hear more, you—

Tom: No, I won't hear more, I'm going out!

Amanda: You come right back in—

Tom: Out, out out! Because I'm—

Amanda: Come back here, Tom Wingfield! I'm not through talking to you!

Tom: Oh, go—

Laura: *(desperately)* Tom!

Amanda: You're going to listen, and no more insolence from you! I'm at the end of my patience! *(He comes back toward her.)*

Tom: What do you think I'm at? Aren't I supposed to have any patience to reach the end of, Mother? I know, I know. It seems unimportant to you, what I'm *doing*—what I *want* to do—having a little *difference* between them! You don't think that—

Amanda: I think you've been doing things that you're ashamed of. That's why you act like this. I don't believe that you go every night to the movies. Nobody goes to the movies night after night. Nobody in their right mind goes to the movies as often as you pretend to. People don't go to the movies at nearly midnight, and movies don't let out at two A.M. Come in stumbling. Muttering to yourself like a maniac! You get three hours' sleep and then go to work. Oh, I can picture the way you're doing down there. Moping, doping, because you're in no condition.

Tom: *(wildly)* No, I'm in no condition!

---

[1]*Mr. Lawrence:* English novelist D. H. Lawrence (1885–1930). The reference is to his 1928 novel *Lady Chatterley's Lover,* which was banned in the United States and England because of its frank treatment of sexuality.

Amanda: What right have you got to jeopardize your job? Jeopardize the security of us all? How do you think we'd manage if you were—

Tom: Listen! You think I'm crazy *about* the *warehouse? (He bends fiercely toward her slight figure.)* You think I'm in love with the Continental Shoemakers? You think I want to spend fifty-five *years* down there in that—*celotex interior!* with—*fluorescent—tubes!* Look! I'd rather somebody picked up a crowbar and battered out my brains—than go back mornings! I *go!* Every time you come in yelling that God damn *"Rise and Shine!" "Rise and Shine!"* I say to myself "How *lucky dead* people are!" But I get up. I *go!* For sixty-five dollars a month I give up all that I dream of doing and being *ever!* And you say self—*self's* all I ever think of. Why, listen, if self is what I thought of, Mother, I'd be where he is—GONE! *(Pointing to father's picture.)* As far as the system of transportation reaches! *(He starts past her. She grabs his arm.)* Don't grab at me, Mother!

Amanda: Where are you going?

Tom: I'm going to the *movies!*

Amanda: I don't believe that lie!

Tom: *(crouching toward her, overtowering her tiny figure. She backs away, gasping)* I'm going to opium dens! Yes, opium dens, dens of vice and criminals' hang-outs, Mother. I've joined the Hogan gang, I'm a hired assassin, I carry a tommy-gun in a violin case! I run a string of cat-houses in the Valley! They call me Killer, Killer Wingfield, I'm leading a double-life, a simple, honest warehouse worker by day, by night a dynamic *czar of the underworld, Mother.* I go to gambling casinos, I spin away fortunes on the roulette table! I wear a patch over one eye and a false mustache, sometimes I put on green whiskers. On those occasions they call me—*El Diablo!* Oh, I could tell you things to make you sleepless! My enemies plan to dynamite this place. They're going to blow us all sky-high some night! I'll be glad, very happy, and so will you! You'll go up, up on a broomstick, over Blue Mountain with seventeen gentlemen callers! You ugly—babbling old—*witch. ... (He goes through a series of violent, clumsy movements, seizing his overcoat, lunging to the door, pulling it fiercely open. The women watch him, aghast. His arm catches in the sleeve of the coat as he struggles to pull it on. For a moment he is pinioned by the bulky garment. With an outraged groan he tears the coat off again, splitting the shoulders of it, and hurls it across the room. It strikes against the shelf of Laura's glass collection, there is a tinkle of shattering glass. Laura cries out as if wounded.)*

Music Legend: "The Glass Menagerie."

Laura: My *glass!*—menagerie. . . . *(She covers her face and turns away.)*

But Amanda is still stunned and stupefied by the "ugly witch" so that she barely notices this occurrence. Now she recovers her speech.

Amanda: *(in an awful voice) I won't speak to you—until you apologize! (She crosses through portieres and draws them together behind her. Tom is left with Laura. Laura clings weakly to the mantel with her face averted. Tom stares at her* *stupidly for a moment. Then he crosses to shelf. Drops awkwardly to his knees to collect the fallen glass, glancing at Laura as if he would speak but couldn't.)*

"The Glass Menagerie" steals in as The Scene Dims Out.

SCENE 4

The interior is dark. Faint in the alley.

A deep-voiced bell in a church is tolling the hour of five as the scene commences.

Tom appears at the top of the alley. After each solemn boom of the bell in the tower, he shakes a little noise-maker or rattle as if to express the tiny spasm of man in contrast to the sustained power and dignity of the Almighty. This and the unsteadiness of his advance make it evident that he has been drinking.

As he climbs the few steps to the fire-escape landing light steals up inside. Laura appears in night-dress, observing Tom's empty bed in the front room.

Tom fishes in his pockets for the door-key, removing a motley assortment of articles in the search, including a perfect shower of movie-ticket stubs and an empty bottle. At last he finds the key, but just as he is about to insert it, it slips from his fingers. He strikes a match and crouches below the door.

Tom: *(bitterly)* One crack—and it falls through!

Laura opens the door.

Laura: Tom! Tom, what are you doing?

Tom: Looking for a door-key.

Laura: Where have you been all this time?

Tom: I have been to the movies.

Laura: All this time at the movies?

Tom: There was a very long program. There was a Garbo picture and a Mickey Mouse and a travelogue and a newsreel and a preview of coming attractions. And there was an organ solo and a collection for the milk-fund—simultaneously—which ended up in a terrible fight between a fat lady and an usher!

Laura: *(innocently)* Did you have to stay through everything?

Tom: Of course! And, oh, I forgot! There was a big stage show! The head-liner on this stage show was Malvolio the Magician. He performed wonderful tricks, many of them, such as pouring water back and forth between pitchers. First it turned to wine and then it turned to beer and then it turned to whiskey. I know it was whiskey it finally turned into because he needed somebody to come up out of the audience to help him, and I came up—both shows! It was Kentucky Straight Bourbon. A very generous fellow, he gave souvenirs. *(He pulls from his back pocket a shimmering rainbow-colored scarf.)* He gave me this. This is his magic scarf. You can have it, Laura. You wave it over a canary cage and you get a bowl of gold-fish. You wave it over the gold-fish bowl and they fly away canaries. . . . But the wonderfullest trick of all was the coffin trick. We nailed him into a coffin and he got out of the coffin without removing one nail. *(He has come inside.)* There is a trick that would come in handy for me—get me out of this 2 by 4 situation! *(Flops onto bed and starts removing shoes.)*

Laura: Tom—Shhh!

Tom: What you shushing me for?

Laura: You'll wake up Mother.

Tom: Goody, goody! Pay 'er back for all those "Rise an' Shines." *(Lies down, groaning.)* You know it don't take much intelligence to get yourself into a nailed-up coffin, Laura. But who in hell ever got himself out of one without removing one nail?

As if in answer, the father's grinning photograph lights up.

Scene Dims Out.

Immediately following: The church bell is heard striking six. At the sixth stroke the alarm clock goes off in Amanda's room, and after a few moments we hear her calling: "Rise and Shine! Rise and Shine! Laura, go tell your brother to rise and shine!"

Tom: *(sitting up slowly)* I'll rise—but I won't shine.

The light increases.

Amanda: Laura, tell your brother his coffee is ready.

Laura slips into front room.

Laura: Tom! It's nearly seven. Don't make Mother nervous. *(He stares at her stupidly. Beseechingly.)* Tom, speak to Mother this morning. Make up with her, apologize, speak to her!

Tom: She won't to me. It's her that started not speaking.

Laura: If you just say you're sorry she'll start speaking.

Tom: Her not speaking—is that such a tragedy?

Laura: Please—please!

Amanda: *(calling from kitchenette)* Laura, are you going to do what I asked you to do, or do I have to get dressed and go out myself?

Laura: Going, going—soon as I get on my coat! *(She pulls on a shapeless felt hat with nervous, jerky movement, pleadingly glancing at Tom. Rushes awkwardly for coat. The coat is one of Amanda's inaccurately made-over, the sleeves too short for Laura.)* Butter and what else?

Amanda: *(entering upstage)* Just butter. Tell them to charge it.

Laura: Mother, they make such faces when I do that.

Amanda: Sticks and stones may break my bones, but the expression on Mr. Garfinkel's face won't harm us! Tell your brother his coffee is getting cold.

Laura: *(at door)* Do what I asked you, will you, will you, Tom?

He looks sullenly away.

Amanda: Laura, go now or just don't go at all!

Laura: *(rushing out)* Going—going! *(A second later she cries out. Tom springs up and crosses to the door. Amanda rushes anxiously in. Tom opens the door.)*

Tom: Laura?

Laura: I'm all right. I slipped, but I'm all right.

Amanda: *(peering anxiously after her)* If anyone breaks a leg on those fire-escape steps, the landlord ought to be sued for every cent he possesses! *(She shuts door. Remembers she isn't speaking and returns to other room.)*

As Tom enters listlessly for his coffee, she turns her back to him and stands rigidly facing the window on the gloomy gray vault of the areaway. Its light on her face with its aged but childish features is cruelly sharp, satirical as a Daumier print.

Music Under: "Ave Maria."

Tom glances sheepishly but sullenly at her averted figure and slumps at the table. The coffee is scalding hot; he sips it and gasps and spits it back in the cup. At his gasp, Amanda catches her breath and half turns. Then catches herself and turns back to window.

Tom blows on his coffee, glancing sidewise at his mother. She clears her throat. Tom clears his. He starts to rise. Sinks back down again, scratches his head, clears his throat again. Amanda coughs. Tom raises his cup in both hands to blow on it, his eyes staring over the rim of it at his mother for several moments. Then he slowly sets the cup down and awkwardly and hesitantly rises from the chair.

Tom: *(hoarsely)* Mother. I—I apologize. Mother. *(Amanda draws a quick, shuddering breath. Her face works grotesquely. She breaks into childlike tears.)* I'm sorry for what I said, for everything that I said, I didn't mean it.

Amanda: *(sobbingly)* My devotion has made me a witch and so I make myself hateful to my children!

Tom: No, you *don't*.

Amanda: I worry so much, don't sleep, it makes me nervous!

Tom: *(gently)* I understand that.

Amanda: I've had to put up a solitary battle all these years. But you're my right-hand bower! Don't fall down, don't fail!

Tom: *(gently)* I try, Mother.

Amanda: *(with great enthusiasm)* Try and you will SUCCEED! *(The notion makes her breathless.)* Why, you—you're just *full* of natural endowments! Both of my children—they're *unusual* children! Don't you think I know it? I'm so—*proud!* Happy and—feel I've—so much to be thankful for but—Promise me one thing, son!

Tom: What, Mother?

Amanda: Promise, son, you'll—never be a drunkard!

Tom: *(turns to her grinning)* I will never be a drunkard, Mother.

Amanda: That's what frightened me so, that you'd be drinking! Eat a bowl of Purina!

Tom: Just coffee, Mother.

Amanda: Shredded wheat biscuit?

Tom: No. No, Mother, just coffee.

Amanda: You can't put in a day's work on an empty stomach. You've got ten minutes—don't gulp! Drinking too-hot liquids makes cancer of the stomach. ... Put cream in.

Tom: No, thank you.

Amanda: To cool it.

Tom: No! No, thank you, I want it black.

Amanda: I know, but it's not good for you. We have to do all that we can to build ourselves up. In these trying times we live in, all that we have to cling to is—each other. . . . That's why it's so important to—Tom, I—I sent out your sister so I could discuss something with you. If you hadn't spoken I would have spoken to you. *(Sits down.)*

Tom: *(gently)* What is it, Mother, that you want to discuss?

Amanda: Laura!

Tom puts his cup down slowly.

Legend On Screen: "Laura."

Music: "The Glass Menagerie."

Tom: —Oh.—Laura . . .

Amanda: *(touching his sleeve)* You know how Laura is. So quiet but—still water runs deep! She notices things and I think she—broods about them. *(Tom looks up.)* A few days ago I came in and she was crying.

Tom: What about?

Amanda: You.

Tom: Me?

Amanda: She has an idea that you're not happy here.

Tom: What gave her that idea?

Amanda: What gives her any idea? However, you do act strangely. I—I'm not criticizing, understand *that!* I know your ambitions do not lie in the warehouse, that like everybody in the whole wide world—you've had to—make sacrifices, but—Tom—Tom—life's not easy, it calls for—Spartan endurance! There's so many things in my heart that I cannot describe to you! I've never told you but I—*loved* your father. . . .

Tom: (gently) I know that, Mother.

Amanda: And you—when I see you taking after his ways! Staying out late—and—well, you *had* been drinking the night you were in that—terrifying condition! Laura says that you hate the apartment and that you go out nights to get away from it! Is that true, Tom?

Tom: No. You say there's so much in your heart that you can't describe to me. That's true of me, too. There's so much in my heart that I can't describe to *you!* So let's respect each other's—

Amanda: But, why—*why*, Tom—are you always so *restless?* Where do you go to, nights?

Tom: I—go to the movies.

Amanda: Why do you go to the movies so much, Tom?

Tom: I go to the movies because—I like adventure. Adventure is something I don't have much of at work, so I go to the movies.

Amanda: But, Tom, you go to the movies *entirely* too *much!*

Tom: I like a lot of adventure.

Amanda looks baffled, then hurt. As the familiar inquisition resumes he becomes hard and impatient again. Amanda slips back into her querulous attitude toward him.

Image On Screen: Sailing Vessel With Jolly Roger.

Amanda: Most young men find adventure in their careers.

Tom: Then most young men are not employed in a warehouse.

Amanda: The world is full of young men employed in warehouses and offices and factories.

Tom: Do all of them find adventure in their careers?

Amanda: They do or they do without it! Not everybody has a craze for adventure.

Tom: Man is by instinct a lover, a hunter, a fighter, and none of those instincts are given much play at the warehouse!

Amanda: Man is by instinct! Don't quote instinct to me! Instinct is something that people have got away from! It belongs to animals! Christian adults don't want it!

Tom: What do Christian adults want, then, Mother?

Amanda: Superior things! Things of the mind and the spirit! Only animals have to satisfy instincts! Surely your aims are somewhat higher than theirs! Than monkeys—pigs—

Tom: I reckon they're not.

Amanda: You're joking. However, that isn't what I wanted to discuss.

Tom: *(rising)* I haven't much time.

Amanda: *(pushing his shoulders)* Sit down.

Tom: You want me to punch in red at the warehouse, Mother?

Amanda: You have five minutes. I want to talk about Laura.

Legend: "Plans And Provisions."

Tom: All right! What about Laura?

Amanda: We have to be making plans and provisions for her. She's older than you, two years, and nothing has happened. She just drifts along doing nothing. It frightens me terribly how she just drifts along.

Tom: I guess she's the type that people call home-girls.

Amanda: There's no such type, and if there is, it's a pity! That is unless the home is hers, with a husband!

Tom: What?

Amanda: Oh, I can see the handwriting on the wall as plain as I see the nose in front of my face! It's terrifying! More and more you remind me of your father! He was out all hours without explanation—Then *left!*

Good-bye! And me with the bag to hold. I saw that letter you got from the Merchant Marine. I know what you're dreaming of. I'm not standing here blindfolded. Very well, then. Then *do* it! But not till there's somebody to take your place.

Tom: What do you mean?

Amanda: I mean that as soon as Laura has got somebody to take care of her, married, a home of her own, independent—why, then you'll be free to go wherever you please, on land, on sea, whichever way the wind blows! But until that time you've got to look out for your sister. I don't say me because I'm old and don't matter! I say for your sister because she's young and dependent. I put her in business college—a dismal failure! Frightened her so it made her sick to her stomach. I took her over to the Young People's League at the church. Another fiasco. She spoke to nobody, nobody spoke to her. Now all she does is fool with those pieces of glass and play those worn-out records. What kind of a life is that for a girl to lead!

Tom: What can I do about it?

Amanda: Overcome selfishness! Self, self, self is all that you ever think of! *(Tom springs up and crosses to get his coat. It is ugly and bulky. He pulls on a cap with earmuffs.)* Where is your muffler? Put your wool muffler on! *(He snatches it angrily from the closet and tosses it around his neck and pulls both ends tight.)* Tom! I haven't said what I had in mind to ask you.

Tom: I'm too late to—

Amanda: *(catching his arms—very importunately. Then shyly)* Down at the warehouse, aren't there some—nice young men?

Tom: No!

Amanda: There *must* be—*some* . . .

Tom: Mother—

Gesture.

Amanda: Find out one that's clean-living—doesn't drink and—ask him out for sister!

Tom: What?

Amanda: For *sister!* To *meet!* Get *acquainted!*

Tom: *(stamping to door)* Oh, my *go-osh!*

Amanda: Will you? *(He opens door. Imploringly.)* Will you? *(He starts down.)* Will you? *Will* you, dear?

Tom: *(calling back)* YES!

Amanda closes the door hesitantly and with a troubled but faintly hopeful expression.

(Screen Image: A Glamour Magazine Cover.)

Spot Amanda at phone.

Amanda: Ella Cartwright? This is Amanda Wingfield! How are you, honey? How is that kidney condition? *(Count five.) Horrors! (Count five.)* You're a Christian martyr, yes, honey, that's what you are, a Christian martyr! Well, I just happened to notice in my little red book that your subscription to the *Companion* has just run out! I knew that you wouldn't want to miss out on the wonderful serial starting in this new issue. It's by Bessie Mae Hopper, the first thing she's written since *Honeymoon for Three*. Wasn't that a strange and interesting story? Well, this one is even lovelier, I believe. It has a sophisticated society background. It's all about the horsey set on Long Island!

Fade Out.

SCENE 5

(Legend On Screen: "Annunciation.") Fade with music.

It is early dusk of a spring evening. Supper has just been finished in the Wingfield apartment. Amanda and Laura in light colored dresses are removing dishes from the table, in the upstage area, which is shadowy, their movements formalized almost as a dance or ritual, their moving forms as pale and silent as moths.

Tom, in white shirt and trousers, rises from the table and crosses toward the fire-escape.

Amanda: *(as he passes her)* Son, will you do me a favor?

Tom: What?

Amanda: Comb your hair! You look so pretty when your hair is combed! *(Tom slouches on sofa with evening paper. Enormous caption "Franco Triumphs.")* There is only one respect in which I would like you to emulate your father.

Tom: What respect is that?

Amanda: The care he always took of his appearance. He never allowed himself to look untidy. *(He throws down the paper and crosses to fire-escape.)* Where are you going?

Tom: I'm going out to smoke.

Amanda: You smoke too much. A pack a day at fifteen cents a pack. How much would that amount to in a month? Thirty times fifteen is how much, Tom? Figure it out and you will be astounded at what you could save. Enough to give you a night-school course in accounting at Washington U! Just think what a wonderful thing that would be for you, son!

Tom is unmoved by the thought.

Tom: I'd rather smoke. *(He steps out on landing, letting the screen door slam.)*

Amanda: *(sharply)* I know! That's the tragedy of it. . . . *(Alone, she turns to look at her husband's picture.)*

Dance Music: "All The World Is Waiting For The Sunrise!"

Tom: (*to the audience*) Across the alley from us was the Paradise Dance Hall. On evenings in spring the windows and doors were open and the music came outdoors. Sometimes the lights were turned out except for a large glass sphere that hung from the ceiling. It would turn slowly about and filter the dusk with delicate rainbow colors. Then the orchestra played a waltz or a tango, something that had a slow and sensuous rhythm. Couples would come outside, to the relative privacy of the alley. You could see them kissing behind ash-pits and telephone poles. This was the compensation for lives that passed like mine, without any change or adventure. Adventure and change were imminent in this year. They were waiting around the corner for all these kids. Suspended in the mist over Berchtesgaden,[1] caught in the folds of Chamberlain's umbrella[2]—In Spain there was Guernica! But here there was only hot swing music and liquor, dance halls, bars, and movies, and sex that hung in the gloom like a chandelier and flooded the world with brief, deceptive rainbows. . . . All the world was waiting for bombardments!

Amanda turns from the picture and comes outside.

Amanda: (*sighing*) A fire-escape landing's a poor excuse for a porch. (*She spreads a newspaper on a step and sits down, gracefully and demurely as if she were settling into a swing on a Mississippi veranda.*) What are you looking at?

Tom: The moon.

Amanda: Is there a moon this evening?

Tom: It's rising over Garfinkel's Delicatessen.

Amanda: So it is! A little silver slipper of a moon. Have you made a wish on it yet?

Tom: Um-hum.

Amanda: What did you wish for?

Tom: That's a secret.

Amanda: A secret, huh? Well, I won't tell mine either. I will be just as mysterious as you.

Tom: I bet I can guess what yours is.

Amanda: Is my head so transparent?

Tom: You're not a sphinx.

Amanda: No, I don't have secrets. I'll tell you what I wished for on the moon. Success and happiness for my precious children! I wish for that whenever there's a moon, and when there isn't a moon, I wish for it, too.

Tom: I thought perhaps you wished for a gentleman caller.

---

[1] *Berchtesgaden:* A resort in Germany, in the Bavarian Alps; the site of Adolf Hitler's fortified retreat, the Berghof.

[2] *Chamberlain's umbrella:* (Arthur) Neville Chamberlain (1869–1940)—Conservative Party prime minister of England (1937–1940) who advocated a policy of appeasement toward Hitler. Political cartoons often showed him carrying an umbrella.

Amanda: Why do you say that?

Tom: Don't you remember asking me to fetch one?

Amanda: I remember suggesting that it would be nice for your sister if you brought home some nice young man from the warehouse. I think I've made that suggestion more than once.

Tom: Yes, you have made it repeatedly.

Amanda: Well?

Tom: We are going to have one.

Amanda: What?

Tom: A gentleman caller!

The Annunciation Is Celebrated With Music.

Amanda rises.

Image On Screen: Caller With Bouquet.

Amanda: You mean you have asked some nice young man to come over?

Tom: Yep. I've asked him to dinner.

Amanda: You really did?

Tom: I did!

Amanda: You did, and did he—*accept?*

Tom: He did!

Amanda: Well, well—well, well! That's—lovely!

Tom: I thought that you would be pleased.

Amanda: It's definite, then?

Tom: Very definite.

Amanda: Soon?

Tom: Very soon.

Amanda: For heaven's sake, stop putting on and tell me some things, will you?

Tom: What things do you want me to tell you?

Amanda: Naturally I would like to know when he's *coming!*

Tom: He's coming tomorrow.

Amanda: *Tomorrow?*

Tom: Yep. Tomorrow.

Amanda: But, Tom!

Tom: Yes, Mother?

Amanda: Tomorrow gives me no time!

Tom: Time for what?

Amanda: Preparations! Why didn't you phone me at once, as soon as you asked him, the minute that he accepted? Then, don't you see, I could have been getting ready!

Tom: You don't have to make any fuss.

Amanda: Oh, Tom, Tom, Tom, of course I have to make a fuss! I want things nice, not sloppy! Not thrown together. I'll certainly have to do some fast thinking, won't I?

Tom: I don't see why you have to think at all.

Amanda: You just don't know. We can't have a gentleman caller in a pig-sty! All my wedding silver has to be polished, the monogrammed table linen ought to be laundered! The windows have to be washed and fresh curtains put up. And how about clothes? We have to *wear* something, don't we?

Tom: Mother, this boy is no one to make a fuss over!

Amanda: Do you realize he's the first young man we've introduced to your sister? It's terrible, dreadful, disgraceful that poor little sister has never received a single gentleman caller! Tom, come inside! *(She opens the screen door.)*

Tom: What for?

Amanda: I want to ask you some things.

Tom: If you're going to make such a fuss, I'll call it off, I'll tell him not to come.

Amanda: You certainly won't do anything of the kind. Nothing offends people worse than broken engagements. It simply means I'll have to work like a Turk! We won't be brilliant, but we'll pass inspection. Come on inside. *(Tom follows, groaning.)* Sit down.

Tom: Any particular place you would like me to sit?

Amanda: Thank heavens I've got that new sofa! I'm also making payments on a floor lamp I'll have sent out! And put the chintz covers on, they'll brighten things up! Of course I'd hoped to have these walls re-papered. . . . What is the young man's name?

Tom: His name is O'Connor.

Amanda: That, of course, means fish—tomorrow is Friday! I'll have that salmon loaf—with Durkee's dressing! What does he do? He works at the warehouse?

Tom: Of course! How else would I—

Amanda: Tom, he—doesn't drink?

Tom: Why do you ask me that?

Amanda: Your father *did!*

Tom: Don't get started on that!

Amanda: He *does* drink, then?

Tom: Not that I know of!

Amanda: Make sure, be certain! The last thing I want for my daughter's a boy who drinks!

Tom: Aren't you being a little premature? Mr. O'Connor has not yet appeared on the scene!

Amanda: But will tomorrow. To meet your sister, and what do I know about his character? Nothing! Old maids are better off than wives of drunkards!

Tom: Oh, my God!

Amanda: Be still!

Tom: *(leaning forward to whisper)* Lots of fellows meet girls whom they don't marry!

Amanda: Oh, talk sensibly, Tom—and don't be sarcastic! *(She has gotten a hairbrush.)*

Tom: What are you doing?

Amanda: I'm brushing that cow-lick down! What is this young man's position at the warehouse?

Tom: *(submitting grimly to the brush and the interrogation)* This young man's position is that of a shipping clerk, Mother.

Amanda: Sounds to me like a fairly responsible job, the sort of a job *you* would be in if you just had more *get-up*. What is his salary? Have you got any idea?

Tom: I would judge it to be approximately eighty-five dollars a month.

Amanda: Well—not princely, but—

Tom: Twenty more than I make.

Amanda: Yes, how well I know! But for a family man, eighty-five dollars a month is not much more than you can just get by on. . . .

Tom: Yes, but Mr. O'Connor is not a family man.

Amanda: He might be, mightn't he? Some time in the future?

Tom: I see. Plans and provisions.

Amanda: You are the only young man that I know of who ignores the fact that the future becomes the present, the present the past, and the past turns into everlasting regret if you don't plan for it!

Tom: I will think that over and see what I can make of it.

Amanda: Don't be supercilious with your mother! Tell me some more about this—what do you call him?

Tom: James D. O'Connor. The D. is for Delaney.

Amanda: Irish on *both* sides! *Gracious!* And doesn't drink?

Tom: Shall I call him up and ask him right this minute?

Amanda: The only way to find out about those things is to make discreet inquiries at the proper moment. When I was a girl in Blue Mountain and it was suspected that a young man drank, the girl whose attentions he had been receiving, if any girl *was*, would sometimes speak to the minister of his church, or rather her father would if her father was living, and sort of feel him out on the young man's character. That is the way such things are discreetly handled to keep a young woman from making a tragic mistake!

Tom: Then how did you happen to make a tragic mistake?

Amanda: That innocent look of your father's had everyone fooled! He *smiled*—the world was *enchanted!* No girl can do worse than put herself at the mercy of a handsome appearance! I hope that Mr. O'Connor is not too good-looking.

Tom: No, he's not too good-looking. He's covered with freckles and hasn't too much of a nose.

Amanda: He's not right-down homely, though?

Tom: Not right-down homely. Just medium homely, I'd say.

Amanda: Character's what to look for in a man.

Tom: That's what I've always said, Mother.

Amanda: You've never said anything of the kind and I suspect you would never give it a thought.

Tom: Don't be suspicious of me.

Amanda: At least I hope he's the type that's up and coming.

Tom: I think he really goes in for self-improvement.

Amanda: What reason have you to think so?

Tom: He goes to night school.

Amanda: *(beaming)* Splendid! What does he do, I mean study?

Tom: Radio engineering and public speaking!

Amanda: Then he has visions of being advanced in the world! Any young man who studies public speaking is aiming to have an executive job some day! And radio engineering? A thing for the future! Both of these facts are very illuminating. Those are the sort of things that a mother should know concerning any young man who comes to call on her daughter. Seriously or—not.

Tom: One little warning. He doesn't know about Laura. I didn't let on that we had dark ulterior motives. I just said, why don't you come have dinner with us? He said okay and that was the whole conversation.

Amanda: I bet it was! You're eloquent as an oyster. However, he'll know about Laura when he gets here. When he sees how lovely and sweet and pretty she is, he'll thank his lucky stars he was asked to dinner.

Tom: Mother, you mustn't expect too much of Laura.

Amanda: What do you mean?

Tom: Laura seems all those things to you and me because she's ours and we love her. We don't even notice she's crippled any more.

Amanda: Don't say crippled! You know that I never allow that word to be used!

Tom: But face facts, Mother. She is and—that's not all—

Amanda: What do you mean "not all"?

Tom: Laura is very different from other girls.

Amanda: I think the difference is all to her advantage.

Tom: Not quite all—in the eyes of others—strangers—she's terribly shy and lives in a world of her own and those things make her seem a little peculiar to people outside the house.

Amanda: Don't say peculiar.

Tom: Face the facts. She is.

The Dance-Hall Music Changes To A Tango That Has A Minor And Somewhat Ominous Tone.

Amanda: In what way is she peculiar—may I ask?

Tom: *(gently)* She lives in a world of her own—a world of—little glass ornaments, Mother. . . . *(Gets up. Amanda remains holding brush, looking at him, troubled.)* She plays old phonograph records and—that's about all— *(He glances at himself in the mirror and crosses to door.)*

Amanda: *(sharply)* Where are you going?

Tom: I'm going to the movies. *(Out screen door.)*

Amanda: Not to the movies, every night to the movies! *(Follows quickly to screen door.)* I don't believe you always go to the movies! *(He is gone.*

Amanda looks worriedly after him for a moment. Then vitality and optimism return and she turns from the door. Crossing to portieres.) Laura! Laura! *(Laura answers from kitchenette.)*

Laura: Yes, Mother.

Amanda: Let those dishes go and come in front! *(Laura appears with dish towel. Gaily.)* Laura, come here and make a wish on the moon!

Laura: *(entering)* Moon—moon?

Amanda: A little silver slipper of a moon. Look over your left shoulder, Laura, and make a wish! *(Laura looks faintly puzzled as if called out of sleep. Amanda seizes her shoulders and turns her at an angle by the door.)* Now! Now, darling, *wish!*

Laura: What shall I wish for, Mother?

Amanda: *(her voice trembling and her eyes suddenly filling with tears)* Happiness! Good Fortune!

The violin rises and the stage dims out.

SCENE 6

Image: High-School Hero.

Tom: And so the following evening I brought Jim home to dinner. I had known Jim slightly in high school. In high school Jim was a hero. He had tremendous Irish good nature and vitality with the scrubbed and polished look of white chinaware. He seemed to move in a continual spotlight. He was a star in basketball, captain of the debating club, president of the senior class and the glee club and he sang the male lead in the annual light operas. He was always running or bounding, never just walking. He seemed always at the point of defeating the law of gravity. He was shooting with such velocity through his adolescence that you would logically expect him to arrive at nothing short of the White House by the time he was thirty. But Jim apparently ran into more interference after his graduation from Soldan. His speed had definitely slowed. Six years after he left high school he was holding a job that wasn't much better than mine.

Image: Clerk.

He was the only one at the warehouse with whom I was on friendly terms. I was valuable to him as someone who could remember his former glory, who had seen him win basketball games and the silver cup in debating. He knew of my secret practice of retiring to a cabinet of the washroom to work on poems when business was slack in the warehouse. He called me Shakespeare. And while the other boys in the warehouse regarded me with suspicious hostility, Jim took a humorous attitude toward me. Gradually his attitude affected the others, their hostility wore off and they also began to smile at me as people smile at an oddly fashioned dog who trots across their path at some distance.

I knew that Jim and Laura had known each other at Soldan, and I had heard Laura speak admiringly of his voice. I didn't know if Jim remembered her or not. In high school Laura had been as unobtrusive as Jim had been astonishing. If he did remember Laura, it was not as my sister, for when I asked him to dinner, he grinned and said, "You know, Shakespeare, I never thought of you as having folks!" He was about to discover that I did. . . .

Light Up Stage.

Legend On Screen: "The Accent Of A Coming Foot."

Friday evening. It is about five o'clock of a late spring evening which comes "scattering poems in the sky."

A delicate lemony light is in the Wingfield apartment.

Amanda has worked like a Turk in preparation for the gentleman caller. The results are astonishing. The new floor lamp with its rose-silk shade is in place, a colored paper lantern conceals the broken light fixture in the ceiling, new billowing white curtains are at the windows, chintz covers are on chairs and sofa, a pair of new sofa pillows make their initial appearance.

Open boxes and tissue paper are scattered on the floor.

Laura stands in the middle with lifted arms while Amanda crouches before her, adjusting the hem of the new dress, devout and ritualistic. The dress is colored and designed by memory. The arrangement of Laura's hair is changed; it is softer and more becoming. A fragile, unearthly prettiness has come out in Laura: she is like a piece of translucent glass touched by light, given a momentary radiance, not actual, not lasting.

Amanda: *(impatiently)* Why are you trembling?
Laura: Mother, you've made me so nervous!
Amanda: How have I made you nervous?
Laura: By all this fuss! You make it seem so important!
Amanda: I don't understand you, Laura. You couldn't be satisfied with just sitting home, and yet whenever I try to arrange something for you, you seem to resist it. *(She gets up.)* Now take a look at yourself. No, wait! Wait just a moment—I have an idea!
Laura: What is it now?

Amanda produces two powder puffs which she wraps in handkerchiefs and stuffs in Laura's bosom.

Laura: Mother, what are you doing?
Amanda: They call them "Gay Deceivers"!
Laura: I won't wear them!
Amanda: You will!
Laura: Why should I?

Amanda: Because, to be painfully honest, your chest is flat.
Laura: You make it seem like we were setting a trap.
Amanda: All pretty girls are a trap, a pretty trap, and men expect them to be.

(Legend: "A Pretty Trap.") Now look at yourself, young lady. This is the prettiest you will ever be! I've got to fix myself now! You're going to be surprised by your mother's appearance! (She crosses through portieres, humming gaily.)

Laura moves slowly to the long mirror and stares solemnly at herself.

A wind blows the white curtains inward in a slow, graceful motion and with a faint, sorrowful sighing.

Amanda: *(offstage)* It isn't dark enough yet. *(She turns slowly before the mirror with a troubled look.)*

Legend On Screen: "This Is My Sister: Celebrate Her With Strings!" Music.

Amanda: *(laughing, off)* I'm going to show you something. I'm going to make a spectacular appearance!
Laura: What is it, Mother?
Amanda: Possess your soul in patience—you will see! Something I've resurrected from that old trunk! Styles haven't changed so terribly much after all. . . . *(She parts the portieres.)* Now just look at your mother! *(She wears a girlish frock of yellowed voile with a blue silk sash. She carries a bunch of jonquils—the legend of her youth is nearly revived. Feverishly.)* This is the dress in which I led the cotillion. Won the cakewalk twice at Sunset Hill, wore one spring to the Governor's ball in Jackson! See how I sashayed around the ballroom, Laura? *(She raises her skirt and does a mincing step around the room.)* I wore it on Sundays for my gentlemen callers! I had it on the day I met your father—I had malaria fever all that spring. The change of climate from East Tennessee to the Delta—weakened resistance—I had a little temperature all the time—not enough to be serious—just enough to make me restless and giddy! Invitations poured in—parties all over the Delta!—"Stay in bed," said Mother, "you have fever!"—but I just wouldn't.—I took quinine but kept on going, going!—Evenings, dances!—Afternoons, long, long rides! Picnics—lovely!—So lovely, that country in May. All lacy with dogwood, literally flooded with jonquils!—That was the spring I had the craze for jonquils. Jonquils became an absolute obsession. Mother said, "Honey, there's no more room for jonquils." And still I kept bringing in more jonquils. Whenever, wherever I saw them, I'd say, "Stop! Stop! I see jonquils!" I made the young men help me gather the jonquils! It was a joke, Amanda and her jonquils! Finally there were no more vases to hold them, every available space was filled with jonquils. No vases to hold them? All right, I'll hold them myself! And then I—*(She stops in front of the picture.) (Music)* met your father! Malaria fever and jonquils and then—this—boy. . . . *(She switches on the rose-colored lamp.)* I hope

they get here before it starts to rain. *(She crosses upstage and places the jonquils in bowl on table.)* I gave your brother a little extra change so he and Mr. O'Connor could take the service car home.

Laura: *(with altered look)* What did you say his name was?

Amanda: O'Connor.

Laura: What is his first name?

Amanda: I don't remember. Oh, yes, I do. It was—Jim!

Laura sways slightly and catches hold of a chair.

Legend On Screen: "Not Jim!"

Laura: *(faintly)* Not—Jim!

Amanda: Yes, that was it, it was Jim! I've never known a Jim that wasn't nice!

Music: Ominous.

Laura: Are you sure his name is Jim O'Connor?

Amanda: Yes. Why?

Laura: Is he the one that Tom used to know in high school?

Amanda: He didn't say so. I think he just got to know him at the warehouse.

Laura: There was a Jim O'Connor we both knew in high school—*(Then, with effort.)* If that is the one that Tom is bringing to dinner—you'll have to excuse me, I won't come to the table.

Amanda: What sort of nonsense is this?

Laura: You asked me once if I'd ever liked a boy. Don't you remember I showed you this boy's picture?

Amanda: You mean the boy you showed me in the year book?

Laura: Yes, that boy.

Amanda: Laura, Laura, were you in love with that boy?

Laura: I don't know, Mother. All I know is I couldn't sit at the table if it was him!

Amanda: It won't be him! It isn't the least bit likely. But whether it is or not, you will come to the table. You will not be excused.

Laura: I'll have to be, Mother.

Amanda: I don't intend to humor your silliness, Laura. I've had too much from you and your brother, both! So just sit down and compose yourself till they come. Tom has forgotten his key so you'll have to let them in, when they arrive.

Laura: *(panicky)* Oh, Mother—*you* answer the door!

Amanda: *(lightly)* I'll be in the kitchen—busy!

Laura: Oh, Mother, please answer the door, don't make me do it!

Amanda: *(crossing into kitchenette)* I've got to fix the dressing for the salmon. Fuss, fuss—silliness!—over a gentleman caller!

Door swings shut. Laura is left alone.

Legend: "Terror!"

She utters a low moan and turns off the lamp—sits stiffly on the edge of the sofa, knotting her fingers together.

Legend On Screen: "The Opening Of A Door!"

Tom and Jim appear on the fire-escape steps and climb to landing. Hearing their approach, Laura rises with a panicky gesture. She retreats to the portieres.

The doorbell. Laura catches her breath and touches her throat. Low drums.

Amanda: *(calling)* Laura, sweetheart! The door!

Laura stares at it without moving.

Jim: I think we just beat the rain.
Tom: Uh-huh. *(He rings again, nervously. Jim whistles and fishes for a cigarette.)*
Amanda: *(very, very gaily)* Laura, that is your brother and Mr. O'Connor! Will you let them in, darling?

Laura crosses toward kitchenette door.

Laura: *(breathlessly)* Mother—you go to the door!

Amanda steps out of kitchenette and stares furiously at Laura. She points imperiously at the door.

Laura: Please, please!
Amanda: *(in a fierce whisper)* What is the matter with you, you silly thing?
Laura: *(desperately)* Please, you answer it, *please!*
Amanda: I told you I wasn't going to humor you, Laura. Why have you chosen this moment to lose your mind?
Laura: Please, please, please, you go!
Amanda: You'll have to go to the door because I can't!
Laura: *(despairingly)* I can't either!
Amanda: Why?
Laura: I'm *sick!*
Amanda: I'm sick, too—of your nonsense! Why can't you and your brother be normal people? Fantastic whims and behavior! *(Tom gives a long ring.)* Preposterous goings on! Can you give me one reason— *(Calls out lyrically.)* COMING! JUST ONE SECOND!—why should you be afraid to open a door? Now you answer it, Laura!
Laura: Oh, oh, oh . . . *(She returns through the portieres. Darts to the Victrola and winds it frantically and turns it on.)*
Amanda: Laura Wingfield, you march right to that door!
Laura: Yes—yes, Mother!

A faraway, scratchy rendition of "Dardanella" softens the air and gives her strength to move through it. She slips to the door and draws it cautiously open. Tom enters with the caller, Jim O'Connor.

Tom: Laura, this is Jim. Jim, this is my sister, Laura.

Jim: *(stepping inside)* I didn't know that Shakespeare had a sister!

Laura: *(retreating stiff and trembling from the door)* How—how do you do?

Jim: *(heartily extending his hand)* Okay!

Laura touches it hesitantly with hers.

Jim: Your hand's *cold*, Laura!

Laura: Yes, well—I've been playing the Victrola. . . .

Jim: Must have been playing classical music on it! You ought to play a little hot swing music to warm you up!

Laura: Excuse me—I haven't finished playing the Victrola. . . .

She turns awkwardly and hurries into the front room. She pauses a second by the Victrola. Then catches her breath and darts through the portieres like a frightened deer.

Jim: *(grinning)* What was the matter?

Tom: Oh—with Laura? Laura is—terribly shy.

Jim: Shy, huh? It's unusual to meet a shy girl nowadays. I don't believe you ever mentioned you had a sister.

Tom: Well, now you know. I have one. Here is the *Post Dispatch*. You want a piece of it?

Jim: Uh-huh.

Tom: What piece? The comics?

Jim: Sports! *(Glances at it.)* Ole Dizzy Dean[1] is on his bad behavior.

Tom: *(disinterested)* Yeah? *(Lights cigarette and crosses back to fire-escape door.)*

Jim: Where are *you* going?

Tom: I'm going out on the terrace.

Jim: *(goes after him)* You know, Shakespeare—I'm going to sell you a bill of goods!

Tom: What goods?

Jim: A course I'm taking.

Tom: Huh?

Jim: In public speaking! You and me, we're not the warehouse type.

Tom: Thanks—that's good news. But what has public speaking got to do with it?

Jim: It fits you for—executive positions!

Tom: Awww.

Jim: I tell you it's done a helluva lot for me.

Image: Executive At Desk.

Tom: In what respect?

---

[1]*Dizzy Dean:* Jay Hanna Dean (1910–1974), American baseball player who pitched for the St. Louis Cardinals (1930, 1932–1937), winning 30 games in 1934 and averaging 24 wins in his first five full seasons. From 1938 to 1941, he played for the Chicago Cubs.

Jim: In every! Ask yourself what is the difference between you an' me and men in the office down front? Brains?—No!—Ability?—No! Then what? Just one little thing—

Tom: What is that one little thing?

Jim: Primarily it amounts to—social poise! Being able to square up to people and hold your own on any social level!

Amanda: *(offstage)* Tom?

Tom: Yes, Mother?

Amanda: Is that you and Mr. O'Connor?

Tom: Yes, Mother.

Amanda: Well, you just make yourselves comfortable in there.

Tom: Yes, Mother.

Amanda: Ask Mr. O'Connor if he would like to wash his hands.

Jim: Aw—no—thank you—I took care of that at the warehouse. Tom—

Tom: Yes?

Jim: Mr. Mendoza was speaking to me about you.

Tom: Favorably?

Jim: What do you think?

Tom: Well—

Jim: You're going to be out of a job if you don't wake up.

Tom: I am waking up—

Jim: You show no signs.

Tom: The signs are interior.

Image On Screen: The Sailing Vessel With Jolly Roger Again.

Tom: I'm planning to change. *(He leans over the rail speaking with quiet exhilaration. The incandescent marquees and signs of the first-run movie houses light his face from across the alley. He looks like a voyager.)* I'm right at the point of committing myself to a future that doesn't include the warehouse and Mr. Mendoza or even a night-school course in public speaking.

Jim: What are you gassing about?

Tom: I'm tired of the movies.

Jim: Movies!

Tom: Yes, movies! Look at them— *(A wave toward the marvels of Grand Avenue.)* All of those glamorous people—having adventures—hogging it all, gobbling the whole thing up! You know what happens? People go to the *movies instead of moving!* Hollywood characters are supposed to have all the adventures for everybody in America, while everybody in America sits in a dark room and watches them have them! Yes, until there's a war. That's when adventure becomes available to the masses! *Everyone's* dish, not only Gable's! Then the people in the dark room come out of the dark room to have some adventures themselves—Goody, goody—It's our turn now, to go to the South Sea Island—to make a safari—to be exotic, far-off—But I'm not patient. I don't want to wait till then. I'm tired of the *movies* and I am *about* to *move!*

Jim: *(incredulously)* Move?
Tom: Yes.
Jim: When?
Tom: Soon!
Jim: Where? Where?

Theme three music seems to answer the question, while Tom thinks it over. He searches among his pockets.

Tom: I'm starting to boil inside. I know I seem dreary, but inside—well, I'm boiling! Whenever I pick up a shoe, I shudder a little thinking how short life is and what I am doing!—Whatever that means. I know it doesn't mean shoes—except as something to wear on a traveler's feet! *(Finds paper.)* Look—
Jim: What?
Tom: I'm a member.
Jim: *(reading)* The Union of Merchant Seamen.
Tom: I paid my dues this month, instead of the light bill.
Jim: You will regret it when they turn the lights off.
Tom: I won't be here.
Jim: How about your mother?
Tom: I'm like my father. The bastard son of a bastard! See how he grins? And he's been absent going on sixteen years!
Jim: You're just talking, you drip. How does your mother feel about it?
Tom: Shhh—Here comes Mother! Mother is not acquainted with my plans!
Amanda: *(enters portieres)* Where are you all?
Tom: On the terrace, Mother.

They start inside. She advances to them. Tom is distinctly shocked at her appearance. Even Jim blinks a little. He is making his first contact with girlish Southern vivacity and in spite of the night-school course in public speaking is somewhat thrown off the beam by the unexpected outlay of social charm.

Certain responses are attempted by Jim but are swept aside by Amanda's gay laughter and chatter. Tom is embarrassed but after the first shock Jim reacts very warmly. Grins and chuckles, is altogether won over.

Image: Amanda As A Girl.

Amanda: *(coyly smiling, shaking her girlish ringlets)* Well, well, well, so this is Mr. O'Connor. Introductions entirely unnecessary. I've heard so much about you from my boy. I finally said to him, Tom—good gracious!—why don't you bring this paragon to supper? I'd like to meet this nice young man at the warehouse!—Instead of just hearing him sing your praises so much! I don't know why my son is so stand-offish—that's not Southern behavior! Let's sit down and—I think we could stand a little more air in here! Tom, leave the door open. I felt a nice fresh breeze a moment ago. Where has it gone? Mmm, so warm already! And not quite summer, even. We're going to burn up when summer really gets started. However, we're having—we're having a very light supper. I think light things are better fo' this time of year. The same as light clothes are. Light clothes an' light food are what warm weather calls fo'. You know our blood gets so thick during th' winter—it takes a while fo' us to *adjust* ou'selves!—when the season changes . . . It's come so quick this year. I wasn't prepared. All of a sudden—heavens! Already summer!—I ran to the trunk an' pulled out this light dress—Terribly old! Historical almost! But feels so good—so good an' co-ol, y'know. . . .

Tom: Mother—

Amanda: Yes, honey?

Tom: How about—supper?

Amanda: Honey, you go ask Sister if supper is ready! You know that Sister is in full charge of supper! Tell her you hungry boys are waiting for it. *(To Jim.)* Have you met Laura?

Jim: She—

Amanda: Let you in? Oh, good, you've met already! It's rare for a girl as sweet an' pretty as Laura to be domestic! But Laura is, thank heavens, not only pretty but also very domestic. I'm not at all. I never was a bit. I never could make a thing but angel-food cake. Well, in the South we had so many servants. Gone, gone, gone. All vestiges of gracious living! Gone completely! I wasn't prepared for what the future brought me. All of my gentlemen callers were sons of planters and so of course I assumed that I would be married to one and raise my family on a large piece of land with plenty of servants. But man proposes—and woman accepts the proposal!—To vary that old, old saying a little bit—I married no planter! I married a man who worked for the telephone company!—that gallantly smiling gentleman over there! *(Points to the picture.)* A telephone man who—fell in love with long-distance!—Now he travels and I don't even know where!—But what am I going on for about my—tribulations? Tell me yours—I hope you don't have any! Tom?

Tom: *(returning)* Yes, Mother?

Amanda: Is supper nearly ready?

Tom: It looks to me like supper is on the table.

Amanda: Let me look—*(She rises prettily and looks through portieres.)* Oh, lovely—But where is Sister?

Tom: Laura is not feeling well and says that she thinks she'd better not come to the table.

Amanda: What?—Nonsense!—Laura? Oh, Laura!

Laura: *(offstage, faintly)* Yes, Mother.

Amanda: You really must come to the table. We won't be seated until you come to the table! Come in, Mr. O'Connor. You sit over there and I'll—Laura? Laura Wingfield! You're keeping us waiting, honey! We can't say grace until you come to the table!

The back door is pushed weakly open and Laura comes in. She is obviously quite faint, her lips trembling, her eyes wide and staring. She moves unsteadily toward the table.

Legend: "Terror!"

Outside a summer storm is coming abruptly. The white curtains billow inward at the windows and there is a sorrowful murmur and deep blue dusk.

Laura suddenly stumbles—She catches at a chair with a faint moan.

Tom: Laura!

Amanda: Laura! *(There is a clap of thunder.) (Legend: "Ah!") (Despairingly.)* Why, Laura, you are sick, darling! Tom, help your sister into the living room, dear! Sit in the living room, Laura—rest on the sofa. Well! *(To the gentleman caller.)* Standing over the hot stove made her ill!—I told her that it was just too warm this evening, but—*(Tom comes back in. Laura is on the sofa.)* Is Laura all right now?

Tom: Yes.

Amanda: What *is* that? Rain? A nice cool rain has come up! *(She gives the gentleman caller a frightened look.)* I think we may—have grace—now . . . *(Tom looks at her stupidly.)* Tom, honey—you say grace!

Tom: Oh . . . "For these and all thy mercies—" *(They bow their heads, Amanda stealing a nervous glance at Jim. In the living room Laura, stretched on the sofa, clenches her hand to her lips, to hold back a shuddering sob.)* God's Holy Name be praised—

The Scene Dims Out.

SCENE 7

A Souvenir.

Half an hour later. Dinner is just being finished in the upstage area which is concealed by the drawn portieres.

As the curtain rises Laura is still huddled upon the sofa, her feet drawn under her, her head resting on a pale blue pillow, her eyes wide and mysteriously watchful. The new floor lamp with its shade of rose-colored silk gives a soft, becoming light to her face, bringing out the fragile, unearthly prettiness which usually escapes attention. There is a steady murmur of rain, but it is slackening and stops soon after the scene begins; the air outside becomes pale and luminous as the moon breaks out.

A moment after the curtain rises, the lights in both rooms flicker and go out.

Jim: Hey, there, Mr. Light Bulb!

Amanda laughs nervously.

Legend: "Suspension Of A Public Service."

Amanda: Where was Moses when the lights went out? Ha-ha. Do you know the answer to that one, Mr. O'Connor?

Jim: No, Ma'am, what's the answer?

Amanda: In the dark! *(Jim laughs appreciatively.)* Everybody sit still. I'll light the candles. Isn't it lucky we have them on the table? Where's a match? Which of you gentlemen can provide a match?

Jim: Here.

Amanda: Thank you, sir.

Jim: Not at all, Ma'am!

Amanda: I guess the fuse has burnt out. Mr. O'Connor, can you tell a burnt-out fuse? I know I can't and Tom is a total loss when it comes to mechanics. *(Sound: Getting Up: Voices Recede A Little To Kitchenette.)* Oh, be careful you don't bump into something. We don't want our gentleman caller to break his neck. Now wouldn't that be a fine howdy-do?

Jim: Ha-ha! Where is the fuse-box?

Amanda: Right here next to the stove. Can you see anything?

Jim: Just a minute.

Amanda: Isn't electricity a mysterious thing? Wasn't it Benjamin Franklin who tied a key to a kite? We live in such a mysterious universe, don't we? Some people say that science clears up all the mysteries for us. In my opinion it only creates more! Have you found it yet?

Jim: No, Ma'am. All these fuses look okay to me.

Amanda: Tom!

Tom: Yes, Mother?

Amanda: That light bill I gave you several days ago. The one I told you we got the notices about?

Tom: Oh.—Yeah.

Legend: "Ha!"

Amanda: You didn't neglect to pay it by any chance?

Tom: Why, I—

Amanda: Didn't! I might have known it!

Jim: Shakespeare probably wrote a poem on that light bill, Mrs. Wingfield.

Amanda: I might have known better than to trust him with it! There's such a high price for negligence in this world!

Jim: Maybe the poem will win a ten-dollar prize.

Amanda: We'll just have to spend the remainder of the evening in the nineteenth century, before Mr. Edison made the Mazda lamp!

Jim: Candlelight is my favorite kind of light.

Amanda: That shows you're romantic! But that's no excuse for Tom. Well, we got through dinner. Very considerate of them to let us get through dinner before they plunged us into everlasting darkness, wasn't it, Mr. O'Connor?

Jim: Ha-ha!

Amanda: Tom, as a penalty for your carelessness you can help me with the dishes.

Jim: Let me give you a hand.

Amanda: Indeed you will not!

Jim: I ought to be good for something.

Amanda: Good for something? *(Her tone is rhapsodic.) You?* Why, Mr. O'Connor, nobody, *nobody's* given me this much entertainment in years—as you have!

Jim: Aw, now, Mrs. Wingfield!

Amanda: I'm not exaggerating, not one bit! But Sister is all by her lonesome. You go keep her company in the parlor! I'll give you this lovely old candelabrum that used to be on the altar at the church of the Heavenly Rest. It was melted a little out of shape when the church burnt down. Lightning struck it one spring. Gypsy Jones was holding a revival at the time and he intimated that the church was destroyed because the Episcopalians gave card parties.

Jim: Ha-ha.

Amanda: And how about coaxing Sister to drink a little wine? I think it would be good for her! Can you carry both at once?

Jim: Sure. I'm Superman!

Amanda: Now, Thomas, get into this apron!

The door of kitchenette swings closed on Amanda's gay laughter; the flickering light approaches the portieres.

Laura sits up nervously as he enters. Her speech at first is low and breathless from the almost intolerable strain of being alone with a stranger.

The Legend: "I Don't Suppose You Remember Me At All!"

In her first speeches in this scene, before Jim's warmth overcomes her paralyzing shyness, Laura's voice is thin and breathless as though she has run up a steep flight of stairs.

Jim's attitude is gently humorous. In playing this scene it should be stressed that while the incident is apparently unimportant, it is to Laura the climax of her secret life.

Jim: Hello, there, Laura.

Laura: *(faintly)* Hello. *(She clears her throat.)*

Jim: How are you feeling now? Better?

Laura: Yes. Yes, thank you.

Jim: This is for you. A little dandelion wine. *(He extends it toward her with extravagant gallantry.)*

Laura: Thank you.

Jim: Drink it—but don't get drunk! *(He laughs heartily. Laura takes the glass uncertainly; laughs shyly.)* Where shall I set the candles?

Laura: Oh—oh, anywhere . . .

Jim: How about here on the floor? Any objections?

Laura: No.

Jim: I'll spread a newspaper under to catch the drippings. I like to sit on the floor. Mind if I do?

Laura: Oh, no.

Jim: Give me a pillow?

Laura: What?

Jim: A pillow!

Laura: Oh . . . *(Hands him one quickly.)*

Jim: How about you? Don't you like to sit on the floor?

Laura: Oh—yes.

Jim: Why don't you, then?

Laura: I—will.

Jim: Take a pillow! *(Laura does. Sits on the other side of the candelabrum. Jim crosses his legs and smiles engagingly at her.)* I can't hardly see you sitting way over there.

Laura: I can—see you.

Jim: I know, but that's not fair, I'm in the limelight. *(Laura moves her pillow closer.)* Good! Now I can see you! Comfortable?

Laura: Yes.

Jim: So am I. Comfortable as a cow. Will you have some gum?

Laura: No, thank you.

Jim: I think that I will indulge, with your permission. *(Musingly unwraps it and holds it up.)* Think of the fortune made by the guy that invented the first piece of chewing gum. Amazing, huh? The Wrigley Building is one of the sights of Chicago.—I saw it summer before last when I went up to the Century of Progress. Did you take in the Century of Progress?

Laura: No, I didn't.

Jim: Well, it was quite a wonderful exposition. What impressed me most was the Hall of Science. Gives you an idea of what the future will be in America, even more wonderful than the present time is! *(Pause. Smiling at her.)* Your brother tells me you're shy. Is that right, Laura?

Laura: I—don't know.

Jim: I judge you to be an old-fashioned type of girl. Well, I think that's a pretty good type to be. Hope you don't think I'm being too personal—do you?

Laura: *(hastily, out of embarrassment)* I believe I *will* take a piece of gum, if you—don't mind. *(Clearing her throat.)* Mr. O'Connor, have you—kept up with your singing?

Jim: Singing? Me?

Laura: Yes. I remember what a beautiful voice you had.

Jim: When did you hear me sing?

Voice Offstage In The Pause.

Voice *(offstage)*:

O blow, ye winds, heigh-ho,
A-roving I will go!

I'm off to my love
With a boxing glove—
Ten thousand miles away!

Jim: You say you've heard me sing?

Laura: Oh, yes! Yes, very often . . . I—don't suppose you remember me—at all?

Jim: *(smiling doubtfully)* You know I have an idea I've seen you before. I had that idea soon as you opened the door. It seemed almost like I was about to remember your name. But the name that I started to call you—wasn't a name! And so I stopped myself before I said it.

Laura: Wasn't it—Blue Roses?

Jim: *(springs up, grinning)* Blue Roses! My gosh, yes—Blue Roses! That's what I had on my tongue when you opened the door! Isn't it funny what tricks your memory plays? I didn't connect you with the high school somehow or other. But that's where it was; it was high school. I didn't even know you were Shakespeare's sister! Gosh, I'm sorry.

Laura: I didn't expect you to. You—barely knew me!

Jim: But we did have a speaking acquaintance, huh?

Laura: Yes, we—spoke to each other.

Jim: When did you recognize me?

Laura: Oh, right away!

Jim: Soon as I came in the door?

Laura: When I heard your name I thought it was probably you. I knew that Tom used to know you a little in high school. So when you came in the door—Well, then I was—sure.

Jim: Why didn't you *say* something, then?

Laura: *(breathlessly)* I didn't know what to say, I was—too surprised!

Jim: For goodness' sakes! You know, this sure is funny!

Laura: Yes! Yes, isn't it, though . . .

Jim: Didn't we have a class in something together?

Laura: Yes, we did.

Jim: What class was that?

Laura: It was—singing—Chorus!

Jim: Aw!

Laura: I sat across the aisle from you in the Aud.

Jim: Aw.

Laura: Mondays, Wednesdays and Fridays.

Jim: Now I remember—you always came in late.

Laura: Yes, it was so hard for me, getting upstairs. I had that brace on my leg—it clumped so loud!

Jim: I never heard any clumping.

Laura: *(wincing at the recollection)* To me it sounded like—thunder!

Jim: Well, well, well. I never even noticed.

Laura: And everybody was seated before I came in. I had to walk in front of all those people. My seat was in the back row. I had to go clumping all the way up the aisle with everyone watching!

Jim: You shouldn't have been self-conscious.

Laura: I know, but I was. It was always such a relief when the singing started.

Jim: Aw, yes, I've placed you now! I used to call you Blue Roses. How was it that I got started calling you that?

Laura: I was out of school a little while with pleurosis. When I came back you asked me what was the matter. I said I had pleurosis—you thought I said Blue Roses. That's what you always called me after that!

Jim: I hope you didn't mind.

Laura: Oh, no—I liked it. You see, I wasn't acquainted with many—people. . . .

Jim: As I remember you sort of stuck by yourself.

Laura: I—I—never had much luck at—making friends.

Jim: I don't see why you wouldn't.

Laura: Well, I—started out badly.

Jim: You mean being—

Laura: Yes, it sort of—stood between me—

Jim: You shouldn't have let it!

Laura: I know, but it did, and—

Jim: You were shy with people!

Laura: I tried not to be but never could—

Jim: Overcome it?

Laura: No, I—I never could!

Jim: I guess being shy is something you have to work out of kind of gradually.

Laura: *(sorrowfully)* Yes—I guess it—

Jim: Takes time!

Laura: Yes—

Jim: People are not so dreadful when you know them. That's what you have to remember! And everybody has problems, not just you, but practically everybody has got some problems. You think of yourself as having the only problems, as being the only one who is disappointed. But just look around you and you will see lots of people as disappointed as you are. For instance, I hoped when I was going to high school that I would be further along at this time, six years later, than I am now—You remember that wonderful write-up I had in *The Torch?*

Laura: Yes! *(She rises and crosses to table.)*

Jim: It said I was bound to succeed in anything I went into! *(Laura returns with the annual.)* Holy Jeez! *The Torch! (He accepts it reverently. They smile across it with mutual wonder. Laura crouches beside him and they begin to turn through it. Laura's shyness is dissolving in his warmth.)*

Laura: Here you are in *Pirates of Penzance!*

Jim: *(wistfully)* I sang the baritone lead in that operetta.

Laura: *(rapidly)* So—*beautifully!*

Jim: *(protesting)* Aw—

Laura: Yes, yes—beautifully—beautifully!

Jim: You heard me?

Laura: All three times!
Jim: No!
Laura: Yes!
Jim: All three performances?
Laura: *(looking down)* Yes.
Jim: Why?
Laura: I—wanted to ask you to—autograph my program.
Jim: Why didn't you ask me to?
Laura: You were always surrounded by your own friends so much that I never had a chance to.
Jim: You should have just—
Laura: Well, I—thought you might think I was—
Jim: Thought I might think you was—what?
Laura: Oh—
Jim: *(with reflective relish)* I was beleaguered by females in those days.
Laura: You were terribly popular!
Jim: Yeah—
Laura: You had such a—friendly way—
Jim: I was spoiled in high school.
Laura: Everybody—liked you!
Jim: Including you?
Laura: I—yes, I—I did, too— *(She gently closes the book in her lap.)*
Jim: Well, well, well!—Give me that program, Laura. *(She hands it to him. He signs it with a flourish.)* There you are—better late than never!
Laura: Oh, I—what a—surprise!
Jim: My signature isn't worth very much right now. But some day—maybe—it will increase in value! Being disappointed is one thing and being discouraged is something else. I am disappointed but I'm not discouraged. I'm twenty-three years old. How old are you?
Laura: I'll be twenty-four in June.
Jim: That's not old age!
Laura: No, but—
Jim: You finished high school?
Laura: *(with difficulty)* I didn't go back.
Jim: You mean you dropped out?
Laura: I made bad grades in my final examinations. *(She rises and replaces the book and the program. Her voice strained.)* How is—Emily Meisenbach getting along?
Jim: Oh, that kraut-head!
Laura: Why do you call her that?
Jim: That's what she was.
Laura: You're not still—going with her?
Jim: I never see her.
Laura: It said in the Personal Section that you were—engaged!
Jim: I know, but I wasn't impressed by that—propaganda!

Laura: It wasn't—the truth?

Jim: Only in Emily's optimistic opinion!

Laura: Oh—

Legend: "What Have You Done Since High School?"

Jim lights a cigarette and leans indolently back on his elbows smiling at Laura with a warmth and charm which light her inwardly with altar candles. She remains by the table and turns in her hands a piece of glass to cover her tumult.

Jim: *(after several reflective puffs on a cigarette)* What have you done since high school? *(She seems not to hear him.)* Huh? *(Laura looks up.)* I said what have you done since high school, Laura?

Laura: Nothing much.

Jim: You must have been doing something these six long years.

Laura: Yes.

Jim: Well, then, such as what?

Laura: I took a business course at business college—

Jim: How did that work out?

Laura: Well, not very—well—I had to drop out, it gave me—indigestion—

Jim laughs gently.

Jim: What are you doing now?

Laura: I don't do anything—much. Oh, please don't think I sit around doing nothing! My glass collection takes up a good deal of my time. Glass is something you have to take good care of.

Jim: What did you say—about glass?

Laura: Collection I said—I have one— *(She clears her throat and turns away again, acutely shy.)*

Jim: *(abruptly)* You know what I judge to be the trouble with you? Inferiority complex! Know what that is? That's what they call it when someone low-rates himself! I understand it because I had it, too. Although my case was not so aggravated as yours seems to be. I had it until I took up public speaking, developed my voice, and learned that I had an aptitude for science. Before that time I never thought of myself as being outstanding in any way whatsoever! Now I've never made a regular study of it, but I have a friend who says I can analyze people better than doctors that make a profession of it. I don't claim that to be necessarily true, but I can sure guess a person's psychology, Laura! *(Takes out his gum.)* Excuse me, Laura. I always take it out when the flavor is gone. I'll use this scrap of paper to wrap it in. I know how it is to get it stuck on a shoe. Yep—that's what I judge to be your principal trouble. A lack of confidence in yourself as a person. You don't have the proper amount of faith in yourself. I'm basing that fact on a number of your remarks and also on certain observations I've made. For instance that clumping you thought was so awful in high school. You say that you even dreaded to walk into class. You see what you did? You dropped out of school, you gave up an education because of a clump, which as far as I know was practically nonexistent! A little physical defect is what you have. Hardly noticeable even! Magnified thousands of times by imagination! You know what my strong advice to you is? Think of yourself as *superior* in some way!

Laura: In what way would I think?

Jim: Why, man alive, Laura! Just look about you a little. What do you see? A world full of common people! All of 'em born and all of 'em going to die! Which of them has one-tenth of your good points! Or mine! Or anyone else's, as far as that goes—Gosh! Everybody excels in some one thing. Some in many! *(Unconsciously glances at himself in the mirror.)* All you've got to do is discover in *what!* Take me, for instance. *(He adjusts his tie at the mirror.)* My interest happens to lie in electro-dynamics. I'm taking a course in radio engineering at night school, Laura, on top of a fairly responsible job at the warehouse. I'm taking that course and studying public speaking.

Laura: Ohhhh.

Jim: Because I believe in the future of television! *(Turning back to her.)* I wish to be ready to go up right along with it. Therefore I'm planning to get in on the ground floor. In fact, I've already made the right connections and all that remains is for the industry itself to get underway! Full steam— *(His eyes are starry.)* *Knowledge*—Zzzzzp! *Money*—Zzzzzzp!—*Power!* That's the cycle democracy is built on! *(His attitude is convincingly dynamic. Laura stares at him, even her shyness eclipsed in her absolute wonder. He suddenly grins.)* I guess you think I think a lot of myself!

Laura: No—o-o-o, I—

Jim: Now how about you? Isn't there something you take more interest in than anything else?

Laura: Well, I do—as I said—have my—glass collection—

A peal of girlish laughter from the kitchen.

Jim: I'm not right sure I know what you're talking about. What kind of glass is it?

Laura: Little articles of it, they're ornaments mostly! Most of them are little animals made out of glass, the tiniest little animals in the world. Mother calls them a glass menagerie! Here's an example of one, if you'd like to see it! This one is one of the oldest. It's nearly thirteen. *(He stretches out his hand.)* *(Music: "The Glass Menagerie.")* Oh, be careful—if you breathe, it breaks!

Jim: I'd better not take it. I'm pretty clumsy with things.

Laura: Go on, I trust you with him! *(Places it in his palm.)* There now—you're holding him gently! Hold him over the light, he loves the light! You see how the light shines through him?

Jim: It sure does shine!

Laura: I shouldn't be partial, but he is my favorite one.

Jim: What kind of a thing is this one supposed to be?

Laura: Haven't you noticed the single horn on his forehead?

Jim: A unicorn, huh?

Laura: Mmm-hmmm!

Jim: Unicorns, aren't they extinct in the modern world?

Laura: I know!

Jim: Poor little fellow, he must feel sort of lonesome.

Laura: *(smiling)* Well, if he does he doesn't complain about it. He stays on a shelf with some horses that don't have horns and all of them seem to get along nicely together.

Jim: How do you know?

Laura: *(lightly)* I haven't heard any arguments among them!

Jim: *(grinning)* No arguments, huh? Well, that's a pretty good sign! Where shall I set him?

Laura: Put him on the table. They all like a change of scenery once in a while!

Jim: *(stretching)* Well, well, well, well—Look how big my shadow is when I stretch!

Laura: Oh, oh, yes—it stretches across the ceiling!

Jim: *(crossing to door)* I think it's stopped raining. *(Opens fire-escape door.)* Where does the music come from?

Laura: From the Paradise Dance Hall across the alley.

Jim: How about cutting the rug a little, Miss Wingfield?

Laura: Oh, I—

Jim: Or is your program filled up? Let me have a look at it. *(Grasps imaginary card.)* Why, every dance is taken! I'll just have to scratch some out. *(Waltz Music: "La Golondrina.")* Ahhh, a waltz! *(He executes some sweeping turns by himself, then holds his arms toward Laura.)*

Laura: *(breathlessly)* I—can't dance!

Jim: There you go, that inferiority stuff!

Laura: I've never danced in my life!

Jim: Come on, try!

Laura: Oh, but I'd step on you!

Jim: I'm not made out of glass.

Laura: How—how—how do we start?

Jim: Just leave it to me. You hold your arms out a little.

Laura: Like this?

Jim: A little bit higher. Right. Now don't tighten up, that's the main thing about it—relax.

Laura: *(laughing breathlessly)* It's hard not to.

Jim: Okay.

Laura: I'm afraid you can't budge me.

Jim: What do you bet I can't? *(He swings her into motion.)*

Laura: Goodness, yes, you can!

Jim: Let yourself go, now, Laura, just let yourself go.

Laura: I'm—

Jim: Come on!
Laura: Trying!
Jim: Not so stiff—Easy does it!
Laura: I know but I'm—
Jim: Loosen th' backbone! There now, that's a lot better.
Laura: Am I?
Jim: Lots, lots better! *(He moves her about the room in a clumsy waltz.)*
Laura: Oh, my!
Jim: Ha-ha!
Laura: Goodness, yes you can!
Jim: Ha-ha-ha! *(They suddenly bump into the table, Jim stops.)* What did we hit on?
Laura: Table.
Jim: Did something fall off it? I think—
Laura: Yes.
Jim: I hope that it wasn't the little glass horse with the horn!
Laura: Yes.
Jim: Aw, aw, aw. Is it broken?
Laura: Now it is just like all the other horses.
Jim: It's lost its—
Laura: Horn! It doesn't matter. Maybe it's a blessing in disguise.
Jim: You'll never forgive me. I bet that that was your favorite piece of glass.
Laura: I don't have favorites much. It's no tragedy, Freckles. Glass breaks so easily. No matter how careful you are. The traffic jars the shelves and things fall off them.
Jim: Still I'm awfully sorry that I was the cause.
Laura: *(smiling)* I'll just imagine he had an operation. The horn was removed to make him feel less—freakish! *(They both laugh.)* Now he will feel more at home with the other horses, the ones that don't have horns . . .
Jim: Ha-ha, that's very funny! *(Suddenly serious.)* I'm glad to see that you have a sense of humor. You know—you're—well—very different! Surprisingly different from anyone else I know! *(His voice becomes soft and hesitant with a genuine feeling.)* Do you mind me telling you that? *(Laura is abashed beyond speech.)* You make me feel sort of—I don't know how to put it! I'm usually pretty good at expressing things, but—This is something that I don't know how to say! *(Laura touches her throat and clears it—turns the broken unicorn in her hands.) (Even softer.)* Has anyone ever told you that you were pretty? *(Pause: Music.) (Laura looks up slowly, with wonder, and shakes her head.)* Well, you are! In a very different way from anyone else. And all the nicer because of the difference, too. *(His voice becomes low and husky. Laura turns away, nearly faint with the novelty of her emotions.)* I wish you were my sister. I'd teach you to have some confidence in yourself. The different people are not like other people, but being different is nothing to be ashamed of. Because other people are not such wonderful people. They're one hundred times one thousand. You're

Laura in the arms of the gentleman caller while Tom and Amanda look on in Tennessee Williams's *The Glass Menagerie* presented at the Williamstown Theatre festival

one times one! They walk all over the earth. You just stay here. They're common as—weeds, but—you—well, you're—*Blue Roses!*

Image On Screen: Blue Roses.

Music Changes.

Laura: But blue is wrong for—roses . . .
Jim: It's right for you—You're—pretty!
Laura: In what respect am I pretty?
Jim: In all respects—believe me! Your eyes—your hair—are pretty! Your hands are pretty! *(He catches hold of her hand.)* You think I'm making this up because I'm invited to dinner and have to be nice. Oh, I could do that! I could put on an act for you, Laura, and say lots of things without being very sincere. But this time I am. I'm talking to you sincerely. I happened to notice you had this inferiority complex that keeps you from feeling comfortable with people. Somebody needs to build your confidence up and make you proud instead of shy and turning away and—blushing—Somebody ought to—ought to—*kiss* you, Laura! *(His hand slips slowly up her arm to her shoulder.) (Music Swells Tumultuously.) (He suddenly turns her about and kisses her on the lips. When he releases her Laura sinks on the sofa with a bright, dazed look. Jim backs away and fishes in his pocket for a cigarette.) (Legend On Screen: "Souvenir.")* Stumble-john! *(He lights the cigarette, avoiding her look. There is a peal of girlish laughter from Amanda in the kitchen. Laura slowly raises and opens her hand. It still contains the little broken glass animal. She looks at it with a tender, bewildered expression.)* Stumble-john! I shouldn't have done that—That was way off the beam. You don't smoke, do you? *(She looks up, smiling,*

not hearing the question. He sits beside her a little gingerly. She looks at him speechlessly—waiting. He coughs decorously and moves a little farther aside as he considers the situation and senses her feelings, dimly, with perturbation. Gently.) Would you—care for a—mint? *(She doesn't seem to hear him but her look grows brighter even.)* Peppermint—Life Saver? My pocket's a regular drug store—wherever I go . . . *(He pops a mint in his mouth. Then gulps and decides to make a clean breast of it. He speaks slowly and gingerly.)* Laura, you know, if I had a sister like you, I'd do the same thing as Tom, I'd bring out fellows—introduce her to them. The right type of boys of a type to—appreciate her. Only—well—he made a mistake about me. Maybe I've got no call to be saying this. That may not have been the idea in having me over. But what if it was? There's nothing wrong about that. The only trouble is that in my case—I'm not in a situation to do the right thing. I can't take down your number and say I'll phone. I can't call up next week and—ask for a date. I thought I had better explain the situation in case you misunderstood it and—hurt your feelings. . . . *(Pause. Slowly, very slowly, Laura's look changes, her eyes returning slowly from his to the ornament in her palm.)*

Amanda utters another gay laugh in the kitchen.

Laura: *(faintly)* You—won't—call again?

Jim: No, Laura. I can't. *(He rises from the sofa.)* As I was just explaining, I've—got strings on me, Laura, I've—been going steady! I go out all the time with a girl named Betty. She's a home-girl like you, and Catholic, and Irish, and in a great many ways we—get along fine. I met her last summer on a moonlight boat trip up the river to Alton, on the *Majestic*. Well—right away from the start it was—love! *(Legend: Love!) (Laura sways slightly forward and grips the arm of the sofa. He fails to notice, now enrapt in his own comfortable being.)* Being in love has made a new man of me! *(Leaning stiffly forward, clutching the arm of the sofa, Laura struggles visibly with her storm. But Jim is oblivious, she is a long way off.)* The power of love is really pretty tremendous! Love is something that—changes the whole world, Laura! *(The storm abates a little and Laura leans back. He notices her again.)* It happened that Betty's aunt took sick, she got a wire and had to go to Centralia. So Tom—when he asked me to dinner—I naturally just accepted the invitation, not knowing that you—that he—that I—*(He stops awkwardly.)* Huh—I'm a stumble-john! *(He flops back on the sofa. The holy candles in the altar of Laura's face have been snuffed out! There is a look of almost infinite desolation. Jim glances at her uneasily.)* I wish that you would—say something. *(She bites her lip which was trembling and then bravely smiles. She opens her hand again on the broken glass ornament. Then she gently takes his hand and raises it level with her own. She carefully places the unicorn in the palm of his hand, then pushes his fingers closed upon it.)* What are you—doing that for? You want me to have him?—Laura? *(She nods.)* What for?

Laura: A—souvenir . . .

She rises unsteadily and crouches beside the Victrola to wind it up.

Legend On Screen: "Things Have A Way Of Turning Out So Badly."

Or Image: "Gentleman Caller Waving Good-bye!—Gaily."

At this moment Amanda rushes brightly back in the front room. She bears a pitcher of fruit punch in an old-fashioned cut-glass pitcher and a plate of macaroons. The plate has a gold border and poppies painted on it.

Amanda: Well, well, well! Isn't the air delightful after the shower? I've made you children a little liquid refreshment. *(Turns gaily to the gentleman caller.)* Jim, do you know that song about lemonade?

"Lemonade, lemonade
Made in the shade and stirred with a spade—
Good enough for any old maid!"

Jim: *(uneasily)* Ha-ha! No—I never heard it.

Amanda: Why, Laura! You look so serious!

Jim: We were having a serious conversation.

Amanda: Good! Now you're better acquainted!

Jim: *(uncertainly)* Ha-ha! Yes.

Amanda: You modern young people are much more serious-minded than my generation. I was so gay as a girl!

Jim: You haven't changed, Mrs. Wingfield.

Amanda: Tonight I'm rejuvenated! The gaiety of the occasion, Mr. O'Connor! *(She tosses her head with a peal of laughter. Spills lemonade.)* Oooo! I'm baptizing myself!

Jim: Here—let me—

Amanda: *(setting the pitcher down)* There now. I discovered we had some maraschino cherries. I dumped them in, juice and all!

Jim: You shouldn't have gone to that trouble. Mrs. Wingfield.

Scene from *The Glass Menagerie*, with Rita Moreno (as Amanda Wakefield) and Terrence Riordan (as The Gentleman Caller), from 2006

San Francisco Chronicle/Hearst Newspapers via Getty Images/Getty Images

Amanda: Trouble, trouble? Why it was loads of fun! Didn't you hear me cutting up in the kitchen? I bet your ears were burning! I told Tom how outdone with him I was for keeping you to himself so long a time! He should have brought you over much, much sooner! Well, now that you've found your way, I want you to be a very frequent caller! Not just occasional but all the time. Oh, we're going to have a lot of gay times together! I see them coming! Mmm, just breathe that air! So fresh, and the moon's so pretty! I'll skip back out—I know where my place is when young folks are having a—serious conversation!

Jim: Oh, don't go out, Mrs. Wingfield. The fact of the matter is I've got to be going.

Amanda: Going, now? You're joking! Why, it's only the shank of the evening, Mr. O'Connor!

Jim: Well, you know how it is.

Amanda: You mean you're a young workingman and have to keep workingmen's hours. We'll let you off early tonight. But only on the condition that next time you stay later. What's the best night for you? Isn't Saturday night the best night for you workingmen?

Jim: I have a couple of time-clocks to punch, Mrs. Wingfield. One at morning, another one at night!

Amanda: My, but you are ambitious! You work at night, too?

Jim: No, Ma'am, not work but—Betty! *(He crosses deliberately to pick up his hat. The band at the Paradise Dance Hall goes into a tender waltz.)*

Amanda: Betty? Betty? Who's Betty! *(There is an ominous cracking sound in the sky.)*

Jim: Oh, just a girl. The girl I go steady with! *(He smiles charmingly. The sky falls.)*

Legend: "The Sky Falls."

Amanda: *(a long-drawn exhalation)* Ohhhh . . . Is it a serious romance Mr. O'Connor?

Jim: We're going to be married the second Sunday in June.

Amanda: Ohhhh—how nice! Tom didn't mention that you were engaged to be married.

Jim: The cat's not out of the bag at the warehouse yet. You know how they are. They call you Romeo and stuff like that. *(He stops at the oval mirror to put on his hat. He carefully shapes the brim and the crown to give a discreetly dashing effect.)* It's been a wonderful evening, Mrs. Wingfield. I guess this is what they mean by Southern hospitality.

Amanda: It really wasn't anything at all.

Jim: I hope it don't seem like I'm rushing off. But I promised Betty I'd pick her up at the Wabash depot, an' by the time I get my jalopy down there her train'll be in. Some women are pretty upset if you keep 'em waiting.

Amanda: Yes, I know—The tyranny of women! *(Extends her hand.)* Good-bye, Mr. O'Connor. I wish you luck—and happiness—and success! All three of them, and so does Laura!—Don't you, Laura?

Laura: Yes!

Jim: *(taking her hand)* Good-bye, Laura. I'm certainly going to treasure that souvenir. And don't you forget the good advice I gave you. *(Raises his voice to a cheery shout.)* So long, Shakespeare! Thanks again, ladies—Good night!

He grins and ducks jauntily out.

Still bravely grimacing, Amanda closes the door on the gentleman caller. Then she turns back to the room with a puzzled expression. She and Laura don't dare to face each other. Laura crouches beside the Victrola to wind it.

Amanda: *(faintly)* Things have a way of turning out so badly. I don't believe that I would play the Victrola. Well, well—well—Our gentleman caller was engaged to be married! Tom!

Tom: *(from back)* Yes, Mother?

Amanda: Come in here a minute. I want to tell you something awfully funny.

Tom: *(enters with macaroon and a glass of the lemonade)* Has the gentleman caller gotten away already?

Amanda: The gentleman caller has made an early departure. What a wonderful joke you played on us!

Tom: How do you mean?

Amanda: You didn't mention that he was engaged to be married.

Tom: Jim? Engaged?

Amanda: That's what he just informed us.

Tom: I'll be jiggered! I didn't know about that.

Amanda: That seems very peculiar.

Tom: What's peculiar about it?

Amanda: Didn't you call him your best friend down at the warehouse?

Tom: He is, but how did I know?

Amanda: It seems extremely peculiar that you wouldn't know your best friend was going to be married!

Tom: The warehouse is where I work, not where I know things about people!

Amanda: You don't know things anywhere! You live in a dream; you manufacture illusions! *(He crosses to door.)* Where are you going?

Tom: I'm going to the movies.

Amanda: That's right, now that you've had us make such fools of ourselves. The effort, the preparations, all the expense! The new floor lamp, the rug, the clothes for Laura! All for what? To entertain some other girl's fiancé! Go to the movies, go! Don't think about us, a mother deserted, an unmarried sister who's crippled and has no job! Don't let anything interfere with your selfish pleasure! Just go, go, go—to the movies!

Tom: All right, I will! The more you shout about my selfishness to me the quicker I'll go, and I won't go to the movies!

Amanda: Go, then! Then go to the moon—you selfish dreamer!

Tom smashes his glass on the floor. He plunges out on the fire-escape, slamming the door. Laura screams—cut by door.

Dance-hall music up. Tom goes to the rail and grips it desperately, lifting his face in the chill white moonlight penetrating the narrow abyss of the alley.

Legend On Screen: "And So Good-bye . . ."

Tom's closing speech is timed with the interior pantomime. The interior scene is played as though viewed through sound-proof glass. Amanda appears to be making a comforting speech to Laura who is huddled upon the sofa. Now that we cannot hear the mother's speech, her silliness is gone and she has dignity and tragic beauty. Laura's dark hair hides her face until at the end of the speech she lifts it to smile at her mother. Amanda's gestures are slow and graceful, almost dancelike, as she comforts the daughter. At the end of her speech she glances a moment at the father's picture—then withdraws through the portieres. At close of Tom's speech, Laura blows out the candles, ending the play.

Tom: I didn't go to the moon, I went much further—for time is the longest distance between two places— Not long after that I was fired for writing a poem on the lid of a shoe-box. I left Saint Louis. I descended the steps of this fire-escape for a last time and followed, from then on, in my father's footsteps, attempting to find in motion what was lost in space—I traveled around a great deal. The cities swept about me like dead leaves, leaves that were brightly colored but torn away from the branches. I would have stopped, but was pursued by something. It always came upon me unawares, taking me altogether by surprise. Perhaps it was a familiar bit of music. Perhaps it was only a piece of transparent glass. Perhaps I am walking along a street at night, in some strange city, before I have found companions. I pass the lighted window of a shop where perfume is sold. The window is filled with pieces of colored glass, tiny transparent bottles in delicate colors, like bits of a shattered rainbow. Then all at once my sister touches my shoulder. I turn around and look into her eyes . . . Oh, Laura, Laura, I tried to leave you behind me, but I am more faithful than I intended to be! I reach for a cigarette, I cross the street, I run into the movies or a bar, I buy a drink, I speak to the nearest stranger—anything that can blow your candles out! *(Laura bends over the candles.)* —for nowadays the world is lit by lightning! Blow out your candles, Laura—and so good-bye . . .

She blows the candles out.

The Scene Dissolves.

* * *

Reading and Reacting

1. Whom do you think this play is really about—Tom, Laura, or Amanda? Why?
2. What role is played by the absent father? In what sense is he a character in the play?

3. Besides serving as a possible suitor for Laura, what other roles does Jim play?
4. Identify references to historical events occurring at the time of the play's action. How are these events related to the play's central theme?
5. Does Tom function primarily as an actor, a character, a playwright, or a narrator? Explain.
6. What do the music, the lighting and the words and pictures projected on slides—which Tennessee Williams called "extra-literary accents"—contribute to the play's action? Do you see them as essential? (Note that at the urging of the director, Williams eliminated these "accents" when the play opened on Broadway.)
7. In his production notes, Williams calls *The Glass Menagerie* a "memory play." What do you think he meant?
8. Consider the picture of the father, the Victrola, the fire escape, the telephone, the alarm clock, the high-school yearbook, the unicorn, and the candles. How do these props help to develop the play's themes?
9. What events and dialogue foreshadow Tom's escape? Do you see this escape as inevitable? Do you see it as successful? Explain.
10. Do Amanda and Laura change during the play? What do you think will happen to them after the play is over? What is the significance of Laura's blowing out the candles at the end of the play?
11. **Journal Entry** Do you think Tom's decision to leave his family is a sign of strength or weakness? Why?
12. **Critical Perspective** In "Irony and Distance in *The Glass Menagerie*, critic Thomas L. King examines the issue of who is the play's central character, making the following claim:

    > Tennessee Williams's *the Glass Menagerie*, though it has achieved a firmly established position in the canon of American plays, is often distorted, if not misunderstood, by readers, diretors, and audiences. This distortion results from an overemphasis on the scenes involving Laura and Amanda and their plight, so that the play becomes a sentimental tract on the trapped misery of two women in St. Louis.

    He continues:

    > The play... is not Amanda's. Amanda is a striking and a powerful character, but the play is Tom's. Tom opens the play and he closes it; he also opens the second act and two further scenes in the first act—his is the first word and the last. Indeed, Amanda, Laura, and the Gentleman Caller do yot appear in the play at all as separate characters.

    Do you agree with King's assessment? If so, how would you further support his view that "the play is Tom's"? Could you make a case for another character?

Related Works: "A&P" (p. 179), "Barn Burning" (p. 265), "The Road Not Taken" (p. 605), "Elegy for My Father, Who Is Not Dead" (p. 676), "The Soul selects her own Society—" (p. 712), *Fences* (p. 1222)

Bettmann/Getty Images

WILLIAM SHAKESPEARE (1564–1616) is recognized as the greatest of English writers, but many details about his life are based on conjecture or tradition. The earliest dependable information concerning Shakespeare is found in the parish registers of Stratford-upon-Avon's Holy Trinity Church, where his baptism was recorded on April 26, 1564. Although his date of birth cannot be determined with certainty, tradition has assigned it to April 23, 1564. Little is known about his early life, but reliable information about significant events is available in church documents. For example, he married Ann Hathaway in 1582 and had three children—Susanna in 1583 and the twins Judith and Hamnet in 1585.

Soon after the birth of his children, Shakespeare left Stratford for London. Upon his arrival in the capital, he set out to establish himself in London's literary world. His first step toward achieving this goal occurred in 1592, when he published his narrative poem *Venus and Adonis*; the following year, he published a second poem, *The Rape of Lucrece*.

By 1594, Shakespeare had become quite involved with the London stage. For approximately twenty years, he enjoyed a successful professional career in London—as actor, playwright, shareholder in the Lord Chamberlain's Men (an acting company), part owner of the Globe Theatre (from 1599), and author of at least thirty-six plays. The income derived from these activities brought him significant wealth and enabled him, sometime between 1610 and 1613, to retire from the theater and to return to Stratford-upon-Avon, where he owned considerable property. On April 23, 1616, Shakespeare died at age fifty-two in Stratford and was buried two days later in Holy Trinity Church.

It is difficult to date many of Shakespeare's plays exactly because they must be dated by records of their first performance (often hard to come by) and by topical references in the text. Shakespeare's company probably first staged *Hamlet* at the Globe Theatre in 1600 or 1601, but some scholars believe the play was composed as early as 1598.

An audience at the reconstructed Globe Theatre in London

Andreas Hub/laif/Redux

Hamlet has been called Shakespeare's most complex and most confusing play, yet it is also the play most frequently performed, read, and written about. Shakespeare's audience would have recognized *Hamlet* as a revenge tragedy—a play in which the hero discovers that a close relative has been murdered, experiences considerable trouble in identifying the murderer, and, after overcoming numerous obstacles, avenges the death by killing the murderer. In Shakespeare's time, revenge tragedies often featured murders, physical mutilations, and ghosts, all enacted with grand style and bold rhetoric. These plays were extremely popular productions that were the action movies of their day.

Hamlet, however, is different from the typical revenge tragedy. Because the ghost gives him the necessary information, Hamlet has no need to search for the cause of his father's death or find the murderer. In fact, the only impediments to Hamlet's revenge are those he himself creates. And, by the time the delay ends and Hamlet avenges his father's death, the loss is immense: his mother, the woman he loves, her father and brother, and Hamlet himself are all dead. Although the argument that there would be no play if Hamlet had immediately avenged his father may be valid, it fails to satisfy those who ponder the tragic cost of Hamlet's inaction.

Cultural Context The appearance of a ghost was a longstanding tradition in Renaissance drama. The ghost appeared in Elizabethan revenge tragedies as a plot device to help further the action and prompt a reaction from the hero. For a Renaissance audience, the dramatic representation of a ghost from purgatory would evoke a rich context of legends and lore derived from paintings, illuminated manuscripts, prints, and narratives. Moreover, stories involving ghosts were a frequent element of medieval sermons. However, the ghost in *Hamlet* transcends the traditions of the revenge tragedy. Here, Shakespeare's use of the ghost not only as a plot device but also as a character who may or may not be telling the truth adds depth and complexity to the play.

Hamlet (c. 1600)

Prince of Denmark[1]

CHARACTERS

Claudius, *King of Denmark*
Hamlet, *son to the former and nephew to the present King*
Polonius, *Lord Chamberlain*
Horatio, *friend to Hamlet*
Laertes, *son to Polonius*
Courtiers: **Voltimand**, **Cornelius**, **Rosencrantz**, **Guildenstern**, **Osric**
A Gentleman
A Priest
Francisco, *a soldier*
Officers: **Marcellus**, **Bernardo**
Reynaldo, *servant to Polonius*
Players
Two Clowns, *grave-diggers*
Fortinbras, *Prince of Norway*
A Captain
English Ambassadors
Ghost of Hamlet's Father
Gertrude, *Queen of Denmark and mother of Hamlet*
Ophelia, *daughter to Polonius*
Lords, Ladies, Officers, Soldiers, Sailors, Messengers, and other Attendants

[1]Note that individual lines are numbered in the following play. When a line is shared by one or more characters, it is counted as one line.

Richard Burton as Hamlet
Bettmann/Getty Images

Laurence Olivier as Hamlet
Bettmann/Getty Images

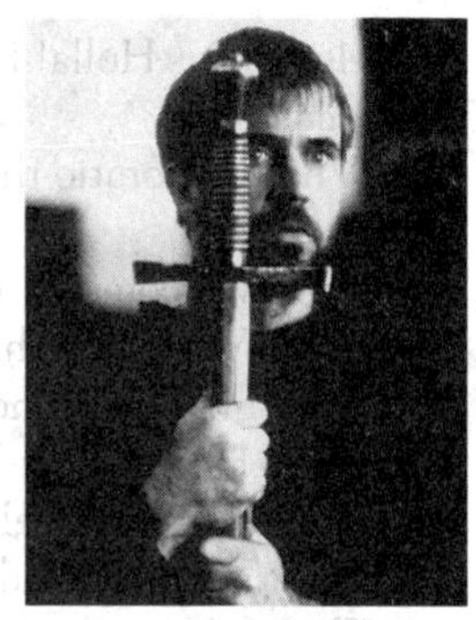

Mel Gibson as Hamlet
United Archives GmbH/Alamy Stock Photo

ACT 1

SCENE 1

Elsinore. A platform before the castle.

Francisco at his post. Enter to him Bernardo.

Bernardo: Who's there?
Francisco: Nay, answer me: stand, and unfold yourself.
Bernardo: Long live the king!
Francisco: Bernardo?
Bernardo: He.
Francisco: You come most carefully upon your hour.
Bernardo: 'Tis now struck twelve; get thee to bed, Francisco.
Francisco: For this relief much thanks: 'tis bitter cold, And I am sick at heart.
Bernardo: Have you had quiet guard?
Francisco: Not a mouse stirring.
Bernardo: Well, good-night.
If you do meet Horatio and Marcellus,
The rivals of my watch, bid them make haste.
Francisco: I think I hear them.—Stand, ho! Who is there?

Enter Horatio and Marcellus.

Horatio: Friends to this ground.
Marcellus: And liegemen to the Dane.
Francisco: Give you good-night.
Marcellus: O, farewell, honest soldier:
Who hath reliev'd you?
Francisco: Bernardo has my place.
Give you good-night.

Exit.

Marcellus: Holla! Bernardo!
Bernardo: Say.
What, is Horatio there?
Horatio: A piece of him.
Bernardo: Welcome, Horatio:—welcome, good Marcellus.
Marcellus: What, has this thing appear'd again to-night?
Bernardo: I have seen nothing.
Marcellus: Horatio says 'tis but our fantasy,
And will not let belief take hold of him
Touching this dreaded sight, twice seen of us:
Therefore I have entreated him along
With us to watch the minutes of this night;
That, if again this apparition come
He may approve our eyes and speak to it.
Horatio: Tush, tush, 'twill not appear.
Bernardo: Sit down awhile,
And let us once again assail your ears,
That are so fortified against our story,
What we two nights have seen.
Horatio: Well, sit we down,
And let us hear Bernardo speak of this.
Bernardo: Last night of all,
When yon same star that's westward from the pole
Had made his course to illume that part of heaven
Where now it burns, Marcellus and myself,
The bell then beating one,—
Marcellus: Peace, break thee off; look where it comes again!

Enter Ghost, armed.

Bernardo: In the same figure, like the king that's dead.
Marcellus: Thou art a scholar; speak to it, Horatio.
Bernardo: Looks it not like the king? mark it, Horatio.
Horatio: Most like:—it harrows me with fear and wonder.
Bernardo: It would be spoke to.
Marcellus: Question it, Horatio.
Horatio: What art thou, that usurp'st this time of night,
Together with that fair and warlike form
In which the majesty of buried Denmark
Did sometimes march? by heaven I charge thee, speak!
Marcellus: It is offended.
Bernardo: See, it stalks away!
Horatio: Stay! speak, speak! I charge thee, speak!

Exit Ghost.

Marcellus: 'Tis gone, and will not answer.
Bernardo: How now, Horatio! you tremble and look pale:
Is not this something more than fantasy?
What think you on't?
Horatio: Before my God, I might not this believe
Without the sensible and true avouch
Of mine own eyes.
Marcellus: Is it not like the king?
Horatio: As thou art to thyself:
Such was the very armor he had on
When he the ambitious Norway combated;
So frown'd he once when, in an angry parle,[1]
He smote the sledded Polacks on the ice.
'Tis strange.
Marcellus: Thus twice before, and just at this dead hour,
With martial stalk hath he gone by our watch.
Horatio: In what particular thought to work I know not;
But, in the gross and scope of my opinion,
This bodes some strange eruption to our state.
Marcellus: Good now, sit down, and tell me, he that knows,
Why this same strict and most observant watch
So nightly toils the subject of the land;
And why such daily cast of brazen cannon,
And foreign mart for implements of war;
Why such impress of shipwrights, whose sore task
Does not divide the Sunday from the week;
What might be toward, that this sweaty haste
Doth make the night joint-laborer with the day:
Who is't that can inform me?
Horatio: That can I;
At least, the whisper goes so. Our last king,
Whose image even but now appear'd to us,
Was, as you know, by Fortinbras of Norway,
Thereto prick'd on by a most emulate pride,
Dar'd to the combat; in which our valiant Hamlet,—
For so this side of our known world esteem'd him,—
Did slay this Fortinbras; who, by a seal'd compact,
Well ratified by law and heraldry,
Did forfeit, with his life, all those his lands.

---

[1]*parle:* Parley, or conference.

Which he stood seiz'd of,[2] to the conqueror:
Against the which, a moiety competent[3]
Was gagéd[4] by our king; which had return'd
To the inheritance of Fortinbras,
Had he been vanquisher; as by the same cov'nant,
And carriage of the article design'd,
His fell to Hamlet. Now, sir, young Fortinbras,
Of unimproved mettle hot and full,
Hath in the skirts of Norway, here and there,
Shark'd up a list of landless resolutes,
For food and diet, to some enterprise
That hath a stomach in't: which is no other,—
As it doth well appear unto our state,—
But to recover of us by strong hand,
And terms compulsatory, those foresaid lands
So by his father lost: and this, I take it,
Is the main motive of our preparations,
The source of this our watch, and the chief head
Of this post-haste and romage[5] in the land.

Bernardo: I think it be no other, but e'en so:
Well may it sort that this portentous figure
Comes armed through our watch; so like the king
That was and is the question of these wars.

Horatio: A mote it is to trouble the mind's eye.
In the most high and palmy state of Rome,
A little ere the mightiest Julius fell,
The graves stood tenantless, and the sheeted dead
Did squeak and gibber in the Roman streets:
As, stars with trains of fire and dews of blood,
Disasters in the sun; and the moist star,
Upon whose influence Neptune's empire stands,
Was sick almost to doomsday with eclipse:
And even the like precurse of fierce events,—
As harbingers preceding still the fates,
And prologue to the omen coming on,—
Have heaven and earth together demonstrated
Unto our climature and countrymen.—
But, soft, behold! lo, where it comes again!

Re-enter Ghost.

I'll cross it, though it blast me.—Stay, illusion!
If thou hast any sound or use of voice,
Speak to me:

---

[2] *seiz'd of:* Possessed.
[3] *moiety competent:* A sufficient portion of his lands.
[4] *gagéd:* Engaged or pledged.
[5] *post-haste and romage:* General activity.

If there be any good thing to be done,
That may to thee do ease, and grace to me,
Speak to me:
If thou art privy to thy country's fate,
Which, happily,[6] foreknowing may avoid,
O, speak!
Or if thou has uphoarded in thy life
Extorted treasure in the womb of earth,
For which, they say, you spirits oft walk in death,

Cock crows.

Speak of it:—stay, and speak!—Stop it, Marcellus.
Marcellus: Shall I strike at it with my partisan?[7]
Horatio: Do, if it will not stand.
Bernardo: 'Tis here!
Horatio: 'Tis here!
Marcellus: 'Tis gone!

Exit Ghost.

We do it wrong, being so majestical,
To offer it the show of violence;
For it is, as the air, invulnerable,
And our vain blows malicious mockery.
Bernardo: It was about to speak when the cock crew.
Horatio: And then it started like a guilty thing
Upon a fearful summons. I have heard,
The cock, that is the trumpet to the morn,
Doth with his lofty and shrill-sounding throat
Awake the god of day; and at his warning,
Whether in sea or fire, in earth or air,
The extravagant and erring spirit hies
To his confine: and of the truth herein
This present object made probation.[8]
Marcellus: It faded on the crowing of the cock.
Some say that ever 'gainst that season comes
Wherein our Saviour's birth is celebrated,
The bird of dawning singeth all night long:
And then, they say, no spirit can walk abroad;
The nights are wholesome; then no planets strike,
No fairy takes, nor witch hath power to charm;
So hallow'd and so gracious is the time.
Horatio: So have I heard, and do in part believe.
But, look, the morn, in russet mantle clad,
Walks o'er the dew of yon high eastern hill:

[6] *happily:* Haply, or perhaps. [7] *partisan:* Pike. [8] *probation:* Proof.

Break we our watch up: and, by my advice,
Let us impart what we have seen to-night
Unto young Hamlet; for, upon my life,
This spirit, dumb to us, will speak to him:
Do you consent we shall acquaint him with it,
As needful in our loves, fitting our duty?

Marcellus: Let's do't, I pray; and I this morning know
Where we shall find him most conveniently.

Exeunt.

SCENE 2

Elsinore. A room of state in the castle.

Enter the King, Queen, Hamlet, Polonius, Laertes, Voltimand, Cornelius, Lords, and Attendants.

King: Though yet of Hamlet our dear brother's death
The memory be green; and that it us befitted
To bear our hearts in grief, and our whole kingdom
To be contracted in one brow of woe;
Yet so far hath discretion fought with nature
That we with wisest sorrow think on him,
Together with remembrance of ourselves.
Therefore our sometime sister, now our queen,
The imperial jointress of this warlike state,
Have we, as 'twere with defeated joy,—
With one auspicious and one dropping eye,
With mirth and funeral, and with dirge in marriage,
In equal scale weighing delight and dole,—
Taken to wife: nor have we herein barr'd
Your better wisdoms, which have freely gone
With this affair along:—for all, our thanks.
Now follows that you know, young Fortinbras,
Holding a weak supposal of our worth,
Or thinking by our late dear brother's death
Our state to be disjoint and out of frame,
Colleagued with the dream of his advantage,
He hath not fail'd to pester us with message,
Importing the surrender of those lands
Lost by his father, with all bonds of law,
To our most valiant brother. So much for him.—
Now for ourself, and for this time of meeting:
Thus much the business is:—we have here writ
To Norway, uncle of young Fortinbras,—
Who, impotent and bed-rid, scarcely hears
Of this his nephew's purpose,—to suppress

His further gait herein; in that the levies,
The lists, and full proportions, are all made
Out of his subject:—and we here despatch
You, good Cornelius, and you, Voltimand,
For bearers of this greeting to old Norway;
Giving to you no further personal power
To business with the king more than the scope
Of these dilated articles allow.
Farewell; and let your haste commend your duty.
Cornelius and Voltimand: In that and all things will we show our duty.
King: We doubt it nothing: heartily farewell.

Exeunt Voltimand and Cornelius.

And now, Laertes, what's the news with you?
You told us of some suit; what is't, Laertes?
You cannot speak of reason to the Dane,
And lose your voice: what wouldst thou beg, Laertes,
That shall not be my offer, nor thy asking?
The head is not more native to the heart,
The hand more instrumental to the mouth,
Than is the throne of Denmark to thy father.
What wouldst thou have, Laertes?
Laertes: Dread my lord,
Your leave and favor to return to France;
From whence though willingly I came to Denmark,
To show my duty in your coronation;
Yet now, I must confess, that duty done,
My thoughts and wishes bend again toward France.
And bow them to your gracious leave and pardon.
King: Have you your father's leave? What says Polonius?
Polonius: He hath, my lord, wrung from me my slow leave
By laborsome petition; and at last
Upon his will I seal'd my hard consent:
I do beseech you, give him leave to go.
King: Take thy fair hour, Laertes; time be thine,
And thy best graces spend it at thy will!—
But now, my cousin Hamlet, and my son,—
Hamlet: [*Aside*] A little more than kin, and less than kind.
King: How is it that the clouds still hang on you?
Hamlet: Not so, my lord; I am too much i' the sun.
Queen: Good Hamlet, cast thy nighted color off,
And let thine eye look like a friend on Denmark.
Do not for ever with thy vailed[1] lids
Seek for thy noble father in the dust:

[1] *vailed:* Downcast.

Thou know'st 'tis common,—all that live must die,
Passing through nature to eternity.
Hamlet: Ay, madam, it is common.
Queen: If it be,
Why seems it so particular with thee?
Hamlet: Seems, madam! nay, it is; I know not seems.
'Tis not alone my inky cloak, good mother,
Nor customary suits of solemn black,
Nor windy suspiration of forc'd breath,
No, nor the fruitful river in the eye,
Nor the dejected 'havior of the visage,
Together with all forms, moods, shows of grief,
That can denote me truly: these, indeed, seem;
For they are actions that a man might play:
But I have that within which passeth show;
These but the trappings and the suits of woe.
King: 'Tis sweet and cómmendable in your nature, Hamlet,
To give these mourning duties to your father:
But, you must know, your father lost a father;
That father lost, lost his; and the survivor bound,
In filial obligation, for some term
To do obsequious sorrow: but to persever
In obstinate condolement is a course
Of impious stubbornness; 'tis unmanly grief:
It shows a will most incorrect to heaven;
A heart unfortified, a mind impatient;
An understanding simple and unschool'd:
For what we know must be, and is as common
As any the most vulgar thing to sense,[2]
Why should we, in our peevish opposition,
Take it to heart? Fie! 'tis a fault to heaven,
A fault against the dead, a fault to nature,
To reason most absurd; whose common theme
Is death of fathers, and who still[3] hath cried,
From the first corse till he that died to-day,
This must be so. We pray you, throw to earth
This unprevailing woe; and think of us
As of a father: for let the world take note
You are the most immediate to our throne;
And with no less nobility of love
Than that which dearest father bears his son
Do I impart toward you. For your intent
In going back to school in Wittenberg,

[2]*any … sense:* Anything that is very commonly seen or heard.

[3]*still:* Ever, or always.

It is most retrograde to our desire:
And we beseech you bend you to remain
Here, in the cheer and comfort of our eye,
Our chiefest courtier, cousin, and our son.

Queen: Let not thy mother lose her prayers, HAMLET.
I pray thee, stay with us; go not to Wittenberg.

Hamlet: I shall in all my best obey you, madam.

King: Why, 'tis a loving and a fair reply:
Be as ourself in Denmark.—Madam, come;
This gentle and unforc'd accord of Hamlet
Sits smiling to my heart: in grace whereof,
No jocund health that Denmark drinks to-day
But the great cannon to the clouds shall tell;
And the king's rouse[4] the heavens shall bruit[5] again,
Re-speaking earthly thunder. Come away.

Exeunt all but Hamlet.

Hamlet: O, that this too too solid flesh would melt,
Thaw, and resolve itself into a dew!
Or that the Everlasting had not fix'd
His canon 'gainst self-slaughter! O God! O God!
How weary, stale, flat, and unprofitable
Seem to me all the uses of this world!
Fie on't! O fie! 'tis an unweeded garden,
That grows to seed; things rank and gross in nature
Possess it merely. That it should come to this!
But two months dead!—nay, not so much, not two:
So excellent a king; that was, to this,
Hyperion[6] to a satyr: so loving to my mother,
That he might not beteem the winds of heaven
Visit her face too roughly. Heaven and earth!
Must I remember? why, she would hang on him
As if increase of appetite had grown
By what it fed on: and yet, within a month,—
Let me not think on't,—Frailty, thy name is woman!—
A little month; or ere those shoes were old
With which she follow'd my poor father's body
Like Niobe, all tears;—why she, even she,—
O God! a beast, that wants discourse of reason,
Would have mourn'd longer,—married with mine uncle,
My father's brother; but no more like my father

[4]*rouse:* Drink. [5]*bruit:* Echo.

[6]*Hyperion:* The Greek sun-god, the brightest and most beautiful of the gods.

Than I to Hercules: within a month;
Ere yet the salt of most unrighteous tears
Had left the flushing in her galled eyes,
She married:—O, most wicked speed, to post
With such dexterity to incestuous sheets!
It is not, nor it cannot come to good;
But break, my heart,—for I must hold my tongue!

Enter Horatio, Marcellus, and Bernardo.

Horatio: Hail to your lordship!
Hamlet: I am glad to see you well:
Horatio,—or I do forget myself.
Horatio: The same, my lord, and your poor servant ever.
Hamlet: Sir, my good friend; I'll change that name with you:
And what make you from Wittenberg, Horatio?—Marcellus?
Marcellus: My good lord,—
Hamlet: I am very glad to see you.—Good even, sir.—
But what, in faith, make you from Wittenberg?
Horatio: A truant disposition, good my lord.
Hamlet: I would not hear your enemy say so;
Nor shall you do mine ear that violence,
To make it truster of your own report
Against yourself: I know you are no truant.
But what is your affair in Elsinore?
We'll teach you to drink deep ere you depart.
Horatio: My lord, I came to see your father's funeral.
Hamlet: I pray thee, do not mock me, fellow-student;
I think it was to see my mother's wedding.
Horatio: Indeed, my lord, it follow'd hard upon.
Hamlet: Thrift, thrift, Horatio! the funeral-bak'd meats
Did coldly furnish forth the marriage tables.
Would I had met my dearest foe[7] in heaven
Ere I had ever seen that day, Horatio!—
My father,—methinks I see my father.
Horatio: Where, my lord?
Hamlet: In my mind's eye, Horatio.
Horatio: I saw him once; he was a goodly[8] king.
Hamlet: He was a man, take him for all in all,
I shall not look upon his like again.
Horatio: My lord, I think I saw him yester-night.
Hamlet: Saw who?
Horatio: My lord, the king your father.

---

[7] *Dearest foe:* Worst enemy.

[8] *goodly:* Handsome.

Hamlet: The king my father!
Horatio: Season your admiration[9] for awhile
With an attent ear, till I may deliver,
Upon the witness of these gentlemen,
This marvel to you.
Hamlet: For God's love, let me hear.
Horatio: Two nights together had these gentlemen,
Marcellus and Bernardo, in their watch,
In the dead vast and middle of the night,
Been thus encounter'd. A figure like your father,
Arm'd at all points exactly, cap-a-pe,[10]
Appears before them, and with solemn march
Goes slow and stately by them: thrice he walk'd
By their oppress'd[11] and fear-surprised eyes,
Within his truncheon's length; whilst they, distill'd
Almost to jelly with the act of fear,
Stand dumb, and speak not to him. This to me
In dreadful secrecy impart they did;
And I with them the third night kept the watch:
Where, as they had deliver'd, both in time,
Form of the thing, each word made true and good,
The apparition comes: I knew your father;
These hands are not more like.
Hamlet: But where was this?
Marcellus: My lord, upon the platform where we watch'd.
Hamlet: Did you not speak to it?
Horatio: My lord, I did;
But answer made it none: yet once methought
It lifted up its head, and did address
Itself to motion, like as it would speak:
But even then the morning cock crew loud,
And at the sound it shrunk in haste away,
And vanish'd from our sight.
Hamlet: 'Tis very strange.
Horatio: As I do live, my honor'd lord, 'tis true;
And we did think it writ down in our duty
To let you know of it.
Hamlet: Indeed, indeed, sirs, but this troubles me.
Hold you the watch to-night?
Marcellus and Bernardo: We do, my lord.
Hamlet: Arm'd, say you?

---

[9] *admiration:* Astonishment.
[10] *cap-a-pe:* From head to toe.
[11] *oppress'd:* Overwhelmed.

Marcellus and Bernardo: Arm'd, my lord.
Hamlet: From top to toe?
Marcellus and Bernardo: My lord, from head to foot.
Hamlet: Then saw you not his face?
Horatio: O yes, my lord; he wore his beaver up.
Hamlet: What, look'd he frowningly?
Horatio: A countenance more in sorrow than in anger.
Hamlet: Pale or red?
Horatio: Nay, very pale.
Hamlet: And fix'd his eyes upon you?
Horatio: Most constantly.
Hamlet: I would I had been there.
Horatio: It would have much amaz'd you.
Hamlet: Very like, very like. Stay'd it long?
Horatio: While one with moderate haste might tell[12] a hundred.
Marcellus and Bernardo: Longer, longer.
Horatio: Not when I saw't.
Hamlet: His beard was grizzled,—no?
Horatio: It was, as I have seen it in his life,
A sable silver'd.
Hamlet: I will watch to-night;
Perchance 'twill walk again.
Horatio: I warrant it will.
Hamlet: If it assume my noble father's person
I'll speak to it, though hell itself should gape
And bid me hold my peace. I pray you all,
If you have hitherto conceal'd this sight,
Let it be tenable in your silence still;
And whatsoever else shall hap to-night,
Give it an understanding, but no tongue:
I will requite your loves. So, fare ye well:
Upon the platform, 'twixt eleven and twelve,
I'll visit you.
All: Our duty to your honor.
Hamlet: Your loves, as mine to you: farewell.

Exeunt Horatio, Marcellus, and Bernardo.

My father's spirit in arms; all is not well;
I doubt some foul play: would the night were come!
Till then sit still, my soul: foul deeds will rise,
Though all the earth o'erwhelm them, to men's eyes.

Exit.

---

[12]*tell:* Count

SCENE 3

A room in Polonius' house.

Enter Laertes and Ophelia.

Laertes: My necessaries are embark'd: farewell:
And, sister, as the winds give benefit,
And convoy[1] is assistant, do not sleep,
But let me hear from you.
Ophelia: Do you doubt that?
Laertes: For Hamlet, and the trifling of his favor,
Hold it a fashion and a toy in blood:
A violet in the youth of primy nature,
Forward, not permanent, sweet, not lasting,
The perfume and suppliance of a minute;
No more.
Ophelia: No more but so?
Laertes: Think it no more:
For nature, crescent,[2] does not grow alone
In thews and bulk; but as this temple[3] waxes,
The inward service of the mind and soul
Grows wide withal. Perhaps he loves you now;
And now no soil nor cautel[4] doth besmirch
The virtue of his will: but you must fear,
His greatness weigh'd, his will is not his own;
For he himself is subject to his birth:
He may not, as unvalu'd persons do,
Carve for himself; for on his choice depends
The safety and the health of the whole state;
And therefore must his choice be circumscrib'd
Unto the voice and yielding of that body
Whereof he is the head. Then if he says he loves you,
It fits your wisdom so far to believe it
As he in his particular act and place
May give his saying deed; which is no further
Than the main[5] voice of Denmark goes withal.
Then weigh what loss your honor may sustain
If with too credent ear you list his songs,
Or lose your heart, or your chaste treasure open
To his unmaster'd importunity.
Fear it, Ophelia, fear it, my dear sister;
And keep within the rear of your affection,
Out of the shot and danger of desire.

---

[1]*convoy:* Means of conveyance. [2]*crescent:* Growing. [3]*temple:* Body.
[4]*cautel:* Deceit. [5]*main:* Strong, or mighty.

The chariest maid is prodigal enough
If she unmask her beauty to the moon:
Virtue itself scrapes not calumnious strokes:
The canker galls the infants of the spring
Too oft before their buttons be disclos'd;
And in the morn and liquid dew of youth
Contagious blastments are most imminent.
Be wary, then; best safety lies in fear:
Youth to itself rebels, though none else near.

Ophelia: I shall the effect of this good lesson keep
As watchman to my heart. But, good my brother,
Do not, as some ungracious pastors do,
Show me the steep and thorny way to heaven;
Whilst like a puff'd and reckless libertine,
Himself the primrose path of dalliance treads,
And recks not his own rede.[6]

Laertes: O, fear me not.
I stay too long:—but here my father comes.

Enter Polonius.

A double blessing is a double grace;
Occasion smiles upon a second leave.

Polonius: Yet here, Laertes! aboard, aboard, for shame!
The wind sits in the shoulder of your sail,
And you are stay'd for. There,—my blessing with you!

Laying his hand on Laertes' head.

And these few precepts in thy memory
See thou character.[7] Give thy thoughts no tongue,
Nor any unproportion'd thought his act.
Be thou familiar, but by no means vulgar.
The friends thou hast, and their adoption tried,
Grapple them to thy soul with hoops of steel;
But do not dull thy palm with entertainment
Of each new-hatch'd, unfledg'd comrade. Beware
Of entrance to a quarrel; but, being in,
Bear't that the opposéd may beware of thee.
Give every man thine ear, but few thy voice:
Take each man's censure,[8] but reserve thy judgment.
Costly thy habit as thy purse can buy,
But not express'd in fancy; rich, not gaudy:
For the apparel oft proclaims the man;

---

[6]*rede:* Counsel. [7]*in . . . character:* Engrave in your mind. [8]*censure:* Opinion.

And they in France of the best rank and station
Are most select and generous chief in that.
Neither a borrower nor a lender be:
For a loan oft loses both itself and friend;
And borrowing dulls the edge of husbandry.
This above all,—to thine own self be true;
And it must follow, as the night the day,
Thou canst not then be false to any man.
Farewell: my blessing season this in thee!
Laertes: Most humbly do I take my leave, my lord.
Polonius: The time invites you; go, your servants tend.[9]
Laertes: Farewell, Ophelia; and remember well
What I have said to you.
Ophelia: 'Tis in my memory lock'd,
And you yourself shall keep the key of it.
Laertes: Farewell. [*Exit.*]
Polonius: What is't, Ophelia, he hath said to you?
Ophelia: So please you, something touching the Lord Hamlet.
Polonius: Marry, well bethought:
'Tis told me he hath very oft of late
Given private time to you; and you yourself
Have of your audience been most free and bounteous:
If it be so,—as so 'tis put on me,
And that in way of caution,—I must tell you,
You do not understand yourself so clearly
As it behoves my daughter and your honor.
What is between you? give me up the truth.
Ophelia: He hath, my lord, of late made many tenders
Of his affection to me.
Polonius: Affection! pooh! you speak like a green girl,
Unsifted in such perilous circumstance.
Do you believe his tenders,[10] as you call them?
Ophelia: I do not know, my lord, what I should think.
Polonius: Marry, I'll teach you: think yourself a baby;
That you have ta'en these tenders for true pay,
Which are not sterling. Tender yourself more dearly;
Or,—not to crack the wind of the poor phrase,
Wronging it thus,—you'll tender me a fool.
Ophelia: My lord, he hath impórtun'd me with love
In honorable fashion.
Polonius: Ay, fashion you may call it; go to, go to.
Ophelia: And hath given countenance to his speech, my lord,

---

[9] *tend:* Wait. [10] *tenders:* Offers.

With almost all the holy vows of heaven.
Polonius: Ay, springes to catch woodcocks. I do know,
When the blood burns, how prodigal the soul
Lends the tongue vows: these blazes, daughter,
Giving more light than heat,—extinct in both,
Even in their promise, as it is a-making,—
You must not take for fire. From this time
Be somewhat scanter of your maiden presence;
Set your entreatments at a higher rate
Than a command to parley. For Lord Hamlet,
Believe so much in him, that he is young;
And with a larger tether may he walk
Than may be given you: in few, Ophelia,
Do not believe his vows; for they are brokers,[11]—
Not of that die which their investments show,
But mere implorators of unholy suits,
Breathing like sanctified and pious bawds,
The better to beguile. This is for all,—
I would not, in plain terms, from this time forth,
Have you so slander any moment leisure
As to give words or talk with the Lord Hamlet.
Look to't, I charge you; come your ways.
Ophelia: I shall obey, my lord.

Exeunt.

SCENE 4

The platform.

Enter Hamlet, Horatio, and Marcellus.

Hamlet: The air bites shrewdly; it is very cold.
Horatio: It is a nipping and an eager air.
Hamlet: What hour now?
Horatio: I think it lacks of twelve.
Marcellus: No, it is struck.
Horatio: Indeed? I heard it not: then it draws near the season
Wherein the spirit held his wont to walk.

A flourish of trumpets, and ordnance shot off within.

What does this mean, my lord?
Hamlet: The king doth wake to-night, and takes his rouse,

[11] *brokers:* Procurers.

Keeps wassail, and the swaggering upspring[1] reels;
And, as he drains his draughts of Rhenish down,
The kettle-drum and trumpet thus bray out
The triumph of his pledge.[2]

Horatio: Is it a custom?

Hamlet: Ay, marry, is't:
But to my mind,—though I am native here,
And to the manner born,—it is a custom
More honor'd in the breach than the observance.
This heavy-headed revel east and west
Makes us traduc'd and tax'd of other nations:
They clepe us drunkards, and with swinish phrase
Soil our addition;[3] and, indeed, it takes
From our achievements, though perform'd at height,
The pith and marrow of our attribute.
So oft it chances in particular men
That, for some vicious mole of nature in them,
As in their birth,—wherein they are not guilty,
Since nature cannot choose his origin,—
By the o'ergrowth of some complexion,
Oft breaking down the pales and forts of reason;
Or by some habit, that too much o'erleavens
The form of plausive[4] manners;—that these men,—
Carrying, I say, the stamp of one defect,
Being nature's livery or fortune's star,—
Their virtues else,—be they as pure as grace,
As infinite as man may undergo,—
Shall in the general censure take corruption
From that particular fault: the dram of evil
Doth all the noble substance of a doubt
To his own scandal.

Horatio: Look, my lord, it comes!

Enter Ghost.

Hamlet: Angels and ministers of grace defend us!—
Be thou a spirit of health or goblin damn'd,
Bring with thee airs from heaven or blasts from hell,
Be thy intents wicked or charitable,
Thou com'st in such a questionable shape
That I will speak to thee: I'll call thee Hamlet,
King, father, royal Dane: O, answer me!

---

[1]*upspring:* A dance.

[2]*triumph … pledge:* The glory of his toasts.

[3]*addition:* Reputation.

[4]*plausive:* Pleasing.

Let me not burst in ignorance; but tell
Why thy canóniz'd bones, hearsèd in death,
Have burst their cerements;[5] why the sepulchre,
Wherein we saw thee quietly in-urn'd,
Hath op'd his ponderous and marble jaws
To cast thee up again! What may this mean,
That thou, dead corpse, again in còmplete steel,
Revisit'st thus the glimpses of the moon,
Making night hideous and we[6] fools of nature
So horridly to shake our disposition
With thoughts beyond the reaches of our souls?
Say, why is this? wherefore? what should we do?

Ghost beckons Hamlet.

Horatio: It beckons you to go away with it,
As if it some impartment did desire
To you alone.
Marcellus: Look, with what courteous action
It waves you to a more removed ground:
But do not go with it.
Horatio: No, by no means.
Hamlet: It will not speak; then will I follow it.
Horatio: Do not, my lord.
Hamlet: Why, what should be the fear?
I do not set my life at a pin's fee;
And for my soul, what can it do to that,
Being a thing immortal as itself?
It waves me forth again;—I'll follow it.
Horatio: What if it tempt you toward the flood, my lord.
Or to the dreadful summit of the cliff
That beetles o'er his base into the sea,
And there assume some other horrible form,
Which might deprive your sovereignty of reason,
And draw you into madness? think of it:
The very place puts toys of desperation,
Without more motive, into every brain
That looks so many fathoms to the sea
And hears it roar beneath.
Hamlet: It waves me still.—
Go on; I'll follow thee.
Marcellus: You shall not go, my lord.
Hamlet: Hold off your hands.

[5]*cements:* Burial garments. [6]*we:* Us.

Horatio: Be rul'd; you shall not go.
Hamlet: My fate cries out,
And makes each petty artery in this body
As hardy as the Némean lion's[7] nerve.—

Ghost beckons.

Still am I call'd;—unhand me, gentlemen;—[*Breaking from them*]
By heaven, I'll make a ghost of him that lets[8] me.
I say, away!—Go on; I'll follow thee.

Exeunt Ghost and Hamlet.

Horatio: He waxes desperate with imagination.
Marcellus: Let's follow; 'tis not fit thus to obey him.
Horatio: Have after.—To what issue will this come?
Marcellus: Something is rotten in the state of Denmark.
Horatio: Heaven will direct it.
Marcellus: Nay, let's follow him.

Exeunt.

Scene 5

A more remote part of the platform.

Enter Ghost and Hamlet.

Hamlet: Where wilt thou lead me? speak, I'll go no further.
Ghost: Mark me.
Hamlet: I will.
Ghost: My hour is almost come,
When I to sulphurous and tormenting flames
Must render up myself.
Hamlet: Alas, poor ghost!
Ghost: Pity me not, but lend thy serious hearing
To what I shall unfold.
Hamlet: Speak; I am bound to hear.
Ghost: So art thou to revenge, when thou shalt hear.
Hamlet: What?
Ghost: I am thy father's spirit;
Doom'd for a certain term to walk the night,
And, for the day, confin'd to waste in fires

[7] *Némean lion's:* The fierce lion that Hercules was called upon to slay as one of his "twelve labors."

[8] *lets:* Hinders.

Till the foul crimes[1] done in my days of nature
Are burnt and purg'd away. But that I am forbid
To tell the secrets of my prison-house,
I could a tale unfold whose lightest word
Would harrow up thy soul; freeze thy young blood;
Make thy two eyes, like stars, start from their spheres;
Thy knotted and combined locks to part,
And each particular hair to stand on end,
Like quills upon the fretful porcupine:
But this eternal blazon[2] must not be
To ears of flesh and blood.—List, list, O, list!—
If thou didst ever thy dear father love,—

Hamlet: O God!

Ghost: Revenge his foul and most unnatural murder.

Hamlet: Murder!

Ghost: Murder—most foul, as in the best it is;
But this most foul, strange, and unnatural.

Hamlet: Haste me to know't, that I, with wings as swift
As meditation or the thoughts of love,
May sweep to my revenge.

Ghost: I find thee apt;
And duller shouldst thou be than the fat weed
That rots itself in ease on Lethe[3] wharf,
Wouldst thou not stir in this. Now, Hamlet,
'Tis given out that, sleeping in mine orchard,
A serpent stung me; so the whole ear of Denmark
Is by a forged process of my death
Rankly abus'd: but know, thou noble youth,
The serpent that did sting thy father's life
Now wears his crown.

Hamlet: O my prophetic soul! mine uncle!

Ghost: Ay, that incestuous, that adulterate beast,
With witchcraft of his wit, with traitorous gifts,—
O wicked wit and gifts that have the power
So to seduce!—won to his shameful lust
The will of my most seeming virtuous queen:
O Hamlet, what a falling-off was there!
From me, whose love was of that dignity
That it went hand in hand even with the vow
I made to her in marriage: and to decline

---

[1] *foul crimes:* Sins or faults.

[2] *eternal blazon:* Disclosure of information concerning the other world.

[3] *Lethe:* The river of forgetfulness of the past, out of which the dead drink.

Upon a wretch whose natural gifts were poor
To those of mine!
But virtue, as it never will be mov'd,
Though lewdness court it in a shape of heaven;
So lust, though to a radiant angel link'd,
Will sate itself in a celestial bed
And prey on garbage.
But, soft! methinks I scent the morning air;
Brief let me be.—Sleeping within mine orchard,
My custom always in the afternoon,
Upon my sécure hour thy uncle stole,
With juice of cursed hebenon[4] in a vial,
And in the porches of mine ears did pour
The leperous distilment; whose effect
Holds such an enmity with blood of man
That, swift as quicksilver, it courses through
The natural gates and alleys of the body;
And with a sudden vigor it doth posset[5]
And curd, like eager[6] droppings into milk,
The thin and wholesome blood: so did it mine;
And a most instant tetter bark'd about,
Most lazar-like,[7] with vile and loathsome crust,
All my smooth body.
Thus was I, sleeping, by a brother's hand,
Of life, of crown, of queen, at once despatch'd:
Cut off even in the blossoms of my sin,
Unhousel'd, unanointed, unanel'd;
No reckoning made, but sent to my account
With all my imperfections on my head:
O, horrible! O, horrible! most horrible!
If thou hast nature in thee, bear it not;
Let not the royal bed of Denmark be
A couch for luxury[8] and damned incest.
But, howsoever thou pursu'st this act,
Taint not thy mind, nor let thy soul contrive
Against thy mother aught: leave her to heaven,
And to those thorns that in her bosom lodge,
To prick and sting her. Fare thee well at once!
The glowworm shows the matin to be near,
And 'gins to pale his uneffectual fire:
Adieu, adieu! Hamlet, remember me. [*Exit.*]

---

[4]*hebenon:* Ebony. [5]*posset:* Coagulate. [6]*eager:* Acid.
[7]*lazar-like:* Like a leper, whose skin is rough. [8]*luxury:* Lechery.

Hamlet: O all you host of heaven! O earth! what else?
And shall I couple hell?—O, fie!—Hold, my heart;
And you, my sinews, grow not instant old,
But bear me stiffly up.—Remember thee!
Ay, thou poor ghost, while memory holds a seat
In this distracted globe. Remember thee!
Yea, from the table of my memory
I'll wipe away all trivial fond[9] recórds,
All saws of books, all forms, all pressures past,
That youth and observation copied there;
And thy commandment all alone shall live
Within the book and volume of my brain,
Unmix'd with baser matter: yes, by heaven.—
O most pernicious woman!
O villain, villain, smiling, damned villain!
My tables,—meet it is I set it down,
That one may smile, and smile, and be a villain;
At least, I am sure, it may be so in Denmark:

Writing.

So, uncle, there you are. Now to my word;
It is, adieu, adieu! Remember me:
I have sworn't.
Horatio: [*Within*] My lord, my lord,—
Marcellus: [*Within*] Lord Hamlet,—
Horatio: [*Within*] Heaven secure him!
Marcellus: [*Within*] So be it!
Horatio: [*Within*] Illo, ho, ho, my lord!
Hamlet: Hillo, ho, ho, boy! come, bird, come.[10]

Enter Horatio and Marcellus.

Marcellus: How is't, my noble lord?
Horatio: What news, my lord?
Hamlet: O, wonderful!
Horatio: Good my lord, tell it.
Hamlet: No; you'll reveal it.
Horatio: Not I, my lord, by heaven.
Marcellus: Nor I, my lord.
Hamlet: How say you, then; would heart of man once think it?—
But you'll be secret?
Horatio and Marcellus: Ay, by heaven, my lord.
Hamlet: There's ne'er a villain dwelling in all Denmark
But he's an arrant knave.

[9] *fond:* Foolish.
[10] *Hillo . . . come:* Hamlet uses the word "bird" because this is a falconer's call.

Horatio: There needs no ghost, my lord, come from the grave
To tell us this.
Hamlet: Why, right; you are i' the right;
And so, without more circumstance at all,
I hold it fit that we shake hands and part:
You, as your business and desire shall point you,—
For every man has business and desire,
Such as it is;—and for mine own poor part,
Look you, I'll go pray.
Horatio: These are but wild and whirling words, my lord.
Hamlet: I'm sorry they offend you, heartily;
Yes, faith, heartily.
Horatio: There's no offence, my lord.
Hamlet: Yes, by Saint Patrick, but there is, Horatio,
And much offence too. Touching this vision here,—
It is an honest ghost, that let me tell you:
For you desire to know what is between us,
O'ermaster't as you may. And now, good friends,
As you are friends, scholars, and soldiers,
Give me one poor request.
Horatio: What is't, my lord? we will.
Hamlet: Never make known what you have seen to-night.
Horatio and Marcellus: My lord, we will not.
Hamlet: Nay, but swear't.
Horatio: In faith,
My lord, not I.
Marcellus: Nor I, my lord, in faith.
Hamlet: Upon my sword.
Marcellus: We have sworn, my lord, already.
Hamlet: Indeed, upon my sword, indeed.
Ghost: [*Beneath*] Swear.
Hamlet: Ha, ha, boy! say'st thou so? art thou there, truepenny?—
Come on,—you hear this fellow in the cellarage,—
Consent to swear.
Horatio: Propose the oath, my lord.
Hamlet: Never to speak of this that you have seen,
Swear by my sword.
Ghost: [*Beneath*] Swear.
Hamlet: *Hic et ubique?*[11] then we'll shift our ground.—
Come hither, gentlemen,
And lay your hands again upon my sword:
Never to speak of this that you have heard,
Swear by my sword.

[11]*Hic et ubique?*: "Here and everywhere" (Latin).

Ghost: [*Beneath*] Swear.
Hamlet: Well said! old mole! canst work i' the earth so fast?
A worthy pioneer![12]—Once more remove, good friends.
Horatio: O day and night, but this is wondrous strange!
Hamlet: And therefore as a stranger give it welcome.
There are more things in heaven and earth, Horatio,
Than are dreamt of in your philosophy.
But come;—
Here, as before, never, so help you mercy,
How strange or odd soe'er I bear myself,—
As I, perchance, hereafter shall think meet
To put an antic disposition on,—
That you, at such times seeing me, never shall,
With arms encumber'd[13] thus, or this headshake,
Or by pronouncing of some doubtful phrase,
As, *Well, well, we know;*—or, *We could, an if we would;*—
Or, *If we list to speak;*—or, *There be, an if they might;*—
Or such ambiguous giving out, to note
That you know aught of me:—this not to do,
So grace and mercy at your most need help you,
Swear.
Ghost: [*Beneath*] Swear.
Hamlet: Rest, rest, perturbed spirit!—So, gentlemen,
With all my love I do commend to you:
And what so poor a man as Hamlet is
May do, to express his love and friending to you,
God willing, shall not lack. Let us go in together;
And still your fingers on your lips, I pray.
The time is out of joint:—O cursed spite,
That ever I was born to set it right!—
Nay, come, let's go together.

Exeunt.

ACT 2

SCENE 1

A room in Polonius' house.

Enter Polonius and Reynaldo.

Polonius: Give him this money and these notes, Reynaldo.

---

[12]*pioneer:* A soldier who digs trenches and undermines fortresses.
[13]*encumber'd:* Folded.

Reynaldo: I will, my lord.
Polonius: You shall do marvelous wisely, good Reynaldo,
Before you visit him, to make inquiry
On his behavior.
Reynaldo: My lord, I did intend it.
Polonius: Marry, well said; very well said. Look you, sir,
Inquire me first what Danskers[1] are in Paris;
And how, and who, what means, and where they keep,
What company, at what expense; and finding,
By this encompassment and drift of question,
That they do know my son, come you more nearer
Than your particular demands will touch it:
Take you, as 'twere, some distant knowledge of him;
As thus, *I know his father and his friends,*
And in part him;—do you mark this, Reynaldo?
Reynaldo: Ay, very well, my lord.
Polonius: *And in part him;—but, you may say, not well:*
But if't be he I mean, he's very wild;
Addicted so and so; and there put on him
What forgeries you please; marry, none so rank
As may dishonor him; take heed of that;
But, sir, such wanton, wild, and usual slips
As are companions noted and most known
To youth and liberty.
Reynaldo: As gaming, my lord.
Polonius: Ay, or drinking, fencing, swearing, quarreling,
Drabbing: [2]—you may go so far.
Reynaldo: My lord, that would dishonor him.
Polonius: Faith, no; as you may season it in the charge.
You must not put another scandal on him,
That he is open to incontinency;
That's not my meaning: but breathe his faults so quaintly
That they may seem the taints of liberty;
The flash and outbreak of a fiery mind;
A savageness in unreclaimed blood,
Of general assault.
Reynaldo: But, my good lord,—
Polonius: Wherefore should you do this?
Reynaldo: Ay, my lord,
I would know that.
Polonius: Marry, sir, here's my drift;
And I believe it is a fetch of warrant:[3]

[1] *Danskers:* Danes.
[2] *Drabbing:* Going about with loose women.
[3] *fetch of warrant:* A good device.

You laying these slight sullies on my son.
As 'twere a thing a little soil'd i' the working,
Mark you,
Your party in converse, him you would sound,
Having ever seen in the prenominate crimes
The youth you breathe of guilty, be assur'd
He closes with you in this consequence;
Good sir, or so; or *friend*, or *gentleman*,—
According to the phrase or the addition[4]
Of man and country.

Reynaldo: Very good, my lord.

Polonius: And then, sir, does he this,—he does,—
What was I about to say?—By the mass, I was
About to say something:—where did I leave?

Reynaldo: At *closes in the consequence*,
At *friend or so*, and *gentleman*.

Polonius: At—closes in the consequence,—ay, marry;
He closes with you thus:—I know the gentleman;
I saw him yesterday, or t'other day,
Or then, or then; with such, or such; and, as you say,
There was he gaming; there o'ertook in's rouse;
There falling out at tennis: or perchance,
I saw him enter such a house of sale,—
Videlicet,[5] a brothel,—or so forth.—
See you now;
Your bait of falsehood takes this carp of truth:
And thus do we of wisdom and of reach,
With windlasses, and with assays of bias,
By indirections find directions out:
So, by my former lecture and advice,
Shall you my son. You have me, have you not?

Reynaldo: My lord, I have.

Polonius: God b' wi' you; fare you well.

Reynaldo: Good my lord!

Polonius: Observe his inclination in yourself.

Reynaldo: I shall, my lord.

Polonius: And let him ply his music.

Reynaldo: Well, my lord.

Polonius: Farewell!

Exit Reynaldo.

[4] *addition:* Form of address.

[5] *Videlicet:* That is; namely (Latin).

Enter Ophelia.

How now, Ophelia! what's the matter?
Ophelia: Alas, my lord, I have been so affrighted.
Polonius: With what, i' the name of God?
Ophelia: My lord, as I was sewing in my chamber,
Lord Hamlet,—with his doublet all unbrac'd;
No hat upon his head; his stockings foul'd,
Ungarter'd, and down-gyved[6] to his ankle;
Pale as his shirt; his knees knocking each other;
And with a look so piteous in purport
As if he had been loosed out of hell
To speak of horrors,—he comes before me.
Polonius: Mad for thy love?
Ophelia: My lord, I do not know;
But truly I do fear it.
Polonius: What said he?
Ophelia: He took me by the wrist, and held me hard;
Then goes he to the length of all his arm;
And with his other hand thus o'er his brow,
He falls to such perusal of my face
As he would draw it. Long stay'd he so;
At last,—a little shaking of mine arm,
And thrice his head thus waving up and down,—
He rais'd a sigh so piteous and profound
That it did seem to shatter all his bulk
And end his being; that done, he lets me go:
And, with his head over his shoulder turn'd,
He seem'd to find his way without his eyes;
For out o' doors he went without their help,
And to the last bended their light on me.
Polonius: Come, go with me: I will go seek the king.
This is the very ecstasy[7] of love;
Whose violent property fordoes itself,[8]
And leads the will to desperate undertakings,
As oft as any passion under heaven
That does afflict our nature. I am sorry,—
What, have you given him any hard words of late?
Ophelia: No, my good lord; but, as you did command,
I did repel his letters, and denied
His access to me.
Polonius: That hath made him mad.

---

[6]*down-gyved:* Dangling like chains. [7]*ecstasy:* Madness. [8]*fordoes itself:* Destroys itself.

I am sorry that with better heed and judgment
I had not quoted him: I fear'd he did but trifle,
And meant to wreck thee; but, beshrew my jealousy!
It seems it is as proper to our age
To cast beyond ourselves in our opinions
As it is common for the younger sort
To lack discretion. Come, go we to the king:
This must be known; which, being kept close, might move
More grief to hide than hate to utter love.

Exeunt.

SCENE 2

A room in the castle.

Enter King, Queen, Rosencrantz, Guildenstern, and Attendants.

King: Welcome, dear Rosencrantz and Guildenstern!
Moreover that we much did long to see you,
The need we have to use you did provoke
Our hasty sending. Something have you heard
Of Hamlet's transformation; so I call it,
Since nor the exterior nor the inward man
Resembles that it was. What it should be,
More than his father's death, that thus hath put him
So much from the understanding of himself,
I cannot dream of: I entreat you both,
That being of so young days brought up with him,
And since so neighbor'd to his youth and humor,
That you vouchsafe your rest here in our court
Some little time: so by your companies
To draw him on to pleasures, and to gather,
So much as from occasion you may glean,
Whether aught, to us unknown, afflicts him thus,
That, open'd, lies within our remedy.
Queen: Good gentlemen, he hath much talk'd of you;
And sure I am two men there are not living
To whom he more adheres. If it will please you
To show us so much gentry and good-will
As to expend your time with us awhile,
For the supply and profit of our hope,
Your visitation shall receive such thanks
As fits a king's remembrance.
Rosencrantz: Both your majesties
Might, by the sovereign power you have of us,

Put your dread pleasures more into command
Than to entreaty.

Guildenstern: We both obey,
And here give up ourselves, in the full bent,
To lay our service freely at your feet,
To be commanded.

King: Thanks, Rosencrantz and gentle Guildenstern.

Queen: Thanks, Guildenstern and gentle ROSENCRANTZ
And I beseech you instantly to visit
My too-much-changed son.—Go, some of you,
And bring these gentlemen where Hamlet is.

Guildenstern: Heavens make our presence and our practices
Pleasant and helpful to him!

Queen: Ay, amen!

Exeunt Rosencrantz, Guildenstern, and some Attendants.

Enter Polonius.

Polonius: The ambassadors from Norway, my good lord,
Are joyfully return'd.

King: Thou still has been the father of good news.

Polonius: Have I, my lord? Assure you, my good liege,
I hold my duty, as I hold my soul,
Both to my God and to my gracious king:
And I do think,—or else this brain of mine
Hunts not the trail of policy[1] so sure
As it hath us'd to do,—that I have found
The very cause of Hamlet's lunacy.

King: O, speak of that; that do I long to hear.

Polonius: Give first admittance to the ambassadors;
My news shall be the fruit to that great feast.

King: Thyself do grace to them, and bring them in.

Exit Polonius.

He tells me, my sweet queen, that he hath found
The head and source of all your son's distemper.

Queen: I doubt it is no other but the main,—
His father's death and our o'erhasty marriage.

King: Well, we shall sift him.

Re-enter Polonius, with Voltimand and Cornelius.

Welcome, my good friends!
Say, Voltimand, what from our brother Norway?

---

[1] *trail of policy:* Statecraft.

Voltimand: Most fair return of greetings and desires.
Upon our first, he sent out to suppress
His nephew's levies; which to him appear'd
To be a preparation 'gainst the Polack;
But, better look'd into, he truly found
It was against your highness: whereat griev'd,—
That so his sickness, age, and impotence
Was falsely borne in hand,—sends out arrests
On Fortinbras; which he, in brief, obeys;
Receives rebuke from Norway; and, in fine,
Makes vows before his uncle never more
To give the assay of arms against your majesty.
Whereon old Norway, overcome with joy,
Gives him three thousand crowns in annual fee;
And his commission to employ those soldiers,
So levied as before, against the Polack:
With an entreaty, herein further shown, [*gives a paper*]
That it might please you to give quiet pass
Through your dominions for this enterprise,
On such regards of safety and allowance
As therein are set down.
King: It likes us well;
And at our more consider'd time we'll read,
Answer, and think upon this business.
Meantime we thank you for your well-took labor:
Go to your rest; at night we'll feast together:
Most welcome home!

Exeunt Voltimand and Cornelius.

Polonius: This business is well ended.—
My liege, and madam,—to expostulate
What majesty should be, what duty is,
Why day is day, night night, and time is time,
Were nothing but to waste night, day, and time.
Therefore, since brevity is the soul of wit,
And tediousness the limbs and outward flourishes,
I will be brief:—your noble son is mad:
Mad call I it; for to define true madness,
What is't but to be nothing else but mad?
But let that go.
Queen: More matter with less art.
Polonius: Madam, I swear I use no art at all.
That he is mad, 'tis true 'tis pity;
And pity 'tis 'tis true: a foolish figure;
But farewell it, for I will use no art.
Mad let us grant him, then: and now remains
That we find out the cause of this effect;

Or rather say, the cause of this defect,
For this effect defective comes by cause:
Thus it remains, and the remainder thus.
Perpend.
I have a daughter,—have whilst she is mine,—
Who, in her duty and obedience, mark,
Hath given me this: now gather, and surmise

[Reads]

To the celestial, and my soul's idol, the most beautified Ophelia,—

That's an ill phrase, a vile phrase,—beautified is a vile phrase: but you shall hear. Thus:

[Reads]

In her excellent white bosom, these, &c.

Queen: Came this from Hamlet to her?
Polonius: Good madam, stay a while; I will be faithful.

[Reads]

Doubt thou the stars are fire;
Doubt that the sun doth move;
Doubt truth to be a liar;
But never doubt I love.

O dear Ophelia, I am ill at these numbers, I have not art to reckon my groans: but
that I love thee best, O most best, believe it. Adieu.
Thine evermore, most dear lady, whilst this machine is to him,
Hamlet

This, in obedience, hath my daughter show'd me:
And more above, hath his solicitings,
As they fell out by time, by means, and place,
All given to mine ear.
King: But how hath she
Receiv'd his love?
Polonius: What do you think of me?
King: As of a man faithful and honorable.
Polonius: I would fain prove so. But what might you think,
When I had seen this hot love on the wing,—
As I perceiv'd it, I must tell you that,
Before my daughter told me,—what might you,
Or my dear majesty your queen here, think,
If I had play'd the desk or table-book;[2]
Or given my heart a winking, mute and dumb;

[2] *table-book:* Memorandum pad.

Or look'd upon this love with idle sight;—
What might you think? No, I went round to work,
And my young mistress thus I did bespeak:
Lord Hamlet is a prince out of thy sphere;
This must not be: and then I precepts gave her,
That she should lock herself from his resort,
Admit no messengers, receive no tokens.
Which done, she took the fruits of my advice;
And he, repulsed,—a short tale to make,—
Fell into a sadness; then into a fast;
Thence to a watch; thence into a weakness;
Thence to a lightness; and, by this declension,
Into the madness wherein now he raves
And all we wail for.

King: Do you think 'tis this?

Queen: It may be, very likely.

Polonius: Hath there been such a time,—I'd fain know that,—
That I have positively said, *'Tis so,*
When it prov'd otherwise?

King: Not that I know.

Polonius: Take this from this, if this be otherwise: [*Pointing to his head and shoulder*]
If circumstances lead me, I will find
Where truth is hid, though it were hid indeed
Within the center.

King: How may we try it further?

Polonius: You know, sometimes he walks four hours together
Here in the lobby.

Queen: So he does, indeed.

Polonius: At such a time I'll loose my daughter to him:
Be you and I behind an arras[3] then;
Mark the encounter: if he love her not,
And be not from his reason fall'n thereon,
Let me be no assistant for a state,
But keep a farm and carters.

King: We will try it.

Queen: But look, where sadly the poor wretch comes reading.

Polonius: Away, I do beseech you, both away:
I'll board[4] him presently:—O, give me leave.

Exeunt King, Queen, and Attendants.

Enter Hamlet, reading.

How does my good Lord Hamlet?

Hamlet: Well, God-a-mercy.

[3]*arras:* Tapestry, hung some distance away from a wall. [4]*board:* Address.

Polonius: Do you know me, my lord?
Hamlet: Excellent, excellent well; you're a fishmonger.
Polonius: Not I, my lord.
Hamlet: Then I would you were so honest a man.
Polonius: Honest, my lord!
Hamlet: Ay, sir; to be honest, as this world goes, is to be one man picked out of ten thousand.
Polonius: That's very true, my lord.
Hamlet: For if the sun breed maggots in a dead dog, being a god kissing carrion,—Have you a daughter?
Polonius: I have, my lord.
Hamlet: Let her not walk i' the sun: conception is a blessing; but not as your daughter may conceive:—friend, look to't.
Polonius: How say you by that?—[*Aside*] Still harping on my daughter:— yet he knew me not at first; he said I was a fishmonger: he is far gone, far gone: and truly in my youth I suffered much extremity for love; very near this. I'll speak to him again.—What do you read, my lord?
Hamlet: Words, words, words.
Polonius: What is the matter, my lord?
Hamlet: Between who?
Polonius: I mean, the matter that you read, my lord.
Hamlet: Slanders, sir: for the satirical slave says here that old men have gray beards; that their faces are wrinkled; their eyes purging thick amber and plum-tree gum; and that they have a plentiful lack of wit, together with most weak hams: all which, sir, though I most powerfully and potently believe, yet I hold it not honesty to have it thus set down; for you yourself, sir, should be old as I am, if, like a crab, you could go backward.
Polonius: [*Aside*] Though this be madness, yet there is method in't.—ill you walk out of the air, my lord?
Hamlet: Into my grave?
Polonius: Indeed, that is out o' the air.—[*Aside*] How pregnant[5] sometimes his replies are! a happiness that often madness hits on, which reason and sanity could not so prosperously be delivered of. I will leave him, and suddenly contrive the means of meeting between him and my daughter.—More honorable lord, I will most humbly take my leave of you.
Hamlet: You cannot, sir, take from me anything that I will more willingly part withal,—except my life, except my life, except my life.
Polonius: Fare you well, my lord.
Hamlet: These tedious old fools!

Enter Rosencrantz and Guildenstern.

Polonius: You go to seek the Lord Hamlet; there he is.
Rosencrantz: [*To Polonius*] God save you, sir!

Exit Polonius.

---

[5]*pregnant:* Ready, and clever.

Guildenstern: Mine honored lord!

Rosencrantz: My most dear lord!

Hamlet: My excellent good friends! How dost thou, Guildenstern? Ah, Rosencrantz? Good lads, how do ye both?

Rosencrantz: As the indifferent children of the earth.

Guildenstern: Happy in that we are not overhappy; on fortune's cap we are not the very button.

Hamlet: Nor the soles of her shoe?

Rosencrantz: Neither, my lord.

Hamlet: Then you live about her waist, or in the middle of her favors?

Guildenstern: Faith, her privates we.

Hamlet: In the secret parts of fortune? O, most true; she is a strumpet. What's the news?

Rosencrantz: None, my lord, but that the world's grown honest.

Hamlet: Then is doomsday near: but your news is not true. Let me question more in particular: what have you, my good friends, deserved at the hands of fortune, that she sends you to prison hither?

Guildenstern: Prison, my lord!

Hamlet: Denmark's a prison.

Rosencrantz: Then is the world one.

Hamlet: A goodly one; in which there are many confines, wards, and dungeons, Denmark being one o' the worst.

Rosencrantz: We think not so, my lord.

Hamlet: Why, then, 'tis none to you; for there is nothing either good or bad, but thinking makes it so: to me it is a prison.

Rosencrantz: Why, then, your ambition makes it one; 'tis too narrow for your mind.

Hamlet: O God, I could be bounded in a nutshell, and count myself a king of infinite space, were it not that I have bad dreams.

Guildenstern: Which dreams, indeed, are ambition; for the very substance of the ambitious is merely the shadow of a dream.

Hamlet: A dream itself is but a shadow.

Rosencrantz: Truly, and I hold ambition of so airy and light a quality that it is but a shadow's shadow.

Hamlet: Then are our beggars bodies, and our monarchs and outstretched heroes the beggars' shadows. Shall we to the court? for, by my fay, I cannot reason.

Rosencrantz and Guildenstern: We'll wait upon you.

Hamlet: No such matter: I will not sort you with the rest of my servants, for, to speak to you like an honest man, I am most dreadfully attended. But, in the beaten way of friendship, what make you at Elsinore?

Rosencrantz: To visit you, my lord; no other occasion.

Hamlet: Beggar that I am, I am even poor in thanks; but I thank you: and sure, dear friends, my thanks are too dear a halfpenny. Were you not sent for? Is it your own inclining? Is it a free visitation? Come, deal justly with me: come, come; nay, speak.

Guildenstern: What should we say, my lord?

Hamlet: Why, anything—but to the purpose. You were sent for; and there is a kind of confession in your looks, which your modesties have not craft enough to color: I know the good king and queen have sent for you.

Rosencrantz: To what end, my lord?

Hamlet: That you must teach me. But let me conjure you, by the rights of our fellowship, by the consonancy of our youth, by the obligation of our ever-preserved love, and by what more dear a better proposer could charge you withal, be even and direct with me, whether you were sent for or no?

Rosencrantz: What say you? [*To Guildenstern*]

Hamlet: [*Aside*] Nay, then, I have an eye of you.—If you love me, hold not off.

Guildenstern: My lord, we were sent for.

Hamlet: I will tell you why; so shall my anticipation prevent your discovery, and your secrecy to the king and queen moult no feather. I have of late,—but wherefore I know not,—lost all my mirth, forgone all custom of exercises; and, indeed, it goes so heavily with my disposition that this goodly frame, the earth, seems to me a sterile promontory; this most excellent canopy, the air, look you, this brave o'erhanging firmament, this majestical roof fretted[6] with golden fire,—why, it appears no other thing to me than a foul and pestilent congregation of vapors. What a piece of work is man! How noble in reason! how infinite in faculties! in form and moving, how express and admirable! in action, how like an angel! in apprehension, how like a god! the beauty of the world! the paragon of animals! And yet, to me, what is this quintessence of dust? man delights not me; no, nor woman neither, though by your smiling you seem to say so.

Rosencrantz: My lord, there was no such stuff in my thoughts.

Hamlet: Why did you laugh, then, when I said, *Man delights not me*?

Rosencrantz: To think, my lord, if you delight not in man, what lenten entertainment[7] the players shall receive from you: we coted[8] them on the way; and hither are they coming, to offer you service.

Hamlet: He that plays the king shall be welcome,—his majesty shall have tribute of me; the adventurous knight shall use his foil and target; the lover shall not sigh gratis; the humorous[9] man shall end his part in peace; the clown shall make those laugh whose lungs are tickled o' the sere;[10] and the lady shall say her mind freely, or the blank verse shall halt[11] for't.—What players are they?

Rosencrantz: Even those you were wont to take delight in,—the tragedians of the city.

Hamlet: How chances it they travel? their residence, both in reputation and profit, was better both ways.

Rosencrantz: I think their inhibition[12] comes by the means of the late innovation.

---

[6] *roof fretted:* A roof with fretwork.

[7] *lenten entertainment:* Poor reception.

[8] *coted:* Passed.

[9] *humorous:* Eccentric.

[10] *whose lungs … sere:* Whose lungs, for laughter, are easily tickled.

[11] *halt:* Limp.

[12] *inhibition:* Difficulty, preventing them from remaining in the capital.

Hamlet: Do they hold the same estimation they did when I was in the city? Are they so followed?

Rosencrantz: No, indeed, they are not.

Hamlet: How comes it? do they grow rusty?

Rosencrantz: Nay, their endeavor keeps in the wonted pace; but there is, sir, an aery[13] of children, little eyases,[14] that cry out on the top of question, and are most tyrannically clapped for't: these are now the fashion; and so berattle the common stages,—so they call them,— that many wearing rapiers are afraid of goose-quills, and dare scarce come thither.

Hamlet: What, are they children? who maintains 'em? how are they escoted?[15] Will they pursue the quality[16] no longer than they can sing? will they not say afterwards, if they should grow themselves to common players,—as it is most like, if their means are no better,—their writers do them wrong, to make them exclaim against their own succession?

Rosencrantz: Faith, there has been much to do on both sides; and the nation holds it no sin to tarre[17] them to controversy: there was for awhile no money bid for argument, unless the poet and the player went to cuffs in the question.

Hamlet: Is't possible?

Guildenstern: O, there has been much throwing about of brains.

Hamlet: Do the boys carry it away?

Rosencrantz: Ay, that they do, my lord; Hercules and his load[18] too.

Hamlet: It is not strange; for mine uncle is king of Denmark, and those that would make mouths at him while my father lived, give twenty, forty, fifty, an hundred ducats a-piece for his picture in little. 'Sblood, there is something in this more than natural, if philosophy could find it out.

Flourish of trumpets within.

Guildenstern: There are the players.

Hamlet: Gentlemen, you are welcome to Elsinore. Your hands, come: the appurtenance of welcome is fashion and ceremony: let me comply with you in this garb; lest my extent[19] to the players, which, I tell you, must show fairly outward, should more appear like entertainment[20] than yours. You are welcome: but my uncle-father and aunt-mother are deceived.

Guildenstern: In what, my dear lord?

Hamlet: I am but mad north-north-west: when the wind is southerly I know a hawk from a handsaw.

Enter Polonius.

Polonius: Well be with you, gentlemen!

Hamlet: Hark you, Guildenstern;—and you too;—at each ear a hearer: that great baby you see there is not yet out of his swathing-clouts.

---

[13]*aery:* Brood of birds of prey.

[14]*little eyases:* Young hawks; a reference to the boys' companies that became popular rivals of Shakespeare's company of players.

[15]*escoted:* Financially supported.

[16]*quality:* Profession.

[17]*to tarre:* To egg them on.

[18]*his load:* The globe, or the world.

[19]*extent:* Show of friendliness.

[20]*entertainment:* Welcome.

Rosencrantz: Happily he's the second time come to them; for they say an old man is twice a child.

Hamlet: I will prophesy he comes to tell me of the players; mark it. You say right, sir: o' Monday morning; 'twas so indeed.

Polonius: My lord, I have news to tell you.

Hamlet: My lord, I have news to tell you. When Roscius was an actor in Rome,—

Polonius: The actors are come hither, my lord.

Hamlet: Buzz, buzz!

Polonius: Upon mine honor,—

Hamlet: Then came each actor on his ass,—

Polonius: The best actors in the world, either for tragedy, comedy, history, pastoral, pastoral-comical, historical-pastoral, tragical-historical, tragical-comical-historical-pastoral, scene individable,[21] or poem unlimited:[22] Seneca cannot be too heavy nor Plautus too light. For the law of writ and the liberty,[23] these are the only men.

Hamlet: O Jephthah, judge of Israel, what a treasure hadst thou!

Polonius: What a treasure had he, my lord?

Hamlet: Why—

One fair daughter, and no more,
The which he loved passing well.

Polonius: [*Aside*] Still on my daughter.

Hamlet: Am I not i' the right, old Jephthah?

Polonius: If you call me Jephthah, my lord, I have a daughter that I love passing well.

Hamlet: Nay, that follows not.

Polonius: What follows, then, my lord?

Hamlet: Why—

As by lot, God wot,
and then, you know,
It came to pass, as most like it was,
the first row of the pious chanson will show you more; for look where my abridgement comes.

Enter four or five Players.

You are welcome, masters; welcome, all:—I am glad to see thee well:—welcome, good friends.—O, my old friend! Thy face is valanced since I saw thee last; comest thou to beard me in Denmark?—What, my young lady and mistress! By'r lady, your ladyship is nearer heaven than when I saw you last, by the altitude of a chopine.[24] Pray God, your voice, like a piece of uncurrent gold, be

---

[21] *scene individable:* A play that observes the unities of time and place.

[22] *poem unlimited:* A typical multiscene Elizabethan drama, not restricted by the unities; examples are *Hamlet, Macbeth, King Lear,* and nearly any other play by Shakespeare.

[23] *For the law … liberty:* For the laws of the unities and for playwriting that is not so restricted.

[24] *chopine:* A wooden stilt more than a foot high used under a woman's shoe; a Venetian fashion introduced into England.

not cracked within the ring.—Masters, you are all welcome. We'll e'en to't like French falconers, fly at anything we see: we'll have a speech straight: come, give us a taste of your quality; come, a passionate speech.

1st Player: What speech, my lord?

Hamlet: I heard thee speak me a speech once,—but it was never acted; or, if it was, not above once; for the play, I remember, pleased not the million; 'twas caviare to the general: but it was,—as I received it, and others whose judgments in such matters cried in the topof mine,—an excellent play, well digested in the scenes, set down with as much modesty as cunning. I remember, one said there were no sallets in the lines to make the matter savory, nor no matter in the phrase that might indite the author of affectation; but called it an honest method, as wholesome as sweet, and by very much morehandsome than fine. One speech in it I chiefly loved: 'twas Aeneas' tale to Dido; and thereabout of it especially where he speaks of Priam's slaughter: if it live in your memory, begin at this line;—let me see, let me see:—

The rugged Pyrrhus, like the Hyrcanian beast,[25]

—it is not so:—it begins with Pyrrhus: —

The rugged Pyrrhus,—he whose sable arms,
Black as his purpose, did the night resemble
When he lay couched in the ominous horse,—
Hath now this dread and black complexion smear'd
With heraldry more dismal; head to foot
Now is he total gules; horridly trick'd
With blood of fathers, mothers, daughters, sons,
Bak'd and impasted with the parching streets,
That lend a tyrannous and damned light
To their vile murders: roasted in wrath and fire,
And thus o'er-sized with coagulate gore,
With eyes like carbuncles, the hellish Pyrrhus
Old grandsire Priam seeks.—

So proceed you.

Polonius: 'Fore God, my lord, well spoken, with good accent and good discretion.

1st Player: Anon he finds him
Striking too short at Greeks; his antique sword,
Rebellious to his arm, lies where it falls,
Repugnant to command: unequal match'd,
Pyrrhus at Priam drives; in rage strikes wide;
But with the whiff and wind of his fell sword

[25] *The rugged . . . :* This speech is an example of the declamatory style of drama, which Shakespeare surely must have considered outmoded.

The unnerved father falls. Then senseless Ilium,
Seeming to feel this blow, with flaming top
Stoops to his base; and with a hideous crash
Takes prisoner Pyrrhus' ear: for, lo! his sword,
Which was declining on the milky head
Of reverend Priam, seem'd i' the air to stick:
So, as a painted tyrant, Pyrrhus stood;
And, like a neutral to his will and matter,
Did nothing.
But as we often see, against some storm,
A silence in the heavens, the rack stand still,
The blood winds speechless, and the orb below
As hush as death, anon the dreadful thunder
Doth rend the region; so, after Pyrrhus' pause,
A roused vengeance sets him new a-work;
And never did the Cyclops' hammers fall
On Mars his armor, forg'd for proof eterne,
With less remorse than Pyrrhus' bleeding sword
Now falls on Priam.—
Out, out, thou strumpet, Fortune! All you gods,
In general synod, take away her power;
Break all the spokes and fellies from her wheel,
And bowl the round knave down the hill of heaven,
As low as to the fiends!

Polonius: This is too long.

Hamlet: It shall to the barber's, with your beard.—Pr'ythee, say on.—He's for a jig, or a tale of bawdry, or he sleeps:—say on; come to Hecuba.

1st Player: But who, O, who had seen the mobled queen,—

Hamlet: *The mobled queen?*

Polonius: That's good; *mobled queen* is good.

1st Player: Run barefoot up and down, threatening the flames
With bissom rheum; a clout upon that head
Where late the diadem stood; and, for a robe,
About her lank and all o'er-teemed loins,
A blanket, in the alarm of fear caught up;—
Who this had seen, with tongue in venom steep'd,
'Gainst Fortune's state would treason have pronounc'd:
But if the gods themselves did see her then,
When she saw Pyrrhus make malicious sport
In mincing with his sword her husband's limbs,
The instant burst of clamor that she made,—
Unless things mortal move them not at all,—
Would have made milch the burning eyes of heaven,
And passion in the gods.

Polonius: Look, whether he has not turn'd his color, and has tears in's eyes.—Pray you, no more.

Hamlet: 'Tis well; I'll have thee speak out the rest soon.—Good my lord, will you see the players well bestowed? Do you hear, let them be well used; for they are the abstracts and brief chronicles of the time; after your death you were better have a bad epitaph than their ill report while you live.

Polonius: My lord, I will use them according to their desert.

Hamlet: God's bodikin, man, better: use every man after his desert, and who should scape whipping? Use them after your own honor and dignity: the less they deserve the more merit is in your bounty. Take them in.

Polonius: Come, sirs.

Hamlet: Follow him, friends: we'll hear a play to-morrow.

Exit Polonius with all the Players but the First.

Dost thou hear me, old friend; can you play the Murder of Gonzago?

1st Player: Ay, my lord.

Hamlet: We'll ha't to-morrow night. You could, for a need, study a speech of some dozen or sixteen lines which I would set down and insert in't? could you not?

1st Player: Ay, my lord.

Hamlet: Very well.—Follow that lord; and look you mock him not.

Exit First Player.

—My good friends, [to Rosencrantz and Guildenstern] I'll leave you till night: you are welcome to Elsinore.

Rosencrantz: Good my lord!

Exeunt Rosencrantz and Guildenstern.

Hamlet: Ay, so God b' wi' ye!—Now I am alone.
O, what a rogue[26] and peasant slave am I!
Is it not monstrous that this player here,
But in a fiction, in a dream of passion,
Could force his soul so to his own conceit[27]
That from her working all his visage wan'd;
Tears in his eyes, distraction in's aspéct,
A broken voice, and his whole function suiting
With forms to his conceit? And all for nothing!
For Hecuba?
What's Hecuba to him or he to Hecuba,
That he should weep for her? What would he do,
Had he the motive and the cue for passion
That I have? He would drown the stage with tears,
And cleave the general ear with horrid speech;
Make mad the guilty, and appal the free;
Confound the ignorant, and amaze, indeed,

---

[26]*rogue:* Wretched creature. [27]*conceit:* Conception.

The very faculties of eyes and ears.
Yet I,
A dull and muddy-mettled rascal, peak,
Like John-a-dreams, unpregnant of my cause,
And can say nothing; no, not for a king
Upon whose property and most dear life
A damn'd defeat was made. Am I a coward?
Who calls me villain? breaks my pate across?
Plucks off my beard and blows it in my face?
Tweaks me by the nose? gives me the lie i' the throat,
As deep as to the lungs? who does me this, ha?
'Swounds, I should take it: for it cannot be
But I am pigeon-liver'd, and lack gall
To make oppression bitter; or ere this
I should have fatted all the region kites
With this slave's offal:—bloody, bawdy villain!
Remorseless, treacherous, lecherous, kindless villain!
O, vengeance!
Why, what an ass am I! This is most brave,
That I, the son of a dear father murder'd,
Prompted to my revenge by heaven and hell,
Must, like a whore, unpack my heart with words,
And fall a-cursing like a very drab,
A scullion!
Fie upon't! foh!—About, my brain! I have heard
That guilty creatures, sitting at a play,
Have by the very cunning of the scene
Been struck so to the soul that presently
They have proclaim'd their malefactions;
For murder, though it have no tongue, will speak
With most miraculous organ. I'll have these players
Play something like the murder of my father
Before mine uncle: I'll observe his looks;
I'll tent[28] him to the quick: if he but blench,
I know my course. The spirit that I have seen
May be the devil: and the devil hath power
To assume a pleasing shape; yea, and perhaps
Out of my weakness and my melancholy,—
As he is very potent with such spirits,—
Abuses me to damn me: I'll have grounds
More relative than this:—the play's the thing
Wherein I'll catch the conscience of the king. [*Exit.*]

---

[28] *tent:* Probe.

ACT 3

SCENE 1

A room in the castle.

Enter King, Queen, Polonius, Ophelia, Rosencrantz, and Guildenstern.

King: And can you, by no drift of circumstance,
Get from him why he puts on this confusion,
Grating so harshly all his days of quiet
With turbulent and dangerous lunacy?
Rosencrantz: He does confess he feels himself distracted;
But from what cause he will by no means speak.
Guildenstern: Nor do we find him forward to be sounded;
But, with a crafty madness, keeps aloof
When we would bring him on to some confession
Of his true state.
Queen: Did he receive you well?
Rosencrantz: Most like a gentleman.
Guildenstern: But with much forcing of his disposition.
Rosencrantz: Niggard of question; but, of our demands,
Most free in his reply.
Queen: Did you assay him
To any pastime?
Rosencrantz: Madam, it so fell out that certain players
We o'er-raught on the way: of these we told him;
And there did seem in him a kind of joy
To hear of it: they are about the court;
And, as I think, they have already order
This night to play before him.
Polonius: 'Tis most true:
And he beseech'd me to entreat your majesties
To hear and see the matter.
King: With all my heart; and it doth much content me
To hear him so inclin'd.
Good gentlemen, give him a further edge,
And drive his purpose on to these delights.
Rosencrantz: We shall, my lord.

Exeunt Rosencrantz and Guildenstern.

King: Sweet Gertrude, leave us too;
For we have closely sent for Hamlet hither
That he, as 'twere by accident, may here
Affront Ophelia:
Her father and myself,—lawful espials,[1]—

---

[1] *espials:* Spies.

Will so bestow ourselves that, seeing, unseen,
We may of their encounter frankly judge;
And gather by him, as he is behav'd,
If't be the affliction of his love or no
That thus he suffers for.

Queen: I shall obey you:—
And for your part, Ophelia, I do wish
That your good beauties be the happy cause
Of Hamlet's wildness: so shall I hope your virtues
Will bring him to his wonted way again,
To both your honors.

Ophelia: Madam, I wish it may.

Exit Queen.

Polonius: Ophelia, walk you here.—Gracious, so please you,
We will bestow ourselves.—[*To Ophelia*] Read on this book;
That show of such an exercise may color
Your loneliness.—We are oft to blame in this,—
'Tis too much prov'd,—that with devotion's visage
And pious action we do sugar o'er
The devil himself.

King: [*Aside*] O, 'tis too true!
How smart a lash that speech doth give my conscience!
The harlot's cheek, beautied with plastering art,
Is not more ugly to the thing that helps it
Than is my deed to my most painted word:
O heavy burden!

Polonius: I hear him coming: let's withdraw, my lord.

Exeunt King and Polonius.

Enter Hamlet.

Hamlet: To be, or not to be,—that is the question:
Whether 'tis nobler in the mind to suffer
The slings and arrows of outrageous fortune,
Or to take arms against a sea of troubles,
And by opposing end them?—To die,—to sleep,—
No more; and by a sleep to say we end
The heart-ache and the thousand natural shocks
That flesh is heir to,—'tis a consummation
Devoutly to be wish'd. To die,—to sleep;—
To sleep! perchance to dream:—ay, there's the rub;
For in that sleep of death what dreams may come,
When we have shuffled off this mortal coil,
Must give us pause: there's the respect

That makes a calamity of so long life;
For who would bear the whips and scorns of time,
The oppressor's wrong, the proud man's contumely,
The pangs of déspis'd love, the law's delay,
The insolence of office, and the spurns
That patient merit of the unworthy takes,
When he himself might his quietus make
With a bare bodkin?[2] who would fardels[3] bear,
To grunt[4] and sweat under a weary life,
But that the dread of something after death,—
The undiscover'd country, from whose bourn[5]
No traveler returns,—puzzles the will,
And makes us rather bear those ills we have
Than to fly to others that we know not of?
Thus conscience does make cowards of us all;
And thus the native hue of resolution
Is sicklied o'er with the pale cast of thought;
And enterprises of great pith and moment,
With this regard, their currents turn awry,
And lose the name of action.—Soft you now!
The fair Ophelia.—Nymph, in thy orisons[6]
Be all my sins remember'd.

Ophelia: Good my lord,
How does your honor for this many a day?

Hamlet: I humbly thank you; well, well, well.

Ophelia: My lord, I have remembrances of yours,
That I have longed long to re-deliver;
I pray you, now receive them.

Hamlet: No, not I;
I never gave you aught.

Ophelia: My honor'd lord, you know right well you did;
And with them, words of so sweet breath compos'd
As made the things more rich: their perfume lost,
Take these again; for to the noble mind
Rich gifts wax poor when givers prove unkind.
There, my lord.

Hamlet: Ha, ha! are you honest?

Ophelia: My lord?

Hamlet: Are you fair?

Ophelia: What means your lordship?

Hamlet: That if you be honest and fair, your honesty should admit no discourse to your beauty.

---

[2] *bodkin:* Stiletto. [3] *fardels:* Burdens. [4] *grunt:* Groan. [5] *bourn:* Boundary.
[6] *orisons:* Prayers.

Ophelia: Could beauty, my lord, have better commerce than with honesty?

Hamlet: Ay, truly; for the power of beauty will sooner transform honesty from what it is to a bawd than the force of honesty can translate beauty into his likeness: this was sometime a paradox, but now the time gives it proof. I did love you once.

Ophelia: Indeed, my lord, you made me believe so.

Hamlet: You should not have believed me; for virtue cannot so inoculate our old stock but we shall relish of it: I loved you not.

Ophelia: I was the more deceived.

Hamlet: Get thee to a nunnery: why wouldst thou be a breeder of sinners? I am myself indifferent[7] honest; but yet I could accuse me of such things that it were better my mother had not borne me: I am very proud, revengeful, ambitious; with more offences at my beck than I have thoughts to put them in, imagination to give them shape, or time to act them in. What should such fellows as I do crawling between heaven and earth? We are arrant knaves, all; believe none of us. Go thy ways to a nunnery. Where's your father?

Opheli: At home, my lord.

Hamlet: Let the doors be shut upon him, that he may play the fool nowhere but in's own house. Farewell.

Ophelia: O, help him, you sweet heavens!

Hamlet: If thou dost marry, I'll give thee this plague for thy dowry,—be thou as chaste as ice, as pure as snow, thou shalt not escape calumny. Get thee to a nunnery, go: farewell. Or, if thou wilt needs marry, marry a fool; for wise men know well enough what monsters you make of them. To a nunnery, go; and quickly too. Farewell.

Ophelia: O heavenly powers, restore him!

Hamlet: I have heard of your paintings too, well enough; God has given you one face and you make yourselves another: you jig, you amble, and you lisp, and nickname God's creatures, and make your wantonness your ignorance. Go to, I'll no more on't; it hath made me mad. I say, we will have no more marriages: those that are married already, all but one, shall live; the rest shall keep as they are. To a nunnery, go. [*Exit.*]

Ophelia: O, what a noble mind is here o'erthrown!
The courtier's, soldier's, scholar's eye, tongue, sword:
The expectancy and rose of the fair state,
The glass of fashion and the mould of form,
The observ'd of all observers,—quite, quite down!
And I, of ladies most deject and wretched
That suck'd the honey of his music vows,
Now see that noble and most sovereign reason,
Like sweet bells jangled, out of tune and harsh;
That unmatch'd form and feature of blown[8] youth

[7] *indifferent:* Tolerably. [8] *blown:* Full-blown.

Blasted with ecstasy: O, woe is me,
To have seen what I have seen, see what I see!

Re-enter King and Polonius.

King: Love! his affections do not that way tend;
Nor what he spake, though it lack'd form a little,
Was not like madness. There's something in his soul
O'er which his melancholy sits on brood;
And I do doubt[9] the hatch and the disclose
Will be some danger: which for to prevent,
I have in quick determination
Thus set it down:—he shall with speed to England
For the demand of our neglected tribute:
Haply, the seas and countries different,
With variable objects, shall expel
This something-settled matter in his heart;
Whereon his brains still beating puts him thus
From fashion of himself. What think you on't?
Polonius: It shall do well: but yet do I believe
The origin and commencement of his grief
Sprung from neglected love.—How now, Ophelia!
You need not tell us what Lord Hamlet said;
We heard it all.—My lord, do as you please;
But if you hold it fit, after the play,
Let his queen mother all alone entreat him
To show his grief: let her be round with him;
And I'll be plac'd, so please you, in the ear
Of all their conference. If she finds him not,[10]
To England send him; or confine him where
Your wisdom best shall think.
King: It shall be so:
Madness in great ones must not unwatch'd go.

Exeunt.

SCENE 2

A hall in the castle.

Enter Hamlet and certain Players.

Hamlet: Speak the speech, I pray you, as I pronounced it to you, trippingly on the tongue: but if you mouth it, as many of your players do, I had as lief the town-crier spoke my lines. Nor do not saw the air too much with

[9]*doubt:* Fear.

[10]*finds him not:* Does not find him out.

your hand, thus; but use all gently: for in the very torrent, tempest, and, as I may say, the whirlwind of passion, you must acquire and beget a temperance that may give it smoothness. O, it offends me to the soul, to hear a robustious periwigpated fellow tear a passion to tatters, to very rags, to split the earsof the groundlings, who, for the most part, are capable of nothing but inexplicable dumb shows and noise: I could have such a fellow whipped for o'erdoing Termagant;[1] it out-herods Herod:[2] pray you, avoid it.

1st Player: I warrant your honor.

Hamlet: Be not too tame neither, but let your own discretion be your tutor; suit the action to the word, the word to the action; with this special observance, that you o'erstep not the modesty of nature: for anything so overdone is from the purpose of playing, whose end, both at the first and now, was and is, to hold, as 'twere, the mirror up to nature; to show virtue her own feature, scorn her own image, and the very age and body of the time his form and pressure. Now, this overdone or come tardy off, though it make the unskilful laugh, cannot but make the judicious grieve; the censure of the which one must, in your allowance, o'erweigh a whole theater of others. O, there be players that I have seen play,—and heard others praise, and that highly,—not to speak it profanely, that, neither having the accent of Christians, nor the gait of Christian, pagan, nor man, have so strutted and bellowed that I have thought some of nature's journeymen had made men, and not made them well, they imitated humanity so abominably.

1st Player: I hope we have reformed that indifferently with us, sir.

Hamlet: O, reform it altogether. And let those that play your clowns speak no more than is set down for them: for there be of them that will themselves laugh, to set on some quantity of barren spectators to laugh too; though, in the meantime, some necessary question of the play be then to be considered: that's villainous, and shows a most pitiful ambition in the fool that uses it. Go, make you ready.

Exeunt Players.

Enter Polonius, Rosencrantz, and Guildenstern.

How now, my lord! will the king hear this piece of work?

Polonius: And the queen, too, and that presently.

Hamlet: Bid the players make haste.

Exit Polonius.

Will you two help to hasten them?

Rosencrantz and Guildenstern: We will, my lord. [*Exeunt.*]

Hamlet: What, ho, Horatio!

---

[1] *Termagant:* A violent pagan deity, supposedly Mohammedan.

[2] *out-herods Herod:* Outrants the ranting Herod, who figures in medieval drama.

Enter Horatio.

Horatio: Here, sweet lord, at your service.
Hamlet: Horatio, thou art e'en as just a man
As e'er my conversation cop'd withal.
Horatio: O, my dear lord,—
Hamlet: Nay, do not think I flatter;
For what advancement may I hope from thee,
That no revénue hast, but thy good spirits,
To feed and clothe thee? Why should the poor be flatter'd?
No, let the candied tongue lick ábsurd pomp;
And crook the pregnant hinges of the knee
Where thrift may follow fawning. Dost thou hear?
Since my dear soul was mistress of her choice,
And could of men distinguish, her election
Hath seal'd thee for herself: for thou hast been
As one, in suffering all, that suffers nothing;
A man that Fortune's buffets and rewards
Hast ta'en with equal thanks: and bless'd are those
Whose blood and judgment are so well commingled
That they are not a pipe for Fortune's finger
To sound what stop she please. Give me that man
That is not passion's slave, and I will wear him
In my heart's core, ay, in my heart of heart,
As I do thee.—Something too much of this.—
There is a play to-night before the king;
One scene of it comes near the circumstance
Which I have told thee of my father's death:
I pr'ythee, when thou see'st that act a-foot,
Even with the very comment of thy soul
Observe mine uncle: if this his occulted guilt
Do not itself unkennel in one speech,
It is a damned ghost that we have seen;
And my imaginations are as foul
As Vulcan's stithy.[3] Give him heedful note:
For I mine eyes will rivet to his face;
And, after, we will both our judgments join
In censure of his seeming.
Horatio: Well, my lord:
If he steal aught the whilst this play is playing,
And scape detecting, I will pay the theft.
Hamlet: They are coming to the play; I must be idle:[4]
Get you a place.

[3]*stithy:* Smithy. [4]*idle:* Foolish.

Danish march. A flourish. Enter King, Queen, Polonius, Ophelia, Rosencrantz, Guildenstern, and others.

King: How fares our cousin Hamlet?

Hamlet: Excellent, i'faith; of the chameleon's dish: I eat the air,[5] promise-crammed: you cannot feed capons so.

King: I have nothing with this answer, Hamlet; these words are not mine.

Hamlet: No, nor mine now. [*To Polonius*] My lord, you played once i' the university, you say?

Polonius: That did I, my lord, and was accounted a good actor.

Hamlet: And what did you enact?

Polonius: I did enact Julius CAESAR: I was killed i' the Capitol; Brutus killed me.

Hamlet: It was a brute part of him to kill so capital a calf there.—Be the players ready.

Rosencrantz: Ay, my lord; they stay upon your patience.

Queen: Come hither, my good Hamlet, sit by me.

Hamlet: No, good mother, here's metal more attractive.

Polonius: O, ho! do you mark that? [*To the King*]

Hamlet: Lady, shall I lie in your lap? [*Lying down at Ophelia's feet*]

Ophelia: No, my lord.

Hamlet: I mean, my head upon your lap?

Ophelia: Ay, my lord.

Hamlet: Do you think I meant country matters?

Ophelia: I think nothing, my lord.

Hamlet: That's a fair thought to lie between maids' legs.

Ophelia: What is, my lord?

Hamlet: Nothing.

Ophelia: You are merry, my lord.

Hamlet: Who, I?

Ophelia: Ay, my lord.

Hamlet: O, your only jig-maker. What should a man do but be merry? for, look you, how cheerfully my mother looks, and my father died within's two hours.

Ophelia: Nay, 'tis twice two months, my lord.

Hamlet: So long? Nay, then, let the devil wear black, for I'll have a suit of sables. O heavens! die two months ago, and not forgotten yet? Then there's hope a great man's memory may outlive his life half a year: but, by'r lady, he must build churches, then; or else shall he suffer not thinking on, with the hobby-horse, whose epitaph is, *For, O, for, O, the hobby-horse is forgot.*

Trumpets sound. The dumb show enters.

---

[5]*of the chameleon's … the air:* Chameleons were believed to live on air.

Enter a King and a Queen, very lovingly; the Queen embracing him and he her. She kneels, and makes show of protestation unto him. He takes her up, and declines his head upon her neck: lays him down upon a bank of flowers: she, seeing him asleep, leaves him. Anon comes in a fellow, takes off his crown, kisses it, and pours poison in the King's ears, and exit. The Queen returns; finds the King dead, and makes passionate action. The Poisoner, with some two or three Mutes, comes in again, seeming to lament with her. The dead body is carried away. The Poisoner woos the Queen with gifts: she seems loth and unwilling awhile, but in the end accepts his love.

Exeunt.

Ophelia: What means this, my lord?
Hamlet: Marry, this is miching mallecho;[6] it means mischief.
Ophelia: Belike this show imports the argument of the play.

Enter Prologue.

Hamlet: We shall know by this fellow: the players cannot keep counsel; they'll tell all.
Ophelia: Will he tell us what this show meant?
Hamlet: Ay, or any show that you'll show him: be not you ashamed to show, he'll not shame to tell you what it means.
Ophelia: You are naught, you are naught: I'll mark the play.
Prologue:

For us, and for our tragedy,
Here stooping to your clemency,
We beg your hearing patiently.

Hamlet: Is this a prologue, or the posy[7] of a ring?
Ophelia: 'Tis brief, my lord.
Hamlet: As woman's love.

Enter a King and a Queen.

Prologue King: Full thirty times hath Phoebus' cart gone round
Neptune's salt wash and Tellus' orbed ground,[8]
And thirty dozen moons with borrow'd sheen
About the world have times twelve thirties been,
Since love our hearts, and Hymen did our hands
Unite commutual in most sacred bands.
Prologue Queen: So many journeys may the sun and moon
Make us again count o'er ere love be done!
But, woe is me, you are so sick of late,
So far from cheer and from your former state

[6]*miching mallecho:* A sneaking misdeed. [7]*posy:* Motto or inscription.
[8]*orbed ground:* The globe.

That I distrust you.[9] Yet, though I distrust,
Discomfort you, my lord, it nothing must:
For women's fear and love holds quantity,[10]
In neither aught, or in extremity.
Now, what my love is, proof hath made you know;
And as my love is siz'd, my fear is so:
Where love is great, the littlest doubts are fear;
Where little fears grow great, great love grows there.

Prologue King: Faith, I must leave thee, love, and shortly too;
My operant powers their functions leave[11] to do:
And thou shalt live in this fair world behind,
Honor'd, belov'd; and haply one as kind
For husband shalt thou,—

Prologue Queen: O, confound the rest!
Such love must needs be treason in my breast:
In second husband let me be accurst!
None wed the second but who kill'd the first.

Hamlet [*Aside*] Wormwood, wormwood.

Prologue Queen: The instances that second marriage move
Are base respects of thrift, but none of love:
A second time I kill my husband, dead,
When second husband kisses me in bed.

Prologue King: I do believe you think what now you speak;
But what we do determine oft we break.
Purpose is but the slave to memory;
Of violent birth, but poor validity:
Which now, like fruit unripe, sticks on the tree;
But fall unshaken when they mellow be.
Most necessary 'tis that we forget
To pay ourselves what to ourselves is debt:
What to ourselves in passion we propose,
The passion ending, doth the purpose lose.
The violence of either grief or joy
Their own enactures with themselves destroy:
Where joy most revels grief doth most lament;
Grief joys, joy grieves, on slender accident.
This world is not for aye; nor 'tis not strange
That even our loves should with our fortunes change;
For 'tis a question left us yet to prove
Whether love lead fortune or else fortune love.
The great man down, you mark his favorite flies;
The poor advanc'd makes friends of enemies.
And hitherto doth love on fortune tend:

---

[9] *distrust you:* Worry about you. [10] *holds quantity:* Correspond in degree. [11] *leave:* Cease.

For who not needs shall never lack a friend;
And who in want a hollow friend doth try,
Directly seasons him his enemy.
But, orderly to end where I begun,—
Our wills and fates do so contrary run
That our devices still are overthrown;
Our thoughts are ours, their ends none of our own:
So think thou wilt no second husband wed;
But die thy thoughts when thy first lord is dead.

Prologue Queen: Nor earth to me give food, nor heaven light!
Sport and repose lock from me day and night!
To desperation turn my trust and hope!
An anchor's[12] cheer in prison be my scope!
Each opposite, that blanks the face of joy,
Meet what I would have well, and it destroy!
Both here and hence, pursue me lasting strife,
If, once a widow, ever I be wife!

Hamlet: If she should break it now! [*To Ophelia*]

Prologue King: 'Tis deeply sworn. Sweet, leave me here awhile;
My spirits grow dull, and fain I would beguile
The tedious day with sleep. [*Sleeps*]

Prologue Queen: Sleep rock thy brain,
And never come mischance between us twain! [*Exit.*]

Hamlet: Madam, how like you this play?

Queen: The lady doth protest too much, methinks.

Hamlet: O, but she'll keep her word.

King: Have you heard the argument? Is there no offence in't?

Hamlet: No, no, they do but jest, poison in jest; no offence i' the world.

King: What do you call the play?

Hamlet: The Mouse-trap. Marry, how? Tropically.[13] This play is the image of a murder done in Vienna: Gonzago is the duke's name: his wife, Baptista: you shall see anon; 'tis a knavish piece of work: but what o' that? your majesty, and we that have free souls, it touches us not: let the galled jade wince, our withers are unwrung.

Enter Lucianus.

This is one Lucianus, nephew to the king.

Ophelia: You are a good chorus, my lord.

Hamlet: I could interpret between you and your love, if I could see the puppets dallying.

---

[12] *anchor's:* Anchorite's, or hermit's.

[13] *Tropically:* Figuratively, or metaphorically; by means of a "trope."

Ophelia: You are keen, my lord, you are keen.

Hamlet: It would cost you a groaning to take off my edge.

Ophelia: Still better, and worse.

Hamlet: So you must take your husbands.—Begin, murderer; pox, leave thy damnable faces and begin. COME:—*The croaking raven doth bellow for revenge.*

Lucianus: Thoughts black, hands apt, drugs fit, and time agreeing;
Confederate season, else no creature seeing;
Thou mixture rank, of midnight weeds collected,
With Hecate's ban[14] thrice blasted, thrice infected,
Thy natural magic and dire property
On wholesome life usurp immediately.

Pours the poison into the sleeper's ears.

Hamlet: He poisons him i' the garden for's estate. His name's Gonzago: the story is extant, and writ in choice Italian: you shall see anon how the murderer gets the love of Gonzago's wife.

Ophelia: The king rises.

Hamlet: What, frighted with false fire!

Queen: How fares my lord?

Polonius: Give o'er the play.

King: Give me some light:—away!

All: Lights, lights, lights!

Exeunt all but Hamlet and Horatio.

Hamlet:

Why, let the stricken deer go weep,
The hart ungalled play;
For some must watch, while some must sleep:
So runs the world away.—

Would not this, sir, and a forest of feathers, if the rest of my fortunes turn Turk with me, with two Provencial roses on my razed shoes, get me a fellowship in a cry[15] of players, sir?

Horatio: Half a share.

Hamlet: A whole one, I.
For thou dost know, O Damon dear,
This realm dismantled was
Of Jove himself; and now reigns here
A very, very—pajock.[16]

---

[14]*Hecate's ban:* The spell of the goddess of witchcraft.

[15]*cry:* Company. [16]*pajock:* Peacock.

Horatio: You might have rhymed.
Hamlet: O good Horatio, I'll take the ghost's word for a thousand pound. Didst perceive?
Horatio: Very well, my lord.
Hamlet: Upon the talk of the poisoning,—
Horatio: I did very well note him.
Hamlet: Ah, ha!—Come, some music! come, the recorders!—

For if the king like not the comedy,
Why, then, belike,—he likes it not, perdy.

Come, some music!

Re-enter Rosencrantz and Guildenstern.

Guildenstern: Good my lord, vouchsafe me a word with you.
Hamlet: Sir, a whole history.
Guildenstern: The king, sir,—
Hamlet: Ay, sir, what of him?
Guildenstern: Is, in his retirement, marvelous distempered.
Hamlet: With drink, sir?
Guildenstern: No, my lord, rather with choler.
Hamlet: Your wisdom should show itself more richer to signify this to his doctor; for, for me to put him to his purgation would perhaps plunge him into far more choler.
Guildenstern: Good my lord, put your discourse into some frame, and start not so wildly from my affair.
Hamlet: I am tame, sir:—pronounce.
Guildenstern: The queen, your mother, in most great affliction of spirit, hath sent me to you.
Hamlet: You are welcome.
Guildenstern: Nay, good my lord, this courtesy is not of the right breed. If it shall please you to make me a wholesome answer, I will do you mother's commandment: if not, your pardon and my return shall be the end of my business.
Hamlet: Sir, I cannot.
Guildenstern: What, my lord?
Hamlet: Make you a wholesome answer; my wit's diseas'd: but, sir, such answer as I can make, you shall command; or, rather, as you say, my mother: therefore no more, but to the matter: my mother, you say,—
Rosencrantz: Then thus she says: your behavior hath struck her into amazement and admiration.
Hamlet: O wonderful son, that can so astonish a mother!—But is there no sequel at the heels of this mother's admiration?

Rosencrantz: She desires to speak with you in her closet[17] ere you go to bed.

Hamlet: We shall obey, were she ten times our mother. Have you any further trade with us?

Rosencrantz: My lord, you once did love me.

Hamlet: So I do still, by these pickers and stealers.[18]

Rosencrantz: Good, my lord, what is your cause of distemper? you do, surely, bar the door upon your own liberty if you deny your griefs to your friend.

Hamlet: Sir, I lack advancement.

Rosencrantz: How can that be, when you have the voice of the king himself for your succession in Denmark?

Hamlet: Ay, but While the grass grows,—the proverb is something musty.

Re-enter the Players, with recorders.

O, the recorders:—let me see one.—To withdraw with you:—why do you go about to recover the wind of me, as if you would drive me into a toil?

Guildenstern: O, my lord, if my duty be too bold, my love is too unmannerly.

Hamlet: I do not well understand that. Will you play upon this pipe?

Guildenstern: My lord, I cannot.

Hamlet: I pray you.

Guildenstern: Believe me, I cannot.

Hamlet: I do beseech you.

Guildenstern: I know no touch of it, my lord.

Hamlet: 'Tis as easy as lying: govern these ventages[19] with your finger and thumb, give it breath with your mouth, and it will discourse most eloquent music. Look you, these are the stops.

Guildenstern: But these cannot I command to any utterance of harmony; I have not the skill.

Hamlet: Why, look you now, how unworthy a thing you make of me! You would play upon me; you would seem to know my stops; you would pluck out the heart of my mystery; you would sound me from my lowest note to the top of my compass: and there is much music, excellent voice, in this little organ; yet cannot you make it speak. 'Sblood, do you think that I am easier to be played on than a pipe? Call me what instrument you will, though you can fret me you cannot play upon me.

Enter Polonius.

God bless you, sir!

Polonius: My lord, the queen would speak with you, and presently.

Hamlet: Do you see yonder cloud that's almost in shape of a camel?

Polonius: By the mass, and 'tis like a camel indeed.

---

[17] *closet:* Boudoir.   [18] *pickers and stealers:* Fingers.   [19] *ventages:* Holes.

Hamlet: Methinks it is like a weasel.
Polonius: It is backed like a weasel.
Hamlet: Or like a whale?
Polonius: Very like a whale.
Hamlet: Then will I come to my mother by and by.—They fool me to the top of my bent.—I will come by and by.
Polonius: I will say so.
Hamlet: By and by is easily said.

Exit Polonius.

Leave me, friends.

Exeunt Rosencrantz, Guildenstern, Horatio, and Players.

'Tis now the very witching time of night,
When churchyards yawn, and hell itself breathes out
Contagion to this world: now could I drink hot blood,
And do such bitter business as the day
Would quake to look on. Soft! now to my mother.—
O heart, lose not thy nature; let not ever
The soul of Nero[20] enter this firm bosom:
Let me be cruel, not unnatural:
I will speak daggers to her, but use none;
My tongue and soul in this be hypocrites,—
How in my words soever she be shent,
To give them seals never, my soul, consent! [*Exit.*]

SCENE 3

A room in the castle.

Enter King, Rosencrantz, and Guildenstern.

King: I like him not; nor stands it safe with us
To let his madness range. Therefore prepare you;
I your commission with forthwith despatch,
And he to England shall along with you:
The terms of our estate may not endure
Hazard so dangerous as doth hourly grow
Out of his lunacies.
Guildenstern: We will ourselves provide:
Most holy and religious fear it is
To keep those many many bodies safe
That live and feed upon your majesty.

[20] *Nero:* The Roman emperor Nero killed his mother, a crime of which Hamlet does not want to be guilty.

Rosencrantz: The single and peculiar life is bound,
With all the strength and armor of the mind,
To keep itself from 'noyance; but much more
That spirit upon whose weal depend and rest
The lives of many. The cease of majesty
Dies not alone; but like a gulf doth draw
What's near it with it: it is a massy wheel,
Fix'd on the summit of the highest mount,
To whose huge spokes ten thousand lesser things
Are mortis'd and adjoin'd; which, when it falls,
Each small annexment, petty consequence,
Attends the boisterous ruin. Never alone
Did the king sigh, but with a general groan.
King: Arm you, I pray you, to this speedy voyage;
For we will fetters put upon this fear,
Which now goes too free-footed.
Rosencrantz and Guildenstern: We will haste us.

Exeunt Rosencrantz and Guildenstern.

Enter Polonius.

Polonius: My lord, he's going to his mother's closet:
Behind the arras I'll convey myself
To hear the process; I'll warrant she'll tax him home:[1]
And, as you said, and wisely was it said,
'Tis meet that some more audience than a mother,
Since nature makes them partial, should o'erhear
The speech, of vantage. Fare you well, my liege:
I'll call upon you ere you go to bed,
And tell you what I know.
King: Thanks, dear my lord.

Exit Polonius.

O, my offence is rank, it smells to heaven;
It hath the primal eldest curse upon't,—
A brother's murder!—Pray can I not,
Though inclination be as sharp as will:
My stronger guilt defeats my strong intent;
And, like a man to double business bound,
I stand in pause where I shall first begin,
And both neglect. What if this cursed hand
Were thicker than itself with brother's blood,—

---

[1] *tax him home:* Reprove him properly.

Is there not rain enough in the sweet heavens
To wash it white as snow? Whereto serves mercy
But to confront the visage of offence?
And what's in prayer but this twofold force,—
To be forestalled ere we come to fall,
Or pardon'd being down? Then I'll look up;
My fault is past. But, O, what form of prayer
Can serve my turn? Forgive me my foul murder?—
That cannot be; since I am still possess'd
Of those effects for which I did the murder,—
My crown, mine own ambition, and my queen.
May one be pardon'd and retain the offence?[2]
In the corrupted currents of this world
Offence's gilded hand may shove by justice;
And oft 'tis seen the wicked prize itself
Buys out the law: but 'tis not so above;
There is no shuffling,—there the action lies
In his true nature; and we ourselves compell'd,
Even to the teeth and forehead of our faults,
To give in evidence. What then? what rests?[3]
Try what repentance can: what can it not?
Yet what can it when one can not repent?
O wretched state! O bosom black as death!
O limed[4] soul, that, struggling to be free,
Art more engag'd! Help, angels! make assay:
Bow, stubborn knees; and, heart, with strings of steel,
Be soft as sinews of the new-born babe!
All may be well. [*Retires and kneels*]

Enter Hamlet.

Hamlet: Now might I do it pat, now he is praying;
And now I'll do't—and so he goes to heaven;
And so am I reveng'd:—that would be scann'd:
A villain kills my father; and for that,
I, his sole son, do this same villain send
To heaven.
O, this is hire and salary, not revenge.
He took my father grossly, full of bread;
With all his crimes broad blown, as flush as May;
And how his audit stands who knows save heaven?
But in our circumstance and course of thought

---

[2]*retain the offence:* Retain the gains won by the offense. [3]*rests:* Remains.
[4]*limed:* Snared.

'Tis heavy with him: and am I, then, reveng'd,
To take him in the purging of his soul,
When he is fit and season'd for his passage?
No.
Up, sword; and know thou a more horrid hent:[5]
When he is drunk, asleep, or in his rage;
Or in the incestuous pleasure of his bed;
At gaming, swearing; or about some act
That has no relish of salvation in't;—
Then trip him, that his heels may kick at heaven;
And that his soul may be as damn'd and black
As hell, whereto it goes. My mother stays:
This physic but prolongs thy sickly days. [*Exit.*]

The King rises and advances.

King: My words fly up, my thoughts remain below:
Words without thoughts never to heaven go. [*Exit.*]

SCENE 4

Another room in the castle.

Enter Queen and Polonius.

Polonius: He will come straight. Look you lay home to him:
Tell him his pranks have been too broad to bear with,
And that your grace hath screen'd and stood between
Much heat and him. I'll silence me e'en here.
Pray you, be round with him.
Hamlet: [*Within*] Mother, mother, mother!
Queen: I'll warrant you:
Fear me not:—withdraw, I hear him coming.

Polonius goes behind the arras.

Enter Hamlet.

Hamlet: Now, mother, what's the matter?
Queen: Hamlet, thou hast thy father much offended.
Hamlet: Mother, you have my father much offended.
Queen: Come, come, you answer with an idle tongue.
Hamlet: Go, go, you question with a wicked tongue.
Queen: Why, how now, Hamlet!

---

[5] *hent:* Opportunity.

Hamlet: What's the matter now?
Queen: Have you forgot me?
Hamlet: No, by the rood, not so:
You are the queen, your husband's brother's wife;
And,—would it were not so!—you are my mother.
Queen: Nay, then, I'll set those to you that can speak.
Hamlet: Come, come, and sit you down; you shall not budge;
You go not till I set you up a glass
Where you may see the inmost part of you.
Queen: What wilt thou do? thou wilt not murder me?—
Help, help, ho!
Polonius: [*Behind*] What, ho! help, help, help!
Hamlet: How now! a rat?

[Draws.]

Dead, for a ducat, dead! [*Makes a pass through the arras*]
Polonius: [*Behind*] O, I am slain! [*Falls and dies.*]
Queen: O me, what hast thou done?
Hamlet: Nay, I know not:
Is it the king? [*Draws forth Polonius*]
Queen: O, what a rash and bloody deed is this!
Hamlet: A bloody deed!—almost as bad, good mother,
As kill a king and marry with his brother.
Queen: As kill a king!
Hamlet: Ay, lady, 'twas my word.—
Thou wretched, rash, intruding fool, farewell! [*To Polonius*]
I took thee for thy better: take thy fortune;
Thou find'st to be too busy is some danger.—
Leave wringing of your hands: peace; sit you down,
And let me wring your heart: for so I shall,
If it be made of penetrable stuff;
If damned custom have not braz'd it so
That it is proof and bulwark against sense.
Queen: What have I done, that thou dar'st wag thy tongue
In noise so rude against me?
Hamlet: Such an act
That blurs the grace and blush of modesty;
Calls virtue hypocrite; takes off the rose
From the fair forehead of an innocent love,
And sets a blister there; makes marriage-vows
As false as dicers' oaths: O, such a deed
As from the body of contraction plucks
The very soul, and sweet religion makes
A rhapsody of words: heaven's face doth glow;

Yea, this solidity and compound mass,
With tristful[1] visage, as against the doom,
Is thought-sick at the act.

Queen: Ah me, what act,
That roars so loud, and thunders in the index?

Hamlet: Look here upon this picture and on this,—
The counterfeit presentment of two brothers.
See what grace was seated on this brow;
Hyperion's curls; the front of Jove himself;
An eye like Mars, to threaten and command;
A station like the herald Mercury
New-lighted on a heaven-kissing hill;
A combination and a form, indeed,
Where every god did seem to set his seal,
To give the world assurance of a man:
This was your husband.—Look you now, what follows:
Here is your husband, like a mildew'd ear
Blasting his wholesome brother. Have you eyes?
Could you on this fair mountain leave to feed,
And batten on this moor? Ha! have you eyes?
You cannot call it love; for at your age
The hey-day in the blood is tame, it's humble,
And waits upon the judgment: and what judgment
Would step from this to this? Sense, sure, you have,
Else could you not have motion: but sure that sense
Is apoplex'd: for madness would not err;
Nor sense to ecstasy was ne'er so thrill'd
But it reserv'd some quantity of choice
To serve in such a difference. What devil was't
That thus hath cozen'd you at hoodman-blind?[2]
Eyes without feeling, feeling without sight,
Ears without hand or eyes, smelling sans all,
Or but a sickly part of one true sense
Could not so mope.
O shame! where is thy blush! Rebellious hell,
If thou canst mutine in a matron's bones,
To flaming youth let virtue be as wax,
And melt in her own fire: proclaim no shame
When the compulsive ardor gives the charge,

---

[1] *tristful:* Gloomy.
[2] *cozen'd … hoodman-blind:* Tricked you at blindman's buff.

Since frost itself as actively doth burn,
And reason panders[3] will.
Queen: O Hamlet, speak no more:
Thou turn'st mine eyes into my very soul;
And there I see such black and grained spots
As will not leave their tinct.[4]
Hamlet: Nay, but to live
In the rank sweat of an enseamed bed,
Stew'd in corruption, honeying and making love
Over the nasty sty,—
Queen: O, speak to me no more;
These words like daggers enter in mine ears;
No more, sweet Hamlet.
Hamlet: A murderer and a villain;
A slave that is not twentieth part the tithe
Of your precedent lord; a vice of kings;[5]
A cutpurse of the empire and the rule,
That from a shelf the precious diadem stole,
And put it in his pocket!
Queen: No more.
Hamlet: A king of shreds and patches,—

Enter Ghost.

Save me, and hover o'er me with your wings,
You heavenly guards!—What would your gracious figure?
Queen: Alas, he's mad!
Hamlet: Do you not come your tardy son to chide,
That, laps'd in time and passion, lets go by
The important acting of your dread command?
O, say!
Ghost: Do not forget: this visitation
Is but to whet thy almost blunted purpose.
But, look, amazement on thy mother sits:
O, step between her and her fighting soul,—
Conceit in weakest bodies strongest works,—
Speak to her, Hamlet.
Hamlet: How is it with you, lady?
Queen: Alas, how is't with you,
That you do bend your eye on vacancy,
And with the incorporal air do hold discourse?
Forth at your eyes your spirits wildly peep;
And, as the sleeping soldiers in the alarm,
Your bedded hair, like life in excrements,[6]

[3]*panders:* Becomes subservient to.
[4]*a vice of kings:* A buffoon among kings; the character "Vice" in morality plays.
[5]*in excrements:* In outgrowths or extremities.
[6]*As will not … tinct:* As will not yield up their color.

Starts up and stands on end. O gentle son,
Upon the heat and flame of thy distemper
Sprinkle cool patience. Whereon do you look?

Hamlet: On him, on him! Look you, how pale he glares!
His form and cause conjoin'd, preaching to stones,
Would make them capable.—Do not look upon me;
Lest with this piteous action you convert
My stern effects: then what I have to do
Will want true color; tears perchance for blood.

Queen: To whom do you speak this?

Hamlet: Do you see nothing there?

Queen: Nothing at all; yet all that is I see.

Hamlet: Nor did you nothing hear?

Queen: No, nothing but ourselves.

Hamlet: Why, look you there! look, how it steals away!
My father, in his habit as he liv'd!
Look, where he goes, even now, out at the portal!

Exit Ghost.

Queen: This is the very coinage of your brain:
This bodiless creation ecstasy
Is very cunning in.

Hamlet: Ecstasy!
My pulse, as yours, doth temperately keep time.
And makes as healthful music: it is not madness
That I have utter'd: bring me to the test,
And I the matter will re-word; which madness
Would gambol from. Mother, for love of grace,
Lay not that flattering unction to your soul,
That not your trespass, but my madness speaks:
It will but skin and film the ulcerous place,
Whilst rank corruption, mining all within,
Infects unseen. Confess yourself to Heaven;
Repent what's past; avoid what is to come;
And do not spread the compost on the weeds,
To make them ranker. Forgive me this my virtue;
For in the fatness[7] of these pursy times
Virtue itself of vice must pardon beg,
Yea, curb and woo for leave to do him good.

Queen: O Hamlet, thou hast cleft my heart in twain.

Hamlet: O, throw away the worser part of it,
And live the purer with the other half.
Good-night: but go not to mine uncle's bed;
Assume a virtue, if you have it not.

[7] *fatness:* Corruption.

That monster custom, who all sense doth eat,
Of habits devil, is angel yet in this,—
That to the use of actions fair and good
He likewise gives a frock or livery
That aptly is put on. Refrain to-night;
And that shall lend a kind of easiness
To the next abstinence: the next more easy;
For use almost can change the stamp of nature,
And either curb the devil, or throw him out
With wondrous potency. Once more, good-night:
And when you are desirous to be bless'd,
I'll blessing beg of you.—For this same lord [*pointing to Polonius*]
I do repent: but Heaven hath pleas'd it so,
To punish me with this, and this with me,
That I must be their[8] scourge and minister.
I will bestow him, and will answer well
The death I gave him. So, again, good-night.—
I must be cruel only to be kind:
Thus bad begins and worse remains behind.—
One word more, good lady.

Queen: What shall I do?

Hamlet: Not this, by no means, that I bid you do:
Let the bloat king tempt you again to bed;
Pinch wanton on your cheek; call you his mouse;
And let him, for a pair of reechy kisses,
Or paddling in your neck with his damn'd fingers,
Make you to ravel all this matter out,
That I essentially am not in madness,
But mad in craft. 'Twere good you let him know;
For who that's but a queen, fair, sober, wise,
Would from a paddock,[9] from a bat, a gib,[10]
Such dear concernings hide? who would do so?
No, in despite of sense and secrecy,
Unpeg the basket on the house's top,
Let the birds fly, and, like the famous ape,
To try conclusions, in the basket creep,
And break your own neck down.

Queen: Be thou assur'd, if words be made of breath
And breath of life, I have not life to breathe
What thou hast said to me.

Hamlet: I must to England; you know that?

Queen: Alack,
I had forgot: 'tis so concluded on.

---

[8]*their:* Heaven's, or the heavens'. [9]*paddock:* Toad. [10]*gib:* Tomcat.

Hamlet: There's letters seal'd: and my two school-fellows,—
Whom I will trust as I will adders fang'd,
They bear the mandate; they must sweep my way,
And marshal me to knavery. Let it work;
For 'tis the sport to have the éngineer
Hoist with his own petard: and't shall go hard
But I will delve one yard below their mines,
And blow them at the moon: O, 'tis most sweet,
When in one line two crafts directly meet.—
This man shall set me packing:
I'll lug the guts into the neighbor room.—
Mother, good-night.—Indeed, this counsellor
Is now most still, most secret, and most grave,
Who was in life a foolish prating knave.
Come, sir, to draw toward an end with you:—
Good-night, mother.

Exeunt severally; Hamlet dragging out Polonius.

ACT 4

SCENE 1

A room in the castle.

Enter King, Queen, Rosencrantz, and Guildenstern.

King: There's matter in these sighs, these prófound heaves:
You must translate: 'tis fit we understand them.
Where is your son?
Queen: Bestow this place on us a little while. [*To Rosencrantz and Guildenstern, who go out*]
Ah, my good lord, what have I seen to-night!
King: What, Gertrude? How does Hamlet?
Queen: Mad as the sea and wind, when both contend
Which is the mightier: in his lawless fit,
Behind the arras hearing something stir,
He whips his rapier out, and cries, A *rat, a rat*!
And, in this brainish apprehension,[1] kills
The unseen good old man.
King: O heavy deed!
It had been so with us had we been there:
His liberty is full of threats to all;
To you yourself, to us, to every one.
Alas, how shall this bloody deed be answer'd?

---

[1] *brainish apprehension:* Mad notion.

It will be laid to us, whose providence
Should have kept short, restrain'd, and out of haunt
This mad young man: but so much was our love,
We would not understand what was most fit;
But, like the owner of a foul disease,
To keep it from divulging, let it feed
Even on the pith of life. Where is he gone?

Queen: To draw apart the body he hath kill'd:
O'er whom his very madness, like some ore
Among a mineral of metals base,
Shows itself pure; he weeps for what is done.

King: O Gertrude, come away!
The sun no sooner shall the mountains touch
But we will ship him hence: and this vile deed
We must, with all our majesty and skill,
Both countenance and excuse.—Ho, Guildenstern!

Enter Rosencrantz and Guildenstern.

Friends both, go join you with some further aid:
Hamlet in madness hath Polonius slain,
And from his mother's closet hath he dragg'd him:
Go seek him out; speak fair, and bring the body
Into the chapel. I pray you, haste in this.

Exeunt Rosencrantz and Guildenstern.

Come, Gertrude, we'll call up our wisest friends;
And let them know both what we mean to do
And what's untimely done: so haply slander,—
Whose whisper o'er the world's diameter,
As level as the cannon to his blank,
Transports his poison'd shot,—may amiss our name,
And hit the woundless air.—O, come away!
My soul is full of discord and dismay.

Exeunt.

SCENE 2

Another room in the castle.

Enter Hamlet.

Hamlet: Safely stowed.

Rosencrantz and Guildenstern: [*Within*] Hamlet! Lord Hamlet!

Hamlet: What noise? who calls on Hamlet?
O, here they come.

Enter Rosencrantz and Guildenstern.

Rosencrantz: What have you done, my lord, with the dead body?
Hamlet: Compounded it with dust, whereto 'tis kin.
Rosencrantz: Tell us where 'tis, that we may take it thence,
And bear it to the chapel.
Hamlet: Do not believe it.
Rosencrantz: Believe what?
Hamlet: That I can keep your counsel, and not mine own. Besides, to be demanded of a sponge!—what replication should be made by the son of a king?
Rosencrantz: Take you me for a sponge, my lord?
Hamlet: Ay, sir; that soaks up the king's countenance, his rewards, his authorities. But such officers do the king best service in the end: he keeps them, like an ape, in the corner of his jaw; first mouthed, to be last swallowed: when he needs what you have gleaned, it is but squeezing you, and, sponge, you shall be dry again.
Rosencrantz: I understand you not, my lord.
Hamlet: I am glad of it: a knavish speech sleeps in a foolish ear.
Rosencrantz: My lord, you must tell us where the body is, and go with us to the king.
Hamlet: The body is with the king, but the king is not with the body. The king is a thing,—
Guildenstern: A thing, my lord!
Hamlet: Of nothing: bring me to him.
Hide fox, and all after.

Exeunt.

SCENE 3

Another room in the castle.

Enter King, attended.

King: I have sent to seek him, and to find the body.
How dangerous is it that this man goes loose!
Yet must not we put the strong law on him:
He's lov'd of the distracted multitude,
Who like not in their judgment, but their eyes;
And where 'tis so, the offender's scourge is weigh'd,
But never the offence. To bear all smooth and even,
This sudden sending him away must seem
Deliberate pause: diseases desperate grown
By desperate appliance are reliev'd,
Or not at all.

Enter Rosencrantz.

How now! what hath befallen!

Rosencrantz: Where the dead body is bestow'd, my lord,
We cannot get from him.
King: But where is he?
Rosencrantz: Without, my lord; guarded, to know your pleasure.
King: Bring him before us.
Rosencrantz: Ho, Guildenstern! bring in my lord.

Enter Hamlet and Guildenstern.

King: Now, Hamlet, where's Polonius?
Hamlet: At supper.
King: At supper! where?
Hamlet: Not where he eats, but where he is eaten: a certain convocation of politic worms are e'en at him. Your worm is your only emperor for diet: we fat all creatures else to fat us, and we fat ourselves for maggots: your fat king and your lean beggar is but variable service,—two dishes, but to one table: that's the end.
King: Alas, alas!
Hamlet: A man may fish with the worm that hath eat of a king, and eat of the fish that hath fed of that worm.
King: What does thou mean by this?
Hamlet: Nothing but to show you how a king may go a progress through the guts of a beggar.
King: Where is Polonius?
Hamlet: In heaven; send thither to see: if your messenger find him not there, seek him i' the other place yourself. But, indeed, if you find him not within this month, you shall nose him as you go up the stairs into the lobby.
King: Go seek him there. [*To some Attendants*]
Hamlet: He will stay till ye come.

Exeunt Attendants.

King: Hamlet, this deed, for thine especial safety,—
Which we do tender, as we dearly grieve
For that which thou hast done,—must send thee hence
With fiery quickness: therefore prepare thyself;
The bark is ready, and the wind at help,
The associates tend, and everything is bent
For England.
Hamlet: For England!
King: Ay, Hamlet.
Hamlet: Good.
King: So is it, if thou knew'st our purposes.
Hamlet: I see a cherub that sees them.—But, come; for England!—
Farewell, dear mother.
King: Thy loving father, Hamlet.
Hamlet: My mother: father and mother is man and wife; man and wife is one flesh; and so, my mother.—Come, for England! [*Exit.*]

King: Follow him at foot; tempt him with speed aboard;
Delay it not; I'll have him hence to-night:
Away! for everything is seal'd and done
That else leans on the affair, pray you, make haste.

Exeunt Rosencrantz and Guildenstern.

And, England, if my love thou hold'st at aught,—
As my great power thereof may give the sense,
Since yet thy cicatrice looks raw and red
After the Danish sword, and thy free awe
Pays homage to us,—thou mayst not coldly set
Our sovereign process; which imports at full,
By letters conjuring to that effect,
The present death of Hamlet. Do it, England;
For like the hectic in my blood he rages,
And thou must cure me: till I know 'tis done,
Howe'er my haps, my joys will ne'er begin. [*Exit.*]

SCENE 4

A plain in Denmark.

Enter Fortinbras, and Forces marching.

Fortinbras: Go, from me greet the Danish king:
Tell him that, by his license, Fortinbras
Craves the conveyance of a promis'd march
Over his kingdom. You know the rendezvous,
If that his majesty would aught with us,
We shall express our duty in his eye,
And let him know so.
Captain: I will do't, my lord.
Fortinbras: Go softly on.

Exeunt Fortinbras and Forces.

Enter Hamlet, Rosencrantz, Guildenstern, &c.

Hamlet: Good sir, whose powers are these?
Captain: They are of Norway, sir.
Hamlet: How purpos'd, sir, I pray you?
Captain: Against some part of Poland.
Hamlet: Who commands them, sir?
Captain: The nephew to old Norway, Fortinbras.
Hamlet: Goes it against the main of Poland, sir,
Or for some frontier?
Captain: Truly to speak, and with no addition,
We go to gain a little patch of ground
That hath in it no profit but the name.
To pay five ducats, five, I would not farm it;

Nor will it yield to Norway or the Pole
A ranker[1] rate should it be sold in fee.
Hamlet: Why, then the Polack never will defend it.
Captain: Yes, it is already garrison'd.
Hamlet: Two thousand souls and twenty thousand ducats
Will not debate the question of this straw:
This is the imposthume[2] of much wealth and peace,
That inward breaks, and shows no cause without
Why the man dies.—I humbly thank you, sir.
Captain: God b' wi' you, sir. [*Exit.*]
Rosencrantz: Will't please you go, my lord?
Hamlet: I'll be with you straight. Go a little before.

Exeunt all but Hamlet.

How all occasions do inform against me,
And spur my dull revenge! What is a man,
If his chief good and market of his time
Be but to sleep and feed? a beast, no more.
Sure he that made us with such large discourse,[3]
Looking before and after, gave us not
That capability and godlike reason
To fust[4] in us unus'd. Now, whether it be
Bestial oblivion or some craven scruple
Of thinking too precisely on the event,—
A thought which, quarter'd, hath but one part wisdom
And ever three parts coward,—I do not know
Why yet I live to say, *This thing's to do*;
Sith[5] I have cause, and will, and strength, and means
To do't. Examples, gross as earth, exhort me:
Witness this army, of such mass and charge,
Led by a delicate and tender prince;
Whose spirit, with divine ambition puff'd,
Makes mouths at the invisible event;
Exposing what is mortal and unsure
To all that fortune, death, and danger dare,
Even for an egg-shell. Rightly to be great
Is not to stir without great argument,
But greatly to find quarrel in a straw
When honor's at the stake. How stand I, then,
That have a father kill'd, a mother stain'd,
Excitements of my reason and my blood,
And let all sleep? while, to my shame, I see
The imminent death of twenty thousand men,
That, for a fantasy and trick of fame,

[1]*ranker:* Dearer. [2]*imposthume:* Ulcer. [3]*discourse:* Reasoning faculty.
[4]*fust:* Grow musty. [5]*Sith:* Since.

Go to their graves like beds; fight for a plot
Whereon the numbers cannot try the cause,
Which is not tomb enough and continent[6]
To hide the slain?—O, from this time forth,
My thoughts be bloody, or be nothing worth! [*Exit.*]

Scene 5

Elsinore. A room in the castle.

Enter Queen and Horatio.

Queen: I will not speak with her.
Horatio: She is importunate; indeed, distract:
Her mood will needs be pitied.
Queen: What would she have?
Horatio: She speaks much of her father; says she hears
There's tricks i' the world; and hems, and beats her heart;
Spurns enviously at straws; speaks things in doubt,
That carry but half sense: her speech is nothing,
Yet the unshapéd use of it doth move
The hearers to collection; they aim at it,
And botch the words up fit to their own thoughts;
Which, as her winks, and nods, and gestures yield them,
Indeed would make one think there might be thought,
Though nothing sure, yet much unhappily.
'Twere good she were spoken with; for she may strew
Dangerous conjectures in ill-breeding minds.
Queen: Let her come in.

Exit Horatio.

To my sick soul, as sin's true nature is,
Each toy seems prologue to some great amiss:
So full of artless jealousy is guilt,
It spills itself in fearing to be spilt.

Re-enter Horatio and Ophelia.

Ophelia: Where is the beauteous majesty of Denmark?
Queen: How now, Ophelia!
Ophelia: [*Sings*]
How should I your true love know
From another one?
By his cockle hat and staff,
And his sandal shoon.

Queen: Alas, sweet lady, what imports this song?
Ophelia: Say you? nay, pray you, mark.

[6] *continent:* Container.

[Sings]

He is dead and gone, lady,
He is dead and gone;
At his head a grass green turf,
At his heels a stone.

Queen: Nay, but, Ophelia,—
Ophelia: Pray you, mark.

[Sings]

White his shroud as the mountain snow,

Enter King.

Queen: Alas, look here, my lord.
Ophelia: [*Sings*]
Larded with sweet flowers;
Which bewept to the grave did go
With true-love showers.

King: How do you, pretty lady?
Ophelia: Well, God 'ild you![1] They say the owl was a baker's daughter. Lord, we know what we are, but know not what we may be. God be at your table!
King: Conceit upon her father.
Ophelia: Pray you, let's have no words of this; but when they ask you what it means, say you this:

[Sings.]

To-morrow is Saint Valentine's day
All in the morning betime,
And I a maid at your window,
To be your Valentine.
Then up he rose, and donn'd his clothes,
And dupp'd the chamber-door;
Let in the maid, that out a maid
Never departed more.

King: Pretty Ophelia!
Ophelia: Indeed, la, without an oath, I'll make an end on't;

[Sings]

By Gis[2] and by Saint Charity,
Alack, and fie for shame!
Young men will do't, if they come to't;
By cock, they are to blame.
Quoth she, before you tumbled me,
You promis'd me to wed.

[1] *ild you:* Yield you—i.e., reward you.
[2] *Gis:* A contraction for "by Jesus."

So would I ha' done, by yonder sun,
An thou hadst not come to my bed.

King: How long hath she been thus?

Ophelia: I hope all will be well. We must be patient: but I cannot choose but weep, to think they should lay him i' the cold ground. My brother shall know of it: and so I thank you; for your good counsel.—Come, my coach!— Good-night, ladies; good-night, sweet ladies; good-night, good-night. [*Exit.*]

King: Follow her close; give her good watch, I pray you.

Exit Horatio.

O, this is the poison of deep grief; it springs
All from her father's death. O Gertrude, Gertrude,
When sorrows come, they come not single spies,
But in battalions! First, her father slain:
Next, your son gone; and he most violent author
Of his own just remove: the people muddied,
Thick and unwholesome in their thoughts and whispers
For good Polonius' death; and we have done but greenly
In hugger-mugger[3] to inter him: poor Ophelia
Divided from herself and her fair judgment,
Without the which we are pictures, or mere beasts:
Last, and as much containing as all these,
Her brother is in secret come from France;
Feeds on his wonder, keeps himself in clouds,
And wants not buzzers to infect his ear
With pestilent speeches of his father's death;
Wherein necessity, of matter beggar'd,
Will nothing stick our person to arraign
In ear and ear. O my dear Gertrude, this,
Like to a murdering piece,[4] in many places
Gives me superfluous death.

A noise within.

Queen: Alack, what noise is this?

King: Where are my Switzers?[5] let them guard the door.

Enter a Gentleman.

What is the matter?

Gentleman: Save yourself, my lord:
The ocean, overpeering of his list,
Eats not the flats with more impetuous haste
Than young Laertes, in a riotous head,
O'erbears your officers. The rabble call him lord;

[3]*in hugger-mugger:* In great secrecy and haste.
[4]*murdering piece:* A cannon.
[5]*Switzers:* Bodyguard of Swiss mercenaries.

And, as the world were now but to begin,
Antiquity forgot, custom not known,
The ratifiers and props of every word,
They cry, *Choose we, Laertes shall be king!*
Caps, hands, and tongues applaud it to the clouds,
Laertes shall be king, Laertes king!

Queen: How cheerfully on the false trail they cry!
O, this is counter, you false Danish dogs!

King: The doors are broke.

Noise within.

Enter Laertes armed; Danes following.

Laertes: Where is this king?—Sirs, stand you all without.

Danes: No, let's come in.

Laertes: I pray you, give me leave.

Danes: We will, we will. [*They retire without the door.*]

Laertes: I thank you:—keep the door.—O thou vile king,
Give me my father!

Queen: Calmly, good Laertes.

Laertes: That drop of blood that's calm proclaims me bastard;
Cries cuckold to my father; brands the harlot
Even here, between the chaste unsmirched brow
Of my true mother.

King: What is the cause, Laertes,
That thy rebellion looks so giant-like?—
Let him go, Gertrude; do not fear our person:
There's such divinity doth hedge a king,
That treason can but peep to what it would,
Acts little of his will.—Tell me, Laertes,
Why thou art thus incens'd.—Let him go, Gertrude:—
Speak, man.

Laertes: Where is my father?

King: Dead.

Queen: But not by him.

King: Let him demand his fill.

Laertes: How came he dead? I'll not be juggled with:
To hell, allegiance! vows, to the blackest devil!
Conscience and grace, to the profoundest pit!
I dare damnation:—to this point I stand,—
That both the worlds I give to negligence,
Let come what comes; only I'll be reveng'd
Most thoroughly for my father.

King: Who shall stay you?

Laertes: My will, not all the world:
And for my means, I'll husband them so well,
They shall go far with little.

King: Good Laertes,
If you desire to know the certainty
Of your dear father's death, is't writ in your revenge
That, sweepstake, you will draw both friend and foe,
Winner or loser?
Laertes: None but his enemies.
King: Will you know them, then?
Laertes: To his good friends thus wide I'll ope my arms;
And, like the kind life-rendering pelican,[6]
Repast them with my blood.
King: Why, now you speak
Like a good child and a true gentleman.
That I am guiltless of your father's death,
And am most sensible in grief for it,
It shall as level to your judgment pierce
As day does to your eye.
Danes: [*Within*] Let her come in.
Laertes: How now! what noise is that?

Re-enter Ophelia, fantastically dressed with straws and flowers.

O heat, dry up my brains! tears seven times salt
Burn out the sense and virtue of mine eyes!—
By heaven, thy madness shall be paid by weight
Till our scale turn the beam. O rose of May!
Dear maid, kind sister, sweet Ophelia!—
O heavens! is't possible a young maid's wits
Should be as mortal as an old man's life!
Nature is fine in love; and where 'tis fine
It sends some precious instance of itself
After the thing it loves.
Ophelia: [*Sings*]

They bore him barefac'd on the bier;
Hey no nonny, nonny, hey nonny;
And on his grave rain'd many a tear,—
Fare you well, my dove!

Laertes: Hadst thou thy wits, and didst persuade revenge,
It could not move thus.
Ophelia: You must sing, *Down-a-down, and you call him a-down-a.* O, how the wheel becomes it! It is the false steward, that stole his master's daughter.
Laertes: This nothing's more than matter.
Ophelia: There's rosemary, that's for remembrance; pray, love, remember: and there is pansies that's for thoughts.
Laertes: A document in madness,—thoughts and remembrance fitted.

---

[6]*life-rendering pelican:* The mother pelican was believed to draw blood from herself to feed her young.

Ophelia: There's fennel for you, and columbines:—there's rue for you; and here's some for me:—we may call it herb-grace o' Sundays: — O, you must wear your rue with a difference.—There's a daisy:—I would give you some violets, but they withered all when my father died:—they say, he made a good end,—

[Sings]

For bonny sweet Robin is all my joy,—

Laertes: Thoughts and affliction, passion, hell itself,
She turns to favor and to prettiness.

Ophelia: *[Sings]*

And will he not come again?
And will he not come again?
No, no, he is dead,
Go to thy death-bed,
He never will come again.
His beard was as white as snow
All flaxen was his poll:
He is gone, he is gone,
And we cast away moan:
God ha' mercy on his soul!
And of all Christian souls, I pray God.—God b' wi' ye. [*Exit.*]

Laertes: Do you see this, O God?

King: Laertes, I must commune with your grief,
Or you deny me right. Go but apart,
Make choice of whom your wisest friends you will,
And they shall hear and judge 'twixt you and me:
If by direct or by collateral hand
They find us touch'd, we will our kingdom give,
Our crown, our life, and all that we call ours,
To you in satisfaction; but if not,
Be you content to lend your patience to us,
And we shall jointly labor with your soul
To give it due content.

Laertes: Let this be so;
His means of death, his obscure burial,—
No trophy, sword, nor hatchment[7] o'er his bones
No noble rite nor formal ostentation,—
Cry to be heard, as 'twere from heaven to earth,
That I must call't in question.

King: So you shall;
And where the offence is, let the great axe fall.
I pray you, go with me.

Exeunt.

[7] *hatchment:* A tablet with coat of arms.

SCENE 6

Another room in the castle.

Enter Horatio and a Servant.

Horatio: What are they that would speak with me?
Servant: Sailors, sir: they say they have letters for you.
Horatio: Let them come in.—

Exit Servant.

I do not know from what part of the world
I should be greeted, if not from Lord Hamlet.

Enter Sailors.

1st Sailor: God bless you, sir.
Horatio: Let him bless thee too.
1st Sailor: He shall, sir, an't please him. There's a letter for you, sir; it comes from the ambassador that was bound for England; if your name be Horatio, as I am let to know it is.
Horatio: [*Reads*] *Horatio, when thou shalt have overlooked this, give these fellows some means to the king: they have letters for him. Ere we were two days old at sea, a pirate of very warlike appointment gave us chase. Finding ourselves too slow of sail, we put on a compelled valor; and in the grapple I boarded them; on the instant they got clear of our ship; so I alone became their prisoner. They have dealt with me like thieves of mercy: but they knew what they did; I am to do a good turn for them. Let the king have the letters I have sent; and repair thou to me with as much haste as thou wouldst fly death. I have words to speak in thine ear will make thee dumb; yet are they much too light for the bore of the matter. These good fellows will bring thee where I am. Rosencrantz and Guildenstern hold their course for England: of them I have much to tell thee. Farewell. He that thou knowest thine.*

Hamlet

Come, I will give you way for these your letters;
And do't the speedier, that you may direct me
To him from whom you brought them.

Exeunt.

SCENE 7

Another room in the castle.

Enter King and Laertes.

King: Now must your conscience my acquittance seal,
And you must put me in your heart for friend,
Sith you have heard, and with a knowing ear,

That he which hath your noble father slain
Pursu'd my life.

Laertes: It well appears:—but tell me
Why you proceeded not against these feats,
So crimeful and so capital in nature.
As by your safety, wisdom, all things else,
You mainly were stirr'd up.

King: O, for two special reasons;
Which may to you, perhaps, seem much unsinew'd,
But yet to me they are strong. The queen his mother
Lives almost by his looks; and for myself,—
My virtue or my plague, be it either which,—
She's so conjunctive to my life and soul,
That, as the star moves not but in his sphere,
I could not but by her. The other motive,
Why to a public count I might not go,
Is the great love the general gender bear him;
Who, dipping all his faults in their affection,
Would, like the spring that turneth wood to stone,
Convert his gyves to graces; so that my arrows,
Too slightly timber'd for so loud a wind,
Would have reverted to my bow again,
And not where I had aim'd them.

Laertes: And so have I a noble father lost;
A sister driven into desperate terms,—
Whose worth, if praises may go back again,
Stood challenger on mount of all the age
For her perfections:—but my revenge will come.

King: Break not your sleeps for that: you must not think
That we are made of stuff so flat and dull
That we can let our beard be shook with danger,
And think it pastime. You shortly shall hear more:
I lov'd your father, and we love ourself;
And that, I hope, will teach you to imagine,—

Enter a Messenger.

How now! what news?

Messenger: Letters, my lord, from Hamlet:
This to your majesty; this to the queen.

King: From Hamlet! Who brought them?

Messenger: Sailors, my lord, they say; I saw them not:
They were given me by Claudio,—he receiv'd them
Of him that brought them.

King: Laertes, you shall hear them.—Leave us.

Exit Messenger.

[*Reads*] *High and mighty,—You shall know I am set naked on your kingdom. To morrow shall I beg leave to see your kingly eyes: when I shall, first asking your pardon thereunto, recount the occasions of my sudden and more strange return.*

Hamlet

What should this mean? Are all the rest come back?
Or is it some abuse,[1] and no such thing?
Laertes: Know you the hand?
King: 'Tis Hamlet's character:[2]—*Naked,*—
And in a postscript here, he says, *alone.*
Can you advise me?
Laertes: I am lost in it, my lord. But let him come;
It warms the very sickness in my heart,
That I shall live, and tell him to his teeth,
Thus diddest thou.
King: If it be so, Laertes,—
As how should it be so? how otherwise?—
Will you be rul'd by me?
Laertes: Ay, my lord:
So you will not o'errule me to a peace.
King: To thine own peace. If he be now return'd,—
As checking at his voyage, and that he means
No more to undertake it,—I will work him
To an exploit, now ripe in my device,
Under the which he shall not choose but fall:
And for his death no wind of blame shall breathe;
But even his mother shall uncharge the practice
And call it accident.
Laertes: My lord, I will be rul'd;
The rather if you could devise it so
That I might be the organ.
King: It falls right.
You have been talk'd of since your travel much,
And that in Hamlet's hearing, for a quality
Wherein they say you shine: your sum of parts
Did not together pluck such envy from him
As did that one; and that, in my regard,
Of the unworthiest siege.
Laertes: What part is that, my lord?
King: A very riband in the cap of youth,
Yet needful too; for youth no less becomes
The light and careless livery that it wears

[1]*abuse:* Ruse. [2]*character:* Handwriting.

Than settled age his sables and his weeds,
Importing health and graveness.—Two months since,
Here was a gentleman of Normandy,—
I've seen myself, and serv'd against, the French,
And they can well on horseback: but this gallant
Had witchcraft in't; he grew unto his seat;
And to such wondrous doing brought his horse,
As he had been incorps'd and demi-natur'd[3]
With the brave beast: so far he topp'd my thought,
That I, in forgery of shapes and tricks,[4]
Come short of what he did.

Laertes: A Norman was't?

King: A Norman.

Laertes: Upon my life, Lamond.

King: The very same.

Laertes: I know him well: he is the brooch, indeed,
And gem of all the nation.

King: He made confession of you;
And gave you such a masterly report
For art and exercise in your defence,
And for your rapier most especially,
That he cried out, 'twould be a sight indeed
If one could match you: the scrimers[5] of their nation,
He swore, had neither motion, guard, nor eye,
If you oppos'd them. Sir, this report of his
Did Hamlet so envenom with his envy,
That he could nothing do but wish and beg
Your sudden coming o'er, to play with him.
Now, out of this,—

Laertes: What out of this, my lord?

King: Laertes, was your father dear to you?
Or are you like the painting of a sorrow,
A face without a heart?

Laertes: Why ask you this?

King: Not that I think you did not love your father;
But that I know love is begun by time;
And that I see, in passages of proof,[6]
Time qualifies the spark and fire of it.
There lives within the very flame of love
A kind of wick or snuff that will abate it;
And nothing is at a like goodness still;
For goodness, growing to a pleurisy,[7]

---

[3]*As … demi-natur'd:* Made as one body and formed into half man, half horse—or centaur.

[4]*in forgery … tricks:* In imagining tricks of horsemanship.

[5]*scrimers:* Fencers.

[6]*passages of proof:* The evidence of experience.

[7]*pleurisy:* Plethora, an excess of blood.

Dies in his own too much: that we would do
We should do when we would; for this *would* changes,
And hath abatements and delays as many
As there are tongues, or hands, or accidents;
And then this *should* is like a spendthrift sigh
That hurts by easing. But to the quick o' the ulcer:
Hamlet comes back: what would you undertake
To show yourself your father's son in deed
More than in words?

Laertes: To cut his throat i' the church.

King: No place, indeed, should murder sanctuarize;
Revenge should have no bounds. But, good Laertes,
Will you do this, keep close within your chamber.
Hamlet return'd shall know you are come home:
We'll put on those shall praise your excellence,
And set a double varnish on the fame
The Frenchman gave you; bring you, in fine, together,
And wager on yours heads: he, being remiss,[8]
Most generous, and free from all contriving,
Will not peruse the foils; so that, with ease,
Or with a little shuffling, you may choose
A sword unbated, and, in a pass of practice,
Requite him for your father.

Laertes: I will do't it:
And, for that purpose, I'll anoint my sword.
I bought an unction of a mountebank,
So mortal that but dip a knife in it,
Where it draws blood no cataplasm so rare,[9]
Collected from all simples that have virtue
Under the moon, can save the thing from death
That is but scratch'd withal: I'll touch my point
With this contagion, that, if I gall him slightly,
It may be death.

King: Let's further think of this;
Weigh what convenience both of time and means
May fit us to our shape: if this should fail,
And that our drift look through our bad performance,
'Twere better not assay'd: therefore this project
Should have a back or second, that might hold
If this should blast in proof. Soft! let me see:—
We'll make a solemn wager on your cunnings,—
I ha't:
When in your motion you are hot and dry,—

---

[8] *remiss:* Unguarded and free from suspicion.

[9] *no cataplasm so rare:* No poultice, however remarkably efficacious.

As make your bouts more violent to that end,—
And that he calls for drink, I'll have prepar'd him
A chalice for the nonce;[10] whereon but sipping,
If he by chance escape your venom'd stuck
Our purpose may hold there.

Enter Queen.

How now, sweet queen!

Queen: One woe doth tread upon another's heel,
So fast they follow:—your sister's drown'd, Laertes.

Laertes: Drown'd! O, where?

Queen: There is a willow grows aslant a brook,
That shows his hoar leaves in the glassy stream;
There with fantastic garlands did she come
Of crowflowers, nettles, daisies, and long purples,
That liberal shepherds give a grosser name,
But our cold maids do dead men's fingers call them.
There, on the pendant boughs her coronet weeds
Clambering to hang, an envious[11] sliver broke;
When down her weedy trophies and herself
Fell in the weeping brook. Her clothes spread wide;
And, mermaid-like, awhile they bore her up:
Which time she chanted snatches of old tunes;
As one incapable of her own distress,
Or like a creature native and indu'd
Unto that element: but long it could not be
Till that her garments, heavy with their drink,
Pull'd the poor wretch from her melodious lay
To muddy death.

Laertes: Alas, then, she is drown'd?

Queen: Drown'd, drown'd.

Laertes: Too much of water hast thou, poor Ophelia,
And therefore I forbid my tears: but yet
It is our trick; nature her custom holds,
Let shame say what it will: when these are gone,
The woman will be out.[12]—Adieu, my lord:
I have a speech of fire, that fain would blaze,
But that this folly douts it.[13] [*Exit.*]

King: Let's follow, Gertrude;
How much I had to do to calm his rage!
Now fear I this will give it start again;
Therefore let's follow.

Exeunt.

---

[10]*nonce:* Purpose. [11]*envious:* Malicious. [12]*The woman ... out:* I.e., "I shall be ruthless."
[13]*douts it:* Drowns it.

ACT 5

SCENE 1

A churchyard.

Enter two Clowns[1] with spades, &c.

1st Clown: Is she to be buried in Christian burial that wilfully seeks her own salvation?

2nd Clown: I tell thee she is; and therefore make her grave straight: the crowner[2] hath sat on her, and finds it Christian burial.

1st Clown: How can that be, unless she drowned herself in her own defence?

2nd Clown: Why, 'tis found so.

1st Clown: It must be se *offendendo,*[3] it cannot be else. For here lies the point: if I drown myself wittingly, it argues an act: and an act hath three branches; it is to act, to do, and to perform: argal,[4] she drowned herself wittingly.

2nd Clown: Nay, but hear you, goodman delver,—

1st Clown: Give me leave. Here lies the water; good: here stands the man; good: if the man go to this water and drown himself, it is, will he, nill he, he goes,—mark you that: but if the water come to him and drown him, he drowns not himself: argal, he that is not guilty of his own death shortens not his own life.

2nd Clown: But is this law?

1st Clown: Ay, marry, is't; crowner's quest law.

2nd Clown: Will you ha' the truth on't? If this had not been a gentlewoman she should have been buried out of Christian burial.

1st Clown: Why, there thou say'st: and the more pity that great folks should have countenance in this world to drown or hang themselves more than their even-Christian.[5]—Come, my spade. There is no ancient gentlemen but gardeners, ditchers, and grave-makers; they hold up Adam's profession.

2nd Clown: Was he a gentleman?

1st Clown: He was the first that ever bore arms.

2nd Clown: Why, he had none.

1st Clown: What, art a heathen? How dost thou understand the Scripture? The Scripture says, Adam digged: could he dig without arms? I'll put another question to thee: if thou answerest me not to the purpose, confess thyself,[6]—

2nd Clown: Go to.

1st Clown: What is he that builds stronger than either the mason, the shipwright, or the carpenter?

2nd Clown: The gallows-maker; for that frame outlives a thousand tenants.

1st Clown: I like thy wit well, in good faith: the gallows does well; but how does it well? it does well to those that do ill: now thou dost ill to say the gallows is built stronger than the church: argal, the gallows may do well to thee. To't again, come.

---

[1] *Clowns:* Rustic fellows. [2] *crowner:* Coroner.

[3] *se offendendo:* In self-offense; he means *se defendendo,* in self-defense.

[4] *argal:* He means *ergo,* therefore. [5] *even-Christian:* Fellow Christian.

[6] *confess thyself:* "Confess thyself an ass," perhaps.

2nd Clown: Who builds stronger than a mason, a shipwright, or a carpenter?
1st Clown: Ay, tell me that, and unyoke.
2nd Clown: Marry, now I can tell.
1st Clown: To't.
2nd Clown: Mass, I cannot tell.

Enter Hamlet and Horatio, at a distance.

1st Clown: Cudgel thy brains no more about it, for your dull ass will not mend his pace with beating; and when you are asked this question next, say a grave-maker; the houses that he makes last till doomsday. Go, get thee to Yaughan: fetch me a stoup of liquor.

Exit Second Clown.

Digs and sings.

In youth, when I did love, did love,
Methought it was very sweet,
To contract, O, the time, for, ah, my behove,[7]
O, methought there was nothing meet.

Hamlet: Has this fellow no feeling of his business, that he sings at grave-making?
Horatio: Custom hath made it in him a property of easiness.
Hamlet: 'Tis e'en so: the hand of little employment hath the daintier sense.
1st Clown: [*Sings*]

But age, with his stealing steps,
Hath claw'd me in his clutch,
And hath shipp'd me intil the land,
As if I had never been such.

Throws up a skull.

Hamlet: That skull had a tongue in it, and could sing once: how the knave joels[8] it to the ground, as if it were Cain's jawbone, that did the first murder! This might be the pate of a politician, which this ass now o'erreaches; one that would circumvent God, might it not?
Horatio: It might, my lord.
Hamlet: Or of a courtier; which could say, *Good-morrow, sweet lord! How dost thou, good lord?* This might be my lord such-a-one, that praised my lord such-a-one's horse, when he meant to beg it,—might it not?
Horatio: Ay, my lord.
Hamlet: Why, e'en so: and now my Lady Worm's; chapless,[9] and knocked about the mazard[10] with a sexton's spade: here's fine revolution, an we had the trick to see't. Did these bones cost no more the breeding but to play at loggats[11] with 'em? Mine ache to think on't.

---

[7] *behove:* Behoof, or advantage. [8] *joels:* Throws. [9] *chapless:* Without a lower jaw.
[10] *mazard:* Head. [11] *loggats:* A game in which small pieces of wood are hurled at a stake.

1st Clown: [*Sings*]

A pick-axe and a spade, a spade,
For and a shrouding sheet:
O, a pit of clay for to be made
For such a guest is meet.

Throws up another.

Hamlet: There's another: why may not that be the skull of a lawyer? Where be his quiddits[12] now, his quillets,[13] his cases, his tenures, and his tricks? why does he suffer this rude knave now to knock him about the sconce with a dirty shovel, and will not tell him of his action of battery? Hum! This fellow might be in's time a great buyer of land, with his statutes, his recognizances, his fines, his double vouchers, his recoveries: is this the fine of his fines, and the recovery of his recoveries, to have his fine pate full of fine dirt? will his vouchers vouch him no more of his purchases, and double ones too, than the length and breadth of a pair of indentures? The very conveyances of his lands will hardly lie in this box; and must the inheritor himself have no more, ha?

Horatio: Not a jot more, my lord.

Hamlet: Is not parchment made of sheep-skins?

Horatio: Ay, my lord, and of calf-skins too.

Hamlet: They are sheep and calves which seek out assurance in that. I will speak to this fellow.—Whose grave's this, sir?

1st Clown: Mine, sir.—[*Sings*]

O, a pit of clay for to be made
For such a guest is meet.

Hamlet: I think it be thine indeed; for thou liest in't.

1st Clown: You lie out on't, sir, and therefore it is not yours: for my part, I do not lie in't, and yet it is mine.

Hamlet: Thou dost lie in't, to be in't, and say it is thine: 'tis for the dead, not for the quick; therefore thou liest.

1st Clown: 'Tis a quick lie, sir: 'twill away again from me to you.

Hamlet: What man dost thou dig it for?

1st Clown: For no man, sir.

Hamlet: What woman, then?

1st Clown: For none, neither.

Hamlet: Who is to be buried in't?

1st Clown: One that was a woman, sir; but, rest her soul, she's dead.

Hamlet: How absolute the knave is! we must speak by the card, or equivocation will undo us. By the Lord, Horatio, these three years I have taken note of it; the age is grown so picked[14] that the toe of the peasant comes so near the heel of the courtier, he galls his kibe.[15]—How long hast thou been a grave-maker?

---

[12]*quiddits:* Quiddities, "whatnesses"—that is, hair-splittings. [13]*quillets:* Quibbling distinctions.

[14]*picked:* Refined or educated.

[15]*galls his kibe:* Rubs and irritates the chilblain sore on the courtier's heel.

1st Clown: Of all the days i' the year, I came to't that day that our last King Hamlet o'ercame Fortinbras.

Hamlet: How long is that since?

1st Clown: Cannot you tell that? every fool can tell that: it was the very day that young Hamlet was born,—he that is mad, and sent into England.

Hamlet: Ay, marry, why was he sent into England?

1st Clown: Why, because he was mad: he shall recover his wits there; or, if he do not, it's no great matter there.

Hamlet: Why?

1st Clown: 'Twill not be seen in him there; there the men are as mad as he.

Hamlet: How came he mad?

1st Clown: Very strangely, they say.

Hamlet: How strangely?

1st Clown: Faith, e'en with losing his wits.

Hamlet: Upon what ground?

1st Clown: Why, here in Denmark: I have been sexton here, man and boy, thirty years.

Hamlet: How long will a man lie i' the earth ere he rot?

1st Clown: Faith, if he be not rotten before he die,—as we have many pocky corses now-a-days, that will scarce hold the laying in,—he will last you some eight year or nine year: a tanner will last you nine year.

Hamlet: Why he more than another?

1st Clown: Why, sir, his hide is so tanned with his trade that he will keep out water a great while; and your water is a sore decayer of your whoreson dead body. Here's a skull now; this skull has lain in the earth three-and-twenty years.

Hamlet: Whose was it?

1st Clown: A whoreson mad fellow's it was: whose do you think it was?

Hamlet: Nay, I know not.

1st Clown: A pestilence on him for a mad rogue! 'a poured a flagon of Rhenish on my head once. This same skull, sir, was Yorick's skull, the king's jester.

Hamlet: This?

1st Clown: E'en that.

Hamlet: Let me see. [*Takes the skull*]—Alas, poor Yorick!—I knew him, Horatio; a fellow of infinite jest, of most excellent fancy: he hath borne me on his back a thousand times; and now, how abhorred in my imagination it is! my gorge rises at it. Here hung those lips that I have kissed I know not how oft. Where be your gibes now? your gambols? your songs? your flashes of merriment, that were wont to set the table on a roar? Not one now, to mock your own grinning? quite chap-fallen? Now get you to my lady's chamber, and tell her, let her paint an inch thick, to this favor[16] she must come; make her laugh at that.—Pr'ythee, Horatio, tell me one thing.

Horatio: What's that, my lord?

---

[16]*favor:* Face.

Hamlet: Dost thou think Alexander looked o' this fashion i' the earth?

Horatio: E'en so.

Hamlet: And smelt so? pah! [*Throws down the skull*]

Horatio: E'en so, my lord.

Hamlet: To what base uses we may return, Horatio! Why may not imagination trace the noble dust of Alexander till he find it stopping a bung-hole?

Horatio: 'Twere to consider too curiously to consider so.

Hamlet: No, faith, not a jot; but to follow him thither with modesty enough, and likelihood to lead it: as thus; Alexander died, Alexander was buried, Alexander returneth into dust; the dust is earth; of earth we make loam; and why of that loam whereto he was converted might they not stop a beer-barrel?

Imperious Caesar, dead and turn'd to clay,
Might stop a hole to keep the wind away:
O, that that earth which kept the world in awe
Should patch a wall to expel the winter's flaw!—

But soft! but soft! aside.—Here comes the king.

Enter Priests, &c., in procession; the corpse of Ophelia, Laertes and Mourners following; King, Queen, their Trains, &c.

The queen, the courtiers: who is that they follow?
And with such maimed rites? This doth betoken
The corpse they follow did with desperate hand
Fordo its own life: 'twas of some estate.
Couch we awhile and mark. [*Retiring with Horatio*]

Laertes: What ceremony else?

Hamlet: That is Laertes,
A very noble youth: mark.

Laertes: What ceremony else?

1st Priest: Her obsequies have been as far enlarg'd
As we have warrantise: her death was doubtful,
And, but that great command o'ersways the order,
She should in ground unsanctified have lodg'd
Till the last trumpet; for charitable prayers,
Shards, flints, and pebbles, should be thrown on her,
Yet here she is allowed her virgin rites,
Her maiden strewments, and the bringing home
Of bell and burial.

Laertes: Must there no more be done?

1st Priest: No more be done:
We should profane the service of the dead
To sing a requiem, and such rest to her
As to peace-parted souls.

Laertes: Lay her i' the earth;—
And from her fair and unpolluted flesh
May violets spring!—I tell thee, churlish priest,
A ministering angel shall my sister be
When thou liest howling.
Hamlet: What, the fair Ophelia!
Queen: Sweets to the sweet: farewell! [*Scattering flowers*]
I hop'd thou shouldst have been my Hamlet's wife;
I thought thy bride-bed to have deck'd, sweet maid,
And not have strew'd thy grave.
Laertes: O, treble woe
Fall ten times treble on that cursed head
Whose wicked deed thy most ingenious sense
Depriv'd thee of!—Hold off the earth awhile,
Till I have caught her once more in mine arms:

Leaps into the grave.

Now pile your dust upon the quick and dead,
Till of this flat a mountain you have made,
To o'er-top old Pelion[17] or the skyish head
Of blue Olympus.
Hamlet: [*Advancing*] What is he whose grief
Bears such an emphasis? whose phrase of sorrow
Conjures the wandering stars, and makes them stand
Like wonder-wounded hearers? this is I, Hamlet the
Dane. [*Leaps into the grave*]
Laertes: The devil take thy soul! [*Grappling with him*]
Hamlet: Thou pray'st not well.
I pr'ythee, take thy fingers from my throat;
For, though I am not splenitive and rash,
Yet have I in me something dangerous,
Which let thy wiseness fear: away thy hand.
King: Pluck them asunder.
Queen: Hamlet! Hamlet!
All: Gentlemen,—
Horatio: Good my lord, be quiet.

The Attendants part them, and they come out of the grave.

Hamlet: Why, I will fight with him upon this theme
Until my eyelids will no longer wag.
Queen: O my son, what theme?
Hamlet: I lov'd Ophelia; forty thousand brothers
Could not, with all their quantity of love,

[17] *Pelion:* A mountain in Greece.

Make up my sum.—What wilt thou do for her?
King: O, he is mad, Laertes.
Queen: For love of God, forbear him.
Hamlet: 'Swounds, show me what thou'lt do:
Woul't weep? woul't fight? woul't fast? woul't tear thyself?
Woul't drink up eisel?[18] eat a crocodile?
I'll do't.—Dost thou come here to whine?
To outface me with leaping in her grave?
Be buried quick[19] with her, and so will I:
And, if thou prate of mountains, let them throw
Millions of acres on us, till our ground,
Singeing his pate against the burning zone,[20]
Make Ossa[21] like a wart! Nay, an thou'lt mouth,
I'll rant as well as thou.
Queen: This is mere madness:
And thus awhile the fit will work on him;
Anon, as patient as the female dove,
When that her golden couplets are disclos'd,[22]
His silence will sit drooping.
Hamlet: Hear you, sir;
What is the reason that you use me thus?
I lov'd you ever: but it is no matter;
Let Hercules himself do what he may,
The cat will mew, and dog will have his day. [*Exit.*]
King: I pray thee, good Horatio, wait upon him.—

Exit Horatio.

[*To Laertes*] Strengthen your patience in our last night's speech;
We'll put the matter to the present push.—
Good Gertrude, set some watch over your son.—
This grave shall have a living monument:
An hour of quiet shortly shall we see;
Till then, in patience our proceeding be.

Exeunt.

SCENE 2

A hall in the castle.

Enter Hamlet and Horatio.

Hamlet: So much for this, sir: now let me see the other;
You do remember all the circumstance?

---

[18]*eisel:* Vinegar. [19]*quick:* Alive. [20]*burning zone:* The fiery zone of the celestial sphere.
[21]*Ossa:* A high mountain in Greece. [22]*When … are disclos'd:* When the golden twins are hatched.

Horatio: Remember it, my lord!
Hamlet: Sir, in my heart there was a kind of fighting
That would not let me sleep: methought I lay
Worse than the mutines in the bilboes.[1] Rashly,
And prais'd be rashness for it,—let us know,
Our indiscretion sometimes serves us well,
When our deep plots do fail: and that should teach us
There's a divinity that shapes our ends,
Rough-hew them how we will.
Horatio: This is most certain.
Hamlet: Up from my cabin,
My sea-gown scarf'd about me, in the dark
Grop'd I to find out them: had my desire;
Finger'd their packet; and, in fine, withdrew
To mine own room again: making so bold,
My fears forgetting manners, to unseal
Their grand commission; where I found, Horatio,
O royal knavery! an exact command,—
Larded with many several sorts of reasons,
Importing Denmark's health and England's too,
With, ho! such bugs[2] and goblins in my life,—
That, on the supervise, no leisure bated,
No, not to stay the grinding of the axe,
My head should be struck off.
Horatio: Is't possible?
Hamlet: Here's the commission: read it at more leisure.
But wilt thou hear me how I did proceed?
Horatio: I beseech you.
Hamlet: Being thus benetted round with villainies,—
Ere I could make a prologue to my brains,
They had begun the play,—I sat me down;
Devis'd a new commission; wrote it fair:
I once did hold it, as our statists do,
A baseness to write fair, and labor'd much
How to forget that learning; but, sir, now
It did me yeoman's service. Wilt thou know
The effect of what I wrote?
Horatio: Ay, good my lord.
Hamlet: An earnest conjuration from the king,—
As England was his faithful tributary;
As love between them like the palm might flourish;
As peace should still her wheaten garland wear

[1] *mutines . . . bilboes:* Mutineers in the iron stocks on board ship.
[2] *bugs:* Bugbears.

And stand a comma[3] 'tween their amities;
And many such like as's of great charge,—
That, on the view and know of these contents,
Without debatement further, more or less,
He should the bearers put to sudden death,
Not shriving-time allow'd.

Horatio: How was this seal'd?

Hamlet: Why, even in that was heaven ordinant.
I had my father's signet in my purse,
Which was the model of that Danish seal:
Folded the writ up in form of the other;
Subscrib'd it; gav't the impression; plac'd it safely,
The changeling never known. Now, the next day
Was our sea-fight; and what to this was sequent
Thou know'st already.

Horatio: So Guildenstern and Rosencrantz go to't.

Hamlet: Why, man, they did make love to this employment;
They are not near my conscience; their defeat
Does by their own insinuation[4] grow:
'Tis dangerous when the baser nature[5] comes
Between the pass and fell[6] incensed points
Of mighty opposites.

Horatio: Why, what a king is this!

Hamlet: Does it not, think'st thee, stand me now upon,[7]
He that hath kill'd my king and whor'd my mother;
Popp'd in between the election and my hopes;
Thrown out his angle for my proper life,
And with such cozenage,[8]—is't not perfect conscience
To quit him with this arm? and is't not to be damn'd,
To let this canker of our nature come
In further evil?

Horatio: It must be shortly known to him from England
What is the issue of the business there.

Hamlet: It will be short: the interim is mine;
And a man's life's no more than to say One.
But I am very sorry, good Horatio,
That to Laertes I forgot myself;
For by the image of my cause I see
The portraiture of his: I'll court his favors:
But, sure, the bravery[9] of his grief did put me
Into a towering passion.

---

[3]*comma:* Link. [4]*insinuation:* By their own "sticking their noses" into the business.

[5]*baser nature:* Men of lower rank. [6]*fell:* Fierce.

[7]*Does . . . upon:* I.e., "Don't you think it is my duty?" [8]*cozenage:* Deceit. [9]*bravery:* Ostentation.

Horatio: Peace; who comes here?

Enter Osric.

Osric: Your lordship is right welcome back to Denmark.

Hamlet: I humbly thank you, sir.—Dost know this water-fly?

Horatio: No, my good lord.

Hamlet: Thy state is the more gracious; for 'tis a vice to know him. He hath much land, and fertile: let a beast be lord of beasts, and his crib shall stand at the king's mess: 'tis a chough;[10] but, as I say, spacious in the possession of dirt.

Osric: Sweet lord, if your lordship were at leisure, I should impart a thing to you from his majesty.

Hamlet: I will receive it with all diligence of spirit. Put your bonnet to his right use; 'tis for the head.

Osric: I thank your lordship, 'tis very hot.

Hamlet: No, believe me, 'tis very cold; the wind is northerly.

Osric: It is indifferent cold, my lord, indeed.

Hamlet: Methinks it is very sultry and hot for my complexion.

Osric: Exceedingly, my lord; it is very sultry,—as't were,—I cannot tell how.—But, my lord, his majesty bade me signify to you that he has laid a great wager on your head. Sir, this is the matter,—

Hamlet: I beseech you, remember,—

Hamlet moves him to put on his hat.

Osric: Nay, in good faith; for mine ease, in good faith. Sir, here is newly come to court Laertes; believe me, an absolute gentleman, full of most excellent differences, of very soft society and great showing: indeed, to speak feelingly of him, he is the card or calendar of gentry, for you shall find in him the continent of what part a gentleman would see.

Hamlet: Sir, his definement suffers no perdition in you;—though, I know, to divide him inventorially would dizzy the arithmetic of memory, and yet but yaw neither, in respect of his quick sail. But, in the verity of extolment, I take him to be a soul of great article; and his infusion of such dearth[11] and rareness as, to make true diction of him, his semblable is his mirror; and who else would trace him, his umbrage,[12] nothing more.

Osric: Your lordship speaks most infallibly of him.

Hamlet: The concernancy, sir? why do we wrap the gentleman in our more rawer breath?

Osric: Sir?

Horatio: Is't not possible to understand in another tongue? You will do't sir, really.

Hamlet: What imports the nomination[13] of this gentleman?

Osric: Of Laertes?

---

[10]*his crib … chough:* He shall have his trough at the king's table: he is a chattering fool.

[11]*dearth:* Rareness, or excellence. [12]*umbrage:* Shadow. [13]*nomination:* Naming.

Horatio: His purse is empty already; all's golden words are spent.

Hamlet: Of him, sir.

Osric: I know, you are not ignorant,—

Hamlet: I would you did, sir; yet, in faith, if you did, it would not much approve me.[14] —Well, sir.

Osric: You are not ignorant of what excellence Laertes is,—

Hamlet: I dare not confess that, lest I should compare with him in excellence; but to know a man well were to know himself.

Osric: I mean, sir, for his weapon; but in the imputation laid on him by them, in his meed he's unfellowed.[15]

Hamlet: What's his weapon?

Osric: Rapier and dagger.

Hamlet: That's two of his weapons: but, well.

Osric: The king, sir, hath wagered with him six Barbary horses: against the which he has imponed,[16] as I take it, six French rapiers and poniards, with their assigns, as girdle, hangers, and so: three of the carriages, in faith, are very dear to fancy, very responsive to the hilts, most delicate carriages, and of very liberal conceit.

Hamlet: What call you the carriages?

Horatio: I knew you must be edified by the margent[17] ere you had done.

Osric: The carriages, sir, are the hangers.

Hamlet: The phrase would be more german to the matter if we could carry cannon by our sides: I would it might be hangers till then. But, on: six Barbary horses against six French swords, their assigns, and three liberal conceited carriages; that's the French bet against the DANISH: why is this imponed, as you call it?

Osric: The king, sir, hath laid, that in a dozen passes between you and him he shall not exceed you three hits: he hath laid on twelve for nine; and it would come to immediate trial if your lordship would vouchsafe the answer.

Hamlet: How if I answer no?

Osric: I mean, my lord, the opposition of your person in trial.[18]

Hamlet: Sir, I will walk here in the hall: if it please his majesty, it is the breathing time of day with me: let the foils be brought, the gentleman willing, and the king hold his purpose, I will win for him if I can; if not, I will gain nothing but my shame and the odd hits.

Osric: Shall I re-deliver you[19] e'en so?

Hamlet: To this effect, sir; after what flourish your nature will.

---

[14] *if you ... approve me:* If you, who are a fool, thought me not ignorant, that would not be particularly to my credit.

[15] *in ... unfellowed:* In his worth, he has no equal.

[16] *imponed:* Staked.

[17] *edified ... margent:* Informed by a note in the margin of your instructions.

[18] *the opposition ... trial:* The presence of your person as Laertes' opponent in the fencing contest.

[19] *re-deliver you:* Carry back your answer.

Osric: I commend my duty to your lordship.
Hamlet: Yours, yours.

Exit Osric.

He does well to commend it himself; there are no tongues else for's turn.
Horatio: This lapwing runs away with the shell on his head.[20]
Hamlet: He did comply with his dug before he sucked it.[21] Thus has he,—and many more of the same bevy, that I know the drossy age dotes on,—only got the tune of the time, and outward habit of encounter; a kind of yesty collection,[22] which carries them through and through the most fanned and winnowed opinions; and do but blow them to their trial, the bubbles are out.

Enter a Lord.

Lord: My lord, his majesty commended him to you by young Osric, who brings back to him that you attend him in the hall: he sends to know if your pleasure hold to play with Laertes, or that you will take longer time.
Hamlet: I am constant to my purposes; they follow the king's pleasure: if his fitness speaks, mine is ready; now or whensoever, provided I be so able as now.
Lord: The king and queen and all are coming down.
Hamlet: In happy time.
Lord: The queen desires you to use some gentle entertainment to Laertes before you fall to play.
Hamlet: She well instructs me.

Exit Lord.

Horatio: You will lose this wager, my lord.
Hamlet: I do not think so; since he went into France I have been in continual practice: I shall win at the odds. But thou wouldst not think how ill all's here about my heart: but it is no matter.
Horatio: Nay, good my lord,—
Hamlet: It is but foolery; but it is such a kind of gain-giving[23] as would perhaps trouble a woman.
Horatio: If your mind dislike anything, obey it: I will forestall their repair hither, and say you are not fit.
Hamlet: Not a whit, we defy augury: there's a special providence in the fall of a sparrow. If it be now, 'tis not to come; if it be not to come, it will be now; if it be not now, yet it will come: the readiness is all. Since no man has aught of what he leaves, what is't to leave betimes?[24]

---

[20] *This lapwing … head:* This precocious fellow is like a lapwing that starts running when it is barely out of the shell.

[21] *He … sucked it:* He paid compliments to his mother's breast before he sucked it.

[22] *yesty collection:* Yeasty or frothy affair.

[23] *gain-giving:* Misgiving.

[24] *what … betimes?:* What does an early death matter?

Enter King, Queen, Laertes, Lords, Osric, and Attendants with foils, &c.

King: Come, Hamlet, come, and take this hand from me.

The King puts Laertes' hand into Hamlet's.

Hamlet: Give me your pardon, sir: I have done you wrong: But pardon't, as you are a gentleman.
This presence knows, and you must needs have heard,
How I am punish'd with sore distraction.
What I have done,
That might your nature, honor, and exception
Roughly awake, I here proclaim was madness.
Was't Hamlet wrong'd Laertes? Never Hamlet:
If Hamlet from himself be ta'en away,
And when he's not himself does wrong Laertes,
Then Hamlet does it not, Hamlet denies it.
Who does it, then? His madness: if't be so,
Hamlet is of the faction that is wrong'd;
His madness is poor Hamlet's enemy.
Sir, in this audience,
Let my disclaiming from a purpos'd evil
Free me so far in your most generous thoughts
That I have shot mine arrow o'er the house
And hurt my brother.
Laertes: I am satisfied in nature,
Whose motive, in this case, should stir me most
To my revenge: but in my terms of honor
I stand aloof; and will no reconcilement
Till by some elder masters of known honor
I have a voice and precedent of peace
To keep my name ungor'd. But till that time
I do receive your offer'd love like love,
And will not wrong it.
Hamlet: I embrace it freely;
And will this brother's wager frankly play.[25]—
Give us the foils; come on.
Laertes: Come, one for me.
Hamlet: I'll be your foil, Laertes; in mine ignorance
Your skill shall, like a star in the darkest night,
Stick fiery off indeed.
Laertes: You mock me, sir.
Hamlet: No, by this hand.
King: Give them the foils, young Osric.
Cousin Hamlet,
You know the wager?

[25] *frankly play:* Fence with a heart free from resentment.

Hamlet: Very well, my lord;
Your grace hath laid the odds o' the weaker side.
King: I do not fear it; I have seen you both;
But since he's better'd, we have therefore odds.
Laertes: This is too heavy, let me see another.
Hamlet: This likes me well. These foils have all a length?

They prepare to play.

Osric: Ay, my good lord.
King: Set me the stoups of wine upon that table,—
If Hamlet give the first or second hit,
Or quit in answer of the third exchange,
Let all the battlements their ordnance fire;
The king shall drink to Hamlet's better breath;
And in the cup an union[26] shall he throw,
Richer than that which four successive kings
In Denmark's crown have worn. Give me the cups;
And let the kettle[27] to the trumpet speak,
The trumpet to the cannoneer without,
The cannons to the heavens, the heavens to earth,
Now the king drinks to Hamlet.—Come, begin;—
And you, the judges, bear a wary eye.
Hamlet: Come on, sir.
Laertes: Come, my lord.

They play.

Hamlet: One.
Laertes: No.
Hamlet: Judgment.
Osric: A hit, a very palpable hit.
Laertes: Well;—again.
King: Stay, give me a drink.—Hamlet, this pearl is thine;
Here's to thy health.—

Trumpets sound, and cannon shot off within.

Give him the cup.
Hamlet: I'll play this bout first; set it by awhile.—
Come.—Another hit; what say you?

They play.

Laertes: A touch, a touch, I do confess.
King: Our son shall win.
Queen: He's fat, and scant of breath.—

[26]*an union:* A pearl. [27]*kettle:* Kettledrum.

Here, Hamlet, take my napkin, rub thy brows:
The queen carouses to thy fortune, Hamlet.
Hamlet: Good madam!
King: Gertrude, do not drink.
Queen: I will, my lord; I pray you, pardon me.
King: [*Aside*] It is the poison'd cup; it is too late.
Hamlet: I dare not drink yet, madam; by and by.
Queen: Come, let me wipe thy face.
Laertes: My lord, I'll hit him now.
King: I do not think't.
Laertes: [*Aside*] And yet 'tis almost 'gainst my conscience.
Hamlet: Come, for the third, Laertes: you but dally;
I pray you, pass with your best violence:
I am afeard you make a wanton of me.
Laertes: Say you so? come on.

They play.

Osric: Nothing, neither way.
Laertes: Have at you now!

Laertes wounds Hamlet; then, in scuffling, they change rapiers, and Hamlet wounds Laertes.

King: Part them; they are incens'd.
Hamlet: Nay, come, again.

The Queen falls.

Osric: Look to the queen there, ho!
Horatio: They bleed on both sides.—How is it, my lord?
Osric: How is't, Laertes?
Laertes: Why, as a woodcock to my own springe, Osric;
I am justly kill'd with mine own treachery.
Hamlet: How does the queen?
King: She swoons to see them bleed.
Queen: No, no, the drink, the drink,—O my dear Hamlet,—
The drink, the drink!—I am poison'd. [*Dies.*]
Hamlet: O villainy!—Ho! let the door be lock'd: Treachery! seek it out.

Laertes falls.

Laertes: It is here, Hamlet: Hamlet, thou art slain;
No medicine in the world can do thee good;
In thee there is not half an hour of life;
The treacherous instrument is in thy hand,
Unbated and envenom'd: the foul practice
Hath turn'd itself on me; lo, here I lie,
Never to rise again: thy mother's poison'd:
I can no more:—the king, the king's to blame.

Hamlet: The point envenom'd too!—
Then venom to thy work. [*Stabs the King.*]
Osric and Lords: Treason! treason!
King: O, yet defend me, friends; I am but hurt.
Hamlet: Here, thou incestuous, murderous, damned Dane,
Drink off this potion.—Is thy union here?
Follow my mother.

King dies.

Laertes: He is justly serv'd;
It is a poison temper'd by himself.—
Exchange forgiveness with me, noble Hamlet:
Mine and my father's death come not upon thee,
Nor thine on me! [*Dies.*]
Hamlet: Heaven make thee free of it! I follow thee.—
I am dead, Horatio.—Wretched queen, adieu!—
You that look pale and tremble at this chance,
That art but mutes or audience to this act,
Had I but time,—as this fell sergeant, death,
Is strict in his arrest,—O, I could tell you,—
But let it be.—Horatio, I am dead;
Thou liv'st; report me and my cause aright
To the unsatisfied.[28]
Horatio: Never believe it: I am more an antique Roman than a Dane,—
Here's yet some liquor left.
Hamlet: As thou'rt a man,
Give me the cup; let go; by heaven, I'll have't.—
O good Horatio, what a wounded name,
Things standing thus unknown, shall live behind me!
If thou didst ever hold me in thy heart,
Absent thee from felicity awhile,
And in this harsh world draw thy breath in pain,
To tell my story.—

March afar off, and shot within.

What warlike noise is this?
Osric: Young Fortinbras, with conquest come from Poland,
To the ambassadors of England gives
This warlike volley.
Hamlet: O, I die, Horatio;
The potent poison quite o'er-crows my spirit:
I cannot live to hear the news from England;
But I do prophesy the election lights

[28]*the unsatisfied:* The uninformed.

On Fortinbras: he has my dying voice;
So tell him, with the occurrents, more and less,
Which have solicited.[29]—The rest is silence. [*Dies.*]
Horatio: Now cracks a noble heart.—Good-night, sweet prince,
And flights of angels sing thee to thy rest!
Why does the drum come hither?

March within. Enter Fortinbras, the English Ambassadors, and others.

Fortinbras: Where is this sight?
Horatio: What is it you would see?
If aught of woe or wonder, cease your search.
Fortinbras: This quarry cries on havoc.[30]—O proud death,
What feast is toward in thine eternal cell,
That thou so many princes at a shot
So bloodily hast struck?
1st Ambassador: The sight is dismal;
And our affairs from England come too late:
The ears are senseless that should give us hearing,
To tell him his commandment is fulfill'd,
That Rosencrantz and Guildenstern are dead:
Where should we have our thanks?
Horatio: Not from his mouth,
Had it the ability of life to thank you:
He never gave commandment for their death.
But since, so jump[31] upon this bloody question,
You from the Polack wars, and you from England,
Are here arriv'd, give order that these bodies
High on a stage be placed to the view;
And let me speak to the yet unknowing world
How these things came about: so shall you hear
Of carnal, bloody, and unnatural acts;
Of accidental judgments, casual slaughters;
Of deaths put on by cunning and forc'd cause;
And, in this upshot, purposes mistook
Fall'n on the inventors' heads: all this can I
Truly deliver.
Fortinbras: Let us haste to hear it,
And call the noblest to the audience.
For me, with sorrow I embrace my fortune:
I have some rights of memory in this kingdom,[32]
Which now to claim my vantage doth invite me.

---

[29] *So tell him … solicited:* So tell him, together with the events, more or less, that have brought on this tragic affair.

[30] *This quarry … havoc:* This collection of dead bodies cries out havoc.

[31] *so jump:* So opportunely.

[32] *I have … kingdom:* I have some unforgotten rights to this kingdom.

Horatio: Of that I shall have also cause to speak,
And from his mouth whose voice will draw on more:
But let this same be presently perform'd,
Even while men's minds are wild: lest more mischance
On plots and errors happen.
Fortinbras: Let four captains
Bear Hamlet like a soldier to the stage;
For he was likely, had he been put on,[33]
To have prov'd most royally: and, for his passage,
The soldier's music and the rites of war
Speak loudly for him.—
Take up the bodies.—Such a sight as this
Becomes the field, but here shows much amiss.
Go, bid the soldiers shoot.

A dead march.

Exeunt, bearing off the dead bodies: after which a peal of ordnance is shot off.

* * *

Reading and Reacting

1. What are Hamlet's most notable character traits? Do you see these traits as generally positive or negative?
2. Review each of Hamlet's soliloquies. Do you believe his assessments of his own problems are accurate? Are his assessments of other characters' behavior accurate? Point to examples from the soliloquies that reveal Hamlet's insight or lack of insight.
3. Is Hamlet a sympathetic character? Where (if anywhere) do you find yourself growing impatient with him or disagreeing with him?
4. Why does Hamlet behave so cruelly toward Ophelia after his "To be or not to be" soliloquy (Act 3, Scene 1)? How does this behavior affect your view of his character?
5. What do other characters' comments reveal about Hamlet's character *before* the key events in the play begin to unfold? For example, how has Hamlet changed since he returned to the castle and found out about his father's death?
6. Claudius is presented as the play's villain. Is he all bad, or does he have any redeeming qualities?
7. List those in the play whom you believe to be flat characters. Why do you characterize each individual in this way? What does each of these flat characters contribute to the play?
8. Is Fortinbras simply Hamlet's foil, or does he have another essential role? Explain.

[33]*put on:* Tested by succession to the throne.

9. Each of the play's major characters has one or more character flaws that influence plot development. What specific weaknesses do you see in Claudius, Gertrude, Polonius, Laertes, Ophelia, and Hamlet himself? Through what words or actions is each weakness revealed? How does each weakness contribute to the play's plot?
10. Why doesn't Hamlet kill Claudius as soon as the ghost tells him what Claudius did? Why doesn't he kill him when he has the chance in Act 3? What words and actions reveal Hamlet's motivation for hesitating? What are the implications of his failure to act?
11. Why does Hamlet pretend to be insane? Why does he arrange for the "play within a play" to be performed? Why does he agree to the duel with Laertes? In each case, what words or actions reveal his motivation to the audience?
12. Is the ghost an essential character, or could the information he reveals and the reactions he arouses come from another source? Explain. (Keep in mind that the ghost is a stock character in Elizabethan revenge tragedies.)
13. Describe Hamlet's relationship with his mother. Do you consider this a typical mother/son relationship? Why, or why not?
14. In the graveyard scene (Act 5, Scene 1), the gravediggers make many ironic comments. How do these comments shed light on the events taking place in the play?
15. **Journal Entry** Both Gertrude and Ophelia are usually seen as weak women, firmly under the influence of the men in their lives. Do you think this characterization of them as passive and dependent is accurate? Explain your views.
16. **Critical Perspective** In *The Meaning of Shakespeare*, Harold Goddard reads *Hamlet* as, in part, a play about war, with a grimly ironic conclusion in that "all the Elder Hamlet's conquests have been for nothing—for less than nothing. Fortinbras, his former enemy, is to inherit the kingdom! Such is the end to which the ghost's thirst for vengeance has led." Goddard goes on to describe the play's ending:

    The dead Hamlet is borne out "like a soldier" and the last rites over his body are to be the rites of war. The final word of the text is "shoot." The last sounds we hear are a dead march and the reverberations of ordnance being shot off. The end crowns the whole. The sarcasm of fate could go no further. Hamlet, who aspired to nobler things, is treated at death as if he were the mere image of his father: a warrior. Shakespeare knew what he was about in making the conclusion of his play martial. Its theme has been war as well as revenge. It is the story of the Minotaur over again, of that monster who from the beginning of human strife has exacted his annual tribute of youth. No sacrifice ever offered to it was more precious than Hamlet. But he was not the last.

    If ever a play seems expressly written for the twentieth century, it is Hamlet. It should be unnecessary to underscore its pertinence to an age in which, twice within three decades, the older generation has called on the younger generation to settle a quarrel with the making of which it had nothing to do. So taken, Hamlet is an allegory of our time. Imagination or violence, Shakespeare seems to say, there is no other alternative.

Can you find other evidence in the play to support the idea that war (and, more specifically, the futility of war) is one of its major themes? Do you agree that the play is, in this respect, "an allegory of our time"?

Related Works: "The Cask of Amontillado" (p. 258), "Young Goodman Brown" (p. 354), "Shakespearean Sonnet" (p. 660), *Oedipus the King* (p. 1137)

WRITING SUGGESTIONS: Character

1. In *The Glass Menagerie* (p. 958), both Tom and Jim pursue versions of the American Dream. Define their different concepts of the American Dream, and explain how each tries to make that dream a reality. In each case, consider the obstacles that are encountered, and try to predict the character's success or lack of success. If you like, you may also consider characters in other works in which the American Dream is central—for example, "Two Kinds" (p. 471), *The Cuban Swimmer* (p. 1122), or *Fences* (p. 1222).
2. In both plays in this chapter, an absent father plays a key role even though neither of them appears in the play. Write an essay in which you discuss the importance of the absent fathers in these two plays.
3. Minor characters are often flat characters; in many cases, their sole function is to advance the plot or to highlight a particular trait in a major character. Sometimes, however, minor characters may be of more than minor importance. Choose one minor character from a play in this chapter (or from a play in another chapter), and write an essay in which you discuss what this character contributes and how the play would be different without that character.
4. Watch a film version of one of the plays in this chapter, and write an essay in which you evaluate an actor's interpretation of a key character.
5. Both *The Glass Menagerie* and *Hamlet* explore the complex relationships between parents and their children. Write an essay in which you analyze Amanda's relationships with her son and daughter or Hamlet's relationship with his mother.
6. In several other plays in this anthology, as in *Hamlet*, the past is an important influence on characters' lives in the present. Write an essay in which you discuss the impact of the past on the present in *Hamlet* and one or two other plays—for example, *A Doll's House* (p. 834) or *Oedipus the King* (p. 1137).

Chapter 31

Staging

Milcha Sanchez-Scott
Milcha Sanchez-Scott

Sophocles
Bettmann/Getty Images

Learning Objectives

After reading this chapter, you will be able to. . .

- Define staging.
- Describe the importance of stage directions.
- Outline the elements of staging.
- Understand the significance of costumes and props.
- Analyze a work of drama for its use of lighting, music, and sound effects.
- Identify a play's theme based on its staging.

Staging refers to the physical elements of a play's production that determine how the play looks and sounds to an audience. It encompasses the **stage settings**, or **sets**—furnishings, scenery, props, and lighting—as well as the costumes, sound effects, and music that bring the play to life on the stage. In short, staging is everything that goes into making a written script a performance.

The play's **director** is primarily responsible for its staging. The director chooses actors, works with set and costume designers, interacts with choreographers and musicians, decides on lighting, oversees rehearsals, and helps the actors interpret their characters. Of course, the actors will have their own ideas about the characters they play, and the director will work closely with them to determine the characters' motivations and actions (see "Actors' Interpretations," p. 954). Once the play opens, the director hands responsibility over to the **stage manager**, who oversees all backstage activity during performances.

Contemporary staging in the West has traditionally concentrated on recreating the real world. This concept of staging, which has dominated Western theatrical productions for centuries, would seem alien in many non-Western theaters. Japanese **Kabuki dramas** and **No plays**, for example, depend on staging conventions that make no attempt to mirror reality. Scenery and costumes are largely symbolic, and often actors wear highly stylized makeup or masks. Although some European and American playwrights have been strongly influenced by non-Western staging, the majority of plays being produced in the West still try to create the illusion of reality.

Stage Directions

Usually a playwright presents instructions for the staging of a play in **stage directions**—notes that comment on the scenery, the movements of the performers, the lighting, and the placement of props. (In the absence of detailed

A scene from *Waiting for Godot,* performed at Théâtre Hébertot in Paris, France in 1956

Lipnitzki/Roger Viollet/Getty Images

stage directions, dialogue can provide information about staging.) Sometimes these stage directions are quite simple, leaving much to the discretion (and imagination) of the director. Consider how little specific information about the setting of the play is provided in these stage directions from Act 1 of Samuel Beckett's 1952 absurdist play *Waiting for Godot:*

> *A country road. A tree. Evening.*

Often, however, playwrights furnish more detailed information about staging. Consider these stage directions from Act 1 of Anton Chekhov's *The Cherry Orchard:*

> *A room, which has always been called the nursery. One of the doors leads into Anya's room. Dawn, sun rises during the scene. May, the cherry trees in flower, but it is cold in the garden with the frost of the early morning. Windows closed.*
>
> *Enter Dunyasha with a candle and Lopahin with a book in his hand.*

These comments indicate that the first act takes place in a room with more than one door and that several windows reveal cherry trees in bloom. They also specify that the lighting should simulate the sun rising at dawn and that characters should enter carrying certain props. Still, Chekhov leaves it up to those staging the play to decide on the costumes for the characters and the furniture to be placed around the room.

Some stage directions are even more specific. Irish playwright George Bernard Shaw's long, complex stage directions are legendary in the theater. Note the degree of detail he provides in these stage directions from his 1906 comedy *The Doctor's Dilemma:*

> *The consulting-room has two windows looking on Queen Anne Street. Between the two is a marble-topped console, with haunched gilt legs ending in sphinx claws. The huge pier-glass [a long narrow mirror that fits between two windows] which surmounts it is mostly disabled from reflection by elaborate painting on its surface of palms, ferns, lilies, tulips, and sunflowers. The adjoining wall contains the fireplace, with two arm-chairs before it. As we happen to face the corner we see nothing of the other two walls. On the right of the fireplace, or rather on the right of any person facing the fireplace, is the door. On the left is the writing-table at which Redpenny [a medical student] sits. It is an untidy table with a microscope, several test tubes, and a spirit lamp [an alcohol burner] standing up through its litter of papers. There is a couch in the middle of the room, at right angles to the console, and parallel to the fireplace. A chair stands between the couch and the window. Another in the corner. Another at the other end of the windowed wall.... The wallpaper and carpets are mostly green.... The house, in fact, was so well furnished in the middle of the XIXth century that it stands unaltered to this day and is still quite presentable.*

Not only does Shaw indicate exactly what furniture is to be placed on stage, but he also includes a good deal of physical description—specifying, for example, "gilt legs ending in sphinx claws" and "test tubes and a spirit lamp" that clutter the writing table. In addition, he defines furniture placement and specifies color.

Regardless of how detailed the stage directions are, they do not eliminate the need for creative interpretations on the part of the producer, director, set designers, and actors. Many directors see stage directions as simply suggestions, not

A production of Tennessee Williams's *The Glass Menagerie* outside his childhood home in St. Louis, Missouri
Whitney Curtis/The New York Time

requirements, and some consider them more confusing than helpful. Therefore, some directors may choose to interpret a play's stage directions quite loosely—or even ignore them entirely. For example, in 2007, the Classical Theater of Harlem staged Samuel Beckett's 1952 existentialist drama *Waiting for Godot* in New Orleans. The performances were held outdoors in areas of the city that had been seriously damaged by Hurricane Katrina, and the still-devastated setting gave new power to Beckett's drama of characters' search for meaning against a backdrop of emptiness and despair. Another example occurred in 2021 when a production of Tennessee Williams's *The Glass Menagerie* was staged in front of Williams's childhood home in St. Louis. The set consisted of a small stage in the parking lot as well as fire escapes and metal walkways that covered the side of the building.

The Uses of Staging

Various elements of staging provide important information about characters and their motivations as well as about the play's theme.

Costumes

Costumes establish the historical period in which a play is set and provide insight into the characters who wear them. For example, when Hamlet first appears on stage, he is profoundly disillusioned and quite melancholy. This fact was immediately apparent to Shakespeare's audience because Hamlet is dressed in sable, which to the Elizabethans signified a melancholy nature. In Tennessee Williams's *The Glass Menagerie* (p. 958), Laura's dress of soft violet material and her hair ribbon reflect her delicate, childlike innocence. In contrast, her mother's "*imitation velvety-looking cloth [coat] with imitation fur collar*" and her "*enormous black patent-leather pocketbook*" reveal her somewhat pathetic attempt to achieve respectability. Later in the play, awaiting the "gentleman caller," Laura's mother wears a dress that is both outdated and inappropriately youthful, suggesting both her need to relive her own past and her increasingly desperate desire to marry off her daughter.

Props and Furnishings

Props (short for *properties*) can also help audiences interpret a play's characters and themes. For example, the handkerchief in Shakespeare's *Othello* gains significance as the play progresses: it begins as an innocent object and ends as the piece of evidence that convinces Othello his wife is committing adultery. Sometimes props can have symbolic significance. During the Renaissance, for example, flowers had symbolic meaning. In Act 4 of *Hamlet*, Ophelia, who is mad, gives flowers to various characters. In a note to the play, the critic Thomas Parrott points out the symbolic significance of her gifts: to Claudius, the murderer of Hamlet's father, she gives fennel and columbines, which signify flattery and ingratitude; to the Queen, she gives rue and daisies, which symbolize sadness and unfaithfulness. Although modern audiences would not understand the significance of these flowers, many people in Shakespeare's Elizabethan audience would have been aware of their meaning.

The **furnishings** in a room can also reveal a lot about a play's characters and themes. Willy Loman's house in Arthur Miller's *Death of a Salesman* is sparsely furnished, revealing the declining financial status of the family. The kitchen contains a table and three chairs and the bedroom only a brass bed and a straight chair. Over the bed on a shelf is Willy's son's silver athletic trophy, a constant reminder of his loss of status. Like Willie Loman's house, the Helmer's living room in *A Doll's House* (p. 834), suggests its inhabitants' social status. The furnishings are typical of "respectable" middle-class families in nineteenth-century Norway. According to the stage directions, the living room is, "A comfortable, tastefully but not expensively furnished room." Everything in it—from the round table with an armchair, to the porcelain stove, to the carpeted floor—is practical and efficient. These furnishings immediately convey to audiences the stability of the family as well as its core values.

Scenery and Lighting

Playwrights often use **scenery** and **lighting** to create imaginative stage settings. As the curtain rises at the beginning of *The Glass Menagerie*, the audience sees "the dark, grim rear wall of the Wingfield tenement" that "runs parallel to the footlights" and is flanked by alleyways and "murkey canons of tangled clotheslines." After Tom's opening monologue, the wall of the tenement slowly fades, revealing the interior of The Windfield's ground floor apartment. (This effect is achieved by using a **scrim**, a curtain that appears solid when illuminated from the front but transparent when illuminated from the back.) During the play, shafts of light draw attention to various characters, and in one instance a "clear pool of light" illuminates Laura throughout an entire scene, emphasizing her innocence and fragility. Lighting also enables the audience to discern the mental state of characters. For example, when Amanda angrily confronts Tom, "gesticulating shadows are cast on the ceiling" in a "fiery glow."

Contemporary playwrights often use sets that combine realistic and nonrealistic elements. In his Tony Award–winning play M. *Butterfly*, for example, David Henry Hwang employs a large red lacquered ramp that runs from the bottom to the top of the stage. The action takes place beneath, on, and above the ramp, creating an effect not unlike that created by Shakespeare's multiple stages. At several points in the play, a character who acts as the narrator sits beneath the ramp, addressing the audience, while at the same time a character on top of the ramp acts out the narrator's words.

Music and Sound Effects

Staging involves more than visual elements such as costumes and scenery; it also involves **music** and **sound effects**. The stage directions for *Death of a Salesman*, for example, begin, "*A melody is heard, played upon a flute*." Although not specifically identified, the music is described as "*small and fine, telling of grass and trees and the horizon*." Significantly, this music stands in stark contrast to the claustrophobic urban setting of the play. Music also plays a major role in *The Glass Menagerie*, where a single recurring tune, like circus music, weaves in and out of the play. This musical motif gives emotional impact to certain lines and suggests the fantasy world into which Laura has retreated.

Sound effects play an important part in Henrik Ibsen's *A Doll's House*. At the very end of the play, after his wife has left him, Torvald Helmer sits alone on the stage. In the following stage directions, the final sound effect cuts short Torvald's attempt at self-deluding optimism:

Torvald: *(sinks down on a chair at the door and buries his face in his hands)* Nora! Nora! *(looks round and rises)* Empty. She's gone. *(a glimmer of hope flashes across his face)* The greatest miracle of all—?

(the sound of a door shutting is heard from below)

When you read a play, it may be difficult to appreciate the effect that staging can have on a performance. As you read, pay particular attention to the stage directions, and use your imagination to visualize the scenes the playwright describes. In addition, try to imagine the play's sights and sounds, and consider the options for staging that are suggested as characters speak to one another. Although careful reading cannot substitute for seeing a play performed, it can help you imagine the play as it might appear on the stage.

A Final Note

Because of a play's limited performance time, and because of space and financial limitations, not every action or event can be represented on stage. Frequently, incidents that would involve many actors or require elaborate scenery are only suggested. For example, a violent riot may be suggested by a single scuffle, a full-scale wedding by the kiss between bride and groom, a gala evening at the opera by a well-dressed group in box seats, and a trip to an exotic locale by a departure scene. Other events may be suggested by sounds offstage—for example, the roar of a crowd may suggest an athletic event.

Checklist Writing about Staging

- What information about staging is specified in the stage directions of the play?
- What information about staging is suggested by the play's dialogue?
- What information about staging is left to the imagination?
- How might different decisions about staging change the play?
- Do the stage directions provide information about how characters are supposed to look or behave?
- What costumes are specified? In what ways do costumes provide insight into the characters who wear them?
- What props play an important part in the play? Do these props have symbolic meaning?
- Is the scenery special or unusual in any way?
- What kind of lighting is specified by the stage directions? In what way does this lighting affect your reaction to the play?
- How are music and sound effects used in the play? Are musical themes associated with any characters? Do music or sound effects heighten the emotional impact of certain lines?
- What events occur offstage? Why? How are they suggested?
- How does staging help to communicate the play's themes?

Milcha Sanchez-Scott

MILCHA SANCHEZ-SCOTT (1953–) is a Los Angeles–based writer of plays that include *Dog Lady* and *The Cuban Swimmer,* both one-act plays (1984); *Roosters,* published in *On New Ground: Contemporary Hispanic American Plays* (1987) and adapted into the 1993 feature film of the same name; and *Stone Wedding,* produced at the Los Angeles Theater Center (1988). Also produced by the Los Angeles Theater Center was her play *Carmen,* adapted from Georges Bizet's opera of the same title.

Born in Bali, Sanchez-Scott is the daughter of an Indonesian mother and a Colombian Mexican father. Her early childhood was spent in Mexico, South America, and Britain; her family moved to San Diego when she was fourteen.

Writing in *Time* magazine, William A. Henry observes that the visionary or hallucinatory elements in Sanchez-Scott's plays derive from the Latin American "magic realism" tradition of Jorge Luis Borges and Gabriel García Márquez. For example, Henry notes that in *Roosters,* what seems "a straightforward depiction of the life of farmlands gives way to mysterious visitations, symbolic cockfights enacted by dancers, virginal girls wearing wings, archetypal confrontations between father and son."

In 1984, the New York production of *The Cuban Swimmer* was noteworthy for an ingeniously designed set that realistically re-created on stage Pacific Ocean waves, a helicopter, and a boat. According to the *New York Times,* "The audience [could] almost feel the resisting tides and the California oil slick . . . represented by a watery-blue floor and curtain." Jeannette Mirabel, as the Cuban swimmer, made an "auspicious" debut in the play, according to the *Times:* "In a tour de force of balletic movements, she [kept] her arms fluttering in the imaginary waters throughout the play."

Cultural Context In 1980, in the wake of numerous incidences of dissent and rebellion, Fidel Castro deported a large number of Cubans and encouraged many others to leave. In the resulting exodus, which became known as the Mariel boatlift, more than 120,000 Cuban refugees arrived in Florida, placing tremendous strain on United States resources. In 1984, an agreement was made between the two countries that limited the number of Cuban immigrants to 20,000 per year. Over time, the United States relaxed this quota, but the resulting abundance of refugees prompted the United States government to reinstate the quota in the mid-1990s. In 1996, the Cuban Adjustment Act was passed, stating that Cubans who reached dry land would be allowed to become permanent residents of the United States, but those who were intercepted while still at sea would be returned to Cuba. In 1999, the plight of Cuban refugees was reflected in the story of Elian Gonzalez, a six-year-old boy who was found clinging to an inner tube but was later returned to Cuba in accordance with the 1996 act. Starting in 2009, President Barack Obama, in an effort to open a dialogue with Cuba, eased some travel and economic restrictions.

The Cuban Swimmer (1984)

CHARACTERS

Margarita Suárez, *the swimmer*
Eduardo Suárez, *her father, the coach*
Simón Suárez, *her brother*
Aída Suárez, *her mother*
Abuela, *her grandmother*
Voice of Mel Munson
Voice of Mary Beth White
Voice of Radio Operator

SETTING

The Pacific Ocean between San Pedro and Catalina Island.

TIME

Summer.

Live conga drums can be used to punctuate the action of the play.

SCENE 1

Pacific Ocean. Midday. On the horizon, in perspective, a small boat enters upstage left, crosses to upstage right, and exits. Pause. Lower on the horizon, the same boat, in larger perspective, enters upstage right, crosses and exits upstage left. Blackout.

SCENE 2

Pacific Ocean. Midday. The swimmer, Margarita Suárez, is swimming. On the boat following behind her are her father, Eduardo Suárez, holding a megaphone, and Simón, her brother, sitting on top of the cabin with his shirt off, punk sunglasses on, binoculars hanging on his chest.

Eduardo: *(leaning forward, shouting in time to Margarita's swimming) Uno, dos, uno, dos. Y uno, dos...* keep your shoulders parallel to the water.

Simón: I'm gonna take these glasses off and look straight into the sun.

Joanna Liao as Margarita Suárez in a production of *The Cuban Swimmer*

Eduardo: *(through megaphone) Muy bien, muy bien…* but punch those arms in, baby.

Simón: *(looking directly at the sun through binoculars)* Come on, come on, zap me. Show me something. *(He looks behind at the shoreline and ahead at the sea.)* Stop! Stop, *Papi!* Stop!

Aída Suárez and Abuela, the swimmer's mother and grandmother, enter running from the back of the boat.

Aída and Abuela: *Qué? Qué es?*

Aída: *Es un* shark?

Eduardo: Eh?

Abuela: *Que es un* shark *dicen?*

Eduardo blows whistle. Margarita looks up at the boat.

Simón: No, *Papi*, no shark, no shark. We've reached the halfway mark.

Abuela: *(looking into the water)* A dónde está?

Aída: It's not in the water.

Abuela: Oh, no? Oh, no?

Aída: No! A *poco* do you think they're gonna have signs in the water to say you are halfway to Santa Catalina? No. It's done very scientific. A *ver, hijo*, explain it to your grandma.

Simón: Well, you see, Abuela—*(He points behind.)* There's San Pedro. *(He points ahead.)* And there's Santa Catalina. Looks halfway to me.

Abuela shakes her head and is looking back and forth, trying to make the decision, when suddenly the sound of a helicopter is heard.

Abuela: *(looking up) Virgencita de la Caridad del Cobre. Qué es eso?*

Sound of helicopter gets closer. Margarita looks up.

Margarita: *Papi, Papi!*

A small commotion on the boat, with everybody pointing at the helicopter above. Shadows of the helicopter fall on the boat. Simón looks up at it through binoculars.

Papi—qué es? What is it?

Eduardo: *(through megaphone)* Uh… uh… uh, *un momentico… mi hija….* Your *papi's* got everything under control, understand? Uh… you just keep stroking. And stay… uh… close to the boat.

Simón: Wow, *Papi!* We're on TV, man! Holy Christ, we're all over the fucking U.S.A.! It's Mel Munson and Mary Beth White!

Aída: *Por Dios!* Simón, don't swear. And put on your shirt.

Aída fluffs her hair, puts on her sunglasses and waves to the helicopter. Simón leans over the side of the boat and yells to Margarita.

Simón: Yo, Margo! You're on TV, man.

Eduardo: Leave your sister alone. Turn on the radio.

Margarita: Papi! Qué está pasando?

Abuela: Que es la televisión dicen? *(She shakes her head.)* Porque como yo no puedo ver nada sin mis espejuelos.

Abuela rummages through the boat, looking for her glasses. Voices of Mel Munson and Mary Beth White are heard over the boat's radio.

Mel's Voice: As we take a closer look at the gallant crew of *La Havana* ... and there... yes, there she is... the little Cuban swimmer from Long Beach, California, nineteen-year-old Margarita Suárez. The unknown swimmer is our Cinderella entry... a bundle of tenacity, battling her way through the choppy, murky waters of the cold Pacific to reach the Island of Romance... Santa Catalina... where should she be the first to arrive, two thousand dollars and a gold cup will be waiting for her.

Aída: Doesn't even cover our expenses.

Abuela: *Qué dice?*

Eduardo: Shhhh!

Mary Beth's Voice: This is really a family effort, Mel, and—

Mel's Voice: Indeed it is. Her trainer, her coach, her mentor, is her father, Eduardo Suárez. Not a swimmer himself, it says here, Mr. Suárez is head usher of the Holy Name Society and the owner-operator of Suárez Treasures of the Sea and Salvage Yard. I guess it's one of those places—

Mary Beth's Voice: If I might interject a fact here, Mel, assisting in this swim is Mrs. Suárez, who is a former Miss Cuba.

Mel's Voice: And a beautiful woman in her own right. Let's try and get a closer look.

Helicopter sound gets louder. Margarita, frightened, looks up again.

Margarita: *Papi!*

Eduardo: *(through megaphone) Mi hija*, don't get nervous... it's the press. I'm handling it.

Aída: I see how you're handling it.

Eduardo: *(through megaphone)* Do you hear? Everything is under control. Get back into your rhythm. Keep your elbows high and kick and kick and kick and kick...

Abuela: *(finds her glasses and puts them on) Ay sí, es la televisión... (She points to helicopter.) Qué lindo mira... (She fluffs her hair, gives a big wave.) Aló América! Viva mi Margarita, viva todo los Cubanos en los Estados Unidos!*

Aída: *Ay por Dios*, Cecilia, the man didn't come all this way in his helicopter to look at you jumping up and down, making a fool of yourself.

Abuela: I don't care. I'm proud.

Aída: He can't understand you anyway.

Abuela: Viva... *(She stops.)* Simón, comó se dice viva?

Simón: Hurray.

Abuela: Hurray for *mi Margarita y* for all the Cubans living *en* the United States, *y un abrazo... Simón, abrazo...*

Simón: A big hug.

Abuela: *Sí*, a big hug to all my friends in Miami, Long Beach, Union City, except for my son Carlos, who lives in New York in sin! He lives… *(she crosses herself)* in Brooklyn with a Puerto Rican woman in sin! *No decente…*

Simón: Decent.

Abuela: Carlos, *no decente*. This family, *decente*.

Aída: Cecilia, *por Dios*.

Mel's Voice: Look at that enthusiasm. The whole family has turned out to cheer little Margarita on to victory! I hope they won't be too disappointed.

Mary Beth's Voice: She seems to be making good time, Mel.

Mel's Voice: Yes, it takes all kinds to make a race. And it's a testimonial to the all-encompassing fairness… the greatness of this, the Wrigley Invitational Women's Swim to Catalina, where among all the professionals there is still room for the amateurs… like these, the simple people we see below us on the ragtag *La Havana*, taking their long-shot chance to victory. *Vaya con Dios!*

Helicopter sound fading as family, including Margarita, watch silently. Static as Simón turns radio off. Eduardo walks to bow of boat, looks out on the horizon.

Eduardo: *(to himself)* Amateurs.

Aída: Eduardo, that person insulted us. Did you hear, Eduardo? That he called us a simple people in a ragtag boat? Did you hear…?

Abuela: *(clenching her fist at departing helicopter) Mal-Rayo los parta!*

Simón: *(same gesture)* Asshole!

Aída follows Eduardo as he goes to side of boat and stares at Margarita.

Aída: This person comes in his helicopter to insult your wife, your family, your daughter…

Margarita: *(pops her head out of the water)* Papi?

Aída: Do you hear me, Eduardo? I am not simple.

Abuela: *Sí.*

Aída: I am complicated.

Abuela: *Sí, demasiada complicada.*

Aída: Me and my family are not so simple.

Simón: Mom, the guy's an asshole.

Abuela: *(shaking her fist at helicopter)* Asshole!

Aída: If my daughter was simple, she would not be in that water swimming.

Margarita: Simple? *Papi…?*

Aída: *Ahora*, Eduardo, this is what I want you to do. When we get to Santa Catalina, I want you to call the TV station and demand an apology.

Eduardo: *Cállete mujer! Aquí mando yo.* I will decide what is to be done.

Margarita: *Papi*, tell me what's going on.

Eduardo: Do you understand what I am saying to you, Aída?

Simón: *(leaning over side of boat, to Margarita)* Yo Margo! You know that Mel Munson guy on TV? He called you a simple amateur and said you didn't have a chance.

Abuela: *(leaning directly behind Simón.) Mi hija, insultó a la familia. Desgraciado!*

Aída: *(leaning in behind Abuela)* He called us peasants! And your father is not doing anything about it. He just knows how to yell at me.

Eduardo: *(through megaphone)* Shut up! All of you! Do you want to break her concentration? Is that what you are after? Eh?

Abuela, Aída, and Simón shrink back. Eduardo paces before them.

Swimming is rhythm and concentration. You win a race *aquí*. *(Pointing to his head.)* Now... *(to Simón)* you, take care of the boat, *Aída y Mama*... do something. Anything. Something practical.

Abuela and Aída get on knees and pray in Spanish.

Hija, give it everything, eh?... *por la familia. Uno... dos....* You must win.

Simón goes into cabin. The prayers continue as lights change to indicate bright sunlight, later in the afternoon.

SCENE 3

Tableau for a couple of beats. Eduardo on bow with timer in one hand as he counts strokes per minute. Simón is in the cabin steering, wearing his sunglasses, baseball cap on backward. Abuela and Aída are at the side of the boat, heads down, hands folded, still muttering prayers in Spanish.

Aída and Abuela: *(crossing themselves) En el nombre del Padre, del Hijo y del Espíritu Santo amén.*

Eduardo: *(through megaphone)* You're stroking seventy-two!

Simón: *(singing)* Mama's stroking, Mama's stroking seventy-two....

Eduardo: *(through megaphone)* You comfortable with it?

Simón: *(singing)* Seventy-two, seventy-two, seventy-two for you.

Aída: *(looking at the heavens)* Ay, Eduardo, *ven acá*, we should be grateful that *Nuestro Señor* gave us such a beautiful day.

Abuela: *(crosses herself) Si, gracias a Dios.*

Eduardo: She's stroking seventy-two, with no problem. *(He throws a kiss to the sky.)* It's a beautiful day to win.

Aída: *Qué hermoso!* So clear and bright. Not a cloud in the sky. *Mira! Mira!* Even rainbows on the water... a sign from God.

Simón: *(singing)* Rainbows on the water... you in my arms...

Abuela and Eduardo: *(Looking the wrong way.)* Dónde?

Aída: *(pointing toward Margarita)* There, dancing in front of Margarita, leading her on...

Eduardo: Rainbows on... Ay *coño!* It's an oil slick! You... you... *(To Simón.)* Stop the boat. *(Runs to bow, yelling.)* Margarita! Margarita!

On the next stroke, Margarita comes up all covered in black oil.

Margarita: *Papi! Papi… !*

Everybody goes to the side and stares at Margarita, who stares back. Eduardo freezes.

Aída: *Apúrate*, Eduardo, move… what's wrong with you… *no me oíste*, get my daughter out of the water.
Eduardo: *(softly)* We can't touch her. If we touch her, she's disqualified.
Aída: But I'm her mother.
Eduardo: Not even by her own mother. Especially by her own mother…. You always want the rules to be different for you, you always want to be the exception. *(To Simón.)* And you… you didn't see it, eh? You were playing again?
Simón: *Papi*, I was watching…
Aída: *(interrupting) Pues*, do something Eduardo. You are the big coach, the monitor.
Simón: Mentor! Mentor!
Eduardo: How can a person think around you? *(He walks off to bow, puts head in hands.)*
Abuela: *(looking over side) Mira como todos los* little birds are dead. *(She crosses herself.)*
Aída: Their little wings are glued to their sides.
Simón: Christ, this is like the La Brea tar pits.
Aída: They can't move their little wings.
Abuela: *Esa niña tiene que moverse.*
Simón: Yeah, Margo, you gotta move, man.

Abuela and Simón gesture for Margarita to move. Aída gestures for her to swim.

Abuela: *Anda niña, muévete.*
Aída: Swim, *hija*, swim or the *aceite* will stick to your wings.
Margarita: *Papi?*
Abuela: *(taking megaphone)* Your *papi* say "move it!"

Margarita with difficulty starts moving.

Abuela, Aída and Simón: *(laboriously counting) Uno, dos… uno, dos …. anda… uno, dos.*
Eduardo: *(running to take megaphone from Abuela) Uno, dos…*

Simón races into cabin and starts the engine. Abuela, Aída and Eduardo count together.

Simón: *(looking ahead) Papi*, it's over there!
Eduardo: Eh?
Simón: *(pointing ahead and to the right)* It's getting clearer over there.
Eduardo: *(through megaphone)* Now pay attention to me. Go to the right.

Simón, Abuela, Aída and Eduardo all lean over side. They point ahead and to the right, except Abuela, who points to the left.

Family: *(shouting together) Para yá! Para yá!*

Lights go down on boat. A special light on Margarita, swimming through the oil, and on Abuela, watching her.

Abuela: *Sangre de mi sangre*, you will be another to save us. *En* Bolondron, where your great-grandmother Luz Suárez was born, they say one day it rained blood. All the people, they run into their houses. They cry, they pray, *pero* your great-grandmother Luz she had *cojones* like a man. She run outside. She look straight at the sky. She shake her fist. And she say to the evil one, "*Mira... (beating her chest) coño, Diablo, aquí estoy si me quieres.*" And she open her mouth, and she drunk the blood.

Blackout

SCENE 4

Lights up on boat. Aída and Eduardo are on deck watching Margarita swim. We hear the gentle, rhythmic lap, lap, lap of the water, then the sound of inhaling and exhaling as Margarita's breathing becomes louder. Then Margarita's heartbeat is heard, with the lapping of the water and the breathing under it. These sounds continue beneath the dialogue to the end of the scene.

Aída: *Dios mío*. Look how she moves through the water....

Eduardo: You see, it's very simple. It is a matter of concentration.

Aída: The first time I put her in water she came to life, she grew before my eyes. She moved, she smiled, she loved it more than me. She didn't want my breast any longer. She wanted the water.

Eduardo: And of course, the rhythm. The rhythm takes away the pain and helps the concentration.

Pause. Aída and Eduardo watch Margarita.

Aída: Is that my child or a seal....

Eduardo: Ah, a seal, the reason for that is that she's keeping her arms very close to her body. She cups her hands, and then she reaches and digs, reaches and digs.

Aída: To think that a daughter of mine...

Eduardo: It's the training, the hours in the water. I used to tie weights around her little wrists and ankles.

Aída: A spirit, an ocean spirit, must have entered my body when I was carrying her.

Eduardo: *(to Margarita)* Your stroke is slowing down.

Pause. We hear Margarita's heartbeat with the breathing under, faster now.

Aída: Eduardo, that night, the night on the boat...

Eduardo: Ah, the night on the boat again… the moon was…

Aída: The moon was full. We were coming to America…. *Qué romantico.*

Heartbeat and breathing continue.

Eduardo: We were cold, afraid, with no money, and on top of everything, you were hysterical, yelling at me, tearing at me with your nails. *(Opens his shirt, points to the base of his neck.)* Look, I still bear the scars… telling me that I didn't know what I was doing… saying that we were going to die….

Aída: You took me, you stole me from my home… you didn't give me a chance to prepare. You just said we have to go now, now! Now, you said. You didn't let me take anything. I left everything behind…. I left everything behind.

Eduardo: Saying that I wasn't good enough, that your father didn't raise you so that I could drown you in the sea.

Aída: You didn't let me say even a good-bye. You took me, you stole me, you tore me from my home.

Eduardo: I took you so we could be married.

Aída: That was in Miami. But that night on the boat, Eduardo…. We were not married, that night on the boat.

Eduardo: *No pasó nada!* Once and for all get it out of your head, it was cold, you hated me, and we were afraid….

Aída: Mentiroso!

Eduardo: A man can't do it when he is afraid.

Aída: Liar! You did it very well.

Eduardo: I did?

Aída: *Sí.* Gentle. You were so gentle and then strong… my passion for you so deep. Standing next to you… I would ache… looking at your hands I would forget to breathe, you were irresistible.

Eduardo: I was?

Aída: You took me into your arms, you touched my face with your fingertips… you kissed my eyes… *la esquina de la boca y*…

Eduardo: *Sí, sí*, and then…

Aída: I look at your face on top of mine, and I see the lights of Havana in your eyes. That's when you seduced me.

Eduardo: Shhh, they're gonna hear you.

Lights go down. Special on Aída.

Aída: That was the night. A woman doesn't forget those things… and later that night was the dream… the dream of a big country with fields of fertile land and big, giant things growing. And there by a green, slimy pond I found a giant pea pod and when I opened it, it was full of little, tiny baby frogs.

Aída crosses herself as she watches Margarita. We hear louder breathing and heartbeat.

Margarita: Santa Teresa. Little Flower of God, pray for me. San Martín de Porres, pray for me. Santa Rosa de Lima, *Virgencita de la Caridad del Cobre*, pray for me.... Mother pray for me.

SCENE 5

Loud howling of wind is heard, as lights change to indicate unstable weather, fog and mist. Family on deck, braced and huddled against the wind. Simón is at the helm.

Aída: *Ay Dios mío, qué viento.*

Eduardo: *(through megaphone)* Don't drift out... that wind is pushing you out. *(To Simón.)* You! Slow down. Can't you see your sister is drifting out?

Simón: It's the wind, *Papi.*

Aída: Baby, don't go so far....

Abuela: *(to heaven) Ay Gran Poder de Dios, quita este maldito viento.*

Simón: Margo! Margo! Stay close to the boat.

Eduardo: Dig in. Dig in hard.... Reach down from your guts and dig in.

Abuela: *(to heaven) Ay Virgen de la Caridad del Cobre, por lo más tú quieres a pararla.*

Aída: *(putting her hand out, reaching for Margarita)* Baby, don't go far.

Abuela crosses herself. Action freezes. Lights get dimmer, special on Margarita. She keeps swimming, stops, starts again, stops, then, finally exhausted, stops altogether. The boat stops moving.

Eduardo: What's going on here? Why are we stopping?

Simón: *Papi*, she's not moving! Yo Margo!

The family all run to the side.

Eduardo: *Hija!... Hijita!* You're tired, eh?

Aída: *Por supuesto* she's tired. I like to see you get in the water, waving your arms and legs from San Pedro to Santa Catalina. A person isn't a machine, a person has to rest.

Simón: Yo, Mama! Cool out, it ain't fucking brain surgery.

Eduardo: *(to Simón)* Shut up, you. *(Louder to Margarita.)* I guess your mother's right for once, huh?... I guess you had to stop, eh?... Give your brother, the idiot... a chance to catch up with you.

Simón: *(clowning like Mortimer Snerd)* Dum dee dum dee dum ooops, ah shucks...

Eduardo: I don't think he's Cuban.

Simón: *(like Ricky Ricardo)* Oye, Lucy! I'm home! Ba ba lu!

Eduardo: *(joins in clowning, grabbing Simón in a headlock)* What am I gonna do with this idiot, eh? I don't understand this idiot. He's not like us, Margarita. *(Laughing.)* You think if we put him into your bathing suit with a cap on his head... *(He laughs hysterically.)* You think anyone would know... huh? Do you think anyone would know? *(Laughs.)*

Simón: *(vamping)* Ay, *mi amor*. Anybody looking for tits would know.

Eduardo slaps Simón across the face, knocking him down. Aída runs to Simón's aid. Abuela holds Eduardo back.

Margarita: *Mía culpa! Mía culpa!*

Abuela: *Qué dices hija?*

Margarita: *Papi*, it's my fault, it's all my fault.... I'm so cold, I can't move.... I put my face in the water... and I hear them whispering .... laughing at me....

Aída: Who is laughing at you?

Margarita: The fish are all biting me... they hate me... they whisper about me. She can't swim, they say. She can't glide. She has no grace.... Yellowtails, bonita, tuna, man-o'-war, snub-nose sharks, *los baracudas*... they all hate me... only the dolphins care... and sometimes I hear the whales crying... she is lost, she is dead. I'm so numb, I can't feel. *Papi! Papi!* Am I dead?

Eduardo: *Vamos*, baby, punch those arms in. Come on... do you hear me?

Margarita: *Papi... Papi...* forgive me....

All is silent on the boat. Eduardo drops his megaphone, his head bent down in dejection. Abuela, Aída, Simón, all leaning over the side of the boat. Simón slowly walks away.

Aída: *Mi hija, qué tienes?*

Simón: Oh, Christ, don't make her say it. Please don't make her say it.

Abuela: Say what? *Qué cosa?*

Simón: She wants to quit, can't you see she's had enough?

Abuela: *Mira, para eso. Esta niña* is turning blue.

Aída: *Oyeme, mi hija.* Do you want to come out of the water?

Margarita: *Papi?*

Simón: *(to Eduardo)* She won't come out until *you* tell her.

Aída: Eduardo... answer your daughter.

Eduardo: *Le dije* to concentrate... concentrate on your rhythm. Then the rhythm would carry her... ay, it's a beautiful thing, Aída. It's like yoga, like meditation, the mind over matter... the mind controlling the body... that's how the great things in the world have been done. I wish you... I wish my wife could understand.

Margarita: *Papi?*

Simón: *(to Margarita)* Forget him.

Aída: *(imploring)* Eduardo, *por favor*.

Eduardo: *(walking in circles)* Why didn't you let her concentrate? Don't you understand, the concentration, the rhythm is everything. But no, you wouldn't listen. *(Screaming to the ocean.)* Goddamn Cubans, why, God, why do you make us go everywhere with our families? *(He goes to back of boat.)*

Aída: *(opening her arms)* *Mi hija, ven*, come to Mami. (Rocking.) Your *mami* knows.

Abuela has taken the training bottle, puts it in a net. She and Simón lower it to Margarita.

Simón: Take this. Drink it. *(As Margarita drinks, Abuela crosses herself.)*
Abuela: *Sangre de mi sangre.*

Music comes up softly. Margarita drinks, gives the bottle back, stretches out her arms, as if on a cross. Floats on her back. She begins a graceful backstroke. Lights fade on boat as special lights come up on Margarita. She stops. Slowly turns over and starts to swim, gradually picking up speed. Suddenly as if in pain she stops, tries again, then stops in pain again. She becomes disoriented and falls to the bottom of the sea. Special on Margarita at the bottom of the sea.

Margarita: Ya no puedo… I can't.… A person isn't a machine… *es mi culpa…* Father forgive me… *Papi! Papi!* One, two. *Uno, dos. (Pause.) Papi! A dónde estás? (Pause.)* One, two, one, two. *Papi! Ay, Papi!* Where are you… ? Don't leave me.… Why don't you answer me? *(Pause. She starts to swim, slowly.) Uno, dos, uno, dos.* Dig in, dig in. *(Stops swimming.) Por favor, Papi! (Starts to swim again.)* One, two, one, two. Kick from your hip, kick from your hip. *(Stops swimming. Starts to cry.)* Oh God, please.… *(Pause.)* Hail Mary, full of grace… dig in, dig in… the Lord is with thee.… *(She swims to the rhythm of her Hail Mary.)* Hail Mary, full of grace… dig in, dig in… the Lord is with thee… dig in, dig in.… Blessed art thou among women.… *Mami,* it hurts. You let go of my hand. I'm lost.… And blessed is the fruit of thy womb, now and at the hour of our death. Amen. I don't want to die, I don't want to die.

Margarita is still swimming. Blackout. She is gone.

SCENE 6

Lights up on boat, we hear radio static. There is a heavy mist. On deck we see only black outline of Abuela with shawl over her head. We hear the voices of Eduardo, Aída, and Radio Operator.

Eduardo's Voice: *La Havana!* Coming from San Pedro. Over.
Radio Operator's Voice: Right, DT6-6, you say you've lost a swimmer.
Aída's Voice: Our child, our only daughter… listen to me. Her name is Margarita Inez Suárez, she is wearing a black one-piece bathing suit cut high in the legs with a white racing stripe down the sides, a white bathing cap with goggles and her whole body covered with a … with a…
Eduardo's Voice: With lanolin and paraffin.
Aída's Voice: *Sí… con* lanolin and paraffin.

More radio static. Special on Simón, on the edge of the boat.

Simón: Margo! Yo Margo! *(Pause.)* Man don't do this. *(Pause.)* Come on.… Come on.… *(Pause.)* God, why does everything have to be so hard? *(Pause.)* Stupid. You know you're not supposed to die for this. Stupid. It's his dream and he can't even swim. *(Pause.)* Punch those arms in. Come home. Come home. I'm your little brother. Don't forget what Mama said. You're not supposed to leave me behind. *Vamos*, Margarita, take your little brother, hold his hand tight when you cross the street. He's so little. *(Pause.)* Oh, Christ, give us a sign.... I know! I know! Margo, I'll send you a message... like mental telepathy. I'll hold my breath, close my eyes, and I'll bring you home. *(He takes a deep breath; a few beats.)* This time I'll beep... I'll send out sonar signals like a dolphin. *(He imitates dolphin sounds.)*

The sound of real dolphins takes over from Simón, then fades into sound of Abuela saying the Hail Mary in Spanish, as full lights come up slowly.

SCENE 7

Eduardo coming out of cabin, sobbing, Aída holding him. Simón anxiously scanning the horizon. Abuela looking calmly ahead.

Eduardo: *Es mi culpa, sí, es mi culpa. (He hits his chest.)*

Aída: *Ya, ya viejo*... it was my sin... I left my home.

Eduardo: Forgive me, forgive me. I've lost our daughter, our sister, our granddaughter, *mi carne, mi sangre, mis ilusiones. (To heaven.) Dios mío*, take me... take me, I say... Goddammit, take me!

Simón: I'm going in.

Aída and Eduardo: No!

Eduardo: *(grabbing and holding Simón, speaking to heaven)* God, take me, not my children. They are my dreams, my illusions... and not this one, this one is my mystery... he has my secret dreams. In him are the parts of me I cannot see.

Eduardo embraces Simón. Radio static becomes louder.

Aída: I... I think I see her.

Simón: No, it's just a seal.

Abuela: *(looking out with binoculars) Mi nietacita, dónde estás? (She feels her heart.)* I don't feel the knife in my heart... my little fish is not lost.

Radio crackles with static. As lights dim on boat, Voices of Mel and Mary Beth are heard over the radio.

Mel's Voice: Tragedy has marred the face of the Wrigley Invitational Women's Race to Catalina. The Cuban swimmer, little Margarita Suárez, has reportedly been lost at sea. Coast Guard and divers are looking for her as we speak. Yet in spite of this tragedy the race must go on because...

Mary Beth's Voice: *(interrupting loudly)* Mel!

Mel's Voice: *(startled)* What!

Mary Beth's Voice: Ah… excuse me, Mel… we have a winner. We've just received word from Catalina that one of the swimmers is just fifty yards from the breakers… it's, oh, it's… Margarita Suárez!

Special on family in cabin listening to radio.

Mel's Voice: What? I thought she died!

Special on Margarita, taking off bathing cap, trophy in hand, walking on the water.

Mary Beth's Voice: Ahh… unless… unless this is a tragic… No …. there she is, Mel. Margarita Suárez! The only one in the race wearing a black bathing suit cut high in the legs with a racing stripe down the side.

Family cheering, embracing.

Simón: *(screaming)* Way to go, Margo!

Mel's Voice: This is indeed a miracle! It's a resurrection! Margarita Suárez, with a flotilla of boats to meet her, is now walking on the waters, through the breakers… onto the beach, with crowds of people cheering her on. What a jubilation! This is a miracle!

Sound of crowds cheering. Lights and cheering sounds fade.

Blackout

* * *

Reading and Reacting

1. What lighting and sound effects do the stage directions specify? In what way do these effects advance the action of the play? How do they help to communicate the play's theme?
2. Although most of the play is in English, the characters frequently speak Spanish. What are the advantages and disadvantages of this use of Spanish? How does the mixing of English and Spanish reflect one of the play's themes?
3. What function do the voices of Mel and Mary Beth serve in the play?
4. What conflicts develop among the family members as the play proceeds? Do you think these conflicts are meant to represent the problems of other immigrant groups?
5. In what sense is Mel's final comment "This is a miracle!" true? In what sense is it ironic?
6. Could this play be seen as an allegory? What is the value of seeing it in this way?
7. During much of the play, Margarita is swimming in full view of the audience. Suggest three ways in which a director could convey this effect on stage. Which way would you choose if you were directing the play? Why?

8. As the headnote to the play explains, the 1984 New York production of *The Cuban Swimmer* had an extremely realistic set. Could the play be staged unrealistically, with the characters on a raised platform instead of a boat? How do you think this kind of set would change the audience's reaction?
9. **Journal Entry** Are you able to empathize with Margarita's struggle? What elements of the play make it easy (or difficult) for you to do so?
10. **Critical Perspective** In a 1998 article in the *New York Times*, theater critic Brooks Atkinson said, "Nothing is better for good actors than a stage with no scenery."

    How do you interpret Atkinson's comment? Do you think this remark could be applied to the staging of *The Cuban Swimmer*?

Related Works: "The Secret Lion" (p. 222), "Two Kinds" (p. 471), "Baca Grande" (p. 532), "Harlem" (p. 561), "Isla" (p. 654)

Bettmann/Getty Images

SOPHOCLES (496–406 B.C.), along with Aeschylus and Euripides, is one of the three great ancient Greek tragic dramatists. He lived during the flowering and subsequent decline of fifth-century B.C. Athens—the high point of Greek civilization. Born as Greece struggled against the Persian Empire and moved to adopt democracy, he lived as an adult under Pericles during the golden age of Athens and died as it became clear that Athens would lose the Peloponnesian War. Sophocles was an active participant in the public life of Athens, serving as a collector of tribute from Athenian subjects and later as a general. He wrote at least 120 plays, but only seven have survived, including three plays about Oedipus: *Oedipus the King* (c. 430 B.C.), *Oedipus at Colonus* (411? B.C.), and *Antigone* (441 B.C.).

Oedipus the King, or *Oedipus Rex* (sometimes called *Oedipus the Tyrant*), was performed shortly after a great plague in Athens (probably in 429 or 425 B.C.) and as Athens was falling into decline. The play opens with an account of a plague in Thebes, Oedipus's kingdom. Over the years, *Oedipus the King* has attracted impressive critical attention, from Aristotle's use of it as a model for his definition of tragedy to Freud's use of it when he discusses the Oedipus complex.

Cultural Context During the period in which *Oedipus* was written, the Greeks were especially interested in the relationship between greatness and *hubris*, the excessive pride and ambition that leads to the downfall of a hero in classical tragedy. They were fascinated by the idea that hubris can bring destruction: that the same traits that can elevate a person to greatness can also cause ruin. This theme recurs throughout classical literature and was especially relevant between 431 and 404 B.C. when the second Peloponnesian War (which Athens lost) was being fought between Athens and Sparta. After a Spartan army invaded Attica in 431 B.C., the Athenians retreated behind the walls of their city while the Athenian fleet began raids. Between 430 and 428 B.C., a plague (which the Athenians believed was inflicted upon them by the gods) wiped out at least a quarter of the Athenian population. It was during this tumultuous time that Sophocles wrote of Oedipus and his troubles.

Oedipus the King (429 BC)

Translated by Ian Johnston

DRAMATIS PERSONAE

Oedipus: *king of Thebes*
Priest: *the high priest of Thebes*
Creon: *Oedipus' brother-in-law*
Chorus *of Theban elders*
Teiresias: *an old blind prophet*
Boy: *attendant on Teiresias*
Jocasta: *wife of Oedipus, sister of Creon*
Messenger: *an old man*
Servant: *an old shepherd*
Second Messenger: *a servant of Oedipus*
Antigone: *daughter of Oedipus and Jocasta, a child*
Ismene: *daughter of Oedipus and Jocasta, a child*
Servants and **Attendants** *on Oedipus and Jocasta*

The action takes place in Thebes in front of the royal palace. The main doors are directly facing the audience. There are altars beside the doors. A crowd of citizens carrying laurel branches garlanded with wool and led by the PRIEST has gathered in front of the altars, with some people sitting on the altar steps. OEDIPUS enters through the palace doors.

Laurence Olivier as Oedipus
Merlyn Severn/Picture Post/Getty Images

Oedipus: My children, latest generation born from Cadmus,
why are you sitting here with wreathed sticks
in supplication to me, while the city
fills with incense, chants, and cries of pain?[1]
Children, it would not be appropriate for me
to learn of this from any other source,
so I have come in person—I, Oedipus,

[1] *cries of pain*: Cadmus was the legendary founder of Thebes. Hence, the citizens of Thebes were often called children of Cadmus or Cadmeians.

whose fame all men acknowledge. But you there,
old man, tell me—you seem to be the one
who ought to speak for those assembled here.
What feeling brings you to me—fear or desire?
You can be confident that I will help.
I shall assist you willingly in every way.
I would be a hard-hearted man indeed,
if I did not pity suppliants like these.

Priest: Oedipus, ruler of my native land,
you see how people here of every age
are crouching down around your altars,
some fledglings barely strong enough to fly
and others bent by age, with priests as well—
for I'm priest of Zeus—and these ones here,
the pick of all our youth. The other groups
sit in the market place with suppliant branches
or else in front of Pallas' two shrines,
or where Ismenus prophesies with fire.[2]
For our city, as you yourself can see,
is badly shaken—she cannot raise her head
above the depths of so much surging death.
Disease infects fruit blossoms in our land,
disease infects our herds of grazing cattle,
makes women in labour lose their children,
and deadly pestilence, that fiery god,
swoops down to blast the city, emptying
the House of Cadmus, and fills black Hades
with groans and howls. These children and myself
now sit here by your home, not because we think
you're equal to the gods. No. We judge you
the first of men in what happens in this life
and in our interactions with the gods.
For you came here, to our Cadmeian city,
and freed us from the tribute we were paying
to that cruel singer—and yet you knew
no more than we did and had not been taught.[3]
In their stories, the people testify
how, with gods' help, you gave us back our lives.

---

[2] *or else… with fire: Pallas Athena.* There were two shrines to her in Thebes. *Ismenus*: A temple to Apollo Ismenios where burnt offerings were the basis for the priest's divination.

[3] *cruel singer… been taught*: A reference to the Sphinx, a monster with the body of a lion, wings, and the head and torso of a woman. After the death of king Laius, the Sphinx tyrannized Thebes by not letting anyone into or out of the city, unless the person could answer the following riddle: "What walks on four legs in the morning, on two legs at noon, and three legs in the evening?" Those who could not answer were killed and eaten. Oedipus provided the answer (a human being), and thus saved the city. The Sphinx then died by suicide.

So now, Oedipus, our king, most powerful
in all men's eyes, we're here as suppliants,
all begging you to find some help for us,
either by listening to a heavenly voice,
or learning from some other human being.
For, in my view, men of experience
provide advice that gives the best results.
So now, you best of men, raise up our state.
Act to consolidate your fame, for now,
thanks to your eagerness in earlier days,
the city celebrates you as its saviour.
Don't let our memory of your ruling here
declare that we were first set right again
and later fell. No. Restore our city,
so that it stands secure. In those times past
you brought us joy—and with good omens, too.
Be that same man today. If you're to rule
as you are doing now, better to be king
in a land of men than in a desert.
An empty ship or city wall is nothing
if no men share a life together there.

Oedipus: My poor children, I know why you have come—
I am not ignorant of what you yearn for.
For I understand that you are ill, and yet,
sick as you are, there is not one of you
whose illness equals mine. Your agony
comes to each one of you as his alone,
a special pain for him and no one else.
But here in my heart, I sorrow for myself,
and for the city, and for you—all together.
You are not rousing me from a deep sleep.
You must know I've been shedding many tears
and, in my wandering thoughts, exploring
many pathways. After a careful search
I grasped the only help that I could find
and acted on it. So I have sent away
my brother-in-law, son of Menoeceus,
Creon, to Pythian Apollo's shrine,
to learn from him what I might do or say
to save our city. But when I count the days—
the time he's been away—I now worry
what he's doing. For he's been gone too long,
well past the time he should have taken.
But when he comes, I'll be a wicked man
if I do not act on all the god reveals.

Priest: What you have said is most appropriate,
for these men here have just informed me
that Creon is approaching.
Oedipus: Lord Apollo,
as he returns may fine shining fortune,
bright as his countenance, attend on him.
Priest: It seems the news he brings is good—if not,
he would not wear that wreath around his head,
a laurel thickly packed with berries.[4]
Oedipus: We'll know soon enough—he's within earshot.

Enter CREON. OEDIPUS calls to him as he approaches.

My royal kinsman, child of Menoeceus,
what message do you bring us from the god?
Creon: Good news, I tell you. If things work out well,
then these troubles, so difficult to bear,
will end up bringing us great benefits.
Oedipus: What is the oracle? So far your words
inspire in me no confidence or fear.
Creon: If you wish to hear the news in public,
I'm prepared to speak. Or we could step inside.
Oedipus: Speak out to everyone. The grief I feel
for these citizens is even greater
than any pain I feel for my own life.
Creon: Then let me report what I heard from the god.
Lord Phoebus clearly orders us to drive away
the polluting stain this land has harboured.
It will not be healed if we keep nursing it.
Oedipus: What sort of cleansing? And this disaster—
how did it happen?
Creon: By banishment—
or atone for murder by shedding blood again,
for blood brings on the storm which blasts our state.
Oedipus: And the one whose fate the god revealed—
what sort of man is he?
Creon: Before you came, my lord,
to steer our ship of state, Laius ruled this land.
Oedipus: I have heard that, but I never saw the man.
Creon: Laius was killed. And now the god is clear:
those murderers, he tells us, must be punished,
whoever they may be.
Oedipus: And where are they?
In what country? Where am I to find a trace
of this ancient crime? It will be hard to track.

[4]*berries*: a suppliant to Apollo's shrine characteristically wore such a garland if he received favourable news.

Creon: Here in Thebes, so said the god. What is sought
is found, but what is overlooked escapes.
Oedipus: When Laius fell in bloody death, where was he—
at home, or in his fields, or in another land?
Creon: He was abroad, on his way to Delphi—
that's what he told us. He began the trip,
but did not return.
Oedipus: Was there no messenger—
no companion who made the journey with him
and witnessed what took place—a person
who might provide some knowledge men could use?
Creon: They all died—except for one who was afraid
and ran away. There was only one thing
he could inform us of with confidence
about the things he saw.
Oedipus: What was that?
We might get somewhere if we had one fact—
we could find many things, if we possessed
some slender hope to get us going.
Creon: He told us it was robbers who attacked them—
not just a single man, a gang of them—
they came on with force and killed him.
Oedipus: How would a thief have dared to do this,
unless he had financial help from Thebes?
Creon: That's what we guessed. But once Laius was dead
we were in trouble, so no one sought revenge.
Oedipus: When the ruling king had fallen in this way,
what bad trouble blocked your path, preventing you
from looking into it?
Creon: It was the Sphinx—
she sang her cryptic song and so forced us
to put aside something we found obscure
to look into the problem we now faced.
Oedipus: Then I will start afresh, and once again
shed light on darkness. It is most fitting
that Apollo demonstrates his care
for the dead man, and worthy of you, too.
And so you'll see how I will work with you,
as is right, seeking vengeance for this land,
as well as for the god. This polluting stain
I will remove, not for some distant friends,
but for myself. For whoever killed this man
may soon enough desire to turn his hand
to punish me in the same way, as well.
Thus, in avenging Laius, I serve myself.
But now, my children, quickly as you can

stand up from these altar steps and raise
your suppliant branches. Someone must call
the Theban people to assemble here.
I'll do everything I can. With the god's help
this will all come to light successfully,
or else will prove our common ruin.

OEDIPUS and CREON go into the palace.

Priest: Let us get up, children. For this man
has willingly declared just what we came for.
And may Phoebus, who sent this oracle,
come as our saviour and end our sickness.

The PRIEST and the CITIZENS leave. Enter the CHORUS OF THEBAN ELDERS.

Chorus: O sweet speaking voice of Zeus,
you have come to glorious Thebes from golden Pytho—
but what is your intent?
My fearful heart twists on the rack and shakes with fear.
O Delian healer, for whom we cry aloud
in holy awe, what obligation
will you demand from me, a thing unknown
or now renewed with the revolving years?
Immortal voice, O child of golden Hope,
speak to me!
First I call on you, Athena the immortal,
daughter of Zeus, and on your sister, too,
Artemis, who guards our land and sits
on her glorious round throne in our market place,
and on Phoebus, who shoots from far away.
O you three guardians against death,
appear to me!
If before now you have ever driven off
a fiery plague to keep disaster
from the city and have banished it,
then come to us this time as well!
Alas, the pains I bear are numberless—
my people now all sick with plague,
our minds can find no weapons
to help with our defence. Now the offspring
of our splendid earth no longer grow,
nor do our women crying out in labour
get their relief from a living new-born child.
As you can see—one by one they swoop away,
off to the shores of the evening god, like birds
faster than fire which no one can resist.

Our city dies—we've lost count of all the dead.
Her sons lie in the dirt unpitied, unlamented.
Corpses spread the pestilence, while youthful wives
and grey-haired mothers on the altar steps
wail everywhere and cry in supplication,
seeking to relieve their agonizing pain.
Their solemn chants ring out—
they mingle with the voices of lament.
O Zeus' golden daughter,
send your support and strength,
your lovely countenance!
And that ravenous Ares, god of killing,
who now consumes me as he charges on
with no bronze shield but howling battle cries,
let him turn his back and quickly leave this land,
with a fair following wind to carry him
to the great chamber of Amphitrite
or inhospitable waves of Thrace.[5]
For if destruction does not come at night,
then day arrives to see it does its work.
O you who wield that mighty flash of fire,
O father Zeus, with your lighting blast
let Ares be destroyed!
O Lycean lord, how I wish those arrows
from the golden string of your bent bow
with their all-conquering force would wing out
to champion us against our enemy,
and I pray for those blazing fires of Artemis
with which she races through the Lycian hills.[6]
I call the god who binds his hair with gold,
the one whose name our country shares,
the one to whom the Maenads shout their cries,
Dionysus with his radiant face—
may he come to us with his flaming torchlight,
our ally against Ares,
a god dishonoured among gods.[7]

Enter OEDIPUS from the palace.

Oedipus: You pray. But if you listen now to me,
you'll get your wish. Hear what I have to say
and treat your own disease—then you may hope

[5] *and that ravenous… waves of Thrace*: *Ares*: God of war and killing, was often disapproved of by the major Olympian deities. *Amphitrite*: Was a goddess of the sea, married to Poseidon.

[6] *Lyceian hills*: The "Lyceian Lord" addressed here is a reference to Apollo, god of light.

[7] *… among gods*: Dionysus was also called Bacchus, and Thebes was sometimes called Baccheia (belonging to Bacchus). The *Maenads* are the followers of Dionysus.

to find relief from your distress. I speak
as one who is a stranger to the story,
a stranger to the crime. If I alone
were tracking down this act, I'd not get far
without a single clue. But as things stand,
for it was after the event that I became
a citizen of Thebes, I now proclaim
the following to all of you Cadmeians:
Whoever among you knows the man it was
who murdered Laius, son of Labdacus,
I order him to reveal it all to me.
And if the killer is afraid, I tell him
to avoid the danger of the major charge
by speaking out against himself. If so,
he will be sent out from this land unhurt
and undergo no further punishment.
If someone knows the killer is a stranger,
from some other state, let him not stay mute.
As well as a reward, he'll earn my thanks.
But if he remains quiet, if anyone,
through fear, hides himself or a friend of his
against my orders, here's what I shall do—
so listen to my words. For I decree
that no one in this land, in which I rule
as your own king, shall give that killer shelter
or talk to him, whoever he may be,
or act in concert with him during prayers,
or sacrifice, or sharing lustral water.[8]
Ban him from your homes, every one of you,
for he is our pollution, as the Pythian god
In this, I'm acting as an ally of the god
and also of dead Laius. And I pray
whoever the man is who did this crime,
one unknown person acting on his own
or with companions, the worst of agonies
will wear out his wretched life. I pray, too,
that, if he should become an honoured guest
in my own home and with my knowledge,
I may suffer all those things I've just called down
upon the killers. And I urge you now
to make sure all these orders take effect,
for my sake, for the sake of the god,
and for our barren, godless, ruined land.

[8] *lustral water:* Water purified in a communal religious ritual.

For in this matter, even if a god
were not urging us, it would not be right
for you to simply leave things as they are
and not to purify the murder of a man
who was so noble and who was your king.
You should have looked into it. But now I
possess the ruling power which Laius held
in earlier days. I have his bed and wife—
she would have borne his children, if his hopes
to have a son had not been disappointed.
Children from a common mother might have linked
Laius and myself. But as it turned out,
Fate swooped down onto his head. So now,
I'll fight on his behalf, as if this matter
concerned my own father, and I will strive
to do everything I can to find him,
the man who spilled his blood, and thus avenge
the son of Labdacus and Polydorus,
of Cadmus and Agenor from old times.[9]
As for those who do not follow what I urge,
I pray the gods send them no fertile land,
no, nor any children in their women's wombs—
may they all perish in our present fate
or one more hateful still. To you others,
you Cadmeians who support my efforts,
may Justice, our ally, and all the gods
attend on us with kindness all our days.

Chorus Leader: My lord, since you extend your oath to me,
I will say this. I am not the murderer,
nor can I tell you who the killer is.
As for what you're seeking, it's for Apollo,
who launched this search, to state who did it.

Oedipus: That is well said. But no man has power
to force the gods to speak against their will.

Chorus Leader: May I then suggest what seems to me
the next best course of action?

Oedipus: You may indeed,
and if there is a third course, too, don't hesitate
to let me know.

Chorus Leader: Our lord Teiresias,
I know, can see into things, like lord Apollo.
From him, my king, a man investigating this
might well find out clear details of the crime.

---

[9]*and thus avenge… Agenor from old times*: Agenor was the founder of the Theban royal family; his son *Cadmus* moved from Sidon in Asia Minor to Greece and founded Thebes. *Polydorus*: Son of Cadmus, father of Labdacus, and hence grandfather of Laius.

Oedipus: I've taken care of that—it's not something
I could overlook. At Creon's urging,
I have dispatched two messengers to him
and have been wondering for some time now
why he has not come.
Chorus Leader: Apart from that,
there are rumours—but inconclusive ones
from a long time ago.
Oedipus: What kind of rumours?
I'm looking into every story.
Chorus Leader: It was said
that Laius was killed by certain travellers.
Oedipus: Yes, I heard as much. But no one has seen
the one who did it.
Chorus Leader: Well, if the killer
has any fears, once he hears your curses on him,
he will not hold back, for they are serious.
Oedipus: When a man has no fear of doing the act,
he's not afraid of words.
Chorus Leader: No, not in the case
where no one stands there to convict him.
But at last Teiresias is being guided here,
our god-like prophet, in whom truth resides
more so than in all other men.

Enter TEIRESIAS led by a small BOY.

Oedipus: Teiresias,
you who understand all things—what can be taught
and what cannot be spoken of, what goes on
in heaven and here on the earth—you know,
although you cannot see, how sick our state is.
And so we find in you alone, great seer,
our shield and saviour. For Phoebus Apollo,
in case you have not heard the news, has sent us
an answer to our question: the only cure
for this infecting pestilence is to find
the men who murdered Laius and kill them
or else expel them from this land as exiles.
So do not withhold from us your prophecies
from voices of the birds or by some other means.
Save this city and yourself. Rescue me.
Deliver us from all pollution by the dead.
We are in your hands. For a mortal man
the finest labour he can do is help
with all his power other human beings.
Teiresias: Alas, alas! How dreadful it can be
to have wisdom when it brings no benefit

to the man possessing it. This I knew,
but it had slipped my mind. Otherwise,
I would not have journeyed here.
Oedipus: What is wrong? You have come, but seem distressed.
Teiresias: Let me go home. You must bear your burden
to the very end, and I will carry mine,
if you'll agree with me.
Oedipus: What you are saying
is not customary and shows little love
toward the city state which nurtured you,
if you deny us your prophetic voice.
Teiresias: I see your words are also out of place.
I do not speak for fear of doing the same.
Oedipus: If you know something, then, by the gods,
do not turn away. We are your suppliants—
all of us—we bend our knees to you.
Teiresias: You are all ignorant. I will not reveal
the troubling things inside me, nor will I state
they are your griefs as well.
Oedipus: What are you saying?
Do you know and will not say? Do you intend
to betray me and destroy the city?
Teiresias: I will cause neither me nor you distress.
Why do you vainly question me like this?
You will not learn a thing from me.
Oedipus: You most disgraceful of disgraceful men!
You would move something made of stone to rage!
Will you not speak out? Will your stubbornness
never have an end?
Teiresias: You blame my nature,
but do not see the temper you possess.
Instead, you're finding fault with me.
Oedipus: What man who listened to these words of yours
would not be enraged—you insult the city!
Teiresias: Yet events will still unfold, for all my silence.
Oedipus: Since they will come, you must inform me.
Teiresias: I will say nothing more. Fume on about it,
if you wish, as fiercely as you can.
Oedipus: I will. In my anger I will not conceal
just what I make of this. You should know
I get the feeling you conspired in the act
and played your part, as much as you could do,
short of killing him with your own hands.
If you could use your eyes, I would have said
that you had done this work all by yourself.
Teiresias: Is that so? Then I would ask you to stand by
the very words which you yourself proclaimed

and from now on not speak to these men or me.
For the accursed polluter of this land is you.
Oedipus: You dare to utter shameful words like this?
Do you think you can get away with it?
Teiresias: I am getting away with it. The truth
within me makes me strong.
Oedipus: Who taught you this?
It could not have been your craft.
Teiresias: You did.
I did not want to speak, but you incited me.
Oedipus: What do you mean? Speak it again,
so I can understand you more precisely.
Teiresias: Did you not grasp my words before,
or are you trying to test me with your question?
Oedipus: I did not fully understand your words.
Tell me again.
Teiresias: I say that you yourself
are the very man you're looking for.
Oedipus: That's twice you've stated that disgraceful lie—
something you'll regret.
Teiresias: Shall I tell you more,
so you can grow even more enraged?
Oedipus: As much as you desire. It will be useless.
Teiresias: I say that with your dearest family,
unknown to you, you are living in disgrace.
You have no idea how bad things are.
Oedipus: Do you really think you can just speak out,
say things like this, and still remain unpunished?
Teiresias: Yes, I can, if the truth has any strength.
Oedipus: It does, but not for you. Truth is not in you—
for your ears, your mind, your eyes are blind!
Teiresias: You are a wretched fool to use harsh words
which all men soon enough will use to curse you.
Oedipus: You live in endless darkness of the night,
so you can never injure me or any man
who can glimpse daylight.
Teiresias: It is not your fate
to fall because of me. Lord Apollo
will make that happen. He will be enough.
Oedipus: Is this something Creon has devised,
or is it your invention?
Teiresias: Creon is no threat.
You have made this trouble on your own.
Oedipus: O wealth and ruling power, skill after skill
surpassing all in life's rich rivalries,
how much envy you must carry with you,

if, for this kingly office—which the city
gave me, for I did not seek it out—
Creon, my old trusted family friend,
has secretly conspired to overthrow me
and paid off a double-dealing quack like this,
a crafty bogus priest, who can only see
his own advantage, who in his special art
is absolutely blind. Come on, tell me
how you have ever given evidence
of your wise prophecy. When the Sphinx,
that singing bitch, was here, you said nothing
to set the people free. Why not? Her riddle
was not something the first man to stroll along
could solve—a prophet was required. And there
the people saw your knowledge was no use—
nothing from birds or picked up from the gods.
But then I came, Oedipus, who knew nothing.
Yet I finished her off, using my wits
rather than relying on birds. That's the man
you want to overthrow, hoping, no doubt,
to stand up there with Creon, once he's king.
But I think you and your conspirator in this
will regret trying to drive me from the state.
If you did not look so old, you'd find out
the punishment your arrogance deserves.

Chorus Leader: To us it sounds as if Teiresias
has spoken in anger, and, Oedipus,
you have done so, too. That isn't what we need.
Instead we should be looking into this:
How can we best act on the god's decree?

Teiresias: You may be king, but I do have the right
to answer you—and I control that right,
for I am not your slave. I serve Apollo,
and thus will never stand with Creon,
signed up as his man. So I say this to you,
since you have chosen to insult my blindness—
you have your eyesight, and you do not see
how miserable you are, or where you live,
or who it is who shares your household.
Do you know the family you come from?
Without your knowledge you have turned into
the enemy of your own relatives,
those in the world below and those up here,
and the dreadful scourge of that two-edged curse
of father and mother will one day drive you
from this land in exile. Those eyes of yours,

which now can see so clearly, will be dark.
What harbour will not echo with your cries?
Where on Cithaeron will they not soon be heard,
once you have learned the truth about the wedding
by which you sailed into this royal house—
a lovely voyage, but the harbour's doomed?[10]
You have no notion of the quantity
of other troubles which will render you
and your own children equals. So go on—
keep insulting Creon and my prophecies,
for among all living mortals nobody
will be destroyed more wretchedly than you.

Oedipus: Must I tolerate this insolence from him?
Get out, and may the plague get rid of you!
Off with you! Now! Turn your back and go!
And don't come back here to my home again.

Teiresias: I would not have come, but you summoned me.

Oedipus: I did not know you would speak so stupidly.
If I had, you would have waited a long time
before I called you here.

Teiresias: I was born like this.
You think I am a fool, but to your parents,
the ones who made you, I was wise enough.

Oedipus: Wait! My parents? Who was my father?

Teiresias: This day will reveal that and destroy you.

Oedipus: Everything you speak is all so cryptic—
like a riddle.

Teiresias: Well, in solving riddles,
are you not the best there is?

Oedipus: Mock my excellence,
but you will find out I am truly great.

Teiresias: That success of yours has been your ruin.

Oedipus: I do not care, if I have saved the city.

Teiresias: I will go now. Boy, lead me away.

Oedipus: Yes, let him guide you back. You're in the way.
If you stay, you will provoke me. Once you're gone,
you won't annoy me further.

Teiresias: I'm going.
But first I shall tell you why I came.
I do not fear the face of your displeasure—
there is no way you can destroy me. I tell you,
the man you have been seeking all this time,
while proclaiming threats and issuing orders
about the one who murdered Laius—

[10] *Where on... harbour's doomed*: Cithaeron references the sacred mountain outside Thebes.

that man is here. According to reports,
he is a stranger who lives here in Thebes.
But he will prove to be a native Theban.
From that change he will derive no pleasure.
He will be blind, although he now can see.
He will be a poor, although he now is rich.
He will set off for a foreign country,
groping the ground before him with a stick.
And he will turn out to be the brother
of the children in his house—their father, too,
both at once, and the husband and the son
of the very woman who gave birth to him.
He sowed the same womb as his father
and murdered him. Go in and think on this.
If you discover I have spoken falsely,
you can say I lack all skill in prophecy.

Exit TEIRESIAS led off by the BOY. OEDIPUS turns and goes back into the palace.

Chorus: Speaking from the Delphic rock
the oracular voice[11] intoned a name.
But who is the man, the one
who with his blood-red hands
has done unspeakable brutality?
The time has come for him to flee—
to move his powerful foot
more swiftly than those hooves
of horses riding like a storm.
Against him Zeus' son now springs,
armed with lightning fire and leading on
the inexorable and terrifying Furies.[12]
From the snowy peaks of Mount Parnassus[13]
the message has just flashed, ordering all
to seek the one whom no one knows.
Like a wild bull he wanders now,
hidden in the untamed wood,
through rocks and caves, alone
with his despair on joyless feet,
keeping his distance from that doom
uttered at earth's central navel stone.
But that fatal oracle still lives,

[11]*oracular voice*: The Oracle of Delphi was a high priestess of Apollo who delivered prophesies whispered to her by the god. She was consulted by figures throughout the ancient world and is frequently referenced in classical texts.

[12]*Against him... terrifying Furies*: "Zeus' son" is a reference to Apollo. The *Furies* are the goddesses of blood revenge.

[13]*Parnassus*: A famous mountain some distance from Thebes but visible from the city.

hovering above his head forever.
That wise interpreter of prophecies
stirs up my fears, unsettling dread.
I cannot approve of what he said
and I cannot deny it.
I am confused. What shall I say?
My hopes are fluttering here and there,
with no clear glimpse of past or future.
I have never heard of any quarrelling,
past or present, between those two,
the house of Labdacus and Polybus' son,
which could give me evidence enough
to undermine the fame of Oedipus,
as he seeks vengeance for the unsolved murder
in the family line of Labdacus.[14]
Apollo and Zeus are truly wise—
they understand what humans do.
But there is no sure way to ascertain
if human prophets grasp things any more
than I do, although in wisdom one man
may leave another far behind.
But until I see the words confirmed,
I will not approve of any man
who censures Oedipus, for it was clear
when that winged Sphinx went after him
he was a wise man then. We witnessed it.
He passed the test and endeared himself
to all the city. So in my thinking now
he never will be guilty of a crime.

Enter CREON.

Creon: You citizens, I have just discovered
that Oedipus, our king, has levelled charges
against me, disturbing allegations.
That I cannot bear, so I have come here.
In these present troubles, if he believes
that he has suffered injury from me,
in word or deed, then I have no desire
to keep on living into ripe old age
still bearing his reproach. For me
the injury produced by this report
is not a single isolated matter—
no, it has the greatest scope of all,

[14] *the house of… line of Labdacus*: Polybus was the ruler of Corinth, who raised Oedipus and is thus believed to be his father. The house of Labdacus is the Theban royal family (i.e., Laius, Jocasta, and Creon).

if I end up being called a wicked man
here in the city, a bad citizen,
by you and by my friends.

Chorus Leader: Perhaps he charged you
spurred on by the rash power of his rage,
rather than his mind's true judgment.

Creon: Was it publicized that my persuasion
convinced Teiresias to utter lies?

Chorus Leader: That's what was said. I have no idea
just what that meant.

Creon: Did he accuse me
and announce the charges with a steady gaze,
in a normal state of mind?

Chorus Leader: I do not know.
What those in power do I do not see.
But he's approaching from the palace—
here he comes in person.

Enter OEDIPUS from the palace.

Oedipus: You! How did you get here?
Have you grown so bold-faced that you now come
to my own home—you who are obviously
the murderer of the man whose house it was,
a thief who clearly wants to steal my throne?
Come, in the name of all the gods, tell me this—
did you plan to do it because you thought
I was a coward or a fool? Or did you think
I would not learn about your actions
as they crept up on me with such deceit—
or that, if I knew, I could not deflect them?
This attempt of yours, is it not madness—
to chase after the king's place without friends,
without a horde of men, to seek a goal
which only gold or factions could attain?

Creon: Will you listen to me? It's your turn now
to let me make a suitable response.
Once you hear that, then judge me for yourself.

Oedipus: You are a clever talker. But from you
I will learn little. I know you now—
a troublemaker, an enemy of mine.

Creon: At least first listen to what I have to say.

Oedipus: Do not bother trying to convince me
that you have done no wrong.

Creon: If you think being stubborn
and forgetting common sense is wise,
then you're not thinking as you should.

Oedipus: And if you think you can try to harm
a man who is a relative of yours
and escape without a penalty
then you have not been thinking wisely.
Creon: I agree. What you've just said makes sense.
So tell me the nature of the damage
you claim you're suffering because of me.
Oedipus: Did you or did you not persuade me
to send for Teiresias, that prophet?
Creon: Yes. And I'd still give you the same advice.
Oedipus: How long is it since Laius … *[pauses]*
Creon: Did what?
What's Laius got to do with anything?
Oedipus: … since Laius was carried off and disappeared,
since he was killed so brutally?
Creon: A long time—
many years have passed since then.
Oedipus: At that time,
was Teiresias as skilled in prophecy?
Creon: Then, as now, he was honoured for his wisdom.
Oedipus: And back then did he ever mention me?
Creon: No, never—not while I was with him.
Oedipus: Did you not investigate the killing?
Creon: Yes, of course we did. But we found nothing.
Oedipus: Why did this man, this wise man, not speak up?
Creon: I do not know. And when I don't know something,
I like to hold my tongue.
Oedipus: You know enough—
at least you understand enough to say …
Creon: What? If I really do know something
I will not deny it.
Oedipus: If Teiresias
were not working with you, he would not name me
as the one who murdered Laius.
Creon: If he says this,
well, you're the one who knows. But I think
the time has come for me to question you
the way that you've been questioning me.
Oedipus: Ask whatever you wish. You'll never prove
that I'm the murderer.
Creon: Then tell me this—
are you not married to my sister?
Oedipus: Since you ask me, yes. I don't deny that.
Creon: And you two rule this land as equals?
Oedipus: Whatever she desires, she gets from me.

Creon: And am I not third, equal to you both?
Oedipus: That's what makes your friendship so deceitful.
Creon: No, not if you think this through, as I do.
First, consider this. In your view, would anyone
prefer to rule and have to cope with fear
rather than live in peace, carefree and safe,
if his powers were the same? I, for one,
have no natural desire to be king
in preference to performing royal acts.
The same is true of any other man
whose understanding grasps things properly.
For now I get everything I want from you,
but without the fear. If I were king myself,
I'd be doing many things against my will.
So how can being a king be sweeter to me
than royal power without anxiety?
I am not yet so mistaken in my mind
that I want things which bring no benefits.
Now all men are my friends and wish me well,
and those who seek to get something from you
now flatter me, since I'm the one who brings
success in what they want. So why would I
give up such benefits for something else?
A mind that's wise will not turn treacherous.
It's not my nature to love such policies.
And if another man pursued such things,
I would not work with him. I could not bear to.
If you want proof of this, then go to Delphi.
Ask the prophet if I brought back to you
exactly what was said. At that point,
if you discover I have planned something,
that I've conspired with Teiresias,
then arrest me and have me put to death,
not merely on your own authority,
but on mine as well, a double judgment.
Do not condemn me on an unproved charge.
It's not fair to judge these things by guesswork,
to assume bad men are good or good men bad.
I say a man who throws away a noble friend
is like a man who parts with his own life,
the thing most dear to him. Give it some time.
Then you will see clearly, since only time
can fully validate a man who's true.
A bad man is exposed in just one day.
Chorus Leader: For a man concerned about being killed,

my lord, he has spoken eloquently.
Those who are unreliable give rash advice.

Oedipus: If some conspirator moves against me,
in secret and with speed, I must be quick
to make my counter plans. If I just rest
and wait for him to act, then he'll succeed
in what he wants to do, and I'll be finished.

Creon: What do you want—to exile me from here?

Oedipus: No. I want you to die, not just run off—
so I can demonstrate what envy means.

Creon: You are determined not to change your mind
or listen to me?

Oedipus: You'll not convince me,
for there's no way that I can trust you.

Creon: I can see that you've become unbalanced.[15]

Oedipus: I'm sane enough to defend my interests.

Creon: You should be protecting mine as well.

Oedipus: But you're a treacherous man. It's your nature.

Creon: What if you're wrong?

Oedipus: I still have to govern.

Creon: Not if you do it badly.

Oedipus: O Thebes—
my city!

Creon: I, too, have some rights in Thebes—
it is not yours alone.

The palace doors open.

Chorus Leader: My lords, an end to this.
I see Jocasta coming from the palace,
and just in time. With her assistance
you should bring this quarrel to a close.

Enter JOCASTA from the palace.

Jocasta: You foolish men, why are you arguing
in such a stupid way? With our land so sick,
aren't you ashamed to start a private fight?
You, Oedipus, go in the house, and you,
Creon, return to yours. Why inflate
a trivial matter into something huge?

Creon: Sister, your husband Oedipus intends
to punish me in one of two dreadful ways—

[15]*you've... unbalanced*: There is some argument about who speaks which lines in 622-626 of the Greek text. I follow Sir Richard Jebb's suggestions, ascribing 625 to Creon, to whom it seems clearly to belong (in spite of the manuscripts) and adding a line to indicate Oedipus' response.

to banish me from my fathers' country
or arrest me and then have me killed.
Oedipus: That's right.
Lady, I caught him committing treason,
an vicious crime against me personally.
Creon: Let me not prosper but die a man accursed,
if I have done what you accuse me of.
Jocasta: Oedipus,
for the sake of the gods, trust him in this.
Respect that oath he made before all heaven—
do it for my sake and for those around you.
Chorus Leader: I beg you, my lord, consent to this—
agree with her.
Oedipus: What is it then
you're asking me to do?
Chorus Leader: Pay Creon due respect.
He has not been foolish in the past, and now
that oath he's sworn has power.
Oedipus: Are you aware
just what you're asking?
Chorus Leader: Yes. I understand.
Oedipus: Then tell me clearly what you mean to say.
Chorus Leader: You should not accuse a friend of yours
and thus dishonour him with a mere story
which may be false, when he has sworn an oath
and therefore could be subject to a curse.
Oedipus: By this point you should clearly understand,
what you are doing when you request this—
seeking to exile me from Thebes or kill me.
Chorus Leader: No, no, by sacred Helios, the god
who stands pre-eminent before the rest!
May I die the most miserable of deaths,
abandoned by the gods and by my friends,
if I have ever harboured such a thought!
But the destruction of our land wears down
my troubled heart—and so does this quarrel,
if you two add new problems to the ones
which have for so long been afflicting us.
Oedipus: Let him go, then, even though it means
I must be killed or sent from here in exile,
forced out in disgrace. I have been moved
to act compassionately by what you said,
not by Creon's words. But if he stays here,
he will be hateful to me.

Creon: You are stubborn—
obviously unhappy to concede,
and when you lose your temper, you go too far.
But men like that find it most difficult
to tolerate themselves. In that there's justice.
Oedipus: Why not go—just leave me alone?
Creon: I'll leave—
since I see you do not understand me.
But these men here know I'm a reasonable man.

Exit CREON away from the palace, leaving OEDIPUS and JOCASTA and the CHORUS on stage.

Chorus Leader: Lady, will you escort our king inside?
Jocasta: Yes, once I have learned what happened here.
Chorus Leader: They talked—
their words gave rise to uninformed suspicions,
but even unjust words inflict sore wounds.
Jocasta: From both of them?
Chorus Leader: Yes.
Jocasta: What caused it?
Chorus Leader: With our country already in distress,
it is enough, it seems to me, enough
to leave things as they are.
Oedipus: Now do you see
the point you've reached thanks to your noble wish
to dissolve and dull what I felt in my heart?
Chorus Leader: My lord, I have declared it more than once,
so you must know it would have been quite mad
if I abandoned you, who, when this land,
my cherished Thebes, was in great trouble,
set it right again and who, in these harsh times
should prove a trusty and successful guide.
Jocasta: By all the gods, my king, please let me know
why in this present matter you now feel
such unremitting rage.
Oedipus: To you I'll speak, lady,
since I respect you more than I do these men.
It's Creon's fault. He conspired against me.
Jocasta: In this quarrel what was said? Tell me.
Oedipus: Creon claims that I'm the murderer—
that I killed Laius.
Jocasta: Does he know this first hand,
or has he picked it up from someone else?
Oedipus: No. He set up that treasonous prophet.
What he says himself all sounds quite innocent.

Jocasta: All right, forget about those things you've said.
Listen to me, and ease your mind with this—
no human being has skill in prophecy.
I'll show you why with this example.
King Laius once received a oracle.
I won't say it came straight from Apollo,
but it was from those who do assist the god.
It said Laius was fated to be killed
by a child of ours, one born to him and me.
Now, at least according to the story,
one day Laius was killed by foreigners,
by robbers, at a place where three roads meet.
Besides, before our child was three days old,
Laius pinned his ankles tight together
and ordered other men to throw him out
on a mountain rock where no one ever goes.
And so Apollo's plan that he'd become
the one who killed his father didn't work,
and Laius never suffered what he feared,
that his own son would be his murderer,
although that's what the oracle had claimed.
So don't concern yourself with prophecies.
Whatever gods intend to bring about
they themselves make known quite easily.
Oedipus: Lady, as I listen to these words of yours,
my soul is shaken, my mind confused …
Jocasta: Why do you say that? What's worrying you?
Oedipus: I thought I heard you say that Laius
was murdered at a place where three roads meet.
Jocasta: That's what was said and people still believe.
Oedipus: Where is this place? Where did it happen?
Jocasta: In a land called Phocis. Two roads lead there—
one from Delphi and one from Daulia.
Oedipus: How long is it since these events took place?
Jocasta: The story was reported in the city
just before you took over royal power
here in Thebes.
Oedipus: O Zeus, what have you done?
What have you planned for me?
Jocasta: What is it,
Oedipus? Why is your spirit so troubled?
Oedipus: Not yet,
no questions yet. Tell me this—Laius,
how tall was he? How old a man?
Jocasta: He was big—with hair starting to turn white.
In shape he was not all that unlike you.

Oedipus: The worse for me! I may have set myself
under a dreadful curse without my knowledge!
Jocasta: What do you mean? As I look at you, my king,
I start to tremble.
Oedipus: I am afraid,
full of terrible fears the prophet sees.
But you can reveal this better if you now
will tell me one thing more.
Jocasta: I'm shaking,
but if you ask me, I will answer you.
Oedipus: Did Laius have a small escort with him
or a troop of soldiers, like a royal king?
Jocasta: Five men, including a herald, went with him.
A carriage carried Laius.
Oedipus: Alas! Alas!
It's all too clear! Lady, who told you this?
Jocasta: A slave—the only one who got away.
He came back here.
Oedipus: Is there any chance
he's in our household now?
Jocasta: No.
Once he returned and understood that you
had now assumed the power of slaughtered Laius,
he clasped my hands, begged me to send him off
to where our animals graze in the fields,
so he could be as far away as possible
from the sight of town. And so I sent him.
He was a slave but he'd earned my gratitude.
He deserved an even greater favour.
Oedipus: I'd like him to return back here to us,
and quickly, too.
Jocasta: That can be arranged—
but why's that something you would want to do?
Oedipus: Lady, I'm afraid I may have said too much.
That's why I want to see him here before me.
Jocasta: Then he will be here. But now, my lord,
I deserve to know why you are so distressed.
Oedipus: My forebodings now have grown so great
I will not keep them from you, for who is there
I should confide in rather than in you
about such a twisted turn of fortune.
My father was Polybus of Corinth,
my mother Merope, a Dorian.
There I was regarded as the finest man
in all the city, until, as chance would have it,

something most astonishing took place,
though it was not worth what it made me to do.
At dinner there a man who was quite drunk
from too much wine began to shout at me,
claiming I was not my father's real son.
That troubled me, but for a day at least
I said nothing, though it was difficult.
The next day I went to ask my parents,
my father and mother. They were angry
at the man who had insulted them this way,
so I was reassured. But nonetheless,
the accusation always troubled me—
the story had become known everywhere.
And so I went in secret off to Delphi.
I didn't tell my mother or my father.
Apollo sent me back without an answer,
so I didn't learn what I had come to find.
But when he spoke he uttered monstrous things,
strange terrors and horrific miseries—
my fate was to defile my mother's bed,
to bring forth to men a human family
that people could not bear to look upon,
and slay the father who engendered me.
When I heard that, I ran away from Corinth.
From then on I thought of it just as a place
beneath the stars. I went to other lands,
so I would never see that prophecy fulfilled,
the abomination of my evil fate.
In my travelling I came across that place
in which you say your king was murdered.
And now, lady, I will tell you the truth.
As I was on the move, I passed close by
a spot where three roads meet, and in that place
I met a herald and a horse-drawn carriage,
with a man inside, just as you described.
The guide there tried to force me off the road—
and the old man, too, got personally involved.
In my rage, I lashed out at the driver,
who was shoving me aside. The old man,
seeing me walking past him in the carriage,
kept his eye on me, and with his double whip
struck me on the head, right here on top.
Well, I retaliated in good measure—
with the staff I held I hit him a quick blow
and knocked him from his carriage to the road.

He lay there on his back. Then I killed them all.
If that stranger was somehow linked to Laius,
who is now more unfortunate than me?
What man could be more hateful to the gods?
No stranger and no citizen can welcome him
into their lives or speak to him. Instead,
they must keep him from their doors, a curse
I laid upon myself. With these hands of mine,
these killer's hands, I now contaminate
the dead man's bed. Am I not depraved?
Am I not utterly abhorrent?
Now I must fly into exile and there,
a fugitive, never see my people,
never set foot in my native land again—
or else I must get married to my mother
and kill my father, Polybus, who raised me,
the man who gave me life. If anyone
claimed this came from some malevolent god,
would he not be right? O you gods,
you pure, blessed gods, may I not see that day!
Let me rather vanish from the sight of men,
before I see a fate like that engulf me!

Chorus Leader: My lord, to us these things are ominous.
But you must sustain your hope until you hear
the servant who was present at the time.

Oedipus: I do have some hope left, at least enough
to wait for the man we've summoned from the fields.

Jocasta: Once he comes, what do you hope to hear?

Oedipus: I'll tell you. If we discover what he says
matches what you say, then I'll escape disaster.

Jocasta: What was so remarkable in what I said?

Oedipus: You said that in his story the man claimed
Laius was murdered by a band of thieves.
If he still says that there were several men,
then I was not the killer, since one man
could never be mistaken for a crowd.
But if he says it was a single man,
the scales of justice guilt sink down on me.

Jocasta: Well, that's certainly what he reported then.
He cannot now withdraw what he once said.
The whole city heard him, not just me alone.
But even if he changes that old news,
he cannot ever demonstrate, my lord,
that Laius' murder fits the prophecy.
For Apollo clearly said the man would die
at the hands of an infant born from me.

Now, how did that unhappy son of ours
kill Laius, when he'd perished long before?
As far as these predictions go, from now on
I would not look for confirmation anywhere.

Oedipus: You're right in what you say. But nonetheless,
send for that peasant. Don't fail to do that.

Jocasta: I'll call him here as quickly as I can.
Let's go inside. I'll not do anything
which does not meet with your approval.

OEDIPUS and JOCASTA go into the palace together.

Chorus: I pray fate still finds me worthy,
demonstrating piety and reverence
in all I say and do—in everything
our loftiest traditions consecrate,
those laws engendered in the heavenly skies,
whose only father is Olympus.
They were not born from mortal men,
nor will they sleep and be forgotten.
In them lives an ageless mighty god.
Insolence gives birth to tyranny—
that insolence which vainly crams itself
and overflows with so much wealth
beyond what's right or beneficial,
that once it's climbed the highest rooftop,
it's hurled down by force—such a quick fall
there's no safe landing on one's feet.
But I pray the god never will abolish
the type of rivalry that helps our state.
That god I will hold onto always,
the one who stands as our protector.[16]
But if a man conducts himself
disdainfully in what he says and does,
and manifests no fear of righteousness,
no reverence for the statues of the gods,
may miserable fate seize such a man
for his disastrous arrogance,
if he does not behave with justice
when he strives to benefit himself,
appropriates all things impiously,
and, like a fool, profanes the sacred.
What man is there who does such things

[16]*the one… protector.* This part of the choral song makes an important distinction between two forms of self-assertive action: the first breeds self-aggrandizement and greed; the second is necessary for the protection of the state.

who can still claim he will ward off
the arrow of the gods aimed at his heart?
If such actions are considered worthy,
why should we dance to honour god?
No longer will I go in reverence
to the sacred stone, earth's very centre,
or to the temple at Abae or Olympia,
if these prophecies fail to be fulfilled
and manifest themselves to mortal men.
But you, all-conquering, all-ruling Zeus,
if by right those names belong to you,
let this not evade you and your ageless might.
For ancient oracles which dealt with Laius
are withering—men now set them aside.
Nowhere is Apollo honoured publicly,
and our religious faith is dying away.

JOCASTA enters from the palace and moves to an altar to Apollo which stands outside the palace doors.

She is accompanied by one or two SERVANTS.

Jocasta: You leading citizens of Thebes, I think
it is appropriate for me to visit
our gods' sacred shrines, bearing in my hands
this garland and an offering of incense.
For Oedipus has let excessive pain
seize on his heart and does not understand
what's happening now by thinking of the past,
like a man with sense. Instead he listens to
whoever speaks to him of dreadful things.
I can do nothing more with my advice,
and so, Lyceian Apollo, I come to you,
who stand here beside us, a suppliant,
with offerings and prayers for you to find
some way of cleansing what corrupts us.
For now we are afraid, just like those
who on a ship see their helmsman terrified.

JOCASTA sets her offerings on the altar. A MESSENGER enters, an older man.

Messenger: Strangers, can you tell me where I find
the house of Oedipus, your king? Better yet,
if you know, can you tell me where he is?
Chorus Leader: His home is here, stranger, and he's inside.
This lady is the mother of his children.
Messenger: May her happy home always be blessed,
for she is his queen, true mistress of his house.

Jocasta: I wish the same for you, stranger. Your fine words
make you deserve as much. But tell us now
why you have come. Do you seek information,
or do you wish to give us some report?
Messenger: Lady, I have good news for your whole house—
and for your husband, too.
Jocasta: What news is that?
Where have you come from?
Messenger: I've come from Corinth.
I'll give you my report at once, and then
you will, no doubt, be glad, although perhaps
you will be sad, as well.
Jocasta: What is your news?
How can it have two such effects at once?
Messenger: The people who live there, in the lands
beside the Isthmus[17], will make him their king.
They have announced it.
Jocasta: What are you saying?
Is old man Polybus no longer king?
Messenger: No. He is dead and in his grave.
Jocasta: What?
Has Oedipus' father died?
Messenger: Yes.
If what I'm telling you is not the truth,
then I deserve to die.
Jocasta: *[to a servant]*
You there—
go at once and tell this to your master.

SERVANT goes into the palace.

O you oracles of the gods, so much for you.
Oedipus has for so long been afraid
that he would murder him. He ran away.
And now Polybus has died, killed by Fate
and not by Oedipus.

Enter OEDIPUS from the palace.

Oedipus: Ah, Jocasta,
my dearest wife, why have you summoned me
to leave our home and come out here?
Jocasta: You must hear this man, and as you listen,
decide for yourself what these prophecies,
these solemn proclamations from the gods,
amount to.

---

[17] *Isthmus*: The city of Corinth stood on the narrow stretch of land (the Isthmus) connecting the Peloponnese with mainland Greece, a very strategic position.

Oedipus: Who is this man? What report
does he have for me?
Jocasta: He comes from Corinth,
bringing news that Polybus, your father,
no longer is alive. He's dead.
Oedipus: What?
Stranger, let me hear from you in person.
Messenger: If I must first report my news quite plainly,
then I should let you know that Polybus
has passed away. He's gone.
Oedipus: By treachery,
or was it the result of some disease?
Messenger: With old bodies a slight weight on the scales
brings final peace.
Oedipus: Apparently his death
was from an illness?
Messenger: Yes, and from old age.
Oedipus: Alas! Indeed, lady, why should any man
pay due reverence to Apollo's shrine,
where his prophet lives, or to those birds
which scream out overhead? For they foretold
that I was going to murder my own father.
But now he's dead and lies beneath the earth,
and I am here. I never touched my spear.
Perhaps he died from a desire to see me—
so in that sense I brought about his death.
But as for those prophetic oracles,
they're worthless. Polybus has taken them
to Hades, where he lies.
Jocasta: Was I not the one
who predicted this some time ago?
Oedipus: You did,
but then I was misguided by my fears.
Jocasta: You must not keep on filling up your heart
with all these things.
Oedipus: But my mother's bed—
Surely I should still be afraid of that?
Jocasta: Why should a man whose life seems ruled by chance
live in fear—a man who never looks ahead,
who has no certain vision of his future?
It's best to live haphazardly, as best one can.
Do not worry you will wed your mother.
It's true that in their dreams a lot of men
have slept with their own mothers, but someone
who ignores all this bears life more easily.
Oedipus: Everything you say would be commendable,
if my mother were not still alive.

But since she is, I must remain afraid,
though all that you have said is right.
Jocasta: But still,
your father's death is a great comfort to us.
Oedipus: Yes, it is good, I know. But I do fear
that lady—she is still alive.
Messenger: This one you fear,
what kind of woman is she?
Oedipus: Old man,
her name is Merope, wife to Polybus.
Messenger: And what in her makes you so fearful?
Oedipus: Stranger,
a dreadful prophecy sent from the god.
Messenger: Is it well known? Or something private,
which other people have no right to know?
Oedipus: No, no. It's public knowledge. Loxias[18]
once said it was my fate that I would marry
my own mother and shed my father's blood
with my own hands. That's why, many years ago,
I left my home in Corinth. Things turned out well,
but nonetheless it gives the sweetest joy
to look into the eyes of one's own parents.
Messenger: And because you were afraid of her
you stayed away from Corinth?
Oedipus: And because
I did not want to be my father's killer.
Messenger: My lord, since I came to make you happy,
why do I not relieve you of this fear?
Oedipus: You would receive from me a worthy thanks.
Messenger: That's really why I came—so your return
might prove a benefit to me back home.
Oedipus: But I will never go back to my parents.
Messenger: My son, it is so clear you've no idea
what you are doing …
Oedipus: *[interrupting]*
What do you mean, old man?
In the name of all the gods, tell me.
Messenger: … if that's the reason you're a fugitive
and won't go home.
Oedipus: I feared Apollo's prophecy
might reveal itself in me.
Messenger: You were afraid
you might become corrupted through your parents?
Oedipus: That's right, old man. That was my constant fear.

[18]*Loxias*: A common name for Apollo.

Messenger: Are you aware these fears of yours are groundless?
Oedipus: And why is that? If I was born their child ...
Messenger: Because you and Polybus were not related.
Oedipus: What do you mean? Was not Polybus my father?
Messenger: He was as much your father as this man here,
no more, no less.
Oedipus: But how can any man
who means nothing to me be just the same
as my own father?
Messenger: But Polybus
was not your father, no more than I am.
Oedipus: Then why did he call me his son?
Messenger: If you must know,
he received you as a gift many years ago.
I gave you to him.
Oedipus: He really loved me.
How could he if I came from someone else?
Messenger: Because before you came, he had no children—
that made him love you.
Oedipus: When you gave me to him,
had you bought me or discovered me by chance?
Messenger: I found you in Cithaeron's forest valleys.
Oedipus: What were you doing wandering up there?
Messenger: I was looking after flocks of sheep.
Oedipus: You were a shepherd, just a hired servant
roaming here and there?
Messenger: Yes, my son, I was.
But at that time I was the one who saved you.
Oedipus: When you picked me up and took me off,
what sort of suffering did you save me from?
Messenger: The ankles on your feet could tell you that.
Oedipus: Ah, my old misfortune. Why mention that?
Messenger: Your ankles had been pierced and pinned together.
I set them free.
Oedipus: My dreadful mark of shame—
I've had that scar there since I was a child.
Messenger: That's why fortune gave you your very name,
the one which you still carry.[19]
Oedipus: Tell me,
in the name of heaven, did my parents,
my father or my mother, do this to me?
Messenger: I don't know. The man who gave you to me

---

[19] ... *still carry.* The name *Oedipus* can be construed to mean either "swollen feet" or "knowledge of one's feet." Both terms evoke a strongly ironic sense of how Oedipus, for all his fame as a man of knowledge, is ignorant about his origin.

knows more of that than I do.
Oedipus: You mean to say
you got me from someone else? It wasn't you
who stumbled on me?
Messenger: No, it wasn't me.
Another shepherd gave you to me.
Oedipus: Who?
Who was he? Do you know? Can you tell me
any details, things you are quite sure of?
Messenger: Well, I think he was one of Laius' servants—
that's what people said.
Oedipus: You mean king Laius,
the one who ruled this country years ago?
Messenger: That's right. He was one of the king's shepherds.
Oedipus: Is he still alive? Can I still see him?
Messenger: You people live here. You'd best answer that.
Oedipus: *[turning to the Chorus]*
Do any of you here now know the man,
this shepherd he describes? Have you seen him,
either in the fields or here in Thebes?
Answer me. It's critical, time at last
to find out what this means.
Chorus Leader: The man he mentioned
is, I think, the very peasant from the fields
you wanted to see earlier. But of this
Jocasta could tell more than anyone.
Oedipus: Lady, do you know the man we sent for—
just minutes ago—the one we summoned here?
Is he the one this messenger refers to?
Jocasta: Why ask me what he means? Forget all that.
There's no point trying to sort out what he said.
Oedipus: With all these indications of the truth
here in my grasp, I cannot end this now.
I must reveal the details of my birth.
Jocasta: In the name of the gods, no! If you have
some concern for your own life, then stop!
Do not keep on investigating this.
I will suffer—that will be enough.
Oedipus: Be brave. Even if I should turn out to be
born from a shameful mother, whose family
for three generations have been slaves,
you will still have your noble lineage.
Jocasta: Listen to me, I beg you. Do not do this.
Oedipus: I will not be convinced I should not learn
the whole truth of what these facts amount to.
Jocasta: But I care about your own well being—

what I tell you is for your benefit.
Oedipus: What you're telling me for my own good
just brings me more distress.
Jocasta: O you unhappy man!
May you never find out who you really are!
Oedipus: *[to Chorus]*
Go, one of you, and bring that shepherd here.
Leave the lady to enjoy her noble line.
Jocasta: Alas, you poor miserable man!
There's nothing more that I can say to you.
I'll never speak another word again.

JOCASTA runs into the palace.

Chorus Leader: Why has the queen rushed off, Oedipus,
so full of grief? I fear a disastrous storm
will soon break through her silence.
Oedipus: Then let it break,
whatever it is. As for myself,
no matter how base born my family,
I wish to know the seed from where I came.
Perhaps my queen is now ashamed of me
and of my insignificant origin—
she likes to play the noble lady.
But I will never feel myself dishonoured.
I see myself as a child of Fortune—
and she is generous, that mother of mine
from whom I spring, and the months, my siblings,
have seen me by turns both small and great.
That's how I was born. I cannot prove false
to my own nature, nor can I ever cease
from seeking out the facts of my own birth.
Chorus: If I have any power of prophecy
or skill in knowing things,
then, by the Olympian deities,
you, Cithaeron, at tomorrow's moon
will surely know that Oedipus
pays tribute to you as his native land
both as his mother and his nurse,
and that our choral dance and song
acknowledge you because you are
so pleasing to our king.
O Phoebus, we cry out to you—
may our song fill you with delight!
Who gave birth to you, my child?
Which one of the immortal gods
bore you to your father Pan,

who roams the mountainsides?
Was it some bedmate of Apollo,
the god who loves all country fields?
Perhaps Cyllene's royal king?
Or was it the Bacchanalian god
dwelling on the mountain tops
who took you as a new-born joy
from maiden nymphs of Helicon
with whom he often romps and plays?[20]

Oedipus: *[looking out away from the palace]*
You elders, though I've never seen the man
we've been seeking for a long time now,
if I had to guess, I think I see him.
He's coming here. He looks very old—
as is appropriate, if he's the one.
And I know the people coming with him,
servants of mine. But if you've seen him before,
you'll recognize him better than I will.

Chorus Leader: Yes, I recognize the man. There's no doubt.
He worked for Laius—a trusty shepherd.

Enter SERVANT, an old shepherd.

Oedipus: Stranger from Corinth, let me first ask you—
is this the man you spoke of?

Messenger: Yes, he is—
he's the man you see in front of you.

Oedipus: You, old man, over here. Look at me.
Now answer what I ask. Some time ago
did you work for Laius?

Servant: Yes, as a slave.
But I was not bought. I grew up in his house.

Oedipus: How did you live? What was the work you did?

Servant: Most of my life I've spent looking after sheep.

Oedipus: Whereabouts? In what specific places?

Servant: On Cithaeron or the neighbouring lands.

Oedipus: Do you know if you came across this man
anywhere up there?

Servant: Doing what?
What man do you mean?

Oedipus: The man over here—
this one. Have you ever met him before?

Servant: Right now I can't say I remember him.

---

[20] *with... and plays*: Cyllene's king is the god Hermes, who was born on Mount Cyllene; the Bacchanalian god is Dionysus.

Messenger: My lord, that's surely not surprising.
Let me refresh his failing memory.
I think he will remember all too well
the time we spent around Cithaeron.
He had two flocks of sheep and I had one.
I was with him there for six months at a stretch,
from early spring until the autumn season.
In winter I'd drive my sheep down to my folds,
and he'd take his to pens that Laius owned.
Isn't that what happened—what I just said?
Servant: You spoke the truth. But it was long ago.
Messenger: All right, then. Now, tell me if you recall
how you gave me a child, an infant boy,
for me to raise as my own foster son.
Servant: What? Why ask about that?
Messenger: This man here, my friend,
was that young child back then.
Servant: Damn you!
Can't you keep quiet about it!
Oedipus: Hold on, old man.
Don't criticize him. What you have said
is more objectionable than his account.
Servant: My noble master, what have I done wrong?
Oedipus: You did not tell us of that infant boy,
the one he asked about.
Servant: That's what he says,
but he knows nothing—a useless busybody.
Oedipus: If you won't tell us of your own free will,
once we start to hurt you, you will talk.
Servant: By all the gods, don't torture an old man!
Oedipus: One of you there, tie up this fellow's hands.
Servant: Why are you doing this? It's too much for me!
What is it you want to know?
Oedipus: That child he mentioned—
did you give it to him?
Servant: I did. How I wish
I'd died that day!
Oedipus: Well, you are going to die
if you don't speak the truth.
Servant: And if I do,
the death I suffer will be even worse.
Oedipus: It seems to me the man is trying to stall.
Servant: No, no, I'm not. I've already told you—
I did give him the child.
Oedipus: Where did you get it?
Did it come from your home or somewhere else?

Servant: It was not mine—I got it from someone.
Oedipus: Which of our citizens? Whose home was it?
Servant: In the name of the gods, my lord, don't ask!
Please, no more questions!
Oedipus: If I have to ask again,
then you will die.
Servant: The child was born in Laius' house.
Oedipus: From a slave or from some relative of his?
Servant: Alas, what I'm about to say now …
it's horrible.
Oedipus: It may be horrible,
but nonetheless I have to hear it.
Servant: If you must know, they said the child was his.
But your wife inside the palace is the one
who could best tell you what was going on.
Oedipus: You mean she gave the child to you?
Servant: Yes, my lord.
Oedipus: Why did she do that?
Servant: So I would kill it.
Oedipus: That wretched woman was the mother?
Servant: Yes.
She was afraid of dreadful prophecies.
Oedipus: What sort of prophecies?
Servant: The story went
that he would kill his father.
Oedipus: If that was true,
why did you give the child to this old man?
Servant: I pitied the boy, master, and I thought
he'd take the child off to a foreign land
where he was from. But he rescued him,
only to save him for the greatest grief of all.
For if you are who this man says you are
you know your birth carried an awful fate.
Oedipus: Ah, so it all came true. It's so clear now.
O light, let me look at you one final time,
a man who stands revealed as cursed by birth,
cursed by my own family, and cursed
by murder where I should not kill.

OEDIPUS moves into the palace.

Chorus: O generations of mortal men,
how I count your life as scarcely living.
What man is there, what human being,
who attains a greater happiness
than mere appearances, a joy
which seems to fade away to nothing?
Poor wretched Oedipus, your fate

stands here to demonstrate for me
how no mortal man is ever blessed.
Here was a man who fired his arrows well—
his skill was matchless—and he won
the highest happiness in everything.
For, Zeus, he slaughtered the hook-taloned Sphinx
and stilled her cryptic song. For our state,
he stood there like a tower against death,
and from that moment, Oedipus,
we have called you our king
and honoured you above all other men,
the one who rules in mighty Thebes.
But now who is there whose story
is more terrible to hear? Whose life
has been so changed by trouble,
by such ferocious agonies?
Alas for celebrated Oedipus,
the same spacious place of refuge
served you both as child and father,
the place you entered as a new bridegroom.
How could the furrow where your father planted,
poor wretched man, have tolerated you
in such silence for so long?
Time, which watches everything
and uncovered you against your will,
now sits in judgment of that fatal marriage,
where child and parent have been joined so long.
O child of Laius, how I wish
I'd never seen you—now I wail
like one whose mouth pours forth laments.
To tell it right, it was through you
I found my life and breathed again,
and then through you the darkness veils my eyes.

The Second Messenger enters from the palace.

Second Messenger: O you most honoured citizens of Thebes,
what actions you will hear about and see,
what sorrows you will bear, if, as natives here,
you are still loyal to the house of Labdacus!
I do not think the Ister or the Phasis rivers
could cleanse this house. It conceals too much
and soon will bring to light the vilest things,
brought on by choice and not by accident.[21]
What we do to ourselves brings us most pain.

[21] *brought… accident.* This line refers, not the entire story, but to what Jocasta and Oedipus have just done to themselves.

Chorus Leader: The calamities we knew about before
were hard enough to bear. What can you say
to make them worse?
Second Messenger: I'll waste no words—
know this—noble Jocasta, our queen, is dead.
Chorus Leader: That poor unhappy lady! How did she die?
Second Messenger: She killed herself. You did not witness it,
so you'll be spared the worst of what went on.
But from what I recall of what I saw
you'll learn how that poor woman suffered.
She left here frantic and rushed inside,
the fingers of both hands clenched in her hair.
She ran through the hall straight to her marriage bed.
She went in, slamming both doors shut behind her
and crying out to Laius, who's been a corpse
a long time now. She was remembering
that child of theirs born many years ago—
the one who killed his father, who left her
to conceive cursed children with that son.
She lay moaning beside the bed, where she,
poor woman, had given birth twice over—
a husband from a husband, children from a child.
How she died after that I don't fully know.
With a scream Oedipus came bursting in.
He would not let us see her suffering,
her final pain. We watched him charge around,
back and forth. As he moved, he kept asking us
to give him a sword, as he tried to find
that wife who was no wife—whose mother's womb
had given birth to him and to his children.
As he raved, some immortal power led him on—
no human in the room came close to him.
With a dreadful howl, as if someone
had pushed him, he leapt at the double doors,
bent the bolts by force out of their sockets,
and burst into the room. Then we saw her.
She was hanging there, swaying, with twisted cords
roped round her neck. When Oedipus saw her,
with a dreadful groan he took her body
from the noose in which she hung, and then,
when the poor woman was lying on the ground—
what happened next was a horrific sight—
from her clothes he ripped the golden brooches
she wore as ornaments, raised them high,
and drove them deep into his eyeballs,
crying as he did so: "You will no longer see

all those atrocious things I suffered,
the dreadful things I did! No. You have seen
what you never should have looked upon,
and what I wished to know you did not see.
So now and for all future time be dark!"
With these words he raised his hand and struck,
not once, but many times, right in the sockets.
With every blow blood spurted from his eyes
down on his beard, and not in single drops,
but showers of dark blood spattering like hail.
So what these two have done has overwhelmed
not one alone—this disaster swallows up
a man and wife together. That old happiness
they had before in their rich ancestry
was truly joy, but now lament and ruin,
death and shame, and all calamities
which men can name are theirs to keep.

Chorus Leader: And has that suffering man found some relief
to ease his pain?

Second Messenger: He shouts at everyone
to open up the gates and thus reveal
to all Cadmeians his father's killer,
his mother's … but I must not say those words.
He wants them to cast him out of Thebes,
so the curse he laid will not come on this house
if he still lives inside. But he is weak
and needs someone to lead him on his way.
His agony is more than he can bear—
as he will show you—for on the palace doors
the bolts are being pulled back. Soon you will see
a sight which even a man filled with disgust
would have to pity.

OEDIPUS enters through the palace doors.

Chorus Leader: An awful fate for human eyes to witness,
an appalling sight—the worst I've ever seen.
O you poor man, what madness came on you?
What eternal force pounced on your life
and, springing further than the longest leap,
brought you this fearful doom? Alas! Alas!
You unhappy man! I cannot look at you.
I want to ask you many things—there's much
I wish to learn. You fill me with such horror,
yet there is so much I must see.

Oedipus: Aaaiiii, aaaiii … Alas! Alas!
How miserable I am … such wretchedness …

Where do I go? How can the wings of air
sweep up my voice? O my destiny,
how far you have sprung now!

Chorus Leader: To a fearful place from which men turn away,
a place they hate to look upon.

Oedipus: O the dark horror engulfing me,
this nameless visitor I can't resist
swept here by fair and fatal winds.
Alas for me! And yet again, alas for me!
The pain of stabbing brooches pierces me!
The memory of agonizing shame!

Chorus Leader: In your distress it's not astonishing
you bear a double load of suffering,
a double load of pain.

Oedipus: Ah, my friend,
so you still care for me, as always,
and with patience nurse me now I'm blind.
Alas! Alas! You are not hidden from me—
I recognize you all too clearly.
Though I am blind, I know that voice so well.

Chorus Leader: You have carried out such dreadful things—
how could you dare to blind yourself this way?
What god drove you to it?

Oedipus: It was Apollo, friends.
It was Apollo. He brought on these troubles—
the awful things I suffer. But the hand
which stabbed out my eyes was mine alone.
In my wretched life, why should I have eyes
when there was nothing sweet for me to see?

Chorus Leader: What you have said is true enough.

Oedipus: What is there for me to see, my friends?
What can I love? Whose greeting can I hear
and feel delight? Hurry now, my friends,
lead me away from Thebes—take me somewhere,
a man completely lost, utterly accursed,
the mortal man the gods despise the most.

Chorus Leader: Unhappy in your fate and in your mind
which now knows all. Would I had never known you!

Oedipus: Whoever the man is who freed my feet,
who released me from that cruel shackle
and rescued me from death, may that man die!
It was a thankless act. Had I perished then,
I would not have brought such agony
to myself or to my friends.

Chorus Leader: I agree—
I, too, would have preferred if you had died.

Oedipus: I would not have come to kill my father,
and men would not see in me the husband
of the woman who gave birth to me.
Now I am abandoned by the gods,
the son of a corrupted mother,
conceiving children with the woman
who gave me my own miserable life.
If there is some horrific suffering
worse than all the rest, then it too belongs
in the fate of Oedipus.

Chorus Leader: I do not believe
what you did to yourself is for the best.
Better to be dead than alive and blind.

Oedipus: Don't tell me what I've done is not the best.
And from now on spare me your advice.
If I could see, I don't know how my eyes
could look at my own father when I come
to Hades or at my wretched mother.
Against those two I have committed acts
so vile that even if I hanged myself
that would not be sufficient punishment.
Perhaps you think the sight of my own children
might give me joy? No! Look how they were born!
They could never bring delight to eyes of mine.
Nor could the city or its massive walls,
or the sacred images of its gods.
I am the most abhorred of men, I,
the finest man of all those bred in Thebes,
I have condemned myself, telling everyone
they had to banish for impiety
the man the gods have now exposed
as sacrilegious—a son of Laius, too.
With such polluting stains upon me,
could I set eyes on you and hold your gaze?
No. And if I could somehow block my ears
and kill my hearing, I would not hold back.
I'd make a dungeon of this wretched body,
so I would never see or hear again.
For there is joy in isolated thought,
completely sealed off from a world of pain.
O Cithaeron, why did you shelter me?
Why, when I was handed over to you,
did you not do away with me at once,
so I would never then reveal to men
the nature of my birth? Ah Polybus
and Corinth, the place men called my home,
my father's ancient house, you raised me well—

so fine to look at, so corrupt inside!
Now I've been exposed as something gross,
contaminated in my origins.
O you three roads and hidden forest grove,
you thicket and defile where three paths meet,
you who swallowed down my father's blood
from my own hands, do you remember me,
what I did there in front of you and then
what else I did when I came here to Thebes?
Ah, you marriage rites—you gave birth to me,
and when I was born, you gave birth again,
children from the child of that same womb,
creating an incestuous blood family
of fathers, brothers, children, brides,
wives and mothers—the most atrocious act
that human beings commit! But it is wrong
to talk about what it is wrong to do,
so in the name of all the gods, act quickly—
hide me somewhere far from the land of Thebes,
or slaughter me, or hurl me in the sea,
where you will never gaze on me again.
Come, allow yourself to touch a wretched man.
Listen to me, and do not be afraid—
for this disease infects no one but me.

Chorus Leader: Creon is coming. He is just in time
to plan and carry out what you propose.
With you gone he's the only one still left
to act as guardian of Thebes.

Oedipus: Alas,
how will I talk to him? How can I ask him
to put his trust in me? Not long ago
I showed I had no faith in him at all.

Enter Creon.

Creon: Oedipus, I have not come here to mock
or blame you for disasters in the past.
But if you can no longer value human beings,
at least respect our lord the Sun, whose light
makes all things grow, and do not put on show
pollution of this kind in such a public way,
for neither earth nor light nor sacred rain
can welcome such a sight.

Creon speaks to the attending servants.

Take him inside the house
as quickly as you can. The kindest thing

would be for members of his family
to be the only ones to see and hear him.

Oedipus: By all the gods, since you are acting now
so differently from what I would expect
and have come here to treat me graciously,
the very worst of men, do what I ask.
I will speak for your own benefit, not mine.

Creon: What are you so keen to get from me?

Oedipus: Cast me out as quickly as you can,
away from Thebes, to a place where no one,
no living human being, will cross my path.

Creon: That is something I could do, of course,
but first I wish to know what the god says
about what I should do.

Oedipus: But what he said
was all so clear—the man who killed his father
must be destroyed. And that corrupted man
is me.

Creon: Yes, that is what was said. But now,
with things the way they are, the wisest thing
is to ascertain quite clearly what to do.

Oedipus: Will you then be making a request
on my behalf when I am so depraved?

Creon: I will. For even you must now trust in the gods.

Oedipus: Yes, I do. And I have a task for you
as I make this plea—that woman in the house,
please bury her as you see fit. You are the one
to give your own the proper funeral rites.
But never let my father's city be condemned
to have me living here while I still live.
Let me make my home up in the mountains
by Cithaeron, whose fame is now my own.
When my father and mother were alive,
they chose it as my special burying place—
and thus, when I die, I shall be following
the orders of the ones who tried to kill me.
And yet I know this much—no disease
nor any other suffering can kill me—
for I would never have been saved from death
unless I was to suffer a strange destiny.
But wherever my fate leads, just let it go.
As for my two sons, Creon, there's no need
for you to care for them on my behalf.
They are men, and, no matter where they are,

they'll always have enough to live on.[22]
But my two poor daughters have never known
my dining table placed away from them
or lacked their father's presence. They shared
everything I touched—so it has always been.
So take care of them for me. But first let me
feel them with my hands and then I'll grieve.
O my lord, you noble heart, let me do that—
if my hands could touch them it would seem
as if I were with them when I still could see.

Some SERVANTS lead ANTIGONE and ISMENE out of the palace.

What's this? By all the gods I hear something—
is it my two dear children crying … ?
Has Creon taken pity on me
and sent out the children, my dear treasures?
Is that what's happening?

Creon: Yes. I sent for them.
I know the joy they've always given you—
the joy which you feel now.

Oedipus: I wish you well.
And for this act, may the god watch over you
and treat you better than he treated me.
Ah, my children, where are you? Come here,
come into my arms—you are my sisters now—
feel these hands which turned your father's eyes,
once so bright, into what you see now,
these empty sockets. He was a man who,
seeing nothing, knowing nothing, fathered you
with the woman who had given birth to him.
I weep for you. Although I cannot see,
I think about your life in days to come,
the bitter life which men will force on you.
What citizens will associate with you?
What feasts will you attend and not come home
in tears, with no share in the rejoicing?
When you're mature enough for marriage,
who will be there for you, my children,
what husband ready to assume the shame
tainting my children and their children, too?
What perversion is not manifest in us?
Your father killed his father, and then ploughed

[22]*they'll… live on*: Oedipus' two sons, Eteocles and Polyneices, would probably be fifteen or sixteen years old at this time, not old enough to succeed Oedipus.

his mother's womb—where he himself was born—
conceiving you where he, too, was conceived.
Those are the insults they will hurl at you.
Who, then, will marry you? No one, my children.
You must wither, barren and unmarried.
Son of Menoeceus, with both parents gone,
you alone remain these children's father.
Do not let them live as vagrant paupers,
wandering around unmarried. You are
a relative of theirs—don't let them sink
to lives of desperation like my own.
Have pity. You see them now at their young age
deprived of everything except a share
in what you are. Promise me, you noble soul,
you will extend your hand to them. And you,
my children, if your minds were now mature,
there's so much I could say. But I urge you—
pray that you may live as best you can
and lead your destined life more happily
than your own father.

Creon: You have grieved enough.
Now go into the house.

Oedipus: I must obey,
although that's not what I desire.

Creon: In due time
all things will work out for the best.

Oedipus: I will go.
But you know there are conditions.

Creon: Tell me.
Once I hear them, I'll know what they are.

Oedipus: Send me away to live outside of Thebes.

Creon: Only the god can give you what you ask.

Oedipus: But I've become abhorrent to the gods.

Creon: Then you should quickly get what you desire.

Oedipus: So you agree?

Creon: I don't like to speak
thoughtlessly and say what I don't mean.

Oedipus: Come then, lead me off.

Creon: All right,
but let go of the children.

Oedipus: No, no!
Do not take them away from me.

Creon: Don't try to keep control of everything.
You have lost the power your life once had.

CREON, OEDIPUS, ANTIGONE, ISMENE, and ATTENDANTS all enter the palace[23].

Chorus: You residents of Thebes, our native land,
look on this man, this Oedipus, the one
who understood that celebrated riddle.
He was the most powerful of men.
All citizens who witnessed this man's wealth
were envious. Now what a surging tide
of terrible disaster sweeps around him.
So while we wait to see that final day,
we cannot call a mortal being happy
before he's passed beyond life free from pain.

* * *

Reading and Reacting

1. The ancient Greeks used no scenery in their theatrical productions. In the absence of scenery, how is the setting established at the beginning of *Oedipus the King*?
2. In some recent productions of *Oedipus the King*, actors wear copies of ancient Greek masks. What are the advantages and disadvantages of using such masks in a contemporary production of the play?
3. In the ancient Greek theater, the chorus chanted as it danced across the stage. If you were staging the play today, would you retain the chorus or do away with it entirely? What would be gained or lost with each alternative?
4. Why does Sophocles have Oedipus blind himself offstage? What would be the effect of having Oedipus perform this act in full view of the audience?
5. How does Sophocles observe the unities of time, place, and action? How does Sophocles manage to present information about what happened years before the action of the play while still maintaining the three unities?
6. The ancient Greek audience that viewed *Oedipus the King* was familiar with the plot of the play. Given this situation, how does Sophocles create suspense? What are the advantages and disadvantages of using a story that the audience already knows?
7. By the end of the play, what has Oedipus learned about himself? about the gods? about the quest for truth? Is he a tragic or a pathetic figure?

---

[23]*...all enter the palace]*: It is not entirely clear from these final lines whether Oedipus now leaves Thebes or not. According to Jebb's commentary (line 1519), in the traditional story on which Sophocles is relying, Oedipus was involuntarily held at Thebes for some time before the citizens and Creon expelled him from the city. Creon's lines suggest he is going to wait to hear from the oracle before deciding about Oedipus. However, there is a powerful dramatic logic in having Oedipus stumble off away from the palace. In Book 23 of the *Iliad*, Homer indicates that Oedipus died at Thebes, and there were funeral games held in his honor in that city.

8. Today, many directors employ **color-blind casting**—that is, they cast an actor in a role without regard to race. Do you think this practice could be used in casting *Oedipus the King*? How, for example, would you react to an African American Oedipus or to an Asian Creon?
9. **Journal Entry** Do you think Oedipus deserves his fate? Why, or why not?
10. **Critical Perspective** In "On Misunderstanding the *Oedipus Rex*," F. R. Dodds argues that Sophocles did not intend that Oedipus's tragedy be seen as rising from a "grave moral flaw." Neither, says Dodds, was Oedipus a "mere puppet" of the gods. Rather, "what fascinates us is the spectacle of a man freely choosing, from the highest motives, a series of actions which lead to his own ruin":

    > Oedipus is great, not in virtue of a great worldly position—for his worldly position is an illusion which will vanish like a dream—but in virtue of his inner strength: strength to pursue the truth at whatever personal cost, and strength to accept and endure it when found.... Oedipus is great because he accepts the responsibility for all his acts, including those which are objectively most horrible, though subjectively innocent.

    Do you agree with Dodds's arguments? Do you see Oedipus as someone who has inner strength or as a morally flawed victim of the gods?

Related Works: "Barn Burning" (p. 265), "Young Goodman Brown" (p. 354), "Out, Out—" (p. 577), "Leda and the Swan" (p. 664), "Ulysses" (p. 739), *Hamlet* (p. 1012)

WRITING SUGGESTIONS: Staging

1. Discuss the problems that the original staging of *Oedipus the King* poses for contemporary audiences and offer some possible solutions.
2. The simplicity of the ancient Greek theater was one of its main strengths. If a scene called for a particular setting—a palace, for example—the setting could be established with dialogue. Find some examples of this technique and write an essay in which you discuss whether or not such suggestions are as effective in the staging of *Oedipus the King* than special effects or realistic settings would be.
3. Discuss and analyze the staging options for a play that is not in this chapter, such as *Beauty* (p. 785) or *Applicant* (p. 807).
4. Choose a short story that appears in this anthology and explain how you would stage it if it were a play. What furnishings, props, costumes, lighting, and sound effects would you choose? What events would occur offstage? Possible subjects for this essay might include "The Story of an Hour" (p. 151), "A&P" (p. 179), or "The Storm" (p. 216).
5. Assume you have a very limited budget for staging *The Cuban Swimmer*. What challenges would you face? Write an essay in which you outline your plans for staging *The Cuban Swimmer*.

Chapter

32

Theme

Sophocles

Bettmann/Getty Images

August Wilson

AP Images

Learning Objectives

After reading this chapter, you will be able to. . .

- Define theme as it relates to drama.
- Interpret the theme of a work of drama based on its title.
- Identify how conflict suggests the theme of a work of drama.
- Describe how dialogue suggests the theme of a work of drama
- Explain how characters convey the themes in a work of drama.
- Explain how staging suggests the theme of a work of drama.
- Describe the relation of genre and theme in drama.

Like a short story or a poem, a play is open to interpretation. Readers' reactions are influenced by the language of the text, and audiences' reactions are influenced by the performance on stage. As in all works of literature, every element of a play—its title, its conflicts, its dialogue, its characters, and its staging—can shed light on its themes.

Titles

The **title** of a play can provide insight into its themes. The ironic title of Susan Glaspell's *Trifles* (p. 820), for example, suggests that women's concerns with "trifles" may get to the truth more effectively than the preoccupations of self-important men. Lorraine Hansberry's *A Raisin in the Sun* (1959) is another title that offers clues to the theme of a play. An allusion to Langston Hughes's poem "Harlem" (p. 561)—which asks, "what happens to a dream deferred? / Does it dry up / like a raisin in the sun?"—the title suggests what happens to an African American family whose dreams are repeatedly crushed. Likewise, the title *Fences* (p. 1222) offers clues to a major theme of August Wilson's play, suggesting that the main character is kept from his goals by barriers that are constructed by himself as well as by society. Finally, the title of Anton Chekhov's *The Brute* (p. 769) calls attention to the play's ideas about male–female relationships. The title may refer to Smirnov, who says that he has never liked women—whom he characterizes as "creatures of poetry and romance." Or, it may refer to Mrs. Popov's late husband, to whose memory she has dedicated her life despite the fact that he was unfaithful. Either alternative reinforces the play's tongue-in-cheek characterization of men as "brutes."

Conflicts

The unfolding plot of a play—especially the **conflicts** that develop—can reveal the play's themes. In Henrik Ibsen's *A Doll's House* (p. 834), for example, at least three major conflicts are present: one between Nora and her husband Torvald, one between Nora and Krogstad (an old acquaintance), and one between Nora and society. Each of these conflicts sheds light on the themes of the play.

Scene from *A Doll's House* with Dominic Rowan (as Torvald Helmer) and Hattie Morahan (as Nora) at the Young Vic in London, UK
Robbie Jack/Corbis Historical/Getty Images

Through Nora's conflict with Torvald, Ibsen examines the constraints placed on women and men by marriage in the nineteenth century. Both Nora and Torvald are imprisoned within their respective roles: Nora must be passive and childlike, and Torvald must be honorable and always in control. Nora, therefore, expects her husband to be noble and generous and, in a crisis, to sacrifice himself for her. When he fails to live up to her high expectations, she is profoundly disillusioned.

Nora's conflict with Krogstad underscores Ibsen's criticisms of the class system in nineteenth-century Norway. At the beginning of the play, Nora finds it "very funny to think that we—that Torvald has so much power over … people." Krogstad, a bank clerk who is in the employ of Torvald, visits Nora in Act 1 to enlist her aid in saving his job. It is clear that she sees him as her social inferior. For example, when Krogstad questions her about a woman with whom he has seen her, she replies, "How dare you question me, Mr. Krogstad…You, one of my husband's subordinates." Nora does not realize that she and Krogstad are, ironically, very much alike: both occupy subordinate positions and therefore have no power to determine their own destinies.

Finally, through Nora's conflict with society, Ibsen examines the destructive nature of the forces that subjugate women. Nineteenth-century society was male dominated. A married woman had the same legal status as one of her children. She could not borrow money without her husband's signature, own real estate in her own name, or enter into contracts. In addition, all her assets—including inheritances and trust funds—automatically became the property of her husband at the time of marriage. As a result of her sheltered life, Nora at the beginning of the play is completely unaware of the consequences of her actions. Most readers share Dr. Rank's confusion when he asks Nora, "Why do you laugh at what I said? Do you really understand what society means?" It is Nora's disillusionment at finding out that Torvald and the rest of society are not what she has been led to believe they are that ultimately causes her to rebel. By walking out the door at the end of the play, Nora rejects not only her husband and her children (to whom she has no legal right once she leaves), but also society and its laws.

These three conflicts underscore many of the themes that dominate *A Doll's House*. First, the conflicts show that marriage in the nineteenth century imprisons both men and women in narrow, constricting roles. They also show that middle-class Norwegian society is narrow, smug, and judgmental. (Krogstad is looked down upon for a crime years after he committed it, and Nora is looked down upon because she borrows money to save her husband's life.) Finally, the conflicts show that society does not offer individuals—especially women—the freedom to lead happy and fulfilling lives. Only when the social and economic conditions that govern society change, Ibsen suggests, can both women and men live together in mutual esteem.

Dialogue

Dialogue can also give insight into a play's themes. Sometimes a character suggests—or even explicitly states—a theme. In Act 3 of *A Doll's House*, for example, Nora's friend, Mrs. Linde, comes as close as any character to expressing the central concern of the play when she says, "Torvald must find out all about it. This painful secret must be revealed. They must come to a complete understanding between themselves. That is impossible with all this deception, this hiding of the truth." As the play goes on to demonstrate, the lies that exist both in marriage and in society are obstacles to love and happiness.

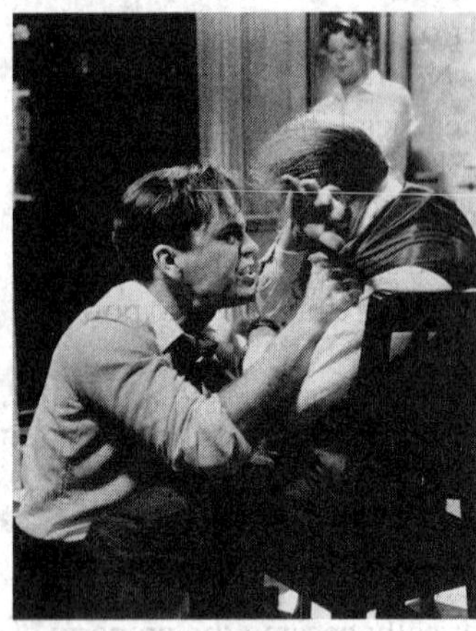

Scene from *Death of a Salesman,* with John Malkovich (as Biff) in a final confrontation with Dustin Hoffman (as Willy Loman), and Stephen Lang (as Happy) looking on

Bettmann/Getty Images

One of the main themes of Arthur Miller's *Death of a Salesman*—the questionable validity of the American Dream, given the nation's social, political, and economic realities—is suggested by the play's dialogue. As his son Biff points out, Willy Loman's stubborn belief in upward mobility and material success is based more on fantasy than on fact:

Willy: *(with hatred, threatening)* The door of your life is wide open!

Biff: Pop! I am a dime a dozen, and so are you!

Willy: *(turning on him now in an uncontrolled outburst)* I am not a dime a dozen! I am Willy Loman, and you are Biff Loman!

Biff starts for Willy, but is blocked by Happy. In his fury, Biff seems on the verge of attacking his father.

Biff: I am not a leader of men, Willy, and neither are you. You were never anything but a hard-working drummer who landed in the ash can like all the rest of them! I'm one dollar an hour, Willy! I tried seven states and couldn't raise it. A buck an hour! Do you gather my meaning? I'm not bringing home any prizes any more, and you're going to stop waiting for me to bring them home!

Although it does not explicitly state the theme of the play, this exchange strongly suggests that Biff rejects the American dream of success to which Willy desperate clings.

Characters

Because a dramatic work focuses on a central character, or **protagonist**, the development of this character can shed light on a play's themes. Nora in *A Doll's House* changes a great deal during the course of the play. At the beginning, she is more her husband's possession than an adult capable of shaping her own destiny. Nora's status becomes apparent in Act 1 when Torvald gently scolds his "Little Miss Extravagant" and refers to her as his "little lark" and his "little squirrel." She is reduced to childish deceptions, such as hiding her macaroons when her husband enters the room. After Krogstad accuses her of committing forgery and threatens to expose her, she expects her husband to rise to the occasion and take the blame for her. When Torvald instead accuses her of being a hypocrite, a liar, and a criminal, Nora's neat little world comes crashing down. As a result of this experience, Nora changes; no longer is she the submissive and obedient wife. Instead, she becomes assertive—even rebellious—ultimately telling Torvald that their marriage is a sham and that she can no longer stay with him. This abrupt shift in Nora's personality gives the audience a clear understanding of the major themes of the play.

Unlike Nora, Antigone in Sophocles's *Antigone* (p. 1191) is a character who changes very little during the course of the play. Fiercely devoted to her brother, Antigone decides to bury her brother's body in violation of Creon's decree that his corpse must be left to rot. Antigone's loyalty to her brother and to the gods makes it impossible for her to compromise. Her stubborn refusal to bend to the will of the king causes her downfall as well as her death. Antigone's inability to change highlights the central conflict of the play: Is a person's main duty to the king, to the gods, or to themselves?

Staging

Various staging elements, such as props and furnishings, may also convey the themes of a play. The miniature animals in *The Glass Menagerie* (p. 958) suggest the fragility of Laura's character and the futility of her efforts to fit into the modern world. And, in *Trifles*, the depressing farmhouse, the broken birdcage, and the dead canary hint at Mrs. Wright's misery and the reason she murdered her husband.

Special lighting effects and music can also suggest a play's themes. Throughout *The Glass Menagerie*, for example, words and pictures are projected onto a section of the set between the front room and dining room walls. In Scene 1, as Tom's mother, Amanda, tells him about her experiences with her "gentlemen callers," an image of her as a girl greeting callers appears on the screen. As Amanda continues, the words "*Où sont Les Neiges*"—"Where are the snows [of yesteryear]?"—appear on the screen. Later in the play, when Laura and her mother discuss a boy Laura knew, his picture is projected on the screen, showing him as a high school hero carrying a silver cup. In addition to the slides, Williams uses music—a recurring tune, dance music, and "Ave Maria"—to increase the emotional impact of certain scenes. He also uses shafts of light focused on selected areas or characters to create a dreamlike atmosphere for the play. Collectively, the slides, music, and lighting reinforce the theme that those who retreat into the past inevitably become estranged from the present.

A Final Note

As you read, your own values and beliefs influence your interpretation of a play's themes. For example, your interest in the changing status of women could lead you to focus on the submissive, almost passive, role of Nora in *A Doll's House*. As a result, you could conclude that the play shows how, in nineteenth century Norway—as well as in the United States—women like Nora often sacrificed their own happiness for that of their husbands'. Remember, however, that the play itself, not just your own feelings or assumptions about it, must support your interpretation.

Checklist Writing about Theme

- What is the central theme of the play?
- What other themes can you identify?
- Does the title of the play suggest a theme?
- What conflicts exist in the play? How do they shed light on the themes of the play?
- Do any characters' statements express or imply a theme of the play?
- Do any characters change during the play? How do these changes suggest the play's themes?
- Do certain characters resist change? How does their failure to change suggest a theme of the play?
- Do scenery and props help to communicate the play's themes?
- Does music reinforce certain ideas in the play?
- Does lighting underscore the themes of the play?

SOPHOCLES (496–406 B.C.) (picture and biography on p. 1136) was one of nine generals elected for a military campaign against Samos, a Greek island that was in revolt against Athens. Sophocles' election was due at least in part to the popularity of his play *Antigone.* (Greek plays often centered on problems of the city-state, and the theater was in many ways the center of the state's religious and political life.)

Even though it was written long before *Oedipus the King, Antigone* traces the events that befall Oedipus's younger daughter after his banishment from Thebes. Caught between the laws of the gods and the edict of her uncle the king, Antigone follows her conscience despite the fatal consequences to herself. In the 1960s, the story of Antigone was especially meaningful to those Americans who engaged in civil disobedience in struggles for civil rights and in protest against the war in Vietnam.

Cultural Context The central struggle in this play revolves around Antigone's desire to bury her brother in an honorable way. The ancient Greeks believed that at the moment of death, the spirit of the dead person left the body as a little puff of wind. The body was then prepared for burial according to certain rituals, which were primarily performed by female relatives. The burial rituals consisted of three parts: the *prothesis,* or laying out of the body; the *ekphora,* or funeral procession; and the interment of the body or cremated remains of the deceased. Coins were placed over the eyelids of the deceased as payment for the ferryman who would usher the body across the River Styx and into the underworld. The ancient Greeks believed that if the correct methods of burial were not followed, the soul of the deceased would roam between worlds until the proscribed rites were completed.

Antigone* (441 B.C.)

Translated by Dudley Fitts and Robert Fitzgerald

CHARACTERS

Antigone	**Teiresias**
Ismene	**A Sentry**
Eurydice	**A Messenger**
Creon	**Chorus**
Haimon	

SCENE

Before the palace of Creon, King of Thebes. A central double door, and two lateral doors. A platform extends the length of the facade, and from this platform three steps lead down into the "orchestra," or chorus-ground.

TIME

Dawn of the day after the repulse of the Argive army from the assault on Thebes.

Scene from a 1999 production of *Antigone* at London's Old Vic Theater

Photo by John Haynes/Lebrecht Music & Arts

*Note that individual lines are numbered in the following play. When a line is shared by two or more characters, it is counted as one line.

PROLOGUE[1]

Antigone and Ismene enter from the central door of the palace.

Antigone: Ismene, dear sister,
You would think that we had already suffered enough
For the curse on Oedipus.[2]
I cannot imagine any grief
That you and I have not gone through. And now—
Have they told you of the new decree of our King Creon?
Ismene: I have heard nothing: I know
That two sisters lost two brothers, a double death
In a single hour; and I know that the Argive army
Fled in the night; but beyond this, nothing.
Antigone: I thought so. And that is why I wanted you
To come out here with me. There is something we must do.
Ismene: Why do you speak so strangely?
Antigone: Listen, Ismene: Creon buried our brother Eteocles
With military honors, gave him a soldier's funeral,
And it was right that he should; but Polyneices,
Who fought as bravely and died as miserably,—
They say that Creon has sworn
No one shall bury him, no one mourn for him,
But his body must lie in the fields, a sweet treasure
For carrion birds to find as they search for food.
That is what they say, and our good Creon is coming here
To announce it publicly; and the penalty—
Stoning to death in the public square!
There it is,
And now you can prove what you are:
A true sister, or a traitor to your family.
Ismene: Antigone, you are mad! What could I possibly do?
Antigone: You must decide whether you will help me or not.
Ismene: I do not understand you. Help you in what?
Antigone: Ismene, I am going to bury him. Will you come?

---

[1]*Prologue:* The portion of the play containing the exposition, or explanation, of what has gone before and what is now happening.

[2]*the curse on Oedipus:* As Sophocles tells in *Oedipus the King,* the king of Thebes discovered that he had lived his life under a curse. Unknowingly, he had slain his father and married his mother. On realizing this terrible truth, Oedipus put out his own eyes and departed into exile. Now, years later, as *Antigone* opens, Antigone and Ismene, daughters of Oedipus, are recalling how their two brothers died. After the abdication of their father, the brothers ruled Thebes together, but they fell to quarreling. When Eteocles expelled Polyneices, the latter returned with an army and attacked the city. The two brothers killed each other in combat, leaving the throne to Creon. The new king of Thebes buried Eteocles with full honors but, calling Polyneices a traitor, decreed that Polyneices' body be left to the crows. This was an especially terrible decree, for a rotting corpse might offend Zeus, bring down plague, blight, and barrenness upon Thebes, and prevent the soul of a dead hero from entering the Elysian Fields, abode of those favored by the gods.

Ismene: Bury him! You have just said the new law forbids it.
Antigone: He is my brother. And he is your brother, too.
Ismene: But think of the danger! Think what Creon will do!
Antigone: Creon is not strong enough to stand in my way.
Ismene: Ah sister!
Oedipus died, everyone hating him
For what his own search brought to light, his eyes
Ripped out by his own hand; and Jocasta died,
His mother and wife at once: she twisted the cords
That strangled her life; and our two brothers died,
Each killed by the other's sword. And we are left:
But oh, Antigone,
Think how much more terrible than these
Our own death would be if we should go against Creon
And do what he has forbidden! We are only women,
We cannot fight with men, Antigone!
The law is strong, we must give in to the law
In this thing, and in worse. I beg the Dead
To forgive me, but I am helpless: I must yield
To those in authority. And I think it is dangerous business
To be always meddling.
Antigone: If that is what you think,
I should not want you, even if you asked to come.
You have made your choice, you can be what you want to be.
But I will bury him; and if I must die,
I say that this crime is holy: I shall lie down
With him in death, and I shall be as dear
To him as he to me.
It is the dead,
Not the living, who make the longest demands:
We die for ever . . .
You may do as you like,
Since apparently the laws of the gods mean nothing to you.
Ismene: They mean a great deal to me; but I have no strength
To break laws that were made for the public good.
Antigone: That must be your excuse, I suppose. But as for me,
I will bury the brother I love.
Ismene: Antigone,
I am so afraid for you!
Antigone: You need not be:
You have yourself to consider, after all.
Ismene: But no one must hear of this, you must tell no one!
I will keep it a secret, I promise!
Antigone: O tell it! Tell everyone!
Think how they'll hate you when it all comes out
If they learn that you knew about it all the time!

Ismene: So fiery! You should be cold with fear.
Antigone: Perhaps. But I am doing only what I must.
Ismene: But can you do it? I say that you cannot.
Antigone: Very well: when my strength gives out,
I shall do no more.
Ismene: Impossible things should not be tried at all.
Antigone: Go away, Ismene:
I shall be hating you soon, and the dead will too,
For your words are hateful. Leave me my foolish plan:
I am not afraid of the danger; if it means death,
It will not be the worst of deaths—death without honor.
Ismene: Go then, if you feel that you must.
You are unwise,
But a loyal friend indeed to those who love you.

Exit into the palace. Antigone goes off, left. Enter the Chorus.

PARODOS[1]

STROPHE 1

Chorus: Now the long blade of the sun, lying
Level east to west, touches with glory
Thebes of the Seven Gates. Open, unlidded
Eye of golden day! O marching light
Across the eddy and rush of Dirce's stream,[2]
Striking the white shields of the enemy
Thrown headlong backward from the blaze of morning!
Choragos:[3] Polyneices their commander
Roused them with windy phrases,
He the wild eagle screaming
Insults above our land,
His wings their shields of snow,
His crest their marshalled helms.

ANTISTROPHE 1

Chorus: Against our seven gates in a yawning ring
The famished spears came onward in the night;
But before his jaws were sated with our blood,
Or pinefire took the garland of our towers,
He was thrown back; and as he turned, great Thebes—

---

[1]*Parodos:* A song sung by the Chorus on the entering. Its *strophe* (according to scholarly theory) was sung while the Chorus danced from stage right to stage left; its *antistrophe,* while the Chorus danced back again. Another parodos follows the prologue of *Oedipus the King.*
[2]*Dirce's stream:* A river near Thebes.
[3]*Choragos:* Leader of the Chorus and principal commentator on the play's action.

No tender victim for his noisy power—
Rose like a dragon behind him, shouting war.
Choragos: For God hates utterly
The bray of bragging tongues;
And when he beheld their smiling,
Their swagger of golden helms,
The frown of his thunder blasted
Their first man from our walls.

STROPHE 2

Chorus: We heard his shout of triumph high in the air
Turn to a scream; far out in a flaming arc
He fell with his windy torch, and the earth struck him.
And others storming in fury no less than his
Found shock of death in the dusty joy of battle.
Choragos: Seven captains at seven gates
Yielded their clanging arms to the god
That bends the battle-line and breaks it.
These two only, brothers in blood,
Face to face in matchless rage,
Mirroring each the other's death,
Clashed in long combat.

ANTISTROPHE 2

Chorus: But now in the beautiful morning of victory
Let Thebes of the many chariots sing for joy!
With hearts for dancing we'll take leave of war:
Our temples shall be sweet with hymns of praise,
And the long nights shall echo with our chorus.

SCENE 1

Choragos: But now at last our new King is coming:
Creon of Thebes, Menoeceus' son.
In this auspicious dawn of his reign
What are the new complexities
That shifting Fate has woven for him?
What is his counsel? Why has he summoned
The old men to hear him?

Enter Creon from the palace, center. He addresses the Chorus from the top step.

Creon: Gentlemen: I have the honor to inform you that our Ship of State, which recent storms have threatened to destroy, has come safely to harbor at last, guided by the merciful wisdom of Heaven. I have summoned you here this morning because I know that I can depend upon you: your devotion to King Laius was absolute; you never hesitated in your duty to our late ruler Oedipus; and when Oedipus died, your loyalty was transferred to his children. Unfortunately, as you know, his two sons, the princes Eteocles and Polyneices, have killed each other in battle; and I, as the next in blood, have succeeded to the full power of the throne.

I am aware, of course, that no Ruler can expect complete loyalty from his subjects until he has been tested in office. Nevertheless, I say to you at the very outset that I have nothing but contempt for the kind of Governor who is afraid, for whatever reason, to follow the course that he knows is best for the State; and as for the man who sets private friendship above the public welfare,—I have no use for him, either. I call God to witness that I saw my country headed for ruin, I should not be afraid to speak out plainly; and I need hardly remind you that I would never have any dealings with an enemy of the people. No one values friendship more highly than I; but we must remember that friends made at the risk of wrecking our Ship are not real friends at all.

These are my principles, at any rate, and that is why I have made the following decision concerning the sons of Oedipus: Eteocles, who died as a man should die, fighting for his country, is to be buried with full military honors, with all the ceremony that is usual when the greatest heroes die; but his brother Polyneices, who broke his exile to come back with fire and sword against his native city and the shrines of his fathers' gods, whose one idea was to spill the blood of his blood and sell his own people into slavery—Polyneices, I say, is to have no burial: no man is to touch him or say the least prayer for him; he shall lie on the plain, unburied; and the birds and the scavenging dogs can do with him whatever they like.

This is my command, and you can see the wisdom behind it. As long as I am King, no traitor is going to be honored with the loyal man. But whoever shows by word and deed that he is on the side of the State,—he shall have my respect while he is living and my reverence when he is dead.

Choragos: If that is your will, Creon son of Menoeceus,
You have the right to enforce it: we are yours.

Creon: That is my will. Take care that you do your part.

Choragos: We are old men: let the younger ones carry it out.

Creon: I do not mean that: the sentries have been appointed.

Choragos: Then what is it that you would have us do?

Creon: You will give no support to whoever breaks this law.

Choragos: Only a crazy man is in love with death!

Creon: And death it is; yet money talks, and the wisest
Have sometimes been known to count a few coins too many.

Enter Sentry from left.

Sentry: I'll not say that I'm out of breath from running, King, because every time I stopped to think about what I have to tell you, I felt like going back. And all the time a voice kept saying, "You fool, don't you know you're walking straight into trouble?"; and then another voice: "Yes, but if you let somebody else get the news to Creon first, it will be even worse than that for you!" But good sense won out, at least I hope it was good sense, and here I am with a story that makes no sense at all; but I'll tell it anyhow, because, as they say, what's going to happen's going to happen and—

Creon: Come to the point. What have you to say?

Sentry: I did not do it. I did not see who did it. You must not punish me for what someone else has done.

Creon: A comprehensive defense! More effective, perhaps,
If I knew its purpose. Come: what is it?

Sentry: A dreadful thing . . . I don't know how to put it—

Creon: Out with it!

Sentry: Well, then;
The dead man—
Polyneices—

Pause. The Sentry is overcome, fumbles for words. Creon waits impassively.

out there—
someone,—
New dust on the slimy flesh!

Pause. No sign from Creon.

Someone has given it burial that way, and
Gone . . .

Long pause. Creon finally speaks with deadly control.

Creon: And the man who dared do this?

Sentry: I swear I
Do not know! You must believe me!
Listen:
The ground was dry, not a sign of digging, no,
Not a wheeltrack in the dust, no trace of anyone.
It was when they relieved us this morning: and one of them,
The corporal, pointed to it.
There it was,
The strangest—
Look:
The body, just mounded over with light dust: you see?
Not buried really, but as if they'd covered it
Just enough for the ghost's peace. And no sign
Of dogs or any wild animal that had been there.
And then what a scene there was! Every man of us
Accusing the other: we all proved the other man did it,
We all had proof that we could not have done it.

We were ready to take hot iron in our hands,
Walk through fire, swear by all the gods,
It was not I!
I do not know who it was, but it was not I!

Creon's rage has been mounting steadily, but the Sentry is too intent upon his story to notice it.

And then, when this came to nothing, someone said
A thing that silenced us and made us stare
Down at the ground: you had to be told the news,
And one of us had to do it! We threw the dice,
And the bad luck fell to me. So here I am,
No happier to be here than you are to have me:
Nobody likes the man who brings bad news.

Choragos: I have been wondering, King: can it be that the gods have done this?

Creon: *(Furiously)* Stop!
Must you doddering wrecks
Go out of your heads entirely? "The gods"!
Intolerable!
The gods favor this corpse? Why? How had he served them?
Tried to loot their temples, burn their images,
Yes, and the whole State, and its laws with it!
Is it your senile opinion that the gods love to honor bad men?
A pious thought!—
No, from the very beginning
There have been those who have whispered together,
Stiff-necked anarchists, putting their heads together,
Scheming against me in alleys. These are the men,
And they have bribed my own guard to do this thing.
(Sententiously) Money!
There's nothing in the world so demoralizing as money.
Down go your cities,
Homes gone, men gone, honest hearts corrupted,
Crookedness of all kinds, and all for money!
(To Sentry) But you—
I swear by God and by the throne of God,
The man who has done this thing shall pay for it!
Find that man, bring him here to me, or your death
Will be the least of your problems: I'll string you up
Alive, and there will be certain ways to make you
Discover your employer before you die;
And the process may teach you a lesson you seem to have missed:
The dearest profit is sometimes all too dear:
That depends on the source. Do you understand me?
A fortune won is often misfortune.

Sentry: King, may I speak?

Creon: Your very voice distresses me.
Sentry: Are you sure that it is my voice, and not your conscience?
Creon: By God, he wants to analyze me now!
Sentry: It is not what I say, but what has been done, that hurts you.
Creon: You talk too much.
Sentry: Maybe; but I've done nothing.
Creon: Sold your soul for some silver: that's all you've done.
Sentry: How dreadful it is when the right judge judges wrong!
Creon: Your figures of speech
May entertain you now; but unless you bring me the man,
You will get little profit from them in the end.

Exit Creon into the palace.

Sentry: "Bring me the man"—!
I'd like nothing better than bringing him the man!
But bring him or not, you have seen the last of me here.
At any rate, I am safe!

Exit Sentry.

ODE 1[1]

STROPHE 1

Chorus: Numberless are the world's wonders, but none
More wonderful than man; the stormgray sea
Yields to his prows, the huge crests bear him high;
Earth, holy and inexhaustible, is graven
With shining furrows where his plows have gone
Year after year, the timeless labor of stallions.

ANTISTROPHE 1

The lightboned birds and beasts that cling to cover,
The lithe fish lighting their reaches of dim water,
All are taken, tamed in the net of his mind;
The lion on the hill, the wild horse windy-maned,
Resign to him; and his blunt yoke has broken
The sultry shoulders of the mountain bull.

STROPHE 2

Words also, and thought as rapid as air,
He fashions to his good use; statecraft is his,
And his the skill that deflects the arrows of snow,
The spears of winter rain: from every wind
He has made himself secure—from all but one:
In the late wind of death he cannot stand.

[1] *Ode 1:* The first song sung by the Chorus, who at the same time danced. Here again, as in the *parodos, strophe* and *antistrophe* probably divide the song into two movements of the dance: right to left, then left to right.

ANTISTROPHE 2

O clear intelligence, force beyond all measure!
O fate of man, working both good and evil!
When the laws are kept, how proudly his city stands!
When the laws are broken, what of his city then?
Never may the anárchic man find rest at my hearth,
Never be it said that my thoughts are his thoughts.

SCENE 2

Reenter Sentry leading Antigone.

Choragos: What does this mean? Surely this captive woman
Is the Princess, Antigone. Why should she be taken?
Sentry: Here is the one who did it! We caught her
In the very act of burying him.—Where is Creon?
Choragos: Just coming from the house.

Enter Creon, center.

Creon: What has happened?
Why have you come back so soon?
Sentry: *(Expansively)* O King,
A man should never be too sure of anything:
I would have sworn
That you'd not see me here again: your anger
Frightened me so, and the things you threatened me with;
But how could I tell then
That I'd be able to solve the case so soon?
No dice-throwing this time: I was only too glad to come!
Here is this woman. She is the guilty one:
We found her trying to bury him.
Take her, then; question her; judge her as you will.
I am through with the whole thing now, and glad of it.
Creon: But this is Antigone! Why have you brought her here?
Sentry: She was burying him, I tell you!
Creon: *(Severely)* Is this the truth?
Sentry: I saw her with my own eyes. Can I say more?
Creon: The details: come, tell me quickly!
Sentry: It was like this:
After those terrible threats of yours, King,
We went back and brushed the dust away from the body.
The flesh was soft by now, and stinking,
So we sat on a hill to windward and kept guard.
No napping this time! We kept each other awake.
But nothing happened until the white round sun
Whirled in the center of the round sky over us:
Then, suddenly,

A storm of dust roared up from the earth, and the sky
Went out, the plain vanished with all its tress
In the stinging dark. We closed our eyes and endured it.
The whirlwind lasted a long time, but it passed;
And then we looked, and there was Antigone!
I have seen
A mother bird come back to a stripped nest, heard
Her crying bitterly a broken note or two
For the young ones stolen. Just so, when this girl
Found the bare corpse, and all her love's work wasted,
She wept, and cried on heaven to damn the hands
That had done this thing.
And then she brought more dust
And sprinkled wine three times for her brother's ghost.
We ran and took her at once. She was not afraid,
Not even when we charged her with what she had done.
She denied nothing.
And this was a comfort to me,
And some uneasiness: for it is a good thing
To escape from death, but it is no great pleasure
To bring death to a friend.
Yet I always say
There is nothing so comfortable as your own safe skin!

Creon: *(Slowly, dangerously)* And you, Antigone,
You with your head hanging,—do you confess this thing?

Antigone: I do. I deny nothing.

Creon: *(To Sentry)* You may go.

Exit Sentry.

(To Antigone.) Tell me, tell me briefly:
Had you heard my proclamation touching this matter?

Antigone: It was public. Could I help hearing it?

Creon: And yet you dared defy the law.

Antigone: I dared.
It was not God's proclamation. That final Justice
That rules the world below makes no such laws.
Your edict, King, was strong,
But all your strength is weakness itself against
The immortal unrecorded laws of God.
They are not merely now: they were, and shall be,
Operative for ever, beyond man utterly.
I knew I must die, even without your decree:
I am only mortal. And if I must die
Now, before it is my time to die,
Surely this is no hardship: can anyone

Living, as I live, with evil all about me,
Think Death less than a friend? This death of mine
Is of no importance; but if I had left my brother
Lying in death unburied, I should have suffered.
Now I do not.
You smile at me. Ah Creon,
Think me a fool, if you like; but it may well be
That a fool convicts me of folly.
Choragos: Like father, like daughter: both headstrong, deaf to reason!
She has never learned to yield:
Creon: She has much to learn.
The inflexible heart breaks first, the toughest iron
Cracks first, and the wildest horses bend their necks
At the pull of the smallest curb.
Pride? In a slave?
This girl is guilty of a double insolence,
Breaking the given laws and boasting of it.
Who is the man here,
She or I, if this crime goes unpunished?
Sister's child, or more than sister's child,
Or closer yet in blood—she and her sister
Win bitter death for this!
(To Servants) Go, some of you,
Arrest Ismene. I accuse her equally.
Bring her: you will find her sniffling in the house there.
Her mind's a traitor: crimes kept in the dark
Cry for light, and the guardian brain shudders;
But how much worse than this
Is brazen boasting of barefaced anarchy!
Antigone: Creon, what more do you want than my death?
Creon: Nothing.
That gives me everything.
Antigone: Then I beg you: kill me.
This talking is a great weariness: your words
Are distasteful to me, and I am sure that mine
Seem so to you. And yet they should not seem so:
I should have praise and honor for what I have done.
All these men here would praise me
Were their lips not frozen shut with fear of you.
(Bitterly) Ah the good fortune of kings,
Licensed to say and do whatever they please!
Creon: You are alone here in that opinion.
Antigone: No, they are with me. But they keep their tongues in leash.
Creon: Maybe. But you are guilty, and they are not.
Antigone: There is no guilt in reverence for the dead.

Creon: But Eteocles—was he not your brother too?
Antigone: My brother too.
Creon: And you insult his memory?
Antigone: *(Softly)* The dead man would not say that I insult it.
Creon: He would: for you honor a traitor as much as him.
Antigone: His own brother, traitor or not, and equal in blood.
Creon: He made war on his country. Eteocles defended it.
Antigone: Nevertheless, there are honors due all the dead.
Creon: But not the same for the wicked as for the just.
Antigone: Ah Creon, Creon.
Which of us can say what the gods hold wicked?
Creon: An enemy is an enemy, even dead.
Antigone: It is my nature to join in love, not hate.
Creon: *(Finally losing patience)* Go join them then; if you must have your love,
Find it in hell!
Choragos: But see, Ismene comes:

Enter Ismene, guarded.

Those tears are sisterly, the cloud
That shadows her eyes rains down gentle sorrow.
Creon: You too, Ismene,
Snake in my ordered house, sucking my blood
Stealthily—and all the time I never knew
That these two sisters were aiming at my throne!
Ismene,
Do you confess your share in this crime, or deny it?
Answer me.
Ismene: Yes, if she will let me say so. I am guilty.
Antigone: *(Coldly)* No, Ismene. You have no right to say so.
You would not help me, and I will not have you help me.
Ismene: But now I know what you meant; and I am here
To join you, to take my share of punishment.
Antigone: The dead man and the gods who rule the dead
Know whose act this was. Words are not friends.
Ismene: Do you refuse me, Antigone? I want to die with you:
I too have a duty that I must discharge to the dead.
Antigone: You shall not lessen my death by sharing it.
Ismene: What do I care for life when you are dead?
Antigone: Ask Creon. You're always hanging on his opinions.
Ismene: You are laughing at me. Why, Antigone?
Antigone: It's a joyless laughter, Ismene.
Ismene: But can I do nothing?
Antigone: Yes. Save yourself. I shall not envy you.
There are those who will praise you; I shall have honor, too.
Ismene: But we are equally guilty!

Antigone: No more, Ismene.
You are alive, but I belong to Death.
Creon: *(to the Chorus)* Gentlemen, I beg you to observe these girls:
One has just now lost her mind; the other
It seems, has never had a mind at all.
Ismene: Grief teaches the steadiest minds to waver, King.
Creon: Yours certainly did, when you assumed guilt with the guilty!
Ismene: But how could I go on living without her?
Creon: You are. She is already dead.
Ismene: But your own son's bride!
Creon: There are places enough for him to push his plow.
I want no wicked women for my sons!
Ismene: O dearest Haimon, how your father wrongs you!
Creon: I've had enough of your childish talk of marriage!
Choragos: Do you really intend to steal this girl from your son?
Creon: No; Death will do that for me.
Choragos: Then she must die?
Creon: *(Ironically)* You dazzle me.
—But enough of this talk!
(To Guards) You, there, take them away and guard them well:
For they are but women, and even brave men run
When they see Death coming.

Exeunt Ismene, Antigone, and Guards.

ODE 2

STROPHE 1

Chorus: Fortunate is the man who has never tasted God's vengeance!
Where once the anger of heaven has struck, that house is shaken
For ever: damnation rises behind each child
Like a wave cresting out of the black northeast,
When the long darkness under sea roars up
And bursts drumming death upon the windwhipped sand.

ANTISTROPHE 1

I have seen this gathering sorrow from time long past
Loom upon Oedipus' children: generation from generation
Takes the compulsive rage of the enemy god.
So lately this last flower of Oedipus' line
Drank the sunlight! but now a passionate word
And a handful of dust have closed up all its beauty.

STROPHE 2

What mortal arrogance
Transcends the wrath of Zeus?

Sleep cannot lull him nor the effortless long months
Of the timeless gods: but he is young for ever,
And his house is the shining day of high Olympos.
    All that is and shall be,
    And all the past, is his.
No pride on earth is free of the curse of heaven.

ANTISTROPHE 2

The straying dreams of men
    May bring them ghosts of joy:
But as they drowse, the waking embers burn them;
Or they walk with fixed eyes, as blind men walk.
But the ancient wisdom speaks for our own time:
    Fate works most for woe
    With Folly's fairest show.
Man's little pleasure is the spring of sorrow.

SCENE 3

Choragos: But here is Haimon, King, the last of all your sons.
    Is it grief for Antigone that brings him here,
    And bitterness at being robbed of his bride?

Enter Haimon.

Creon: We shall soon see, and no need of diviners.
                                        —Son,
    You have heard my final judgment on that girl:
    Have you come here hating me, or have you come
    With deference and with love, whatever I do?
Haimon: I am your son, father. You are my guide.
    You make things clear for me, and I obey you.
    No marriage means more to me than your continuing wisdom.
Creon: Good. That is the way to behave: subordinate
    Everything else, my son, to your father's will.
    This is what a man prays for, that he may get
    Sons attentive and dutiful in his house,
    Each one hating his father's enemies,
    Honoring his father's friends. But if his sons
    Fail him, if they turn out unprofitably,
    What has he fathered but trouble for himself
    And amusement for the malicious?
                            So you are right
    Not to lose your head over this woman.
    Your pleasure with her would soon grow cold, Haimon,
    And then you'd have a hellcat in bed and elsewhere.
    Let her find her husband in Hell!

Of all the people in this city, only she
Has had contempt for my law and broken it.
Do you want me to show myself weak before the people?
Or to break my sworn word? No, and I will not.
The woman dies.
I suppose she'll plead "family ties." Well, let her.
If I permit my own family to rebel,
How shall I earn the world's obedience?
Show me the man who keeps his house in hand,
He's fit for public authority.
I'll have no dealings
With lawbreakers, critics of the government:
Whoever is chosen to govern should be obeyed—
Must be obeyed, in all things, great and small,
Just and unjust! O Haimon,
The man who knows how to obey, and that man only,
Knows how to give commands when the time comes.
You can depend on him, no matter how fast
The spears come: he's a good soldier, he'll stick it out.
Anarchy, anarchy! Show me a greater evil!
This is why cities tumble and the great houses rain down,
This is what scatters armies!
No, no: good lives are made so by discipline.
We keep the laws then, and the lawmakers,
And no woman shall seduce us. If we must lose,
Let's lose to a man, at least! Is a woman stronger than we?

Choragos: Unless time has rusted my wits,
What you say, King, is said with point and dignity.

Haimon: *(Boyishly earnest)* Father:
Reason is God's crowning gift to man, and you are right
To warn me against losing mine. I cannot say—
I hope that I shall never want to say!—that you
Have reasoned badly. Yet there are other men
Who can reason, too; and their opinions might be helpful.
You are not in a position to know everything
That people say or do, or what they feel:
Your temper terrifies—everyone
Will tell you only what you like to hear.
But I, at any rate, can listen; and I have heard them
Muttering and whispering in the dark about this girl.
They say no woman has ever, so unreasonably,
Died so shameful a death for a generous act:
"She covered her brother's body. Is this indecent?
She kept him from dogs and vultures. Is this a crime?
Death?—She should have all the honor that we can give her!"
This is the way they talk out there in the city.

You must believe me:
Nothing is closer to me than your happiness.
What could be closer? Must not any son
Value his father's fortune as his father does his?
I beg you, do not be unchangeable:
Do not believe that you alone can be right.
The man who thinks that,
The man who maintains that only he has the power
To reason correctly, the gift to speak, the soul—
A man like that, when you know him, turns out empty.
It is not reason never to yield to reason!
In flood time you can see how some trees bend,
And because they bend, even their twigs are safe,
While stubborn trees are torn up, roots and all.
And the same thing happens in sailing:
Make your sheet fast, never slacken,—and over you go,
Head over heels and under: and there's your voyage.
Forget you are angry! Let yourself be moved!
I know I am young; but please let me say this:
The ideal condition
Would be, I admit, that men should be right by instinct;
But since we are all too likely to go astray,
The reasonable thing is to learn from those who can teach.

Choragos: You will do well to listen to him, King,
If what he says is sensible. And you, Haimon,
Must listen to your father.—Both speak well.

Creon: You consider it right for a man of my years and experience
To go to school to a boy?

Haimon: It is not right
If I am wrong. But if I am young, and right,
What does my age matter?

Creon: You think it right to stand up for an anarchist?

Haimon: Not at all. I pay no respect to criminals.

Creon: Then she is not a criminal?

Haimon: The City would deny it, to a man.

Creon: And the City proposes to teach me how to rule?

Haimon: Ah. Who is it that's talking like a boy now?

Creon: My voice is the one voice giving orders in this City!

Haimon: It is no City if it takes orders from one voice.

Creon: The State is the King!

Haimon: Yes, if the State is a desert.

Pause.

Creon: This boy, it seems, has sold out to a woman.

Haimon: If you are a woman: my concern is only for you.

Creon: So? Your "concern"! In a public brawl with your father!

Haimon: How about you, in a public brawl with justice?
Creon: With justice, when all that I do is within my rights?
Haimon: You have no right to trample on God's right.
Creon: *(Completely out of control)* Fool, adolescent fool! Taken in by a woman!
Haimon: You'll never see me taken in by anything vile.
Creon: Every word you say is for her!
Haimon: *(Quietly, darkly)* And for you.
And for me. And for the gods under the earth.
Creon: You'll never marry her while she lives.
Haimon: Then she must die.—But her death will cause another.
Creon: Another?
Have you lost your senses? Is this an open threat?
Haimon: There is no threat in speaking to emptiness.
Creon: I swear you'll regret this superior tone of yours!
You are the empty one!
Haimon: If you were not my father,
I'd say you were perverse.
Creon: You girl-struck fool, don't play at words with me!
Haimon: I am sorry. You prefer silence.
Creon: Now, by God—
I swear, by all the gods in heaven above us,
You'll watch it, I swear you shall!
(To the Servants) Bring her out!
Bring the woman out! Let her die before his eyes!
Here, this instant, with her bridegroom beside her!
Haimon: Not here, no; she will not die here, King.
And you will never see my face again.
Go on raving as long as you've a friend to endure you.

Exit Haimon.

Choragos: Gone, gone.
Creon, a young man in a rage is dangerous!
Creon: Let him do, or dream to do, more than a man can.
He shall not save these girls from death.
Choragos: These girls?
You have sentenced them both?
Creon: No, you are right.
I will not kill the one whose hands are clean.
Choragos: But Antigone?
Creon: *(Somberly)* I will carry her far away
Out there in the wilderness, and lock her
Living in a vault of stone. She shall have food,
As the custom is, to absolve the State of her death.

And there let her pray to the gods of hell:
They are her only gods:
Perhaps they will show her an escape from death,
Or she may learn,
though late,
That piety shown the dead is pity in vain.

Exit Creon.

ODE 3

STROPHE

Chorus: Love, unconquerable
Waster of rich men, keeper
Of warm lights and all-night vigil
In the soft face of a girl:
Sea-wanderer, forest-visitor!
Even the pure Immortals cannot escape you,
And mortal man, in his one day's dusk,
Trembles before your glory.

ANTISTROPHE

Surely you swerve upon ruin
The just man's consenting heart,
As here you have made bright anger
Strike between father and son—
And none has conquered but Love!
A girl's glánce wórking the will of heaven:
Pleasure to her alone who mocks us,
Merciless Aphrodite.[1]

SCENE 4

Choragos: *(As Antigone enters guarded)* But I can no longer stand in awe of this,
Nor, seeing what I see, keep back my tears.
Here is Antigone, passing to that chamber
Where all find sleep at last.

STROPHE 1

Antigone: Look upon me, friends, and pity me
Turning back at the night's edge to say
Good-by to the sun that shines for me no longer;
Now sleepy Death

[1]*Aphrodite:* Goddess of love and beauty.

Summons me down to Acheron,[1] that cold shore:
There is no bridesong there, nor any music.
Chorus: Yet not unpraised, not without a kind of honor,
You walk at last into the underworld;
Untouched by sickness, broken by no sword.
What woman has ever found your way to death?

ANTISTROPHE 1

Antigone: How often I have heard the story of Niobe,[2]
Tantalos' wretched daughter, how the stone
Clung fast about her, ivy-close: and they say
The rain falls endlessly
And sifting soft snow; her tears are never done.
I feel the loneliness of her death in mine.
Chorus: But she was born of heaven, and you
Are woman, woman-born. If her death is yours,
A mortal woman's, is this not for you
Glory in our world and in the world beyond?

STROPHE 2

Antigone: You laugh at me. Ah, friends, friends,
Can you not wait until I am dead? O Thebes,
O men many-charioted, in love with Fortune,
Dear springs of Dirce, sacred Theban grove,
Be witnesses for me, denied all pity,
Unjustly judged! and think a word of love
For her whose path turns
Under dark earth, where there are no more tears.
Chorus: You have passed beyond human daring and come at last
Into a place of stone where Justice sits.
I cannot tell
What shape of your father's guilt appears in this.

ANTISTROPHE 2

Antigone: You have touched it at last: that bridal bed
Unspeakable, horror of son and mother mingling:
Their crime, infection of all our family!
O Oedipus, father and brother!
Your marriage strikes from the grave to murder mine.
I have been a stranger here in my own land:
All my life
The blasphemy of my birth has followed me.
Chorus: Reverence is a virtue, but strength
Lives in established law: that must prevail.
You have made your choice,
Your death is the doing of your conscious hand.

---

[1] *Acheron:* A river in Hades, domain of the dead.

[2] *story of Niobe:* When her fourteen children were slain, Niobe wept so copiously that she was transformed into a stone on Mount Sipylus. Her tears became the mountain's streams.

EPODE

Antigone: Then let me go, since all your words are bitter,
And the very light of the sun is cold to me.
Lead me to my vigil, where I must have
Neither love nor lamentation; no song, but silence.

Creon interrupts impatiently.

Creon: If dirges and planned lamentations could put off death,
Men would be singing for ever.
(*To the Servants*) Take her, go!
You know your orders: take her to the vault
And leave her alone there. And if she lives or dies,
That's her affair, not ours: our hands are clean.
Antigone: O tomb, vaulted bride-bed in eternal rock,
Soon I shall be with my own again
Where Persephone[1] welcomes the thin ghosts underground:
And I shall see my father again, and you, mother,
And dearest Polyneices—
dearest indeed
To me, since it was my hand
That washed him clean and poured the ritual wine:
And my reward is death before my time!
And yet, as men's hearts know, I have done no wrong,
I have not sinned before God. Or if I have,
I shall know the truth in death. But if the guilt
Lies upon Creon who judged me, then, I pray,
May his punishment equal my own.
Choragos: O passionate heart,
Unyielding, tormented still by the same winds!
Creon: Her guards shall have good cause to regret their delaying.
Antigone: Ah! That voice is like the voice of death!
Creon: I can give you no reason to think you are mistaken.
Antigone: Thebes, and you my fathers' gods,
And rulers of Thebes, you see me now, the last
Unhappy daughter of a line of kings,
Your kings, led away to death. You will remember
What things I suffer, and at what men's hands,
Because I would not transgress the laws of heaven.
(To the Guards, simply) Come: let us wait no longer.

Exit Antigone, left, guarded.

---

[1]*Persephone:* Pluto, god of the underworld, abducted her to be his queen.

ODE 4

STROPHE 1

Chorus: All Danae's beauty was locked away
In a brazen cell where the sunlight could not come:
A small room still as any grave, enclosed her.
Yet she was a princess too,
And Zeus in a rain of gold poured love upon her.[1]
O child, child,
No power in wealth or war
Or tough sea-blackened ships
Can prevail against untiring Destiny!

ANTISTROPHE 1

And Dryas' son[2] also, that furious king,
Bore the god's prisoning anger for his pride:
Sealed up by Dionysos in deaf stone,
His madness died among echoes.
So at the last he learned what dreadful power
His tongue had mocked:
For he had profaned the revels,
And fired the wrath of the nine
Implacable Sisters[3] that love the sound of the flute.

STROPHE 2

And old men tell a half-remembered tale
Of horror[4] where a dark ledge splits the sea
And a double surf beats on the gráy shóres:
How a king's new woman, sick
With hatred for the queen he had imprisoned,
Ripped out his two sons' eyes with her bloody hands
While grinning Ares watched the shuttle plunge
Four times: four blind wounds crying for revenge,

ANTISTROPHE 2

Crying, tears and blood mingled.—Piteously born,
Those sons whose mother was of heavenly birth!
Her father was the god of the North Wind

---

[1] *All Danae's beauty . . . poured love upon her:* In legend, when an oracle told Acrisius, king of Argos, that his daughter Danae would bear a son who would grow up to slay him, he locked the princess into a chamber made of bronze, lest any man impregnate her. But Zeus, father of the gods, entered Danae's prison in a shower of gold. The resultant child, the hero Perseus, was accidentally to fulfill the prophecy by killing Acrisius with an ill-aimed discus throw.

[2] *Dryas' son:* King Lycurgus of Thrace, whom Dionysos, god of wine, caused to be stricken with madness.

[3] *Sisters:* The Muses, nine sister-goddesses who presided over poetry and music, arts and sciences.

[4] *a half-remembered tale Of horror:* As the Chorus recalls in the rest of this song, the point of this tale is that being nobly born will not save one from disaster. King Phineas cast off his first wife Cleopatra (not the later Egyptian queen but the daughter of Boreas, god of the north wind) and imprisoned her in a cave. Out of hatred for Cleopatra, the cruel Eidothea, second wife of the king, blinded her stepsons. Ares, god of war, was said to gloat over bloodshed.

And she was cradled by gales,
She raced with young colts on the glittering hills
And walked untrammeled in the open light:
But in her marriage deathless Fate found means
To build a tomb like yours for all her joy.

SCENE 5

Enter blind Teiresias, led by a boy. The opening speeches of Teiresias should be in singsong contrast to the realistic lines of Creon.

Teiresias: This is the way the blind man comes, Princes, Princes,
Lockstep, two heads lit by the eyes of one.
Creon: What new thing have you to tell us, old Teiresias?
Teiresias: I have much to tell you: listen to the prophet, Creon.
Creon: I am not aware that I have ever failed to listen.
Teiresias: Then you have done wisely, King, and ruled well.
Creon: I admit my debt to you. But what have you to say?
Teiresias: This, Creon: you stand once more on the edge of fate.
Creon: What do you mean? Your words are a kind of dread.
Teiresias: Listen, Creon:
I was sitting in my chair of augury, at the place
Where the birds gather about me. They were all a-chatter,
As is their habit, when suddenly I heard
A strange note in their jangling, a scream, a
Whirring fury; I knew that they were fighting,
Tearing each other, dying
In a whirlwind of wings clashing. And I was afraid.
I began the rites of burnt-offering at the altar,
But Hephaistos[1] failed me: instead of bright flame,
There was only the sputtering slime of the fat thigh-flesh
Melting: the entrails dissolved in gray smoke,
The bare bone burst from the welter. And no blaze!
This was a sign from heaven. My boy described it,
Seeing for me as I see for others.
I tell you, Creon, you yourself have brought
This new calamity upon us. Our hearths and altars
Are stained with the corruption of dogs and carrion birds
That glut themselves on the corpse of Oedipus' son.
The gods are deaf when we pray to them, their fire
Recoils from our offering, their birds of omen
Have no cry of comfort, for they are gorged
With the thick blood of the dead.
O my son,
These are no trifles! Think: all men make mistakes,
But a good man yields when he knows his course is wrong,

---

[1] *Hephaistos:* God of fire.

And repairs the evil. The only crime is pride.
Give in to the dead man, then: do not fight with a corpse—
What glory is it to kill a man who is dead?
Think, I beg you:
It is for your own good that I speak as I do.
You should be able to yield for your own good.

Creon: It seems that prophets have made me their especial province.
All my life long
I have been a kind of butt for the dull arrows
Of doddering fortune-tellers!
No, Teiresias:
If your birds—if the great eagles of God himself
Should carry him stinking bit by bit to heaven,
I would not yield. I am not afraid of pollution:
No man can defile the gods.
Do what you will,
Go into business, make money, speculate
An India gold or that synthetic gold from Sardis,
Get rich otherwise than by my consent to bury him.
Teiresias, it is a sorry thing when a wise man
Sells his wisdom, lets out his words for hire!

Teiresias: Ah Creon! Is there no man left in the world—

Creon: To do what?—Come, let's have the aphorism!

Teiresias: No man who knows that wisdom outweighs any wealth?

Creon: As surely as bribes are baser than any baseness.

Teiresias: You are sick, Creon! You are deathly sick!

Creon: As you say: it is not my place to challenge a prophet.

Teiresias: Yet you have said my prophecy is for sale.

Creon: The generation of prophets has always loved gold.

Teiresias: The generation of kings has always loved brass.

Creon: You forget yourself! You are speaking to your King.

Teiresias: I know it. You are a king because of me.

Creon: You have a certain skill; but you have sold out.

Teiresias: King, you will drive me to words that—

Creon: Say them, say them!
Only remember: I will not pay you for them.

Teiresias: No, you will find them too costly.

Creon: No doubt. Speak:
Whatever you say, you will not change my will.

Teiresias: Then take this, and take it to heart!
The time is not far off when you shall pay back
Corpse for corpse, flesh of your own flesh.
You have thrust the child of this world into living night,
You have kept from the gods below the child that is theirs:
The one in a grave before her death, the other,
Dead, denied the grave. This is your crime:
And the Furies and the dark gods of Hell

Are swift with terrible punishment for you.
Do you want to buy me now, Creon?
Not many days,
And your house will be full of men and women weeping,
And curses will be hurled at you from far
Cities grieving for sons unburied, left to rot
Before the walls of Thebes.
There are my arrows, Creon: they are all for you.
(To Boy) But come, child: lead me home.
Let him waste his fine anger upon younger men.
Maybe he will learn at last
To control a wiser tongue in a better head.

Exit Teiresias.

Choragos: The old man has gone, King, but his words
Remain to plague us. I am old, too,
But I cannot remember that he was ever false.
Creon: That is true. . . . It troubles me.
Oh it is hard to give in! but it is worse
To risk everything for stubborn pride.
Choragos: Creon: take my advice.
Creon: What shall I do?
Choragos: Go quickly: free Antigone from her vault
And build a tomb for the body of Polyneices.
Creon: You would have me do this!
Choragos: Creon, yes!
And it must be done at once: God moves
Swiftly to cancel the folly of stubborn men.
Creon: It is hard to deny the heart! But I
Will do it: I will not fight with destiny.
Choragos: You must go yourself, you cannot leave it to others.
Creon: I will go.
—Bring axes, servants:
Come with me to the tomb. I buried her, I
Will set her free.
Oh quickly!
My mind misgives—
The laws of the gods are mighty, and a man must serve them
To the last day of his life!

Exit Creon.

PAEAN[1]

STROPHE 1

Choragos: God of many names
Chorus: O Iacchos
son

[1]*Paean:* A song of praise or prayer, here to Dionysos, god of wine.

of Kadmeian Sémele
O born of the Thunder!
Guardian of the West
Regent
Of Eleusis' plain
O Prince of maenad Thebes
and the Dragon Field by rippling Ismenós:[2]

ANTISTROPHE 1

Choragos: God of many names
Chorus: the flame of torches
flares on our hills
the nymphs of Iacchos
dance at the spring of Castalia:[3]
from the vine-close mountain
come ah come in ivy:
Evohé evohé![4] sings through the streets of Thebes

STROPHE 2

Choragos: God of many names
Chorus: Iacchos of Thebes
heavenly Child
of Sémele bride of the Thunderer!
The shadow of plague is upon us:
come
with clement feet
oh come from Parnasos
down the long slopes
across the lamenting water

ANTISTROPHE 2

Choragos: Io[5] Fire! Chorister of the throbbing stars!
O purest among the voices of the night!
Thou son of God, blaze for us!

---

[2]*God of many names . . . Dragon Field by rippling Ismenós:* Dionysos was also called Iacchos (or, by the Romans, Bacchus). He was the son of Zeus ("the Thunderer") and of Sémele, daughter of Kadmos (or Cadmus), legendary founder of Thebes. "Regent of Eleusis' plain" is another name for Dionysos, honored in secret rites at Eleusis, a town northwest of Athens. "Prince of maenad Thebes" is yet another: the Maenads were women of Thebes said to worship Dionysos with wild orgiastic rites. Kadmos, so the story goes, sowed dragon's teeth in a field beside the river Ismenós. Up sprang a crop of fierce warriors who fought among themselves until only five remained. These victors became the first Thebans.

[3]*Castalia:* A spring on Mount Parnassus, named for a maiden who drowned herself in it to avoid rape by the god Apollo. She became a nymph, or nature spirit, dwelling in its waters. In the temple of Delphi, at the mountain's foot, priestesses of Dionysos (the "nymphs of Iacchos") used the spring's waters in rites of purification.

[4]*Evohé evohé!:* The cry of the Maenads in supplicating Dionysos: "Come forth, come forth!"

[5]*Io:* "Hail" or "Praise be to. . . ."

Chorus: Come with choric rapture of circling Maenads
Who cry Iô Iacche!
God of many names!

EXODOS[1]

Enter Messenger from left.

Messenger: Men of the line of Kadmos, you who live
Near Amphion's citadel,[2]
I cannot say
Of any condition of human life "This is fixed,
This is clearly good, or bad." Fate raises up,
And Fate casts down the happy and unhappy alike:
No man can foretell his Fate.
Take the case of Creon:
Creon was happy once, as I count happiness:
Victorious in battle, sole governor of the land,
Fortunate father of children nobly born.
And now it has all gone from him! Who can say
That a man is still alive when his life's joy fails?
He is a walking dead man. Grant him rich,
Let him live like a king in his great house:
If his pleasure is gone, I would not give
So much as the shadow of smoke for all he owns.
Choragos: Your words hint at sorrow: what is your news for us?
Messenger: They are dead. The living are guilty of their death.
Choragos: Who is guilty? Who is dead? Speak!
Messenger: Haimon.
Haimon is dead; and the hand that killed him
Is his own hand.
Choragos: His father's? or his own?
Messenger: His own, driven mad by the murder his father had done.
Choragos: Teiresias, Teiresias, how clearly you saw it all!
Messenger: This is my news: you must draw what conclusions you can from it.
Choragos: But look: Eurydice, our Queen:
Has she overheard us?

Enter Eurydice from the palace, center.

Eurydice: I have heard something, friends:
As I was unlocking the gate of Pallas'[3] shrine,
For I needed her help today, I heard a voice
Telling of some new sorrow. And I fainted

---

[1] *Exodos:* The final scene, containing the play's resolution.
[2] *Amphion's citadel:* A name for Thebes. Amphion, son of Zeus, had built a wall around the city by playing so beautifully on his lyre that the charmed stones leaped into their slots.
[3] *Pallas':* Pallas Athene, goddess of wisdom, and hence an excellent source of advice.

There at the temple with all my maidens about me.
But speak again: whatever it is, I can bear it:
Grief and I are no strangers.

Messenger: Dearest Lady,
I will tell you plainly all that I have seen.
I shall not try to comfort you: what is the use,
Since comfort could lie only in what is not true?
The truth is always best.
I went with Creon
To the outer plain where Polyneices was lying,
No friend to pity him, his body shredded by dogs.
We made our prayers in that place to Hecate
And Pluto,[4] that they would be merciful. And we bathed
The corpse with holy water, and we brought
Fresh-broken branches to burn what was left of it,
And upon the urn we heaped up a towering barrow
Of the earth of his own land.
When we were done, we ran
To the vault where Antigone lay on her couch of stone.
One of the servants had gone ahead,
And while he was yet far off he heard a voice
Grieving within the chamber, and he came back
And told Creon. And as the King went closer,
The air was full of wailing, the words lost,
And he begged us to make all haste. "Am I a prophet?"
He said, weeping, "And must I walk this road,
The saddest of all that I have gone before?
My son's voice calls me on. Oh quickly, quickly!
Look through the crevice there, and tell me
If it is Haimon, or some deception of the gods!"
We obeyed; and in the cavern's farthest corner
We saw her lying:
She had made a noose of her fine linen veil
And hanged herself. Haimon lay beside her,
His arms about her waist, lamenting her,
His love lost under ground, crying out
That his father had stolen her away from him.
When Creon saw him the tears rushed to his eyes
And he called to him: "What have you done, child? Speak to me.
What are you thinking that makes your eyes so strange?
O my son, my son, I come to you on my knees!"
But Haimon spat in his face. He said not a word,
Staring—
And suddenly drew his sword

[4]*Hecate And Pluto:* Two fearful divinities—the goddess of witchcraft and sorcery and the king of Hades, underworld of the dead.

And lunged. Creon shrank back, the blade missed; and the boy,
Desperate against himself, drove it half its length
Into his own side, and fell. And as he died
He gathered Antigone close in his arms again,
Choking, his blood bright red on her white cheek.
And now he lies dead with the dead, and she is his
At last, his bride in the house of the dead.

Exit Eurydice into the palace.

Choragos: She has left us without a word. What can this mean?
Messenger: It troubles me, too; yet she knows what is best,
Her grief is too great for public lamentation,
And doubtless she has gone to her chamber to weep
For her dead son, leading her maidens in his dirge.

Pause.

Choragos: It may be so: but I fear this deep silence.
Messenger: I will see what she is doing. I will go in.

Exit Messenger into the palace.

Enter Creon with attendants, bearing Haimon's body.

Choragos: But here is the king himself: oh look at him,
Bearing his own damnation in his arms.
Creon: Nothing you say can touch me any more.
My own blind heart has brought me
From darkness to final darkness. Here you see
The father murdering, the murdered son—
And all my civic wisdom!
Haimon my son, so young, so young to die,
I was the fool, not you; and you died for me.
Choragos: That is the truth; but you were late in learning it.
Creon: This truth is hard to bear. Surely a god
Has crushed me beneath the hugest weight of heaven,
And driven me headlong a barbaric way
To trample out the thing I held most dear.
The pains that men will take to come to pain!

Enter Messenger from the palace.

Messenger: The burden you carry in your hands is heavy,
But it is not all: you will find more in your house.
Creon: What burden worse than this shall I find there?
Messenger: The Queen is dead.
Creon: O port of death, deaf world,
Is there no pity for me? And you, Angel of evil,
I was dead, and your words are death again.
Is it true, boy? Can it be true?

Is my wife dead? Has death bred death?
Messenger: You can see for yourself.

The doors are opened and the body of Eurydice is disclosed within.

Creon: Oh pity!
All true, all true, and more than I can bear!
O my wife, my son!
Messenger: She stood before the altar, and her heart
Welcomed the knife her own hand guided,
And a great cry burst from her lips for Megareus[5] dead,
And for Haimon dead, her sons; and her last breath
Was a curse for their father, the murderer of her sons.
And she fell, and the dark flowed in through her closing eyes.
Creon: O God, I am sick with fear.
Are there no swords here? Has no one a blow for me?
Messenger: Her curse is upon you for the deaths of both.
Creon: It is right that it should be. I alone am guilty.
I know it, and I say it. Lead me in,
Quickly, friends.
I have neither life nor substance. Lead me in.
Choragos: You are right, if there can be right in so much wrong.
The briefest way is best in a world of sorrow.
Creon: Let it come,
Let death come quickly, and be kind to me.
I would not ever see the sun again.
Choragos: All that will come when it will; but we, meanwhile,
Have much to do. Leave the future to itself.
Creon: All my heart was in that prayer!
Choragos: Then do not pray any more: the sky is deaf.
Creon: Lead me away. I have been rash and foolish.
I have killed my son and my wife.
I look for comfort; my comfort lies here dead.
Whatever my hands have touched has come to nothing.
Fate has brought all my pride to a thought of dust.

As Creon is being led into the house, the Choragos advances and speaks directly to the audience.

Choragos: There is no happiness where there is no wisdom;
No wisdom but in submission to the gods.
Big words are always punished,
And proud men in old age learn to be wise.

* * *

[5]*Megareus:* Son of Creon and brother of Haimon, Megareus was slain in the unsuccessful attack on Thebes.

Reading and Reacting

1. What ideas does *Antigone* express about duty? About obedience? How do these ideas conform (or fail to conform) to your own concepts of duty and obedience?
2. According to Aristotle, the main characters in tragedies possess flaws that lead to their downfall. What is Antigone's tragic flaw? How does this flaw set up (or make inevitable) the series events that lead to the tragic resolution of the play?
3. What is Creon's fatal flaw? How does this flaw lead to the tragic resolution of the play?
4. Both Creon and Antigone defend rights that they believe are sacred. What rights are in conflict? Is there any room for compromise? Do you sympathize with Antigone or with Creon? Explain.
5. Aristotle believed that to be effective, tragic heroes must have elements of both good and evil. Does Antigone conform to Aristotle's requirement? Explain.
6. As the play progresses, do Creon and Antigone change, or do they remain essentially unchanged by events?
7. At the very end of *Antigone*, the Chorus says, "Big words are always punished, / And proud men in old age learn to be wise." Do you think Creon has gained wisdom from his experiences? Why or why not?
8. How does Antigone's gender affect her actions? How does it determine how she is treated? Are the play's attitudes toward women consistent with those of contemporary American society? Explain.
9. **Journal Entry** If you were Antigone, would you have stuck to your principles, or would you have given in? Explain your reasoning.
10. **Critical Perspective** In *Sophocles the Playwright*, S. M. Adams argues that, to the ancient Greek audience, Antigone and Creon were both tragic heroes. Do you agree? If so, do you see the fact that the play has two tragic heroes as a problem?

Related Works: "A Worn Path" (p. 370), "Do not go gentle into that good night" (p. 676), "Medgar Evers" (p. 706), *Hamlet* (p. 1012), *Oedipus the King* (p. 1137)

AP Images

AUGUST WILSON (1945–2005) was born in Pittsburgh, Pennsylvania, to a German immigrant father and a Black mother and lived in a Black neighborhood known as the Hill District. After leaving school at fifteen when he was accused of plagiarizing a paper, he participated in the Black Arts movement in Pittsburgh, submitting poems to local publications. In 1969, Wilson and his friend Rob Penny founded the Black Horizons Theatre Company, for which Wilson produced and directed plays. Although Wilson wrote plays while living in Pittsburgh, his work began to gain recognition only after 1978, when he moved to St. Paul, Minnesota. There, in 1982, Lloyd Richards, dean of the Yale School of Drama and artistic director of the Yale Repertory Company, staged a performance of Wilson's *Ma Rainey's Black Bottom.*

Wilson's achievement was epic. Beginning with *Ma Rainey's Black Bottom* in 1984, he wrote a ten-play cycle that chronicled the African American experience in the United States decade by decade. In addition to *Ma Rainey's Black Bottom,* a Tony Award winner, the plays in this cycle include *Fences* (1985), which won a Pulitzer Prize in 1987; *Joe Turner's Come and Gone* (1986); *Two Trains Running* (1989), which won Wilson his fifth New York Drama Critics Circle Award; *The Piano Lesson* (1987), which won a second Pulitzer Prize for Wilson in 1990; *Seven Guitars* (1996); and *Radio Golf,* the last play in the cycle, which opened in 2005, the year of Wilson's death. To honor his achievements, Broadway's Virginia Theater was renamed the August Wilson Theater.

Fences explores how the long-upheld color barrier in professional baseball affected the main character, Troy, who struggles with the pain of never realizing his dream of becoming a big-league player. Throughout the play, Troy retreats behind literal and figurative barriers that impair his relationships with his family.

Cultural Context The history of African Americans in baseball began in the period between emancipation and the civil rights movement. Banned from professional baseball, African American players formed the Negro Leagues, with stars such as Satchel Paige and Josh Gibson emerging in the 1930s. Then, in 1946, Branch Rickey, the club president and general manager of the Brooklyn Dodgers, changed everything when he set out to sign the Negro Leagues' top players to his team. The first player he chose was Jackie Robinson, who broke the racial barrier and debuted at first base for the Dodgers on April 15, 1947, at the age of 28. Robinson's performance earned him the Rookie of the Year award. In 1957, the year in which *Fences* is set, Robinson announced his retirement from baseball after he was traded to the New York Giants. In 1962, he was inducted into the Baseball Hall of Fame.

Fences (1985)

CHARACTERS

Troy Maxson
Jim Bono, *Troy's friend*
Rose, *Troy's wife*
Lyons, *Troy's oldest son by previous marriage*
Gabriel, *Troy's brother*
Cory, *Troy and Rose's son*
Raynell, *Troy's daughter*

SETTING

The setting is the yard which fronts the only entrance to the Maxson household, an ancient two-story brick house set back off a small alley in a big-city neighborhood. The entrance to the house is gained by two or three steps leading to a wooden porch badly in need of paint.

A relatively recent addition to the house and running its full width, the porch lacks congruence. It is a sturdy porch with a flat roof. One or two chairs of dubious value sit at one end where the kitchen window opens onto the porch. An old-fashioned icebox stands silent guard at the opposite end.

The yard is a small dirt yard, partially fenced, except for the last scene, with a wooden sawhorse, a pile of lumber, and other fence-building equipment set off to the side. Opposite is a tree from which hangs a ball made of rags. A baseball bat leans against the tree. Two oil drums serve as garbage receptacles and sit near the house at right to complete the setting.

THE PLAY

Near the turn of the century, the destitute of Europe sprang on the city with tenacious claws and an honest and solid dream. The city devoured them. They swelled its belly until it burst into a thousand furnaces and sewing machines, a thousand butcher shops and bakers' ovens, a thousand churches and hospitals and funeral parlors and money-lenders. The city grew. It nourished itself and offered each man a partnership limited only by his talent, his guile, and his willingness and capacity for hard work. For the immigrants of Europe, a dream dared and won true.

The descendants of African slaves were offered no such welcome or participation. They came from places called the Carolinas and the Virginias, Georgia, Alabama, Mississippi, and Tennessee. They came strong, eager, searching. The city rejected them and they fled and settled along the riverbanks and under bridges in shallow, ramshackle houses made of sticks and tarpaper. They collected rags and wood. They sold the use of their muscles and their bodies. They cleaned houses and washed clothes, they shined shoes, and in quiet desperation and vengeful pride, they stole, and lived in pursuit of their own dream. That they could breathe free, finally, and stand to meet life with the force of dignity and whatever eloquence the heart could call upon.

By 1957, the hard-won victories of the European immigrants had solidified the industrial might of America. War had been confronted and won with new energies that used loyalty and patriotism as its fuel. Life was rich, full, and flourishing. The Milwaukee Braves won the World Series, and the hot winds of change that would make the sixties a turbulent, racing, dangerous, and provocative decade had not yet begun to blow full.

ACT 1

SCENE 1

It is 1957. Troy and Bono enter the yard, engaged in conversation. Troy is fifty-three years old, a large man with thick, heavy hands; it is this largeness that he strives to fill out and make an accommodation with. Together with his blackness, his largeness informs his sensibilities and the choices he has made in his life.

Of the two men, Bono is obviously the follower. His commitment to their friendship of thirty-odd years is rooted in his admiration of Troy's honesty, capacity for hard work, and his strength, which Bono seeks to emulate.

It is Friday night, payday, and the one night of the week the two men engage in a ritual of talk and drink. Troy is usually the most talkative and at times he can be crude and almost vulgar, though he is capable of rising to profound heights of expression. The men carry lunch buckets and wear or carry burlap aprons and are dressed in clothes suitable to their jobs as garbage collectors.

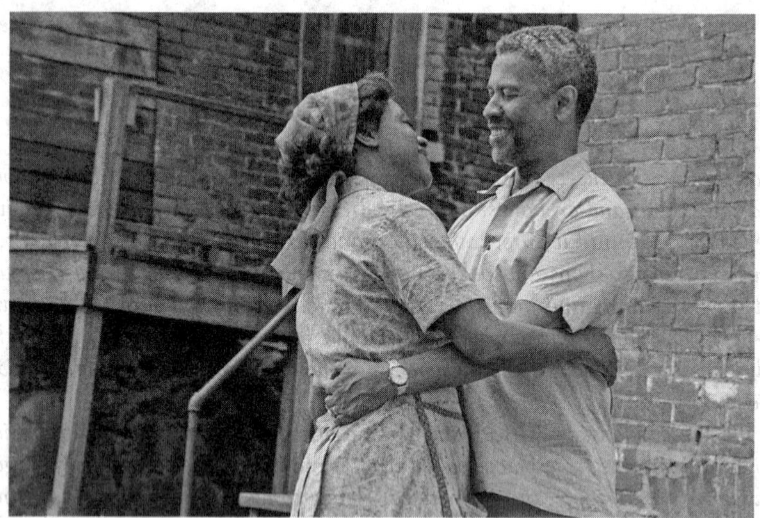

Scene from the 2016 film *Fences* with Viola Davis (as Rose Maxson) and Denzel Washington (as Troy)

Pictorial Press Ltd/Alamy Stock Photo

Bono: Troy, you ought to stop that lying!

Troy: I ain't lying! The nigger had a watermelon this big. *(He indicates with his hands.)* Talking about … "What watermelon, Mr. Rand?" I liked to fell out! "What watermelon, Mr. Rand?"…. And it sitting there big as life.

Bono: What did Mr. Rand say?

Troy: Ain't said nothing. Figure if the nigger too dumb to know he carrying a watermelon, he wasn't gonna get much sense out of him. Trying to hide that great big old watermelon under his coat. Afraid to let the white man see him carry it home.

Bono: I'm like you … I ain't got no time for them kind of people.

Troy: Now what he look like getting mad 'cause he see the man from the union talking to Mr. Rand?

Bono: He come to me talking about … "Maxson gonna get us fired." I told him to get away from me with that. He walked away from me calling you a troublemaker. What Mr. Rand say?

Troy: Ain't said nothing. He told me to go down the Commissioner's office next Friday. They called me down there to see them.

Bono: Well, as long as you got your complaint filed, they can't fire you. That's what one of them white fellows tell me.

Troy: I ain't worried about them firing me. They gonna fire me 'cause I asked a question? That's all I did. I went to Mr. Rand and asked him, "Why? Why you got the white mens driving and the colored lifting?" Told him, "what's the matter, don't I count? You think only white fellows got sense enough to drive a truck. That ain't no paper job! Hell, anybody can drive a truck. How come you got all whites driving and the colored lifting?" He told me "take it to the union." Well, hell, that's what I done! Now they wanna come up with this pack of lies.

Bono: I told Brownie if the man come and ask him any questions ... just tell the truth! It ain't nothing but something they done trumped up on you 'cause you filed a complaint on them.

Troy: Brownie don't understand nothing. All I want them to do is change the job description. Give everybody a chance to drive the truck. Brownie can't see that. He ain't got that much sense.

Bono: How you figure he be making out with that gal be up at Taylors' all the time ... that Alberta gal?

Troy: Same as you and me. Getting just as much as we is. Which is to say nothing.

Bono: It is, huh? I figure you doing a little better than me ... and I ain't saying what I'm doing.

Troy: Aw, nigger, look here ... I know you. If you had got anywhere near that gal, twenty minutes later you be looking to tell somebody. And the first one you gonna tell ... that you gonna want to brag to . . . is me.

Bono: I ain't saying that. I see where you be eyeing her.

Troy: I eye all the women. I don't miss nothing. Don't never let nobody tell you Troy Maxson don't eye the women.

Bono: You been doing more than eyeing her. You done bought her a drink or two.

Troy: Hell yeah, I bought her a drink! What that mean? I bought you one, too. What that mean 'cause I buy her a drink? I'm just being polite.

Bono: It's all right to buy her one drink. That's what you call being polite. But when you wanna be buying two or three ... that's what you call eyeing her.

Troy: Look here, as long as you known me ... you ever known me to chase after women?

Bono: Hell yeah! Long as I done known you. You forgetting I knew you when.

Troy: Naw, I'm talking about since I been married to Rose?

Bono: Oh, not since you been married to Rose. Now, that's the truth, there. I can say that.

Troy: All right then! Case closed.

Bono: I see you be walking up around Alberta's house. You supposed to be at Taylors' and you be walking up around there.

Troy: What you watching where I'm walking for? I ain't watching after you.

Bono: I seen you walking around there more than once.

Troy: Hell, you liable to see me walking anywhere! That don't mean nothing cause you see me walking around there.

Bono: Where she come from anyway? She just kinda showed up one day.

Troy: Tallahassee. You can look at her and tell she one of them Florida gals. They got some big healthy women down there. Grow them right up out the ground. Got a little bit of Indian in her. Most of them niggers down in Florida got some Indian in them.

Bono: I don't know about that Indian part. But she damn sure big and healthy. Woman wear some big stockings. Got them great big old legs and hips as wide as the Mississippi River.

Troy: Legs don't mean nothing. You don't do nothing but push them out of the way. But them hips cushion the ride!

Bono: Troy, you ain't got no sense.

Troy: It's the truth! Like you riding on Goodyears!

Rose enters from the house. She is ten years younger than Troy, her devotion to him stems from her recognition of the possibilities of her life without him: a succession of abusive men and their babies, a life of partying and running the streets, the Church, or aloneness with its attendant pain and frustration. She recognizes Troy's spirit as a fine and illuminating one and she either ignores or forgives his faults, only some of which she recognizes. Though she doesn't drink, her presence is an integral part of the Friday night rituals. She alternates between the porch and the kitchen, where supper preparations are under way.

Rose: What you all out here getting into?

Troy: What you worried about what we getting into for? This is men talk, woman.

Rose: What I care what you all talking about? Bono, you gonna stay for supper?

Bono: No, I thank you, Rose. But Lucille say she cooking up a pot of pigfeet.

Troy: Pigfeet! Hell, I'm going home with you! Might even stay the night if you got some pigfeet. You got something in there to top them pigfeet, Rose?

Rose: I'm cooking up some chicken. I got some chicken and collard greens.[1]

Troy: Well, go on back in the house and let me and Bono finish what we was talking about. This is men talk. I got some talk for you later. You know what kind of talk I mean. You go on and powder it up.

Rose: Troy Maxson, don't you start that now!

Troy: *(puts his arm around her)* Aw, woman ... come here. Look here, Bono ... when I met this woman ... I got out that place, say, "Hitch up my pony, saddle up my mare ... there's a woman out there for me somewhere. I looked here. Looked there. Saw Rose and latched on to her." I latched on to her and told her—I'm gonna tell you the truth—I told her, "Baby, I don't wanna marry, I just wanna be your man." Rose told me ... tell him what you told me, Rose.

Rose: I told him if he wasn't the marrying kind, then move out the way so the marrying kind could find me.

Troy: That's what she told me. "Nigger, you in my way. You blocking the view! Move out the way so I can find me a husband." I thought it over two or three days. Come back—

Rose: Ain't no two or three days nothing. You was back the same night.

---

[1] *collard greens:* A leafy green vegetable.

Troy: Come back, told her … "Okay, baby … but I'm gonna buy me a banty rooster and put him out there in the backyard … and when he see a stranger come, he'll flap his wings and crow … " Look here, Bono, I could watch the front door by myself … it was that back door I was worried about.

Rose: Troy, you ought not talk like that. Troy ain't doing nothing but telling a lie.

Troy: Only thing is … when we first got married … forget the rooster … we ain't had no yard!

Bono: I hear you tell it. Me and Lucille was staying down there on Logan Street. Had two rooms with the outhouse in the back. I ain't mind the outhouse none. But when that goddamn wind blow through there in the winter … that's what I'm talking about! To this day I wonder why in the hell I ever stayed down there for six long years. But see, I didn't know I could do no better. I thought only white folks had inside toilets and things.

Rose: There's a lot of people don't know they can do no better than they doing now. That's just something you got to learn. A lot of folks still shop at Bella's.

Troy: Ain't nothing wrong with shopping at Bella's. She got fresh food.

Rose: I ain't said nothing about if she got fresh food. I'm talking about what she charge. She charge ten cents more than the A&P.

Troy: The A&P ain't never done nothing for me. I spends my money where I'm treated right.
I go down to Bella, say, "I need a loaf of bread, I'll pay you Friday." She give it to me.
What sense that make when I got money to go and spend it somewhere else and ignore the person who done right by me? That ain't in the Bible.

Rose: We ain't talking about what's in the Bible. What sense it make to shop there when she overcharge?

Troy: You shop where you want to. I'll do my shopping where the people been good to me.

Rose: Well, I don't think it's right for her to overcharge. That's all I was saying.

Bono: Look here … I got to get on. Lucille going be raising all kind of hell.

Troy: Where you going, nigger? We ain't finished this pint. Come here, finish this pint.

Bono: Well, hell, I am … if you ever turn the bottle loose.

Troy: *(hands him the bottle)* The only thing I say about the A&P is I'm glad Cory got that job down there. Help him take care of his school clothes and things. Gabe done moved out and things getting tight around here. He got that job … He can start to look out for himself.

Rose: Cory done went and got recruited by a college football team.

Troy: I told that boy about that football stuff. The white man ain't gonna let him get nowhere with that football. I told him when he first come to me with it. Now you come telling me he done went and got more tied up in it. He ought to go and get recruited in how to fix cars or something where he can make a living.

Rose: He ain't talking about making no living playing football. It's just something the boys in school do. They gonna send a recruiter by to talk to you. He'll tell you he ain't talking about making no living playing football. It's a honor to be recruited.

Troy: It ain't gonna get him nowhere. Bono'll tell you that.

Bono: If he be like you in the sports ... he's gonna be all right. Ain't but two men ever played baseball as good as you. That's Babe Ruth[2] and Josh Gibson.[3] Them's the only two men ever hit more home runs than you.

Troy: What it ever get me? Ain't got a pot to piss in or a window to throw it out of.

Rose: Times have changed since you was playing baseball, Troy. That was before the war. Times have changed a lot since then.

Troy: How in hell they done changed?

Rose: They got lots of colored boys playing ball now. Baseball and football.

Bono: You right about that, Rose. Times have changed, Troy. You just come along too early.

Troy: There ought not never have been no time called too early! Now you take that fellow ... what's that fellow they had playing right field for the Yankees back then? You know who I'm talking about, Bono. Used to play right field for the Yankees.

Rose: Selkirk?

Troy: Selkirk! That's it! Man batting .269, understand? .269. What kind of sense that make? I was hitting .432 with thirty-seven home runs! Man batting .269 and playing right field for the Yankees! I saw Josh Gibson's daughter yesterday. She walking around with raggedy shoes on her feet. Now I bet you Selkirk's daughter ain't walking around with raggedy shoes on her feet! I bet you that!

Rose: They got a lot of colored baseball players now. Jackie Robinson[4] was the first. Folks had to wait for Jackie Robinson.

Troy: I done seen a hundred niggers play baseball better than Jackie Robinson. Hell, I know some teams Jackie Robinson couldn't even make! What you talking about Jackie Robinson. Jackie Robinson wasn't nobody. I'm talking about if you could play ball then they ought to have let you play. Don't care what color you were. Come telling me I come along too early. If you could play ... then they ought to have let you play.

---

[2]*Babe Ruth:* George Herman Ruth (1895–1948), American baseball player. He played for the New York Yankees during the 1910s and 1920s and is remembered for his home-run hitting and flamboyant lifestyle.

[3]*Josh Gibson:* (1911–1947), American baseball player. He played in the Negro Leagues between the 1920s and 1940s and was known as "the Negro Babe Ruth." An unwritten rule against hiring black players kept him out of the major leagues.

[4]*Jackie Robinson:* John Roosevelt Robinson (1919–1972). He became the first African American to play major-league baseball when he was hired by the Brooklyn Dodgers in 1947.

Troy takes a long drink from the bottle.

Rose: You gonna drink yourself to death. You don't need to be drinking like that.

Troy: Death ain't nothing. I done seen him. Done wrassled with him. You can't tell me nothing about death. Death ain't nothing but a fastball on the outside corner. And you know what I'll do to that! Lookee here, Bono … am I lying? You get one of them fastballs, about waist high, over the outside corner of the plate where you can get the meat of the bat on it … and good god! You can kiss it goodbye. Now, am I lying?

Bono: Naw, you telling the truth there. I seen you do it.

Troy: If I'm lying … that 450 feet worth of lying! *(Pause.)* That's all death is to me. A fastball on the outside corner.

Rose: I don't know why you want to get on talking about death.

Troy: Ain't nothing wrong with talking about death. That's part of life. Everybody gonna die. You gonna die, I'm gonna die. Bono's gonna die. Hell, we all gonna die.

Rose: But you ain't got to talk about it. I don't like to talk about it.

Troy: You the one brought it up. Me and Bono was talking about baseball … you tell me I'm gonna drink myself to death. Ain't that right, Bono? You know I don't drink this but one night out of the week. That's Friday night. I'm gonna drink just enough to where I can handle it. Then I cuts it loose. I leave it alone. So don't you worry about me drinking myself to death. 'Cause I ain't worried about Death. I done seen him. I done wrestled with him.

Look here, Bono … I looked up one day and Death was marching straight at me. Like Soldiers on Parade! The Army of Death was marching straight at me. The middle of July, 1941. It got real cold just like it be winter. It seem like Death himself reached out and touched me on the shoulder. He touch me just like I touch you. I got cold as ice and Death standing there grinning at me.

Rose: Troy, why don't you hush that talk.

Troy: I say … what you want, Mr. Death? You be wanting me? You done brought your army to be getting me? I looked him dead in the eye. I wasn't fearing nothing. I was ready to tangle. Just like I'm ready to tangle now. The Bible say be ever vigilant. That's why I don't get but so drunk. I got to keep watch.

Rose: Troy was right down there in Mercy Hospital. You remember he had pneumonia? Laying there with a fever talking plumb out of his head.

Troy: Death standing there staring at me … carrying that sickle in his hand. Finally he say, "You want bound over for another year?" See, just like that … "You want bound over for another year?" I told him, "Bound over hell! Let's settle this now!"

It seem like he kinda fell back when I said that, and all the cold went out of me. I reached down and grabbed that sickle and threw it just as far as I could throw it … and me and him commenced to wrestling.

We wrestled for three days and three nights. I can't say where I found the strength from. Every time it seemed like he was gonna get the best of me, I'd reach way down deep inside myself and find the strength to do him one better.

Rose: Every time Troy tell that story he find different ways to tell it. Different things to make up about it.

Troy: I ain't making up nothing. I'm telling you the facts of what happened. I wrestled with Death for three days and three nights and I'm standing here to tell you about it. *(Pause.)* All right. At the end of the third night we done weakened each other to where we can't hardly move. Death stood up, throwed on his robe . . . had him a white robe with a hood on it. He throwed on that robe and went off to look for his sickle. Say, "I'll be back." Just like that. "I'll be back." I told him, say, "Yeah, but … you gonna have to find me!" I wasn't no fool. I wan't going looking for him. Death ain't nothing to play with. And I know he's gonna get me. I know I got to join his army … his camp followers. But as long as I keep my strength and see him coming … as long as I keep up my vigilance … he's gonna have to fight to get me. I ain't going easy.

Bono: Well, look here, since you got to keep up your vigilance . . . let me have the bottle.

Troy: Aw hell, I shouldn't have told you that part. I should have left out that part.

Rose: Troy be talking that stuff and half the time don't even know what he be talking about.

Troy: Bono know me better than that.

Bono: That's right. I know you. I know you got some Uncle Remus[5] in your blood. You got more stories than the devil got sinners.

Troy: Aw hell, I done seen him too! Done talked with the devil.

Rose: Troy, don't nobody wanna be hearing all that stuff.

Lyons enters the yard from the street. Thirty-four years old, Troy's son by a previous marriage, he sports a neatly trimmed goatee, sport coat, white shirt, tieless and buttoned at the collar. Though he fancies himself a musician, he is more caught up in the rituals and "idea" of being a musician than in the actual practice of the music. He has come to borrow money from Troy, and while he knows he will be successful, he is uncertain as to what extent his lifestyle will be held up to scrutiny and ridicule.

Lyons: Hey, Pop.

Troy: What you come "Hey, Popping" me for?

Lyons: How you doing, Rose? *(He kisses her.)* Mr. Bono. How you doing?

Bono: Hey, Lyons … how you been?

---

[5]*Uncle Remus:* The fictional narrator of *Uncle Remus: His Songs and His Sayings* (1880) and a number of sequels by Joel Chandler Harris. Uncle Remus tells tales about characters such as Brer Rabbit and the Tarbaby in exaggerated dialect, now widely considered to be a derogatory representation of African Americans.

Troy: He must have been doing all right. I ain't seen him around here last week.

Rose: Troy, leave your boy alone. He come by to see you and you wanna start all that nonsense.

Troy: I ain't bothering Lyons. *(Offers him the bottle.)* Here … get you a drink. We got an understanding. I know why he come by to see me and he know I know.

Lyons: Come on, Pop … I just stopped by to say hi … see how you was doing.

Troy: You ain't stopped by yesterday.

Rose: You gonna stay for supper, Lyons? I got some chicken cooking in the oven.

Lyons: No, Rose … thanks. I was just in the neighborhood and thought I'd stop by for a minute.

Troy: You was in the neighborhood all right, nigger. You telling the truth there. You was in the neighborhood cause it's my payday.

Lyons: Well, hell, since you mentioned it … let me have ten dollars.

Troy: I'll be damned! I'll die and go to hell and play blackjack with the devil before I give you ten dollars.

Bono: That's what I wanna know about … that devil you done seen.

Lyons: What … Pop done seen the devil? You too much, Pops.

Troy: Yeah, I done seen him. Talked to him too!

Rose: You ain't seen no devil. I done told you that man ain't had nothing to do with the devil. Anything you can't understand, you want to call it the devil.

Troy: Look here, Bono … I went down to see Hertzberger about some furniture. Got three rooms for two-ninety-eight. That what it say on the radio. "Three rooms … two-ninety-eight." Even made up a little song about it. Go down there … man tell me I can't get no credit. I'm working every day and can't get no credit. What to do? I got an empty house with some raggedy furniture in it. Cory ain't got no bed. He's sleeping on a pile of rags on the floor. Working every day and can't get no credit. Come back here—Rose'll tell you—madder than hell. Sit down … try to figure what I'm gonna do. Come a knock on the door. Ain't been living here but three days. Who know I'm here? Open the door … devil standing there bigger than life. White fellow … white fellow … got on good clothes and everything. Standing there with a clipboard in his hand. I ain't had to say nothing. First words come out of his mouth was … "I understand you need some furniture and can't get no credit." I liked to fell over. He say, "I'll give you all the credit you want, but you got to pay the interest on it." I told him, "Give me three rooms worth and charge whatever you want." Next day a truck pulled up here and two men unloaded them three rooms. Man what drove the truck give me a book. Say send ten dollars, first of every month to the address in the book and everything will be all right. Say if I miss a payment the devil was coming back and it'll be hell to pay. That was fifteen years ago. To this day … the first of the month I send my ten dollars, Rose'll tell you.

Rose: Troy lying.

Troy: I ain't never seen that man since. Now you tell me who else that could have been but the devil? I ain't sold my soul or nothing like that, you understand. Naw, I wouldn't have truck with the devil about nothing like that. I got my furniture and pays my ten dollars the first of the month just like clockwork.

Bono: How long you say you been paying this ten dollars a month?

Troy: Fifteen years!

Bono: Hell, ain't you finished paying for it yet? How much the man done charged you?

Troy: Ah hell, I done paid for it. I done paid for it ten times over! The fact is I'm scared to stop paying it.

Rose: Troy lying. We got that furniture from Mr. Glickman. He ain't paying no ten dollars a month to nobody.

Troy: Aw hell, woman. Bono know I ain't that big a fool.

Lyons: I was just getting ready to say ... I know where there's a bridge for sale.

Troy: Look here, I'll tell you this ... it don't matter to me if he was the devil. It don't matter if the devil give credit. Somebody has got to give it.

Rose: It ought to matter. You going around talking about having truck with the devil ... God's the one you gonna have to answer to. He's the one gonna be at the Judgment.

Lyons: Yeah, well, look here, Pop ... let me have that ten dollars. I'll give it back to you. Bonnie got a job working at the hospital.

Troy: What I tell you, Bono? The only time I see this nigger is when he wants something. That's the only time I see him.

Lyons: Come on, Pop, Mr. Bono don't want to hear all that. Let me have the ten dollars. I told you Bonnie working.

Troy: What that mean to me? "Bonnie working." I don't care if she working. Go ask her for the ten dollars if she working. Talking about "Bonnie working." Why ain't you working?

Lyons: Aw, Pop, you know I can't find no decent job. Where am I gonna get a job at? You know I can't get no job.

Troy: I told you I know some people down there. I can get you on the rubbish if you want to work. I told you that the last time you came by here asking me for something.

Lyons: Naw, Pop ... thanks. That ain't for me. I don't wanna be carrying nobody's rubbish. I don't wanna be punching nobody's time clock.

Troy: What's the matter, you too good to carry people's rubbish? Where you think that ten dollars you talking about come from? I'm just supposed to haul people's rubbish and give my money to you 'cause you too lazy to work. You too lazy to work and wanna know why you ain't got what I got.

Rose: What hospital Bonnie working at? Mercy?

Lyons: She's down at Passavant working in the laundry.

Troy: I ain't got nothing as it is. I give you that ten dollars and I got to eat beans the rest of the week. Naw ... you ain't getting no ten dollars here.

Lyons: You ain't got to be eating no beans. I don't know why you wanna say that.

Troy: I ain't got no extra money. Gabe done moved over to Miss Pearl's paying her the rent and things done got tight around here. I can't afford to be giving you every payday.

Lyons: I ain't asked you to give me nothing. I asked you to loan me ten dollars. I know you got ten dollars.

Troy: Yeah, I got it. You know why I got it? 'Cause I don't throw my money away out there in the streets. You living the fast life … wanna be a musician … running around in them clubs and things … then, you learn to take care of yourself. You ain't gonna find me going and asking nobody for nothing. I done spent too many years without.

Lyons: You and me is two different people, Pop.

Troy: I done learned my mistake and learned to do what's right by it. You still trying to get something for nothing. Life don't owe you nothing. You owe it to yourself. Ask Bono. He'll tell you I'm right.

Lyons: You got your way of dealing with the world … I got mine. The only thing that matters to me is the music.

Troy: Yeah, I can see that! It don't matter how you gonna eat … where your next dollar is coming from. You telling the truth there.

Lyons: I know I got to eat. But I got to live too. I need something that gonna help me to get out of the bed in the morning. Make me feel like I belong in the world. I don't bother nobody.

I just stay with the music 'cause that's the only way I can find to live in the world. Otherwise there ain't no telling what I might do. Now I don't come criticizing you and how you live. I just come by to ask you for ten dollars. I don't wanna hear all that about how I live.

Troy: Boy, your mama did a hell of a job raising you.

Lyons: You can't change me, Pop. I'm thirty-four years old. If you wanted to change me, you should have been there when I was growing up. I come by to see you … ask for ten dollars and you want to talk about how I was raised. You don't know nothing about how I was raised.

Rose: Let the boy have ten dollars, Troy.

Troy: *(to Lyons)* What the hell you looking at me for? I ain't got no ten dollars. You know what I do with my money. *(To Rose.)* Give him ten dollars if you want him to have it.

Rose: I will. Just as soon as you turn it loose.

Troy: *(handing Rose the money)* There it is. Seventy-six dollars and forty-two cents. You see this, Bono? Now, I ain't gonna get but six of that back.

Rose: You ought to stop telling that lie. Here, Lyons. *(She hands him the money.)*

Lyons: Thanks, Rose. Look … I got to run … I'll see you later.

Troy: Wait a minute. You gonna say "thanks, Rose" and ain't gonna look to see where she got that ten dollars from? See how they do me, Bono?

Lyons: I know she got it from you, Pop. Thanks. I'll give it back to you.

Troy: There he go telling another lie. Time I see that ten dollars … he'll be owing me thirty more.

Lyons: See you, Mr. Bono.

Bono: Take care, Lyons!

Lyons: Thanks, Pop. I'll see you again.

Lyons exits the yard.

Troy: I don't know why he don't go and get him a decent job and take care of that woman he got.

Bono: He'll be all right, Troy. The boy is still young.

Troy: The *boy* is thirty-four years old.

Rose: Let's not get off into all that.

Bono: Look here … I got to be going. I got to be getting on. Lucille gonna be waiting.

Troy: *(puts his arm around Rose)* See this woman, Bono? I love this woman. I love this woman so much it hurts. I love her so much … I done run out of ways of loving her. So I got to go back to basics. Don't you come by my house Monday morning talking about time to go to work … 'cause I'm still gonna be stroking!

Rose: Troy! Stop it now!

Bono: I ain't paying him no mind, Rose. That ain't nothing but gin-talk. Go on, Troy. I'll see you Monday.

Troy: Don't you come by my house, nigger! I done told you what I'm gonna be doing.

The lights go down to black.

SCENE 2

The lights come up on Rose hanging up clothes. She hums and sings softly to herself. It is the following morning.

Rose: *(sings)*

Jesus, be a fence all around me every day
Jesus, I want you to protect me as I travel on my way.
Jesus, be a fence all around me every day.

Troy enters from the house.

Jesus, I want you to protect me
As I travel on my way.

(To Troy.) 'Morning, You ready for breakfast? I can fix it soon as I finish hanging up these clothes?

Troy: I got the coffee on. That'll be all right. I'll just drink some of that this morning.

Rose: That 651 hit yesterday. That's the second time this month. Miss Pearl hit for a dollar … seem like those that need the least always get lucky. Poor folks can't get nothing.

Troy: Them numbers don't know nobody. I don't know why you fool with them. You and Lyons both.

Rose: It's something to do.

Troy: You ain't doing nothing but throwing your money away.

Rose: Troy, you know I don't play foolishly. I just play a nickel here and a nickel there.

Troy: That's two nickels you done thrown away.

Rose: Now I hit sometimes … that makes up for it. It always comes in handy when I do hit. I don't hear you complaining then.

Troy: I ain't complaining now. I just say it's foolish. Trying to guess out of six hundred ways which way the number gonna come. If I had all the money niggers, these Negroes, throw away on numbers for one week—just one week—I'd be a rich man.

Rose: Well, you wishing and calling it foolish ain't gonna stop folks from playing numbers. That's one thing for sure. Besides … some good things come from playing numbers. Look where Pope done bought him that restaurant off of numbers.

Troy: I can't stand niggers like that. Man ain't had two dimes to rub together. He walking around with his shoes all run over bumming money for cigarettes. All right. Got lucky there and hit the numbers …

Rose: Troy, I know all about it.

Troy: Had good sense, I'll say that for him. He ain't throwing his money away. I seen niggers hit the numbers and go through two thousand dollars in four days. Man bought him that restaurant down there … fixed it up real nice … and then didn't want nobody to come in it! A Negro go in there and can't get no kind of service. I seen a white fellow come in there and order a bowl of stew. Pope picked all the meat out the pot for him. Man ain't had nothing but a bowl of meat! Negro come behind him and ain't got nothing but the potatoes and carrots. Talking about what numbers do for people, you picked a wrong example. Ain't done nothing but make a worser fool out of him than he was before.

Rose: Troy, you ought to stop worrying about what happened at work yesterday.

Troy: I ain't worried. Just told me to be down there at the Commissioner's office on Friday. Everybody think they gonna fire me. I ain't worried about them firing me. You ain't got to worry about that. *(Pause.)* Where's Cory? Cory in the house? *(Calls.)* Cory?

Rose: He gone out.

Troy: Out, huh? He gone out 'cause he know I want him to help me with this fence. I know how he is. That boy scared of work.

Gabriel enters. He comes halfway down the alley and, hearing Troy's voice, stops.

Troy: *(continues)* He ain't done a lick of work in his life.

Rose: He had to go to football practice. Coach wanted them to get in a little extra practice before the season start.

Troy: I got his practice … running out of here before he get his chores done.

Rose: Troy, what is wrong with you this morning? Don't nothing set right with you. Go on back in there and go to bed … get up on the other side.

Troy: Why something got to be wrong with me? I ain't said nothing wrong with me.

Rose: You got something to say about everything. First it's the numbers … then it's the way the man runs his restaurant … then you done got on Cory. What's it gonna be next? Take a look up there and see if the weather suits you … or is it gonna be how you gonna put up the fence with the clothes hanging in the yard.

Troy: You hit the nail on the head then.

Rose: I know you like I know the back of my hand. Go on in there and get you some coffee … see if that straighten you up. 'Cause you ain't right this morning.

Troy starts into the house and sees Gabriel. Gabriel starts singing. Troy's brother, he is seven years younger than Troy. Injured in World War II, he has a metal plate in his head. He carries an old trumpet tied around his waist and believes with every fiber of his being that he is the Archangel Gabriel.[1] *He carries a chipped basket with an assortment of discarded fruits and vegetables he has picked up in the strip district and which he attempts to sell.*

Gabriel: *(singing)*

Yes, ma'am, I got plums
You ask me how I sell them
Oh ten cents apiece
Three for a quarter
Come and buy now
'Cause I'm here today
And tomorrow I'll be gone

Gabriel enters.

Hey, Rose!

Rose: How you doing, Gabe?

Gabriel: There's Troy … Hey, Troy!

Troy: Hey, Gabe.

Exit into kitchen.

Rose: *(To Gabriel.)* What you got there?

Gabriel: You know what I got, Rose. I got fruits and vegetables.

Rose: *(looking in basket)* Where's all these plums you talking about?

Gabriel: I ain't got no plums today, Rose. I was just singing that. Have some tomorrow. Put me in a big order for plums. Have enough plums tomorrow for St. Peter and everybody.

---

[1] *Archangel Gabriel:* A messenger of God.

Troy reenters from kitchen, crosses to steps.

(To Rose.) Troy's mad at me.

Troy: I ain't mad at you. What I got to be mad at you about? You ain't done nothing to me.

Gabriel: I just moved over to Miss Pearl's to keep out from in your way. I ain't mean no harm by it.

Troy: Who said anything about that? I ain't said anything about that.

Gabriel: You ain't mad at me, is you?

Troy: Naw … I ain't mad at you, Gabe. If I was mad at you I'd tell you about it.

Gabriel: Got me two rooms. In the basement. Got my own door too. Wanna see my key? *(He holds up a key.)* That's my own key! Ain't nobody else got a key like that. That's my key! My two rooms!

Troy: Well, that's good, Gabe. You got your own key … that's good.

Rose: You hungry, Gabe? I was just fixing to cook Troy his breakfast.

Gabriel: I'll take some biscuits. You got some biscuits? Did you know when I was in heaven … every morning me and St. Peter[2] would sit down by the gate and eat some big fat biscuits? Oh, yeah! We had us a good time. We'd sit there and eat us them biscuits and then St. Peter would go off to sleep and tell me to wake him up when it's time to open the gates for the judgment.

Rose: Well, come on … I'll make up a batch of biscuits.

Rose exits into the house.

Gabriel: Troy … St. Peter got your name in the book. I seen it. It say … Troy Maxson. I say … I know him! He got the same name like what I got. That's my brother!

Troy: How many times you gonna tell me that, Gabe?

Gabriel: Ain't got my name in the book. Don't have to have my name. I done died and went to heaven. He got your name though. One morning St. Peter was looking at his book … marking it up for the judgment … and he let me see your name. Got it in there under M. Got Rose's name … I ain't seen it like I seen yours … but I know it's in there. He got a great big book. Got everybody's name what was ever been born. That's what he told me. But I seen your name. Seen it with my own eyes.

Troy: Go on in the house there. Rose going to fix you something to eat.

Gabriel: Oh, I ain't hungry. I done had breakfast with Aunt Jemima. She come by and cooked me up a whole mess of flapjacks. Remember how we used to eat them flapjacks?

Troy: Go on in the house and get you something to eat now.

Gabriel: I got to sell my plums. I done sold some tomatoes. Got me two quarters. Wanna see? *(He shows Troy his quarters.)* I'm gonna save them and buy me a new horn so St. Peter can hear me when it's time to open the

[2]*St. Peter:* Disciple of Christ, believed to be the guard at the gates of heaven.

gates. *(Gabriel stops suddenly. Listens.)* Hear that? That's the hellhounds. I got to chase them out of here. Go on get out of here! Get out!

Gabriel exits singing.

Better get ready for the Judgment
Better get ready for the Judgment
My Lord is coming down

Rose enters from the house.

Troy: He's gone off somewhere.
Gabriel: *(offstage)*

Better get ready for the Judgment
Better get ready for the Judgment morning
Better get ready for the Judgment
My God is coming down

Rose: He ain't eating right. Miss Pearl say she can't get him to eat nothing.
Troy: What you want me to do about it, Rose? I done did everything I can for the man. I can't make him get well. Man got half his head blown away … what you expect?
Rose: Seem like something ought to be done to help him.
Troy: Man don't bother nobody. He just mixed up from that metal plate he got in his head. Ain't no sense for him to go back into the hospital.
Rose: Least he be eating right. They can help him take care of himself.
Troy: Don't nobody wanna be locked up, Rose. What you wanna lock him up for? Man go over there and fight the war … messin' around with them Japs, get half his head blown off … and they give him a lousy three thousand dollars. And I had to swoop down on that.
Rose: Is you fixing to go into that again?
Troy: That's the only way I got a roof over my head … 'cause of that metal plate.
Rose: Ain't no sense you blaming yourself for nothing. Gabe wasn't in no condition to manage that money. You done what was right by him. Can't nobody say you ain't done what was right by him. Look how long you took care of him … till he wanted to have his own place and moved over there with Miss Pearl.
Troy: That ain't what I'm saying, woman! I'm just stating the facts. If my brother didn't have that metal plate in his head … I wouldn't have a pot to piss in or a window to throw it out of. And I'm fifty-three years old. Now see if you can understand that!

Troy gets up from the porch and starts to exit the yard.

Rose: Where you going off to? You been running out of here every Saturday for weeks. I thought you was gonna work on this fence?

Troy: I'm gonna walk down to Taylors'. Listen to the ball game. I'll be back in a bit. I'll work on it when I get back.

He exits the yard. The lights go to black.

SCENE 3

The lights come up on the yard. It is four hours later. Rose is taking down the clothes from the line. Cory enters carrying his football equipment.

Rose: Your daddy like to had a fit with you running out of here this morning without doing your chores.

Cory: I told you I had to go to practice.

Rose: He say you were supposed to help him with this fence.

Cory: He been saying that the last four or five Saturdays, and then he don't never do nothing, but go down to Taylors'. Did you tell him about the recruiter?

Rose: Yeah, I told him.

Cory: What he say?

Rose: He ain't said nothing too much. You get in there and get started on your chores before he gets back. Go on and scrub down them steps before he gets back here hollering and carrying on.

Cory: I'm hungry. What you got to eat, Mama?

Rose: Go on and get started on your chores. I got some meat loaf in there. Go on and make you a sandwich ... and don't leave no mess in there.

Cory exits into the house. Rose continues to take down the clothes. Troy enters the yard and sneaks up and grabs her from behind.

Troy! Go on, now. You liked to scared me to death. What was the score of the game? Lucille had me on the phone and I couldn't keep up with it.

Troy: What I care about the game? Come here, woman. *(He tries to kiss her.)*

Rose: I thought you went down Taylors' to listen to the game. Go on, Troy! You supposed to be putting up this fence.

Troy: *(attempting to kiss her again)* I'll put it up when I finish with what is at hand.

Rose: Go on, Troy. I ain't studying you.

Troy: *(chasing after her)* I'm studying you ... fixing to do my homework!

Rose: Troy, you better leave me alone.

Troy: Where's Cory? That boy brought his butt home yet?

Rose: He's in the house doing his chores.

Troy: *(calling)* Cory! Get your butt out here, boy!

Rose exits into the house with the laundry. Troy goes over to the pile of wood, picks up a board, and starts sawing. Cory enters from the house.

Troy: You just now coming in here from leaving this morning?

Cory: Yeah, I had to go to football practice.

Troy: Yeah, what?

Cory: Yessir.

Troy: I ain't but two seconds off you noway. The garbage sitting in there overflowing ... you ain't done none of your chores ... and you come in here talking about "Yeah."

Cory: I was just getting ready to do my chores now, Pop ...

Troy: Your first chore is to help me with this fence on Saturday. Everything else come after that. Now get that saw and cut them boards.

Cory takes the saw and begins cutting the boards. Troy continues working. There is a long pause.

Cory: Hey, Pop ... why don't you buy a TV?

Troy: What I want with a TV? What I want one of them for?

Cory: Everybody got one. Earl, Ba Bra ... Jesse!

Troy: I ain't asked you who had one. I say what I want with one?

Cory: So you can watch it. They got lots of things on TV. Baseball games and everything. We could watch the World Series.

Troy: Yeah ... and how much this TV cost?

Cory: I don't know. They got them on sale for around two hundred dollars.

Troy: Two hundred dollars, huh?

Cory: That ain't that much, Pop.

Troy: Naw, it's just two hundred dollars. See that roof you got over your head at night? Let me tell you something about that roof. It's been over ten years since that roof was last tarred. See now ... the snow comes this winter and sit up there on that roof like it is ... and it's gonna seep inside. It's just gonna be a little bit ... ain't gonna hardly notice it. Then the next thing you know, it's gonna be leaking all over the house. Then the wood rot from all that water and you gonna need a whole new roof. Now, how much you think it cost to get that roof tarred?

Cory: I don't know.

Troy: Two hundred and sixty-four dollars ... cash money. While you thinking about a TV, I got to be thinking about the roof ... and whatever else go wrong here. Now if you had two hundred dollars, what would you do ... fix the roof or buy a TV?

Cory: I'd buy a TV. Then when the roof started to leak ... when it needed fixing ... I'd fix it.

Troy: Where you gonna get the money from? You done spent it for a TV. You gonna sit up and watch the water run all over your brand new TV.

Cory: Aw, Pop. You got money. I know you do.

Troy: Where I got it at, huh?

Cory: You got it in the bank.

Troy: You wanna see my bankbook? You wanna see that seventy-three dollars and twenty-two cents I got sitting up in there.

Cory: You ain't got to pay for it all at one time. You can put a down payment on it and carry it on home with you.

Troy: Not me. I ain't gonna owe nobody nothing if I can help it. Miss a payment and they come and snatch it right out your house. Then what you got? Now, soon as I get two hundred dollars clear, then I'll buy a TV. Right now, as soon as I get two hundred and sixty-four dollars, I'm gonna have this roof tarred.

Cory: Aw … Pop!

Troy: You go on and get you two hundred and buy one if ya want it. I got better things to do with my money.

Cory: I can't get no two hundred dollars. I ain't never seen two hundred dollars.

Troy: I'll tell you what … you get you a hundred dollars and I'll put the other hundred with it.

Cory: All right, I'm gonna show you.

Troy: You gonna show me how you can cut them boards right now.

Cory begins to cut the boards. There is a long pause.

Cory: The Pirates won today. That makes five in a row.

Troy: I ain't thinking about the Pirates. Got an all-white team. Got that boy … that Puerto Rican boy … Clemente.[1] Don't even half-play him. That boy could be something if they give him a chance. Play him one day and sit him on the bench the next.

Cory: He gets a lot of chances to play.

Troy: I'm talking about playing regular. Playing every day so you can get your timing. That's what I'm talking about.

Cory: They got some white guys on the team that don't play every day. You can't play everybody at the same time.

Troy: If they got a white fellow sitting on the bench … you can bet your last dollar he can't play! The colored guy got to be twice as good before he get on the team. That's why I don't want you to get all tied up in them sports. Man on the team and what it get him? They got colored on the team and don't use them. Same as not having them. All them teams the same.

Cory: The Braves got Hank Aaron[2] and Wes Covington.[3] Hank Aaron hit two home runs today. That makes forty-three.

Troy: Hank Aaron ain't nobody. That what you supposed to do. That's how you supposed to play the game. Ain't nothing to it. It's just a matter of

---

[1] *Clemente:* Roberto Clemente (1934–1972), Major League baseball player for the Pittsburg Pirates, known as much for his humanitarianism as his unique batting style and ability. Clemente received the Most Valuable Player Award in 1966 and died in a plane crash in 1972 while shuttling supplies to Nicaraguan earthquake victims.

[2] *Hank Aaron:* Henry Aaron (1934–2021), American baseball player who broke Babe Ruth's career home run record with a lifetime total of 755 home runs. The holder of 12 other Major League records, Aaron spent his Major League career with the Braves, first in Milwaukee and later in their hometown of Atlanta.

[3] *Wes Covington:* John Wesley Covington (1932–2011), American baseball player known for his ability to frustrate pitchers by wasting time at the plate. In an eleven-year career, Covington played for six Major League teams, beginning with the Milwaukee Braves and retiring with the Los Angeles Dodgers in 1966.

timing … getting the right follow-through. Hell, I can hit forty-three home runs right now!

Cory: Not off no major-league pitching, you couldn't.

Troy: We had better pitching in the Negro leagues. I hit seven home runs off of Satchel Paige.[4] You can't get no better than that!

Cory: Sandy Koufax.[5] He's leading the league in strikeouts.

Troy: I ain't thinking of no Sandy Koufax.

Cory: You got Warren Spahn[6] and Lew Burdette.[7] I bet you couldn't hit no home runs off of Warren Spahn.

Troy: I'm through with it now. You go on and cut them boards. *(Pause.)* Your mama tell me you done got recruited by a college football team? Is that right?

Cory: Yeah. Coach Zellman say the recruiter gonna be coming by to talk to you. Get you to sign the permission papers.

Troy: I thought you supposed to be working down there at the A&P. Ain't you suppose to be working down there after school?

Cory: Mr. Stawicki say he gonna hold my job for me until after the football season. Say starting next week I can work weekends.

Troy: I thought we had an understanding about this football stuff? You suppose to keep up with your chores and hold that job down at the A&P. Ain't been around here all day on a Saturday. Ain't none of your chores done … and now you telling me you done quit your job.

Cory: I'm going to be working weekends.

Troy: You damn right you are! And ain't no need for nobody coming around here to talk to me about signing nothing.

Cory: Hey, Pop … you can't do that. He's coming all the way from North Carolina.

Troy: I don't care where he coming from. The white man ain't gonna let you get nowhere with that football noway. You go on and get your book-learning so you can work yourself up in that A&P or learn how to fix cars or build houses or something, get you a trade. That way you have something can't nobody take away from you. You go on and learn how to put your hands to some good use. Besides hauling people's garbage.

---

[4] *Satchel Page:* Leroy Robert Paige (1906–1982), American baseball player. He played in the Negro Leagues from the 1920s until 1948, when he joined the Cleveland Indians; he reportedly pitched 55 no-hit games during his career. Joe DiMaggio called him "the best pitcher I have ever faced."

[5] *Sandy Koufax:* Sanford Koufax (1935–), left-handed pitcher who won 129 games and lost only 47 for the Los Angeles Dodgers in the six seasons between 1961 and 1966; he won three Cy Young Awards and pitched four no-hit games, the last of which (1965) was a perfect game.

[6] *Warren Spahn:* (1921–2003), left-handed pitcher who at the time of his retirement in 1966 held the National League record of 363 wins; he won 20 or more games in four consecutive seasons (1947–1950) and in several other seasons during the 1950s.

[7] *Lew Burdette:* Selva Lewis Burdette (1926–2007), American baseball player who pitched and won three games for the Milwaukee Braves against the New York Yankees in the 1957 World Series; for that Series, his ERA was an amazingly low .067.

Cory: I get good grades, Pop. That's why the recruiter wants to talk with you. You got to keep up your grades to get recruited. This way I'll be going to college. I'll get a chance …

Troy: First you gonna get your butt down there to the A&P and get your job back.

Cory: Mr. Stawicki done already hired somebody else 'cause I told him I was playing football.

Troy: You a bigger fool than I thought … to let somebody take away your job so you can play some football. Where you gonna get your money to take out your girlfriend and whatnot? What kind of foolishness is that to let somebody take away your job?

Cory: I'm still gonna be working weekends.

Troy: Naw … naw. You getting your butt out of here and finding you another job.

Cory: Come on, Pop! I got to practice. I can't work after school and play football too. The team needs me. That's what Coach Zellman say . . .

Troy: I don't care what nobody else say. I'm the boss … you understand? I'm the boss around here. I do the only saying what counts.

Cory: Come on, Pop!

Troy: I asked you … did you understand?

Cory: Yeah …

Troy: What?!

Cory: Yessir.

Troy: You go on down there to that A&P and see if you can get your job back. If you can't do both … then you quit the football team. You've got to take the crookeds with the straights.

Cory: Yessir. (*Pause.*) Can I ask you a question?

Troy: What the hell you wanna ask me? Mr. Stawicki the one you got the questions for.

Cory: How come you ain't never liked me?

Troy: Liked you? Who the hell say I got to like you? What law is there say I got to like you? Wanna stand up in my face and ask a damn fool-ass question like that. Talking about liking somebody. Come here, boy, when I talk to you.

Cory comes over to where Troy is working. He stands slouched over and Troy shoves him on his shoulder.

Straighten up, goddammit! I asked you a question … what law is there say I got to like you?

Cory: None.

Troy: Well, all right then! Don't you eat every day? (*Pause.*) Answer me when I talk to you! Don't you eat every day?

Cory: Yeah.

Troy: Nigger, as long as you in my house, you put that sir on the end of it when you talk to me!

Cory: Yes ... sir.

Troy: You eat every day.

Cory: Yessir!

Troy: Got a roof over your head.

Cory: Yessir!

Troy: Got clothes on your back.

Cory: Yessir.

Troy: Why you think that is?

Cory: 'Cause of you.

Troy: Ah, hell I know it's 'cause of me ... but why do you think that is?

Cory: *(hesitant)* 'Cause you like me.

Troy: Like you? I go out of here every morning ... bust my butt ... putting up with them crackers[8] every day ... 'cause I like you? You are the biggest fool I ever saw. *(Pause.)* It's my job. It's my responsibility! You understand that? A man got to take care of his family. You live in my house ... sleep you behind on my bedclothes ... fill you belly up with my food ... 'cause you my son. You my flesh and blood. Not 'cause I like you! 'Cause it's my duty to take care of you. I owe a responsibility to you! Let's get this straight right here ... before it go along any further ... I ain't got to like you. Mr. Rand don't give me my money come payday cause he likes me. He give me 'cause he owe me. I done give you everything I had to give you. I gave you your life! Me and your mama worked that out between us. And liking your black ass wasn't part of the bargain. Don't you try and go through life worrying about if somebody like you or not. You best be making sure they doing right by you. You understand what I'm saying, boy?

Cory: Yessir.

Troy: Then get the hell out of my face, and get on down to that A&P.

Rose has been standing behind the screen door for much of the scene. She enters as Cory exits.

Rose: Why don't you let the boy go ahead and play football, Troy? Ain't no harm in that. He's just trying to be like you with the sports.

Troy: I don't want him to be like me! I want him to move as far away from my life as he can get. You the only decent thing that ever happened to me. I wish him that. But I don't wish him a thing else from my life. I decided seventeen years ago that boy wasn't getting involved in no sports. Not after what they did to me in the sports.

Rose: Troy, why don't you admit you was too old to play in the major leagues? For once ... why don't you admit that?

Troy: What do you mean too old? Don't come telling me I was too old. I just wasn't the right color. Hell, I'm fifty-three years old and can do better than Selkirk's .269 right now!

---

[8] *crackers:* Derogatory term for white people, generally poor southern whites.

Rose: How's was you gonna play ball when you were over forty? Sometimes I can't go no sense out of you.

Troy: I got good sense, woman. I got sense enough not to let my boy get hurt over playing no sports. You been mothering that boy too much. Worried about if people like him.

Rose: Everything that boy do … he do for you. He wants you to say "Good job, son." That's all.

Troy: Rose, I ain't got time for that. He's alive. He's healthy. He's got to make his own way. I made mine. Ain't nobody gonna hold his hand when he get out there in that world.

Rose: Times have changed from when you was young, Troy. People change. The world's changing around you and you can't even see it.

Troy: *(slow, methodical)* Woman … I do the best I can do. I come in here every Friday. I carry a sack of potatoes and a bucket of lard. You all line up at the door with your hands out. I give you the lint from my pockets. I give you my sweat and my blood. I ain't got no tears. I done spent them. We go upstairs in that room at night … and I fall down on you and try to blast a hole into forever. I get up Monday morning … find my lunch on the table. I go out. Make my way. Find my strength to carry me through to the next Friday. *(Pause.)* That's all I got, Rose. That's all I got to give. I can't give nothing else.

Troy exits into the house. The lights go down to black.

SCENE 4

It is Friday. Two weeks later. Cory starts out of the house with his football equipment. The phone rings.

Cory: *(calling)* I got it! *(He answers the phone and stands in the screen door talking.)* Hello? Hey, Jesse. Naw … I was just getting ready to leave now.

Rose: *(calling)* Cory!

Cory: I told you, man, them spikes[1] is all tore up. You can use them if you want, but they ain't no good. Earl got some spikes.

Rose: *(calling)* Cory!

Cory: *(calling to Rose)* Mam? I'm talking to Jesse. *(Into phone.)* When she say that? *(Pause.)* Aw, you lying, man. I'm gonna tell her you said that.

Rose: *(calling)* Cory, don't you go nowhere!

Cory: I got to go to the game, Ma! *(Into the phone.)* Yeah, hey, look, I'll talk to you later. Yeah, I'll meet you over Earl's house. Later. Bye, Ma.

Cory exits the house and starts out the yard.

Rose: Cory, where you going off to? You got that stuff all pulled out and thrown all over your room.

---

[1] *spikes:* Athletic shoes with sharp metal grips set into the soles.

Cory: *(in the yard)* I was looking for my spikes. Jesse wanted to borrow my spikes.

Rose: Get up there and get that cleaned up before your daddy get back in here.

Cory: I got to go to the game! I'll clean it up *when I get back.*

Cory exits.

Rose: That's all he need to do is see that room all messed up.

Rose exits into the house. Troy and Bono enter the yard. Troy is dressed in clothes other than his work clothes.

Bono: He told him the same thing he told you. Take it to the union.

Troy: Brownie ain't got that much sense. Man wasn't thinking about nothing. He wait until I confront them on it ... then he wanna come crying seniority. *(Calls.)* Hey, Rose!

Bono: I wish I could have seen Mr. Rand's face when he told you.

Troy: He couldn't get it out of his mouth! Liked to bit his tongue! When they called me down there to the Commissioner's office ... he thought they was gonna fire me. Like everybody else.

Bono: I didn't think they was gonna fire you. I thought they was gonna put you on the warning paper.

Troy: Hey, Rose! *(To Bono.)* Yeah, Mr. Rand like to bit his tongue.

Troy breaks the seal on the bottle, takes a drink, and hands it to Bono.

Bono: I see you run right down to Taylors' and told that Alberta gal.

Troy: *(calling)* Hey, Rose! *(To Bono.)* I told everybody. Hey, Rose! I went down there to cash my check.

Rose: *(entering from the house)* Hush all that hollering, man! I know you out here. What they say down there at the Commissioner's office?

Troy: You supposed to come when I call you, woman. Bono'll tell you that. *(To Bono.)* Don't Lucille come when you call her?

Rose: Man, hush your mouth, I ain't no dog ... talk about "come when you call me."

Troy: *(puts his arm around Rose)* You hear this, Bono? I had me an old dog used to get uppity like that. You say, "C'mere, Blue!" ... and he just lay there and look at you. End up getting a stick and chasing him away trying to make him come.

Rose: I ain't studying you and your dog. I remember you used to sing that old song.

Troy: (he sings)

> Hear it ring! Hear it ring!
> I had a dog his name was Blue.

Rose: Don't nobody wanna hear you sing that old song.

Troy: *(sings)*

> You know Blue was mighty true.

Rose: Used to have Cory running around here singing that song.

Bono: Hell, I remember that song myself.

Troy: *(sings)*

> You know Blue was a good old dog.
> Blue treed a possum in a hollow log.

That was my daddy's song. My daddy made up that song.

Rose: I don't care who made it up. Don't nobody wanna hear you sing it.

Troy: *(makes a song like calling a dog)* Come here, woman.

Rose: You come in here carrying on, I reckon they ain't fired you. What they say down there at the Commissioner's office?

Troy: Look here, Rose … Mr. Rand called me into his office today when I got back from talking to them people down there … it come from up top … he called me in and told me they was making me a driver.

Rose: Troy, you kidding!

Troy: No I ain't. Ask Bono.

Rose: Well, that's great, Troy. Now you don't have to hassle them people no more.

Lyons enters from the street.

Troy: Aw hell, I wasn't looking to see you today. I thought you was in jail. Got it all over the front page of the *Courier* about them raiding Sefus's place … where you be hanging out with all them thugs.

Lyons: Hey, Pop … that ain't got nothing to do with me. I don't go down there gambling. I go down there to sit in with the band. I ain't got nothing to do with the gambling part. They got some good music down there.

Troy: They got some rogues … is what they got.

Lyons: How you been, Mr. Bono? Hi, Rose.

Bono: I see where you playing down at the Crawford Grill tonight.

Rose: How come you ain't brought Bonnie like I told you? You should have brought Bonnie with you, she ain't been over in a month of Sundays.

Lyons: I was just in the neighborhood … thought I'd stop by.

Troy: Here he come . . .

Bono: Your daddy got a promotion on the rubbish. He's gonna be the first colored driver. Ain't got to do nothing but sit up there and read the paper like them white fellows.

Lyons: Hey, Pop … if you knew how to read you'd be all right.

Bono: Naw … naw … you mean if the nigger knew how to *drive* he'd be all right. Been fighting with them people about driving and ain't even got a license. Mr. Rand know you ain't got no driver's license?

Troy: Driving ain't nothing. All you do is point the truck where you want it to go. Driving ain't nothing.

Bono: Do Mr. Rand know you ain't got no driver's license? That's what I'm talking about. I ain't asked if driving was easy. I asked if Mr. Rand know you ain't got no driver's license.

Troy: He ain't got to know. The man ain't got to know my business. Time he find out, I have two or three driver's licenses.

Lyons: *(going into his pocket)* Say, look here, Pop …

Troy: I knew it was coming. Didn't I tell you, Bono? I know what kind of "Look here, Pop" that was. The nigger fixing to ask me for some money. It's Friday night. It's my payday. All them rogues down there on the avenue … the ones that ain't in jail … and Lyons is hopping in his shoes to get down there with them.

Lyons: See, Pop … if you give somebody else a chance to talk sometimes, you'd see that I was fixing to pay you back your ten dollars like I told you. Here … I told you I'd pay you when Bonnie got paid.

Troy: Naw … you go ahead and keep that ten dollars. Put it in the bank. The next time you feel like you wanna come by here and ask me for something … you go on down there and get that.

Lyons: Here's your ten dollars, Pop. I told you I don't want you to give me nothing. I just wanted to borrow ten dollars.

Troy: Naw … you go on and keep that for the next time you want to ask me.

Lyons: Come on, Pop … here go your ten dollars.

Rose: Why don't you go on and let the boy pay you back, Troy?

Lyons: Here you go, Rose. If you don't take it I'm gonna have to hear about it for the next six months. *(He hands her the money.)*

Rose: You can hand yours over here too, Troy.

Troy: You see this, Bono. You see how they do me.

Bono: Yeah, Lucille do me the same way.

Gabriel is heard singing offstage. He enters.

Gabriel: Better get ready for the Judgment! Better get ready for … Hey! … Hey! … There's Troy's boy!

Lyons: How are you doing, Uncle Gabe?

Gabriel: Lyons … The King of the Jungle! Rose … hey, Rose. Got a flower for you. *(He takes a rose from his pocket.)* Picked it myself. That's the same rose like you is!

Rose: That's right nice of you, Gabe.

Lyons: What you been doing, Uncle Gabe?

Gabriel: Oh, I been chasing hellhounds and waiting on the time to tell St. Peter to open the gates.

Lyons: You been chasing hellhounds, huh? Well … you doing the right thing, Uncle Gabe. Somebody got to chase them.

Gabriel: Oh, yeah … I know it. The devil's strong. The devil ain't no pushover. Hellhounds snipping at everybody's heels. But I got my trumpet waiting on the judgment time.

Lyons: Waiting on the Battle of Armageddon, huh?

Gabriel: Ain't gonna be too much of a battle when God get to waving that Judgment sword. But the people's gonna have a hell of a time trying to get into heaven if them gates ain't open.

Lyons: *(putting his arm around Gabriel)* You hear this, Pop. Uncle Gabe, you all right!

Gabriel: *(laughing with Lyons)* Lyons! King of the Jungle.

Rose: You gonna stay for supper, Gabe? Want me to fix you a plate?

Gabriel: I'll take a sandwich, Rose. Don't want no plate. Just wanna eat with my hands. I'll take a sandwich.

Rose: How about you, Lyons? You staying? Got some short ribs cooking.

Lyons: Naw, I won't eat nothing till after we finished playing. *(Pause.)* You ought to come down and listen to me play, Pop.

Troy: I don't like that Chinese music. All that noise.

Rose: Go on in the house and wash up, Gabe … I'll fix you a sandwich.

Gabriel: *(to Lyons, as he exits)* Troy's mad at me.

Lyons: What you mad at Uncle Gabe for, Pop?

Rose: He thinks Troy's mad at him cause he moved over to Miss Pearl's.

Troy: I ain't mad at the man. He can live where he want to live at.

Lyons: What he move over there for? Miss Pearl don't like nobody.

Rose: She don't mind him none. She treats him real nice. She just don't allow all that singing.

Troy: She don't mind that rent he be paying … that's what she don't mind.

Rose: Troy, I ain't going through that with you no more. He's over there cause he want to have his own place. He can come and go as he please.

Troy: Hell, he could come and go as he please here. I wasn't stopping him. I ain't put no rules on him.

Rose: It ain't the same thing, Troy. And you know it.

Gabriel comes to the door.

Now, that's the last I wanna hear about that. I don't wanna hear nothing else about Gabe and Miss Pearl. And next week …

Gabriel: I'm ready for my sandwich, Rose.

Rose: And next week … when that recruiter come from that school … I want you to sign that paper and go on and let Cory play football. Then that'll be the last I have to hear about that.

Troy: *(to Rose as she exits into the house)* I ain't thinking about Cory nothing.

Lyons: What … Cory got recruited? What school he going to?

Troy: That boy walking around here smelling his piss … thinking he's grown. Thinking he's gonna do what he want, irrespective of what I say. Look here, Bono … I left the Commissioner's office and went down to the A&P … that boy ain't working down there. He lying to me. Telling me he got his job back … telling me he working weekends … telling me he working after school … Mr. Stawicki tell me he ain't working down there at all!

Lyons: Cory just growing up. He's just busting at the seams trying to fill out your shoes.

Troy: I don't care what he's doing. When he get to the point where he wanna disobey me … then it's time for him to move on. Bono'll tell you that. I bet he ain't never disobeyed his daddy without paying the consequences.

Bono: I ain't never had a chance. My daddy came on through ... but I ain't never knew him to see him ... or what he had on his mind or where he went. Just moving on through. Searching out the New Land. That's what the old folks used to call it. See a fellow moving around from place to place ... woman to woman ... called it searching out the New Land. Can't say if he ever found it. I come along, didn't want no kids. Didn't know if I was gonna be in one place long enough to fix on them right as their daddy. I figured I was going searching too. As it turned out I been hooked up with Lucille near about as long as your daddy been with Rose. Going on sixteen years.

Troy: Sometimes I wish I hadn't known my daddy. He ain't cared nothing about no kids. A kid to him wasn't nothing. All he wanted was for you to learn how to walk so he could start you to working. When it come time for eating ... he ate first. If there was anything left over, that's what you got. Man would sit down and eat two chickens and give you the wing.

Lyons: You ought to stop that, Pop. Everybody feed their kids. No matter how hard times is ... everybody care about their kids. Make sure they have something to eat.

Troy: The only thing my daddy cared about was getting them bales of cotton in to Mr. Lubin. That's the only thing that mattered to him. Sometimes I used to wonder why he was living. Wonder why the devil hadn't come and got him. "Get them bales of cotton in to Mr. Lubin" and find out he owe him money ...

Lyons: He should have just went on and left when he saw he couldn't get nowhere. That's what I would have done.

Troy: How he gonna leave with eleven kids? And where he gonna go? He ain't knew how to do nothing but farm. No, he was trapped and I think he knew it. But I'll say this for him ... he felt a responsibility toward us. Maybe he ain't treated us the way I felt he should have ... but without that responsibility he could have walked off and left us . . .made his own way.

Bono: A lot of them did. Back in those days what you talking about ... they walk out their front door and just take on down one road or another and keep on walking.

Lyons: There you go? That's what I'm talking about.

Bono: Just keep on walking till you come to something else. Ain't you never heard of nobody having the walking blues? Well, that's what you call it when you just take off like that.

Troy: My daddy ain't had them walking blues! What you talking about? He stayed right there with his family. But he was just as evil as he could be. My mama couldn't stand him. Couldn't stand that evilness. She run off when I was about eight. She sneaked off one night after he had gone to sleep. Told me she was coming back for me. I ain't never seen her no more. All his women run off and left him. He wasn't good for nobody.

When my turn come to head out, I was fourteen and got to sniffing around Joe Canewell's daughter. Had us an old mule we called Greyboy.

My daddy sent me out to do some plowing and tied up Greyboy and went to fooling around with Joe Canewell's daughter. We done found us a nice little spot, got real cozy with each other. She about thirteen and we done figured we was grown anyway … so we down there enjoying ourselves … ain't thinking about nothing. We didn't know Greyboy had got loose and wandered back to the house and my daddy was looking for me. We down there by the creek enjoying ourselves when my daddy come up on us. Surprised us. He had them leather straps off the mule and commenced to whupping me like there was no tomorrow. I jumped up, mad and embarrassed. I was scared of my daddy. When he commenced to whupping on me … quite naturally I run to get out of the way. *(Pause.)* Now I thought he was mad 'cause I ain't done my work. But I see where he was chasing me off so he could have that gal for himself. When I see what the matter of it was, I lost all fear of my daddy. Right there is where I become a man … at fourteen years of age. *(Pause.)* Now it was my turn to run him off. I picked up them same reins that he had used on me. I picked up them reins and commenced to whupping on him. The gal jumped up and run off … and when my daddy turned to face me, I could see why the devil had never come to get him … cause he was the devil himself. I don't know what happened. When I woke up, I was laying right there by the creek, and Blue … this old dog we had … was licking my face. I thought I was blind. I couldn't see nothing. Both my eyes were swollen shut. I laid there and cried. I didn't know what I was gonna do. The only thing I knew was the time had come for me to leave my daddy's house. And right there the world suddenly got big. And it was a long time before I could cut it down to where I could handle it.

Part of that cutting down was when I got to the place where I could feel him kicking in my blood and knew that the only thing that separated us was the matter of a few years.

Gabriel enters from the house with a sandwich.

Lyons: What you got there, Uncle Gabe?

Gabriel: Got me a ham sandwich. Rose gave me a ham sandwich.

Troy: I don't know what happened to him. I done lost touch with everybody except Gabriel. But I hope he's dead. I hope he found some peace.

Lyons: That's a heavy story, Pop. I didn't know you left home when you was fourteen.

Troy: And didn't know nothing. The only part of the world I knew was the forty-two acres of Mr. Lubin's land. That's all I knew about life.

Lyons: Fourteen's kinda young to be out on your own. *(Phone rings.)* I don't even think I was ready to be out on my own at fourteen. I don't know what I would have done.

Troy: I got up from the creek and walked on down to Mobile.[2] I was through with farming. Figured I could do better in the city. So I walked the two hundred miles to Mobile.

---

[2] *Mobile:* City and seaport in southwestern Alabama.

Lyons: Wait a minute … you ain't walked no two hundred miles, Pop. Ain't nobody gonna walk no two hundred miles. You talking about some walking there.

Bono: That's the only way you got anywhere back in them days.

Lyons: Shhh. Damn if I wouldn't have hitched a ride with somebody!

Troy: Who you gonna hitch it with? They ain't got no cars and things like they got now. We talking about 1918.

Rose: *(entering)* What you all out here getting into?

Troy: *(to Rose)* I'm telling Lyons how good he got it. He don't know nothing about this I'm talking.

Rose: Lyons, that was Bonnie on the phone. She say you supposed to pick her up.

Lyons: Yeah, okay, Rose.

Troy: I walked on down to Mobile and hitched up with some of them fellows that was heading this way. Got up here and found out … not only couldn't you get a job … you couldn't find no place to live. I thought I was in freedom. Shhh. Colored folks living down there on the riverbanks in whatever kind of shelter they could find for themselves. Right down there under the Brady Street Bridge. Living in shacks made of sticks and tarpaper. Messed around there and went from bad to worse. Started stealing. First it was food. Then I figured, hell, if I steal money I can buy me some food. Buy me some shoes too! One thing led to another. Met your mama. I was young and anxious to be a man. Met your mama and had you. What I do that for? Now I got to worry about feeding you and her. Got to steal three times as much. Went out one day looking for somebody to rob … that's what I was, a robber. I'll tell you the truth. I'm ashamed of it today. But it's the truth. Went to rob this fellow … pulled out my knife … and he pulled out a gun. Shot me in the chest. I felt just like somebody had taken a hot branding iron and laid it on me. When he shot me I jumped at him with my knife. They told me I killed him and they put me in the penitentiary and locked me up for fifteen years. That's where I met Bono. That's where I learned how to play baseball. Got out that place and your mama had taken you and went on to make life without me. Fifteen years was a long time for her to wait. But that fifteen years cured me of that robbing stuff. Rose'll tell you. She asked me when I met her if I had gotten all that foolishness out of my system. And I told her, "Baby, it's you and baseball all what count with me." You hear me, Bono? I meant it too. She say, "Which one comes first?" I told her, "Baby, ain't no doubt it's baseball … but you stick and get old with me and we'll both outlive this baseball." Am I right, Rose? And it's true.

Rose: Man, hush your mouth. You ain't said no such thing. Talking about "Baby, you know you'll always be number one with me." That's what you was talking.

Troy: You hear that, Bono. That's why I love her.

Bono: Rose'll keep you straight. You get off the track, she'll straighten you up.

Rose: Lyons, you better get on up and get Bonnie. She waiting on you.

Lyons: *(gets up to go)* Hey, Pop, why don't you come on down to the Grill and hear me play.

Troy: I ain't going down there. I'm too old to be sitting around in them clubs.

Bono: You got to be good to play down at the Grill.

Lyons: Come on, Pop …

Troy: I got to get up in the morning.

Lyons: You ain't got to stay long.

Troy: Naw, I'm gonna get my supper and go on to bed.

Lyons: Well, I got to go. I'll see you again.

Troy: Don't you come around my house on my payday.

Rose: Pick up the phone and let somebody know you coming. And bring Bonnie with you. You know I'm always glad to see her.

Lyons: Yeah, I'll do that, Rose. You take care now. See you, Pop. See you, Mr. Bono. See you, Uncle Gabe.

Gabriel: Lyons! King of the Jungle!

Lyons exits.

Troy: Is supper ready, woman? Me and you got some business to take care of. I'm gonna tear it up too.

Rose: Troy, I done told you now!

Troy: *(puts his arm around Bono)* Aw hell, woman … this is Bono. Bono like family. I done known this nigger since … how long I done know you?

Bono: It's been a long time.

Troy: I done know this nigger since Skippy was a pup. Me and him done been through some times.

Bono: You sure right about that.

Troy: Hell, I done know him longer than I known you. And we still standing shoulder to shoulder. Hey, look here, Bono … a man can't ask for no more than that. *(Drinks to him.)* I love you, nigger.

Bono: Hell, I love you too … I got to get home see my woman. You got yours in hand. I got to go get mine.

Bono starts to exit as Cory enters the yard, dressed in his football uniform. He gives Troy a hard, uncompromising look.

Cory: What you do that for, Pop?

He throws his helmet down in the direction of Troy.

Rose: What's the matter? Cory … what's the matter?

Cory: Papa done went up to the school and told Coach Zellman I can't play football no more. Wouldn't even let me play the game. Told him to tell the recruiter not to come.

Rose: Troy …

Troy: What you Troying me for. Yeah, I did it. And the boy know why I did it.

Cory: Why you wanna do that to me? That was the one chance I had.

Rose: Ain't nothing wrong with Cory playing football, Troy.

Troy: The boy lied to me. I told the nigger if he wanna play football … to keep up his chores and hold down that job at the A&P. That was the conditions. Stopped down there to see Mr. Stawicki …

Cory: I can't work after school during the football season, Pop! I tried to tell you that Mr. Stawicki's holding my job for me. You don't never want to listen to nobody. And then you wanna go and do this to me!

Troy: I ain't done nothing to you. You done it to yourself.

Cory: Just cause you didn't have a chance! You just scared I'm gonna be better than you, that's all.

Troy: Come here.

Rose: Troy …

Cory reluctantly crosses over to Troy.

Troy: All right! See. You done made a mistake.

Cory: I didn't even do nothing!

Troy: I'm gonna tell you what your mistake was. See … you swung at the ball and didn't hit it. That's strike one. See, you in the batter's box now. You swung and you missed. That's strike one. Don't you strike out!

Lights fade to black.

ACT 2

SCENE 1

The following morning. Cory is at the tree hitting the ball with the bat. He tries to mimic Troy, but his swing is awkward, less sure. Rose enters from the house.

Rose: Cory, I want you to help me with this cupboard.

Cory: I ain't quitting the team. I don't care what Poppa say.

Rose: I'll talk to him when he gets back. He had to go see about your Uncle Gabe. The police done arrested him. Say he was disturbing the peace. He'll be back directly. Come on in here and help me clean out the top of this cupboard.

Cory exits into the house. Rose sees Troy and Bono coming down the alley.

Troy … what they say down there?

Troy: Ain't said nothing. I give them fifty dollars and they let him go. I'll talk to you about it. Where's Cory?

Rose: He's in there helping me clean out these cupboards.

Troy: Tell him to get his butt out here.

Troy and Bono go over to the pile of wood. Bono picks up the saw and begins sawing.

Troy: *(to Bono)* All they want is the money. That makes six or seven times I done went down there and got him. See me coming they stick out their *hands.*

Bono: Yeah. I know what you mean. That's all they care about … that money. They don't care about what's right. *(Pause.)* Nigger, why you got to go and get some hard wood? You ain't doing nothing but building a little old fence. Get you some soft pine wood. That's all you need.

Troy: I know what I'm doing. This is outside wood. You put pine wood inside the house. Pine wood is inside wood. This here is outside wood. Now you tell me where the fence is gonna be?

Bono: You don't need this wood. You can put it up with pine wood and it'll stand as long as you gonna be here looking at it.

Troy: How you know how long I'm gonna be here, nigger? Hell, I might just live forever. Live longer than old man Horsely.

Bono: That's what Magee used to say.

Troy: Magee's a damn fool. Now you tell me who you ever heard of gonna pull their own teeth with a pair of rusty pliers.

Bono: The old folks … my granddaddy used to pull his teeth with pliers. They ain't had no dentists for the colored folks back then.

Troy: Get clean pliers! You understand? Clean pliers! Sterilize them! Besides we ain't living back then. All Magee had to do was walk over to Doc Goldblum's.

Bono: I see where you and that Tallahassee gal … that Alberta … I see where you all done got tight.

Troy: What you mean "got tight"?

Bono: I see where you be laughing and joking with her all the time.

Troy: I laughs and jokes with all of them, Bono. You know me.

Bono: That ain't the kind of laughing and joking I'm talking about.

Cory enters from the house.

Cory: How you doing, Mr. Bono?

Troy: Cory? Get that saw from Bono and cut some wood. He talking about the wood's too hard to cut. Stand back there, Jim, and let that young boy show you how it's done.

Bono: He's sure welcome to it.

Cory takes the saw and begins to cut the wood.

Whew-e-e! Look at that. Big old strong boy. Look like Joe Louis.[1] Hell, must be getting old the way I'm watching that boy whip through that wood.

Cory: I don't see why Mama want a fence around the yard noways.

Troy: Damn if I know either. What the hell she keeping out with it? She ain't got nothing nobody want.

Bono: Some people build fences to keep people out … and other people build fences to keep people in. Rose wants to hold on to you all. She loves you.

---

[1]*Joe Louis:* Joseph Louis Barrow (1914–1981), American boxer known as the "Brown Bomber." In 1937, he became the youngest boxer ever to win the Heavyweight Championship, which he defended twenty-five times; he retired undefeated in 1949.

Troy: Hell, nigger, I don't need nobody to tell me my wife loves me. Cory ... go on in the house and see if you can find that other saw.

Cory: Where's it at?

Troy: I said find it! Look for it till you find it!

Cory exits into the house.

What's that supposed to mean? Wanna keep us in?

Bono: Troy ... I done known you seem like damn near my whole life. You and Rose both. I done know both of you all for a long time. I remember when you met Rose. When you was hitting them baseballs out the park. A lot of them gals was after you then. You had the pick of the litter. When you picked Rose, I was happy for you. That was the first time I knew you had any sense. I said ... My man Troy knows what he's doing ... I'm gonna follow this nigger ... he might take me somewhere. I been following you too. I done learned a whole heap of things about life watching you. I done learned how to tell where the shit lies. How to tell it from the alfalfa. You done learned me a lot of things. You showed me how to not make the same mistakes ... to take life as it comes along and keep putting one foot in front of the other. *(Pause.)* Rose a good woman, Troy.

Troy: Hell, nigger, I know she a good woman. I been married to her for eighteen years. What you got on your mind, Bono?

Bono: I just say she a good woman. Just like I say anything. I ain't got to have nothing on my mind.

Troy: You just gonna say she a good woman and leave it hanging out there like that? Why you telling me she a good woman?

Bono: She loves you, Troy. Rose loves you.

Troy: You saying I don't measure up. That's what you trying to say. I don't measure up 'cause I'm seeing this other gal. I know what you trying to say.

Bono: I know what Rose means to you, Troy. I'm just trying to say I don't want to see you mess up.

Troy: Yeah, I appreciate that, Bono. If you was messing around on Lucille I'd be telling you the same thing.

Bono: Well, that's all I got to say. I just say that because I love you both.

Troy: Hell, you know me ... I wasn't out there looking for nothing. You can't find a better woman than Rose. I know that. But seems like this woman just stuck onto me where I can't shake her loose. I done wrestled with it, tried to throw her off me ... but she just stuck on tighter. Now she's stuck on for good.

Bono: You's in control ... that's what you tell me all the time. You responsible for what you do.

Troy: I ain't ducking the responsibility of it. As long as it sets right in my heart ... then I'm okay. 'Cause that's all I listen to. It'll tell me right from wrong every time. And I ain't talking about doing Rose no bad turn. I love Rose. She done carried me a long ways and I love and respect her for that.

Bono: I know you do. That's why I don't want to see you hurt her. But what you gonna do when she find out? What you got then? If you try and juggle both of them … sooner or later you gonna drop one of them. That's common sense.

Troy: Yeah, I hear what you saying, Bono. I been trying to figure a way to work it out.

Bono: Work it out right, Troy. I don't want to be getting all up between you and Rose's business … but work it so it come out right.

Troy: Ah hell, I get all up between you and Lucille's business. When you gonna get that woman that refrigerator she been wanting? Don't tell me you ain't got no money now. I know who your banker is. Mellon don't need that money bad as Lucille want that refrigerator. I'll tell you that.

Bono: Tell you what I'll do … when you finish building this fence for Rose … I'll buy Lucille that refrigerator.

Troy: You done stuck your foot in your mouth now!

Troy grabs up a board and begins to saw. Bono starts to walk out the yard.

Hey, nigger … where you going?

Bono: I'm going home. I know you don't expect me to help you now. I'm protecting my money. I wanna see you put that fence up by yourself. That's what I want to see. You'll be here another six months without me.

Troy: Nigger, you ain't right.

Bono: When it comes to my money … I'm right as fireworks on the Fourth of July.

Troy: All right, we gonna see now. You better get out your bankbook.

Bono exits, and Troy continues to work. Rose enters from the house.

Rose: What they say down there? What's happening with Gabe?

Troy: I went down there and got him out. Cost me fifty dollars. Say he was disturbing the peace. Judge set up a hearing for him in three weeks. Say to show cause why he shouldn't be recommitted.

Rose: What was he doing that cause them to arrest him?

Troy: Some kids were teasing him and he run them off home. Say he was howling and carrying on. Some folks seen him and called the police. That's all it was.

Rose: Well, what's you say? What'd you tell the judge?

Troy: Told him I'd look after him. It didn't make no sense to recommit the man. He stuck out his big greasy palm and told me to give him fifty dollars and take him on home.

Rose: Where's he at now? Where'd he go off to?

Troy: He's gone about his business. He don't need nobody to hold his hand.

Rose: Well, I don't know. Seem like that would be the best place for him if they did put him into the hospital. I know what you're gonna say. But that's what I think would be best.

Troy: The man done had his life ruined fighting for what? And they wanna take and lock him up. Let him be free. He don't bother nobody.

Rose: Well, everybody got their own way of looking at it I guess. Come on and get your lunch. I got a bowl of lima beans and some cornbread in the oven. Come and get something to eat. Ain't no sense you fretting over Gabe.

Rose turns to go into the house.

Troy: Rose … got something to tell you.
Rose: Well, come on … wait till I get this food on the table.
Troy: Rose!

She stops and turns around.

I don't know how to say this. *(Pause.)* I can't explain it none. It just sort of grows on you till it gets out of hand. It starts out like a little bush … and the next thing you know it's a whole forest.
Rose: Troy … what is you talking about?
Troy: I'm talking, woman, let me talk. I'm trying to find a way to tell you … I'm gonna be a daddy. I'm gonna be somebody's daddy.
Rose: Troy … you're not telling me this? You're gonna be … what?
Troy: Rose … now … see …
Rose: You telling me you gonna be somebody's daddy? You telling your *wife* this?

Gabriel enters from the street. He carries a rose in his hand.

Gabriel: Hey, Troy! Hey, Rose!
Rose: I have to wait eighteen years to hear something like this.
Gabriel: Hey, Rose … I got a flower for you. *(He hands it to her.)* That's a rose. Same rose like you is.
Rose: Thanks, Gabe.
Gabriel: Troy, you ain't mad at me is you? Them bad mens come and put me away. You ain't mad at me is you?
Troy: Naw, Gabe, I ain't mad at you.
Rose: Eighteen years and you wanna come with this.
Gabriel: *(takes a quarter out of his pocket)* See what I got? Got a brand new quarter.
Troy: Rose … it's just …
Rose: Ain't nothing you can say, Troy. Ain't no way of explaining that.
Gabriel: Fellow that give me this quarter had a whole mess of them. I'm gonna keep this quarter till it stop shining.
Rose: Gabe, go on in the house there. I got some watermelon in the Frigidaire. Go on and get you a piece.
Gabriel: Say, Rose … you know I was chasing hellhounds and them bad mens come and get me and take me away. Troy helped me. He come down there and told them they better let me go before he beat them up. Yeah, he did!
Rose: You go on and get you a piece of watermelon, Gabe. Them bad mens is gone now.

Gabriel: Okay, Rose … gonna get me some watermelon. The kind with the stripes on it.

Gabriel exits into the house.

Rose: Why, Troy? Why? After all these years to come dragging this in to me now. It don't make no sense at your age. I could have expected this ten or fifteen years ago, but not now.

Troy: Age ain't got nothing to do with it, Rose.

Rose: I done tried to be everything a wife should be. Everything a wife could be. Been married eighteen years and I got to live to see the day you tell me you been seeing another woman and done fathered a child by her. And you know I ain't never wanted no half nothing in my family. My whole family is half. Everybody got different fathers and mothers … my two sisters and my brother. Can't hardly tell who's who. Can't never sit down and talk about Papa and Mama. It's your papa and your mama and my papa and my mama …

Troy: Rose … stop it now.

Rose: I ain't never wanted that for none of my children. And now you wanna drag your behind in here and tell me something like this.

Troy: You ought to know. It's time for you to know.

Rose: Well, I don't want to know, goddamn it!

Troy: I can't just make it go away. It's done now. I can't wish the circumstance of the thing away.

Rose: And you don't want to either. Maybe you want to wish me and my boy away. Maybe that's what you want? Well, you can't wish us away. I've got eighteen years of my life invested in you. You ought to have stayed upstairs in my bed where you belong.

Troy: Rose … now listen to me … we can get a handle on this thing. We can talk this out … come to an understanding.

Rose: All of a sudden it's "we." Where was "we" at when you was down there rolling around with some godforsaken woman? "We" should have come to an understanding before you started making a damn fool of yourself. You're a day late and a dollar short when it comes to an understanding with me.

Troy: It's just … She gives me a different idea … a different understanding about myself. I can step out of this house and get away from the pressures and problems … be a different man. I ain't got to wonder how I'm gonna pay the bills or get the roof fixed. I can just be a part of myself that I ain't never been.

Rose: What I want to know … is do you plan to continue seeing her. That's all you can say to me.

Troy: I can sit up in her house and laugh. Do you understand what I'm saying. I can laugh out loud … and it feels good. It reaches all the way down to the bottom of my shoes. *(Pause.)* Rose, I can't give that up.

Rose: Maybe you ought to go on and stay down there with her … if she's a better woman than me.

Troy: It ain't about nobody being a better woman or nothing. Rose, you ain't the blame.

A man couldn't ask for no woman to be a better wife than you've been. I'm responsible for it. I done locked myself into a pattern trying to take care of you all that I forgot about myself.

Rose: What the hell was I there for? That was my job, not somebody else's.

Troy: Rose, I done tried all my life to live decent … to live a clean … hard … useful life. I tried to be a good husband to you. In every way I knew how. Maybe I come into the world backwards, I don't know. But … you born with two strikes on you before you come to the plate. You got to guard it closely … always looking for the curve ball on the inside corner. You can't afford to let none get past you. You can't afford a call strike. If you going down … you going down swinging. Everything lined up against you. What you gonna do. I fooled them, Rose. I bunted. When I found you and Cory and a halfway decent job … I was safe. Couldn't nothing touch me. I wasn't gonna strike out no more. I wasn't going back to the penitentiary. I wasn't gonna lay in the streets with a bottle of wine. I was safe. I had me a family. A job. I wasn't gonna get that last strike. I was on first looking for one of them boys to knock me in. To get me home.

Rose: You should have stayed in my bed, Troy.

Troy: Then when I saw that gal … she firmed up my backbone. And I got to thinking that if I tried … I just might be able to steal second. Do you understand after eighteen years I wanted to steal second.

Rose: You should have held me tight. You should have grabbed me and held on.

Troy: I stood on first base for eighteen years and I thought … well, goddamn it … go on for it!

Rose: We're not talking about baseball! We're talking about you going off to lay in bed with another woman … and then bring it home to me. That's what we're talking about. We ain't talking about no baseball.

Troy: Rose, you're not listening to me. I'm trying the best I can to explain it to you. It's not easy for me to admit that I been standing in the same place for eighteen years.

Rose: I been standing with you! I been right here with you, Troy. I got a life too. I gave eighteen years of my life to stand in the same spot with you. Don't you think I ever wanted other things? Don't you think I had dreams and hopes? What about my life? What about me. Don't you think it ever crossed my mind to want to know other men? That I wanted to lay up somewhere and forget about my responsibilities? That I wanted someone to make me laugh so I could feel good? You not the only one who's got wants and needs. But I held on to you, Troy. I took all my feelings, my wants and needs, my dreams … and I buried them inside you. I planted a seed and watched and prayed over it. I planted myself inside you and waited to bloom. And it didn't take me no eighteen years to find out the soil was hard and rocky and it wasn't never gonna bloom.

But I held on to you, Troy. I held you tighter. You was my husband. I owed you everything I had. Every part of me I could find to give you. And upstairs in that room … with the darkness falling in on me … I gave everything I had to try and erase the doubt that you wasn't the finest man in the world. And wherever you was going … I wanted to be there with you. 'Cause you was my husband. 'Cause that's the only way I was gonna survive as your wife. You always talking about what you give … and what you don't have to give. But you take too. You take … and don't even know nobody's giving!

Rose turns to exit into the house; Troy grabs her arm.

Troy: You say I take and don't give!
Rose: Troy! You're hurting me!
Troy: You say I take and don't give!
Rose: Troy … you're hurting my arm! Let go!
Troy: I done give you everything I got. Don't you tell that lie on me.
Rose: Troy!
Troy: Don't you tell that lie on me!

Cory enters from the house.

Cory: Mama!
Rose: Troy. You're hurting me.
Troy: Don't you tell me about no taking and giving.

Cory comes up behind Troy and grabs him. Troy, surprised, is thrown off balance just as Cory throws a glancing blow that catches him on the chest and knocks him down. Troy is stunned, as is Cory.

Rose: Troy. Troy. No!

Troy gets to his feet and starts at Cory.

Troy … no. Please! Troy!

Rose pulls on Troy to hold him back. Troy stops himself.

Troy: *(to Cory)* All right. That's strike two. You stay away from around me, boy. Don't you strike out. You living with a full count. Don't you strike out.

Troy exits out the yard as the lights go down.

SCENE 2

It is six months later, early afternoon. Troy enters from the house and starts to exit the yard. Rose enters from the house.

Rose: Troy, I want to talk to you.
Troy: All of a sudden, after all this time, you want to talk to me, huh? You ain't wanted to talk to me for months. You ain't wanted to talk to me last

night. You ain't wanted no part of me then. What you wanna talk to me about now?

Rose: Tomorrow's Friday.

Troy: I know what day tomorrow is. You think I don't know tomorrow's Friday? My whole life I ain't done nothing but look to see Friday coming and you got to tell me it's Friday.

Rose: I want to know if you're coming home.

Troy: I always come home, Rose. You know that. There ain't never been a night I ain't come home.

Rose: That ain't what I mean … and you know it. I want to know if you're coming straight home after work.

Troy: I figure I'd cash my check … hang out at Taylors' with the boys … maybe play a game of checkers …

Rose: Troy, I can't live like this. I won't live like this. You livin' on borrowed time with me. It's been going on six months now you ain't been coming home.

Troy: I be here every Friday. Every night of the year. That's 365 days.

Rose: I want you to come home tomorrow after work.

Troy: Rose … I don't mess up my pay. You know that now. I take my pay and I give it to you. I don't have no money but what you give me back. I just want to have a little time to myself … a little time to enjoy life.

Rose: What about me? When's my time to enjoy life?

Troy: I don't know what to tell you, Rose. I'm doing the best I can.

Rose: You ain't been home from work but time enough to change your clothes and run out … and you wanna call that the best you can do?

Troy: I'm going over to the hospital to see Alberta. She went into the hospital this afternoon. Look like she might have the baby early. I won't be gone long.

Rose: Well, you ought to know. They went over to Miss Pearl's and got Gabe today. She said you told them to go ahead and lock him up.

Troy: I ain't said no such thing. Whoever told you that is telling a lie. Pearl ain't doing nothing but telling a big fat lie.

Rose: She ain't had to tell me. I read it on the papers.

Troy: I ain't told them nothing of the kind.

Rose: I saw it right there on the papers.

Troy: What it say, huh?

Rose: It said you told them to take him.

Troy: Then they screwed that up, just the way they screw up everything. I ain't worried about what they got on the paper.

Rose: Say the government send part of his check to the hospital and the other part to you.

Troy: I ain't got nothing to do with that if that's the way it works. I ain't made up the rules about how it work.

Rose: You did Gabe just like you did Cory. You wouldn't sign the paper for Cory … but you signed for Gabe. You signed that paper.

The telephone is heard ringing inside the house.

Troy: I told you I ain't signed nothing, woman! The only thing I signed was the release form. Hell, I can't read. I don't know what they had on that paper! I ain't signed nothing about sending Gabe away.

Rose: I said send him to the hospital … you said let him be free … now you done went down there and signed him to the hospital for half his money. You went back on yourself, Troy. You gonna have to answer for that.

Troy: See now … you been over there talking to Miss Pearl. She done got mad cause she ain't getting Gabe's rent money. That's all it is. She's liable to say anything.

Rose: Troy, I seen where you signed the paper.

Troy: You ain't seen nothing I signed. What she doing got papers on my brother anyway? Miss Pearl telling a big fat lie. And I'm gonna tell her about it too! You ain't seen nothing I signed. Say … you ain't seen nothing I signed.

Rose exits into the house to answer the telephone. Presently she returns.

Rose: Troy … that was the hospital. Alberta had the baby.

Troy: What she have? What is it?

Rose: It's a girl.

Troy: I better get on down to the hospital to see her.

Rose: Troy …

Troy: Rose … I got to go see her now. That's only right … what's the matter … the baby's all right, ain't it?

Rose: Alberta died having the baby.

Troy: Died … you say she's dead? Alberta's dead?

Rose: They said they done all they could. They couldn't do nothing for her.

Troy: The baby? How's the baby?

Rose: They say it's healthy. I wonder who's gonna bury her.

Troy: She had family, Rose. She wasn't living in the world by herself.

Rose: I know she wasn't living in the world by herself.

Troy: Next thing you gonna want to know if she had any insurance.

Rose: Troy, you ain't got to talk like that.

Troy: That's the first thing that jumped out your mouth. "Who's gonna bury her?" Like I'm fixing to take on that task for myself.

Rose: I am your wife. Don't push me away.

Troy: I ain't pushing nobody away. Just give me some space. That's all. Just give me some room to breathe.

Rose exits into the house. Troy walks about the yard.

Troy: *(with a quiet rage that threatens to consume him)* All right … Mr. Death. See now … I'm gonna tell you what I'm gonna do. I'm gonna take and build me a fence around this yard. See? I'm gonna build me a fence around what belongs to me. And then I want you to stay on the other side. See? You stay over there until you're ready for me. Then you come on. Bring your army. Bring your sickle. Bring your wrestling clothes. I ain't gonna fall down on my vigilance this time. You ain't gonna sneak up on me no more. When you ready for me ... when the top of your list say Troy Maxson ... that's when you come around here. You come up and knock on the front door. Ain't nobody else got nothing to do with this. This is between you and me. Man to man. You stay on the other side of the fence until you ready for me. Then you come up and knock on the front door. Anytime you want. I'll be ready for you.

The lights go down to black.

SCENE 3

The lights come up on the porch. It is late evening three days later. Rose sits listening to the ball game waiting for Troy. The final out of the game is made and Rose switches off the radio. Troy enters the yard carrying an infant wrapped in blankets. He stands back from the house and calls.

Rose enters and stands on the porch. There is a long, awkward silence, the weight of which grows heavier with each passing second.

Troy: Rose ... I'm standing here with my daughter in my arms. She ain't but a wee bittie little old thing. She don't know nothing about grownups' business. She innocent ... and she ain't got no mama.

Rose: What you telling me for, Troy?

She turns and exits into the house.

Troy: Well ... I guess we'll just sit out here on the porch.

He sits down on the porch. There is an awkward indelicateness about the way he handles the baby. His largeness engulfs and seems to swallow it. He speaks loud enough for Rose to hear.

A man's got to do what's right for him. I ain't sorry for nothing I done. It felt right in my heart. *(To the baby.)* What you smiling at? Your daddy's a big man. Got these great big old hands. But sometimes he's scared. And right now your daddy's scared 'cause we sitting out here and ain't got no home. Oh, I been homeless before. I ain't had no little baby with me. But I been homeless. You just be out on the road by your lonesome and you see one of them trains coming and you just kinda go like this ...

He sings a lullaby.

Please, Mr. Engineer let a man ride the line
Please, Mr. Engineer let a man ride the line
I ain't got no ticket please let me ride the blinds

Rose enters from the house. Troy, hearing her steps behind him, stands and faces her.

She's my daughter, Rose. My own flesh and blood. I can't deny her no more than I can deny them boys. *(Pause.)* You and them boys is my family. You and them and this child is all I got in the world. So I guess what I'm saying is … I'd appreciate it if you'd help me take care of her.

Rose: Okay, Troy … you're right. I'll take care of your baby for you …'cause … like you say … she's innocent … and you can't visit the sins of the father upon the child. A motherless child has got a hard time. *(She takes the baby from him.)* From right now … this child got a mother. But you a womanless man.

Rose turns and exits into the house with the baby. Lights go down to black.

SCENE 4

It is two months later. Lyons enters from the street. He knocks on the door and calls.

Lyons: Hey, Rose! *(Pause)* Rose!

Rose: *(from inside the house)* Stop that yelling. You gonna wake up Raynell. I just got her to sleep.

Lyons: I just stopped by to pay Papa this twenty dollars I owe him. Where's Papa at?

Rose: He should be here in a minute. I'm getting ready to go down to the church. Sit down and wait on him.

Lyons: I got to go pick up Bonnie over her mother's house.

Rose: Well, sit it down there on the table. He'll get it.

Lyons: *(enters the house and sets the money on the table)* Tell Papa I said thanks. I'll see you again.

Rose: All right, Lyons. We'll see you.

Lyons starts to exit as Cory enters.

Cory: Hey, Lyons.

Lyons: What's happening, Cory? Say man, I'm sorry I missed your graduation. You know I had a gig and couldn't get away. Otherwise, I would have been there, man. So what you doing?

Cory: I'm trying to find a job.

Lyons: Yeah I know how that go, man. It's rough out there. Jobs are scarce.

Cory: Yeah, I know.

Lyons: Look here, I got to run. Talk to Papa … he know some people. He'll be able to help get you a job. Talk to him … see what he say.

Cory: Yeah … all right, Lyons.

Lyons: You take care. I'll talk to you soon. We'll find some time to talk.

Lyons exits the yard. Cory wanders over to the tree, picks up the bat, and assumes a batting stance. He studies an imaginary pitcher and swings. Dissatisfied with the result, he tries again. Troy enters. They eye each other for a beat. Cory puts the bat down and exits the yard. Troy starts into the house as Rose exits with Raynell. She is carrying a cake.

Troy: I'm coming in and everybody's going out.

Rose: I'm taking this cake down to the church for the bake sale. Lyons was by to see you. He stopped by to pay you your twenty dollars. It's laying in there on the table.

Troy: *(going into his pocket)* Well ... here go this money.

Rose: Put it in there on the table, Troy. I'll get it.

Troy: What time you coming back?

Rose: Ain't no use in you studying me. It don't matter what time I come back.

Troy: I just asked you a question, woman. What's the matter ... can't I ask you a question?

Rose: Troy, I don't want to go into it. Your dinner's in there on the stove. All you got to do is heat it up. And don't you be eating the rest of them cakes in there. I'm coming back for them. We having a bake sale at the church tomorrow.

Rose exits the yard. Troy sits down on the steps, takes a pint bottle from his pocket, opens it, and drinks. He begins to sing.

Troy:

Hear it ring! Hear it ring!
Had an old dog his name was Blue
You know Blue was mighty true
You know Blue was a good old dog
Blue treed a possum in a hollow log
You know from that he was a good old dog

Bono enters the yard.

Bono: Hey, Troy.

Troy: Hey, what's happening, Bono?

Bono: I just thought I'd stop by to see you.

Troy: What you stop by and see me for? You ain't stopped by in a month of Sundays. Hell, I must owe you money or something.

Bono: Since you got your promotion I can't keep up with you. Used to see you every day. Now I don't even know what route you working.

Troy: They keep switching me around. Got me out in Greentree now ... hauling white folks' garbage.

Bono: Greentree, huh? You lucky, at least you ain't got to be lifting them barrels. Damn if they ain't getting heavier. I'm gonna put in my two years and call it quits.

Troy: I'm thinking about retiring myself.

Bono: You got it easy. You can *drive* for another five years.

Troy: It ain't the same, Bono. It ain't like working the back of the truck. Ain't got nobody to talk to ... feel like you working by yourself. Naw, I'm thinking about retiring. How's Lucille?

Bono: She all right. Her arthritis get to acting up on her sometime. Saw Rose on my way in. She going down to the church, huh?

Troy: Yeah, she took up going down there. All them preachers looking for somebody to fatten their pockets. *(Pause.)* Got some gin here.

Bono: Naw, thanks. I just stopped by to say hello.

Troy: Hell, nigger … you can take a drink. I ain't never known you to say no to a drink. You ain't got to work tomorrow.

Bono: I just stopped by. I'm fixing to go over to Skinner's. We got us a domino game going over his house every Friday.

Troy: Nigger, you can't play no dominoes. I used to whup you four games out of five.

Bono: Well, that learned me. I'm getting better.

Troy: Yeah? Well, that's all right.

Bono: Look here … I got to be getting on. Stop by sometime, huh?

Troy: Yeah, I'll do that, Bono. Lucille told Rose you bought her a new refrigerator.

Bono: Yeah, Rose told Lucille you had finally built your fence … so I figured we'd call it even.

Troy: I knew you would.

Bono: Yeah … okay. I'll be talking to you.

Troy: Yeah, take care, Bono. Good to see you. I'm gonna stop over.

Bono: Yeah. Okay, Troy.

Bono exits. Troy drinks from the bottle.

Troy: Old Blue died and I dig his grave
Let him down with a golden chain
Every night when I hear old Blue bark
I know Blue treed a possum in Noah's Ark[1].
Hear it ring! Hear it ring!

Cory enters the yard. They eye each other for a beat. Troy is sitting in the middle of the steps. Cory walks over.

Cory: I got to get by.

Troy: Say what? What's you say?

Cory: You in my way. I got to get by.

Troy: You got to get by where? This is my house. Bought and paid for. In full. Took me fifteen years. And if you wanna go in my house and I'm sitting on the steps … you say excuse me. Like your mama taught you.

Cory: Come on, Pop … I got to get by.

Cory starts to maneuver his way past Troy. Troy grabs his leg and shoves him back.

Troy: You just gonna walk over top of me?

Cory: I live here too!

---

[1]*Noah's Ark:* See Genesis 6.14–20.

Troy: *(advancing toward him)* You just gonna walk over top of me in my own house?

Cory: I ain't scared of you.

Troy: I ain't asked if you was scared of me. I asked you if you was fixing to walk over top of me in my own house? That's the question. You ain't gonna say excuse me? You just gonna walk over top of me?

Cory: If you wanna put it like that.

Troy: How else am I gonna put it?

Cory: I was walking by you to go into the house 'cause you sitting on the steps drunk, singing to yourself. You can put it like that.

Troy: Without saying excuse me???

Cory doesn't respond.

I asked you a question. Without saying excuse me???

Cory: I ain't got to say excuse me to you. You don't count around here no more.

Troy: Oh, I see … I don't count around here no more. You ain't got to say excuse me to your daddy. All of a sudden you done got so grown that your daddy don't count around here no more … Around here in his own house and yard that he done paid for with the sweat of his brow. You done got so grown to where you gonna take over. You gonna take over my house. Is that right? You gonna wear my pants. You gonna go in there and stretch out on my bed. You ain't got to say excuse me 'cause I don't count around here no more. Is that right?

Cory: That's right. You always talking this dumb stuff. Now, why don't you just get out my way?

Troy: I guess you got someplace to sleep and something to put in your belly. You got that, huh? You got that? That's what you need. You got that, huh?

Cory: You don't know what I got. You ain't got to worry about what I got.

Troy: You right! You one hundred percent right! I done spent the last seventeen years worrying about what you got. Now it's your turn, see? I'll tell you what to do. You grown … we done established that. You a man. Now, let's see you act like one. Turn your behind around and walk out this yard. And when you get out there in the alley … you can forget about this house. See? 'Cause this is my house. You go on and be a man and get your own house. You can forget about this. 'Cause this is mine. You go on and get yours 'cause I'm through with doing for you.

Cory: You talking about what you did for me … what'd you ever give me?

Troy: Them feet and bones! That pumping heart, nigger! I give you more than anybody else is ever gonna give you.

Cory: You ain't never gave me nothing! You ain't never done nothing but hold me back. Afraid I was gonna be better than you. All you ever did was try and make me scared of you. I used to tremble every time you called my name. Every time I heard your footsteps in the house. Wondering all the time … what's Papa gonna say if I do this? … What's he gonna say if I do that? … What's Papa gonna say if I turn on the radio? And Mama, too … she tries … but she's scared of you.

Troy: You leave your mama out of this. She ain't got nothing to do with this.

Cory: I don't know how she stand you … after what you did to her.

Troy: I told you to leave your mama out of this!

He advances toward Cory.

Cory: What you gonna do … give me a whupping? You can't whup me no more. You're too old. You just an old man.

Troy: *(shoves him on his shoulder)* Nigger! That's what you are. You just another nigger on the street to me!

Cory: You crazy! You know that?

Troy: Go on now! You got the devil in you. Get on away from me!

Cory: You just a crazy old man … talking about I got the devil in me.

Troy: Yeah, I'm crazy! If you don't get on the other side of that yard … I'm gonna show you how crazy I am! Go on … get the hell out of my yard.

Cory: It ain't your yard. You took Uncle Gabe's money he got from the army to buy this house and then you put him out.

Troy: *(advances on Cory)* Get your black ass out of my yard!

Troy's advance backs Cory up against the tree. Cory grabs up the bat.

Cory: I ain't going nowhere! Come on … put me out! I ain't scared of you.

Troy: That's my bat!

Cory: Come on!

Troy: Put my bat down!

Cory: Come on, put me out.

Cory swings at Troy, who backs across the yard.

What's the matter? You so bad … put me out!

Troy advances toward Cory.

Cory: *(backing up)* Come on! Come on!

Troy: You're gonna have to use it! You wanna draw that bat back on me … you're gonna have to use it.

Cory: Come on! … Come on!

Cory swings the bat at Troy a second time. He misses. Troy continues to advance toward him.

Troy: You're gonna have to kill me! You wanna draw that bat back on me. You're gonna have to kill me.

Cory, backed up against the tree, can go no farther. Troy taunts him. He sticks out his head and offers him a target.

Come on! Come on!

Cory is unable to swing the bat. Troy grabs it.

Troy: Then I'll show you.

Cory and Troy struggle over the bat. The struggle is fierce and fully engaged. Troy ultimately is the stronger and takes the bat away from Cory and stands over him ready to swing. He stops himself.

Go on and get away from around my house.

Cory, stung by his defeat, picks himself up, walks slowly out of the yard and up the alley.

Cory: Tell Mama I'll be back for my things.
Troy: They'll be on the other side of that fence.

Cory exits.

Troy: I can't taste nothing. Helluljah! I can't taste nothing no more. *(Troy assumes a batting posture and begins to taunt Death, the fastball on the outside corner.)* Come on! It's between you and me now! Come on! Anytime you want! Come on! I be ready for you … but I ain't gonna be easy.

The lights go down on the scene.

SCENE 5

The time is 1965. The lights come up in the yard. It is the morning of Troy's funeral. A funeral plaque with a light hangs beside the door. There is a small garden plot off to the side. There is noise and activity in the house as Rose, Gabriel, and Bono have gathered. The door opens and Raynell, seven years old, enters dressed in a flannel nightgown. She crosses to the garden and pokes around with a stick. Rose calls from the house.

Rose: Raynell!
Raynell: Mam?
Rose: What you doing out there?
Raynell: Nothing.

Rose comes to the door.

Rose: Girl, get in here and get dressed. What you doing?
Raynell: Seeing if my garden growed.
Rose: I told you it ain't gonna grow overnight. You got to wait.
Raynell: It don't look like it never gonna grow. Dag!
Rose: I told you a watched pot never boils. Get in here and get dressed.
Raynell: This ain't even no pot, Mama.
Rose: You just have to give it a chance. It'll grow. Now you come on and do what I told you. We got to be getting ready. This ain't no morning to be playing around. You hear me?
Raynell: Yes, mam.

Rose exits into the house. Raynell continues to poke at her garden with a stick. Cory enters. He is dressed in a Marine corporal's uniform, and carries a duffel bag. His posture is that of a military man, and his speech has a clipped sternness.

Cory: *(to Raynell)* Hi. *(Pause.)* I bet your name is Raynell.
Raynell: Uh huh.
Cory: Is your mama home?

Raynell runs up on the porch and calls through the screen door.

Raynell: Mama … there's some man out here. Mama?

Rose comes to the door.

Rose: Cory? Lord have mercy! Look here, you all!

Rose and Cory embrace in a tearful reunion as Bono and Lyons enter from the house dressed in funeral clothes.

Bono: Aw, looka here …
Rose: Done got all grown up!
Cory: Don't cry, Mama. What you crying about?
Rose: I'm just so glad you made it.
Cory: Hey Lyons. How you doing, Mr. Bono.

Lyons goes to embrace Cory.

Lyons: Look at you, man. Look at you. Don't he look good, Rose. Got them Corporal stripes.
Rose: What took you so long?
Cory: You know how the Marines are, Mama. They got to get all their paperwork straight before they let you do anything.
Rose: Well, I'm sure glad you made it. They let Lyons come. Your Uncle Gabe's still in the hospital. They don't know if they gonna let him out or not. I just talked to them a little while ago.
Lyons: A Corporal in the United States Marines.
Bono: Your daddy knew you had it in you. He used to tell me all the time.
Lyons: Don't he look good, Mr. Bono?
Bono: Yeah, he remind me of Troy when I first met him. *(Pause.)* Say, Rose, Lucille's down at the church with the choir. I'm gonna go down and get the pallbearers lined up. I'll be back to get you all.
Rose: Thanks, Jim.
Cory: See you, Mr. Bono.
Lyons: *(with his arm around Raynell)* Cory … look at Raynell. Ain't she precious? She gonna break a whole lot of hearts.
Rose: Raynell, come and say hello to your brother. This is your brother, Cory. You remember Cory.
Raynell: No, Mam.

Cory: She don't remember me, Mama.

Rose: Well, we talk about you. She heard us talk about you. *(To Raynell.)* This is your brother, Cory. Come on and say hello.

Raynell: Hi.

Cory: Hi. So you're Raynell. Mama told me a lot about you.

Rose: You all come on into the house and let me fix you some breakfast. Keep up your strength.

Cory: I ain't hungry, Mama.

Lyons: You can fix me something, Rose. I'll be in there in a minute.

Rose: Cory, you sure you don't want nothing? I know they ain't feeding you right.

Cory: No, Mama … thanks. I don't feel like eating. I'll get something later.

Rose: Raynell … get on upstairs and get that dress on like I told you.

Rose and Raynell exit into the house.

Lyons: So … I hear you thinking about getting married.

Cory: Yeah, I done found the right one, Lyons. It's about time.

Lyons: Me and Bonnie been split up about four years now. About the time Papa retired. I guess she just got tired of all them changes I was putting her through. *(Pause.)* I always knew you was gonna make something out yourself. Your head was always in the right direction. So … you gonna stay in … make it a career … put in your twenty years?

Cory: I don't know. I got six already, I think that's enough.

Lyons: Stick with Uncle Sam and retire early. Ain't nothing out here. I guess Rose told you what happened with me. They got me down the workhouse. I thought I was being slick cashing other people's checks.

Cory: How much time you doing?

Lyons: They give me three years. I got that beat now. I ain't got but nine more months. It ain't so bad. You learn to deal with it like anything else. You got to take the crookeds with the straights. That's what Papa used to say. He used to say that when he struck out. I seen him strike out three times in a row … and the next time up he hit the ball over the grandstand. Right out there in Homestead Field. He wasn't satisfied hitting in the seats … he want to hit it over everything! After the game he had two hundred people standing around waiting to shake his hand. You got to take the crookeds with the straights. Yeah, Papa was something else.

Cory: You still playing?

Lyons: Cory … you know I'm gonna do that. There's some fellows down there we got us a band … we gonna try and stay together when we get out … but yeah, I'm still playing. It still helps me to get out of bed in the morning. As long as it do that I'm gonna be right there playing and trying to make some sense out of it.

Rose: *(calling)* Lyons, I got these eggs in the pan.

Lyons: Let me go on and get these eggs, man. Get ready to go bury Papa. *(Pause.)* How you doing? You doing all right?

Cory nods. Lyons touches him on the shoulder and they share a moment of silent grief. Lyons exits into the house. Cory wanders about the yard. Raynell enters.

Raynell: Hi.

Cory: Hi.

Raynell: Did you used to sleep in my room?

Cory: Yeah … that used to be my room.

Raynell: That's what Papa call it. "Cory's room." It got your football in the closet.

Rose comes to the door.

Rose: Raynell, get in there and get them good shoes on.

Raynell: Mama, can't I wear these? Them other ones hurt my feet.

Rose: Well, they just gonna have to hurt your feet for a while. You ain't said they hurt your feet when you went down to the store and got them.

Raynell: They didn't hurt then. My feet done got bigger.

Rose: Don't you give me no backtalk now. You get in there and get them shoes on.

Raynell exits into the house.

Ain't too much changed. He still got that piece of rag tied to that tree. He was out here swinging that bat. I was just ready to go back in the house. He swung that bat and then he just fell over. Seem like he swung it and stood there with this grin on his face … and then he just fell over. They carried him on down to the hospital, but I knew there wasn't no need … why don't you come on in the house?

Cory: Mama … I got something to tell you. I don't know how to tell you this … but I've got to tell you … I'm not going to Papa's funeral.

Rose: Boy, hush your mouth. That's your daddy you talking about. I don't want hear that kind of talk this morning. I done raised you to come to this? You standing there all healthy and grown talking about you ain't going to your daddy's funeral?

Cory: Mama … listen …

Rose: I don't want to hear it, Cory. You just get that thought out of your head.

Cory: I can't drag Papa with me everywhere I go. I've got to say no to him. One time in my life I've got to say no.

Rose: Don't nobody have to listen to nothing like that. I know you and your daddy ain't seen eye to eye, but I ain't got to listen to that kind of talk this morning. Whatever was between you and your daddy … the time has come to put it aside. Just take it and set it over there on the shelf and forget about it. Disrespecting your daddy ain't gonna make you a man, Cory. You got to find a way to come to that on your own. Not going to your daddy's funeral ain't gonna make you a man.

Cory: The whole time I was growing up … living in his house … Papa was like a shadow that followed you everywhere. It weighed on you and sunk into your flesh. It would wrap around you and lay there until you couldn't tell which one was you anymore. That shadow digging in your flesh. Trying to crawl in. Trying to live through you. Everywhere I looked, Troy Maxson was staring back at me … hiding under the bed … in the closet. I'm just saying I've got to find a way to get rid of that shadow, Mama.

Rose: You just like him. You got him in you good.

Cory: Don't tell me that, Mama.

Rose: You Troy Maxson all over again.

Cory: I don't want to be Troy Maxson. I want to be me.

Rose: You can't be nobody but who you are, Cory. That shadow wasn't nothing but you growing into yourself. You either got to grow into it or cut it down to fit you. But that's all you got to make life with. That's all you got to measure yourself against that world out there. Your daddy wanted you to be everything he wasn't … and at the same time he tried to make you into everything he was. I don't know if he was right or wrong … but I do know he meant to do more good than he meant to do harm. He wasn't always right. Sometimes when he touched he bruised. And sometimes when he took me in his arms he cut.

When I first met your daddy I thought … Here is a man I can lay down with and make a baby. That's the first thing I thought when I seen him. I was thirty years old and had done seen my share of men. But when he walked up to me and said, "I can dance a waltz that'll make you dizzy." I thought, Rose Lee, here is a man that you can open yourself up to and be filled to bursting. Here is a man that can fill all them empty spaces you been tipping around the edges of. One of them empty spaces was being somebody's mother.

I married your daddy and settled down to cooking his supper and keeping clean sheets on the bed. When your daddy walked through the house he was so big he filled it up. That was my first mistake. Not to make him leave some room for me. For my part in the matter. But at that time I wanted that. I wanted a house that I could sing in. And that's what your daddy gave me. I didn't know to keep up his strength I had to give up little pieces of mine. I did that. I took on his life as mine and mixed up the pieces so that you couldn't hardly tell which was which anymore. It was my choice. It was my life and I didn't have to live it like that. But that's what life offered me in the way of being a woman and I took it. I grabbed hold of it with both hands.

By the time Raynell came into the house, me and your daddy had done lost touch with one another. I didn't want to make my blessing off of nobody's misfortune … but I took on to Raynell like she was all them babies I had wanted and never had.

The phone rings.

Like I'd been blessed to relive a part of my life. And if the Lord see fit to keep up my strength ... I'm gonna do her just like your daddy did you ... I'm gonna give her the best of what's in me.

Raynell: *(entering, still with her old shoes)* Mama ... Reverend Tollivier on the phone.

Rose exits into the house.

Raynell: Hi.

Cory: Hi.

Raynell: You in the Army or the Marines?

Cory: Marines.

Raynell: Papa said it was the Army. Did you know Blue?

Cory: Blue? Who's Blue?

Raynell: Papa's dog what he sing about all the time.

Cory: (singing)

Hear it ring! Hear it ring!
I had a dog his name was Blue
You know Blue was mighty true
You know Blue was a good old dog
Blue treed a possum in a hollow log
You know from that he was a good old dog.
Hear it ring! Hear it ring!

Raynell joins in singing.

Cory and Raynell:

Blue treed a possum out on a limb
Blue looked at me and I looked at him
Grabbed that possum and put him in a sack
Blue stayed there till I came back
Old Blue's feets was big and round
Never allowed a possum to touch the ground.
Old Blue died and I dug his grave
I dug his grave with a silver spade
Let him down with a golden chain
And every night I call his name
Go on Blue, you good dog you
Go on Blue, you good dog you

Raynell:

Blue laid down and died like a man
Blue laid down and died ...

Both:

Blue laid down and died like a man
Now he's treeing possums in the Promised Land
I'm gonna tell you this to let you know

Blue's gone where the good dogs go
When I hear old Blue bark
When I hear old Blue bark
Blue treed a possum in Noah's Ark
Blue treed a possum in Noah's Ark.

Rose comes to the screen door.

Rose: Cory, we gonna be ready to go in a minute.
Cory: *(to Raynell)* You go on in the house and change them shoes like Mama told you so we can go to Papa's funeral.
Raynell: Okay, I'll be back.

Raynell exits into the house. Cory gets up and crosses over to the tree. Rose stands in the screen door watching him. Gabriel enters from the alley.

Gabriel: *(calling)* Hey, Rose!
Rose: Gabe?
Gabriel: I'm here, Rose. Hey Rose, I'm here!

Rose enters from the house.

Rose: Lord ... Look here, Lyons!
Lyons: See, I told you, Rose ... I told you they'd let him come.
Cory: How you doing, Uncle Gabe?
Lyons: How you doing, Uncle Gabe?
Gabriel: Hey, Rose. It's time. It's time to tell St. Peter to open the gates. Troy, you ready? You ready, Troy. I'm gonna tell St. Peter to open the gates. You get ready now.

Gabriel, with great fanfare, braces himself to blow. The trumpet is without a mouthpiece. He puts the end of it into his mouth and blows with great force, like a man who has been waiting some twenty-odd years for this single moment. No sound comes out of the trumpet. He braces himself and blows again with the same result. A third time he blows. There is a weight of impossible description that falls away and leaves him bare and exposed to a frightful realization. It is a trauma that a sane and normal mind would be unable to withstand. He begins to dance. A slow, strange dance, eerie and life-giving. A dance of atavistic signature and ritual. Lyons attempts to embrace him. Gabriel pushes Lyons away. He begins to howl in what is an attempt at song, or perhaps a song turning back into itself in an attempt at speech. He finishes his dance and the gates of heaven stand open as wide as God's closet.

That's the way that go!

*   *   *

Reading and Reacting

1. Fences are a central metaphor in this play. To what different kinds of fences does the play's title refer?
2. How are the fathers and sons in this play alike? How are they different? Does the play imply that sons must inevitably follow in their fathers' footsteps?
3. This play is set in 1957. Given the racial climate of the country at that time, how realistic are Cory's ambitions? Compare the development of this theme in *Fences* and in another play in this book—for example, *Antigone* (p. 1191), *The Cuban Swimmer*, (p. 1122) or *Hamlet* (p. 1012)?
4. How has Troy's character been shaped by his contact with the white world?
5. Is Troy a tragic hero? If so, what is his flaw?
6. Which of the play's characters, if any, do you consider stereotypes? What comment do you think the play makes about stereotypes?
7. How does the conflict between Troy and Cory reflect conflicts within the Black community? Does the play suggest any possibilities for compromise?
8. Is the message of this play to be optimistic or pessimistic? Explain.
9. **Journal Entry** Which characters do you like? Which do you dislike? Why?
10. **Critical Perspective** Robert Brustein, theater critic and artistic director of Harvard's American Repertory Theater, has criticized Wilson on the ground that "his recurrent theme is the familiar American charge of victimization"; in *Fences*, he argues, "Wilson's larger purpose depends on his conviction that Troy's potential was stunted not [by] 'his own behavior' but by centuries of racist oppression."

    Do you see the central theme of *Fences* as "the familiar American charge of victimization," or do you think another theme is more important?

Related Works: "Discovering America" (p. 114), "Big Black Good Man" (p. 246), "The White City" (p. 512), "What Shall I Give My Children" (p. 538), "Yet Do I Marvel" (p. 662), *A Doll's House* (p. 834)

WRITING SUGGESTIONS: Theme

1. Both *Fences* and *Antigone* focus on compelling characters, but they also deal with social and political issues. Write an essay in which you examine how these social and political issues impact the main characters of each play.
2. *Antigone* explores the theme of obedience to authority: Antigone is executed for denying Creon's orders and thus defying the authority of the state. Do you think she was right to act as she did, or do you think she should have compromised her principles?
3. One of the themes of *Fences* is the dream parents have for their children. Compare the development of this theme in *Fences* and in another play in this book—for example, *The Cuban Swimmer* (p. 1122) or *Hamlet* (p. 1012).

Appendix

Using Literary Criticism in Your Writing

As you become aware of various schools of literary criticism, you see new ways to think—and to write—about fiction, poetry, and drama. Just as you value the opinions of your peers and your instructors, you also will find that the ideas of literary critics can enrich your own reactions to and evaluations of literature. Keep in mind that no single school of literary criticism offers the "right" way of approaching what you read; moreover, no single critic provides the definitive analysis of any short story, poem, or play. As you become aware of the richly varied possibilities of literary criticism, you will begin to ask new questions and discover new insights about the works you read.

Contents

Formalism and New Criticism

Formalism stresses the importance of literary form to the meaning of a work. Formalist scholars consider each work of literature in isolation. They consider biographical, historical, and social matters to be irrelevant to the real meaning of a play, short story, novel, or poem. For example, a formalist would see the relationship between Adam and Eve in *Paradise Lost* as entirely unrelated to John Milton's own marital concerns, and they would view theological themes in the same work as entirely separate from Milton's deep involvement with the Puritan religious and political cause in seventeenth-century England. Formalists would also regard Milton's intentions and readers' responses to the epic poem as irrelevant. Instead, formalists would read the text closely, paying attention to organization and structure, to verbal nuances (suggested by word choice and use of figurative language), and to multiple meanings (often created through the writer's use of paradox and irony). Formalist critics try to reconcile the tensions and oppositions inherent in the text to develop a unified reading.

The formalist movement in English-language criticism began in England with I. A. Richards's *Practical Criticism* (1929). To explain and introduce his theory, Richards asked students to interpret famous poems without telling them the poets' names. This strategy encouraged close reading of the text rather than reliance on information about a poet's reputation, the details of a poet's life, or the poem's historical context. The American formalist movement, called **New Criticism**, was made popular by college instructors who realized that formalist criticism provided a useful way for students to work along with an instructor in interpreting a literary work rather than passively listening to a lecture on biographical, literary, and historical influences. The New Critical theorists Cleanth Brooks and Robert Penn Warren put together a series of textbooks (*Understanding Poetry, Understanding Fiction,* and *Understanding Drama,* first published in the late 1930s) that were used in colleges for years. After the 1950s, many New Critics began to reevaluate their theories and to broaden their approaches. Although few scholars currently maintain a strictly formalist approach, nearly every critical movement, including feminist, Marxist, psychoanalytic, structuralist, and deconstructionist criticism, owes a debt to the close reading techniques introduced by the formalists.

A New Critical Reading: Kate Chopin's "The Storm" (p. 216)

If you were to apply formalist criticism to Chopin's "The Storm," you might begin by noting the story's three distinctive sections. What relationship do the sections bear to one another? What do we learn from the word choice, the figures of speech, and the symbols in these sections? And, most important, how do these considerations lead readers to a unified view of the story?

> In the first section of "The Storm," readers meet Bobinôt and his son Bibi. The description of the approaching clouds as "sombre," "sinister," and "sullen" (216) suggests an atmosphere of foreboding, yet the alliteration of these words also introduces a poetic tone. The conversation between father and son in the final part of this section contrasts, yet does not conflict, with the rather formal language of the introduction. Both Bobinôt and Bibi speak

in Cajun dialect, and their words have a rhythm that echoes the poetic notes struck in the description of the storm. As the section closes, Bobinôt, thinking of his wife Calixta at home, buys a can of the shrimp he knows she likes and holds the treasure "stolidly" (216), ironically suggesting the protection he cannot offer his wife in his separation from her during the coming storm.

The long second section brings readers to the story's central events. Calixta, as she watches the rain, sees her former lover, Alcée, riding up to seek shelter. As in the first section, the language of the narrator is somewhat formal and always poetic, filled with sensuous diction and images. For example, we see Calixta "unfasten[ing] her white sacque at the throat" (217) and, later, Alcée envisions her lips "as red and moist as pomegranate seed" (218). The lovemaking that follows, then, seems both natural and poetic. There is nothing sordid about this interlude and, as the final sections of the story suggest through their rather ordinary, matter-of-fact language, nothing has been harmed by Calixta and Alcée's yielding to passion.

In the third section, Bobinôt brings home the shrimp, a symbol of his love for Calixta, and, although we recognize the tension between Bobinôt's shy, gentle approach and Alcée's passion, readers can accept the final sentence as literal rather than ironic. The "storms" (both the rain and the storm of passion) have passed, and no one has been hurt. The threat suggested in the opening sentences has been diffused; both the power and the danger evoked by the poetic diction of the first two sections have disappeared, to be replaced entirely by the rhythms of daily life and speech.

For Further Reading: Formalism and New Criticism

Brooks, Cleanth. *The Well Wrought Urn*. 1947.
Empson, William. *Seven Types of Ambiguity*. 1930.
Hartman, Geoffrey H. *Beyond Formalism*. 1970.
Stallman, Robert W. *Critiques and Essays in Criticism. 1920–1948*. 1949.
Wellek, René. *A History of Modern Criticism*. Vol. 6. 1986.
Wimsatt, W. K. *The Verbal Icon*. 1954.

Reader-Response Criticism

Reader-response criticism opposes formalism, seeing the reader's interaction with the text as central to interpretation. Unlike formalists, reader-response critics do not believe that a work of literature exists as a separate, closed entity. Instead, they consider the reader's contribution to the text as essential. A poem, short story, novel, or play is not a solid piece of fabric but rather a series of threads separated by gaps that readers must fill in, drawing on their own experiences and knowledge.

As readers approach a literary text, they contribute their own interpretations. As they read one sentence and then the next, they develop expectations; and, in realistic stories, these expectations are generally met. Nevertheless, nearly every reader supplies personal meanings and observations, making each reader's experience of a work unique and distinctive from every other reader's experience of the same work. For example, imagine Shakespeare's *Romeo and Juliet* as it might be read by a fourteen-year-old high school student and by her father. The young woman, whose age is the same as Juliet's, is almost certain to identify closely with the female protagonist and to "read" Lord Capulet, Juliet's father, as overbearing and rigid. The young reader's father, however, may be drawn to the poignant passage where Capulet talks with a prospective suitor, urging that he wait while Juliet has time to enjoy her youth. Capulet describes the loss of his other children and calls Juliet "the hopeful lady of my earth." Although the young woman reading this line may interpret it as yet another indication of Capulet's possessiveness, her father may see it as a sign of love and even generosity. The twenty-first-century father may read Capulet as a man willing to risk offending a friend to keep his daughter safe from the rigors of early marriage (and early childbearing). Whose interpretation is correct? Reader-response theorists would say that both readings are entirely plausible and therefore equally "right."

The differing interpretations produced by different readers can be seen as simply the effect of the different personalities and personal histories involved in constructing meaning from the same series of clues. Not only do readers "create" the work of literature, but the literature itself may work on readers, altering their experience and thus their interpretation. For example, the father reading *Romeo and Juliet* may alter his sympathetic view of Capulet as he continues through the play and observes Capulet's later, angry exchanges with Juliet.

Reader-response theorists believe in the importance of **recursive reading**—that is, reading and rereading with the idea that no interpretation is carved in stone. A second or third interaction with the text may well produce a new interpretation. This changing view is particularly likely when the rereading takes place significantly later than the initial reading. For example, if the young woman just described rereads *Romeo and Juliet* when she is middle-aged and herself the mother of teenage children, her reaction to Capulet might be different from her reaction when she read the work at age fourteen.

In one application of reader-response theory, called **reception theory**, the idea of developing readings is applied to the general reading public rather than to individual readers. Reception theory, as proposed by Hans Robert Jauss ("Literary History as a Challenge to Literary Theory," *New Literary History*, Vol. 2 [1970–1971]), suggests that each new generation reads the same works of literature differently. Because each generation of readers has experienced different historical events, read different books, and been aware of different critical theories, each generation will view the same works very differently from its predecessors.

Reader-response criticism has received serious attention since the 1960s, when Norman Holland formulated the theory in *The Dynamics of Literary Response* (1968). The German critic Wolfgang Iser (*The Implied Reader*, 1974) argued that to be an effective reader, one must be familiar with the conventions of writing. This, then, is one reason for studying literature in a classroom: not to produce approved interpretations but to develop strategies and information that will help readers to make sense of a text. Stanley Fish, an American critic, goes even further, arguing that there may not be any "objective" text at all (*Is There a Text in This Class?* 1980). Fish says that no two readers read the same book, though readers can be trained to have relatively similar responses to a text if they have had relatively similar life experiences. For example, readers who went to college and took an Introduction to Literature course in which they learned to respond to the various elements of literature, such as character, theme, irony, and figurative language, are likely to have similar responses to a text.

Reader-Response Readings: Kate Chopin's "The Storm" (p. 216)

To demonstrate possible reader-response readings, we can look at the same story previously considered from a formalist perspective. (Of course, if several formalist critics read the story, they too would each write a somewhat different interpretation.)

Written by a twenty-five-year-old man who has studied American literature

> In Kate Chopin's "The Storm," attention must be paid to the two adult male characters, Bobinôt and Alcée. Usually, in a love triangle situation, one man is portrayed more sympathetically than the other. However, Chopin provides us with a dilemma. Alcée is not a cavalier seducer; he genuinely cares for Calixta. Neither is he a brooding hero. There is nothing gruff or angry about Alcée, and he returns to his family home with no apparent harm done following the passionate interlude. On the other hand, Bobinôt is not a cruel or abusive husband. We can see no clear reason for Calixta's affair except for her desire to fulfill a sexual longing for Alcée.

Written by an eighteen-year-old male student in a first-year literature course

> Bibi doesn't seem to be a very important character in the story, but we should pay attention to him as a reflection of his father. At the beginning of the story, Bibi worries about his mother and he expresses his concern to his father. Bobinôt tries to reassure his son, but he gets up and buys a treat for Calixta as much to comfort himself as to get something for her. Then Bibi sits with his father, and it seems as if he has transferred all his worries

to Bobinôt. In the third section of the story, after Calixta and Alcée have had their love affair, Bibi and Bobinôt come home. They both seem like children, worried about how Calixta will react. She, of course, is nice to them because she feels so guilty. At the end of the third section, both father and son are happy and enjoying themselves. You can't help but feel great sympathy for them both because they are so loving and because they have been betrayed by Calixta, who has not behaved the way a loving mother and wife should.

Written by a forty-five-year-old woman who has studied Kate Chopin's life and work

A decade after the controversial novel *The Awakening* was published in 1899, one critic protested, "To think of Kate Chopin, who once contented herself with mild yarns about genteel Creole life ... blowing us a hot blast like that!" (qtd. in Gilbert and Gubar, 1981). This literary observer was shocked, as one might expect from an early-twentieth-century reader, by Chopin's frank picture of sexual relations, and particularly of the sexual feelings of the novel's heroine. One cannot help but wonder, however, whether the scandalized reader was widely acquainted with Chopin.

Certainly, he could not have read "The Storm." This short story is surprising for many reasons, but primarily because it defies the sexual mores of the late nineteenth century by showing a woman who is neither evil nor doomed enjoying, even glorying in, her sexuality. Calixta is presented as a good wife and loving mother, concerned about her husband and son who are away from home during the storm. Yet her connection to Bobinôt and Bibi does not keep her from passionately enjoying her interlude with Alcée. She goes to his arms unhesitatingly, with no false modesty or guilt (feigned or real) to hold her back.

For Further Reading: Reader-Response Criticism

Bleich, David. *Subjective Criticism*. 1978.
Fish, Stanley. *Is There a Text in This Class?* 1980.
Holland, Norman. *The Dynamics of Literary Response*. 1968.
Iser, Wolfgang. *The Implied Reader*. 1974.
———. *The Act of Reading: A Theory of Aesthetic Response*. 1978.
Rosenblatt, Louise. *The Reader, the Text, the Poem*. 1978.
Sulleiman, Susan, and Inge Crosman, eds. *The Reader in the Text*. 1980.
Tomkins, Jane P., ed. *Reader-Response Criticism*. 1980.

Feminist Criticism

Throughout the nineteenth century, women such as the Brontë sisters, George Eliot (Mary Ann Evans), Elizabeth Barrett Browning, and Christina Rossetti struggled for the right to be taken as seriously as their male counterparts. Then, in 1929, Virginia Woolf, an experimental novelist and literary critic, published *A Room of One's Own*, which described the difficulties that women writers faced and defined a tradition of literature written by women.

Feminist criticism emerged as a distinct approach to literature only in the late 1960s. Modern feminist criticism began with works such as Mary Ellman's *Thinking about Women* (1968), which focuses on the negative female stereotypes in books authored by men and points out alternative female characteristics suggested by women authors. Another pioneering feminist work was Kate Millet's *Sexual Politics* (1969), which analyzes the societal mechanisms that perpetuate male domination of women. Since that time, feminist writings, though not unified in one theory or methodology, have appeared in ever-growing numbers. Some feminist critics have adapted psychoanalytic, Marxist, or other poststructuralist theories, and others have broken new ground. In general, feminist critics take the view that our culture—and by extension our literature—is primarily patriarchal (reinforcing systems that favor men as the dominant social group).

According to feminist critics, what is at issue is not anatomical sex but gender. As Simone de Beauvoir explained, a person is not born feminine, as our society defines it, but rather becomes so because of cultural conditioning. According to feminist critics, patriarchal Western culture has defined the feminine as "other" to the male, as passive and emotional in opposition to the dominating and rational masculine.

Feminist critics claim that patriarchal cultural stereotypes pervade works of literature in the **canon**—those works generally acknowledged to be the best and most significant. Feminists point out that the traditional canon typically consisted of works written by males and about male experiences. Female characters, when they did appear, were often subordinated to male characters. A female reader of these works must either identify with the male protagonist or accept a marginalized role.

One response of feminist critics is to reinterpret works in the traditional canon. As Judith Fetterley explains in *The Resisting Reader* (1978), the reader "revisions" the text, focusing on the covert sexual bias in a literary work. For example, a feminist scholar studying Shakespeare's *Macbeth* might look closely at the role played by Lady Macbeth and argue that she was not simply a cold-hearted villain but a victim of the circumstances of her time: women in her day were not permitted to follow their own ambitions but were relegated to supporting roles, living their lives vicariously through the achievements of their husbands and sons.

A second focus of feminist scholars has been the redefinition of the canon. By seeking out, analyzing, and evaluating little-known works by women, feminist scholars have rediscovered women writers who were ignored or shunned by the reading public and by critics of their own times. Thus, writers such as Kate Chopin and Charlotte Perkins Gilman (see "The Yellow Wallpaper," p. 315), who wrote during the late nineteenth and early twentieth centuries, are now recognized as worthy of serious consideration and study.

A Feminist Reading: Tillie Olsen's "I Stand Here Ironing" (p. 227)

To approach Tillie Olsen's "I Stand Here Ironing" from a feminist perspective, you might focus on the passages in which the narrator describes her relationships and encounters with men.

> Some readings of Tillie Olsen's "I Stand Here Ironing" suggest that the narrator made choices that doomed her oldest daughter to a life of confusion. If we look at the narrator's relationships with the men in her life, however, we can see that she herself is the story's primary victim.
>
> At nineteen, the narrator was a mother abandoned by her husband, who left her a note saying that he "could no longer endure ... sharing want" (228) with his wife and infant daughter. This is the first desertion we hear about in the narrator's life, and although she agonizingly describes her painful decisions and the mistakes she made with her daughter Emily, we cannot help but recognize that she was the one who stayed and tried to make things right. Her actions contrast sharply with those of her husband, who ran away, saying that his wife and daughter were burdens too great for him to bear.
>
> The second abandonment is more subtle than the first but no less devastating. After the narrator remarried, she was again left alone to cope with a growing family when her second husband went off to war. True, this desertion was for a "noble" purpose and probably was not voluntary, but the narrator, nevertheless, had to seek one of the low-paying jobs available to women to supplement her allotment checks. She was again forced to leave her children because her husband had to serve the needs of the military establishment.
>
> The narrator was alone at crucial points in Emily's life and had to turn away from her daughter to survive. She has been brought up in a world that teaches women to depend on men, but she learns that she is ultimately alone. Although the desertions she endured were not always intentional, she had to bear the brunt of circumstances that were not her choice but were foisted on her by the patriarchal society in which she lived.

For Further Reading: Feminist Criticism

Benstock, Shari, ed. *Feminist Issues in Literary Scholarship*. 1987.

Engleton, Mary, ed. *Feminist Issues in Literary Theory: A Reader*. 1986.

Gilbert, Sandra, and Susan Gubar. *The Madwoman in the Attic*. 1979.

———, *No Man's Land*. 3 vols. 1988, 1989, 1994.

———, eds. *The Norton Anthology of Literature by Women*. 1985.

Heilbrun, Carolyn G. *Hamlet's Mother and Other Women*. 1990.

Jacobus, Mary. *Reading Woman: Essays in Feminist Criticism*. 1986.

Miller, Nancy, K., ed. *The Poetics of Gender*. 1986.

———. *Subject to Change*. 1988.

Showalter, Elaine. *A Literature of Their Own*. 1977.

———. *Sister's Choice: Tradition and Change in American Women's Writing*. 1991.

Marxist Criticism

Marxist criticism bases interpretations of literature on the social and economic theories of Karl Marx (*Das Kapital*, 1867–1894) and his colleague and coauthor Friedrich Engels (*The Communist Manifesto*, 1884). Marx and Engels believed that the dominant capitalist middle class would eventually be challenged and overthrown by the working class. In the meantime, however, middle-class capitalists would continue to exploit the working class, who produce excess products and profits yet do not share in the benefits of their labor. Marx and Engels further regarded all parts of the society in which they lived—religious, legal, educational, governmental—as tainted by what they saw as the corrupt values of middle-class capitalists.

Marxist critics apply these views about class struggle to their readings of poetry, fiction, and drama. They tend to analyze the literary works of any historical era as products of the ideology, or network of concepts, that supports the interests of the cultural elite and suppresses those of the working class. Some Marxist critics see all Western literature as distorted by the privileged views of the elite class, but most believe that a few creative writers reject the distorted views of their society and see clearly the wrongs to which working-class people have been subjected. For example, George Lukacs, a Hungarian Marxist critic, proposed that great works of literature create their own worlds and reflect life with clarity. These great works, though not written by Marxists, can be studied for their revealing examples of class conflict and other Marxist concerns. A Marxist critic would look with favor on Charles Dickens, who in nearly every novel pointed out inequities in the political, legal, and educational establishments of his time. Readers who remember Oliver Twist's pitiful plea for "more" workhouse porridge (refused by evil Mr. Bumble, who skims money from funds intended to feed the impoverished inmates) cannot help but see fertile ground for the Marxist critic, who would certainly applaud Dickens's scathing criticism of Victorian social and economic inequality.

Marxist criticism developed in the 1920s and 1930s in Germany and the Soviet Union. Since 1960, British and American Marxism has received greatest attention, with works such as Raymond Williams's *Culture and Society, 1780–1950* (1960) and Terry Eagleton's *Criticism and Ideology* (1976).

A Marxist Reading: Tillie Olsen's "I Stand Here Ironing" (p. 227)

In a Marxist reading of Tillie Olsen's "I Stand Here Ironing," you might concentrate on events that demonstrate how the narrator's and Emily's fates have been directly affected by the capitalist society of the United States.

> Tillie Olsen's "I Stand Here Ironing" stands as a powerful indictment of the capitalist system. The narrator and her daughter Emily are repeatedly exploited and defeated by the pressures of the economic system in which they live.

The narrator's first child, Emily, is born into the world of the 1930s depression—an economic disaster brought on by the excesses and greed of Wall Street. When the young mother is deserted by her first husband, there are no government programs in place to help her. She says it was the "pre-relief, pre-WPA world of the depression" that forced her away from her child and into "a job hashing at night" (228). Although she is willing to work, she is paid so poorly that she must finally send Emily to live with her husband's family. Raising the money to bring Emily back takes a long time; and after this separation, Emily's health, both physical and emotional, is precarious.

When Emily gets the measles, we get a hard look at what the few social programs that existed during the Depression were like. The child is sent—at the urging of a government social worker—to a convalescent home. The narrator notes bitterly, "They still send children to that place. I see pictures on the society page of sleek young women planning affairs to raise money for it, or dancing at the affairs, or decorating Easter eggs or filling Christmas stockings for the children" (230). The privileged class basks in the artificial glow of their charity work for the poor, yet the newspapers never show pictures of the hospitalized children who are kept isolated from everyone they loved and forced to eat "runny eggs ... or mush with lumps" (230). Once again, the mother is separated from her daughter by a system that discriminates against the poor. Because the family cannot afford private treatment, Emily is forced to undergo treatment in a public institution that not only denies her any contact with her family but also cruelly forbids her to save the letters she receives from home. Normal family relationships are severely disrupted by an uncaring economic structure that only grudgingly offers aid to the poor.

It is clear that the division between mother and daughter is created and worsened by the social conditions in which they live. Because they are poor, they are separated at crucial times and therefore never get to know each other fully. Thus, neither can truly understand the ordeals the other has been forced to endure.

For Further Reading: Marxist Criticism

Agger, Ben. *The Discourse of Domination*. 1992.

Bullock, Chris, and David Peck, eds. *Guide to Marxist Literary Criticism*. 1980.

Eagleton, Terry. *Marxism and Literary Criticism*. 1976.

Frow, John. *Marxism and Literary History*. 1986.

Holub, Renate, and Antonio Gramsci. *Beyond Marxism and Postmodernism*. 1992.

Jameson, Fredric. *Marxism and Form*. 1971.

Lentricchia, Frank. *Criticism and Social Change*. 1983.

Ohmann, Richard M. *Politics of Letters*. 1987.

Strelka, Joseph P., ed. *Literary Criticism and Sociology*. 1973.

Williams, Raymond. *Culture and Society, 1780–1950*. 1960.

———. *Marxism and Literature*. 1977.

Psychoanalytic Criticism

Psychoanalytic criticism focuses on a work of literature as an expression in fictional form of the inner workings of the human mind. The premises and procedures used in psychoanalytic criticism were developed by Sigmund Freud (1846–1939), though some critics disagree strongly with his conclusions and their therapeutic and literary applications. Feminists, for example, take issue with Freud's notion that women are inherently masochistic.

Some of the major points of Freud's theories depend on the idea that much of what is most significant to us does not take place in our conscious life. Freud believed that we are forced (mostly by the rigors of having to live in harmony with other people) to repress much of our experience and many of our desires in order to coexist peacefully with others. Some of this repressed experience Freud saw as available to us through dreams and other unconscious structures. He believed that literature could often be interpreted as the reflection of our unconscious life.

Freud was among the first psychoanalytic critics, often using techniques developed for interpreting dreams to interpret literature. Among other analyses, he wrote an insightful study of Dostoevsky's *The Brothers Karamazov* as well as brief commentaries on several of Shakespeare's plays, including *A Midsummer Night's Dream*, *Macbeth*, *King Lear*, and *Hamlet*. The study of *Hamlet* may have inspired a classic of psychoanalytic criticism: Ernest Jones's *Hamlet and Oedipus* (1949), in which Jones explains Hamlet's strange reluctance to act against his uncle Claudius as resulting from Hamlet's unresolved longings for his mother and subsequent drive to eliminate his father. Because Hamlet's own father is dead, Jones argues, Claudius becomes, in the young man's subconscious mind, a father substitute. Hamlet, then, cannot make up his mind to kill his uncle because he sees not a simple case of revenge (for Claudius's murder of his father) but rather a complex web that includes incestuous desire for his own mother (now wed to Claudius). Jones extends his analysis to include the suggestion that Shakespeare himself experienced such a conflict and reflected his own Oedipal feelings in *Hamlet*.

A French psychoanalyst, Jacques Lacan (1901–1981), combined Freudian theories with structuralist literary theories to argue that the essential alienating experience of the human psyche is the acquisition of language. Lacan believed that once you can name yourself and distinguish yourself from others, you enter the difficult social world that requires you to repress your instincts. Like Lacan, who modified and adapted psychoanalytic criticism to connect it to structuralism, many twentieth-century literary scholars, including Marxists and feminists, have found useful approaches in psychoanalytic literary theory (for example, see Mary Jacobus's *Reading Woman: Essays in Feminist Criticism*, 1986).

Psychoanalytic Terms

To fully appreciate psychoanalytic criticism, readers need to understand the following terms:

- *id*—The part of the mind that determines sexual drives and other unconscious compulsions that urge individuals to unthinking gratification.
- *ego*—The conscious mind that strives to deal with the demands of the id and to balance its needs with messages from the superego.
- *superego*—The part of the unconscious that seeks to repress the demands of the id and to prevent gratification of basic physical appetites. The superego is a type of censor that represents the prohibitions of society, religion, family beliefs, and so on.
- *condensation*—A process that takes place in dreams (and in literature) when several elements from the repressed unconscious are linked together to form a new yet disguised whole.
- *symbolism*—The use of representative objects to stand for forbidden (often sexual) objects. This process takes place in dreams and in literature. For example, a pole, knife, or gun may stand for the penis.
- *displacement*—The substitution of a socially acceptable desire for a desire that is not acceptable. This process takes place in dreams or in literature. For example, a woman who experiences sexual desires for her son may instead dream of being intimate with a neighbor who has the same first name as (or who looks like) her son.
- *Oedipus complex*—The repressed desire of a son to unite sexually with his mother and kill his father. According to Freud, all young boys go through this stage, but most resolve these conflicts before puberty.
- *projection*—A defense mechanism in which people mistakenly see in others antisocial impulses they fail to recognize in themselves.
- *subject*—The term used in Lacanian theory to designate a speaking person or a person who has assumed a position within language. The Lacanian subject of language is split or characterized by unresolvable tension between the conscious perception of the self (Freud's ego) and the unconscious desires that motivate behavior.

A Psychoanalytic Reading: Edgar Allan Poe's "The Cask of Amontillado" (p. 258)

Edgar Allan Poe died in 1849, six years before Freud was born, so Poe could not possibly have known Freud's work. Nevertheless, psychoanalytic critics argue that the principles discovered by Freud and those who followed him are inherent in human nature. Therefore, they believe it is perfectly plausible to use modern psychiatric terms when analyzing a work written before their invention. If you approached Poe's "The Cask of Amontillado" from a psychoanalytic perspective, you might write the following interpretation.

> Montresor, the protagonist of Poe's "The Cask of Amontillado," has long fascinated readers who have puzzled over his motives for the story's climactic action when he imprisons his rival, Fortunato, and leaves him to die. Montresor claims that Fortunato insulted him and dealt him a "thousand injuries" (258). Yet when we meet Fortunato, although he appears something of a pompous fool, none of his actions—or even his comments—seems powerful enough to motivate Montresor's thirst for revenge.
>
> If, however, we consider a defense mechanism, first named "projection" and described by Sigmund Freud, we gain a clearer picture of Montresor. Those who employ projection are often people who experience antisocial impulses yet are not conscious of these impulses. It seems highly likely that Fortunato did not persecute Montresor; rather, Montresor himself experienced the impulse to act in a hostile manner toward Fortunato. We know, for example, that Fortunato belongs to the exclusive Order of Masons because he gives Montresor the secret Masonic sign. Montresor's failure to recognize the sign shows that he is a mason only in the grimmest literal sense. Montresor clearly resents Fortunato's high standing and projects onto Fortunato his own hostility toward those who (he thinks) have more or know more than he does. Thus, he imagines that Fortunato's main business in life is to persecute and insult him.
>
> Montresor's obsessive behavior further indicates his pathology. He plans Fortunato's punishment with the cunning one might ordinarily reserve for a major battle, cleverly figuring out a way to keep his servants from the house and to lure the ironically named Fortunato to his death. Each step of the revenge is carefully plotted. This is no sudden crime of passion but rather the diabolically planned act of a deeply disturbed mind.
>
> If we understand Montresor's need to take all the hatred and anger that is inside himself and to rid himself of those socially unacceptable emotions by projecting them onto someone else, then we can see how he rationalizes a crime that seems otherwise nearly unmotivated. By killing Fortunato, Montresor symbolically kills the evil in himself. It is interesting to note that the final lines of the story support this reading. Montresor observes that "For the half of a century no mortal has disturbed" the bones (263). In other words, the unacceptable emotions have not again been aroused. His last words, a Latin phrase from the Mass for the Dead meaning "rest in peace," suggest that only through his heinous crime has he found release from the torment of his own hatred.

For Further Reading: Psychoanalytic Criticism

Freud, Sigmund. *The Interpretation of Dreams*. 1900.

Gardner, Shirley N., ed. *The (M)other Tongue: Essays in Feminist Psychoanalytic Interpretation*. 1985.

Hartman, Geoffrey H., ed. *Psychoanalysis and the Question of the Text*. 1979.

Kris, Ernst. *Psychoanalytic Explorations in Art*. 1952.
Kristeva, Julia. *Desire in Language*. 1980.
Nelson, Benjamin, ed. *Sigmund Freud on Creativity and the Unconscious*. 1958.
Wright, Elizabeth. *Psychoanalytic Criticism: Theory in Practice*. 1984.

Structuralism

Structuralism, a literary movement with roots in linguistics and anthropology, concentrates on literature as a system of signs that have no inherent meaning except in their agreed-upon or conventional relation to one another. Structuralism is usually described by its proponents not as a new way to interpret literary works but rather as a way to understand how works of literature come to have meaning. Because structuralism developed from linguistic theory, some structuralists use linguistic approaches to literature. When they talk about literary texts, they use the terms such as *morpheme* and *phoneme* that linguists use as they study the nature of language. Many structuralists, however, use the linguistic model as an analogy. To understand the analogy, you need to know a bit of linguistic theory.

The French linguist Ferdinand de Saussure (*Course in General Linguistics*, 1915) suggested that the relationship between an object and the name we use to designate it is purely arbitrary. What, for example, makes "C-A-T" signify a small, furry animal with pointed ears and whiskers? Only our learned expectation makes us associate *cat* with the family feline pet. Had we grown up in France, we would make the same association with *chat*, or in Mexico with *gato*. The words we use to designate objects (linguists call these words *signs*) make sense only within the large context of our entire language system and will not be understood as meaningful by someone who does not know that language system. Further, Saussure pointed out, signs become truly useful when designating difference. For example, the word *cat* becomes useful when we want to differentiate a small furry animal that meows from a small furry animal that barks. Saussure was interested in how language, as a structure of conventions, worked. He asked intriguing questions about the underlying rules that allow this made-up structure of signs to work, and, as a result, his pioneering study caught the interest of scholars in many fields.

Many literary scholars saw linguistic structuralism as analogous to the study of literary works. Literary structuralism leads readers to think of poems, short stories, novels, and plays not as self-contained and individual entities that have inherent meaning but rather as part of a larger literary system. To fully appreciate and analyze the work, readers must understand the system within which it operates. Like linguistic structuralism, literary structuralism focuses on the importance of difference. We must, for example, understand the difference between the structure of poetry and the structure of prose before we can make sense of William Carlos Williams's "Red Wheelbarrow" (p. 547):

> so much depends
> upon
> a red wheel
> barrow

Readers unacquainted with the conventions of poetry would find those lines meaningless and confusing, although if they knew the conventions of prose, they would readily understand this sentence:

> So much depends upon a red wheelbarrow.

The way we interpret any group of "signs," then, depends on how they are structured and on the way we understand the system that governs their structure.

Structuralists believe that literature is basically artificial because although it uses the same "signs" as everyday language, whose purpose is to give information, the purpose of literature is *not* primarily to relay data. For example, a poem like Dylan Thomas's "Do not go gentle into that good night" (p. 676) is written in the linguistic form of a series of commands, yet the poem goes much further than that. Its meaning is created not only by our understanding the lines as a series of commands but also by our recognition of the poetic form, the rhyming conventions, and the figures of speech that Thomas uses. We can only fully discuss the poem within the larger context of our literary knowledge.

Structuralism also provides the foundation for poststructuralism, a theoretical movement that informs the fields of deconstructionist and New Historicist criticism and has influenced the work of many psychoanalytic and sociological critics. Although structuralists claim that language functions by arbitrarily connecting words (signifiers) to ideas (signifieds), poststructuralists develop the implications of this claim, arguing that because the connection of a word to an idea is purely arbitrary, any operation of language is inherently unstable. Poststructuralists believe that to study a literary text is to study a continuously shifting set of meanings.

A Structuralist Reading: William Faulkner's "Barn Burning" (p. 265)

A structuralist reading tries to bring to light some of the assumptions about language and form that we are likely to take for granted. Looking at the opening paragraph of Faulkner's "Barn Burning," from the point of view of structuralist criticism, you might first look at an interpretation that reads the passage as a stream of Sarty's thoughts. The structuralist critic might then consider the assumptions a reader would have to make to see what Faulkner has written as the thoughts of an illiterate child. Next, the structuralist might look at evidence to suggest the language in this section operates outside the system of language that would be available to Sarty and that, therefore, "Barn Burning" opens not with a simple recounting of the main character's thoughts but rather with something far more complex.

> The opening paragraph of William Faulkner's "Barn Burning" is often read as an excursion into the mind of Sarty, the story's young protagonist. When we read the passage closely, however, we note that a supposedly simple consciousness is represented in a highly complex way. For Sarty—uneducated and illiterate—the "scarlet devils" and "silver curve of fish" on the labels of food tins serve as direct signs appealing to his hunger. It is unlikely, however, that Sarty could consciously understand what he sees and express it as metaphor. We cannot, then, read this opening passage as a recounting of the thoughts that pass through Sarty's mind. Instead, these complex sentences and images offer possibilities that reach beyond the limits of Sarty's linguistic system.
>
> Because our own knowledge is wider than Sarty's, the visual images the narrator describes take on meanings for us that are unavailable to the young boy. For example, like Sarty, we know that the "scarlet devils" stand for deviled ham. Yet the devils also carry another possible connotation. They may indicate evil and thus serve to emphasize the despair and grief Sarty feels are ever present. We are given images that flash through the mind of an illiterate young boy, apparently intended to suggest his poverty and ignorance (he cannot read the words on the labels), yet we are led to see a highly complicated set of meanings. When we encounter later in the passage Sarty's articulated thought, "*our enemy … ourn! mine and hisn both! …*," his dialect shows clearly the sharp distinction between the system of language the narrator uses to describe Sarty's view of the store shelves and the system of language Sarty uses to describe what he sees and feels.

For Further Reading: Structuralism

Barthes, Roland. *Critical Essays*. 1964.
Culler, Jonathan. *Structuralist Poetics*. 1975.
Greimas, A. J. *Structured Semantics: An Attempt at a Method*. Trans. McDowell, Schleifer, and Velie. 1983.
Hawkes, Terence. *Structuralism and Semiotics*. 1977.
Lentricchia, Frank. *After the New Criticism*. 1980.
Pettit, Philip. *The Concept of Structuralism: A Critical Analysis*. 1975.
Scholes, Robert. *Structuralism in Literature: An Introduction*. 1974.

Deconstruction

Deconstruction is a literary movement that developed from structuralism. Deconstructionists argue that every text contains within it some ingredient undermining its purported system of meaning. In other words, the structure that seems to hold the text together is unstable because it depends on the conclusions of a particular ideology (for example, patriarchal views that women are inferior to men or classist beliefs that peasants are content existing in a system of wealth disparity), conclusions that are not as natural as the text may pretend. The practice of finding the point at which the text falls apart because of these internal inconsistencies is called deconstruction.

Deconstructive theorists share with formalists and structuralists a concern for the work itself rather than for biographical, historical, or ideological influences. Like formalists, deconstructionists focus on possibilities for multiple meanings within texts. However, while formalists seek to explain paradox by discovering tensions and ironies that can lead to a unified reading, deconstructionists insist on the primacy of multiple possibilities. They maintain that any given text can yield many divergent readings, all of which are equally valid yet may in some way undermine and oppose one another.

Like structuralists, deconstructionists see literary texts as part of larger systems of discourse. A key structuralist technique is identifying opposites to show the structure of language used in a work. Having identified the opposites, the structuralist rests the case. Deconstructionists, however, go further. Jacques Derrida, a French philosopher, noticed that these oppositions do not simply reflect linguistic structures but are the linguistic response to the way people deal with their ideologies. For example, if you believe strongly that democracy is the best possible form of government, you tend to lump other forms of government into the category "nondemocracies." If a government is nondemocratic, that—not its other distinguishing characteristics—would be significant to you. This typical ideological response operates in all kinds of areas of belief, even ones we are not aware of. Deconstructionists contend that texts tend to give away their ideological biases by means of this opposition.

Derrida called this distinction between "A" and "Not-A" (rather than between "A" and "B") *différance*, a word he coined to suggest a concept represented by the French verb *différer*, which has two meanings: "to be different" and "to defer." (Note that in Derrida's new term an *a* is substituted for an *e*—a distinction that can be seen in writing but not heard in speaking.) When deconstructionists uncover *différance* through careful examination of a text, they also find an (often unwitting) ideological bias. Deconstructionists argue that the reader must transcend such ideological biases and must instead acknowledge contradictory possibilities as equally worthy of consideration. No one meaning can or should be designated as correct.

Deconstruction, then, is not really a system of criticism (and, in fact, deconstructionists resist being labeled as a school of criticism). Rather, deconstruction offers a way to take apart a literary text and thereby reveal its separate layers. Deconstructionists often focus on the metaphorical nature of language, claiming that all language is basically metaphoric because the sign we use to designate any given object or action stands apart from the object itself. In fact, deconstructionists believe that all writing is essentially literary and metaphorical because language, by its very nature, can only *stand for* what we call reality or truth; it cannot *be* reality or truth.

A major contribution of deconstructive critics lies in their playful approach to language and to literary criticism. They refuse to accept as absolute any one way of reading poetry, fiction, or drama, and they guard against what they see as the fixed conclusions and arbitrary operating assumptions of many schools of criticism.

A Deconstructionist Reading: Flannery O'Connor's "A Good Man Is Hard to Find" (p. 302)

A deconstructionist reading of Flannery O'Connor's "A Good Man Is Hard to Find" might challenge the essentially religious interpretations the author offered of her own stories in essays and letters. If you were applying deconstructionist criticism to the story, you might argue that the author's reading of the story is no more valid than anyone else's, and that the story can just as legitimately be read as an investigation of the functions of irony in language.

> Flannery O'Connor explained that the grotesque and violent aspects of her stories are intended to shock readers into recognizing the inhospitable nature of the world and thereby recognizing the universal human need for divine grace. The last sentence of "A Good Man Is Hard to Find" is spoken by The Misfit, who has just murdered a family of travelers: "It's no real pleasure in life" (314). However, the language of O'Connor's stories is extremely ironic—that is, her narrators and characters often say one thing but mean another. So, it is possible that their statements are not empirically true but are representations of a persona or elements of a story they have created using language.
>
> The Grandmother, for example, lives almost entirely in fictions—newspaper clippings, stories for the grandchildren, her belief that The Misfit is a good man. In contrast, The Misfit is more literal than the Grandmother in his perception of reality. He knows, for example, whether the car turned over once or twice. But he, too, is posing, at first as the tough guy who rejects religious and societal norms by saying, "... it's nothing for you to do but enjoy the few minutes you got left the best way you can—by killing somebody or burning down his house or doing some other meanness to him. No pleasure but meanness ..." (313). Finally, he poses as the pessimist—or, according to O'Connor's reading, the Christian—who claims, "It's no real pleasure in life." The contradictions in The Misfit's language make it impossible to tell which of these facades is "real."

For Further Reading: Deconstruction

Abrams, M. H. "Rationality and the Imagination in Cultural History." *Critical Inquiry* 2 (1976): 447–64. (Abrams claims deconstructionists are parasites who depend on other critics to come up with interpretations that can be deconstructed.)

Arac, Jonathan, Wlad Godzich, *and Wallace Martin, eds. The Yale Critics: Deconstruction in America.* 1983.

Berman, Art. *From the New Criticism to Deconstruction*. 1988.

Culler, Jonathan. *On Deconstruction: Theory and Criticism after Structuralism*. 1982.

Jefferson, Ann. "*Structuralism and Post-Structuralism*." *Modern Literary Theory: A Comparative Introduction*. 1982.

Johnson, Barbara. *The Critical Difference: Essays in the Contemporary Rhetoric of Reading*. 1980.

Leitsch, Vincent B. *Deconstructive Theory and Practice*. 1982.

Lynn, Steven. "A Passage into Critical Theory." *College English* 52 (1990): 258–71.

Miller, J. Hillis. "The Critic as Host." *Deconstruction and Criticism*. Ed. Harold Bloom et al. 1979. (a response to Abrams's article, listed above)

Norris, Christopher. *Deconstruction: Theory and Practice*. 1982.

Cultural Studies

Cultural studies is a particularly difficult field of criticism to define for a number of reasons. Chief among these is the scope of the field. Literary theory has typically focused on literature—however defined—while bringing in knowledge about a work's historical context or the life and views of the author as a means of better understanding the work. Cultural studies, on the other hand, treats any and all objects produced by a society as worthy of the same kind of analysis that literary texts receive. Thus, the advertisements for Arthur Miller's *Death of a Salesman*, or the diary of an actual traveling salesman might, to a cultural critic, be as interesting and complex as Miller's play itself.

Given that the work of art no longer occupies a privileged position relative to other artifacts, it is not surprising that cultural critics have tended to call into question the relative merit of what we have traditionally thought of as masterpieces. To say that one work is "better" than another, such critics would argue, is an almost meaningless statement, and one that reveals more about the values of the person making it than about the work itself. Many cultural critics would therefore reject altogether the idea of a literary canon, or a list of great works that an educated person should know. At the very least, cultural critics would argue, any canon must be subject to constant examination and revision.

Cultural studies has roots in both the French structuralism of critics such as Roland Barthes and the Cultural Materialism of British critics such as Raymond Williams. In his classic text *Mythologies* (1957), Barthes began to apply structural analysis not simply to texts but to phenomena in popular culture—professional wrestling, for example. Williams came at similar subject matter from a different angle. Mass culture has traditionally been viewed by Marxists as something imposed on the working classes and the disadvantaged by upper and bourgeoisie classes seeking to maintain their own position. Williams, while acknowledging the truth in such an assertion, distinguished between mass culture and popular culture, noting that the latter can be used by those outside of power as a means of self-expression and even rebellion. It is not surprising that there is a distinctly political edge to cultural studies, and that many of its practitioners see themselves as activists and their research as a means to effect social change.

There are a number of distinct schools—New Historicism, postcolonialism, American multiculturalism, and queer theory—that are often, though not always, placed under the heading of cultural studies. Of these four, the broadest is New Historicism. Its assumptions—that a work cannot be discussed in isolation from the culture that gave rise to it—are shared by most critics in the other schools, and it might be described as much as a method as a school. Postcolonialism, American multiculturalism, and queer theory can all be seen as applications of the principles of cultural studies—particularly its awareness of power relationships and its questioning of traditional canons—to specific geographical areas and cultures.

New Historicism

New Historicism relates a text to the historical and cultural contexts of the period in which it was created and the periods in which it was critically evaluated. These contexts are not considered simply as "background" but as integral parts of a text. According to the New Historicists, history is not objective facts; rather, like literature, history is subject to interpretation and reinterpretation depending on the power structure of a society. Louis Althusser, for example, suggests that ideology intrudes in the discourse of an era, subjecting readers to the interests of the ruling establishment. Michel Foucault argues that the discourse of an era defines the nature of "truth" and what behaviors are acceptable, sane, or criminal. "Truth," according to Foucault, is produced by the interaction of power and the systems in which the power flows, and it changes as society changes. Mikhail Bakhtin suggests that all discourse is dialogic, containing within it many independent and sometimes conflicting voices.

Literature, in the opinion of the New Historicist critics, cannot be interpreted without reference to the time and place in which it was written. Criticism likewise cannot be evaluated without reference to the time and place in which it was written. A flaw of much criticism, according to the New Historicists, is the consideration of a literary text as if it were an organic whole. Such an approach ignores the diversity of conflicting voices in a text and in the cultural context in which a text is embedded. Indeed, Stephen Greenblatt prefers the term "cultural poetics" to New Historicism because it acknowledges the integral role that literature and art play in the culture of any era. Works of art and literature, according to Greenblatt, actively foster subversive elements or voices but somehow constrain those forces in ways that defuse challenges to the dominant culture.

New Historicists also point out that readers, like texts, are influenced and shaped by the cultural context of their eras and that a thoroughly objective "reading" of a text is therefore impossible. Acknowledging that all readers to some degree "appropriate" a text, some New Historicists present their criticism of texts as "negotiations" between past and present contexts. Thus, criticism of a particular work of literature would draw from both the cultural context of the era in which the text was written and the critic's present cultural context, and the critic would acknowledge how the latter context influences interpretation of the former.

Since the early 1970s, feminist critics have adopted some New Historicist positions, focusing on male–female power conflicts. And critics interested in multicultural texts have stressed the role of the dominant white culture in suppressing or marginalizing the texts of nonwhite cultures. Marxist critics, including Raymond Williams, have adopted the term "cultural materialism" in discussing their mode of New Historicism, which focuses on the political significance of a literary text.

A New Historicist Reading: Charlotte Perkins Gilman's "The Yellow Wallpaper" (p. 315)

A New Historicist scholar might write an essay about "The Yellow Wallpaper" as an illustration of the destructive effects of the patriarchal culture of the late nineteenth century on women. This reading would be vastly different from that of most nineteenth-century critics, who interpreted the story as a harrowing case study of female mental illness. Even some early-twentieth-century readings posited that the narrator's mental illness is the result of her individual psychological problems. In a New Historicist reading, however, you might focus on the social conventions of the time, which produced conflicting discourses that drove the narrator to madness.

> The female narrator of "The Yellow Wallpaper," who is writing in her private journal (which is the text of the short story), explains that her husband, a physician, has diagnosed her as having a "temporary nervous depression—a slight hysterical tendency" (316). She says she should believe such a physician "of high standing" (316) and cooperate with his treatment, which is to confine her to a room in an isolated country estate and compel her to rest and have no visitors and not to write. The "cure" is intended to reduce her nervousness, she further explains. But as the story unfolds, the narrator reveals that she suspects the treatment will not cure her because it leaves her alone with her thoughts without even her writing to occupy her mind. Her husband's "cure" forces her into a passive role and eliminates any possibility of asserting her own personality. However, she guiltily suggests that her own lack of confidence in her husband's diagnosis may be what is preventing her cure.
>
> The text of "The Yellow Wallpaper" can be divided into at least two conflicting discourses: (1) the masculine discourse of the husband, who has the authority both of a highly respected physician and of a husband, two positions reinforced by the patriarchal culture of the time; and (2) the feminine discourse of the narrator, whose hesitant personal voice contradicts the masculine voice but undermines itself because it keeps reminding her that

women should obey their husbands and their physicians. A third discourse underlies the two dominant ones—that of the gothic horror tale, a popular genre of the late nineteenth century. The narrator in "The Yellow Wallpaper" is isolated against her will in a room with barred windows in an almost deserted palatial country mansion she describes as "The most beautiful place!" (316) She is at the mercy of her captor, in this case her husband. She is not sure whether she is hallucinating, and she thinks the mansion may be haunted. She does not know whom to trust, not being sure whether her husband really wants to "cure" her or to punish her for expressing her rebellion.

The narrator learns to hide her awareness of the conflicting discourses. She avoids mentioning her thoughts and fears about her illness or her fancies about the house being haunted, and she hides her writing. She speaks reasonably and in "a very quiet voice" (323). But this inability to speak freely to anyone is a kind of torture, and alone in her room with the barred windows, she takes up discourse with the wallpaper. At first, she describes it as "One of those sprawling flamboyant patterns committing every artistic sin" (317). But she is fascinated by the pattern, which has been distorted by mildew and by the tearing away of some sections. The narrator begins to strip off the wallpaper to free a woman she thinks is trapped inside; and, eventually, she visualizes herself as that woman, trapped yet freed by the destruction of the wallpaper. The narrator retreats, or escapes into madness, driven there by the multiple discourses she cannot resolve.

For Further Reading: New Historicist Criticism

Brook, Thomas. *The New Historicism and Other Old Fashioned Topics.* 1991.

Coates, Christopher. "What Was the New Historicism?" *Centennial Review* 32.2 (Spring 1993): 267–80.

Geertz, Clifford. "Thick Description: Toward an Interpretive Theory of Culture." *The Interpretation of Cultures.* By Clifford Geertz. 1973.

Greenblatt, Stephen, ed. *Representing the English Renaissance.* 1988.

Levin, David. "American Historicism: Old and New." *American Literary History* 6.3 (Fall 1994): 527–38.

Rabinov, Paul, ed. *The Foucault Reader.* 1986.

Veeser, H. Aram, ed. *The New Historicism.* 1989.

Queer Theory

The roots of queer theory go back to the 1960s and 1970s, when movements for gay liberation and changing attitudes toward sexuality in general made it easier for artists and critics to identify themselves as gay and lesbian and to deal directly with gay and lesbian themes in their work. Critical examination of these subjects intensified during the 1980s, partly in response to the AIDS crisis. By the early 1990s, the term "queer theory," coined by Teresa de Lauretis, came to be used as an umbrella term for the work being done by critics such as Eve Kosofsky Sedgwick and Judith Butler.

The actual scope of queer theory is significantly broader than the name might imply. Queer theorists tend to doubt prevailing notions of sexual identity as something fixed by biology or even by personal inclination since a person might find different means of sexual expression appealing at different points. Queer theory therefore calls into question terms such as *homosexual*, *heterosexual*, *bisexual*, *transsexual*, and *transgender*. It also examines sympathetically those aspects of sexuality that, while not necessarily "queer" in the sense of "gay," have nonetheless been marginalized—crossdressing, for example, or sadomasochism.

When applying queer theory to texts, critics tend to be particularly interested in those ways in which the text blurs or subverts traditional notions of binary sexual identity, notions that tend to rely on "heteronormativity"—the idea that heterosexuality is the statistical, and even moral, standard and that all departures from it are perverse or problematic. These blurrings in the text occur not only in contemporary literature but also in works from the past, where they were perhaps missed because of the ideological prejudices of earlier critics.

Given queer theory's emphasis on gender, there are inevitably points of contact with feminist criticism. Critics such as Judith Butler, however, have argued that feminists have been too quick to regard gender, however defined, as something fixed. Queer theory has connections to gay and lesbian activism, but those connections are sometimes strained because activists are often trying to gain recognition or respect for those with a given sexual identity, while queer theorists are more likely to call into question *all* identities. Like other schools within the field of cultural studies, critics employing queer theory often examine cultural artifacts such as film, music, and television programs, in this case for messages that may subtly subvert heteronormativity. For example, there has been considerable interest within queer studies in the ways that the pop icon Madonna has portrayed sexuality.

In theoretical terms, queer theory's biggest debt has been to the deconstructionists, particularly to Michel Foucault, and to his groundbreaking work, *The History of Sexuality*. Among the foundational works in the field are Butler's *Gender Trouble* and Sedgwick's *Epistemology of the Closet*.

A Queer Theory Reading: Zadie Smith's "The Girl with Bangs" (p. 204)

A queer theory reading of Zadie Smith's "The Girl with Bangs" might focus on the ways in which sexual desire in the story seems related less to gender as it is commonly conceived than to the attraction between individuals. A critic might argue, in fact, that the story calls into question the validity of gender roles.

> In Zadie Smith's "The Girl with Bangs," the narrator begins a relationship with another woman, one that leaves her with a new perspective on sexual relationships and on herself. However, the narrator does not think in terms of gay and straight. Rather, she describes herself as being "a boy" in her relationship with Charlotte Greaves.
>
> Male and female, in the eyes of the narrator, are designations that have less to do with physical gender than with gender roles. Because she is the

one who pursues Charlotte, and because she is the one who figuratively waits beneath Charlotte's window, she sees herself in the male role, that of the pursuer. Because she finds herself helpless to resist Charlotte—a situation she has never encountered with a man—she thinks, "So this is what it's like being a boy" (206). When Maurice comes to ask her to give up Charlotte, she describes their talk—with only partial irony—as "man-to-man."

The narrator agrees to end her relationship with Charlotte, but when she and Maurice go to speak with Charlotte, they find her in bed with another man. Charlotte's sexual openness—she apparently has sex with anyone, of any gender, whenever she wants—represents another challenge to the heteronormativity of society and to its conventions of monogamy. Her eventual marriage to Maurice might seem at first a surrender to that norm, but the story certainly hints that Maurice will regret the marriage because nothing indicates that Charlotte will suddenly stop sleeping with other people.

Interestingly, the story concludes with the narrator identifying not—as she has during the affair with Charlotte—with men, but with a woman, the woman Maurice has been sleeping with in Thailand. For the duration of the affair, she viewed men as helpless, a view at odds with much of the stereotypical rhetoric of manliness—though not with the conventions of traditional courting. She pictured men, and herself with them, as standing beneath the beloved's window, waiting to catch whatever she might throw down. Now she says that "in the real world, or so it seems to me, it is almost always women and not men who are waiting under windows, and they are almost always disappointed. In this matter Charlotte was unusual" (208).

To say that Charlotte was "unusual" is to say that she was, in a broader sense of the word, "queer." What is "queer" about Charlotte, then, may not be her bisexuality or promiscuity, but her ability to remain free of the negative emotional consequences her existence as a woman in a male-dominated society would typically bring with it.

For Further Reading: Queer Theory

Butler, Judith. *Bodies That Matter: On the Discursive Limits of "Sex."* 1993.

Halperin, David. *Homosexuality: A Cultural Construct.* 1990.

———. *One Hundred Years of Homosexuality.* 1990.

Jagose, Annamarie. *Queer Theory: An Introduction.* 1997.

Parker, Andrew. *After Sex?: On Writing Since Queer Theory.* 2007.

Sedgwick, Eve Kosofsky. *Between Men: English Literature and Male Homosocial Desire.* 1985.

Spargo, Tamsin. *Foucault and Queer Theory.* 1999.

Thomas, Calvin (ed.). *Straight with a Twist: Queer Theory and the Subject of Heterosexuality.* 1999.

Postcolonial Studies

In the years following World War II, the period of European colonization ended as first one country and then another gained its independence from the colonial powers that had controlled them; countries like England, France, Spain, The

Netherlands, and Portugal. In most cases, these newly independent countries were substantially different from how they had been prior to colonization; some, in fact, had actually been created by colonization, their borders having been determined by foreign powers. The colonial powers typically introduced their own languages as the languages of government in these countries, and the educational systems they introduced for both the European and native populations of the colonies were likewise modeled on those in Europe.

Writers in former colonies, then, inherited a mix of cultural tools and assumptions. On the one hand, many of them had been educated to appreciate European works of literature, and many of them wrote most naturally in European languages. On the other hand, they saw everywhere around them a culture that was very different from that of its former European colonizers, and which those colonizers tended to regard as inferior and less civilized. The tension that results from this cultural mix is one of the chief subjects of postcolonial theory and research. In addition, although colonialism has more or less formally ended, many critics would argue that European and other western countries continue to dominate their former colonies in a cultural and economic sense, a domination called **neo-colonialism**.

Postcolonial critics do not necessarily restrict themselves to the literatures of those countries that the European powers have left. Australia, New Zealand, and Canada, for example, were all colonies, and some critics would regard any literature produced in such countries, including that by authors of European descent, to be an appropriate subject of study for postcolonialism. Others would argue that such writers belong to a European tradition and would use the adjective *postcolonial* to describe only the works written by authors from the indigenous populations of those countries.

Nor do postcolonial critics restrict themselves to looking at works produced since the end of the colonial period. Canonical European texts are of special interest to these critics, especially for what they reveal about how the colonizers view the colonized. The character of Caliban in Shakespeare's *The Tempest*, for example, has been the focus of much debate about what his brutish nature reveals about the views of Shakespeare and the England in which he lived toward the native peoples being encountered by European explorers.

One of the foundational texts of postcolonialism is Edward Said's *Orientalism* (1978), which examined how Europeans and Americans view, and have viewed, peoples in developing nations. Other important works include *The Location of Culture* (1994) by Homi Bhaba and the essay "Under Western Eyes" (1986) by Chandra Talpade Mohanty.

A Postcolonial Reading: Jhumpa Lahiri's 2000 short story "The Third and Final Continent"

A postcolonial reading of "The Third and Final Continent" by Jhumpa Lahiri might look at the differences the narrator notices between his native culture and those of England and the United States. It might also examine the process of his gradual assimilation to American culture, and his own sense of the cultural distance he has traveled.

Jhumpa Lahiri's short story "The Third and Final Continent" relates the thoughts of an Indian emigrant as he adjusts to western society. As a citizen of a country that gained its independence from Great Britain less than twenty years earlier—and after his own birth—the narrator is very much in the position of a provincial visiting the imperial homeland. He lives with other Indians—specifically with other Bengalis—and they eat Indian food and listen to Indian music, but many of their habits are English. For example, they drink tea, smoke English cigarettes, and watch cricket matches.

The narrator arrives in the United States on the day of the first moon landing. The symbolism of this is particularly appropriate since the American astronauts have literally gone to another world, something the narrator does metaphorically. The moment also marks, again literally, the height of American power. At that moment, America is the most powerful country in the world, much as Great Britain was when it first subjugated India. To plant a flag on a piece of land has traditionally been a way of claiming that land for the country represented by the flag.

In the time the narrator spends with Mrs. Croft each evening while staying in her house, the acknowledgment of American supremacy becomes a kind of religious ritual. Each time Mrs. Croft observes that there is an American flag on the moon, the narrator is expected to reply, loudly enough so that the old women can hear him, "Splendid!" The narrator himself had not thought very much about the moon landing despite the reports of it in the paper—and despite the fact that he is a librarian at the Massachusetts Institute of Technology. His values and the values of the American culture in which he finds himself are very different.

His stay with Mrs. Croft also reveals to him the enormous difference between Indian and American attitudes toward family. It shocks the narrator to learn that a woman one hundred and three years old would be living alone, and the story of her fortitude after the death of her husband is in marked contrast to his own mother's descent into madness after the death of her husband. At the same time, the narrator and Mrs. Croft seem to have a special understanding. The culture he comes from, with its strict rules of propriety, is in some ways reminiscent of the America in which Mrs. Croft lived as a young woman, a point made clear when the old woman, on seeing the narrator's new wife dressed in her traditional Indian clothes, acknowledges that she is truly a lady.

For Further Reading: Postcolonial Studies

Ashcroft, Bill, Gareth Griffiths, and Helen Tiffin. *The Empire Writes Back: Theory and Practice in Post-Colonial Literatures*. 1989.

Chaterjee, Para. *Nationalist Thought in the Colonial World: A Derivative Discourse*. 1993.

Gandhi, Leela. *Postcolonial Theory: A Critical Introduction*. 1998.

Loomba, Ania. *Colonialism/Postcolonialism*. 1998.

Nandy, Ashis. *The Intimate Enemy: Loss and Recovery of Self under Colonialism*. 1983.
Poddar, Prem, and David Johnson. *A Historical Companion of Postcolonial Thought*. 2005.
Said, Edward. *Culture and Imperialism*. 1994.
Williams, Patrick, and Laura Chrisman, eds. *Colonial Discourse and Post-colonial Theory: A Reader*. 1994.
Young, Robert. *Colonial Desire: Hybridity in Theory, Culture, and Race*. 1995.
——— *Postcolonialism: An Historical Introduction*. 2001.

American Multiculturalism

American Multiculturalism examines literature by individuals from all cultures, backgrounds, and experiences within America; further, this field of study seeks to understand literature from points of view that expand upon or are different from those of the dominant culture. One of the primary goals of multicultural literary critics has been to increase the visibility of literature produced by members of marginalized groups in the United States. Another goal has been to create a critical environment in which these works are seen as an essential part of the American literary canon. Since many works by BIPOC (Black, Indigenous, and People of Color) authors are written from a perspective different from that of the dominant culture, such a critical environment cannot simply be assumed.

Studies in Race and Ethnicity, a critical framework within American multiculturalism, examines the relationship between literature and race, ethnicity, and cultural pluralism. Although BIPOC philosophers, writers, and critics have explored the impact of race upon literature and culture since the late nineteenth century, the American Civil Rights Movement of the 1960s and 1970s brought discussions of race and ethnicity into the mainstream of academic discourse.

In *The Souls of Black Folk* (1903), W. E. B. Du Bois writes about a "double consciousness," a condition of "always looking at one's self through the eyes of others." According to Du Bois, to be Black in America is to understand oneself as both a person of African origin and a subject of "contempt" in the eyes of a racist dominant culture. Du Bois understood that race is a construct imposed upon the individual, a construct that defines selfhood, identity, and life experiences. Although Du Bois discusses double consciousness as it relates to Black American identity, the concept has been embraced by other communities as a way of understanding the relationship between race and selfhood.

BIPOC writers have produced literature that seeks to understand the complex relationships between race and selfhood; additionally, their work sees literature as an agent of social and political change. Literature written by authors such as Toni Morrison, Louise Erdrich, Sandra Cisneros, and Maxine Hong

Kingston explores the relationship between the self and the group and the resistance to systems of oppression.

The critical examination of BIPOC literature explores suppressed voices; untold histories, stories and traditions; vernacular traditions; and oral histories. It also examines the value of cross-cultural perspectives. Critics such as Lyla June, Frantz Fanon, and Henry Louis Gates Jr. have articulated the problem of applying "Eurocentric paradigms," or classist systems of thought, to literature written by BIPOC authors.

The study of race and ethnicity in relation to literature often embraces an intersectional approach, the cumulative way in which systems of oppression (such as racism, sexism, and classism) overlap (or intersect) with the experience of marginalized groups or individuals. Therefore, the work of Feminist theorists, Queer theorists, and Postcolonial theorists overlaps with that of the American multicultural theorists. Multicultural studies of literature also overlap with cultural studies in general—for example, both share a willingness to investigate literature traditionally excluded from the canon and a disruption of the categories of "high" and "low" art. Along with Marxist and New Historicist criticism, multicultural critics examine the ways writers and the texts they produce are shaped by social, political, and economic conditions. Even so, it is important to understand that all literary criticism related to race and ethnicity studies should not be grouped into one large category. Each theoretical framework has its own methodologies and areas of particular interest.

An American Multicultural Reading: Alice Walker's "Everyday Use" (p. 346)

A multicultural reading of "Everyday Use" might focus on the quilt that the narrator decides to give to Maggie, rather than to Dee, and on its connection to African American history. Such a reading might also look at the ways in which the narrator's relationship to that history differs from Dee's.

> African American art has often been functional—that is, it is meant to be used. The quilts that become the subject of contention in Alice Walker's "Everyday Use" are an example of this type of art. In fact, the title of the story is a specific reference to the functionality of the handmade things that Dee wants to take with her from her family home. Given Dee's newfound interest in African and African American culture, it is striking that she is unable to appreciate this fact, which seems so obvious to her mother and sister.
>
> Dee seems interested in the history of her people, and of her family, chiefly when she is able to view them as exotic. At times, it seems that she has come to visit her family largely because she sees their home as a kind of museum of Black culture. She wants nearly everything in and around the house that she lays eyes on, but she wants them as curios or decorations, not as the functioning butter churns, dashers, and quilts that they are. She was named after her mother's sister, and after her

grandmother, but she has taken a new, supposedly more African name: Wangero. She wants the artifacts these women have left behind but not their names.

It would be going too far to say that Walker is simply condemning Dee as shallow. Dee does genuinely admire the artifacts she wants to take with her, and she does want them in part because of the connection they have to members of her own family. Her failing—and this is where the story is at its most subtle—is that, in contrast with Maggie, she *needs* these artifacts to maintain a connection with her family's past. What convinces the narrator of the story to save the quilts for Maggie is the way in which Maggie relinquishes her claim to them: "She can have them, Mama ... I can 'member Grandma Dee without the quilts" (352).

Dee's last words to her mother and sister neatly sum up her contradictory relationship to them and to the tradition they represent. After saying that her mother doesn't understand her own heritage, she turns to Maggie and says, "You ought to try to make something of yourself, too, Maggie. It's really a new day for us. But from the way you and mama still live you'd never know it" (352). Dee wants to be free of all the negative aspects that have defined the American Black experience, yet at the same time she wants to position herself as the heir to that culture. It isn't—it can't be—that simple.

For Further Reading: American Multiculturalism

Allen, Paula Gunn. *The Sacred Hoop: Recovering the Feminine in American Indian Traditions*. 1986.

Anzaldúa, Gloria. *Borderlands/La Frontera: The New Mestiza*. 1987.

Appiah, Kwame Anthony. *The Lies That Bind: Rethinking Identity*. 2018.

Awkward, Michael. *Inspiriting Influences: Tradition, Revision, and Afro-American Literature*. 1989.

Bell, Derrick. *Race, Racism and American Law*. 1973.

Berkovitch, Sacvan. *The Rites of Ascent: Transformations in the Symbolic Construction of America*. 1981.

Bernal, Martin. *Black Athena: Afroasiatic Roots of Classical Civilization*. 1987.

Byrd, Jodi. *The Transit of Empire: Indigenous Critiques of Colonialism*. 2011.

Chow, Rey. *Not Like a Native Speaker: On Languaging as a Postcolonial Experience*. 2014.

Dubois, W.E.B. *The Souls of Black Folk*. 1903.

Fanon, Frantz. *The Wretched of the Earth*. 1961.

Ferraro, Thomas J. *Ethnic Passages: Literary Immigrants in Twentieth-Century America*. 1993.

Gates, Henry Louis, Jr. (ed.). *"Race," Writing, and Difference*. 1985.

———. *Who's Black and Why?: A Hidden Chapter from the Eighteenth-Century Invention of Race*. 2022.

Gilroy, Paul. *The Black Atlantic: Modernity and Double Consciousness.* 1993.

Goldberg, David Theo, ed. *Multiculturalism: A Critical Reader.* 1995.

hooks, bell. *Ain't I a Woman: Black Women and Feminism.* 1981.

Krupat, Arnold. *Ethnocriticism: Ethnography, History, Literature.* 1992.

Morrison, Toni. *Playing in the Dark: Whiteness and the Literary Imagination.* 1993.

Pulitano, Elvira. *Toward a Native American Critical Theory.* 2003.

Saldívar, Ramón. *Chicano Narrative: The Dialectics of Difference.* 1990.

Vizenor, Gerald. *Native Liberty: Natural Reason and Cultural Survivance.* 2009.

West, Thomas R. *Signs of Struggle: The Rhetorical Politics of Cultural Difference.* 2002.

Postmodernism

Postmodernism sees reason, logic, objective knowledge, reality, and truth as relative constructs that vary based upon their position in an individual's mind. Postmodern literature is often ironic, intertextual, self-referential, fragmented, and/or absurd. Because postmodern criticism places all objective fact, knowledge, or truth under scrutiny, any attempt to define the term *postmodern* would itself be subject to question.

Postmodern thought is a reaction against the modern condition. Enlightenment humanism, a movement that emerged in eighteenth-century Europe, provided the foundation for the idea that humans have the ability to understand the world around them. The eighteenth and nineteenth centuries produced political frameworks that encouraged "freedom," artistic work that exemplified "creativity," scientific discovery that promoted "progress," and literature that laid bare "knowledge." According to postmodern thought, reality itself is a construct, created in the mind of the individual, and is therefore always shifting, often fragmented, and totally uninterpretable. The literary products of postmodern thought embrace absurdity, reorder time and space, and disregard "reality" as something that we are all inventing. A postmodern critic may look at anything, including texts, as a network of signs, symbols, images, and ideas without any basis in reality. According to postmodernist critics, high art, low art, and popular art are all on the same plane; no one is better than another.

Postmodernism sees the dominant discourses of Western culture and philosophy as arbitrary and relative, disrupting the possibility of any absolute truth, meaning, or reality. Influenced by Marxist theory, postmodernists often argue that all discourse has political and economic agendas; what has been considered "valuable" and "true" and "real" in Western culture has actually been determined by dominant and elite structures of power. If, as postmodernists argue, all value, truth, and reality are arbitrary, marginalized discourses are of equal value to those that have dominated the canon of Western thought and literature.

Hence, in many ways, by considering all knowledge to be equally questionable and unstable, postmodernism provides an inclusive framework that welcomes discourse that exists beyond an elite, Western, Judeo-Christian paradigm.

A Postmodernist Reading: Zadie Smith's "The Girl with Bangs" (p. 204)

A postmodernist reading of Smith's "The Girl with Bangs" might consider how this story destabilizes the love story narrative that has dominated the Western cultural tradition.

> In "The Girl with Bangs," love is described by the narrator in terms of fragmented chunks of a body. Charlotte is only named as the object of the narrator's affection *after* her primary characteristic, her bangs, have been exalted; in fact, the narrator presents pieces of the female body, including hair, a mole, and eyes, as features that inspire love. Not only is Charlotte described in terms of her physical characteristics, but the experience of loving her is similarly "dismembering." Ironically, the objectification that the narrator employs to describe her love for Charlotte recalls a technique in Petrarchan and Shakespearean sonnets in which the male speaker creates a list of physical characteristics to define his love for a female. This objectification of the female body, the focus upon specific body parts rather than on a whole self, has been criticized by feminist scholars who denounce narratives of love that place women and their fragmented and idealized parts, on a pedestal. Smith may be playing with this common trope from love narratives. She could also be destabilizing both the trope and its criticism by presenting both female narrator and female love object as equally fragmented.
>
> Because Smith's narrative does not place value on the tropes that so commonly define love stories, love is not presented as stable, unified, or "true." For example, Charlotte is described as "bad news," "Labyrinthine," and "stumbling"; her allure and the narrator's pursuit of her is, therefore, absurd. Further, the romantic narrative of love making is displaced by Charlotte's messy room, full to the brim with trash. Her space has no time or order, as represented by the absence of a clock or watch; the focal point of a bedroom, the bed, is missing. Finally, Maurice and the narrator understand that they are replaceable and replicable when they realize that Charlotte has another lover whom neither knew about; even so, Maurice marries her. Therefore, Charlotte as a "love object" resists categorization, classification, and monogamy; each lover's experience of her is defined by that lover's perception of her as "real," but she continually redefines that reality through her own actions.
>
> Finally, the repetition of references to film and movie culture throughout the short story reflect a postmodern sensibility. The narrator repeatedly describes her experience of love in relation to films. In defining her love, she praises Charlotte's eyes and recalls an image of a woman stumbling away from a burning city; however, the narrator acknowledges that she had "watched too many films," thereby questioning both her perception of reality and the source of her romantic ideas. The narrator describes Charlotte searching for Maurice in the dining hall as like "those movie time-travelers";

she also compares Maurice's announcement that he plans to marry Charlotte to a scene from a "bad movie." Although the narrator acknowledges that her perception of love may have been determined by her experience with movies, she never refers to a specific film.

All in all, the narrator's experience of love is presented much like images in a kaleidoscope, colorful and confusing fragments from other texts (perhaps sonnets, perhaps films) that she does not determine or define. The reality of this love narrative is as unreliable, unstable, and questionable as any love story that has ever been written or told. In this way, Smith's story resists (and challenges) the construct of "true love" that has dominated Western fictional discourse.

For Further Reading: Postmodernism

Baudrillard, Jean. *Simulacra and Simulation*. 1981.

Lyotard, Jean-François. *The Postmodern Condition: A Report on Knowledge*. 1979.

Habermas, Jürgen. *The Philosophical Discourse of Modernity: Twelve Lectures*. 1985.

Jameson, Frederic. *Postmodernism, or, The Cultural Logic of Late Capitalism*. 1991.

Kristeva, Julia. *Strangers to Ourselves*. 1991.

Posthumanism

Posthumanism is a critical framework that seeks to reimagine the relationship between human beings and nature, sentient and non sentient beings, and technology. Inspired by scientific and technological advancement, but also by environmental and ecological ethics, posthumanist scholars explore the porous boundaries between humans, nature, and technology. Posthumanist study covers a wide range of issues. For example, posthumanist critics might examine genetically engineered life forms and artificial intelligence, or they might study predictions about the imagined future of humans' relationship to machines.

Whatever the focus, posthumanist thought recalibrates the premises of **humanism**. Emerging from the European Renaissance, humanism—inspired by Classical Greek and Roman philosophy and led by thinkers such as Francis Bacon, Thomas Hobbes, and Rene Descartes—emphasized the central position of human beings within the universe. According to humanist thought, human beings are rational observers of the world around them and supervise the natural world and all non sentient beings from a position of authority. In contrast, posthumanism sees human beings as participants within a diverse, fluid, and ever-changing environment. Human action is motivated by physical, chemical, and biological interactions with beings and systems that people do not always understand. Thus, posthumanist discourse dismantles human exceptionalism as the framework for understanding human beings' place in the world.

The origins of posthumanist thought can be traced to the work of Darwin, Marx, and Freud, among other philosophers who sought to understand the relationship between human beings and the natural world. The term emerges from Ihab Hassan's 1977 essay "Prometheus as Performer: Toward a Posthumanist Culture." In this essay, Hassan explores the human imagination as it intersects with myth, science, and technology. Donna Haraway's "The Cyborg Manifesto" (1985) provides another framework for posthumanism; Haraway imagines the possibility of the cyborg, a "cybernetic organism," that works to break down the boundaries between human, animal, and machine; in particular, the cyborg creates the possibility for feminist action to destabilize gendered constructs.

Although science fiction may seem the most logical home for posthumanist literary theory, it strongly aligns with ecocritical scholarship, as well as with animal rights activism. A related movement is **transhumanism**, which advocates for a union of technology and science with the human body to transcend human limitations. For example, transhumanist thinkers explore the implications of an extended lifespan, the elimination of disease, and the possibility of technologically enhanced brain capabilities. Posthumanism seeks to understand the possibilities, both real and imagined, of human bodies and minds flexible enough to change through their interaction with science, technology, and the natural world.

A Posthumanist Reading: Neil Gaiman's "How to Talk to Girls at Parties" (p. 155)

A posthumanist analysis of Gaiman's short story, "How to Talk to Girls at Parties," might explore the interaction of the teenage boys with several "girls" at a party.

> As the story begins, Enn and his friend Vic search for a party. Vic's desire to find the party is premised upon one thing: "Girls! Girls! Girls!" Speaking thirty years later, Enn recalls that as students at an all-boys' school, the two boys primarily understood and interacted with other boys. As Enn follows his friend through the streets of London, his anxiety and discomfort emerge from his own sense of girls and women as "the other"; he does not understand the operations or motivations of women, nor does he understand the social norms of heterosexual courting.
>
> The party begins, as we might expect, with dancing and beer and loud music. Enn notes that some of the beautiful women at the party are "out of [his] league," reflecting his sense of distance and discomfort. He first meets Wain, who immediately shares that she is a "second" and "may not breed." Although he wonders about this statement and notices her six-fingered hand, Enn admits that he has "no idea what she was talking about." However, Enn's perseverance in conversation with Wain may reflect his willingness to seek understanding across differences: he listens as Wain describes her life of travel, and he offers to get her water when she tells him that she's not permitted to dance. His next encounter, with the girl with the gap in her teeth, provides us with more information: she describes visiting the sun, spinning webs through galaxies, and the discomfort of taking form in the

"decaying lump of meat" that is a human body. As readers, we understand that Enn is at a party with non-human life forms; we are not sure if they are sentient or non-sentient, machine or alien. Undeterred, Enn puts his arm around the girl with the gap in her teeth, a move toward a romantic encounter. His final interaction, with Triolet, reveals that this being identifies as a "poem." Although Enn thinks she is speaking "nonsense," Triolet's physical form serves as a manifestation of language that we, from a human perspective, may not be able to understand or imagine. During the party, Enn interacts with beings who have human characteristics but who do not identify as human; they know and have experienced much more than he can imagine; they are agents of their own patterns of thought and desire. Readers may ask if Enn realizes that these "girls" are not human or if it even matters to him. Is there really a difference between his lack of understanding of human females and his lack of understanding of the beings he encounters at the party? Is his drive for sexual experimentation so great that he glosses over what is in front of him? Or is it possible for intimacy to transcend a definitive human-to-human connection?

In the final scene of the story, Vic runs in panic from a physical encounter with Stella. Vic's anger and fear, he suggests, come from his feeling that if he had gone any further, he would not be himself anymore. Has Vic stopped just short of sexual intercourse? Or has he halted intimacy with Stella because her physical form was not "human"? Although Vic is upset, Enn seems almost nostalgic in his recollection of the night. Both Vic and Enn are provoked by physical, chemical, and biological interactions within their given environment, but their responses are quite different. Gaiman asks us to consider the limitations of understanding between human beings and how, if at all, these limitations are different from what we might encounter with nonhuman beings. Is the desire for intimacy restricted to human contact, or could humans find emotional or physical connection with nonhuman forms? And does the "othering" that human beings already inflict upon one another need to extend beyond the human, or are there possibilities there for understanding and intimacy?

For Further Reading: Posthumanism

Bostrom, Nick. *Anthropic Bias: Observation Selection Effects in Science and Philosophy*. 2002.

Braidotti, Rosi. "Posthuman Critical Theory." *Critical Posthumanism and Planetary Futures*, edited by Debashesh Banerji and Makarand R. Paranjape, 2016.

—. *Posthuman Feminism*. 2022.

Fukuyama, Francis. *Our Posthuman Future: Consequences of the Biotechnology Revolution*. 2003.

Haraway, Donna. "Manifesto for Cyborgs: Science, Technology, and Socialist Feminism in the 1980s," *Socialist Review*, 1985.

Hayles, N. Katherine. *Postprint: Books and Becoming Computational*. 2021.

Wolfe, Cary. *What is Posthumanism?* 2009.

Ecocriticism

Ecocriticism is the interdisciplinary study of the relationship between literature and the environment. Sometimes called "literature and the environment" or "environmental criticism," ecocriticism has evolved since its inception as a critical framework in the 1970s. It draws upon subjects such as history, media studies, philosophy, politics, economics, and ethics to examine how literature portrays nature, especially in light of ecological concerns.

Coined in 1978 by William Rueckert in his essay "Literature and Ecology: An Experiment in Ecocriticism," the term *ecocriticism* was revived by Cheryll Glotfelty in 1989. "First-wave" ecocriticism sought to explore the natural world and the wilderness as depicted in literature; this phase of the movement looked back to the writings of William Thoreau and William Wordsworth for inspiration. "Second-wave" ecocriticism saw a new focus on the relationship between imperialism and environmental destruction; the intersection of gender, race, and the natural world; and the autonomy of nonhuman life forms, such as plants and animals. "Third-wave" ecocriticism broadened the scope of the conversation beyond a Western, primarily Anglo-American perspective. This scholarship examines the global implications of the study of literature and the environment, ranging from celebrating the natural world to seeking solutions to contemporary ecological and environmental global concerns.

The word *ecology* refers to the branch of biology that studies living things in relation to their environment. A study of ecology in literature seeks to understand the relationship between human beings and the world in which they live as represented in a literary text. Contemporary ecocriticism examines the relationship between human beings and the environmental challenges we face, such as pollution, climate change, deforestation, and the eradication of animal species. Recently, fiction with a focus on climate change, called "Climate Change Fiction" or "Cli-Fi," has emerged to address scientific, political, and existential questions about the future of our planet. In fact, many ecocritics seek to understand the relationship between people and all other living things in a way that does not prioritize or privilege humans. By embracing the coexistence between humans, machines, and nonhuman life, ecocriticism aligns with the posthumanism. Feminist scholarship also overlaps with ecocriticism, as feminist theorists explore the connections between the historical exploitation of nature and nonhuman life and the patriarchal structures that have historically marginalized women.

An Ecocritical Reading: Joy Harjo's "Invisible Fish" (p. 682)

An ecocritical reading of Joy Harjo's "Invisible Fish" might analyze the poem's depiction of animal life, human beings, and the environment. It would ask how these entities relate to one another and what future this poem imagines.

> "Invisible Fish" may be read as a warning about our planet's future. The poem takes a wide view, exploring the vast scale of planetary evolution

without emotion or bias. The repeated use of "will" to imagine a future state of being indicates that the poem is a prediction. The "invisible fish" may be seen as traces or memories of creatures that once inhabited the sea in abundance but are now diminished to near, or total, extinction. Alternately, readers might imagine the invisibility of the fish as an indication of their powerlessness in the face of human destruction of their habitat, perhaps suggesting that fish might as well not exist, given the way they are disregarded by human beings. Readers may wonder what Harjo means when she predicts that the "fish will learn to walk." Perhaps she imagines a future in which the creatures of the sea morph into versions of creatures on land, whether by evolution or by exposure to toxins. Or, perhaps Harjo's conflation of humans and fish is a statement about the essential interconnectedness between the animal world and the world of human beings. Regardless of the interpretation, the experience of humanity is one of loss and nostalgia as humans are left to "paint dreams" on a "dying shore." Artistic production, Harjo suggests, may be the only source of hope in the face of a wasted planet.

In Harjo's poem, the ocean continues to exist in all its strength and power despite the fate of both animals and people. The "ghost ocean" may be a trace of what it once was, or perhaps the ocean has ironically become a container for the remnants of human production and waste. The "Chevy trucks" that "punctuate" the floor of the ocean are reminders of the trash that inhabits the space where sea creatures used to live. Readers may conclude that no matter what is changing for fish and humans, no matter what litters the floor of the sea, the ocean "described by waves of sand, by water-worn rock" is ageless and timeless, continuing in its power and motion beyond the goings on above and below its surface.

An ecocritical reading of this poem may pose the following questions: What is the relationship between animal and human life and death? How does the relationship between humans and nonhumans evolve as the planet changes? What is the dynamic between sentient beings and the results of human action, symbolized by the "Chevy truck[s]"? Where can we find hope in the face of the current climate crisis?

For Further Reading: Ecocriticism

Association for the Study of Literature and Environment. https://www.asle.org

Buell, Laurence. *The Environmental Imagination*. 1996.

Clark, Timothy. *The Value of Ecocriticism*. 2019.

Fromm, Harold and Cheryll Glotfelty, editors. *The Ecocriticism Reader: Landmarks in Literary Ecology*. 1996.

Garrard, Greg. *Ecocriticism*. 2nd ed., 2012.

Interdisciplinary Studies in Literature and Environment. https://academic.oup.com/isle

Love, Glen. *Practical Ecocriticism: Literature, Biology, and the Environment*. 2003.

Meeker, Joseph. *The Comedy of Survival: Studies in Literary Ecology*. 1974.

Credits

Agha Shahid Ali "The Wolf's Postscript to 'Little Red Riding Hood'". Copyright © 1987 by Agha Shahid Ali, from THE VEILED SUITE: THE COLLECTED POEMS by Agha Shahid Ali. Used by permission of W.W. Norton & Company, Inc.

Margaret Atwood "The City Planners" from THE CIRCLE GAME. Copyright © 1966, 1998 by Margaret Atwood. Reprinted with the permission of House of Anansi Press, Toronto.

W. H. Auden from "In Time of War" Copyright © 1939 by W. H. Auden and Christopher Isherwood. Reprinted by permission of Curtis Brown, Ltd.

W. H. Auden "Musée des Beaux Arts" copyright 1940 and © renewed 1968 by W. H. Auden; from COLLECTED POEMS by W. H. Auden, edited by Edward Mendelson. Used by permission of Random House, an imprint and division of Penguin Random House LLC. All rights reserved.

Matsuo Bashō "Four Haiku" from *The Penguin Book of Japanese Verse* by Anthony Thwaite and Geoffrey Bownas published by Penguin Classics. Translation Copyright © Anthony Thwaite and Geoffrey Bownas 2009. Reprinted by permission of Penguin Books Limited.

Charles Baxter "Gryphon" by Charles Baxter. Copyright © 1985 by Charles Baxter. Originally appeared in Epoch, 1985 and currently collected in *Gryphon: New and Selected Stories* (Vintage, 2012.) Used with permission of Penguin Random House LLC and Darhansoff & Verrill Literary Agents. All rights reserved.

F. J. Bergmann "An Apology" from *180 More: Extraordinary Poems for Every Day*, New York: Random House Trade Paperbacks. Copyright © 2005 by F. J. Bergmann. Reprinted with permission of the author.

Elizabeth Bishop "Sestina" from THE COMPLETE POEMS 1927-1979. Copyright © 1979, 1983 by Alice Helen Methfessel. Reprinted by permission of Farrar, Straus & Giroux, LLC.

T. Coraghessan Boyle "Greasy Lake" from GREASY LAKE AND OTHER STORIES by T. Coraghessan Boyle. Copyright © 1979, 1981, 1982, 1983, 1984, 1985 by T. Coraghessan Boyle. Used by permission of Viking Penguin, a division of Penguin Group (USA) Inc.

Gwendolyn Brooks "The Chicago Defender Send a Man to Little Rock" from BLACKS. Copyright © 1991 by Gwendolyn Brooks Blakely. Reprinted by consent of Brooks Permissions.

Gwendolyn Brooks "Medgar Evers" from BLACKS. Copyright © 1991 by Gwendolyn Brooks Blakely. Reprinted by consent of Brooks Permissions.

Gwendolyn Brooks "Sadie and Maud" from BLACKS. Copyright © 1991 by Gwendolyn Brooks Blakely. Reprinted by consent of Brooks Permissions.

Gwendolyn Brooks "We Real Cool" from BLACKS. Copyright © 1991 by Gwendolyn Brooks Blakely. Reprinted by consent of Brooks Permissions.

Gwendolyn Brooks "What Shall I Give My Children?" from "The Womanhood" from ANNIE ALLEN. Copyright 1949 by Gwendolyn Brooks. Reprinted by consent of Brooks Permissions.

Rafael Campo "My Voice" from *What the Body Told* by Rafael Campo. Copyright © 1996 by Rafael Campo. Reprinted by permission of Georges Borchardt, Inc., for the author.

Lynn Aarti Chandhok "The Carpet Factory" from *The View from Zero Bridge.* Copyright © 2007 by Anhinga Press. Reprinted with permission.

Anton Chekhov "The Brute" from THE BRUTE AND OTHER FARCES, edited by Eric Bentley. Copyright © 1958. Reprinted with the permission of Applause Theatre Books.

Sandra Cisneros "Geraldo No Last Name" from THE HOUSE ON MANGO STREET. Copyright © 1984 by Sandra Cisneros. Published by Vintage Books, a division of Penguin Random House, and in hardcover by Alfred A. Knopf in 1994. By permission of Susan Bergholz Literary Services, New York, NY and Lamy, NM. All rights reserved.

Judith Ortiz Cofer "My Father in the Navy: A Childhood Memory" from REACHING FOR THE MAINLAND & SELECTED NEW POEMS. Reprinted with the permission of Bilingual Press/ Editorial Bilingüe, Arizona State University, Tempe.

Billy Collins "Introduction to Poetry" from THE APPLE THAT ASTONISHED PARIS. Copyright © 1988, 1996 by Billy Collins. Reprinted with the permission of The Permissions Company, Inc. on behalf of the University of Arkansas Press, www.uapress.com.

Stephen Crane "The Open Boat" William Heineman, 1898.

Robert Crumb "A Hunger Artist" from INTRODUCING KAFKA. Text copyright © 1993 by David Zane Mairowitz. Illustrations © 1993 by Robert Crumb. Reprinted by permission of the authors.

Countee Cullen "Incident" from COLOR © 1925 Harper & Bros., NY, renewed 1952 Ida M. Cullen. Copyrights held by Amistad Research Center, Tulane University. Administered by Thompson and Thompson, Brooklyn, NY. By permission.

Countee Cullen "Yet Do I Marvel" from COLOR © 1925 Harper & Bros., NY, renewed 1952 Ida M. Cullen. Copyrights held by Amistad Research Center, Tulane University. Administered by Thompson and Thompson, Brooklyn, NY. By permission.

E. E. Cummings "l(a" Copyright © 1958, 1986, 1991 by the Trustees for the E. E. Cummings Trust, Used by permission of Liveright Publishing Corporation.

E. E. Cummings "next to of course god america i" Copyright 1926, 1954, ©1991 by the Trustees for the E. E. Cummings Trust. Copyright © 1985 by George James Firmage, from COMPLETE POEMS: 1904-1962 by E. E. Cummings, edited by George J. Firmage. Used by permission of Liveright Publishing Corporation.

E. E. Cummings "the sky" Copyright © 1973, 1983, 1991 by the Trustees for the E. E. Cummings Trust. Copyright © 1973, 1983 by George James Firmage, Used by permission of Liveright Publishing Corporation.

Junot Diaz "No Face" from DROWN by Junot Diaz, copyright © 1996 by Junot Diaz. Used by permission of Riverhead Books, an imprint of Penguin Group (USA) Inc.

Emily Dickinson "Because I could not stop for Death" from THE POEMS OF EMILY DICKINSON, edited by Thomas H. Johnson, Cambridge, Mass.: The Belknap Press of Harvard University Press, Copyright © 1951, 1955 by the President and Fellows of Harvard College. Copyright © renewed 1979, 1983 by the President and Fellows of Harvard College. Copyright © 1914, 1918, 1919, 1924,

1929, 1930, 1932, 1935, 1937, 1942, by Martha Dickinson Bianchi. Copyright © 1952, 1957, 1958, 1963, 1965, by Mary L. Hampson. Used by permission.

Emily Dickinson "'Faith' is a fine invention" from THE COMPLETE POEMS OF EMILY DICKINSON, edited by Thomas H. Johnson (Cambridge, Mass.: The Belknap Press of Harvard University Press, 1979).

Emily Dickinson "'Hope' is the thing with feathers?" from THE COMPLETE POEMS OF EMILY DICKINSON, edited by Thomas H. Johnson (Cambridge, Mass.: The Belknap Press of Harvard University Press, 1979).

Emily Dickinson "I heard a Fly buzz – when I died" from THE POEMS OF EMILY DICKINSON, edited by Thomas H. Johnson, Cambridge, Mass.: The Belknap Press of Harvard University Press, Copyright © 1951, 1955 by the President and Fellows of Harvard College. Copyright © renewed 1979, 1983 by the President and Fellows of Harvard College. Copyright © 1914, 1918, 1919, 1924, 1929, 1930, 1932, 1935, 1937, 1942, by Martha Dickinson Bianchi. Copyright © 1952, 1957, 1958, 1963, 1965, by Mary L. Hampson. Used by permission.

Emily Dickinson "I like to see it lap the Miles" from THE POEMS OF EMILY DICKINSON, edited by Thomas H. Johnson, Cambridge, Mass.: The Belknap Press of Harvard University Press, Copyright © 1951, 1955 by the President and Fellows of Harvard College. Copyright © renewed 1979, 1983 by the President and Fellows of Harvard College. Copyright © 1914, 1918, 1919, 1924, 1929, 1930, 1932, 1935, 1937, 1942, by Martha Dickinson Bianchi. Copyright © 1952, 1957, 1958, 1963, 1965, by Mary L. Hampson. Used by permission.

Emily Dickinson "I'm nobody! Who are you" from THE POEMS OF EMILY DICKINSON, edited by Thomas H. Johnson, Cambridge, Mass.: The Belknap Press of Harvard University Press, Copyright © 1951, 1955 by the President and Fellows of Harvard College. Copyright © renewed 1979, 1983 by the President and Fellows of Harvard College. Copyright © 1914, 1918, 1919, 1924, 1929, 1930, 1932, 1935, 1937, 1942, by Martha Dickinson Bianchi. Copyright © 1952, 1957, 1958, 1963, 1965, by Mary L. Hampson. Used by permission.

Emily Dickinson "Much Madness is divinest Sense" from THE POEMS OF EMILY DICKINSON, edited by Thomas H. Johnson, Cambridge, Mass.: The Belknap Press of Harvard University Press, Copyright © 1951, 1955 by the *President and Fellows of Harvard College.* Copyright © renewed 1979, 1983 by the President and Fellows of Harvard College. Copyright © 1914, 1918, 1919, 1924, 1929, 1930, 1932, 1935, 1937, 1942, by Martha Dickinson Bianchi. Copyright © 1952, 1957, 1958, 1963, 1965, by Mary L. Hampson. Used by permission.

Emily Dickinson "The Soul selects her own Society" from THE POEMS OF EMILY DICKINSON, edited by Thomas H. Johnson, Cambridge, Mass.: The Belknap Press of Harvard University Press, Copyright © 1951, 1955 by the President and Fellows of Harvard College. Copyright © renewed 1979, 1983 by the President and Fellows of Harvard College. Copyright © 1914, 1918, 1919, 1924, 1929, 1930, 1932, 1935, 1937, 1942, by Martha Dickinson Bianchi. Copyright © 1952, 1957, 1958, 1963, 1965, by Mary L. Hampson. Used by permission.

Emily Dickinson "There's a certain Slant of light" from THE POEMS OF EMILY DICKINSON, edited by Thomas H. Johnson, Cambridge, Mass.: The Belknap Press of Harvard University Press, Copyright © 1951, 1955 by the President and Fellows of Harvard College. Copyright © renewed 1979, 1983 by the President and Fellows of Harvard College. Copyright © 1914, 1918, 1919, 1924, 1929, 1930, 1932, 1935, 1937, 1942, by Martha Dickinson Bianchi. Copyright © 1952, 1957, 1958, 1963, 1965, by Mary L. Hampson. Used by permission. All rights reserved.

Emily Dickinson "There is no Frigate like a Book" from THE POEMS OF EMILY DICKINSON, edited by Thomas H. Johnson, Cambridge, Mass.: The Belknap Press of Harvard University Press, Copyright © 1951, 1955 by the President and Fellows of Harvard College. Copyright © renewed 1979, 1983 by the President and Fellows of Harvard College. Copyright © 1914, 1918, 1919, 1924, 1929, 1930, 1932, 1935, 1937, 1942, by Martha Dickinson Bianchi. Copyright © 1952, 1957, 1958, 1963, 1965, by Mary L. Hampson. Used by permission. All rights reserved.

Emily Dickinson "This is my letter to the World" Reprinted by permission of the publishers and the Trustees of Amherst College from THE COMPLETE POEMS OF EMILY DICKINSON, Thomas H. Johnson, ed, J258, Cambridge, Mass.: The Belknap Press of Harvard University Press, Copyright © 1951, 1955, 1979, 1983 by the President and Fellows of Harvard College.

Emily Dickinson "Volcanoes be in Sicily" Reprinted by permission of the publishers and the Trustees of Amherst College from THE COMPLETE POEMS OF EMILY DICKINSON, Thomas H. Johnson, ed, J258, Cambridge, Mass.: The Belknap Press of Harvard University Press, Copyright © 1951, 1955, 1979, 1983 by the President and Fellows of Harvard College.

Chitra Banerjee Divakaruni "The Disappearance" copyright © 1995 by Chitra Divakaruni. Reprinted by permission of the author and the Sandra Dijkstra Literary Agency.

Jehanne Dubrow "Before the Deployment" Copyright © 2010 by Jehanne Dubrow. Published 2010 by TriQuarterly Books/Northwestern University Press. All rights reserved.

Dave Eggers "Accident" by Dave Eggers. Copyright © Dave Eggers, used by permission of The Wylie Agency LLC.

T. S. Eliot "The Love Song of J. Alfred Prufrock" from THE COLLECTED POEMS, 1909-1932. Reprinted by permission of Harcourt, Inc. and Faber and Faber, Ltd.

James A. Emanuel "Emmett Till." Copyright © 1968 by James A. Emanuel. Reprinted with the permission of James A. Emanuel.

Louise Erdrich "Indian Boarding School: The Runaways" from *Original Fire* by Louise Erdrich. Copyright © 2003 by Louise Erdrich. Used by permission of HarperCollins Publishers.

Louise Erdrich "The Red Convertible" from *The Red Convertible* by Louise Erdrich. Copyright © 2009 by Louise Erdrich. Used by permission of HarperCollins Publishers.

Martin Espada "The Community College Revises Its Curriculum in Response to Changing Demographics" from A MAYAN ASTRONOMER IN HELL'S KITCHEN by Martin Espada. Copyright © 2000 by Martin Espada. Used by permission of the author and W. W. Norton & Company, Inc.

Martin Espada "Why I Went to College" from A MAYAN ASTRONOMER IS HELL'S KITCHEN. Copyright © 2000 by Martín Espada. Used by permission of the author and W. W. Norton & Company, Inc.

Rhina Espaillat "Bilingual/Bilingüe" from WHERE HORIZONS GO Kirksville, Mo.: Truman State University Press, 1998.

William Faulkner "A Rose for Emily" Copyright 1930 and renewed 1958 by William Faulkner, from COLLECTED STORIES OF WILLIAM FAULKNER by William Faulkner. Used by permission of W. W. Norton & Company, Inc. and Random House, an imprint and division of Penguin Random House LLC.

William Faulkner "Barn Burning" Copyright 1950 by Random House, Inc. Copyright renewed 1977 by Jill Faulkner Summers from COLLECTED STORIES OF WILLIAM FAULKNER by William Faulkner. Used by permission of W. W. Norton & Company, Inc. and Random House, an imprint and division of Penguin Random House LLC.

Lawrence Ferlinghetti "Constantly Risking Absurdity" from A CONEY ISLAND OF THE MIND, copyright ©1958 by Lawrence Ferlinghetti. Reprinted by permission of New Directions Publishing Corp.

Jane Flanders "Cloud Painter" from *Timepiece* by Jane Flanders, © 1988. Reprinted by permission of the University of Pittsburgh Press.

Robert Frost "Birches" from THE POETRY OF ROBERT FROST, edited by Edward Connery Lathem. Copyright 1923, © 1969 by Henry Holt and Company, copyright 1944, 1951 by Robert Frost. Reprinted by permission of Henry Holt and Company LLC.

Robert Frost "Fire and Ice" from THE POETRY OF ROBERT FROST, edited by Edward Connery Lathem. Copyright 1923, © 1969 by Henry Holt and Company, copyright 1944, 1951 by Robert Frost. Reprinted by permission of Henry Holt and Company LLC.

Robert Frost "For Once, Then, Something" from THE POETRY OF ROBERT FROST, edited by Edward Connery Lathem. Copyright 1923, © 1969 by Henry Holt and Company, copyright 1944, 1951 by Robert Frost. Reprinted by permission of Henry Holt and Company LLC.

Robert Frost "Mending Wall" from THE POETRY OF ROBERT FROST, edited by Edward Connery Lathem. Copyright 1923, © 1969 by Henry Holt and Company, copyright 1944, 1951 by Robert Frost. Reprinted by permission of Henry Holt and Company LLC.

Robert Frost "Nothing Gold Can Stay" from THE POETRY OF ROBERT FROST, edited by Edward Connery Lathem. Copyright 1923, © 1969 by Henry Holt and Company, copyright 1944 1951 by Robert Frost. Reprinted by permission of Henry Holt and Company LLC.

Robert Frost "Out, Out—" from THE POETRY OF ROBERT FROST, edited by Edward Connery Lathem. Copyright 1923, © 1969 by Henry Holt and Company, copyright 1944, 1951 by Robert Frost. Reprinted by permission of Henry Holt and Company LLC.

Robert Frost "The Road Not Taken" from THE POETRY OF ROBERT FROST, edited by Edward Connery Lathem. Copyright 1923, © 1969 by Henry Holt and Company, copyright 1944, 1951 by Robert Frost. Reprinted by permission of Henry Holt and Company LLC.

Robert Frost "Stopping by Woods on a Snowy Evening" from THE POETRY OF ROBERT FROST, edited by Edward Connery Lathem. Copyright 1923, © 1969 by Henry Holt and Company, copyright 1944, 1951 by Robert Frost. Reprinted by permission of Henry Holt and Company LLC.

Neil Gaiman "How to Talk to Girls at Parties" reprinted by arrangement with Neil Gaiman c/o Writers House as agent for the proprietor, New York, NY. "How to Talk to Girls at Parties" Copyright © 2006 by Neil Gaiman.

Allen Ginsburg "A Supermarket in California" Originally published in HOWL AND OTHER POEMS, currently collected in *Collected Poems 1947-1997*. Copyright © 1956, 1959, 2006 by the Allen Ginsberg Trust, used by permission of The Wylie Agency LLC and HarperCollins Publishers.

Louise Glück "Gretel in Darkness" from *The First Four Books of Poems* by Louise Glück. Copyright © 1968, 1971, 1972, 1973, 1974, 1975, 1976, 1977, 1978, 1979, 1980, 1985, 1995 by Louise Glück. Used by permission of HarperCollins Publishers and Carcanet Press.

R. S. Gwynn "Shakespearean Sonnet" from *180 More: Extraordinary Poems for Every Day*, New York: Random House Trade Paperbacks, 2005. Reprinted with permission of the author.

Joy Harjo "Invisible Fish" from *Secrets from the Center of the World* by Joy Harjo and Stephen Strom. ©1989 The Arizona Board of Regents. Reprinted by permission of the University of Arizona Press.

Robert Hayden "Those Winter Sundays" Copyright © 1966 by Robert Hayden from COLLECTED POEMS OF ROBERT HAYDEN by Robert Hayden, edited by Frederick Glaysher. Used by permission of Liveright Publishing Corporation.

Seamus Heaney "Digging" from OPENED GROUND: SELECTED POEMS 1966-1996. Copyright © 1998 by Seamus Heaney. Reprinted by permission of Farrar, Straus & Giroux, LLC.

Ernest Hemingway "Hills Like White Elephants" from THE COMPLETE SHORT STORIES OF ERNEST HEMINGWAY by Ernest Hemingway. Copyright © 1927 by Charles Scribner's Sons. Copyright renewed © 1955 by Ernest Hemingway. Reprinted with the permission of Scribner, a division of Simon & Schuster, Inc. All rights reserved.

William Ernest Henley "Invictus" from *The Oxford Book of English Verse: 1250-1900*, ed. Arthur Quiller-Couch, 1919.

David Hernandez "Mosul" from *Hoodwinked*. Copyright © 2011 by David Hernandez. Reprinted with the permission of The Permissions Company, LLC on behalf of Sarabande Books, www.sarabandebooks.org.

Robert Herrick "The Argument of His Book" from Robert Herrick, edited by Douglas Brooks-Davies (Everyman's Library, 1997).

Bob Holman "Beautiful" reprinted with permission of Inkwell Management and the author.

A. E. Housman "Loveliest of Trees" from *Modern British Poetry*, ed. Louis Untermeyer, 1920.

Andrew Hudgins "Elegy for My Father, Who Is Not Dead" from *The Never-Ending* by Andrew Hudgins. Copyright © 1991 by Andrew Hudgins. Used by permission of HarperCollins Publishers.

Robert Huff "Rainbow" in *The Ventriloquist*, Huff, Robert. pp. 39–39. © 1977 by the Rector and Visitors of the University of Virginia. Reprinted by permission of the University of Virginia Press.

Langston Hughes "Birmingham Sunday" from THE COLLECTED POEMS OF LANGSTON HUGHES by Langston Hughes, edited by Arnold Rampersad with David Roessel, Associate Editor, copyright © 1951, 1994, by the Estate of Langston Hughes. Used by permission of Alfred A. Knopf, an imprint of the Knopf Doubleday Publishing Group, a division of Penguin

Random House LLC and Reprinted by permission of Harold Ober Associates.

Langston Hughes "Harlem" from THE COLLECTED POEMS OF LANGSTON HUGHES by Langston Hughes, edited by Arnold Rampersad with David Roessel, Associate Editor, copyright © 1951, 1994, by the Estate of Langston Hughes. Used by permission of Alfred A. Knopf, an imprint of the Knopf Doubleday Publishing Group, a division of Penguin Random House LLC and Reprinted by permission of Harold Ober Associates.

Langston Hughes "Negro" from THE COLLECTED POEMS OF LANGSTON HUGHES by Langston Hughes, edited by Arnold Rampersad with David Roessle, Associate Editor.

Langston Hughes "The Negro Speaks of Rivers" from THE COLLECTED POEMS OF LANGSTON HUGHES by Langston Hughes, edited by Arnold Rampersad with David Roessle, Associate Editor.

Langston Hughes "Theme for English B" from THE COLLECTED POEMS OF LANGSTON HUGHES by Langston Hughes, edited by Arnold Rampersad with David Roessel, Associate Editor, copyright © 1951, 1994, by the Estate of Langston Hughes. Used by permission of Alfred A. Knopf, an imprint of the Knopf Doubleday Publishing Group, a division of Penguin Random House LLC and Reprinted by permission of Harold Ober Associates.

Leigh Hunt "Jenny Kissed Me" from *The Oxford Book of English Verse: 1250-1900*, ed. Arthur Quiller-Couch, 1919.

Henrik Ibsen "A Doll's House" Reproduced from DOLLS HOUSE by Henrik Ibsen - Translated by Nicholas Rudall, published by Ivan R. Dee. © Rowman & Littlefield, 1999, reproduced by arrangement with Ivan R. Dee.

Kobayahi Issa "Not yet Buddha—the mindless old pine" translated by David Lanoue.

Shirley Jackson "The Lottery" from THE LOTTERY AND OTHER STORIES. Copyright 1948, 1949 by Shirley Jackson. Copyright renewed © 1976, 1977 by Laurence Hyman, Barry Hyman, Mrs. Sarah Webster and Mrs. Joanne Schnurer. Reprinted by permission of Farrar, Straus & Giroux, LLC.

Randall Jarrell "The Death of the Ball Turret Gunner" from THE COMPLETE POEMS. Copyright © 1969, renewed 1997 by Mary von S. Jarrell. Reprinted by permission of Farrar, Straus & Giroux, LLC.

Charles Jensen "Poem in Which Words Have Been Left Out" Copyright © 2012 by Charles Jensen. Used with permission of the author.

Bret Anthony Johnston "Encounters with Unexpected Animals." Reprinted with permission. http://www.esquire.com/fiction/encounters-with-unexpected-animals-story-0312.

Stephen Graham Jones "Discovering America" from *Bleed Into Me: A Book of Stories* (139-42) by Stephen Graham Jones by permission of the University of Nebraska Press. Copyright 2005 by Stephen Graham Jones.

James Joyce "Araby" from DUBLINERS (New York: Viking, 1967).

Franz Kafka "A Hunger Artist" from FRANZ KAFKA: THE COMPLETE STORIES, edited by Nahum H. Glazer, translated by Willa and Edwin Muir. Copyright 1946, 1947, 1948, 1949, 1954, © 1958, 1971 by Schocken Books, Inc. Used by permission of Schocken Books, a division of Random House, Inc.

David Michael Kaplan "Doe Season" by David Michael Kaplan; first appeared in *The Atlantic Monthly*; also appeared in COMFORT by David Michael Kaplan, and BEST AMERICAN SHORT STORIES, 1986. Copyright © 1985 by David Michael Kaplan. Used by permission of Brandt & Hochman Literary Agents, Inc.

John Keats, "Ode to a Nightingale" from THE COMPLETE POEMS OF JOHN KEATS (Wordsworth, 1994), pp. 218–220.

Jamaica Kincaid "Girl" from AT THE BOTTOM OF THE RIVER. Copyright © 1983 by Jamaica Kincaid. Reprinted by permission of Farrar, Straus & Giroux, LLC.

Yusef Komunyakaa "Facing It" from NEON VERNACULAR © 1993 by Yusef Komunyakaa. Reprinted with the permission of Wesleyan University Press.

Yusef Komunyakaa "Nude Interrogation" from *Pleasure Dome: New and Collected Poems* © 2001 by Yusef Komunyakaa. Published by Wesleyan University Press. Used by permission.

Steven Korbar "What Are You Going to Be?" © 2013 by Steven Korbar. Reprinted by permission of the author. For performance rights, contact Steven Korbar (stevekorbar1@juno.com).

Ada Limón "The Contract Says: We'd Like the Conversation to Be Bilingual" from *The Carrying*. Copyright © 2018 by Ada Limón. Reprinted with the permission of The Permissions Company LLC on behalf of Milkweed Editions, milkweed.org.

Audre Lorde "Rooming Houses Are Old Women". Copyright © 1964 by Audre Lorde, from THE COLLECTED POEMS OF AUDRE LORDE by Audre Lorde. Used by permission of W. W. Norton & Company, Inc. and Abner Stein Ltd.

Thomas Lux "A Little Tooth" from *New and Selected Poems of Thomas Lux*. Copyright © 1997 by Thomas Lux. Used by permission of HarperCollins Publishers.

Jeri Mahoney "Come Rain or Come Shine" Copyright © 2008 by Jeni Mahoney. Reprinted with permission of the author.

Katherine Mansfield "Miss Brill" from THE SHORT STORIES OF KATHERINE MANSFIELD (New York: Knopf, 1939). Originally collected in The Garden Party and Other Stories (New York: Alfred A. Knopf, 1922).

Jane Martin "Beauty" Copyright © 2001 by Alexander Seeper, Trustee.

James McLindon "Choices" © James McLindon.

Nancy Mercado "Going to Work" from *Poetry After 9/11: An Anthology of New York Poets* (Hoboken: Melville House Pub., 2002).

William Meredith "Dreams of Suicide" Copyright © 1997 by William Meredith. Published 1997 by TriQuarterly Books/Northwestern University Press. All rights reserved.

Harriet Levin Millan "Bucharest 1918" originally appeared in *Narr* © Harriet Levin Millan.

Edna St. Vincent Millay "If I should learn, in some quite casual way" © 1917, 1945 by Edna St. Vincent Millay.

Edna St. Vincent Millay "Love is not all: it is not meat nor drink" from *Collected Poems*. Copyright 1931, © 1958 by Edna St. Vincent Millay and Norma Millay Ellis. Reprinted with the permission of The Permissions Company, LLC on behalf of Holly Peppe, Literary Executor, The Millay Society, www.millay.org.

Arthur Miller "All My Sons" Entire Play from ALL MY SONS by Arthur Miller, copyright 1947, renewed © 1975 by Arthur Miller. Used by permission of Penguin Books, an imprint of Penguin Publishing Group, a division of Penguin

Random House LLC. All rights reserved and used by permission of The Wylie Agency LLC.

N. Scott Momaday "Simile" from *In the Presence of the Sun* by N. Scott Momaday. Copyright © 2009 University of New Mexico Press, 2009.

Frederick Morgan "The Busses" from POEMS FOR PAULA. Copyright © 1999 Red Hen Press.

Pablo Neruda "The United Fruit Co." from NERUDA AND VALLEGO: SELECTED POEMS translated by Robert Bly. Translation Copyright © 1971, 1993 by Robert Bly. Reprinted by permission of Georges Borchardt, Inc., for Robert Bly.

Naomi Shihab Nye "All Things Not Considered" from *19 Varieties of Gazelle* by Naomi Shihab Nye. Text copyright © 2002 Naomi Shihab Nye.

Joyce Carol Oates "Where Are You Going, Where Have You Been?" from *High Lonesome* by Joyce Carol Oates. Copyright © 2006 by The Ontario Review, Inc. Used by permission of HarperCollins Publishers.

Flannery O'Connor "A Good Man Is Hard to Find" from A GOOD MAN IS HARD TO FIND AND OTHER STORIES, copyright 1953 by Flannery O'Connor and renewed © 1981 by Regina O'Connor. Reprinted by permission of Houghton Mifflin Harcourt Publishing Company.

Tillie Olsen "I Stand Here Ironing" from TELL ME A RIDDLE. Copyright © 1961, 2013 by Tillie Olsen. Reprinted by permission of The Frances Goldin Literary Agency and by permission of the University of Nebraska Press.

Wilfred Owen "Dulce et Decorum Est" from THE COMPLETE POEMS AND FRAGMENTS OF WILFRED OWEN, edited by Jon Stallworthy (New York: W. W. Norton & Company, 1984).

Deborah Paredez "Wife's Disaster Manual" from *Poetry*, 200.5 (September 2012, 452-53) © Deborah A Paradez.

Ed Park "Slide to Unlock" Reprinted with permission. *The New Yorker*, 6/10 & 17/13, 62+.

Dorothy Parker "General Review of the Sex Situation" copyright 1926, renewed © 1954 by Dorothy Parker; copyright © 1973, 2006 by The National Assoc. for the Advancement of Colored People, from THE PORTABLE DOROTHY PARKER by Dorothy Parker, edited by Marion Meade. Used by permission of Viking Penguin, a division of Penguin Group (USA) Inc.

Dorothy Parker "News Item" copyright 1926, renewed © 1954 by Dorothy Parker; from THE PORTABLE DOROTHY PARKER by Dorothy Parker, edited by Marion Meade. Used by permission of Viking Books, an imprint of Penguin Publishing Group, a division of Penguin Random House LLC. All rights reserved.

Harold Pinter "Applicant" from REVUE SKETCHES, Excerpt from COMPLETE WORKS, VOL. 3 by Harold Pinter, copyright © 1961 by Harold Pinter. Used by permission of Grove/Atlantic, Inc. and Faber & Faber.

Sylvia Plath "Daddy" from *The Collected Poems*, Sylvia Plath. Copyright © 1960, 1965, 1971, 1981 by the Estate of Sylvia Plath. Editorial material copyright © 1981 by Ted Hughes. Used by permission of HarperCollins Publishers and Faber and Faber Ltd.

Sylvia Plath "Metaphors" from *The Collected Poems*, Sylvia Plath. Copyright © 1960, 1965, 1971, 1981 by the Estate of Sylvia Plath. Editorial material copyright © 1981 by Ted Hughes. Used by permission of HarperCollins Publishers and Faber and Faber Ltd.

Sylvia Plath "Morning Song" from *The Collected Poems*, Sylvia Plath. Copyright © 1960, 1965, 1971, 1981 by the Estate of Sylvia Plath. Editorial material copyright © 1981 by Ted Hughes. Used by permission of HarperCollins Publishers and Faber and Faber Ltd.

Ezra Pound "In a Station of the Metro" from PERSONAE, copyright ©1926 by Ezra Pound. Reprinted by permission of New Directions Publishing Corp.

Adrienne Rich "Aunt Jennifer's Tigers" from THE FACT OF A DOORFRAME: Poems Selected and New, 1950-1984 by Adrienne Rich. Copyright © 1984 by Adrienne Rich. Copyright © 1975, 1978 by W. W. Norton & Company, Inc. Copyright © 1981 by Adrienne Rich. Used by permission of W. W. Norton & Company, Inc.

Adrienne Rich "Living in Sin" Copyright © 1984 by Adrienne Rich. Copyright © 1975, 1978 by W. W. Norton & Company, Inc. Copyright © 1981 by Adrienne Rich, from THE FACT OF A DOORFRAME: Poems Selected and New, 1950-1984 by Adrienne Rich. Used by permission of W. W. Norton & Company, Inc.

Alberto Álvaro Ríos "Nani" from WHISPERING TO FOOL THE WIND. Copyright © 1982 by Alberto Álvaro Ríos. Reprinted with the permission of the author.

Alberto Álvaro Ríos "The Secret Lion" from *The Iguana Killer: Twelve Stories of the Heart*. Copyright © 1984 by Alberto Álvaro Ríos. Reprinted with the permission of The Permissions Company, LLC on behalf of Confluence Press, www.confluencepress.com.

José Rivera "Tape" by José Rivera. Copyright © José Rivera. reprinted with permission of Concord Theatricals.

Edward Arlington Robinson "Richard Cory" from SELECTED POEMS OF EDWIN ARLINGTON ROBINSON, edited by Morton Dauwen Zabel (New York: Macmillan Publishing Company, 1965).

Theodore Roethke "My Papa's Waltz" copyright © 1942 by Hearst Magazines, Inc., copyright © 1966 and renewed 1994 by Beatrice Lushington; from COLLECTED POEMS by Theodore Roethke. Used by permission of Faber and Faber Ltd. and Doubleday, an imprint of the Knopf Doubleday Publishing Group, a division of Penguin Random House LLC. All rights reserved.

Theodore Roethke "The Waking" copyright © 1966 and renewed 1994 by Beatrice Lushington; from COLLECTED POEMS by Theodore Roethke. Used by permission of Faber and Faber Ltd. and Doubleday, an imprint of the Knopf Doubleday Publishing Group, a division of Penguin Random House LLC. All rights reserved.

Jacob Saenz "Evolution of My Block" from *Poetry*, 196.5 (September 2010, 428). © Jacob Saenz.

Jim Sagel "Baca Grande" by Jim Sagel from HISPANICS IN THE UNITED STATES. Reprinted with the permission of Bilingual Press/Editorial Bilingüe, Arizona State University, Tempe, AZ.

Milcha Sanchez-Scott "The Cuban Swimmer" Copyright © 1984, 1988 by Milcha Sanchez-Scott. Reprinted by permission of William Morris Agency, Inc. on behalf of the Author.

Carl Sandburg "Chicago" from *The Complete Poems of Carl Sandburg*. Copyright © 1969, 1970 by Lillian Steichen Sandburg, Trustee. Used by permission of HarperCollins Publishers.

Carl Sandburg "Fog" from *The Complete Poems of Carl Sandburg*. Copyright © 1969, 1970 by Lillian Steichen Sandburg, Trustee. Used by permission of HarperCollins Publishers.

George Saunders "Sticks" from *Tenth of December: Stories* (New York: Random House, 2013, 29-30).

Siegfried Sassoon "Atrocities" from *The War Poems of Siegfried Sassoon*, London: W. Heinemann, 1919.

William Shakespeare "Hamlet" from EVANS. THE RIVERSIDE SHAKESPEARE, 2E. © 1997 Heinle/Arts & Sciences, a part of Cengage Learning, Inc. Reproduced by permission. www.cengage.com/permissions.

Leslie Marmon Silko "Where Mountain Lion Lay Down with Deer" from STORYTELLER by Leslie Marmon Silko, copyright © 1981, 2012 by Leslie Marmon Silko. Used by permission of Viking Books, an imprint of Penguin Publishing Group, a division of Penguin Random House LLC and used by permission of The Wylie Agency LLC. All rights reserved.

Shel Silverstein "Where the Sidewalk Ends" from *Where the Sidewalk Ends* by Shel Silverstein Illustrated By: Shel Silverstein. COPYRIGHT © 1974, renewed 2002 EVIL EYE MUSIC, LLC. Reprinted with permission from the Estate of Shel Silverstein and HarperCollins Children's Books. Used by permission of HarperCollins Publishers and Edite Kroll Literary Agency Inc.

Patricia Smith "Ethel's Sestina" from *Blood Dazzler*. Copyright © 2008 by Patricia Smith. Reprinted with the permission of The Permissions Company, LLC on behalf of Coffee House Press, www.coffeehousepress.org.

Stevie Smith "Not Waving But Drowning" by Stevie Smith, from COLLECTED POEMS OF STEVIE SMITH, copyright ©1957 by Stevie Smith. Reprinted by permission of New Directions Publishing Corp.

Zadie Smith "The Girl with Bangs" by Zadie Smith. Copyright © Zadie Smith. Reproduced by permission of the author c/o Rogers, Coleridge & White Ltd., 20 Powis Mews, London W11 1JN.

Gary Snyder "Some good things to be said for the Iron Age" from REGARDING WAVE, copyright © 1970 by Gary Snyder. Reprinted by permission of New Directions Publishing Corp.

Sophocles "Antigone" from Sophocles, *The Oedipus Cycle*. Translated by Dudley Fitts and Robert Fitzgerald. Copyright © 1949, 1941, 1939 by Harcourt Brace & Company. Copyright renewed 1967 by Dudley Fitts and Robert Fitzgerald. Copyright renewed 1969 by Robert Fitzgerald. Copyright renewed 1977 by Cornelia Fitts and Robert Fitzgerald. Used by permission of HarperCollins Publishers.

Sophocles "Oedipus the King" translated by Ian Johnston of Vancouver Island University.

John Steinbeck "The Chrysanthemums" copyright 1937, renewed © 1965 by John Steinbeck, from THE LONG VALLEY by John Steinbeck. Used by permission of Viking Penguin, a division of Penguin Group (USA) Inc.

Wallace Stevens "The Anecdote of the Jar" from THE COLLECTED POEMS OF WALLACE STEVENS (New York: Alfred A. Knopf, 1954).

Adrienne Su "The English Canon" from SANCTUARY. Originally from NEW LETTERS 65, no 3 (1999). Reprinted with the permission of the author, New Letters and the Curators of the University of Missouri-Kansas City, and Manic D Press, San Francisco.

Virgil Suárez "Isla" from *Guide to the Blue Tongue: Poems*. Copyright 2002 by Virgil Suárez. Used with permission of the University of Illinois Press.

May Swenson "The Watch" by May Swenson, Copyright © 1967 May Swenson. From *Collected Poems* (Library of America 2013).

Used with permission of the Literary Estate of May Swenson. All rights reserved.

May Swenson "Women" Copyright © 1970 May Swenson. From *Collected Poems* (Library of America, 2013). Used with permission of The Literary Estate of May Swenson. All rights reserved.

Wislawa Szymborska "The End and the Beginning" from MIRACLE FAIR, by Wislawa Szymborska, translated by Joanna Trzeciak. Copyright © 2001 by Joanna Trzeciak. Used by permission of W. W. Norton & Company, Inc.

Wislawa Szymborska "Hitler's First Photograph" from *View with a Grain of Sand* by Wislawa Szymborska. English Translation copyright © 1995 by HarperCollins Publishers. Used by permission of HarperCollins Publishers.

Amy Tan "Two Kinds" from THE JOY LUCK CLUB by Amy Tan, copyright © 1989 by Amy Tan. Used by permission of G. P. Putnam's Sons, a division of Penguin Group (USA) Inc.

Dylan Thomas "Do not go gentle into that good night" from THE POEMS OF DYLAN THOMAS, copyright ©1952 by Dylan Thomas. Reprinted by permission of New Directions Publishing Corp.

Jean Toomer "Reapers" from CANE by Jean Toomer. Copyright 1923 by Boni & Liveright, renewed 1951 by Jean Toomer. Used by permission of Liveright Publishing Corporation.

David Trinidad "9773 Comanche Ave." Copyright © 2010 by David Trinidad. Used with permission of the author.

John Updike "A&P" from PIGEON FEATHERS AND OTHER STORIES by John Updike, copyright © 1962, and renewed 1990 by John Updike. Used by permission of Alfred A. Knopf, a division of Random House, Inc.

Luisa Valenzuela "All about Suicide" from *Strange Things Happen Here* by Luisa Valenzuela, translated by Helen Lane. Harcourt Brace Jovanovich, 1979. Used by permission of HarperCollins Publishers.

Alice Walker "Everyday Use" from *In Love & Trouble: Stories of Black Women* by Alice Walker. Copyright © 1973, renewed 2001 by Alice Walker (compilation copyright). Used by permission of HarperCollins Publishers and The Joy Harris Literary Agency, Inc.

Eudora Welty "A Worn Path" from *A Curtain of Green* by Eudora Welty. Copyright © 1941 and renewed 1969 by Eudora Welty (compilation copyright). Used by permission of HarperCollins Publishers and Russell & Volkening as agents for The Eudora Welty LLC.

Tennessee Williams "The Glass Menagerie" Copyright © 1945, renewed 1973 The University of the South. Reprinted by permission of Georges Borchardt, Inc. for the Estate of Tennessee Williams.

William Carlos Williams "The Great Figure" from THE COLLECTED POEMS: Volume I, 1909-1939, copyright © 1938 by New Directions Publishing Corp. Reprinted by permission of New Directions Publishing Corp.

William Carlos Williams "The Red Wheelbarrow" from THE COLLECTED POEMS: Volume I, 1909-1939, copyright © 1938 by New Directions Publishing Corp. Reprinted by permission of New Directions Publishing Corp.

William Carlos Williams "Spring and All, Section I" from THE COLLECTED POEMS: Volume I, 1909-1939, copyright ©1938 by New Directions Publishing Corp. Reprinted by permission of New Directions Publishing Corp.

August Wilson Entire Play from FENCES by August Wilson, copyright ©

1986 by August Wilson. Used by permission of New American Library, an imprint of Penguin Publishing Group, a division of Penguin Random House LLC and Reprinted by permission of Penguin Books Limited.

Richard Wright "Big Black Good Man" from *Eight Men* by Richard Wright. Copyright © 1940, 1957, 1961 by Richard Wright; renewed © 1989 by Ellen Wright. Introduction copyright © 1996 by Paul Gilroy. Used by permission of HarperCollins Publishers and permission of John Hawkins and Associates, Inc.

Mitsuye Yamada "The Night Before Goodbye" from CAMP NOTES AND OTHER WRITINGS. Copyright © 1998 by Mitsuye Yamada. Reprinted with the permission of Rutgers University Press.

William Butler Yeats "Leda and the Swan" from THE COLLECTED WORKS OF W. B. YEATS, VOLUME I: THE POEMS, REVISED by W. B. Yeats, edited by Richard J. Finneran. Copyright © 1928 by The Macmillan Company, renewed 1956 by Georgie Yeats. Reprinted with the permission of Scribner, a division of Simon & Schuster, Inc.

William Butler Yeats "The Lake Isle of Innisfree" Reprinted with the permission of Scribner, a Division of Simon & Schuster, Inc. from THE COLLECTED WORKS OF W. B. YEATS, VOLUME I: THE POEMS, REVISED by W. B. Yeats, edited by Richard J. Finneran. (New York: Scribner, 1997).

William Butler Yeats "The Second Coming" from THE COLLECTED WORKS OF W. B. YEATS, VOLUME I: THE POEMS, REVISED by W. B. Yeats, edited by Richard J. Finneran. Copyright © 1924 by The Macmillan Company, renewed 1952 by Bertha Georgie Yeats. Reprinted with the permission of Scribner, a division of Simon & Schuster, Inc.

Glossary of Literary Terms

Action What happens in a drama.

Alexandrine Verse with six iambic feet (iambic hexameter), a common form in French poetry but relatively rare in English poetry.

Allegorical figure or framework See **Allegory**.

Allegory Story with two parallel and consistent levels of meaning, one literal and one figurative, in which the figurative level offers a moral or political lesson; John Bunyan's *The Pilgrim's Progress* and Nathaniel Hawthorne's "Young Goodman Brown" are examples of moral allegory. An **allegorical figure** has only one meaning (for example, it may represent good or evil), as opposed to a **symbol**, which may suggest a complex network of meanings. An **allegorical framework** is the system of ideas that conveys the allegory's message.

Alliteration Repetition of consonant sounds (usually the initial sounds) in a series of words, as in Blake's "The Chimney Sweeper": "So your chimneys I sweep, and in soot I sleep." Alliteration may be reinforced by repeated sounds within and at the ends of words.

Allusion Reference, often to literature, history, mythology, or the Bible, that is unacknowledged in the text but the author expects a reader to recognize.

Ambiguity Device in which authors intentionally evoke several possible meanings of a word or grammatical structure by leaving unclear which meaning they intend.

Anapest See **Meter**.

Anaphora Deliberate repetition of words or phrases typically used consecutively at the beginning of sentences or clauses. Anaphora is a device that stylizes prose, poetry, or speeches, which allows the writer or speaker to create emphasis, emotional resonance, or a sense of urgency for their audience. Sometimes anaphora can appear in two lines, such as in Lewis Carroll's "A Boat Beneath a Sunny Sky", which repeats, "Drowning as the days go by, / Drowning as the summers die." Other times, anaphora occurs more frequently throughout the entire piece, such as in the repetition of the article a/an at the beginning of many clauses in Robert Herrick's "Delight in Disorder".

Antagonist Character who is in conflict with or opposition to the protagonist, the villain. Sometimes the antagonist may be a force or situation (war or poverty) rather than a person.

Antihero Modern character who possesses the opposite attributes of a hero. Rather than being dignified and powerful, the antihero tends to be passive and ineffectual. Hamlet, the main character in Shakespeare's *Hamlet, Prince of Denmark*, is an antihero.

Apostrophe Figure of speech in which an absent character or a personified force or object is addressed directly, as if it were present or could comprehend: "O Rose, thou art sick!"

Archetype Image or symbol that is so common or important that it seems to have universal significance. Many archetypes appear in classical myths (for example, a journey to the underworld).

Arena stage Stage on which the actors are surrounded by the audience; also called **theater in the round**.

Aside Brief comment spoken by an actor to the audience (such as, "Here she comes. I'll play a fine trick on her now!") and assumed not to be heard by the other characters.

Assonance Repetition of the same or similar vowel sounds in a series of words: "creep three feet."

Atmosphere Tone or mood of a literary work, often established by the setting and language. Atmosphere is the emotional aura that determines readers' expectations about a work—for example, the sense of doom established at the beginning of Shakespeare's *Macbeth*.

Aubade Poem about morning, usually celebrating the dawn.

Ballad Narrative poem, rooted in an oral tradition, usually arranged in quatrains rhyming *abcb* and containing a refrain.

Ballad stanza See **Stanza**.

Beast fable Short tale, usually including a moral, in which animals assume human characteristics—for example, Aesop's "The Tortoise and the Hare."

Beginning rhyme See **Rhyme**.

Black comedy Comedy that relies on the morbid and absurd. Often black comedies (also called *dark comedies*) are so satiric that they become ironic and tragic; examples are Joseph Heller's novel *Catch 22* and Edward Albee's play *The Sandbox*.

Blank verse Unrhymed iambic pentameter verse in no particular stanzaic form. Because iambic pentameter resembles the rhythms of ordinary English speech, blank verse is often unobtrusive; for example, Shakespeare's noble characters usually use it, though they may seem to us at first reading to be speaking in prose. See **Meter**.

Blocking Decisions about how characters move and where they stand on stage in a dramatic production.

Box set Stage setting that gives the audience the illusion of looking into a room.

Cacophony Harsh or unpleasant spoken sound created by clashing consonants such as "The vorpal blade went snicker-snack!" in Lewis Carroll's "Jabberwocky."

Caesura Strong or long pause in the middle of a poetic line, created by punctuation or by the sense of the poem, as in Yeats's "Leda and the Swan": "And Agamemnon dead. Being so caught up. …"

Carpe diem Latin for "seize the day"; the philosophy arguing that one should enjoy life today before it passes by, as seen in Herrick's "To the Virgins, to Make Much of Time."

Catastrophe The moment in a tragedy after the climax, when the rising action has ended and the falling action has begun, when protagonists begin to understand the implications of events that will lead to their downfall.

Catharsis Aristotle's term for the emotional reaction or "purgation" that takes place in an audience watching a tragedy.

Character Fictional representation of a person, usually but not necessarily in a psychologically realistic way. E. M. Forster classified characters as **round** (well developed, closely involved in the action and responsive to it) or **flat** (static, stereotypical, or operating as **foils** for the protagonist). Characters can also be classified as **dynamic** (growing and changing) or **static** (remaining unchanged).

Characterization Way in which writers develop their characters and reveal those characters' traits to readers.

Choragos See **Chorus**.

Chorus Group of actors in classical Greek drama who comment in unison on the action and the hero; they are led by the **Choragos**.

Classicism Attitude toward art that values symmetry, clarity, discipline, and objectivity. **Neoclassicism**, practiced in eighteenth-century Europe, appreciated those qualities as found in Greek and Roman art and culture.

Cliché Overused phrase or expression.

Climax Point of greatest tension or importance, where the decisive action of a play or story takes place.

Closed form Type of poetic structure that has a recognizable rhyme scheme, meter, or stanzaic pattern; also called *fixed form*.

Closet drama Play meant to be read instead of performed—for example, Shelley's *Prometheus Unbound*.

Comedy Any literary work, but especially a play, in which events end happily, a character's fortunes are reversed for the better, and a community is drawn more closely together, often by the marriage of one or more protagonists at the end.

Comedy of humours Comedy that focuses on characters whose behavior is controlled by a single characteristic trait, or humour, such as *Volpone* (1606) by Ben Jonson.

Comedy of manners Satiric comedy that achieved great popularity in the nineteenth century. This form focuses on the manners and customs of society and directs its satire against the characters who violate its social conventions and norms. *The Importance of Being Earnest* (1895) by Oscar Wilde is a comedy of manners.

Common measure See **Stanza**.

Conceit See **Metaphor**.

Concrete poem Poem whose typographical appearance on the page reinforces its theme, as with George Herbert's "Easter Wings."

Conflict Struggle between opposing forces (protagonist and antagonist) in a work of literature.

Connotation Meaning that a word suggests beyond its literal, dictionary meaning; its emotional associations, judgments, or opinions. Connotations can be positive, neutral, or negative.

Consonance See **Rhyme**.

Convention See **Literary convention**.

Conventional symbol See **Symbol**.

Cosmic irony See **Irony**.

Couplet See **Stanza**.

Crisis Point at which the decisive action of the plot occurs.

Dactyl See **Meter**.

Denotation Dictionary meaning of a word; its explicit, literal meaning.

Denouement See **Resolution**.

Deus ex machina Latin for "God from a machine"; any improbable resolution of plot involving the intervention of some force or agent from outside the story.

Dialect Particular regional variety of language, which may differ from the more widely used standard or written language in its pronunciation, grammar, or vocabulary. Calixta's Creole dialect in Kate Chopin's short story "The Storm" is an example.

Dialogue Conversation between two or more characters.

Diction Word choice that determines the level of language used in a piece of literature. **Formal diction** is lofty and elaborate (typical of Shakespearean nobility); **informal diction** is idiomatic and relaxed (like the narrative in John Updike's "A&P"). **Jargon** is the specialized diction of a professional or occupational group (such as computer scientists).

Idioms are the colloquial expressions, including slang, of a particular group or society.

Didactic poetry Poetry whose purpose is to make a point or teach a lesson, particularly common in the eighteenth century.

Double entendre Phrase or word with a deliberate double meaning, one of which is usually sexual.

Double plot See **Plot**.

Drama Literature written to be performed.

Dramatic irony See **Irony**.

Dramatic monologue Type of poem perfected by Robert Browning that consists of a single speaker talking to one or more listeners and often revealing much more about the speaker than they seem to intend; Browning's "My Last Duchess" is an example of this form.

Dramatis personae Characters in a play.

Dynamic character See **Character**.

Elegy Poem commemorating someone's death, usually in a reflective or mournful tone, such as A. E. Housman's "To an Athlete Dying Young."

Elision Leaving out an unstressed syllable or vowel, usually to maintain a regular meter in a line of poetry ("o'er" instead of "over," for example).

End rhyme See **Rhyme**.

End-stopped line Line of poetry that has a full pause at the end, typically indicated by a period or semicolon.

Enjambment See **Run-on line**.

Envoi Three-line conclusion to a sestina that includes all six of the poem's key words, three placed at the ends of lines and three within the lines. See **Sestina**.

Epic Long narrative poem, such as the *Iliad* or the *Aeneid*, recounting the adventures of heroes on whose actions the fate of a nation or race depends. Frequently the gods or other supernatural beings take active interest in the events.

Epigram Short pithy poem or statement—for example, Dorothy Parker's sarcastic comment on an actress's performance, "She runs the gamut of emotions from A to B."

Epiphany Term first applied to literature by James Joyce to describe a sudden moment of revelation about the deep meaning of something, such as the boy's realization at the end of "Araby."

Euphemism Word consciously chosen for its pleasant **connotations**; often used for subjects such as sex and death, whose frank discussion is somewhat taboo in our society. For example, a euphemism for *die* is *pass away*.

Euphony Pleasant spoken sound created by smooth consonants such as "ripple" or "pleasure."

Exposition First stage of a plot, where the author presents the information about characters or setting that a reader or viewer will need to understand the subsequent action.

Expressionism Artistic and literary movement that attempts to portray inner experience. It moves away from realistic portrayals of life and is characterized by violent exaggeration of objective reality and extremes of mood and feeling. In drama, expressionistic stage sets mirror the inner states of the character.

Extended metaphor See **Metaphor**.

Extended simile See **Metaphor**. Also see **Conceit**.

Eye rhyme See **Rhyme**.

Fable Short tale, often involving animals or supernatural beings and stressing plot above character development, whose object is to teach a pragmatic or moral lesson. See **Beast fable**.

Fairy tale See **Folktale**.

Falling action Stage in a play's plot during which the intensity of the climax subsides.

Falling meter Trochaic and dactylic meters, so called because they move from stressed to unstressed syllables. See **Rising meter**.

Fantasy Work of literature that takes place in an unreal world or contains unreal or incredible characters. J. R. R. Tolkien's *The Lord of the Rings* is one example.

Farce Comedy in which stereotypical characters engage in boisterous horseplay and slapstick humor, as in Chekhov's *The Brute*.

Feminine rhyme See **Rhyme**.

Fiction Form of narrative that is primarily imaginative although its form may resemble types of factual writing such as history and biography.

Figures of speech Expressions—such as **hyperbole, metaphor, metonymy, personification, simile, synechdoche**, and **understatement**—that use words to achieve effects beyond ordinary language.

Flashback Departure from chronological order that presents an event or situation that occurred before the time in which the story's action takes place.

Flat character See **Character**.

Foil Minor characters whose role is to highlight the main characters by presenting a contrast with them.

Folktale Contemporary version of an old, even ancient, oral tale that can be traced back centuries through many different cultures. Folktales include fairy tales, myths, and fables.

Foot See **Meter**.

Foreshadowing Introduction early in a story of situations, characters, or objects that seem to have no special importance but in fact are later revealed to have great significance.

Form Structure or shape of a literary work; the way a work's parts fit together to form a whole. In poetry, form is described in terms of the presence (or absence) of elements like rhyme, meter, and stanzaic pattern. See **Open form** and **Closed form**.

Formal diction See **Diction**.

Free verse See **Open form**.

Freytag's pyramid In his *Technique of the Drama* (1863), Gustav Freytag suggested that the stages of a classic dramatic plot resemble a pyramid, with rising action leading to the climax and giving way to falling action.

Genre Category of literature. Fiction, drama, and poetry are the three major genres; subgenres include the novel, the farce, and the lyric poem.

Haiku Seventeen-syllable, three-line form of Japanese verse that almost always uses concrete imagery and deals with the natural world.

Hamartia Aristotle's term for the "tragic flaw" in characters that eventually causes their downfall in Greek tragedy.

Hermeneutics Traditionally, the use of the Bible to interpret other historical or current events; in current critical theory, the principles and procedures followed to determine the meaning of a text.

Heroic couplet See **Stanza**.

High comedy Term introduced in 1877 by George Meredith to denote comedy that appeals to the intellect, such as Shakespeare's *As You Like It*. See **Low comedy**.

Hubris Tragic flaw of overwhelming pride that exists in the protagonist of a tragedy.

Hyperbole Figurative language that depends on intentional overstatement; Mark Twain often used it to create humor; Jonathan Swift used it for **satire**.

Iamb See **Meter**.

Imagery Words and phrases that describe the concrete experience of the five senses, most often sight. A **pattern of imagery** is a group of related images developed throughout a work. **Synesthesia** is a form of imagery that mixes the experience of the senses (hearing something visual, smelling something audible, and so on): "He smelled the blue fumes of her scent." **Static imagery** freezes the moment to give it the timeless quality of painting or sculpture. **Kinetic imagery** attempts to show motion or change.

Imagism Movement in modern poetry stressing terseness and concrete imagery. **Imagists** were a group of early twentieth-century American poets, including Ezra Pound, William Carlos Williams, and Amy Lowell, who focused on visual images and created new rhythms and meters.

Imperfect rhyme See **Rhyme**.

In medias res Latin phrase describing works like Virgil's *Aeneid* that begin in the middle of the action to catch a reader's interest.

Informal diction See **Diction**.

Internal rhyme See **Rhyme**.

Irony Literary device or situation that depends on the existence of at least two separate and contrasting levels of meaning or experience. **Dramatic** or **tragic irony**, such as that found in *Oedipus the King*, depends on the audience's knowing something the protagonist has not yet realized. **Situational irony** exists when what happens is at odds with what the story's situation leads readers to expect will happen, as in Browning's "Porphyria's Lover." **Cosmic irony** (or irony of fate) exists when fate frustrates any effort a character might make to control or reverse destiny. **Verbal irony** occurs when what is said is in contrast with what is meant. Verbal irony can be expressed as **understatement, hyperbole**, or **sarcasm**.

Jargon Specialized language associated with a particular trade or profession.

Kinetic imagery Imagery that attempts to show motion or change. See, for example, William Carlos Williams's "The Great Figure." See **Static imagery**.

Literary canon Group of literary works generally acknowledged by critics and teachers to be the best and most significant to have emerged from our history. In the twentieth century, the canon began to be expanded to include works by writers from traditionally marginalized groups.

Literary convention Something whose meaning is so widely understood within a society that authors can expect their audiences to accept it unquestioningly—for example, the division of plays into acts or the fact that stepmothers in fairy tales are likely to be wicked.

Literary criticism Descriptions, analyses, interpretations, or evaluations of works of literature by experts in the field.

Literary symbol See **Symbol**.

Low comedy Introduced by George Meredith, it refers to comedy with little or no intellectual appeal. Low comedy is used as comic relief in *Macbeth*. See **High comedy**.

Lyric Form of poetry, usually brief and intense, that expresses a poet's subjective response to the world. In classical times, lyrics were set to music. The romantic poets, particularly Keats, often wrote lyrics about love, death, and nature.

Masculine rhyme See **Rhyme**.

Meditation Lyric poem that focuses on a physical object—for example, Keats's "Ode on a Grecian Urn"—using this object as a vehicle for considering larger issues.

Melodrama A type of play that appeals shamelessly to the emotions, contains elements of tragedy but ends happily, and often relies on set plots and stock characters.

Metaphor Concise form of comparison equating two things that may at first seem completely dissimilar, often an abstraction and a concrete image—for example, "My love's a fortress." An **extended metaphor** (or **conceit**) is a comparison used throughout a work;

in Tillie Olsen's "I Stand Here Ironing," the mother compares her daughter to a dress waiting to be ironed, thus conveying her daughter's passivity and vulnerability. See **Simile**.

Meter Regular pattern of stressed and unstressed syllables, each repeated unit of which is called a **foot**: an **anapest** has three syllables, two unstressed and the third stressed; a **dactyl** has three syllables, the first stressed and the subsequent ones unstressed. An **iamb** has two syllables, unstressed followed by stressed; a **trochee** has a stressed syllable followed by an unstressed one; a **spondee** has two stressed syllables; and a **pyrrhic** has two unstressed syllables. A poem's meter is described in terms of the kind of foot (anapest, for example) and the number of feet found in each line. The number of feet is designated by the Greek prefix for the number, so one foot per line is called *monometer*, two feet is *dimeter*, followed by *trimeter*, *tetrameter*, *pentameter*, *hexameter*, and so on. The most common meter in English is *iambic pentameter*. See also **Rising meter** and **Falling meter**.

Metonymy Figure of speech in which the term for one thing can be applied to another with which it is closely associated—for example, using "defend the flag" to mean "defend the nation."

Mimesis Aristotle's term for the purpose of literature, which he felt was "imitation" of life.

Monologue Extended speech by one character.

Mood Atmosphere created by the elements of a literary work (setting, characterization, imagery, tone, and so on).

Morality play Medieval Christian allegory, in which personified abstractions, such as Selfishness and Pride, struggle for a person's soul.

Motivation Reasons behind a character's behavior that make us accept or believe that character.

Mystery play Medieval play depicting biblical stories.

Myth Anonymous story reflecting the religious and social values of a culture or explaining natural phenomena, often involving gods and heroes.

Narrative The "storytelling" of a piece of fiction; the forward-moving recounting of episode and description. When an event that occurred earlier is told during a later sequence of events, it is called a **flashback**; suggesting earlier in a narration something that will occur later is called **foreshadowing**.

Narrator Person who tells the story. See **Point of view**.

Naturalism Nineteenth-century movement whose followers believed that life should not be idealized when depicted in literature. Rather, literature should show that human experience is a continual (and for the most part losing) struggle against the natural world. Émile Zola, Jack London, and Stephen Crane are important practitioners of naturalism.

New Comedy Greek comedies of the fourth and third centuries B.C. that followed **Old Comedy**. They were comedies of romance with stock characters and conventional settings. They lacked the satire, abusive language, and bawdiness of Old Comedy.

Novel A book-length fictional narrative, traditionally realistic, relating a series of events or following the history of a character or group of characters through a period of time.

Novella A piece of prose fiction that is longer than a short story but shorter than a novel. Franz Kafka's "The Metamorphosis" is a novella.

Octave See **Sonnet**.

Ode Relatively long lyric poem, common in antiquity and adapted by the romantic poets, for whom it was a serious poem of formal diction, often addressed to some significant object (such as a nightingale or the west wind) that has stimulated the poet's imagination.

Old Comedy The first comedies, written in Greece in the fifth century B.C., which heavily satirized the religious and social issues of the day. The chief practitioner of Old Comedy was Aristophanes. See **New Comedy**.

Onomatopoeia Word whose sound resembles what it describes: "snap, crackle, pop." Lewis Carroll's "Jabberwocky" uses onomatopoeia.

Open form Form of poetry that makes use of varying line lengths, abandoning stanzaic divisions, breaking lines in unexpected places, and even dispensing with any pretense of formal structure. Sometimes called *free verse* or *vers libre*. See **Form**.

Ottava rima See **Stanza**.

Oxymoron Phrase combining two seemingly incompatible elements: "crashing silence."

Parable Story that teaches a lesson, such as the parable of the prodigal son in the New Testament.

Paradox Seemingly contradictory situation. Adrienne Rich's "A Woman Mourned by Daughters" uses paradox.

Parody Exaggerated imitation of a serious piece of literature for humorous effect. Shakespeare's "My mistress' eyes are nothing like the sun" is a parody of traditional Renaissance love poetry.

Pastoral Literary work, such as Christopher Marlowe's lyric poem "The Passionate Shepherd to His Love," that deals nostalgically and usually unrealistically with a simple, preindustrial rural life; the name comes from the fact that traditionally pastorals feature shepherds.

Pastoral romance Prose tale set in an idealized rural world; popular in Renaissance England.

Pathos Suffering that exists simply to satisfy the sentimental or morbid sensibilities of the audience.

Pattern of imagery See **Imagery**.

Perfect rhyme See **Rhyme**.

Persona Narrator or speaker of a poem or story; in Greek tragedy, a persona was a mask worn by an actor.

Personification A figure of speech that endows inanimate objects or abstract ideas with life or human characteristics: "the river wept."

Petrarchan conceit A type of metaphor in which the author draws exaggerated comparisons between their beloved and a physical object; for example, the sun, a flower, or a precious jewel. This device is common in Renaissance writing, and its name is derived from the Italian poet, Petrarch (1304–1374).

Petrarchan sonnet See **Sonnet**.

Picaresque Episodic, often satirical work, presenting the life story of a rogue or rascal—for example, Cervantes' *Don Quixote*. The form emerged in sixteenth-century Spain.

Picture-frame stage Stage that looks like a room with a missing fourth wall through which the audience views the play. The **proscenium arch** separates the audience from the play.

Plot Way in which the events of the story are arranged. When there are two stories of more or less equal importance, the work has a **double plot**; when there is more than one story, but one string of events is clearly the most significant, the other stories are called **subplots**. Plot in fiction often follows the pattern of action in drama, rising to a **climax** and then falling to a **resolution**.

Poetic rhythm See **Rhythm**.

Point of view Perspective from which a story is told. The storyteller may be a major character in the story or a character who witnesses the story's events (*first-person narrator*) or someone who does not figure in the action at all (*third-person narrator*), in which case they may know the actions and internal doings of everyone in the story (*omniscient narrator*) or just some part of these (*limited omniscient narrator*).

The narrator may be an *observer* or a *participant*. If a narrator is untrustworthy (stupid or bad, for example), the story has an *unreliable narrator*; narrators who are unreliable because they do not understand what they are reporting (children, for example) are called *naive narrators*. If the perspective on the events is the same as one would get by simply watching the action unfold on stage, the point of view is *dramatic* or *objective*.

Popular fiction Works aimed at a mass audience.

Prologue First part of a play (originally of a Greek tragedy) in which the actor gives the background or explanations that the audience needs to follow the rest of the drama.

Props (short for **properties**) Pictures, furnishings, and so on that decorate the stage for a play.

Proscenium arch Arch that surrounds the opening in a **picture-frame stage**; through this arch the audience views the performances.

Prose poem Open form poem whose long lines appear to be prose set in paragraphs—for example, Yusef Komunyakaa's "Nude Interrogation."

Protagonist Principal character of a drama or a work of fiction; the hero. The *tragic hero* is the noble protagonist in classical Greek drama who falls because of a tragic flaw.

Pyrrhic See **Meter**.

Quatrain See **Stanza**.

Realism Writing that depicts life as it really is. Realism relies on careful description of setting and the trappings of daily life, psychological probability, and the lives of ordinary people. Ibsen's *A Doll's House* is an example.

Resolution Also called the **denouement**, this is the final stage in the plot of a drama or work of fiction. Here the action comes to an end, and remaining loose ends are tied up.

Rhyme Repetition of concluding sounds in different words, often intentionally used at the ends of poetic lines. In **masculine rhyme** (also called *rising rhyme*) single syllables correspond. In **feminine rhyme** (also called *double rhyme* or *falling rhyme*) two syllables correspond, the second of which is stressed. In **triple rhyme**, three syllables correspond. **Eye rhyme** occurs when words look as though they should rhyme but are pronounced differently ("cough / tough"). In **perfect rhyme**, the corresponding vowel and consonant sounds of accented syllables must be preceded by different consonants—for example, the *b* and *h* in "born" and "horn." **Imperfect rhyme**, also called *near rhyme*, *slant rhyme*, or *consonance* occurs when consonants in two words are the same but intervening vowels are different—for example, "pick / pack," "lads / lids." The most common type of rhyme within a poem is **end rhyme**, where the rhyming syllables are placed at the end of a line. **Internal rhyme** consists of rhyming words found within a line of poetry. **Beginning rhyme** occurs in the first syllable or syllables of a line.

Rhyme royal See **Stanza**.

Rhythm Regular recurrence of sounds in a poem. Ordinarily, rhythm is determined by the arrangement of metrical feet in a line, but sometimes *sprung rhythm*, introduced by Gerard

Manley Hopkins, is used. In this type of rhythm, the number of strong stresses in a line determines the rhythm, regardless of how many weak stresses there might be.

Rising action Stage in a play's plot during which the action builds in intensity. See **Freytag's pyramid**.

Rising meter Iambic and anapestic meters, so called because they move from unstressed to stressed syllables. See **Falling meter**.

Romance Type of narrative that deals with love and adventure in a nonrealistic way, most popular in the Middle Ages but sometimes used by more modern authors, such as Hawthorne.

Romantic comedy Comedy such as Shakespeare's *Much Ado about Nothing* in which love is the main subject and idealized lovers endure great difficulties to get to the inevitable happy ending.

Romanticism Eighteenth- and nineteenth-century literary movement that valued subjectivity, individuality, the imagination, nature, excess, the exotic, and the mysterious.

Round character See **Character**.

Run-on line Line of poetry that ends with no punctuation or natural pause and consequently runs over into the next line; also called *enjambment*.

Sarcasm Form of irony in which apparent praise is used to convey strong, bitter criticism.

Satire Literary attack on folly or vanity by means of humor; usually intended to improve society.

Scansion Process of determining the meter of a poem by analyzing the strong and weak stresses in a line to find the unit of **meter** (each recurring pattern of stresses) and the number of these units (or **feet**) in each line.

Scrim Curtain that when illuminated from the front appears solid but when lit from the back becomes transparent.

Sentimental comedy Reaction against the **comedy of manners**. This type of comedy relies on sentimental emotion rather than on wit or humor and focuses on the virtues of life.

Sestet See **Sonnet**.

Sestina Poem composed of six six-line stanzas and a three-line conclusion called an **envoi**. Each line ends with one of six key words. The alternation of these six words in different positions—but always at the ends of lines—in the poem's six stanzas creates a rhythmic verbal pattern that unifies the poem.

Setting Background against which the action of a work takes place: the historical time, locale, season, time of day, weather, and so on.

Shakespearean sonnet See **Sonnet**.

Short-short story Short fictional narrative that is generally under five pages (or fifteen hundred words) in length.

Short story Fictional narrative centered on one climatic event, usually developing only one character in depth; its scope is narrower than that of the **novel**, and it often uses setting and characterization more directly to make its theme clear.

Simile Comparison of two seemingly unlike things using the words *like* or *as*: "My love is like an arrow through my heart." See **Metaphor**.

Situational irony See **Irony**.

Soliloquy Convention of drama in which a character speaks directly to the audience, revealing thoughts and feelings that other characters present on stage are assumed not to hear.

Sonnet Fourteen-line poem, usually a **lyric** in *iambic pentameter* (see **Meter**). It has a strict rhyme scheme in one of two forms: the *Italian*, or **Petrarchan sonnet** (an eight-line **octave** rhymed *abba / abba* with a six-line **sestet** rhymed *cdc / cdc* or a variation) and the *English*, or **Shakespearean sonnet** (three quatrains rhymed *abab* / *cdcd* / *efef* with a concluding couplet rhymed *gg*).

Speaker See **Persona**.

Spenserian stanza See **Stanza**.

Spondee See **Meter**.

Stage directions Words in a play that describe an actor's role apart from the dialogue, dealing with movements, attitudes, and so on.

Stage setting (set) Scenery and props in the production of a play. In *expressionist* stage settings, scenery and props are exaggerated and distorted to reflect the workings of a troubled, even abnormal mind. *Surrealistic* stage settings are designed to mirror the uncontrolled images of dreams or nightmares. See **Staging**.

Staging Overall production of a play in performance: the sets, costumes, lighting, sound, music, and so on.

Stanza Group of lines in a poem that forms a metrical or thematic unit. Each stanza is usually separated from others by a blank space on the page. Some common stanzaic forms are the **couplet** (two lines), **tercet** (three lines), **quatrain** (four lines), **sestet** (six lines), and **octave** (eight lines). The **heroic couplet**, first used by Chaucer and especially popular throughout the eighteenth century, notably in Alexander Pope's poetry, consists of two rhymed lines of iambic pentameter, with a weak pause after the first line and a strong pause after the second. **Terza rima**, a form used by Dante, has a rhyme scheme (*aba*, *bcb*, *ded*) that creates an interlocking series of stanzas. The **ballad stanza** alternates lines of eight and six syllables. Typically, only the second and fourth lines rhyme. **Common measure** is a four-line stanzaic pattern closely related to the ballad stanza. It differs in that its rhyme scheme is *abab* rather than *abcb*. **Rhyme royal** is a seven-line stanza (*ababbcc*) set in iambic pentameter. **Ottava rima** is an eight-line stanza (*abababcc*) set in iambic pentameter. The **Spenserian stanza** is a nine-line form (*ababbcbcc*) with the first eight lines in iambic pentameter and the last line in iambic hexameter.

Static character See **Character**.

Static imagery Imagery that freezes a moment to give it the timeless quality of painting or sculpture. Much visual imagery is static. See **Kinetic imagery**.

Stock character Stereotypical character who behaves consistently and whom the audience of a play can recognize and classify instantly: the town drunk, the nerd, and so on.

Stream of consciousness Form of narration controlled not by external events but by the thoughts and subjective impressions of the narrator, commonly found in modern literature, such as the work of Virginia Woolf and James Joyce.

Stress Accent or emphasis, either strong or weak, given to each syllable in a piece of writing, as determined by conventional pronunciation (cárpět, not cârpét) and intended emphasis ("going dowń, dowń, dowń tŏ thĕ bóttŏm ŏf thĕ ócĕan"). Strong stresses are marked with a ´ and weak ones with a ˇ.

Structure Formal pattern or arrangement of elements to form a whole in a piece of literature.

Style How an author selects and arranges words to express ideas and, ultimately, theme.

Subplot See **Plot**.

Surrealism Literary movement that allows unconventional use of syntax; chronology; juxtaposition; and bizarre, dreamlike images in prose and poetry.

Symbol Person, object, action, or idea whose meaning transcends its literal or denotative sense in a complex way. A symbol is invested with significance beyond what it could carry on its own. **Universal symbols**, such as the grim reaper, may be called **archetypes; conventional symbols**, such as national flags, evoke a general and agreed-upon response from most people. There are also *private symbols*, such as the "gyre" created by Yeats, which the poet himself invested with extraordinary significance.

Synecdoche Figure of speech in which a part of something is used to represent the whole—for example, "hired hand" represents a laborer.

Synesthesia See **Imagery.**

Tale Short story often involving mysterious atmosphere and supernatural or inexplicable events, such as "The Tell-Tale Heart" by Edgar Allan Poe.

Ten-minute play Short play that can be performed in ten minutes or less.

Tercet See **Stanza.**

Terza rima See **Stanza.**

Theater in the round See **Arena stage.**

Theater of the Absurd Type of drama that discards conventions of plot, character, and motivation to depict a world in which nothing makes sense. Edward Albee's *The Sandbox* is an example.

Theme Central or dominant idea of a piece of literature, made concrete by the details and emphasis in the work itself.

Thrust stage Stage that juts out into the audience so the action may be viewed from three sides.

Tone Attitude of the speaker or author of a work toward the subject itself or the audience, as determined by the word choice and structure of the piece.

Tragedy Literary work, especially a play, that recounts the downfall of an individual. *Greek tragedy* demanded a noble protagonist whose fall could be traced to a *tragic personal flaw*. *Shakespearean tragedy* also treats noble figures, but the reasons for their tragedies may be less clear-cut than in Greek drama. *Domestic* or *modern tragedy* tends to deal with the fates of ordinary people.

Tragic irony See **Irony.**

Tragicomedy Type of Elizabethan and Jacobean drama that uses elements of both tragedy and comedy.

Triple rhyme See **Rhyme.**

Trochee See **Meter.**

Understatement Intentional downplaying of a situation's significance, often for ironic or humorous effect, as in Mark Twain's famous comment on reading his own obituary, "The reports of my death are greatly exaggerated."

Unities Rules that require a dramatic work to be unified in terms of its time, place, and action. *Oedipus the King* illustrates the three unities.

Universal symbol See **Symbol.**

Verbal irony See **Irony.**

Villanelle A nineteen-line poem composed of five tercets and a concluding quatrain; its rhyme scheme is *aba aba aba aba aba abaa*. Two different lines are systematically repeated in the poem: line 1 appears again in lines 6, 12, and 18, and line 3 reappears as lines 9, 15, and 19. Thus, each tercet concludes with an exact (or close) duplication of either line 1 or line 3, and the final quatrain concludes by repeating both line 1 and line 3.

Visual poetry Poetry that focuses as much on the words' appearance on the page as on what the words say, using a combination of media that may include video, photography, and even sound as well as text.

Wagons Sets mounted on wheels, which make rapid changes of scenery possible.

Index of First Lines of Poetry

Index of Authors and Titles

Index of Literary Terms